Exploring Science

The Exploring Science series is designed to familiarize young students with science topics taught in grades 4–9. The topics in each book are divided into knowledge and understanding sections, followed by exploration by means of simple projects or experiments. The topics are also sequenced from easiest to more complex, and should be worked through until the correct level of attainment for the age and ability of the student is reached. Carefully planned Test Yourself questions at the end of each topic allow the student to gain a sense of achievement on mastering the subject.

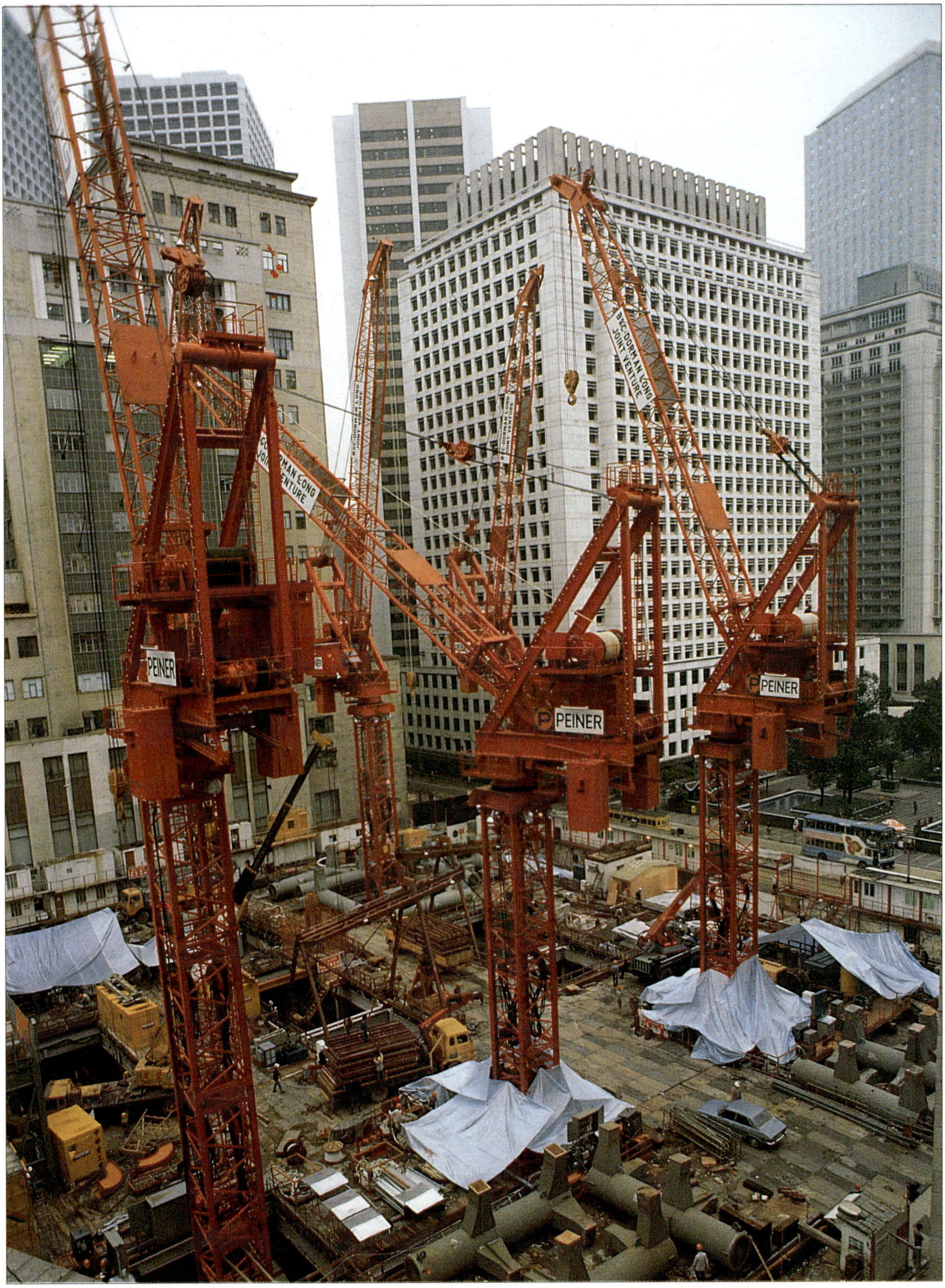
PEINER
PEINER
PEINER
B&C-DORMAN LONG
JOINT VENTURE

EXPLORING
FORCES AND STRUCTURES

Keith Bardon

Illustrated by Marilyn Clay

**RAINTREE
STECK-VAUGHN**
L I B R A R Y
The Steck-Vaughn Company

Austin, Texas

Exploring Science

Earth in Space
Electricity
Energy Sources
Forces and Structures
The Human Body
Light

Magnets
Plants
Soil and Rocks
Sound
Uses of Energy
Weather

©Copyright 1992, text, Steck-Vaughn Company

All rights reserved. No reproduction, copy, or transmission of this publication may be made without written permission of the publisher.

Library of Congress Cataloging-in-Publication Data

Bardon, Keith.
   Forces and structures / Keith Bardon; illustrated by Marilyn Clay.
     p.   cm. — (Exploring science)
   Includes bibliographical references and index.
   Summary: Text and experiments explore various forces and their effect on the world, including friction, resistance, gravity, and movement.
   ISBN 0-8114-2602-5
   1. Force and energy—Juvenile literature.   [1. Force and energy-Experiments.   2. Experiments.]   I. Clay, Marilyn, ill.   II. Title.
III. Series.
QC73.4.B37   1992   91-38318
531—dc20   CIP
                                                                AC

Cover illustrations:
Left The forces created at the launch of the space shuttle are enormous.
Right above A spider's web is one of nature's greatest feats of engineering. It is able to withstand very strong forces.
Right below A diagram showing a bridge, with the forces that act on it.

Frontispiece Tall buildings have to be carefully constructed. They often have a wider base, to prevent toppling.

Editor: Elizabeth Spiers
Editor, American Edition: Susan Wilson
Series Designer: Ross George
Book designer: Jenny Hughes

Typeset by Multifacit Graphics, Keyport, NJ
Printed in Italy by G. Canale & C.S.p.A.,Turin
Bound in the United States by Lake Book, Melrose Park, IL

1 2 3 4 5 6 7 8 9 0 Ca 96 95 94 93 92

Contents

What Is a Force?	6
Forces All Around Us	8
Making Things Move	10
Floating and Sinking	12
Magnetic Forces	14
Electrostatic Forces	16
Gravity	18
Balance	20
Friction	22
Resistance	24
Flying High	26
Speeding Up and Slowing Down	28
Materials	30
Measuring Force	32
Surface Tension	34
Nature, the Builder	36
Across the Gap	38
Making Things Easy	40
Under Pressure	42
Bricks and Mortar	44
Glossary	46
Books to Read	47
Index	48

WHAT IS A FORCE?

Sir Isaac Newton is famous for his work on forces.

Have you ever felt "forced" to do something you did not want or intend to do? Think about slipping on a frozen puddle and falling over, or having to chase something that has blown away on a windy day. We all experience forces constantly. Often we do not notice them, but at other times, such as when two cars collide, they are obvious.

You cannot see forces, but you can observe their effects. What is a force? The easiest way to think of a force is as a push or pull. Forces make objects start moving and keep them going. They also slow moving things down or bring them to a stop. In addition, forces change the direction or speed of movement.

Think about a bicycle traveling over a level surface. To get it started, you have to exert a pushing force on the pedals. You must continue pushing the pedals to keep the bicycle going. To slow the bicycle down or make it stop, you have to pull on the brakes. You can make the bicycle change direction by pushing and pulling the handlebars. To make it go faster, you have to exert more force on the pedals.

Forces can bring about changes in shape and size. A piece of clay can be molded into a new shape by pushing and pulling it. Old cars can be squashed into very small, dense blocks by pushing on them with a strong force, using a hydraulic ram.

Much of what is known about forces was learned long ago. An ancient Greek named Aristotle was one of the first to study forces. Other theories come from the work of Sir Isaac Newton, who lived about 300 years ago. You may have heard the story of how he arrived at his ideas about gravity after being hit on the head by an apple falling from a tree. Newton's Laws of Motion are still used today to explain how and why things move.

ACTIVITY

YOU NEED

- **paper**
- **a pen or pencil**

1 Pick a simple task from the list below:
  - changing your shoes
  - getting something out of a drawer
  - putting a record on a record player (or a cassette in a cassette player)
2 Guess how many pushes and pulls will be needed to perform the task.
3 Perform the task. As you do it, make a note every time a force is needed and tell whether it is a push or a pull.
4 Count the pushes and pulls needed to perform this simple task.
5 How close was your guess?

Forces can bring about changes in shape. As these children bounce, the force of their weight changes the shape of the "moon walk."

TEST YOURSELF

1. What can forces do?
2. What do you do to the pedals of a bicycle to make it move?
3. Who is the scientist whose Laws of Motion are still used today?

FORCES ALL AROUND US

Different forces produce different effects. They are easy to spot when you know what to look for.

Gravity is the name given to the force that pulls objects toward the Earth. This force causes a book to fall when it is pushed over the edge of a table, and a ball to roll down a hill. It is also the force that enables us to keep our feet planted firmly on the ground.

When surfaces rub against each other, they create a force called friction. The friction between your shoes and the floor stops you from slipping when you run, but it also causes the soles and heels of your shoes to wear out (see page 22).

When two people play "tug-of-war," they are putting the rope under a force called tension. The person causing the most tension will win the game. The force that is the opposite of tension is called compression. If you push on or squash an empty can, you have compressed it.

Magnetic force, as the name suggests, deals with magnets and the pushes and pulls they can produce. The Earth has lines of magnetic force running around it. We use these lines to find direction with a compass (see page 14).

Static electricity causes electrostatic force. Sometimes, when you are taking off clothing made of nylon, you can feel the tiny hairs on your arms stand up. Electrostatic force causes this. (page 16).

Forces often go unnoticed because they act against each other. A book resting on a table will stay there without moving for as long as you leave it. We know that gravity pulls the book toward the Earth, so why does it not move? The answer is that the table itself exerts a force. This force acts upward to balance exactly the weight of the book. Thus, as the book pushes down, the table pushes back and the book stays where it is. Of course, if the book exerts too much force, the table will break.

When coal mines are dug underground, special supports called pit props must be used. These help resist the forces that would otherwise cause the tunnels to collapse.

ACTIVITY

YOU NEED

- **a large piece of modeling clay**

1. Warm the clay in your hands so that it is soft. Roll it into three identical balls.

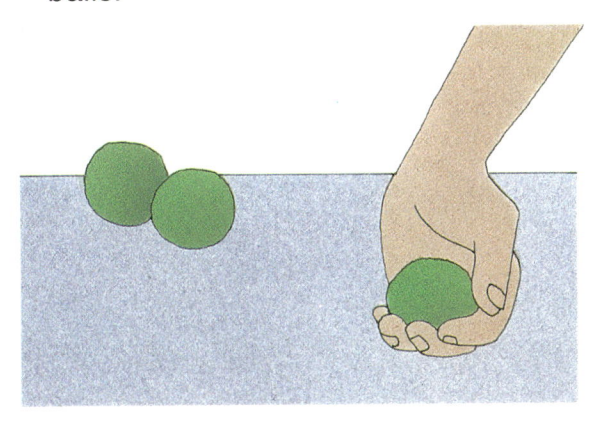

2. Drop one of the balls of clay on the floor from the height of your knee.

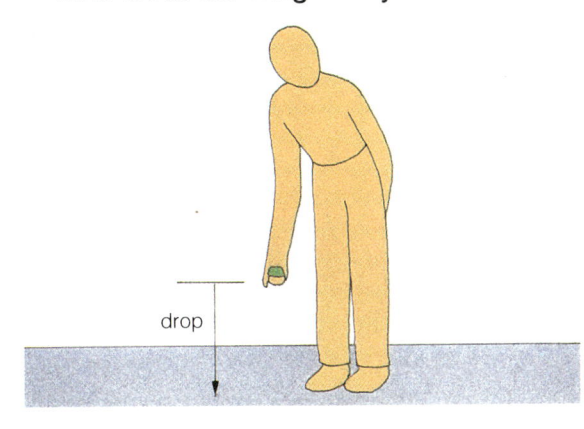

3. Pick up the clay carefully and examine it. What has happened to it? What forces have acted on the clay to make this happen?

4. Drop the second ball of clay from the height of your shoulder.

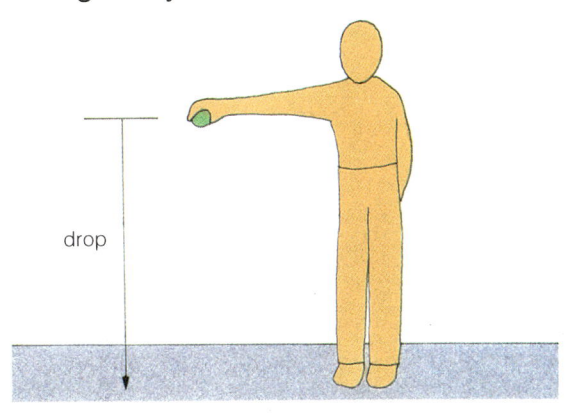

5. Drop the third ball from as high as you can reach.

6. Compare all three balls. What do you notice? Why are they different?

TEST YOURSELF

1. What type of force results from surfaces rubbing against each other?
2. What causes electrostatic force?
3. If two equal forces work against each other, what will happen?

MAKING THINGS MOVE

The launch of the space shuttle. A huge pushing force must be created in order for the spacecraft to escape the Earth's gravitational pull. In space, the engines can be switched off and the craft will continue to move.

What makes something that is stationary (not moving) start to move? Often, movement is brought about by direct contact. For example, to make a shopping cart move, you push it, and to remove a stopper from a bottle, you pull it. In other cases, we use motors or engines to start something moving. The most common cause of movement is gravity. Gravity, motors, and pushing all involve force. To start an object moving, a force is needed.

If an object has been made to move by a force, what happens when that force stops? The pushing force used to launch a simple paper airplane stops when the airplane is released, but the airplane does not stop. It continues to fly until air friction (see page 26) and gravity eventually stop it.

It is difficult to think about what happens after a force that has caused an object to move, stops. This is because on Earth, whenever anything moves, gravity and friction always act upon it. We have to use our imagination to think of a situation where these two forces do not exist. Imagine a spaceship in deep space where there was absolutely nothing: no planets to cause gravity and no matter to cause friction. Once the spaceship got there, it could switch off its engines and continue in the same direction at exactly the same speed. This is because there would be nothing to slow it down or stop it. Even in space, however, gravity acts on objects.

These are the kinds of questions that Sir Isaac Newton asked himself. His answers are considered to be scientific laws:

"An object that is stationary will start to move only when forces are applied to it."

and

"Once an object has been made to move, it will continue at the same speed and in the same direction unless other forces cause it to change speed, stop or alter its direction."

ACTIVITY
TESTING NEWTON'S LAWS OF MOTION

YOU NEED

- **a toy car**
- **a ramp**
- **rubber bands**

1 Use different methods (pushing, catapulting, rolling down the ramp) to start the toy car moving. Can you say what forces made it move in each case?
2 Repeat each method. This time, describe the forces that make the vehicle slow down or stop.
3 What ways can you think of to make the vehicle change direction?
4 Look at your answers. Do you agree with Sir Isaac Newton?

push

TEST YOURSELF

1. What is the most common cause of movement?
2. Which two forces always act when objects move on Earth?
3. Why would a spaceship's speed or direction change in deep space if its engines were turned off?

FLOATING AND SINKING

Enormous vessels, such as this cargo ship, can float because of their shape. This ship produces a large displacement of water, so the upthrust is strong enough to keep it afloat.

Have you ever noticed, when you get into the bathtub, how the water level rises? It happens because some of the water has been displaced (pushed out of the way). This is the key to an understanding of why some things float while others sink.

The link between floating, sinking, and displacement is best thought of in terms of pushing forces. If you have ever had to push your way through a crowd, you will have felt forces similar to those acting on a floating block of wood. When the wood is placed in water, it pushes aside a certain amount of water. The water that has been pushed aside pushes back, just as the people in the crowd do. The force created by the displaced water pushing back is given a special name—it is buoyant force. This means we have two pushing forces: the weight of the wood pushing down and the upthrust of the water pushing up. If these two opposite forces are equal, they balance each other and the wood floats.

Whenever an object is placed in a liquid (or gas), there is always an upthrust, even if it sinks. If a block of steel the same size as the wood were placed in the water, it would sink. This is because the weight of the block of steel is too large a force for the upthrust of the water to counterbalance.

Why, then, does a block of steel sink, but a steel ship that may weigh thousands of tons float? It is because of the air-filled hull. This shape makes the ship displace far more water than if it had been left in a solid block. If the shape produces a large displacement, the upthrust created will be strong enough to make the ship float.

ACTIVITY

MEASURING BUOYANT FORCE

YOU NEED

- string
- a stone
- a block of wood
- a spring scale (see page 32)
- a large plastic container
- water

1 Tie a string to the stone and the block of wood. Loop the end of each string so that it can be hung from the scale.

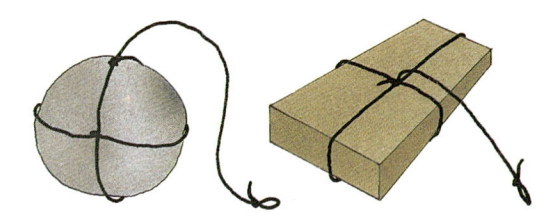

2 Hang the stone from the spring scale and weigh it. Record the weight.

3 Leave the stone attached to the spring scale and lower it into the container of water until it is completely underwater.

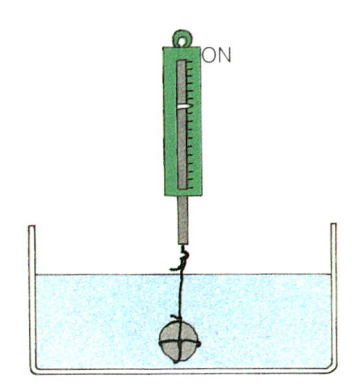

4 Take the reading on the spring scale. Can you calculate how much buoyant force the water is producing?

5 Hang the block of wood from the spring scale and weigh it.

6 Leave the block of wood attached to the spring scale and lower it into the container of water. What happens to the reading on the spring scale? Can you explain why this has happened?

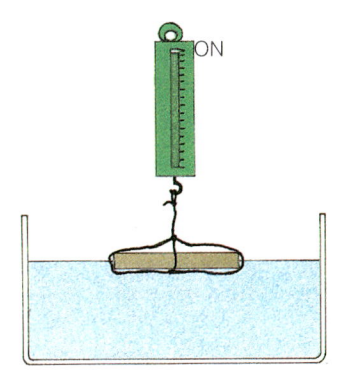

TEST YOURSELF

1. What does the word displaced mean?
2. What is the pushing force that displaced liquids and gases produce?
3. A 5-inch cube of softwood will float in water, but a 5-inch cube of steel will sink. Why is this?

MAGNETIC FORCES

Making use of magnetic force is not a new idea. The ancient Chinese knew about it and used a magnetic rock called lodestone as a simple compass to tell direction. Magnetism is a very difficult force to explain, but its effects are fairly obvious: pushing and pulling force that affects some materials and not others.

Iron and steel are by far the most common magnetic materials in use today. The property of iron and the other magnetic materials to become magnets, or to be attracted to them, is rather special. An ordinary piece of iron is made up of millions of tiny magnets but, because they are all mixed up, they work against each other. So you do not notice that they are there. When the piece of iron is magnetized, all the tiny magnets are turned so that they face the same way. Then they work together to create the force called magnetism.

Iron filings are attracted to the pole of a bar magnet.

The Earth acts like a huge bar magnet, with north and south poles.

Magnets are many different shapes—for example, bar, horseshoe, ring, and cylindrical. Bar magnets have two very distinct ends: a north pole and a south pole. Two north poles, or two south poles, placed close together will produce a pushing force called repulsion. A north and a south pole placed close together will exert a pulling force called attraction. This rule works every time: "like poles repel and unlike poles attract."

A small paper clip placed close to a magnet and released will jump the gap between them. This shows that the force of attraction extends out from the magnet. This extending out of the force is called the magnetic field and the stronger the magnet, the larger the field.

The Earth itself acts like a huge bar magnet. It has a magnetic field and north and south poles. It is the Earth's magnetic field that we detect with a directional compass in order to find our way.

ACTIVITY
PLOTTING THE MAGNETIC FIELD

YOU NEED

- a strong bar magnet
- masking tape
- a piece of thin cardboard
- a compass
- a pencil

1. Tape the magnet to the underside of the cardboard.
2. Place the compass on top of the cardboard, near one of the poles of the magnet. 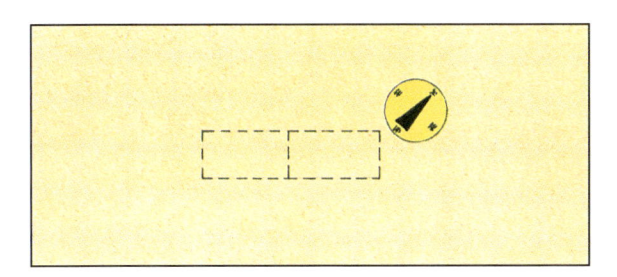
3. Mark the position of the north pole of the compass needle with a pencil dot. 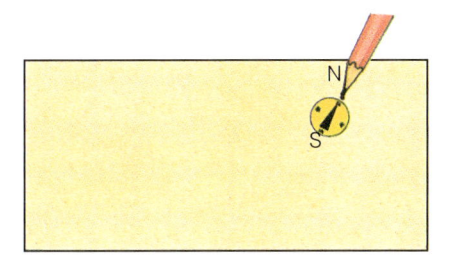
4. Move the compass until the south pole is touching the dot you have just made. 
5. Mark the new position of the north pole of the compass needle.
6. Repeat this until you have a line of dots from one end of the magnet to the other. Join the dots with a smooth curve. 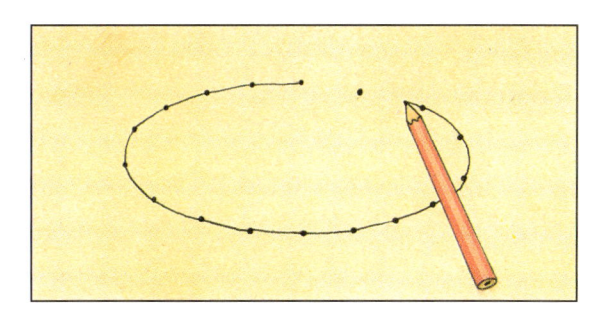
7. What you have traced is one line of force. Other lines can be traced by varying the starting place slightly. Trace enough lines and a picture of the whole magnetic field will appear.

TEST YOURSELF

1. Name three metals that have magnetic properties.
2. According to the rules of science, what do like and unlike poles do?
3. What do we call the area of magnetic force that surrounds a magnet?

ELECTROSTATIC FORCES

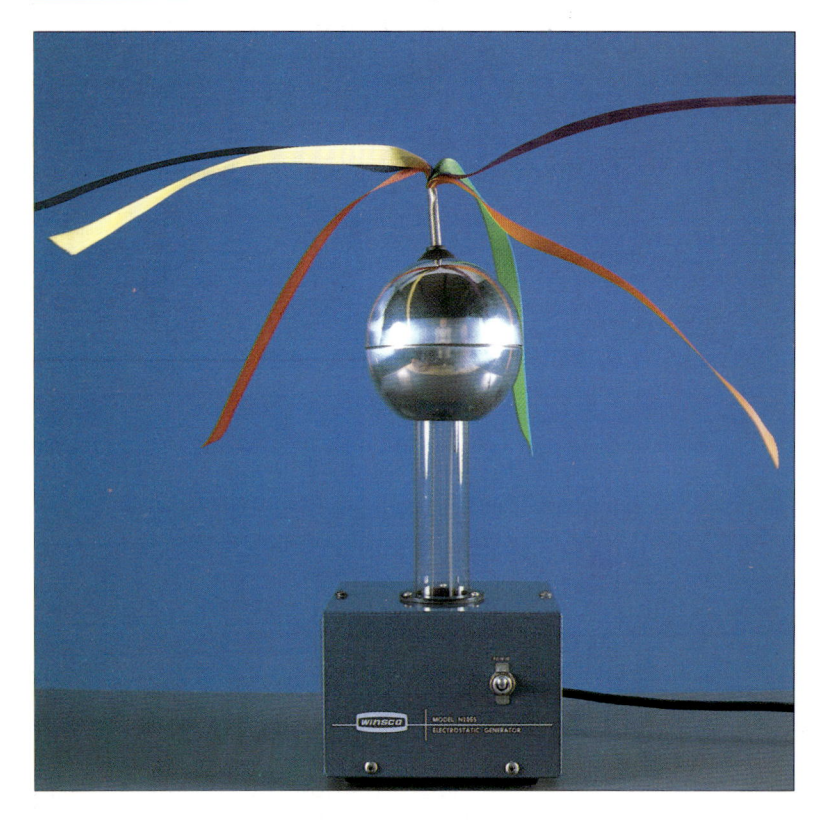

The strips of plastic attached to this electrostatic generator have picked up a static charge from the metal dome. They are all carrying the same type of charge, so they repel each other and the metal dome of the generator.

Electrostatic is a word made from two others. The "electro" part refers to electrical charge and "static" means standing still. Electrostatic forces are created by electricity that is not moving. This is different from current electricity, which "flows" through anything that will carry it.

Static electricity is very common. It causes dust to stick to a television screen and lightning to flash across the sky during a thunderstorm. It can even make your hair stand on end.

How are electrostatic forces created? Every substance is made up of tiny particles called atoms. If you grip a plastic bag firmly in one hand and quickly pull it through with the other, it will stick to you afterwards. This happens because the rubbing causes some particles from the atoms in your hand to "jump off" onto the plastic. Your hand and the plastic then have different electrical charges. These attract each other in the same way that unlike poles of a magnet attract. This causes the two substances to stick together. The static charge does not last very long, and the two soon become "unattracted."

There are many other ways of showing electrostatic attraction. Inflated balloons can be stuck to walls if they are first rubbed on a wool sweater.

When two objects carry the same charge, they will repel each other. If two balloons are suspended by thread so that they hang level and are just touching, and are rubbed with a piece of wool cloth, they will jump apart as the like charges repel each other.

ACTIVITY

YOU NEED

- **a small ball of modeling clay**
- **a long dressmaking pin**
- **a 1-inch square of paper**
- **rods of various materials (plastic, glass, metal, wood)**
- **pieces of cloth of various materials (cotton, wool, nylon)**

1 Flatten one side of the ball of clay so that it cannot roll.

2 Push the pin point first into the clay until it is firmly in place.

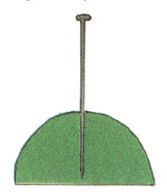

3 Fold the sheet of paper in half and then open it into a V shape.

4 Balance the sheet of paper on the head of the pin so that the V is upside down. You have made a simple static charge detector.

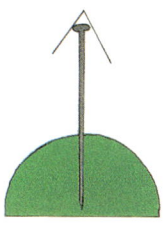

5 Rub a plastic rod with the wool cloth, place it close to the detector, and watch what happens. This will occur with any substance that is charged.

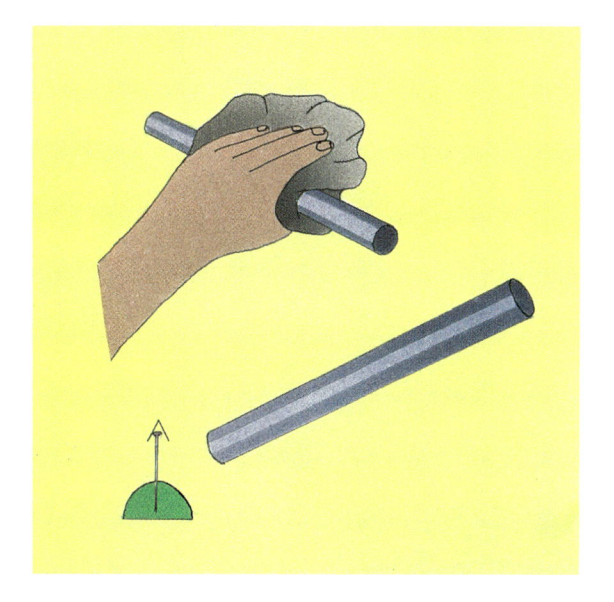

6 Try different combinations of rod and cloth to see which will produce an electrostatic charge.

TEST YOURSELF

1. What is the difference between static and current electricity?
2. What is the name of the tiny particles from which all substances are made?
3. What are the two rules of electrostatic charge?

GRAVITY

Christa McAuliffe, an astronaut, floats around a training capsule, where the effect of gravity has been removed. This was practice for conditions in space.

Gravity is a force that acts upon us continually throughout our lives, but what is it and where does it come from? If you ask the question "What is gravity?" the most common answer you will get is "The pull of the Earth."

In fact, everything that has mass (the amount of substance in an object) exerts a gravitational pulling force. This book is exerting a pull on you and you are exerting a pull on the book. The reason that neither you nor the book moves toward each other is that the force is very weak. It is only when an object has a very large mass, like the Earth, that its gravitational pull can be felt.

The Earth's gravitational pull extends out into space, but the farther away you get the weaker it becomes, until its effect can no longer be felt. The area over which the gravitational pull can be felt is called the gravitational field, and the pull is always toward the center of the Earth.

All large bodies in space, such as planets and stars, have gravitational fields. The larger the body, the stronger the field. Gravity on the moon is only one-sixth of that on Earth. That is why, when you see a film of astronauts on the moon, they move so strangely. The sun's gravity is far greater than the Earth's. That is why the Earth stays in orbit around it. This is true not only for our own solar system but for the entire universe. It is gravity that keeps all the suns, planets, and moons of the universe in place.

What happens when there is no gravity? You have probably seen pictures of "weightless" astronauts floating about inside their spaceship. This is exactly the same effect that someone would experience if he or she went into deep space, far away from any large masses. In such a situation, the person would really be weightless, because weight is the force caused by gravity acting on a mass.

ACTIVITY

YOU NEED

- **scissors**
- **thin string**
- **large, flat, metal washers**

1. Cut a 20-inch length of string.
2. Tie the washer to one end of the string.
3. Hold the string up and check that the washer is heavy enough to pull it taut. If it isn't, add another washer.
4. You have made a simple but very useful device called a plumb line. If it is held up and allowed to hang freely, gravity will pull it downward toward the center of the Earth.
5. Many things are made to be perfectly vertical. Walls, doors, window frames, and wallpaper are examples. Use your plumb line to find out if the things around you that are supposed to be vertical have been built accurately.

TEST YOURSELF

1. If everything that has mass exerts a gravitational pull, why is everything on this planet not stuck together?
2. What is a gravitational field?
3. Why is the sun's gravity far greater than the Earth's?

BALANCE

Have you ever tried to make a seesaw work with someone much heavier sitting at the other end? You probably spent most of the time stuck up in the air! This is because the forces involved are out of balance. Gravity is pulling on the other person with greater force than it is on you, so there is greater force at one end of the seesaw than at the other. You know by now that if there is a large force working against a small force, the large force always wins.

If you sat on the seesaw with someone of equal weight at the other end, it could be balanced in a horizontal position. A seesaw is an example of an equal-arm balance. You have probably seen other examples of equal-arm balances at home or school. You may know them as "weighing" scales of the type that you put "weights" on. The forces that make an equal-arm balance move are called turning forces, because they make the balance arms turn on the pivot point.

Every object has a point through which its mass seems to be concentrated. This point is called the center of gravity and it determines the stability of an object. A cereal box has a high center of gravity, so you do not have to tip it far before gravity takes hold and pulls it over. A double-decker bus has a low center of gravity, so that it can lean over quite far before becoming unstable and falling over.

An object's center of gravity is determined by its shape and the area where most of its mass is located. A tall, thin object with most of its mass at the top will be very unstable. An object with a wide base and most of its mass at the base will be very stable. You can test this by trying to balance a new pencil first on its point and then on its eraser. Which is easier and why?

These children are using turning forces, created by their leg muscles to make the seesaw turn around its pivot (balance) point.

ACTIVITY

YOU NEED

- a small plastic bottle with a screw-top cap
- water
- a medium-sized nail
- a golf-ball-sized piece of clay
- 2 teaspoons

1 Fill the bottle with water and screw on the cap.

2 Carefully push the head of the nail into the clay, but leave the point sticking out.

3 Insert the two spoons at opposite sides of the ball of clay, so that they look like a penguin's wings when the penguin is walking.

4 Put your model on the bottle cap and adjust the spoons until the model balances on the nail point.

5 Once the model is balanced properly, push it gently. Watch it rock back and forth without falling off.

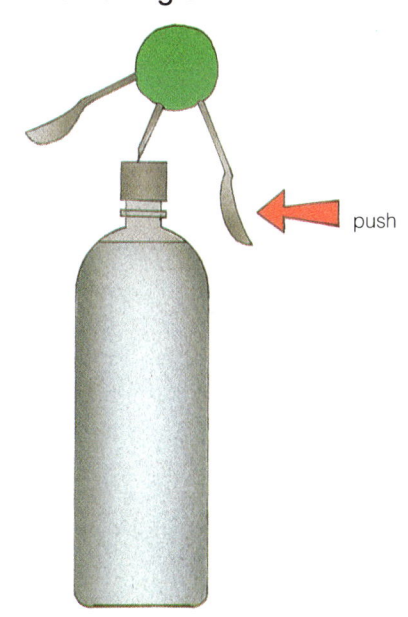

TEST YOURSELF

1. A seesaw is an example of what kind of balance?
2. What is meant by the term "center of gravity"?
3. Which is easier to balance: something with a high center of gravity or something with a low one?

FRICTION

All surfaces are uneven. Even those that feel smooth to the touch look like bumpy roads or broken glass under a microscope. Because of this, they rub when they move against each other. It is this rubbing that causes friction, and rough surfaces create more friction than smoother ones.

If gravity is the most common cause of movement, then friction must be the force that most often resists movement. It slows down objects that are already moving and eventually brings them to a complete standstill. It also generates heat—test this by rubbing your hands together.

Moving parts always generate friction. Some machines have so many working parts that they will not work at all unless something is done to reduce the friction. A car engine constantly needs to be lubricated with oil if it is to last a long time and work efficiently. Lubricants such as oil, grease, and soft wax all work in the same way. They run over the surface and fill in the uneven places, making it smooth.

Many machines have bearings to help reduce friction. Try pushing a book across a table, then put marbles under it and push it again. This is a demonstration of one of the most common types of bearing—the ball bearing. In machines, metal balls or rollers are used instead of marbles, but the principle is the same.

Although friction is often thought of as a nuisance, life would be very difficult without it. If there were no friction, how could a moving object be stopped? Brake blocks are made from rubber, so that when a bicycle's brakes are applied the friction produced slows it down. Rubber is also used to make tires that grip the road, and shoe soles are made from "rubbery" materials. Surface shape can also be important, which is why tires have tread patterns molded into them.

Above *Ice skaters take advantage of the low friction of the surface of the ice.*

Right *Tires have raised areas of tread to increase the friction between the road and the tire.*

ACTIVITY
SOLES THAT GRIP

YOU NEED

- **a pencil**
- **a yardstick**
- **a variety of shoes**
- **a 3-foot ramp made from a slippery material, such as plastic laminate**

1 Make a mark with the pencil, about 1 foot from one end of the ramp.
2 Place one of the shoes on the ramp, with its toe touching the mark.

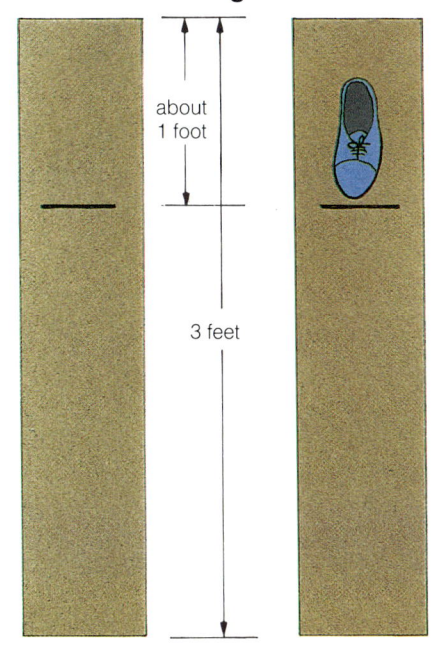

3 Raise the ramp at the marked end until the shoe begins to slide down.
4 Hold the ramp in that position and measure how high it had to be raised before the shoe moved. Record the measurements.

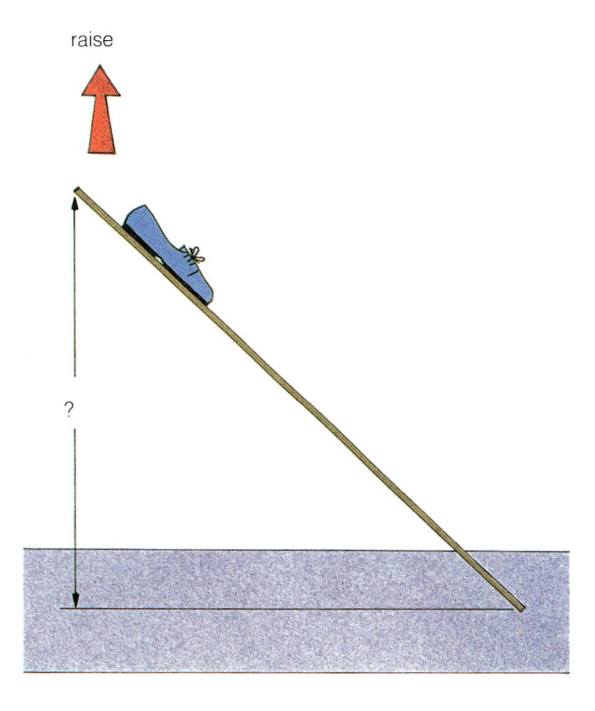

5 Repeat these steps with all the shoes.
6 Compare the measurements. Which shoe had the most grip?
7 Compare the various shoes with the measurements they gave. Can you say anything about the soles and the amount of grip they had?

TEST YOURSELF

1. What is the cause of friction?
2. Why is it important to check the oil level in a car engine regularly?
3. When is friction a useful force?

RESISTANCE

Left *This hydrofoil cuts down on water resistance by lifting its hull completely out of the water as it travels.*

Below *This parachutist relies on air resistance to reach the ground safely.*

In the previous section, you learned about the frictional force generated by solids, but liquids and gases also produce a type of friction. Friction in liquids and gases is called resistance. We talk about air and water resistance because it describes what they do—they resist movement.

The effects produced by resistance are almost the same as those produced by friction. For example, anything moving very quickly through air gets hot. The Earth is constantly bombarded from space by meteors, but they do little or no damage because the resistance created as they enter the atmosphere causes them to burn up. The moon has no atmosphere to protect it, which is why it is covered with craters.

To reduce air resistance (sometimes called "drag"), aircraft have very smooth shapes, designed to cut through air rather than to push it out of the way. This design is called streamlining.

However, cutting through air at high speed is not always desirable. People who jump out of aircraft use parachutes to increase their overall air resistance. Parachutes work on the principle of opposing forces. The two forces—gravity and air resistance—never cancel each other out. Gravity is always the slight winner, but the parachute creates enough air resistance to ensure a safe rate of descent.

Water resists movement even more than air. This makes designing the shape of a ship's hull a very skilled operation, often involving the use of modern computers. Hydrofoils eliminate as much resistance as possible by raising the hull completely out of the water and skimming across the surface on structures that look and work like water skis.

ACTIVITY

YOU NEED

- nylon fishing line
- 6 feet of rain gutter fitted with watertight end stops, one with a shallow groove cut in it
- cellophane tape
- a small hook
- water
- various boat shapes cut from softwood and fitted with screw-in eyelets
- a hanging mass (1/2 ounce) or fishing line sinker
- a stopwatch

1. Cut a 7-foot length of fishing line. Use the cellophane tape to attach one end of the line to the grooved end stop of the gutter.
2. Attach the hook to the other end of the fishing line. 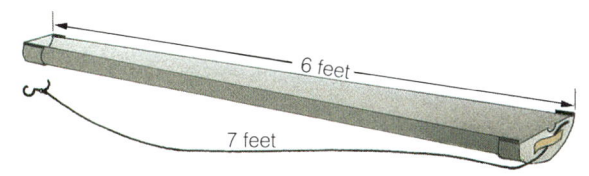
3. Place the gutter on a flat surface at least 3 feet from the floor, with the grooved end overhanging slightly. Fill the gutter three-quarters full of water. 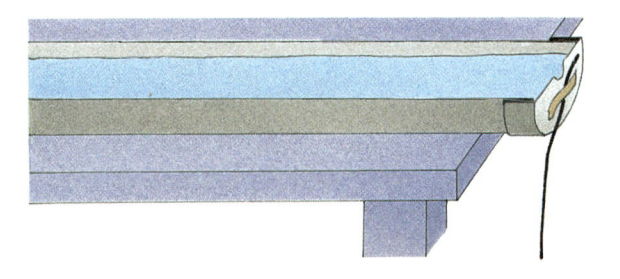
4. Place one of the boat shapes at the ungrooved end and hook the fishing line to it.
5. Set the fishing line in the groove. Make a loop at the grooved end.
6. Hang the mass or the sinker from the loop of fishing line. Set the stopwatch and let go of the boat. Time how long the boat shape takes to "sail" down the gutter. 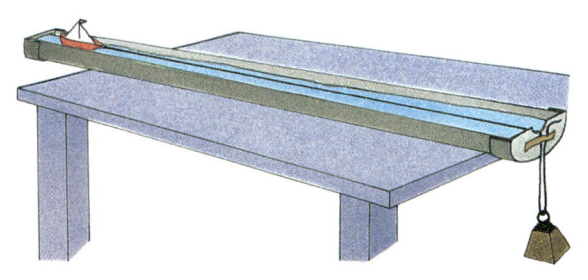
7. Repeat the test using the other boat shapes.
8. Put the boat shapes in order, starting with the one that encounters the least water resistance and ending with the one that encounters the most.

TEST YOURSELF

1. Why are there far more craters on the moon than on Earth?
2. Why are aircraft and boats streamlined?
3. What are the two main forces encountered by parachutists?

FLYING HIGH

Flight has always fascinated humans, but early attempts to fly like a bird were always doomed to failure. If early "aviators" had thought about the forces involved, they would soon have realized their mistake. Humans are too heavy, the wrong shape, and lack the muscle structure to fly like birds. When planning to build something that will rise into the air and move forward without falling back to Earth, two pairs of forces have to be taken into account.

In order to overcome gravity, an opposite force called "lift" has to be produced. The shape of the wings is very important in achieving lift. If you could take a slice of a wing and look at it, you would see that it has a special shape called an airfoil. It is curved across its upper surface, but the bottom surface is almost flat. As the airplane moves forward, the air flowing over the top surface has farther to go than the air flowing past the bottom surface. This difference in air flow produces the lift.

You have already found out that

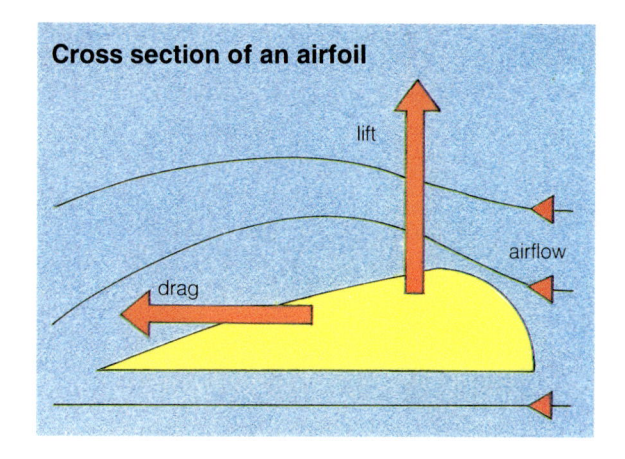

Cross section of an airfoil

anything that moves through the air experiences a frictional force called air resistance, or "drag." An aircraft's streamlined shape helps to reduce the amount of drag, but the engines provide the thrust to move it forward. You have probably inflated a balloon and then released it, letting it fly around the room. The balloon is powered by the air rushing out—jet engines work in a similar way. Fans suck air into the engine and compress (squash) it. This makes the air very hot. When it is sprayed with fuel, the mixture of air and fuel burns fiercely. The burning gases expand and rush out the back of the engine, pushing the airplane forward.

Although air resistance can be a nuisance in forward flight, it is essential for the control of the aircraft. Flaps on the wings (called ailerons) and on the tail (called elevators), along with the rudder, enable the pilot to control the direction and angle of flight. Large flaps on the wings also act as brakes—essential when you remember that a large jet comes in to land at over 200 miles per hour.

This fighter plane is streamlined to reduce air resistance.

ACTIVITY

YOU NEED

- **a sheet of paper**
- **scissors**
- **ruler**

1. Make a simple paper airplane by
   - folding the paper in half
   - folding the corners toward the center at one end
   - folding the edges of the triangles to the center
   - folding in half again and then bending back the edges to make wings.

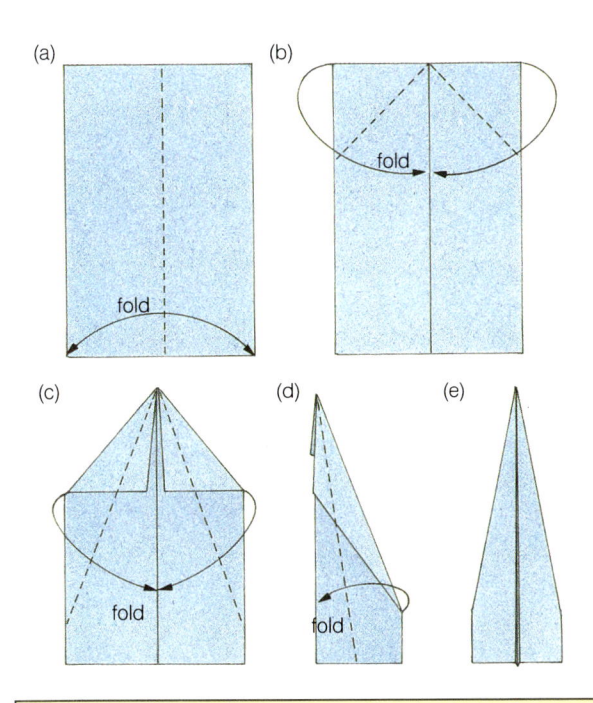

2. Test your airplane to make sure it flies straight.
3. Make two 1/2-inch deep cuts 2 inches apart at the rear of each wing.
4. Fold between the cuts to make flaps. 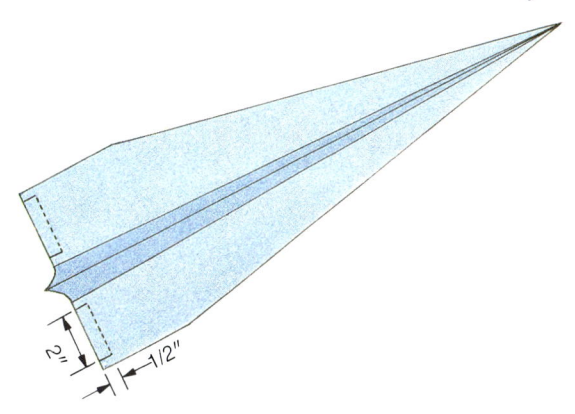
5. Investigate what happens to the flight of your airplane when both flaps are up; both are down; one is up and one is down.
6. Further investigations can be carried out by making airplanes with different-sized or different-shaped flaps. 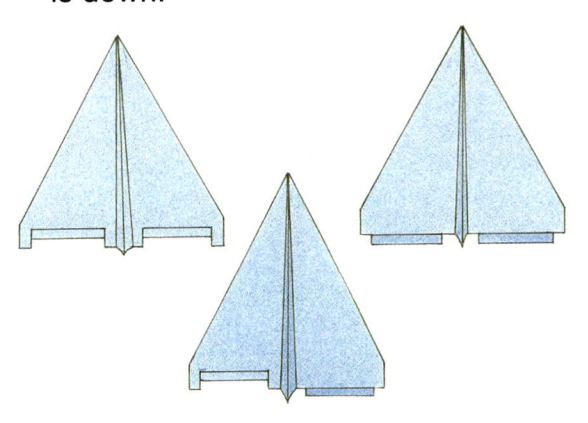

TEST YOURSELF

1. Why is it that a human cannot strap on a pair of wings and fly like a bird?
2. What are the two pairs of forces that most affect flight?
3. How does a jet engine work?

27

SPEEDING UP AND SLOWING DOWN

Speed, the measure of the distance traveled in a certain time, is something you cannot help being aware of. Our roads are full of speed-related signs. Those with numbers give the maximum speed allowed; others warn of hazards that require a speed reduction.

In some sports, speed is extremely important. An automobile-racing commentator constantly bombards the audience with statistics: "That car has a top speed of 200 miles per hour," or "The new lap record is 150 miles per hour." The reason for the different figures is that speed is measured in a number of different ways. The top speed mentioned is the fastest the car can travel, and it probably cannot run at that speed for long. The lap record is an average speed taken over one lap. At some time during the lap, the car will have been traveling faster than 150 miles per hour, but at other times (when going around corners, for instance), it will have been traveling more slowly. A third measurement is that of constant speed. This is difficult to achieve on modern roads, but it is sometimes possible to bring a car up to a certain speed and maintain it.

Speed is related to the forces that create or resist a movement. If you have ever ridden a bicycle, you have probably noticed that bringing it to a standstill from a high speed needs far more braking force than when traveling slowly.

Another speed-related term is acceleration. This is a measure of how quickly speed is increasing. If a sprinter leaves the block and has reached a speed of 30 feet per second after 5 seconds, it can be said that the average increase in speed has been 6 feet per second for every second of running. This is the acceleration.

The Indianapolis-500 is one of the most famous automobile races. The cars are specially shaped to reduce "drag." These cars are able to reach very high speeds.

ACTIVITY

YOU NEED

- a 5-foot ramp
- protractor
- a toy truck
- a yardstick or tape measure
- a 1/2-pound mass
- a 1-pound mass
- a 2-pound mass

1. Set the ramp on the floor at an angle of 25° to 30°.
2. Place the toy truck at the top of the ramp and release it. 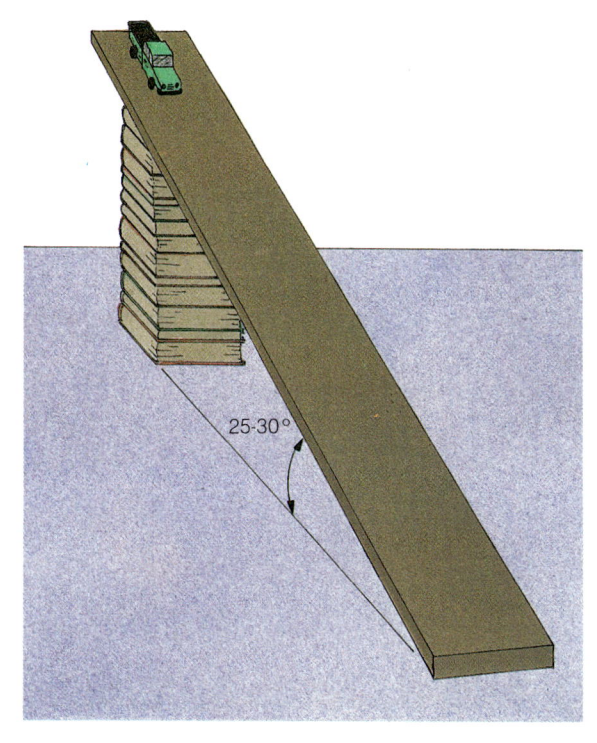
3. Measure the distance the truck traveled after it left the ramp. 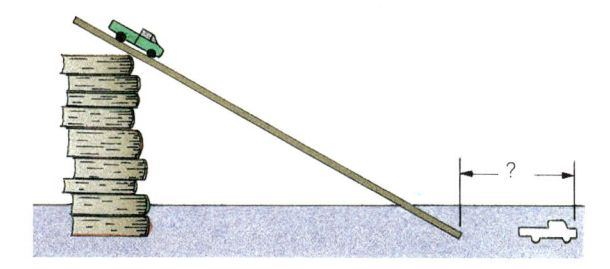
4. Put the 1/2-pound mass in the truck.
5. Predict whether the loaded truck will go farther or not as far.
6. Repeat steps 2 and 3. 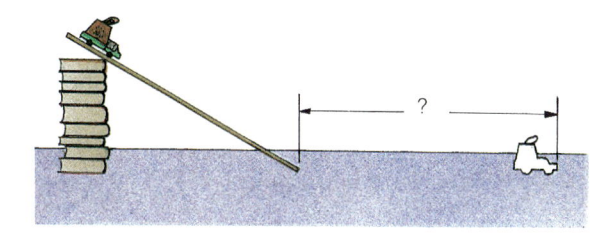
7. Was your prediction correct?
8. Repeat the test with the truck loaded with the 1-pound mass, then the 1/2-pound mass.
9. Look at your results and predict how far you think the truck would go if it were loaded with 1½ pounds.
10. Load the truck with 1½ pounds and test your prediction.
11. From your results, which generates more force: a family car traveling at 50 miles per hour, or a large, loaded truck traveling at the same speed?

TEST YOURSELF

1. What is speed?
2. What is the difference between maximum speed and average speed?
3. What is acceleration?

MATERIALS

The idea that all substances are made up of tiny units goes back more than 2,000 years, but it was not taken seriously until the early 1800s. At that time, the English scientist John Dalton based his atomic theory on the idea that all atoms of the same element, or substance, are exactly the same size and shape. Why is this so? Again we have to look at forces to provide us with an answer.

An atom is made up of a center, called the nucleus, and tiny particles that spin around the center, called electrons. Particles in the nucleus, called protons, have a positive charge and electrons have a negative charge. You found out (see page 16) how objects that have different charges attract each other. The force of attraction between the protons and the electrons gives the atom its fixed size and shape.

The atoms of different elements can combine, using the force of attraction, and form new material called compounds. When some compounds form, one becomes positively charged and the other becomes negatively charged. Because unlike charges attract each other, the two substances bond together to form a new material. If you look around you, most of the things you see are compounds. Some of them, such as water and table salt, are very simple compounds. Others, such as sugar and nylon, are far more complicated.

Some compounds such as sugar and salt, have a special property: they form crystals. These form when the atoms that make up the substance all bond together in a set pattern. In the case of salt, for instance, the pattern is always a cube. The crystal structure of some substances, such as diamond, makes them very hard and long-lasting.

Two materials that form crystals—fluorite **(bottom)** and diamond **(top)**.

Below A diagram of an atom.

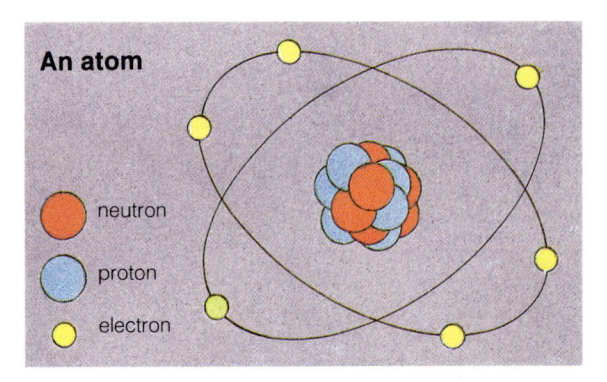

ACTIVITY
GROWING CRYSTALS

> **YOU NEED**
> - **a jam jar**
> - **warm water**
> - **alum (potassium aluminum sulfate)**
> - **a spoon**
> - **a pencil**
> - **nylon sewing thread**
> - **a piece of fine wire mesh or netting**

1. Half fill the jam jar with warm water.
2. Add small quantities of alum to the water and stir until no more will dissolve.

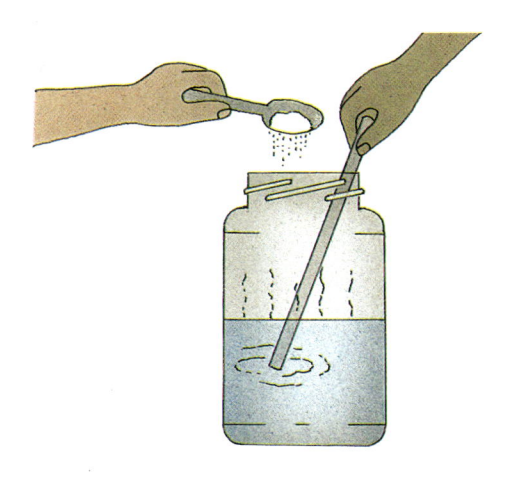

3. Allow the solution to get cold.
4. Select a small alum crystal and tie it to the pencil with a length of thread.

5. Place the pencil across the top of the jar. Adjust the thread until the crystal is suspended in the middle of the solution.

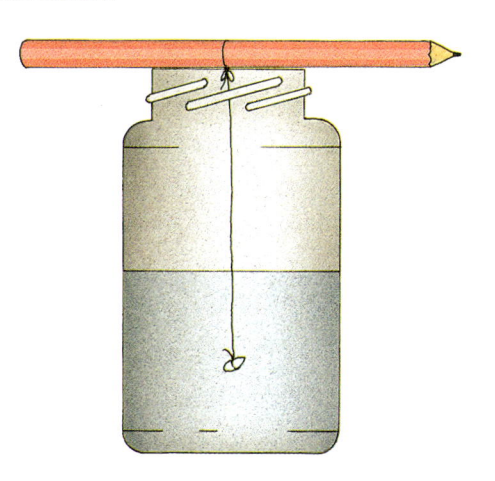

6. Cover the top of the jar with the wire mesh. Put the jar in a draft-free place that has an even temperature.

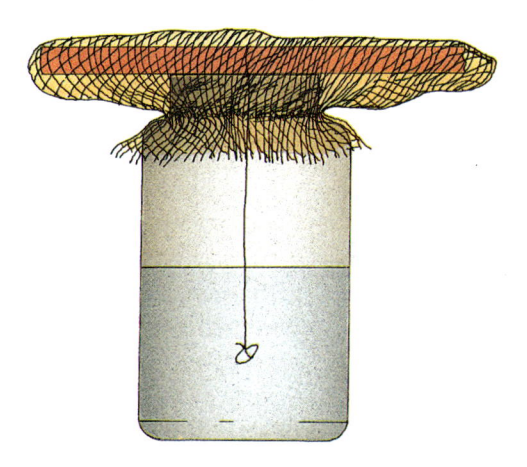

7. As the level of the solution drops, make more to add to it. The longer it is left, the larger the crystal will grow.

TEST YOURSELF

1. What is the center of an atom called?
2. What holds the components of a compound together?
3. Describe how you would grow a crystal.

MEASURING FORCE

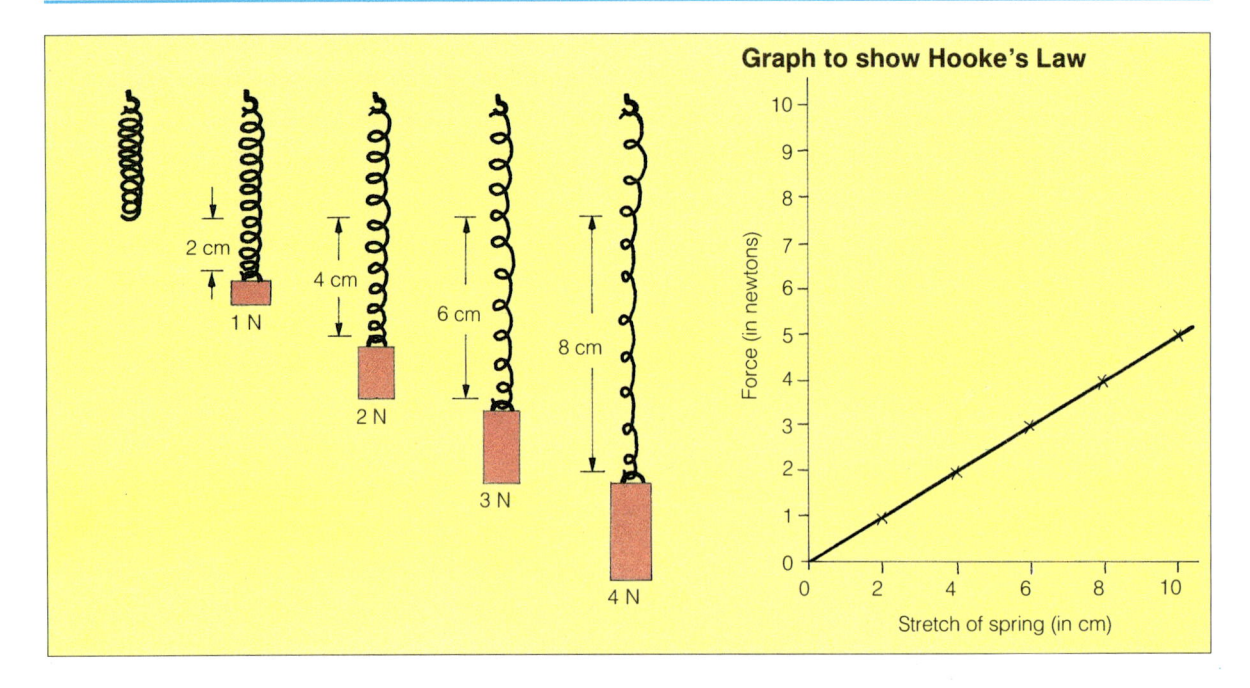

Graph to show Hooke's Law

The name of Sir Isaac Newton was chosen to represent the unit of force we all use. Force is measured in newtons, or N.

On Earth, gravity pulls on every 1 kg (2.2 pounds) of mass with a force of almost exactly 10 N. This means that gravity will exert a force of 10 N on a 1 kg bag of apples, or 600 N on a 60 kg person.

Instruments used to measure force in newtons are called spring scales. These are often very simple devices made up of a coiled spring and a scale. A scientist called Robert Hooke discovered that there is a link between the stretch of a spring and the force causing it. If, for instance, a 1 N force causes a spring to stretch 2 cm, then a 2 N force will cause a 4 cm stretch in the same spring. A 3 N force will cause a 6 cm stretch and so on. This rule, known as Hooke's Law, will continue to work as long as you do not overstretch the spring.

The rule also works if you squash the spring instead of stretching it. The common type of bathroom scale has a spring inside that compresses when you stand on it. The heavier a person, the more the spring compresses and the higher the reading. A bathroom scale can be used to measure other forces. Place the scale upright against a wall, lie flat on your back and push as hard as you can on the scale with your feet. The reading you get will be the force you are capable of exerting with your legs.

Two terms that people often confuse are weight and mass. It is important to remember that weight is a force related to the pull of gravity. Mass is related to the amount of material from which something is made. When someone says "I think it is time I went on a diet to lose weight," it really means he or she wants to lose mass. The only way to lose weight is to go to a place where the gravitational pull is not as strong as it is on Earth—a day trip to the moon, perhaps!

ACTIVITY

YOU NEED

- 2 pieces of softwood— 40 cm × 10 cm
- plain white paper
- double-sided cellophane tape
- a hammer
- small nails
- a 15-cm coil spring
- white correcting fluid
- different masses

1. Cover one side of one of the pieces of softwood with white paper, using the double-sided tape.
2. Hammer a nail into one end of the piece of wood until it holds firm.
3. Hook one end of the spring over the nail. 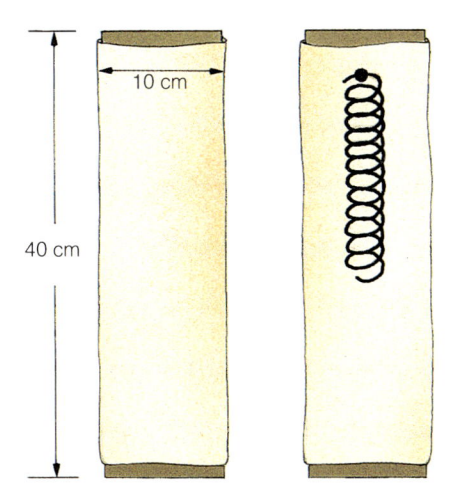
4. Attach the second piece of wood to form a base, so that the spring hangs freely when the apparatus is stood upright.
5. Use the white correcting fluid to make an easily visible mark on the bottom coil of the spring. Make a pencil mark on the paper opposite the white mark. Label it 0 N. 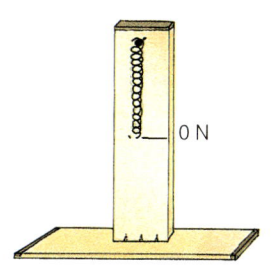
6. Hang a 100-g mass on the spring. Make a pencil mark opposite the white mark. Label it 1 N. 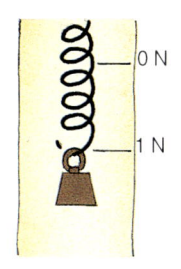
7. Repeat this with 200-g mass, but this time label it 2 N.
8. Continue increasing the mass 100 g at a time, and labeling appropriately, until the scale has reached 10 N.
9. Now use the spring scale you have made to find the weight exerted by some of the objects around you.

TEST YOURSELF

1. How much gravitational force does the Earth exert on 5-kg of potatoes?
2. What is weight?
3. What does Hooke's Law tell us about springs?

SURFACE TENSION

Insects called pond skaters use surface tension to skim across the surface of water.

Have you noticed that, when a tumbler is filled to the brim, the surface of the liquid is curved rather than flat? There appears to be a skin across the surface. What you are observing is the effect produced by a force called surface tension.

Surface tension is not a strong force, but it can be important. To some creatures, it is a way of life. Pond skaters are insects that skim across the surface of ponds and slow-moving rivers. Their light bodies and widespread legs prevent them from sinking through the surface tension.

Meniscus

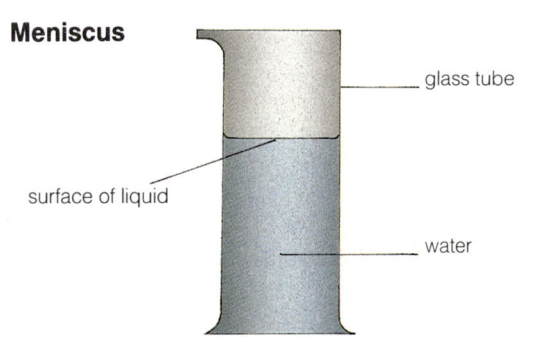

glass tube
surface of liquid
water

All the molecules in a liquid attract each other, and it is this attraction at the surface of a liquid that creates surface tension. When molecules of the same type attract each other in this way, they are said to be cohesive.

Molecules of a liquid may also be attracted to the molecules of a different substance. This type of attraction is called adhesion. Adhesives are substances that attract others with so much force that they are difficult to separate.

Cohesion and adhesion are often in conflict. In most cases, the adhesive forces are stronger. When you pour water into a flask or other glass container, the level always takes the shape of a curve called the meniscus. This is caused by adhesion between the water and the glass pulling at the edge of the water.

ACTIVITY

A BUBBLE BLOWER

YOU NEED

- a 6-inch piece of uncovered copper wire
- sewing thread
- dish-washing liquid
- 1/2 cup of warm water in a beaker or jar
- a sharp pencil

1. Pour enough dish-washing liquid into the water to make a strong solution.
2. Make a "bubble blower" by bending the copper wire into the shape of a letter P.

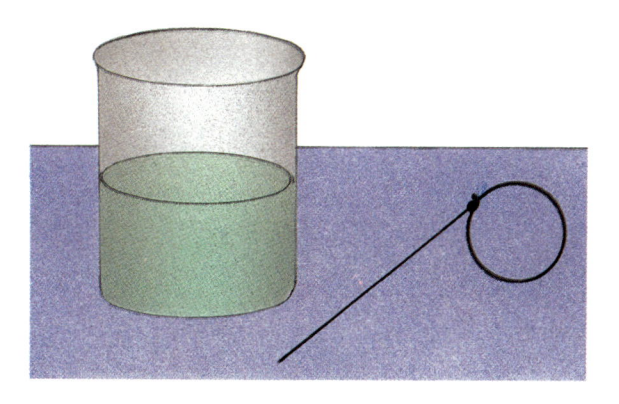

3. Tie a piece of sewing thread loosely across the middle of the bubble blower.

4. Dip the bubble blower into the dish-washing solution. Lift it out carefully so that the bubble does not burst.
5. Using the sharp pencil, burst the bubble at one side of the thread. What shape has the thread taken? What has caused the thread to react this way?

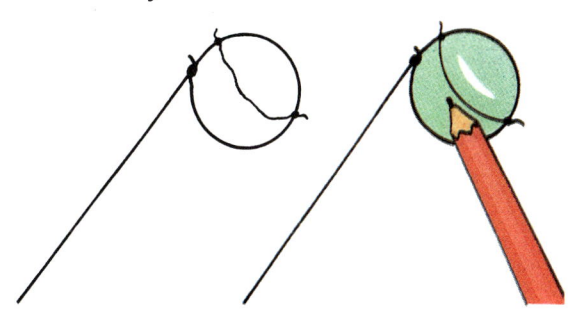

6. Wash the bubble blower and reposition the thread so that it forms a loop.

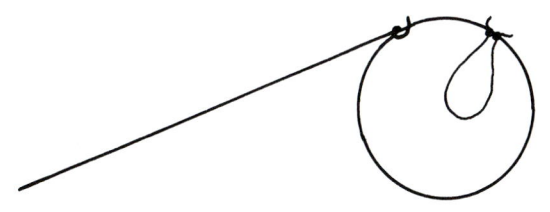

7. Place the bubble blower into the dish-washing solution and again lift it out carefully so the bubble does not burst.
8. Take the sharp pencil and burst the part of the bubble that is inside the loop. What shape has the thread taken up this time?

TEST YOURSELF

1. What causes the effect produced by surface tension?
2. What is adhesion?
3. Why is the liquid level in a flask always curved? What special name is given to this curve?

NATURE, THE BUILDER

*Spiders' webs (**left**) and honeycombs (**above**) are two of nature's most extraordinary feats of engineering. They are both able to withstand very strong forces.*

All living things are made from basic building blocks called cells. Very simple living things are made up of just one cell or several cells of the same type. But most living things are made up of many different types of cells. Very complex living things, such as humans, are made up of millions of cells of many different types, each with a particular job to do.

Have you ever wondered why there are no butterflies the size of eagles, or why spiders do not grow as large as elephants? One important reason has to do with the structure of the skeleton. Butterflies and spiders do not have a skeleton of bone inside their bodies. Instead, they are protected and supported by a hard covering called an exoskeleton. Humans and many other animals have an internal skeleton. This is much stronger and can support a much larger animal. Many of the bones of a human skeleton are hollow—this reduces weight and gives strength. Hollow bone is stronger than solid bone.

Trees are among the strongest of nature's structures. Some of them can withstand the weather for hundreds of years. One of the reasons for a tree's strength can be found around each cell. The cells are kept firmly in shape by a cell wall made of a substance called cellulose, as well as by the pressure of the sap inside. As the cells at the center of the tree get older, they die and form a hard, central column. This then acts as the tree's "backbone."

Nature has produced some wonderful engineers. Spiders construct delicate yet strong webs across wide spans, providing the building materials from within their own bodies. Bees build a honeycomb from what seems to be an impossible construction material—wax. A honeycomb is such a successful structure that it is capable of holding fifty times its own weight in honey. These are just two examples of nature's builders. There are many more that construct nests, dens, and burrows to very high engineering standards.

ACTIVITY

YOU NEED

- 2 hard-boiled eggs in shells
- a small triangular file
- a small knife
- a small spoon
- cellophane tape
- a 6-inch square of rigid board
- a selection of masses

1. Score around the center of both eggs, using the file.

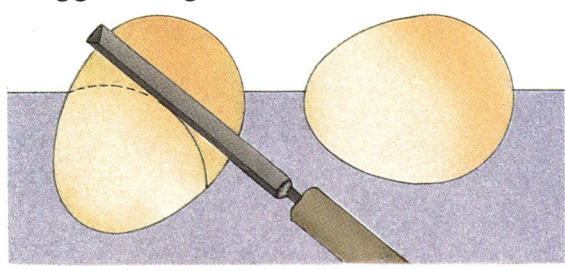

2. Cut the eggs in half, being careful to avoid cracking the shells.
3. Carefully scrape the eggs out of the shells.
4. Strengthen the cut edges of the shells with cellophane tape. 
5. Place the shells round side up on the table and place the board on top. Estimate what force you think the eggshells will be able to withstand. 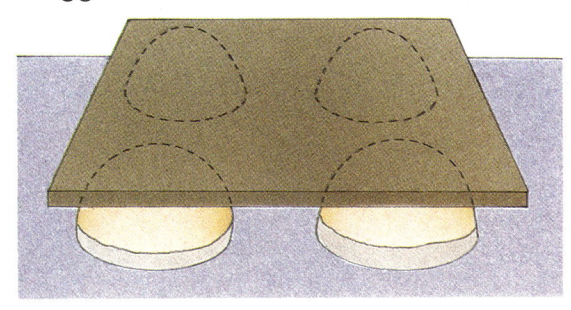
6. Starting with the smallest one, place the masses on the board so that the weight pressing on the eggshells gradually increases.
7. How much force did the eggshells withstand before they broke? How accurate was your estimate? 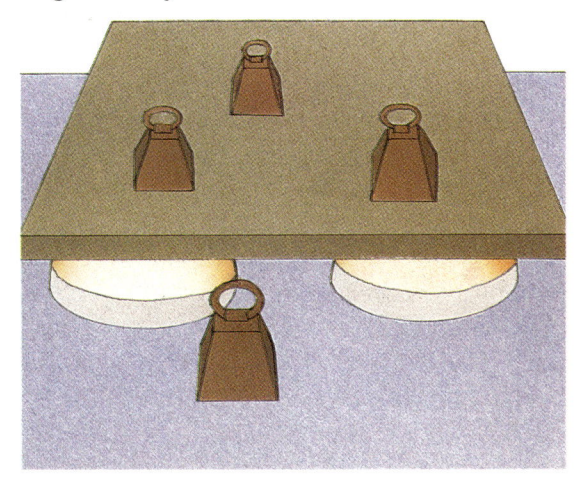

TEST YOURSELF

1. What is the name of the basic units from which all living things are made?
2. What type of skeleton does a spider have?
3. From what material is the cell wall of a plant made?

ACROSS THE GAP

Since very early times, humans have used beams to span gaps and to give strength to buildings. These beams were originally very simple, such as fallen trees. Today, beam technology is much more complex.

Many load-carrying beams are not solid, but hollow, shaped like a letter I. This makes them lighter and cheaper, but are they as strong? When a load is applied to a beam it bends, even though this may not always be easy to see. As it bends, the top of the beam is compressed and the bottom is put under tension. However, the middle section is unaffected, so removing it does not reduce the strength of the beam.

The strength of a beam also depends on the material from which it is made. When a concrete beam bends under a load, the lower surface becomes weaker. This is because concrete is not as strong under tension as it is under compression. To compensate for this, the lower surfaces of concrete beams are often reinforced (strengthened) with steel rods, because steel is strong under tension.

Early beam bridges were made from fallen trees or large flat stones. In this type of bridge, the load is taken by the foundations and support pillars. Modern beam bridges are made from box girders or reinforced concrete.

An arch bridge needs strong supports at its ends because this is where most of the force acts. Arch bridges made from stone and brick have to be built over a temporary framework, which limits the length of span that can be constructed. Modern arch bridges are made of steel and have much longer spans.

Cantilevers have beams resting on structures that act like huge shelf brackets. Basically, the forces pushing down on the central span are balanced by those pushing down on the "bracket" ends.

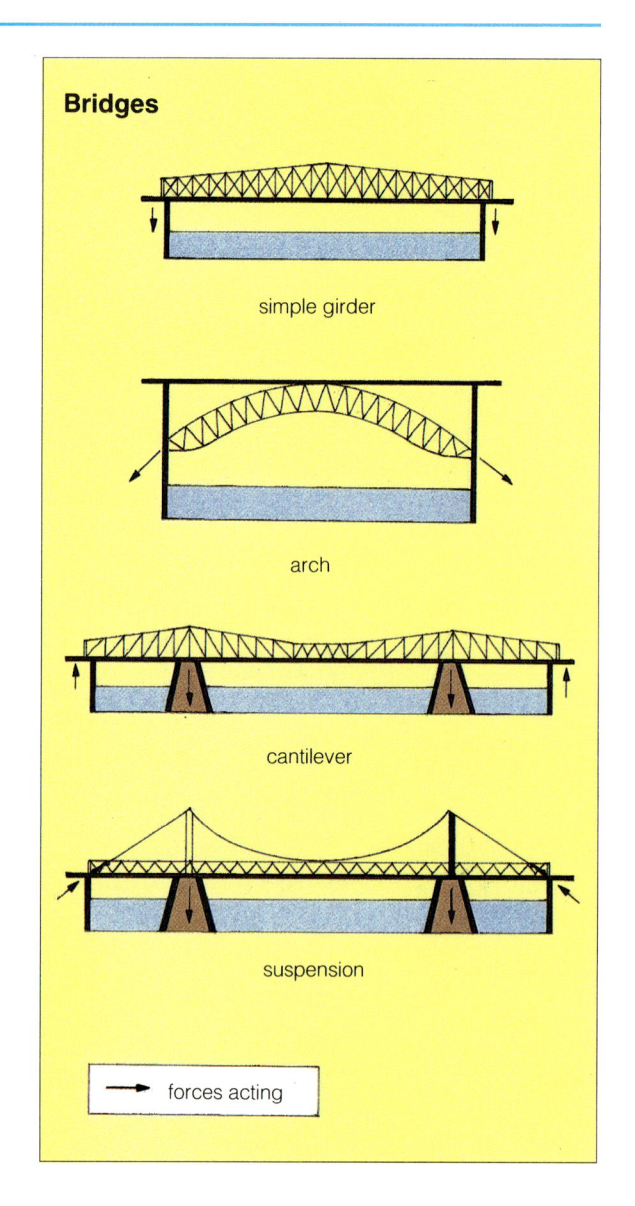

Today, large gaps such as river estuaries are spanned by suspension bridges. Here, the roadway is suspended from cables supported by two towers and anchored into the bank at either end. The tension in the cables balances the force produced by the load.

Bridges

simple girder

arch

cantilever

suspension

→ forces acting

ACTIVITY

YOU NEED

- a yardstick
- 3 rulers
- a selection of masses
- a small toy car

1. Place two tables 2 feet apart.
2. Place two of the rulers facing each other across the space between the tables, with a 4-inch gap between them. Place a small mass on the end of each ruler to hold it in place.
3. Place a third ruler across the gap between the other two. If the bridge is unstable, increase the support masses at either end.
4. Place the toy car in the middle of the bridge. Increase the support masses until the bridge holds.
5. Look carefully at the structure you have made. It is a cantilever bridge. Try to work out how all the forces involved are acting to support the structure.

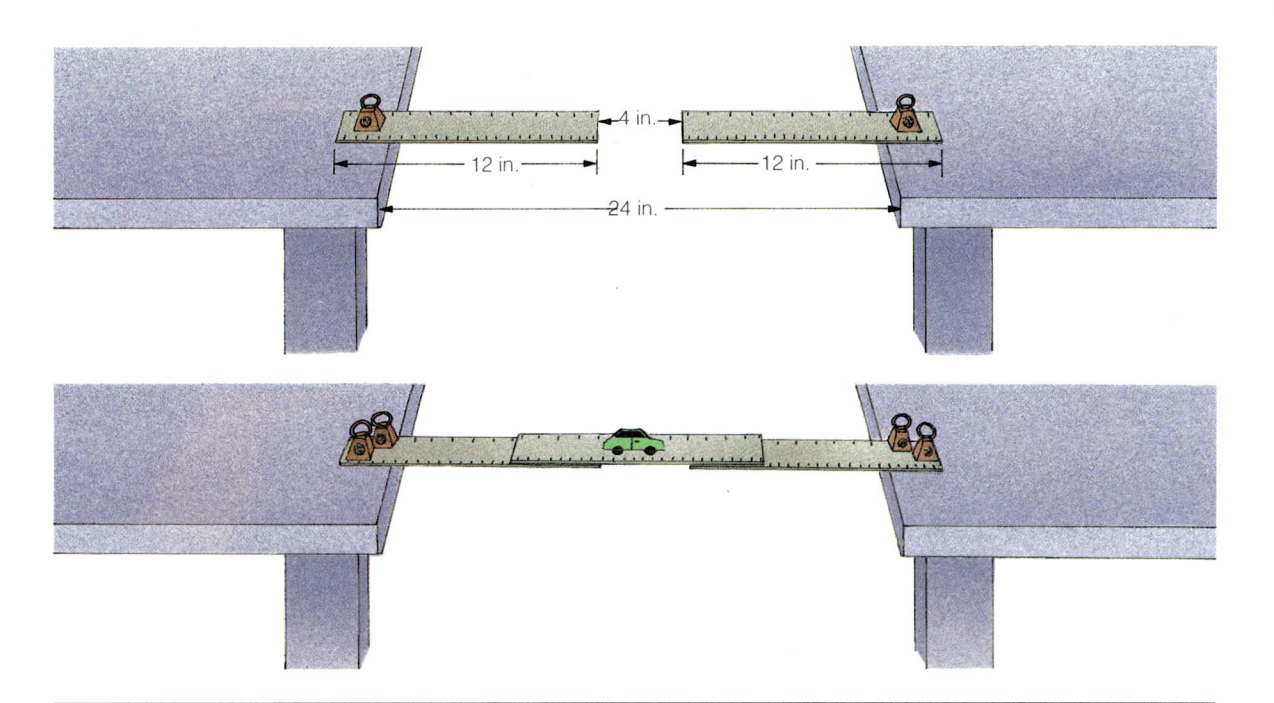

TEST YOURSELF

1. Why is an I-shaped beam as strong as a solid beam of the same material?
2. What is reinforced concrete?
3. Name the four types of bridge construction.

MAKING THINGS EASY

Some machines are very complex. Others are much simpler. Levers are among the simplest but most reliable and effective of all machines. Scissors, hammers, wheelbarrows, and tweezers are all examples of levers in everyday use.

All levers have the same three features: a place where the load is applied, a place where the effort is applied, and a pivot point. The load is whatever needs to be moved by the lever. The effort is the force that is being applied to the lever. The pivot point, or fulcrum, is the point around which the lever turns. The type of lever depends on the positions of these three features. For example, if you want to remove the lid from a can of paint, a long screwdriver will be easier than a short one.

There is an old saying that applies to machines as well as to other things: "You only get out what you put in." However, this may not seem to be the case with levers. If using a lever enables you to get out more force than is put in, something else must be lost. Remember that a lever is a machine and machines do work. The work the screwdriver was doing did not just involve force, but also the distances moved. At the load end, the force applied was large but the distance moved was small, whereas at the effort end, the force applied was small but the distance moved was large. The result is that the amount of work done at both ends was the same.

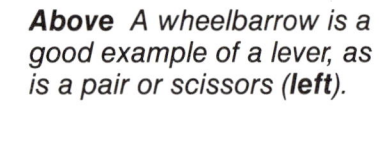

Above *A wheelbarrow is a good example of a lever, as is a pair or scissors* **(left)**.

ACTIVITY

YOU NEED

- assorted masses up to 1 kg
- a rigid strip of wood with a hole drilled in one end
- a triangular block of wood
- a spring scale
- small nails

1. Place a 1-kg mass at the undrilled end of the rigid strip of wood. The 1-kg mass will be exerting a force of 10 N. This is the load.

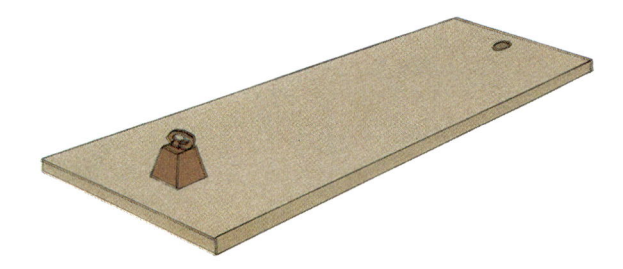

2. Use the triangular block of wood as a fulcrum by sliding it under the strip as close to the 1-kg mass as it will go.

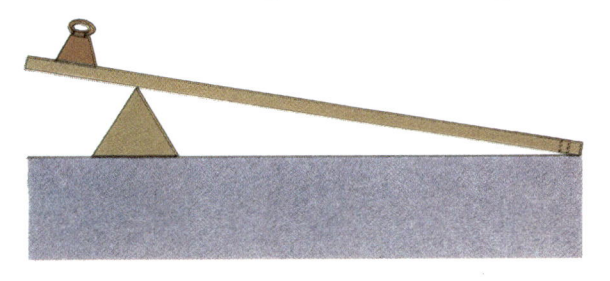

3. Hook the spring scale through the hole in the other end of the strip of wood. Pull until the 1-kg mass begins to move. This is the effort.

4. How much effort was needed to overcome the load? Did you use more, or less, effort with the lever?

5. Repeat the investigation, using different-sized masses as the load. Look at the results carefully. What do you observe?

TEST YOURSELF

1. Give three examples of everyday levers.
2. What are the three components of a lever?
3. Explain why, with a lever, "you only get out what you put in."

41

UNDER PRESSURE

Left *Knife blades, used for cutting, are very thin. The force created by the person who is cutting is concentrated over a very small area, so the pressure is very high.*

Below *This boy sucks his drink up the straw by creating pressure with his tongue.*

At the entrance to some buildings, you used to find notices asking people not to enter wearing stiletto-shoes. Obviously, the owners feared that this type of heel would damage the floor. To understand why, we need to look at the forces that are being exerted and the area over which they act. Stiletto heels are very thin, so the total weight of the person is concentrated over a very small area. If the same person were wearing flat-soled shoes, the force would be spread over a much larger area and therefore less likely to cause damage.

This relationship between a force and its area of action is called pressure. The same force can produce different pressures, as we have seen from the example above.

The amount of pressure is calculated by dividing the force by the area over which it acts. The standard unit of pressure is the pascal (Pa), named after the French scientist Blaise Pascal. To calculate any pressure in pascal units, you divide the force in newtons by the area in square meters.

All substances have weight, so they exert pressure. In liquids, the pressure increases with depth because, as you go deeper, the amount of water pressing down increases. This is why dam walls are thicker at the bottom than they are at the top.

Pressure is also created by the air that surrounds us. This is called atmospheric pressure and it averages 100,000 Pa at sea level. Variations in atmospheric pressure influence the weather and that is why they are of interest to weather forecasters.

ACTIVITY

> **YOU NEED**
> - **a bathroom scale**
> - **a piece of cm-squared paper**
> - **a pencil**

1 Weigh yourself in newtons (1 kg = 10 N).

2 Remove your shoes. Place both feet on the squared paper and carefully draw around them with a pencil.

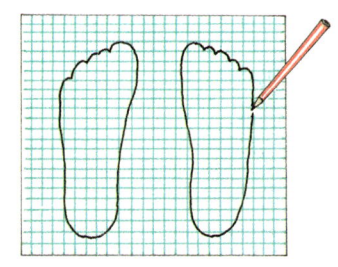

3 Shade in the shape of your feet.

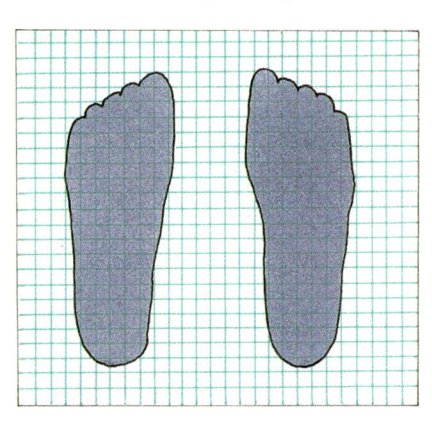

4 Count the squares to find the area covered by your feet. Any squares that are less than half-shaded should be ignored and any that are half or more should be counted as whole.

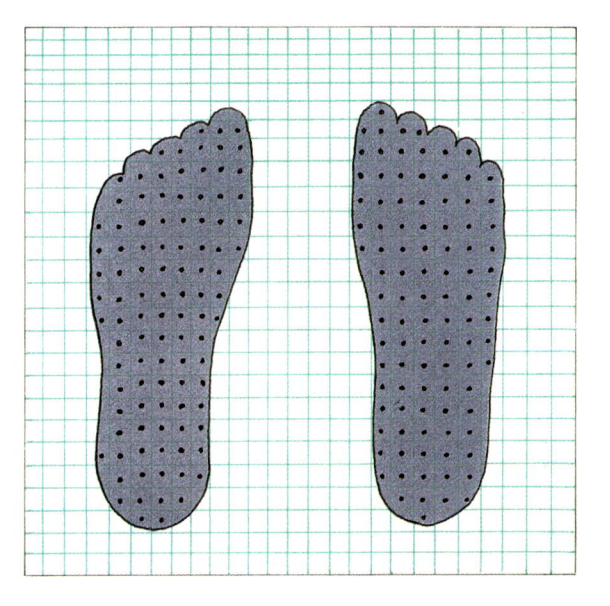

5 You now have the information needed to calculate how much pressure your body is exerting when you are standing upright. The formula to use is:

$$\text{pressure} = \frac{\text{weight in newtons} \times 10{,}000}{\text{area in sq cm}}$$

(the 10,000 is used to convert sq cm into sq m)

6 Now find out how much pressure you exert on a chair when you sit on it?

> **TEST YOURSELF**
> 1. Why are stiletto heels likely to cause more damage to a floor than flat soles?
> 2. What is the relationship between force, area, and pressure, and what is the standard unit of pressure?
> 3. Why does a dam wall have to be thicker at the bottom than at the top?

BRICKS AND MORTAR

Left *Limestone is quarried so that it can be used to make cement.*

Below *Diagrams showing different types of brick bonding.*

When traveling through the countryside, you may come across a place where a hillside has been cut away to expose white rock. This is a limestone quarry, and the material being removed will be made into an important building material—cement.

When cement is mixed with sand and water and left to dry, it undergoes a chemical change. It changes from a soft powder into a hard, rocklike substance with excellent bonding (sticking) properties. This is the mortar that is used to bind bricks and stones together into strong walls. Small stones added at the mixing stage make concrete. This is even stronger than cement mix. The strength of concrete comes from the crystals that form as the chemical change takes place.

Concrete is used to make a building's foundations. But why does the building need a foundation? If you take a ruler and push one end of it into sand, it goes in quite easily. However, if you try to push it in flat, it is far more difficult because the force created by the ruler is spread over a much greater area (see page 42). Foundations spread the force created by the building and prevent it from sinking.

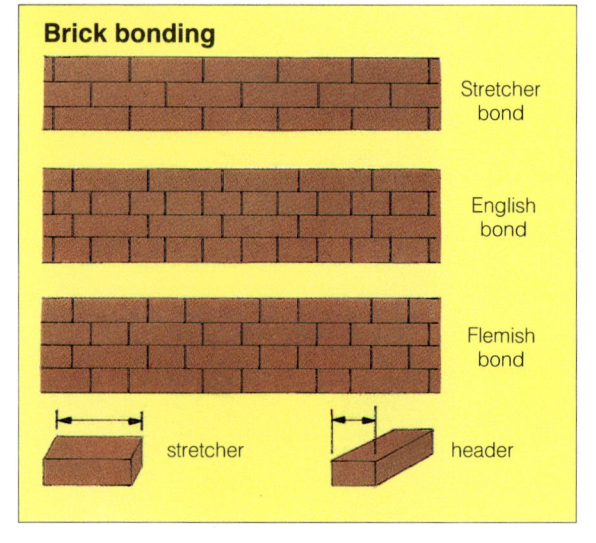

Brick bonding

Stretcher bond

English bond

Flemish bond

stretcher   header

When constructing a wall, a bricklayer will build a layer at a time so that the stones or bricks overlap each other. This is called bonding and prevents vertical lines of weakness from occurring in the wall. Bricks are a regular shape and particular patterns of bonding are used for particular situations. In the most common pattern, the bricks are laid with an overlap of exactly half their length. This is called the stretcher bond, but others, such as the English and Flemish bonds, are often used.

ACTIVITY
TESTING CONCRETE BEAMS

YOU NEED

- a mixing board
- an old egg cup
- cement
- sand
- fine gravel
- 4 molds (12" × 1" × 1")
- water
- thick string
- a safety mat
- assorted masses

1 Using the egg cup as a measure, make enough concrete mixture of 1 part cement to 2 parts sand to 3 parts gravel, to overfill a mold.
2 Add water to the concrete mixture, mix thoroughly, and pour into the mold. 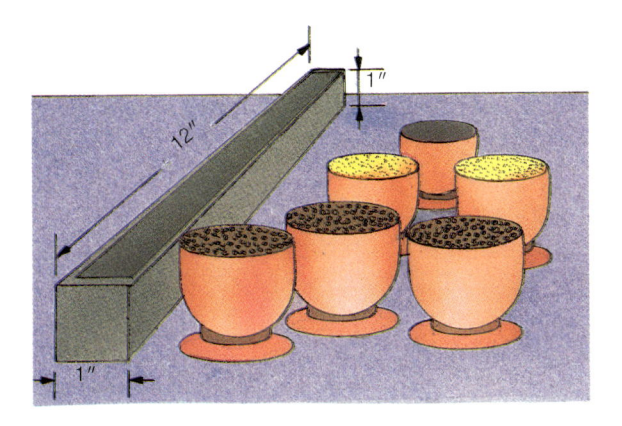
3 Fill the other three molds in a similar way, but use the following mixtures:
   - 1 cement / 4 sand / 8 gravel
   - 1 cement / 8 sand / 4 gravel
   - 3 cement / 2 sand / 1 gravel
4 Allow the mixtures to set hard and then remove the concrete beams.
5 Place 2 tables parallel to each other, 8 inches apart.
6 Make a strong harness, using several loops of thick string. Thread it onto one of the beams. 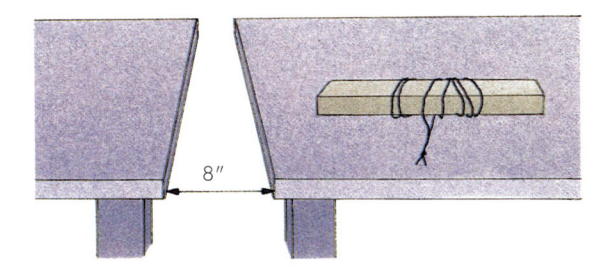
7 Position the beam across the gap and protect the floor with the safety mat.
8 Hang masses from the harness to increase the force exerted on the beam gradually until it breaks. 
9 Test the other three beams in the same way to find out which concrete mixture produced the strongest beam.

TEST YOURSELF

1. Why is limestone so important to the building industry?
2. What is the difference between mortar and concrete?
3. How does a bricklayer bond a wall?

Glossary

Ailerons   Wing flaps that enable a pilot to bank an aircraft in a turn.
Atmosphere   The layer of gases that surrounds the Earth. It is held in place by gravity.
Attract   To pull together.
Box girder   A hollow steel beam with a square or rectangular cross section.
Braking distance   The distance traveled by a vehicle between the application of the brakes and the vehicle stopping.
Buoyant force   The pushing force produced by a liquid or gas when an object is put into it. This force enables some things to float in water.
Cantilever   A support structure that is anchored at only one end. A shelf bracket is a simple cantilever.
Cellulose   A substance, made by plants, that forms a wall around all plant cells.
Coil spring   A piece of spring steel wound into a spiral shape.
Compound   A substance made by chemically combining two or more different elements. Water, table salt, and rust are examples of compounds.
Compression   A pushing force that tends to squash things.
Displacement   The amount of liquid or gas pushed out of the way when an object is put into it.
Efficiency   A measure of how well something works.
Element   A substance in which all the atoms are exactly alike: for example, iron, oxygen, or carbon.
Elevator   A device that enables something to be lifted. On an aircraft, the elevators are flaps on the tail that the pilot can use to make it climb or descend.
Exoskeleton   A skeleton on the outside of the body. This is not usually made of bone, but of shell-like material. The beetle has an exoskeleton.
Hull   The body of a ship or boat.
Hydraulic mechanism   A device that is operated by liquids.
Inflate   To fill with gas (usually air).
Law of Gravity   This was first realized by Sir Isaac Newton. Very simply, it states that all bodies (objects) with mass attract each other.
Lodestone   A magnetic rock with a high iron content.
Lubricant   A substance that reduces the friction between moving parts.
Mass   The amount of material that makes up a body, object, or substance.
Matter   The materials that make up all known substances. These include air, water, living materials, dead materials, stone, metals, glass, and plastics.
Meteor   A piece of rock that travels through space until it falls within the gravitational field of a star or planet.
Molecule   The smallest part of a substance that can exist on its own. All substances, living and nonliving, are made up of molecules.
Orbit   The curved path followed by one object in space (e.g., a planet or satellite) around another, larger object.
Particle   A very small piece of a substance.
Pivot   A turning point.
Principle   The idea that explains how something works or why it happens.
Repel   To push away.
Sap   The liquid part of a plant.
Solution   A solid or gas dissolved in a liquid.
Spring scale   A device for measuring force in units called newtons.

Stability The ability to stay in one place and not fall over.
Statistic A fact or measurement given as a number or set of figures.
Stiletto Long and thin; often used to describe the high heel on ladies' fashion shoes.
Suspended Hanging.
Tension A pulling force that tends to stretch things out.
Unit A quantity used for the purpose of measurement. For example, one of the units of mass is the kilogram.
Vertical Standing upright.

Books to Read

Electricity and Magnetism, Gregory Vogt (Watts, 1985)
Exploring Electricity, Ed Catherall (Steck-Vaughn, 1990)
Isaac Newton: Reluctant Genius, David C. Ipsen (Enslow, 1985)
Machines and How They Work, Harvey Weiss (Harper/Collins, 1983)
Magnets, Laurence Santrey (Troll, 1985)
Movement, Brenda Walpole (Watts, 1987)
Understanding Energy, Neil Ardley (Silver Burdett, 1986)
Understanding Movement, Ralph Hancock (Silver Burdett, 1985)
Understanding Structures and Materials, Robin Kerrod (Silver Burdett, 1986)

Picture Acknowledgments

The author and publishers would like to thank the following for allowing the illustrations to be reproduced in this book: Eye Ubiquitous 20 (above), 40 (below); Geoscience Features 44; Oxford Scientific Films 34; Topham 40 (above); Wayland Picture Library 6; Tim Woodcock 20; ZEFA *cover (both), frontispiece,* 8, 10, 12, 14, 16, 22, 24, 26, 28, 30, 36, 42. All artwork is by Marilyn Clay.

Index

Acceleration 28, 29
Adhesion 34, 35
Airfoil 26
Aircraft 24, 26
Aristotle 6
Atmospheric pressure 42
Atomic theory 30
Atoms 16, 30, 31
Attraction 14, 16, 30

Balance 12, 20, 21
Ball bearings 22
Beams 38, 45
Bicycle 6, 22, 28
Bonding 44
Brakes 6
Bricks 38, 44
Bridges 38-39
Buoyant force 12, 13

Cantilevers 38
Cells 36
Cement 44, 45
Center of gravity 20, 21
Cohesion 34
Compass 8, 14, 15
Compounds 30, 31
Compression 8, 38
Concrete 44, 45
Crystals 30, 31, 44

Dalton, John 30
Diamond 30
Displacement 12, 13
"Drag" 24, 26

Effort 40-41
Electricity 16
Electrons 30
Electrostatic force 8, 9, 16-17
Engines 10
Equal-arm balance 20

Flight 26, 27
Floating 12-13
Foundations 44
Friction 8, 10, 22-23, 24, 26

Gravity 6, 8, 10, 18-19, 20, 22, 24, 26, 32

Hooke, Robert 32
Hooke's Law 32, 33
Hydraulic ram 6
Hydrofoils 24

Jet engines 26, 27

Laws of Motion 6, 7, 10, 11
Levers 40-41
"Lift" 26
Limestone 44
Load 38, 40-41
Lodestone 14
Lubrication 22

Machine 22, 40
Magnetism 8, 14-15
Mass 20, 32
Matter 10
Meniscus 34
Molecules 34
Mortar 44, 45
Motors 10

Newton, Sir Isaac 6, 10, 11, 32
Nucleus 30

Parachutes 24, 25
Pascal, Blaise 42
Pivot point 20, 40
Poles (of magnets) 14, 15, 16
Pressure 42, 43
Protons 30

Reinforced concrete 38, 39
Repulsion 14, 16
Resistance 24-25

Scales 32, 43
Sinking 12-13
Skeleton 36, 37
Speed 6, 10, 28-29
Spring scale 13, 32, 33, 41
Stability 20
Static electricity 8, 16, 17
Streamlining 24, 25
Strength 36, 38
Surface tension 34-35

Tension 38
Tread 22
Turning forces 20

Weight 20, 32, 33, 36, 37, 42

First published in 1990 by Wayland (Publishers) Ltd.
© Copyright 1990 Wayland (Publishers) Ltd

PUBLIC FINANCE

Theory and Practice

PUBLIC FINANCE
Theory and Practice

Michael L. Marlow

The Dryden Press
Harcourt Brace College Publishers

Fort Worth   Philadelphia   San Diego   New York   Orlando   Austin   San Antonio
Toronto   Montreal   London   Sydney   Tokyo

Senior Acquisitions Editor	Rick Hammonds
Senior Developmental Editor	Daryl Fox
Project Editors	Emily Thompson, Amy Schmidt
Art Director	Jeanette Barber
Production Manager	Kelly Cordes
Product Manager	Craig Johnson
Director of Editing, Design & Production	Diane Southworth
Publisher	Elizabeth Widdicombe
Copy Editor	Wanda Giles
Indexer	Sylvia Coates
Compositor	Monotype
Text Type	10/12 Times Roman

Cover Image: "American Flag Concept," M-144; Liaison International © Sandra Baker

Copyright © 1995 by Harcourt Brace & Company

All rights reserved. No part of this publication may be reproduced or transmitted in any form or by any means, electronic or mechanical, including photocopy, recording, or any information storage and retrieval system, without permission in writing from the publisher.

Requests for permission to make copies of any part of the work should be mailed to: Permissions Department, Harcourt Brace & Company, 6277 Sea Harbor Drive, Orlando, FL 32887-6777.

Address for Editorial Correspondence:
The Dryden Press, 301 Commerce Street, Suite 3700, Fort Worth, TX 76102

Address for Orders:
The Dryden Press, 6277 Sea Harbor Drive, Orlando, FL 32887
1-800-782-4479, or 1-800-433-0001 (in Florida)

ISBN: 0-03-096960-3

Library of Congress Catalog Card Number: 94-72113

Printed in the United States of America

4 5 6 7 8 9 0 1 2 3   039   9 8 7 6 5 4 3 2 1

The Dryden Press
Harcourt Brace College Publishers

To Valerie and Emily Chase

The Dryden Press Series in Economics

Asch and Seneca
Government and the Marketplace
Second Edition

Baumol and Blinder
Economics: Principles and Policy
Sixth Edition (also available in micro and macro paperbacks)

Baumol, Panzar, and Willig
Contestable Markets and the Theory of Industry Structure
Revised Edition

Berch
The Endless Day: The Political Economy of Women and Work

Breit and Elzinga
The Antitrust Casebook: Milestones in Economic Regulation
Second Edition

Brue
The Evolution of Economic Thought
Fifth Edition

Demmert
Economics: Understanding the Market Process

Dolan and Lindsey
Economics
Seventh Edition (also available in micro and macro paperbacks)

Edgmand, Moomaw, and Olson
Economics and Contemporary Issues
Second Edition

Gardner
Comparative Economic Systems

Glahe
Microeconomics: Theory and Application
Second Edition

Green
Macroeconomics: Analysis and Applications

Gwartney and Stroup
Economics: Private and Public Choice
Seventh Edition (also available in micro and macro paperbacks)

Gwartney and Stroup
Introduction to Economics: The Wealth and Poverty of Nations

Heilbroner and Singer
The Economic Transformation of America: 1600 to the Present
Second Edition

Hirschey and Pappas
Fundamentals of Managerial Economics
Fifth Edition

Hirschey and Pappas
Managerial Economics
Seventh Edition

Hyman
Public Finance: A Contemporary Application of Theory to Policy
Fourth Edition

Kahn
The Economic Approach to the Environment and Natural Resources

Kaserman and Mayo
Government and Business: The Economics of Antitrust and Regulation

Kaufman
The Economics of Labor Markets
Fourth Edition

Kennett and Lieberman
The Road to Capitalism: The Economic Transformation of Eastern Europe and the Former Soviet Union

Kidwell, Peterson, and Blackwell
Financial Institutions, Markets, and Money
Fifth Edition

Kreinin
International Economics: A Policy Approach
Seventh Edition

Lott and Ray
Applied Econometrics with Data Sets

Marlow
Public Finance: Theory and Practice

Nicholson
Intermediate Microeconomics and Its Application
Sixth Edition

Nicholson
Microeconomic Theory: Basic Principles and Extensions
Sixth Edition

Puth
American Economic History
Third Edition

Ragan and Thomas
Principles of Economics
Second Edition (also available in micro and macro paperbacks)

Ramanathan
Introductory Econometrics with Applications
Third Edition

Rukstad
Corporate Decision Making in the World Economy: Company Case Studies

Rukstad
Macroeconomic Decision Making in the World Economy: Text and Cases
Fourth Edition

Samuelson and Marks
Managerial Economics
Second Edition

Scarth
Macroeconomics: An Introduction to Advanced Methods
Third Edition

Thomas
Economics: Principles and Applications
(also available in micro and macro paperbacks)

Wachtel
Labor and the Economy
Third Edition

Walton and Rockoff
History of the American Economy
Seventh Edition

Welch and Welch
Economics: Theory and Practice
Fifth Edition

Yarbrough and Yarbrough
The World Economy: Trade and Finance
Third Edition

Preface

Public Finance: Theory and Practice thoroughly examines how the public sector influences the allocation of our scarce resources. Not only has the public sector undergone considerable change in this century, it has also expanded dramatically, thereby underscoring the importance of the study of public finance. This textbook develops the fundamental principles of public finance as well as common and not-so-common public finance practices.

Public Finance: Theory and Practice makes many improvements to the study of public finance. First and foremost, it integrates the roles played by voters and policymakers. Voters and policymakers determine public policies, and their roles are the subject of what is commonly referred to as *public choice analysis*. Most other textbooks do not successfully convey the importance of public choice analysis, relegating the topic to one or two short chapters. Unfortunately, this approach may leave students with the mistaken impression that public choice lends little insight to the study of public finance.

Additionally, *Public Finance: Theory and Practice* awards full coverage to the microeconomic analysis of expenditure and tax policies. Several chapters are devoted to transfer programs and social insurance policies, and the textbook also contains separate chapters on health care policy and off-budget policy, as well as a detailed analysis of how the budgetary process influences public expenditures. The chapter devoted entirely to health care policy is clearly warranted by the rapidly growing interest in this policy area. Off-budget credit and insurance policies also deserve a separate chapter because, unless we can completely account for what government does, we may miss many of the allocative and distributive effects of its policies.

Tax policies receive full and current coverage as well. Two chapters examine the theory of tax principles, and four chapters are devoted to taxation and the economic effects of taxation on behavior. A complete chapter on the economics of budget deficits is also included—the vast majority of our students have never experienced a federal budget that was in anything other than a deficit. The coverage extends to important issues surrounding the economic effects of deficits, the causal relationships between spending and taxes, and concerns over whether tax increases do, in fact, lead to higher tax revenues.

Public Finance: Theory and Practice is very strong on historical detail. Numerous graphs display and document the history of spending and tax trends in the United States and other countries. Liberal use of historical charts demonstrates for students how the practice of public finance has changed over time and also provides them with important benchmarks with which to analyze the important policy issues of today. This inclusion contrasts with most other textbooks, which tend to provide the entire history of public programs in an introductory chapter. An initial summary of our country's public programs is provided in Chapter 2 of *Public Finance: Theory and Practice*, but I have found that students gain a greater appreciation of the integration of the economic theory with its practical application when historical analyses are included in later chapters presenting the economic theory behind spending and tax programs.

An understanding of our past also helps us appreciate the overall growth of government—an unmistakable trend in the United States as well as most other industrialized economies. An historical approach utilizes the burgeoning literature on public-sector expansion theories and contributes to an overall understanding of the ever-present policy discussions focusing on whether the public sector tends to expand too much or too little—an issue that has always been fundamental to the study of public finance.

One of the greatest challenges is to write a textbook that carefully and objectively examines the many viewpoints of public finance economists. The multifacetedness of the issues is the very reason why economists find public finance so fascinating and so challenging. Students are drawn to the study of public finance for the very same reasons. My teaching experience also indicates that there is no better way to excite students about the relevance and usefulness of economic theory than to show them its application. This is justification enough for balancing the theory of public finance with its practice.

Structure of the Book

Public Finance: Theory and Practice is divided into seven parts. Part 1 contains two introductory chapters. The subject matter of public finance is introduced in Chapter 1. Chapter 2 summarizes the spending, tax, employment, credit, insurance, legislative, and regulatory policies of the public sector.

Part 2 examines the traditional functions of government policy and therefore focuses on issues relating to efficiency and equity. A framework for analyzing the fundamental differences between private and public resource allocation is presented in Chapter 3. For those instructors who emphasize analysis at the level of intermediate theory, an appendix to Chapter 3 thoroughly discusses efficiency in exchange and production within private markets. Economic analyses of externalities and public goods are provided in Chapters 4 and 5, respectively.

Part 3 examines how the policy process results in public policies, and it introduces public choice analysis. Chapter 6 outlines the roles of voters and policymakers and the institutions within which they interact. Models of voting and an examination of public market structure are discussed in Chapter 7. A demand and supply model of government policy is developed in Chapter 8 and is used to address the important issues related to the size and the growth of the public sector.

Part 4 analyzes the expenditure aspect of public budgets. Chapter 9 examines the allocative and distributive effects of spending policies and discusses how the budgetary process influences public spending. The allocative and distributive effects of credit and insurance off-budget programs are the subject of Chapter 10. Transfer programs for the poor are analyzed in Chapter 11. Chapter 12 discusses social insurance programs (Social Security, Medicare, and unemployment compensation), and Chapter 13 is devoted to health care policy. A thorough discussion of cost-benefit analysis is provided in Chapter 14.

Part 5 introduces the tax and deficit aspects of the public budget. Chapter 15 examines the major alternative principles (benefit versus ability-to-pay) behind the tax policies and examines their influences on resource allocation and income distribution. The economic theories of tax incidence and excess burden are the subject of Chapter 16, and budget deficits are discussed in Chapter 17.

Part 6 presents the practice of taxation as well as its economic effects on behavior. Chapter 18 examines personal income taxation, and its economic effects are the subject of Chapter 19. Chapter 20 studies the corporation tax. The practice and economic effects of taxation of consumption and wealth are developed in Chapter 21.

Part 7, completes with Chapter 22, the study of public finance with an analysis of our federal system of government. How fiscal structures affect the interplay between voters and policymakers is emphasized as an important policy issue.

An appendix to the book provides a refresher course for those students who have already completed an intermediate microeconomic theory course or the appendix can serve as an introduction to intermediate theory for those who have had only a principles course.

Public Finance: Theory and Practice is written at a level that is appropriate for undergraduate- and master-course levels in public finance and for the graduate course level in public administration. Its organization is purposely flexible and therefore easily adaptable to many different courses. Students who have taken an intermediate microeconomics theory course will have studied the primary theoretical tools used in this book. Students who have taken only a principles course in microeconomics will also be able to understand the vast majority of theory developed in the book. For those who have not studied indifference curves and budget constraints, the appendix on microeconomic theory is sufficient for their understanding of the material throughout the textbook.

The table of contents reflects the sequence of topics that I normally present in my public finance course. I fully expect that some professors prefer another sequence; there should be no difficulty in rearranging the chapters into the preferred sequence. The most common difference in approaches involves whether or not to study the expenditure side of the public sector (Chapters 9–14) before studying the tax side (Chapters 15–21). Either approach may easily be taken using this book. Chapters are self-contained and can be easily omitted without any loss of comprehension on the part of students.

Many chapters have boxes that apply the theory of public finance to current issues. The issues chosen will be immediately recognizable to students as important topics of the day. Each chapter contains a marginal glossary, summary, listing of key words, review questions, and discussion questions. The marginal glossary helps students to quickly understand new key terms presented in the text. The summaries reinforce the major ideas studied in each chapter. The listing of key words helps students understand the new concepts introduced in each chapter, and the discussion and review questions solidify their comprehension.

I have written a complete instructor's manual and test bank that provide many helpful suggestions for lecture topics. A thorough study guide, written by Alden Shiers of California Polytechnic State University in San Luis Obispo, is also available and highly recommended.

Acknowledgments

I am grateful for the many insights and full-fledged encouragement provided by my many colleagues and friends over the years. Alden Shiers, Angelo R. Mascaro

(Congressional Budget Office), David Joulfaian (U.S. Treasury Department), William T. Orzechowski (Tobacco Institute), Gordon L. Brady (Sweet Briar College), and Robert N. Mottice (U.S. Senate) commented on various chapters or in many other ways contributed to my understanding and appreciation of the issues of public finance.

I fully appreciate the many fine recommendations offered by the formal reviewers of my book:

Gary M. Anderson, California State University, Northridge
Gary V. Engelhardt, Dartmouth College
Roger L. Faith, Arizona State University
Dennis Patrick Leyden, University of North Carolina at Greensboro
Stephen E. Lile, Western Kentucky University
Matthew N. Murray, University of Tennessee, at Knoxville
Kevin M. O'Brien, Bradley University
David D. Ramsey, Illinois State University
Edward M. Sabella, Augsburg College
Larry D. Singell, University of Oregon
Ira Smolowitz, American International College
William F. Stine, Clarion University of Pennsylvania
John Wade, Western Carolina University
Anne E. Winkler, University of Missouri-St. Louis

I have been most impressed with the professional staff at The Dryden Press, including Rick Hammonds, Daryl Fox, Amy Schmidt, Emily Thompson, Jeanette Barber, and Kelly Cordes, and I appreciate the excellent editorial advice of free-lance copy editor Wanda Giles. I am especially grateful for the painstaking and skilled guidance of Emily Thompson.

Michael L. Marlow
August 1994

About the Author

Michael L. Marlow is Professor of Economics at California Polytechnic State University, San Luis Obispo, where he has taught Public Finance since 1988. In 1990, the students of Cal Poly named him the "Most Outstanding Professor" in the business school. Professor Marlow is a *Phi Beta Kappa* graduate of the George Washington University. He received his Ph.D. from Virginia Polytechnic Institute and State University in 1978, and subsequently taught at the George Washington University in Washington, D.C. From 1983 to 1988, Professor Marlow was Senior Financial Economist at the U.S. Department of the Treasury in the offices of the Undersecretary for Monetary Affairs and the Assistant Secretary for Economic Policy. He has been published extensively in such journals as the *Review of Economics and Statistics, Economic Inquiry, Public Finance, Public Choice, Economics Letters,* and the *Southern Economic Journal.* He currently referees for more than ten scholarly journals. Professor Marlow lives in San Luis Obispo, Calif. with his wife Valerie and daughter Emily Chase.

Contents in Brief

Preface ix

Part 1 What Is the Public Sector? 1
Chapter 1   Introduction 3
Chapter 2   Policies of the Public Sector 19

Part 2 The Role of the Public Sector 35
Chapter 3   Private or Public Markets? 37
Appendix   Efficiency in Exchange and Production 64
Chapter 4   Externalities 80
Appendix   Regulation and the Savings and Loan Crisis 112
Chapter 5   Public Goods 117

Part 3 The Policy Process 149
Chapter 6   Voters and Policymakers in the Policy Process 151
Appendix   Public Exchange under Dictatorships 180
Chapter 7   Voting Models and Public Market Structure 182
Chapter 8   The Demand and Supply of Government 213

Part 4 Expenditure, Credit, and Insurance Programs 235
Chapter 9   Expenditure Policies of the Federal Government 237
Chapter 10 Off-Budget Government: Credit and Insurance Policies 269
Chapter 11 Transfer Programs for the Poor 301
Chapter 12 Social Insurance Programs 331
Chapter 13 Health Care Policy 364
Chapter 14 Cost-Benefit Analysis 382

Part 5 Financing Government Activities 411
Chapter 15 Financing Public Expenditures: An Introduction 413
Chapter 16 Principles of Tax Analysis 436
Chapter 17 Financing Expenditures through Budget Deficits 463

Part 6 The Practice of Taxation 491
Chapter 18 The Personal Income Tax 493
Chapter 19 Income Taxation and Behavior 517
Chapter 20 The Corporation Tax 537
Chapter 21 Taxation of Consumption and Wealth 555

Part 7 Intergovernmental Finance 575
Chapter 22 Fiscal Federalism 577

Appendix   Review of Microeconomic Theory 603
References 626
Glossary   637
Index   644

Contents

Part 1   What Is the Public Sector?   1

Chapter 1   Introduction   3

What Is Public Finance?   3
Benefits and Costs of Policies   4
   Beneficiaries of Policies   4
   Everyone Pays for Policies   5
Private or Public Markets?   6
   Private Markets   6
   Public Markets   7
   Choices and the Public Sector   8
The Health Insurance Debate: What Is the Role of Government?   9
Positive and Normative Analysis   10
Studying Voters and Policymakers   11
   Behaviors of Policymakers   12
   Behaviors of Voters   12
Functions of the Public Sector   13
   Protection   13
   Allocation   13
   Distribution   14
   Stabilization   15
Public Sector: Small or Large?   15
   Supporters of Large Government   15
   Supporters of Small Government   15
The Usefulness of Public Finance   16
Summary   17
Review Questions   17
Discussion Questions   17
Key Words   18

Chapter 2   Policies of the Public Sector   19

The Size of the Public Sector   19
Spending Policies   19
   Total Government Spending   19
   Private Sector Spending   20
Areas of Public Spending   20
   Federal and Nonfederal Spending   21
Financing Activities   21
   Government Revenues, Budgetary Deficits, and Surpluses   21
   Sources of Revenues   24

Public Sector Employment   26
Federal Credit and Insurance Programs   26
Legislative Output of Congress   28
   Measures Introduced and Enacted   28
   Legislation   29
   Regulatory Agencies   30
Public Sectors of Other Countries   30
Reinventing Government? The Gore Plan   32
A Growing Public Sector   33
Summary   33
Review Questions   34
Discussion Questions   34
Key Words   34

Part 2 The Role of the Public Sector   35

Chapter 3 *Private or Public Markets?*   37
Private and Public Markets   37
Focus on Society as a Collection of Individuals   38
Efficiency in Resource Allocation   39
   Total Net Benefits to Society   39
   Total Benefit and Cost Analysis   40
   Total Net Benefit Analysis   41
   Marginal Benefit and Marginal Cost Analysis   42
   Market Equilibrium and Efficiency   43
   Efficiency and Changes in Market Conditions   44
   Private Market Equilibrium and Consumer Surplus   45
Restrictions on Market Equilibrium   47
   Rent Control and Resource Allocation   47
      Who Gains from Rent Control Policies?   47
      Who Loses from Rent Control Policies?   48
      Evaluation of Rent Control Policies   49
How Upper-Income Professionals Gain from Rent Control   50
   Private Markets Often Work against Public Intervention   50
Welfare Economics   51
   Pareto Efficient Allocations   52
   Equity versus Efficiency in Resource Allocation   53
   Compensation Tests   54
      Reallocations with Compensation   54
      Reallocations without Compensation   55
   Unanimity Test   56

Social Welfare Functions 56
   Maximization of Social Welfare 57
Welfare Economics in Practice 58
   Large Numbers as Constraints on Viability 58
   Individuals Consider Net Changes of All Reallocations 58
   Importance of the Process by which Reallocations Are Chosen 58

Role of the Public Sector 58
Externalities 59
Public Goods 59
Allocative Efficiency and Monopoly 59
Imperfect Information and Resource Allocation 60
Equity Goals of Society 60
Stabilization Policies 61

Market Failure or Government Failure? 61

Summary 62

Review Questions 62

Discussion Questions 62

Key Words 63

Chapter 3 Appendix   Efficiency in Exchange and Production 64
Efficiency in Exchange 64
   Trades along the Football 65
   Trades outside the Football 66
   Trades within the Football 66
   Conditions for Pareto Efficiency 66
   Contract Curve 67
   Utility Possibilities Curve 68
Efficiency in Production 69
   Production Possibilities Curve 69
   Marginal Rate of Transformation 70
   Efficient Production of Goods 71
Overall Efficiency 72
   Grand Utility Possibilities Curve 74
Private Markets, Competition, and Overall Efficiency 75
   Perfect Competition and Efficiency in Exchange 75
   Perfect Competition and Efficiency in Production 75
   Perfect Competition and Efficiency in Exchange and Production 76
   Monopoly and Efficiency in Exchange and Production 76
   Comparison of Perfect Competition and Monopoly 77

Chapter 4   Externalities   80
What Are Externalities? 80
Negative Externalities 81
   Concept of Negative Externalities 81

   Allocative Efficiency and Negative Externalities 81
   Market Prices and Negative Externalities 82
   Property Right Assignments 83
    The Case of African Elephants 83
   The Coase Theorem 85
    Assignment to Michael 86
    Assignment to David 87
   Implications of the Coase Theorem 88
    Allocative Efficiency Requires Assignment of Property Rights 88
    Assignment of Property Rights Influences Wealth Distribution 88
    Transactions Costs and the Role of Government 89

Sell the Whale? 90
   Negative Externalities and the Prisoners' Dilemma 91
   Do Property Rights Transcend Geographical Boundaries? 92

Government Intervention and Negative Externalities 92
   Corrective Taxation 92
    Net Gains to Society 94
    Income Distributional Issues 95
    Difficulties of Implementing Tax Policy 96
   Subsidies 96
   Regulation 98
    Incentives to Innovation and Productivity 99
    Market Incentives 99
   Pollution Permits 100

Positive Externalities 101
   Concept of Positive Externalities 101

Pollution Credits for Old Cars? 102
   Positive Externalities and Allocative Efficiency 103
   Subsidies and Allocative Efficiency 104
   Is Government Intervention Necessarily Better? 104
   Inframarginal Positive Externalities 105
   Can Subsidies Cause Overproduction? 106

Resource Allocation in an Imperfect World 108
Summary 110
Review Questions 110
Discussion Questions 110
Key Words 111

Chapter 4 Appendix *Regulation and the S&L Crisis* 112
 Overview 112
 Benefits of Regulation 113
 Costs of Regulation 114

Root Causes of the S&L Crisis   115
Assessment of Regulatory Policy   115

Chapter 5   Public Goods   117

What Are Public Goods?   118
   Nonrivalry in Consumption   118
   Zero Marginal Costs of Provision   118
   Exclusion Characteristics   118

All Goods Produced by the Public Sector Are Not Public Goods   119
   Public Goods Produced in Private Markets   119
   Private Goods Produced in Public Markets   119
   Public Goods Produced in Private and Public Markets   120
   Between Private and Public Goods   120

Market Failure and Public Goods   120
   Free Rider Effect   120
   Zero Marginal Costs of Provision   122

Optimal Provision of Pure Public Goods   122
   Correction of Market Failure   122
   Market Demand for Private Goods   123
   Market Demand for Public Goods   123
   Efficient Quantities of Public Goods   123
      Financing Public Goods   125
   Lindahl Equilibrium   125

Private Market Provision of Public Goods   126
   Theory of Clubs   127
      Incentives to Form Clubs   127
   Sizes of Clubs   128
      Congestion and Optimal Membership Size   128
      Mechanisms for Excluding Free Riders   128
      Efficiency of Club Arrangements   128

Special Interest Groups as Clubs   129
   What Are Special Interest Groups?   129
   Special Interest Groups Also Influence the Private Sector   130
   Incentives to Form Special Interest Groups   131
   Political Action Committees   132
   The Public Good Nature of Special Interest Groups   133

Cases for Public Sector Provision of Public Goods   134
   Pure Public Goods   134
   Economies of Scale   134
      Centralization and Decentralization   135
   Public Goods Characterized by Externalities   135
      Special Interest Groups and Negative Externalities   135
      Special Interest Groups and Positive Externalities   136
   Private Clubs Limit Membership   136

Community Associations as Clubs   137
   Assignment and Enforcement of Property Rights   138
Cases for Private Sector Provision of Public Goods   139
   Taxation in Practice: Taxation versus Lindahl Pricing   139
      Tax Policy Based on Efficiency   139
      Tax Policy Based on Equity   141
   Coercion versus Voluntary Agreements   141
   Monopoly Government Arguments   142
Public Sector Provision in Practice   143
   Private and Public Markets Are Less than Ideal   143
   Cost Differences between Public and Private Provision   143
   Subsidies of Nonprofits   145
   Are Special Interest Groups Too Powerful?   145
   Common-Pool Problems   146
Summary   147
Review Questions   147
Discussion Questions   147
Key Words   148

Part 3   The Policy Process   149

Chapter 6   *Voters and Policymakers in the Policy Process*   151
Why Study Voters and Policymakers?   151
Modeling the Policy Process   152
   Behavioral Assumptions   152
   Positive Dimensions of Model Building   152
What Motivates Voters?   153
   Political Participation   153
   Self-Interest: Narrow and Broad Definitions   153
   Special Interest Groups   155
   Policy Intentions versus Policy Results   156
   Rational Ignorance   156
   Are Voters Well Informed?   159
   Voting Participation   160
   Institutional Factors   160
   Behavioral Factors   162
   Is Voting Participation High or Low?   164
      The United States   164
      Other Countries   164
      Comparison of the United States with Other Countries   164
Policymakers: Who Are They?   165
   Policymakers and the Policy Process   165

Institutional Factors   166
Characteristics of Members of Congress   167
  Experience   167
  Reelection Rates   167
  Employment   169
Behavioral Factors   169
  Importance of Reelection   169
  "Very Narrow" Self-Interests of Policymakers   169
Narrow Self-Interests of Policymakers   171
  Constituencies of Elected Policymakers   171
  Credit Claiming and Position Taking   172
Broad Self-Interests of Policymakers   173
  Ideal versus Actual Behaviors of Policymakers   173

When Promises and Votes Diverge   174
  Power and Self-Interest   175
  Ideology and Self-Interest   175
Constraints on Self-Interests   175
Nonelected Policymakers   176
  Constituencies of Nonelected Policymakers   176

Institutional Differences between Public Markets   177
Summary   178
Review Questions   179
Discussion Questions   179
Key Words   179

Chapter 6 Appendix   Public Exchange under Dictatorships   180

Chapter 7   *Voting Models and Public Market Structure*   182
Unanimity Rules of Voting   182
  Characteristics   182
Majority Voting Rules   184
  Optimal Majority Rules   184
    Optimal Majority in the Private Sector   186
Simple Majority Voting Rules   187
  Implications of Median Voter Model for Provision of Public Goods   189
  Implications of the Median Voter Model for Representative Democracy   189
Existence of Majority Voting Equilibrium   192
  Single-Peaked Preferences and Majority Voting   194
  How Prevalent Are Double-Peaked Preferences?   196
  Logrolling with Multiple Issues   196
Majority Voting Rules, Externalities, and Property Rights   198

Private Sector 199
Public Sector 199

Public Market Structure and Exchange 200
   Voice and Exit as Properties Affecting Public Exchange 201
   Voice Options 201
      Advantages of Being an Incumbent 201
      Gerrymandering 202
   Exit Options 202
      The Benevolent Policymaker View 203
      The Leviathan View 203
      Implications for the Policymaker Role 204

Bureaucracy Theory 205

Special Interest Groups and Policymakers 207

Removing Plums with Twig Scars and Sunburn Spots from the Marketplace 209

Final Observations 210

Summary 211

Review Questions 211

Discussion Questions 211

Key Words 212

Chapter 8   *The Demand and Supply of Government* 213

Equilibrium Size of the Public Sector 215
   Demand and Supply Framework 215
   Demanders of Public Programs 215
   Suppliers of Public Programs 217
   Changes in the Equilibrium Size of the Public Sector 217

Demand-Side Explanations 220
   Urbanization 220
   Demand for Income Redistribution 221
   Demand by Public Sector Employees 221
   Fiscal Illusion 222

Supply-Side Explanations 223
   Bureaucracy Theory 223

The Agriculture Department: Bureaucracy Theory in Action? 225
   Public Sector Centralization 225
   Taxes Cause Spending 226

Implications of Theories for Policy Process 228
   Expansion as a Result of Government Monopoly 228
   Expansion as a Result of Special Interest Groups 228
   Expansion as a Result of Misperceptions 229

Public Sector Expansion and Economic Growth   230
Final Analysis   232
Summary   233
Review Questions   233
Discussion Questions   233
Key Words   234

Part 4   Expenditure, Credit, and Insurance Programs   235

Chapter 9   Expenditure Policies of the Federal Government   237

Analysis of Expenditure Policies   237
Allocational Effects   237
Distributional Effects   238

Costs of Public Spending   239
A Static World   239
Allocations along the Frontier   239
Allocations within the Frontier   239
A Dynamic World   241

Trends in Expenditure Policies   242
General Trends: Purchases versus Transfers   242
Defense Spending and the End of the Cold War   244
Transfers   246
Purchases as Transfers: Pork Barrel Spending   246

Net Interest Expenditures   248
Net Interest Expenditures Reflect Past Spending Programs   250
  Are Program Benefits Long-Lived?   250
Crowding Out of Discretionary Spending Programs   251
Incentives for Policymakers   251

Federal Budget Process   252
Federal Budget Process before 1974   253
Impoundment Act of 1974   254
  Leverage over Spending   254
  When Spending Increases Are Called Spending Cuts   255
Gramm-Rudman-Hollings Deficit Reduction Act   258
Budget Enforcement Act of 1990   260

Reform of the Federal Budget Process   261
Fiscal Rules   261
  Line-Item Veto   261
  Balanced Budget Amendment   263
  Evidence from State Governments   264

Capital Budget 264
    What Is a Capital Budget? 264
    Too Little Capital Spending on Infrastructure? 265
    A Capital Budget for the U.S. Government? 265
Final Thoughts 266
Summary 267
Review Questions 267
Discussion Questions 267
Key Words 268

Chapter 10   Off-Budget Government: Credit and Insurance Policies   269

Allocational and Distributive Effects 270
    Role of Risk in Private Credit and Insurance Markets 270
        Risk and Resource Allocation: Two Effects 273
    Four Rationales for Credit and Insurance Policies 273
Allocative Effects 275
    Direct Allocative Effects 275
        Indirect Allocative Effects 276
        Direct and Indirect Allocative Effects: The Case of Deposit Insurance 276
    Distributional Effects 276
How Off-Budget Policies Affect Risk 277
    Policies Focus on High-Risk Transactions 277
    Moral Hazard and Risk Liabilities 277
        When Moral Hazard Occurs 278
    VA Loan Program and Moral Hazard 279
    Cases in which Moral Hazard Does Not Exist 280
    Adverse Selection 281
Federal Deposit Insurance Policy 281
    Deposit Insurance 281
    Moral Hazard and Liabilities 282
        Does Policy Control Risk? 283
    Costs of Regulatory Forbearance 284
    Economic Effects of Deposit Insurance Policy 285
        Allocational Effects 285
        Distributional Effects 286
    Other Insurance Programs 286
        Federal Exposure to Losses 286
        Allocation and Distribution Effects 288
Government-Sponsored Enterprises 288
    Implications of Implicit Federal Guarantee 289
    Capital Requirements of GSEs 289
    Allocative and Distributive Effects 290

GSEs and the Thrift Bailout 291
New Role for GSEs? 291

Direct Loans, Guarantees, and Credit Policies 292
Federal Participation in Credit Markets 293

Credit and Insurance Policy Reform? 293

Potential Costs of Federal Credit and Insurance Programs 293
Reforms 294
Accounting Methods 294
Risk Adjustment 296
Bottom Line with Reforms 296

Final Thoughts 297

The Expanding Off-Budget Sector of State and Local Governments 298

Summary 299

Review Questions 299

Discussion Questions 299

Key Words 300

Chapter 11 Transfer Programs for the Poor 301

The Role of Government in Income Redistribution 303
Private Market Charity 303
Goals of Redistribution Policy 304
Useful Distinctions 305

Distribution of Income 306
Measurement of Income 306
Real Median Family Income 307
Level versus Distribution of Income 308
Poverty Thresholds 310
The Middle Class 310
Cautionary Notes 311

Description of Means-Tested Transfers 313
Cash Transfers 313
Noncash Transfers 314

Economic Effects of Transfers 315
Cash versus Noncash Transfers 315
Case 1 315
Case 2 317
Welfare Costs 318
Excise Subsidies 319
Market Perspective 319
Individual Perspective 320
Conclusion 321
Choice of Transfer Programs 322

Transfers and the Work–Leisure Trade-Off 322
    Moral Hazard and Adverse Selection 323
    Negative Income Tax Policy 324
Alternative Views of Poverty 325
Workfare: A Radical Proposal? 327
    Policy Reforms That May Attract a Wide Audience 328
Summary 329
Review Questions 329
Discussion Questions 329
Key Words 330

Chapter 12   Social Insurance Programs   331

Historical Perspective 333
Rationales for Social Insurance Policies 334
    Lack of Private Markets 334
    Promotion of Equity Goals of Society 335
    Paternalism 335
Social Security 336
    Private Pensions 336
    Social Security Taxes 337
    Social Security Benefits 337
    Trust Funds 339
    Booming Trust Funds until 2050 341
    Implications of Changes in Trust Funds 342
Social Security Is a Transfer Program 344
    Intragenerational Transfers 345
    Intergenerational Transfers 345
    Transfer Function of Government 346
Current Social Security Issues 347
    Does Social Security Influence Saving? 347
    Effects on the Federal Budget 348
        Where Do Surpluses Go? 348
        Measurement of Overall Budget Deficit 349
Reforming Social Security 350
    Generational Accounting 350
    Cutting the Payroll Tax 351
    Privatization 352
Medicare 353
    Background on Health Care Costs 353
    Rationales for Public Health Insurance 354
    Characteristics of Medicare 355
    Medicare Trust Funds 355
Unemployment Insurance 357

Rationales for Public Unemployment Insurance   357
Characteristics of Unemployment Insurance   357
How Unemployment Insurance Transfers Income   358
Economic Effects of Unemployment Insurance   359

Concluding Observations   360

Summary   361

Review Questions   362

Discussion Questions   362

Key Words   363

Chapter 13   *Health Care Policy*   *364*

Introduction   364

An Expanding Health Care Sector   364
How Much Do We Spend?   364
Expansion of Public Health Care Spending   366
Is There a Health Care Crisis?   368

Implications of Rising Health Care Costs   369
Reduced Access to Health Insurance   369
    Why Are Some Americans Uninsured?   369
    Rising Costs Reduce Insurance Access   370
Health Cost Escalation: Slower Wage Growth?   370
Rising Costs Dampen Tax Revenues   371

Why Such Rapid Growth?   371
An Aging Society   371
Rising National Income   372
Imperfect Information of Consumers   372
Third-Party Payments   372
    Moral Hazard in Medical Insurance?   373
    Does Medical Technology Growth Push Demand?   375
Tax Expenditures Promote Health Care Spending   375

Health Care Reform Proposals   377
Managed Competition   377
Play-or-Pay   378
    Rate Setting: A Cure for Cost Escalation?   378
National Health Insurance   380

Summary   380

Review Questions   381

Discussion Questions   381

Key Words   381

Chapter 14   *Cost-Benefit Analysis*   *382*

Cost-Benefit Analysis and Allocative Efficiency   383

Allocative Efficiency 383
Alternative Time Frameworks for Cost-Benefit Analysis 384

Present Value Framework 385
What Is Present Value? 385
- Two-Year Analysis 386
- *n*-Period Analysis 386

Comparing Projects Using the Present Value Framework 387
Two Implications of Present Value Analysis 387
Application: Present Value of a Professional Athlete's Salary 388
Effects of Inflation on Present Values 390
- Present Value When There Is Inflation 392
- Implications of Inflation for Present Value Calculations 393

Methods for Choosing between Projects 393
Maximum Present Value of Net Benefits 394
Internal Rates of Discount 396
Benefit-Cost Ratios 396

Application of Cost-Benefit Analysis 397
Measuring Benefits 397
- Common Errors in Measuring Benefits 399

Valuing Life 400
Measuring Costs 400
Measurement Problems and Cost-Benefit Analysis 401
What Discount Rate Should Government Use? 402
- Opportunity Cost of Not Allowing Private Sector to Allocate Resources 402
- Income Taxes and the Discount Rate 402
- Risk and the Discount Rate 403

A Lower Discount Rate for Public Projects? 403
- Shortsighted Policies? 404
- Policies Addressing Market Failures 404
- Redistributional Arguments 404

The Policy Process and Cost-Benefit Analysis 405
Incentives to Use Cost-Benefit Analysis 405
Voters, Interest Groups, and Cost-Benefit Analysis 405
- Marketing Orders of the U.S. Department of Agriculture 405
- The Audit Function of Policymakers 406

Does Cost-Benefit Analysis Lead to Pareto Efficient Policies? 408

Cost-Benefit Analysis in an Imperfect Public Sector 408
Summary 409
Review Questions 409
Discussion Questions 409
Key Words 410

Part 5 Financing Government Activities 411

Chapter 15 Financing Public Expenditures: An Introduction 413

Financing Trends 414
- Aggregate Financing Trends 414
- Changing Tax Sources 414
- Tax Trends of Other Countries 416

Benefits as a Principle of Tax Policy 416
- Benefit Principle in Private Markets 416
- Benefit Principle in Public Markets: Application to Private Goods 418
  - Tax-Earmarking 419
- Benefit Principle in Public Markets: Application to Public Goods 419

The Benefit Principle Is Often Incompatible with Public Policy 420
- Possible Inconsistencies 420
- The Benefit Principle and Cost-Benefit Analysis 421

Ability to Pay: An Alternative Principle 422
- Overview 422
- Defining Ability to Pay: Horizontal Equity 423
- Defining Ability to Pay: Vertical Equity 424

Transferring Income through Tax Policy 425
- Positive and Negative Transfers 426
- Assessing the Performance of Transfer Policies 427
- Who Receives Transfers? 428

Tax Expenditures 428
- Important Distinction: Tax Rate versus Tax Base 429
- Allocational Effects 430
- Distributional Effects 430
- Substitutability with Expenditure Programs 431
- Tax Expenditure Estimates Are Imperfect 432
- Outlay Equivalence of Tax Expenditures 433

Summary 434

Review Questions 434

Discussion Questions 435

Key Words 435

Chapter 16 Principles of Tax Analysis 436

Tax Incidence: General Issues 436

Unit Taxes 437
- Unit Tax on Suppliers 437
- Unit Tax on Demanders 438
- Economic Incidence Is Unrelated to Statutory Incidence 439

Incidence and Elasticities of Supply and Demand 441
    Demand Elasticities 441
    Supply Elasticities 442
    Implications of Elasticity for Tax Policy 443

Ad Valorem Taxes 444

Taxes on Monopolists 444

Taxes on Labor 446

General Equilibrium Analysis of Tax Incidence 447
  Two-Good World 447
  Implications for Tax Incidence 448
  Complications 449

Excess Burden of Taxation 449
  What Is Excess Burden? 449
  Excess Burden and the Individual 451
  Excess Burden and Elasticity 452
  Measuring Excess Burdens of Unit Taxes 453
  Minimization of Excess Burden 455

Other Costs of Taxation 456
  Administrative Costs 456
  Compliance Costs 456
  Tax Shelters 457
  Lobbying Costs of Rent Seeking Activities 458

Tax Evasion and Amnesties 458
  Tax Evasion 458

Tax Law Instability: Another Cost of Taxation? 459
  Tax Amnesties 459

Tax Principles and the Policy Process 460

Summary 461

Review Questions 462

Discussion Questions 462

Key Words 462

Chapter 17   Financing Expenditures through Budget Deficits   463

Budget Deficits and the National Debt 463
  What Are Budget Deficits? 463
  National Debt 465
  Components of the National Debt 466
  Re-Funding of the National Debt 467

Measurement Issues 468
  Budget Deficit Is a Residual 468
  Inflation and the Real Value of Debt 468

Capital and Noncapital Goods Are Not Separated 469
Unfunded Liabilities of Credit and Insurance Programs Are Not Reflected 470
Unfunded Liabilities of Trust Funds Are Not Reflected 471

Economic Effects of Public Debt 471
Does the Foreign Share of the Debt Matter? 472
Intergenerational Burdens from Public Debt? 473
The Ricardian Equivalence Proposition 474
Theoretical Criticisms of the Ricardian Equivalence Proposition 476
Evidence on Burdens Associated with Public Debt 477

Policy Issues 478
Undertaxation or Overspending? 479
Two Views of Budget Deficits and Government Expansion 480
  Fiscal Illusion Hypothesis 480
  Ricardian Equivalence Proposition 481
Do Tax Increases Lead to Deficit Reduction? 482
Can Tax Legislation Increase Tax Collections? 484
A Political Disequilibrium? 486

Summary 488
Review Questions 488
Discussion Questions 489
Key Words 489

Part 6 The Practice of Taxation 491

Chapter 18 The Personal Income Tax 493

Defining Taxable Income: Theory 493
What Is Income? 493
Defining a Comprehensive Measure of Income 494
Problems in Defining a Comprehensive Measure of Income 496
Why Economists Advocate a Comprehensive Definition 496

Taxing Free Parking 497

Defining Taxable Income: Practice 498
Step 1: Calculation of Gross Income 498
Step 2: Calculation of Adjusted Gross Income 499
Step 3: Calculation of Taxable Income 499
  Exemptions 500
  Deductions 500
Step 4: Calculating Tax Liability 501
Step 5: Lowering Tax Liability through Tax Credits 502
  The Alternative Minimum Tax 503

Income Tax Policy Reform 504

xxxii Contents

    Economic Recovery Tax Act of 1981   504
    Social Security Amendments of 1983   504
    Tax Reform Act of 1986   504
    Omnibus Budget Reconciliation Acts of 1990 and 1993   506
    What Has Tax Reform Achieved?   507
        Simplification?   507
        Changes in Marginal Tax Rates   507
        Base Broadening   508
        Equity   509

Marriage Tax   511

Inflation and Tax Burdens   513
    Labor Income   513
    Interest Income and Interest Expenses   514
    Capital Gains   514
    Political Responses   514

Summary   515

Review Questions   516

Discussion Questions   516

Key Words   516

Chapter 19   Income Taxation and Behavior   517

Income Taxation and Labor Supply   517
    Income–Leisure Model   517
    Incidence of Income Taxation on Labor Income   519
        Vertical Labor Supply   520
        Upward-Sloping Labor Supply   521
    Excess Burden of Income Taxation on Labor Income   522
        Vertical Labor Supply   522
    Empirical Evidence   523

Labor Supply and the Laffer Curve   524
    Theory   524

Does the Tax Code Influence a Couple's Wedding Date?   525
    Policy Implications   527
    Empirical Evidence   527

Income Taxation and Saving Behavior   528
    A Model of Intertemporal Choice   528
    Taxation of Interest Earnings and Intertemporal Choice   530
        Substitution Effects   530
        Income Effects   530
        Net Effect on Saving   531
        Empirical Evidence   531
    Tax Shifting by Savers   531
        Inelastic Savings Supply   532
        Upward-Sloping Savings Supply   532

Implications of Savings Supply Elasticity   533
Excess Burdens   533
Behavior When There Are Interest Expense Deductions   533
Allocation of Saving Activities   534

Summary   535

Review Questions   536

Discussion Questions   536

Key Words   536

Chapter 20   The Corporation Tax   537

Defining Taxable Income: Deductions   537
Gross Income   537
Wages   538
Interest Costs   538
Depreciation   539
Expensing   539
Straight-Line Depreciation   539
Depreciation Rates and Tax Lives   540
Depreciation and Inflation   541

Tax Rates and Tax Credits   542
Statutory Tax Rates   542
Effective Tax Rates   542
Tax Credits   543

Tax Policy and Corporate Behavior   543
Financing through Debt versus Equity   544
Dividends versus Retained Earnings   545
Depreciation and the Choice of Capital Resources   545

Incidence of the Corporation Tax   546
Short-Run Incidence   546
Long-Run Incidence   548
Implications for Long-Run Incidence   550
Excess Burden   551

Reform of the Corporation Tax   552
Why Tax Corporations?   552
Which Directions for Reform?   552

Summary   553

Review Questions   554

Discussion Questions   554

Key Words   554

Chapter 21   Taxation of Consumption and Wealth   555

Consumption Taxes   555
Sales Tax Collections   555

National Consumption Taxation   557
   Arguments in Favor   557
How Well Do We Really Want "Sin" Taxes to Work?   558
   Arguments Against   559
   Assessment of the Issues   560
   Are Consumption Taxes Regressive?   561
Value-Added Taxes   562
   Mechanics of a VAT   562
   Advantages of a VAT   563
   The VAT's Taxable Base   564
   Little Support for a VAT in the United States   565
Wealth Taxation: Estate and Gift Taxes   566
   Estate and Gift Taxation   567
Wealth Taxation: The Property Tax   568
   A Uniform Property Tax   568
   Extension to a System of Nonuniform Property Taxes   571
Summary   572
Review Questions   573
Discussion Questions   573
Key Words   573

Part 7   Intergovernmental Finance   575

Chapter 22   Fiscal Federalism   577

Trends in Fiscal Structure   578
   Numbers of Governments   578
   Centralization of Spending Policy   580
   Centralization by Spending Area   580
   Revenues of State and Local Governments   580
Advantages of Federalism   582
   Better Correspondence to Demand Variations   582
   Can an Optimal Federal System Be Designed?   585
   Tiebout Model: A Solution   586
      Local Communities as Clubs   588
   State and Local Governments as Laboratories   588
Just How Mobile Are Americans?   589
   Controls Rent Seeking   590
Disadvantages of Federalism   590
   Economies of Scale   590
      Complications   591
   Interjurisdictional Externalities   593

      Uniformity of Provision   593
      Redistribution   594
      Avoidance of Tax Wars   594
      Stabilization Policies   595

Intergovernmental Grants   595
      Trends   595
      Rationales   596
      Economic Effects of Unconditional Grants   597
      Matching and Nonmatching Conditional Grants   598

Grant Policy   599
      Why Offer Matching Grants?   599
      Equalization of the Income Distribution   600

Summary   601
Review Questions   601
Discussion Questions   602
Key Words   602

Appendix   Review of Microeconomic Theory   603

Exchange in Private Markets   603
Consumer Theory   603
      Utility Theory   603
      Preference Orderings between Goods   605
      Indifference Schedules and Curves   605
      Budget Constraints   610
      Consumer Equilibrium   611
      Changes in Income and Consumer Equilibrium   613
      Changes in Prices and Consumer Equilibrium   614
      Deriving Demand Curves from Price Consumption Curves   616
      Substitution and Income Effects   617
          Substitution Effects   617
          Income Effects   619
      Market Demand Curves   619

Producer Theory   620
      Role of Profits   620
      Production Costs and Supply Curves   620

Market Equilibrium: Supply and Demand Analysis   622
Price Elasticity of Demand and Supply   624
      Price Elasticity of Demand   624
      Price Elasticity of Supply   624

References   626
Glossary   637
Index   644

PART 1

What Is the Public Sector?

Chapter 1
Introduction

Chapter 2
Policies of the Public Sector

CHAPTER 1

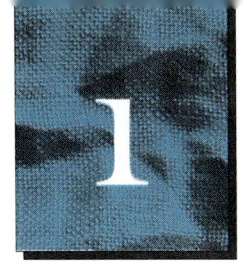

Introduction

What Is Public Finance?

Very few areas of our lives are untouched by the public sector. All policies of the public sector confer benefits upon and exact costs from members of society. Public policies determine the quantity and quality of public works, such as schools, libraries, parks, playgrounds, bridges, and roads. They also establish the role of the police and military services in our society, set standards for medical research and health care, and provide for myriad other public services that we care about. In addition, the public sector regulates many private-sector entities, such as banks, airlines, and the construction industry, and controls many of our personal activities. Speed limits, legal drinking ages, prohibitions on drug use—these are just a few of the areas over which the public sector exercises controls on personal behavior.

In examining how governments influence our economic lives, **public finance** addresses one fundamental issue: Why do we want the public sector to exert such powerful influences over our lives? Public finance, a subdiscipline of economics (also known as *public sector economics* or just *public economics*), provides us with a framework for understanding, changing, and improving the ways in which the public sector influences our lives.

Public finance is the study of how spending and tax policies influence our economic lives.

In public finance we look for answers to such questions as

- ❑ Are there areas in which the private sector does a poor job of allocating our resources?
- ❑ Which functions should the public sector perform? Which dimensions of our lives are best left to the private sector?
- ❑ How do we evaluate the benefits and costs of public policies?
- ❑ Who should receive the benefits of policies—and who should pay their costs?
- ❑ What do we expect from the public sector? How will it allocate our resources?
- ❑ Are there many areas where reasonable individuals might disagree about the appropriate role of the public sector in our economy?
- ❑ Can we recommend improvements in existing policies?

In this chapter we survey the study of public finance in general. After a brief discussion of the ways in which public spending and taxation policies influence our lives, we look at the roles of voters and policymakers as integral determinants of the policies of the public sector. By focusing on the wide range of options for organizing our resources, we underscore the need for a framework that allows us to make informed choices about what role we want the public sector to assume in allocating resources. Finally, we discuss why some people prefer a fairly large public sector while others prefer a small public sector.

Benefits and Costs of Policies

Beneficiaries of Policies

We all benefit from public policies. Consider Table 1-1, which indicates that since 1950, U.S. citizens experienced a more than threefold increase in per capita spending of federal, state, and local governments. This expansion in public spending has undoubtedly provided substantial benefits to citizens. Expansion of spending indicates an increasing influence of the public sector on our lives and, as the breakdown in Table 1-1 indicates, the federal government plays the dominant role in the public sector. An expanding public sector is not unique to the United States; all industrialized countries have experienced growing public sectors.

An important focus in the study of public finance is the examination of the ways in which individuals benefit from public policies. Given the broad range of policies, all individuals receive substantial benefits from one or more policies; therefore, as beneficiaries of policies, all citizens have personal stakes in policies undertaken by the public sector. But, clearly, not all citizens receive identical benefits from each of the many public policies; some policies affect the well-being of some individuals more than others. This is no great surprise since even such broadly beneficial policies as highway construction confer different levels of benefits to different individuals. Those who, for example, drive many miles to work each day feel the greatest benefits. Other beneficiaries

TABLE 1-1
Per-Capita Spending of Governments
Real Dollars (1982–84)

Year	Total	Federal	State and Local
1950	$1,673	$1,163	$ 513
1960	1,730	1,730	743
1970	3,674	2,459	1,214
1980	4,460	3,157	1,300
1990	5,550	3,849	1,701
1993	5,882	4,005	1,877

Note: The consumer price index (CPI), 1982–84 = 100, is used to calculate real spending dollars.

Source: Economic Report of the President, 1994.

include those individuals who win construction contracts or supply the resources (for example, asphalt, heavy equipment, and labor) to construct highways. Individuals who walk to work, travel infrequently, or are not employed by the highway construction industry receive less immediate benefits from highway construction policies.

Everyone Pays for Policies

The flip side to benefiting from public policies is that we must also pay for them. Rising spending must be matched by rising tax bills. (Another way to finance policies is deficit financing, the subject of Chapter 17.) Taxes are levied on incomes of individuals and corporations, on sales of goods and services, and on personal and real property items such as boats, automobiles, and houses.

Table 1-2 demonstrates the expanding nature of *tax burdens* placed on U.S. citizens. *Tax freedom day* is an estimate of the earliest date in the calendar year on which an average person has earned enough income to pay for his or her share of federal, state, and local taxes. Since 1929, tax freedom day has moved more and more deeply into the year—from February 9 to May 5. *Tax bite in the eight-hour day* is a similar concept that estimates the amount of time out of each workday the average worker must devote toward paying tax bills. The tax bite in the eight-hour day has risen from 52 minutes to 2 hours and 45 minutes, or from 11 percent of the workday to 34 percent of the workday, over the same period.

All citizens do not equally share benefits associated with spending programs, and similarly, they are not assessed identical tax bills. In some cases, citizens pay for policies of which they themselves are primary beneficiaries, but in others, citizens pay for policies that confer benefits mostly to others. The **progressive income tax** is characterized by individual tax bills that rise faster than income. Progressive tax policies are one means by which tax policies address various **equity,** or fairness, goals of society. Irrespective of benefits derived from spending policies, progressive tax policies assess tax bills that rise with incomes of taxpayers.

Progressive income tax is a tax system in which tax bills rise faster than income.

Equity is a criterion for allocating resources on the basis of fairness.

TABLE 1-2
Tax Freedom Day and Tax Bite in the Eight-Hour Day

		Tax Bite in the Eight-Hour Day (Hours:Minutes)		
Year	Tax Freedom Day	Total	Federal	State and Local
1929	February 9	:52	:19	:33
1940	March 8	1:29	:45	:44
1950	April 3	2:02	1:30	:32
1960	April 17	2:22	1:40	:42
1970	April 28	2:34	1:40	:54
1980	May 1	2:39	1:48	:51
1990	May 5	2:45	1:47	:58

Source: Table A17, Tax Foundation, *Facts and Figures on Government Finance,* 1991 Edition (Baltimore/London: The Johns Hopkins University Press, 1991).

Taxes may also take the form of *tolls,* in which tax burdens are placed directly on beneficiaries of policies. Tolls are often charged to users of public roads, tunnels, and bridges. Those who do not use the roads, tunnels, and bridges do not pay tolls. Often in attempts by society to discourage consumption of various goods and services, taxes are levied on highly visible groups in society, such as consumers of tobacco and alcohol. The goal, besides money making, is to change certain behaviors of individuals.

Since individuals do not equally share in the burdens of financing the public sector, some taxes hurt more than others. In public finance, just as economists study who receives benefits associated with public policies, they also carefully examine the issue of who can and should bear the burdens of taxation.

Private or Public Markets?

All economists understand that we live in a world of scarce resources and endless wants. They therefore study resource allocation by the public sector within a world of unlimited and competing consumption goals. Resource scarcity ensures that because of our unlimited wants, we will never be entirely satisfied with our economic and social conditions. There will always be more goods and services that we wish to consume or social problems we would like to remedy through public policy. Each individual therefore has a personal stake in the intelligent allocation of scarce resources, so that the many available consumption and production opportunities available are considered carefully.

Opportunity cost is measured by what is lost by not pursuing the next-best alternative.

Choices are necessary because resources are scarce. **Opportunity cost** is a concept used to inform us about the desirability of competing opportunities. The opportunity cost of an activity is the cost of *not* pursuing the next best activity with those same resources. Whenever one good or service is chosen over another, we incur an opportunity cost. When we enroll in an economics class, for instance, we give up many other uses of our time and money. We cannot enroll in other classes that meet at that time, either in the economics department, in other departments of the same school, or in other schools. We forgo opportunities to work and earn income during class and study time and are unable to purchase other goods and services with tuition fees. The world is filled with economic constraints, and examination of opportunity costs informs us about the choices we have.

All economies, those organized by private markets and those directed by the public sector, must make three fundamental choices. These are

❏ *Which* goods and services to produce
❏ *How* scarce resources are to be organized in production and
❏ *Who* will receive the goods and services

Allocation of resources resolves these three fundamental choices.

Private Markets

The price system allocates resources in private markets, and in microeconomics we study the ways in which the interactions of consumers (demanders) and producers (suppliers) determine prices and output. Success, or profitability, of producers is intimately linked to their ability to satisfy desires of consumers. In a competitive system, consumers generally select producers who supply what they desire at the lowest prices. Producers who organize resources efficiently also are characterized by low prices and high quality, and over the long run these producers are the most profitable as well. Price changes are the signals that direct resource allocations. In the automobile market, for example, rising demand for a certain type of car leads to higher prices and, consequently, more resources allocated to production of that car. At the same time, fewer resources are allocated to production of other cars. Producers who do not base resource allocation decisions on the basis of price signals will be out of step with consumer desires. Consumers and producers together determine quantities, models (compact, midsize, luxury), colors, and prices of cars produced in a given year. The sum of all such decisions in every U.S. market comprises the gross domestic product (GDP), which is the total value of all goods and services produced in the United States during a given year.

Price changes also signal how to organize production. If, for example, wage rates are rising, producers may use fewer workers and more automated capital equipment in their production process. Similarly, rising input costs may impel perceptive producers to substitute cheaper inputs. Producers who do not heed the messages contained in price signals are unable to compete with producers who allocate resources on the basis of price signals.

Final distribution of goods and services is a function of each consumer's command over resources. This function of economic systems determines who consumes the goods and services produced by the private sector. Individuals whose skills are in somewhat short supply tend to receive above-average wages and salaries. The purchasing power of these individuals tends to be higher than that of those individuals whose skills are neither so scarce nor so valuable to employers. Salaries therefore reflect resource scarcity and demands for the goods and services supplied in the various occupations, with those in short supply and high demand offering the highest salaries. The higher the salary an individual commands, the greater an individual's ability to consume goods and services produced in the private sector.

Public Markets

A logical rationale for the existence of public policy is to provide goods and services that the private market either does not provide or does not provide in quantities or qualities determined to be appropriate according to various social criteria. Consider the following possibilities, for example:

- Private markets produce too many eight-cylinder and too few four-cylinder automobiles.
- Private markets provide more "fat farms" for the overweight than food programs for the poor and elderly.
- Private markets offer more generous compensation to rock stars and sports figures than to teachers.
- Private markets allocate more resources to television "sitcoms" than to the arts and theater.

Market failure
occurs when the private market fails to produce an efficient or equitable outcome.

We use the concept of **market failure** to convey the idea that private markets do not always allocate resources the way that society judges appropriate. Although several criteria may be considered when allocating resources in the public sector, the two major criteria are *equity* and *economic efficiency*.

The first of these criteria, equity, has to do with what is fair. One individual may argue, for example, that lawyers should not earn more than civil engineers, a judgment based on that individual's view of what an equitable salary structure would be. Progressive tax structures are also based on the concept of what constitutes equity in taxation. A progressive income tax system imposes tax bills on the basis of income, but it ignores benefits received by taxpayers.

The other criterion, economic efficiency, is an evaluative one in which resources are allocated according to their highest-valued uses. Many subtleties help to define economic efficiency and the study of public finance devotes considerable attention to this most important criterion for allocating resources. In general, public policies are often deemed to be appropriate whenever the private sector fails to meet the **Pareto efficiency** criterion: *One or more individuals cannot be made better off without at least one individual becoming worse off.*

Pareto efficiency
characterizes resource allocation in which no individual can be made better off without making any other individual worse off.

Policy process
is the interaction of voters and policymakers to determine public policies.

Choices and the Public Sector

In a representative democracy, voters and policymakers decide, through the **policy process,** when to have the public sector allocate resources. The policy process is the forum through which voters signal to policymakers their demands for public policies. Within the policy process, choices are made concerning how many of our resources should be directed by the private sector and how many should be directed by the public sector. Choices do not normally lie in either extreme but, rather, address whether the economy should be primarily market driven or government driven. Economies whose resources are primarily directed by private markets include those of the United States, Japan, Germany, and Canada. At the other extreme are the economies of many African nations and, at least until recently, the former Soviet Union, in which the public sector allocates a majority of resources.

How does the public sector determine where to allocate its resources? Should more or fewer resources go toward construction of roads and bridges? Should education or national defense be allocated more resources? These questions are questions of choice. That is, after a particular policy goal is chosen, many alternative policies may be used to achieve that goal. For example, any of the following policies may foster a goal of higher rates of home ownership:

- spending programs that build low-cost housing
- interest rate controls on mortgages
- Federal Housing Administration (FHA) loan programs
- tax credits for builders of low-income housing
- tax deductions for homeowners

For every policy goal, there exist many alternative policies, and the concept of opportunity cost helps us evaluate the many policies that may be used to accomplish our policy goals.

The Health Insurance Debate: What Is the Role of Government?

In October 1993, President Bill Clinton unveiled his blueprint for health insurance reform.

> We all look back now in American history [and] remember 1935 as the year that the American people adopted Social Security; 1965 is the year the American people adopted Medicare," he said. "I believe that 1994 will go down in history as the year when, after decades and decades of false starts and lame excuses and being overcome by special interests, the American people finally—finally—had health care security for all.

What precipitated this bold proposal for reform? One factor is that 37 million Americans have no health insurance. Even with health insurance, the savings of families can be wiped out when a family member becomes seriously ill. Another factor is that spending on health care currently consumes 14 percent of gross domestic product. Current trends suggest that by early in the next century, health care spending may absorb 20 percent of gross domestic product.

Hillary Rodham Clinton is the chief architect of this ambitious proposal. It promises to control the escalation of health care costs, maintain health care quality, and expand coverage to all Americans. A brief summary of the many initiatives considered would include emphasis on the early prevention and treatment of diseases, promotion of health maintenance organizations (HMOs), incentives to doctors to become general practitioners rather than specialists, control costs on prescriptions and medical procedures, and the requirement of portable insurance coverage, so that when workers change jobs, they will not experience periods without health insurance.

Source: David Lauter, "President Delivers Health Care Pep Talk," *Los Angeles Times,* January 4, 1994, A14.

Analysis

Our introduction to public finance has emphasized that all public policies have benefits and costs. Clearly, those who were previously uninsured benefit from having health insurance provided through this plan. Improving the quality of health insurance also benefits those who already have health insurance if under the plan they receive better insurance coverage or pay lower premiums. Costs arise because the plan extends coverage to those who previously did not have health insurance. Costs also arise because public employees are needed to oversee implementation of the plan.

The plan addresses the allocation function of government because it influences the allocation of health care resources in our economy. It redirects resources (e.g., into early prevention versus later treatment of diseases), increases resource allocation in certain areas (e.g., toward those who were previously without health insurance coverage) and, because it promises to reverse the escalation of costs, lowers the overall allocation of resources toward health care in the future. The plan is also motivated by the distribution function of government because it addresses the issue of who should bear the costs of health insurance. In 1993–94 various proposals were forwarded, but financing was an unresolved issue. Proposed sources included many sources, smokers and higher-income Americans among them.

It is not surprising that so much controversy has surrounded the health care proposal. Early reports, for example, estimated that up to 45 percent of Americans would end up paying higher insurance premiums under the plan than

continued on next page

> *continued from previous page*
> with previous arrangements. While some believe this is appropriate because the plan would improve the health care system, others have questioned whether promised benefits would ever materialize. Representative Dick Armey, a Ph.D. economist representing the state of Texas, for example, calls the plan a "bureaucratic nightmare that will kill jobs." Another Texan and Ph.D. economist, Senator Phil Gramm, declared, "I am not going to support the President's effort to have the government take over and run the health care system." Critics often suggested that a solution to the health care problem should come from the private market rather than from an increase in the government's role in allocating resources. One proposal, for example, would require that all Americans purchase their own health insurance, as they do their auto insurance. This approach clearly represents voters and policymakers who are committed to maintaining a small role for government in our economy. In contrast, the Clinton plan represents that segment of the public which believes in an active, large role for government in allocating our resources.
>
> Clearly, health care is a complex issue, and we cannot cover all relevant issues here. It is likely to continue in the public limelight for many years to come.

How we design our public institutions is another important choice. The following are a few of the relevant choices that underlie the institutional structure of the policy process:

- Who is allowed to vote?
- How often are elections held?
- Must governments operate under a balanced budget rule?
- Are elected policymakers subject to term limitations?
- Are there ceilings on campaign contributions?

In public finance we examine the relevant trade-offs associated with the various ways in which our public institutions are designed; for when we design our institutions one way, we of course incur an opportunity cost of not designing our institutions in other ways.

The institutional structure of the policy process influences the ability of voters to determine policies. At one extreme, some elections are held with only one candidate. In such a case, the institutional structure of the policy process may deny voters power; whereas when they may choose between two or more well-qualified candidates, voters may have considerable influence. The important point here is that the institutional structure of the policy process influences the outcomes of the policy process and, for this reason, is an important issue examined in public finance.

Positive and Normative Analysis

Positive analysis is analysis based on pure scientific prediction.

There are two dimensions of economic analysis: positive analysis and normative analysis. **Positive analysis** focuses on pure scientific prediction, or developing predictions from alternative models of the economy. Positive analysis predicts, for instance, that a surplus will develop whenever a market has a price above equilibrium. This prediction follows directly from models of supply and demand. A common application of this prediction is to the case of minimum wage laws, in which unemployment is predicted to rise whenever wages are set above market equilibrium. A general consensus among the analysts' predictions tends to characterize positive analysis.

Normative analysis offers policy analysts the luxury of allowing value judgments to enter into their analyses. Judgments are made about how our economic system *should* allocate resources. Because value judgments are diverse, normative analyses tend to vary widely among public finance economists. Let us return to minimum wage policy. As in all policy debates, many important issues are involved in evaluating the costs and benefits of the proposed policy. One economist may think that the higher wages earned by those who continue working justify the jobs lost by those the policy puts out of work. But another economist may believe that lost jobs do not justify higher wages earned by those fortunate enough to have kept their jobs.

> **Normative analysis** is analysis based on value judgments.

As evidence of the normative dimension of policy analysis, consider the lack of consensus evident from a survey of 936 economists.[1] For each question, three responses were allowed: "generally agree"; "agree with provisions"; and "generally disagree." Of the 27 questions, the highest consensus was 68.5 percent (and a response of "generally disagree") for a statement proposing: "Wage-price controls should be used to control inflation." Only seven questions posted a consensus greater than 50 percent; of those, only three posted a consensus over 60 percent.

Because all economists do not share common values, it is important for us to distinguish between positive and normative dimensions of policy analysis. Different values of different economists affect their normative analyses of economic issues; as a consequence, analysts tend to differ considerably about policy prescriptions. Individual differences in value judgments explain why much of public discussion of policy issues is subject to persistent controversy and debate. Note, however, that this is not to argue that normative prescriptions are not informed by positive analysis. Positive analysis allows us to evaluate the trade-offs between various policy options even though policies must be chosen on the basis of someone's normative preferences, including the value-based preferences of voters and policymakers. The act of choosing between available policy alternatives, however well analyzed, therefore must contain a substantial normative element, and so the policy arena will always be subject to dissension among voters, policymakers, and economists.

Studying Voters and Policymakers

A significant challenge of public finance, and hence much of its usefulness, lies in the ability of economists to understand what determines the policies of the public sector. The following are fundamental issues concerning voters and policymakers in the study of public finance:

❏ What is the framework by which policy goals are chosen?

❏ How do we arrive at policy goals?

---

[1] Bruno S. Frey, Werner W. Pommerehne, Friedrich Schneider and Guy Gilbert, "Consensus and Dissension among Economists: An Empirical Inquiry," *American Economic Review* 74 (December 1984): 986–994.

- Why does the public sector pursue policy A and not policy B?
- Why are some goals awarded greater priority than other goals?
- Why do policies change over time?

You will recall that policies are determined through the policy process. A simple model of the policy process in a representative democracy is

$$\text{voter} \Rightarrow \text{policymaker} \Rightarrow \text{public policy}$$

Voters signal their desires to policymakers, who in turn enact policies. Whereas resources are allocated by consumers and producers in private markets, voters and policymakers allocate resources in public markets. Voter and policymaker behaviors are therefore essential factors to be examined in public finance.

Behaviors of Policymakers

Self-interest is concern with one's own well-being.

With few exceptions, microeconomists assume that **self-interest** motivates consumers and producers. Consumers are assumed to maximize utility and producers to maximize profits. We can briefly define self-interested behavior as being concerned with the well-being of oneself. An individual's self-interest may also be defined to include the well-being of those close to that individual. For example, a wife and mother is probably interested in the well-being of her husband, children, parents, friends, relatives, and so on. (See Chapter 6.) Little, if any, debate exists among microeconomists on their modeling of consumers and producers as self-interested agents of the private market system.

Public spirit is concern for pursuing policies that benefit all of society.

No such consensus exists in public finance, in which the behaviors of voters and policymakers are contentious topics. In contrast to microeconomics, public finance is an arena of lively debate among those economists who believe that policymakers are motivated by **public spirit** and those who believe that policymakers display behaviors that are primarily self-interested. Public-spirited policymakers are assumed to be interested in pursing policies that benefit all of society. Self-interested policymakers, in contrast, are presumed to be interested in pursuing policies that benefit a narrower subset of society. Because different economists hold different views of policymakers, it should come as no surprise that the examination of policymakers in public finance is one of its liveliest areas.

Behaviors of Voters

One important reason for structuring political systems as representative democracies is to give voters, through the election of policymakers, a procedure for allocating resources in the public sector. Controversies over whether voters act according to public spirit or self-interest thus mirror the debate over what motivates behaviors of policymakers. But several other critical issues surround the behavior of voters. One issue is how well-informed voters are about policy issues. Because voters are both beneficiaries and financiers of public policies they have incentives to acquire information about policy issues. However, other factors tend to diminish incentives to acquire information. The very fact that many more policies exist today than ever before in history suggests that accumulating good information on policy issues involves increasing costs. The sheer size of the federal budget document may be enough to overwhelm many voters. One look at it can cause voters to decide that examining it carefully would be a waste of their valuable time and energies. For example, the *Budget of the United States Government, Fiscal Year 1994* is more than 2,000 pages long, weighs over five pounds, and costs $43. This is clearly a great deal more than bedside reading for the average voter. The costs of reading about state and local government policies are similar. Furthermore, the average voter who wants to be well informed is inundated with twenty-four hour television news programs, pages and pages of government documents, and a multitude of speeches by policymakers, lobbyists, and other parties interested in public policy.

Different perceptions of how well informed voters are may explain one reason for the widespread disagreements about policy. For example, some analysts believe that average voters are misinformed or lack essential information about certain policy issues. These analysts might therefore recommend that better-informed policymakers be awarded greater leverage in the policy process and voter leverage be decreased by limiting the frequency of elections and lengthening the terms of office for policymakers. Such changes would alter the institutional structure of the policy process. If, however, other analysts believe that voters are reasonably well informed, they might recommend that voters be given more leverage in the policy process and advise that elections be held more frequently and that terms of office be shortened.

Functions of the Public Sector

There are four primary functions of the public sector: protection, allocation, distribution, and stabilization.

Protection

Protection function is the safeguarding of the personal property and rights of individuals by the public sector.

The public sector provides a **protection function** when it safeguards the personal property and rights of individuals. Police, the military, and the courts protect the rights of individuals to own property, enforce contracts, and exercise freedoms of religion and speech. Private market economies are predominantly characterized by individual ownership of resources, and individuals are therefore the stewards, or guardians, of resources. Private owners assign values on their resources and determine their usage. For example, market suppliers and demanders determine which plots of land are developed into housing developments as well as the purchase price of each homesite. However, even in economies dominated by private ownership of resources, some resources such as air, water, and national parks are often jointly owned by all citizens. An example of a jointly owned resource is Yosemite National Park, which occupies 1,183 square miles in east-central California. Yosemite National Park comes under stewardship of the public sector and therefore the values and usage (e.g., what admission fees will be charged, which portions of the park will be developed for tourism and so on) of this resource are determined within the public sector.

Allocation

Allocation function is the shifting of resources into preferred (and out of nonpreferred) areas.

The public sector also performs an **allocation function.** Public spending on highway construction, defense spending, and medical research programs represent policies that perform an allocation function. Such policies are aimed at shifting resources into "preferred" areas and, since resources are scarce, out of other less well-favored areas. An increase in spending on health care, for example, necessarily implies less spending in some other area, such as defense.

Free riders and negative externalities are two problems associated with private markets that the public sector attempts to address with its allocation function. A free rider problem occurs when some individuals are able to avoid paying for goods they consume. One example would be the case of national defense: it is difficult, or impossible, to exclude free riders from enjoying the benefits of a well-protected nation. It is commonly believed that because free riders would cause resources to be under allocated in the private sector, the public sector should allocate resources when private markets are characterized by many free riders.

Negative externalities arise whenever the private sector does not assign appropriate values on economic resources. Clean air and water are often argued to be resources that private markets undervalue. Because private sector companies do not consider the full social costs of emitting pollutants into the air and water when they calculate profits, the private sector is believed to generate too many negative externalities. Government regulation or taxation of polluters is often prescribed to correct the private sector's miscalculation of the resource values of clean air and water.

Some individuals may also argue that the private sector undervalues resources when, for instance, private developers want to build a new shopping center or housing development on property on or adjoining a Civil War battlefield. This, in fact, has been a point of controversy in the community of Manassas, Virginia, where some local citizens have attempted, via the court system, to prevent private developers from building a new shopping center on land adjacent to the Bull Run battlefield. Critics of the shopping center argue that the land value is greater as a historic landmark than if it were developed.

Distribution

Distribution function is the changing of the final recipients of goods and services produced by the economy.

The **distribution function** is aimed at changing the final recipients of the goods and services produced by the economy. The primary goal of this function is to provide an equitable distribution of income. The essential issue that the distribution function addresses is whether the distribution policies of the public sector lead to a better or worse distribution of income than when the private sector allocates our resources. Progressive income tax policies, guaranteed loans provided to students and farmers, and programs that subsidize agriculture and automotive industries are examples of policies that influence the distribution of income in the economy.

Because reasonable people have diverse perceptions regarding what constitutes a fair or equitable distribution of income, the distributive role is an area of considerable controversy. While positive analysis may show how various policies may affect different measures of the income distribution, a sizable portion of the analysis must be normative in nature. Our judgments about who should receive the benefits of public programs and who should pay for them emerge from the interactions of voters and policymakers in the policy process.

Stabilization

Stabilization function is the smoothing out of the ups and downs of the macroeconomy.

The **stabilization function** of the public sector is carried out by monetary and fiscal policymakers who attempt to smooth out ups and downs in the macroeconomy. One of the most divisive macroeconomic debates in the twentieth century is over the question of how stable or unstable the private macroeconomy is. On one side are economists who believe that the private market is inherently stable and that in the event of recessions and high unemployment, market forces quickly stabilize the macroeconomy. The other side argues that although the price system of the private economy is a natural stabilizing device, periods of instability can dominate the economy. Textbooks on macroeconomics address these fundamental issues of stability and the theories and the evidence on which they are based.

There is considerable debate over how well the public sector performs the stabilization function. Although we do not address the important controversies in macroeconomics here, it is important to realize that these same controversies underlie the study of the protection, allocation, and distribution roles of the public sector. The essential issues are identical: Does the public sector improve the allocation of resources over what occurs when the private sector allocates our resources? Do policies improve the distribution of income over the distribution provided by the private sector? Do allocative policies aimed at remedying private underproduction of goods and services lead to optimal production or to overproduction of those goods and services?

Public Sector: Small or Large?

Supporters of Large Government

The public sector can play a large or a small role in our economy, and there are many different viewpoints on this issue of what the appropriate role is. Advocates of fairly large government tend to believe that many cases of market failure exist, that the policy process is an efficient means by which voters and policymakers organize resources, and that policymakers are driven by public spirit. Proponents of a fairly large public sector may also believe that policymakers should base their policies on **paternalism.** That is, in cases where policymakers believe that citizens make unwise choices, policies may be aimed at restricting choices. Prohibitions on what may be produced (e.g., licensing and regulation of suppliers) and consumed (e.g., liquor, tobacco, and drugs) are sometimes advocated by calls for paternalism in policymaking. Clearly, perceptions of what motivates behaviors of voters and policymakers and issues regarding the quantity and quality of information at the disposal of voters and policymakers influence how strongly one advocates paternalistic influences in public policy.

Paternalism is a characterization of a belief that policies should be provided that would not necessarily be freely chosen by voters.

Supporters of Small Government

Another viewpoint emphasizes that while the private sector is not a perfect organizer of resources, the public sector is imperfect as well. The flip side to the notion of

Government failure occurs when a public policy results in an inefficient or inequitable outcome.

market failure is that of **government failure,** which is a condition whereby public policies result in resource allocations that are more inefficient or inequitable than when those resources are organized by the private sector. Inefficiencies and inequities may be the result of technical inabilities of policymakers to improve upon private resource allocations or may result from the self-interested nature of policymakers. Supporters of small government tend to believe that few policies improve upon resource allocations of the private sector.

This viewpoint tends to emphasize the importance of individual liberty and the importance of protecting voters from the coercive powers of the public sector. Supporters therefore tend to reject the validity of a paternalistic influence in public policy as well. While those who reject the validity of paternalism may also believe that some of the choices made by members of society are inappropriate, they tend to believe that few cases arise which justify paternalistic policies.

The Usefulness of Public Finance

It is human nature to want to change things that affect our lives—including public policy. However, without a good understanding of how private and public sectors operate, it is difficult or impossible to adopt changes in public policy that result in improvements in our economic well-being. We should not dismiss the possibilities that public policies can result in a world that would be less desirable than before.

Policy choices necessarily entail many trade-offs and a great deal of analysis and thought. Economists cannot be expected to make appropriate value judgments about which policy tools and goals are appropriate for society. Rather, it is up to voters and policymakers to choose policies on the basis of positive and normative analyses. To the extent allowed by the institutional structure of the policy process, dissatisfied voters may reject policymakers who fail to perform to their satisfaction. We must also be careful to distinguish among the roles of economists, voters, and policymakers as we study public finance. An understanding of public finance can give awareness of the ways in which the private and public sectors of the economy operate and, given various policy goals, it can lead to recommendations on the means by which policies can achieve these goals. The role of the economist is not to give us policy goals, but, rather, to comment on the ways in which alternative policies contribute toward the achievement of policy goals.

Continuing study will provide us with an appreciation of the many complexities in understanding the policy process between voters and policymakers and the role that economists play in the formation of public policy. At first glance, the relationship of voters, policymakers, and economists may seem pretty simple. However, once we understand the many competing theories on the behaviors of voters and policymakers and when we see that analysis necessarily entails a normative dimension, we appreciate the challenge and complexity of our study. While public policy may not be the panacea that allows us to correct every social and economic problem, the study of public finance is an important step toward being able to make wise decisions about how, where, and to what extent the public sector allocates our scarce resources.

Summary

- The study of public finance provides a framework for understanding and improving the ways in which spending and tax policies of the public sector influence our economic lives.
- Because resources are scarce, choices are made regarding what role the public sector should be awarded in influencing resource allocation. The notion of opportunity cost informs us about the costs of pursuing one public policy over another.
- The concept of market failure conveys the idea that private markets do not always result in resource allocations that society believes is appropriate. Economic efficiency and equity are two criteria for influencing resource allocations by the public sector.
- Voters and policymakers decide, through the policy process, policies of the public sector. The institutional structure of the policy process comprises such features as who is allowed to vote, how often elections are held, how many policymakers are elected, how long policymakers may serve in public office, and whether there are ceilings on campaign contributions.
- Positive economic analysis focuses on pure scientific prediction. Normative economic analysis is based on the values of the analyst.
- The four primary functions of the public sector are protection, allocation, distribution, and stabilization.

Review Questions

1. What is the subject matter of public finance?
2. What does tax freedom day measure?
3. What is meant by the term opportunity cost?
4. What is market failure? What is government failure? How do the two concepts differ?
5. What is the difference between positive and normative economic analysis?
6. What is the policy process?
7. What are the four major functions of the public sector? Give an example of each.

Discussion Questions

1. How would you determine your total tax bill for this year?
2. Name three government programs in which you are a primary beneficiary. Name five government programs in which you receive few or no benefits. Can you name many programs in which you have taken the benefits of those programs for granted?
3. Discuss at least four ways in which public policy could be designed to accomplish the policy goal of improving the country's network of roads. Discuss whether all ways are equally beneficial to you.
4. It is often difficult for analysts to arrive at one answer or solution to any specific policy issue. Discuss the reasons for the fact that even when a well-defined policy goal, such as eliminating poverty, exists, consensus among policy analysts regarding the appropriate policy solution to achieve the policy goal will not arise.
5. What is the difference between *discussing* policy options and *choosing* one policy option over another?
6. Discuss the following statement: Every public policy entails a cost.
7. Why would different people hold different views regarding what is the appropriate size of government? Which functions of the public sector would you expect to cause the most agreement concerning their validity as functions the public sector should provide? Which functions of government would you expect to cause considerable disagreement as to their appropriateness?

Key Words

Public finance
Progressive income tax
Equity
Opportunity cost
Market failure
Pareto efficiency
Policy process
Positive analysis
Normative analysis

Self-interest
Public spirit
Protection function
Allocation function
Distribution function
Stabilization function
Paternalism
Government failure

CHAPTER 2

Policies of the Public Sector

The Size of the Public Sector

The influence of the public sector on our lives comes in many forms and includes spending and loan programs, tax laws, regulations on consumers and businesses, and insurance and credit programs. An accounting of the many policies provides us with an understanding of the size of the public sector. Public finance examines public sector size because an adequate description of the many policies provides a starting point for later chapters that delve into the details of how individual policies influence resource allocation and the distribution of income in our economy.

Three general conclusions are drawn from this chapter:

❑ Public policies influence almost every facet of our economic lives.
❑ Measuring the size of the public sector is a challenging endeavor.
❑ The influence of the public sector on our lives is growing.

Spending Policies

Total Government Spending

Spending is the most commonly used measure of the size of the public sector. (The spending budgets of governments are measured over *fiscal years*. The fiscal year of the federal government begins on October 1 of each year, and fiscal years of most state governments begin on July 1 of each year.) Figure 2-1 displays public spending as a share of gross domestic product, or GDP, which measures annual economic output. Public spending is therefore placed within the perspective of the overall economy since it indicates the spending share of the economy awarded to the public sector. In 1940, federal, state, and local governments spent $18.4 billion, which when divided by GDP of $100.4 billion, amounted to an 18.3 percent share of the economy. By 1993, public spending accounted for 34.4 percent of GDP. Therefore, the public spending share of the economy has almost doubled since 1940.

Public spending during World War II rose to unprecedented levels and at its highest point, in 1944, commanded 48 percent of GDP. During wartime, demands for military hardware and service personnel rapidly increases public spending. Public spending tends to drop swiftly after wartime; in the case of World War II, which ended in 1945, public spending fell to 18 percent of GDP by 1947. However, despite various ups and downs in its spending share, a positive trend characterizes public spending in years following World War II.

Private Sector Spending

The economy can be divided into two components: public and private sectors. Growth in the share controlled by the public sector therefore implies that the share controlled by the private sector has shrunk over this time period. In other words, when one sector allocates more of our resources, the other sector must allocate fewer. Figure 2-2 displays the falling importance of the private sector's role in allocating economic resources. Starting at 81.7 percent of GDP in 1940, the spending share of the private sector fell to 65.6 percent of GDP in 1993. That is, $82 out of $100 were allocated by the private sector in 1940, but now that allocation has fallen to $66 out of every $100.

Areas of Public Spending

Table 2-1 presents a breakdown of public spending into thirteen policy areas. The listing is very broad in nature, but it indicates the thrust, or general direction, of public policies. These thirteen areas nicely summarize the general direction of thousands of

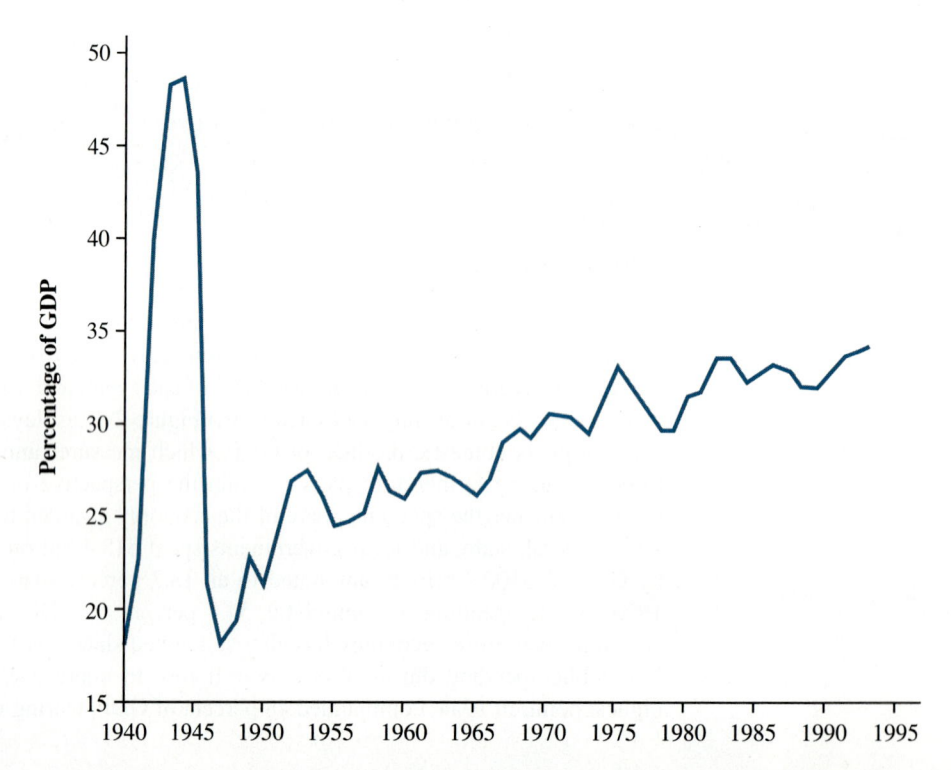

FIGURE 2-1
Public Spending in the United States as a Share of GDP

Sources: Facts and Figures on Government Finance, 1991; and Budget of the United States Government, 1994.

**FIGURE 2-2
Private Spending in
the United States as
a Share of GDP**

*Sources: Facts and
Figures on Government
Finance, 1991; and
Budget of the United
States Government, 1994.*

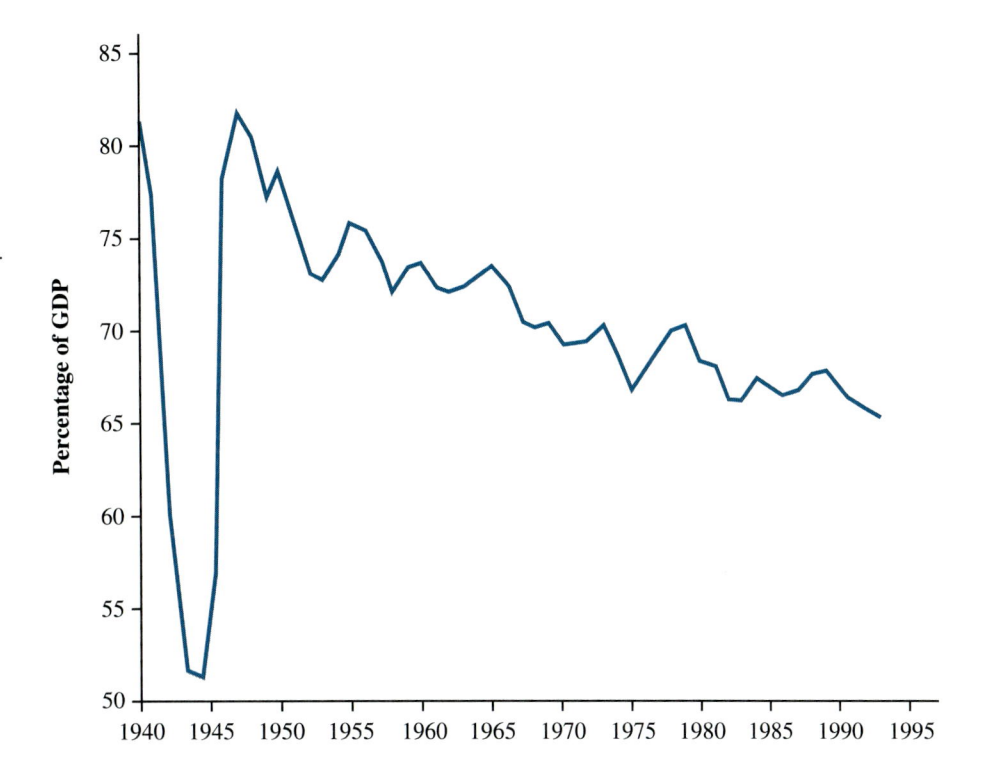

different spending programs of federal, state, and local governments. Insurance trusts, which constitute 21 percent of public spending, rank first in spending levels. These programs include Social Security and unemployment compensation; because they transfer income from one individual to another, they reflect the distributive function of the public sector. National defense and international relations are the second largest spending area.

Federal and Nonfederal Spending

Figure 2-3 separates public spending into its federal and nonfederal components. Since 1950, both federal and nonfederal governments have been allocating expanding shares of GDP. The federal government share of GDP grew from 16 percent to 23.4 percent between 1950 and 1993. Over the same period, the state and local government share of GDP rose from 7.1 percent to 11 percent.

Financing Activities

Government Revenues, Budgetary Deficits, and Surpluses

The public sector must have the means of paying for its spending policies. Two primary means of financing public spending exist: taxes and borrowing. Figure 2-4

TABLE 2-1
Spending of All Governments by Area
Fiscal Year 1988

Area	Total ($Millions)	Total Spending (%)
Insurance trusts	$ 388,505	21%
National defense and international relations	329,993	18
Education	256,960	14
Social service	219,554	12
Interest on general debt	202,437	11
Environment and housing	152,679	8
Transportation	70,274	4
Public safety	67,542	4
Utility expenditures	67,214	4
Governmental administration	48,110	3
Postal service	33,892	2
Space research and technology	8,866	0[a]
Liquor store expenditures	2,837	0[a]
SUM	$1,920,413	100

[a] Less than 1 percent.

Source: Table A7, Tax Foundation, *Facts and Figures on Government Finance,* 1991 Edition (Baltimore/London: The Johns Hopkins Press, 1991).

shows tax revenues as a share of GDP.[1] It should not be surprising that tax revenues grow in tandem with public spending. The figure also displays the breakdown of tax revenues into federal and nonfederal components.

When tax revenues do not perfectly mirror changes in public spending, public budgets are unbalanced. Figure 2-5 displays public budget deficits/surpluses since 1950. A **budget deficit** occurs when public spending exceeds tax revenues, and a **budget surplus** occurs when public spending is less than tax revenues.

Notice the dissimilar funding experiences of federal and nonfederal (state and local) governments. Since the early 1970s, the total budgetary picture of federal, state, and local governments indicates growing budget deficits. However, over this period, the nonfederal sector has experienced gradual and growing budget surpluses, while the federal sector has experienced continual and growing budget deficits. In fact, the last time the federal budget was not in deficit was 1969. All past unpaid, or outstanding, federal debt is called the national debt, and in 1993 it stood at $4,410,475 million,

Budget deficit
occurs when public spending exceeds tax revenues.

Budget surplus
occurs when tax revenues exceed public spending.

---

[1] When we view the share of GDP that is allocated to tax revenues, we are viewing GDP as the sum of all incomes in an economy. This difference demonstrates the differences between public spending and taxation. Spending may be viewed as the purchase of goods and services while taxation may be viewed as the share of taxpayers' income that finances the spending of governments.

**FIGURE 2-3
Public Spending in
the United States**
*Composition by
Government*

Source: Budget of
the United States
Government, 1994.

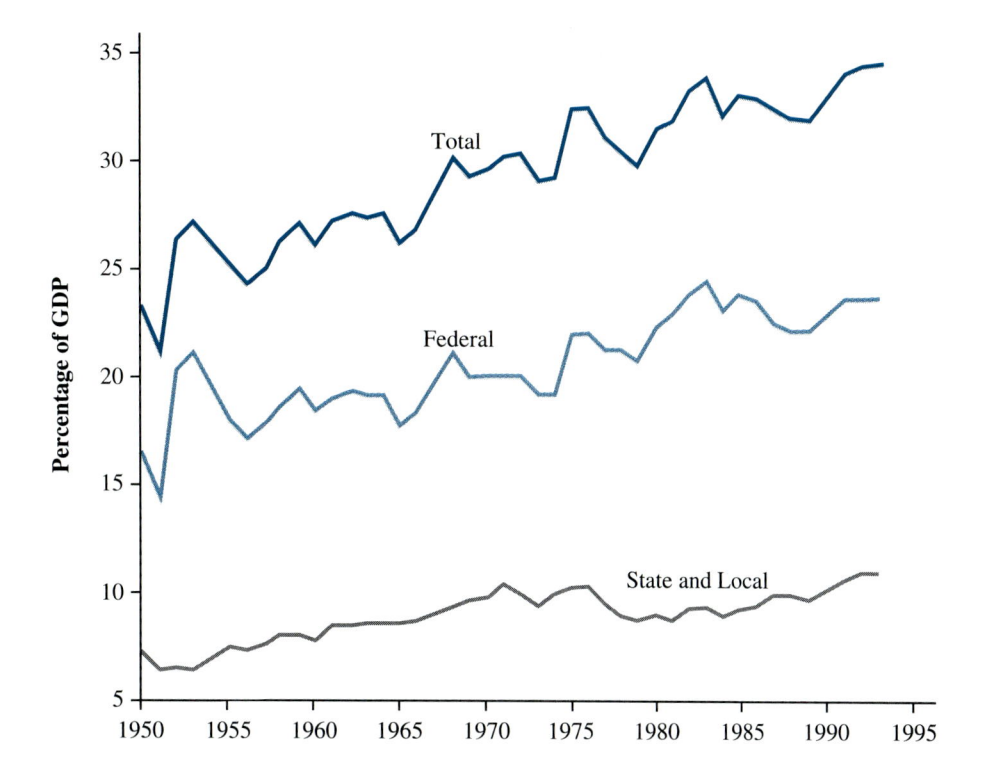

**FIGURE 2-4
Tax Collection in the
United States**
*Composition by
Government*

Source: Budget of
the United States
Government, 1994.

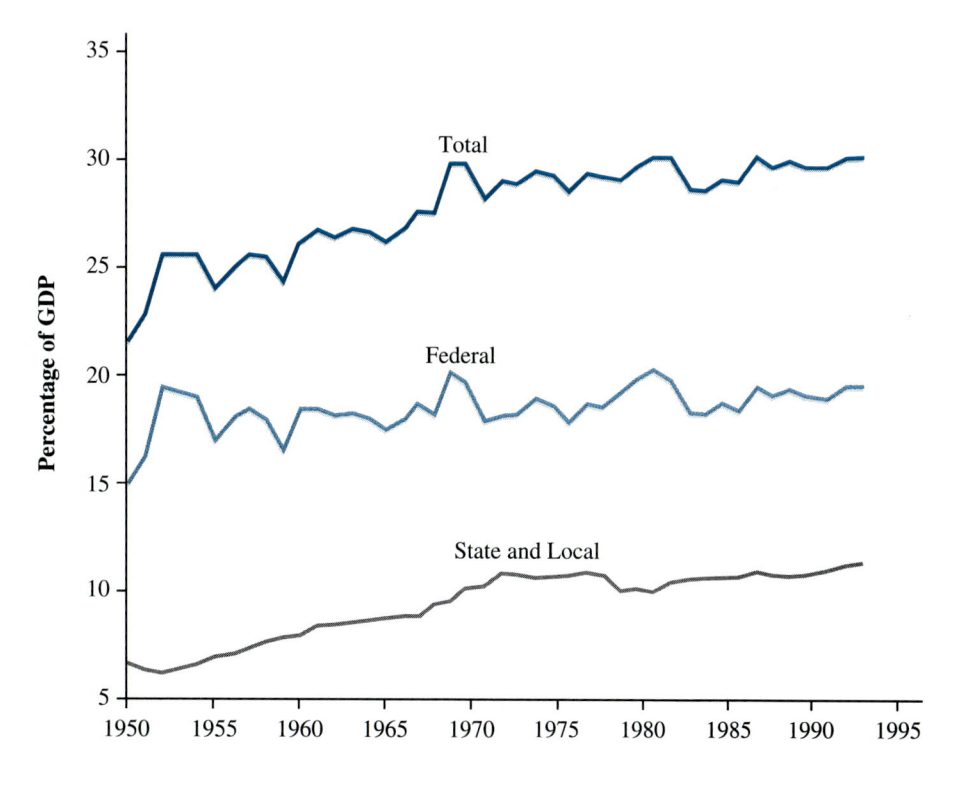

FIGURE 2-5
Budget Deficits (−) and Surpluses (+)

Source: Budget of the United States Government, 1994.

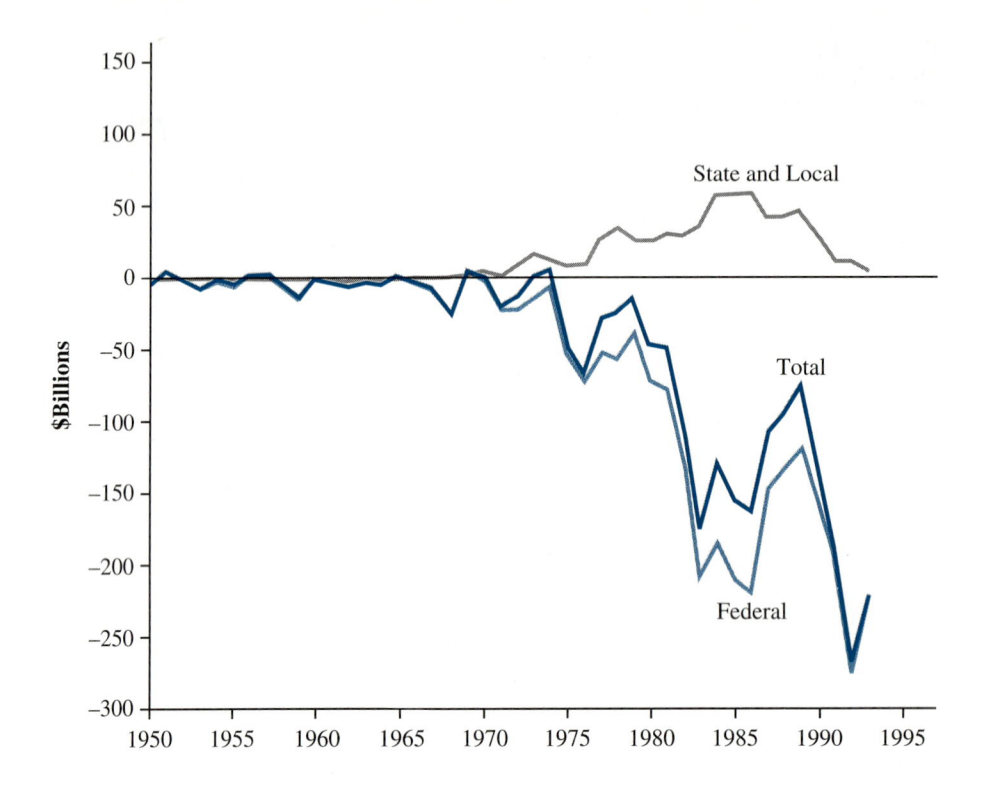

or about 71 percent of GDP.[2] The term "outstanding" is used to describe all dollar commitments still in existence, that is, all previously made commitments that have not been retired plus any new additional commitments made in the current year.

Prior to the 1970s, both federal and nonfederal governments ran budget surpluses about as often as budget deficits. Changes in policy priorities between financing spending through taxation versus borrowing have occurred since the 1970s.

Sources of Revenues

Many sources of revenue are available to governments. Table 2-2, which presents twenty-three sources of revenue, provides an overview of this dimension of the public budget. A partial list of the different groups of taxpayers includes private workers, public employees, corporations, retirees, users of toll bridges and highways as well as consumers of tobacco, liquor, gasoline, air travel, and luxury automobiles. Personal income taxation accounts for 27.6 percent of revenues of all governments. The second largest revenue source is associated with insurance trusts and, within this category, Social Security taxes (OASDIH) are the largest revenue source.

---

[2] Data from *Budget of the United States Government,* 1994. This is the number for "gross federal debt." Chapter 17 on budget deficits examines alternative definitions of public debt.

TABLE 2-2
Revenues of All Governments by Source
Fiscal Year 1988

Source	Total ($Millions)	Total %
General Taxes		**41.6%**
Property	$ 132,240	7.4
Individual income	489,530	27.6
Corporate income	117,936	6.6
Sales and Gross Receipts		**14.4**
Custom duties	16,317	0.9
Sales and gross receipts	105,168	5.9
Motor fuel	30,649	1.7
Alcohol	9,311	0.5
Tobacco	9,523	0.5
Public utility	16,202	0.9
Other	21,691	1.2
Motor vehicle and license	10,291	0.6
Death and gift	10,868	0.6
All other general	28,549	1.6
Insurance Trust Taxes		**18.6**
Unemployment compensation	17,468	1.0
OASDIH	310,023	17.4
Railroad retirement	4,423	0.2
Nontax Revenues		**19.9**
Current charges[a]	174,639	9.8
Miscellaneous general[b]	126,324	7.1
Utilities	49,226	2.8
Liquor store	3,290	0.2
Insurance Trust Receipts[c]		**5.3**
Employee retirement	82,262	4.6
Veterans' life insurance	703	0.1
Other	9,749	0.6
SUM	$1,776,382	100.0

[a] Amounts received from the public for performance of specific services benefiting the person charged; includes fees, toll charges, tuition, and other categories.

[b] Includes special assessments, sale of property, interest earnings, etc.

[c] Includes co-payments for benefits received.

Source: Table A12, Tax Foundation, *Facts and Figures on Government Finance,* 1991 Edition (Baltimore/London: The Johns Hopkins Press, 1991).

Public Sector Employment

Another measure of the size of the public sector is its number of employees. Figure 2-6 places civilian government employment within the perspective of the entire nonmilitary work force of the economy. While total government employment as a percentage of the U.S. work force rose to a high of approximately 17 percent in the 1975, it has recently dropped to 15.8 percent. Employment trends of federal and nonfederal governments, however, are dissimilar for this period. Since 1950, the federal share of employment fell from 3.3 percent to 2.4 percent of the work force. In this same period, the nonfederal share of employment expanded from 7.0 percent to 13.3 percent.

Federal Credit and Insurance Programs

The federal government is the largest creditor in the country, as well its largest underwriter of risk. About one-half of nonfederal borrowing is influenced by programs of the federal government. **Credit and insurance policies** direct resources into various areas of the economy. For example, in order to improve the chances that low-income, gifted individuals go to college, the federal government may try to increase the likelihood that these individuals can borrow funds for tuition payments and other expenses associated with college education at a low cost. Federal policies that increase the supply of college loans will result in greater availability of loans, and these loans will carry lower interest rates than if the federal policies did not reallocate

Credit and insurance policies reallocate resources in credit and insurance markets.

**FIGURE 2-6
Government
Employees**
Composition by Government

Source: Economic Report of the President, 1994.

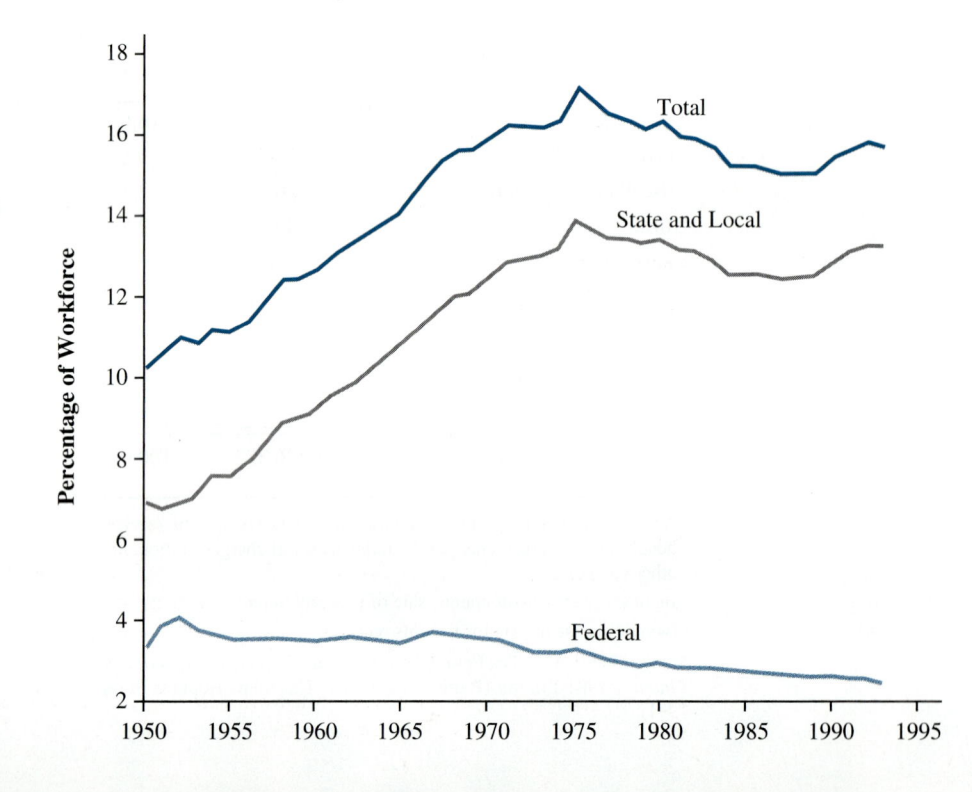

funds into this credit market. Policies that lower interest rates on loans are in effect subsidizing college educations, and therefore, are policies that increase the share of resources allocated to education.

Table 2-3 displays the growth in the outstanding value of federal credit and insurance policies. These policies are designed to increase the allocation of resources into credit and insurance markets. The largest program, Deposit Insurance, accounts for 45.5 percent of credit and insurance policies and is administered by the Federal Deposit Insurance Corporation (FDIC). Up to a maximum of $100,000 per account, this policy insures deposits at commercial banks, savings and loans, and credit unions. Other insurance programs account for 27.2 percent of federal credit and insurance programs and have experienced a 678 percent increase over this same period. These programs include private pension insurance, flood insurance, crop insurance, nuclear risk insurance, and many others.

Government-sponsored enterprises (GSEs) are off-budget government agencies that reallocate resources in credit markets.

Accounting for 13.8 percent of programs, GSE loans are loans by **government-sponsored enterprises (GSEs)**—firms that are created, chartered, and regulated by the federal government. These firms sell debt that carries an implicit perception that the federal government guarantees payment of principal and interest if they are unable to repay their investors. GSEs act like financial institutions and are primarily involved in the housing, education, and agricultural sectors of the economy. GSEs include

- Federal National Mortgage Association (Fannie Mae), created in 1938 to help buyers of home mortgages.
- Federal Home Loan Mortgage Corporation (Freddie Mac), created in 1970 to help buyers of home mortgages.
- Student Loan Marketing Association (Sallie Mae), created in 1972 to help college students.
- College Construction Loan Insurance Association (Connie Lee), created in 1986 to facilitate new construction and renovation of college buildings.

TABLE 2-3
Federal Credit and Insurance Outstanding
$Billions

Program	1970	1975	1980	1985	1990	Percent Increase 1970–90
Deposit insurance	$476	$ 855	$1,456	$2,342	$2,815	491%
Other insurance	216	187	831	1,031	1,681	678
GSE loans	24	49	151	370	855	3,462
Loan guarantees	125	189	299	410	630	404
Direct loans	51	74	164	257	210	312
TOTAL	$892	$1,354	$2,901	$4,410	$6,191	594%

Source: Table A1, *Budget of the United States Government,* 1991.

Experiencing the largest percentage increase (3,462 percent) of credit and insurance programs, GSE loans and their tremendous expansions demonstrate the rapidly growing role of the federal government in financial markets.

The associated liabilities of credit and insurance programs is an important issue. Because these programs are liabilities of governments, they are liabilities of taxpayers as well. To the extent that liabilities come due (as in the case of a loan default), some means of funding these liabilities must be made. While private market firms, such as insurers, must establish contingency funds for meeting future expected liabilities, governments do not always operate under similar funding constraints. When no ongoing public fund exists to meet future liabilities of a program, that program is unfunded or underfunded. To the extent that liabilities are underfunded, additional tax dollars, public sector borrowing, or reduced spending may be used to finance claims on these liabilities. This is expected to be a growing policy issue, for a recent Treasury Department study finds: "Some GSEs are among the most thinly capitalized of major U.S. financial entities."[3]

Loan guarantees represent 10.2 percent of federal credit and insurance programs and include Federal Housing Administration (FHA) and the Department of Veterans Affairs (VA) mortgage loans, Small Business Administration (SBA) loans, and guaranteed student loans. **Direct loans** are the smallest category and are offered in diverse areas, among them agriculture, rural electrification, and loans for exporters and importers of goods and services. This category has grown far more slowly than any other federal credit and insurance program.

Many important issues are related to credit and insurance policies. One is their **off-budget policy** nature. An **on-budget policy** is the previously discussed spending, tax, and deficit policies of the public sector. Even though off-budget policies influence resource allocations, these policies, with the exception of direct loans, do not immediately show up on on-budget books of the public sector.

Loan guarantees are loans guaranteed by the public sector.

Direct loans are loans made directly by the public sector.

Off-budget policies are credit and insurance policies that do not directly show up on the government budget.

On-budget policies are spending and tax policies that show up directly on the government budget.

Legislative Output of Congress

Measures Introduced and Enacted

Among the laws enacted by the U.S. Congress are policies that allocate resources in our economy. Before spending, tax, credit, and insurance policies may be implemented, Congress must introduce and pass authorizing legislation. Table 2-4 displays a history of this aspect of Congress. While the number of measures introduced has fallen steadily since the 1970s, Congress continues to introduce and enact a large body of laws. In recent years, it is not uncommon for the U.S. Congress to introduce close to 6,700 new laws in its two-year session and to enact over 600 of these measures into legislation.

The information provided in Table 2-4 quantifies one aspect of the legislative activities of the federal public sector. Unfortunately, it is difficult to analyze the implications of these activities on resource allocation within our economy. For example, one measure may legislate November 2 of each year as National Pickle Day, whereas

---

[3] *Report of the Secretary of the Treasury on Government Sponsored Enterprises,* May 1990, 8.

TABLE 2-4
Measures Introduced and Enacted by Congress

Session	Introduced	Enacted
92nd, 1971–72	22,969	768
93rd, 1973–74	23,396	774
94th, 1975–76	21,096	729
95th, 1977–78	19,387	803
96th, 1979–80	12,583	736
97th, 1981–82	11,490	529
98th, 1983–84	10,134	677
99th, 1985–86	9,885	483
100th, 1987–88	9,558	761
101st, 1989–90	6,664	666
102nd, 1991–92	6,775	609

Source: Statistical Abstract of the United States, 1993.

another measure may lower tax rates on certain types of investment activity. The two different measures exert very different influences on resource allocations. Congressional measures, therefore, do not offer a clear documentation of the many ways in which Congress influences resource allocations.

Legislation

The following are a few of the laws enacted by the U.S. Congress:

- The *National Labor Relations Act of 1935* allows employees the right to organize in labor unions and engage in collective bargaining with employers.
- The *Minimum Wage Act of 1938* sets wage and overtime standards.
- The *Equal Pay Act of 1963* requires that men and women receive the same pay for the same jobs.
- The *Civil Rights Act of 1964* bars discrimination in the workplace and across all U.S. society.
- The *Age Discrimination Act of 1967* bars discrimination based on age in employment and promotion and protects workers from forced employment.
- The *Occupational Safety and Health Act of 1970* sets health and safety standards for the workplace.

Laws alter the resource allocations of the private sector. The justification for reallocation is often the market failure argument that the private sector does not produce appropriate quantities or qualities of various goods and services. Consider the case of the Occupational Safety and Health Act (OSH Act) of 1970, which attempts to increase the allocation of resources devoted to the control of occupational injuries above that of the private sector. The OSH Act requires that firms adopt specified safety and health regulations in the workplace. For example, there are regulations on the numbers and locations of fire extinguishers in the firm, as well as on maximum noise exposure for workers. Compliance means that firms may have to purchase more fire extinguishers, less noisy machinery, and more earplugs. To ensure compliance with regulations, Congress awards the public sector powers of inspection and, for those firms which do not comply with the regulations, the power to penalize recalcitrant firms. The OSH Act therefore influences the resource allocations of private firms and directs more of the economy's resources than was the case before 1970 toward improving health and safety in the workplace.

Regulatory Agencies

Regulatory agencies are government agencies that monitor and enforce Congressional regulations.

Congress also influences resource allocation through the creation of **regulatory agencies,** which enforce regulations. The late 1960s saw the creation of a large number of health and safety regulatory agencies designed to protect consumers from environmental and product quality problems. Based on market failure arguments, Congress creates regulatory agencies to correct various perceived flaws in private market allocations of resources. These regulatory agencies include:

- The *Occupational Safety and Health Administration (OSHA),* which promotes health and safety in the workplace.
- The *Consumer Product Safety Commission (CPSC),* which regulates the safety of products.
- The *National Highway Traffic Safety Administration (NHTSA),* which promotes safety of U.S. highways.
- The *Environmental Protection Agency (EPA),* which regulates the environment.

The primary tools of agencies are inspection programs, product labeling requirements, and such quality requirements as mandatory seat belts in cars, prohibition of flammable materials in clothing made for children, and rules stating the number, types, and locations of fire extinguishers in the workplace.

All of this suggests the difficulty of separating the influences of the private and public sectors on the allocations of our resources. For example, even though we may purchase a new automobile from a private dealer, the car we buy reflects decisions made in both private and public sectors. Decisions to produce 500 red six-cylinder automobiles is primarily a decision stemming from the supplies and demands in the private market. The public sector, however, may require that the automobiles be produced with seat belts and pollution control devices. While the automobiles are produced within the private market, the public sector also plays a significant role in allocating resources to it.

Public Sectors of Other Countries

Table 2-5 displays the sizes of public sectors of the Organization for Economic Cooperation and Development (OECD) countries. Public sector size is measured by the ratio of tax revenue to GDP. All OECD countries are experiencing growing public

TABLE 2-5
Sizes of Public Sectors in OECD Countries
Tax Revenues as a Percentage of Gross Domestic Product

	1965	1975	1985	1987
Australia	23.2	27.6	30.4	31.3
Austria	34.7	38.6	43.1	42.3
Canada	25.4	32.4	32.9	34.5
Germany	31.6	35.7	38.0	37.6
Switzerland	20.7	29.6	32.0	32.0
United States	25.9	29.0	29.2	30.0
Belgium	30.8	41.1	46.5	46.1
Denmark	29.9	41.4	49.0	52.0
Finland	29.5	35.1	36.8	35.9
France	34.5	36.9	44.5	44.8
Greece	20.6	24.6	35.2	37.4
Ireland	26.0	31.5	38.4	39.9
Italy	25.5	26.2	34.4	36.2
Japan	18.3	20.9	28.0	30.2
Luxembourg	30.4	39.2	43.6	43.8
Netherlands	33.2	43.7	44.9	48.0
New Zealand	24.7	31.3	33.9	38.6
Norway	33.3	44.9	47.6	48.3
Portugal	18.4	24.7	31.6	31.4
Spain	14.5	19.6	29.1	33.0
Sweden	35.4	43.9	50.6	56.7
Turkey	15.0	20.7	19.7	24.1
United Kingdom	30.4	35.7	37.8	37.5
AVERAGE	23.2	24.4	34.0	35.5

Source: Table 1, *Significant Features of Fiscal Federalism,* vol. 2, Advisory Commission on Intergovernmental Relations, 1991.

sectors and, between 1965 and 1987, public sectors have expanded, on average, from 23.2 percent to 35 percent of GDP. The largest public sector, Sweden, allocates well over one-half of the resources of its economy. Turkey, which has the smallest public sector, allocates approximately one-fourth of the resources of its economy. Notice that the United States has one of the smallest public sectors of any OECD country. We must be careful, however, to remember that these comparisons are based solely on tax revenue measures of public sector size. More extensive examination and comparison of all policy areas (spending, deficits and surpluses, laws, regulations, credit and insurance policies) would be required to complete a more thorough comparison of public sector sizes across these countries.

Reinventing Government? The Gore Plan

American voters seem increasingly dissatisfied with the ways in which government operates, to the point where recent polls show that only 20 percent of Americans trust the federal government to do "the right thing most of the time." This is down from 76 percent of Americans polled thirty years ago. Moreover, polls indicate that Americans believe that 48 percent of all tax dollars are wasted by the federal government.

As a way of dealing with increasing discontent of voters, the Clinton administration launched its National Performance Review in 1993. The general conclusion of the review is clear from the following statement in its final report: "It is almost as if federal programs were *designed* not to work. In truth, few are 'designed' at all; the legislative process simply churns them out, one after another, year after year." This review process, often called the Reinventing Government Plan, has been headed by Vice President Al Gore. It promises to meet two goals: to make government work better and to make it cost less.

Gore's commission collected an immense list of problem areas in government policies. A few—from many—examples suggest the silliness of some current practices. The best known are probably the ten pages of government specifications for the types of ash trays, or, as they are known by the government, "ash receivers, tobacco (desk type)," that may be purchased. Vice President Gore demonstrated some of the "receiver" specifications on news programs—and also on David Letterman's late night talk show. One branch office of the Department of Agriculture serves only seventeen farmers. Procurement rules can run to 1,600 pages, and signature after signature is required before anything may be purchased. Buying a desktop computer, for example, takes about one year and leads many workers to complain that the computers are obsolete by the time they arrive.

Running 168 pages, the report lists 800 recommendations for reinventing government. These include streamlining procurement practices, adopting a two-year budget cycle, simplifying tax forms, allowing taxes to be paid by credit cards, reducing the federal work force through early retirement incentives, increasing debt collection efforts, eliminating incentives to spend excess money at the end of fiscal years, and eliminating some branch offices of the Departments of Agriculture and Housing and Urban Development. Overall, the plan promises to save $108 billion over 5 years and to double, to 200,000, the planned reduction in the federal work force.

Source: George J. Church, "Gorezilla Zaps the System: Al Gore Seeks to 'Reinvent Government,' but Beware the Bureaucracy's Seasoned Heel Draggers," *Time,* September 13, 1993, 25–28.

Analysis

Many times in the past there have been calls to end "waste, fraud and abuse" in government. The Grace Commission, for instance, was created by President Ronald Reagan in 1982 to meet the same goals as the 1993 National Performance Review. Providing 2,500 specific recommendations, the Grace Commission recommended that federal spending be cut by $400 billion over a period of three years. Interestingly, many of the Grace Commission recommendations are echoed in the National Performance Review because they have never been implemented.

If all of the Gore recommendations are enacted, only about 1.3 percent of federal spending would be cut over a period of five years. Clearly, this is little in comparison to the growth rate of public spending. Even so, there may be reason to suspect that budgetary savings are far less than promised. Analysis by the Congressional Budget Office (CBO), which appeared a month after the Gore report, estimates that reforms would save

continued on next page

continued from previous page
less than $500 million over the five-year period—about 8 percent of the promised 1.3 percent of savings. The Gore report may have fallen victim to the same problems that have done in previous attempts at reinventing government.

This is not to argue that elected policymakers are insincere in their desire to make government more efficient and leaner. Our discussion, however, does suggest the importance of understanding how the policy process operates. A thorough understanding of the ways in which voters and policymakers operate within government institutions provides us with a better understanding of the government policies we receive.

A Growing Public Sector

Public policies come in many varieties, and the influence of the public sector on our lives is growing. Spending and taxation policies are the traditional and highly visible measures of the size of the public sector. The less visible measures, such as credit, insurance, and legislative and regulatory policies, have also grown. All such policies influence resource allocations within our economy.

Our survey suggests that a degree of substitutability exists among various policies. The following policies, for instance, all attempt to direct more resources into education:

- Public spending of $50 million on new school buildings
- A law that requires all students to pass standardized tests in mathematics
- A law that raises the minimum certification level for teachers of economics
- A program that offers low-interest loans to students to attend public universities
- A program that funds teachers in secondary schools to return to school and earn advanced degrees in their field of expertise

These are only a few of the policies that may be used to advance the goal of improving education in the United States, and it should be clear that they allocate resources in many different ways.

Our ability to control the size of the public sector is a subject of continuing debate in light of recent, controversial growth in federal budget deficits. Balanced budget rules, changes in budgetary accounting rules, line-item veto powers for the President, and term limitations on incumbent policymakers are a few of the proposals that public finance economists have discussed as methods of improving control over the size of the public sector.

Summary

- Spending is the most commonly used measure of the size of the public sector. Public policies, however, include many expenditure, tax, legislative, regulatory, credit, and insurance policies.

- Public spending, as a share of the economy, has grown rapidly since World War II. Insurance trusts, which include Social Security, Medicare, and unemployment insurance, constitute roughly

- one-fifth of total public spending. Spending on defense and international relations is the second largest spending area.
- Public spending may be separated into spending by federal and nonfederal (state and local) governments. Spending by both levels of governments have grown as shares of the overall economy. The federal government outspends the nonfederal sector at a rate of more than two to one.
- Personal income taxation is the largest tax revenue source of governments. The second largest revenue source is provided by insurance trusts, which include Social Security taxes.
- Budget deficits occur when public spending exceeds tax revenues, and budget surpluses occur when public spending is less than tax revenues. While the nonfederal sector has recently operated under growing levels of surplus, the federal government has operated under budgetary deficit since the 1970s.
- The federal government is the largest creditor in the country and the largest underwriter of risk. Taxpayer liabilities associated with credit and insurance programs have rapidly expanded in recent years and are often referred to as off-budget programs of government because they do not usually directly show up on the budget of the government at the time when the policies are legislated by Congress.

Review Questions

1. What is meant by the term "public sector size"?
2. What are the definitions of budget deficits and surpluses?
3. What are the major sources of taxation?
4. What are the major federal credit and insurance programs?
5. What is the legislative output of Congress? Why is it important in the study of public finance?

Discussion Questions

1. Discuss what makes it difficult to measure the "size" of government. Explain why, even given these difficulties, it is important to attempt to make this measurement.
2. Explain why some activities of the public sector are more directly recognizable as public sector activities than others. Discuss several examples of both types of activities, those that are directly recognizable and those that are less visible.
3. Discuss three different ways in which the public sector may provide policies that increase resources directed toward sports activities.
4. To what extent is the United States a market-driven economy? How has the private/public share changed over time? How does the United States differ from the other countries mentioned in this chapter?
5. Explain how Congress influences resource allocations in the United States.

Key Words

Budget deficit
Budget surplus
Credit and insurance policies
Government-sponsored enterprises (GSEs)
Loan guarantees
Direct loans
Off-budget policy
On-budget policy
Regulatory agencies

PART 2

The Role of the Public Sector

Chapter 3
Private or Public Markets?

Chapter 4
Externalities

Chapter 5
Public Goods

CHAPTER 3

Private or Public Markets?

Private and Public Markets

Private markets are characterized by resource allocation through the price system.

Public markets are characterized by resource allocation through the interaction of voters and policymakers in the policy process.

The processes by which scarce resources are allocated and goods and services are exchanged may take place within either **private markets** or **public markets.** Private markets exist so that we can purchase goods and services, such as groceries and dental care from supermarkets and dentists; they operate wherever exchanges between consumers and producers take place. Workers furnish their labor in private markets and exchange the wages and salaries they receive from employers for food, housing, medical care, and recreation in other private markets. Public markets provide such goods as national defense and highways; they exist anyplace that exchanges between voters and policymakers take place.

Through private and public markets, society answers the following three questions, which all economies must determine:

❏ Which goods and services will the economy produce?
❏ How will our goods and services be produced?
❏ Who receives the goods and services produced by our economy?

Because the processes through which private and public markets allocate resources differ, an important dimension of public finance is a comparison of how these two markets allocate resources.

The study of the public sector requires a thorough understanding of the ways and means by which private markets allocate resources. Examination of exchanges between consumers and producers informs us about the allocation of resources in private markets and provides a starting point, or benchmark, for our examination of the public sector. To argue that either private or public markets are better at allocating resources, we must first understand their differences. It is an empty argument, for instance, to say that private markets are inefficient or inequitable unless we can make a strong case that public markets perform a better job of resource allocation. Likewise it is unproductive to criticize the performance of the public sector without making a case that demonstrates how and why private markets would provide an improvement in resource allocation.

The following key questions are addressed in this chapter.

- What constitutes efficiency in resource allocation?
- Can private markets achieve efficiency in resource allocation?
- What constitutes equity in resource allocation?
- Is there a trade-off between efficiency and equity?
- Are there cases in which public markets improve efficiency or equity?
- Are there differences between theory and practice in the ability of the public sector to improve upon the resource allocations of the private sector?
- Do the institutional structures of private and public markets influence resource allocation?

Focus on Society as a Collection of Individuals

From the outset, it is essential to accept the premise that private and public markets are about exchanges among *individuals*.[1] Thus, it is always individuals who behave, make choices, consume, and produce within both private and public markets. This view is often called **methodological individualism,** which—in its purest form—argues that all choices over resource allocation rest with individuals in private markets and with *collections of individuals* in public markets. While it is convenient to refer to collections of individuals as "society," we should try not to subscribe to the notion that there exists a single, homogeneous group of individuals that can be called society. Society does not behave, make choices, consume, or produce. Rather, it is the choices and behaviors of individuals that determine resource allocations. Individuals come in all shapes and sizes with preferences and tastes of varying characteristics. If we lose sight of the fact that society is composed of many unique individuals who allocate resources and exchange with one another in private and public markets, we lose sight of the many behaviors of many different individuals that must be understood when we study resource allocation in our economy. Final resource allocations in society are a result of the many choices of a diverse collection of individuals.

In the same vein, we must be very careful when we measure the performance by which resources are allocated in our economy. Concepts of social well-being and allocative performance are meaningful only so long as they examine the roles of individuals and collections of individuals in private and public markets. Economists define allocative performance, or *efficiency,* from the point of view of individuals. If the collection of individuals that form society is diverse, it is difficult to summarize and compare the well-being of one individual to the well-being of the collection of individuals that make up society.

A focus on individuals indicates, for instance, that although the proponents of a policy that increases public expenditures on parks may claim that it improves efficiency in the economy, this claim is, at best, ambiguous when one or more individuals would be hurt by the policy. For example, any individual who must pay for new parks

Methodological individualism is the concept that all choices over resource allocation rest with individuals in private markets and with collections of individuals in public markets.

---

[1] For a discussion of this issue, see James M. Buchanan, "The Domain of Constitutional Economics," *Constitutional Political Economy* 1 (1990): 1–18.

but does not receive benefits from them may be hurt by the policy. To claim that society is better off requires either that some individuals gain and none lose, or that the gains received by some individuals are somehow more important than the losses borne by others. Note that there would be little or no debate between affected individuals if the former claim were true; thus, under most circumstances, individuals would need little convincing to agree to a policy that increases public expenditures on, say, parks. The latter claim, that some individuals are worth more than others, is even more troublesome, since it assumes a clear means for comparing the gains and losses of individuals affected by the policy.

In this book we will use the word *society*, but strictly as a convenient means of referring to the diverse collection of individuals involved in private and public markets. It may be human nature to resort to thinking of society as "us" or "them," but this approach lacks descriptive content if we are interested in understanding the viewpoints of many individuals. Many different individuals comprise society, and gaining an in-depth understanding of the ways in which resource allocations affect each member of society is the best way to examine the performance by which resources are allocated in the economy.

Efficiency in Resource Allocation

Adam Smith (1723–90), who is considered the father of modern economics, argued that the self-interests of consumers and producers result in the most efficient way of allocating resources for the good of society.[2] Ironically, no consumer or producer intends to pursue the interests of society. Nonetheless, the interests of society—and therefore of all individuals who make up society—are promoted as if guided by the invisible hand of the private market. This means that allocative efficiency cannot be improved upon when utility-maximizing consumers and profit-maximizing producers allocate resources in private markets. Now the question is: What is meant by "efficiency"?

Total Net Benefits to Society

Efficiency in resource allocation occurs when no other allocations offer greater total net benefits to the collection of individuals who comprise society. The concept of net benefits is used in this definition because resource allocations both confer benefits on and exact costs from individuals. **Total net benefits** thus are equal to the difference between total benefits and total costs, or

Total net benefits are total benefits less total costs.

$$TNB = TB - TC \qquad (3\text{-}1)$$

where *TNB* is total net benefits, *TB* is total benefits, and *TC* is total opportunity costs of production. Equation (3-1) provides a useful framework for analyzing the efficiency characteristics of the resource allocations of any market. Because benefits and costs characterize usage of resources by society, these may also be called, respectively, *social benefits* and *social costs*.

---

[2] Adam Smith, *The Wealth of Nations,* edited by Andrew Skinner (Middlesex, U.K.: Penguin Books, 1974).

We can measure the total benefits that society derives from consuming goods produced in dollars. When we are willing to pay money—say $1 for a cup of coffee and $.50 for a newspaper—we are placing monetary figures on benefits derived from allocating resources to the production of these goods. Thus we have a readily available—and quantifiable—source of information that can be summarized by demand curves. For example, at a price of $30 per bushel, the market demand for apples shows how many bushels of apples consumers are willing to purchase. Prices that consumers willingly pay for various quantities of goods provide a useful measure of the benefits their purchases confer. The higher the price, the higher are the social benefits associated with allocating resources toward production of this good. Social benefits, then, may be directly measured by the information contained in market demand curves.

Society also bears costs when resources are allocated to the production of any good. For example, the costs of producing more apples include the loss of other goods that consumers could have enjoyed if those same resources had been allocated elsewhere. This concept, called opportunity cost, is a measure of the cost as compared to the benefits derived from consumption of other goods. The opportunity costs of producing one more bushel of apples, then, are the benefits that consumers would receive if those same resources were allocated to the next best alternative. If the next best resource allocation is the production of ten comic books, then the opportunity cost of one more bushel of apples is the benefit consumers would receive from consuming ten more comic books. Benefits are reflected in the prices consumers are willing to pay for goods; therefore, if consumers are willing to pay $20 for ten more comic books, the opportunity cost of producing one more bushel of apples is $20. The greater the benefits consumers place on comic books, the higher are the opportunity costs of producing one more bushel of apples. Opportunity costs may thus be easily compared against benefits.

Total net benefits, *TNB*, associated with allocating resources toward production of one more bushel of apples can now be determined. If consumers are willing to pay $30 (*TB*) for one more bushel of apples and $20 (*TC*) for ten more comic books, total net benefits are *TB* − *TC* = *TNB* or $30 − $20 = $10. Our next question is: What level of apple production is consistent with allocative efficiency? That is, what is the most efficient level of apple production for society? All three panels of Figure 3-1 show, in different frameworks, what constitutes efficient apple production for society.

Total Benefit and Cost Analysis

Figure 3-1a displays hypothetical total benefit and total cost curves for the apple market. Because consumers enjoy eating apples, total benefits (*TB*) rise as more resources are devoted to the production of apples. Total opportunity costs (*TC*) also tend to rise with greater apple production because each additional bushel of apples requires that more and more resources be taken from the production of other goods. As each additional bushel takes away more production of other goods, the benefits derived from those goods will also rise; therefore, opportunity costs of producing apples tend to rise. As other goods become scarcer, the benefits lost tend to rise as reflected by movements up the demand curves for these goods. Allocative efficiency occurs at the maximum distance between *TC* and *TB*, which is also *TNB*. Total net benefits are greatest at *A**, which is therefore the efficient level of apple production for society.

FIGURE 3-1
Efficiency in
Resource Allocation

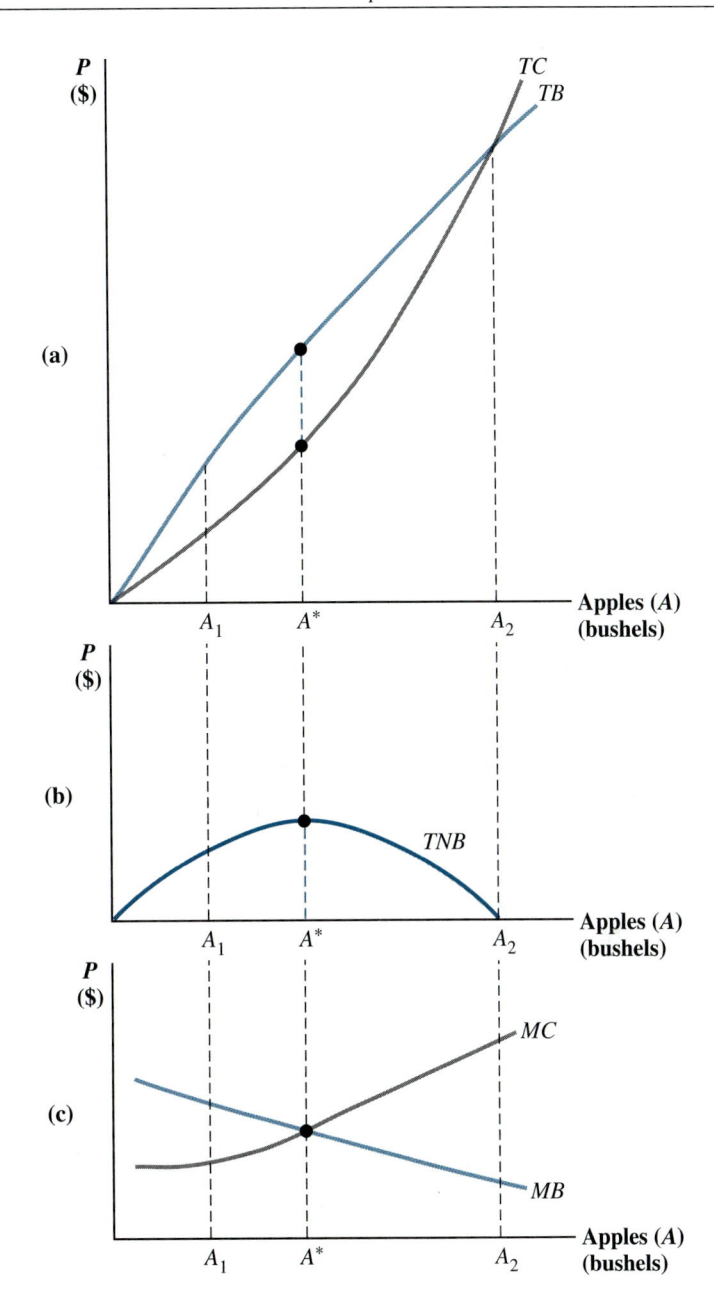

Underutilization of resources occurs at any level of apple production below A^*, and overutilization occurs at any level greater than A^*.

Total Net Benefit Analysis

An alternative way of showing that A^* is the most efficient level is shown in Figure 3-1b, which plots the total net benefit curve (*TNB*) for apple production. This curve is simply the difference between the *TC* and *TB* curves in Figure 3-1a and clearly shows that, for $A \neq A^*$, total net benefits are not maximized. Level A_1 is not efficient since increased allocation of resources in apple production yields higher total net benefits to society. Therefore, for levels below A^*, too few resources are employed in apple production, and too many resources are employed in production of other goods. At A_2, too many resources are employed in apple production; therefore, when resources are shifted from production of apples to other goods, total net benefits rise. Level A^* is the efficient allocation of resources because only at A^* will reallocation of resources between production of goods not result in higher total net benefits to society.

Marginal Benefit and Marginal Cost Analysis

Marginal benefits are the change in total benefits divided by the change in consumption.

Marginal opportunity costs are the change in total opportunity costs divided by the change in consumption.

Economists often prefer to solve for allocative efficiency by equating **marginal benefits** to **marginal opportunity costs.** *Marginal* means additional or incremental and, in the cases of apple production, these concepts are defined as

$$MB = \frac{\Delta TB}{\Delta A} \qquad (3\text{-}2)$$

$$MC = \frac{\Delta TC}{\Delta A} \qquad (3\text{-}3)$$

where *MB* is marginal benefit, *MC* is marginal opportunity cost, Δ means change in, and *A* is the quantity of apples. If an increase from 5 to 6 bushels of apples raises total benefits from $15 to $17, then $MB = (\$17 - \$15)/(6 - 5) = \$2$. If associated total costs rise from $9 to $10, then $MC = (\$10 - \$9)/(6 - 5) = \$1$.

Marginal analysis is closer to reality than the two previous approaches in the sense that individuals usually base their decisions "on the margin." For example, in preparing for a test in one subject, students usually have to decide whether to study an additional hour or more in that subject or to spend that time in other ways. Applied to apple production, the decision is whether total net benefits will rise or fall with one more or one less bushel of apples.

Figure 3-1c plots marginal benefit and marginal cost curves for the production of apples. While total benefits rise with greater apple production, each additional bushel results in a smaller addition to total benefits.[3] Because additional bushels of apples mean that fewer and fewer other goods may be produced, marginal opportunity costs of apple production rise with greater apple production. Curves *MB* and *MC* intersect at point A^*, which means that allocative efficiency is achieved when

$$MB = MC \qquad (3\text{-}4)$$

To see why $MB = MC$ implies allocative efficiency, consider production of A_1 where $MB > MC$. If, for example, $MB = \$15$ and $MC = \$10$, then one additional bushel of apples increases total benefits by $15 but costs only an additional $10. It is efficient to expand apple production in this case because benefits ($15) placed on the additional bushel outweigh opportunity costs ($10), as measured by the benefits derived when

---

[3] The appendix at the end of the book discusses the law of diminishing marginal utility, which explains why marginal benefits decline with greater consumption of any good.

the same resources are devoted to production of the next best alternative to apples. In other words, at A_1, no better use for these resources exists.

The opposite occurs at A_2, where $MB < MC$. If $MB = \$5$ and $MC = \$20$, the benefits (\$5) placed on an additional bushel of apples are less than the opportunity cost (\$20), as measured by the benefits derived when those resources are devoted to production of the next best alternative. In this case allocative efficiency requires that resources be moved out of the apple market and into the next best alternative markets where, at the margin, consumers place greater values on those goods.

Only when $MB = MC$ can resource allocations not be altered in ways that increase total net benefits to society.

Market Equilibrium and Efficiency

Market equilibrium occurs when market demand and market supply intersect.

The demand and supply framework of microeconomics shows that private markets are efficient allocators of resources at **market equilibrium**—which occurs at the intersection of supply and demand. It also demonstrates that allocative efficiency results when consumers and producers are free to allocate society's resources. To see that allocative efficiency is the result of voluntary exchanges between consumers and producers, notice that the MB and MC curves in Figure 3-1c may be relabeled demand (D) and supply (S) curves. Because benefits that consumers derive from consumption are reflected by the prices they are willing to pay for goods, demand curves are really marginal benefit curves; thus, in Figure 3-2, the market demand curve for apples is also the marginal benefit curve for apples ($D = MB$). For A_1, consumers attach a maximum benefit of \$10 per bushel and, for larger quantity A_2, they attach a lower maximum benefit of \$1 per bushel. (These are maximum prices, since consumers would prefer to pay lower prices than \$10 per pound for A_1 and \$1 per pound for A_2.) While consumers still attach positive total benefits to greater consumption of apples, the inverse relationship between price and quantity demanded means that each additional bushel yields lower marginal benefits to consumers.

Marginal opportunity costs of production measure what it costs society to produce an additional unit of any good. This same information is summarized along supply curves, since supply curves show the minimum prices at which producers are willing to sell different levels of output. To sell A_1, producers must receive a minimum price of \$1 per bushel, a minimum price in the sense that they would prefer to receive more than \$1 per pound. At prices less than \$1, profit-maximizing suppliers earn higher profits by shifting resources into production of other goods.

Marginal benefits that consumers derive from consumption in these alternative markets define the marginal opportunity costs for producers. A marginal opportunity cost of \$1 per bushel means that the resources required to produce A_1, earn \$1 when devoted to production in the next best market. At prices (P) less than \$1 per bushel for A_1, producers will shift their resources out of the apple market and into other markets where consumers place a higher value (\$1) on those resources. Because prices along supply curves reflect the marginal opportunity costs of production, the supply curve in Figure 3-2 is also the marginal opportunity cost curve for society ($S = MC$).

Thus, A^* reflects allocative efficiency in the apple market since, only at this output level does $MB = MC$. Because A^* is also equilibrium (e) output for this market, the equation describing allocative efficiency may be rewritten as:

FIGURE 3-2
Market Equilibrium and Efficiency

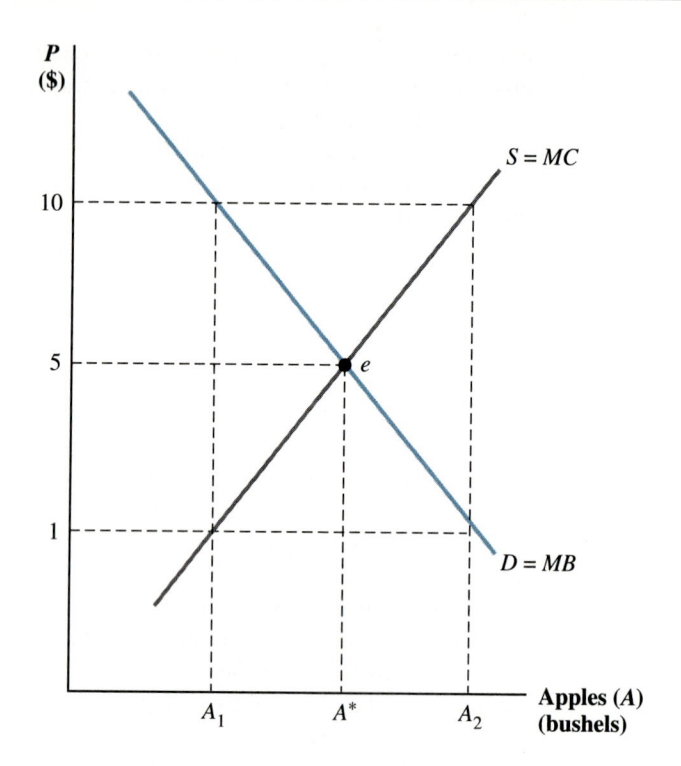

$$P = MB = MC \qquad (3\text{-}5)$$

Equation (3-5) shows that resource allocative efficiency requires that consumers pay prices equal to marginal benefits and marginal opportunity costs of production. Inefficient allocations are associated with shortages or surpluses that are removed by price changes; therefore, allocative efficiency is a natural tendency of private markets.

Efficiency and Changes in Market Conditions

Long-term efficiency in resource allocation requires that private markets quickly adapt to the many possible changes in the economy that may shift market demand and supply curves. Consider the effects on allocative efficiency when a news report persuades consumers that eating apples is beneficial to good health. This report may be expected to increase market demand from D_1^A to D_2^A as shown in Figure 3-3a. Before the increase in demand, allocative efficiency is achieved at the market equilibrium described by P_e and A_e. When demand increases, resources are no longer efficiently allocated since, at A_e, $P_e = MC < MB$. Marginal benefits are now described by point a. Allocative inefficiency is short-lived however, because market prices rise in response to the shortage reflected by distance $e1b$ until, at new equilibrium $e2$, allocative efficiency is once again achieved. In other words, the collection of individuals who comprise this market adjust to the health report by efficiently shifting resources from other markets into the apple market.

Figure 3-3b shows how private markets adapt to higher resource prices that cause the market supply of apples to decrease. At initial equilibrium $e1$, resources are efficiently allocated by producing A_e and setting $P_e = MB = MC$. When supply decreases from S_1^A to S_2^A, resources are inefficiently allocated because, at A_e, $P_e = MB < MC$. Marginal costs exceed prices and marginal benefits by distance $e1a$. However, the resulting shortage of $be1$ is only temporary, since prices will rise until the new equilibrium combination P'_e and A'_e are achieved at $e2$ where, once again, $P = MB = MC$. The private market restores allocative efficiency by reallocating resources from the apple market to other markets.

Private Market Equilibrium and Consumer Surplus

Consumer surplus is a concept used to measure how well markets treat consumers. It follows from the notion that consumers are usually willing to pay more for their purchases than they actually do. Although demand curves show the relationship between the *maximum* prices consumers are willing to pay for each additional unit of good,

Consumer surplus is the difference between maximum possible expenditures and actual expenditures

FIGURE 3-3 Efficiency and Changes in Market Equilibrium

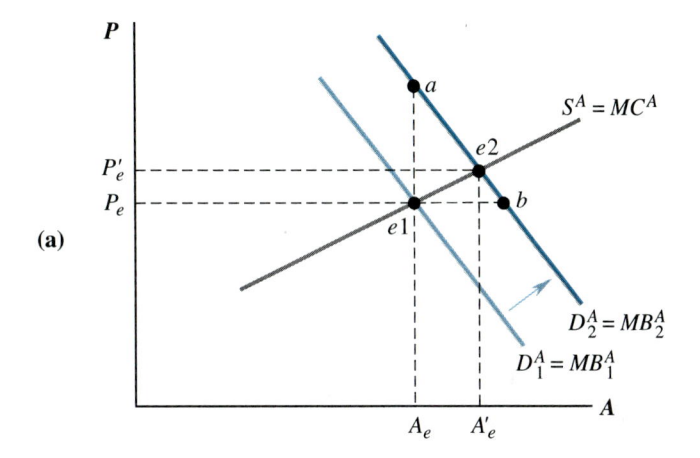

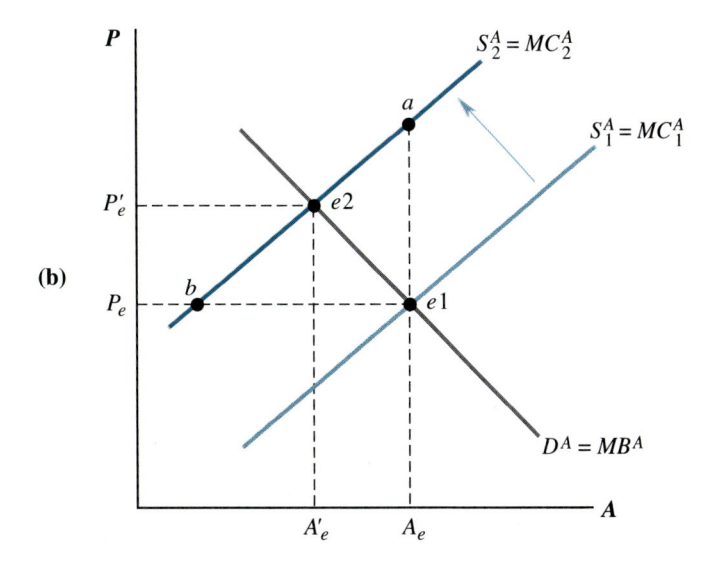

consumers still prefer to pay the lowest price possible for each additional unit. Consider the market demand curve for corn shown in Figure 3-4. Each price along the demand curve represents the highest price that consumers are willing to pay for each additional bushel of corn. For quantity C_1, consumers are willing pay P_1 and, for the additional quantity C_2, consumers are willing to pay P_2. If consumers were walked down the demand curve and charged each successive price associated with each successive unit of corn, consumers would pay a different price for each additional bushel of corn. In fact, maximum total expenditures of consumers are equal to the entire *area under the demand curve*, up to the final quantity of consumption. Thus for C_2, total maximum expenditures would equal the area OP_4fC_2. (Prices and quantities must, of course, be changed in infinitesimally small units in order to extract every cent of expenditure from consumers.)

Consumers are rarely charged more than one price for any one good. Vending machines, for example, charge a constant price for each can of soft drink purchased, and consumers may purchase thousands of products in supermarkets at uniform prices. In our example, when a uniform price of P_2 is charged for C_2, expenditures equal area OP_2fC_2. The maximum they are willing to pay, however, is area OP_4fC_2. The difference between the two, area P_2P_4f, is the consumer surplus associated with this private market.

When corn production occurs in a private market, the consumer surplus is determined by the difference between maximum expenditures and actual expenditures.

**FIGURE 3-4
Market Equilibrium and Consumer Surplus**

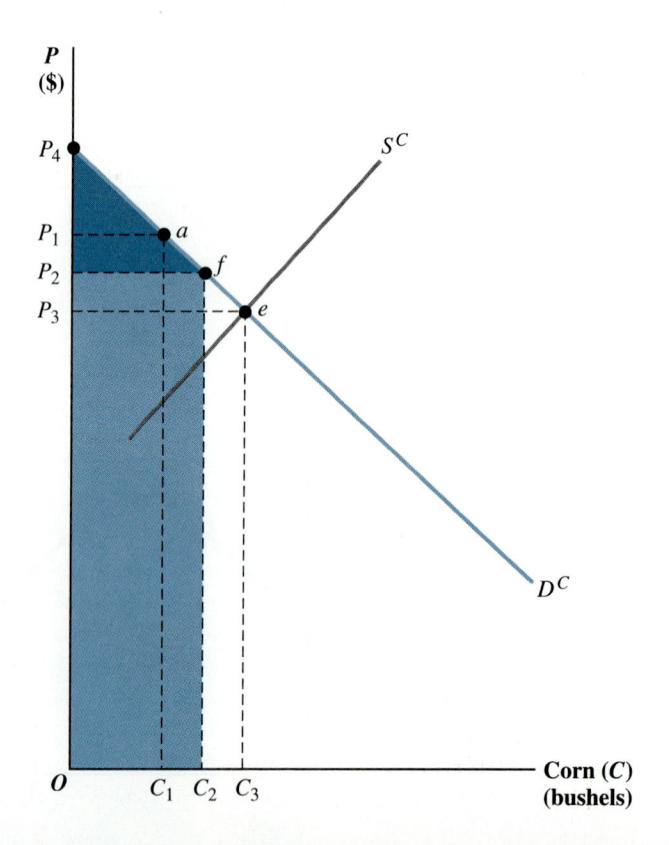

Thus if market supply S^C, intersects D^C at e, then the market equilibrium price is $P_e = P_3$ and consumer surplus is area $P_3 P_4 e$. The lower the price of any market, the larger is consumer surplus.

Restrictions on Market Equilibrium

Rent controls
are the artifacts of public policies that set the maximum rents landlords may charge renters.

Even though private markets may achieve allocative efficiency, society may believe that other criteria should guide resource allocation. Public policies seek to change the outcomes of private markets. For example, **rent controls** are public policies that prohibit the private market from setting rents at equilibrium levels by setting maximum, or ceiling, prices that renters may pay their landlords. These policies are imposed in many of the larger cities in the United States and are often many hundreds of dollars below the monthly rents that are charged for comparable, uncontrolled rental units. The rationale for rent control is that private markets set rents "too high" and that it is "fair" to set rents below equilibrium levels. Intended primarily for low-income individuals, such controls reflect the distribution function of the public sector. Similar restrictions have been placed on the prices of gasoline, heating oil, and natural gas; and, during wartime, controls have been placed on all goods. Nor is war the only emergency that may create conditions indicating a need for such policies: In 1971 President Richard Nixon imposed price and wage controls in response to inflationary pressures.

Rent Control and Resource Allocation

The demand and supply curves in Figure 3-5 demonstrate the resource allocative effects of rent controls. If the private market were allowed to set rental prices (R), allocative efficiency would be achieved at an equilibrium combination of R_e and Q_e. With rent control set at R_c, this market experiences a permanent shortage of $Q_1 Q_2$ rental units since rent controls increase the number of renters and decrease the number of units available for rent. Allocative inefficiency results because, at the number of units (Q_1) provided, marginal benefits (a) exceed marginal costs of production (b).

Rent controls exert a public influence on what otherwise would be a private market. The resulting market becomes a quasi-public or mixed market in the sense that it is a hybrid of private and public markets. The market is not totally private, since consumers and producers no longer have unlimited power to set prices. Nor is it totally public, since the public sector does not provide all of the good or regulate all aspects of consumption and production in the market.

Who Gains from Rent Control Policies?

Because rental prices are below private market levels, it is primarily the occupants of controlled rental units who benefit from the policy. The further the ceiling is below equilibrium, the larger are these direct benefits. When occupants are primarily lower income, taxpayers may gain because the benefits that flow to this low-income group may reduce their dependence on other income-support policies offered by the public sector. Policymakers who promote these polices, therefore, are perceived to be effectively improving the lives of their constituents and hence gain political support. Finally, because rents paid by occupants of rent-controlled housing are below-market

FIGURE 3-5
Rent Control and Resource Allocation

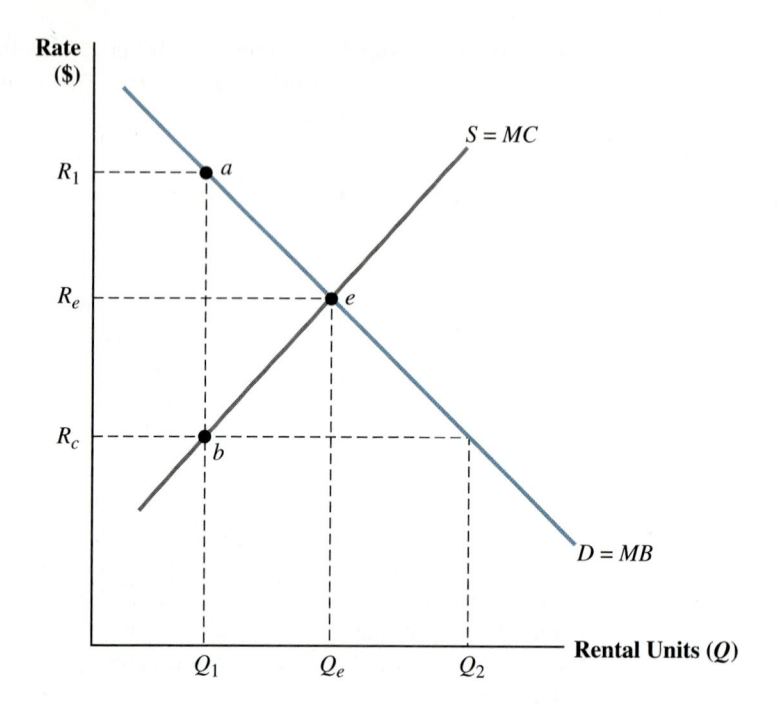

rates, some renters may also gain by subletting their apartments to others, profiting by charging rents close to the market equilibrium level.

Who Loses from Rent Control Policies?

One of the principles of economics is that resources must be rationed because they are scarce. Private competitive markets ration on the basis of prices: Price increases eliminate shortages and price decreases eliminate surpluses. We have seen that price rationing also results in allocative efficiency and, for this reason, is highly praised by economists. When prices cannot ration resources, some other rationing device must take their place. The rationing issue in a rent-controlled market is: Which individuals are allowed to rent, and which are placed on waiting lists? Individuals who are not able to rent in the market are placed on waiting lists. The shortage is so acute in New York City, for example, that native New Yorkers have been known to contend that the only way to get a rent-controlled apartment is to read the obituaries at night and be the first in line the following morning to apply for newly vacated units.

Favoritism or racial, gender, or ethnic discrimination become rationing devices when landlords choose applicants on the basis of characteristics they prefer to see in tenants. Thus, potential tenants lose when landlords decide to rent to relatives or choose one ethnic group over another. Landlords also lose income to rent controls, so they may attempt to regain those losses by requiring all renters to lease furniture at above-market prices. Or they may solicit bribes of money or gifts by applicants. Thus it can be argued that raising effective rental prices creates a black market for rent-controlled units. Lower-income individuals who cannot pay bribes may end up on permanent waiting lists. To the extent that lower-income individuals are excluded from this market, side effects on income support and public housing expenditures may result, placing higher burdens on the taxpayers who finance these programs.

Landlords may also recoup income losses from rent control restrictions by reducing maintenance expenditures. For every renter who complains about a badly kept up apartment, there are many individuals who would be willing to take that unit. Rent control laws are therefore often linked to a deteriorating rental housing stock in rent-controlled sections of cities. Landlords also have an incentive to convert rental units into condominiums and cooperatives, which are not subject to rent controls. (Some cities have countered these enterprises by restricting the conversion of apartments to condominiums or cooperatives.) As the supply of rental units decreases, shortages—and therefore waiting lists—grow. Because of the below-market rate of return, the policy may also persuade potential investors not to enter these markets and thereby further contribute to a decreasing supply of rental housing.

Evaluation of Rent Control Policies

The effects of public policies are often much more complicated than they appear at first glance.[4] Rent controls, to continue our example, may be little more than an attempt to lower the rents of low-income renters. But in practice they turn into a complex web of resource reallocations that are difficult to organize for study. Private competitive markets provide benchmarks with which to examine the effects of rent control policies, but there can be no simple answer to the question of whether these policies are good or bad for society. Similar ambiguities arise with minimum wage laws, which set minimum wage floors that employers may pay certain workers.[5] If the criterion is allocative efficiency, these policies clearly misallocate resources. If the criterion is equity, however, the situation is no longer clear; the combination of gains and losses borne by individuals requires careful examination before the policy can be assessed.

So far our discussion of rent control laws has been long on positive analysis, but short on normative. Positive analysis shows us the facts—that rent controls cause a deviation from allocative efficiency and that some gain and others lose when the policy is enacted. Individuals affected by this policy are diverse, though; so final recommendations regarding social desirability are not within the scope of positive analysis.

Normative analysis, however, requires value judgments to answer the question of whether the loss in allocative efficiency is worth the change in the well-being of the individuals who gain and lose from the policy. If younger renters, for instance, tend to get rent-controlled units and the elderly tend to stay on waiting lists, normative analysis must question whether the gains conferred on the young offset the losses suffered by the elderly. Furthermore, if such policies as rent control also affect public housing and income-support policies, then the resulting changes in tax burdens must also be weighed against other effects of this policy.

---

[4] See Steven N. S. Cheung, "Roofs or Stars: The Stated Intents and Actual Effects of a Rents Ordinance," *Economic Inquiry* 13 (March 1975): 1–21.

[5] See Charles Brown, "Minimum Wage Laws: Are They Overrated?" *Journal of Economic Perspectives* 2 (Summer 1988): 133–45. His conclusion is that the benefits do not seem to outweigh the typical economist's aversion to the resource misallocative effects of these laws.

How Upper-Income Professionals Gain from Rent Control

The primary goal of rent control policies is laudable: to lower rents for low-income individuals and families. However, the intended results of public policies do not always occur. When they do not, the outcome can be unfortunate.

Rolf Goetze, a housing consultant, examined who occupies rent controlled housing in Cambridge, Massachusetts. The general conclusion is that "the largest concentration of people in rent controlled apartments seems to be white-collar professionals in their 30s and 40s." The same conclusion is reached by Michael St. John, after examining the rent control issue in Berkeley, California: professional, white-collar workers have a disproportionately large share of the rent controlled market. Lower-income, young, and elderly individuals, in contrast, occupy relatively few rent controlled units.

Source: William Tucker, "A Model for Destroying a City," *Wall Street Journal*, March 12, 1993, A10.

Analysis

Why do so few lower-income individuals and families benefit from rent control laws? Goetze suggests that "rent controlled units are not concentrated in any particular neighborhood. It's just that, wherever they are, professional people seem to be more skillful at ferreting them out." Professionals may have better contacts and connections with which to track down rent controlled units. They may also benefit from the fact that their high incomes award them special status when they apply for rent controlled units. Landlords, for instance, are more likely to rent to higher-income individuals because they are less likely to experience periods of difficulty meeting monthly rent payments. There is also the possibility that higher-income individuals offer higher side payments, or bribes, to landlords than their lower-income counterparts.

This discussion demonstrates that the intentions of policies do not always guarantee the desired outcomes. The trick, therefore, is to design policies that correctly match intentions with outcomes.

It is also important to compare the resource allocative effects of alternative policies that may provide the poor with places to live. Rent control is, after all, only one type of policy that addresses the issue of housing. While its goal may be noble, it is important to determine whether other types of public policies could achieve the goal of low-cost housing more quickly and cheaply. Direct payments to the poor or the building of public housing, for example, are substitutes that may be more effective in meeting this goal.

Private Markets Often Work against Public Intervention

Policies are often designed to change the behaviors of one or more individuals (consumers or producers) by imposing rules and regulations on their behavior. Rent control provides a clear example of the many ways in which consumers and producers, to some extent, circumvent the goals of public policy. It makes sense that when policy is an attempt to alter behavior the individuals affected will expend resources to maneuver around some of the constraints imposed upon them. Individuals may object to policies for a variety of reasons. Landlords object to constraints placed on rental prices because those constraints limit profits. They may also broadly object to the goal of equity underlying the policy, or they may believe that other policies would meet the equity goals better than rent controls. Consumers of rental housing may object to the waiting lists that result from the policy or to methods of rationing that can involve racial or ethnic discrimination, bribes, or favoritism.

Numerous other examples of other policies elicit similar responses by market participants.[6] Taxpayers commonly exploit tax loopholes and tax shelters to evade tax policies. Liquor and tobacco smuggling from high-tax states to low-tax states has a long history. When price controls have been placed on gasoline and other products, black markets have rationed the resulting shortages. Illegal underground drug markets arise in response to policies making drug use illegal. Drivers routinely violate speed limits. And laws that set minimums on wages, the amount of alcohol individuals may consume before operating motor vehicles, and ages for recruitment into the armed forces are also frequently broken.

Public policies obviously fail to achieve their intended goals on some occasions. The achievement of goals depends upon the ways in which market participants react to policies and the abilities of policymakers to enforce them. The success of policies may also be influenced by the skill and clarity with which the rules or regulations are written. For instance, laws that forbid "offensive" behavior are bound to be ineffective when they do not define specifically what constitutes offensive behavior. Similarly, laws forbidding "unfair" prices may not influence consumer prices when such laws do not define what a fair price is.

The more burdensome policies are, the greater are the incentives to circumvent them. Policies that do not factor in these attempts at circumvention, therefore, will likely fail to achieve their purposes, whether the failure has been poorly written laws, attempts to minimize the burdens of those laws, or weak law enforcement.

Welfare Economics

Welfare economics is the study of the efficiency and equity of resource allocation.

Pareto efficiency characterizes resource allocation in which no individual can be made better off without making any other individual worse off.

Measurement of the welfare of the collection of individuals who make up society is, at best, difficult, and economists spend a great deal of time studying how to do it. **Welfare economics** is the study of the efficiency and equity of resource allocation. Allocative efficiency is the point at which allocations maximize total net benefits of society. **Pareto efficiency,** or *optimality,* is another way to measure efficiency—one that helps to clarify the differences between efficiency and equity in resource allocation. Developed by Vilfredo Pareto (1848–1923), Pareto efficient allocations of goods occur when no other possible allocation makes at least one individual better off without making anyone else worse off. Pareto efficiency analysis therefore uses individuals as the basis of evaluation and argues that no matter how many individuals gain

---

[6] For greater discussion, see Edgar L. Feige, *The Underground Economies: Tax Evasion and Information Distortion* (Cambridge, U.K.: Cambridge University Press, 1989).

from a reallocation, those reallocations that make one or more individuals worse off cannot be recommended on the basis of efficiency.

The concept of equity is quite different from Pareto efficiency because it evaluates the final *distribution* of goods in society. Reallocations that benefit one or more individuals may at times be recommended even though one or more individuals in society may lose from them. Distributive justice, or fairness, is the underlying criterion for rating equity in society.

Pareto Efficient Allocations

Consider a society that contains fixed amounts of two goods, 10 loaves of bread and 20 gallons of water, and two individuals, Mark and Beth. There are many possible allocations of bread and water for the society composed of Mark and Beth. All bread and water could be awarded to one individual, each individual could receive half of the goods, or some other allocation could divide available bread and water. Welfare economics examines whether one or more of these allocations are Pareto efficient.

A **utility possibilities curve** plots the maximum utility for each individual, holding constant the utility of the other individual (see chapter appendix). Given the many possible allocations of bread and water, Figure 3-6 plots the appropriate utility possibilities curve UU' for Mark and Beth. Each point along UU' represents the separate well-beings of Mark and Beth associated with different allocations of bread and water. Interior points, such as *a* correspond to allocations that sum less than 20 gallons of water and 10 loaves of bread. Points such as *b*, which are on the exterior of UU', correspond to bread and water combinations that exceed the fixed quantities of goods. All points along UU' represent maximum attainable utilities to Mark and Beth and therefore reflect complete allocations of water and bread.

Utility possibilities curve is a plot of the maximum utility for one individual, holding constant the utility of another individual.

**FIGURE 3-6
Utility Possibilities Curve**

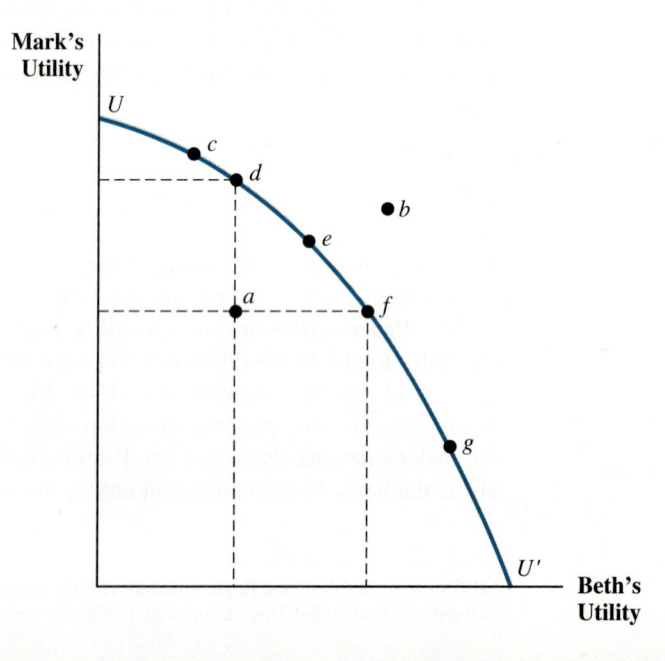

Pareto superior move
is a resource reallocation in which one individual is made better off without making any other individual worse off.

Pareto inefficiency
characterizes a resource allocation whereby another allocation exists that would make at least one individual better off and no individual worse off.

❏ *Points interior to utility possibilities curves are not Pareto efficient.* At point *a*, for instance, allocations exist that improve the well-being of one individual without lowering the well-being of the other individual. A vertical move from *a* to *d* is called a **Pareto superior move,** since it allows one person, Mark, to experience higher utility without lowering the utility of the other person, Beth. A horizontal move from *a* to *f* is another Pareto superior move since Beth experiences higher utility without lowering Mark's utility. A move from *a* to *e* is yet another Pareto superior move, except in this case, the utilities of both improve with reallocation. In general, all points within the interior of utility possibilities curves are **Pareto inefficient,** and the triangular area defined by vertical and horizontal segments at the initial Pareto inefficient point defines all points that are Pareto superior to that point. For *UU'*, all points defined by area *adf* are Pareto superior to *a*.

❏ *All points along utility possibilities curves are Pareto efficient.* At point *e*, a move to *d* increases Mark's well-being and lowers Beth's. A move from *e* to *f* results in the opposite, higher well-being for Beth and lower well-being for Mark. Because any move along the utility possibilities curve results in increased well-being for one individual and diminished well-being for the other, all points along the curve are Pareto efficient. Efficiency in allocation therefore means that Mark and Beth receive allocations that correspond to points along *UU'* and that once a point along a utility possibilities curve is reached, any change from that point is a Pareto inefficient move for society.

❏ *Private markets achieve Pareto efficient allocations of resources* (see the chapter appendix). Since private markets are the result of the voluntary exchanges of individuals, no person can be coerced into accepting allocations that reduce individual well-being. The limits of gains from reallocations are reached with Pareto efficient allocations, which occur only on utility possibilities curves. Thus, utility-maximizing individuals can be expected to voluntarily exchange among themselves until a Pareto efficient point is achieved. (There are circumstances in which private markets do not achieve Pareto efficient allocations of resources, but they are discussed later in the chapter.)

❏ *While all points along utility possibilities curves are efficient, the Pareto efficiency framework cannot recommend all Pareto efficient allocations over Pareto inefficient allocations.* Suppose point *a* reflects the current allocation of bread and water for Mark and Beth. Even though point *a* is not Pareto efficient, it cannot be argued that efficiency is enhanced when reallocations result in, say, point *c*, which raises Mark's well-being at the expense of Beth's, or point *g*, which raises Beth's well-being at the expense of Mark's. For point *a*, the Pareto efficiency framework limits the options for increasing efficiency to the points described by area *adf*.

Equity versus Efficiency in Resource Allocation

The criterion of Pareto efficiency does not allow us to judge which Pareto efficient point is most equitable. Without further information on what constitutes an equitable distribution of bread and water, this framework cannot address which Pareto efficient point represents the most equitable distribution for Mark and Beth. To the extent that equity is defined as equality of distribution, policies that reallocate bread and water toward the middle of utility possibilities curve *UU'* may be viewed as equitable.

While one of the attractions to using the Pareto efficiency criterion is that it does not require interpersonal utility comparisons, it necessarily places a straitjacket, so to speak, on those who wish to make recommendations based on judgments regarding equity. Recommendations of reallocations based on equity criteria necessarily involve interpersonal utility comparisons. To argue that c is more equitable than d or a is to argue that what Mark gains in utility more than outweighs any loss suffered by Beth. At Pareto efficient point c, some may argue (especially Beth) that it is not fair that Beth's well-being is lower than Mark's. But how can such interpersonal utility comparisons be made?

Interpersonal utility comparisons are the province of normative economic analysis, since a value system must determine what constitutes an equitable distribution of goods in society. The role that equity plays in policy discussion is obvious to anyone with even a casual introduction to public policy debates, and it is clear that Pareto efficiency is not always the ultimate test of how well society allocates its goods among its citizens.

In welfare economics both efficiency and equity must be studied, and it is not clear which attribute is more important. The concept of equity, however, necessarily rejects the concept of methodological individualism in favor of basing resource usage on a comparison of the gains or losses suffered by the collection of individuals that comprise society. Where Pareto efficiency requires that no individual be harmed by any reallocation, a reallocation that harms some individuals and benefits others may be supported on the grounds that it promotes a more equitable distribution of goods in society.

Compensation Tests

Compensation test is a test of resource reallocations based on measurable increases in net social benefits.

A commonly made criticism of the Pareto efficiency criterion is that it unduly rejects, on the basis of efficiency, many reallocations that might enhance social welfare. The **compensation test** removes some of the roadblocks imposed by the Pareto efficiency criterion on reallocations that are believed to be better for society.[7] The underlying assumption of the compensation test is that the gains and losses associated with reallocations of goods between individuals may be measured or valued in dollars. We remember that similar comparisons are made in the construction of demand curves where the prices that consumers are willing to pay for additional quantities of goods reflect marginal benefits. For example, an additional gallon of water may be valued at $10 by Mark and $25 by Beth. Therefore, if a move from c to e results in a gain of $300 to Beth and a loss of $100 to Mark, net social benefits are argued to increase by $200. Moves that result in increases in net social benefits are said to pass the compensation test.

Reallocations with Compensation

Whether compensation is awarded to the losers of reallocations that pass the compensation test is an interesting issue. Clearly, whenever compensation of losers results

---

[7] For example, see Nicholas Kaldor, "Welfare Propositions of Economics and Interpersonal Comparisons of Utility," *Economic Journal* 49 (September 1939): 549–562; and T. Scitovsky, "A Note on Welfare Propositions in Economics," *Review of Economic Studies* 9 (November 1941): 77–88.

either in no change or in an increase in their well-being, such moves become Pareto superior moves and will be approved by any individual. Returning to our previous example, when at least $100 is awarded to Mark, the move from c to e becomes a Pareto superior move and therefore meets the criteria of both Pareto efficiency and the compensation test. So long as each individual is compensated for losses suffered during reallocation, these reallocations also conform to the notion of methodological individualism, and analysis is focused on the point of view of each individual within society.

Reallocations without Compensation

But can moves that meet the compensation test still be recommended when compensation is not part of the deal? Some critics of the Pareto efficiency criterion argue that the compensation test is too restrictive because high transaction costs associated with compensation will unduly hinder implementation of many reallocations that would improve social welfare. It is virtually impossible, for instance, to compensate all individuals who do not directly gain from a new public housing project in a town of 50,000 people. Such a policy reallocates resources from taxpayers to those who directly benefit from the housing project. (When tax burdens vary positively with income, this reflects a reallocation from the rich to the poor.) If there are 25,000 taxpayers and 14,000 of them do not believe that they directly gain from the project, the latter group experiences lower well-being if the housing project is built. Administrative and information costs involved in compensating these taxpayers, however, may be expected to prevent the reallocation of taxpayer money for public housing (when compensation is required), even when the project may improve social welfare on the basis of the compensation test.

Arguments that the project results in greater social welfare rests on many controversial points. The argument that social welfare increases is based on the assumption that it is appropriate to *aggregate* the dollars gained and lost from all affected individuals. This viewpoint rejects methodological individualism in favor of the viewpoint that as long as the sum of the well-beings of all individuals improves, it is appropriate to recommend policies that lower at least one individual's well-being. The logic of this argument suggests that

$$SW = u_1 + u_2 + \cdots + u_{50,000} \tag{3-6}$$

where SW is social welfare and u_i is the well-being (measured in dollars) of each of 50,000 individuals. But is it appropriate to measure changes in social welfare as the sum of the gains and losses stemming from the project? For example, if Mark were to gain $450 and Beth were to lose $400, would social welfare, in fact, rise by $50?

The compensation test also assumes that a dollar's utility is equal for all individuals. That is, for example, that the contribution to social welfare of a dollar's increase for Beth is exactly equal to the contribution to social welfare of a dollar's increase for Mark. Because this implies that social welfare improves when a rich person gains $100 and a poor individual loses $99, the compensation test may violate some notions of what constitutes appropriate income distribution in society. This approach also assumes that information is readily available on the dollar values of gains and losses for all affected individuals. As the collection of affected individuals grows and becomes more diverse, it of course becomes more difficult to assess this conglomerate of information.

For all of these reasons, recommendations of reallocations without compensation are likely to rest on assumptions that many find difficult to support and are therefore likely to be contentious topics. However, it should be obvious that a consensus will not emerge when proposed reallocations are based on some criteria other than Pareto efficiency.

Unanimity Test

Unanimity test is a test of resource reallocations based on approval by all parties.

In the late 1800s, Knut Wicksell (1851–1926) offered the **unanimity** (or *consensus*) **test** as a partial way around the strict confines of the Pareto efficiency framework.[8] Because unanimous approval of reallocations suggests a Pareto superior move, Wicksell argued that such approval must occur before any such move is deemed to improve social welfare. Without unanimity, such moves lower social welfare and therefore cannot be recommended by public finance economists. It is clear that the unanimity test rejects the aggregative nature of the social welfare function described in equation (3-6) and recommends only those reallocations which harm no individual as reallocations that unambiguously result in a better distribution of goods for society.

It is also reasonable to expect individuals to agree among themselves (and reach unanimity) on reallocations that meet the criteria of the compensation test, since it should be fairly obvious to each individual whether moves that are not initially Pareto superior become Pareto superior when gainers compensate losers. If a move from c to e really results in a gain of $300 to Beth and a loss of $100 to Mark, then Beth may be expected to offer Mark adequate compensation of at least $100, thus making this move acceptable to him. A problem develops, however, when society consists of a large number of diverse individuals. As the number of individuals grows, transactions and information costs involved may make it impossible for many Pareto superior moves to evolve within this framework of unanimity.

Social Welfare Functions

Social welfare function indicates the changes in a society's welfare as each member experiences changes in personal well-being.

A **social welfare function** indicates how society's welfare changes as all the members of society experience changes in their well-being. The general form of social welfare functions for a society composed of n individuals is

$$SW = f(U_1, U_2, U_3, \ldots, U_n) \qquad (3\text{-}7)$$

where $f(\ )$ is the functional form and U_i is the well-being of each of n individuals. The specific form of the function depends upon the weights society places on each individual's utility. The greater the weight attached to a person's attainment of utility, the more deserving the individual is believed to be. (Equation (3-6) is a specific form of a social welfare that *sums* each individual's welfare and therefore assigns equal weight to each person's utility.)

---

[8] See James M. Buchanan, "Constitutional Economics," in *The World of Economics,* eds. John Eatwell, Murray Milgate, and Peter Newman (New York: W. W. Norton, 1991). First published in *The New Palgrave: A Dictionary of Economics* (London: Macmillan, 1987).

Maximization of Social Welfare

Figure 3-7 plots three social indifference curves (I^S) for the two-person society of Mark and Beth. Each has the property that social welfare does not change for movements along a curve. These curves have negative slopes, which mean that in order for society to remain indifferent between combinations along the curve, one person's gain in utility must be offset by the other's losses. Preference levels rise with distance from the origin, and of the three curves shown, I_3^S yields the highest level and I_1^S the lowest level of welfare for society. Combined with utility possibilities curve UU' for Mark and Beth, the distribution of individual well-being that maximizes social welfare may be determined. While points *a, b,* and *c* are all Pareto efficient, social indifference curves allow us to recommend one Pareto efficient point over another. By inspection, *b* is the Pareto efficient point that provides the highest social welfare and therefore the welfare distribution that welfare economists recommend for society. Any other Pareto efficient point along the utility possibilities curve yields a lower level of social welfare.

This approach has great appeal for welfare economists who believe they should recommend which Pareto efficient point is most appropriate for society. But some obvious problems hinder the validity of this approach. The ability to argue, for example, that *b* is socially preferable to *a* requires (1) adequate compensation for Mark, the loser in the reallocation, (2) Mark's willingness to contribute to Beth even though he loses from the reallocation, or (3) an unambiguous method of making interpersonal utility comparisons that justifies forcing Mark to give up goods so that Beth may experience higher well-being. The second of these conditions is the rationale for private charity and indicates that losers understand that although they personally lose from one or more reallocations, the good of society, or social welfare, improves by the

FIGURE 3-7
Maximization of Social Welfare

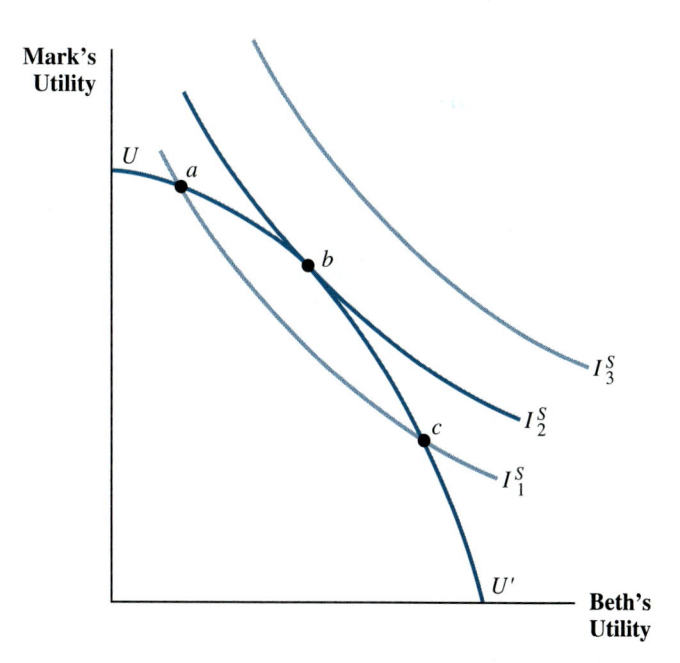

reallocation. Because of these difficulties, the usefulness of the social welfare function approach rests more on its theoretical nature than on its practical application.

Welfare Economics in Practice

Large Numbers as Constraints on Viability

What is a fairly simple matter when society consists solely of Mark and Beth becomes a complex problem when welfare economists attempt to provide recommendations to societies consisting of more than a few individuals. What happens when there are 200 individuals or, in the United States, more than 250 million members of society? It takes a long stretch of imagination to believe that welfare economists can determine how individuals of so complex and so large a population are individually affected by reallocations. The difference between the merits of a reallocation based on the compensation test involving two individuals and the merits when large numbers of individuals are involved is significant.

The same problem exists for reallocations based on social welfare functions. Even if it is assumed that social indifference curves can be constructed, their application becomes increasingly difficult when societies comprise large numbers of individuals. The costs of acquiring the information necessary to measure net gains to society from reallocations may grow so quickly with population that it becomes increasingly unlikely that welfare economists will be able to make strong cases for one allocation over another. The larger and more diverse society is, the more likely it is that recommendations regarding the social desirability of reallocations will follow from the normative "gut feelings" of the analyst.

Individuals Consider Net Changes of All Reallocations

Even if losers from one or more reallocations believe that social welfare is not enhanced, they may vote for those reallocations if net improvements to their individual well-beings result. In other words, individuals may be willing to balance out losses incurred from a public housing project with gains received from, say, a new football stadium. Therefore, individuals may tend to consider the whole picture of reallocation policy and tolerate some losses in anticipation of gains in other reallocations.

Importance of the Process by Which Reallocations Are Chosen

Policymaking often involves analysis based on compensation tests and social welfare functions, and it is extremely important to understand the *process* by which decisions regarding the social desirability of reallocations are made. While most enacted reallocations result in both losers and gainers, it is important to understand the degree to which both losers and gainers contribute to the decisions regarding those policies.

Role of the Public Sector

There are six general areas in which cases may be made that the public sector improves the well-being of individuals in society. Although much controversy surrounds the role of the public sector and issues surrounding the behaviors of voters and policymakers are integral to our understanding of how well the public sector operates, an overview of these six cases will set the stage for more detailed discussions.

Externalities

Competitive private markets do not allocate resources efficiently when private benefits and costs diverge from social benefits and costs. Such divergences are likely to result when some individuals are affected by market allocations but do not have a direct influence on the consumers and producers who are exchanging with one another in private markets. These affected individuals are called "third parties," and when they are adversely influenced by market outcomes, a *negative externality* exists. Air and water pollution are examples of negative externalities resulting from the allocation of resources by private competitive markets. While private competitive markets allocate resources so that marginal private benefits and marginal private costs are equated, true allocative efficiency for society occurs when marginal social benefits are equated to marginal social costs.

Private and social benefits may also diverge in private markets when market participants do not fully account for the benefits to society of their actions. When third parties are positively affected by the actions of market participants, a *positive externality* exists. A common example is education because its beneficiaries, in addition to students and their families, include all of society. Because social benefits outweigh private benefits, private markets are believed to underproduce education.

Many public policies are used to address divergences between social and private benefits and costs. Regulation, fines, and taxes are imposed on markets characterized by negative externalities, and public provision and subsidization of such goods as education are often based on arguments that some goods provide positive externalities to society.

Public Goods

Public goods have two characteristics. The first is that it is difficult or impossible to prevent those who do not pay for the good from receiving the benefits attached to that good. National defense is an example of such a good, for those who do not pay for it still receive its benefits. The second characteristic is that public goods are nonrival in consumption. When the United States gains another citizen, for example, no other citizen experiences lower consumption of national defense.

Private markets tend to underproduce public goods because individual producers have little desire to market something from which consumers will benefit but for which they have little incentive to pay. However, because marginal costs of providing public goods to additional consumers are zero, allocative efficiency requires that more of the good be produced than the level that private markets will provide. Because private markets tend to underproduce these goods, public production is a means of improving allocative efficiency.

Allocative Efficiency and Monopoly

Private competitive markets have been shown to maximize total net benefits by setting prices at marginal costs of production ($P = MC$). Monopolists are sole sellers of goods and therefore have the ability to set prices above marginal costs; resources will thus not be allocated efficiently when monopolists control production. In comparison to competitive markets, monopolies charge higher prices, produce fewer goods, and allocate resources inefficiently. The extent to which resources are inefficiently allocated is called the *welfare loss* of monopoly power and, in comparison to competitive markets, consumer surplus is lower when monopolists allocate resources. Solutions to the welfare losses associated with monopoly that have been suggested or used include antitrust laws, which break up large monopolies into smaller competitive firms, and regulation, which attempts to make monopolies perform like competitive firms.

Imperfect Information and Resource Allocation

In our discussion of private markets we have argued that consumers signal their demands to producers who, given an incentive to maximize profits, have an incentive to deliver low-price, high-quality goods to consumers. While the ability of consumers to determine the goods that producers provide is usually viewed as an important and favorable characteristic of private markets, it may be argued that consumers do not always possess the information necessary to make appropriate decisions regarding which goods should be produced in the economy. For instance, farmers may not fully understand the risks of working with some pesticides, or consumers may not fully realize that certain over-the-counter drugs do not effect the cures that manufacturers claim. In these cases, **imperfect information** results in consumer behavior that would differ if consumers were more fully informed. Because such cases sometimes result in resource misallocations, some economists argue that public policy should address the information imperfections that characterize various markets.

> **Imperfect information** is lack of complete information.

Policies that expand information to consumers may allow consumers to send signals that are more in line with allocative efficiency to producers. Another policy may be to regulate or forbid various consumption behaviors that policymakers believe are the result of too little or wrong consumer information. This regulatory role, consistent with a paternalistic role of government, underlies polices that prohibit tobacco firms from advertising on television and radio and prevents the domestic sale of DDT. Clearly controversial, such policies raise important questions about how much power the public sector should be awarded when it comes to allocating resources in the U.S. economy.

It is also important to realize that policymakers, like consumers, are subject to imperfect and scarce information; it is therefore unlikely that consumers (voters) or policymakers will ever make perfect decisions.

Equity Goals of Society

Efficiency and equity are not synonymous and, with various exceptions, private competitive markets can be expected to achieve only the former. When various private market outcomes are viewed as unfair or inequitable, policies may be developed that attempt to alter the allocations of private markets with the goal of improving the well-being of society. As our discussion of rent controls shows, the analysis of equity issues involves normative as well as positive dimensions; therefore, fairness issues are always highly debatable subjects among citizens and policymakers. Nonetheless, equity goals are perennial topics of public policy, and the tools of welfare economics

Stabilization Policies

The field of economics includes several major debates regarding private versus public markets. One concerns the stability of the private market. Some economists believe that private markets are inherently unstable and that when private markets are allowed to allocate too many of society's resources, the economy will suffer harsh swings in employment, inflation, interest rates, and real growth. Other economists tend to believe that private markets are generally stable and that the economy, when left alone, allocates resources efficiently and is characterized by great stability.

Another important debate concerns whether stabilization policies do, in fact, produce more stability than if they were not pursued. Some economists—often referred to as Keynesians (for John Maynard Keynes, a theorist of the 1930s and early 1940s)—believe that monetary and fiscal policies can increase economic stability. Other economists—often referred to as monetarists and neoclassicalists—believe that stabilization policies often create instability in the economy. These issues and debates are traditionally discussed in macroeconomics courses.

Market Failure or Government Failure?

Under various ideal conditions related to competition, information, and absence of externalities or public goods, private competitive markets allocate resources efficiently. For government to play a legitimate role, then, either ideal conditions must not be present or efficiency must not be the most important criterion for directing resource allocation in the economy. Monopolies, externalities, public goods, and policies related to issues of equity, and stabilization are all cases in which public markets may improve upon the resource allocations of private markets. The general term **market failure** is used to describe these circumstances in which the public sector may be able to correct various allocative inefficiencies, instabilities, or inequities that result from resource allocations by private markets. The next logical step for our study of the public sector is to examine what tools are available to correct cases identified as market failures.

Market failure occurs when the private market fails to produce an efficient or equitable outcome.

An important issue must also be investigated along with our examination of these tools: If private markets are believed to provide inefficient, inequitable, or unstable outcomes, is it necessarily true that public markets do a better job? This is clearly not an easy question to answer, but it is of vital concern to the study of public finance. Rent control is one example of a well-intentioned policy aimed at improving the well-being of the poor that may result in reallocations of resources that partially mitigate the goal of the policy. It might be nice to believe that policymakers could wave a magic wand and solve various perceived problems, but the real world is obviously not supplied with that kind of wand.

Government failure occurs when a public policy results in an inefficient or inequitable outcome.

Government failure is the obverse of private market failure. It is always inappropriate to view either the private or the public sector with rose-colored glasses. The role that policymakers may play in improving allocative efficiency or promoting the equity goals of society is subject to much debate, and it is folly to assume that resource allocation is always enhanced when policies are enacted and implemented through the policy process. Government may fail in several ways.

Two questions form the basis of our investigation of how well public markets perform. First, do applications of policy tools actually correct market failures that are identified by welfare economists? (In other words, do policy tools actually do what they are supposed to do?) Second, can the policy process be expected to enact and implement policies that correct market failures?

Summary

- Resources are allocated within either private or public markets. The price system allocates resources in private markets, and the policy process allocates resources in public markets.
- Methodological individualism is the concept that all choices over resource allocation rest with individuals in private markets and with collections of individuals in public markets. This concept demonstrates that we must be careful to undertake in-depth analysis of the ways in which public policies affect each individual in society.
- Allocative efficiency occurs whenever marginal benefits and marginal costs are equal, and thus total net benefits are maximized. Under an idealized private market setting, allocative efficiency occurs when markets are allowed to set prices and quantities at market equilibrium.
- Welfare economics is the study of the efficiency and equity of resource allocation. Pareto efficiency occurs whenever no other possible allocation of resources makes at least one individual better off without making any other individual worse off. Under various conditions, private markets achieve Pareto efficient allocations of resources. The concept of equity evaluates the final distribution of goods in society. Pareto efficient allocations are not necessarily the most equitable.
- Social welfare functions indicate how society's welfare changes as each member of society experiences changes in individual well-being. The usefulness of these functions rests more on their theoretical nature than on their practical application.
- Market failures indicate cases in which private market allocations of resources fail to achieve allocative efficiency (as with externalities, public goods, imperfect competition, and imperfect information) or fail to meet various equity goals. However, the possibility exists that policies aimed at correcting market failures may also misallocate resources, and in these cases government failures are said to result.

Review Questions

1. What is the primary difference between private and public markets?
2. What is meant by methodological individualism? How does it relate to the use of the word "society" in the study of public finance?
3. What is an efficient allocation of resources?
4. What is the subject matter of welfare economics?
5. What is a Pareto efficient allocation of resources?
6. What is the compensation test?

Discussion Questions

1. Economists argue that competitive private markets often result in allocative efficiency. Explain how this result does not imply that resource allocations are equitable.
2. Assume that the rental housing market in your town is subject to rent controls that are placed several hundred dollars below market-determined rents. Show the reasons that placement of rent

controls will not lead to maximization of total social net benefits in the rental housing market.

3. If a new public park were to be built and its total social benefits exceeded its total social costs, is it efficient for a community to build the park?

4. Minimum wage legislation sets a wage floor that employers may legally pay their employees. Examine the effects of a minimum wage law on the efficiency of resource allocation in the labor market. Discuss who is expected to gain and who is expected to lose from these policies.

5. Discuss the importance of individuals in the definition of Pareto efficiency. How does this definition separate the concepts of efficiency and equity?

6. Suppose that a community of 20,000 citizens is considering building a new swimming pool and financing it through higher property taxes. Under what circumstances would this new project be a Pareto superior move for the community?

7. Reconsider the previous question, applying the compensation test criteria to your answer.

8. Explain the similarities between resource allocations in the private sector and those in the public sector when the rule of unanimity is chosen to decide which public projects are undertaken.

Key Words

Private markets
Public markets
Methodological individualism
Total net benefits
Marginal benefits
Marginal opportunity costs
Market equilibrium

Consumer surplus
Rent controls
Welfare economics
Pareto efficiency
Utility possibilities curve
Pareto superior allocation
Pareto inefficiency

Compensation test
Unanimity test
Social welfare function
Imperfect information
Market failure
Government failure

APPENDIX 3

Efficiency in Exchange and Production

Resources are efficiently allocated when private competitive markets are allowed to operate.[1] Efficiency is measured in both exchange and production, and overall efficiency requires that both occur at the same time. **Efficiency in exchange** occurs when final allocations of all goods (apples, bananas, bicycles, cars, houses, and so on) are awarded to each individual in society so that no other allocation exists that makes at least one individual better off without making anyone else worse off. If apples and oranges may be reallocated in such a way that at least one individual gains and none loses, then the current distribution of apples and oranges is not efficient. **Efficiency in production** occurs whenever allocations of inputs are such that no other allocations increase production of any good without lowering production of any other good. An economy that produces twenty cars and thirty trucks, for instance, is inefficient if it can rearrange those same resources and produce twenty-two cars and thirty-one trucks.

Efficiency in Exchange

Consider a society that consists of Mark and Beth, so that the welfare of society is based on the allocations received by these two individuals. Further assume that this is a pure exchange economy, one in which production decisions regarding its two goods, bread and water, have already been determined and therefore, for the moment, lie outside our examination. Welfare economics evaluates the allocations received by Mark and Beth and determines whether other allocations of bread and water are more efficient for society (Mark and Beth).

The exchanges that may take place between Mark and Beth in their two-person, two-good economy are described by the Edgeworth-Bowley box in Figure 3A-1, where fixed quantities of bread and water are plotted along the axes. The lengths of each axis are equal to the fixed quantities of bread and water; the quantity allocated to Mark is measured by the distance from point O and, for Beth, from point O'. Mark's

---

[1] Readers who are not familiar with indifference curve theory should read the appendix at the end of the book, which summarizes microeconomic theory.

FIGURE 3A-1
Edgeworth-Bowley Box

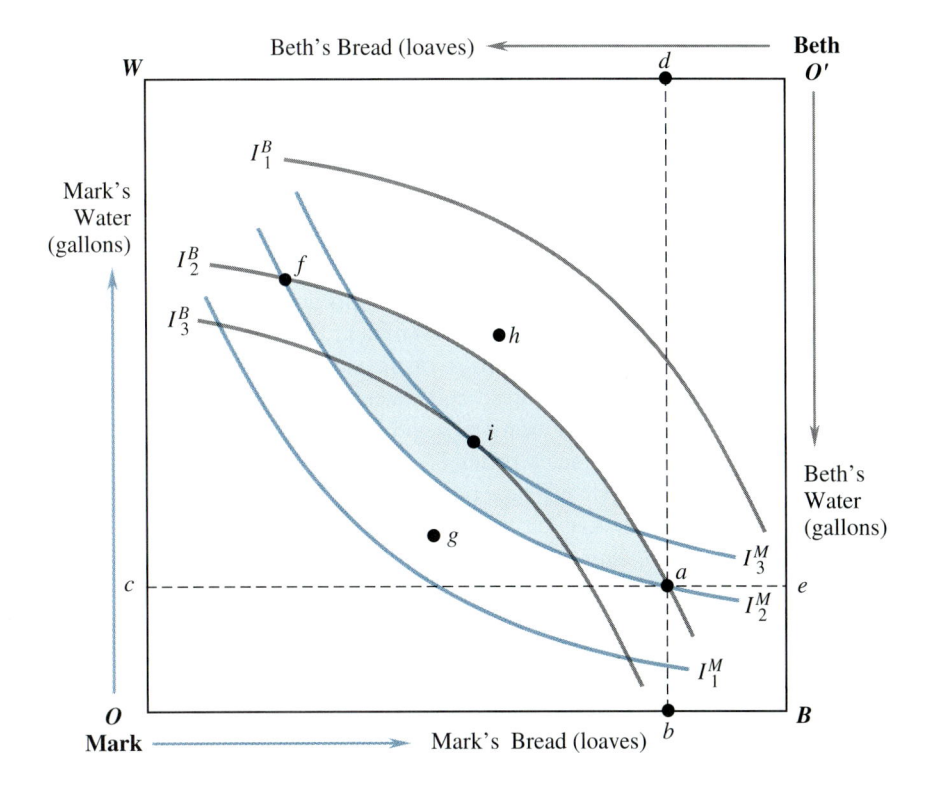

allocation is therefore shown in relation to the southwestern corner, and Beth's allocation is shown in relation to the northeastern corner of the box. Appropriate origins for Mark and Beth are O and O', respectively, and any point within the box results in a unique allocation of goods. Thus, allocation a distributes Oc gallons of water and Ob loaves of bread to Mark and $O'e$ gallons of water and $O'd$ loaves of bread to Beth. Note that the sum of allocations of each good equals the fixed quantity of each good: $Ob + O'd = OB$ loaves of bread and $Oc + O'e = OW$ gallons of water.

The scope of exchange possibilities between Mark and Beth is a function of their preferences for bread and water. Indifference curves (I) summarize their personal preferences for the two goods and have the traditional property of convexity to the appropriate origin. Only a few of the many indifference curves are shown in the box, and these display the conventional property that the further the curve is from its origin, the greater the utility received from any combination of bread and water on the curve. For example, Mark prefers any combination along I_2^M to any combination on I_1^M, and Beth prefers any combination along I_3^B to any combination on I_2^B. Preference levels rise as allocations move in the northeast direction for Mark, and for Beth preference levels rise as allocations move in the southwestern direction.

Trades along the Football

To show the range of exchange possibilities, consider allocation a as our initial point of reference and examine how changes from a influence the utilities of Mark and

Beth. Any upward movement along I_2^B toward allocation f results in higher utility for Mark and no change in utility for Beth. This is true because, as Mark receives allocations that lie on indifference curves above I_2^M, Beth receives allocations that remain on I_2^B, and she is therefore indifferent between any of these allocations. Therefore, Mark gains when he trades some of his bread for water. Any upward movement along I_2^M toward allocation f results in the opposite situation. Beth receives allocations on higher indifference curves and Mark receives allocations that remain on I_2^M. Beth gains when she trades some of her water for bread and, at the same time, Mark is indifferent between those allocations and a.

Note that both Mark and Beth are indifferent between a and f, since f is formed by the intersection of the same indifference curves that form a. With f, trades that reallocate bread and water along the football-shaped area (defined by I_2^M and I_2^B and within allocations a and f) toward a yield combinations that make at least one of the individuals better off and neither worse off. Therefore, allocations a and f are not Pareto efficient because there are allocations of bread and water that improve the utility of at least one of these individuals without making either worse off. Reallocations *along* the football-shaped area result in combinations of bread and water that yield higher utility for either Mark or Beth and, at the same time, do not lower the utility for either individual. All combinations of bread and water that lie along this football-shaped area are therefore Pareto superior to a and f.

Trades outside the Football

Using points a and f as reference points again, how do you suppose Mark and Beth perceive g and h? Even though g results in higher utility for Beth, Mark is opposed to this reallocation of bread and water because it yields lower utility for him. The opposite occurs with allocation h: higher utility for Mark and lower utility for Beth. Trades therefore will not develop outside the football-shaped area defined by I_2^M and I_2^B and allocations a and f.

Trades within the Football

What about trades *within* the football-shaped area defined by a and f? All allocations are associated with higher utility levels for both Mark and Beth and therefore all are Pareto superior to a and f. Consider allocation tangent point i which lies on both I_3^M and I_3^B and is therefore clearly Pareto superior to a and f. Are there any allocations Pareto superior to i? The answer is no, because any other allocation would result in a combination of bread and water that lowers the utility of either Mark or Beth. Allocation i is Pareto efficient since any other reallocation would yield an improvement in the utility of one person that is necessarily associated with a worsening in utility of the other individual. Since no other allocation raises Mark's or Beth's utility without lowering the utility of either individual, Pareto efficient allocations occur at the point of tangency between the indifference curves of Mark and Beth.

Conditions for Pareto Efficiency

At a point of tangency between two curves, the slopes of the two curves are equal. Economists call the slope of an indifference curve the **marginal rate of substitution (MRS)**, which indicates the rate at which individuals are willing to trade one good for the other as they remain indifferent between combinations of the goods. The condition for Pareto efficiency is therefore

$$MRS^M_{BW} = MRS^B_{BW} \tag{3A-1}$$

where the superscripts M and B refer to Mark and Beth, respectively, and the subscripts BW refer to trades of bread and water between Mark and Beth. Equation (3A-1) tells us that efficient exchange requires that no rearrangement of bread and water between Mark and Beth may take place that improves either person's utility without making either individual worse off.

Contract Curve

There is no reason to believe that a or f would be the initial allocation of bread and water in this economy. A **contract curve** represents all the Pareto efficient combinations of bread and water that occur at all points of tangency between Mark and Beth's indifference curves. In other words, for each possible initial allocation of bread and water, there exists a different Pareto efficient allocation for the society composed of Mark and Beth. In Figure 3A-2, the contract curve OO' shows all possible tangencies of indifference curves and therefore lists all Pareto efficient allocations for society.

The welfare economist uses the contract curve to assess the efficiency of exchange in society. When allocations of bread and water do not fall on the contract curve, the contract curve allows welfare economists to show which reallocations are

**FIGURE 3A-2
Contract Curve**

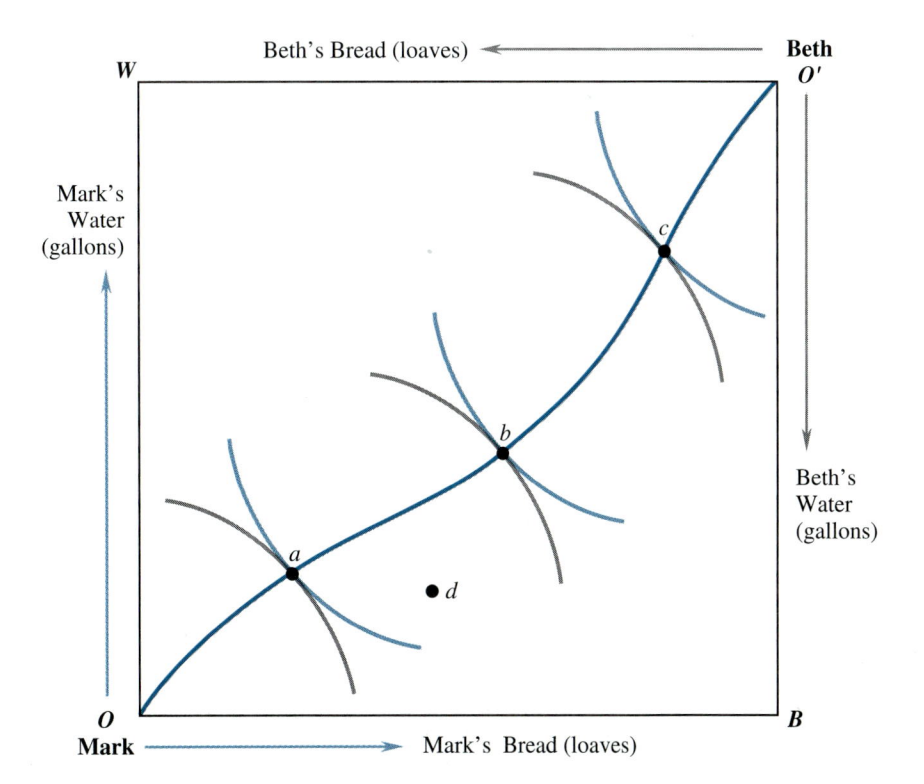

Pareto superior and Pareto efficient. Such reallocations are socially desirable in the sense that they improve the welfare of at least one individual in society without reducing the welfare of any other individual.

Utility Possibilities Curve

The contract curve is a plot of all the Pareto efficient combinations of bread and water available for society. These combinations are determined by the tastes that Mark and Beth have for the fixed quantities of bread and water in the economy. It should also be noted that each point along the contract curve is associated with different utility levels for Mark and Beth. A **utility possibilities curve** plots the maximum utility for each individual, holding constant the utility of the other individual. The information required for construction of the utility possibilities curve comes directly from the contract curve. Figure 3A-3, then, plots the trade-off between the utility of Mark and Beth. Using the points *a, b,* and *c* from the contract curve in Figure 3A-2, the utility possibilities curve *AB* for Mark and Beth is plotted in Figure 3A-3. Notice that *a* in both Figure 3A-2 and Figure 3A-3 corresponds to relatively high utility for Beth and low utility for Mark. Point *c* corresponds to the opposite.

Because point *d* is not Pareto efficient and therefore lies *off* the contract curve in Figure 3A-2, it is plotted on the *inside* of the utility possibilities curve in Figure 3A-3. That is, the utility of one person may be raised without lowering the utility of the other. There are allocations that are Pareto superior to *d;* these are shown in the area defined by *def* in Figure 3A-3. Reallocations within *def* improve efficiency; they therefore define the limits of welfare economists to recommend reallocations that

FIGURE 3A-3
Utility Possibilities Curve

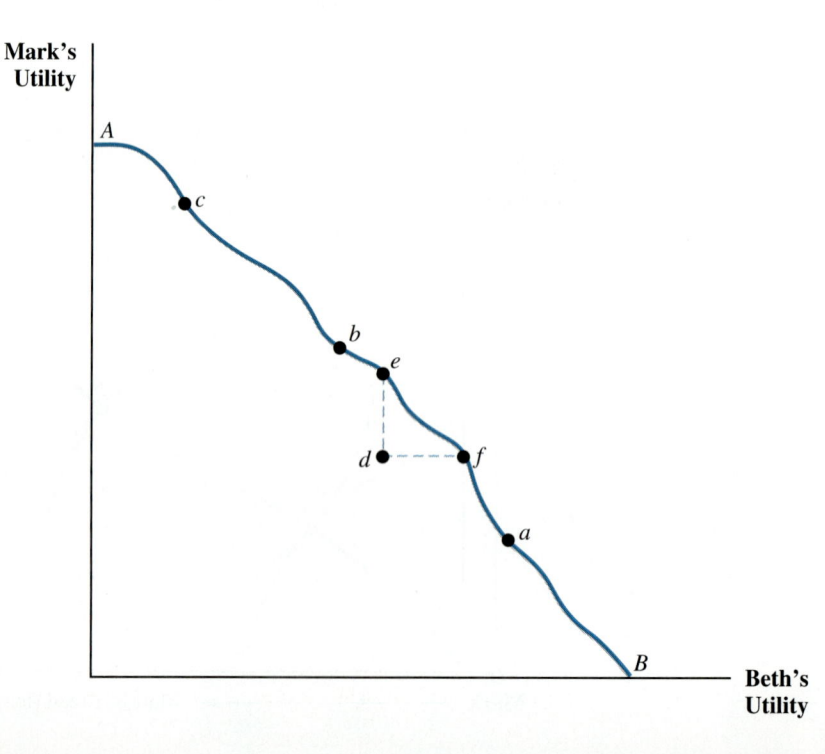

enhance exchange efficiency. It is clear, for example, that exchange efficiency is not enhanced by reallocating from *d* to *a, b,* or *c,* since such reallocations lower the welfare of either Mark or Beth. We see similar violations of the definition of efficiency when reallocations occur *along* the utility possibilities curve since these result in combinations of bread and water that lower individual welfare. While all points along the utility possibilities curve are Pareto efficient, our framework does not allow us to judge which Pareto efficient point is best for society.

Efficiency in Production

What if bread and water are not in fixed supply? Are there other bread and water combinations that utilize society's resources better? Resources are not efficiently used when more of any good can be produced without decreasing production of any other good. When this condition holds, there is efficiency in production, or what is also called a Pareto efficient use of resources.

Production Possibilities Curve

Production possibilities curves[2] indicate the maximum quantities of two goods that can be produced in the economy when the supply of resources and technology is fixed. Combinations of goods along the production possibilities curve are assumed to be the result of state-of-the-art production technologies. Figure 3A-4 shows what a production possibilities curve for bread and water may look like in the society composed of Mark and Beth. Any point along curve *AB* shows the maximum gallons of water that can be produced for any given level of bread production and vice versa. Combinations of bread and water that lie within the interior of *AB,* such as *a,* are the result of less-than-full employment of resources or less than state-of-the-art technology. All combinations outside of the curve, such as *b,* are unattainable under current resources or technology constraints.

Production possibilities curves list the production choices that are available for society. In effect, our previous discussion of efficiency in exchange assumed that quantities of bread and water were one of many possible combinations shown in Figure 3A-4. For example, combination *D,* with W_1 gallons of water and B_1 loaves of bread, may have been the fixed levels of water and bread that defined the length of the axes of the Edgeworth-Bowley box in Figure 3A-1. We now see that, in addition to *D* in Figure 3A-4, many other quantities of bread and water fall within the productive limits of society. (Points, such as *a,* which lie on the interior of the production possibilities curve may also have defined the fixed quantities of bread and water. However, we will show that such bread and water combinations are not overall efficient in both exchange and production.) Production possibilities curves list all available combinations, and our next step is to compare the productive efficiency characteristics of these combinations.

---

[2] Production possibilities curves are derived from Edgeworth-Bowley box diagrams, which determine the most efficient combinations of fixed quantities of inputs to produce two goods. Efficient combinations are input combinations that cannot be changed without decreasing the quantity of one of the goods. Interested readers should consult an intermediate microeconomics textbook for this derivation.

**FIGURE 3A-4
Production
Possibilities Curve**

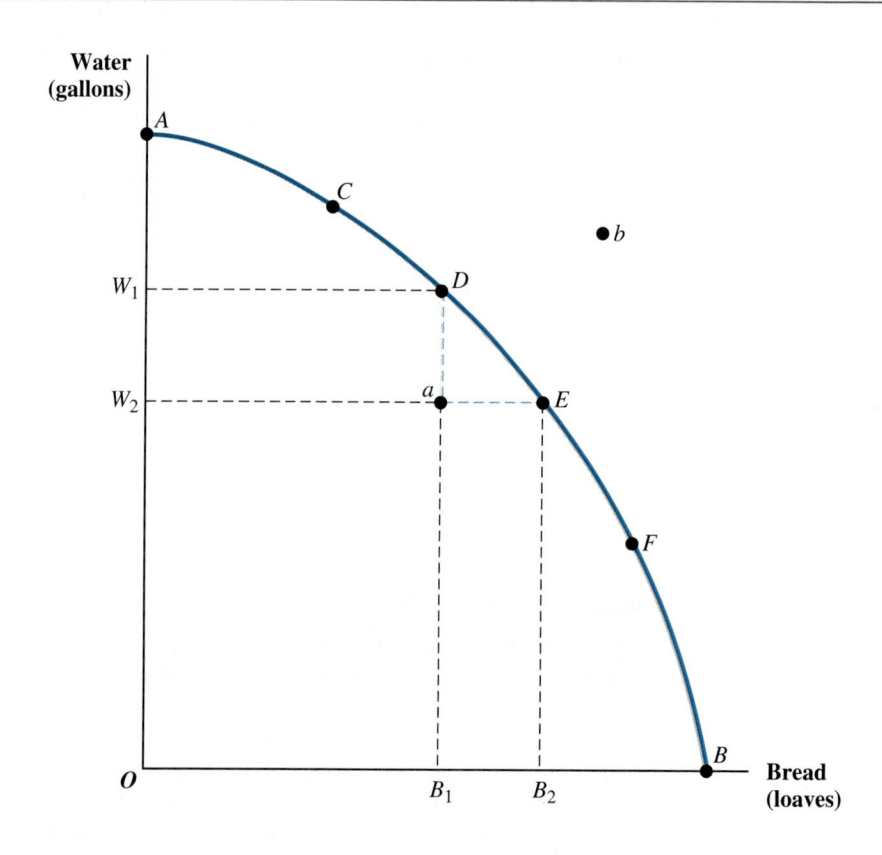

Marginal Rate of Transformation

The slope of the production possibilities curve is called the **marginal rate of transformation (MRT)**. The MRT is negative. In other words, as more bread is produced, fewer units of water may be produced. At the extremes of the production possibilities curve AB all resources are devoted to only one of the goods. Allocation A occurs when all resources are devoted to the production of water, and allocation B is the result of the employment of all resources in the production of bread.

The MRT_{BW} measures the benefits and costs associated with changing production of bread and water along the production possibilities curve. If the combination of bread and water is moved from D to E, society gains B_1B_2 loaves of bread and loses W_1W_2 gallons of water. This trade-off is the ratio $\Delta W / \Delta B$, which is also the formula for MRT_{BW}.

The MRT also measures the **marginal costs (MC)** of production for society. Marginal costs are defined as changes in total costs associated with expanding output. With a world of just two goods, bread and water, the marginal cost of an additional loaf of bread is the water that must be given up to produce the additional loaf of bread. The marginal cost of an additional gallon of water is just the opposite: the loaves of bread that must be given up to produce the additional gallon of water. Therefore, along segment D to E, the marginal cost of producing B_1B_2 more bread is W_1W_2 gallons of water, and the marginal cost of producing W_1W_2 more water is B_1B_2 bread.

Therefore, we can rewrite the slope, or MRT_{BW}, of the production possibilities curve as

$$MRT_{BW} = \frac{MC_B}{MC_W} \qquad (3A\text{-}2)$$

Production possibilities curves are concave to the origin; therefore for movements down the curve, the MRT_{BW} rises. The primary reason for this rising slope is the heterogeneity of scarce resources. As resources are transferred from production of water to bread, producers are increasingly forced to use resources that are not so productive in making bread; therefore, for each unit fall in water production, fewer and fewer units of bread may be made.

Rising MRT_{BW}, then, means that more and more water must be given up as society expands production of bread. Another way of saying this is to say that the costs of expanding bread production rise because more and more water must be given up. This is the notion of opportunity costs—the use of resources to produce bread means fewer resources to produce water. The rising MRT_{BW} indicates that this opportunity cost rises as we move down the production possibilities curve. The rate at which the opportunity cost is rising is indicated by the MRT_{BW}, which rises as fewer gallons of water and more loaves of bread are produced. (This also holds for changes in production that move up the production possibilities curve.) This characteristic of production processes is so pervasive that it has been dubbed the **law of increasing cost;** that is, expanded production of most goods comes at increasing costs to society. As is clear from production possibilities curves that are concave to the origin, each unit increase in bread comes at a higher loss (cost) of water production.

Efficient Production of Goods

- *Combinations of goods that fall inside the production possibilities curve are not the result of efficient utilization of resources.* In Figure 3A-4, consider combination *a*, which contains W_2 gallons of water and B_1 loaves of bread and lies on the interior of the production possibilities curve. Combinations *D* and *E* are characterized by more efficient uses of resources since, in either case, more of one of each good may be produced without decreasing production of the other. A move from *a* to *D* results in more water and no loss of bread, and from *a* to *E*, society produces more bread and experiences no loss in water. Either change is feasible within the resource constraints of society; therefore both combinations are the result of more efficient uses of society's resources. Combination *a* is therefore a result of an inefficient use of society's resources; thus, by inspection, all combinations defined by area *aDE* represent combinations of bread and water that are more efficient than *a*.

- *Combinations of goods that lie on production possibilities curves are the result of efficient resource allocations.* This follows from the observations that for all combinations below *AB*, production of at least one of the goods may be expanded without reducing production of any good. Therefore, all efficient uses of resources produce combinations of goods that lie on the production possibilities curve.

- *No combination of goods along the production possibilities curve is more efficient than any other.* To see this, consider point *C* and notice that any movement along the curve necessarily increases one good and decreases the other good. Without a framework for judging the social desirability of one good over another, we cannot tell whether the increase in one good (and decrease in the other) produces greater productive efficiency for society. Therefore, with the information supplied by the production possibilities framework, welfare economists have no way of arguing the relative efficiency of any combination along a society's production possibilities curve. We can only point out the trade-offs that lie along the production possibilities curve.

❏ *Combinations of goods that lie within the interior of production possibilities curves are not always less efficient than points along the curves.* Is combination C the result of greater efficiency in production than combination a? Combination C meets our definition of efficiency in production, but we cannot say that it is a result of more efficient resource allocation than the goods combination described by a. The move from a to C necessarily results in lower bread production and without imposing value judgments about the desirability of gaining water, we cannot claim that C is more efficient than a. The limit to our comparison of relative efficiencies is to argue that all combinations defined by the *aDE* area represent more efficient resource utilizations than a.

Overall Efficiency

Overall economic efficiency occurs when exchanges and production are efficient at the same time. Efficient exchange requires that no further rearrangement of society's goods among individuals may take place unless one's gain in utility causes another to lose utility. Technically, efficiency in exchange requires equality of marginal rates of substitution among all individuals in society. Efficient production requires that resources be allocated in such a way as to produce a combination of goods that lies on society's production possibilities curve. We now show that for a given combination of goods along the production possibilities curve, not all exchanges defined by the contract curve are Pareto efficient in the overall sense of exchange and production.

Figure 3A-5 plots the production possibilities curve *EF* for our example economy, listing all its points of efficient production. For output combination *O'*, the appropriate Edgeworth-Bowley box facing Mark and Beth may be defined. Output combination *O'* is efficient in the sense that resources cannot be rearranged such that increases in the production of any good occur without decreasing production of any other good. Because combination *O'* defines *OW* gallons of water and *OB* loaves of bread, box *OWO'B* defines the appropriate Edgeworth-Bowley box for this economy. As before, *O* and *O'* are the respective origins for Mark and Beth. The contract curve *OO'* lists all allocations that result in Pareto efficiency in exchange.

While all points along the contract curve reflect Pareto efficiency in exchange, not all allocations along the contract curve reflect overall efficiency in *both* exchange and production. Remember that *MRS* measures the rate at which individuals trade one good for another along indifference curves, and *MRT* measures the rate at which one good may be exchanged for another along production possibilities curves. Also note that, while along any contract curve $MRS_{BW}^M = MRS_{BW}^B$, the *MRS* values are not necessarily uniform. For example, at point *a*, it could be the case that $MRS_{BW}^M = MRS_{BW}^B = 2$ and, at point *f*, $MRS_{BW}^M = MRS_{BW}^B = 4$. Finally, note that

FIGURE 3A-5
Overall Economic Efficiency

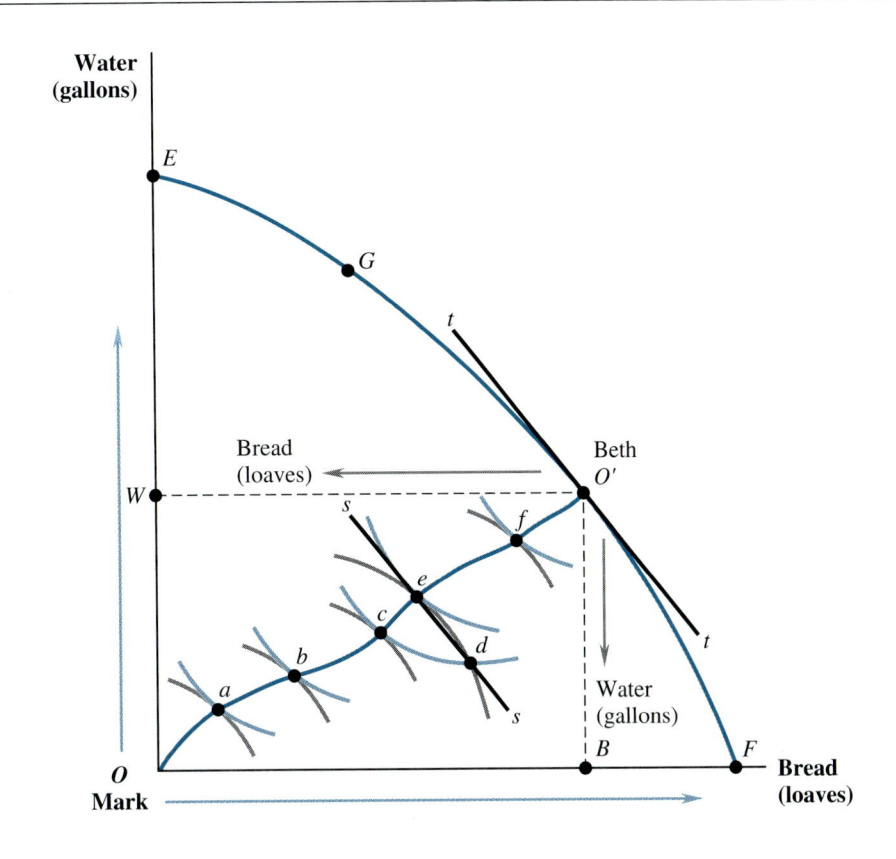

production possibilities curves are concave to the origin; their *MRT* values rise and are therefore not uniform for movements down the curve.

In order to achieve overall economic efficiency in exchange and production, output combination O' needs to be allocated between Mark and Beth in such a way that

$$MRS_{BW}^{M} = MRS_{BW}^{B} = MRT_{BW} \qquad (3A\text{-}3)$$

To show why equation (3A-3) is the condition for overall efficiency, consider the case where $MRT_{BW} > MRS_{BW}^{M} = MRS_{BW}^{B}$. Here the rate at which bread may be substituted into water exceeds the rate at which Mark and Beth require additional water as compensation for reduced consumption of bread. For example, consider $MRT_{BW} = 3$ and $MRS_{BS}^{M} = MRS_{BW}^{B} = 1$. With $MRT_{BW} = 3$, three additional gallons of water may be produced by switching the resources required to produce one additional loaf of bread. If Mark is to remain indifferent, he must give up one loaf of bread for each additional gallon of water. Therefore, Mark would be better off by converting one loaf of bread into three more gallons of water. The two gallons of water above the necessary one gallon that keeps him on his indifference curve may either be used by Mark or given to Beth. In either case, at least one person's utility rises without adverse effects on anyone's utility. Therefore, as long as trades like this exist, the economy is not in overall efficiency of exchange and production, and social welfare is enhanced by changing the exchange and production allocations in this economy. As long as $MRT_{BW} > MRS^M_{BW} = MRS^B_{BW}$, changes exist that may improve Beth's and/or Mark's utility without adverse effects on anyone else's well-being; therefore, only when $MRS^M_{BW} = MRS^B_{BW} = MRT_{BW}$ does overall efficiency in exchange and production exist.

Overall efficiency in exchange and production may also be demonstrated in Figure 3A-5. Taking the slope of line *tt*, which is tangent to *O'*, we have the appropriate *MRT*, which must equal $MRS^M_{BW} = MRS^B_{BW}$ along contract curve *OO'*. Taking the slope of line *ss*, which measures the *MRS* where two indifference curves are tangent at *e*, we see one allocation of bread and water between Mark and Beth that meets the condition that $MRS^M_{BW} = MRS^B_{BW} = MRT_{BW}$. Therefore, although all allocations along the contract curve *OO'* are Pareto efficient in exchange, only allocation *e* results in overall efficiency in exchange and production.

Grand Utility Possibilities Curve

Overall efficiency in exchange and production has been discussed in terms of a given point along the production possibilities curve. Thus we can see in our example that allocation *e* is the result of overall efficiency when point *O'* defines the fixed output opportunities for society. We also note that each point along the contract curve is associated with different utility levels for Mark and Beth; from this, we can construct a utility possibilities curve, which plots the maximum utility for each individual, holding constant the utility of the other individual. Now we can conceive a way to arrive at the condition of overall efficiency in exchange and production for another point, such as *G*, along the production possibilities curve in Figure 3A-5. From an Edgeworth-Bowley box defined by *G*, we would choose the allocation along its corresponding contract curve that meets the overall efficiency condition $MRS^M_{BW} = MRS^B_{BW} = MRT_{BW}$. From this contract curve, there is also a corresponding utility possibilities curve. However, as in the above case where we are at point *O'* on the production possibilities curve, overall efficiency in exchange and production is consistent with only one point along the utility possibilities curve.

Theoretically, we can arrive at points of efficiency in exchange and production for each point along the production possibilities curve and construct a **grand utility possibilities curve**.[3] In effect, it chooses those points along the contract curves associated with each point along the production possibilities curve that meet the efficiency conditions for exchange and production. All points along a grand utility possibilities curve represent efficiency in exchange and production; therefore, at each point, reallocations of exchange and production that enhance one person's utility must make someone else worse off.

---

[3] A grand utility possibilities curve is not shown here because, while it may be an interesting theoretical construct, it appears to have little practical significance when society consists of a large and diverse collection of individuals. The concept of maximization of social welfare is fraught with many problems that necessarily carry over to our ability to argue that one or more points along a grand utility possibilities curve is more or less desirable than any other.

Private Markets, Competition, and Overall Efficiency

Perfect Competition and Efficiency in Exchange

Under perfect competition, private markets allocate resources that achieve overall efficiency in exchange and production. Perfectly competitive firms are price takers and produce a homogeneous product; the demand curve facing individual firms is therefore *perfectly elastic*. Perfectly elastic demand curves indicate that all consumers face the same prices for the goods that they wish to consume. For example, if Mark must pay $2 for a loaf of bread, Beth also pays $2. As discussed in the appendix at the end of the book, consumers maximize utility by purchasing combinations of goods such that the ratio of marginal utilities is equal to price ratios. Or, in terms of bread and water and Mark and Beth, this result may be written as

$$\frac{MU_B^M}{MU_W^M} = \frac{MU_B^B}{MU_W^B} = \frac{P_B}{P_W} \tag{3A-4}$$

Because the ratio MU_B/MU_W is also the definition of MRS_{BW}, we may rewrite (3A-4) as (3A-5) and see that consumers in perfectly competitive markets equate their *MRS* to the ratio of prices:

$$MRS_{BW}^M = MRS_{BW}^B = \frac{P_B}{P_W} \tag{3A-5}$$

Because P_B/P_W is the same for both Mark and Beth, we may rewrite (3A-5) as

$$MRS_{BW}^M = MRS_{BW}^B \tag{3A-6}$$

which is the condition for efficiency in exchange. Therefore, we have just demonstrated that perfectly competitive markets result in efficient exchange.

Perfect Competition and Efficiency in Production

Perfectly competitive firms maximize profits by selling the quantity of output where marginal revenue *(MR)* is equal to marginal cost *(MC)*, or

$$MR = MC \tag{3A-7}$$

Equation (3A-7) is the condition for profit maximization, and marginal revenue is defined as the change in total revenue *(TR)* divided by a change in quantity sold, or $MR = \Delta TR/\Delta Q$. Because the demand curves facing perfectly competitive firms are perfectly elastic, all additional units are sold at the same price and therefore P will equal MR. (Because $TR = PQ$, $MR = \Delta TR/\Delta Q$ may be rewritten as $MR = P\Delta Q/\Delta Q = P$.) Because $P = MR$, we may rewrite the condition of profit maximization (3A-7) as $P = MC$. Using our bread and water example,

$$P_B = MC_B \text{ and } P_W = MC_W \tag{3A-8}$$

are the conditions of profit maximization for bread and water suppliers, respectively.

Profit maximization also implies that

$$\frac{P_B}{P_W} = \frac{MC_B}{MC_W} \qquad (3A\text{-}9)$$

Remember that equation (3A-2) demonstrated that the *MRT* along the production possibilities curve is equal to the ratio of marginal costs of production; therefore, by substituting $MRT_{BW} = MC_B/MC_W$ from (3A-2) we may rewrite (3A-9) as

$$MRT_{BW} = \frac{P_B}{P_W} \qquad (3A\text{-}10)$$

which means that profit maximizing, perfectly competitive markets produce combinations of products that are defined by the point on the production possibilities curve where *MRT* equals the ratio of product prices.

Perfect Competition and Efficiency in Exchange and Production

We have just shown that consumers in perfectly competitive markets set $MRS^M_{BW} = MRS^B_{BW} = P_B/P_W$ and that producers allocate resources on the basis of $MRT_{BW} = P_B/P_W$. Because both consumers and producers base behavior on the ratio of prices, P_B/P_W, we see that

$$MRS^M_{BW} = MRS^B_{BW} = MRT_{BW} \qquad (3A\text{-}11)$$

in perfectly competitive markets. Since (3A-11) is the condition for overall efficiency in exchange and production, we have just demonstrated that competitive markets produce overall efficiency in exchange and production, which therefore leads to socially desirable results.

Monopoly and Efficiency in Exchange and Production

Monopolists are price setters, not price takers, as in the model of perfect competition. Monopolists are, by definition, sole sellers of output, and therefore the demand curves facing them will not be perfectly elastic with respect to price. This less-than-perfect elasticity is a result of having no close substitutes in consumption; therefore, when monopolists raise their prices, they do not lose all their customers. Profit-maximizing monopolists produce that output at which $MR = MC$, so price exceeds *MC*:

$$P > MC \qquad (3A\text{-}12)$$

Therefore, when monopolists produce bread and water,

$$P_B > MC_B \text{ and } P_W > MC_W \qquad (3A\text{-}13)$$

profit maximization results in prices greater than marginal costs:[4]

---

[4] This is not necessarily true, as the following example indicates. With $P_B = \$1$, $MC_B = \$0.50$, $P_W = \$0.60$ and $MC_W = \$0.30$, $P_B > MC_B$ and $P_W > MC_W$, but $P_B/P_W = MC_B/MC_W = \$1.66$. In other words, it is possible for $MRT_{BW} = MRS_{BW}$, but efficiency is still not achieved because a monopolist still produces a smaller level of output than a competitive firm. Therefore monopoly production occurs inside the production possibilities curve.

$$\frac{P_B}{P_W} > \frac{MC_B}{MC_W} \tag{3A-14}$$

Because $MC_B/MC_W = MRT_{BW}$, we see that markets organized by monopolists will produce where prices are greater than marginal costs and the ratio of prices will be greater than the MRT_{BW} of the production possibilities curve:

$$\frac{P_B}{P_W} > MRT_{BW} \tag{3A-15}$$

On the consumption side of the market, utility maximizing consumer behaviors do not differ between perfect competition and monopoly; therefore, as previously shown in (3A-5), they purchase combinations of bread and water such that

$$MRS_{BW}^M = MRS_{BW}^B = \frac{P_B}{P_W}$$

Thus, comparing the relationships to P_B/P_W, we see that (3A-15) and (3A-5) imply that

$$MRS_{BW}^M = MRS_{BW}^B \neq MRT_{BW} \tag{3A-16}$$

in markets organized by monopolists. Equation (3A-16) therefore demonstrates that private markets do not achieve overall efficiency in consumption and production when they are not perfectly competitive.

The litmus test for overall efficiency in markets is the relationship of price to marginal cost. When $P = MC$, as in perfect competition, overall efficiency is achieved. When $P > MC$, as in monopoly, overall efficiency is not achieved.

Comparison of Perfect Competition and Monopoly

Figure 3A-6 exhibits the demand curve ($D = MB$), marginal revenue *(MR)*, and marginal cost *(MC)* curves facing a typical monopolist. Because monopolists have no competitors, they have power to set prices that maximize profits. Profits are maximized at quantities where marginal revenues are equal to marginal costs, or[5]

$$MR = MC \tag{3A-17}$$

Marginal revenue is defined as the change in total revenue divided by a change in quantity sold, or $\Delta TR/\Delta Q$. Because prices must fall as the monopolist sells more output, the marginal revenue associated with successive increases in units sold will fall as shown by the *MR* curve in Figure 3A-6. Note that the *MR* curve of the monopolist always lies below its demand curve. Marginal opportunity costs curves are assumed to be the same as when competitive firms organize the production of this market.

---

[5] To understand why $MR = MC$ is a requirement of profit maximization, consider the implications for profits when $MR \neq MC$. When $MR > MC$, monopolists can sell an additional unit of output and increase profit; and, when $MR < MC$, monopolists may sell one fewer unit and raise profits. Because only at $MR = MC$ can monopolists not alter the number of units sold and increase profitability at the same time, this conditions indicates profit maximization.

FIGURE 3A-6
Comparison of Competition and Monopoly

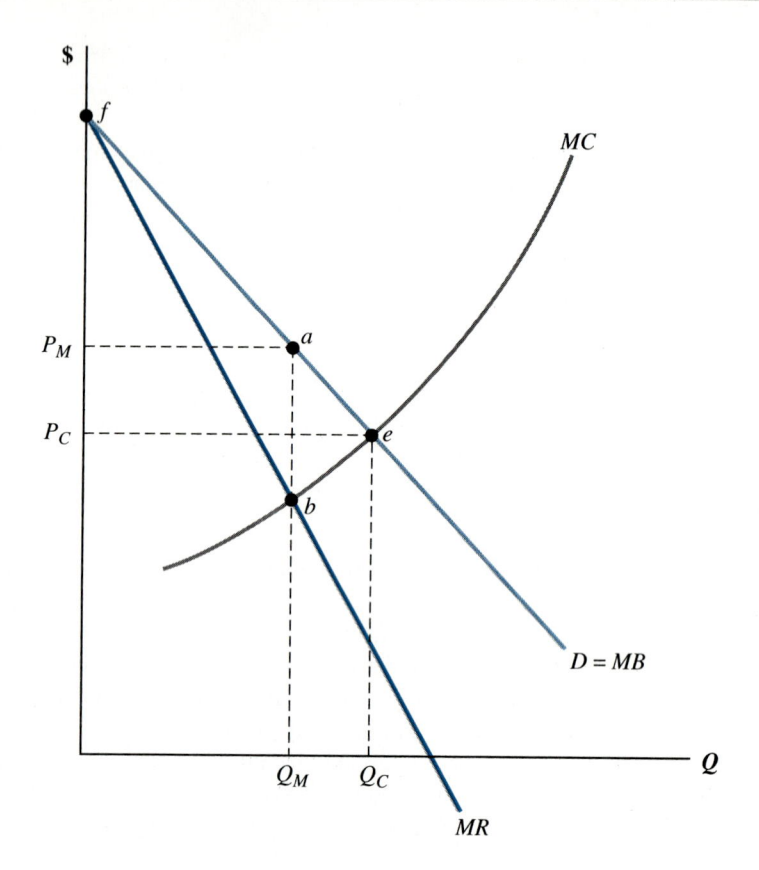

By setting $MR = MC$ at point b, this monopolist maximizes profit by selling output Q_M. The highest price that Q_M may be sold for is P_M, which can be determined by drawing a vertical line, $Q_M a$, to the demand curve. Monopolists therefore set prices above marginal costs, or

$$P_M > MC \qquad (3A\text{-}18)$$

In Figure 3A-6, this difference is distance ab. Because the demand and marginal revenue curves of monopolists are not identical, equation (3A-18) also indicates that at the profit-maximizing price and output,

$$MB > MC \qquad (3A\text{-}19)$$

which means that if monopolists produced more goods, total net benefits of society would rise. In contrast, perfectly competitive firms are price takers and must sell all their output at a uniform price determined by the intersection of market supply and demand curves. Competitive market equilibrium, which occurs at e, is characterized by P_C and Q_C.

We can now compare the resource allocative characteristics of the two types of market structure shown in Figure 3A-6:

❏ *Monopolists charge higher prices than firms in perfectly competitive markets.* For the same product, monopolists and perfect competitors charge P_M and P_C, respectively. The price differential $P_M P_C$ is an important difference between the two market structures.

❏ *Monopolists sell smaller quantities to consumers than firms in perfectly competitive markets.* While perfectly competitive firms produce Q_C, a monopolist maximizes profit by producing Q_M.

❏ *Monopoly production results in lower consumer surplus.* Under a monopoly, consumer surplus is much smaller ($P_M fa$) than is the case under competitive markets ($P_C fe$). In this sense, consumers enjoy greater benefits when production is organized by perfect competitors.

❏ *Monopolists allocate resources inefficiently.* Monopolists do not maximize total net benefits of society because $P_M > MC$ and therefore $MB > MC$. If more resources were allocated in their markets, society would benefit from higher output. In contrast, competitive markets allocate resources until $P_C = MB = MC$ and therefore allocate resources efficiently for society.

The extent to which resources are inefficiently allocated is called the *welfare loss* of monopoly and is sometimes measured as the amount by which consumer surpluses differ between monopoly and competitive markets. Various solutions to the welfare losses associated with monopoly have been suggested. One approach uses antitrust laws to break up large monopolies into smaller, competitive firms. Another approach is to regulate monopolies and attempt to make them perform like competitive firms.

CHAPTER 4

Externalities

What Are Externalities?

Our lives are affected by the actions of many individuals, and as much as we would like to control our lives, some factors are clearly beyond our own control. The time we spend commuting to our jobs is affected by how many other people decide to leave at the same time. It is easier to fall asleep at night when our neighbors (and their dogs) are quiet. The actions of others may also be beneficial. Medical scientists who find new cures for illnesses and quiet neighbors who keep tidy lawns exert positive influences on our lives. In this chapter we discuss how markets allocate resources when the actions of other individuals affect our lives.

Private markets can be efficient allocators of society's resources only when market participants consider all the benefits and costs of their actions. When individuals do not pay for all the resources that they use, **negative externalities,** or external costs, are said to exist. A negative externality may arise, for example, when homeowners are subjected to the noise created by a nearby factory. That factory is imposing a cost (noise) on homeowners that is not paid for by factory owners and therefore allocates too many resources in this market.

Negative externalities occur when private markets fail to allocate resources on the basis of full social costs.

Positive externalities occur when private markets fail to allocate resources on the basis of full social benefits.

Positive externalities occur whenever private markets fail to allocate resources on the basis of full social benefits. While all the neighbors' property values rise because the Smiths keep a tidy lawn, those neighbors do not have to pay the Smiths for those higher values. The Smiths, however, may not consider the beneficial effects on others when they make decisions about the quantity of resources to allocate in maintaining a tidy lawn. Private markets allocate too few resources to activities when individuals do not fully take account of the benefits of their actions on others.

This chapter addresses the following issues regarding resource allocations when externalities are present.

❑ Why do private markets fail to allocate resources efficiently when externalities exist?

❑ Why are property rights an important dimension to the study of externalities?

❑ In what way are externalities reciprocal in nature?

❑ Can assignment of property rights solve the problems associated with externalities?

❑ Does it matter who is assigned property rights?

❑ What forms of government intervention may improve allocative efficiency?
❑ Will government intervention necessarily result in greater allocational efficiency?

Negative Externalities

Concept of Negative Externalities

Michael, an aspiring rock musician, practices electric guitar every day for four hours in his house in the suburbs. When Michael's neighbor, David, does not enjoy listening to the ear-shattering guitar notes, Michael's practice time may differ from what is efficient for society. The musician determines how many hours to practice based on the benefits and costs of that activity. Future fame and wealth determine the expected benefits from practicing. Costs include time, which could be spent at a paying job, and money for purchasing guitars, strings, picks, music sheets, and an amplifier capable of filling a 100,000-seat stadium with his music. In addition to these costs, though, an external cost, as measured by the discomfort that Michael imposes on David, is involved. In effect, the musician is polluting the atmosphere for David because when David dislikes his playing, a by-product of the musician's activity is noise pollution. Air is a resource used in the production of practice time, but Michael does not pay for the air space he uses.

A divergence between private and social costs emerges when the full costs of producing a product, such as practice time, are not fully considered by the producer. **Private costs** include only those paid by the producer and therefore do not necessarily include the costs of all resources used in production. **Social costs** include all resource costs and therefore, in the example of the aspiring rock musician, the difference between private and social costs is the discomfort that Michael imposes on David. This difference between private and social costs measures the extent of negative externality, or external cost, and reflects resource costs not charged to any individual. David, however, loses quiet air space, sleeping and nap time, and possibly a lower property value when Michael practices guitar.

Private costs are costs incurred by private parties.

Social costs are those incurred by private parties in addition to any other costs borne by other members of society.

Allocative Efficiency and Negative Externalities

When private and social costs diverge, private markets do not allocate resources efficiently. Figure 4-1 shows marginal social benefits *(MSB)*, marginal private opportunity costs *(MPC)*, and marginal social opportunity costs *(MSC)* for Michael's practice time. Marginal benefit and demand curves are identical, of course, as are marginal cost and supply curves. Because there are two cost curves, we have two supply curves: *PS* is private costs and *SS* is social costs. When Michael does not pay for the costs inflicted on David, total net benefits are maximized at T_1, because *MSB = MPC*. However, because the air space has many alternative uses—like listening to classical music or the pure pleasure of sleeping in peace—air space is not efficiently allocated when Michael does not consider its value. In other words, while T_1 is efficient from Michael's point of view, it is not efficient for the society composed of Michael and David.

The *MSC* of practice time is constructed by adding the value of air space plus *MPC*. The value of the air space in the next best use measures the opportunity cost of

**FIGURE 4-1
A Market with a Negative Externality**

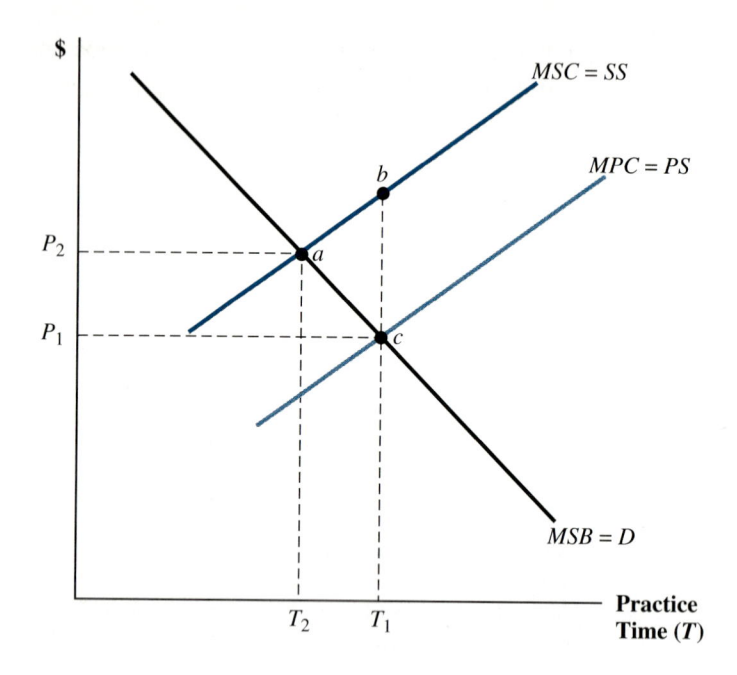

that resource. The difference between *MSC* and *MPC* is distance *bc* per unit; it measures the size of the negative externality. (For simplicity, it is assumed that the gap between *MPC* and *MSC*, the negative externality, does not change as Michael spends more time in practice.) Allocative efficiency occurs at practice time T_2, where net social benefits are maximized or

$$MSB = MSC \qquad (4\text{-}1)$$

At the private market output of T_1, net social benefits are not maximized because *MSB* < *MSC* (that is, *c* < *b*), and in this case too many resources are devoted to practicing guitar since shifting resources out of practice time and into other uses results in higher net social benefits. Only at *MSB* = *MSC* are there no other allocations that can expand net social benefits.

Distance T_2T_1 is the amount by which Michael practices too much when he does not pay for the air space he uses. Marginal net social benefits are equal to the difference between *MSB* and *MSC*; therefore, for changes in time spent in practice, they are measured by the distance between *MSB* and *MSC* curves. By reducing time spent in practice from T_1 to T_2, area *abc* is equal to the rise in net social benefits that results when the market fully accounts for costs of all resources used in the market.

Market Prices and Negative Externalities

We remember that private markets allocate resources efficiently when prices are equal to marginal social costs and marginal social benefits. In Figure 4-1, we see that market prices are determined by the intersection of marginal social benefits and marginal cost curves. However, when *MPC* and *MSC* curves diverge, there are two supply curves. Supply PS does not reflect the externality but supply SS does. When the negative externality is not included in the costs of production, price P_1 is placed on practice and

$$P = MSB = MPC < MSC \qquad (4\text{-}2)$$

Equation (4-2) shows that market price P_1 is set below MSC and is therefore inconsistent with maximizing total net benefits of society.

When externalities are reflected in costs,

$$P = MSB = MSC > MPC \qquad (4\text{-}3)$$

Equation (4-3) shows that market price P_2 achieves allocative efficiency because marginal social benefits are equal to marginal social costs. In other words, prices must reflect marginal social costs in order for private markets to achieve allocative efficiency. Where negative externalities are present, one or more resources are not being priced appropriately by the market.

Property Right Assignments

In addition to our example of the aspiring rock star, many other examples of negative externalities come to mind. Air and water pollution produced by chemical plants, the barking of a neighbor's dogs, the fidgets of children attending a classical musical performance are all cases in which the full costs borne by members of society may not be reflected in resource allocations of private markets. A common characteristic shared by externalities is that no individual is assigned property rights for all the resources used by the market. The air space, for instance, is not owned by any individual and Michael, therefore, does not have to pay anyone for the right to spoil David's air space. A chemical plant may not have to pay anyone for air and water resources it pollutes during the production of chemicals. Parents with noisy children do not have to compensate music lovers when their children run up and down the aisles of concert halls.

The Case of African Elephants

It is instructive to examine how property right assignments affect resource allocation.[1] Consider African elephants, for example. Some countries permit citizens to "own" elephants and assign property rights to villagers but other countries do not. Southern Africa, where a property rights approach is used, has seen an annual increase of elephant herds of about 5 percent. In Zimbabwe, for example, property rights are held by approximately two dozen villages, which earn roughly $5 million a year by selling hunting rights on their communal lands to safari operations. Because elephants provide revenue, villagers have powerful incentives to prevent poaching and to care

---

[1] This discussion is based on Gordon L. Brady and Michael L. Marlow, "The Political Economy of Endangered Species Management: The Case of Elephants," *Journal of Public Finance and Public Choice* (1991): 29–39. For similar insights into the relationship between property right assignments and resource usage, see Richard J. Angello and Lawrence P. Donnelley, "Property Rights and Efficiency in the Oyster Industry," *Journal of Law and Economics* 18 (October 1975): 521–533; and Harold Demsetz, "Toward a Theory of Property Rights," *American Economic Review* 57 (May 1967): 347–359.

for sick animals. In the ten years ending in 1991, the elephant population of Zimbabwe had grown from 30,000 to 43,000. Botswana, whose elephant population increased from 20,000 to 51,000 over the same period, has a similar success story. In contrast, consider eastern and central African countries, where no private ownership rights in elephants are assigned. These countries have experienced dramatic herd reductions and, according to various worst-case forecasts, elephants in these regions could be practically extinct by 1995.

Why is assignment of property rights to villagers an important factor behind the growing herds? People will not usually invest in the protection of elephants when protection fails to yield economic benefits. When villagers own elephants, they have strong incentives to be good stewards of their property since the well-being of the herd directly influences the well-being of the village. Resources that are well cared for are more valuable today and tomorrow than resources that suffer neglect or bad stewardship. In contrast, when villagers are not allowed to own elephants, they have few incentives to take good care of them. Further, if unowned elephants destroy crops, villagers are likely to kill the elephants, which have no ownership value and also destroy resources. While it is possible to manage elephant populations without providing ownership to villagers, no one has much economic incentive to provide this service free of charge.

The leaders of those countries that prohibit hunting and private ownership of elephants believe, in effect, that the appropriate number that should be hunted is zero. However, without private ownership of elephants there can be no private market for this resource, thus, this approach charges poachers a price of zero for each elephant they poach. With an effective price of zero, poachers hunt elephants until marginal benefits cease to be greater than zero.

Consider Figure 4-2 which shows the marginal social benefits and marginal social costs of hunting elephants. When ownership is not vested in private hands, poachers will hunt E_2 elephants, which is the quantity at which marginal benefits are zero. (Assume, for the moment, that the public sector does not fine or effectively deter poaching.) Therefore, in addition to leaving villagers no incentive to manage and care for herds, lack of private ownership may also (unintentionally) *promote* the extinction of elephants, which are potential resources, by allowing them to be taken at zero price—clearly not a reflection of their true resource value. In contrast, private ownership forces the market to consider the marginal social costs of this valuable resource and results in an equilibrium combination of price P_E and quantity E_1.

Comparison of these two systems of property rights suggests that private ownership is the system that results in maximization of total net social benefits since $MSB = MSC$ only at E_1. Where private ownership is prohibited, private markets are not allowed to charge resource users the marginal social costs of their actions; therefore resources are overutilized, as shown by consumption of E_2.

An alternative way by which private markets may be forced to pay full social costs for elephants, without assigning property rights to villagers, is for governments to fine poachers. The expected cost to poachers would become the probability of getting caught times the fine, which, if set high enough, could equal the efficient market equilibrium price. However, as the countries that use this regulatory approach have found out, funding for enforcement and detection programs is far below a resource

**FIGURE 4-2
Analysis of the
Elephant Market**

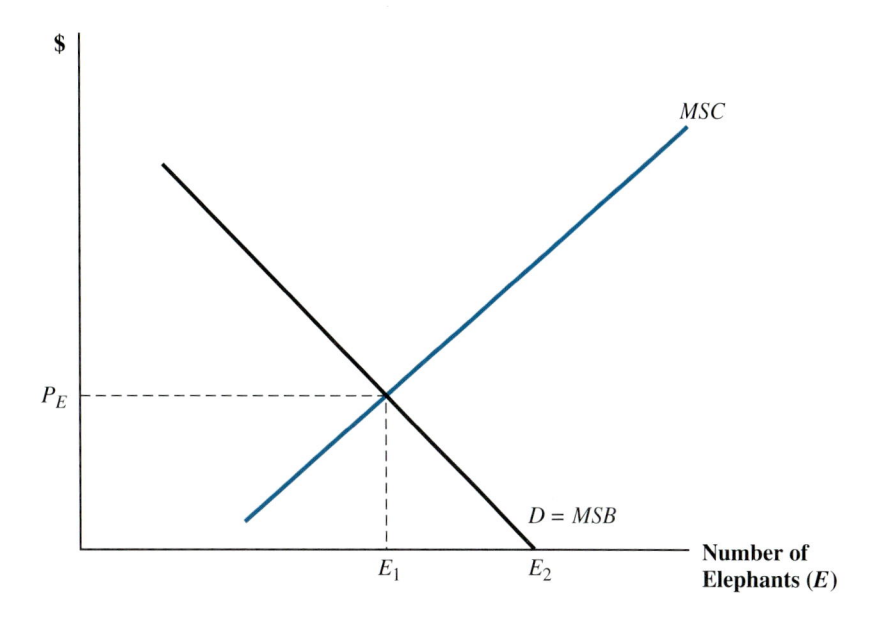

level that would effectively create a credible deterrent to poaching. These public programs have therefore not been able to stop the rapid depletion of elephants.

The plight of elephants is a serious matter, and this discussion does not suggest that private ownership would solve all the problems society believes attend that plight. If the hunting of elephants is perceived to be immoral, then it may not be appropriate for any village to own elephant herds. Similar logic can be used to explain why no private individual owns the Washington Monument or Grand Canyon National Park. Prohibition of ownership rights does not, however, solve the many problems associated with poaching when no one has an incentive to provide good stewardship of these valuable resources. A long-known truth is that, when private markets are not allowed to ration scarce and valuable resources through the price system, some other means of rationing will take over, and as in the case of rent controls, the results may be quite different from those intended. In the case of elephants, stewardship over certain resources is sometimes assigned to the public sector, which through regulation or prohibition, seeks to manage these valuable resources.

The Coase Theorem

No one can claim payment for resource usage when property rights are not well defined, but this does not imply that prices cannot be assigned to those resources. An example of an auction market for property rights is the case of New York City, which awards ownership of the rights to operate taxicabs to only 11,787 individuals. These licenses are called medallions and are required for operation of all taxicabs.[2] Because

---

[2] For a recent discussion of the medallion system, see "New York's Taxis," *The Economist*, March 9, 1991, 28.

the regulator, the city's Taxi and Limousine Commission, has not increased the number of medallions since 1937, these medallions are worth many dollars to their owners. Over the years, growing demand for taxicabs has driven up the value of the fixed supply of medallions because New York is a city in which it is convenient to travel by cabs. Owners can sell or lease the rights to operate taxicabs, and these ownership rights reached a record level of $144,000 in 1989.[3] Thus we see that, even though resources (medallions) may be regulated by government, they are nonetheless priced according to values placed upon them by owners.

Let us return now to our discussion of Michael and David and question whether a value may be placed on the air space they both use. It might be considered just good manners or neighborly for Michael and David to try to work out a solution acceptable to both parties, but there is also an economic incentive for both parties to want to come to some mutually beneficial agreement over usage of air space. Beneficial agreements will be based on the way each party values the scarce resource in question.

Externality relationships are reciprocal in nature, that is, there are two valid and relevant points of view that can work to solve the problem. Michael appears to impose negative externalities on David, who does not enjoy his practicing. But David imposes negative externalities on Michael because David wants to limit practicing time, which is important to Michael's future fame and wealth. Two issues concerning Michael and David are now examined: (1) what is the efficient use of air space by society? and (2) does it matter who is given property right over air space?

Ronald Coase, recipient of the 1991 Nobel Prize in economics, published a seminal article in 1960 in which he proposed what is now called the **Coase theorem.** He argued that as long as there are two conditions—zero transaction costs and clear assignment of property rights to all resources—private markets achieve allocative efficiency in cases involving negative externalities.[4] The first of these conditions, that transaction costs be zero, means that information is perfect and the costs of bargaining and enforcing contracts between parties is zero.[5] In other words, all information summarized by *MSB* and *MSC* curves is known by all parties, and it is costless for parties to negotiate settlement over resource usage. The other condition, that property rights to all resources be clearly assigned, means that private owners of resources may charge for the use of their resources. Thus ownership rights to resources are transferable and exclusive.

Coase theorem is a proposition that resources are allocated efficiently so long as there are well-defined property rights and transactions costs are negligible.

Assignment to Michael

Consider how Michael and David might negotiate with each other when property rights over the air space are assigned to Michael. When Michael owns the air space,

---

[3] For a discussion of the way in which property right assignments provide only transitional gains to the owners of these medallions, see Gordon Tullock, "The Transitional Gains Trap," *Bell Journal of Economics* 6 (Autumn 1975): 671–678.

[4] Ronald H. Coase, "The Problem of Social Cost," *Journal of Law and Economics* 3 (October 1960): 1–44. In his memoirs, 1982 Nobel laureate George Stigler tells of the time in 1960 when Ronald Coase was invited to give his arguments before an audience of twenty nonbelievers from the University of Chicago. Before the evening was through, all became believers in the Coase theorem and, since then, it has been one of the most important insights in economics. See George J. Stigler, *Memoirs of an Unregulated Economist* (New York: Basic Books, 1988), 75–80.

[5] For a discussion of how transactions costs influence creation of firms, see Ronald Coase, "The Nature of the Firm," *Economica* 4 (1937): 386–405.

David must pay for greater peace and quiet. Michael is willing to reduce practice time by an hour so long as David provides compensation greater than his net gain from that hour. Michael's loss per hour is the difference between *MSB* and *MPC*. David is willing to compensate those losses so long as payments are no greater than the losses that he suffers. These losses may be measured by the size of the externality, or on a per unit basis, the difference between *MSC* and *MPC*. Michael is therefore willing to quit practice early whenever the externality exceeds what Michael loses by not practicing. (There are, of course, other ways to negotiate: Michael could soundproof his walls or buy practice headphones, whereas David could also soundproof and buy earplugs.)

From inspection of Figure 4-3, we see that David prefers that Michael never practice, but he is unable to offer sufficient compensation for any hours less than T_2. At T_3, for example, the most that David is willing to offer is *ab,* which is less than the net gain of *ae* that Michael would lose if he quit practice even earlier. At T_1, however, David is willing to compensate Michael *cd,* which because *MSB = MPC,* far exceeds Michael's net gain of zero. Bargaining between the affected parties will result in T_2 practice hours and will occur where the net gain from practicing is equal to the externality. Note also that T_2 reflects allocative efficiency as well, since *MSB = MSC*.

Assignment to David

Now consider what happens when property rights are assigned to David, in which case Michael must pay David for the right to practice. As long as compensation equals or exceeds the value of the externality, David is willing to suffer Michael's practicing. This is true for all practice hours less than or equal to T_2. At T_3, for example, *ae* is the most that Michael is willing to pay and far exceeds *ab* which represents the

FIGURE 4-3
The Reciprocal Nature of Externality

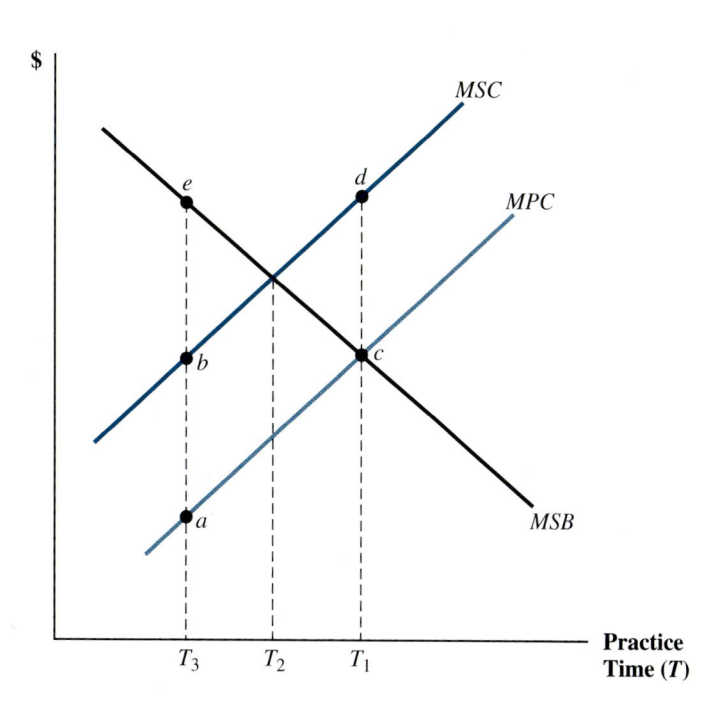

minimum David is willing to take for suffering through the practice. Beyond T_2, however, it is no longer possible for Michael to compensate David enough to justify use of air space since the externality far exceeds any net gain Michael would experience with further practicing. As in the opposite assignment of property rights, both parties will agree to T_2.

Implications of the Coase Theorem

The Coase theorem indicates that irrespective of who owns the property right, resources are allocated to those who place the most value on those resources. Whether Michael is or is not assigned ownership of the air space, Michael practices T_2 hours. When Michael owns the air space, he is willing to pay David for the right to practice up to T_2, and when David owns the air space, David is willing to pay Michael to cut back his practice time to T_2. In either case, values placed on the air space by affected parties determine the use of that scarce resource. For all levels below T_2, Michael values the resource more than David, and for all levels greater than T_2 David values the air space more. When allocative efficiency is reached through trades between affected parties, **internalization of costs** is said to occur, meaning in this case that the negative externality is said to be corrected through the private market system.

Internalization of costs is the allocation of resources by private markets on the basis of full social costs.

Also note that all exchanges between Michael and David are Pareto superior moves since at least one party gains and none loses when both parties engage in mutually beneficial trade. Because private competitive markets achieve allocative efficiency in the presence of negative externalities, the Coase theorem demonstrates that as long as property rights are assigned and no transactions costs exist, government intervention cannot enhance allocative efficiency when negative externalities are present. Let us now explore why the Coase theorem requires the assignment of property rights and low transactions costs.

Allocative Efficiency Requires Assignment of Property Rights

Michael and David's ability to engage in Pareto superior moves is dependent upon the assignment of ownership to the air space. Ownership must be assigned to individuals so that payments may be collected for use of resources. The Coase theorem therefore also implies a role for government in the creation and preservation of well-defined property rights.

Assignment of Property Rights Influences Wealth Distribution

As in the example of African elephants, assignment of property rights also gives the owners of resources an incentive to maintain the quality of resources. Thus, when Michael owns the air space, he has an incentive to maintain its quality by keeping out rival guitarists who may practice at levels that hinder his own. When David owns the air space, he has an incentive to provide an air space that Michael finds conducive to practicing. Otherwise, Michael may not find it beneficial to pay David for its use.

For allocative efficiency it does not matter who is assigned ownership, but it does matter to individuals. We can expect that Michael prefers to own the air space and collect compensation from David. Similar logic indicates that David also prefers to own the air space and earn income, selling the resource to Michael.

Assignment of property rights can be changed through public policy. When this occurs, important changes in income distribution result, affecting the well-being of individuals in society. One of the uses of land along highways, for instance, is the placement of billboards.[6] Land with a gently rising slope along a well-traveled highway brings many dollars to landowners who rent billboard space. Starting in 1958, however, the federal government implemented a policy designed to force state governments to enact laws placing restrictions on the placement of billboards on private land. In 1965, Congress passed the Highway Beautification Act, heavily lobbied by President Lyndon Johnson and Lady Bird Johnson. This law allowed federal payments from highway trust funds to be reduced if states did not ban billboards along certain areas of federally financed highways. As a result, many states banned billboards within 660 feet of rural highways. This is an example of a public policy that reassigns property rights by placing restrictions on how owners of property may use their resources (even though owners of land reacted by putting up larger signs outside the 660-foot limit). Some members of Congress have proposed a Visual Pollution Control Act, which would allow state and local governments to condemn, without compensation, existing billboards and ban all new billboards along 90 percent of federally funded highways. To the extent that changes in property rights reduce the value of property to its owners and the owners are not compensated, the changes affect the distribution of income in society. In this case, property owners suffer income losses when they are prohibited from renting billboard space.

Another example of a case in which changes in property rights have important implications for income distribution is the case of zoning laws. For example, landowners may experience sharp increases in the value of their land when zoning is changed from residential to commercial or industrial.

Transactions Costs and the Role of Government

The lower are transactions costs, the greater are potential gains from trading among affected parties. While transactions costs are never zero, they may at times be sufficiently low to foster Pareto superior trades among individuals. In the example of Michael and David, transactions costs associated with negotiating use of the air space should be fairly trivial. It takes little time or effort for two affected parties to meet with each other and agree upon an efficient use of the air space. David has a fairly good idea about how much damage he suffers when Michael practices and Michael is also aware of his gains and losses. In general, then, the smaller the number of affected parties, the lower are the transactions costs associated with negotiating resource usage. It also follows that the smaller are transactions costs, the greater the incentive for Pareto superior moves to develop that eventually result in efficient resource allocation. Similar logic suggests that the smaller are the numbers of affected parties and the

---

[6] See, for example, James Bovard, "Billboard Ban: Road to Ruin for Property Rights," *Wall Street Journal*, April 2, 1991, A12.

Sell the Whale?

What causes the debate over saving the whale? Is it a product of the whale's being an attractive mammal, or does it arise because whales are actually in danger of extinction? A conflict clearly exists between those who wish to hunt whales and those who want to protect them from hunting. Governments often find themselves caught between these two viewpoints, and it appears that the days when they could reach workable compromises are rapidly drawing to a close.

Auctioning of the property rights to whales is one solution that would allow owners of whales rights to determine whether their whales may be hunted or must be protected. A quota, for example, could be set up by which the ownership rights to 2,000 whales could be auctioned to the highest bidders. If environmentalists outbid hunters, they may protect these whales simply by exercising their right not to hunt them. When hunters outbid environmentalists, hunters place the highest values on whales. Bidders who value whales the most also determine whether they should be protected or hunted.

Source: "Sell the Whale," *The Economist*, June 27, 1992, 16.

Analysis

The Coase theorem demonstrates that when transactions costs are small and property rights are assigned, resources are allocated in an efficient manner. As in the case of elephants, it is essential that scarce resources be owned by someone if those resources are to be allocated efficiently. The same is true of whales. Moreover, it does not matter who is initially assigned property rights so long as those rights are assigned, enforced, and well defined. Auctioning is the means that unlocks the power of the Coase theorem, and it results in an efficient allocation of resources in this resource market.

Governments could themselves get into the bidding and, in this way, speak for voters who do not have the private means with which to determine whether whales are hunted or preserved. If a majority of citizens favor protection, then governments would bid for the right to protect whales. Governments could also bid with the intent of allowing citizens to hunt them when their constitutents favor hunting.

Auctioning off property rights to the highest bidders certainly does not appeal to all individuals. Some will argue that the optimal quantity of hunting is zero. Note, however, that revenues that governments gain from selling whales could be used for conservation policies that pave the path toward a larger number of whales in the future.

It should also be considered that environmentalists may have a vested interest in obtaining policies prohibiting the hunting of whales. Such policies mean that they do not expend their monies in bidding wars with hunters for the rights to determine ownership. In other words, environmentalists would prefer to be assigned ownership at no cost. In this case, they no longer must outbid hunters and, except for lobbying costs, do not expend their scarce resources in obtaining policies they desire.

lower are transactions costs, the less likely that government intervention could improve the efficiency of markets in which all resources are privately owned.

The larger are transactions costs, the smaller the potential gains from trading among affected parties. As an example of negative externalities that affect a large number of parties, consider the case of a chemical plant that pollutes the air space occupied by 200,000 individuals within an area of 100 square miles. It becomes less likely that 200,000 diverse and widely dispersed individuals have enough in common to come together and jointly begin a trading process among themselves and the owners of the chemical plant. Because the level of negative externality is likely to be nonuniform across individuals, information requirements involved will also be a major impediment to formation of Pareto superior moves that result in allocative efficiency. It may also be difficult for 200,000 individuals to agree on much of anything, another way of saying that transactions costs are likely to be high. In general, the greater the number of affected parties, the higher are transactions costs and the less likely it is that private competitive markets will achieve allocative efficiency in cases of negative externalities. In these cases, government intervention may be more likely to improve allocative efficiency.

Negative Externalities and the Prisoners' Dilemma

In addition to cases in which transaction costs are not low or property rights are not well defined, private competitive markets may not achieve allocative efficiency when market participants do not act independently of one another. In these cases, voluntary agreements to internalize negative externalities may not always turn out to be mutually advantageous for all parties. The classic case of **prisoners' dilemma** illustrates this possibility. Two people, Rob and Mary, are accused of robbing a liquor store. The district attorney informs them of the possible sentences they face: If both confess, they both will receive five years in prison; if neither confesses, they each receive two years; if only one confesses, the confessor receives one year and the other (who claims innocence) receives ten years in prison.

What Rob and Mary do depends upon whether they have time to formulate a joint strategy. When acting together, Rob and Mary will both decide to claim innocence and therefore each receive two years in prison. But what if the district attorney segregates them from each other, so that they cannot jointly formulate their strategy? Here each individual must formulate an independent strategy separate from that of the other and will find it advantageous to own up to the robbery. In this case, both serve five years in prison.

This discussion indicates that voluntary agreements among affected parties do not necessarily turn out to be advantageous for all parties. There are two implications for the role that the number of affected parties plays on efficiency of market outcomes. When few individuals are affected, the higher is the incentive of each to form a strategy based on a belief as to what the other is going to do. In other words, the smaller the number of individuals, the more likely the market will stray from the competitive assumption that all market participants act independently of one another. The other implication is that the larger the number of affected parties, the more difficult or costly it is for affected parties to work together and form mutually advantageous trades. This is the same point made above with respect to the role that numbers of participants play on the ability of markets to internalize negative externalities. The concept of prisoners' dilemma suggests that voluntary agreements among all participants need not always perfectly internalize negative externalities.

Prisoners' dilemma is a situation in which two parties may gain from cooperation but are destined to act independently of each other.

Do Property Rights Transcend Geographical Boundaries?

In January 1991, JC Penney was not able to use its trademark in Singapore because a Singapore company had earlier registered itself as "JC Penny Collections."[7] While JC Penney could sell its products in Singapore, sales could not be made under the name JC Penney. Recent attention has also been drawn to foreign-made copies of blue jeans, designer watches, and clothing and at issue is whether property rights can transcend political jurisdictions. Assignment of property rights over information stored on computers has also been gaining great attention. For example, do firms have the right to sell information about your income, education, buying habits, age, address, and phone numbers? Computerized databases are profitable items and without property right assignment to an individual, firms may profit by not having to pay anyone for those valuable resources. Because widespread computer use is a relatively recent phenomenon, no existing property right law governs this case. However, because of the valuable nature of these resources, many individuals are likely to attempt to gain ownership through court cases and legislation.

A related issue is whether citizens of other countries should be allowed to purchase property and businesses in the United States. For example, when Matsushita, a large Japanese firm, bought the U.S. company Yosemite Park and Curry Company that ran many of the concessions in Yosemite Park, many Americans were troubled that the National Park Service, through the U.S. Department of Interior, would allow a foreign firm to operate the business.[8] In other words, should only Americans be allowed to operate this business and therefore own property in this country?

We cannot give a complete response on these issues, but it is important to realize that assignment or reassignment of property rights has important implications for allocative efficiency and income distribution in society. As long as property rights are not established for resources, those resources will not be allocated efficiently in private markets, and where property rights are introduced or reassigned, new owners of those resources gain income. The importance of understanding the role of government in the assignment of property rights is clear.

Government Intervention and Negative Externalities

Government intervention may attempt to internalize negative externalities and enhance allocative efficiency. Policies may be suggested in cases whose transactions costs are too high for the Coase theorem to work or for cases in which it is difficult or impossible to assign property rights over resources. Many types of intervention are available, with four especially common.

Corrective Taxation

Corrective taxation is tax policy that forces market participants to account for the opportunity costs of all resources.

Corrective taxation of negative externalities forces market participants to account for the opportunity costs of all resources allocated in private markets. Figure 4-4 depicts the relevant benefit and cost curves for a competitive market for plastic toys,

---

[7] William M. Borchard, "Trademark Piracy at Home and Abroad," *Wall Street Journal,* May 7, 1991, A12.
[8] Jeanne McDowell, "Fighting for Yosemite's Future," *Time,* January 14, 1991, 46.

FIGURE 4-4
Corrective Taxation of Externality

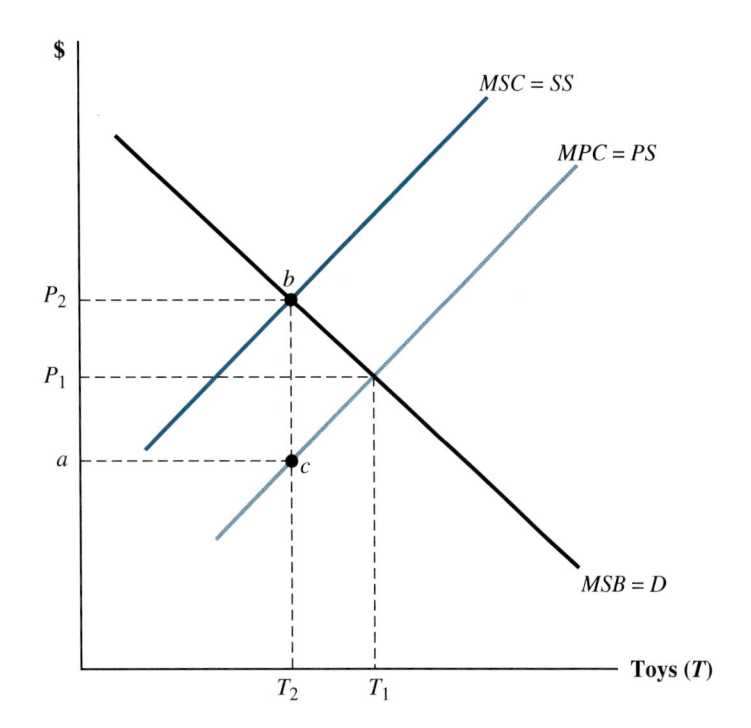

where a by-product of production is emission of a rotten-egg smell that fouls the air for 2,000 homeowners. (We assume that all the firms in this competitive market are located in this same general area.) Assume that property rights are not issued for the air space, and therefore neither toy manufacturers or homeowners may charge the other for use of scarce air space. Because toy manufacturers can use free air, they will set *MPC = MSB*, produce T_1, and charge a per unit price of P_1. This is an efficient output level from the point of view of toy manufacturers, but market price reflects the opportunity costs of all allocated resources except those of the air space. Socially efficient production of toys is determined where *MSC = MSB* and occurs at T_2 with a higher per unit price of P_2.

A Pigouvian tax, named after British economist Arthur C. Pigou (1877–1959), is one means of internalizing the negative externality so that a socially efficient level of toys is produced.[9] By imposing a tax equal to the level of the externality, or *MSC − MPC*, public policy forces manufacturers to fully account for all resources used in production. When the externality is added to producers' costs, that difference, which on a per unit basis is equal to *bc*, forces manufacturers to base their production decisions on marginal social cost. In effect, tax imposition replaces *MPC* with the higher *MSC*, which is now the relevant cost curve for toy manufacturers. After the tax

---

[9] For a more detailed treatment of various options, see William J. Baumol and Wallace E. Oates, *Economics, Environmental Policy, and the Quality of Life*, 2d ed. (New York: Harcourt Brace Jovanovich, 1982).

is imposed, toy manufacturers produce T_2 toys at a price per unit of P_2 and, from society's point of view, resources are efficiently allocated.

The tax internalizes the negative externality and results in a smaller output and a higher price that fully reflect the costs to society of resources used in this market. Tax policies yield tax revenues equal to the tax rate times the level of output produced, or, in our case, aP_2bc. This could be a substantial sum; for example, with a tax rate of $2 applied to 150,000 toys, tax revenues equal $300,000.

Net Gains to Society

Let us consider who gains and who loses when the tax is imposed on manufacturers and tax funds are not allocated to either party. Figure 4-5, which reproduces the curves of Figure 4-4, allows us to see this issue more clearly. When the corrective tax causes production to fall from T_1 to T_2, manufacturers are losers, since they must pay higher costs; and homeowners are gainers, since they breathe cleaner air. The loss to manufacturers is equal to area *abd*, which is equal to the reduction in net gains caused by cutting back production in response to a tax equal to the negative externality. Homeowners gain area *abcd*, which is equal to the overall reduction in negative externality.

When we assume that both parties value dollars equally and that social welfare may be measured as the sum of gains and losses of all affected parties, the net gain to society is *bcd*. As long as gains are large enough to offset the losses suffered by losers, the corrective tax may result in a Pareto superior move for society when sufficient compensation is awarded to all losers.

**FIGURE 4-5
Gains and Losses from Corrective Taxation**

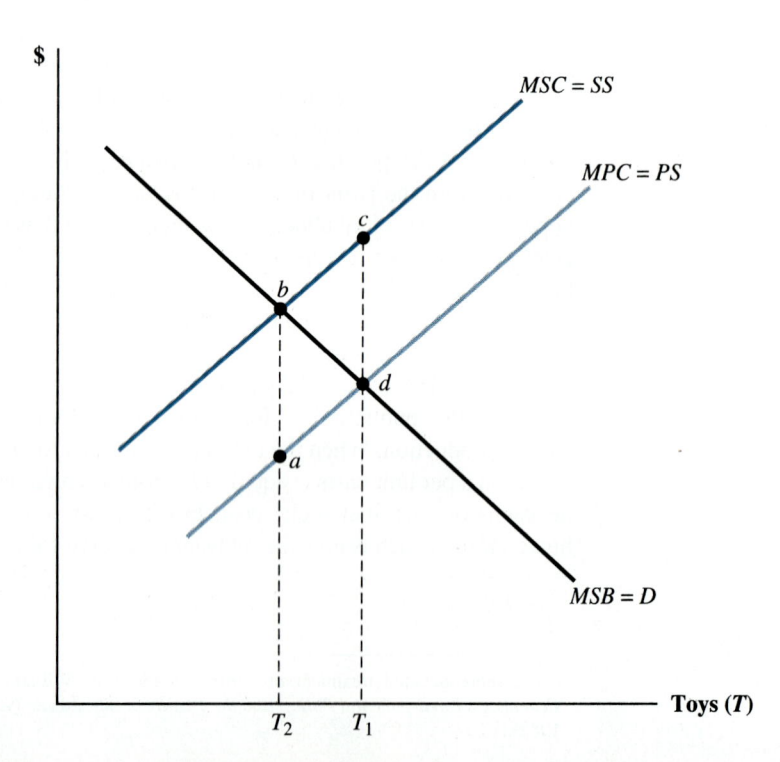

Income Distributional Issues

An issue of compensation revolves around the disposition of tax revenues. Although, as in the case of property rights assignments, corrective taxes may lead to an efficient level of output for this industry, the disposition of tax revenues affects income distribution, and it should not be surprising that there will be many different views regarding who should be the recipient of the tax revenues. Discussion of the different compensation programs helps explain who will tend to support each of the possible programs and whether the policy results in a Pareto superior move for society.

When compensation is part of the policy, the government is in effect assigning property rights to the air space to the recipients of the tax revenues. When one party is given the property right to a valuable and scarce resource—for example, ownership over tax payments—that party is awarded the right to collect payment from those who must pay the tax.

Options for disposition of the funds include compensation for the 2,000 homeowners who must breathe air that is polluted when T_2 toys are produced or compensation of toy manufacturers who now must pay for air space; or, revenues may flow to the government's treasury, where they may be used to fund higher government spending or to lower tax burdens. When homeowners are awarded tax revenues, property rights are assigned to them. It should also be noted that to the extent that property values rise by the decrease in the negative externality, homeowners will have already received an amount of compensation equal to the reduction in negative externality resulting from the tax policy. Substantial evidence, for example, shows that because air pollution exerts adverse effects on property values, policies that reduce air pollution will raise the values of properties.[10]

Property rights are awarded to producers when they are awarded tax revenues. When private markets are competitive, taxes levied on firms are also shifted, to some degree, to consumers and may be considered payments to resource owners for higher-quality air.

Finally, if tax revenues are used to fund government programs or lower existing taxes in other areas, property rights are awarded to the recipients of higher government spending or lower tax burdens. Revenues could also flow to a regulatory agency that could be used to cover administrative costs and/or compensate individuals for remaining levels of externalities or firms that pay the taxes.[11] These tax revenues could also be used to fund policies in pollution control and in research and development of pollution control equipment, or the revenues could also fund unrelated projects or could lower income taxes.

While all compensation options yield identical production levels, assignment of property rights through corrective taxation bestows income to certain individuals in society; assignment of property rights is therefore bound to be a contentious issue.

---

[10] See, for example, A. M. Freeman III, *The Benefits of Environmental Improvement* (Baltimore: Johns Hopkins University Press, 1979).

[11] An issue arises here over whether a regulatory agency has an incentive to set tax rates above the level of the externality. Bureaucracy theory argues that regulators will attempt to set tax rates at levels that maximize tax revenues. See, for example, Paul B. Downing, *Environmental Economics and Policy* (Boston: Little, Brown and Company, 1984), 216–218.

Note, however, that as long as sufficient compensation is offered to losers, corrective taxes may also provide Pareto superior moves for society.

Difficulties of Implementing Tax Policy

Many issues add great complexity to what so far appears to be a fairly simple exercise in forcing private markets to internalize negative externalities. It is too simple to believe that levels of negative externalities are equal across all participants in the market. Some firms may be rather new, with modern, well-maintained pollution control equipment, but other firms may use outdated, poorly maintained pollution control equipment. It is not efficient for all firms to carry identical burdens since firms that discharge little or no pollution should carry lower tax rates than firms that discharge a great deal of pollution. It may not be possible, however, for the policy process to implement policies that create greater burdens on some firms than on others. For example, if firms that discharge the most pollution are situated primarily in states that are also suffering high unemployment, considerations of the ways in which tax policies affect the overall economies of those states may make it politically nonfeasible to implement tax rates equal to rates of discharge.

Even if it is agreed that losers should be compensated when corrective taxes are used, further complications arise to hinder the ability of corrective tax policies to result in Pareto superior moves. Compensation of homeowners, for example, is bound to be a complex issue when not all homeowners suffer identical harm. Studies must be performed to determine the extent of externalities and decisions made about what constitutes appropriate tax levels. The information necessary to assign appropriate damage compensation may be too costly to justify implementation of this policy. Moreover, compensation policies may also create a perverse incentive for individuals or firms to move into areas for the sole purpose of receiving compensation payments.

Subsidies

Subsidies result from policies that pay firms for not producing negative externalities.

Efficient levels of production may also result from policies that offer **subsidies,** or payments to firms for not producing negative externalities. In our example of the toy market, firms could be awarded property rights for air space they use, and payment for cleaner air comes from taxpayers who pay the subsidies provided by the policy.

To illustrate a policy of subsidies, consider Figure 4-6, which shows the relevant cost and benefit curves for this market. Before the subsidy program, firms produce T_1 toys, which is where $MPC = MSB$. In order to lower production to the socially efficient level of T_2, a subsidy must be offered which sets the firms' marginal opportunity costs equal to marginal social benefits at T_2. The subsidy becomes an additional opportunity cost since for each unit they decide to produce, they give up a subsidy. For example, if the subsidy is equal to $2 per toy, then reduction of production from 10,000 to 9,000 toys yields a $2,000 subsidy payment. This opportunity cost is added to all other opportunity costs and forces the toy manufacturers to base production decisions on *MSC*, not *MPC*.

A subsidy equal to the difference between *MPC* and *MSC* creates incentives for firms to internalize the negative externality in this market. At T_1, for example, a per unit subsidy of *eg* raises marginal opportunity costs to *Ob*. Because marginal opportunity

FIGURE 4-6
Corrective Subsidy of Externality

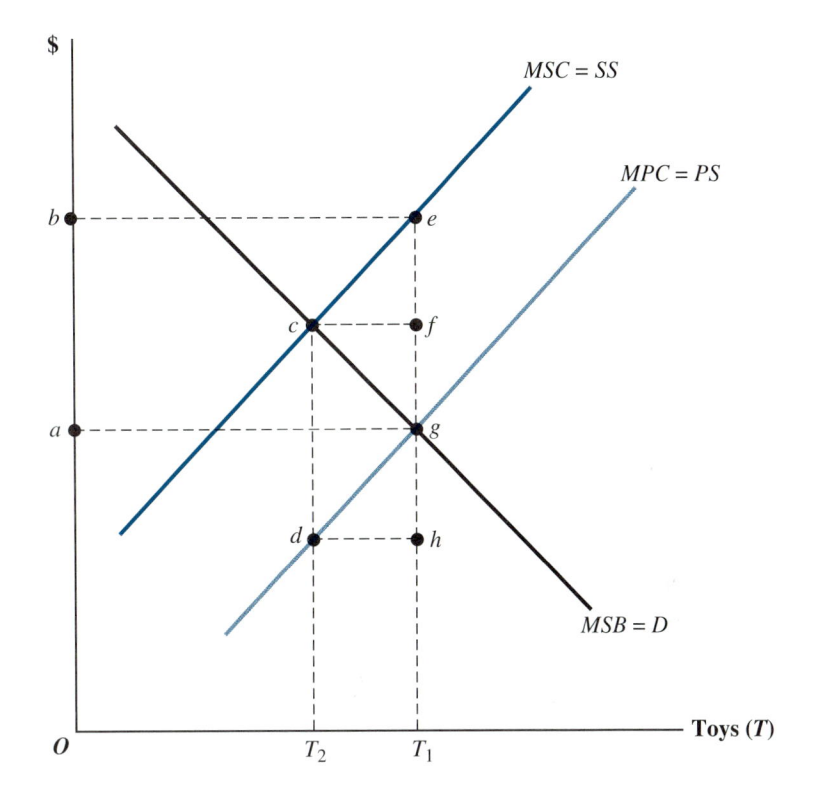

costs exceed marginal benefits of *Oa,* firms increase profits by cutting back production to where marginal opportunity costs are equal to marginal benefits. This equality occurs at T_2, which is the socially efficient level of production. Firms lower production to socially efficient levels and receive subsidies equal to *dcfh,* which equals the subsidy rate times the reduced number of toys produced.

Firms gain income equal to their share of the subsidy. These gains, however, must be weighed against the losses suffered by taxpayers who fund this policy. Some homeowners may actually be net gainers when they pay relatively low taxes and at the same time live in an area where the reduction in the harm they suffer is great. In this case, homeowners receive gains in excess of their tax burdens. To the extent that taxpayers fund the subsidy and do not directly benefit from lower levels of externality, they are net losers. Unless compensation is sufficient to make up for the losses of all taxpayers, this policy does not represent a Pareto superior trade among toy manufacturers and homeowners.

Other considerations may suggest problems with a policy of subsidies. Some may argue that it is inappropriate, or even immoral, to pay firms in order to keep them from creating negative externalities. It has also been suggested that because subsidies lower production costs, they may entice more firms to produce in this area. Firms may also find it disadvantageous to use pollution control technology because a greater capacity to pollute results in larger subsidies. Or, firms may claim that they would produce more just to receive higher subsidy payments.

Regulation

Regulation
is a form of command-and-control policy aimed at restricting, influencing, or defining behavior that produces negative externalities.

Regulation is another means by which public policy attempts to deal with negative externalities. Often referred to as "command and control" policy, regulation *commands* various firms and individuals to *control* behavior that creates negative externalities. Policy may, for example, require that all cars be equipped with catalytic converters or that all factories utilize specific types of pollution control equipment, such as smokestack scrubbers. Or laws may require recycling, which is one way to reduce the negative externalities caused by garbage. Regulation is very different from tax and subsidy policies because rather than charging for externalities (tax policy) or paying for externalities not created (subsidy policy), regulation sets minimum environmental quality levels or maximum allowable levels of externalities.

Because of high informational and transactions costs involved in tailoring regulation to all the differences that exist among sources of pollution, regulation usually provides uniform standards across very large areas—which is not efficient. Take cars, for instance. All cars are required to have catalytic converters, but not all cars emit the same level of externality. It has been estimated that most pollution produced by cars is generated by pre-1980 models. If this is correct, it may be cheaper to buy up and dispose of older cars than to set emission standards for old and new cars alike. Even if all cars pollute equally, some cars are operated in areas with low pollution and others in areas of high pollution. Air pollution districts, however, are often large areas where uniform standards are applied, and within each district there exists wide diversity of levels and sources of emissions.

It may be efficient for standards to be set on the basis of benefits and costs of externality control, but standards must be set within the policy process. In other words, standards are influenced by many individuals who are affected by regulation. While individuals who are adversely affected by externalities prefer strict regulation, those that have to carry the burden of meeting standards will tend to prefer weak regulation.[12] Firms in the United States, for instance, spend a large sum of money on pollution abatement; in 1990, these expenditures were estimated at $90 billion.[13]

Polluters, then, can be expected to exert strong pressures on policymakers to lessen burdens imposed upon them by regulation. However, because individuals who are adversely affected by pollution are widely dispersed and because transaction and information costs associated with organizing are great, it has been argued that those whom pollution harms cannot provide as effective a voice in the policy process as can polluters.

Regulations also require enforcement. It is one thing to describe regulation in theory and quite another to implement it. Regulators have no magic wands to wave over firms and ensure compliance. The ability to enforce standards, however, is dependent on the resources of the enforcement agency and the will of the policymakers to enforce policies. Enforcement requires methods of inspections to detect violations.

---

[12] However, firms may use regulation as a means of restricting entry into industries that now require new firms to purchase expensive pollution control equipment. For this argument, see James M. Buchanan and Gordon Tullock, "Polluters' Profits and Political Response: Direct Controls versus Taxes," *American Economic Review* 65 (March 1975): 139–147.

[13] Table 377, "Pollution Abatement and Control Expenditures," *Statistical Abstract of the United States,* 1991, 213.

And when enforcement budgets are low, inspection activities may not efficiently deter individuals and firms not in compliance with standards. In fact, lack of budgetary resources has caused some regulatory agencies to allow firms to monitor their own air and water pollution emissions. But this does not result in perfect compliance. Just as drivers violate speed limits more often when local police do not enforce speed limits, polluting companies may violate standards when no one is looking. Policymakers may also not be interested in enforcing regulations to the letter of the law. If the local police enforce speed limits so stringently that a certain town becomes known as a speed trap, tourists may simply stop visiting and spending money there. Lack of enforcement may therefore reflect either low budgets or the regulators' lack of will, but it really does not matter to the violator which is the case. It has been estimated that weak enforcement of many standards has led to low compliance and rendered many regulations ineffective.[14]

Incentives to Innovation and Productivity

Regulation may reduce incentives of affected parties to be innovative as, for example, in regulations that require a certain type of pollution abatement equipment. Writing a particular type of equipment into a standard creates a disincentive for anyone to introduce cheaper, more effective equipment. The Occupational Safety and Health Administration (OSHA), for instance, in a widely publicized case, forced firms to install expensive noise-absorbing mufflers on their equipment instead of requiring employers to make their employees wear lower-cost, but equally effective, earplugs. (OSHA's argument was that many employees would not wear earplugs, thus necessitating the muffler standard.)

Costs of regulation are arguably a significant deterrent to overall economic growth, therefore any associated reduction in macroeconomic growth should also be weighed against gains in reducing levels of various negative externalities. A great many examples suggest that standards impose various inefficiencies that reduce incentives to innovate and create new technology. The 1990 Clean Air Act, for example, has been estimated to create an additional burden on businesses of $25 billion a year.[15] In response to past regulatory growth and declines in productivity, deregulation and bans on new regulations have become a recent trend. During 1981, for example, President Ronald Reagan ordered a two-month ban on new regulations, and in 1992 President George Bush proposed a three-month moratorium on new regulations.

Market Incentives

One criticism of regulation is that it cannot replace the incentives for efficiency present in private competitive markets. The appendix to this chapter, "Regulation and the Savings and Loan Crisis" provides an example of a case in which regulation has been used in an attempt to take over many of the functions of private markets.

---

[14] See, for example, Michael L. Marlow, "The Economics of Enforcement: The Case of OSHA," *Journal of Economics and Business* 34 (1982): 165–171; and Paul B. Downing and James N. Kimball, "Enforcing Pollution Control Laws in the United States," *Policy Studies Journal* 11 (September 1982): 55–64.

[15] Bob Davis, "Bush Plans to Unveil a 90-Day Moratorium on New Regulations," *Wall Street Journal*, January 20, 1992, A1.

Pollution Permits

Pollution permits are transferable property rights to pollute up to a specified maximum level of pollution.

The selling of **pollution permits** is one way to introduce market-based incentives into public policy regarding negative externalities. Recently applied to air pollution, this policy sells transferable property rights to pollute up to some maximum level of pollution.[16] Thus environmental regulation imposes standards on all firms, but it is up to the firms to decide how to meet them. Policymakers establish a maximum level of allowable pollution, and then a sufficient number of permits to meet this maximum are auctioned to the highest bidders.

Under the 1990 Clean Air Act, a market-based program was developed to compel power plants to cut emissions of sulfur dioxide, starting in 1995. This approach sets national goals for reducing sulfur dioxide pollution, which is a major contributor to acid rain, from approximately 19 million tons annually, to 9 million tons by the year 2000. Whereas traditional command and control regulation would force all power stations to reduce pollution, this market-based approach allows the owners of each power station to determine the most cost-effective means of achieving the national combined goal. The Environmental Protection Agency will issue enough permits, so that by the year 2000, all power stations will have received their share to use or sell to other power plants. Each permit allows the discharge of one ton annually, and the number of permits received is based on how much a firm currently pollutes. Some firms will find it advantageous to reduce their emissions and sell some of their permits, whereas others may find it cheaper to purchase those of others rather than buy new equipment. Because there are large differences in technology, plant age, and fuel use among power plants, there will certainly be both buyers and sellers of pollution permits. The potential for this approach is so great that southern California is developing a plan to sell pollution permits to the major culprits in smog production.

An obvious advantage to this policy is that, unlike command and control regulatory policy, it allows firms to profit from the sale of their permits when they reduce emissions below current levels. Since selling permits is profitable, firms have an incentive to lower pollution as well as to create new technology in pollution-control devices. Because it does not mandate the means by which pollution control is to be achieved and because it allows firms to decide how much pollution they find it profitable to reduce, this plan encourages firms to use their ingenuity to lower pollution.

Permit policies, however, can convert small polluters into large polluters and *vice versa*. Such policies can also occasion distributional issues. Mixed feelings, therefore, have been expressed about their desirability. Large changes in the distribution of air pollution may, for example, result in large changes in property values. Property owners who experience higher values will tend to be more in favor of these policies than owners who experience lower property values. Distributional issues also arise when firms are induced to change the fuels they use. For example, some states such as West Virginia, Kentucky, and Ohio—where high-sulfur coal is mined—are attempting to stop the federal program since they may lose income and jobs if their power plants

---

[16] For more detail on pollution permits, see J. H. Dales, *Pollution, Property, and Prices* (Toronto: University of Toronto Press, 1968); "Pollution Control: Unshackling the Invisible Hand," *The Economist*, January 4, 1992, 66; and Jeffrey Taylor, "Smog Swapping: New Rules Harness Power of Free Markets to Curb Air Pollution," *Wall Street Journal*, April 14, 1992, A1, A9.

shift from high-sulfur to low-sulfur coal. Even though this policy may contribute to better air quality in these states, at the margin, overall costs of improved air quality may prove much greater than benefits.

Another criticism of this approach is that firms may find it advantageous to increase levels of pollution in order to increase their allotment of permits. Permits are valuable resources that add to the profitability of the firm. Given a pollution permit policy, then, firms may be encouraged to increase their number of permits by degrading the environment more than they would have had the policy not been implemented. That is, the worse polluters are given the most permits, so they have an incentive to become worse yet. We can see this phenomenon in other cases, too. Consider, for example, the city of San Luis Obispo, California. In 1989, in response to four consecutive years of below-normal rainfall, this municipality implemented a water-rationing system. Because each homeowner's quota was based on the previous two year's water usage, homeowners who had worked diligently to conserve water in those two years were granted much lower water usage than those who did not conserve. That is, homeowners who had a history of high water usage were rewarded while those that conserved were, in effect, punished. In this case, however, unlike that of pollution permit policy, property rights to water usage were not transferable, and therefore no homeowner could gain by selling water rights on the open market. (Sale of property did convey the homeowner's water quota; therefore, the policy could possibly have affected housing values. That is, properties with higher quotas would have been worth more than those with lower quotas.)

A further criticism of permit policies is that they are effective only when pollution is relatively easy to monitor and the number of participants is relatively small. Cars offer a good illustration of this point: They emit air pollution, but there are too many of them and the difficulties in monitoring these nonstationary sources of pollution are too great for permits to work well. Finally, some individuals may find it unethical to sell the rights to pollute. In this case, such objections must be weighed against the feasibility of the available alternatives. While many such objections have been raised in the past, public recognition of the growing problems of environmental pollution may lead to a reconsideration of the merits of a permit policy.

Positive Externalities

Concept of Positive Externalities

Positive externalities occur whenever private markets fail to allocate resources on the basis of full social benefits. Immunization against communicable diseases is a common example of a good that produces positive externalities—individuals who do not consume the good benefit because inoculations decrease the number of individuals who may transmit diseases. Private markets do not take account of the benefits that flow to those who are not inoculated. However, those benefits, which are external to the market exchange, are part of the benefits that society receives when resources are allocated to immunization.

Individuals who are external to the market exchange are not required to pay for benefits they receive when individuals pay for such goods as inoculations in the private market. This is similar to the case of negative externalities in which individuals

Pollution Credits for Old Cars?

The Air Quality Management District (AQMD) of southern California adopted, in 1993, the nation's first pollution control program that allows firms to trade in old cars for pollution credits. Old cars are notorious for their heavy emissions and for causing much of southern California's infamous smog. Any car produced before 1982 qualifies for the program, and in a region with an estimated 1.9 million old cars and trucks, there is clearly much room for advancement of this program.

The program works very simply. Firms participate in the program by buying old cars, taking them to dismantlers, who crush them, and then receiving certificates, which they trade to the AQMD for emission credits. Credits are determined by a formula based on the estimated level of hydrocarbon and nitrogen emissions that would have been produced if the car remained on the road. Emission credits last for three years, which is the average remaining life of older cars.

Source: Maria L. LaGanga, "Firms Can Earn Pollution Credits by Buying Old Cars," *Los Angeles Times,* January 9, 1993, A1.

Analysis

An obvious advantage of this program is that it is a cost-effective means of lowering air pollution. If it is cheaper for firms to purchase new control equipment or adopt new technology, then they will not participate in the program. For some firms, however, it is cheaper, for a given reduction in emissions, to exchange older cars than to adopt changes in their operations. Some wholeheartedly endorse the program. In the words of Joseph Goffman, an attorney for the Environmental Defense Fund, "We think, as environmentalists, if we're going to be arguing for ambitious pollution control programs, we have to really support every effort to find the cheapest reductions to comply with those programs."

But others take the exchange program to task. One criticism is that it discriminates against the poor because they are the ones who tend to own older clunkers. Although they benefit when they receive higher prices for their cars as demand rises (for scrapping purposes), a reduced supply of these cars occurs as they are exchanged for emission credits. Antique and classic car buffs are not happy either, because scrapping older cars results in higher prices for auto parts.

Finally, some environmentalists are unhappy because the exchange program does not lower emissions of polluting firms. For example, Daniel F. Becker, an officer of the Sierra Club, argues that "the pollution continues after the auto is gone.... If someone's grandmother leaves them a '66 Buick that wasn't driven for 15 years but was registered and scrapped, would that offset pollution from a factory?"

This argument clearly states that the program is unacceptable because it allows polluting firms to lower emissions that they themselves did not create. But does it really matter whether emissions are lowered through scrapping of old clunkers or changes in technology by firms? If we believe that polluters should be responsible only for what they emit, we can make a case against the exchange program. The answer is no, however, if we are interested in lowering total emissions within the AQMD.

who are adversely affected by the actions of others do not influence resource allocations in private markets. But while negative externalities result in too much production of goods, positive externalities result in too little production because individuals who receive benefits outside the private market cannot influence resource allocations of private markets.

Positive Externalities and Allocative Efficiency

Marginal social benefits *(MSB)* exceed marginal private benefits *(MPB)* whenever benefits derived from consumption of goods positively influence others who are not part of the market exchange. The condition for allocative efficiency can be stated as

$$MSC = MSB \qquad (4\text{-}4)$$

When positive externalities are present, *MSB > MPB;* therefore, private competitive markets do not allocate resources efficiently.

To see how positive externalities affect resource allocations, consider Figure 4-7, which shows the private market for education. Marginal private benefits of education flow to those who are in school, and when the private market allocates resources into education, resources are allocated until $MPB = MSC$ at E_1. However, if everyone in society benefits from an educated citizenry, positive externalities are associated with the education market. Marginal external benefits that flow to those who are not in school are measured as $MSB - MPB$ (distance *ce* at E_1), and therefore, at E_1,

FIGURE 4-7
Market with a Positive Externality

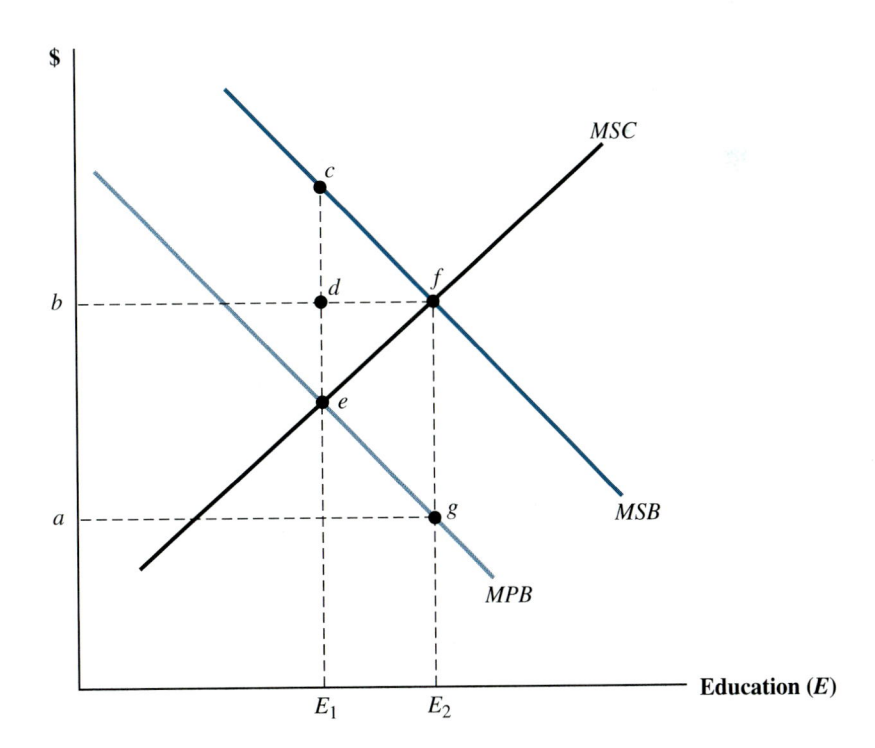

$MSB > MPB$. Allocative efficiency, however, occurs at E_2, where $MSC = MSB$, and therefore the private market for education underproduces education by E_1E_2.

Subsidies and Allocative Efficiency

Subsidies are often used when private markets do not take full consideration of positive externalities. In Figure 4-7, for example, a subsidy rate of *fg* at the optimal level of education E_2 results in raising *MPB* up to *MSB*. Area *abfg* measures the tax subsidy that taxpayers provide for education.

The National Science Foundation (NSF) is one federal government agency that subsidizes scientific research in many fields. During 1993, for instance, $2.3 billion in research subsidies was awarded to researchers in the biological sciences, computer and information services, engineering, geosciences, physical sciences, social sciences, and many other areas.[17] As in the example of immunization programs, subsidies for these research areas are justified by arguments that the private sector tends to underproduce research in these areas. Other programs that are argued to produce positive externalities include research on energy supply and the development of technologies in solar energy, windmill farms, and other renewable energy sources. In 1993, for example, the U.S. Department of Energy had a budget of $3.7 billion to finance new technologies and improve existing energy technologies.[18]

Is Government Intervention Necessarily Better?

Arguments that research activities provide positive externalities are based on the hypothesis that, in addition to the firms that develop new technologies, individuals and firms outside of the market for new products also receive benefits when resources are allocated to developing new technologies. In other words, when ACME Energy develops a new technology for harnessing solar power to run automobiles, this same technology may be used in other markets, such as home heating, electric utilities, or national defense.

We must be careful, however, not to carry too far the notion that many products provide positive externalities. Remember that negative externalities result in inefficient resource allocations because well-defined and transferable property rights are lacking. Similarly, private markets can be expected to be inefficient when the producers of goods that produce positive externalities cannot charge for the benefits that flow outside their principal markets. To some degree, patent and copyright laws protect the ownership rights of the producer of goods characterized by positive externalities. For example, if ACME Energy carries a patent on its new technology, it will be able to charge other firms for the use of that technology in other private markets. Theoretically, if ACME Energy is able to charge all who use its new technology, the benefits it receives—its marginal private benefits—from new technology development are identical to marginal social benefits. Thus ACME will allocate resources toward technology development until $MSB = MSC$. Therefore, the private market allocates

---

[17] Estimates for 1993 as provided in *Budget of the United States Government, Fiscal Year 1993*.
[18] Estimates for 1993 as provided in *Budget of the United States Government, Fiscal Year 1993*.

resources efficiently when it can charge all who benefit from its development of technology.

There are still more reasons why private markets may not achieve allocative efficiency when positive externalities are present. As we have seen, protection of property rights is difficult when property rights do not transcend political jurisdictions. JC Penney in Singapore, for example, was not awarded property rights over its name in that country. We have also seen that new technology may become the source of debate about who should be awarded property rights over the resulting new resources. Transaction costs are also important determinants of how efficiently private markets are able to allocate resources in the presence of positive externalities. It may not be an easy matter for ACME Energy, for instance, to determine which firms and individuals are benefiting from its new technology. In addition to the high information costs of finding out who the beneficiaries are, ACME Energy may also be affected by high transaction costs incurred when it must fight court battles before it can bill those beneficiaries and collect payment from them. It may be the case, for instance, that many of them are very small and that it is not profitable for ACME Energy to collect payment from each beneficiary.

Clearly, when goods are characterized by positive externalities, certain factors may lead private markets away from the efficient allocation of resources. We must not assume, however, that government intervention will necessarily result in an improvement in the ways in which society's resources are allocated just because private markets do not always efficiently allocate resources. We have already shown, for example, how regulation of goods characterized by negative externalities does not always result in allocative efficiency. While it may be perfectly clear how to set the appropriate subsidy when we know all of the relevant curves regarding education, as in Figure 4-6, the real world is never that simple.

Inframarginal Positive Externalities

We have so far assumed that the level of externalities—positive or negative—does not vary with the quantities of goods produced in private markets. But that is not always the case. **Inframarginal externalities** occur whenever externalities disappear at production levels consistent with private market allocations of resources. Consider, for instance, the argument that education provides positive externalities to individuals who are no longer in school. It may be arguable that society gains whenever its citizens gain an elementary or a high school education, but it becomes less clear that continued education beyond high school is associated with positive externalities. The clearly valuable fundamentals of education—reading, writing, and arithmetic—are taught at the elementary/secondary level, but it is not so clear that many of the skills and much of the knowledge taught at the post-secondary level exert positive externalities on those not in college. Pushing the thesis even further, it is very difficult to argue that society is better off when a large number of its citizens earn graduate degrees and are able to understand the calculus, read Shakespeare in twelve languages, and remember the names of all the children born to U.S. presidents. While these may be admirable achievements that some in society find useful, we must also remember that education policies, which subsidize this learning, also use scarce resources that could be used to produce other goods.

Inframarginal externalities occur whenever externalities disappear at production levels consistent with private market allocations of resources.

**FIGURE 4-8
Market with an Inframarginal Positive Externality**

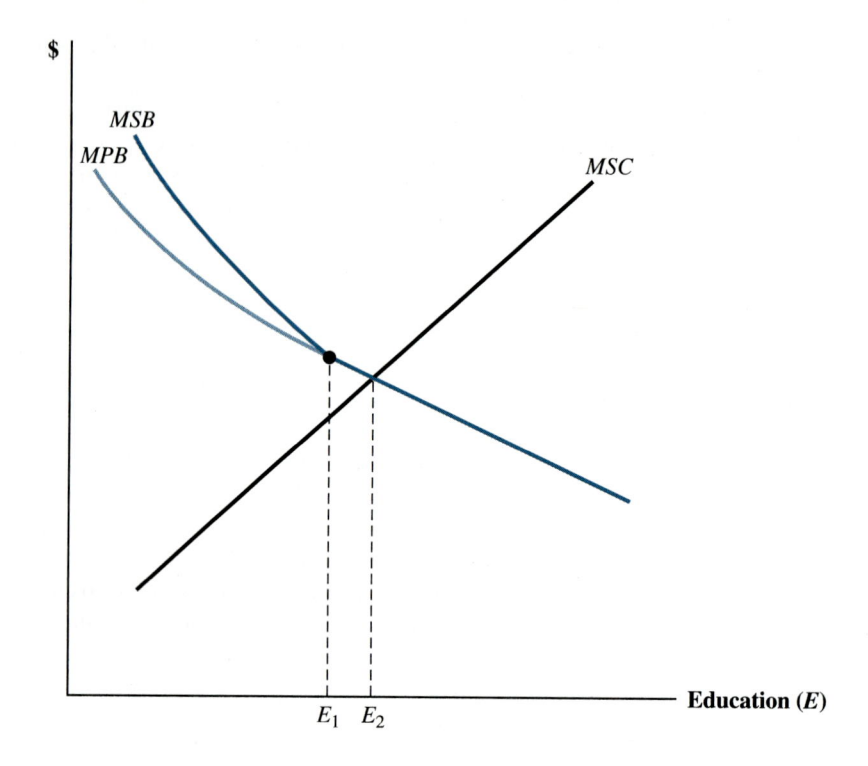

We see in Figure 4-8 the case where education produces inframarginal positive externalities. For low levels of education, marginal social benefits are shown to outweigh marginal private benefits. However, with continued increases in education production, the difference between *MSB* and *MPB* decreases, until at E_1, marginal values of positive externalities are zero. Therefore, up to E_1, *MSB* > *MPB* and, after E_1, *MSB* = *MPB*. Because private markets produce E_2, where *MSB* = *MPB*, there is no need for the public sector to correct for cases of inframarginal positive externalities.

Note that, while education production beyond E_2 continues to provide positive marginal benefits to society, the associated marginal social costs are too high to justify additional resource usage. In other words, allocative efficiency does not justify, as in our earlier example, a citizenry that understands the calculus, reads Shakespeare in twelve languages, and remembers the names of all the children born to U.S. presidents. Rather, resources may be used to produce other goods that society perceives to be more useful.

Can Subsidies Cause Overproduction?

The case of inframarginal externalities suggests that we must be careful to not overemphasize arguments for subsidization that are based on the presence of positive externalities. Another point that requires elaboration is that in order to set subsidies correctly, policymakers must have all the appropriate information on the costs and benefits of a good. But it is one thing to determine optimal subsidies based on the hypothetical benefit and cost curves shown in Figure 4-7, and quite another to calculate the true benefits and costs of education. Policymakers can make only educated guesses on what the true costs and benefits are, and it is therefore possible for underproduction or overproduction of goods to result from subsidization policies.

Consider, for example, the private market for housing. Arguments are commonly made that homeowners produce positive externalities for others in their neighborhoods. Pride of ownership is said to offer incentives for maintaining the quality and appearances of homes so that benefits accrue not only to the homeowners who maintain their homes but to nearby homeowners as well. We frequently see, for example, newspaper listings of homes for sale that include such descriptions as "well-maintained" and "immaculate" neighborhoods as reasons for the high value of some houses. Now look at Figure 4-9. When positive externalities are not captured in the private market, H_1 houses would be produced. This is socially inefficient, however, because the private market underestimates the benefits by the amount of the positive externality. If marginal social benefits of private home ownership are identified by *MSB*, allocative efficiency occurs when policymakers subsidize homeowners at a level that achieves H_3 homes.

But what if policymakers incorrectly guess the size of positive externalities in this market? Consider, for instance, what happens if they estimate that MSB_1 is the appropriate marginal social benefit for home ownership. While subsidy policies that provide H_2 houses result in more home ownership than there would be without subsidies, or

FIGURE 4-9
A Subsidy That Promotes Overproduction

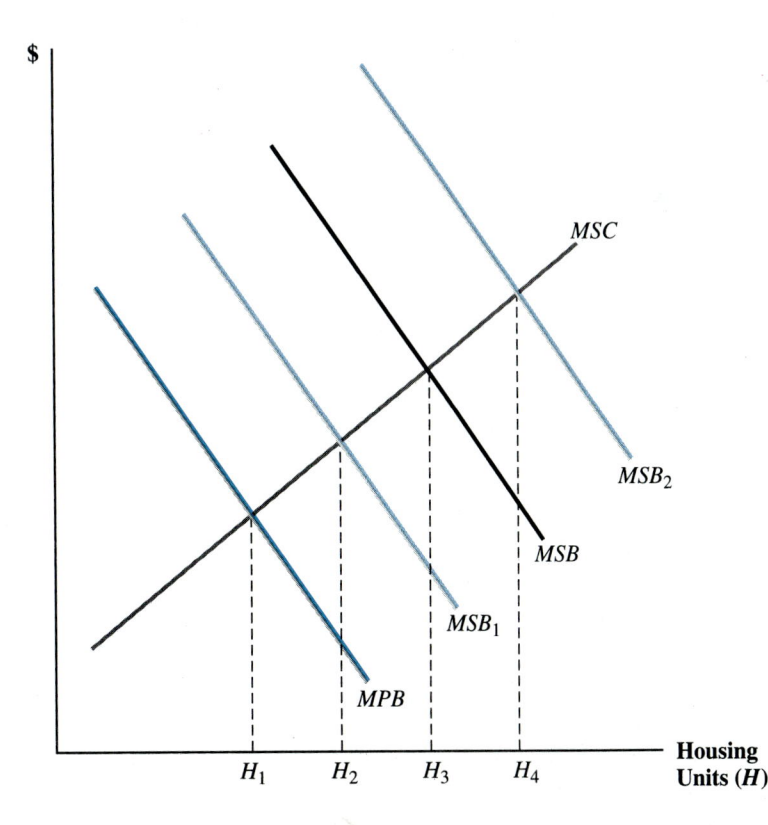

H_1, housing remains underproduced. Although this result may not appear to be particularly bad, it is also possible that marginal social benefits are overestimated at MSB_2. In this case, subsidies result in overproduction of housing when H_4 houses are produced.

Homeowners comprise one of the largest groups of recipients of government subsidies. A significant portion of the subsidy is financed through the deductibility of mortgage interest on owner-occupied homes. This subsidy, which amounted to $43 billion in 1993, lowers the costs of home ownership, so it is instrumental in raising many Americans' power to purchase their own homes.[19] According to one study the effect of housing subsidies has been to increase the share of housing in the U.S. capital stock by one-third.[20] To the extent that housing is oversubsidized, too many resources are allocated in the housing market and too few resources are allocated in other markets. The additional dollars that subsidies send to the housing market means fewer dollars available for other uses such as vacations, food, and health care, as well as public programs for the homeless, the elderly, and children.

The important point is that although private markets arguably underproduce goods characterized by positive externalities, government intervention into those markets may cause overproduction of those goods. We have suggested two reasons why public intervention may result in overproduction. First, as discussed in the example of goods characterized by inframarginal positive externalities, policymakers may overestimate the positive externalities of certain goods. Second, the term *overproduction* is defined in terms of allocative efficiency; and when other criteria, such as equity, are important, society may believe that resources should be allocated in various markets beyond ranges indicated by allocative efficiency. (The issue of who pays for subsidies is also important. Only when losers are fully compensated can subsidy policies result in Pareto superior moves for society.) Housing, for example, has long been integrally associated with the American dream, it is therefore not surprising that the public sector directs many resources into this market.

Resource Allocation in an Imperfect World

The world is imperfect, so private competitive markets do not always achieve allocative efficiency. Negative and positive externalities are two cases of imperfection that prevent private markets from allocating resources efficiently. Externalities are often present when no individual is assigned ownership over a scarce resource. When private markets disregard the costs and benefits of using those resources, markets allocate too many or too few resources to goods.

The Coase theorem demonstrates that when private individuals are assigned ownership rights over resources, and transaction costs are not high, private markets allocate resources efficiently. When transaction costs are high or when it is difficult to assign property rights, government intervention is often prescribed as a means of compelling private markets to correctly internalize externalities.

---

[19] Estimates for 1993 as provided in *Budget of the United States Government, Fiscal Year 1993*.
[20] Edwin Mills, "Has the U.S. Overinvested in Housing?" *Business Review,* April 1987, 13–23.

The world of government intervention is imperfect as well. While it is easy to show textbook examples of the ways that intervention achieves the desired goals of policy, the real world of public policy shares a common characteristic with the real world of private markets—again, imperfection. One's approach to solving the problems of externalities is likely to be influenced by viewpoints about the role of government in society. Those who believe in the efficiency of private markets are likely to view the problems associated with externalities as problems best corrected through assignment of property rights, lowering of transaction costs, or market-based policies such as pollution permits. Within this view, cases for government intervention may lose some of their charm if, as is surely the case, it is likely that policymakers will imperfectly estimate marginal social benefits or, for that matter, marginal social costs. If government policies are likely to result in either underproduction or overproduction of goods as well, the desirability of this intervention decreases. Persons who adopt this view argue that society is better off when government clearly defines and enforces property rights and places significant emphasis on lowering transaction costs in the economy.

Even when property rights are not well-defined, private markets have a mechanism for dealing with negative externalities. Environmentally conscious investment funds offer investments in firms sensitive to environmental issues. That these funds have been growing in popularity suggests that private citizens may be becoming more interested in dealing firsthand with the control of negative externalities. Likewise, when consumers do not care for the ways in which firms allocate resources, they may choose not to purchase their products. While these behaviors of individuals do not necessarily solve all the problems associated with negative externalities, some individuals in society find it mutually advantageous to address these problems through private markets.

Others tend to see private markets as relatively clumsy in their efforts to deal with externalities and therefore tend to look toward the public sector for solutions. Because of the difficulties in assigning property rights to such resources as air and water and because of the high transaction costs associated with dealing with the many people who are affected by externalities, corrective taxes, subsidies, or regulation are viewed as appropriate solutions to externalities. The problems associated with public intervention are often viewed as preferable to the problems associated with private market allocations of resources—and the hope is that, over time, better public policies will further improve efficiency in the economy. Proponents of this view stress that market failure is a more serious problem than government failure.

Apart from debates regarding the appropriate role of government in society, it is important to understand that policies that seek to address externalities have implications for the distribution of income in society. While the Coase theorem shows that choice of who is assigned property rights does not affect allocative efficiency, those who are assigned property rights are better off as a result of being able to charge others for the use of their resources. It has also been shown that government intervention in the forms of corrective taxes, subsidies, regulation, and pollution permits also have important implications for income distribution. Through its ability to assign and reassign property rights and to intervene in private markets, government has the ability to change the income distribution of members of society.

Summary

- Negative externalities occur when private markets fail to allocate resources on the basis of full social costs. When private and social costs diverge, producers overallocate resources because they are not required to pay full social costs of resources.
- Positive externalities occur when private markets fail to allocate resources on the basis of full social benefits. When private and social benefits diverge, producers underallocate resources since they do not collect full social benefits.
- The Coase theorem shows that as long as transactions costs are low and property rights to resources are well defined and protected, private markets allocate resources in an efficient manner. This result holds no matter which individuals are assigned property rights. However, actual assignments influence the distribution of income in the economy.
- There are four general approaches by which governments may attempt to improve allocative efficiency when there are negative externalities. Corrective taxation raises the costs of using resources. Subsidies pay creators of externalities to reduce resource usage. Regulation, often called command and control policy, forces firms either to adopt alternative production technology or in some other way control behavior that results in negative externalities. Pollution permits are transferable property rights to pollute up to some maximum level of pollution. Each approach results in different economic influences on resource allocation and the distribution of income.
- Subsidies are often used to promote allocative efficiency in cases of positive externalities.

Review Questions

1. What is a negative externality? Give two examples.
2. What is a positive externality? Give two examples.
3. What is the Coase theorem? Under what assumptions does it foster an efficient allocation of resources?
4. What is meant by corrective taxation of a negative externality?
5. How does a subsidy lead to an efficient allocation of resources in a case of a negative externality?
6. What is an inframarginal negative externality?

Discussion Questions

1. Explain how the presence of externalities may prevent private markets from achieving allocative efficiency.
2. Explain how externalities are reciprocal in nature.
3. Why are the assignment of property rights and the size of transactions costs important requirements for the internalization of externalities by private markets?
4. Provide examples in which the assignment of property rights is likely to result in a complete internalization of externalities by private markets. Provide other examples in which this is not likely to be a viable strategy. Explain.
5. Suppose that a local airport serves a community of 20,000 citizens who live within a 20-square-mile area. Explain how a corrective tax may provide an efficient allocation of resources when it corrects an externality associated with air traffic noise for all who live near the airport.
6. Reconsider the previous question, and discuss under what circumstances corrective taxation results in a net gain for society.
7. We have discussed pollution permits as a way for public intervention to correct market failures due to externalities. Provide three other examples in which the issuance of permits might result in allocative efficiency.
8. Explain why public subsidies may cause overproduction of goods that are characterized by inframarginal positive externalities.

Key Words

Negative externalities
Positive externalities
Private costs
Social costs
Coase theorem
Internalization of costs

Prisoners' dilemma
Corrective taxation
Subsidies
Regulation
Pollution permits
Inframarginal externalities

APPENDIX 4

Regulation and the Savings and Loan Crisis

Overview

The regulation of savings and loans institutions (S&Ls) provides an interesting study of the complexity of issues underlying regulatory policy. Regulation of financial firms has a long history in the United States and much of the modern-day regulatory structure was put into place following the many bank failures of the Great Depression of the 1930s. Almost 10,000 banks failed during those years, leaving an indelible mark on the minds and financial holdings of many Americans. In view of a widely held belief that private markets failed to provide sufficient stability, regulation of financial firms was argued to offer better regulation of firms than could be offered by the depositors themselves. In other words, the notion was that financial markets were subject to market failure, with regulation prescribed as an attempt to protect depositors from insolvent firms.

It could also be argued that to the extent that some bankers follow unsound practices, the failure of their firms would result in a domino effect which would cause many sound banks to fail. Even though technically solvent, the fractional reserve system of banking means that banks keep only a small percentage of their deposits within the institution, so that the rest may be invested and earn income with which to pay interest to depositors. While investments may be liquidated over a short period of time, bank runs could quickly lead to a majority of the firms' being unable to meet withdrawal demands. Therefore, some people believe that unsound firms exert negative externalities on sound ones, and therefore their depositors as well. The ability of market competition to allow efficient firms to drive out inefficient firms is viewed as beneficial to consumers, but the effect of financial market regulation has been to drive out competitive forces that were believed to result in bank runs and therefore eliminate chances of a replay of the Great Depression.

Although many important issues figure in a responsible discussion of the S&L crisis, the role of deposit insurance in regulatory policy is our focus here. (Other important areas are capital requirements, merger guidelines, budgets of regulators, and changes in liability and asset restrictions.) The Federal Savings and Loan

Insurance Corporation (FSLIC) was created in 1934 to provide insurance for the depositors of S&Ls. (FSLIC has since been replaced, in 1989, by the the Savings Association Insurance Fund). Insurance coverage was initially $5,000 per depositor; over the years it has grown to $100,000 per depositor. Annual insurance premiums, which are paid by insured institutions, have decreased from 1/4 of 1% of total insured deposits to approximately 5/24 of 1% in 1990.[1] Federal deposit insurance premiums have never been adjusted for the risk characteristics of financial firms, even though it can be argued that firms with the highest risks should pay the highest premiums. In contrast, it is common practice for private insurance companies to adjust premiums for the risk characteristics of their clients. For instance, drivers with a long history of speeding violations and accidents are charged higher insurance rates than drivers with clean records.

Implementation of risk-based premiums for deposit insurance poses several problems for regulators. One problem is that risk-based insurance premiums raise the costs of financially weak firms and may lead to their immediate failure. Another problem is that such a system would send signals regarding the health of S&Ls to depositors. That is, a policy of risk-based insurance premiums would provide information on the risk characteristics of financial firms, and the domino effect might lead to runs on all institutions.

The overall thrust of regulation has been to replace the competitive nature of private markets with a regulated market which has tight controls on new firm entry, assets and liabilities, and controls on interest rates that may be offered to depositors (mostly eliminated in the early 1980s). The result of regulation has been to instill a sense of great security in the minds of depositors. And until recently, another result was the virtual absence of firm failures. By limiting entry and controlling the ability of these firms to compete, regulation attempts to substitute itself for the scrutiny and oversight normally allocated to consumers (depositors) in financial markets. In contrast, consider the level of scrutiny a typical investor would exercise when contemplating investment of money in a nonfinancial institution listed on the stock market. Investors constantly read reports on the activities of the firms they wish to invest in, and changes in their opinions about the quality of firms lead to changes in stock prices. For S&Ls, however, depositors seek little information because no matter how poorly managed the institution is, federal deposit insurance guarantees that they will not lose their money. In contrast, poorly managed nondepository firms erode the investments of stockholders, thereby creating an incentive for investors to scrutinize their activities and, when they lose confidence in management, to invest elsewhere.

Benefits of Regulation

The result of regulatory policy has been to remove from the minds of depositors curiosity over their bank's management of deposits and to replace their scrutiny of

---

[1] For additional special assessments levied on savings and loans, see Appendix F in James R. Barth, *The Great Savings and Loan Debacle* (Washington, D.C.: AEI Press, 1991).

bank management with that of a regulatory agency. Benefits are therefore awarded to depositors who either do not wish to scrutinize the activities of their S&Ls or do not feel competent to do so. To the extent that regulation lessens the anxieties that depositors may feel when they deposit their funds in an S&L, depositors benefit from regulatory policy. If deposit insurance also serves to lower the risk of bank runs, sound firms and depositors also gain from policies that control the negative externalities imposed by unsound firms.

Costs of Regulation

Extensive literature indicates that regulation of financial institutions causes depository institutions to provide fewer operating hours, charge higher fees for such services as cashiers checks and safety deposit boxes, charge higher interest rates on loans, provide lower interest rates on deposits, and earn higher profits.[2] Depositors therefore lose whenever firms operate less efficiently than when private markets are allowed to weed out inefficient firms.

Most economists agree that regulatory policy has played an important role in causing the S&L crisis. The term *moral hazard* is applied to cases in which policy (private or public) fosters behaviors that are the opposite of those intended by policy. It is argued, for instance, that car insurance leads some drivers to operate their cars more recklessly than if they were unable to obtain insurance. Without insurance, the full liabilities of accidents would fall on drivers and create an incentive for drivers to exercise extreme caution. Similarly, the existence of federal deposit insurance may create incentives for insured institutions to follow unsound banking practices.

Two perverse effects may exist. One effect is that absence of risk based premiums may lead some firms to invest in higher-risk investments than when such investment would result in higher insurance premiums. In pursuit of higher returns, then, deposit insurance lowers the costs of pursuing high-risk, but higher-yielding, investments. However, when insured institutions follow these practices, the likelihood of insolvency rises, as well, which is the opposite of the goal of regulatory policy. Another effect is that insured institutions become less concerned about safeguarding the deposits of their customers when they know that when deposits are lost on high-risk investments, their depositors do not lose their money. In this case, the chances of losing their customers' deposits become negligible, and management may become less interested in following prudent investment strategies.

Government policy has also allowed institutions to keep operating after they have become insolvent. In other words, firms that are insolvent are allowed to remain open, collect deposits, and invest. The term applied to this policy is *mutual forbearance*. Many insolvent S&Ls were known by regulators to be insolvent for many years before action was taken either to close the institutions or merge them with healthier institutions. In part the reason behind the delay in resolving insolvent firms is that the

---

[2] See, for example, Michael L. Marlow, John P. Link, and Robert P. Trost, "Market Structure and Rivalry: New Evidence with a Nonlinear Model," *Review of Economics and Statistics* (November 1984): 678–682.

deposit insurance fund has been empty since the mid-1980s. Many debates have been waged concerning how to pay for drains on the deposit insurance fund. However, as insolvent firms are allowed to continue operating, they continue to collect deposits and invest them. Insolvency also means that since the owners of firms have no equity in these firms, they also have little incentive to invest those funds in conservative, low-yielding investments. As a Congressional Budget Office study observes, "Having lost all of their equity, owners had nothing more to lose. Institutions gambled for resurrection by taking inordinate risks."[3] Though 489 insolvent firms were resolved by 1988, 517 insolvent firms continued to operate in 1989.[4] Delaying resolution of these insolvent firms has been a significant cost of the bailout.

Root Causes of the S&L Crisis

There are two views about blame for the S&L crisis. One is that it is a result of the greedy and unsound practices of the managers of savings and loans. This view is consistent with the market-failure concept, which involves the belief that private markets cannot provide stability and security to depositors. Proponents of this view offer regulation as the correction, and the usual prescription for greater stability in this market is increased regulation of firms. Interestingly, while fraud did play a role in the crisis, this explanation is usually assigned a fairly small weight, about 3 percent to 10 percent, as the cause of the crisis.[5]

An opposing view is that private markets are not perfect, but regulation cannot substitute for the powerful scrutiny that private markets impose on financial firms. This view of government failure is the opposite of market failure. Its advocates consider moral hazard and mutual forbearance aspects of regulatory policy to be extremely important causes of the crisis.

Proponents of this view emphasize the liabilities that government policies impose on taxpayers. As seen by the growing bailout cost of the S&L crisis, insurance premiums have not been set at levels that yield sufficient reserves for covering the costs of failures. The costs of insufficient reserves and various government failures are primarily borne by taxpayers, and recent estimates are that the per capita liabilities of every individual in the United States are likely to exceed $1,200.

Assessment of Regulatory Policy

One's view of the merits of regulatory policy is related to one's beliefs regarding market failure versus government failure as explanations for the crisis. There are legitimately different viewpoints regarding the relative abilities of private and public

---

[3] Congressional Budget Office, "The Economic Effects of the Savings and Loan Crisis: A CBO Study," January 1992, 8.
[4] James R. Barth, *The Great Savings and Loan Debacle* (Washington, D.C.: AEI Press, 1991), 62.
[5] Congressional Budget Office, "The Economic Effects of the Savings and Loan Crisis: A CBO Study," January 1992, 5.

markets to allocate resources efficiently. Those who view the private market as a clumsy, inefficient allocator of resources tend to view the crisis in terms of market failure, but those who view the public sector as clumsy and inefficient tend to see the crisis in terms of government failure.

The distribution of benefits and costs is also an important factor in one's view of regulatory policy, since the list of affected parties includes depositors, taxpayers, incumbent management of S&Ls, and regulators. Each of these parties may be expected to receive different allocations of benefits and costs, making it extremely difficult to tie up the merits of this regulatory policy in terms of one tidy package. Rather, each of these groups is likely to experience changes in well-being. Therefore, one final assessment of this policy (for all groups together) is impossible unless we assume that a simple social welfare function exists, as well as ample accurate information on all costs and benefits.

CHAPTER 5

Public Goods

The very fact that most governments—in the United States and elsewhere—provide certain goods, such as national defense, roads, museums, and parks, suggests that these goods are best provided by the public sector. Goods like these are often called *public,* or *collective,* goods, because all citizens share the benefits they confer. But what characteristics define public goods and what are the necessary implications of public goods for the role of government? Our discussion of public goods takes us one step further in developing a framework for assessing the public sector's role in our economy.

We have already seen that the public sector may allocate resources when there are external costs and benefits that are not considered in private market transactions. We have also discussed government's interventionist role in achieving allocative efficiency by means of taxes, subsidies, regulation, or changes in property-rights assignments. In examining the topic of public goods, however, we are primarily concerned with government as provider of goods and services. In this role the public sector does not simply intervene to reallocate resources in the private sector; rather, its activities may expand to include, in some cases, a complete takeover of production in various markets.

Now we need a framework that lets us distinguish between goods the public sector should provide and those that should be left to the private sector. In this chapter we therefore address the following issues:

❑ What distinguishes public goods from private?
❑ What quantities of public goods should the public sector provide?
❑ Can the private sector provide public goods?
❑ Can subsidies compel the private sector to provide optimal quantities of public goods?
❑ What has been the experience of having the public sector provide public goods?

What Are Public Goods?

Nonrivalry in Consumption

Public goods are nonrival in consumption.

A **public good** is *nonrival in consumption;* that is, when additional citizens consume the good, others do not have to reduce their consumption of that good.[1] When new citizens are born in the United States, for instance, their enjoyment of a strong national defense does not prevent anyone else from benefiting from it. When lights are placed on top of high mountains, the fact that additional aircraft pilots use the lights for navigational purposes does not prevent any other pilot from reaping those benefits. Because many individuals may collectively share in the consumption of public goods, they are sometimes called *collective goods.*

Private goods are rival in consumption.

In contrast, a **private good** is *rival in consumption;* that is, the act of consumption necessarily prevents others from consuming the good. When Alice buys and eats a pizza, no one else can consume that same pizza. When you buy twenty gallons of gasoline for your car, you are obtaining a private good, since no one else may use that gasoline. Thus, private goods provide ownership only to the purchaser of goods. It follows, then, that the amount of a private good available for consumption must be divided among all consumers. For example, if 100 bicycles are produced in an economy composed of 101 individuals, at least one individual will not be able to own a bicycle. Public goods, on the other hand, are equally available to all consumers.

Zero Marginal Costs of Provision

Zero marginal cost of provision occurs when one or more citizens may consume a good with zero additional costs.

Because public goods are nonrival in consumption, the marginal costs of providing these goods to additional citizens are zero once they are produced. **Zero marginal cost of provision** means, for example, that the costs of allowing one more citizen to enjoy the benefits of a well-protected nation or to let one more pilot use the warning lights on mountains are nothing. When goods are nonrival in consumption, additional resources are not expended when additional persons enjoy their benefits. (But note that this rule holds as long as the quantity of public goods is held constant. If, however, three more tanks are used for national defense, marginal costs rise by the costs of the three tanks. But after three more tanks are supplied, the costs of defending additional citizens are zero.)

In contrast, the marginal costs of providing benefits to one more consumer of private goods, such as pizza or gasoline, are greater than zero. When one more person orders pizza, additional resources must be expended to supply it. When goods are rival in consumption, the very act of allowing one more individual to consume those goods requires additional resources.

Exclusion Characteristics

Lack of exclusion is a characteristic of public goods making it difficult or impossible to restrict the enjoyment of benefits to any individual.

The ability to exclude others from enjoying benefits of goods is another distinguishing characteristic between private and public goods. **Lack of exclusion** characterizes

---

[1] For seminal work on public goods, see Paul Samuelson, "The Pure Theory of Public Expenditure," *Review of Economics and Statistics* 36 (November 1954): 387–389; and Paul Samuelson, "Diagrammatic Exposition of the Theory of Public Expenditure," *Review of Economics and Statistics* 37 (November 1955): 350–356.

many public goods. Radio signals, for example, may be considered public goods because they are available to everyone within certain transmitting areas, and unless radio stations somehow jam frequencies, no one can be excluded. National defense is another example of a good from whose benefits it is virtually impossible to exclude one or more individuals. It is highly implausible that a country could implement a national defense program that somehow prevented some citizens from enjoying its defense of the country's borders.

In contrast, the ability to exclude individuals from enjoying the benefits of goods is a characteristic of many private goods. The cable television industry excludes individuals from using its services when it scrambles signals to all who do not purchase cable boxes. (It is true, of course, that this is imperfect when descrambler devices are available from private suppliers, but cable companies allocate many resources to ensure that this activity is minimized.) Grocery store owners prosecute shoplifters, and amusement parks and movie theaters exclude those who do not buy tickets. Even in the case of fire protection, private fire companies have been known to ignore fires that burn down properties whose owners do not pay the fees required.

All Goods Produced by the Public Sector Are Not Public Goods

Public Goods Produced in Private Markets

The distinction between private and public goods is not always clear-cut. Goods provided in private markets may share some characteristics of public goods. As long as there are empty seats, movie theaters, for instance, are nonrival in consumption because the admission of one or more additional customers would not prevent anyone else from watching the movie. Additional customers do not affect the costs of running movie theaters either, and therefore the marginal costs of additional provision are zero. Swimming pools, sporting events, fireworks displays, and parades are also public goods that are often produced in the private sector, even though they tend to exhibit nonrivalry and zero marginal costs.

But there are limits to this similarity, since not all uses of these public goods are equally desirable. It is important to note, therefore, that even public goods may *become* rival in consumption. Not all movie theater seats are equally desirable, as everyone knows who has had the misfortune to get the last seat in a theater. By the time a swimming pool reaches its capacity, not every swimmer is able to swim in a favorite section of the pool. Someone who likes to perform on the diving board, for instance, may find space only in the wading pool. Flight traffic may become congested when too many pilots use the warning lights atop a particular mountain.

Private Goods Produced in Public Markets

Some goods that are provided in public markets have characteristics of private goods. When a family lives in a public housing unit, no other family is able to live in the same unit. When retirees receive monthly Social Security payments, they are given ownership rights over those payments. When an individual checks out a book at the local public library, no one else may use that book for that time. Thus it is incorrect to believe that all goods provided by the public sector perfectly fit the definition of public goods. Likewise, it is incorrect to believe that all goods provided by the private sector perfectly fit the definition of private goods. It is therefore important to distinguish between goods that fit definitions of private and public goods and goods that are produced in the private and public sectors. Clearly, both private and public goods may be produced in either sector of the economy.

Public Goods Produced in Private and Public Markets

Home security is one example of a good produced by both private and public sectors. The public sector provides police protection and a system of laws and courts. However, publicly provided home security has aspects that are both rival and nonrival in consumption. Rivalry occurs when, for example, patrol cars cruise one neighborhood and cannot, at the same time, visit other neighborhoods. However, police protection is nonrival in nature when its well-recognized presence on city streets lends protection to all neighborhoods. Because it is illegal for homeowners not to pay for taxes that fund police departments, police protection is a good for which all homeowners must pay. But the private market also provides home security, as evidenced by the lively market for locks, guard dogs, strategically placed lights, and alarm systems.

Between Private and Public Goods

It is convenient to classify goods along a continuum of privateness or publicness. Cable television, food and beverages, clothing, computers, and cars belong on the private end of the continuum. Goods that lie in the middle include movie theaters, swimming pools, and sporting events. Goods that lie on the public end of the continuum include national defense, navigational lights on mountains, and lighthouses. A good that lies on one end or the other of the continuum is called a *pure private good* or a *pure public good*. Nonrivalry in consumption is viewed as the important distinguishing dimension, although lack of exclusion is considered equally important by some economists. As goods become more private in nature, they are characterized by growing rivalry in consumption or partial excludability in benefits.

Market Failure and Public Goods

We have used the term *market failure* to describe situations in which private markets do not achieve allocational efficiency. In the case of public goods, two interrelated reasons suggest that market failures occur when the private sector produces public goods.

Free Rider Effect

Suppose you want to buy a $20,000 car, and you have a choice between two ways of obtaining the car. Option A is to pay the producer of the car $20,000, and Option B allows you to buy the same car for $0. Why would most people choose Option B? It is human nature for consumers with scarce resources to find alternative uses for their income that yield positive marginal benefits. In a world of scarcity, there is no end to the many good uses of our income, and therefore it is not surprising that consumers generally prefer to pay lower, not higher, prices for the goods they desire. In fact, this is simply a restatement of the law of demand, that is: For any good, an inverse relation exists between price and quantity demanded, *ceteris paribus.*

There is also a natural tendency for some individuals to want to pay nothing for the public goods they consume. If, for example, we were able to enjoy the benefits of a well-protected nation and not have to pay for the costs of defending the nation, many people would choose to pay nothing. Because lack of exclusion characterizes many public goods, an individual may well choose to be a **free rider.** Free ridership means literally that one or more individuals choose to let others pay for goods that they themselves plan to consume. Thus, they get to ride free while others pay.

Free riders are individuals who let others pay for goods they themselves consume.

Even though it is impossible to exclude all free riders from the benefits of public goods supplied in the private market, it is important to realize that one or more individuals do tend to pay for public goods. Consider a neighborhood where several homeowners enjoy having a swing set on a nearby vacant lot. Without a fence or some other means of preventing free riders from using the swing set, the swing set is a public good (though impure) in the sense that it lacks exclusion, and so long as seats remain available, marginal costs of additional provision are zero. (The alternative is that neighbors may individually or collectively decide to place swing sets in their own backyards, thereby providing a means of excluding free riders.) Even though there may be several neighbors who decide to be free riders, it is quite possible that one or more neighbors agree to pay the costs of erecting the swing set.

Market failure occurs when the actions of free riders fail to send appropriate signals to the allocators of resources in markets. Remember that allocative efficiency requires that $MSC = MSB$; therefore allocative efficiency requires that all who benefit from consumption of goods signal those benefits to providers of goods. However, the benefits enjoyed by free riders are in a sense invisible to providers of goods. Intuitively it makes no sense for producers to cater to nonpaying customers, and they will allocate resources only on the basis of paying customers, a practice that can contribute to their profits. Therefore, to the extent that free riders receive benefits from public goods, private markets underestimate social benefits; those goods will therefore be underproduced. In our example of swing sets, neighbors who pay for swing sets consider only their own benefits, and not those of free riders, when they decide how many swing sets to place on the empty lot. Even though one or more homeowners may find it advantageous to pay for the swing set, it is likely that a socially inefficient number of swing sets will be provided.

Goods that lack exclusion tend not to be produced or to be underproduced in the private sector. Conversely, a requirement for the private sector to produce optimal quantities of public goods is that there be some means of excluding free riders. This is really another way of saying that externalities exist whenever market transactions do not fully account for all costs and benefits. In the case of neighborhood provision of swing sets, a lack of exclusion would mean that there are positive externalities, or external benefits, that are not considered by the providers of swing sets. Similarly, when only a subset of the population pays for national defense, private markets extend positive externalities to free riders.

The correction of market failure that results from positive externalities associated with public goods is similar to the positive externalities associated with private goods.

Correction of market failure can be addressed by subsidies and by awarding property rights for resources previously unowned by any individual. While in theory either of these two policies may result in correction of market failure, these methods tend to deal only with the lack of exclusion characteristic of public goods. The other two characteristics, nonrivalry in consumption and zero marginal costs of provision, present further complications, which suggests that public provision of public goods may be preferable to providing subsidies or assignment of property rights. While ownership rights tend to be exclusive and enforceable through admission prices in instances of impure public goods like sporting events and movie theaters, similar characteristics tend to be missing in the cases of pure public goods like national defense. It is not clear, for example, how property rights to the benefits of national defense could be successfully assigned to private firms while all the problems of free ridership were resolved at the same time.

Zero Marginal Costs of Provision

We have argued that one characteristic of public goods is that the marginal costs of providing benefits to additional customers is zero. Because $MSC = MSB$ is the condition for allocative efficiency, resources should be allocated until marginal social benefits become zero as well. In other words, all who gain from provision of public goods should be allowed to consume those goods. Whether they receive $5,000 in benefits from a public good, or 10 cents, this conclusion is relevant for all consumers.

Allocative efficiency therefore suggests universal provision of public goods. Private markets, however, will not provide public goods to all individuals in society, especially in cases where lack of exclusion is present. Private markets overlook the benefits that flow to free riders, and therefore when marginal costs are zero, private markets underallocate resources in public goods markets.

An additional reason that resources tend to be misallocated in these markets is that someone has to pay the initial costs of placing navigational lights atop mountains and a strong national defense. But in order to make a profit, suppliers must charge a price above zero. Those whose marginal benefits are less than price, however, will not choose to consume public goods. Because $MSB > MSC = 0$, misallocative efficiency results when private markets charge prices that recoup initial start-up costs of providing public goods, at least when exclusion is possible. Moreover, because Pareto efficiency requires that no other allocation exist that does not improve anyone's well-being without lowering anyone else's, private markets will not achieve allocative efficiency so long as one or more individuals who benefit from the public good are excluded when they are charged prices in excess of marginal social cost.

Optimal Provision of Pure Public Goods

Correction of Market Failure

Our discussion so far has not suggested that cases of market failure necessarily present a case for public sector intervention or provision. Before we address this important issue, we must determine what levels of public goods are efficient. After determining the extent of market failure, we must answer two important questions.

First, in which cases should public goods be provided by the private sector and in which cases should they be provided by the public sector? Second, does public sector intervention or provision necessarily improve upon the resource allocations of the private sector?

Market Demand for Private Goods

Optimal provision of public goods occurs when marginal social benefits equal marginal social costs, or $MSB = MSC$. There is, however, an important difference between how the marginal social benefits of private and public goods are measured. Market demand curves for private goods are the *horizontal* summation of all individual demand curves (see Appendix). For example, consider a market for a typical private good, say apples, composed of three individuals: Maria, Anne, and Bill. If, at price $2, Maria purchases 2 apples, Anne purchases 3 apples, and Bill purchases 4 apples, then the market purchases 9 apples. Market demand curves, then, are constructed by summing, at each price, the quantity demanded by each individual.

Market Demand for Public Goods

While market demand curves for public goods are also the summation of the demand curves of all individuals, there is one major difference. Pure public goods, by definition, cannot be characterized by rivalry in consumption; therefore, once the market produces a given quantity, all consumers may equally enjoy the benefits that flow from that given quantity. For example, Figure 5-1 shows the demands by Maria, Anne, and Bill for a particular public good. Note that while all consume the same quantity, they do not equally value the public good. When, for instance, Q^* is produced, all three individuals can collectively share in the benefits associated with that level of production. Remember that demand curves *(D)* are also marginal benefit curves and that prices measure the marginal valuations that individuals place on successive quantities of goods. Market demand, then, at Q^* is determined by summing the marginal values that each individual places on Q^*. Quantity Q^* is valued in the following way: Maria ($1), Anne ($2), and Bill ($3). Marginal social benefits at Q^* are constructed by vertically summing the separate valuations of each individual, or ΣMB, and amount to $6. Therefore, to construct market demand for any public good, we *vertically* sum the demand curves of each individual in the market.

Efficient Quantities of Public Goods

Efficient, or optimal, output of a public good is based on comparison of marginal social benefits MSB with marginal social costs MSC. Figure 5-2 superimposes the demand curves from Figure 5-1 onto the marginal cost curve for the public good. For simplicity, it is assumed that MSC is constant at $6 per unit. The optimal output occurs at Q^*, which is where $MSB = MSC$. To see why this is optimal, consider any output less than Q^*. At Q_1, for example, $MSB > MSC$ by distance *ab,* indicating that values placed on this good by society exceed opportunity costs of producing this good. At any output greater than Q^*, the opposite occurs. At Q_2, for example, $MSB < MSC$ by distance *de;* that is, values placed on this good by society are less than the

FIGURE 5-1
Market Demand for a Public Good

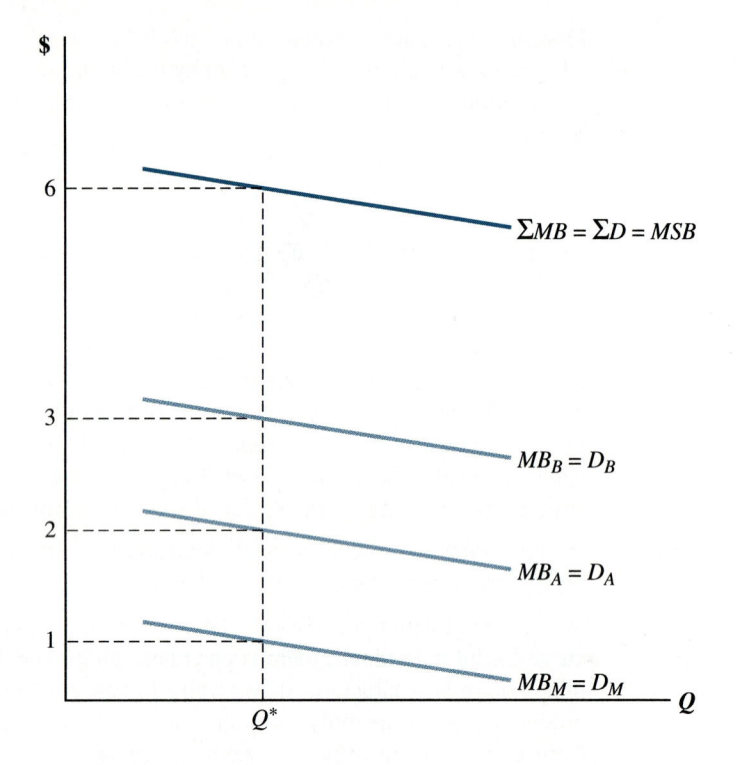

$\Sigma MB = \Sigma D = MSB$

$MB_B = D_B$

$MB_A = D_A$

$MB_M = D_M$

Q^*

FIGURE 5-2
Efficient Quantity of a Public Good

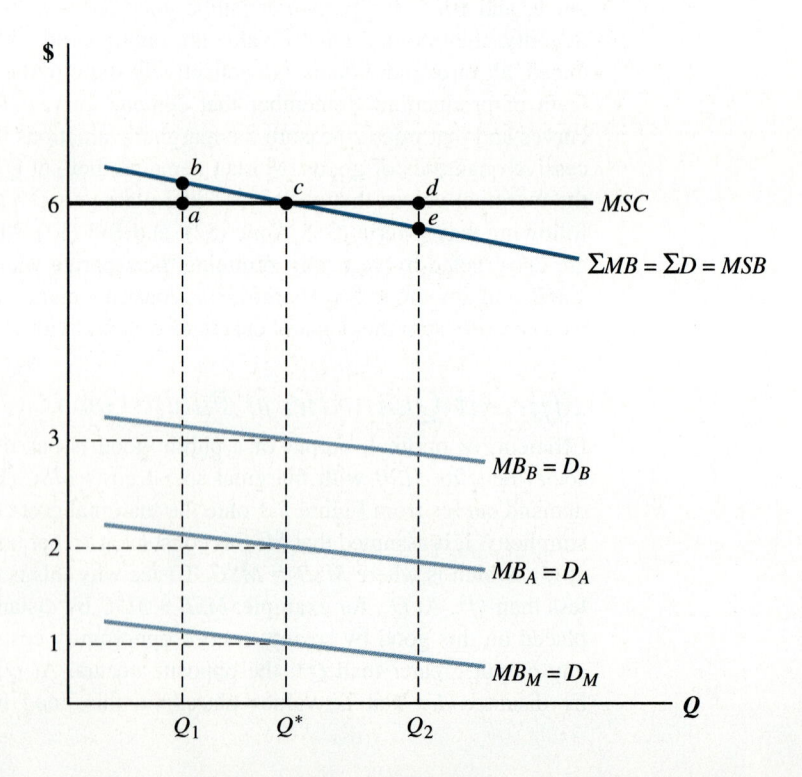

MSC

$\Sigma MB = \Sigma D = MSB$

$MB_B = D_B$

$MB_A = D_A$

$MB_M = D_M$

$Q_1 \quad Q^* \quad Q_2$

opportunity costs of producing this good. Only at c, where $MSB = MSC$, can resources not be reallocated in such a way that expands total net social benefits.

Note that public goods are nonrival in consumption. Unlike the case of private markets, in which quantities of private goods are not equally available to all individuals, all individuals receive equal quantities of public goods. This does not imply that all consumers of public goods receive equal benefits. As demonstrated in Figure 5-1, marginal benefits that each individual receives from any quantity of public good are different.

Financing Public Goods

Now we move to the question of who pays for optimal quantity Q^*. Consider how much each individual is willing to pay to receive the public good in Figure 5-2. For any quantity less than Q^*, $MSB > MSC = \$6$, as would be the case, for instance, where the respective marginal benefits for Maria, Anne, and Bill are respectively $2, $3, and $4. In this case, it is likely they could agree among themselves to make sufficient contributions to meet the marginal cost of $6. An agreement, for instance, whereby each contributes $2 would provide a beneficial arrangement for all three individuals. Equal sharing is only one of many possible financial arrangements, and the actual arrangement is likely to depend upon the bargaining skills of each individual. For example, if Maria and Bill are superior bargainers, respective contributions for Maria, Anne, and Bill might be $1, $3, and $2, respectively. Voluntary consent, however, requires that no one be asked to contribute more than one's own marginal benefit since anyone who is asked to contribute more than that would not be willing to share in the collective payment of the good.

It is also true that, as long as $MSB > MSC$, voluntary bargaining among individuals is likely to result in agreements to purchase more of the public good; voluntary agreement among individuals therefore leads to an increase in net social benefits. Moreover, so long as individuals contribute less then their marginal benefits, it is beneficial for them to contribute more toward the purchase of additional quantities of the public good. Purchase of additional units of the public good in this case will not only improve their *individual* well-being, but, as long as no one is forced to pay more than each individual's marginal benefit, expanded purchase of the public good represents Pareto superior exchanges among *all* individuals.

Voluntary agreements to expand consumption will not occur when $MSB < MSC$. For instance, if the respective marginal benefits of Maria, Anne, and Bill are $1, $2, and $2, respectively, the highest possible total payment that they will agree to provide is just $5, which is less than the additional cost ($6) of acquiring another unit of the public good.

Because $MSB > MSC$ indicates that the individuals will reach voluntary agreement to purchase more of the public good, and because agreements to purchase additional quantities are not possible when $MSB < MSC$, voluntary agreements among individuals will result in purchasing quantities where $MSB = MSC$.

Lindahl prices are prices that equal the marginal benefits individuals receive when they consume optimal quantities of public goods.

Lindahl Equilibrium

Lindahl prices, named after Swedish economist Erik Lindahl, are prices that equal the marginal benefits that each individual receives on consuming optimal quantities of public goods.[2] For Q^* in Figure 5-2, the respective Lindahl prices for Maria, Anne, and Bill are $1, $2, and $3. Note that any other price combination is bound to be rejected by one or more of the individuals. Because these prices are exactly equal to the marginal benefit that each places on Q^*, no individual is willing to accept a higher price. Moreover, because no one can be charged a lower price without charging another a higher price, the only set of prices that will permit voluntary agreement among all individuals to produce Q^* will be Lindahl prices. When Lindahl prices are charged, socially efficient levels of public goods are purchased; thus, because there is no incentive for anyone to want to consume more or less than Q^*, we say that a *Lindahl equilibrium* occurs.

Economists pay great attention to Lindahl equilibrium because it corresponds to the socially optimum quantity of output. Furthermore, when Lindahl prices are charged, voluntary agreement among all individuals in society results in consumption of socially efficient levels of public goods. In this way, Lindahl pricing suggests a guide for the public sector that results in both optimal quantities of public goods and unanimous agreement on how many resources should be devoted to production of public goods.

Because coercion is not required for Lindahl pricing to achieve allocative efficiency, there exists a clear similarity to the way in which resources are allocated in the private market.[3] In essence, Lindahl pricing charges users of public goods prices that are based on the benefits they receive, and voluntary agreement among all individuals results in allocative efficiency.

Private Market Provision of Public Goods

We have seen that public goods are often provided in the private market. Individuals find it mutually advantageous to collectively share the benefits of swimming pools, movie theaters, and radio stations in private markets. Clubs are often formed in private markets by persons with mutual interests, say single parents, swimmers, hikers, golfers, sports enthusiasts, and bridge-players who voluntarily agree to share in the costs of providing activities. Private clubs are, in fact, quite similar to governments, and it may be argued that the relationship between members and officers of private clubs is similar to the relationship between taxpayers and policymakers in governments.

Our examination of the ways in which public goods are produced in the private market naturally leads to issues regarding the efficiency of these voluntary arrangements among individuals. Because voluntary membership suggests gains from trade, or Pareto superior moves among members, it is useful to understand the role of clubs, and hence the private market, in delivering public goods in our economy. While private clubs and governments share many important similarities, their important dissimilarities require examination as well. We will pay specific attention to the question of whether private markets fail to allocate resources efficiently in cases of public

---

[2] Erik Lindahl, "Just Taxation—A Positive Solution," (1919) in *Classics in the Theory of Public Finance*, ed. Richard A. Musgrave and Alan T. Peacock (London: Macmillan, 1958), 168–176.

[3] For complications in generalizing the results of Lindahl pricing from marginal to total analysis, see Richard E. Wagner, *Public Finance: Revenues and Expenditures in a Democratic Society* (Boston: Little, Brown, 1983), 34–37.

goods. This examination then logically allows us to consider the role of the public sector in the provision of public goods.

Theory of Clubs[4]

Theory of clubs explains voluntary cooperation among individuals seeking mutual advantage.

The **theory of clubs** is the theory of voluntary cooperation among individuals seeking mutual advantage. Individuals do not find it advantageous to purchase some goods, such as swimming pools or parks, unless they can find a way of sharing their costs. For example, you may enjoy swimming, but the benefits you receive may be greatly outweighed by the costs of putting a swimming pool in your own backyard. In addition to the fixed costs of building the pool, you must pay maintenance costs, and you must often sacrifice available yard space. The greater these costs are, the greater the cost savings would be from sharing a pool with other individuals. Someone else may enjoy taking long walks in the woods but find it impossible to justify the expenditures necessary to cut a path through undergrowth and trees and then maintain a path that permits pleasant walks. It is also beyond the financial means of most individuals to own the many acres of wooded land required to provide several miles of hiking trails. Thus we see that cost savings are clearly possible when costs are shared among a collection of individuals.

Sharing of goods is likely to occur among individuals with common interests. Swimmers are attracted to swimming clubs, gun owners are attracted to gun clubs, and cardplayers are attracted to bridge or euchre clubs. Voluntary agreement to share costs, then, is most likely to occur when the interests of groups are well defined. For instance, sports lovers are numerous but they do not equally enjoy all sports; therefore, it is more common to see clubs devoted to a particular sport, such as swimming, biking, and football, than all-inclusive sports clubs. Some clubs do provide more than one activity. Country clubs, for instance, provide facilities for tennis, golf, swimming, eating, and dancing. But these clubs usually focus on a different common interest, such as socializing within communities. Voluntary cooperation for mutual advantage is also seen among communities, firms, and countries. Voluntary agreements to limit arms and nuclear arsenals as well as treaties that seek to preserve the environment are applications of the theory of clubs. The point remains that there are strong incentives for individuals with similar tastes to group together and provide public goods within private markets.

Incentives to Form Clubs

A club may be defined as "a voluntary group deriving mutual benefit from sharing one or more of the following: production costs, the members' characteristics, or a good characterized by excludable benefits."[5] Individuals determine whether to join clubs on the basis of the benefits and costs of membership. Benefits associated with membership are measured in the same way that demand, or marginal benefits, for public goods

---

[4] This section follows from the seminal article by James M. Buchanan, "An Economic Theory of Clubs," *Economica* 32 (February 1965): 1–14. The examples of swimming pools, lighthouses, and inoculations against disease are from this article.

[5] Todd Sandler and John T. Tschirhart, "The Economic Theory of Clubs: An Evaluative Survey," *Journal of Economic Literature* 18 (December 1980): 1482.

is measured. For example, the more utility swimmers gain when they swim, the more likely they are to find it advantageous to join a swimming club. Costs of forming clubs include fixed and variable costs and are reflected in initiation and membership fees. Because transaction costs of forming clubs also exist—permit fees, liability insurance, and the costs of getting people to agree—the higher these are, the less likely it becomes that groups will form.

Sizes of Clubs

Congestion and Optimal Membership Size

Although a characteristic of private goods is that only one person can benefit from consuming them (eating an apple or buying a shirt), many people can consume public goods without diminishing the benefits enjoyed by others in the group. But while benefits are initially nonrival, many club activities eventually suffer from congestion. The congestion properties of goods are therefore important determinants of optimal membership size: The more easily congested are the activities of clubs, the smaller is optimal membership size.

When expanded membership results in greater congestion costs, marginal costs of additional provision rise. When we speak of rising marginal costs of provision, we are saying that the activities of clubs become more similar to private goods because the rising marginal costs suggest rivalry in consumption. When rivalry in consumption begins to characterize rising membership, club activities begin to take on the properties of private goods—therefore, an optimal membership size will exist that is less than infinity. In contrast, pure public goods are characterized by zero marginal costs, a condition that characterizes an optimal membership size that approaches infinity.

Mechanisms for Excluding Free Riders

The ability to exclude free riders from the benefits of clubs is one reason that clubs are formed in the first place. Membership initiation fees and dues provide the financial means to pay the costs of providing club activities. Application processes are often important screening devices for excluding individuals who cannot contribute to the goals of the club. For example, membership committees protect the interests of club members by rejecting applicants who are unable to provide credible references and appropriate employment and income histories.

Efficiency of Club Arrangements

Membership in clubs and voluntary agreements between consumers and producers in private markets are clearly similar. The fact that membership is voluntary means that clubs are efficient arrangement that result in Pareto superior moves for its members. The voluntary nature of clubs allows any member who loses from membership to leave the club; therefore, because no one is forced to join or remain a member, no one loses when clubs are formed to deliver public goods. This is really a restatement of the conclusion that competitive private markets result in allocative efficiency and suggests that clubs are an important means by which private markets deliver public goods.

Another important similarity between private market provision of private goods and private market provision of public goods is that in their provision of private goods, profit-maximizing producers (in competitive markets) have an incentive to cater to the needs of their customers. Producers who are able to deliver high-quality, low-cost private goods to consumers are the producers who earn the highest profits. When producers do not cater to the desires of consumers, they run the risk of losing customers, and this oversight ultimately earns them lower profits and increases risks of failure. Similarly, because the profitability, or success, of clubs is dependent upon fees and dues of members, officers of clubs have an incentive to cater to the needs of members. In fact, because the officers are representatives of members, or members themselves, the collective nature of cost sharing gives each club member an incentive to retain the optimal club size.

The voluntary nature of clubs forces dues and fees to resemble Lindahl pricing. In the case of private goods, no one is forced to purchase goods, and it is up to each individual to determine how much of any good to purchase at the market price. Similarly, in private market provision of public goods, individuals who receive no benefits from goods are not required to contribute for production of those goods. Because of this voluntary nature of private markets, club members will be those individuals who are asked to pay no more than their marginal benefits. If they are asked to pay more than their marginal benefits, they resign membership and either seek another club that sets prices more in line with their marginal benefits or decide that they should not purchase the public good at all.

The voluntary nature of membership places a discipline on club officers to provide high-quality, low-cost activities for its members. The important point, therefore, is that when public goods are provided in private markets, the club has an inherent incentive to be well run and accountable to the preferences of its members.

Special Interest Groups as Clubs

What Are Special Interest Groups?

We hear a great deal about special interest groups and the role they play in influencing public policy.[6] **Special interest groups** are voters who are linked by some common bond or interest. They also represent powerful signaling devices on specific issues to policymakers. Myriad interests may unite individuals, and some of the more obvious groupings include charities, producers, consumers, and workers. Table 5-1 lists a few of the many possible groupings of voters into special interest groups at the national level. Many more special interest groups exist on the local level. When special interests are associated with the policy process, they are sometimes called *lobbies*. Agents, or representatives, of special interest groups are called lobbyists—persons who attempt to influence policymakers to approve, design, and modify legislation that improves the well-being of the special interest group. Because special interest groups seek to "pressure" policymakers into approving legislation that benefits the membership, these clubs are often called pressure groups as well.

Special interest groups are associations of voters linked by some common interest.

---

[6] An excellent treatment of special interest groups is Mancur Olson, *The Logic of Collective Action: Public Goods and the Theory of Groups* (Cambridge, Mass: Harvard University Press, 1965).

TABLE 5-1
Number of National Nonprofit Associations

Type	1980	1992
Trade, business, commercial	3,118	3,851
Agriculture	677	1,082
Legal, governmental, public administration, military	529	790
Scientific, engineering, technical	1,039	1,365
Educational	2,376	1,294
Cultural	NA[a]	1,887
Social welfare	994	1,773
Health, medical	1,413	2,290
Public affairs	1,068	2,190
Fraternal, foreign interest, nationality, ethnic	435	561
Religious	797	1,175
Veteran, hereditary, patriotic	208	586
Hobby, avocational	910	1,504
Athletic sports	504	845
Labor unions	235	249
Chambers of commerce	105	168
Greek and non-Greek letter societies	318	339
Fan clubs	NA	506
TOTAL	14,726	22,455

[a] NA = not available.

Source: *Statistical Abstract of the United States,* 1993.

Special Interest Groups Also Influence the Private Sector

The activities of special interest groups are not focused solely on public policy; they also look to the private sector. Labor unions, for instance, wage publicity campaigns with mottoes such as Buy American or Look for the Union Label in the hope of swaying private consumers to buy more of the goods they produce. Charities actively raise funds from the private sector as well as funding from government sources. (It is also interesting to note that publicity campaigns are not solely the province of the private sector. The Pentagon, for example, has more than 1,000 full-time public relations specialists.[7])

While charities, for instance, lobby policymakers to increase funding of those programs that benefit their membership, the benefits they seek from government, or from private contributors, are not always directed specifically toward members of

---

[7] James T. Bennett and Thomas J. DiLorenzo, "How (and Why) Congress Twists Its Own Arm: The Political Economy of Tax Funded Politics," *Public Choice* 55 (1987): 199–213.

their group. Members of the American Heart Association, for example, may not have heart disease, and members of groups interested in ending illiteracy are rarely illiterate themselves. But even though members do not necessarily directly benefit from the success of their efforts, achievement of their goals may yield them considerable pleasure—that is, benefits.

Incentives to Form Special Interest Groups

Individuals join interest groups for the same reasons that they join clubs: They compare the benefits and costs of membership. Benefits include any monetary and psychological gains that are associated with membership. Car and textile manufacturers, for instance, have successfully lobbied policymakers to place quotas and other restrictions on foreign imports. Consumer groups lobby for government standards and regulations that increase the safety of automobiles and children's clothes and require truthful food labels. Labor unions unite workers into special interest groups that lobby policymakers for government regulations that restrict foreign imports (which use foreign labor) and for better working conditions. Members of the American Heart Association gain when they successfully lobby for increased funding for research on heart disease.

One of the benefits of organizing is that special interest groups economize on the costs of gathering information valuable to members of the group. For example, consider the case of senior citizens, a group now believed to be the largest voting bloc in the United States. An inexpensive source of information specifically directed toward their interests is the magazine *Modern Maturity,* published by the American Association of Retired Persons (AARP). With a subscription of 19,301,820, *Modern Maturity* has the largest circulation of any magazine in the United States. In contrast, the well-known news magazine *Time* has a circulation of 4,648,454.[8]

One of the great benefits to grouping together individuals who share common interests is the capacity to produce and consume large quantities of information about public policy issues that affect their well-being. While one individual may not find it advantageous to thumb through the thousands of pages in the federal budget document, a group of voters may cheaply produce excellent information through an informational arm to their organization. When grouped over tens of thousands of members, for example, the costs of providing high-quality information through a few researchers, lobbyists, and other staff may result in fairly small membership fees.

Another reason to join a special interest group is to gain the ability to send an extremely powerful signal to policymakers. While policymakers listen to the preferences and wishes of voters separately, the signal that is sent when voters form special interest groups is undeniable and enhances the power of voters to influence policymakers to introduce and enact favorable legislation. As Figure 5-3 demonstrates, age and voting appear to be positively related, and therefore the magnitude of the signal sent from senior citizens to policymakers is likely to be much more powerful than if they had not formed a special interest group.

---

[8] The sources of the circulation data are "Circulation of Leading Magazines," *The World Almanac and Book of Facts, 1990* (New York: World Almanac, 1989), 363–364.

**FIGURE 5-3
The Correlation between Voting and Age**
Voting-Age Population versus Voting Behavior

Source: Statistical Abstract of the United States, 1993.

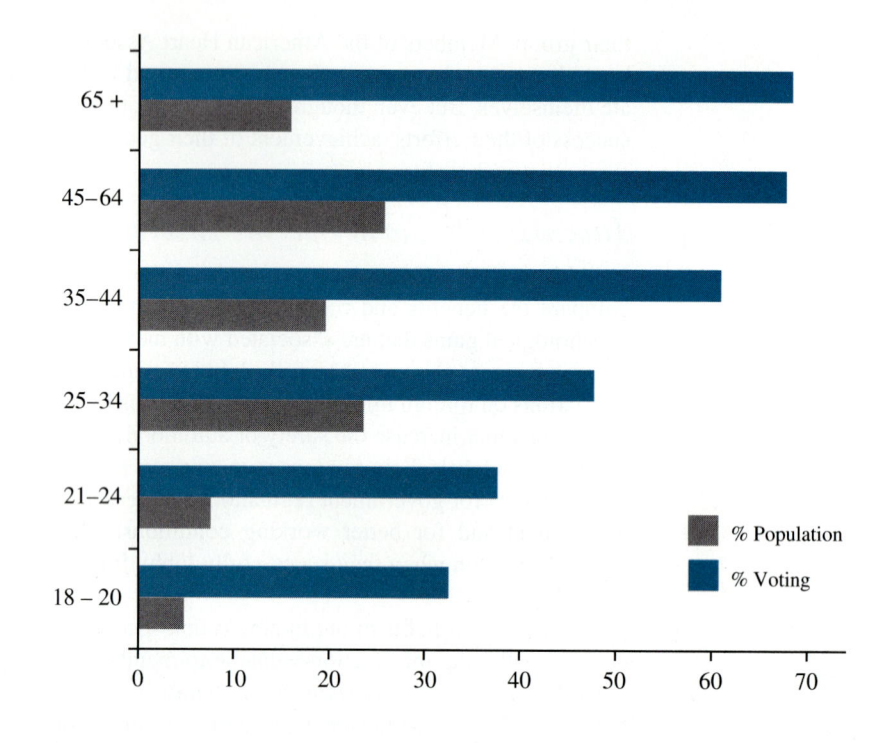

Political Action Committees

Political action committees (PACs) are special interest groups subject to limits on the amount of funds they may contribute to political candidates.

A **political action committee (PAC)** is a specific type of special interest group that plays an important role in the policy process. The Federal Election Campaign Act of 1971 limits individual voters to contributions of no more than $1,000 to any candidate. Organizations, such as corporations or labor unions, are limited to no more than $5,000 in contributions. However, subject to registration with the Federal Elections Commission, PACs may collect up to $5,000 per member of the PAC, and there are no limits on how many candidates a given PAC may contribute to or the number of PACs that an individual candidate may receive contributions from. Over 1987 and 1988, the types of PACs that contributed to Senate candidates were distributed as follows:

- corporate (44 percent)
- trade association (24 percent)
- labor (15 percent)
- nonspecific or "ideological" in nature (17 percent)[9]

Figure 5-4 indicates that the number of PACs has increased approximately sevenfold over the period from 1974 to 1990. The contributions of PACs to political candidates have grown rapidly as well. In 1978, for instance, PAC contributions were $34 million,

---

[9] These data are from Table 465, *Statistical Abstract of the United States,* 1993.

**FIGURE 5-4
Political Action Committees**

Source: Ornstein et al., 1992.

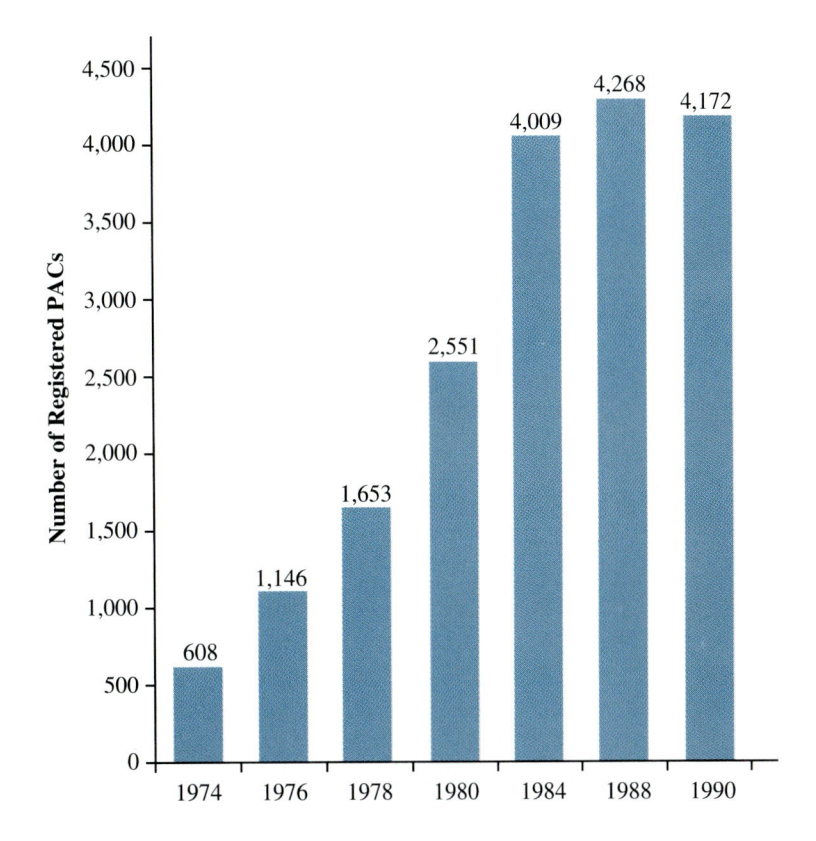

Year	Number of Registered PACs
1974	608
1976	1,146
1978	1,653
1980	2,551
1984	4,009
1988	4,268
1990	4,172

but by 1990, they had risen to $150 million.[10] For 1987–88, at the federal level, PACs accounted for 37 percent of financing for candidates for the House of Representatives and 23 percent for candidates for the Senate.[11]

The Public Good Nature of Special Interest Groups

GAINS FROM LARGE MEMBERSHIP The output of special interest groups has many characteristics in common with public goods. The benefits of achieving preferential legislation tend to be nonrival in consumption; in other words, additional members take no benefits from any other member. These goods tend to be pure public goods, and because additional marginal costs of providing benefits to additional members are negligible, there tend to be no limitations on the number of members. In terms of their ability to form large voting blocs, the greater the number of members, the more powerful the signal that can be sent to policymakers. Because benefits of public goods are nonrival, marginal costs of providing benefits to additional members tend

---

[10] Norman J. Ornstein, Thomas E. Mann, and Michael J. Malbin, *Vital Statistics on Congress, 1991–1992* (Washington, D.C.: Congressional Quarterly, 1992).

[11] From Table 452 in *Statistical Abstract of the United States,* 1990.

to be low or zero. In addition to the gains associated with a large voting bloc, cost savings derived from expanding membership is an additional incentive to add members.

EXCLUSION OF FREE RIDERS In addition to nonrival benefits, many special interest groups provide private goods as well.[12] Membership benefits sometimes represent attempts to reduce incentives to free riding by providing goods that are rival in nature and/or partially excludable. By offering such benefits as technical and advisory services and data collection on items of interest to members, special interest groups discourage free riders and widen their membership. As another means of excluding free riders, special interest groups may lobby to have favorable legislation written in a way that excludes nonmembers. For example, legislation that requires that only union members be used in production may be written for particular industries, such as the garment industry, or even more specifically, for shoes or hats. Consumer regulations that regulate quality of health care, for example, may apply only to certain states or various medical professions.

Cases for Public Sector Provision of Public Goods

Pure Public Goods

The issue of whether private or public sectors should produce public goods is extremely complex. In general, the more pure the public good, the greater the case for public sector provision. But there are few pure public goods characterized by total lack of exclusion and perfect nonrivalry in consumption. Lack of exclusion suggests cases in which it may be appropriate to rely on public markets to produce public goods. A common example is national defense, from which it is impossible to exclude one or more citizens from the benefits of a well-defended country. Because citizens understand that foreign enemies do not decide to invade on the basis of who has contributed to payment of national defense, all citizens benefit from national defense programs. If private clubs produced national defense, for instance, they would have difficulties excluding those that did not pay membership fees. And because private markets would not consider benefits enjoyed by free riders, national defense would not be optimally supplied. Therefore, when exclusion is difficult or impossible, public sector provision of public goods is often viewed as appropriate.

We have also shown that when goods are nonrival in consumption, the marginal cost of extending provision to additional individuals is zero. While zero marginal cost implies that it is socially efficient for all who benefit from the good to receive the good, private suppliers would either not supply these goods or produce less than optimal quantities. It is often recommended that these goods be provided in public markets, so that all who benefit from these goods may consume them. Unlike private clubs, the public sector extends membership rights to all citizens in its provision of these goods.

Economies of scale occur when increased levels of production result in decreased average costs of production.

Economies of Scale

Economies of scale occur whenever higher production results in falling average costs of production. A case for government production may be made on the basis of scale

---

[12] See Olson, *The Logic of Collective Action*, 145.

economies: It is argued that because the private sector underproduces public goods, cost savings are greatest when the public sector takes over production and produces socially efficient levels of public goods. In other words, by providing for a greater number of consumers than is possible under private markets, the public sector is more fully capable of exploiting cost savings associated with scale economies and therefore uses resources more efficiently.

Centralization and Decentralization

Public goods come in many varieties, so it makes sense that they should be provided in many different ways. National defense, for example, is considered a relatively pure public good—it is nonrival in consumption, lacks excludability, and because it is provided by the federal government, it is available equally to all citizens of a country. The argument for production at the federal level is also based on the existence of zero marginal costs, which justifies universal coverage of the benefits of a given level of good to all citizens. Clearly, however, public goods do not always fit the profile of national defense, and it is inappropriate for all public goods to be produced on such a grand scale. State governments, for instance, provide roads and parks on a much smaller scale than that of the federal government. On a smaller scale still, police protection is a public good provided by local governments.

Centralization of public production is often proposed in cases of public goods characterized by scale economies. When average costs continue to drop with increased membership, cost savings may be maximized when only one government unit produces the good. Because government production can better exploit economies of scale by centralizing production into one provider, cost savings are argued to flow to taxpayers—one rationale for having the federal government supply national defense, Social Security, and foreign aid programs.

When benefits tend to be regional in nature, however, purity of public goods diminishes because benefits become partially excludable. Here, production by more than one government may be appropriate. For example, it might not be appropriate for the federal government to run all lighthouses. Similar arguments for decentralized production by more than one government are made when economies of scale do not continue indefinitely.

> **Centralization** is the degree to which policies emanate from central governments.

Public Goods Characterized by Externalities

In the cases of some public goods, problems arise when the private sector cannot capture all of the benefits and costs of allocating resources in those markets. In fact, our discussion of special interest groups indicates that some public goods impose negative or positive externalities upon others who are not directly involved in the market exchange.

Special Interest Groups and Negative Externalities

When special interest groups successfully secure favorable legislation, the benefits they receive are often paid by an external party. For example, when textile manufacturers succeed in outlawing the importation of competitive products, consumers of textile products pay higher prices. When senior citizens secure legislation that increases Social Security payments, taxpayers fund those higher payments. When consumer groups successfully establish policy that requires all automobile manufacturers to include seatbelts in their products, someone must pay for the scarce resources used to produce those seatbelts. If the external costs placed on third parties are not fully considered, the activities of special interest groups will be overproduced, as the theory of negative externalities demonstrates. Markets may therefore fail to allocate resources efficiently when there are incentives for public goods to be provided in private markets by special interest groups.

Special Interest Groups and Positive Externalities

It may also be argued that the activities of special interest groups impose positive externalities on other members of society. Many individuals benefit, for example, when civic groups beautify neighborhoods and cities by planting trees and keeping parks clean. Restoration of historic homes and operation of museums by special interest groups may also positively affect individuals who are not members of those special interest groups. This argument is exemplified by the many public policies that subsidize such special interest groups. For example, as of 1985, there were more than 1.2 million nonprofit groups that had been granted tax-exempt status by the federal government.[13] Of these groups, 497,321 are classified as social welfare, charitable, and religious organizations.

Private Clubs Limit Membership

The theory of clubs is arguably a theory of optimal exclusion as well as optimal inclusion.[14] When exclusion and congestion are possible, it is not optimal to include all individuals into clubs, and because many public goods have congestion possibilities, it is beneficial for private clubs to limit membership. Crowded swimming pools and long lines of golfers diminish benefits to membership. Thus, if a community has fifteen well-defined neighborhoods, for instance, then conceivably all fifteen may have their own private golf and swimming clubs, and all who want to join may do so. If, however, some neighborhoods do not have sufficient resources or enough swimmers and golfers, they may not find it beneficial to form their own clubs. Some may then argue that it is appropriate either that government require all clubs to allow all applicants to join (neighbors or not) or that the public sector provide places for anyone who likes to swim and golf.

One or more club members may also be inclined to exclude applicants from membership on the basis of subjective preferences. Clubs, for instance, have discriminated on the basis of gender, race, and religion. If various members of society find this offensive, then the public sector may be called upon either to require that membership be open to all individuals or to provide the activity itself. For example, if a swimming pool club allows only men to join, the public sector may outlaw this discrimination or provide a swimming pool for all citizens.

---

[13] James T. Bennett and Thomas J. DiLorenzo, *Unfair Competition: The Profits of Nonprofits* (Lanham, Md.: Hamilton Press, 1989), 3.

[14] James M. Buchanan, "An Economic Theory of Clubs."

Community Associations as Clubs

The walled city, popular in medieval times, is making a comeback. According to the Community Associations Institute, there were 130,000 community associations in 1989. While some are small, such as condominium associations, many are quite large. Southern California's Leisure World, for example, claims 21,000 residents, of which most are senior citizens. It is estimated that the average association has 543 housing units and that 80 percent govern communal land as well as buildings.

What are the characteristics of modern walled cities? Many associations have swimming pools, tennis courts, parks, and gyms. Some have their own private security forces that patrol grounds and buildings day and night. Some have security gates that keep out uninvited guests and allow entrance only to those who produce appropriate identification cards. A few even have their own television stations, convenience stores, and bus routes. Some of these associations therefore appear to be viable cities that provide many of the functions of local government.

Source: "Government by the Nice, for the Nice," *The Economist,* July 25, 1992, 25–26.

Analysis

Three main reasons explain why roughly one in eight Americans belongs to a community association: fear of crime, decreased local government services, and rising land prices. The theory of clubs predicts that people with these concerns will join in producing goods and services. Association fees are set in line with benefits; otherwise, we would not see rapid growth in these voluntary organizations. As one manager of a large community association argues, "They know their money is being spent on them." Consequently, association members appear to grumble less about association fees than about taxes paid to their local governments.

There are various criticisms of community associations. Some dislike the many restrictions that are often imposed on members. For example, there are often restrictions on the colors that houses may be painted, on numbers and sizes of pets, and on numbers of cars that may be parked on community streets. Remember, though, that these associations are voluntary and that no coercion is used to gain membership.

Other critics point out that community associations discriminate against lower-income citizens. But the theory of clubs is also a theory of exclusion. Members may join because associations protect the value of their property from problems associated with crime and proximity to lower-priced homes. Moreover, some critics are fearful that by distancing themselves from other citizens, association members may become less willing to pay for local government programs. In fact, some of the larger community associations have attempted to secede from local government jurisdictions and form their own governments, which no longer pay taxes to other local governments. When higher-income individuals flee local governments and join associations, such secessions clearly increase financing burdens on lower-income individuals.

Such conflicts are not surprising when we remember that medieval walled cities were also built as a way of protecting citizens from problems of the outside world. Can the same be said of their modern equivalents?

Assignment and Enforcement of Property Rights

Market failures may also be related to lack of property rights over resources. When ownership is transferable and clearly vested in private individuals, market failure is not likely as long as transaction costs are not too high. Lack of property rights may also contribute to market failures associated with goods for which exclusion is limited or impossible. Consider, for example, lighthouses that guide ships along dangerous coastlines. In the past many economists believed that it was nearly impossible to exclude nonpaying consumers of this good, and there were two different reasons for this belief. First, past technology did not enable owners of lighthouses to monitor which ships were passing by. Today's technology, however, permits lighthouse owners to monitor traffic via video equipment with night vision that spots all passing ships. Second, owners of lighthouses are not assigned property rights over the light that guides passing ships. If lighthouse owners were awarded flexible property rights that prohibited ship captains from free riding on their services, problems related to free riding would be diminished.[15]

Flexible property rights exist when government enforces property rights by requiring that users of goods pay producers of goods. For example, government could require all ship captains to transmit radio signals that can easily be read by lighthouse owners. Further, if proof of payment for the services of lighthouses is made necessary for the (public) license to operate ships, it would be more difficult for ship captains to free ride on the services of lighthouse owners. When flexible property rights are granted and the courts provide lighthouse owners with the ability to collect payments, ship captains will be more inclined to pay for services.

One implication of flexible property rights is that it is more likely lighthouse owners will provide efficient output; alternatively, ship captains will find it advantageous to form a club that provides lighthouse services. In any event, when property rights are flexible and enforced, problems of lack of exclusion and free ridership are reduced and, consequently, the possibility of market failure.

Other cases suggest that flexible property rights do not always easily diminish free riding problems. If all individuals who are inoculated against communicable diseases are authorized to collect payment from all who have not been inoculated, socially efficient levels of inoculation may occur. But in contrast, to the case in which a lighthouse owner is able to monitor all passing ships, the number of individuals who benefit from inoculation programs may be vast. Transaction and information costs of determining who receives external benefits from inoculations and collecting compensation may greatly outweigh benefits from payment collections. Assuming that, for every inoculated individual there are 20,000 noninoculated individuals and marginal benefits are $0.50 per person, potential compensation is worth $10,000. But the transaction and information costs of collecting compensation from 20,000 individuals may greatly exceed this sum. (Note that the decision rule is to equate the marginal benefits to the marginal costs of collecting compensation. This is not an all-or-nothing decision, but one that determines, at the margin, how many individuals to collect payment from.) The degree to which compensation is sought is influenced by the value of the

---

[15] This argument is presented in Buchanan, "An Economic Theory of Clubs."

benefits and the costs associated with collecting payments. In other words, in this case, it is ambiguous whether it is feasible to award flexible property rights as a way of eliminating free riding and market failure.

Cases for Private Sector Provision of Public Goods

Taxation in Practice: Taxation versus Lindahl Pricing

We have seen that Lindahl pricing leads to efficient levels of public goods and Pareto efficient exchanges. If all public goods could be priced along the lines of the Lindahl framework, then little discussion regarding public production of public goods would be necessary. However, once it is decided that public goods should be produced in the public sector, the ways in which those public goods are financed are always controversial. Thus we must address the ability of the public sector to achieve optimal provision of public goods.

Tax Policy Based on Efficiency

Is it likely that a public sector would ever engage in Lindahl pricing? Information is a resource and, like any other resource, it is to some degree scarce. When the public sector attempts to provide public goods on the basis of Lindahl equilibrium, it must know the marginal benefits that each taxpayer receives from consuming public goods. The public sector has two primary ways to produce information regarding marginal benefits. One approach is for policymakers simply to ask all individuals what their marginal benefits are when they consume public goods. However, consumers of public goods may have incentives to lie about their marginal benefits and claim they receive nothing; the amount of public goods they consume is therefore only marginally less than it would be if they were to pay their true marginal benefits.[16] Free riders then would tend to underreport their marginal benefits, thus leading policymakers to underproduce public goods.

Another approach is for policymakers to estimate each individual's marginal benefit and then tax each taxpayer an amount equal to the individual's estimated marginal benefit at the socially optimal level of public good. It is highly doubtful, however, that in practice policymakers could ever come close to measuring true marginal benefits of each of thousands or millions of taxpayers. It is important to understand that the ways in which public markets acquire information on production decisions is vastly different from the ways in which private markets acquire information. While the information that guides efficient production of private goods in private markets is as extensive as that required for public markets to achieve efficient levels of public goods, the former is not the result of planning or estimation by a single group of individuals or policymakers. Resource allocation in the private sector is the product of

---

[16] A fairly technical literature has developed that attempts to circumvent this free rider problem with public goods. For the literature on preference revelation mechanisms (also called demand-revealing processes), see T. Nicolaus Tideman and Gordon Tullock, "A New and Superior Process for Making Social Choices," *Journal of Political Economy* 84 (December 1976): 1145–1160; and Theodore Groves and J. Ledyard, "Optimal Allocation of Public Goods: A Solution to the 'Free Rider' Problem," *Econometrica* 45 (1977): 783–809.

many consumers and producers working independently of one another. In contrast, in order to produce optimal levels of public goods within the framework of Lindahl equilibrium, policymakers must attempt to estimate each individual's marginal benefit curves and then, based on their vertical summation, or ΣMB, derive the market demand for public goods. At the socially efficient level, where $\Sigma MB = MSC$, policymakers then tax each individual according to that person's marginal benefit. As discussed previously, tax policy based on Lindahl equilibrium results in both optimal quantities of public goods and unanimous agreement among taxpayers over how many resources should be devoted to the production of public goods.

Taxation, in practice, is necessarily far removed from Lindahl pricing. Consider the following two scenarios for weekly grocery shopping as a demonstration of how actual tax policy differs from the Lindahl framework:

- Paula walks down the aisles of a supermarket and, based on the benefits associated with each good and the listed prices, chooses from among many thousands of items. At the checkout counter, she receives a final itemized bill that lists the goods chosen and their prices.

- Emily proceeds immediately to the checkout counter and receives a final bill along with a shopping cart full of groceries. She is not allowed to pick and choose the items in the shopping cart or in the store, and the bill is not itemized.

As we can see, Paula's situation is consistent with Lindahl equilibrium because she makes choices about what to purchase based on her own benefits and costs. But Emily's situation defies Lindahl equilibrium, and is more consistent with actual tax policy.

Under current policy, thousands of programs are grouped together, and taxpayers have no choice, other than serving prison time, but to pay for all public programs. Tax prices are often assigned on the basis of income and not on marginal benefits of taxpayers.[17] Taxpayers who greatly enjoy the benefits of programs are not systematically charged more than taxpayers who do not enjoy the benefits of those programs. When taxpayers honestly do not enjoy the benefits of various programs (that is, they are not free riders), they prefer not to fund them. However, tax policies, which are outside the Lindahl framework, do not allow this choice; therefore, when taxpayers are forced to pay for programs they do not want, tax policy used to finance public goods results in Pareto inferior moves.

Present tax policy, however, approximates Lindahl pricing when it finances public good spending through tolls and fees. There are many ways in which tolls and fees could be used to finance public goods. The imposition of tolls on roads, for instance, achieves two important purposes: First, toll booths exclude free riders; and second, users that value the good the most end up paying the most because they are charged each time they use the road. Tolls and fees are also used to finance costs of public

---

[17] When taxes are proportional and the demands by individuals for public goods have unitary price and income elasticities, then income taxation may be a good approximation of Lindahl pricing. When this is not the case, the term *forced riders* may describe all citizens who are forced to pay taxes that exceed the value they place on public goods. See Richard E. Wagner, *Public Finance: Revenues and Expenditures in a Democratic Society* (Boston: Little, Brown, 1983), 40, for a discussion of these issues.

parks, ferries, parking facilities, and museums. However, tolls and fees in fact usually finance only part of the costs of these public goods.

One reason that the public sector does not use this approach very often is that it may be impossible to collect tolls or fees for many public goods. For example, how would tolls be charged for national defense provision or programs that place astronauts on the moon? Another reason is that the transaction costs of operating thousands of public programs through tolls and fees might outweigh the gains associated with basing tax policy on the Lindahl framework.

The implication is that because the public sector will never perfectly know the marginal benefits of individual taxpayers for each and every public good, tax policy, in practice, can never be consistent with the Lindahl framework. This does not necessarily mean that the public sector should not provide public goods. Rather, it introduces a requirement that the case for public sector provision—and its finance—must be demonstrated. That is, it must be shown that although the public sector is imperfect, it does a better job providing public goods than does the private sector. We must closely examine arguments that the transaction and information costs necessary for the public sector to use the Lindahl framework outweigh the case for using the Lindahl framework. Discussion of tax policies must include comparisons with resource allocations in private markets.

Tax Policy Based on Equity

One of the reasons that tax policy is a contentious topic arises from the issue of equity. Efficiency necessarily becomes less important when equity considerations are considered more important dimensions of tax policy. While it may be efficient for public goods to be priced according to marginal benefits received by users, other considerations may suggest that tax policy should seek to meet the equity goals of society. Issues concerning how much each taxpayer should pay in taxes are bound to be complex, occasioning many conflicting views among voters and policymakers.

Coercion versus Voluntary Agreements

The degree to which public intervention is characterized by coercion is a tricky subject. On one hand, whenever Lindahl prices are not charged, a certain level of **coercion** exists, whereby tax policy forces users to pay taxes higher than their marginal benefits. This is likely to be the case when many programs are grouped together so that individuals who do not desire a particular program cannot be excluded from contributing to it.[18] Such policies reflect Pareto inferior moves; therefore, in order to collect payment for these programs, a level of coercion is necessary. Whenever Lindahl pricing does not guide tax policy, unanimity, or perfect consensus among taxpayers, will not

Coercion occurs when individuals are compelled, against their will, to receive and pay for public policies.

---

[18] An argument could also be made that even though one or more taxpayers lose when their tax payments exceed the marginal benefits of various programs, there may also be other programs in which tax payments are less than their marginal benefits. Therefore, when all programs are considered together, some individuals gain, and some lose. Note, however, that contrary to actual tax policy, this logic implies that taxpayers receive tax bills for each and every policy provided by the public sector. Moreover, even if actual policy were to separately charge for each program, calculation of whether society gains or loses assumes an ability to make interpersonal utility comparisons.

characterize policy. In contrast, the fact that private markets achieve Pareto efficient outcomes under various ideal conditions indicates that all agreements are voluntary.

On the other hand, the process that determines policies is always based on some degree of voluntary support. In democratic societies, voters signal their support of public policies; therefore, to some extent policies are the result of **voluntary agreements.** But we must be careful in following the logic of this argument since even in representative democracies, politicians are never elected on the basis of 100 percent of all votes. Because unanimity is not a requirement of most political systems, public policies will have an element of coercion. For example, if a majority voting rule is employed, the only requirement for passage is that a majority of voters agree. This means that when minorities lose an election, they are unable to prevent the implementation of policies that lower their overall well-being.

Just how voluntary, or how coercive, is public policy? This is an extremely important issue that requires an understanding of the process by which decisions are made in the public sector. Specifically, the role of voters and policymakers must be examined in a context that describes their relative abilities to determine policy. If, for example, all voters do not have equal access to the policy process, outcomes may differ from those achieved when voters do have equal access.

Monopoly Government Arguments

Economists increasingly debate whether lack of competition is as much of a problem in the public sector as it is in the private sector.[19] When private markets are not competitive, prices do not equal marginal social costs, and socially inefficient levels of output are therefore produced. Because monopoly is one example in which resources are misallocated in private markets, government intervention into these markets may improve allocative efficiency. Similarly, when the public sector itself has monopoly power, it is appropriate to question whether it may misallocate resources as well. Instances of **monopoly government** production on the federal level include provision of national defense and Social Security, and, on the state level, regulation of liquor stores and lotteries.

Several important issues require discussion. One issue pertains to what motivates policymakers, and we will first consider two extreme assumptions. At one extreme are policymakers who attempt to provide socially optimal quantities of public goods at the lowest possible tax prices to citizens. At the other extreme are policymakers motivated only by the power, prestige, and perquisites associated with being in the public sector. In the case of the former, we would be unconcerned that governments are monopolies and would expect policymakers to try to maximize total net social benefits of citizens. In the latter, we would predict that policymakers who care less about total net social benefits would allocate resources in a manner beneficial to their own narrow interests.

Another important issue involves cost savings associated with government monopolization when production is subject to economies of scale. Because exploitation of scale economies requires some centralization, or monopolization, of

---

[19] See, for example, Geoffrey Brennan and James M. Buchanan, *The Power to Tax: Analytical Foundations of a Fiscal Constitution* (Cambridge, U.K.: Cambridge University Press, 1980).

production, it is appropriate to question whether cost savings that follow from monopolization of production outweigh resource misallocations that may result if governments become monopolies and misallocate resources. Of course, this issue is related to one's assumption about what motivates policymakers.

Public Sector Provision in Practice

Private and Public Markets Are Less than Ideal

Market failures occur when private markets are unable to incorporate all the information that would lead to allocative efficiency. We must therefore address the issue of whether policymakers themselves have sufficient information to correct market failures associated with public goods. Cases for private sector provision are usually based on practical problems of implementing ideal public interventions into private markets. In other words, while private markets do not allocate resources perfectly, public markets cannot perfectly allocate resources either. Appreciation of this fact leads us to examine the practical application of public goods theory.

Cost Differences between Public and Private Provision

After examining fifty studies of cost differences between publicly and privately provided services, Dennis C. Mueller argues, "The evidence that public provision of a service reduces the efficiency of its provision seems overwhelming." (p. 266).[20] In forty studies (and controlling for quality, prices, and costs), public sector provision was found to be vastly more expensive than private sector provision, and in only two cases was the opposite determined. A few of the conclusions of these studies follow:

- The private airline in Australia is 12 to 100 percent more efficient than the public airline.[21]
- Public bus service in West Germany is 160 percent more expensive per kilometer than its private sector counterparts.[22]
- Public sector cleaning services in West Germany are 40 to 60 percent more costly than private sector alternatives.[23]
- The debt collection service of the U.S. government is 200 percent more costly per dollar of debt collected than private debt collection services.[24]

---

[20] Dennis C. Mueller, *Public Choice II* (Cambridge: Cambridge University Press, 1989), 261–266.

[21] D. G. Davies, "The Efficiency of Public versus Private Firms: The Case of Australia's Two Airlines," *Journal of Law and Economics* 14 (April 1971): 149–165; and D. G. Davies, "Property Rights and Economic Efficiency: The Australian Airlines Revisited," *Journal of Law and Economics* 20 (April 1977): 223–226.

[22] W. Oelert, "Reprivatisierung des Öffentlichen Personalverkehrs," *Der Personenverkehr* 4 (1976): 108–114, as cited in Mueller.

[23] Hamburger Senat, *Abschlubbericht des Beauftragten zur Gebäudereinigung*, Hamburg, 1974, 1; and H. Fischer-Menshausen, "Entlastung des Staates durch Privatisierung von Aufgaben," *Wirtschaftsdienst* 55 (1975): 545–552, as cited in Mueller.

[24] James T. Bennett and Manuel H. Johnson, "Tax Reduction without Sacrifice: Private-Sector Production of Public Services," *Public Finance Quarterly* 8 (October 1980): 363–369.

❏ Municipal fire departments in Seattle, Washington are 39 to 88 percent more costly per capita than private sector provision in Scottsdale, Arizona.[25]

❏ Public housing agencies in the United States are 20 percent more costly per housing unit than private firms.[26]

Several important points should be made concerning this evidence. One is that there are some goods the public sector will not produce more cheaply (or of higher or equal quality) than the private sector. Just because the public sector is producing a product does not necessarily imply that it fits the classic definition of a public good. When the public sector produces goods that more closely fit the definition of private goods, there is no reason to expect the public sector to outperform the private sector. Indeed, recent interest and growth of **privatization** is a referendum on this issue. Privatization occurs whenever the public sector either stops producing one or more of its goods or turns over the responsibility of producing goods to the private sector. The President's Commission on Privatization, established in 1987, is commissioned to explore those areas of public production that should be privatized.[27] The following areas were singled out as areas in which some degree of privatization offers potential for improved efficiency and service quality: air traffic control, urban mass transit, postal service, housing, education, and Medicare. It would appear then that these goods are now considered to have various characteristics associated with our definition of private goods.

Another point is that cost differences are common when the purpose of public sector provision is to meet various equity goals of society. The important differences between efficiency and equity make it unsurprising that to the extent that equity motivates government provision, public sector provision is more costly than private sector provision. For example, while it may not be efficient for all homes to have equal access to low-cost telephone services, it may be viewed as inequitable to exclude low-income rural customers from obtaining service that is in line with their income. Similarly, if it is not profitable for bus companies to provide frequent service to low-income neighborhoods, it may be appropriate to subsidize private bus companies or provide public bus service on a more frequent basis. Note, however, that these goods are private in nature, and it is therefore not entirely appropriate to examine them within the theory of public goods. Rather, they may fall within the redistributive role of the public sector.

Finally, cost differences may suggest that few scale economies exist when government takes over production of the goods represented in those studies. Higher costs may also suggest lack of scale economies, called *diseconomies of scale,* as well as the possibility that in comparison to competitive private sector firms, government monopolists are misallocating resources.

Privatization occurs when government responsibilities are shifted to the private sector.

---

[25] R. S. Ahlbrandt, Jr., "Efficiency in the Provision of Fire Services," *Public Choice* 16 (Fall 1973): 1–15.

[26] R. F. Muth, *Public Housing: An Economic Evaluation* (Washington, D.C.: American Enterprise Institute, 1973).

[27] President's Commission on Privatization, *Privatization: Toward More Effective Government,* March 1988.

Subsidies of Nonprofits

It may be argued that the public nature of many private clubs, charitable organizations, and special interest groups requires intervention by the public sector. Most arguments call for subsidization of their activities through grants, subsidies, or various tax deductions. In fact, many of these groups are classified as *nonprofits,* a definition that allows them to take advantage of partial or complete tax exemptions. The result of tax exemptions is identical to that of subsidization as a means of internalizing positive externalities; therefore, by lowering operating costs, outputs of private clubs, charitable organizations, and special interest groups expand beyond levels that would occur without subsidy policies.[28]

Are Special Interest Groups Too Powerful?

Our examination of special interest groups has suggested that they have incentives to form voting blocs in representative democracies. Growth in their numbers and in the magnitude of their contributions suggests that members of special interest groups have interests in common that could be furthered through the policy process. While some critics of special interest groups argue that they are in an unfair position to manipulate policymakers (and thereby impose negative externalities on other voters), others argue that only those with strong feelings about policies will care enough to organize themselves into voting blocs. This latter view suggests that when some interests are not strong enough to elicit membership among many individuals, those interests will not be represented.

It is interesting to apply the compensation test to this issue.[29] If gainers from a new piece of legislation are able to compensate losers, then gainers should be able to expend funds and energies sufficient to win approval of the legislation over the objections of losers. Moreover, if one accepts the compensation test as a valid way of improving social welfare, then, so long as all groups have equal access to policymakers, they should be in favor of special interest groups. If, however, sufficient compensation is not awarded to losers, enactment of such legislation represents a Pareto inferior move for society.

When government subsidies are provided, activities of special interest groups are greater than what the private market would produce. When too large, subsidies promote overproduction of activities of special interest groups, and when too small, activities are underproduced. All policies have income redistribution effects that need to be considered when deciding whether subsidy policies are appropriate. When tax

---

[28] It has recently been argued that there is a fine line, though, between the role that the public sector plays in encouraging the activities of these organizations and the role that these organizations play in encouraging the political careers of policymakers. When hundreds of millions of dollars are given to these organizations, it may be questionable whether these funds contribute back to policymakers in the forms of campaign contributions, lobbying efforts for various political causes and other ways that may affect votes and the reelection efforts of policymakers who are controlling the purse-strings of those grants and subsidies. For a discussion of these issues, see James T. Bennett and Thomas J. DiLorenzo, *Destroying Democracy: How Government Funds Partisan Politics* (Washington, D.C.: Cato Institute, 1985).

[29] See, for example, Gary S. Becker, "Public Policies, Pressure Groups, and Dead Weight Losses," *Journal of Public Economics* 28 (1985): 329–347.

reductions are offered, for example, groups that pay lower taxes gain at the expense of those that must pay higher taxes, assuming that total tax revenues are unchanged. Unless losses to those with higher taxes are offset by external benefits they receive from having special interest groups produce more goods, subsidies foster Pareto inferior moves for society.

Common-Pool Problems

Externalities often arise when resources are not privately owned. Air and water pollution occurs, in part, because private individuals do not own clean air and water resources, and therefore no one can collect payment for the use of those resources. While it may be impractical to award ownership of air and water resources to private individuals, problems occur when tax, subsidy, and regulatory policies are used to correct market failures associated with lack of property rights. When government produces public goods, ownership rights to resources are transferred to the public sector. As our discussion of how private ownership provides good stewardship of African elephants demonstrates, if the public sector is to allocate scarce resources efficiently, it must be a good steward of those resources as well.

Common-pool problems occur when public stewardship of resources allocates resources inefficiently.

A **common-pool problem** occurs when public sector stewardship of resources does not allocate resources efficiently. The following example, offered by Terry L. Anderson and Donald R. Leal, describes a particular case of how public takeover of a natural resource led to its destruction.[30] Mr. and Mrs. Beck privately owned several areas of wooded land outside Seattle, Washington. Starting in 1887, the Becks cultivated and maintained its giant fir trees, some of which were 400 feet high and 20 feet in diameter. They built an outdoor center called Ravenna Park to be used for concerts and nature talks. At a cost of 25 cents a day, the Becks were able to draw up to 10,000 visitors on a busy day. However, after having condemned the land in 1911, the city government paid the Becks $135,663, and took over stewardship of the natural resource. Cutting down the trees and selling them for firewood, city employees had destroyed every tree by 1925, making the place look like any other park with tennis courts and playgrounds. Anderson and Leal argue that contrary to the popular view that government protects natural resources under its care, this is one of many examples in which destruction of resources was permitted under government stewardship.

In order for the public sector to be an efficient steward, it must allocate its resources on the basis of marginal social benefits and costs. In a sense, all resources that are not owned by private individuals are owned by the public sector. Common-pool problems are more likely when it is difficult to monitor and enforce ownership rights. For example, it is easy to monitor and enforce property rights for land and difficult in the cases of air and water. Complexity also arises when damages to property or health that can occur are deferred, as is the case with toxic wastes.

---

[30] Terry L. Anderson and Donald R. Leal, *Free Market Environmentalism* (Boulder, Col.: Westview Press, 1991), 51.

Summary

- Public goods are nonrival in consumption; that is, when additional citizens consume these goods, others do not have to reduce their consumption. Because of nonrivalry in consumption, the marginal costs of providing benefits to additional citizens are zero.

- Two reasons suggest that market failure occurs in cases of public goods and results in resource underallocation. The free rider effect occurs when one or more citizens are able to let others pay (because of lack of exclusion) for goods that they themselves plan to consume. The other reason is that allocative efficiency (because marginal costs are zero) requires that all possible beneficiaries of public goods be allowed to consume them. Private markets, however, only allocate resources on the basis of paying customers.

- Market demand for public goods is determined by summing vertically the marginal values that each individual places on consumption of different levels of public goods. Efficiency occurs when the sum of marginal benefits equals marginal social cost.

- Lindahl prices equal the marginal benefits that each individual receives after consuming optimal quantities of public goods. Under Lindahl pricing, voluntary agreements result in consumption of socially efficient levels of public goods.

- The theory of clubs is the theory of voluntary cooperation between individuals seeking mutual advantage. The ability to exclude free riders from enjoying benefits of clubs is one reason that clubs are formed. Special interest groups are clubs, and their role in the policy process is controversial.

- Overproduction of public goods, common-pool problems, oversubsidization of special interest groups and policies that assign taxes in excess of marginal benefits are government failures that may result when policies attempt to correct market-failures.

Review Questions

1. What are the characteristics of public goods? Give two examples.
2. What is the free rider effect?
3. How does the market demand for private goods differ from the demand for public goods?
4. What is meant by Lindahl equilibrium?
5. What is meant by the theory of clubs?
6. What are special interest groups? Give two examples.

Discussion Questions

1. Explain why all public goods are not produced in the public sector.
2. Explain why production of (pure) public goods in the private sector will generally result in an inefficient level of provision.
3. What factors might lead the public sector to overprovide various public goods? Is it necessarily better for the public sector to overprovide these goods than it is for the private sector to underprovide these goods?
4. For which of two goods, playgrounds and hats, would you expect there to be a greater incentive for individuals to free ride?
5. Explain the differences between efficient production of private and public goods.
6. Under what circumstances are private clubs most likely to provide efficient levels of public goods? Under what circumstances are they likely to provide inefficient levels? Even if private clubs provide efficient levels of public goods, provide

several reasons for why it may be viewed as more appropriate for the public sector to provide these goods.

7. Provide three examples of special interest groups and discuss the relationship of these groups to public goods.

Key Words

Public good
Private good
Zero marginal cost of provision
Lack of exclusion
Free rider
Lindahl prices
Theory of clubs
Special interest groups

Political action committee (PAC)
Economies of scale
Centralization
Coercion
Voluntary agreements
Monopoly government
Privatization
Common-pool problem

PART 3

The Policy Process

Chapter 6
Voters and Policymakers in the Policy Process

Chapter 7
Voting Models and Public Market Structure

Chapter 8
The Demand and Supply of Government

CHAPTER 6

Voters and Policymakers in the Policy Process

Why Study Voters and Policymakers?

Public exchange takes place for the same reason that exchange in private markets does: Exchange partners believe their economic lives will be enhanced. Thus, the goal of voters and policymakers is to improve their economic lives. Like private exchanges, public exchanges may take many forms. Voters may agree with policymakers to exchange such financial resources as taxes and public debt for various policies perceived to be advantageous. In 1994, for example, a $28.8 billion budget for the U.S. Department of Education was funded by voters.[1] Exchanges that do not directly result in taxes or public debt may also take place, such as laws and regulations that reallocate resources in our economy.

Public choice—the branch of public finance that studies the processes by which public exchanges take place—investigates the two agents in the policy process, voters and policymakers, along with the institutions within which their exchanges occur. While the roots of public choice analysis go back to Adam Smith, it is commonly argued that its modern starting point came in the late 1950s and early 1960s with the pioneering works of James M. Buchanan, Gordon Tullock, Duncan Black, and Anthony Downs.[2] These works elevated the study of voters and policymakers to the level of vital inquiry in public finance and introduced a rich and challenging avenue to follow in understanding the public sector.

The tools of public choice analysis are those developed in microeconomic theory; therefore, the exchanges between voters and policymakers are modeled in much the same way that exchanges between consumers and producers in private markets are

Public choice models the public-market exchanges between voters and policymakers much as exchanges between consumers and producers in private markets are modeled.

---

[1] Estimate provided in *Budget of the United States Government, Fiscal Year 1995* (Washington, D.C.: Office of Management and Budget, 1994).

[2] See Adam Smith, *The Wealth of Nations* (New York: Random House, Modern Library Edition, 1937); James M. Buchanan and Gordon Tullock, *The Calculus of Consent: Logical Foundations of Constitutional Democracy* (Ann Arbor, Mich.: University of Michigan Press, 1962); Duncan Black, *The Theory of Committees and Elections* (Cambridge, U.K.: Cambridge University Press, 1958); and Anthony Downs, *An Economic Theory of Democracy* (New York: Harper & Row, 1957).

modeled. Thus, public behaviors are considered to be the products of *choices*—choices that reflect the decisions of voters and policymakers in favor of (or against) various alternatives that lie before them. Public choice analysis is also concerned with alternative ways in which public markets may be structured and how each alternative influences the choices made by voters and policymakers.

Study of voters, policymakers, and institutions is now commonly accepted by public finance economists as crucial to understanding the public sector. In our own study, then, let us examine the following questions:

- Are voters well informed about policies?
- How often do voters vote?
- How active are voters in the policy process?
- Do Americans vote more often than citizens of other countries do?
- What motivates policymakers?
- How important is reelection to incumbent policymakers?
- Are there important differences between elected and nonelected policymakers?
- Who are the constituents of policymakers?

Modeling the Policy Process

Behavioral Assumptions

In representative democracies, exchanges occur between voters and policymakers in public markets (see the chapter appendix for a discussion of public exchange under dictators). The simple model

$$\text{Voters} \Rightarrow \text{Policymakers} \Rightarrow \text{Public policy}$$

describes the possible interactions of voters and policymakers in the formation of public policy. The word *possible* is used since the behaviors of voters and policymakers are not described by this model; rather, it is the role of the public choice analyst to delineate the behaviors of voters and policymakers within this simple model. In the course of our discussion we will make use of various **behavioral assumptions** that suggest the different motivations of participants in the policy process. In this case, *motivation* means what voters and policymakers really care about. Because the policies that result from the exchange process are greatly influenced by the behavioral characteristics of voters and policymakers, we must examine many possibilities.

Behavioral assumptions are predictions of voters' and policymakers' interactions in the policy process.

Positive Dimensions of Model Building

While we may prefer that voters and policymakers behave in a certain manner, we must be careful to not let our value judgments about what is appropriate behavior influence our ability to understand actual behaviors of voters and policymakers. Regardless of whether voters and policymakers behave as we would prefer them to, our primary task is to understand and predict policy outcomes. Positive analysis develops models that describe behaviors not governed by facts. If facts, or absolute truths, described the behaviors of voters and policymakers, then policy outcomes could be absolutely predictable. This is clearly not the case, and behavioral assumptions are the subject of much debate and controversy. Modeling the policy process is a building exercise; that is, we examine how different behavioral assumptions about voters and policymakers lead to different conclusions or predictions of public policy. Model A, for example, may assume that public policy is a product of self-interested policymakers, and model B may assume that policymakers are not motivated by self-interest. After we build alternative models, we then compare their capacities to help us understand and predict public policy. The task of positive analysis is to determine which model, or theory, best describes public policy among all other models.[3]

For public finance economists interested in positive analysis of the policy process, examination of alternative models of the policy process serves two important purposes. First, testing alternative models gives us the ability to choose the model that best describes the policy that results from the exchanges between voters and policymakers. Courageous model builders test their beliefs against many alternative assumptions and take the chance that their beliefs may not be validated by the evidence. Second, for those interested in changing policy, choosing the "best" model increases the likelihood that policy recommendations will result in desired policy outcomes.

What Motivates Voters?

Political Participation

Political participation is the involvement of citizens in the policy process. Of the many ways in which citizens participate, here are some of the most common:

Political participation is the act of contributing to the policy process.

- voting
- writing letters or talking to policymakers
- writing letters to the editor
- writing books and articles
- running for political office
- working for a political party
- working in government
- contributing to political parties or candidates

Research indicates that voting is the most common form of political participation. Survey research has also shown that, in 1984, citizens participated in the following (nonvoting) activities: attempts to persuade others about political views (32 percent); attending political meetings (8 percent); working for a political party or candidate (4 percent); wearing buttons or placing bumper stickers on cars (9 percent); and contributing money to political parties or candidates (12 percent).[4]

Self-Interest: Narrow and Broad Definitions

Narrow self-interest is the desire to enhance one's well-being without regard to the well-being of others.

We hear a lot about self-interest in politics, especially applied to policymakers. However, it is also relevant in the study of voters. Self-interest can be defined in either a narrow or broad sense. **Narrow self-interest** signifies individual behavior driven by

---

[3] Milton Friedman, "The Methodology of Positive Economics," in his *Essays in Positive Economics* (Chicago: University of Chicago Press, 1953).

[4] From Table 1-2 in M. Margaret Conway, *Political Participation in the United States* (Washington, D.C.: Congressional Quarterly Press, 1985); and based on several sources of information cited in that table.

issues and concerns affecting only that individual. As an example, consider a policy that proposes to widen a major road through your town. Under a narrow definition of self-interest, you might perceive the policy to be beneficial only if the expanded road decreases your traveling time or, by rerouting traffic, lowers the annoying traffic noise near your house. More generally, narrow definitions of self-interest may lead us to conclude that all rich citizens oppose anti-poverty programs that redistribute income from the rich to the poor.

Broad self-interest indicates that individuals may be concerned about issues and policies that directly affect other individuals as well as themselves. In addition to himself, a husband and father may genuinely be concerned about the well-being of his wife and children. Parents, grandparents, grandchildren, other relatives, good friends, fellow church members, and respected business associates may also be included in his range of self-interest. There are clearly many possibilities for other people to enter into our perception of what constitutes self-interest. Other factors that may define the range of our broad self-interest include ethnicity, region, and language.[5] In the example of a policy that widens a major road through town, an individual may believe the policy to be beneficial even when it does not alter his or her commuting time or the level of street noise in the neighborhood. As long as individuals believe that a policy improves the well-being of someone they care about, it is beneficial to those individuals and may be interpreted as serving their broad self-interest.

Broad definitions of self-interest may lead us to conclude that many citizens support programs that redistribute income from the rich to the poor. Figure 6-1 demonstrates that private citizens engage in *philanthropy*—charitable contributions intended to increase the welfare of society. Of the $124.8 billion in private philanthropic contributions, private individuals contributed $103.6 billion, or 83 percent, of all funds. Of course, these funds are in addition to the funds allocated through the public sector, and it is clear that the behaviors of some portion of the participants of both private and public markets are activated by broad definitions of self-interest. This is not to say that all participants are equally interested in contributing to others, but that behavior exists that is predicated on broad self-interests.

This discussion of narrow and broad definitions of self-interest suggests that all voters are self-interested. We should not associate the word *self-interest* with selfishness or a derogatory or disparaging notion of individuals or groups. The fact that all voters are self-interested does not suggest that all voters are alike or that their behaviors are identical. Self-interested voters can differ immensely. This should not surprise us for in 1992 the United States had 126,000,000 registered voters, room for plenty of diversity.[6] Some voters deeply care about U.S. public policy on starving people in Africa, but others may not be particularly interested in pursuing policies that seek to improve conditions that seem so remote. It is not particularly useful to debate whether voters are self-interested, in fact, but it may be useful to argue about the broadness of their self-interests. Self-interested voters differ in the extent and degree to which they

> **Broad self-interest** is the desire to enhance one's own well-being as well as that of others with whom one recognizes some literal or figurative kinship.

---

[5] See Donald E. Stokes, "What Decides Elections," in *Democracy at the Polls: A Comparative Study of Competitive Elections,* ed. David Butler, Howard R. Penniman, and Austin Ranney (Washington, D.C.: American Enterprise Institute, 1981).

[6] Table 454, Department of Commerce, Bureau of the Census, *Statistical Abstract of the United States,* 1993.

**FIGURE 6-1
Private Philanthropy Funds**
Allocation of $124.8 Billion in 1991

Source: Table 617, Statistical Abstract of the United States, 1993.

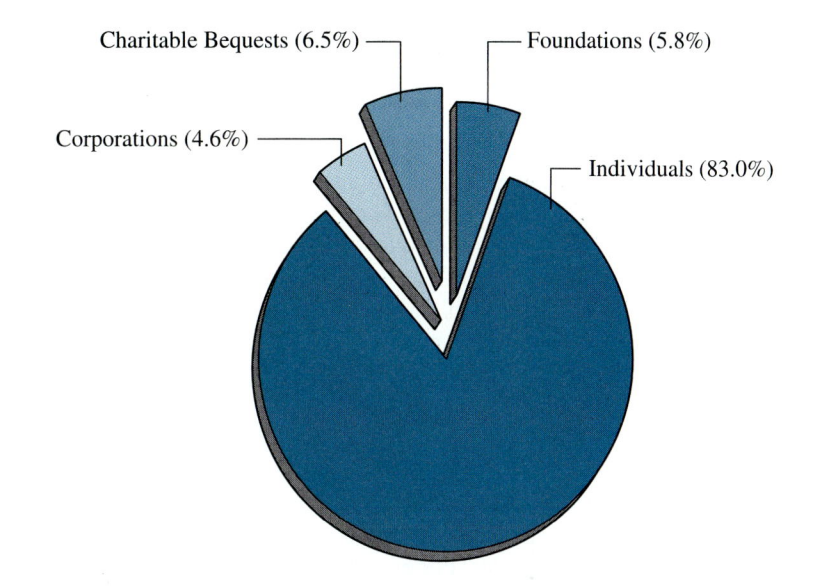

Charitable Bequests (6.5%)
Foundations (5.8%)
Corporations (4.6%)
Individuals (83.0%)

are concerned about others, and the broadness of their self-interest will clearly provide at least a partial explanation of their voting behaviors.

Special Interest Groups

Special interests have been defined as groups of voters linked by some common bond. Under broad definitions of self-interest, voters may organize into special interest groups that represent powerful signaling devices on specific issues to policymakers. Political action committees have also been described as a specific type of special interest group that plays an important role in the policy process. Inclusion of special interests into our model of the policy process adds the following complexity to our framework:

Individual voters, Special interests ⇒ Policymakers ⇒ Public policy

The model now includes two sets of voters, individual and groups, in the process that determines policies. Consistent with our previous discussion of the importance of formulating alternative assumptions about the behaviors of individual voters and policymakers, we must now consider the possible assumptions that we might make about the behaviors of special interest groups.

The following questions emerge when we introduce special interest groups into our examination of the policy process:

❑ How different are the self-interests of special interest groups from those of individual voters?
❑ Are members of special interest groups more likely to vote than voters who are not so strongly aligned?
❑ What signals are special interests likely to send to policymakers, and to what extent do they influence policymakers?

Policy Intentions versus Policy Results

Given that self-interested voters and special interests may care about the well-being of many people, they may direct their energies toward two separate aspects of policy. One aspect concerns *policy intentions*. Voters may support well-intentioned policies they perceive as solutions to problems that the policy process should remedy. This is a perfectly reasonable statement. Otherwise, why would voters promote policies based on bad intentions? Sending aid to drought-ridden countries is a policy characterized by the best of intentions. Clearly, there is no end to the well-intentioned policies that might be enacted through the policy process, since there are always ways to benefit one or more individuals. When policies benefit people included in their broad definition of self-interest, individual voters and special interest groups are inclined to support them.

Another aspect of policy concerns *policy results*. Policy results are defined as actual outcomes. Anti-poverty programs are aimed at helping the poor, and national defense programs are designed to protect a nation from external attack. It can be argued that good intentions *without* good results do not offer sufficient reasons to support policies. For example, if the growth in social spending on the poor did not result in overall improvement in their condition, the policy may be considered a failure. Thus, some believe that no matter how well-intentioned, policies that do not accomplish their intentions are classified as policy failures.

Some controversy exists over how we should weigh the importance of the intentions and results characteristic of policy. Steven Kelman, for example, argues that the policy arena should be a place in which voters can show their concerns for others.[7] Kelman maintains that by setting a good example and showing compassion for others, government—and its policies—serves as a school that helps mold the character of its citizens. Good intentions are a major point of emphasis in this argument. While good results are also considered an important role of policy, this approach may imply that because the good intentions of people promote good policies, policy results will necessarily be good as well.

It is useful to examine the assumptions about behavior that underlie this view. The first assumption is that not only are there some voters whose characters should be molded by government, but that there are also policymakers who know how to accomplish this feat. Policymakers, therefore, are assumed to know which characteristics policymaking should instill into voters. But before continuing these considerations, we must understand how the logic of the argument depends critically upon the assumptions we adopt on the behaviors and characteristics of voters and policymakers.

Rational Ignorance

Rational ignorance is a term that we use to describe the fact that voters are not fully informed about all policy issues. It is important to remember that ignorance means only that individuals have less-than-perfect information, and that lack of information,

Rational ignorance is the result of rational decision making when obtaining complete information is unreasonable, impractical, or unproductive.

---

[7] Steven Kelman, "Public Choice and Public Spirit," *The Public Interest* 87 (1987): 80–94.

or ignorance, is rational behavior on the part of voters. Even if information acquisition is relatively costless and of high quality, voters expend effort only in those areas consistent with their broad self-interests. Only so many issues are of concern to individual voters or special interest groups and information acquisition is costly, so it is rational for voters to willingly maintain ignorance of the total range of policy issues under debate within the policy process. Voters may also decide to be rationally ignorant because they believe that policymakers will make appropriate judgments about particular issues that affect them. This is likely when voters believe that policymakers exhibit similarity in values.

It should not be surprising that rational voters economize on scarce resources such as information and time. Processing of information on policy issues is time-consuming and costly and, in addition to conducting their own research on policy issues, voters receive information provided by various news sources. Television, newspapers, and magazines are important sources of information, but even these sources require voters to expend time and energy analyzing them.[8] One of the benefits of organizing voters into special interest groups is that the costs of gathering information are diminished. Senior citizens, for example, are believed to be the largest special interest group in the United States, and as a bloc this group is a highly efficient disseminator of information to its members (see Chapter 5). Thus, as demonstrated by the high correlation between age and voting, the magnitude of the signal this group sends to policymakers may be more powerful than that of unorganized younger voters.

We can see that the identity of voters suggests what motivates them to acquire and process information about public policies. Voters are taxpayers and, because policies must be financed through their pocketbooks, they have financial incentives to acquire information on the policies they must ultimately finance. Voters are also recipients of public expenditures, and the targets of rules and regulations and thus have further incentives to inform themselves about public policies. Public sector expansion throughout this century suggests a corresponding rising incentive to acquire and process information on the policies that voters finance and receive. Partial evidence in support of the hypothesis that voters are increasingly interested in public policy is shown in Figure 6-2 which indicates that the rate at which citizens send letters and packages to members of the U.S. Congress has accelerated over time. In 1989, for example, citizens sent their congressional representatives 121.8 million letters and packages.[9]

In addition, the technology of information dissemination has undergone tremendous growth in the last decade. Computers, 24-hour cable television, and a wealth of magazines and newsletters provide a large array of information to the voter who wishes to remain informed about policy. Technology also permits voters to monitor

---

[8] See Anthony Smith, "Mass Communications," in *Democracy at the Polls: A Comparative Study of Competitive National Elections,* ed. David Butler, Howard R. Penniman, and Austin Ranney (Washington, D.C.: American Enterprise Institute, 1981).

[9] Table 6-9 in Norman J. Ornstein, Thomas E. Mann, and Michael J. Malbin, *Vital Statistics on Congress, 1991–1992* (Washington, D.C.: Congressional Quarterly, 1992).

**FIGURE 6-2
Volume of Incoming
Mail to Congress**

Source: Ornstein et al., 1992, Table 6-9.

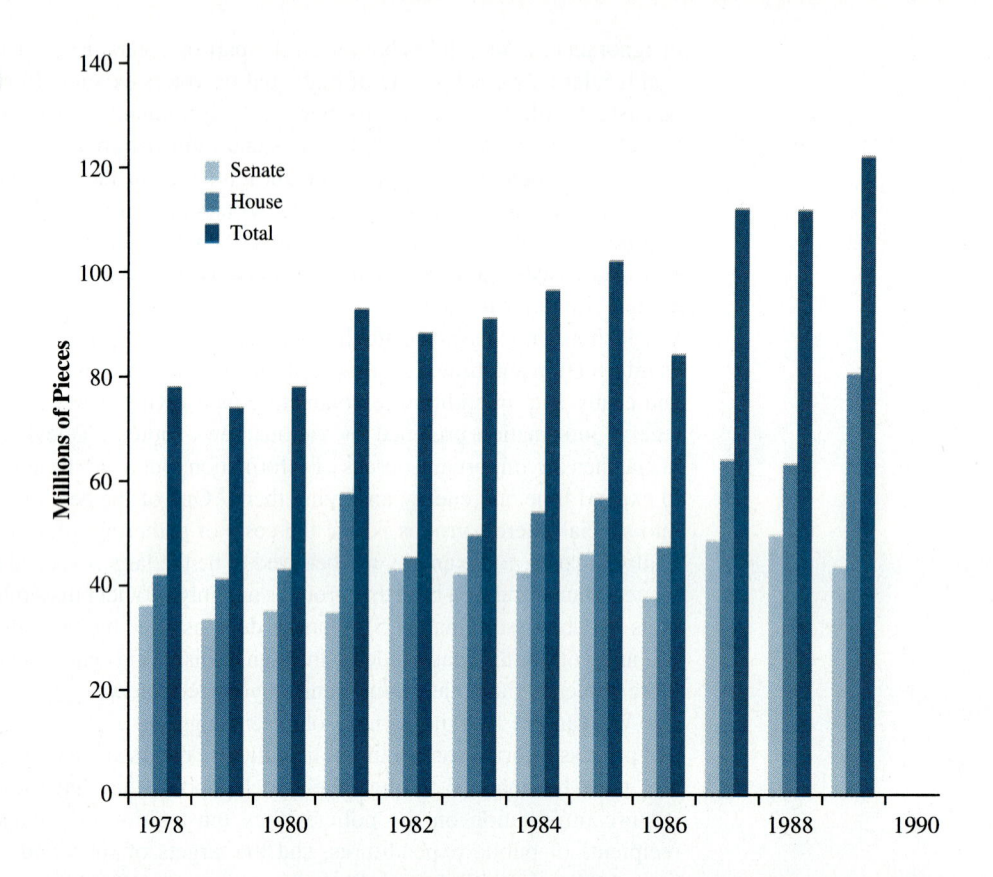

the actions of their legislators. In 1979, the U.S. House of Representatives approved live broadcasts of their proceedings, and, in 1986, the U.S. Senate followed suit.[10]

Many factors, however, diminish the incentives of voters to acquire and process information on public policies. The fact that the number and size of programs have been increasing suggests that the costs of acquiring good information on policy are growing. The sheer size of the federal budget document may be enough to overwhelm many voters and discourage them from using their valuable time and energy to make sense of federal policies. For example, the *Budget of the United States Government, Fiscal Year 1993* contains more than 1,700 pages, weighs over five pounds, and costs $43.00. This is clearly considerably more than bedside reading for the average voter. Similarly daunting are the costs of reading about state and local government policies, perusing pages and pages of government documents, and listening to a multitude of

---

[10] See W. Mark Crain and Brian L. Goff, *Televised Legislatures: Political Information Technology and Public Choice* (Norwell, Mass.: Kluwer Academic Publishers, 1988) for a discussion of the history and influence that televised legislatures had on policy information and policy outcomes. B. H. Abrams, and R. F. Settle, "The Effects of Broadcasting on Political Campaign Spending: An Empirical Investigation," *Journal of Political Economy* 84 (October 1976): 1095–1108 argue that television has lowered the advertising costs borne by presidential candidates.

politicians' speeches. Consider, for example, the *Federal Register*—the federal document that reports all the testimonies before federal regulatory agencies as well as any resulting new laws. The number of pages in this publication has increased more than 20-fold since its first issue in 1936. Moreover, since 1954 the number of Congressional mailings to *constituents*—the voters represented by policymakers—has increased 13-fold.[11] In 1989, for instance, constituents received 598.6 million pieces of mail.

Voters may also be interested in consuming the normative analysis of various commentators and may therefore subscribe to magazines because of the well-known ideological biases of the editors. Some magazines, for instance, are known to present either so-called liberal or conservative viewpoints. Various politically interested organizations also publish their ratings of policymakers and thus provide voters with additional sources of information related to alternative normative viewpoints of policymaking performance of every member of the U.S. Congress.[12]

Given the sheer size and great variety of the information available, it is clearly rational for voters to remain imperfectly informed—that is, ignorant.

Are Voters Well Informed?

Even though it is rational for voters to not be fully informed, it is useful to ask whether voters are well informed. This is not an easy question to answer, since it implies that we know what voters really care about and that we have a means of assessing the quality of their information. It has been shown that most Americans use television as their principal source of policy information. But it has been argued that television news coverage has several weak spots.[13] Because this visual medium tends to emphasize news as crises, the more mundane, but possibly more permanent and important, events are often overlooked.

It has also been argued that elections with several competing political parties may produce political candidates who are quite uniform in their policy views.[14] Moreover, television, it has been claimed, has made it increasingly difficult for political candidates to fool voters with lavish promises that they have neither the intention nor the ability to keep. The greater scrutiny placed on political candidates by technological advances in news reporting and analysis may eventually result in fewer of these pledges. If so, limits on what candidates may promise voters would necessarily lead to even greater uniformity in campaign promises and thereupon to less voter interest in the outcomes of elections with several candidates, none of which differs significantly from the others. With relative uniformity of candidates, it may make less of a

---

[11] From Table 6-8, Ornstein, Mann, and Malbin, *Vital Statistics on Congress, 1991–1992*. There is a noticeable increase in mailings in years in which a presidential election takes place.

[12] For example, Ornstein, Mann, and Malbin list the ACU (American Conservative Union) and ADA (Americans for Democratic Action) ratings of all members of the U.S. Congress. For a discussion of the political biases in the news media, see Anthony Smith, "Mass Communications."

[13] M. Margaret Conway, *Political Participation in the United States* (Washington, D.C.: Congressional Quarterly Press, 1985).

[14] See Anthony Smith, "Mass Communications," for a discussion of the argument that television reporting has led to reduction in the differences of competing political parties. Much of the material in this paragraph follows from this article.

difference to the average voter which politician is elected than in the case where there are few competitors, and the views of the candidates are quite dissimilar.

The nature of the controversies over the relative importance of policy intentions versus policy results suggests that it may be impossible for outside observers to know fully which issues should be of concern to individual voters. The phrasing of the question "Are voters well informed?" also implies that it is possible for voters to be uninformed about issues of which they do not realize they should be aware. This understanding requires the normative analysis of outsiders who believe they know which issues individual voters should care about. Such an outside observer would recognize that uniformed voters are subject to *irrational ignorance*. Many complexities exist as to the kinds of information that voters should have. For the time being, the reader should be aware of what assumptions about voter behavior underlie such questions as "Are voters well informed?"

Voting Participation

Figure 6-3 shows the participation rates of voters in elections of U.S. representatives from 1932.[15] The zigzag of voting behavior reflects the fact that in the United States, Presidential elections have higher voter turnouts than elections that do not include a choice for President on the ballot. For example, in the 1992 election year, 55.2 percent of the voting age population cast votes for the U.S. Presidential electors.[16] That same year, 50.9 percent of registered voters cast ballots for their representatives in Congress. In the non-Presidential election year of 1986, only 33.1 percent of the voters cast ballots for their elected representatives. Figure 6-4 shows the participation rates of voters in Presidential elections.[17]

Institutional Factors

Voting is a primary means for citizens to participate in the political process, and various institutional factors affect this form of political participation. The institutional framework of the voting process is an important determinant of voting behavior, since rules specify eligibility and in general define the abilities of citizens to participate in the policy process.

When property ownership, for instance, was a requirement for voting, those who did not own property were not allowed to vote.[18] This is an institutional factor, not a behavioral one, since it is an outside requirement, or rule, that determines who is eligible to vote. Even if citizens who did not own property wished to vote, institutional factors prevented their voting. Another institutional factor is the 19th Amendment to the U.S. Constitution, passed in 1920, which gives women the right to vote. This is institutional in nature since until 1920 all women were denied voting privileges, and this institutional factor was therefore one of many rules that determined the role

---

[15] Data are from *Statistical Abstract of the United States,* 1993.

[16] *Statistical Abstract of the United States,* 1993.

[17] *Statistical Abstract of the United States,* 1993.

[18] See Conway, *Political Participation in the United States,* 84. Before the American Revolution, individuals had to be members of the businesses that ran the colonies, therefore property ownership (in business) was a prerequisite for voting in local elections.

FIGURE 6-3
Voter Participation Rates in Elections of U.S. Representatives

Source: Statistical Abstract of the United States, 1993.

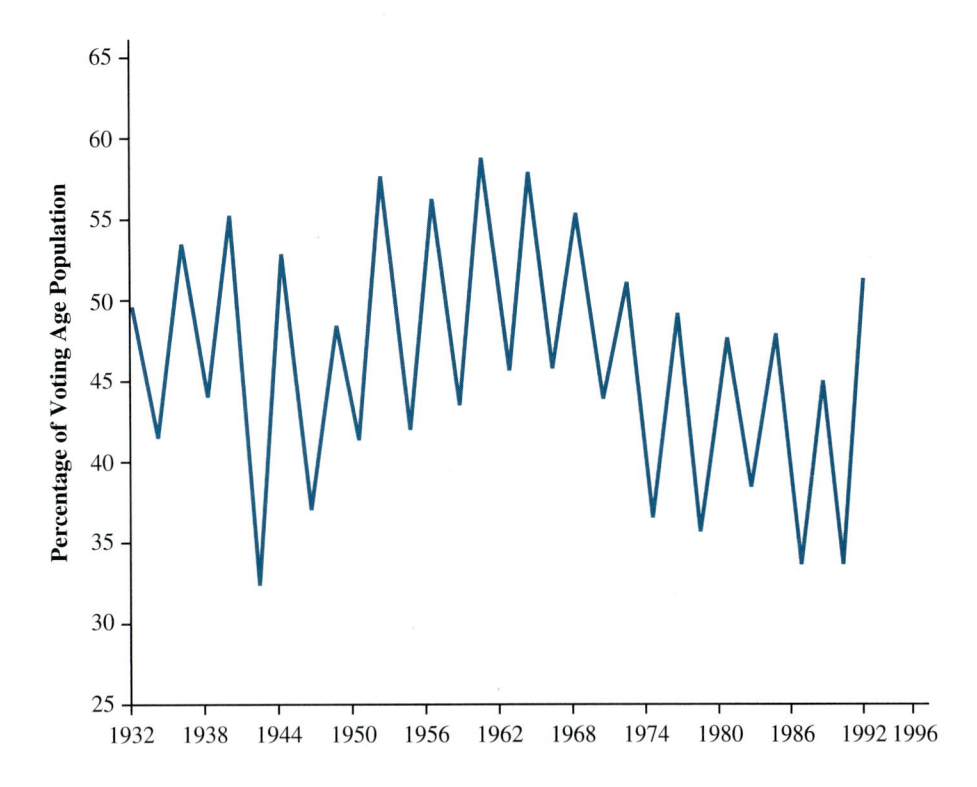

FIGURE 6-4
Voter Participation Rates in the Elections of U.S. Presidents

Source: Statistical Abstract of the United States, 1993.

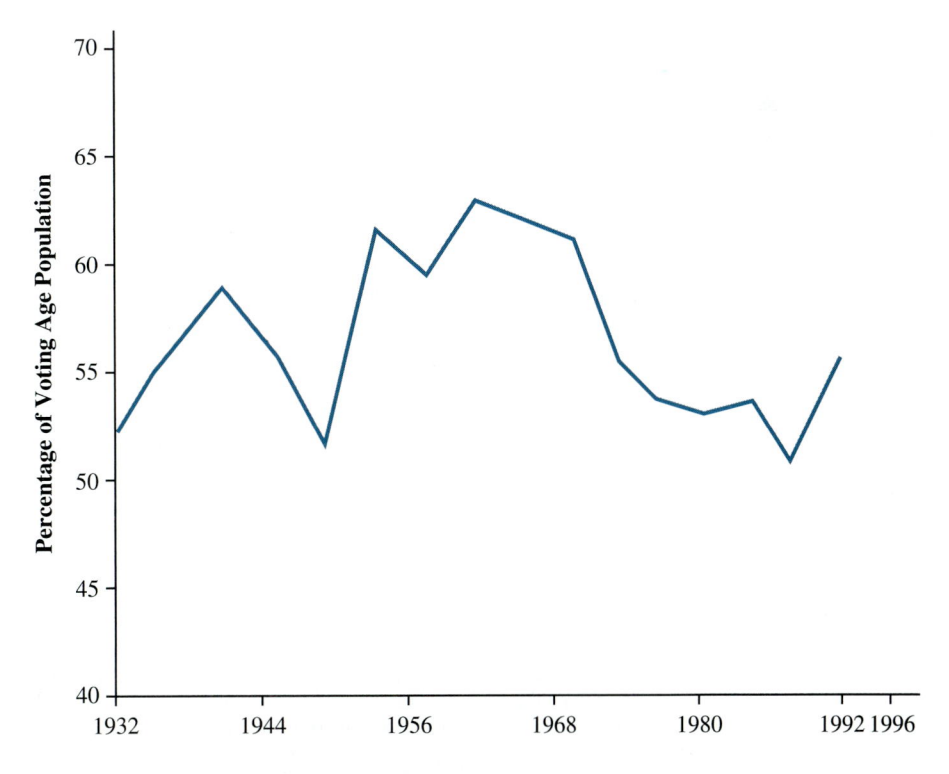

citizens could play in the policy process. Passage of civil rights laws also changed the institutional nature of voting and increased the numbers of U.S. citizens who are eligible to vote.

Registration requirements are also important institutional factors. While the governments of many other countries are heavily engaged in registering citizens and standardizing the requirements for voting at all levels of government (local, provincial, and national), governments in the United States are not as active in registering their citizens or ensuring that requirements are uniform across the various jurisdictions. Different political jurisdictions have different registration requirements and rules with respect to such items as absentee voting and residency requirements, and it appears that these institutional factors exert significant influences on voting participation.[19]

Behavioral Factors

Many behavioral factors explain how often—as well as how—individuals vote. Economists argue that voting behavior is a function of individual benefit-cost calculations.[20] There is some evidence, for instance, that suggests that the closer the race, the higher the likelihood of voting.[21] One plausible explanation for this result is that the closer the race, the greater the likelihood that an individual's vote, at the margin, can influence the outcome of the political contest. In this sense, close political races may be characterized by higher benefits to voting as opposed to the case in which the race is perceived to be lopsided. Other studies suggest that the lower the costs of acquiring information on political contests, the greater is voting participation.[22]

Other factors that may affect benefit-cost calculations of individuals are their wealth and tax brackets, since these may indicate one dimension of a voter's personal financial stake in a political contest. Political contributions are one means of political participation and, as such, should also be related to the factors that influence voting. A recent study finds that political contributions of individuals are related to their wealth, age, and income tax rates.[23] Voting and contributing to political candidates are similar activities since, in both cases, the costs are related to time and informational costs. In the case of voting, one must learn of the upcoming election, be registered, and go to the poll. In the case of contributing to candidates, one must take the time to learn about the laws regulating political contributions, pick a candidate(s), fill in the appropriate form(s), and mail the check(s). The odds of making political contributions are found to rise with age, net worth, and the tax bracket of individuals. These results

---

[19] See Conway, *Political Participation in the United States,* 100.

[20] See William H. Riker and Peter C. Ordeshook, "A Theory of the Calculus of Voting," *American Political Science Review* (1968); and George J. Stigler, "The Theory of Economic Regulation," *Bell Journal of Economics and Management Science* 2 (1971): 3–21.

[21] Ibid.

[22] Robert D. Tollison, W. Mark Crain, and Paul A. Paulter, "Information and Voting: An Empirical Note," *Public Choice* 24 (1975): 43–49.

[23] David Joulfaian and Michael L. Marlow, "Incentives and Political Contributions," *Public Choice* 69 (1991): 351–355. As their measure of contributions, they use data on usage of the dollar-for-dollar tax credit that, prior to the Tax Reform Act of 1986, taxpayers could designate to political candidates and political organizations. Prior to 1987, the U.S. individual income tax laws allowed dollar-for-dollar tax credits for contributions up to $100 for joint filers and $50 for single filers. Since the price is effectively zero, the decision regarding usage of tax credits is similar to the decision regarding voting.

suggest that some individuals not only vote their pocketbooks at the polls but also contribute to politicians accordingly.

The calculations of benefits and costs to voting include such general factors as

- the state of the economy
- whether the election takes place in a time of war or peace
- whether the election day has nice or foul weather
- various socioeconomic characteristics of citizens

A great deal of research exists on the influence of the last factor—socioeconomic characteristics—on the voting behavior of citizens. As we have seen in the case of senior citizens, voting appears to increase with age.[24] Income appears to be a positive determinant of voter turnout.[25] Income also appears to positively influence the rate at which individuals work in political organizations and campaigns and correspond with policymakers.[26] While education and income are highly correlated, education also appears to exert an independent and positive influence on voter turnout and participation in related activities.

One survey indicates the following voter participation rates, by education, for the Presidential election of 1984: grade school (58 percent); high school (66.4 percent); and college (85.5 percent).[27] The following correlations between education and voter turnout have been suggested:[28]

- Education provides knowledge about how the policy process works and improves awareness of how policies affect the lives of citizens.
- Education places citizens under increased peer pressure to vote.
- Education fosters the skills required for participating in many policy-related activities, such as becoming a candidate for elective office and working for candidates and political parties.
- Education increases citizen interest in reading about policy issues in the mass media.

Certain occupations also appear to be more conducive to political activity than others. Farmers, for instance, tend to be relatively politically active.[29] Various studies also conclude that government employees tend to vote more often than the general voting

---

[24] Also see Raymond E. Wolfinger and Steven J. Rosentone, *Who Votes?* (New Haven, Conn.: Yale University Press, 1980).

[25] See Anthony Downs, *An Economic Theory of Democracy* (New York: Harper & Row, 1957); and Bruno Frey, "Why Do High Income People Participate More in Politics?" *Public Choice* 11 (Fall 1971): 101–105.

[26] Conway, *Political Participation in the United States.*

[27] From Conway, Table 2-1, *Political Participation in the United States,* 21. Conway reports that as a result of social pressures dictating that all Americans should vote, respondents in survey data have been found to overstate their participation by as much as 25 percent (p. 11).

[28] Conway, *Political Participation in the United States,* 20–22.

[29] See Michael Lewis-Beck, "Agrarian Political Behavior in the United States," *American Journal of Political Science* 21 (1977): 543–565. He argues that the wealth of farmers is more related to public policy than for most other occupations. For example, farmers receive many forms of government payments, subsidies, and trade agreements that exert a substantial influence on their well-being.

public.[30] Identification with a political party also appears to increase the probability that an individual citizen will vote.[31]

Is Voting Participation High or Low?

The United States

While answers to questions such as whether participation is high or low are seldomly clear-cut, we can place voting participation in the United States in perspective. One perspective is voting participation trends. Figure 6-3 and Figure 6-4 suggest that since the 1970s, voter participation in the United States has exhibited a downward trend. This trend may reflect a long-term decline in voting participation, but it is far from evident that this is true after we examine a longer time span. Between the entire 1932–92 time span, certain periods such as the early 1940s, were similar in low voter participation to the most recent voting years. It may be true, however, that the decline in the early 1940s was short-lived compared to that in 1960–92.

Other Countries

Another perspective compares the U.S. experience with voting participation rates of other countries. Table 6-1 lists the average voter turnout rates of various countries. What can explain these variations? A partial reason may be the intercountry institutional differences in the voting process. In some countries, such as Australia and Belgium, voting is compulsory. There are also intercountry differences in voter registration rules, abilities to mail in votes and vote by proxy, the number of elections, and the numbers of days in which voting booths are open. Other explanations for intercountry variations may include such behavioral factors as differences in income, education, national pride associated with voting, and demographics of the voting age population.

Comparison of the United States with Other Countries

It may be surprising that voters in the United States appear to be less interested in voting than voters in many other countries. But do the data in Table 6-1 indicate that voters in the United States are apathetic about the political process? Or, as an alternative hypothesis, are Americans more content with their political process than voters in other parts of the world? A problem of using data from other geographic areas and political jurisdictions is that it is difficult to test hypotheses that follow from alternative models of voting behavior. It is not necessarily true that higher voter turnouts reflect greater interest in participating in the policy process. Different countries are

---

[30] For evidence in the United States, see James T. Bennett and William P. Orzechowski, "The Voting Behavior of Bureaucrats: Some Empirical Evidence," *Public Choice* 41 (1983): 271–283; and Winston C. Bush and Arthur T. Denzau, "The Voting Behavior of Bureaucrats and Public Sector Growth," in *Budgets and Bureaucrats: The Sources of Government Growth,* ed. Thomas E. Borcherding (Durham, N.C.: Duke University Press, 1977). For evidence on parliamentary elections in the Netherlands, see Bert Jaarsma, Arthur Schram, and Frans Van Winden, "On the Voting Participation of Public Bureaucrats," *Public Choice* 48 (1986): 183–187.

[31] Paul R. Abramson and John H. Aldrich, "The Decline of Electoral Participation in America," *American Political Science Review* 76 (1982): 502–521.

TABLE 6-1
Voter Turnout Rates

Country	Average Turnout	Country	Average Turnout
Australia	95.4%	France	79.3
Netherlands	94.7	Finland	79.0
Austria	94.2	United Kingdom	76.9
Italy	92.6	Canada	76.4
Belgium	92.5	Ireland	74.7
New Zealand	90.4	Japan	73.1
West Germany	86.9	Switzerland	65.4
Sweden	84.9	India	58.7
Israel	81.4	United States	58.5
Norway	80.8		

Source: Table 10-5 in Ivor Crewe, "Electoral Participation," in *Democracy at the Polls: A Comparative Study of Competitive National Elections,* eds. David Butler, Howard R. Penniman, and Austin Ranney, 1981. See the original table for the time spans used for each country and various other issues of comparability between the countries.

not likely to have identical incentives for voters to engage in voting, and simple comparisons of rates of voting turnouts do not therefore offer an unambiguous test that explains differences in voting behavior across countries. And there are also many other ways in which citizens may participate in the policy process; therefore, comparison of voter participation differences is only one of many ways to measure citizen participation in the policy process. Examination of the differences in institutional and behavioral factors in greater detail is necessary before appropriate conclusions may be drawn from the differences in voter turnout rates among the countries displayed in Table 6-1.

Policymakers: Who Are They?

Policymakers and the Policy Process

Our model of the policy process in representative democracies shows that voters and special interest groups signal their preferences about public policies to policymakers:

Voters, Special interests ⇒ Policymakers ⇒ Public policy

The next step is to refine our model in the following way:

Voters, Special interests ⇒ Elected and nonelected policymakers ⇒ Public policy

Elected policymakers are chosen by voters for public office.

Nonelected policymakers are not elected by voters.

Elected policymakers are directly appointed by voters whereas **nonelected policymakers,** often known as civil servants, serve under elected policymakers in the various branches of government. Both are empowered to carry out policy, but it is too simplistic to argue that elected and nonelected policymakers possess identical powers. Thus a detailed examination of both types is essential to our study of the policy process.

Because of the wide diversity in state and local governments, our primary focus here is on the policymakers of the U.S. federal government. Briefly, however, the chief executives of state governments are called governors. There are 1,946 state senators and 5,466 state representatives.[32] In addition to elected policymakers, in 1988 there were 14,476,000 nonelected civilian employees of state and local governments.[33]

In this section we consider the following questions about the role of policymakers in the policy process:

❏ How many policymakers are there?

❏ Which institutional and behavioral factors motivate policymakers?

❏ Do behaviors of elected and nonelected policymakers differ?

Institutional Factors

Institutional factors define the ways in which governments are organized and therefore define the ways in which policymakers may influence the policy process. The Constitution of the United States, approved in 1787, divides the federal government into three branches: legislative, executive, and judicial. Table 6-2 contains a brief description of the organizational structure of the federal government. The **legislative branch** is run by Congress and contains subbranches such as the General Accounting Office, the Library of Congress, the Office of Technological Assessment, and the Congressional Budget Office. The primary task of Congress is to create a body of laws that govern citizens. The two houses of Congress are the Senate and the House of Representatives. Elected for six-year terms, the senators are elected, two from each state, for a total of 100. The House of Representatives has 435 members, who serve two-year terms. Other than minimum ages of thirty for the Senate and twenty-five for the House of Representatives, and various residency requirements, there are few institutional constraints on who may be a member of Congress. While term limits were not initially placed on members of Congress, the appropriateness of limitations has recently received attention, as it does from time to time.[34] In 1992, voters in fourteen states passed term limits on senators of two terms and, for representatives, from three to six terms.

The President, an elected policymaker who is prohibited from serving more than two four-year terms, presides over the **executive branch** of the U.S. government. The President is the chief executive of the U.S. government and oversees the Office of the Vice President (elected running mate of the President), the Cabinet (various departments such as State, Treasury, Defense, Agriculture), and several other offices, including the Office of Management and Budget, the Council of Economic Advisors, the National Security Council, and the Council on Environmental Quality.

*The **legislative branch** of government in the United States is Congress, which consists of the Senate and the House of Representatives.*

*The **executive branch** of government is headed by the President of the United States.*

---

[32] Numbers are approximate and are obtained from *Statistical Abstract of the United States,* 1993.

[33] Table A24, *Facts and Figures on Government Finance,* (Baltimore: Johns Hopkins Press, 1991).

[34] See, for example, James M. Perry, "Movement to Limit Lawmakers' Terms Revs Up and Heads toward Congress," *Wall Street Journal,* July 17, 1991, A10; James C. Miller, III, "Cut Federal Spending—Limit Congressional Terms," *Wall Street Journal,* August 19, 1991, A8; Robert J. Barro, "A Free Marketeer's Case against Term Limits," *Wall Street Journal,* December 24, 1991, A6.

TABLE 6-2
Federal Government Organization

THE CONSTITUTION

Legislative Branch	Executive Branch	Judicial Branch
Congress **Senate and House**	**President** **Vice President**	**Supreme Court**
General Accounting Office Congressional Budget Office Library of Congress Government Printing Office Architect of the Capitol Office of Technology Assessment	Office of Management and Budget Council of Economic Advisors National Security Council White House Office Council on Environmental Quality Office of Science and Technology **Executive Departments** Treasury / Health and Human Services State / Veterans' Affairs Defense / Labor Agriculture / Justice Commerce / Transportation Education / Interior Energy	Court of Appeals District Courts Tax Court Federal Judicial Center Court of Military Appeals Court of International Trade

---

The **judicial branch** of government is the system of courts headed by the Supreme Court.

The **judicial branch** is headed by the Supreme Court of the United States. The Supreme Court is the highest court in the country and, therefore, has jurisdiction over all other courts in the country. The chief justice and the eight associate justices oversee the Supreme Court. All justices are appointed for life terms by the president, subject to Senate approval. Subbranches of the judicial branch include the Court of Appeals, the District Courts, the Claims Court, and Tax Court.

Characteristics of Members of Congress

Experience

Table 6-3, which describes the prior occupations of members of Congress, shows that experience in the fields of business/banking, education, law, and public service/politics are the most common.

Reelection Rates

The rates at which incumbent members of Congress are reelected are shown in Table 6-4. Historical experience suggests that, especially in the House, incumbent members of Congress experience high rates of reelection. The composition of Congress has also become increasingly stable. For example, in the 83rd Congress (1953), the average

TABLE 6-3
Prior Occupations of Representatives and Senators[a]

Occupation	Representative	Senator
Acting/entertainer	2	0
Aeronautics	1	1
Agriculture	20	8
Business/banking	157	32
Clergy	2	1
Education	57	10
Engineering	7	0
Journalism	25	10
Labor leader	3	0
Law	183	61
Law enforcement	5	0
Medicine	5	0
Military	1	1
Professional sports	3	1
Public service/politics	61	5

[a]Some members are listed under several categories.

Source: Table 1-8 and Table 1-11 in Norman J. Ornstein, Thomas E. Mann, and Michael J. Malbin, *Vital Statistics on Congress, 1991–1992*. Data for 1991 (102nd Congress).

TABLE 6-4
Incumbent Reelection Rates

Year	Representatives	Senators
1964	86.6	84.8
1968	96.8	71.4
1972	93.6	74.1
1976	95.8	64.0
1980	90.7	55.2
1984	95.3	89.7
1988	98.3	85.2
1992	88.3	82.1

Source: Statistical Abstract of the United States, 1993. Years displayed are also Presidential election years.

number of years served by representatives and senators was 9.8 years and 8.5 years, respectively.[35] By the 102nd Congress (1991), the average number of years served increased to 12.4 years and 11.1 years, respectively.[36]

Employment

Growth in the staffs of the legislative and executive branches (nonelected) is shown in Table 6-5. There has been an approximate threefold increase in the numbers of nonelected policymakers in the legislative branch. The largest employer, the executive branch, grew more than sixfold since 1929, an increase that includes military employment as the largest component. The judicial branch, the second largest employer, grew from 2,040 in 1918 to 22,071 in 1990.[37]

Behavioral Factors

It is increasingly common for people to believe that politicians are self-interested, in the pejorative sense. However, we have defined self-interest in both narrow and broad contexts, and it is not therefore particularly useful or informative to debate the self-interest of policymakers. It is useful, however, to discuss the degree to which policymakers are narrowly or broadly self-interested.

Importance of Reelection

No matter how broadly we interpret self-interest, it is likely that reelection is the priority for most elected policymakers. Whether policymakers wish to pursue narrow or broad self-interests, they must remain in office if they are to contribute to the policy process. And within the long-term frameworks of policymaking, an important role requires reelection.

"Very Narrow" Self-Interests of Policymakers

In a very narrow definition of self-interest, policymakers are assumed to be interested in the "power, pay, and prestige" associated with policymaking.[38] Although elective policymakers receive pay far below that of high-ranking officers of large corporations, their salaries are much higher than those of most workers.[39] And many perquisites (nicknamed "perks") go along with these salaries. For example, members of Congress enjoy free travel, virtually unlimited free parking in the Washington, D.C., area, free medical prescriptions, subsidized dining at fourteen Senate and House restaurants, haircuts for $5, and their choice of wholesale-or-below prices on such

---

[35] Ornstein, Mann, and Malbin, *Vital Statistics on Congress, 1991–1992,* table 1-6 and table 1-7.
[36] Ornstein, Mann, and Malbin, *Vital Statistics on Congress, 1991–1992,* table 1-6 and table 1-7.
[37] *Facts and Figures on Government Finance,* table C65.
[38] This hypothesis is often associated with William A. Niskanen, Jr., *Bureaucracy and Representative Government* (Chicago: Aldine-Atherton, 1971).
[39] As of 1994, the president earned an annual salary of $200,000, and members of Congress earned $133,600.

TABLE 6-5
Employment in Legislative and Executive Branches

CONGRESSIONAL STAFF

	Personal Staff				Standing Committee Staff		
Year	House	Senate	Total	Year	House	Senate	Total
1957	2,441	1,115	3,556	1960	440	470	910
1967	4,055	1,749	5,804	1970	702	635	1,337
1977	6,942	3,554	10,496	1980	1,917	1,191	3,108
1987	7,515	4,075	11,590	1986	1,954	1,075	3,029

EXECUTIVE BRANCH

Year	Employees	Year	Employees
1929	847,000	1969	6,484,000
1939	3,312,000	1979	5,049,000
1949	3,684,000	1988	5,400,000
1959	5,010,000		

Source: The material on the Legislative Branch is from Table 431 in *Statistical Abstract of the United States,* 1990. The Executive Branch material is from Table A20 in Tax Foundation, *Facts and Figures on Government Finance,* 1991 Edition (Baltimore/London: The Johns Hopkins University Press, 1991).

items as silk neckties, crystal candlesticks, crystal champagne flutes, and fine leather goods at congressional stores.[40]

Narrowly self-interested policymakers are believed to seek power since it allows them to pursue policies that enhance their own selfish interests. One hypothesis is that policymakers—especially those in higher offices—are interested in using political office to increase their own wealth. While there are limits on the annual pay that policymakers may earn, policymaking experience is viewed as a long-term investment in future earning capabilities. Visibility, and the experience of being high-level policymakers, enhances their future employment prospects in the private sector. Many private firms view experience, high visibility, and long lists of personal contacts to be extremely useful assets. A more contentious argument has also been made that in return for votes and favors (such as employment at high salaries) policymakers promote policies that enhance the wealth of various individual voters and special interest groups.[41]

The prestige associated with being a highly visible member of society may also be a compelling reason that explains why some individuals desire to be policymakers. There can be little question that many policymakers, especially elected policymakers, enjoy the limelight and the social aspects of being closely involved with other

---

[40] "Perk City," *Time,* October 14, 1991, 18–20. For example, compared to the $174.99 price tag at a private camera store, the same camera at the congressional stores goes for $99.57.

[41] William M. Landes and Richard A. Posner, "The Independent Judiciary in an Interest-Group Perspective," *Journal of Law and Economics* 18 (December 1975): 875–901.

policymakers and with voters. Television coverage of policy events dominates many nightly news programs and policymakers are often awarded center stage in news reports. Prestige may be a primary reason that elected policymakers endure the constant pressure of being in the spotlight and an unremitting examination of all aspects of their private and public lives. High visibility has been known to bring policymakers both pleasure and pain, but the attendant scrutiny and the long hours of public service are reason enough for many of us never to consider running for office.

Narrow Self-Interests of Policymakers

The abilities of elected policymakers to pursue their very narrow self-interests are quite clearly a function of their abilities to remain in elective office. Elected policymakers may remain in office only with the continuing support of their constituencies.

Constituencies of Elected Policymakers

Individual voters and special interest groups make up the constituencies of policymakers. In terms of range of constituency, the President, who represents all voters, has the widest constituency and is followed, in descending order, by senators and then representatives. In this sense, a President has the broadest self-interest of any policymaker since election and reelection are determined by the largest segment of the voting population.[42] In other words, in order to gain and maintain political office, the President must appeal to the broadest segment of the voting population.

Each state has two senators, and their constituencies are therefore smaller than that of the President, but still larger than the constituencies of the representatives. With 435 representatives spread across the 50 states, each representative is awarded a fairly small constituency that is relatively well defined in comparison to those of senators and the President. Figure 6-5 demonstrates that the placement of representatives is quite elastic to shifts in the populations of voters over time. Consistent with rapid population growth in the West and South, those areas of the country have gained representation by the House of Representatives. On the other hand, because there are always two senators per state, population shifts do not alter the placement of senators in our country.

Because representatives generally serve fewer voters than do senators, there are some important distinctions between the constituencies of representatives and senators. The expression *being senatorial* suggests that senators may spend more of their time and energies on broad issues of interest to their state, or for the nation, than on servicing individual voters and small interest groups within their state. Consider, for instance, a policy that widens a road in Pennsylvania, and for simplicity, assume that no one objects to building the road on the basis of such issues as its impact on the environment or local development. The voters who benefit the most are those who use the road and thus necessarily include those in the district of one representative and, to some degree, those in surrounding districts governed by other representatives. Reflecting the majority of interests in a narrow political district such as that of a representative, the number of voters that benefit from this policy may not constitute a majority of voters in the state. It is more likely then, that the group of voters who

---

[42] Technically, the Electoral College, a body of electors chosen in the popular election, chooses the President and Vice President.

**FIGURE 6-5
Apportionment of
Congressional Seats,
1910 and 1990**

Source: Ornstein et al., 1982.

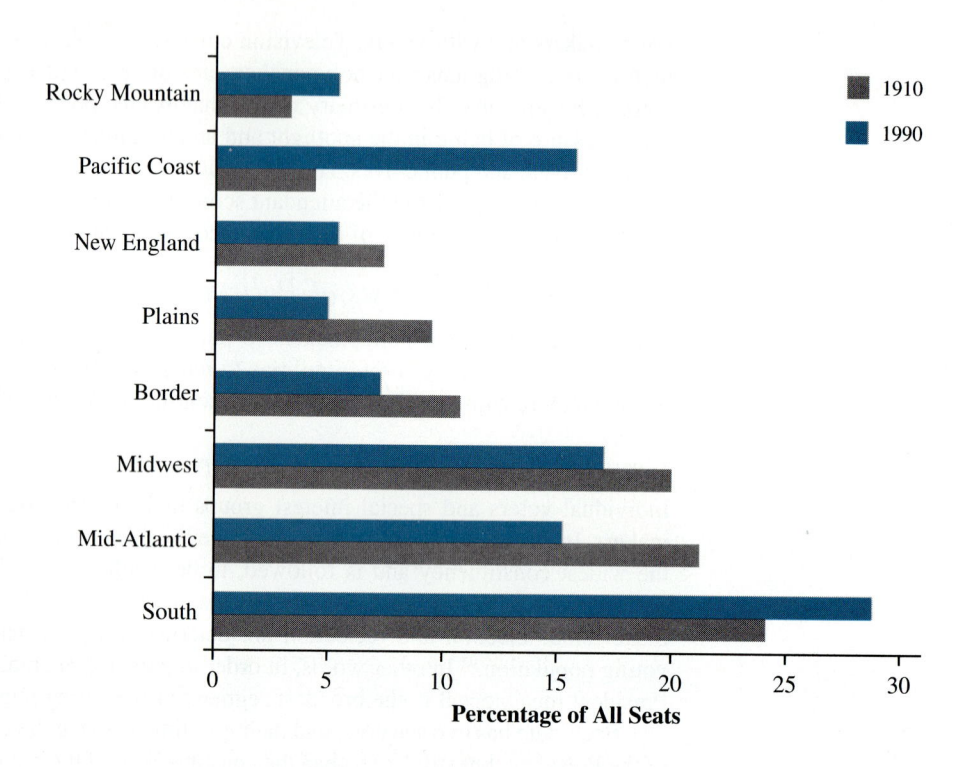

would benefit from the road will be able to persuade their local representative that the public sector should provide the road than it would be to persuade either of their senators or the President.

A final point about constituencies is that it is not necessary to define them simply in terms of the voters in each policymaker's political district. To the extent that individual voters and special interest groups are concerned with the well-being of foreigners, for example, Presidents may include foreigners within the range of individuals included within their broad self-interests. Similarly, certain senators and representatives are known for their supportive views and efforts in various policy issues that know no geographic boundaries. Policies affecting such national or international issues as poverty, education, and health care are frequently advocated by senators and representatives. And even though the benefits from those policies do not entirely flow to the voters in their political districts, they are interested in providing those benefits through the public sector.

Credit Claiming and Position Taking

David R. Mayhew and Morris P. Fiorina argue that "credit claiming" and "position taking" describe the narrowly self-interested behaviors of members of Congress.[43]

---

[43] David R. Mayhew, *Congress: The Electoral Connection* (New Haven, Conn.: Yale University Press, 1974); and Morris P. Fiorina, *Congress: Keystone of Washington,* 2d ed. (New Haven, Conn.: Yale University Press, 1989).

Credit claiming
is declaring responsibility for a successful public policy.

Credit claiming is an attempt to make voters believe that the efforts of their elective representatives are the sole reasons behind any good fortune that comes their way. A relevant hypothesis concerning credit claiming would be that members of Congress will claim responsibility for inflation, interest rates, and unemployment when these economic variables are falling, but will blame their opponents or other factors when these economic variables are rising.

Position taking
is declaring a particular position on a policy issue.

Position taking is the making of a public policy proclamation about an issue of great emotional concern to voters. Policymakers may make speeches denouncing drug dealers but at the same time offer no new policy on the problem. Morris P. Fiorina goes a step further toward description of narrow self-interest by suggesting that Congress may exploit the bad service associated with programs they have legislated.[44] For example, members of Congress may promise to reform the waste in government bureaucracy that they themselves have helped create. Speaking of an extremely narrow form of self-interest, Fiorina argues that members of Congress may have an incentive to promote waste and abuse in government in order to ensure a job for themselves when voters seek policymakers who promise to clean up waste and abuse in government.

Broad Self-Interests of Policymakers

A popular argument is that, while there is no lack of narrow self-interest in government, policymakers pursue the "public interest."[45] This view sees policymakers as mostly interested in making "good" policy; at times, this may require that policymakers rise above their own narrow self-interests and those of their constituencies. To support this view, proponents argue that growth of income redistribution programs for the poor and the creation of safety and health legislation are important cases in which policymakers serve the whole public interest. Steven Kelman has gone so far as to argue that the mere discussion of the narrow self-interest view of policymakers serves to "weaken" the policy process by making narrow self-interest a self-fulfilling prophecy.[46] One policy prescription that follows from this argument is that policymakers should set good examples, thereby providing a means through which the policy process molds the characters of individuals and makes them better citizens.

Ideal versus Actual Behaviors of Policymakers

At first glance, it appears that the public interest model of behavior is quite different from the model of self-interest. However, the broad definition of self-interest and public interest are similar in that, under both behavioral hypotheses, policymakers are concerned about the interests of many citizens. A major departure between the two views, however, is that the public interest view is primarily normative in nature.[47] By

---

[44] This is not to say that Fiorina is arguing that all policy is "bad" or that all members of Congress attempt to create ineffectual government programs. For example, see pp. 107–110, "Clarification 5: Congress Sometimes Adopts 'Good' Policies," in Fiorina, *Congress: Keystone of Washington*, 2d ed.

[45] Steven Kelman, *Making Public Policy: A Hopeful View of American Government* (New York: Basic Books, 1987); and Steven Kelman, " 'Public Choice' and Public Spirit," *The Public Interest* 87 (1987): 80–94.

[46] Kelman, " 'Public Choice' and Public Spirit."

[47] See Fiorina, 104–107.

When Promises and Votes Diverge

On his first day in office, a congressman from a conservative state asked a senior colleague from his home state how he managed to keep being reelected with his liberal voting record. Another congressman immediately explained: "It's easy. Vote liberal. Press release conservative."

Does this anecdote accurately describe policymakers? Do they promise one thing and deliver another? Yes, according to some members of Congress who have attempted to eliminate the secrecy on discharge petitions. There are many intricacies behind House procedures for discharging bills before House committees. One procedure allows members of Congress to claim that they are in support of a policy and, at the same time, refuse to discharge the policy for a vote. In this way, they can claim that they support policies favored by their constituents but be instrumental in blocking them from ultimate approval or rejection in the voting process. Only final votes on policies that are discharged by members become public information. While members may claim they would vote for policies if they were ever put up to vote, some have, in fact, voted against them by rejecting their discharge into the formal voting process.

Source: "Real House Reform," *Wall Street Journal,* October 30, 1993, A18.

Analysis

If one argues that policymakers should be fully accountable and up front with voters, there is little basis for retaining secrecy in discharge petitions. As the *Washington Post* argues, "in a democracy, where elected officials have an obligation to be candid and accountable, there is no reasonable argument against this change." That 384 members voted in favor of eliminating secrecy suggests that there is substantial support in Congress for this view as well.

But are there valid reasons that forty members of Congress voted *against* ending secrecy in discharge petitions? One congressman, John Dingell, argues that this reform would undermine the power of congressional committees. Another view, expressed by House Rules Committee Chairman Joe Moakley, is that secrecy is essential because voters are "virtually impossible to engage in reasonable and thoughtful debate."

The debate on this issue clearly demonstrates opposing views on the quantity and nature of information that policymakers should provide to voters. Those who believe that policymakers should provide clear information on their actions tend to support elimination of secrecy in discharge petitions. Those who believe that policymakers serve the public interest best when they operate under the cloak of secrecy tend to support its retention. Supporters of paternalism in policymaking, who argue that voters are sometimes incapable of knowing what is best for themselves, also tend to support retention of secrecy, though voters may be frustrated and insulted at the same time.

arguing that the policy process should be a means by which policymakers take on a benign, paternalistic role and mold the characters of citizens is to imply that various citizens *need* molding. But this requires value judgments and can be true only if consensus exists on the values that should be promoted. And consensus is unlikely when normative judgments are required.

Power and Self-Interest

It is common for proponents of the self-interest view of policymakers to argue that the desire of policymakers for power supports the hypothesis that behavior is ruled by little else than narrow self-interest. The simple model of the policy process indicates that individual and groups of voters must empower their policymakers with authority in order to make policy. It is not therefore particularly revealing, nor even disparaging, to argue that policymakers are somehow ruled by a desire to wield power over voters. As Milton and Rose Friedman have argued, all policymakers—those ruled by narrow self-interests and those ruled by broad self-interests—have an incentive to expand their power.[48] In the case of a policymaker who wishes to pursue improvements in the well-being of constituents, power is the necessary means by which improvements can be accomplished.

Ideology and Self-Interest

When policymakers vote for legislation consistent with their ideology, an argument can be made that policymaking is not characterized by narrow self-interests. Several studies have found ideology to be an important influence on the way in which members of Congress vote.[49] However, Sam Peltzman maintains that such studies do not necessarily provide support for the public interest hypothesis. In his view, when connections between voting and ideology are determined, ideology may be closely connected to the interests of constituents.[50] The costs of voting against the interest of constituents are found to rise with the relative wealth of constituents; therefore, despite ideologies of policymakers or constituents, the higher the wealth of constituents, the more costly it is for policymakers to promote policies that redistribute wealth away from their constituents.

Constraints on Self-Interests

In the final analysis, two factors influence the degree to which policymakers are narrowly self-interested. One factor is the narrowness or broadness of the self-interests of their constituents. Because voters and special interest groups empower policymakers to provide public policies, the policies promoted by policymakers will in large part be a product of the signals sent by their constituents. Responsive policymakers, then, provide policies that voters and special interest groups desire. The other factor is the degree to which policymakers may override the desires of constituents and provide policies that they themselves desire. In this case, policies are influenced by the narrowness or broadness of the self-interests of policymakers. This second factor also suggests the importance of understanding the institutional nature of the policy

---

[48] Milton Friedman and Rose Friedman, *Tyranny of the Status Quo* (New York: Harcourt Brace Jovanovich, 1983).

[49] See James Kau and Paul Rubin, "Self-Interest, Ideology and Logrolling in Congressional Voting," *Journal of Law and Economics* 22 (October 1979): 365–384; and Joseph Kalt and Mark Zupan, "Capture and Ideology in the Economic Theory of Politics," *American Economic Review* 74 (June 1984): 279–300.

[50] Sam Peltzman, "An Economic Interpretation of the History of Congressional Voting in the Twentieth Century," *American Economic Review* 75 (September 1985): 656–675.

process, since the ability to override the desires of constituents is influenced by the rules defining the process of exchange between voters and policymakers.

Nonelected Policymakers

A major difference between elected and nonelected policymakers is, of course, that only the former must endure the trials of election and reelection. Most nonelected employees of the executive branch have great permanency and stability in their employment. (Before the Civil Service system was created, a system commonly referred to as *political patronage* dominated the employment opportunities of employees of the executive and judicial branches. Under this system, most civil servants were directly appointed by elected policymakers.) Even though the Civil Service system gives a high degree of permanency to the nonelected employees of the executive branch, they are not necessarily unresponsive to elected policymakers or voters.

In contrast to the other two branches of the federal government, the staffs of members of Congress do not enjoy as much permanency in their positions. However, under regulations similar to those of the Civil Service system, the employees of the various agencies of Congress, such as the Library of Congress or the Congressional Budget Office, do enjoy permanency. Staffs of members of Congress are not guaranteed permanency; rather, their continued employment is a function of remaining productive staff members and working for members of Congress who win reelection. As Table 6-4 demonstrates, members of Congress tend to remain in office—this stability is undoubtedly due, in part, to productive efforts of their staff.

Constituencies of Nonelected Policymakers

Both elected and nonelected policymakers may participate in providing policies that benefit voters. Civil servants at the U.S. Department of Health and Human Services (HHS), for instance, may conduct research on improving the nutrition for the poor. The chairperson of the Federal Reserve System is nominated by the President, subject to Senate approval, and is considered to be one of the most important economic officials in the country. These policymakers are nonelected.

Those policymakers such as staffs of members of Congress who are not guaranteed much permanency in employment see that their self-interests are linked to the reelection of their senator or congressperson. To the extent that employment stability is a motivating factor, staff members have an incentive to work toward the reelection of whomever they serve. Civil servants, who are guaranteed greater permanency, may also desire that the elected policymakers under whom they serve be reelected, but reelection is not so directly tied to their employment. In the executive branch, for example, it is not uncommon for civil servants to have voted for losing candidates.

The separation between the interests of the reigning political party and the employees who serve under elective policymakers is a direct outcome of the removal of the political patronage system. To the extent that civil servants are in agreement with the goals of the elected policymakers, the constituencies of elected policymakers become the constituencies of civil servants, but civil servants' own narrow self-interests and various characteristics of their employment make an interesting study, to come later.

With policymakers, elected or nonelected, there is an intriguing hypothesis that the greater the degree to which policymakers are not elected, the more difficult it is for voters to influence policy. This is clearly a contentious hypothesis, characterized by several important assumptions about the behaviors of nonelected policymakers. It is important to realize that the proportion of policymakers who are nonelected is a potentially important factor that influences the role of voters and policymakers in the policy process.

Institutional Differences between Public Markets

Representative democracy is characterized by institutions that provide citizens with the ability to influence public policy through election of policymakers. We have seen, in comparisons of sizes of public sectors in the OECD countries, many differences. In countries such as Denmark and Sweden, public sectors allocate relatively many economic resources, and in other countries, such as the United States and Japan, public sectors allocate relatively few economic resources. But this comparison is not the only way to compare the policy processes of countries.

The institutional structure of policy processes varies across countries, and if we are to understand the public exchanges that take place in representative democracies, we must understand the roles of voters and policymakers in the policy process. Gerald W. Scully and Daniel J. Slottje recently studied the "economic liberty" characteristics of 144 countries.[51] By examining and comparing these characteristics, an analyst may determine the less visible ways in which institutional characteristics of the policy process influence the allocation of resources in various economies. Differences between the economic liberty characteristics of countries mirror important differences in the amount of influence individual citizens and voters may exert in public markets. The following are a few of the attributes that Scully and Slottje considered to be related to individual economic liberty:

- freedom to own property
- freedom of movement
- freedom of information
- freedom of the print media
- freedom from search without a warrant
- freedom of peaceful assembly

Table 6-6 contains a partial list of the 144 countries measured in terms of the Scully-Slottje index.[52] Changes have certainly occurred since the time of the study, as in the case of the breakdown of the former Soviet Union, but this listing suggests that vast differences exist in the degree to which voters and citizens influence the policies of their public sectors. Of the 144 countries studied, Ireland and Luxembourg were determined to be the most free and the former U.S.S.R. and Angola the least free. This ranking structure is far from perfect, but it does allow us to place a large number of

---

[51] Gerald W. Scully, and Daniel J. Slottje, "Ranking Economic Liberty across Countries," *Public Choice* 69 (1991): 121–152.

[52] The average of eight indexes discussed in Scully and Slottje is used for the ranking in Table 6-6.

TABLE 6-6
Countries Ranked according to Liberty Characteristics

Countries with Most Liberty	Countries with Least Liberty
1. Ireland	144. Soviet Union
2. Luxembourg	143. Angola
3. Liechtenstein	142. Albania
4. United States	141. Mongolia
5. Belgium	140. Bulgaria
6. Canada	139. North Korea
7. Switzerland	138. Laos
8. Hong Kong	137. Vietnam
9. Netherlands	136. Mozambique
10. Barbados	135. Seychelle and Somalia
11. Federal Republic of Germany	134. Zaire
12. Austria	133. Romania
13. Bahamas	132. Mauritania
14. Australia	131. Ethiopia
15. Costa Rica	130. Burma

Source: Gerald W. Scully, and Daniel J. Slottje, "Ranking Economic Liberty across Countries," *Public Choice* 69 (1991): 121–152.

countries in the perspective of the relative roles of voters and citizens in allocating resources in their public sectors.

Representative democracies are usually countries with the most liberty, and dictatorships are characterized by the least liberty. As a broad generalization with many unstated implications and assumptions, communist countries and African nations rank near the bottom and European countries near the top of the listing.

Correlation analysis by Scully and Slottje indicates a direct relationship between economic growth and economic liberty. That is, the greater the individual liberty and freedom in a country, the greater is that country's economic growth. Their results do not confirm or indicate a *causal* relationship between economic freedom and economic growth, but Scully and Slottje suggest that their results support the hypothesis that economic freedom is essential for economic development. In this sense, their analysis suggests the importance of public market structure for the standards of living enjoyed by citizens.

Summary

❏ Public choice analysis models those public market exchanges which take place between voters and policymakers in similar fashion to exchanges that take place between consumers and producers in private markets.

❏ Various behavioral assumptions regarding self-interest can be placed on the behaviors of voters and policymakers within the policy process. Narrow self-interest indicates behaviors driven by issues and concerns that affect only one individual.

Broad self-interest, in contrast, indicates a condition in which individuals are concerned with issues and policies that directly affect individuals other than themselves. Considerable controversy surrounds the attribution of motivations of voters and policymakers.

❏ Elected policymakers are directly appointed by voters, and nonelected policymakers, usually known as civil servants, serve under elected policymakers in the various branches of govenment. The three branches of federal government are the executive (President), the legislative (Congress), and the judicial (Supreme Court).

❏ The general institutional framework of the policy process is an extremely important influence on the policies of the public sector.

Review Questions

1. What is public choice?
2. What are behavioral assumptions?
3. What are the major forms of political participation?
4. What is the difference between narrow self-interest and broad self-interest?
5. What is the difference between policy intentions and policy results?
6. What is the institutional framework of the policy process?

Discussion Questions

1. Explain why it is important to examine the roles of both voters and policymakers in the policy process.
2. Discuss what is meant by self-interest in the policy process. Distinguish between narrow and broad definitions of self-interest.
3. What is meant by rational ignorance? Are you rationally ignorant about any policy issues? What might cause you to be more interested in gaining more information on these issues?
4. What is the institutional nature of the policy process?
5. What incentives are there for individuals to vote to elect policymakers? Provide three examples of institutional changes that might raise the incentives of individuals to vote in elections.
6. Provide two examples in which you believe that the distinction between policy intentions and policy results may be a useful distinction to make regarding policy issues.
7. Name three information sources that you use to form opinions about public policies. Is there any evidence of an ideological bias to the information that is provided by these sources?
8. Do you favor a policy that would make it easier for voters to register for voting? Do you believe that easier registration would increase voting participation? If so, how do you believe that this change would affect the outcomes of the policy process?
9. What changes do you believe would occur in the policy process if all elected policymakers were limited to one term in political office?
10. Who is your elected U.S. Representative? Discuss what constituency he/she serves and whether you believe that he/she serves the constituency well.

Key Words

Public choice
Behavioral assumptions
Political participation
Narrow self-interest
Broad self-interest
Rational ignorance
Elected policymakers
Nonelected policymakers
Legislative branch
Executive branch
Judicial branch
Credit claiming
Position taking

APPENDIX 6

Public Exchange under Dictatorships

Dictatorships, in which citizens generally have little capacity to influence policy outcomes, have always been the dominant form of government in the world.[1] According to Gordon Tullock, who specializes in such studies, roughly 80 percent of the world's governments are currently dictatorships, and the share of the world's population under this form of government has increased in recent years.[2] Despite the obvious differences between dictatorships and representative democracies, certain similarities between the two are apparent. Whatever the form of their government, Tullock argues, policymakers are always keenly interested in retaining their positions. In fact, unseating an incumbent politician through an election is analogous to overthrowing a dictator. Tullock recognizes three serious threats against the incumbency of dictators. In order of seriousness, these are (1) officials of the current regime, (2) foreign powers, and (3) popular uprisings. While foreign intervention has historically been the dominant reason for overthrows, Tullock maintains that such foreign interventions have not been prevalent in recent years. Popular uprisings, which are commonly perceived as major factors in felling dictatorial regimes, rarely succeed. Thus, although foreign intervention and popular uprisings send dictators important signals, it is the officials of the reigning regime that constitute the most serious threat and send the strongest signals.

Given that dictatorship is constrained, to some degree, by various threats, a simple model of the exchange process under a dictatorship is

$$\text{Officals} \Rightarrow \text{Dictator} \Rightarrow \text{Public policy}$$

At first glance, the exchange process is quite similar to the case of representative democracy. But important differences exist. One is the degree of influence that officials impose on dictators. It is not clear, for instance, that officials of dictatorial regimes exert the same level of influence as do voters over elected policymakers.

---

[1] Gordon Tullock, *Autocracy* (Dordrecht, The Netherlands: Martinus Nijhoff Publishers, 1987).

[2] Tullock uses the estimates provided in Robert A. Dahl, *Polyarchy Participation and Opposition* (New Haven, Conn.: Yale University Press, 1971). Tullock argues that dictatorships come in two varieties: kingdoms and empires. The main difference between the two types of dictatorship is that kingdoms tend to be hereditary.

Another difference lies in the broadness of influence imposed upon dictators. Tullock argues that "the basic advantage of a democracy is that those people who seek power must seek power by attempting to please a majority of the population. A dictatorship is ruled by people who seek power and must please other people, but the people who must be pleased are a much smaller group."[3] Whereas both representative democracies and dictatorships are systems of public exchange, the final policies that allocate economic resources tend to be quite different.

It would be useful to know whether there are substantial differences between the ways in which representative democracies and dictatorships allocate resources. Unfortunately, little empirical evidence has been assembled to answer this important question. For example, it is commonly believed that representative democracies provide a better standard of living for their citizens, but there is little empirical evidence on this issue. David N. Laband studied the relationship between political structure and economic performance (for example, higher living standards) in 123 countries.[4] One of his conclusions is that it is not clear which direction the relationship might take, since one possibility is that political structure is causally related to economic performance. But it may also be the case that better economic performance and conditions may lead citizens to exert greater pressure for representative forms of government. As usual, questions of causality pervade much of our theoretical and empirical investigations in economics. Another important question is what causes a country to move from dictatorship to representative democracy and vice versa?[5] Surprisingly, this question has received little study in public finance.

---

[3] Tullock, *Autocracy*, 12.

[4] See David N. Laband, "Is There a Relationship between Economic Conditions and Political Structure?" *Public Choice* 42 (1984): 25–37.

[5] See Dennis C. Mueller, *Public Choice II* (Cambridge, U.K.: Cambridge University Press, 1989), 271–273, for a discussion of this important issue.

CHAPTER 7

Voting Models and Public Market Structure

In this chapter we examine the ways in which voting rules and public market structure affect the roles of voters and policymakers in the policy process. Through this voting process, voters signal their demands for policies. Voting rules define the environment within which voters may direct public policies, and because simple majority voting is the most commonly used rule, it is the primary focus in a discussion of voting rules. While voters and policymakers exchange with one another in public markets, the structure of public markets may come in many varieties. Analogous to the treatment of market structure in microeconomic theory, public markets may be modeled as either competitive or monopolistic, and the structure of public markets will be shown to affect the relative powers of voters and policymakers to direct the exchanges that take place in the policy process.

A few issues examined in this chapter follow:

❏ Is it appropriate for voting rules to require unanimous consent?
❏ Is there an optimal rule of majority?
❏ Do voting rules necessarily achieve Pareto efficient exchanges?
❏ Do some public market structures award more power to voters than do others?
❏ Does public market structure influence the size of the public sector?

Unanimity Rules of Voting[1]

Characteristics

We have already explored mechanisms by which citizens would voluntarily agree to share consumption of public goods: Private markets produce many public goods, such as movie theaters, sporting events, and swimming pools. Private clubs are often

---

[1] We assume that votes are taken, one at a time, on separate issues.

Unanimity rules of voting
is a procedure that requires that all individuals must agree to policies before they are passed.

formed to share the costs of public goods among many members. **Unanimity rules of voting** in public markets are the natural analogue to voluntary agreements in the private sector. Under such rules, exchange requires that all voters agree to quantities and qualities of goods as well as prices, or tax shares, paid by individuals. When unanimous consent is required, the decision process is similar to that of private markets: Individuals are never forced to pay for goods that they do not desire, and agreements among all individuals are voluntary.

Lindahl pricing provides an obvious means by which this voting rule results in optimal provision of public goods (see Chapter 5). Optimal provision occurs where $\sum MB = MSC$ and, within the Lindahl framework, voters are assigned prices, or tax shares, according to their marginal benefit when optimal quantities of public goods are provided. Voluntary agreement is consistent with these prices because any other price combination is bound to be rejected by one or more individuals. Lindahl pricing therefore suggests a guide for the public sector that results in optimal quantities of public goods, Pareto efficient exchanges, and unanimous consent over resource allocation in public markets.

In practice, however, problems with implementation of the Lindahl framework indicate that unanimous consent is a cumbersome means to approve exchanges in the public sector. Informational costs are undoubtedly high when public goods must be priced so that each voter pays his or her marginal benefit at the optimal level of provision. Free rider problems may compound these costs when lack of exclusion causes some voters to underreport their marginal benefits in the hope of lowering tax shares. Free riding is therefore likely to result in underproduction of public goods when unanimous consent is the voting rule. Also, time and effort required for unanimous consent may result not only in a public sector that produces too few public goods, but one that may validate the status quo in much the same way as adherence to the Pareto efficiency criterion militates against policies that may improve the well-being of a large and diverse collection of individuals.[2]

Unanimous consent may also thwart application of tax policies aimed at promoting combinations of efficiency and equity criteria.[3] Although it may be efficient for public goods to be priced according to individual marginal benefits, equity considerations may require that tax policies be based on something other than individual marginal benefits. Unless all voters agree to the same equity criteria, unanimous consent among *all* voters is most unlikely to result if one or more voters believe that public policies, and concomitant tax burdens, should address various equity goals. Unanimous consent ensures rejection of all redistribution policies when at least one dissenter votes against policy.

---

[2] This point was made in Duncan Black, *The Theory of Committees and Elections* (Cambridge, U.K.: Cambridge University Press, 1958).

[3] It should also be remembered that it is only relevant to compare unanimity rules with Lindahl pricing when the public sector is providing public goods. However, because the public sector provides many private goods, there is no corresponding reason to believe that unanimous consent could ever occur when private goods are provided by the public sector. For the argument that publicly provided private goods may result in income redistribution, see James M. Buchanan, "Notes for Economic Theory of Socialism," *Public Choice* 81 (Spring 1970): 29–43. For a useful discussion of how redistribution occurs when private goods are publicly provided, see Dennis C. Mueller, *Public Choice II*, 60–62.

While there are many problems in applying rules of unanimity to collective decision making, there is, nonetheless, a distinct advantage with these rules. Those who believe that the policy process should provide only Pareto superior exchanges tend to advocate unanimity rules of voting because coercion of one or more dissenters reflects Pareto inferior exchange. Even though unanimity rules of voting produce only mutually beneficial and voluntary exchange, those who recommend against unanimous consent tend to emphasize the cumbersome nature of these rules, problems associated with free riders, and its possible glorification of the status quo—or they believe that dissenting individuals should be overruled when policies address the equity goals of society.

Majority Voting Rules

Majority rules of voting is a procedure that requires that a majority, simple or otherwise specified, must agree to policies before they are passed.

Simple majority rule is a procedure in which the greatest number of votes wins.

Debates over voting rules are not usually couched in terms of unanimity versus nonunanimity rules of voting. Rather, discussion focuses on **majority rules of voting,** which do not require unanimous consent. Majority rules turn on the definition of *majority.* For instance, a voting rule requiring that all policies be approved by 51 percent of the voters is a rule that defines the majority as a minimum of 51 percent and the minority as a maximum of 49 percent of the voting population. This is also called a **simple majority rule,** and it allows 51 percent of voters to approve policies that are not desired by 49 percent of the voting population. In contrast, unanimous consent requires 100 percent agreement for exchange and therefore defines the majority as all voters. Note also that as long as all individuals have the right to vote, there are no minorities under unanimous consent.

Optimal Majority Rules

Optimal majority rule is one that results in the minimization of the sum of decision and external costs.

James M. Buchanan and Gordon Tullock addressed the issue of optimal majority by assuming that an **optimal majority rule** is one that minimizes costs of collective agreements.[4] Even though Buchanan and Tullock argue that unanimity rules of voting are ideal, because they allow only Pareto superior exchanges, they recognize that decision-making costs in a large and diverse society make it difficult for exchanges to occur in public markets when unanimous consent is required.

Optimal decision rules for reaching collective agreements may be determined by inspection of Figure 7-1 which shows, for a particular policy issue, decision costs (D), external costs (E), and the sum of decision and external costs ($D + E$) associated with different majority rules. The horizontal axis measures the percentage of agreement that is required for passage of any policy considered by voters, and the vertical axis measures costs. The horizontal axis therefore defines the majority required for passage of any policy.

Decision costs occur when resources are expended to persuade voters to agree on proposals.

Decision costs are the costs of getting voters to agree on proposals. These costs should be very low when voting rules allow relatively few individuals the right to determine which policies are passed. It is easier to get one or two individuals to agree on policies that affect 100 individuals than it is to get unanimous agreement among

---

[4] James M. Buchanan and Gordon Tullock, *The Calculus of Consent* (Ann Arbor, Mich.: University of Michigan Press, 1962).

FIGURE 7-1
Model of the Optimal Majority

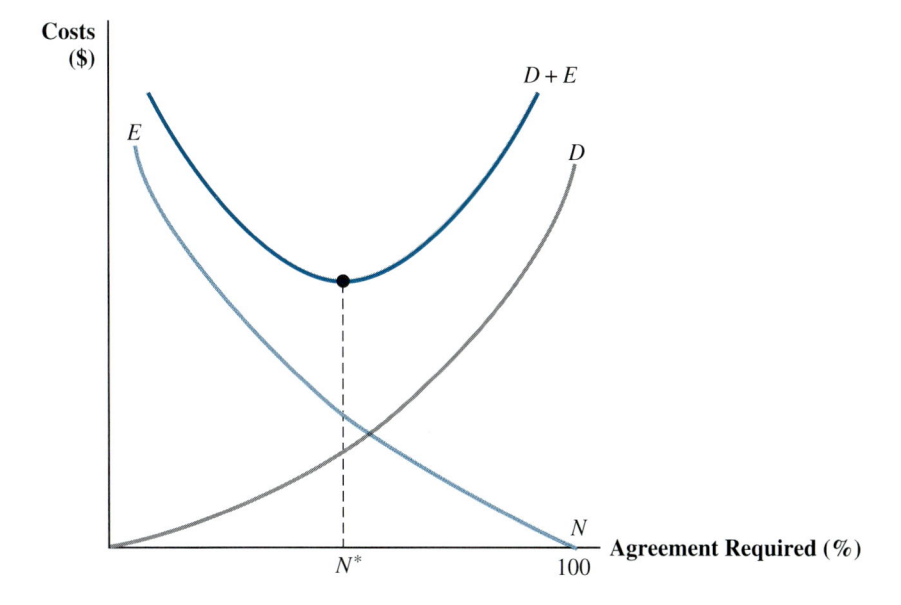

100 individuals. Thus we can see that the higher the percentage required for agreement, the higher are the costs of reaching agreement. Transactions costs of organizing larger numbers of individuals to discuss policy are also likely to rise as the voting rule approaches unanimity.[5] As the definition of majority rises, policies must be tailored to an increasing number of voters' preferences, and it is therefore likely that more trouble occurs as a larger definition of majority is used.

External costs are costs imposed by majorities upon minorities when approved policies impose negative externalities. With heterogeneous preferences, it is likely that the smaller the percentage required for agreement, the easier it is to pass Pareto inferior policies. When passage of policies requires the approval of only 2 percent of the voting population, it is more likely that approved policies will exert external costs than when passage requires approval from 98 percent. When 98 percent is required, external costs borne by the minority of 2 percent are also likely to be much smaller than when approval requires only 2 percent of the voting population. Accordingly, as the definition of majority rises, external costs imposed upon minorities tend to fall. When $E = 0$, that is, when external costs are zero, consent is unanimous, or $N = 100$. Lack of decision costs, therefore, implies that unanimous consent would be optimal.

Separate discussions of decision and external costs suggest the opposite implications for the optimal rule of majority. Because it is difficult to argue that voting rules should impose large negative externalities upon minorities, high external costs suggest that majorities should be relatively large, since the larger the majority requirement, the

External costs are those imposed by majorities on minorities.

---

[5] Two studies, however, suggest that strategic behavior may not cause decision costs to rise as voting rules approach unanimous consent. See Vernon Smith, "Experiments with a Decentralized Mechanism for Public Good Decisions," *American Economic Review* 70 (September 1980): 584–599; and Elizabeth Hoffman and M. L. Spitzer, "Experimental Tests of the Coase Theorem with Large Bargaining Groups," *Journal of Legal Studies* 15 (January 1986): 149–171.

lower the external costs. In contrast, if decision costs rise rapidly with size of majority, then relatively small majorities are required to limit decision costs. The optimal rule, however, is one that efficiently deals with the trade-off between decision and external costs.

Buchanan and Tullock argue that optimal majority is determined by minimizing the sum of decision and external costs. Consider, for example, D, E, and $D + E$ in Figure 7-1. Optimal majority occurs at N^*. Note that N^* does not coincide with a unanimity rule of voting, which occurs at N. Also remember that the curves in Figure 7-1 represent only one issue. Because it is reasonable to expect decision and external costs to vary with issues, it is also reasonable to expect a different optimal majority for each issue. Thus N^* will be different for every issue.

Optimal Majority in the Private Sector

Voting rules chosen by collections of individuals in the private sector demonstrate that rules that require less than unanimity do not always require coercion of the minority. When all members agree to a majority voting rule, the agreement itself is evidence that the majority voting rule is an efficient way of reaching mutually beneficial exchanges. Majority voting rules can be expected when public goods are produced in the private sector.

Consider, for example a private hunting club that has a party each year. The party requires that someone make decisions—or policies—on important issues, such as which day to hold the party and the relatively trivial questions, such as what colors and sizes napkins should be. Clearly, certain members would rather not be involved in picayune details, and it is therefore rational for them to refrain from participating in every decision. Delegation of authority to club officers, or committees, is a voting rule that requires less than unanimity, and committees are efficient means by which private production of public goods reduces the decision costs associated with collective agreements.

External costs are another factor that helps to explain why club members are interested in having a committee of more than one member that can make decisions for the club. It can be expected that external costs are much smaller for issues like the sizes and colors of napkins, for example, than for those relating to new membership requirements. Accordingly, the optimal majority for napkin questions is expected to be much smaller than the optimal majority for membership criteria.

There are strong incentives for private clubs to minimize the decision and external costs associated with collective agreements. If club members believe that, at the margin, benefits of membership exceed costs, they remain club members. Remember, however, that because voting rules define expected external costs, costs of club membership are influenced by the voting rules used by clubs. If rules impose high external costs on (minority) members, membership may fall in such a way that threatens the financial health of the club. Because clubs are formed in part to exploit cost savings from shared consumption, it is in the best interest of all club members to choose voting rules that minimize decision and external costs. The important point here is that in the private sector there is a natural tendency for providers of public goods to minimize the decision and external costs of collective agreement. Whether public goods are purchased separately by individuals or collectively in clubs, exchanges are voluntary.

Majority voting rules therefore do not imply that coercion plays a necessary role in exchange.

Simple Majority Voting Rules

Simple majority voting rules require that all policies be approved by at least one vote over one-half of all the votes. Consider, for example, the case of three homeowners, Antonio, Blanca, and Consuelo, who are deciding the width of a new bridge that connects their properties to a new highway. Antonio drives a small and narrow car, Blanca has a medium-size car, and Consuelo drives a large, wide, four-wheel-drive pickup truck. The costs are to be divided equally among all three homeowners, and each proposes the following widths: Antonio (narrow), Blanca (medium), and Consuelo (wide). Because each homeowner has a different idea about how wide the new bridge should be, all three decide to work out a compromise within the rule of simple majority.

Because all three want a bridge, a narrow bridge is *minimally* acceptable. When voting on whether to increase the width from narrow to medium, the vote is 2 to 1 in favor. When voting on whether to increase the width from medium to wide, the vote is 2 to 1 against, and the medium width therefore is the compromise solution.

Note that the median voter, Blanca, is the one whose preferences are agreed upon in the voting process. The *median voter* is the one who lies between an equal number of voters who prefer one extreme (a narrow bridge) and an equal number who prefer the opposite extreme (a wide bridge). The dominance of the median voter's preferences is so pervasive under simple majority rules that it is called the **median voter theorem** (or model): *Under certain conditions, the preferences of the median voter are selected under simple majority rule.* Note that this model is also applicable to a committee procedure in which three individuals act as representatives of a larger population of voters.[6] For instance, in the previous example of a hunting club, members could select a committee of two or more members who are empowered to make decisions regarding the annual party.[7]

Median voter theorem is the proposition that preferences of the median voter are chosen when several conditions, such as all preferences being single-peaked, are present.

Figure 7-2, which shows demands for bridge widths by Antonio (D_A), Blanca (D_B) and Consuelo (D_C), allows us to see why the median voter's preferences are chosen. We assume that marginal social cost of providing each additional inch of bridge is $300; therefore equal sharing of costs requires that each individual pays $100 per inch, which also equals his or her individual marginal cost (*MC*). (Our assumption of fixed marginal costs of course simplifies the analysis and allows marginal costs to equal average costs.)

Which bridge width is approved? Each individual prefers to have a width whose marginal costs equal his or her own marginal benefits. Thus, faced with marginal costs (*MC*) of $100, Antonio prefers Q_A, Blanca prefers Q_B, and Consuelo prefers Q_C. Note that these quantities are consistent with the widths of their vehicles. However, only one individual's preference may prevail.

---

[6] The classic work here is Black, *The Theory of Committees and Elections*.
[7] When an even number of voters exists, two median voters exists, and one of these must be arbitrarily chosen.

**FIGURE 7-2
The Median
Voter Model**

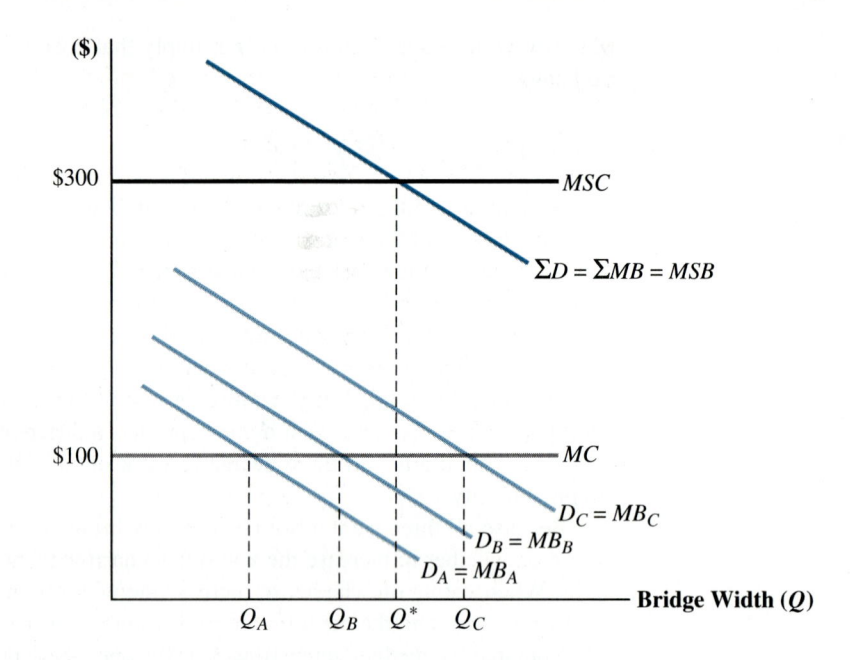

[Figure: Graph with vertical axis in ($) and horizontal axis labeled Bridge Width (Q). Horizontal line at $300 labeled MSC. Horizontal line at $100 labeled MC. Downward-sloping line labeled $\Sigma D = \Sigma MB = MSB$. Three parallel downward-sloping demand curves labeled $D_A = MB_A$, $D_B = MB_B$, $D_C = MB_C$. Quantities marked on horizontal axis: Q_A, Q_B, Q^*, Q_C.]

Let us start the process by voting on the narrow bridge width, Q_A. Because all three individuals find it beneficial to vote in favor of this provision, unanimity exists that width should be a minimum of Q_A. But whereas $MB = \$100$ for Antonio, $MB > \$100$ for Blanca and Consuelo, and these individuals favor a wider bridge. When Blanca, for example, proposes her preferred width of Q_B, the vote is 2 to 1 in favor, and thus there is collective agreement to expand the width of the bridge. Note, however, that Consuelo is unable to win approval to widen the bridge to Q_C, since $MB < \$100$ for Antonio and Blanca, and the vote is 2 to 1 against this proposal.

This voting process results in a voting equilibrium in the sense that, once Q_B is reached, there is no tendency for any new votes to win approval.[8] To understand why this is an equilibrium, consider the outcome when the order of proposals is reversed. Both Antonio and Blanca vote against Q_C since as long as $MB < \$100$, neither individual finds it favorable to vote for this width. When Q_B is put up to vote, support by Blanca and Consuelo passes the proposal. Finally, a proposal to make the bridge narrower, from Q_B to Q_A, is rejected by both Blanca and Consuelo and therefore cannot win majority approval. The order of voting does not affect the final result and, consistent with the median voter model, equilibrium width Q_B represents the preferences of the median voter.

---

[8] This model of equilibrium is developed in Howard R. Bowen, "The Interpretation of Voting in the Allocation of Economic Resources," *Quarterly Journal of Economics* 58 (November 1943): 27–48.

Implications of Median Voter Model for Provision of Public Goods

1. *Even though all voters receive the same level of public good, only the median voter receives output consistent with maximum net benefits.* In our example of bridge widths, only Blanca is able to consume where $MB = MC\ (= \$100)$. In contrast $MB < MC$ for Antonio and $MB > MC$ for Consuelo. Therefore, at the price they face, all voters except for the median voter consume more or less public goods than they prefer, suggesting that the greater the differences in preferences among voters, the less satisfaction voters as a group receive from majority voting.

2. *The majority voting framework does not always translate changes in preferences of voters into changes in policies.* What changes would occur, for example, if Consuelo purchases an even wider pickup truck? Even though her preferences for a wider bridge will rise when she purchases a wider truck, the median voter model demonstrates that collective agreement will not be reached to widen the bridge. Majority voting is therefore not sensitive to changes in preferences of voters other than those of the median voter. Majority voting, in this sense, places other voters at the mercy of the preferences of the median voter because majority voting does not weigh the intensity of preferences of different voters. All yes and no votes of nonmedian voters are of equal value, and none influence exchanges that result from voting. Majority voting focuses on the preferences of the median voter. (But, it is at least possible for Consuelo to bribe Blanca into voting for a wider bridge. In this way, bribes reflect intensity of preferences and are therefore a way around some of the obstacles associated with the median voter model.)

3. *Majority voting does not necessarily result in socially efficient production of public goods.* (The same result can also be shown for the case where majority voting determines the output of private goods.) The point where $\Sigma MB = MSC$ is the socially efficient level of public good and, in our example of bridge widths, occurs at Q^*. Because collective agreement results in production $Q_B < Q^*$, is is clear that there is no inherent tendency for simple majority voting to result in socially efficient levels of public goods. It is also true that, as demonstrated in Figure 7-3, there is no inherent tendency of majority voting to result in underproduction of public goods. Holding costs of production the same, a slightly different set of demands for bridge widths by Antonio, Blanca, and Consuelo can be shown to result in overproduction. While Blanca remains the median voter, her preference for bridge width is now much closer to that of Consuelo. While majority voting is sensitive to changes in the median voter, the socially efficient level of production of Q^* is now less than Q_B, the width chosen by majority rule.

Implications of the Median Voter Model for Representative Democracy

The median voter model provides insights into the policy positions of elected representatives who, under representative democracy, are elected by voters. Not all voters

FIGURE 7-3
Overproduction under Majority Voting

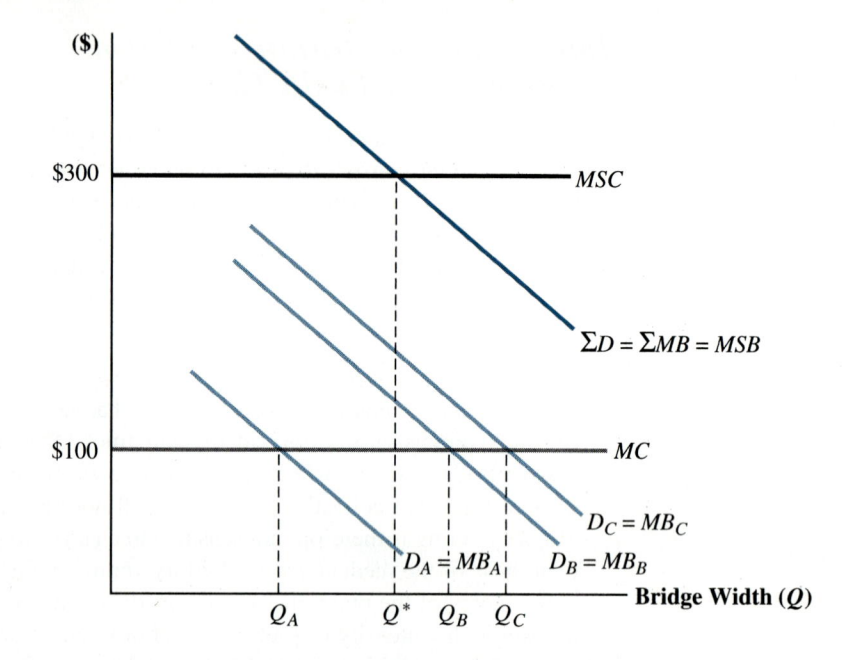

are alike, and elected policymakers must choose which policies to favor—or, to put it on another level of reality—which voters to represent. Because policymakers are elected by simple majority under majority rule, the median voter model demonstrates that positions chosen by policymakers tend to be those of the median voter.

Consider Figure 7-4, which shows the symmetric and single-peaked frequency distribution of voter preferences regarding a single issue.[9] This single issue is described, or ordered, along the stereotypical continuum of left to right and the vertical axis shows the number of voters who support it. For example, the issue may be how much to spend on national defense, with those in support of large expenditures on the right and those in support of small expenditures on the left of the continuum. The median voter is described by position M and, the farther a policymaker's position is from M, the fewer are the voters in support of that policymaker.

Assuming that voters choose policymakers who promote views closest to their own, policymakers who win the most votes are those who propose policies in line with those of median voters. If, for example, a candidate proposes $L1$ policy, that candidate could, at most, win all of the votes to the left of $L1$ and only half of those between $L1$ and M, the median voter, when another candidate proposes policy M. This would surely cause that candidate to lose to any candidate who chooses M, since in addition to all votes to the right of M, that candidate will also win half of those between $L1$ and M. Because the rule of simple majority decides the political race, it is optimal for candidates to choose the policies preferred by the median voter.

---

[9] This model was developed in Harold Hotelling, "Stability in Competition," *Economic Journal* 39 (March 1929): 41–57.

FIGURE 7-4
Frequency Distribution of Voter Preferences

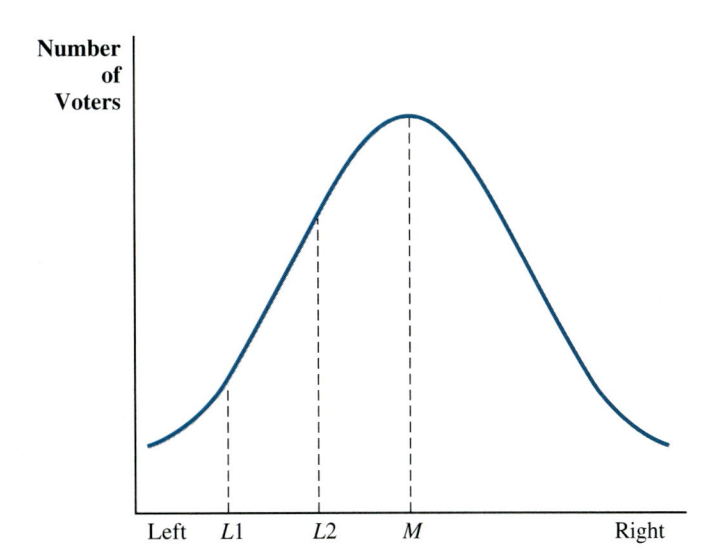

Number of Voters

Left   L1   L2   M   Right

An interesting implication of the median voter model is that the views of candidates tend to be quite similar as they all attempt to promote the views of the median voter. While candidates may claim to be new and different, this model suggests that candidates who really do offer new and different views will lose elections when those new and different views are not those of the median voter. Of course, if the views of the median voter become new and different, then successful candidates must adopt these new and different views as well.

The median voter model predicts that the greater are margins of victory by successful candidates, the further are views of losing candidates from those of the median voter. Consider Table 7-1 which shows percentages of popular votes won by the two major candidates for U.S. President since 1960.[10] The median voter model suggests that, in three races (1960, 1972, and 1984), the views of losing candidates (Senators Barry Goldwater, George McGovern, and Walter Mondale) were relatively far from those of median voters, and the views of winners of those same races (Lyndon B. Johnson, Richard M. Nixon, and Ronald Reagan) were relatively close to those of median voters. In other words, the more extreme are the views of candidates, the less likely that individual is to capture a majority of voters. The median voter model also suggests that because of very narrow margins of victory, the 1960 (John F. Kennedy versus Nixon) and 1968 (Nixon and Hubert Humphrey) races were characterized by candidates who held fairly similar views.

Another implication of the median voter model is that representative democracies tend to be characterized by just two dominant political parties. Consider, for instance, an election in which a third candidate enters a previously two-candidate race.

---

[10] Third-party candidates are not shown. They have not always captured a significant percentage of votes. Obvious exceptions occurred in 1992 when Ross Perot captured 19 percent, and in 1980 when John Anderson won 7 percent of the popular vote for U.S. President.

TABLE 7-1
Popular Vote Cast for U.S. President

Year	Winner	%	Loser	%	Margin
1960	Kennedy	49.7	Nixon	49.5	0.2
1964	Johnson	61.1	Goldwater	38.5	22.6
1968	Nixon	43.4	Humphrey	42.7	0.7
1972	Nixon	60.7	McGovern	37.5	23.2
1976	Carter	50.1	Ford	48.0	2.1
1980	Reagan	50.7	Carter	41.0	9.7
1984	Reagan	58.5	Mondale	40.6	17.9
1988	Bush	53.4	Dukakis	45.6	7.8
1992	Clinton	43.0	Bush	38.0	5.0

Source: Statistical Abstract of the United States, 1993.

Inspection of Figure 7-4 shows that the introduction of a third candidate necessarily reduces support for one of the two original candidates. For example, if a candidate with views in line with *L1* enters a race that was previously dominated by two candidates espousing views *L2* and *M*, the support of candidate with view *L2* must surely be reduced by all voters to the left of *L1* and half of the voters between *L1* and *L2*.

Such reshuffling of support leaves the candidate with views associated with *M* to win by a landslide and suggests that it is to the advantage of any candidate to have a third candidate enter the race so long as that new candidate holds views on the outside of his or her opposition. For example, in a race between candidate with view *L2* and a candidate with view *M*, the candidate with position *M* can only gain (lose) when additional candidates enter the race to the left (right) of *M*. Because this necessarily leads to dominance by the winning party, this situation will not persist when losing candidates are interested in winning elections. Because losing candidates will either leave the political arena or merge their campaigns for public office with that of another candidate, the median voter model predicts that the equilibrium number of political candidates, or parties, is two.

Existence of Majority Voting Equilibrium

Simple majority voting does not always result in voting equilibria. Consider, for instance, Table 7-2, which shows the preferences of Adam, Blake, and Carl for how much to spend on their annual Fourth of July party. They have agreed to share equally in party expenses and have chosen the rule of simple majority to work out a compromise. Adam, for example, prefers to spend $200, but given the choice between $100 and $300, would choose $100 as the second-best alternative. The preference orderings for Blake and Carl are also listed in the table. Let us now examine which agreement results from three alternative initial pairings of options.

TABLE 7-2
Preferences for Party Expenses

	Voter		
Ranking	Adam	Blake	Carl
First	$200	$300	$100
Second	100	200	300
Third	300	100	200

❑ *Initial Pairing 1: $100 versus $200.* If the first pairing is $100 versus $200, the vote is 2 to 1 for $200; therefore, under the voting rule, $200 is judged the winner. When $200 is then paired against $300, the vote is 2 to 1 in favor of $300, and therefore $300 is the compromise.

❑ *Initial Pairing 2: $200 versus $300.* What agreement results when the first pairing is $200 versus $300? In this case, the vote is 2 to 1 in favor of $300 and, when the next round of voting pairs $300 against $100, the winning option is $100.

❑ *Initial Pairing 3: $100 versus $300.* When $100 is initially paired against $300, a vote of 2 to 1 goes in favor of $100. When $100 is then paired against $200, the winning option is $200.

This example demonstrates four important points.

1. *Unique voting equilibria are not guaranteed.* The final outcome is clearly dependent upon which options are initially paired against one another; therefore, no unique equilibrium describes the final outcome of the voting process. In the example of the Fourth of July party, the group appears to agree to options that appear to be *inconsistent* with their individual preferences. The Fourth of July party also provides a case where the preferences of the median voter are not necessarily chosen through simple majority voting.

Voting cycles
occur when no voting equilibrium exists.

2. *Voting cycles can occur when round-robin rules require that approval of any option cannot be final until no other option defeats it.* Voting cycles can occur when there are endless cycles to the voting process. Under our first pairing in which $100 is initially paired against $200, the winning option is $300. However, because $300 is Adam's last choice, a round-robin rule would allow him to force a new pairing of $300 against $100 because he knows that $100—an option that Adam prefers over $300—will win. Not to be outdone, Blake, who awards lowest ranking to $100, may force a new vote between $100 and $200 that then results in a win for $200. Because Carl awards lowest priority to $200, he may find it advantageous to force a new vote between $200 and $300, resulting in a win for $300. Collective decisions may not be reached as long as cycling continues. Evidence suggests that the probability of cycles is high and is positively related to how

different the preferences of voters are.[11] Intuitively, it makes sense that, the more homogeneous are preferences, the lower the likelihood of endless cycling.

3. *Savvy voters find it advantageous to manipulate the ordering of vote taking.* In the case of the party expenses (Table 7-2), it is in Adam's interest, for instance, to suggest that the first pairing be between $100 and $300 in order to achieve a final outcome of $200, which coincides with his preferred outcome. Similarly, Blake prefers for $100 to be initially paired against $200, and Carl prefers a pairing between $200 and $300. This behavior is called **agenda control,** or manipulation; it occurs whenever voters, or committee members, seek to order voting on an issue so as to secure a favorable outcome.[12] Prevalence of agenda control is also more likely when voting does not allow round-robin rules.

4. *Prior knowledge about the ordering of votes may induce strategic behavior by voters.* For example, if Adam understands that an initial pairing of $100 against $200 would eventually result in a decision to spend $300 on the party, he may change his vote in such a way that goes against his true preferences for each possible pairing. Adam, for instance, may decide to vote for $100 against $200, since he recognizes that if he were to reveal his true preference for $200, this would eventually lead to approval of $300. By his voting for $100 over $200, he causes the initial vote to result in $100, which, when pitted against $300, causes $100 to be agreed upon.

Agenda control arises when voters or committee members order voting on issues in such a way as to secure a favorable outcome.

Single-Peaked Preferences and Majority Voting

Table 7-3 shows how a slight change to the preference orderings of Table 7-2 produces a majority voting equilibrium which, in this case, means that no matter what the ordering of voting options, collective agreement is to spend $200 on the Fourth of July party. **Single-peaked preferences** are a requirement for unique voting equilibria.

Single-peaked preferences mean that as options move further away from a voter's most preferred option, those options become less desirable. In Table 7-3, distance between options is measured in dollars; therefore, because Adam's first choice is $100, Adam displays single-peaked preferences when he prefers $200 over $300. Figure 7-5 is a plot of the preference orderings for Adam, Blake, and Carl (as shown in Table 7-3) and demonstrates that all three individuals have single-peaked preferences. Notice that we do not have information on the levels of utility that each individual associates with each option, and we therefore plot the relevant data on the vertical axis to show how each individual perceives the *relative* orderings of each option. For example, it does not matter whether the preference orderings for Adam show a steep fall or a flat fall in utility so long as there is some decline as options move further away from the first preference.

In Blake's case, the further the option is from his most preferred expenditure of $300, the less desirable options become. Because Adam and Blake's first preferences

Single-peaked preferences characterize preferences when, as options move further away from a voter's most preferred option, those preferences or options become less desirable.

---

[11] Mueller, *Public Choice II,* 79–82.

[12] See, for example, Robert J. Mackay and Carolyn L. Weaver, "Agenda Control by Budget Maximizers in a Multi-Bureau Setting," *Public Choice* 37 (1981): 447–472.

TABLE 7-3
Preferences for Party Expenses

Ranking	Adam	Blake	Carl
First	$100	$300	$200
Second	200	200	300
Third	300	100	100

occur at either extreme of the available options, movement away from first preferences is always characterized by falling levels of utility. Carl's preferences are single peaked as well, even though there is an obvious spike at the expenditure that denotes his first preference. His first preference lies in the middle of the extremes, and movements in either direction result in lower utility.

Figure 7-6 plots data from Table 7-2 and therefore shows what preference orderings occur when there are possibilities for vote cycling. While Adam and Blake's preference orderings are single peaked, Carl exhibits **double-peaked preferences** because, while Carl's first preference is $100, he prefers to spend $300 rather than $200. His preference orderings are double peaked since peaks occur at $100 and $300; we may interpret these data as meaning that he prefers spending relatively little or relatively much rather than an option somewhere in the middle.

Double-peaked preferences are a characteristic whereby, as voters move away from most preferred options, utility falls at first, but eventually rises.

**FIGURE 7-5
Preferences for Party Expenses**

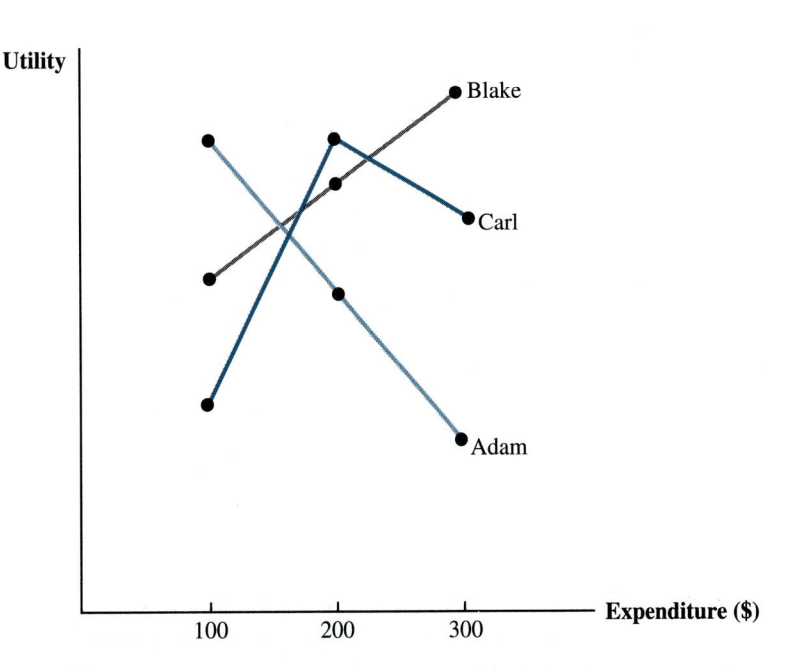

How Prevalent Are Double-Peaked Preferences?

Because double-peaked preferences allow vote cycling to take place, it is important to understand what factors are likely to produce double-peaked preferences. In our example of the Fourth of July party, does it make any sense for Carl to prefer spending much or little over somewhere in between? It does if Carl's behavior tends toward extremes. He may believe, for instance, that parties should have either very little or very much preparation; maybe he considers anything in between to be merely mediocre. Carl may believe that when little is spent, the creative spirits of all three will flourish and create a great party. But he may also believe that if a lot of money is spent, all of the great food and drink that $300 could buy would ensure a great party. Anything in between, however, elicits very little enthusiasm from Carl.

When private goods are provided by the public sector, voters may have double-peaked preferences. Public and private education is one such case. It is often argued that parents would rather send their children to private schools than to poorly funded public schools. Unless public schools are heavily funded, parents prefer to spend very little on public schools. In fact they may prefer minor funding because it lowers their tax burdens and gives them more to spend on private education for their children. Therefore, first preferences of parents may be for large expenditures; but when the choice is between low or medium expenditures, parents choose low expenditures. Other examples of private sector alternatives that may foster double-peaked preferences are police protection, parks, and playgrounds, in which cases, vote cycling may occur.

Logrolling with Multiple Issues

Logrolling is the trading of votes in situations comprising multiple issues where voters are trying to further their well-being. Table 7-4, for example, shows hypothetical benefits that Ashleigh, Bjorn, and Cletus receive if there are collective agreements to build a park, a bridge, and a school. Benefits tend to differ between individuals and, in the cases of the park and school, are related to the number of children they care for; costs reflect how much each individual contributes to funding of these projects. Numbers shown reflect net benefits, equal to benefits minus costs, and therefore total

> **Logrolling** occurs when voters further their well-being by trading votes (on multiple issues) with one another.

TABLE 7-4
Logrolling That Results in Net Gains for Society

| | Net Benefits of Three Projects | | |
| | | Project | |
Voter	Park	Bridge	School
Ashleigh	100	−10	−50
Bjorn	−50	160	−100
Cletus	−20	−15	200
TOTAL NET GAIN	30	135	50

FIGURE 7-6
Single-Peaked versus Double-Peaked Preferences

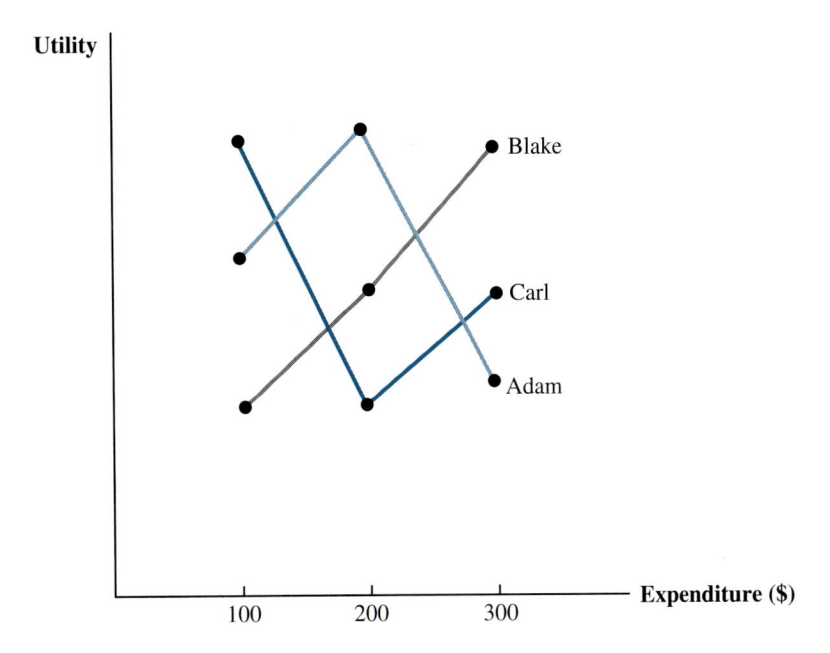

net social benefits equal the sum of net benefits that each individual receives from each project.

It is clear from Table 7-4 that each individual has a strong interest in having one project funded. Ashleigh has a strong interest in having the park, Bjorn in having a new bridge, and Cletus in having a new school. Because only one individual supports any one project, no project is undertaken under a rule of simple majority.

Note, however, that logrolling between Ashleigh and Bjorn can result in a net gain to both parties. By agreeing to vote for both a new park and bridge, Ashleigh and Bjorn experience net gains of 90 and 110, respectively. Inspection of Table 7-4 also shows that when all three trade votes, net gains per individual are: Ashleigh (40), Bjorn (10), and Cletus (165). Logrolling may therefore enhance allocative efficiency and provide for collective agreements that would not occur under simple majority voting.

So what is so awful about logrolling? The "jam" in the story of logrolling is that it does not necessarily produce net gains for society; in fact, inspection of Table 7-5 shows a case in which logrolling between Ashleigh, Bjorn, and Cletus lowers allocative efficiency.

Based on total net gain to society, none of these projects is worthy of funding, and it is clear that in the absence of logrolling, none of them would be approved by a majority of voters. Logrolling, however, may result in approval of two or more of these projects by a majority of voters. Consider Ashleigh, for example, who has a strong interest in a new park. If she and Bjorn agree to trade votes for the park and bridge (which is the only project that Bjorn wants), their coalition claims a majority that can pass both projects. Examination of net gains reveals that Ashleigh gains 80 and Bjorn gains 210 when they trade votes in this manner.

TABLE 7-5
Logrolling That Results in Net Loss for Society

| | Net Benefits of Three Projects | | |
| | Project | | |
Voter	Park	Bridge	School
Ashleigh	100	−20	−70
Bjorn	−100	310	−200
Cletus	−100	−300	200
TOTAL NET GAIN	−100	−10	−70

Table 7-5 also suggests another coalition. A coalition between Ashleigh and Cletus produces respective gains of 30 and 100 when they vote for a park and school. Bjorn on the other hand, suffers a net loss of 300 and is unable to block this winning coalition. Once again, even though funding of these projects results in a total net loss for society, logrolling fosters incentives for two or more voters to support projects they would not support when vote trading was not possible.

We can clearly see who is the loser in these two examples of logrolling. In the first case, Cletus, who has agreed to abide by the will of the majority, is a loser when Ashleigh and Bjorn trade votes. While society loses (net social benefits) 100 and 10, respectively, when a new park and bridge are agreed upon, the primary loser is Cletus who loses 400. In other words, the will of the majority (Ashleigh and Bjorn) is able to pass projects which serve its individual interests at the expense of the minority (Cletus). In the second example of logrolling, gains of the majority (Ashleigh and Cletus) are also at the expense of the minority (Bjorn).

These examples demonstrate that logrolling allows majorities to redistribute income from minorities to themselves. This is only possible, however, as long as minorities cannot fight redistribution by withdrawing from a private club or convincing others to change voting rules in such a way that forbids logrolling.

Majority Voting Rules, Externalities, and Property Rights

Any rule other than unanimous consent clearly allows the reigning majority to exercise power over minorities. While Buchanan and Tullock's model of optimal majority rule serves to minimize the sum of decision and external costs, it is important to realize that majority voting rules result in Pareto superior exchanges only when voters have the right to refuse various external costs, or negative externalities, associated with those rules. In other words, while it may be efficient for individuals to trade off some degree of externality for lower decision-making costs, Buchanan and Tullock's model applies to cases in which voters voluntarily choose to trade off more redistribution for lower decision costs. Choice of voting rule is similar to property rights over scarce resources in the sense that voting rules define property rights over one's economic well-being. The assignment of voting rights has important implications for allocation of scarce resources under collective agreements to provide public goods. We now elaborate upon this point by showing how majority voting rules result in different (externality) redistribution policies in private and public sectors.

Private Sector

Voting rules tend to be voluntarily agreed upon by members of private clubs. A certain degree of redistribution is acceptable to members of clubs because, as described in Buchanan and Tullock's model of optimal majority, minimization of decision and external costs results in optimal majorities that require less than unanimous approval. However, when club members believe that their interests are not furthered by voting rules, either they can successfully argue for changes of rules or they can leave the club. Redistribution that occurs then will be voluntary. Because it is irrational for members to accept Pareto inferior exchanges by maintaining membership, policies adopted by private clubs tend to be Pareto neutral or superior.

Public Sector

The most common voting rule in the public sector is simple majority, which therefore represents an important institutional factor that influences the ability of voters to set policies. (An alternative case would be plurality voting, in which the candidate or option with the greatest percentage of votes wins.) Under a simple majority rule with two candidates, the majority can impose costs upon the other 49 percent, which, when opposed by the minority, represents a negative externality. Negative externalities occur, for example, when the taxes of voting minorities are raised or when expenditures that they found beneficial are cut. Voting rules define the degree to which allocations may be either coercive or voluntary, and it is therefore important to understand the nature of these alternative rules and their implications.

There is no question that redistribution may occur under both voluntary and coercive arrangements. Private charitable contributions clearly represent policies that have the unanimous consent of those who wish to share their own wealth with others. Even though redistributive policies of the public sector may be supported by a majority of voters, such policies at times have both voluntary and coercive elements. These policies are voluntary in the sense that they are supported by a majority of voters. But they may also be partially coercive in nature when some subset of the voting minority does not willingly agree to go along with the majority, even though some of the voters in the minority do not strongly object.

The policy process often results in redistributive measures, and it is useful to examine these in terms of majority voting rules. Here we must remember that Buchanan and Tullock's model of optimal majority indicates that each policy issue has a unique optimal majority because different issues have different decision and external costs. Because most voting rules for deciding collective agreements in the public sector are simple majority (51 percent), the ways in which issues are decided tend to be optimal in very few cases. For example, it could be the case that national defense issues have an optimal majority of 55 percent, and issues regarding social insurance and welfare programs have an optimal majority of 75 percent. Because it can be expected that issues that are explicitly redistributive in nature tend to have the highest external costs, Buchanan and Tullock's model of optimal majority predicts that optimal majorities of these programs tend to be associated with relatively high majorities. But since these are also decided on the basis of simple majority, it is predicted that more redistribution will take place than would be the case if simple majority were replaced by an optimal majority rule.

Simple majority is often selected to decide many collective decisions in the public sector not only because it is too costly to vote on each issue separately, but because it is virtually impossible to determine the optimal majority for each of thousands of single issues. In practice, we vote for one candidate whose platform consists of many issues. Even though it is costly to take separate votes on each issue, however, it may be appropriate to take votes on similar issues. For example, policies relating to income distribution could be grouped together, and policies related to national defense could also be collected to be voted on separately.

It is possible that positive externalities are imposed when, for example, majorities pass policies that end up benefiting the minority. But unless it is assumed that the minorities are not well informed or do not understand how these policies are favorable to them, it is difficult to argue that minorities would be averse to agreeing to beneficial policies. Some believe, for instance, that certain individuals in society (for example, informed voters or policymakers) should play a paternalistic role in public policy. In this case, less than optimal rules of majority may be justified by arguments that members of the minority do not understand that certain policies will improve their welfare or that the costs associated with getting everyone to agree are so great that the policies will either never pass or take too long, despite the fact that they are believed to be truly beneficial.

Public Market Structure and Exchange

Private market structure consists of the institutions through which exchanges between consumers and producers take place.

Private market structure is the set of institutions and mechanisms through which exchanges take place between consumers and producers. Microeconomic theory shows that freely competitive market structures offer consumers lower prices and higher consumption opportunities than markets organized under less competitive circumstances. As a general rule, consumers are more influential in the exchange process when private markets are relatively competitive and less influential when private markets are more monopolistic. There is little disagreement among economists that consumers prefer competitive markets, and producers prefer noncompetitive markets.

Public market structure consists of the institutions through which exchanges between voters and policymakers take place.

Public market structure is the set of institutions and mechanisms through which exchanges take place between voters and policymakers. We have studied the voting process and have shown how voting rules are important determinants of the policies approved by voters. Our examination of the policy process is incomplete, however, and requires examination of how policymakers respond to the wishes of voters. Analogous to the ways in which different market structures affect the power of consumers in private markets, public markets may be structured in many different ways, and it is likely that the design of public market structure influences the power of voters to direct resources in the public sector.

Voice and Exit as Properties Affecting Public Exchange

Voice options allow the expression of demands by voters to policymakers.

Exit options allow voters to reject policies by moving to other political jurisdictions.

Voters must inform or persuade policymakers to provide policies of their choosing. Voters communicate their preferences to policymakers through available **voice options** and **exit options**.[13] Examples of voice options are letters to policymakers, voting, and working in political campaigns. These options are analogous to consumers' letting producers know what they like and dislike about prices, warranties, and product qualities. The exercise of exit options, however, conveys a much stronger statement by voters, since it occurs when voters leave political jurisdictions. It is thus the natural analogue to consumers refusing to do business with certain firms. In private clubs, for instance, members quit whenever they become totally dissatisfied with policies. The exit option is the ultimate threat that voters bring against policymakers because, as in the case of private markets, it means that voters (or consumers) go to other suppliers.

Voice Options

Many factors affect the ability of voters to exercise voice options. Competition in political markets may be stifled, for example, when incumbent policymakers have competitive advantages over challengers. To the extent that incumbents are able to protect themselves from challengers, public markets may be considered monopolistic. Great stability of tenure for elected officials may allow these policymakers to exercise monopoly power, and if this is so, voters may have less influence over policymakers than under a more competitive public market. The following factors indicate that public markets are not entirely competitive.

Advantages of Being an Incumbent

An important advantage of being an incumbent policymaker is that one already has a support staff and public funds with which to fight challengers. Glenn Parker has argued that

> The incumbent's advantage is clear: repeated exposure through trips to the district and mass mailings.... House incumbents have an assortment of resources for promoting their visibility within districts. The perquisites of office provide a member with funds to operate district offices and/or mobile vans that keep the incumbent's name prominent within the district and the local press; these incumbent "enterprises" are staffed and operated at public expense. In addition, House incumbents have use of the congressional frank that permits them to send mail to their constituents also free of charge.[14]

Money may also affect electability, in part because incumbents often outspend challengers, frequently by a factor of two to one.[15] Nevertheless, a survey of the

---

[13] These options were introduced in Albert O. Hirschman, *Exit, Voice and Loyalty* (Cambridge, Mass.: Harvard University Press, 1970).

[14] Glenn R. Parker, "Competition in Congressional Elections," in his *Studies of Congress* (Washington, D.C.: Congressional Quarterly Press, 1985), 4.

[15] Norman J. Ornstein, Thomas E. Mann, and Michael J. Malbin, *Vital Statistics on Congress, 1991–1992* (Washington, D.C.: Congressional Quarterly Press, 1992), table 3-1 and table 3-4.

empirical literature on this issue indicates that while money does buy votes, challengers are able to buy them more easily than incumbents.[16]

Gerrymandering

Gerrymandering is the formation of political districts in such a way as to favor one political party (or incumbent policymaker) over another.[17] The political jurisdictions of U.S. Representatives are redistricted every ten years so as to maintain equal representation across the country in accordance with shifts in the population. After the 1990 Census, for instance, California, along with seven other states, gained seats, and thirteen states lost seats. Political jurisdictions are redrawn every ten years, and even though the law states that all districts must have an equal number of citizens, new districts are determined in many different ways.

In California, for instance, it has been argued that gerrymandering is the principal reason behind the fact that incumbents were defeated only five times in 225 elections of U.S. Representatives during the 1980s. North Carolina, in particular, has received much attention because of its use of gerrymandering. For example, even though one North Carolina district stretches 190 miles, it is sometimes no wider than Interstate 85. Evidence also suggests that gerrymandering dilutes the ability of racial and ethnic minorities to elect their own representatives. Even though the 1965 Voting Rights Act, as amended in 1982, outlawed the use of gerrymandering to discriminate against minority groups, so far, there is little evidence that this kind of discrimination is any less prevalent today than in the past. A commonly cited example of gerrymandering to silence minorities, or at least lessen their influence, is in Mississippi, where, even though 20 percent of its population is black, only 3 percent of its elected congresspersons are black. Similar redistricting has been argued to have diluted the voting power of Hispanics.[18] To the extent that gerrymandering reduces competition for political seats, the ability of dissatisfied voters to oust incumbents from office is diminished.

Exit Options

The exit option manifests itself primarily through fiscal structure, or the intergovernmental arrangements that divide the various functions of the public sector among governments.[19] The United States comprises more than 82,000 individual governments and is referred to as a federalist structure of government. Because there are many different governments under federalist structures, voters may exercise exit options whenever they become dissatisfied with policies of local governments. In response to government policies they disagree with, they have the option to move from one political jurisdiction to another. In this way, then, voters may flee policies they do not like and seek policies more to their liking in other political jurisdictions.

---

[16] Muller, *Public Choice II*, 209–212.

[17] See, for example, "Adios, Gerrymander," *Wall Street Journal,* December 20, 1991, A10; "Political Pornography," *Wall Street Journal,* September 9, 1991, A12; and "Political Pornography—II," *Wall Street Journal,* February 4, 1992, A14.

[18] See, for example, "The Battle of the Pastry Cooks," *The Economist,* May 18, 1991, 27–28.

[19] For a more detailed examination of exit options, see Michael L. Marlow, "Intergovernmental Competition, Voice and Exit Options and the Design of Fiscal Structure," *Constitutional Political Economy* 3 (Winter 1992): 73–87.

Gerrymandering is the formation of political districts so as to favor one political party over another.

In contrast, a unitary system of government is one that has only one government, which is referred to as the central or federal government. This single government handles all operations of the public sector and, in the parlance of microeconomic theory, fiscal structure is monopolistic. Under a monopolistic, or centralized, fiscal structure, voters can exercise exit options only by leaving the country.

Exercise of exit options is often a last resort, either because of loyalty to current policymakers or transaction costs associated with moving. This option is applied when voters believe they cannot effectively influence public policy through voice options. In the case of government monopoly or centralization, lack of exit possibilities may give voters less influence over policymakers than a government structure with many exit possibilities. Since there is much disagreement about this issue, we now discuss two viewpoints about the design of exit options in public markets.

The Benevolent Policymaker View

Benevolent view of government is the belief and theory that policymakers are motivated to maximize the well-being of society.

The **benevolent view of government** assumes that benevolent policymakers wish only to provide policies that enhance allocative efficiency and meet the equity goals of society.[20] Proponents of this view tend to think that allocative efficiency is enhanced through centralization, which can exploit scale economies and decrease production costs better than a system of many governments can. Centralization is often argued to be appropriate for national standardization of such programs as air traffic control, social insurance, and various welfare programs. Public goods whose benefits are primarily local in nature, such as public parks and libraries, are believed to be best allocated to noncentral governments.

Redistributive policies are generally argued to be the province of central governments because the policies of noncentral governments can be self-defeating as long as citizens are mobile; when one noncentral government raises its redistribution from rich to poor, the poor tend to enter the jurisdiction while the rich leave.[21] Because voter mobility thwarts the goals of redistribution, centralized provision, with its lack of exit options, is viewed as an appropriate device that restricts the adverse effects of voter mobility and, at the same time, exploits the scale economies associated with centralized provision.

The Leviathan View

Leviathan view of government is the belief and theory that policymakers are motivated to maximize their narrow self-interests.

The **Leviathan view of government,** named after a huge and monstrous creature of the Old Testament, rests on the premise that centralized government awards primary leverage in the policy process to policymakers.[22] This premise is coupled with the

---

[20] For an early treatment, see Wallace E. Oates, *Fiscal Federalism* (New York: Harcourt Brace Jovanovich, 1972).

[21] Mark V. Pauly, "Income Redistribution as a Local Public Good," *Journal of Public Economics* (1973): 44–62.

[22] See, for example, Geoffrey Brennan and James M. Buchanan, *The Power to Tax: Analytical Foundations of a Fiscal Constitution.* (Cambridge, U.K.: Cambridge University Press, 1980); and Jack Wiseman, "Principles of Political Economy: An Outline Proposal, Illustrated with Application to Fiscal Federalism," *Constitutional Political Economy* 1 (1990): 101–124. The focus of this literature is often the model developed in Charles M. Tiebout, "A Pure Theory of Local Government Expenditures," *Journal of Political Economy* 64 (1956): 416–424.

assumption that policymakers are motivated to serve their own narrow self-interests, and that self-interested policymakers are inclined to further interests that differ from those of average voters. Proponents of the Leviathan view recommend that fiscal constitutions be designed to take account of these assumptions. While the Leviathan view recognizes that a representative democracy, and its voting process, in theory provides voters with appropriate defenses against the narrow self-interests of policymakers, it also acknowledges that lack of competition for public office, gerrymandering, restrictions on government supply, and other factors leave voters without enough leverage in the policy process to constrain the narrow self-interests of policymakers. This view of policymakers suggests the need to design fiscal constitutions that protect taxpayers from coercive policies that they do not desire and cautions against centralizing the powers of policymakers.

Exit options are argued to be vital defenses for protecting voters from self-serving policymakers. While voters may use voice options to influence policies, there are limits to their effectiveness when public markets are not entirely competitive. When voice options fail to provide the policies voters desire, exit options provide the ultimate threat against policymakers. However, because monopolization means restriction or removal of exit options, policymakers are more likely to pursue their narrow self-interests when exit options are incomplete. Restriction or removal of exit options also lower the effectiveness of voice options, since without the ultimate threat of exit, narrowly self-interested policymakers are less inclined to respond to signals sent through voice options.

Implications for the Policymaker Role

An important difference between the Leviathan and the benevolent views stems from their assumptions about what constitutes appropriate roles for policymakers. As a source of similarity, proponents of both views believe that it is appropriate for policymakers to provide policies that are signaled through the exercise of voice options. But a crucial difference clearly surfaces over the role of policymakers when voters do not signal, or voice, demands for policies that policymakers believe they should receive. Under the benevolent view of policymaking, provision of these policies is often justified on the grounds that policymakers have more information than voters do and that voters would demand these policies if they fully understood their full capacity to improve their well-being.[23] Under the Leviathan view, however, the ability to provide policies that voters do not demand opens the door for policies that serve the narrow self-interests of policymakers. We should keep in mind that these views reflect alternative hypotheses about the motivations behind the behaviors of policymakers and it should therefore be unsurprising that they yield divergent conclusions on the role of exit options in the policy process.

The importance of differentiating between these two roles for policymakers becomes apparent when we examine cases in which voters try to avoid or flee policies

---

[23] See S. C. Littlechild and Jack Wiseman, "The Political Economy of Restriction of Choice," *Public Choice* 51 (1986): 161–171, for a discussion of three alternative frameworks (market failure, paternalist, and libertarian) for the political economy of forcing taxpayers to accept government programs.

they do not like. Such a policy may be one that requires that all workers contribute to the Social Security system, that all passengers in automobiles wear seatbelts, or that cigarettes carry an extraordinary excise tax. We know, however, that not all citizens agree that these policies are wise; the many reports of cigarette smuggling from low-tax to high-tax states give evidence in that example. Clearly, in the case of cigarette taxation, a national, or central government, tax policy would remove all incentives to smuggle across state lines and, in this way, remove exit possibilities for smokers who disagree with the tax. While not all proponents of the benevolent view of policymaking believe that policymakers are justified in forcing individuals to accept policies they do not want, the point remains that centralization of policies removes some degree of exit opportunity from the consumer of policies, and hence, to some degree, removes the ability of citizens to control the policies of the public sector.

Under the benevolent view, if voters flee or exit policies, there may be cases in which policymakers believe that voters are actually fleeing welfare-enhancing policies. A case may therefore be made for designing public market structures with controls on the abilities of voters to flee policies designed by benevolent policymakers. Removal of exit possibilities through centralization of government is believed to control the abilities of voters to thwart the beneficent aims of policymakers. In contrast, the Leviathan view raises the possibility that when voters wish to flee policies, they are fleeing policies that in fact do not serve their interests. The widening of exit options, under this view, is therefore predicted to produce policies that better reflect the desires of voters than under a monopolistic public market structure that lacks exit options.

Bureaucracy Theory

Nonelected policymakers, or bureaucrats, who enjoy relatively high permanency and stability in their employment, have the primary responsibility for implementing the policies of the public sector. But why are there so many government employees who are not elected by voters? Before the introduction of the civil service system, nonelected officials were appointed by elected policymakers. This system, called political patronage (or, derogatorily, the "spoils system"), was not popular with voters because it appeared to be corrupt: Politicians were accused of selling political offices and rewarding friends and relatives with high-paying and influential positions. The civil service system, starting with the Pendleton Act of 1883, was developed to replace this system with one based less on political vagaries and more on merit. In order to ensure their independence from the political concerns of elected officials, employees of the civil service system are, for the most part, permanent.[24]

Bureaucracy theory rests on the assumption that civil servants are primarily motivated by the power, pay, and prestige associated with being a government employee.

Bureaucracy theory, often associated with the work of William A. Niskanen, Jr., is the study of the behaviors of bureaucrats. Behavior is modeled as being primarily motivated by the "power, pay, and prestige" that goes along with being a

---

[24] James Q. Wilson, *Bureaucracy: What Government Agencies Do and Why They Do It* (New York: Basic Books, 1989), 239, argues that the civil service system also gives politicians the ability to permanently place individuals of like ideology into civil service positions.

government employee.[25] One hypothesis that follows from this theory is that bureaucrats seek to maximize their budgets. In contrast to the private sector, where managers seek to maximize profitability, civil servants, for whom profitability is not a consideration, are modeled as seeking to maximize something other than profit. Instead of profits, bureaucrats are predicted to try to add to the amenities of the workplace, to advance their ability to gain such perquisites as large, lavishly furnished offices and frequent, nonessential trips, among other things, in order to maximize their budgets.

An implication of this theory is that bureaus expand beyond socially efficient levels. In Figure 7-7a, total social cost (*TC*) and total social benefit *(TB)* curves are shown for a hypothetical government agency. While maximization of total net social benefits corresponds to production of Q_C, bureaucrats produce at a higher level (for example, Q_B) so resources are wasted because it is socially inefficient for output to be any level other than Q_C.

Because sponsors (Congress and the President) set budgets, bureaucracy theory also predicts that bureaucrats serve the interests of sponsors and not voters. Of course, this assumes that the interests of sponsors and voters are not the same, since if they were, bureaucrats would serve the interests of voters as well. Note that because bureaucrats are not necessarily assumed to serve the interests of voters, this theory is similar to the Leviathan view and is therefore inconsistent with the benevolent view of policymakers.

Bureaucracy theory also argues that it is difficult for elected policymakers to force bureaucrats to work for the general interests of voters. Milton and Rose Friedman, for instance, have argued as follows:

> *One other enormously important feature of bureaucracy deserves mention. Bureaucrats in general have very long tenure. It is almost impossible to discharge them. The number of governmental employees discharged in the course of a year is trivial compared to the total number employed. The top bureaucrats were in place long before the current President was elected; they expect to remain in place long after the current President completes his term or terms in office. They have their fingers on the controls; they know where the bodies are buried. They can outwit the current President and the current legislature. Delay is an enormously effective instrument for this purpose and can be deftly exercised by bureaucrats.*[26]

This argument clearly models bureaucrats as government employees who operate at a relatively high level of autonomy from elected policymakers. This autonomy follows from the prediction that because elected policymakers have problems in obtaining useful information on the activities and costs of government bureaus, sponsors operate under a severe informational disadvantage when it comes to monitoring the performance of bureaucrats. Given high monitoring costs and lack of private market counterparts from which to gain comparable information, sponsors may indeed find oversight difficult. Moreover, many programs, such as national defense and

---

[25] William A. Niskanen, Jr., *Bureaucracy and Representative Government* (Chicago: Aldine, 1972); and William A. Niskanen, Jr., "Bureaucrats and Politicians," *Journal of Law and Economics* 18 (December 1975): 617–643. An important earlier work on the economics of bureaucracy is Gordon Tullock, *The Politics of Bureaucracy* (Washington, D.C.: Public Affairs Press, 1965).

[26] Milton Friedman and Rose Friedman, *Tyranny of the Status Quo* (San Diego: Harcourt Brace Jovanovich, 1983), 50.

FIGURE 7-7
Public Output under a Bureaucracy

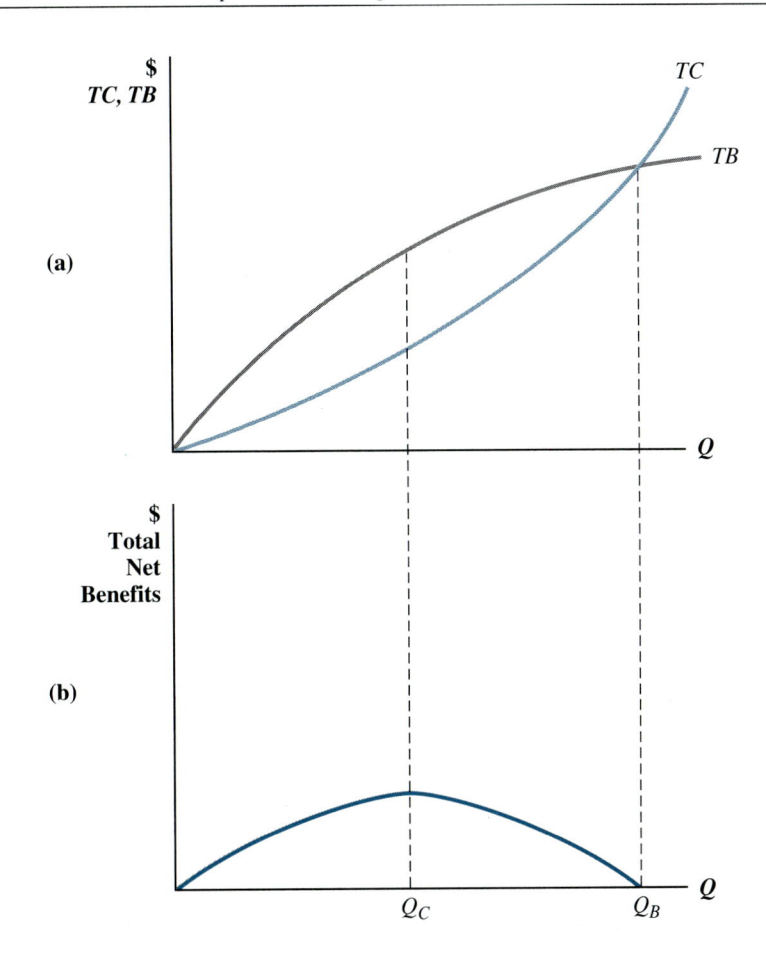

antipoverty policies, for example, are not easy to measure in terms of productivity or efficiency, and, in these areas, control over bureaucrats by elected policymakers is predicted to be rather loose.

An important implication of bureaucracy theory is that separation of policymakers into elected and nonelected workforces introduces monopoly elements into the policy process that result in problems for voters who wish to guide resource allocation in the public sector. Even when elected policymakers are assumed to be benevolent servants of voters, elections will not control the narrow self-interests of bureaucrats when elected policymakers exercise less than perfect control over bureaucrats. The theory of bureaucracy may therefore shed light on the efficiency of bureaucracy as well as on the abilities of voters to receive, through public markets, policies that they desire.

Special Interest Groups and Policymakers

Special interest groups range in size and scope from local farmers to national groups, such as Greenpeace USA, and are capable of sending powerful signals to policymakers. The conduits, or intermediaries, between special interest groups and favorable public policies, are policymakers. The ways in which policymakers filter the demands of special interest groups from those of individual voters are an important issue.

Gordon Tullock writes about the Egg Marketing Board, which has monopoly rights to distribution of all eggs in British Columbia.[27] The Egg Marketing Board is the result of the efforts of a special interest group of roughly 200 egg producers; it has raised the prices all consumers pay for eggs roughly 10 percent above what they would pay without a monopoly distribution policy. While costing every family, on average, an additional $10 per year, this policy has given egg producers an average gain of more than $300,000.

Why did this transfer of income from egg consumers to egg producers occur? The Egg Marketing Board, and the policymakers who sponsor it, claims that it supports "family farms" and stabilizes prices of eggs for families, but Tullock offers the following explanation for why individuals—like special interest groups—have incentives to use policymakers to increase their wealth:

> *The individual who works hard and thinks carefully in order to make money in the market will also work hard and think carefully in order to use the government to increase his wealth. From the individual standpoint, the effort and ingenuity he puts into the project and the return he gets are the important variables, not whether he is using the government or the market for his income. Thus, we should anticipate the effort and ingenuity would be put into using the government for gain, and if we look at the real world we do indeed see such activities.[28]*

The founding fathers of the United States were extremely worried about inherent incentives for special interest groups, or factions, to persuade policymakers to redistribute income from the "many" to the "few" in representative democracies. Called the "violence of the faction" in the *Federalist Papers* by James Madison, redistribution occurs because government policies generally confer substantial benefits on relatively small groups while, at the same time, distributing the costs widely over the population at large. In our example of the Egg Marketing Board, the benefits are high ($300,000 per producer) and flow to few (200 producers), but the costs ($10 per family) are spread thinly across all egg consumers. This phenomenon of income redistribution has been called **rent seeking,** which, in general, occurs when special interest groups attempt to win favors, or rents, from policymakers through the policy process.[29]

Rent seeking is that part of the policy process in which special interest groups try to win favors.

The different incentives facing gainers and losers explain why statesmen like James Madison were so worried about special interest groups' redistribution of income through the policy process. Note how vastly the benefits and costs to supporting or fighting these programs differ. The gainers (200 egg producers) have strong incentives to lobby policymakers for a policy that awards monopoly distribution rights to the Egg Marketing Board. Each individual consumer (loser), however, has

---

[27] This section draws heavily on Gordon Tullock, Welfare for the Well-to-Do (Dallas: Fisher Institute, 1983), which itself draws upon Thomas Borcherding and Gary W. Dorosh, The Egg Marketing Board Simon Fraser University, (Vancouver, B.C.: Simon Fraser University 1981).

[28] Tullock, *Welfare for the Well-to-Do,* 2.

[29] The seminal article here is Gordon Tullock, "The Welfare Costs of Tariffs, Monopolies and Theft," *Western Economic Journal* 5 (June 1967): 224–232.

Removing Plums with Twig Scars and Sunburn Spots from the Marketplace

Marketing orders were created during the Great Depression in response to falling farm incomes. Their aim is clear: By removing produce from markets, government stimulates a price rise, which results in higher incomes for farmers. Over the years, millions of oranges, limes, lemons, and nuts have been removed from the markets through federal marketing orders. Removal usually means either that the produce is left to rot or is purchased by the federal government. Many of these marketing orders were reduced, or eliminated, in the early 1990s, causing a variety of effects on farmers who raise fruit or nuts.

Most plums are grown in California, and in response to the removal of federal marketing orders, plum farmers have recently requested that the state of California govern the plum market through state marketing orders. If "undersize" and "ugly" plums were removed from the market, rising plum prices would improve the incomes of plum farmers. One farmer has requested that all plums with twig scars or sunburn spots be removed from the market. It is estimated that such restrictions would remove roughly 10 percent, or 42,000 half-ton pickup trucks, of the crop from the market each year.

Source: Marshall Fritz, "Protectionist Plum Ripens in California," *Wall Street Journal*, January 7, 1994, A10

Analysis

It is easy to see who gains if marketing orders are reintroduced in the plum market. Since the removal of federal marketing orders, plum prices have experienced the ups and downs that accompany any market that follows ever-changing supplies and demands. Farmers may claim that marketing orders are required to restore stability to the marketplace, but it is not clear that plum farmers should be saved from the ups and downs of the marketplace.

Our discussion of rent seeking suggested that it pays for special interest groups to lobby for policies to raise their income. As one farmer readily admits, "The bottom line, as plum growers: We want more money." Consumers are losers, however, if the marketing orders are approved. With the price increase, they are forced to transfer more of their income to farmers. Consumers will no longer be able to buy small, or blemished, fruit priced below their larger unblemished counterparts. The income transfers that flow from lower-income consumers to farmers are especially interesting. In the words of Debra Saunders of the *San Francisco Chronicle*, "What the poor can't buy, the flies get free."

little incentive to fight, or even become informed about, the redistribution because, even if the consumers fully understood how the policy lowers their income, it would seldom be worth the $10 per year they would (individually) receive if they were to launch a successful policy fight. In these cases, it is likely that consumers choose to be rationally ignorant.

Now consider the different signals that losers (consumers) and gainers (producers) send to policymakers. Policymakers are likely to respond to the powerful and concentrated signals of egg producers (special interest groups) and not the weak and dispersed signals of egg consumers (individual voters). This suggests that the policy process may be captured, to some extent, by special interest groups that favor policies which redistribute income away from nonmembers to themselves. We have, of course, discussed the role of special interest groups several times before. The important new point here, though, is the role of policymakers in providing an avenue for special interest groups through which rent seeking redistributes income through the policy process. The issue of whether policymakers should provide this avenue for redistribution is an open question, but, nonetheless, is an important consideration in our study of public market structure.

Final Observations

The issues regarding resource allocation through the policy process are many and clearly subject to different views of the behaviors of voters and policymakers. As with our discussion of imperfections in private markets, we see that the exchange process of public markets is obviously imperfect as well. The lack of unique voting equilibria in the presence of double-peaked preferences, for example, leads some observers to question the appropriateness of majority voting rules for reaching collective agreement. Logrolling and cycling possibilities make it clear that majority voting does not always result in allocative efficiency. Even under conditions in which policymakers provide the preferences of the median voter, public provision of public goods will not tend to maximize total net social benefits of society.

The choice of what constitutes a voting majority determines which voters guide policy and which voters are in the minority. Voting rules are therefore clearly important in our understanding of the role that voters play in the policy process, as well as the degree to which policies redistribute income and are coercive. Rules are manifestly vital in determining the role of the public sector; for example, those that tend to advocate redistribution as a proper role of government tend to advocate simple majority rules and strongly oppose unanimity rules.

Lack of competition for political office and theories of bureaucracy, Leviathan policymakers, and rent seeking also pose important questions regarding the ability of voters to guide allocations of resources through the policy process. The design of public market structure is an important determinant of the power of policymakers in the policy process and, ultimately, of the role the public sector plays in our economy. The debate over what motivates policymakers is a perennial one and is clearly a significant ingredient in our analysis of the ways in which public market structure affects the policies chosen through the policy process. One way to put these differences into perspective is to frame the issue in terms of the importance of exit options in public market structure. Proponents of the benevolent view of policymakers predict that lack of exit options allows policymakers to provide policies that enhance the well-being of voters. Proponents of the Leviathan view predict that lack of exit options results in policies that serve the narrow self-interests of policymakers.

We do not argue which view is correct. It is important, however, to understand how different assumptions about voters and policymakers lead to different views of the proper role of the public sector in our economy.

Summary

- Voting rules are important determinants of the roles that voters play in the policy process. Under unanimity rules, all individuals must agree to public policies. Unanimous consent, however, is cumbersome and may foster free riders and the status quo.

- An optimal voting rule is one that minimizes decision and external costs of collective agreements. Decision costs are the costs of getting voters to agree on proposals. External costs arise when approved policies impose negative externalities upon minorities.

- A simple majority voting rule allows 51 percent of voters to approve policies that 49 percent of the voting population do not desire. The median voter theorem states that under certain conditions, preferences of the median voter are selected under simple majority rule.

- The median voter theorem has three important implications: (1) Even though all voters receive the same level of public goods, only the median voter receives a quantity consistent with individual maximum net benefits; (2) majority voting does not translate changes in (nonmedian) voter preferences into policy changes; (3) majority voting does not necessarily result in socially efficient production of public goods.

- Simple majority voting does not always result in voting equilibria. Voting cycles may occur when there are endless cycles to the voting process. A requirement for unique voting equilibria is that voter preferences are single peaked.

- Logrolling occurs when in a state of multiple issues voters attempt to further their welfare by trading votes with one another. Logrolling may enhance allocative efficiency, but not always.

- Voters convey information to policymakers on the policies they desire through the voice and exit options available to them. Voice options include letters to policymakers, voting, and working on political campaigns. Voters exercise exit options by leaving one political jurisdiction for another.

- The benevolent view of policymakers is that policymakers pursue policies that best serve the public interest. The Leviathan view is that policymakers pursue policies that serve their narrow self-interests.

- The theory of bureaucracy models the behaviors of civil servants as motivated by the power, pay and, prestige that come with being a government employee. Bureaucracy theory predicts that government expands beyond socially efficient levels.

Review Questions

1. What is meant by a unanimity rule of voting?
2. What is a majority rule of voting? What is an optimal majority voting rule?
3. What is the median voter theorem? What are its major implications?
4. What are the differences between single-peaked preferences and double-peaked preferences?
5. What is meant by logrolling?
6. What are voice and exit options?
7. What are the primary differences between the benevolent and Leviathan views of government?

Discussion Questions

1. It has been argued that because it is unlikely that policies will be agreed to by all voters, the rule of unanimity glorifies the status quo. Do you agree? Can you think of policies under which this would not be true?

2. Consider devising a policy that will address the need for a new public park. Distinguish between the decision (D) and external (E) costs of such a policy, and show how these costs affect where N^* occurs.

3. Using the median voter model, explain why even though all voters receive the same level of public good, only the median voter receives output consistent with maximum net benefits. Explain why the greater are the differences in preferences among voters, the less satisfaction voters as a group receive from majority voting.

4. If cycling continues, collective decisions may never be reached. Explain what vote cycling is, and why it makes intuitive sense that the more homogeneous are preferences, the lower the likelihood of endless cycling.

5. We have argued that examples in which private sector alternatives may foster double-peaked preferences include education, police protection, and parks and playgrounds. We have also noted that in these cases, vote cycling may occur. Can you name other goods and services that might be associated with double-peaked preferences for one or more voters?

6. Would you expect more or less logrolling in committees (for example, in Congress) or logrolling in general elections (for example, presidential elections)?

7. Assess the following statement: The median voter model shows that the views of the "average" voter determine policy.

8. Give examples if you can of policies that policymakers should provide voters even though voters do not recognize that they need them. If such policies exist, are voters irrationally ignorant? Would you recommend that in order to provide these policies, government should eliminate exit possibilities?

9. Give several examples where rent seeking appears to explain policies. Who are the gainers and the losers of these policies? How do the policies gain approval in the policy process?

10. Explain how gerrymandering affects public market structure.

11. What implications about public market structure are drawn from bureaucracy theory?

Key Words

Unanimity rules of voting
Majority rules of voting
Simple majority rule
Optimal majority rule
Decision costs
External costs
Median voter theorem

Voting cycles
Agenda control
Single-peaked preferences
Double-peaked preferences
Logrolling
Private market structure
Public market structure

Voice options
Exit options
Gerrymandering
Benevolent view of government
Leviathan view of government
Bureaucracy theory
Rent seeking

CHAPTER 8

The Demand and Supply of Government

Our study of voters and policymakers provides a framework for determining the role of the public sector in our economy. One measure of that role is the public spending share of gross domestic product (GDP). As Figure 8-1 shows, total public spending during the World War II years (1941–45) rose to unprecedented levels and, at its highest point, commanded close to 50 percent of GDP. Public spending fell to approximately 15 percent of GDP in the years immediately following World War II and currently is about 34 percent of GDP. The figure also shows federal spending, which exhibits trends similar to that of total spending and is now around 25 percent of GDP. Examination of federal and total spending trends demonstrates that despite various ups and downs since World War II, a positive trend characterizes the role of the public sector in our economy.

Thomas Borcherding has placed the issue of public sector expansion in the following way:

> Any scholar of U.S. fiscal history must address one simple, but central point, to wit: Why did Americans, using a highly competitive, democratically organized political framework characterized by much consensus (at least until recently) on the acceptable budgetary process, choose to spend one-twelfth of their income through the public sector at this century's beginning, but over one-third today?[1]

Demanders of public programs are parties (for example, voters and special interest groups) who seek public policies.

Suppliers of public programs are parties (for example, government employees and private contractors) who provide public policies.

It is important to recognize that the United States is not alone when it comes to an expanding public sector. As shown in Chapter 2 (Table 2-5), public sectors of the Organization for Economic Cooperation and Development (OECD) countries have all expanded considerably.

In this chapter we model the size of the public sector within a demand and supply framework. Voters are the **demanders of public programs** in the model. The **suppliers of public programs** are policymakers. This framework allows us to

---

[1] Reprinted from Thomas E. Borcherding, "The Causes of Government Expenditure Growth: A Survey of the U.S. Evidence," *Journal of Public Economics* 28 (1985): 359, with kind permission from Elsevier Science BV, Amsterdam, The Netherlands.

**FIGURE 8-1
Public Spending in the United States as a Share of GDP**

Sources: Facts and Figures on Government Finance, 1991; Budget of the United States Government, 1994.

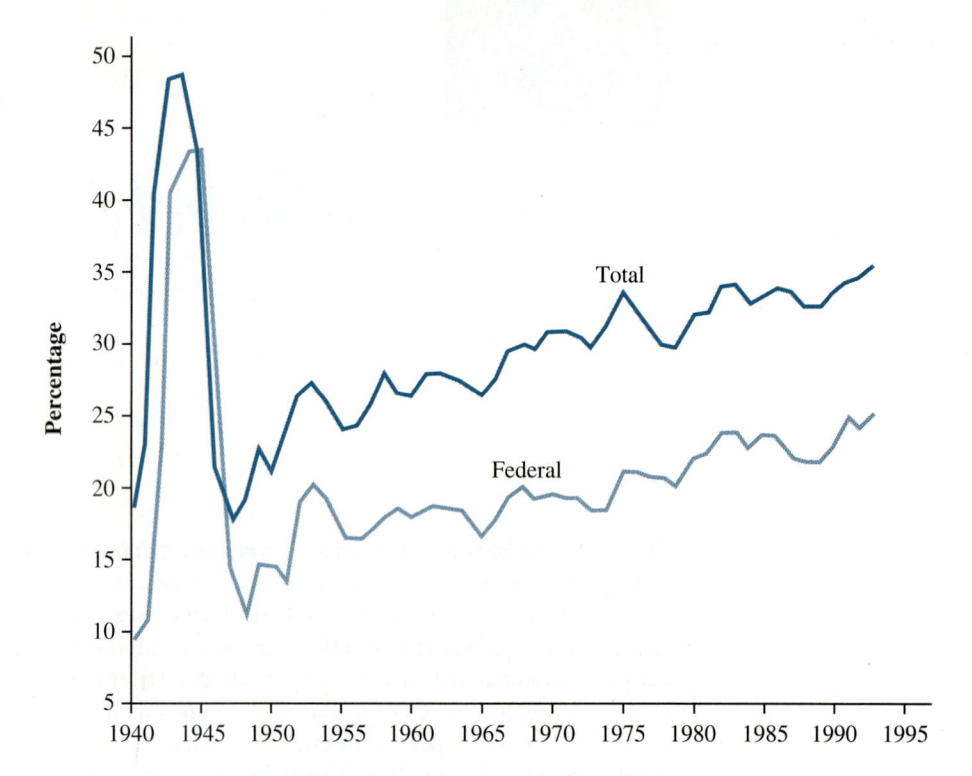

understand how voters and policymakers determine the role of government and its expansion over time. Our study is motivated by the following three facts:

❑ Public sector expansion is universal across countries.[2]
❑ Modern-day (private market-oriented) governments have not experienced permanent reductions in their size.
❑ Consensus is lacking on the causes of public sector expansion.

These three facts frame our modeling of public sector expansion and, while primary emphasis is on the experience of the United States, our discussion is applicable to all countries.

The following issues are addressed in this chapter:

❑ What factors explain the size of the public sector? Which factors are demand related and which factors are supply related?
❑ Does the demand and supply framework clarify the debate over the appropriate size of the public sector? Why do some people believe that the public sector is too small and others believe that it is too large?

---

[2] An early documentation of public sector expansion is G. Warren Nutter, *Growth of Government in the West* (Washington, D.C.: American Enterprise Institute for Public Policy Research, 1978).

❏ What controls might be placed on public sectors to bring expansion more in line with one's view of an appropriate size of the public sector?

Equilibrium Size of the Public Sector

Demand and Supply Framework

The first tools that all economists learn to work with are supply and demand curves. Applied to the problem of explaining the size of the public sector, economists visualize an intersection of supply *(S)* and demand *(D)* curves like that in Figure 8-2, which determines an **equilibrium size of government** G^*. These demand and supply curves are aggregates in the sense that they are the sum of curves that exist in every market in which the public sector allocates resources. There are many markets (for example, spending, credit, and regulation); thus, for simplicity, we examine only the demand and supply for spending programs.

Equilibrium size of government is the size characterized by the intersection of the demand and supply of government.

Just like their private sector counterparts, demand curves for public programs have negative slopes because consumers of those programs are subject to the law of demand. That is, the lower the price of public programs, *ceteris paribus,* the greater the quantity of programs demanded by consumers. Supply curves for public programs have positive slopes because resources are scarce and heterogeneous, just as in the private sector. Our next step examines who the demanders and suppliers of public spending programs are.

Demanders of Public Programs

Voters are demanders of spending programs. Voting rules on what constitutes a majority, who is allowed to vote, and registration requirements are factors that influence the ability of citizens to signal their demands through the policy process. The separation of voters into various collections of demanders, or special interest groups, suggests who demands each program. For example, the elderly demand Social Security payments, parents and teachers demand public education spending, homeowners demand spending on crime prevention, and college students demand low-cost tuition.

Holding income, tastes, and prices of substitute goods constant—the *ceteris paribus* assumption—an inverse relation exists between price and quantity of demand for public spending programs. Let us now explore these factors held constant along demand curves for public programs.

Income is considered an important determinant of the demand for public spending programs. If, for example, public programs are normal goods, increases in income cause demand to rise. Evidence suggests that demands for public programs are income elastic; in other words, for given increases in income, demanders want larger increases in public programs.[3] Introduced in the late nineteenth-century by German economist

---

[3] See, for example, Rati Ram, "Wagner's Hypothesis in Time-Series and Cross-Section Perspectives: Evidence from 'Real' Data for 115 Countries," *Review of Economics and Statistics* 69 (May 1987): 194–204.

FIGURE 8-2
Equilibrium Public Sector Size

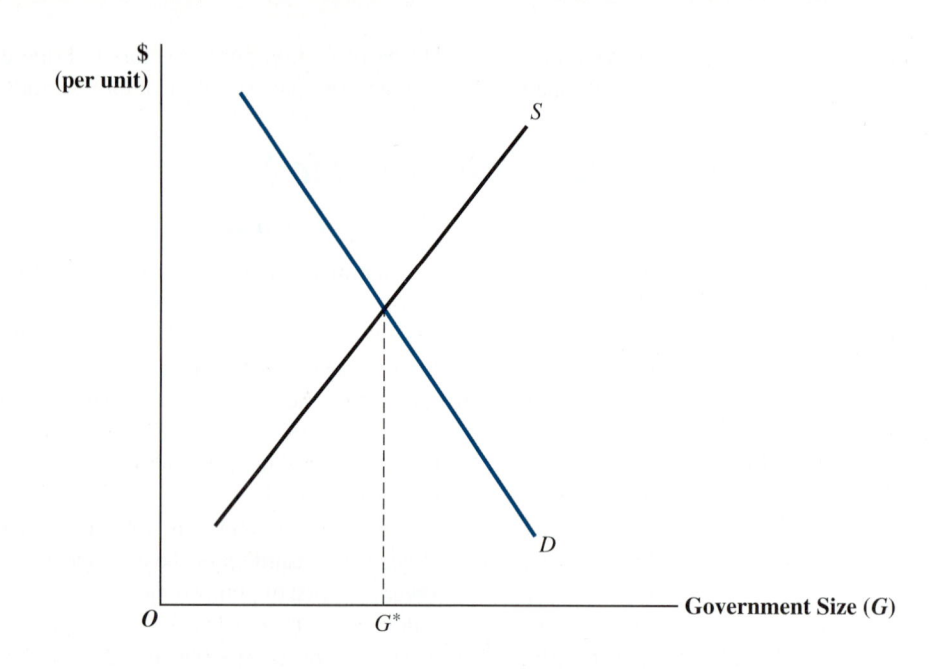

Wagner's law is the theory that public spending increases more quickly than does national income.

Adolph Wagner, this hypothesis is called **Wagner's law.** It was based on the observation that as the standards of living of industrialized economies grow, public sectors tend to grow more quickly.[4] Wagner hypothesized that when industrialized economies experience rising standards of living, pressures for public health, education, and transportation programs grow, and overall public spending therefore tends to rise over time.

Tastes of demanders are also important determinants of demand. Ideology, for instance, is often considered a primary determinant of our tastes for programs and is reflected in public opinion, or attitudes, on permitting the public sector to allocate resources. Simply put, if one's ideology leans toward the belief that the private sector is an efficient allocator of resources, then one tends to be less enthusiastic about public programs than another whose ideology tends toward the belief that the public sector does an excellent job of allocating resources. It is widely believed that public opinion has changed significantly in the last sixty years or so in regard to the resource allocation role of the public sector in the U.S. economy.[5] The depths of the Great Depression of the 1930s and a system called Keynesian economics (and named for John Maynard Keynes) were instrumental in promoting a favorable view of public sector intervention and provision that reflects a pivotal reversal from the earlier laissez-faire view of the role of government. The stronger the faith in, or taste for, public sector intervention, the stronger is voter demand for its programs.

---

[4] *Adolph Wagner Finanzwissenschaft* (1883), partly reproduced in *Classics in Public Finance*, ed. Richard A. Musgrave and Allan T. Peacock (London: Macmillan, 1958).

[5] See, for instance, Herbert McClosky and John Zaller, *The American Ethos: Public Attitudes toward Capitalism and Democracy* (Cambridge, Mass: Harvard University Press, 1984). For a discussion of the ways in which ideology may affect government growth see James B. Kau and Paul H. Rubin, "Self-Interest, Ideology and Logrolling in Congressional Voting," *Journal of Law and Economics* 22 (October 1979): 365–384.

Finally, prices of substitute goods affect the demand for public programs. If, for instance, prices of providing garbage collection or education in the private sector fall relative to similar provision by the public sector, demand for public provision of these goods falls.

Suppliers of Public Programs

Since policymakers are the suppliers of public programs, an elaboration of who they are should promote our understanding of how supply influences the size of the public sector. In addition to elected and nonelected policymakers, private sector consultants and firms also provide goods and services to the public sector. Therefore, the private sector plays an important role in the supply of public programs. Private consultants, for example, provide studies on such issues as the effect of acid rain on the environment and the ways in which new fertilizers may expand crop yields. Private sector firms are major suppliers of defense-related goods and research to the U.S. Department of Defense. Private firms also maintain public roads and buildings and lease office space to all branches of government.

The determinants of supply are technology and resource prices. Technology is the means by which resources are transformed into output. The faster it improves, the more productive resources become, and therefore the quicker supply expands over time. It is commonly hypothesized that because government is less capital intensive than the private sector, the productivity of the public sector tends to lag behind that of the private sector.[6] According to the **price effects hypothesis,** lower productivity follows from the fact that the public sector is oriented toward service and often engages in redistribution, neither of which is particularly capital intensive. An implication of this hypothesis is that even without expansion in the number of public programs, costs of these programs grow faster than costs of private sector goods. In comparison to the private sector, supplies of public programs increase more slowly, since the nature of its production does not take full advantage of technological innovations. Empirical evidence suggests that the price effects hypothesis explains about one-third of U.S. government spending.[7]

Price effects hypothesis theorizes that because rhe public sector is increasingly service-oriented and engaged in transfer policies, government grows more quickly than the economy.

Finally, the higher (lower) are resource costs, *ceteris paribus,* the lower (higher) is the supply of public programs. While resources are the same as in the private sector—land, labor, and capital—the price effects hypothesis suggests that in comparison to the private sector, the public sector tends to be less capital intensive.

Changes in the Equilibrium Size of the Public Sector

Changes in demand and supply explain changes in the size, or growth, of the public sector. Notice that in our examination of public spending, government expansion requires that total expenditures rise over time. Public spending equals total expenditures,

---

[6] William J. Baumol, "The Macroeconomics of Unbalanced Growth: The Anatomy of Urban Crisis," *American Economic Review* 57 (June 1967): 415–426.

[7] Thomas E. Borcherding, "The Causes of Government Expenditures Growth," 359. For a discussion of the literature on this hypothesis, see Dennis C. Mueller, *Public Choice II* (Cambridge, U.K.: Cambridge University Press, 1989), 325–326.

which are determined by multiplying, at equilibrium, price (*P*) times the quantity of public programs (*G*). (For simplicity, we assume that changes in public expenditure do not lead to changes in GDP and that an increase in public spending always leads to a larger share of *GDP* as well.) Figure 8-3 shows what happens to equilibrium public sector size when, assuming no change in supply, demand increases from *D1* to *D2*. Because total expenditures increase from OP_1aG_1 to OP_2bG_2, rising demand is one possible explanation behind an expanding public sector. Similarly, falling demand is one possible explanation for a shrinking public sector.

When supply changes and demand is invariant, two possibilities explain public sector expansion. Let us first consider, as shown in Figure 8-4, an increase in supply. Initial equilibrium expenditures are determined by the intersection of *D1* and *S1* at *a* and therefore are equal to OP_3aG_1. Because price falls, but quantity rises, when supply increases along a given demand curve, the direction that spending follows is determined by the elasticity of demand. Now consider two demand curves: *D1* (relatively price inelastic) and *D2* (relatively price elastic).[8] Observation demonstrates that when supply increases, expenditures rise with price elastic demands (OP_2cG_3) and fall with price inelastic demands (OP_1bG_2).

Figure 8-5 shows how expenditures change when supply falls from *S1* to *S2*. Starting from the initial equilibrium level of expenditures of OP_1aG_3, expenditures rise to OP_3bG_2 with inelastic demand *D1* and fall to OP_2cG_1 with elastic demand *D2*.

Expanding public sectors may now be explained by

- Rising elastic or inelastic demand (holding supply fixed) or
- Rising supply (holding an elastic demand fixed) or
- Falling supply (holding an inelastic demand fixed).

And shrinking public sectors may be explained by

- Falling elastic or inelastic demand (holding supply fixed) or
- Rising supply (holding an inelastic demand fixed) or
- Falling supply (holding an elastic demand fixed).

Because of the importance of demand elasticity in explanations of public sector expansion, it is relevant to question whether demands for public programs tend to be price elastic or inelastic. Studies indicate that elasticity coefficients tend to be around −0.40, which is highly price inelastic.[9] Our model of the demand and supply of public expenditures therefore suggests one of two possible candidates for explaining public sector expansion:

- Rising demand (holding supply fixed) or
- Falling supply (holding an inelastic demand fixed)

---

[8] A discussion of elasticity is provided in the appendix at the end of the book.

[9] See, for example, Theodore C. Bergstrom and Robert P. Goodman, "Private Demands for Public Goods," *American Economic Review* 63 (June 1973): 280–296; and Thomas E. Borcherding and Robert T. Deacon, "The Demand for the Services of Nonfederal Governments," *American Economic Review* 62 (December 1972): 891–901.

**FIGURE 8-3
Increase in Demand
for Government**

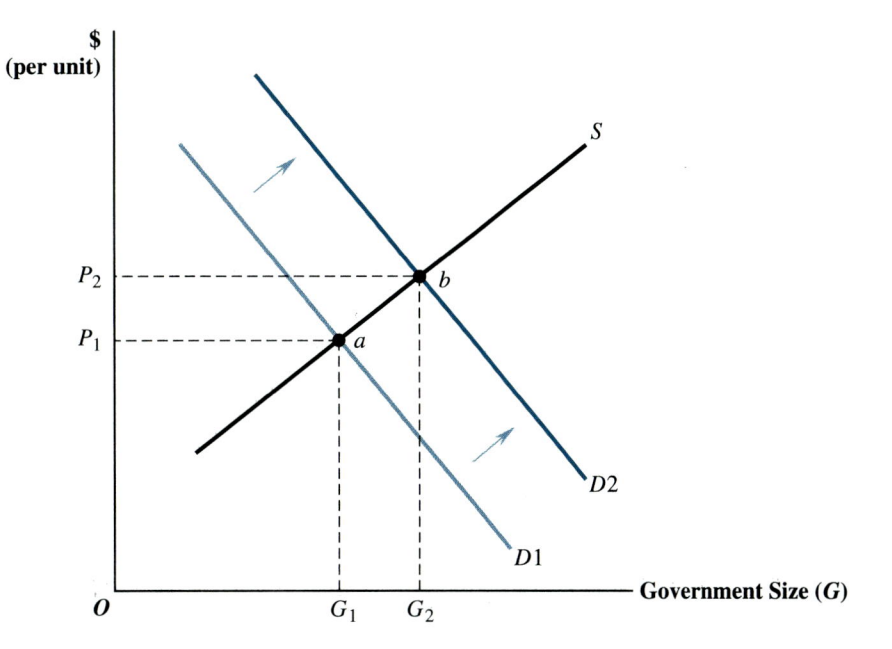

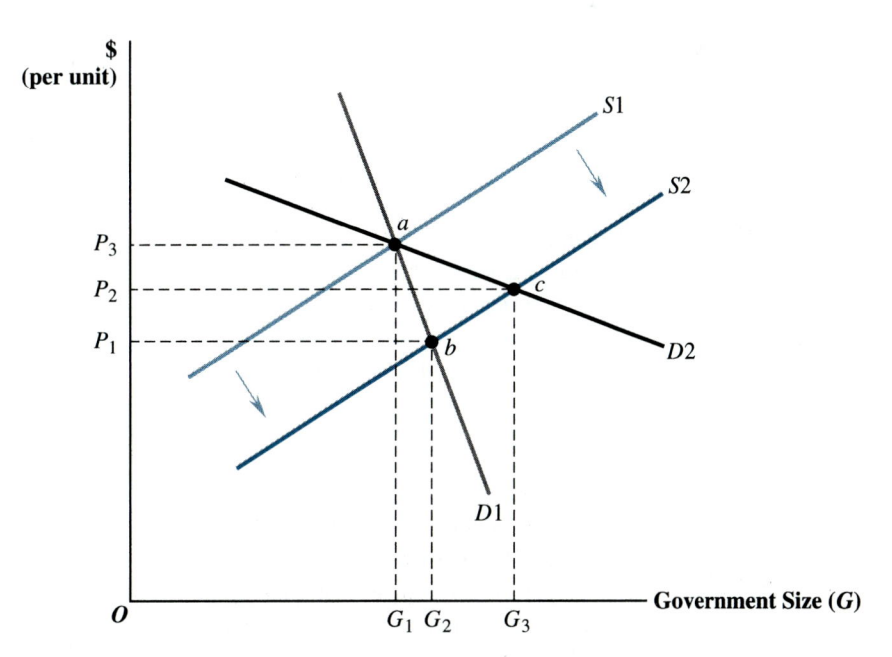

**FIGURE 8-4
Increase in Supply
of Government**

**FIGURE 8-5
Decrease in Supply
of Government**

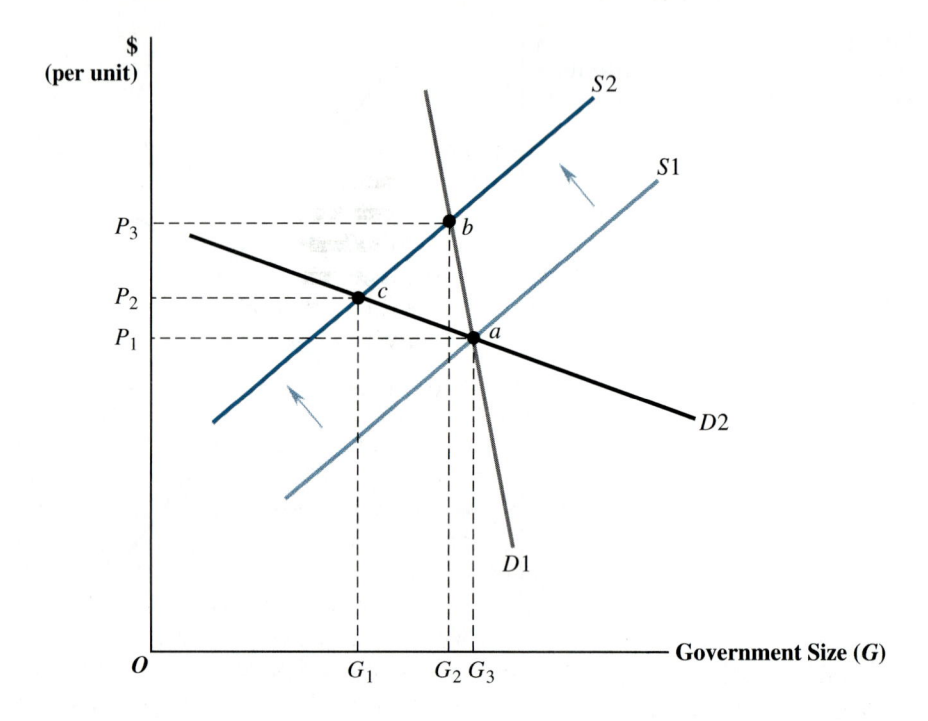

In this section, we have presented several hypotheses to suggest reasons for public sector expansion. Hypotheses regarding changes in ideology, price effects, and rising income predict growth of public sectors through changes in either demand or supply. Over the past twenty-five years, however, many newer theories have been developed so we now look at the important and expanding literature within our supply and demand framework.

Demand-Side Explanations

Urbanization

Urbanization, or the increasing percentage of population in urban areas, has been suggested as a factor that affects public sector demand. Since all developed countries have experienced rising urbanization, this hypothesis deserves some consideration. Two reasons are usually given to support the notion that urbanization contributes to public sector expansion. First, with rising urbanization, increased cost savings from sharing public goods (parks, museums, libraries) raise the demand for these public goods, thereby causing an expansion in the public sector. Second, with increasing urbanization, congestion and other negative externalities rise, resulting in increases in the demand for government intervention. Because the evidence for this theory is largely anecdotal and therefore not prone to produce hard data, this explanation of expansion is awarded little attention. Moreover, it is not the increased provision of public goods that accounts for much of government expansion, but rather, increases in programs that redistribute income among voters.

Demand for Income Redistribution

Redistribution policies have grown more rapidly than all other public policies; this growth is therefore the focus of much attention. Some theorize that special interest groups are the general force behind demands for income redistribution. They adduce evidence that increases in the number and size of special interest groups result in rising demand for policies that redistribute resources to their membership and hence an expanding public sector.[10]

One area of research models the ways in which changes in voting franchises affect the demand for income redistribution by various special interest groups. The median voter model predicts that extension of the voting franchise to citizens with incomes below those of the previous median voter causes the new median voter to determine elections under majority voting. In effect, extending the vote creates a new median voter, which represents a newly created special interest group. Assuming lower-income individuals prefer public programs that distribute income in their favor, extensions of the voting franchise may make government grow because of newly created demands. This thinking therefore leads to two hypotheses: (1) As the voting franchise is extended to lower-income individuals, redistribution policy expands; and (2) the direction of an expanded redistribution policy is from rich to poor. Some evidence supports both hypotheses.[11]

Another theory is that income differences among voters explain public sector expansion. The argument is that greater redistribution occurs when income distribution is uniform than when it is uneven since the more uniform the distribution of income within a given special interest group, the more easily that interest group may capture favors from policymakers. Empirical support for this argument indicates that, contrary to the hypothesis using the median voter model, income redistribution does not always flow from rich to poor but depends critically upon who has the largest special interest group (a function of the lowest transaction costs of organizing as many voters as possible).[12]

Demand by Public Sector Employees

Substantial evidence shows that public sector employees vote not only more often than other citizens, but they also tend to vote for expanding the role of the public sector in the economy.[13] Two opposing motivations may explain why public employees

---

[10] See, for example, Dennis C. Mueller and Peter Murrell, "Interest Groups and the Size of Government," *Public Choice* 48 (1986): 125–145.

[11] See Allan H. Meltzer and Scott F. Richard, "A Rational Theory of the Size of Government," *Journal of Political Economy* 89 (October 1981): 914–927.

[12] Sam Peltzman, "The Growth of Government," *Journal of Law and Economics* 23 (October 1980): 209–288.

[13] For evidence on voting participation, see Winston C. Bush and Arthur T. Denzau, "The Voting Behavior of Bureaucrats and Public Sector Growth," in *Budgets and Bureaucrats: The Sources of Government Growth*, ed. Thomas E. Borcherding (Durham: Duke University Press, 1977); and James T. Bennett and William P. Orzechowski, "The Voting Behavior of Bureaucrats: Some Empirical Evidence," *Public Choice* (1983): 271–283. See Edward M. Gramlich and Daniel L. Rubinfeld, "Voting on Public Spending: Differences between Public Employees, Transfer Receipts, and Private Workers," *Journal of Policy Analysis and Management* 1 (1982): 516–533.

favor such expansion. One view is that public employees may more easily increase their incomes and power when public sectors are expanding than when they are shrinking or maintaining the status quo in resource allocation.[14] The other view is that they genuinely believe in their ability to improve resource allocation in the economy. Even though they assume opposite motivations, both views concur that public employees demand expansion of the public sector. While relatively little research has been performed on the influence of demand by public employees, there is extensive research on public employees as suppliers of public programs.

Fiscal Illusion

Fiscal illusion hypothesis
theorizes that current policies are the result of incorrect perceptions by voters.

The debate about the ability of demanders to understand the costs and benefits of public programs includes the contention that, without perfect information, such demands are sustained by perceptions rather than facts. The **fiscal illusion hypothesis** suggests that demanders tend to underestimate the costs of public programs and therefore argues that voters base their demands on an illusory price—one that is lower than the true price.[15] This underestimation phenomenon may be due, at least in part, to the complexity of the tax system and the fact that, because calculation is costly, voters may exhibit rational ignorance over true tax burdens. The argument is strengthened by the supposition that voters feel they have little recourse with respect to their tax burdens. They may not be inclined to calculate the true costs because they are persuaded that such knowledge cannot significantly change the situation. There is no question that tax sources are plentiful, and little that citizens may not fully recognize their true tax burdens. Consider, for example, that prior to 1942, the Internal Revenue Service collected income tax after the year was over—and that now these taxes are withheld from each paycheck as they are received. Taxes are also collected each time we go to the grocery store, fill our cars with gasoline, purchase liquor, attend sporting events, buy clothes, eat at restaurants, and pay utility bills. Thus taxes have become so much a part of daily life that they are becoming nearly invisible.

It follows that because the net benefit for any public program is measured as the difference between benefits and costs, net benefits must be overestimated whenever costs are underestimated. Within the framework of this hypothesis, then, it is the fiscal illusion that causes an expansion of the public sector because mis- or uninformed voters continue to demand public programs whose net benefits they overestimate.

The hypothesis that voters generally underestimate the costs of public programs financed through budget deficits has been the subject of much controversy within economics.[16] It is known, however, that the U.S. government has greatly expanded the

---

[14] See Gordon Tullock, "Dynamic Hypothesis on Bureaucracy," *Public Choice* 19 (1974): 127–131; and James M. Buchanan and Gordon Tullock, "The Expanding Public Sector: Wagner Squared," *Public Choice* 32 (1977): 147–150.

[15] For evidence in favor, see Richard C. Wagner, "Revenue Structure, Fiscal Illusion, and Budgetary Choice," *Public Choice* 25 (1976): 45–61; and for evidence against, see Kevin V. Greene and Vincent G. Munley, "Generating Growth in Public Expenditures: The Role of Employee and Constituent Demand," *Public Finance Quarterly* 7 (1979): 82–109.

[16] James M. Buchanan and Richard W. Wagner, *Democracy in Deficit: The Political Legacy of Lord Keynes* (New York: Academic Press, 1977).

degree to which it funds spending through deficit finance, as Figure 8-6 shows. If, for example, voters do underestimate future tax burdens associated with deficit finance, they may believe that public programs are cheaper than they really are. Underestimation occurs when voters believe that current taxes cost more than the present value of future taxes required to pay off today's deficit. Misled by this underestimation, voters then overestimate the net benefits of public programs. This error, in turn, leads them to demand more programs than if current spending were financed entirely by current taxes. It may also be the case that voters may estimate tax burdens correctly but fail to care because they wish to make future generations pay the higher future taxes.

Critics of the fiscal illusion theory of deficit finance argue that voters are unlikely to systematically underestimate financing burdens and that expansion of the public sector is therefore unlikely to be a result of fiscal illusion.[17] In their view, fiscal illusion can cause permanent increases in the public sector only so long as it comes up with new illusions that continue to mislead voters. While these theories regarding deficit finance are especially interesting in light of the rise of deficit finance by the U.S. government since the 1970s, little empirical research is available on the influence of deficit spending on public sector expansion. Testing of this hypothesis will likely be the object of increased study in the near future.

Supply-Side Explanations

Bureaucracy Theory

Bureaucracy theory involves the hypothesis that public employees, or bureaucrats, possess sufficient monopoly power over public sector supply to expand spending beyond the levels that voters prefer. Bureaucrats, it is argued, want larger budgets because of the power, pay, and prestige associated with such expansion; associated with this is the premise that public sector provision of goods is usually more costly than private sector provision.[18] Bureaucracy theory may explain why budgets are larger when bureaucrats exercise monopoly power, but it is not clear how this explains the steady increase in the public sector over this century. Only with *increasing* provision of goods by government—that is, perpetual increases in monopoly power—does this theory predict that public spending will continue to rise over time.

Some support, however, for using bureaucracy theory to explain public sector expansion is apparent in the **crisis, or displacement, theory of government**.[19]

Crisis (displacement) theory of government predicts that government expansion occurs as the result of significant, adverse past events.

---

[17] See, for example, Robert J. Barro, "Comments from an Unreconstructed Ricardian," *Journal of Monetary Economics* 4 (August 1978): 569–581.

[18] Evidence in support of the hypothesis that governments act like monopolists is provided in Thomas E. Borcherding, Winston C. Bush, and Robert M. Spann, "The Effects of Public Spending on the Divisibility of Public Outputs in Consumption, Bureaucratic Power, and the Size of the Tax-Sharing Group," in *Budgets and Bureaucrats: The Sources of Government Growth,* ed. Thomas E. Borcherding (Durham, N.C.: Duke University Press, 1977).

[19] This connection to bureaucracy theory follows the discussion in Mueller, *Public Choice II,* 347. The crisis theory was first applied to the United Kingdom in Alan T. Peacock and Jack Wiseman, *The Growth of Public Expenditure in the United Kingdom* (Princeton, N.J.: Princeton University Press, 1961). For an application to the United States, see Robert Higgs, *Crisis and Leviathan: Critical Episodes in the Growth of American Government* (New York: Oxford University Press, 1987).

FIGURE 8-6
Budget Deficits (−) and Surpluses (+)

Source: Budget of the United States Government, 1994.

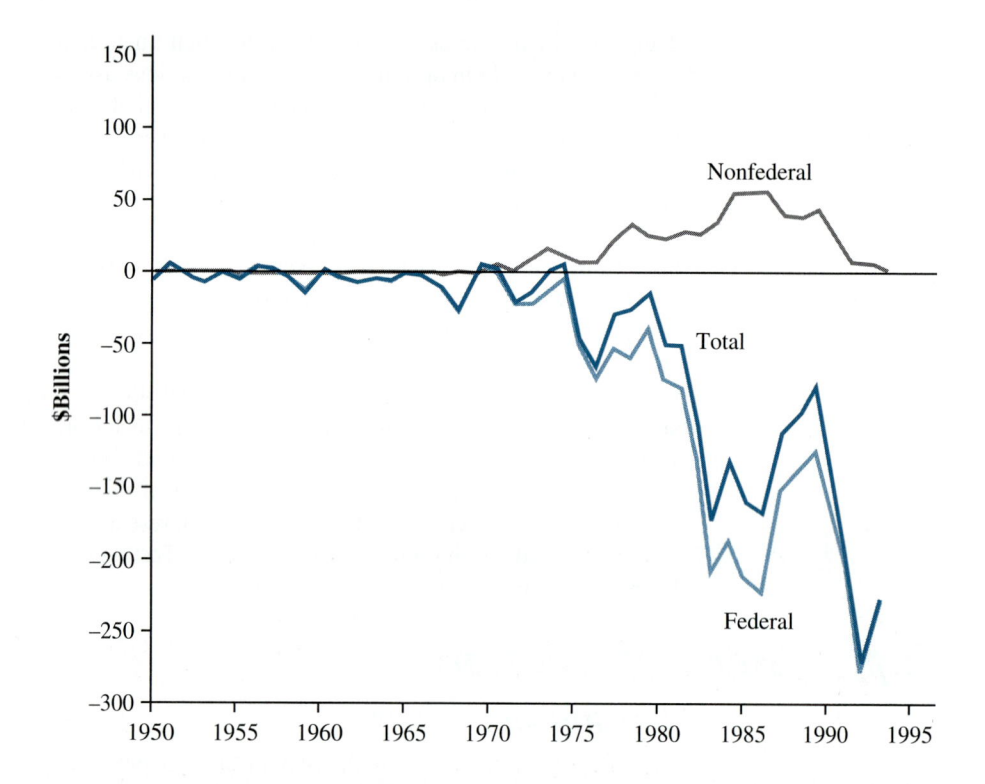

National emergencies, such as wars and depressions, often engender immediate and rapid increases in the role of the public sector. In wartime, for example, private factories are quickly converted to produce defense-related goods such as weapons and aircraft. The crisis theory predicts that normal barriers to public sector expansion, such as lengthy congressional debate before passage of new legislation, are often lowered during crises, and because these barriers are removed, crises can result in a permanent expansion of government. Two conditions create an environment conducive to public sector expansion. First, while the role of the public sector is reduced after emergencies pass, its post-emergency size never falls back to pre-emergency levels. Second, there must be a continuum of emergencies over time that lead to an ongoing expansion over time. When these two conditions are met, bureaucracy theory may explain public sector expansion, since each time the role of the public sector is expanded, budget-maximizing bureaucrats ratchet up budget size over that which existed before the emergency.

While the crisis theory has great intuitive appeal, it is difficult to test a theory that predicts that crises lead to expansion of the public sector. For obvious cases like the Great Depression or World War II, substantial casual evidence supports this theory. But what else constitutes a crisis? While some may argue that the savings and loan industry or health care have been in a state of crisis in recent years, some crises or emergencies are clearly more intense than others. Economists and historians have not yet clearly defined *crisis,* and as a result little effort has been exerted in empirically testing this theory.

The Agriculture Department: Bureaucracy Theory in Action?

The Department of Agriculture is considered by many to be an example of bureaucracy theory in action. Much of its departmental structure was developed in the early 1930s, when many American farmers were battling the Great Depression. In 1932, the department had 32,000 employees, caring for roughly 7 million full-time farmers, or 25 percent of all Americans. Today the Department of Agriculture employs some 110,000 to 154,000 workers, administering to fewer than 400,000 farmers, or roughly 2 percent of all Americans. Interestingly, the Agriculture Department is not even sure how many individuals it employs.

One Department official has recently admitted, "We have tried to get a straight answer to this question for as long as I have been here. Our staff still cannot give us an accurate answer."

Source: "Farming: A Soft Touch," *The Economist*, January 23, 1993, 26–27.

Analysis

Critics question why the Agriculture Department now employs one bureaucrat for every four farmers when, in the 1930s, it employed roughly one bureaucrat for every 218 farmers. It has gained additional responsibilities in various areas (e.g., food stamp and farm subsidy programs), but a recent congressional report concluded that most large farmers "do not need direct government payments and/or subsidies to compete and survive." In fact, farmers' financial positions have never been better: Farmers enjoy incomes that are more than twice the U.S. average, and their average net worth is roughly $700,000.

Does bureaucracy theory help explain the expansion of the agriculture bureaucracy? Its many employees may represent a powerful voice in support of maintaining, if not increasing, its influence on the U.S. economy. But remember that farmers represent a powerful special interest group and, together with Agriculture Department employees, they are a very powerful lobby in Washington as well. The influence of the bureaucracy may explain why attempts in the early 1990s to eliminate 1,000 of the 3,700 department's field offices have been recently changed to a new strategy of attempting to reduce the size of the Washington bureaucracy. Reformers would welcome any reduction, but they have little hope that the new strategy holds much promise of curtailing the influence of this most powerful bureaucracy.

Advocates argue that U.S. farming needs to be protected through subsidies administered by a powerful Department of Agriculture in Washington. This perspective reflects the long tradition of U.S. farming and enjoys the support of many voters.

Public Sector Centralization

The centralization hypothesis addresses the issue of whether governments act as monopolists when competitors are weak or absent.[20] This hypothesis complements

---

[20] Geoffrey Brennan and James M. Buchanan, *The Power to Tax: Analytical Foundations of a Fiscal Constitution* (Cambridge, U.K.: Cambridge University Press, 1980).

bureaucracy theory as it predicts that when governments have monopoly power, they tend to favor the interests of the suppliers of public programs over those of demanders. Proponents of this theory hypothesize that the ability of voters to use exit options is influenced by the degree to which the public sector is monopolized; therefore, the greater is centralization, the less discipline voters can assert over Leviathan policymakers who are motivated by self-interest to promote costly production, expand budgets, and increase taxes. Thus, voter flight from highly taxed, unresponsive political jurisdictions is assumed to be more difficult with each increase in the degree of government centralization, or monopolization.

In Figure 8-7 we see that since the early 1900s, the federal share of total public spending has risen from about 35 percent to roughly 60 percent. In other words, centralization, measured as the federal share of total spending, has grown considerably in that time. Centralization theory predicts that this trend weakens intergovernmental competition between state and local governments, and that this growing centralization results in continued expansion of the public sector. Empirical evidence is mixed, but a growing number of studies lend support for the centralization hypothesis.[21]

Taxes Cause Spending

Tax-spend hypothesis theorizes that spending rises in response to higher tax revenues.

The **tax-spend hypothesis** predicts that revenues determine spending levels; that is, whenever governments increase taxes, public spending rises. The tax-spend model rests on the assumption that there is always a worthwhile program that someone wishes to implement through legislation. Tax increases are predicted to raise expenditures since governments, like individual consumers, are subject to scarce resources; thus there is never any lack of programs that individual voters and special interest groups wish to fund. It makes intuitive sense that it is easier to fund new programs when tax revenues are rising than when they are constant or falling. Moreover, there are always issues such as poverty and unemployment that someone wishes to remedy through the expansion of existing programs or the creation of new ones.

Taxes may rise over time for several reasons. One obvious way is for Congress to pass tax increases. Another way is through inflation, in the process called *bracket creep*. The high inflation of the 1970s, for example, saw tax revenues rise rapidly with inflation. When inflation rises, individual incomes tend to rise, and with a progressive tax system, taxes rise faster than increases in income. One recent estimate is that (inflation-adjusted) taxes go up 6 percent for every increase in inflation of 10 percent.[22] Another reason for rising taxes is the decreasing costs of tax collection caused by technological and structural innovations; computers, for example, have made collection more efficient, and the withholding system, whereby employers collect taxes for governments, has shifted much of the costs of collection to the private sector. Tax collection is clearly easier when employers withhold taxes from paychecks. Private firms also facilitate the collection process when, for instance, gas stations, grocery

---

[21] For a discussion of differences between the many studies see David Joulfaian and Michael L. Marlow, "Centralization and Government Competition," *Applied Economics* 23 (October 1991): 1603–1612.

[22] Lawrence B. Lindsey, *The Growth Experiment: How the New Tax Policy Is Transforming the U.S. Economy* (New York: Basic Books, 1990), 101.

**FIGURE 8-7
Centralization of
Spending**

Sources: Budget of the United States Government, 1994; and Economic Report of the President, 1994.

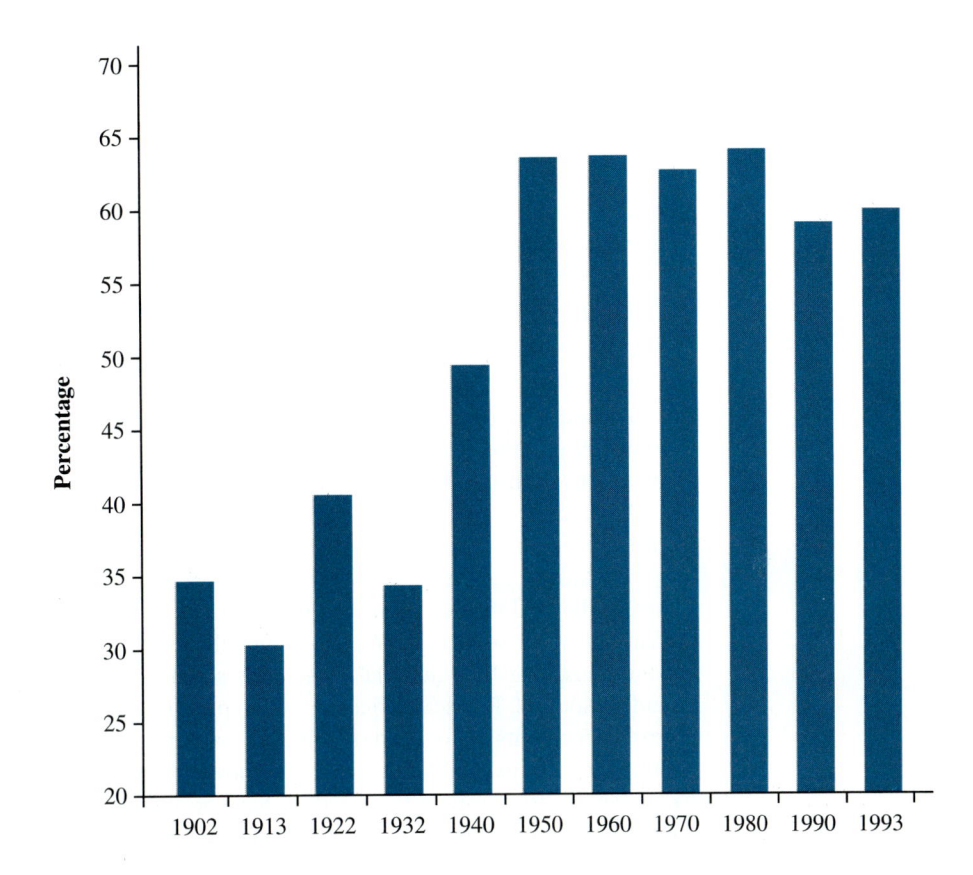

stores, and airlines collect taxes from consumers. In tax-spend theory all this efficiency in tax collection, which causes tax revenues to rise, causes public spending to rise as well.[23]

The tax-spend model calls into question the causal direction of taxes and spending and therefore turns on a behavioral issue concerning what motivates the spenders of public monies. These issues of causality have been tested in a growing literature on the behavior of local, state, and federal governments. Thus far, empirical studies suggest some support for the hypothesis that taxes cause spending.[24]

---

[23] See, for example, James B. Kau and Paul H. Rubin, "The Size of Government," *Public Choice* 37 (1981): 261–274; and Benjamin Ward, "Taxes and the Size of Government," *American Economic Review* 72 (May 1982): 346–350.

[24] For studies in support of the tax-spend hypothesis, see Neela Manage and Michael L. Marlow, "The Causal Relation between Federal Expenditures and Receipts," *Southern Economic Journal* 52 (January 1986): 717–729; and Paul R. Blackley, "Causality between Revenues and Expenditures and the Size of the Federal Budget," *Public Finance Quarterly* 14 (April 1986): 139–156. A study that does not support the hypothesis is George Von Furstenburg, Jeffrey R. Green, and Jin-Ho Jeong, "Tax and Spend or Spend and Tax," *Review of Economics and Statistics* 67 (May 1986): 179–188.

Implications of Theories for Policy Process

Many theories exist and though each attempts to explain public sector expansion, the variety of hypotheses indicates that the roles voters and policymakers play in public sector expansion are complex. By summarizing the many theories into several categories that combine one or more common elements, we can address the controversial, but extremely important, issue of whether public sectors tend to be too small or large.

Expansion as a Result of Government Monopoly

Theories of bureaucracy and centralization represent the Leviathan view of government. Monopoly hypotheses imply that the policy process is lopsided in such a way as to award primary leverage to policymakers. Coupled with an assumption that policymakers are motivated by narrow self-interest, these hypotheses predict that policy institutions with monopolistic elements do not serve the best interests of voters, in much the same way that microeconomic theory predicts that consumers are not well served when goods and services are provided by monopolists.

Leviathan and bureaucratic models of policymakers predict that government expands beyond the desires of voters and that remedies for overexpansion are appropriate. Their proponents emphasize that public institutions should become more competitive and that constitutional constraints should be placed upon the government's funding sources. Political offices, for example, are often held to be ruled by monopolistic incumbents who erect significant barriers to entry by challengers. Gerrymandering, for example, is viewed as a means of maintaining monopoly elements in public markets. Term limitations, then, have been prescribed as one possible means to introduce more competition into political office. Privatization has also been proposed as another possible remedy. If the provision of publicly provided private goods is transferred to the private sector, competing private firms may provide these goods more cheaply to demanders.

Advocates of bureaucracy and centralization theories view the nonelected component of policymaking—that is, the bureaucracy—as monopolistic as well. Their prescriptions for controlling overexpansion thus often emphasize a widening of exit options for demanders. One such prescription is to require public bureaus to compete against one another. If public pension or deposit insurance funds were allowed to compete, for example, it is hypothesized that the result would be goods that are more sensitive to the wishes of demanders. In other words, if demanders of pension funds were able to choose between public pension A or B, it is argued that both pensions A and B would perform better than pension M—a single monopoly pension to which all voters must contribute. In much the same way that decentralization into many small competing governments is hypothesized to inject competition into public markets (as argued in the centralization hypothesis), competition among public agencies is expected to hold the monopolistic power of bureaucracies in check.

Expansion as a Result of Special Interest Groups

Theories of demands for income redistribution, including demands by government employees, suggest that various collections of voters tend to have more voice in the policy process. We have seen that there are significant cost savings that accrue to voters who promote a common cause through formation of special interest groups—their signals to policymakers can be extremely powerful. When the demands of special interest groups are met through a steady stream of tax revenues, the tax-spend hypothesis predicts that the result is a steady stream of new spending for existing and new programs that redistribute income toward their membership.

At issue is whether special interest groups exert undue influence in their role as voters in the policy process. Previous discussion suggests that special interest groups cause overexpansion of the public sector when their activities produce negative externalities. Proposed remedies for overexpansion include limitations on public subsidies for special interest groups and strict restrictions on the amount of money that PACs may contribute to political candidates. Measures that increase the voters' ability to exit coercive policies are also recommended, which may offer individual voters more control over the narrowly self-interested policies that policymakers are pressed to provide. Constitutional restrictions on the ability to raise money may also be appropriate constraints on overexpansion, given the inherent tendency of governments to find new programs to fund when tax revenues rise (tax-spend hypothesis). Tax limits, for instance, may restrain governments from providing policies that serve the narrow self-interests of special interest groups as is the case in six state governments which have placed caps on revenue growth.

If, however, special interest groups are assumed to be sending appropriate signals to policymakers—signals that improve (or exert neutral effects on) the well-being of other voters in society—monopolistic theories imply that the resulting expansion of the public sector may not be excessive. For example, if public employees are able to increase public sector size through their high voting participation, the influence of these public servants on the policy process may be appropriate. In that case public subsidies and fewer restrictions on political contributions are obvious strategies for fostering the beneficial influences that special interest groups may provide in the policy process.

Expansion as a Result of Misperceptions

The fiscal illusion hypothesis rests on the assumption that voters almost inevitably misperceive the costs of public policies. Proponents of this view believe that the complexities in tax policy and/or miscalculation of the burdens associated with deficit finance cause the public sector to expand beyond the true desires of voters. Two possible remedies for such voter misperceptions are simplification of tax policies and constitutional limitations on deficits. Most states have some constitutional or legislative limitations on deficits, but the U.S. government operates under no such rule.

There is, however, a symmetrical argument that fiscal illusion may also occur when voters *underestimate* the benefits of public policies.[25] Proponents of this view maintain that voters tend to demand less government than is desirable; hence the public sector is likely to expand less slowly than would be the case if voters were not subject to this misperception. Other than the implementation of programs that try to inform voters about the true nature of benefits, it is not clear what remedies would

---

[25] Anthony Downs, "Why the Government Budget Is Too Small in a Democracy," *World Politics* 12 (1960): 541–563.

dispel this illusion and permit the public sector to expand commensurately with the true nature of its costs and benefits—although it has been argued that increased centralization may allow a faster expansion that would compensate for public misperceptions.

One recent hypothesis has advanced the notion that decentralization causes government to be too small and that competing governments are forced by businesses and voters to keep taxes lower than necessary to provide an appropriate level of public spending.[26] Under this view, businesses and voters are presumed to care more about low taxes than about the beneficial effects of programs funded by those taxes. If, for example, one state were to raise its taxes to provide some much-needed benefit, that revenue hike would result in taxpayer flight, thereby compromising the state's financial viability. In this view decentralization is responsible for the inability of government to provide adequate services owing to policymakers' fears of losing votes.

One prescription for solving this problem is to have all states share a common tax collection effort, thereby eliminating the ability of voters and businesses to flee from a high-tax state to a low-tax state—that is, closing off exit possibilities. This proposition contains two related assumptions: that the higher monopoly power that results from closing off tax-related competition among states will *not* be exploited by narrowly self-interested policymakers, and that voters and businesses will be forced to pay greater attention to the benefits that different state governments provide their voters. This view—in which the public sector is seen as too small—clearly represents a counterpoint to the Leviathan view of government. In this case policymakers are regarded as benevolent and voters as ill-informed on the benefits of expanded public policies. Thus, for example, voters who use their exit options to force governments to set tax revenues below truly desirable levels are, in effect, militating against their own interests; that is, what they would really desire if they fully understood all the issues.

Public Sector Expansion and Economic Growth

The legacy of John Maynard Keynes (1883–1946) created a lengthy interval in which many economists took for granted the notion that public policies could at the very least lessen the length and severity of business downturns in the economy. Fiscal policies of spending and taxation were the common prescription of Keynesian economists for recessions and depressions. When expansionary fiscal policies are predicted to exert positive influences on macroeconomic performance, little concern is evidenced for the fact that such policies tend to expand the public sector.

Since the 1960s, however, the ability of tax and spend programs to improve upon the growth of the macroeconomy has been increasingly questioned. Moreover, some economists predict that continued expansion of public programs exerts negative influences on macroeconomic growth. This is a troubling idea because, to the extent that public policies reduce the rate at which the economy grows, society's standard of

---

[26] Alice M. Rivlin, *Reviving the American Dream: The Economy, the States and the Federal Government* (Washington, D.C.: Brookings Institution, 1992).

living falls as well. Although some may argue that macroeconomic growth should not be the main focus of public policy, economic growth has important implications for the ability of public sectors to redistribute income among the citizens. It may be easier, for instance, to engage in more redistribution, if the economy is growing fast than if an economy is growing slowly or not at all. Moreover, there is increasing support for the view that it is easier for an economy to allocate resources to such areas as the environment and health care when its economy is expanding than when it is contracting or stagnant.

Often governments finance their expansion through progressive taxation. Public finance economists, however, hypothesize that marginal tax rates influence the incentives of workers to supply their services in the economy—specifically, they argue that workers will work longer and harder, the lower are marginal tax rates. When marginal tax rates on income are 90 percent, for instance, 90 cents of each additional dollar earned is taken away from the worker and transferred to the public sector. If marginal tax rates are lowered to 50 percent, only 50 cents of each additional dollar is transferred to the public sector. As long as it is assumed that workers prefer to keep a larger portion of their income, reductions in marginal tax rates are predicted to increase work effort and lead to higher economic growth.

If public sector expansion is financed through raising marginal tax rates, the claim that such policies slow economic growth must be considered as a possible cost of an expanding public sector. In other words, if higher marginal tax rates finance the building of a new bridge, our calculation of net social benefits associated with the new bridge must consider the detrimental effects (if any) exerted on the macroeconomy. Detrimental effects may, for example, take the form of lost jobs and output. Such costs must be taken into account before we can determine the net benefits of public programs that expand the size of the public sector. (Note also that, in this case, the public sector's share of the economy will tend to rise in response to the reduction in economic growth. That is, if we measure the size of the public sector as *G/GDP*, where *G* = government spending, reductions in *GDP* by itself lead to increases in *G/GDP*.)

Government expansion caused by special interest groups has also recently been argued to hinder overall macroeconomic growth.[27] It has been predicted, for example, that, because relatively young nations have less buildup of special interest groups, these nations experience faster economic growth than do older nations whose special interest groups have accumulated over time. Because lack of special interest groups is argued to reflect less rent-seeking activity, resources are hypothesized to be more efficiently allocated in younger nations. As examples, the post–Civil War South and post–World War II Japan are adduced as evidence of rapid economic growth. This is an interesting hypothesis, but it should be noted that the empirical evidence is mixed.[28]

---

[27] Mancur Olson, *The Rise and Decline of Nations* (New Haven, Conn.: Yale University Press, 1982).

[28] See, for example, Clark Nardinelli, Myles S. Wallace, and John T. Warner, "Explaining Differences in State Growth: Catching Up versus Olson," *Public Choice* 52 (1987): 201–213; and John McCallum, "Government, Special Interest Groups, and Economic Growth," *Public Choice* 54 (1987): 3–18.

Final Analysis

It should be clear by now that the reason that there are so many theories explaining public sector expansion is that there are so many views regarding what motivates the behaviors of voters and policymakers in the policy process. Analysis of these issues leads to many interesting hypotheses that may explain the size and growth of the public sector, and each provides, in one way or another, a possible explanation for the expansion of government over this century.

Demand-side explanations emphasize that voters receive what they demand—that the current size of the public sector, as well as its growth over time, is the result of a policy process that is sensitive to the wishes of voters. Public sector expansion is therefore interpreted as a result of a growing demand by individual voters and special interest groups. While Wagner's law and theories on urbanization and fiscal illusion place primary emphasis on the demands of the average voter, theories regarding demands for income redistribution and demands by public sector employees place primary emphasis on special interest groups as an explanation for increases in voters' demand for public programs.

Supply-side explanations usually see growing public sectors as a result of contractions in supply. The price effects hypothesis predicts that because public policies are increasingly more service oriented and redistributive in nature, public policies are increasingly unable to take advantage of technological innovations and therefore, over time, supply becomes relatively more costly than production in the private sector. Theories of bureaucracy and centralization are theories of monopoly in public sector provision; they predict that as public monopolies expand, supply of public sector output contracts. The tax-spend hypothesis predicts that because tax revenues have an innate proclivity to rise, spending rises in tandem.

A useful by-product of the examination of many theories is the ability to question whether the size of the public sector is too small or too large. For example, if one believes that fiscal illusion causes voters to underestimate tax burdens or that governments act as budget-maximizing Leviathans, then it follows that public sectors tend to overexpand. It is important to realize, however, that other theories predict that the public sector tends to be too small because voters underestimate the benefits that they receive from policies and/or that special interest groups provide positive externalities.

Two final comments are in order. First, it is important to understand the assumptions about voters and policymakers that alternative theories of public sector expansion make. Without a firm understanding of which behavioral assumptions underlie theories, it is impossible to fully understand the relevance of these theories or to compare predictions of alternative theories. In other words, recognition of the assumptions underlying the various theories gives a good sense of the reasons that some theories predict overexpansion and others predict underexpansion of the public sector. Second, although it is useful to compare and debate the many assumptions underlying the different theories, it is important to test and compare the predictions of the alternative theories. Our brief summary of empirical studies indicates that this is still an emerging area of inquiry and is a fertile area for further research.

Summary

- Voters are demanders, and policymakers are suppliers of public programs. Various theories of government growth may be examined within this framework.
- Demand-side explanations of government growth provide a framework that emphasizes that the size of the public sector grows because of a policy process that is sensitive to the wishes of voters. Demand-side explanations include growth in urbanization, the demand for income redistribution, the demand by public sector employees, and fiscal illusion.
- Supply-side explanations of government growth usually explain growing public sectors (in terms of rising expenditures) as the result of contractions in supply. Supply-side explanations include growth in bureaucracy, crisis theory of government, public sector centralization, and the tax-spend hypothesis.
- A highly controversial issue is whether public sectors tend to overexpand or underexpand. Overexpansion is usually related to theories that point to government monopoly, rent-seeking special interest groups, and underestimation of the costs of government programs as the primary causes of government growth. Underexpansion has been argued to occur when voters underestimate the benefits of government programs. The validity of competing theories is an empirical issue and needs further research.

Review Questions

1. What is the equilibrium size of the public sector?
2. Who are the demanders of government programs? Who are the suppliers of government programs?
3. What is the price effects hypothesis of government growth?
4. What are the major demand-side explanations of government growth?
5. What are the major supply-side explanations of government growth?

Discussion Questions

1. Name two public programs and discuss who are the demanders and suppliers of those programs.
2. After naming the demanders and suppliers of these two programs, discuss whether you believe that the size of those programs has expanded, contracted, or stayed invariant over the past ten years. Discuss these changes, if any, in terms of changes in demand or supply for these programs.
3. Should the number of suppliers be listed as a factor that shifts the supply curve of public programs? How would an increase in the number of suppliers, coupled with an inelastic demand curve, affect the size of the public sector?
4. Are there any incentives for special interest groups to form that are based on a common belief that the size of the public sector should be reduced? Do you know of any of these groups?
5. How complex is your tax burden? List the different tax sources which comprise your overall tax burden.
6. Within the context of Leviathan and bureaucracy theories of policymakers, discuss arguments for and against using term limitations on elected policymakers.
7. It is often argued that the question of whether the size of the public sector is too small or large is normative. Do you agree?
8. If you wished to reduce the federal budget deficit, what implications would you draw from the tax-spend hypothesis?

Key Words

Demanders of public programs
Suppliers of public programs
Equilibrium size of government
Wagner's law

Price effects hypothesis
Fiscal illusion hypothesis
Crisis (displacement) theory of government
Tax-spend hypothesis

PART 4

Expenditure, Credit, and Insurance Programs

Chapter 9
Expenditure Policies of the Federal Government

Chapter 10
*Off-Budget Government:
Credit and Insurance Policies*

Chapter 11
Transfer Programs for the Poor

Chapter 12
Social Insurance Programs

Chapter 13
Health Care Policy

Chapter 14
Cost-Benefit Analysis

CHAPTER 9

Expenditure Policies of the Federal Government

The federal government spent roughly $1.48 trillion in fiscal year 1994. This is clearly no small sum, especially when we rewrite it as $1,484,000,000,000, which is roughly $5,936 for each man, woman, and child in the United States. Economists study the effects of expenditure policies on the allocation of economic resources and the distribution of income. The allocation of resources determines the types of goods and services produced in our economy. Policies affect resource allocation in thousands of areas, and because resources are scarce and wants are unlimited, it is important to examine the trade-offs involved when resources are allocated by the public sector. More tanks, for instance, means fewer hospitals, roads, or student loans that could be provided with the same resources. Given a specific allocation of resources, the resulting production of goods and services must be distributed to someone and our study of distribution examines who gets what in the economy.

In this chapter we examine general characteristics of the spending programs of the federal government, and we address the following issues:

❏ How do expenditure policies influence the allocation of resources and distribution of income?
❏ Which expenditure categories are experiencing the greatest changes?
❏ What are the implications of expenditure trends for the functions of government?
❏ What budgetary process determines expenditures?
❏ How important is the budgetary process to our understanding of expenditure trends?
❏ What budgetary reforms might be approved in the future?

Analysis of Expenditure Policies

Allocational Effects

Allocational effects are the ways in which policies influence the use of resources.

Assessment of how the public sector affects resource allocation is not always a simple matter. For instance, consider the **allocational effects** of public spending on education. While education spending increases government's role in resource allocation,

237

education policies affect allocations in many areas of the economy. Some are more direct than others, and it is important to remember that *total* resource allocation is the *sum* of allocations in private and public markets. A direct effect of public spending on education is to increase the allocation of resources into the public market for education. An indirect effect occurs in the private market for education, since the private sector undoubtedly allocates resources toward its production as well. *Increased* public spending on education is likely to reduce, by some amount, private spending on education and therefore *total* resource allocation toward education will not increase by as much as the *increase* in public education spending. Examination of effects on *total* resource allocation requires that we follow the ways in which public spending affects allocations in both private and public markets.

An important determinant of allocative effects is the nature of public spending programs themselves. Public education spending may be directed, for example, toward basic training in mathematics or specialized training in the arts. If the private sector allocates more resources toward the former, an increase in public spending on basic mathematical training is likely to elicit a greater reduction in the resources allocated by the private sector than would an equal increase in public spending on specialized training in the arts. In general, then: *Public spending increases are likely to exert greater effects on total resource allocation when spending is directed toward areas where the private sector allocates relatively few resources.* (This statement assumes that private and public allocations are substitutes for each other. An alternative view is that they are complements; if so, one may predict that increases in public spending may increase private spending as well.)

The study of allocative effects also involves the question of whether spending programs alter economic behavior in such diverse areas as consumption, work, and savings. It has been argued, for instance, that, because the public unemployment benefit program provides income to laid-off workers, it increases the duration of unemployment for workers eligible for this program. Spending on the poor has also been argued to lessen the incentive of welfare recipients to become employed. Some argue that Social Security reduces the personal savings of workers who will receive Social Security payments upon retirement, thus possibly decreasing their incentive to save for retirement. Allocative effects may therefore arise when spending programs alter the economic behaviors of citizens, which also influence the places where resources are allocated in the economy.

Distributional Effects

Distributional effects are the ways in which policies transfer income from one person to another.

The study of **distributional effects** concentrates on how public spending programs redistribute income in the economy. Note that use of the word *redistribute* implies that the distribution of income is changed from some *initial* distribution. The most obvious initial distribution is the one provided by the private sector. We can also ask, for example, how have incomes of various individuals, who are either rich or poor, or from the North or the South, changed as a result of public spending programs.

Consider again public spending on education. Even though allocational analysis may show that public spending on education has increased by $250 million, there are many ways in which this sum may be distributed to members of society. Spending may be distributed equally across all areas of the country or it may be concentrated on

Costs of Public Spending

A Static World

The production possibilities frontier shown in Figure 9-1a places public spending in perspective with the entire economy. Spending on goods may occur either in the private or the public sectors and frontier *AC* shows the possible allocations between these two sectors when resources are fully employed within the best available technology. A purely private economy produces a maximum of *OC* goods, whereas an economy entirely directed by the public sector produces, at most, *OA* goods. Any allocation within these two extremes, such as *B*, defines an economy in which resources are allocated by both public (producing *OH*) and private sectors (producing *OI*).

From a historical perspective, the changing role of the public sector in resource allocation may be pictured as a movement along a production possibilities frontier. Allocation *E*, for example, represents a larger government role (and a smaller private sector role) than allocations such as *F* that lie below it on the same frontier. The public sector's role has expanded over time as Figure 9-1b demonstrates. One aspect of that expansion over time may be pictured as a series of upward movements along frontier *AC* in Figure 9-1a, such as that described by path *F → E → G*.

Allocations along the Frontier

Opportunity costs measure the losses involved in spending and, within our production possibilities model, the costs of public spending are the lost opportunities for private spending. Let us reconsider Figure 9-1a. The opportunity cost of expanding the public sector from point *G* to point *B* is *IK*, which is the private spending lost when public spending is expanded by *JH*.

Locations such as *B* and *G* represent Pareto efficient production levels. Pareto efficiency occurs when no other allocations exist which provide higher production of any good without lowering production of any other good (see Chapter 3). It is therefore impossible to argue, on the basis of available information, whether it is preferable for production to move from *G* to *B* or vice versa. Decisions regarding the desirability of *B* versus *G*, however, are often determined within the policy process. While future decisions may, in theory, go in both directions, past decisions have clearly awarded the public sector an expanding role in the allocation of economic resources.

Allocations within the Frontier

So far, our analysis has assumed that decisions are made on the production possibilities frontier in which all allocations are Pareto efficient. As we learned in Chapter 3—along with several important caveats—voluntary exchanges between demanders and

**FIGURE 9-1
Federal Spending**

Source: Budget of
the United States
Government, 1994.

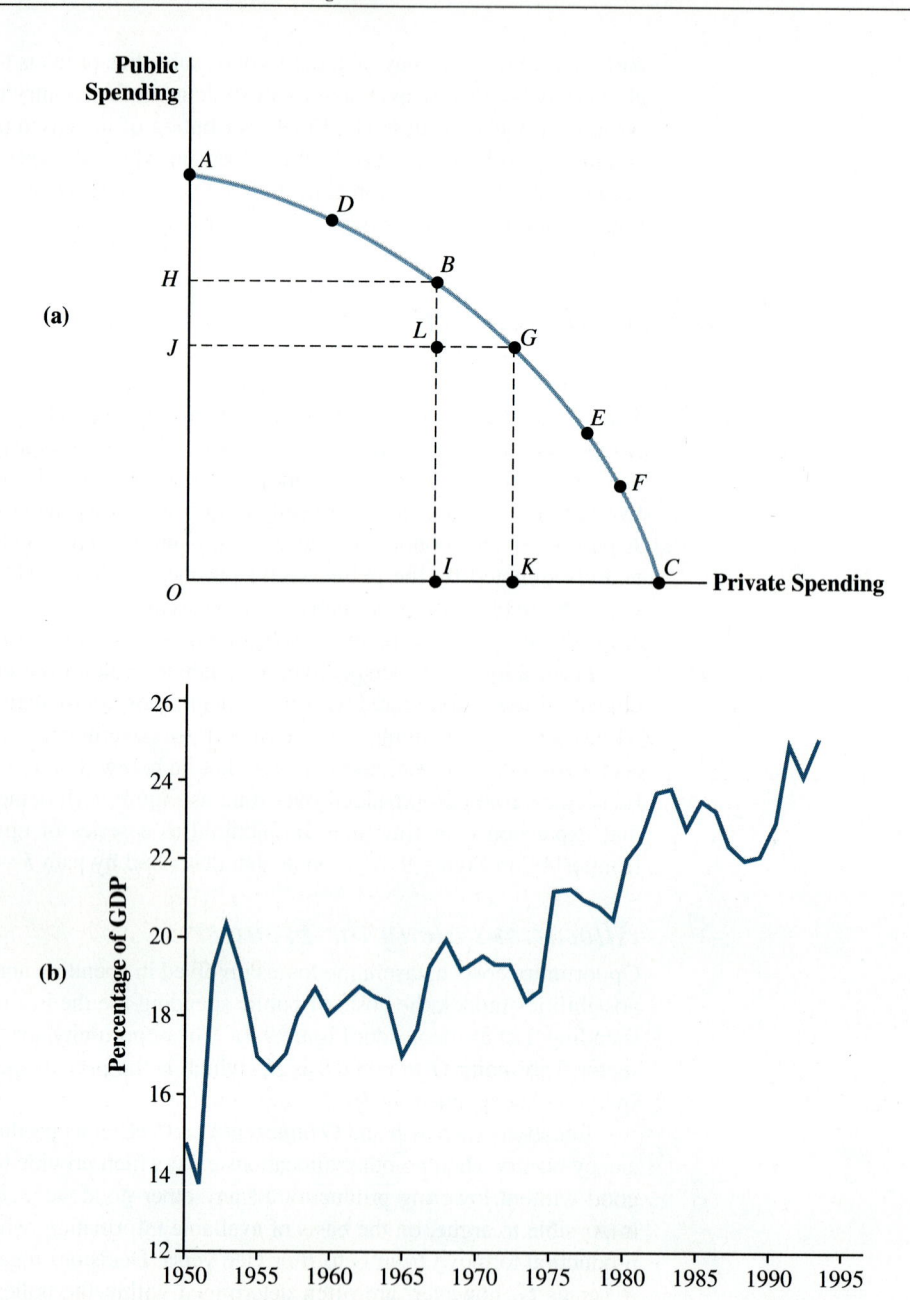

suppliers in private markets result in Pareto efficient outcomes. But no similar reason suggests that the public sector has any tendency to arrive at Pareto efficient outcomes. In fact our study of the policy process suggests that it is unlikely that allocations occur along the frontier. Majority voting rules, the median voter model, logrolling, agenda control, and the noncompetitive aspects of public market structure all suggest that exchanges made through the policy process do not usually result in Pareto-superior exchanges, or for that matter, Pareto efficient outcomes. For example, point L in Figure 9-1a is within the frontier and reflects a Pareto inefficient allocation of resources that might be approved through the policy process.

Consider the case in which the economy operates on point E. If the policy process approves expansion of public spending on medical research, a move from Pareto efficient E to Pareto inefficient L might occur. Even though L represents a Pareto inefficient resource allocation, the policy process may not be able to approve Pareto efficient points, such as B or G. (Note that, while there is no information with which one can argue that B or G are preferred over E, it can be argued that once L is chosen through the policy process, allocations defined within triangle LGB are Pareto superior to L.) If the available policy options are to stay at E or accept L, allocation L may be preferred since it allocates more resources to medical research. Of course, this is the same as saying that lost production opportunities associated with a Pareto inefficient allocation are worth the resulting gains associated with higher spending on medical research.

The point here is that the policy process may determine that allocative efficiency is *not* the final guide for its allocation of resources. Consider, for instance, the Davis-Bacon Act of 1931, which requires that private contractors pay union-scale wages for public contracts, even when there are sufficient numbers of equally qualified, but lower-paid, workers available. The initial purpose was protection of union workers from competition from nonunion workers, but its ultimate effect is to force private contractors to use inefficient combinations of resources. In other words, the Davis-Bacon law forces the economy to operate on the interior of its production possibilities curve.[1] Distributional consequences of the law are clear: more jobs for union labor and fewer jobs for nonunion labor. There have been several temporary suspensions of the law, as for example in 1992 by President George Bush, but the law of sixty years was reinstated by President Bill Clinton in 1993.

A Dynamic World

Figure 9-2 presents a more complex, but also more precise, depiction of the changing roles of the public and private sectors. Here we see how these roles have changed with expansion of the productive capacity of the economy. Remember that frontiers are a function of fully employed resources *given* levels of technology, and therefore tend to expand as resources increase and technology advances. Increases in the frontier are shown to be more generous for the private sector because public production tends to be primarily service and transfer oriented. Technological gains are therefore likely to be less pervasive than in the private sector. Path $A \rightarrow B \rightarrow C$ in Figure 9-2 depicts the case in which expansion of the public sector has outpaced expansion of the

---

[1] Nonunion workers are, or at least tend to be, members of some minority group. Originally, these were such groups as Finns, Irish, and Italians. Later, they became union leaders and were replaced in the ranks by African-Americans and Hispanics. Many economists have suggested that the Davis-Bacon Act is therefore a well-disguised means of promoting racial discrimination in labor markets.

**FIGURE 9-2
Federal Spending in a Dynamic Economy**

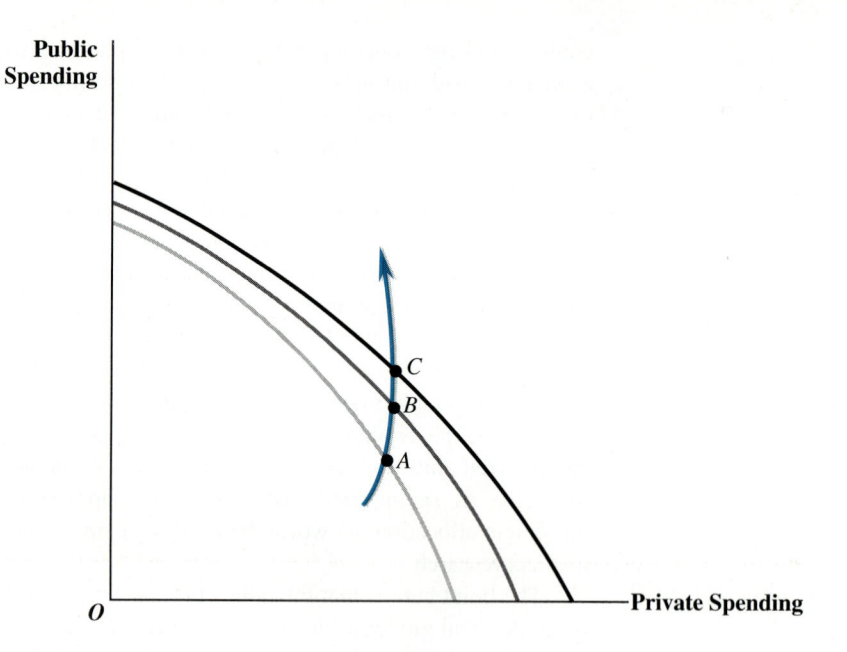

overall economy; this direction is consistent with the historical experience exhibited in Figure 9-1b.

Trends in Expenditure Policies

General Trends: Purchases versus Transfers

The dominant trend in expenditure policy is growth. From its fairly narrowly defined role as the provider of national defense, a system of justice, and such infrastructure as roads, dams, and bridges, government has expanded its responsibilities to include redistribution of income among citizens. Differences in the types of spending fall into two categories: *purchases* and *transfers*. **Government purchases** are purchases of tangible goods and services produced in the economy such as, for example, purchases of tanks and aircraft by the military. **Government transfers,** in contrast, redistribute income from one citizen to another.

Government purchases consist of tangible goods and services purchased by the government.

Government transfers redistribute income.

The changing proportions of purchases and transfers are shown in Figure 9-3a.[2] Starting at a high of 62 percent of all spending in the late 1950s, purchases now account for roughly 25 percent of all spending activities. In contrast, transfers have followed the opposite path, rising from 24 percent to 40 percent of all spending over this period. These clearly significant, and extremely important, changes in the direction of spending policy took place for the most part between the 1960s and mid-1970s.

---

[2] A significant spending category—net interest payments—has been omitted here but discussed later in the chapter.

**FIGURE 9-3
Federal Government Expenditures**

Source: Budget of the United States Government, 1994.

(a) Percentage of Total Federal Spending — Purchases, Transfers (1958–1994)

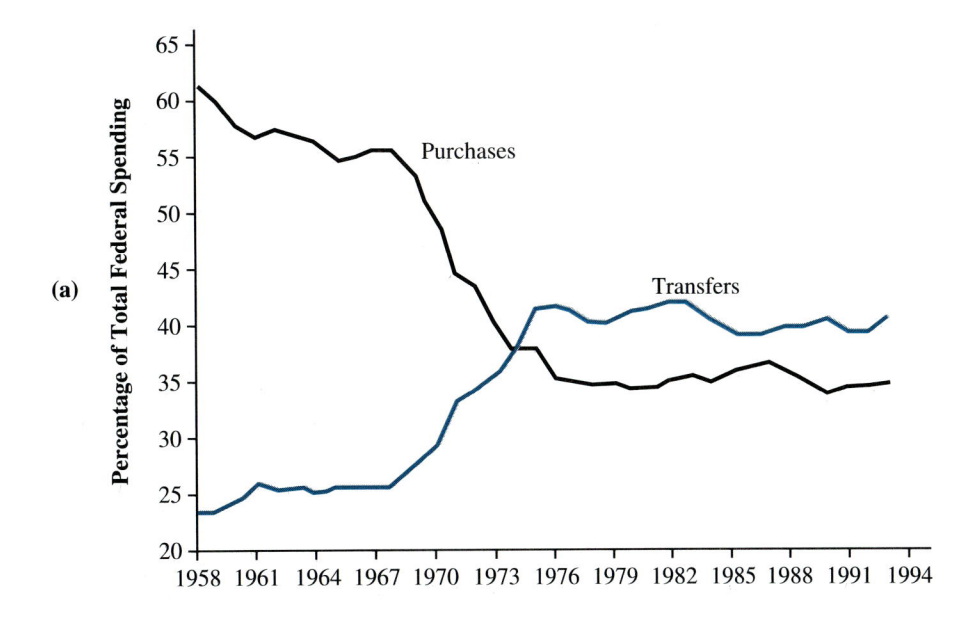

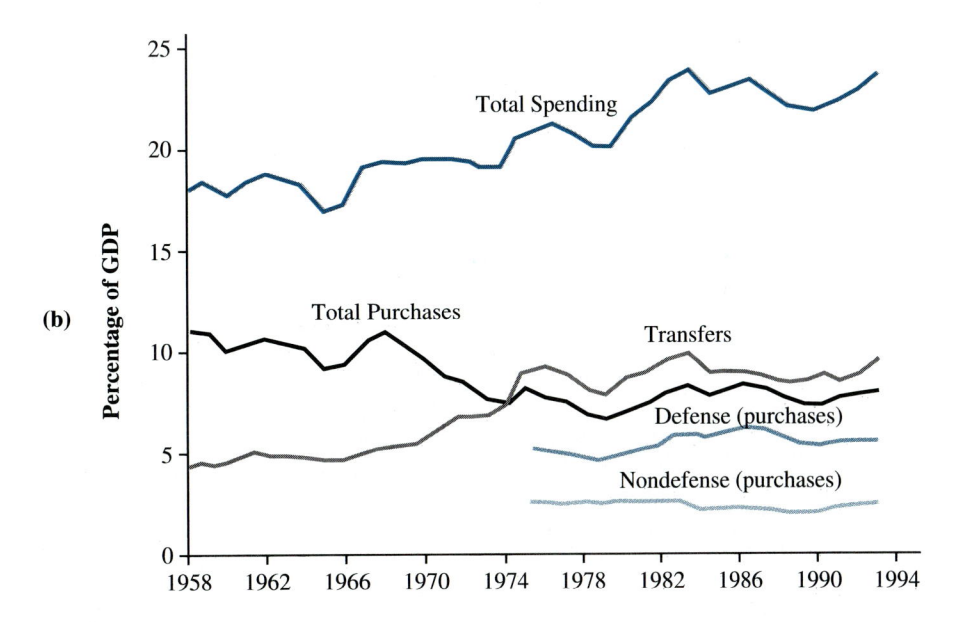

(b) Percentage of GDP — Total Spending, Total Purchases, Transfers, Defense (purchases), Nondefense (purchases) (1958–1994)

Figure 9-3b places these changes in spending in the perspective of a growing economy. When we compare the various spending categories over time, we see that spending changes are less dramatic with respect to the overall economy. To be sure, purchases comprise a falling share of GDP and transfers a rising share; but the former has fallen from 12 percent to 7.5 percent, and the latter has risen from 4 percent to over 9 percent of GDP. It is also clear that much of the turnaround in these categories occurred by the mid-1970s.

Defense spending is the primary component of purchases, and though data have only been disaggregated into defense and nondefense purchases since 1975, several points are clear. Purchases for defense constitute the largest component of total purchases and account for roughly 6 percent of GDP. Nondefense purchases account for roughly 2.5 percent of GDP. A slight defense buildup is evident in the 1980s; however, neither category of purchases has changed very much since the mid-1970s.

Defense Spending and the End of the Cold War

Common perception has it that the 1980s saw an enormous expansion of defense spending. Figure 9-4a, however, indicates that as a percentage of total federal spending, national defense has been allocated an increasingly smaller portion of federal spending.[3] Escalations in defense spending obviously occurred during World War II (1941–45), when defense spending rose to 90 percent of total spending, as well as during the Korean War (1950–53) when it was 70 percent of total spending. But during Ronald Reagan's presidency (1981–89) defense spending rose from roughly 25 percent to just 28 percent of total spending—a modest, but temporary, reversal of the long-term trend of defense in overall spending.[4] The collapse of the Soviet Union on December 25, 1991, and its replacement by twelve independent states (Commonwealth of Independent States), signaled an end to the cold war that has been translated into a smaller role in federal spending.

The long-term trend, therefore, shows a sharply declining role for defense spending, which has recently accounted for 20 percent of federal spending. A long-term decline in defense and corresponding rise of nondefense spending are clearly evident in Figure 9-4b, which places these categories in the perspective of the overall economy.

While many believe that it is appropriate to reduce the share of defense spending, important issues remain regarding the ways in which spending is reduced and the speed at which the reduction is accomplished. Downsizing of defense spending has created both short-run and long-run implications for the economy. In the short run, there are adverse effects on local economies that rely on defense contracts and other defense-related spending for much of their income and employment. In 1992, for example, Southern California is estimated to have lost up to 300,000 jobs as a result of reduced defense spending. Estimates indicate that by 1995, more than 800,000 defense-sector jobs will have been eliminated in the overall economy.[5]

The closing of military bases is a subject of great controversy. Among policymakers a not-in-my-backyard (**NIMBY**) attitude has been apparent and appears to affect equally those who have supported past defense policies as well as those who have been the staunchest opponents. Policymakers are strong opponents of base closures when the bases within their own jurisdictions are on the cut list. It is easy to see why. Consider, for example, Fort Ord in Monterey, California, which has been slated

NIMBY
is the attitude of policymakers and voters characterized by the saying "not in my backyard."

---

[3] This is defense spending on a functional basis and therefore includes all defense-related spending by the Departments of Defense, Energy, Veteran's Affairs, and so on.

[4] Note that spending in one year may be the result of past budgetary decisions. For example, a five-year contract for building a new type of defense equipment will show up over five years, not just in the year in which that budgetary measure is passed.

[5] Congressional Budget Office, *The Economic Effects of Reduced Defense Spending*, March 1992.

**FIGURE 9-4
Defense and
Nondefense
Expenditures**

Source: Budget of the United States Government, 1994.

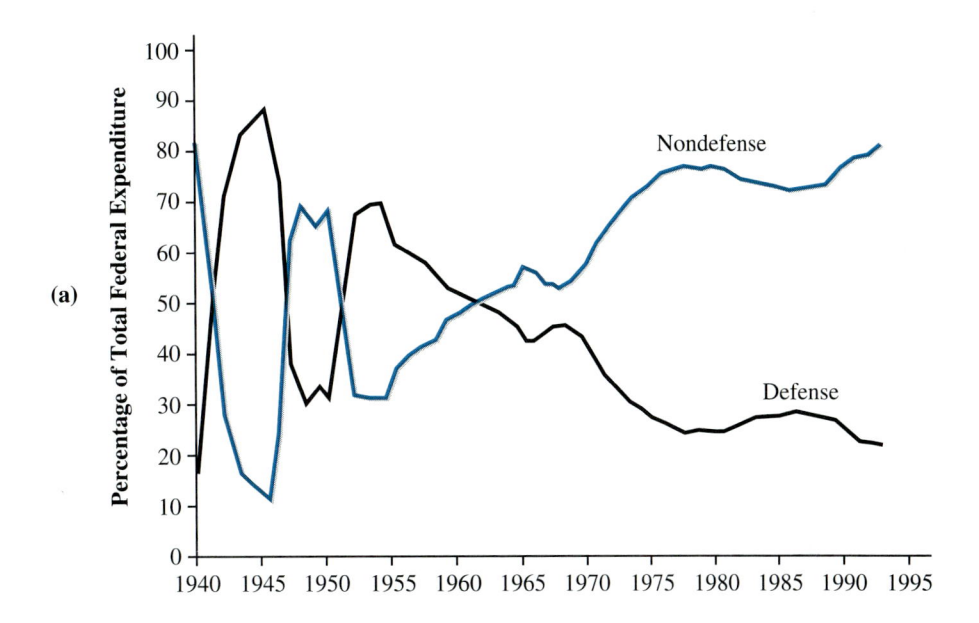

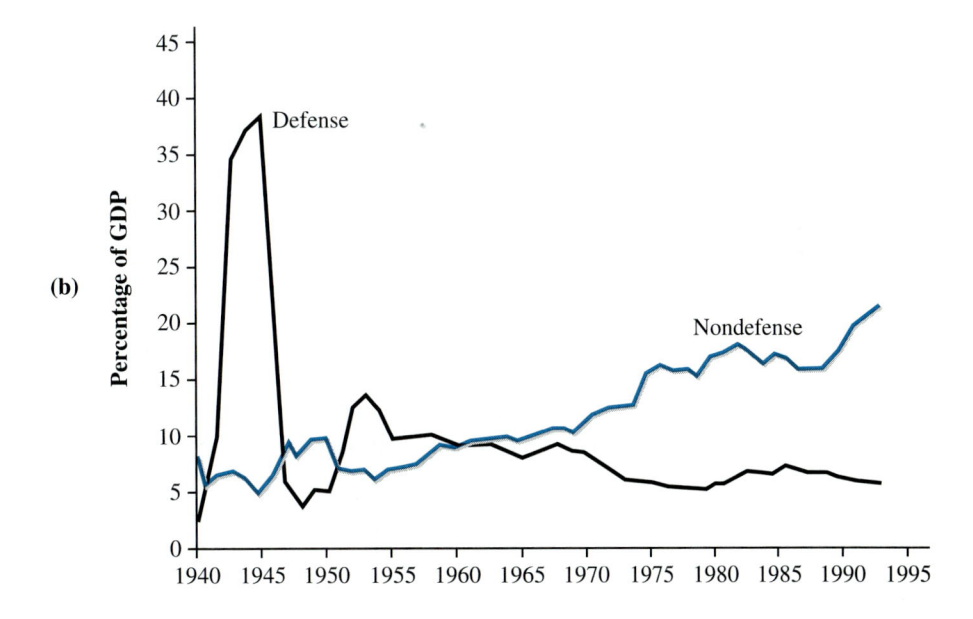

(a) Percentage of Total Federal Expenditure vs. year (1940–1995), showing Defense and Nondefense curves.

(b) Percentage of GDP vs. year (1940–1995), showing Defense and Nondefense curves.

for closure. Approximately 10 percent of the population of Monterey County are in some way connected with Fort Ord and, in 1990, the main post generated roughly 31 percent of the earnings there.[6] With many similar examples across the country, controversy will surround cuts in defense spending, especially those close to home.

---

[6] Congressional Budget Office, *The Economic Effects of Reduced Defense Spending.*

Even with the inevitable debate over which bases to close, and which areas of the country to cut spending from, there is a consensus that the long-run implication of falling defense spending is an improved public allocation of resources. We should also remember that reallocations since the 1950s have awarded defense spending a declining share of GDP and, in the long run, the economy should be well accustomed to surviving changes in the allocation of resources devoted to defense. Several of the recent proposals aimed at easing the transition from defense spending include allowing active-duty military personnel to take up to a one-year leave of absence for education or training, providing early retirement for personnel employed at bases facing closure or reductions, and millions of dollars in grants to communities hard hit by the transition.

Transfers

Spending on transfers is unlike government purchases in that transfers do not constitute payment for the production of any new good or service. When the government purchases a new tank, builds a new road, or hires a new schoolteacher, scarce resources are used up. Transfers, in contrast, simply shift income from one member of society to another.

As shown in Figure 9-3a, transfers have been allocated an increasing priority in federal spending policy. Growth of transfers reflects substantial growth in expenditures for Social Security and income support of children, the elderly, and sick and disabled persons. A huge surge in transfer spending began in the late 1960s, when it rose from 25 percent to 40 percent of all spending by the mid-1970s. Since the mid-1970s, however, transfers have stabilized at roughly 40 percent of total spending. As shown in Figure 9-3b transfers, as a share of GDP, have roughly doubled, from 4 percent to over 8 percent.

Welfare state is a term used to describe a public sector heavily engaged in redistributing income among its citizens.

The rise in transfers primarily reflects accelerations of Social Security and other social program spending having to do with the **welfare state.** The designation of government-as-welfare state describes a public sector that transfers much income among its citizens. Social Security, for instance, was originally envisioned as a way to provide for old age security on a self-financed system, but this program has evolved into the largest transfer program of the federal government. The rising role of transfers reflects a growing redistributive role of government.[7]

Purchases as Transfers: Pork Barrel Spending

Pork barrel spending consists of disbursements that solely benefit a particular locale or special interest group.

Government purchases may also be transfers. Many critics of defense spending, for example, believe that some portion of defense spending has little to do with national security, but rather constitutes favors for constituents. Such spending is often called **pork barrel spending,** which is an old slang term for providing one's constituents with what they want—a big share of money or a special project—without regard for

---

[7] See Carolyn Webber and Aaron Wildavsky, *A History of Taxation and Expenditure in the Western World* (New York: Simon & Schuster, 1986) for the role of transfers in other governments.

the general welfare. Consider the following example in which parochial interests prevailed over the general interests of the population.[8]

In June 1984, the late Representative Claude D. Pepper of Florida defeated a move to excise $500 million from an $18 billion water project that funded new dams, canals, and bridges throughout the country. The $500 million for which Representative Pepper yearned was to be spent for a 110-mile canal to be built across Florida, a project that had been initially proposed in 1942 as a means of protecting shipping from Nazi U-boats. The $500 million project was finally approved, despite opposition from many of the members of Congress.

Similar stories abound, commonly associated with the funding of roads, dams, bridges, hospitals, and post offices. We also frequently hear recurrent discussions about "bailouts" of particular industries and constant wranglings about where to locate government buildings and military bases. While not all of these purchases are clearcut cases of pork barrel politics, there is little question that some portion of government purchases serves mainly to cater to localized special interests at the expense of the broader interests of the citizenry at large.

How much pork barrel spending is there? It is clearly difficult to assess, but some attempts have been made to provide exact estimates. One widely respected attempt was conducted by J. Peter Grace, who was named, in June 1982, chairman of President Ronald Reagan's Private Sector Survey on Cost Control. Preparing more than 40 separate reports and citing more than 2,500 specific examples of pork barrel spending, the Grace Commission (as it came to be known) provided recommendations in January 1984 that cut an estimated $400 billion out of federal spending from 1985 to 1987. Dividing $400 billion into $1,061 billion, the level of federal government purchases over 1985–87, we can infer that the Grace Commission estimated pork barrel spending to be roughly 38 percent of total federal government purchases.

Depending on one's view of the policy process, one might ask

❑ Why is there so *much* pork barrel spending? or
❑ Why is there so *little* pork barrel spending?

Voters and special interest groups in political districts—that is, congressional constituencies—are what matters most to elected policymakers, as we saw in Chapter 6. If we then attribute self-interested motivations both to congressional constituencies and to members of Congress, the phrase "take home the bacon" probably accurately describes the role that Congresspersons play when they wish to please their constituents—and the wording of this phrase goes a long way toward explaining the "pork" in pork barrel spending.

But why would there be enough support for pork barrel spending, which serves mainly the parochial interests of a small number of voters? How, for example, could Representative Claude Pepper win approval of $500 million for the canal project—especially since resources are scarce, and the opportunity costs for this project must be reckoned in terms of $500 million that could be spent either for some other worthy

---

[8] Randall Fitzgerald and Gerald Lipson, *Pork Barrel: The Unexpurgated Grace Commission Story of Congressional Profligacy* (Washington, D.C.: The Cato Institute, 1984), xix.

project, tax relief, or deficit reduction? The answer to this question lies in the process of vote trading, or logrolling, described in Chapter 7. Voters, or in this case, elected policymakers, may trade votes among themselves for projects that serve the interests of several minorities, thereby achieving majority approval for each minority bloc.

In the case of the $500 million canal project, the logrolling worked this way.[9] When opponents of Claude Pepper's canal project attempted to write it out of the spending bill, they were told by the chairman of the Public Works and Transportation Committee that other projects in the same spending bill—projects that would benefit their own districts—would also be withdrawn if they were to eliminate the Florida canal. This tactic was apparently effective since the canal project was fully intact when the bill received final approval.

The results of logrolling are consistent with the widely known attitude that voters display toward Congress. While many citizens tend to hold a predominantly negative image of Congress in general, they tend to be quite pleased with their particular representatives. Often described as "schizophrenia" on the part of voters, this oddly contradictory thinking has been the subject of much concern for those who would like to reduce pork barrel spending in government.

Net Interest Expenditures

We know that expansion of budget deficits has been an important characteristic of the fiscal behavior of the federal government. When taxes do not rise in tandem with public spending, budget deficits are the usual means of making up the shortfall between expenditures and tax receipts. (Another avenue of financing the shortfall between expenditures and tax revenues is inflation.) Even though deficits are a means of postponing payment of current spending, expenditures must be made for borrowing costs; therefore, when budget deficits rise over time, these expenditures tend to rise as well. It comes as no surprise, then, that as a consequence of budget deficit expansion, **net interest expenditures** have become a larger fraction of federal expenditures and now constitute the third largest category of federal spending, exceeded only by spending on defense and Social Security.

Net interest expenditures are the interest expenses from borrowing less the interest fees from lending.

Spending on interest is measured on a *net* basis since the federal government is a major lender of funds as well as a major borrower. The federal government, for example, lends to students to finance college education, and interest payments from students are therefore an income source for the federal government. When a government borrows, interest payments are an expenditure; when it lends, interest payments are counted as revenues.

Although it is possible in theory for the federal government to receive more interest revenue than it pays out for borrowing, Figure 9-5a clearly shows that this has not been the history of federal government finance. As a percentage of total federal spending, there are three important periods in the history of net interest payments.

---

[9] Fitzgerald and Lipson, *Pork Barrel: The Unexpurgated Grace Commission Story of Congressional Profligacy*, xix.

**FIGURE 9-5
Interest Expenditures**

Source: Economic Report of the President, 1994.

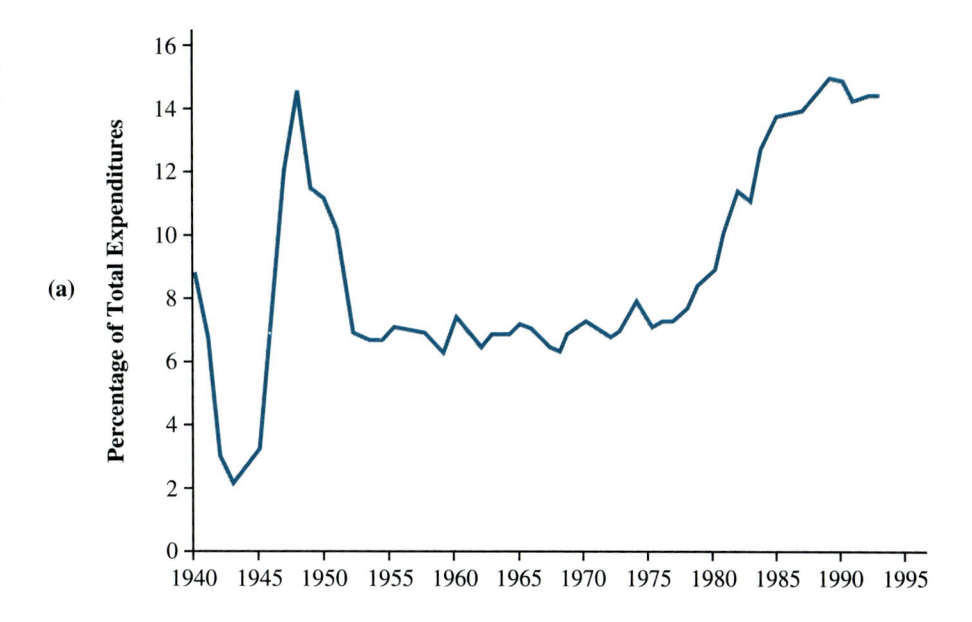

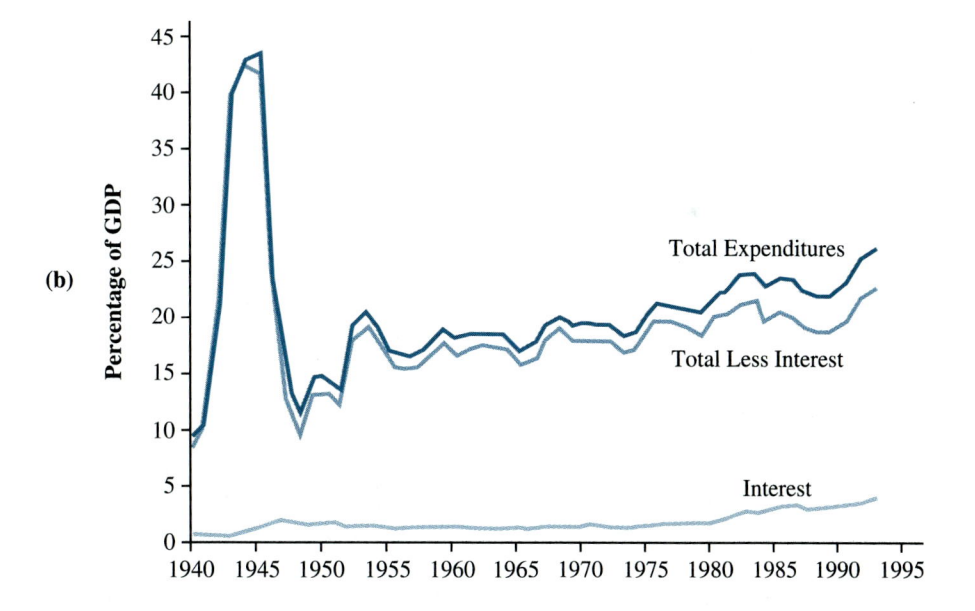

(a) Percentage of Total Expenditures

(b) Percentage of GDP — Total Expenditures, Total Less Interest, Interest

- As deficits were used to pay for much of World War II spending, net interest payments underwent a huge surge, from 2 percent to 14 percent, in the late 1940s.
- In the 1955–70 period little change occurred, as net interest payments averaged 7 percent of total spending.
- Since the late 1970s, net interest payments have surged from 7 percent to 14 percent of total spending.

A slightly different historical record emerges when we consider net interest payments as percentages of GDP in Figure 9-5b. Interest payments show a fairly gradual, but distinct, rise in their share of GDP. Part of the reason that interest payments, as a share of GDP, did not sharply rise during World War II is that the Federal Reserve pegged interest rates on government debt during this period as a way of holding down federal government expenditures.[10] Therefore, because interest payments are a function of both interest rates and the size of debt, total interest payments are lower than they would have been if the Federal Reserve did not pursue policies aimed at lowering the interest expenses of the federal government.

Net Interest Expenditures Reflect Past Spending Programs

In 1994, net interest payments amounted to $203 billion, which in terms of a federal spending budget of $1.48 trillion, accounts for 14 percent of all spending. As shown in Figure 9-5b, as interest payments have risen, a growing gap has grown between total federal expenditures and total federal expenditures *less* net interest payments. Rising interest payments have important implications for spending policies.

As more spending goes toward net interest payments, a greater share of current spending reflects payment for past policies. This reflects the fact that when the government engages in deficit finance of current spending, it postpones payment of those spending programs to the future. As long as the federal government continues to add to its debt, past obligations for past deficit-financed programs are not repaid. In fact, in 1994, debt outstanding was estimated at $4.7 trillion. In other words, the payment of this amount of past spending continued to be postponed. Interest payments on this debt are the borrowing costs associated with continued postponement of these past obligations, and because the federal government has not run a budget surplus since 1969, the federal government continues to postpone payment for a portion of past spending programs.

Are Program Benefits Long-Lived?

An interesting issue regarding this postponement is whether the benefits provided by these programs are short- or long-lived. Few people believe, for instance, that it is improper for private individuals to finance a house over a period of thirty years or for college students to finance their education over a period as long as ten years. The assets that are financed in these cases are long-lived; they return benefits over a period of many years. Short-lived assets, on the other hand, are assets that yield benefits over a rather short period of time. For example, few people would consider it appropriate to finance purchase of shoes, compact disks, or theater tickets over many years. Similarly, appropriate financing of government spending programs may also be determined by the life of the benefits associated with various spending programs. Roads, dams, bridges, and education may be viewed as relatively long-lived assets that some would argue should be financed over many years.

---

[10] For the history of this period, see Milton Friedman and Anna J. Schwartz, *A Monetary History of the United States, 1867–1960* (Princeton, N.J.: Princeton University Press, 1963).

Growing debt burdens and associated net interest payments, then, may reflect optimal behavior on the part of the federal government if it can be shown that a growing percentage of its spending programs are in the form of long-lived assets that provide Americans with many years of benefits. Some believe that government purchases reflect long-lived programs. The record, however, as displayed in Figure 9-3 show that over this period of rising net interest payments, government purchases have been rapidly declining as a share of total spending. Transfers, in contrast, represent a rapidly rising share of expenditures, and it is more difficult to argue that their benefits are as long-lived as purchases.

Crowding Out of Discretionary Spending Programs

For all practical purposes, net interest payments are mandatory in the sense that it is most unlikely that the federal government would ever renege on its promises to pay interest on its debt. Therefore, as net interest payments have been allocated a growing share of total spending, its growth may crowd out spending on other programs. For a given total spending budget, fewer and fewer dollars are able to fund other programs, and in order for funding of noninterest programs to either increase or maintain the same share of total spending, overall growth in total spending is required. However, in an era of concern over public sector expansion, rising net interest payments may force a falling share of spending in other parts of the spending budget.

We will discuss the Budget Enforcement Act (BEA) of 1990 in terms of the ways in which federal spending is separated into programs that involve both **mandatory spending** and **discretionary spending.** While we describe the details of this act below, the main difference between these two types of programs is that mandatory programs are spending policies more or less placed on automatic pilot. The largest mandatory program is Social Security, which accounts for roughly 20 percent of all federal spending. Shrinking from 70 percent of federal spending in the early 1960s, discretionary spending is now allocated 35 percent of all spending. The largest discretionary spending program is national defense, followed by international and domestic programs. Mandatory programs and net interest payments are given higher priority in the spending budget, so their growth has been argued to crowd out the discretionary portion of spending.

Mandatory spending consists of disbursements not subject to annual review or budgeting.

Discretionary spending consists of disbursements subject to annual review and budgeting.

Incentives for Policymakers

Rising net interest payments cause serious problems for public policy over time. At issue is when deficit-financed programs are paid off. Let us view this issue from the point of view of elected policymakers. Public spending today can go in two different, and opposing, directions:

❏ payment for *past* deficit-financed programs

❏ payment for *new* programs or expansion of *current* programs

These two directions clearly have different implications for policymakers and the constituents they serve. Put in a slightly different way, $10 million in spending can either be used to pay off $10 million of past spending or can be used to finance $10 million of a *current* or *new* program.

These two alternatives have very different returns for policymakers and their constituents. If *past* spending is paid off, then the return is the reduction of principal of the same amount plus whatever interest payments no longer need to be made. For policymakers and constituents to believe that this is a wise use of $10 million they must perceive the usefulness of paying off *past* debts (and the offsetting reduction in interest payments) *relative to* benefits they perceive conveyed by increasing *current* spending programs by $10 million. Remembering that resources are always scarce and there are always problems that many policymakers and constituents believe should be remedied through a spending program, the $10 million may more easily flow to promote *current* spending than toward reduction of *past* debts that reflect *past* spending programs. As anyone with sizable credit card debt quickly understands, it is more fun to buy a *new* suit of clothes, eat in a fancy restaurant, or go on a vacation than it is to pay off *past* vacations, meals, or clothing, especially since the restaurant meals and vacations are long gone, and the clothing may have worn out or gone out of fashion.

The dilemma that this behavior promotes is that the longer this pattern of postponing payments for *past* spending occurs, the more rapidly will interest payments pile up. As we saw in 1994, for example, the federal government owed $203 billion in net interest payments. That is, in order to pay off any of its *past* deficit-financed spending programs, it must spend a sum of money over and above $203 billion. Every dollar, however, over and above $203 billion means that one less dollar may be spent on a *new* or existing spending program. As net interest payments rise over time, a greater percentage of total federal spending goes toward payment of interest on *past* deficit financed spending, and therefore it becomes increasingly difficult to allocate funds for retirement of past debt.

Some may argue that it is inappropriate for net interest burdens to rise over time, but what is at issue is what motivates the behaviors of voters and policymakers. Under one scenario, voters and policymakers could be argued to be shifting the costs of *current* and *past* spending onto future generations. In other words, why pay today for *past* and *current* spending when we can force future generations to pay for this spending? Another scenario may be that because it is appropriate to deficit finance long-term spending programs, current policies reflect optimal financing methods. Another scenario is that of fiscal illusion which, as discussed in Chapter 8, predicts that policymakers mislead taxpayers by disguising some of the costs of current spending through deficit finance. It is important to recognize that various economists hold each of these views and that support of their particular view reflects their assumptions regarding the behaviors of voters and policymakers. These issues are therefore likely to remain contentious.

Federal Budget Process

Federal budget process represents the events, decisions, laws, and the influential people that determine federal spending.

The history of U.S. spending trends is, to a great extent, also a history of the **federal budget process.** Government budgeting tends to be numerous and highly complex processes. Ordinary citizens often have great difficulty in understanding the mechanics of government spending. The simple fact is that budgeting by government is very different from budgeting by individuals. For example, governments run on fiscal years, whereas individuals usually budget and pay taxes on a calendar year basis. The fiscal year of the federal government runs from October 1 to September 30, and each budget is named for the ending year of the budget. For example, the 1994 fiscal year started on October 1, 1993, and its end date was September 30, 1994. These differences are fairly obvious. There are less obvious differences, and we must spend time examining some of the more arcane details of the federal budgetary process in order to understand how it has affected public spending over the years. The budgetary process has a life of its own, and it is extremely important to understand specific definitions attached to such words as *budget cuts* and *balanced budget laws*.

Federal Budget Process before 1974[11]

Prior to 1921, each federal agency submitted funding requests for congressional approval. There was no unified federal budget document. The 1921 Budget and Accounting Act required that the President submit executive budgets to Congress for approval and that all agencies submit their spending requests to the President, who, under the newly created Bureau of the Budget, coordinated requests. The 1921 act also created the General Accounting Office (GAO) to help Congress analyze the President's budget. After this, Congress would pass, with majority votes in both the House and Senate, a spending budget, which was a modified version of the President's budget. The President would then either sign or veto Congress's version of the budget. If the latter occurred, the whole process started over.[12] With minor modifications, the 1921 act remained intact until the 1970s. One modification was the creation of the Council of Economic Advisors under the Full Employment Act of 1946, which in addition to an increase in the level of economic analysis and advisement in the White House, led to the publishing of an annual economic report to Congress.

In the early 1970s, many budgetary fights arose between President Richard Nixon and Congress. With Democratic majorities in both the House and Senate, Congress passed many spending bills that contained many individual items that Nixon, a Republican, did not want to approve. While he could have vetoed congressional budget requests, the veto carried a high cost, as it held the public hostage while the President and Congress fought over various esoteric budgetary items. In recent times, when budgets have not been passed on schedule, there have been work furloughs of federal employees and temporary, but embarrassing, shutdowns of such services as tours of the Washington Monument and the White House. Extended shutdowns also become quite problematic for all policymakers, since it can also mean temporary delays in processing Social Security payments and various health services already promised to constituents.

---

[11] A more detailed treatment of this issue is contained in Aaron Wildavsky, *The New Politics of the Budgetary Process* (Glenview, Ill.: Scott, Foresman and Company, 1988).

[12] Interestingly, while the President has ultimate say on the final budget for the Executive Branch, the President is required to accept, without possibility of veto, the spending budget that Congress appropriates for itself (as well as for the Judicial Branch). In other words, the President has no authority over the budget that Congress approves for itself—a budget that in 1992 was approximately $5 million per member.

Impoundment Act of 1974

As a means of avoiding stalemates between Congress and the White House, President Nixon started impounding spending on various funds that had already been authorized in budgets. In effect, Nixon would sign the budget sent to him by Congress and then, because actual disbursement of funds to any government agency must be finally approved by the President, impound some portion of those funds that he did not approve of. While the Congress could authorize more spending than Nixon wanted, final disbursement of authorized spending remained in the hands of the President.

Clearly, Congress objected to the impoundment of any previously authorized funds in the final budget signed by the President. Congress also knew that it had the ultimate power, since only the Legislative Branch can make law, including those pertaining to the budget process. Accordingly, Congress passed the Congressional Budget and **Impoundment Act of 1974** which denies the President the power to impound funds. This act also established specific time tables for spending to occur and created the Congressional Budget Office, an agency which provides budgetary reports to Congress.

While the power of impoundment was taken away from the President, the Impoundment Act allows the President the power of *recision*. When the President believes that a portion of appropriated funds should not be spent, the President may request a recision. However, before a recision is allowed, both houses of Congress must approve it within forty-five days of the President's recommendation. Over the period 1988–92, for example, the President requested approval for 120 recissions for a total of $11.4 billion, and only three of them were approved, totalling $38.1 million, or 0.3 percent of the funding reductions requested by the President.[13] In reality, then, it appears that the act decreased the President's control over public spending.

Leverage over Spending

There is little question that the Impoundment Act created a new budgetary environment for the U.S. government. Many hypothesize that the shift of some power over budgetary matters from the President to Congress has greatly expanded spending. This hypothesis is consistent with the discussion in Chapter 6 of the constituencies of elected policymakers, where the argument was advanced that the President's constituency is the broadest, followed by the constituencies of Senators and then the constituencies of Representatives. The greater the power shift away from the President, the greater spending will be directed toward the narrower self-interests of Senators and Representatives and the constituencies they represent. As possible evidence in support of this view, consider Figure 9-6, which compares spending in the sixteen years before the Impoundment Act of 1974 with the sixteen years immediately following it. Because federal spending rose from an average of 18.5 percent of GDP to slightly over 22 percent of GDP over this period, there may be some empirical support for this view.

The **Impoundment Act of 1974** is a Congressional act that denies the President the power to impound funds.

[13] *Budget of the United States Government, Fiscal Year 1993*, Part 1, 410.

**FIGURE 9-6
Federal Government
Expenditures as a
Percentage of GDP**

*Source: Budget of
the United States
Government, 1994.*

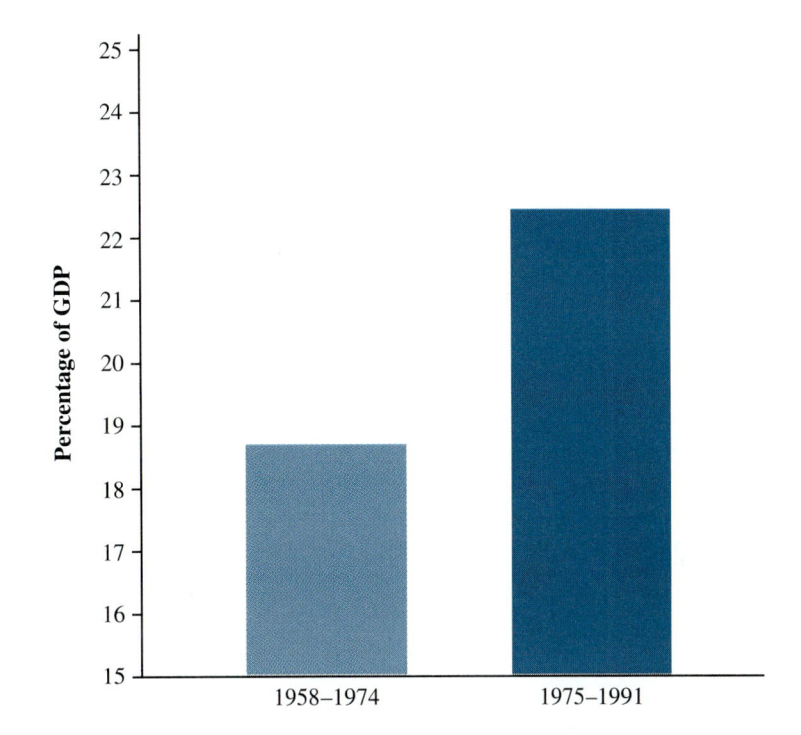

When Spending Increases Are Called Spending Cuts

One of the most important changes introduced in the Impoundment Act was the creation of the **current services budget,** which allows various spending *increases* to be called spending *cuts.* Current services budgets are estimated spending increases that are consistent with current levels of service. That is, what spending levels in a new budget are consistent with the previous budget's level of service? To estimate what constitutes continuation of current services, budget analysts must make various assumptions regarding the economy (for example, inflation, real growth, unemployment, agricultural prices) and public programs (for example, numbers of program beneficiaries). Table 9-1, for example, shows the economic assumptions for 1993–95 made during the budget proposal period for the 1993 budget.

These assumptions about the future are detailed in the President's budget as submitted to Congress and, therefore, at initial stages of examination, Congress considers new budget proposals with spending levels that are *automatically* higher than current budgetary levels. Consider, for example, Table 9-2, which displays actual spending levels in 1991, current service levels (CSs) for 1992, and the percentage change between the two budget years. Given the various assumptions regarding economic and program factors, current service changes range from a low of −26.7 percent (Commerce and Housing credit) to a high of 135 percent (Energy). For the budget as a whole, maintenance of current services requires a 9.6 percent increase in total spending for the 1992 budget.

A **current services budget** allows for automatic spending increases to maintain past levels of service.

TABLE 9-1
Summary of Economic Assumptions, 1993–95

	1993	1994	1995
Constant dollar GDP (% change)	2.8	3.0	3.0
Inflation measures (% change)			
GDP deflator	3.3	3.3	3.3
Consumer price index	3.2	3.2	3.2
Unemployment rate (%)	6.5	6.1	5.8
Interest rates (%)			
91-day Treasury bills	5.0	5.3	5.3
1-year Treasury notes	7.0	6.8	6.6

Source: Budget of the United States Government, Fiscal Year 1993.

TABLE 9-2
Current Services Outlays by Function ($Billions)

	1991 Actual	1992 CSs	Change
Department of Defense—Military	$ 262.4	$ 295.3	12.5%
International affairs	15.9	17.2	8.2
General science, space and technology	16.1	16.4	1.9
Energy	1.7	4.0	135.3
Natural resources and environment	18.6	20.2	8.6
Agriculture	15.2	17.2	13.2
Commerce and housing credit	75.6	55.4	−26.7
Transportation	31.1	34.0	9.3
Community and regional development	6.8	7.9	16.2
Education, employment, and social services	42.8	45.3	5.8
Health	71.2	94.6	32.9
Medicare	104.5	118.7	13.6
Income security	170.8	202.6	18.6
Social Security	269.0	286.7	6.6
Veterans' benefits and services	31.3	33.8	8.0
Administration of justice	12.3	14.0	13.8
General government	11.7	12.8	9.4
Net interest	194.5	200.2	2.9
TOTAL[a]	$1,323.0	$1,450.4	9.6%

[a] Several smaller functional categories have been excluded in this table.

Use of a current services budget therefore defines a budget *cut* as any spending change that is less than continuation of current spending levels and policies. For example, consider the case of Agriculture, where an increase of $2 billion maintains current services. If an increase of $1.1 billion takes place, a budget *cut* of $900 million is said to occur. In terms of the total budget, an increase of anything less than $127.4 billion is labeled a budget cut since spending would fall below $1,450.4 billion.

The original intent of providing current service estimates was to provide a base against which the President's proposal might be compared with that of Congress. There is, however, some merit to the criticism that the estimates bias the budgetary process in favor of spending increases. Consider, for instance, budgetary debates on Capital Hill. If a policymaker wishes to trim spending on any program by advocating an increase that is less than the increase implied by the current services estimate, opponents may claim that the policymaker advocates budget *cuts*. In effect, the current services definition for the 1992 budget shifted the definition of a cut in spending from a *fall* in current spending to any decrease less than a 9.6 percent increase in overall spending.[14] In the early 1980s, President Ronald Reagan was accused of cutting federal spending to the bone when, in fact, he proposed that spending rise by slightly less than the current services budget. Also note that, while President Reagan was a budget cutter in the language of the federal budget process, federal spending continued to rise during his tenure as President.

This budgetary definition may not appear to be inappropriate when one wishes to place spending changes in the perspective of the current baseline of spending. But we should also understand what incentives this budgetary definition may give to those who wish to expand federal spending. The spending of $450 million on a health care program could be budgeted in two very different ways:

❑ Fund a one-year increase of $450 million and disburse it immediately.

❑ Fund $450 million over the next ten years.

While it is often appropriate to fund programs over many years, today's budget only shows that portion of spending disbursed during today's budget year. For example, if the first year commitment is for $3 million, only that sum is placed on the budget for that year. However, the remainder of the commitment of $447 million shows up in the budgets of following years. Therefore, while the immediate impact on spending is only $3 million in this year's budget, much of the approved budget's impact is felt outside the current year's budgetary deliberations. Moreover, while increased spending shows up only in the year in which it is disbursed, estimates of current services in later years *immediately* rise in tandem with higher future spending commitments. As more spending is postponed to the future, tomorrow's definitions of budget *cuts* are based on higher current services budgets.

If it is easier to get other policymakers to agree to spending in the future versus spending today, the budgetary process may bias spending programs so that they are

---

[14] Note how the 9.6 percent increase implied by the current services budget estimate for 1992 calls for an expansion of public spending faster than the economy. The 9.6 percent increase in spending is in excess of the assumed increase in the economy which may be measured as the change in nominal GDP of 6.1 percent (3.3 + 2.8).

not only disbursed over many years, but because they raise estimates of current services, they will increase spending over time at higher rates than without this budgetary rule. Many believe that such changes in budget definitions account for some of the spending expansion that has occurred since the 1974 Impoundment Act.

Gramm-Rudman-Hollings Deficit Reduction Act

The **Gramm-Rudman-Hollings Act** called for automatic spending cuts in order to balance the budget of the federal government by 1991.

A consensus emerged in the early 1980s that the budget deficit was out of control. As shown in Figure 9-7a, deficit expansion began in the early 1970s and, by the mid-1980s, considerable concern on the part of voters and policymakers resulted in various legislation to control the deficit. The Balanced Budget and Deficit Reduction Act of 1985, often referred to as the **Gramm-Rudman-Hollings Act,** placed the budget on a predetermined path toward budgetary balance by 1991. The path set in 1984 is shown in Table 9-3 under the column GRH I (Gramm-Rudman-Hollings I). Failure to meet these deficit targets was to result in automatic cuts, called *sequestrations,* in spending programs.

Inspection of Table 9-3 shows the troubled history of GRH I. Before the ink was barely dry, it was clear that it would be very difficult to enforce its provisions and therefore, after two years of failing to meet its plan, the original law was revised into the 1987 Gramm-Rudman-Hollings Plan. This new plan, GRH II, pushed a balanced budget out to the 1993 budgetary year and was viewed as an unfortunate, but necessary, revision of GRH I. By the time GRH II was approved in 1987, it was also obvious that it would not result in its desired goal of a balanced budget by 1993, and consequently in 1990, the **Budget Enforcement Act of 1990** (BEA) replaced GRH II with a new plan that further pushed the balanced budget deadline out to 1994. As a way of making reparations for previous failures, the Congress promised that the BEA would produce budgetary surpluses in 1994 and 1995. As seen in Table 9-3, this 1990 plan also failed to reach its promised goal.

The **Budget Enforcement Act of 1990** extended the Gramm-Rudman-Hollings budget deadline to 1994.

TABLE 9-3
Deficit Reduction Plans Since 1985 ($Billions)

FY	1985 GRH I	1987 GRH II	1990 BEA	BEA Update[a]	Actual Deficit
1986	$171.9	—	—		$221.2
1987	144.0	—	—		149.7
1988	108.0	$144.0	—		155.1
1989	72.0	136.0	—		161.4
1990	36.0	100.0	—		152.0
1991	0.0	64.0	$253.6		268.5
1992	—	28.0	229.4	$360.0	290.2
1993	—	0.0	129.4	292.0	327.3
1994	—	—	(+16.7)	162.0	—
1995	—	—	(+68.3)	122.0	—

[a] Updated by OMB in August 1991.

**FIGURE 9-7
Federal Budget
Deficit**

*Source: Budget of
the United States
Government,* 1994.

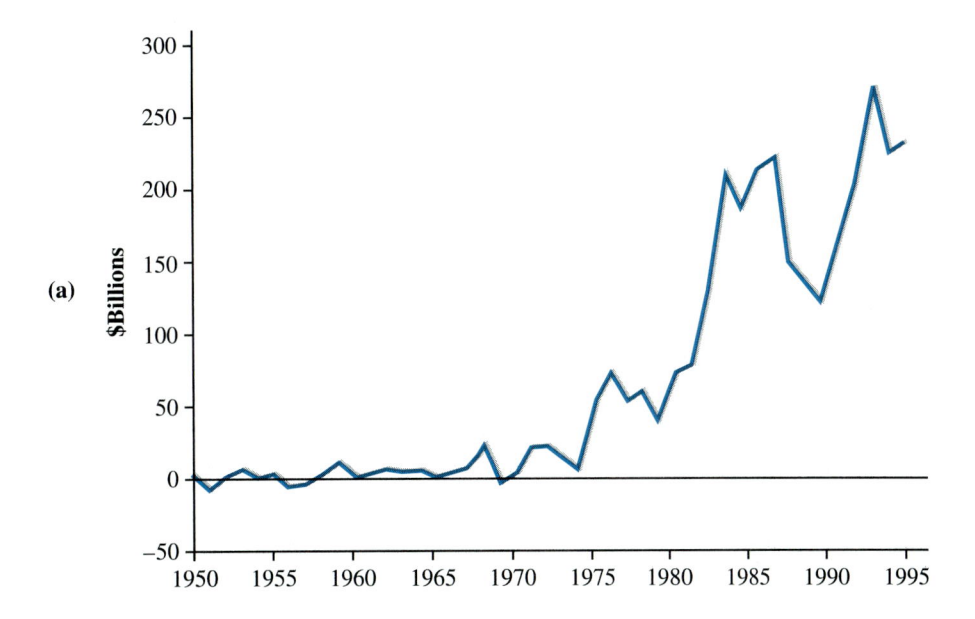

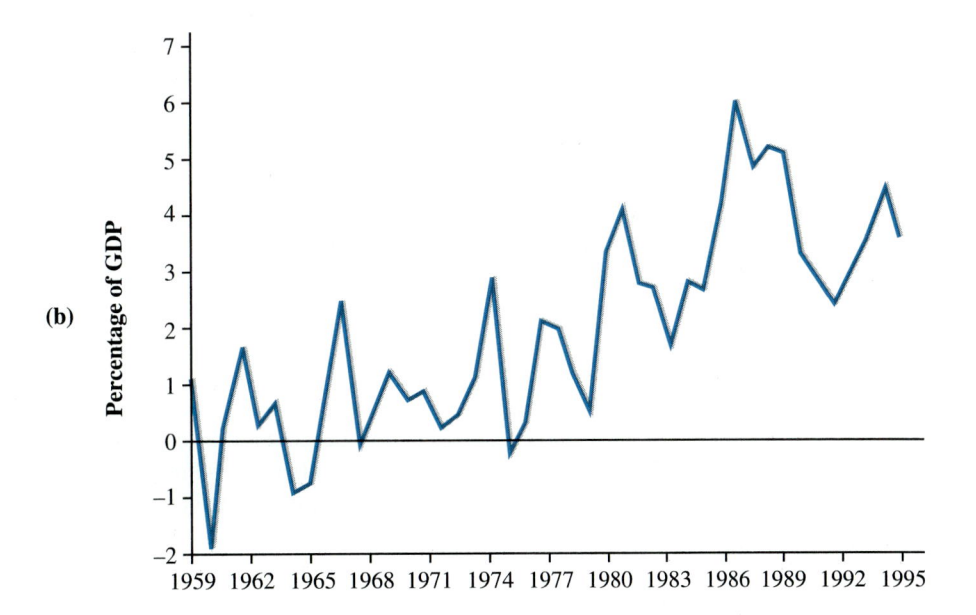

(a)

(b)

An understanding of the budget definitions introduced by the deficit-reduction laws is essential to our understanding why these laws failed to achieve their stated goals. Just as the budgetary process was redefined under the 1974 Impoundment Act, each new balanced budget plan redefined some portion of the budgetary process. One change permitted spending and tax receipts to be shifted between different fiscal years. For example, a Pentagon payday was moved from September 29, 1989, which is in FY89, to October 1, 1989, the first day of FY90. This shift lessened spending by that amount for FY90 and increased, by the same amount, spending in the previous year. GRH I and GRH II made policymakers responsible only for current and future deficit numbers; increases in past levels of budget deficits above targeted levels would therefore not trigger sequestrations of funds. Similarly, farm price support payments during FY90 were shifted back in time to FY89, and this move made it $4 billion easier to reach the FY90 deficit target.

Deficit targets could also be met by taking budgetary savings out of future budgetary years, or *out-years*. For example, if the current policies of a certain spending program called for spending increases of $5 million a year for the next five years, reductions of $1 million during each of five years could be used to decrease current spending levels by the sum of those savings, or $5 million. Under the current budgetary process, promised savings are only promises, and because there is no requirement that promised savings actually occur during the out-years, savings seldom materialize.

The laws also placed little, or no, penalty for failing to meet targets—behavior that may be reinforced by the ease with which new budget deficit reduction plans have been put into place. One reason for this behavior may stem from the fact that many programs were exempt from so-called automatic cuts of the Gramm-Rudman-Hollings Act. These were mainly in the form of **entitlement programs** such as Social Security, food stamps, and federal pensions. Entitlements are legal obligations created through legislation that require the payment of benefits to individuals or state and local governments that meet eligibility requirements established by law. Because close to half of federal spending is for entitlements, the scope of sequestrations affected a fairly narrow portion of federal spending.

Entitlement programs are those which provide benefits to all who meet various eligibility requirements.

Budget Enforcement Act of 1990

The Budget Enforcement Act of 1990 (BEA),[15] which enforces the Omnibus Budget Reconciliation Act of 1990, is the latest major change in the budgetary process. Legislated in October 1990, this plan is often called the Budget Compromise, since it represented a budget deal between Congress and the Bush White House to reduce, over a five-year period, $500 billion from the budget deficit. As they were under the two versions of Gramm-Rudman-Hollings, voters were promised that the BEA would eventually produce a balanced budget because it was to change the budgetary process in a way that eliminated future deadlocks between the President and Congress. Even though the BEA promised a slight budgetary surplus by FY96, within a year of passage of this act, the budget deficit was 30 percent higher than the budgetary target for that year.

As with previous deficit-reduction plans, the BEA produced a new budgetary environment between budget makers. Division of spending into two categories, discretionary and mandatory, was one major change. For 1991–95, the BEA limits discretionary spending and establishes a pay-as-you-go requirement that legislation which increases or decreases mandatory spending (or receipts) above a specified

---

[15] For detailed analysis of this recent change in the budgeting process, see Stanley E. Collender, *The Guide to the Federal Budget, Fiscal 1993* (Washington, D.C.: Urban Institute Press, 1992); and Marvin H. Kosters, ed., *Fiscal Politics and the Budget Enforcement Act* (Washington, D.C.: AEI Press, 1992).

percentage must, in total, be at least deficit neutral.[16] If deficit targets are not met, changes in discretionary spending programs are required to be deficit neutral.[17] As seen in Table 9-3, this newest installment of the drive to balance the budget deficit is off track, and it is likely that Congress will approve a new plan in the near future.[18] Moreover, as more and more of federal spending is placed in mandatory spending status, there exists fewer and fewer spending programs that can be used to meet deficit targets, and within the definition of a current services budget, spending *cuts* often entail substantial expansion beyond today's budget.

Reform of the Federal Budget Process[19]

Fiscal Rules

Fiscal rules
are procedures, such as the line-item veto and balanced budget laws and amendments, that seek to control spending or budget deficits.

Fiscal rules are laws placed upon the agents of the budgetary process. In response to growth of federal budget deficits, considerable attention has been placed on questioning whether imposition of fiscal rules would improve the budgetary process.[20] Critics of the current process point to the fact that 1969 was the last year that the federal government did not operate under a budget deficit. Critics also point to the fact that since Congress passed the Impoundment Act of 1974, budget agreements are rarely settled by the beginning of the fiscal year. This section considers two reforms which have received substantial attention.

Line-Item Veto

Line-item veto
allows the President or governors to eliminate individual spending items from an entire budget.

While many presidents have argued for the power of **line-item veto,** President Reagan is most especially associated with the issue. As we have discussed, passage of a final budget requires that the President sign, *in its entirety*, the latest congressionally approved budget. Presidents have two options when Congress sends them a budget: send it back to Congress or sign it. The line-item veto empowers the President to approve a budget and *then* to remove, line by line, individual components of the entire

---

[16] Deficit-neutral policy is policy under which changes in spending or tax revenues do not change the level of the budget deficit.

[17] Stanley E. Collender, *The Guide to the Federal Budget, Fiscal Year 1993* argues that in contrast to GRH I and GRH II, the BEA does not really have as its ultimate goal a balanced budget. Rather, the primary goals are to control spending growth and to ensure that spending increases are associated with tax revenue increases.

[18] Stephen Moore, "Crime of the Century: The 1990 Budget Deal after Two Years," *Policy Analysis*, no. 182, Cato Institute (Washington, D.C., October 1992) discusses this issue. The BEA was supposed to save $500 billion over five years and lead to a (cumulative) $770 billion deficit over 1991–95. However, it appears that after the BEA was passed, the budget deficit over this period is predicted to be $1.4 trillion. Therefore an additional $500 billion appears to have been added to the deficit. Moore also argues that if GRH I had been faithfully followed, the 1991–95 budget deficit would have been lower by the amount $1.3 trillion.

[19] For an interesting view of economists and the role that they play in the federal budget process, see Alice M. Rivlin, "Economics and the Political Process," *American Economic Review* 77 (March 1987): 1–10.

[20] For example, see Congressional Budget Office, *Balancing the Federal Budget and Limiting Federal Spending: Constitutional and Legislative Approaches* (Washington, D.C., 1983).

spending package.[21] For example, if the President does not believe that spending $2 million on a new fish hatchery in Alabama is appropriate, that provision may be simply removed from the budget. While governors of forty-three states have a line-item veto, the U.S. President currently lacks this power.

The hypothesis behind support for the line-item veto is that the President would be more inclined to veto pork barrel spending sections from the budget. An area of controversy, therefore, is what assumptions are placed upon the behaviors of the Congress and the President. For example, are members of Congress more interested in providing special favors to constituents, or are they most interested in providing spending programs that serve the interests of the voting public at large? We have discussed several related issues that provide some information on this issue. For example, what is the range of self-interests of policymakers? If the interests of Congress are not assumed to reflect narrow self-interests of constituents, then the case for the line-item veto is diminished because it is harder to claim that pork barrel spending plays much of a role in federal spending policy.

The *Federal Budget for Fiscal Year 1993* comments on the importance of a line-item veto in this way:

> *The current system of authorizing spending promotes special interest spending and affords the President little opportunity to control it. The President, as representative of the general interest, should have the power to strike from legislation provisions that reflect only narrow interests. As with any other veto, a veto by the President of an item in a spending or revenue bill would be subject to override by a two-thirds vote in each house of Congress. This essential tool is available to most State Governors, who have used it successfully without unduly shifting the balance of power between the executive and the legislature.*[22]

On the surface, line-item veto powers appear to shift power from Congress to the President, but it is not always clear how changes in the rules of the budgetary process will work themselves out over the years. An important concern surfaces when it is assumed that pork barrel characterizes much of federal spending. Given the history of earlier changes in budgetary rules, we can certainly question whether proponents of pork barrel spending will find ways around the presidential veto. Moreover, we must wonder what happens if the President is willing to trade off various pork barrel programs that Congress wants (and the President does not) for various spending programs that the President wants (and Congress does not). Each presidential administration has various agendas that Congress does not necessarily share, and in order to pass the presidential agenda, Presidents may be willing to overlook various pork barrel programs. In effect, such behavior would represent logrolling between Congress and the President.

---

[21] Usually the President signs roughly thirteen different general appropriations bills, and the decision is whether to sign each of the separate bills or send them back to the Congress. More recently, the Congress has sent one "omnibus" spending bill, representing the entire budget, to the President.

[22] *Budget of the United States Government, Fiscal Year 1993*, Part 1, 410.

Balanced Budget Amendment

Balanced budget amendment is a law that, under most circumstances prohibits policymakers' from running a budget deficit.

A **balanced budget amendment** to the constitution of the United States is another fiscal rule that has been suggested many times. In contrast to the previously discussed plans for reducing the budget deficit, a balanced budget amendment leaves no option other than to balance the federal budget by some specified date. Proponents believe that budgetary agents do not have sufficient incentives to reach a balanced budget and cite evidence regarding the histories of GRH I, GRH II, and BEA in support of this belief. Proponents also argue that state governments do not persistently run budget deficits because, unlike the federal government, a majority of state governments operate under balanced budget rules. Forty-four states require that governors must present balanced budgets to legislatures; thirty-eight states require that legislatures must pass balanced budgets; and thirty-one states require that governors sign balanced budgets.

Congress has considered several versions of balanced budget amendments recently. The following provisions are usually part of them:

- Spending may not exceed total tax receipts, unless three-fifths of both houses approve an exception.
- Tax increases must be approved by a majority of both houses.
- Congress may waive these requirements during wartime.

Critics argue that a balanced budget amendment places the budgetary process on automatic pilot, thus reducing the discretionary role of elected policymakers in economic policy. It is often claimed, for example, that a balanced budget rule unduly ties the hands of policymakers to respond to crises because it limits the ability to enact new spending programs without enacting corresponding, and offsetting, increases in taxes or reductions in spending in other programs. Moreover, while opponents do not often claim that governments should continually run deficits, it is argued at times that deficit spending should play an important role in fiscal policy.

Before we end our discussion of a balanced budget amendment, it is worth remembering that while new rules change the rules of the budgetary game, it is not easy to predict the final results of changes on spending. Balanced budget rules create incentives for policymakers to maneuver around deficit-reduction targets. Recent expansion of off-budget activities is a case in point. In response to GRH I, GRH II and BEA, more policies have been shifted off budget, so that they are not counted under current definitions of spending, revenues, and deficits. This is an extremely important trend, which we cover in the following chapter. For the time being, however, note that it is sufficient to know that a balanced budget amendment may be approved, but it does not necessarily provide a balancing of all the books of the federal government.[23]

---

[23] As discussed in Chapter 17, current definitions of spending do not measure future liabilities, and balancing of annual budgets therefore fails to provide a meaningful measure of the long-run fiscal position of the federal government.

Evidence from State Governments

Two facts are often linked together by supporters of fiscal rules on the federal government:

- Many states have line-item veto and balanced budget requirements.
- Since 1955, state governments, on average, have usually operated under budgetary surpluses.

Whether or not line-item veto and balanced budget requirements cause surpluses is an empirical issue. In a survey of state budget officers, one study concludes that governors seldom use the line-item veto except in states where the political parties of the governor and the legislature differ.[24] Another study finds that states with line-item veto powers tend to have 9 percent lower spending when political parties of the governor and the legislature differ.[25] This same study finds that when political parties are the same, spending is higher by 9 percent in those states with line-item veto powers. In a comprehensive study of the effects of many fiscal rules (for example, balanced budget, line-item veto, and tax and spending limits) on government spending, little or no influence from fiscal rules is found.[26] Another study, however, finds that the presence of these same fiscal rules exerts a constraining force on public spending.[27] The issues examined in these studies are clearly very important, and further examination is certain to be the focus of future study.

Capital Budget

What Is a Capital Budget?

Capital budgets are budgets that distinguish between short-lived and long-lived assets.

A **capital budget** distinguishes between spending on short-lived and long-lived assets. Private firms use accounting methods that depreciate long-lived assets over many years rather than charging them to the year in which they are purchased. Some economists argue that because the federal government purchases capital assets, policymakers overstate the size of the budget deficit, since capital spending yields benefits over time.[28] In contrast, noncapital items such as income transfers or salary payments yield only short-term benefits and therefore should be paid immediately. An implication of this argument is that costs of long-lived assets should be partially borne by future generations. Although this is a relatively uncommon concept at the

---

[24] G. Abney and T. Lauth, "The Line-Item Veto in the States: An Instrument for Fiscal Restraint or an Instrument for Partisanship," *Public Administration Review* 45 (1985): 372–377.

[25] James Alm and Mark Evers, "The Item Veto and State Government Expenditures," *Public Choice* 68 (1991): 1–15.

[26] Burton A. Abrams and William R. Dougan, "The Effects of Constitutional Restraints on Governmental Spending," *Public Choice* 49 (1986): 101–116.

[27] W. Mark Crain and James C. Miller III, "Budget Process and Spending Growth," *William and Mary Law Review* 31 (Spring 1990): 1021–1046.

[28] Robert Eisner and Paul J. Pieper, "A New View of the Federal Debt and Budget Deficits," *American Economic Review* 74 (March 1984): 11–29.

federal level of government, such a distinction is common to local and state levels of governments.[29]

Too Little Capital Spending on Infrastructure?

Provision of infrastructure is believed to be a crucial function of government since it paves the way, sometimes literally, for economic development and growth. Highways, electricity, mass transit, and communications are a few of the capital goods that constitute the infrastructure of the economy. It is obvious, for example, that it is easier for private firms to deliver their products to their customers in an economy characterized by a well-coordinated and maintained transportation system. Production efficiency is also related to a reliable and powerful energy supply. Possible connections between infrastructure and economic growth are many and have engendered a growing debate over what role the public sector should play in capital spending on infrastructure.

Let us examine the argument for public sector provision of infrastructure. Provision of capital goods is often relegated to the public sector because these goods have much in common with the traditional definition of public goods. Lack of exclusion and zero marginal costs of additional provision characterize many of the goods that make up an economy's infrastructure. As Chapter 5 demonstrates, public sector provision of public goods is often recommended on the basis of the prediction that the private sector underallocates resources toward production of public goods. A growing number of analysts have argued that the public sector underinvests in infrastructure and during his 1992 campaign, President Bill Clinton repeated the theme of the United States' "crumbling infrastructure" and promised to redirect public spending toward infrastructure. As a first step, President Clinton proposed spending $80 billion on infrastructure over four years.

Some empirical studies have linked falling public spending on infrastructure to falling productivity and call for increased spending as the key to raising the growth of the private economy.[30] Empirical evidence, however, is mixed and further study therefore is necessary before a direct relationship is established between the size of the public capital stock and private sector growth.[31]

A Capital Budget for the U.S. Government?

One of the reasons that some economists believe that the public sector spends too little on capital goods is that when governments operate under large budget deficits, policymakers tend to reduce capital investments in such areas as construction and

---

[29] An appendix to the federal budget now contains a summary of federal investment spending and reflects the extent to which the federal government considers capital investment in its policies.

[30] See, for example, Benjamin Friedman, *Day of Reckoning* (New York: Random House, 1988); and David A. Aschauer, "Public Investment and Productivity Growth in the Group of Seven," *Economic Perspectives of the Federal Reserve Bank of Chicago* 8 (September–October 1989): 17–25.

[31] See, for example, Jonathan B. Ratner, "Government Capital and the Production Function for U.S. Private Output," *Economics Letters* 25 (1983): 213–217; and David A. Aschauer, "Is Public Expenditure Productive?" *Journal of Monetary Economics* 25 (March 1989): 177–200. It has recently been argued, however, that these previous studies are invalid and that little evidence suggests any relationship; see John A. Tatom, "Public Capital and Private Sector Performance," *Review of the Federal Reserve Bank of St. Louis* 73 (May–June 1991): 3–15.

maintenance of roads and bridges. This is especially damaging when it is considered that, because part of the public capital stock depreciates each year, capital spending is required to maintain the existing capital stock. This logic leads some to argue for capital budgeting that spreads the costs of long-term investment spending across current and future beneficiaries of spending projects. In effect, proponents of capital budgeting seek to divide the budget into operating and capital budgets.

As argued earlier in this chapter, it is important to examine the allocational effects of increased public spending. An appropriate allocational issue is whether higher public capital spending crowds out private sector spending on those same goods. This is really an issue of whether private and public capital goods are substitutes or complements of each other. When substitutes, higher public spending lowers private spending. When complements, the opposite occurs. The evidence remains mixed, and it is therefore unclear to what extent higher public capital spending would actually increase the total (private and public) capital stock of an economy.[32]

Even if it were clear that the public sector underinvested in infrastructure, several factors complicate the implementation of a capital budget. *First*, though it may be easy for a private firm to place a dollar figure on capital assets, it is unclear how the public sector would place values on government office buildings, prisons, tanks, and fighter jets. These assets do not earn profits, and therefore the means by which to measure rates of return to these assets is yet another question. One alternative is to use replacement value, but this is extremely difficult to measure when there are few or no private market alternatives from which to make estimates.

Second, critics argue that greater public spending on infrastructure serves to expand pork barrel spending. It is fairly easy, for instance, for a member of Congress to argue that a new building, road, or bridge is a valuable long-term asset for the nation when in fact it may serve only the narrow constituency of the advocate. As one means of controlling this problem, President Clinton has mentioned the possibility of line-item veto for the President. But our discussion of the current services budget also suggested that spreading the costs of programs over many years is one way to increase the likelihood that projects will be approved by members of Congress. Because a capital budget, for instance, allows divisions to be made between short-term and long-term assets, arguments for public capital goods that are, in fact, pork barrel projects, may appear more attractive when they become part of the capital budget. Our previous discussion, suggests, however, that because they act as transfers, there appears to be little justification for including them in a capital budget.

Final Thoughts

We have covered many topics in our discussion of spending policy. Various trends in spending have been shown, and a framework has been developed to examine the

---

[32] For evidence suggesting they are substitutes, see Robert C. Kormendi, "Government Debt, Government Spending, and Private Sector Behavior," *American Economic Review* 71 (December 1983): 994–1010; and David A. Aschauer, "Fiscal Policy and Aggregate Demand," *American Economic Review* 75 (March 1985): 117–127. For evidence suggesting that they are complements, see James R. Barth, George Iden, and Frank S. Russek, "Government Debt, Government Spending, and Private Sector Behavior: Comment," *American Economic Review* 76 (December 1986): 1158–1167.

allocative and distributive effects of spending. We have also examined the budgetary process in depth; for definitions come and go, but the budgetary process plays an important role in explaining public spending policies. New laws will undoubtedly be passed that will play important roles in determining future federal spending. Balanced budget amendments, line-item veto power for the President, and capital budgeting may define new future budgetary processes, and it will be interesting to see whether they are approved in the near future.

Summary

- Economic analysis of expenditure policies is the study of the effects of policies on the allocation of resources. Allocational effects occur when policies shift resources into one area and out of other areas.

- The dominant trend in expenditure policy is that spending has spread from a fairly narrowly defined role, that of providing national defense, a system of justice, and infrastructure (roads, dams, and bridges) to spending on transfers and income support. Spending has therefore moved from purchases to transfers. Spending on tangible goods reflects purchases, and transfer spending redistributes income among members of society.

- Governments incur interest expenses when they operate under budget deficits. Since the late 1970s, federal interest expenses have doubled, from 7 percent to 14 percent of total spending. As the interest expenses compound, a greater share of current spending reflects payment for past spending policies.

- The Congressional Budget and Impoundment Act of 1974 denied the President the power to impound funds, created the current services budget, established specific time tables for spending to occur, and created the Congressional Budget Office. Creation of the current services budget introduced budgetary terminology that allowed various spending *increases* to be called budget *cuts*.

- Congress has legislated various budgetary laws aimed at reducing budget deficits. None of these laws has met the legislated targets. Some analysts recommend fiscal rules as a means of improving control over budget deficits. Such rules include line-item veto for the President and a balanced budget amendment. Some analysts also call for a capital budget, which distinguishes between spending on short-lived and long-lived assets.

Review Questions

1. What are the allocational effects of expenditure policies?
2. What are the distributional effects of expenditure policies?
3. What is the primary difference between a government purchase and a transfer? Give two examples of each.
4. What are the net interest expenditures of government? In what sense are they defined on a net basis?
5. What is a current services budget?
6. What is a line-item veto? What is a balanced budget amendment?
7. How would a capital budget differ from the budget used by the federal government?

Discussion Questions

1. Our discussion of externalities and public goods in Chapters 4 and 5 shows ways in which public spending may enhance allocative efficiency. Do the spending trends of the federal government suggest a growing public role in improving allocative efficiency?

2. Previous chapters have suggested areas in which allocative efficiency may be enhanced when more resources are allocated into such areas as pollution control (goods with negative externalities), vaccinations (goods with positive externalities), and national defense (public good). Provide examples in which spending programs could improve allocative efficiency in these areas.

3. Is it possible for a spending program to be characterized by a falling share of total public spending but to account for a growing share of GDP?

4. Analyze the allocative and distributive effects of the following recent proposals aimed at easing the ongoing transition away from defense spending: (1) allowing active duty military personnel to take up to a one-year leave of absence for education or training; (2) providing early retirement for personnel who are either employed at bases facing closure or reductions; and (3) spending millions in grants to communities hit hard by the transition to a lower role for defense.

5. We have argued that because of faster technological growth, expansion of the production possibilities frontier favors the private sector. What does this imply about the opportunity cost of expanding the role of the public sector in the economy?

6. The federal government must decide on which geographic location to provide a government contract to produce windows for a new government building. Even though such contracts necessarily imply higher income and jobs for the location selected, does the choice of geographic location necessarily imply that the project contains pork barrel spending? Provide several ways that would safeguard against the possibility of pork barrel spending.

7. Since education spending is an investment in human capital, should it be considered a capital asset or as current spending?

8. Some analysts argue that the federal government should not operate on a single-year budget but, rather, should set spending over two or more year periods. What changes do you predict may occur if a multiyear budget was adopted?

9. It has been argued that a balanced budget amendment would unduly restrict the abilities of policymakers to react to crises and emergencies. Examine this issue from the point of view of someone who wants a balanced budget amendment, but at the same time wants to provide policymakers with powers to enact spending programs in states of emergency or crises. Be sure to define specifically what constitutes crises and emergencies in your budget plan.

10. Do you agree with the following statement? "If logrolling plays a large role in spending policy, the case for a line-item veto becomes stronger."

Key Words

Allocational effects
Distributional effects
Government purchases
Government transfers
NIMBY
Welfare state
Pork barrel spending

Net interest expenditures
Mandatory spending
Discretionary spending
Federal budget process
Impoundment Act of 1974
Current services budget
Gramm-Rudman-Hollings Act

Budget Enforcement Act of 1990
Entitlement programs
Fiscal rules
Line-item veto
Balanced budget amendment
Capital budget

CHAPTER 10

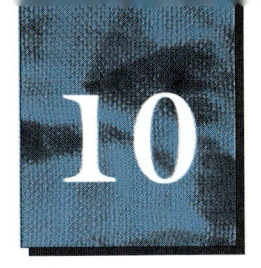

Off-Budget Government: Credit and Insurance Policies

More than half of all borrowing in the United States is influenced by programs of the federal government. Credit policies channel resources into many areas of our economy: Almost all credit in educational and agricultural markets is federally aided, and much of the credit extended to businesses is also influenced by public policies. In education, for example, federal policies lower interest rates on student loans so that low-income, gifted individuals are better able to afford college. Furthermore, the federal government is the largest underwriter of risk, and hence the largest insurer in the country. Deposit insurance is one example of a federal insurance policy that has received considerable attention in recent years.

An interesting aspect of federal credit and insurance policies is that they tend to be *off-budget*—that is, they either do not show up on the accounting books or they show up many years after enactment by Congress. This is in direct contrast to the *on-budget* spending policies we examined in the previous chapter, which show up on the books *directly* and *immediately*.[1] In this chapter we survey the off-budget policies of the federal government.

The following issues are examined in this chapter:

❏ What are off-budget policies?
❏ How do off-budget policies affect resource allocation and income distribution in the U.S. economy?
❏ Are on-budget and off-budget policies substitutes for each other?
❏ What explains the rapid expansion of off-budget policies?
❏ What are the implications of off-budget policies for our control over the public sector?
❏ What changes might improve, or reform, the off-budget policy process?

---

[1] This is not entirely true since, as discussed in Chapter 12, the unfunded future liabilities of programs such as Social Security do not show up on today's budget.

Allocational and Distributive Effects

Off-budget policies, like their on-budget counterparts, have been expanding rapidly in recent years. Since 1970, *credit policies* and *insurance policies* have increased by 603 percent, whereas federal on-budget spending has risen 575%, as we see in Table 10-1, which compares growth in federal credit and insurance outstanding and on-budget spending.[2]

Government policies exert two effects on resource allocation: allocative effects, which channel resources into specific areas of the economy, and distributional effects, which transfer income from one individual or group to another. In this section we briefly discuss how off-budget credit and insurance programs alter the allocation of resources and the distribution of income. (The following sections provide specific details on how programs operate.)

Role of Risk in Private Credit and Insurance Markets

To understand the allocational and distributional effects of off-budget programs, it is important first to understand how resources in credit and insurance markets are allocated in the private sector. Credit markets are institutions from which borrowers obtain loans to purchase such goods as automobiles and houses. Terms of credit transactions include the amount borrowed (or principal), the interest rate, collateral, down payments, and the period over which credit is extended. In insurance markets, individuals, such as owners of homes and automobiles, pay premiums to insurance firms, which in turn guarantee that they will replace some portion of any insured losses these individuals may suffer. For example, insured homeowners may submit claims for replacement or repair of their property when they suffer fire or storm damage.

A primary determinant of the terms by which resources are exchanged in these markets is the degree of risk that lenders or insurers assign to borrowers and insured individuals. In credit markets, for example, lenders believe that collateral and down payments are important determinants of risk. Collateral represents the value of assets lenders may take from borrowers in the event of loan defaults; thus higher collateral reduces risks of borrowers' defaulting on loans. Higher down payments also reduce risk because borrowers have more stake, or equity, in credit transactions. Other factors that influence credit risk are income, credit history, education, and occupations of borrowers. The importance of any of these factors is subject to debate, but it is clear that risk plays an important role in the allocation of resources in credit markets.

Risk also enters into exchanges that take place between insurance firms and insured individuals. The higher the rate at which insured individuals are expected to submit claims to insurance companies, the greater the risk. Anyone who has purchased automobile insurance knows firsthand how insurance companies calculate risks associated with various classes of drivers. Applicants for coverage must supply information on gender, age, residence, type of car, history of accidents and traffic

---

[2] As discussed below, increases in credit and insurance outstanding overestimate growth in taxpayer liability and in this way are unlike the case of federal on-budget spending. However, this comparison still suggests a rapid expansion of off-budget policies.

TABLE 10-1
Federal Credit and Insurance Outstanding ($Billions)

Program	1970	1975	1980	1985	1991	Increase 1970–91
Deposit insurance	$476	$855	$1,456	$2,342	$2,793	487%
Other insurance	216	187	831	1,031	1,650	664
GSE loans	24	49	151	370	1,006	4,091
Loan guarantees	125	189	299	410	649	419
Direct loans	51	74	164	257	174	241
TOTAL	$892	$1,354	$2,901	$4,410	$6,272	603%
Federal Spending	$196	$332	$591	$946	$1,323	575%

Sources: For credit and insurance outstanding, Table A1, *Budget of the United States Government, Fiscal Year 1992*, and Table 13–1, *Budget of the United States Government, Fiscal Year 1993*; for federal spending, *Budget of the United States Government*, 1994.

citations, and they must indicate whether they use their cars for commuting to work or for pleasure. Each of these factors connotes some degree of risk, which influences the expected payout of insurance claims. Similar questioning occurs when we apply for life and health insurance. In any case, private insurers always assess risk before they offer insurance to applicants.

Because analysis is the same for insurance and credit markets, we can concentrate on explaining how risk affects allocations in credit markets. In Figure 10-1, for example, we see a hypothetical credit market for home mortgages for a *given* level of risk. The supply of loanable funds, S_{LF}, has an upward slope, since it becomes more attractive, or profitable, for lenders to offer credit to borrowers as interest rates rise. The demand for loanable funds, D_{LF}, however, represents the point of view of borrowers'; that is, the higher are interest rates, the lower the quantity of credit demanded. Intersection of demand and supply curves determines the equilibrium interest rate, $r_e = 10$ percent, and the equilibrium quantity of credit, $Q_e = \$100$ million, in this mortgage market.

From Figure 10-2, we see how changes in the risk characteristics of borrowers affect interest rates and mortgage lending. When they believe that borrower risk has risen, lenders require, at any level of credit, additional compensation for the increased possibility of default. Such additions to interest charged, called *risk premiums*, may be measured by the vertical rise described by S_{LF} to S'_{LF}. (Actually, this is the *change* in the risk premium, since at the initial equilibrium some element of risk is likely to be perceived by lenders.) In this case we have assumed a constant risk premium which leads to a higher equilibrium interest rate, $r'_e = 12$ percent, and a lower equilibrium quantity of credit, $Q'_e = \$80$ million. (The degree to which the risk premium increases the equilibrium rate of interest is influenced by the elasticity of demand.) Now consider how a reduction in risk affects credit market equilibrium when the supply curve shifts in the opposite direction. The rightward shift in supply from S_{LF} to S''_{LF} leads to a fall in the equilibrium interest rate, $r''_e = 8$ percent, and a rise in equilibrium quantity

FIGURE 10-1
Hypothetical Market for Mortgages

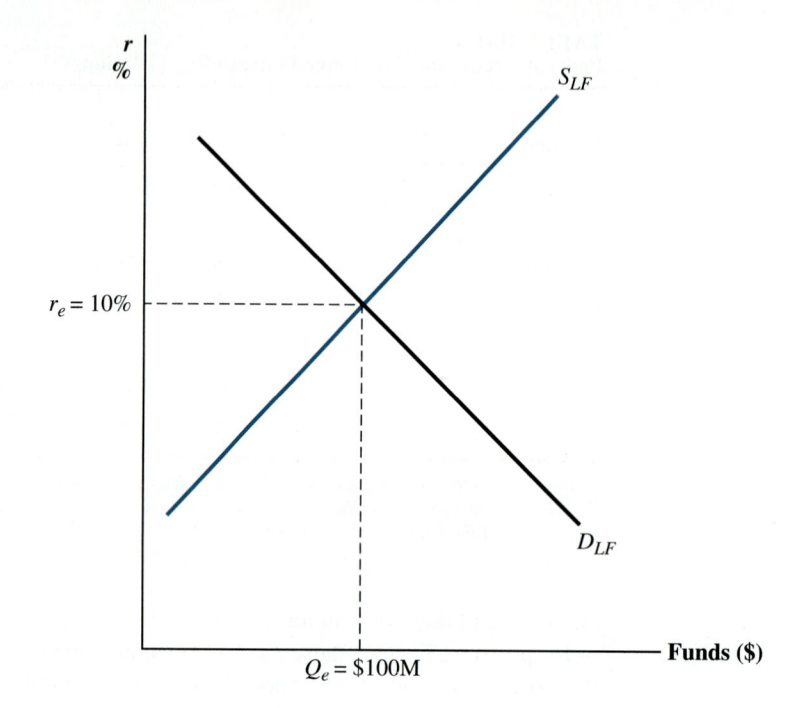

$r_e = 10\%$

$Q_e = \$100M$

S_{LF}, D_{LF}, Funds ($)

FIGURE 10-2
Changes in Risk Characteristics

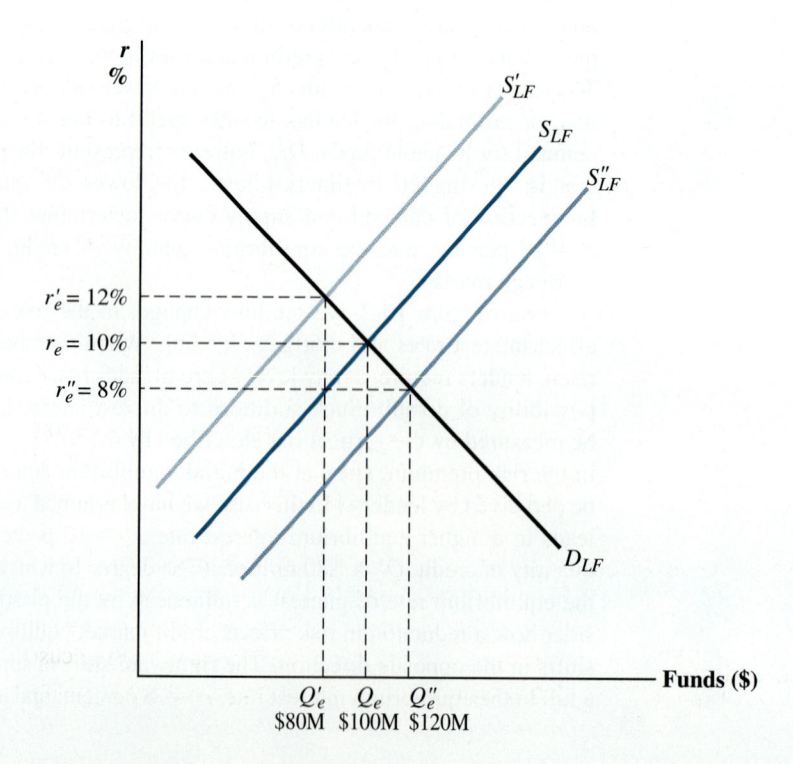

$r'_e = 12\%$
$r_e = 10\%$
$r''_e = 8\%$

Q'_e Q_e Q''_e
$80M $100M $120M

S'_{LF}, S_{LF}, S''_{LF}, D_{LF}, Funds ($)

of credit, $Q''_e = \$120$ million, as Figure 10-2 shows. Lowering the risk premium therefore leads to lower interest rates and a larger quantity of credit.

Risk and Resource Allocation: Two Effects

The exercise of plotting changes in risk demonstrates that risk plays a twofold role in allocating resources in private credit and insurance markets.

1. *Risk positively affects interest rates and premiums charged to borrowers and insured individuals.* The higher (lower) the risk, the higher (lower) interest rates and premiums will be. It is useful to consider how, *holding other factors constant*, credit histories of individuals tend to influence interest rates. A credit history indicates whether a borrower has paid credit card debt, mortgages, and car loans in a timely manner, and a poor credit history is a sign of high default risk. Thus individuals who have poor credit histories tend to pay higher interest rates than do individuals with excellent credit histories. (Changes in other factors, such as collateral, education, and income also affect risk and are considered by creditors as well.)

2. *Changes in risk characteristics lead to changes in resource allocation in credit and insurance markets.* When risk falls, supply rises, resulting in higher equilibrium levels of resources allocated in credit and insurance markets. This effect is symmetric since, when risk rises, supply falls, resulting in lower equilibrium allocations of resources.

Four Rationales for Credit and Insurance Policies

Although private markets allocate resources efficiently, (see Chapter 3), we can identify four reasons to explain why the public sector may be called upon to intervene in credit and insurance markets.

1. *Public intervention may be required to minimize misallocation of resources arising from misperceptions of risk.* In order for private markets to achieve allocative efficiency, market participants must be assumed to have perfect information. Information on risk characteristics is, however, necessarily imperfect, and some economists therefore argue that credit and insurance markets misallocate resources because they misperceive the factors that signal excessive risk. If, for instance, lenders overestimate default risk, they will require higher risk premiums than implied by allocative efficiency, and the resulting higher interest rates will preclude borrowing that might have occurred had the risk been perceived correctly. If, for example, lenders believe that S'_{LF} in Figure 10-2 captures risk when in fact S_{LF} contains an appropriate risk premium, the equilibrium interest rate r'_e will be higher and the equilibrium quantity of funds Q'_e lower, than when resources are efficiently allocated.

It has been argued that overestimation of risk is a result of discrimination on the basis of race, gender, age, and ethnic origin. It is not unknown for lenders or insurers to refuse to lend to, or insure, anyone in a perceived high-risk group. Mortgage lenders, for example, have been accused of **redlining**, which occurs when residents of an entire neighborhood are denied credit because of their common high-risk characteristics. (The word *redlining* comes from the now-illegal

Redlining is the process of denying credit and insurance to residents in certain (redlined) neighborhoods, usually those in high-risk areas.

practice of striking out, in red ink, areas on maps representing neighborhoods in which lenders refused to lend.)

To the extent that risk premiums are based on misperceptions rather than true default risks, public intervention in these markets may enhance allocative efficiency. Critics, however, believe that, because lenders or insurance companies wish only to maximize profits—and must do so using currently available information on risk characteristics—relatively high-risk premiums or refusals to lend are justified because they reflect efficient allocations of resources.

2. *Public intervention into credit and insurance markets may be justified because private sector firms have not fully developed these markets.* It may be argued, for instance, that because private firms do not wish to insure homeowners whose houses are built close to rivers and lakes, no active market in flood insurance exists. Similarly, private insurance companies do not offer U.S. corporations coverage for war-related or political risks when they invest abroad. And students from poor families and inner-city homeowners may be denied many private market sources of credit and insurance.

Such government-sponsored enterprises as Fannie Mae were created because the private secondary market in mortgages was believed to be greatly underdeveloped. A *secondary market* in mortgages—or any credit market for that matter—is one in which previously made loans are bought and sold. Secondary mortgage markets facilitate the relending of funds. Thrifts, for example, need not hold mortgage loans for the full term (commonly 30 years), but may sell those loans to life insurance companies or pension funds. The proceeds from these sales may then be lent again to other borrowers in the mortgage market. An active secondary market is desirable because it increases liquidity and, by allowing more loans to be made, tends to lower interest rates. Public policies that provide for an active secondary market are therefore argued to enhance the efficiency by which markets allocate resources.

3. *Public intervention into credit and insurance markets may be justified on the basis of equity and national priorities.* Let us reconsider Figure 10-1, where the intersection of demand and supply curves for loanable funds determines an equilibrium rate of interest of 10 percent. It may be argued that an interest rate of 10 percent, however efficient, is higher than low-income borrowers can pay. Similarly, an annual insurance premium of $850 may be too high for low-income automobile owners. In these cases the argument for public sector intervention is not based on the premise that lenders or insurance companies are overestimating risk. Rather, the claim is that interest rates and insurance premiums are higher than what would be consistent with the equity goals of society or various national priorities. In the United States, for instance, it has been suggested that home ownership is an important national goal that should be promoted through credit policies.

4. *Public sector intervention into credit and insurance markets may be justified because private markets misallocate resources in cases of public goods and goods that generate externalities.* The private sector has been shown to allocate too few resources in cases of public goods and goods that generate positive externalities. Conversely, the private sector allocates too many resources in cases of goods that

generate negative externalities. Off-budget policies that reallocate resources may enhance efficiency in these cases.

Allocative Effects

Direct Allocative Effects

Off-budget policies reallocate resources by channeling funds into various credit and insurance markets. Consider, for example, Figure 10-3, which demonstrates how public sector guarantees against risk of default by borrowers reallocate resources in mortgage markets. *Before the guarantee*, an equilibrium interest rate of $r_e = 10$ percent and quantity of $Q_e = \$90$ million are determined by intersection of D_{LF} and S_{LF}. Remember that embedded within r_e is a risk premium based on risk characteristics of borrowers.

How do lenders perceive public guarantees of loans? For simplicity, let us assume that lenders have zero transaction costs when borrowers go into default, so that a loan guarantee in effect removes any risk of default. Removal of risk premiums therefore shifts the supply curve of loanable funds to the right (S'_{LF}) and results in a lower interest rate ($r'_e = 8$ percent) and a greater quantity of mortgage lending ($Q'_e = \$100$ million). Note that an off-budget policy could also be proposed that guarantees against losses incurred by insurance companies, in which case the result would be lower insurance premiums and a greater quantity of insurance underwritten by insurance firms.

FIGURE 10-3
Allocative Effects of Public Sector Guarantees

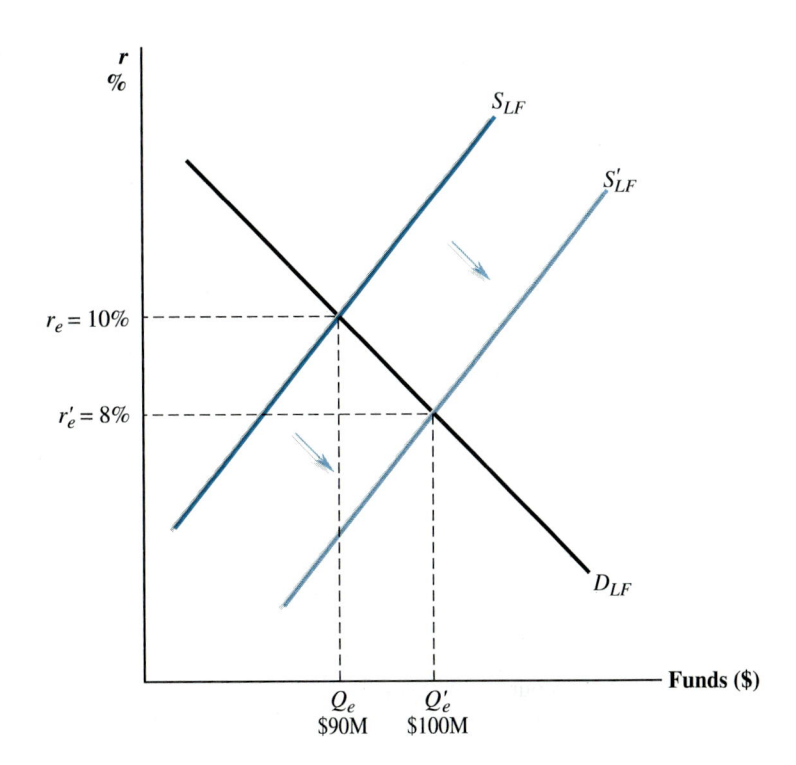

It is inevitable that some allocative effects are more visible than others. A direct effect of guarantees is increased allocation of resources into markets. Consider, for example, the direct allocative effects of a policy that guarantees student loans: Lower risk lowers interest rates so more students can get more loans. This is an effect that will surely be emphasized when proponents make their case for public sector provision of such a policy.

Indirect Allocative Effects

Other allocational effects, however, are less visible and follow from the fact that allocation of additional resources into one market necessarily implies that fewer resources are allocated into other markets. Thus, for example, interest rates rise and the quantity of lending falls in nonmortgage markets as the supply of loanable funds in mortgage markets increases. The extent to which nonmortgage markets experience these effects depends directly on the degree to which the policy succeeds. In other words, the greater the additional allocation of resources into mortgage markets, the fewer funds available in *other* markets.

Direct and Indirect Allocative Effects: The Case of Deposit Insurance

We can similarly examine allocative effects of policies that lower risk in insurance markets. Consider first what a private market for deposit insurance would look like. Insurance companies would set insurance premiums on the basis of portfolio risk of thrifts and commercial banks, and the higher the risk, the higher the premiums. Stockholders of thrifts and commercial banks would also carefully consider risk before they decide whether to invest in institutions, and because risk influences safety of deposits, depositors, as well, are interested in risk characteristics of financial institutions.

Now consider our current deposit insurance market, in which federal policy plays a major role in allocating resources. The government guarantees some portion of deposits. Policy therefore lowers the risk that financial firms will fail and exerts a *direct* allocative effect by inducing depositors and stockholders to allocate more resources into insured, "failure-proof" institutions. Furthermore, the guarantee of deposits also allows insured firms to pay lower interest rates to depositors since the risk of firm failures is reduced. The *indirect* allocative effect is that fewer resources are allocated into other nonpublicly insured markets when more resources are allocated into insured markets.

Distributional Effects

The distributional effects of credit and insurance policies are the ways in which income is redistributed throughout the economy. Income is necessarily redistributed, for instance, when guarantees against borrower default pertain only to low-income borrowers, borrowers of a certain age or ethnic group, or borrowers in a particular section of the country. Consider the primary insurance program of the Federal Housing Administration (FHA): The FHA partially insures against default of first-time mortgage borrowers and thereby lowers interest rates. Income is therefore redistributed toward those that qualify and away from those who do not qualify for this insurance program.

The question of who pays for these policies is integral to our analysis. When loans go into default or insurance claims come due, someone must pay off the guarantees and claims. Some public means of funding these liabilities must be available. Whereas private firms, such as insurers, establish contingency funds for meeting expected future claims, governments do not always operate under similar funding constraints. When no ongoing public fund exists for meeting the liabilities of a program, we call that program *unfunded* or *underfunded*. To the extent that liabilities are underfunded, additional tax dollars, public sector borrowing, or reduced on-budget spending must pay for claims on incurred liabilities.

How Off-Budget Policies Affect Risk

Off-budget policies are primarily concerned with changing risk characteristics of beneficiaries in a way that secures them more favorable credit and insurance terms. By lowering risk, these policies have been shown to affect resource allocation and distribution of income in our economy. But is it true that the risk associated with lending and writing insurance policies has been lowered or eliminated from the economy? Although risk is shifted onto the public sector, cases exist in which risk rises when policies are introduced. We now explore various possibilities.

Policies Focus on High-Risk Transactions

It should not be surprising that policies tend to focus on transactions that carry relatively high risk. High risk may be either the result of overestimation on the part of private lenders and insurance companies or may represent accurate appraisals of future loan defaults or insurance claims. It makes intuitive sense that in its promotion of efficiency and equity goals, the public sector designs policies that focus on lowering risk of transactions in private markets that attract high-risk customers.

Consider, for instance, Table 10-2, which shows delinquency and foreclosure rates for various types of mortgage loans. The *delinquency rate* is the percentage of loans delinquent 30 days or more and the *foreclosure rate* measures the percentage of loans that, at year-end, are in the process of foreclosure. *Conventional loans*, defined as loans other than VA (Department of Veterans Affairs) and FHA loans, represent private market loans that do not carry guarantees by the public sector. When we measure risk by rates of delinquency and foreclosure, the figures in Table 10-2 indicate that conventional loans carry roughly one-half of the risk of VA and FHA loans. In 1992, for instance, the delinquency rate of conventional loans averaged 3.0 percent, and for VA and FHA loans delinquency rates averaged 6.5 percent and 7.1 percent, respectively. Similar differences are evidenced by comparisons measured by foreclosure rates. Although such results appear reasonable for policies that focus on relatively high-risk transactions, it is appropriate to question whether off-budget policies themselves raise risk in credit and insurance markets.

Moral Hazard and Risk Liabilities

The issue of whether policies increase the risk undertaken by recipients of credit and insurance policies has been receiving significant attention in recent years, but before we address it, let us examine behavior in private insurance markets.

TABLE 10-2
Mortgage Delinquency and Foreclosure Rates

	Delinquency Rates			Foreclosure Rates		
	1970	1980	1992	1970	1980	1992
Conventional	1.77	3.09	3.00	0.08	0.17	0.80
VA loans	3.03	5.34	6.50	0.25	0.46	1.30
FHA loans	3.65	6.55	7.10	0.47	0.53	1.40
TOTAL	3.13	4.97	4.60	0.33	0.38	1.00

Source: Statistical Abstract of the United States, 1991 and 1993, U.S. Department of Commerce.

When Moral Hazard Occurs

Moral hazard is the tendency of policies to exert perverse incentives on the behaviors of firms and individuals.

The term **moral hazard** describes the tendency of policies to exert perverse incentives on behaviors of firms and individuals. If, for example, the primary goal of automobile insurance is to protect drivers from accidents, that goal may never be achieved because owners of insurance policies may take greater driving risks than those who are unable to obtain insurance. From the viewpoint of drivers, insurance policies reduce the costs of accidents because they insure against some portion of losses, or medical costs, incurred in accidents. To the extent that insured drivers are induced to undertake greater risks than uninsured drivers, the insured will tend to have more accidents than the latter. When insurance policies produce this adverse effect on risk taking, a moral hazard is said to exist.[3]

Now let us address this issue in the case of off-budget policies. A moral hazard results from off-budget policies when someone increases risky behavior. When public policies insure or guarantee mortgage loans through VA and FHA programs, the liability for risk taking is shifted from private lenders to the public sector. When private lenders are no longer concerned about default risk, they become less interested in assessing borrower risk, and they will make more loans, at lower interest rates, to high-risk borrowers than if FHA and VA programs were unavailable.

As we have seen, risks associated with FHA and VA loans are roughly twice that of conventional loans, and some portion of this difference is undoubtedly due to moral hazard. Another reason that probability of loan default may rise when the public sector intervenes in private credit markets is a lack of commitment to enforcing contracts. Student loans, for instance, are notorious for their high default rates. In 1992, roughly $3 billion in student loan defaults occurred. High default rates are often associated with the low likelihood that the public sector will enforce repayment by borrowers. This phenomenon may be attributed to political pressure, which, in effect, turn these loans into gifts, or to relatively high collection costs.

---

[3] It has been argued that private markets appropriately deal with this issue; see Richard E. Kihlstrom and Mark V. Pauly, "The Role of Insurance in the Allocation of Risk," *American Economic Review* 61 (May 1971): 371–379.

Other examples of moral hazard include deposit and flood insurance programs and guarantees of agricultural loans. In the case of flood insurance, for example, the burdens of paying claims are shifted from private insurance companies to the public sector. Therefore private firms can offer lower insurance premiums to homeowners who, without a public guarantee, would either not be offered insurance or would pay higher premiums.

From an *allocational* standpoint, these policies allocate more resources into credit and insurance markets so that when moral hazard results, a greater number of resources are shifted into riskier activities. Cases of moral hazard, in other words, raise the overall risk associated with resource allocation. From a *distributional* standpoint, taxpayers are responsible not only for incurred liabilities, but moral hazard results in an overall increase in their liabilities (and income loss) as well.

VA Loan Program and Moral Hazard

An example of a loan guarantee policy that increases risk taking by borrowers is the VA loan program. Unlike conventional loans, VA mortgage loans, which are available to veterans, carry no down payment requirements. The primary purpose of these loans is to make it easier for veterans to buy houses, but one effect of this policy is to raise default risk. As we can see in Table 10-2, the default risk of VA loans is roughly twice that of conventional loans, which often require minimum 20 percent down payments for houses.

To understand how the VA program influences probability of default, consider the viewpoint of a borrower who wishes to purchase a $100,000 house. Assume that under a conventional loan, the borrower is offered a 30-year mortgage, an interest rate of 10 percent, and a down payment requirement of 20 percent. In other words, the borrower is offered an $80,000 loan at 10 percent and, according to the down payment requirement, must come up with $20,000 of the purchase price of the house. This contract roughly converts into a monthly mortgage payment of $702. How would the VA program affect the terms the lender would offer this borrower? Remembering that the loan is guaranteed by the government, and assuming zero transactions costs, we see that risk is virtually eliminated from the point of view of the lender. This explains why lenders offer VA loans at rates below those of conventional loans. For example, under VA terms the rate may be 8.5 percent, which, without a down payment requirement, roughly converts into a monthly mortgage payment of $769. From the point of view of the borrower, contract terms are much more attractive; even though the monthly payment is $67 more per month, the borrower does not have to come up with the $20,000 up front. Moreover, the borrower who has $20,000 may earn roughly $1,000 in annual interest income by investing those funds in a savings account that pays 5 percent interest. (For simplicity, we do not consider complexities introduced by such factors as taxation.)

Now the question becomes: Does the policy influence the behavior of the borrower? Consider first how, in the absence of the VA loan program, the private lender would control for default risk. By requiring a down payment of $20,000, the lender shifts some of the risk of the transaction onto the borrower. The down payment represents the initial equity of the borrower, and if the investment goes sour, the borrower stands to lose some or all of the $20,000. The borrower's equity improves the chances that the borrower will maintain the house well—and it reduces the probability that the borrower will default on the loan. If, for whatever reason, the borrower fails to make monthly payments, the lender can foreclose on the house and sell it to pay off some portion of the outstanding loan balance. As long as the house has not depreciated in value, the lender may recoup its loan in full, and after the outstanding loan balance is paid, the borrower receives any residual value. The important point of this discussion is that private lenders have incentives to deal efficiently with risk in their transactions with borrowers.

Now let us return to our discussion of the same borrower, who now receives a VA loan. Zero down payment means zero equity—the borrower therefore has nothing to lose under default. We assume here that loss of home and adverse effects of default on the credit history of borrowers are not a concern. Consider how zero equity creates an incentive for loan default when the house depreciates in value from $100,000 to $90,000. The borrower now holds a property worth $10,000 less than the mortgage contract. And because the loan value far exceeds the house value, an incentive exists for the borrower to default on the investment—sometimes literally, just walking away and mailing the keys to the lender.

We can see why private lenders do not offer zero-down payment mortgage loans. In our example, loan default leaves the lender with an investment that is worth $10,000 less than when the contract was negotiated. With a $20,000 down payment requirement, however, a $10,000 drop in value means only that the borrower's equity has been reduced by that amount. The lender can fully recoup the loan (roughly $80,000, depending on how many payments had been made) by selling the house for $90,000. Because the borrower maintains an equity stake of roughly $10,000 ($90,000 − $80,000, or house value minus loan value) in the house, monthly payments are more likely to continue than if the equity stake was zero, or negative.

When policies guarantee zero-down payment loans, lenders cease to be concerned with default risk. A moral hazard therefore exists not only because the policy shifts risk onto the public sector but because it increases overall risk taking in this market. But is this moral hazard inevitable? The possibility that the public sector could design off-budget policies that do not increase overall risk taking is now explored.

Cases in Which Moral Hazard Does Not Exist

The fact that risk liabilities are transferred to the public sector does not necessarily imply that moral hazards must result from off-budget policies. Policies can be designed, for example, with risk-adjusted insurance premiums or interest rates. In these cases, risks need not rise above what would occur without public intervention. Just as insurance companies charge higher premiums to riskier drivers, public guarantees against flood damage could be written to include premium charges commensurate with risks.

Risk-adjusted premiums, or interest rates, are clearly in the spirit of credit and insurance policies designed to promote activity in areas underdeveloped by private markets. As we shall show, however, such adjustments are not common. Rather, uniform insurance premiums are the typical pricing scheme, and therefore a high likelihood of moral hazard exists in off-budget policies.[4] It should also be understood that when policies are not designed to enhance allocative efficiency, they often promote risk taking. That is, under policies that promote social equity, there is no reason to control risk, which is an efficiency issue.

The proposition that policies which promote risk taking result in lower allocative efficiency deserves further elaboration. We have shown that it is efficient for private insurance and credit firms to charge risk premiums to customers. When private firms control for risks, they are performing an allocative function in the economy. But when credit and insurance policies increase risk taking, the allocative function is weakened and efficiency worsens. Redistribution of income, rather than allocative efficiency, may be the primary goal, however—in which case the direction of redistribution is from taxpayers to policy recipients.

Adverse Selection

Adverse selection is the tendency whereby those at the greatest risk of collecting insurance are also those most likely to purchase insurance.

It is commonly believed that high-risk individuals tend to buy insurance and low-risk individuals tend not to buy insurance; similarly, high-risk individuals are believed to be more interested in borrowing than are low-risk individuals. This tendency results in a phenomenon called **adverse selection**, which poses serious problems to private insurance and credit firms because it threatens their capacity to diversify risks. Firms need to have a mix of high- and low-risk customers in order to remain profitable. Consider what would happen if an automobile insurance firm were to sell policies primarily to high-risk drivers. The resulting poor mix of high- and low-risk drivers could force profits so low that the firm would have to stop offering insurance to anyone. But when public policies remove risk, firms do not have to select insurance or loan applicants on the basis of their risk characteristics. Thus, while more customers can be offered more loans and insurance, a risk pool characterized by a preponderance of high-risk customers increases the probability of claims. Off-budget policies therefore tend to encourage adverse selection, which contributes to high risk taking in insurance and credit markets.

Federal Deposit Insurance Policy

Deposit Insurance

The largest off-budget program is federal deposit insurance, which accounts for roughly 45 percent of federal credit and insurance outstanding. This policy insures, to a maximum of $100,000 per account, private deposits at commercial banks, savings and loans, and credit unions. With $2,793 billion in outstanding liabilities, this insurance program has grown 487 percent since 1970 (see Table 10-1).

Federal deposit insurance arose out of the Great Depression, when banks failed in droves. By what is often described as a domino effect, the banking industry

---

[4] In the case of the FHA mortgage program, for example, policy is to not adjust interest rates on borrower characteristics that commonly signal likelihood of default; see James R. Barth, Joseph J. Cordes, and Anthony M. Yezer, "Federal Government Attempts to Influence the Allocation of Mortgage Credit: FHA Mortgage Insurance and Government Regulations," in Congressional Budget Office, *Conference on the Economics of Federal Credit Activity*, Part 2, 1980.

virtually toppled over when the failure of just a few unsound firms triggered a chain reaction that brought down many healthy firms as well. From 1929 to 1933, roughly 10,000 out of a total of 25,000 banks failed.[5] It is not, therefore, surprising that the public sector was called upon to restore financial market stability at that time. In the 1930s, federal deposit insurance, which was the public sector's primary means of restoring stability to an extremely fragile industry, took the form of two agencies: the *Federal Deposit Insurance Corporation (FDIC),* created to insure deposits in commercial banks, and the *Federal Savings and Loan Insurance Corporation (FSLIC),* established to insure deposits in savings and loan associations (thrifts).

The amount of insurance coverage provided by the FDIC and FSLIC has varied over the years. The largest increase (as well as most recent), however, occurred in 1980 under the Depository Institutions Deregulation and Monetary Control Act, which raised the ceiling from $40,000 to $100,000. At the end of that decade another big change was introduced. The Financial Institutions Reform, Recovery, and Enforcement Act of 1989 (FIRREA) transferred the duties of FSLIC to the *Savings Association Insurance Fund (SAIF),* and the *Bank Insurance Fund (BIF)* was established to insure commercial banks.

In order to be eligible for insurance coverage, depository institutions must meet various capital requirements, and they must pay premiums in return for insurance coverage. These premiums cover administrative costs and, in theory, the costs of current resolutions of troubled firms. Any remaining funds are to be used to increase reserve funds for future resolutions. Such resolutions can take one of two forms: Institutions may be closed or, more commonly, ailing institutions may be merged with or acquired by healthier institutions. Prior to the 1980s, reserve funds were more than sufficient to cover all resolutions.

Moral Hazard and Liabilities

Moral hazard is commonly believed to be a major factor behind the surge in resolution costs during the 1980s. That is, the very act of receiving insurance is suspected of increasing individual or institutional incentives to engage in risky behaviors. In the case of deposit insurance policy, then, it appears that perverse incentives have been created that encourage institutions to choose more risk.

In order to examine the case of deposit insurance in detail, we need to remember the case of auto insurance, in which private insurers control customers who engage in risky behavior by disciplining those whose frequency of accidents is high. High-risk drivers either have problems renewing their policies or they are charged high risk premiums. The incentive for owners of private insurance companies to discipline customers' behavior is clearly strong. And because low-risk customers do not wish to subsidize high-risk customers, they will exert some discipline, in turn, upon insurance companies; low-risk customers tend to price-shop for companies that set premiums according to risk. It is now appropriate to ask: Is there a similar mechanism that controls risk taking when federal deposit insurance is offered to financial institutions?"

---

[5] Milton Friedman and Rose Friedman, *Free to Choose* (New York: Harcourt Brace Jovanovich, 1989), 84.

Does Policy Control Risk?

To answer this question, we examine three possible sources of discipline—regulators, depositors, and stockholders.

1. REGULATORS Do regulators discipline the high-risk activities of insured institutions? In general, the answer is no, because insurance premiums are set at *uniform* rates.[6] Insured institutions that choose high-risk investment portfolios are charged premiums no higher than those of institutions that select low-risk portfolios. High risk-taking by insured institutions is therefore not penalized by higher insurance premiums. In theory, risk taking of management is controlled by federal regulators, but there is little question that regulators are limited in the practical effort to contain risk taking by insured institutions.[7]

Another regulatory policy deserves mention here—the practice of lowering capital requirements, which are the equity stakes of owners of firms. In the event of failure, capital requirements represent the personal liability of owners; therefore, lower capital requirements reduce the equity of owners and increase the likelihood of failure.[8] In the early 1980s capital requirements were roughly 5 percent of assets, but in 1982 they were lowered to 3 percent. Moreover, more liberal definitions of what counted as capital were also applied in that decade. Thus the equity stakes of owners have been lowered over time, thereby increasing risk taking by insured institutions.

2. DEPOSITORS When deposits are insured, what incentives do depositors have to discipline the imprudent investment policies of management? Even though insurance policies clearly state that deposits are insured to a maximum of $100,000 only, it is commonly believed that all deposits are fully covered. This notion arises out of fears that the domino effect may be triggered by rumors that depositors are unable to withdraw funds. Another common belief is that government is committed to a policy of "too big to fail"—that is, regulators will never close down large, high-profile insured institutions because the resulting domino effect would cripple other, healthier institutions. In effect, deposit ceilings approach infinity in the minds of the public, and the safety of their funds is of little concern to depositors.

3. STOCKHOLDERS[9] Unlike owners of tool or computer manufacturers, stockholders have had few concerns about losses because the rate of failure of insured depository institutions has historically been extremely low. In fact, there have been

---

[6] An initial move toward risk-based premiums was introduced in January 1, 1993. Premiums for banks and thrifts now range from 23 cents per $100 of deposits for the healthiest firms to 31 cents for the weakest.

[7] For a discussion of changes that have limited the ability of regulators to contain the risk taking of depository institutions, see James R. Barth, *The Great Savings and Loan Debacle* (Washington, D.C.: AEI Press, 1991).

[8] In fact, insolvency means there is zero capital and implies that further risk taking carries no personal liability.

[9] As discussed in Barth, *The Great Savings and Loan Debacle*, an increasing number of thrifts were operated within stock form, as opposed to mutual. In fact, roughly three-fourths of the resolution costs of thrifts are due to stock ownership. This follows from the fact that stock ownership carries less liability for owners than does mutual ownership.

many cases in which thrifts that were technically insolvent had stock prices greater than zero. In other words, because of the strong backing of these institutions by the public sector, the fortunes of stockholders are partially guaranteed; therefore, stockholders have fewer incentives to worry about the management practices of these insured firms than about those of other corporations in which they have invested. With little equity to lose and insurance premiums that are not linked to portfolio risk, stockholders themselves may encourage higher risk taking by management. Moreover, stockholders expect that regulators will allow firms to continue operation and/or arrange mergers with healthier institutions in the event of insolvency.

For these reasons, it is commonly believed that the net result of deposit insurance policy is to raise the level of risk undertaken by depository institutions. Moral hazard is therefore an integral by-product of this policy and, as we saw in our previous examples, there are important allocational and distributional effects on resources in the U.S. economy.

Costs of Regulatory Forbearance

Regulatory forbearance occurs whenever a regulator does not enforce an existing rule.

The Congressional Budget Office estimates that **regulatory forbearance** has increased the costs of the thrift bailout by at least $66 billion.[10] Regulatory forbearance occurs whenever a regulator does not enforce an existing rule. In this case, the standing rule is that when a firm becomes insolvent, the regulator will close it down or arrange a merger with a healthier firm. Another option, however, is to allow it to keep operating in the hope that the firm will eventually return to good health. In 1982, roughly 85 percent of all thrifts, or 2,793 firms, reported negative net income and, under most definitions, were insolvent. At the time, many observers believed that the poor health of the industry was due to a weak economy and high interest rates and that with time and new legislation, the industry would eventually turn healthy again. In retrospect, we see that very few insolvent firms recovered; on the contrary, most entered into a period of rapid decline.

Two reasons support the view that insolvent firms should be allowed to continue operation. One reason was that the reserves of the FSLIC were insufficient to meet closure costs and that in order to close these firms and pay off claims of depositors, federal on-budget spending would have to rise. However, rapidly rising federal budget deficits swayed many in Congress to follow a policy of regulatory forbearance, and regulators therefore had little choice but to keep insolvent firms open.[11] A second reason for this policy was that closures of insolvent thrifts would exert adverse impacts on local economies. It is not surprising, therefore, that constituents of policymakers strongly signaled their concerns to influential members of Congress, who exerted substantial pressure for forbearance.

---

[10] Congressional Budget Office, "The Cost of Forbearance during the Thrift Crisis," CBO Staff Memorandum, June 1991. Note that this figure is in 1990 dollars.

[11] Interestingly, the option of increasing insurance premiums as a means of paying for the resolutions of failed institutions was dismissed because it was believed that if insurance premiums were increased to pay for closures, higher insurance costs would have resulted in a greater number of insolvencies. Similarly, policymakers also greatly opposed increased capital requirements because of their fear that the increases would further weaken the financial health of thrifts.

By 1987, 80 percent of thrifts were insolvent, and only 26 percent had been resolved.[12] There was also, on average, a 38-month lag between the time a firm became insolvent and its resolution through the regulatory framework. By 1990, the average lag grew to 49 months, and the Congressional Budget Office has estimated that the cost of keeping an insolvent firm open increases 37 percent for each year it is allowed to remain open. This leads to an estimate of $66 billion in higher costs as a result of regulatory forbearance.

Economic Effects of Deposit Insurance Policy

Allocational Effects

Deposit insurance policy clearly influences resource allocation. It encourages individuals to deposit more of their wealth into insured depository institutions than in riskier alternative investments such as bonds, stocks, and real estate because risk is effectively zero.

The original justification for creation, and favorable regulatory treatment, of thrifts was to ensure a large and cheap source of lending for home mortgages. Before 1980, for example, 80 percent of the assets of thrifts were required to be in residential mortgages. The Garn–St. Germain Act of 1982 lowered the requirement to roughly 60 percent of assets; then, under the Financial Institutions Reform, Recovery, and Enforcement Act of 1989, it was raised to roughly 70 percent. By directing funds into thrifts, deposit insurance policy allocates funds into housing markets, and thus fewer funds are allocated into nonhousing markets.[13]

Deposit insurance allocates a greater proportion of resources into high-risk institutions. Regulatory forbearance created an industry characterized by insolvent, but open, institutions that advertised deposit rates in excess of those offered by healthy institutions. Over time, then, more funds have been diverted to insolvent firms. With zero equity in their firms, owners attempted to "win at the races," gambling on investments with the highest returns and the higher risks. In addition to offering higher returns on deposits, managers of failing institutions were forced to invest in riskier investments in order to pay the high interest rates promised to depositors. At the same time they tried to rescue their firms by earning higher income on portfolios comprising ever-riskier investments. The Congressional Budget Office has argued that policy has promoted investment into "inefficient and sometimes worthless projects, rather than into productive investments such as new factories and new equipment."[14] Because a reduction in the quantity and quality of the nation's capital stock causes gross domestic product to be lower than it would be otherwise, deposit insurance may be a factor that makes the U.S. economy grow more slowly over time.

---

[12] Congressional Budget Office, "The Cost of Forbearance during the Thrift Crisis."

[13] Commercial banks have been required to direct a large portion of their assets into loans for businesses and therefore, under similar reasoning, deposit insurance channels more funds into these markets and less into others.

[14] Congressional Budget Office, *The Economic Effects of the Savings and Loan Crisis*, January 1992.

Distributional Effects

Insurance subsidizes risk taking by insured institutions. The value of this subsidy may be measured in terms of how much the policy reduces the costs of funds for insured institutions.[15] Insured institutions can attract funds more cheaply as a result of deposit insurance because deposits become risk free from the viewpoint of depositors. The Office of Management and Budget has estimated a subsidy cost of $14 to $32 billion over 1992–97.[16] A redistribution of income, as measured by the subsidy, flows to insured institutions.

To the extent that deposit insurance policy creates unfunded liabilities, taxpayers are called upon to bail out insolvent firms. This is a distributive effect because insurance policy becomes a transfer policy that draws from the public sector to stabilize the wealth of depositors. A recent estimate of the present-value cost of resolving the S&L crisis is $215 billion in 1990 dollars—an estimate that yields roughly $800 for every man, woman, and child in the United States.[17]

Other Insurance Programs

As we see in Table 10-1, "other" insurance programs account for 26 percent of federal credit and insurance outstanding, and since 1970 these policies have increased by 664 percent. These programs include private pension insurance, flood insurance, crop insurance, and nuclear risk insurance programs. Table 10-3 shows the liabilities associated with these programs. Flood and crop insurance provide protection for damages to real estate from floods and crop losses due to bad weather. War risk insurance protects air and maritime carriers from loss of their ships or aircraft during war or national emergency. The Overseas Private Investment Corporation (OPIC) insures foreign investment against political risk arising from inconvertibility of currency, political violence, or expropriations. Veterans' life insurance helps veterans and active military personnel purchase insurance policies when combat risks or health problems make it difficult for them to obtain private insurance. Nuclear risk insurance protects against losses associated with nuclear power. Finally, the Pension Benefit Guaranty Corporation (PBGC, or Pennie Bennie) guarantees the private pensions of more than 65,000 private pension funds.

Federal Exposure to Losses

We can identify three problems that expose the public sector to high risk when it provides these insurance policies. First, like deposit insurance, these policies create incentives for insured firms and individuals to undertake risky ventures. For example, flood insurance creates a moral hazard whereby homeowners tend to build more often

---

[15] For a detailed analysis of subsidies, see William G. Gale, "Economic Effects of Federal Credit Programs," *American Economic Review* 81 (March 1991): 133–152.

[16] Table 13.1, *Budget of the United States Government, Fiscal Year 1993*. Also note that this is understated because it only reflects its effect on on-budget government spending. In our examination of government-sponsored enterprises, we will show how some portion of these costs are financed off budget.

[17] Congressional Budget Office, *The Economic and Budget Outlook: An Update*, August 1991, 63–69.

TABLE 10-3
Outstanding Liabilities of Other Major Insurance Programs ($Billions)

Program	1970	1980	1990
Flood insurance	—	$ 88	$ 203
Federal crop insurance	$ 1	3	13
Aviation war risk insurance	53	185	474
Maritime war risk insurance	17	22	11
Veterans' life insurance	38	33	27
Overseas Private Investment Corporation	8	5	10
Nuclear risk insurance	100	89	—
Pension Benefit Guaranty Corporation	—	405	943
TOTAL	$217	$830	$1,681

Source: Budget of the United States Government, Fiscal Year 1992.

on flood plains than they would if they could not purchase flood insurance. While the private sector can limit its exposure to moral hazard by charging risk-based premiums, the public sector often increases its exposure to risk when its premiums do not fully reflect risk.

The *second* problem is one of adverse selection. Because only high-risk firms and individuals purchase insurance, the risk pool carries high probability of claims. Earthquake insurance, for instance, attracts only applicants, whether firms or individuals, who believe they are at risk for damage by earthquakes. When premiums are not risk adjusted and priced below what private insurance firms would charge, the moral hazard problem compounds the problem of adverse selection, since the policy itself tends to increase risky behavior on the part of the insured. When flood insurance subsidizes building along flood plains, for example, more houses are built along flood plains, and, at the same time, the risk pool of the insurance fund rises.

Third, policies that subsidize certain types of risk taking also may increase risk taking by uninsured individuals. For example, in the event of emergencies the federal government often grants disaster relief to insured and uninsured alike. Even when offered subsidized premiums, some people or firms may not buy insurance. In the case of federal crop insurance, for instance, disaster relief bills of $7 billion were enacted in 1983, 1986, 1988, and 1989, and a high portion of payments flowed to uninsured farmers.[18] And in 1992 the hurricane that devastated much of south Florida was the occasion of government-granted disaster relief to all affected individuals and firms. A moral hazard may therefore exist for the uninsured, as well as for the insured.

---

[18] *Budget of the United States Government, Fiscal Year 1992*, Part 2, 217.

Allocation and Distribution Effects

The allocational and distributional effects of nondeposit insurance programs are similar to those discussed under federal deposit insurance.[19] Subsidization of risk taking channels more resources into risk-prone markets and, to the extent that moral hazard is created, raises the general level of risk taking in the economy. More houses are built along flood plains, more managers take higher risks with pensions funds, and more buildings are located on fault lines. This, of course, also means that fewer resources are directed to nonsubsidized markets and, to the extent that resources are misallocated, the overall efficiency of the economy falls, resulting in slower economic growth.

These policies also redistribute income. Various firms and individuals benefit when their risk taking is subsidized through public insurance programs. When policies lead to unfunded liabilities, the distribution of income also changes so that those who bear the costs suffer income losses at the expense of those who receive the gains but have no liability. The unfunded liability of the private pension insurance program operated by Pennie Bennie, for example, has recently prompted concerns that a large federal bailout is imminent. Estimates of the true nature of these liabilities are surely debatable, but some estimates put the amount in excess of $50 billion.[20]

Government-Sponsored Enterprises

Accounting for 16 percent of federal credit and insurance outstanding (see Table 10-1), GSE loans are loans of government-sponsored enterprises (GSEs)—firms that are created, chartered, and regulated by the federal government. GSEs direct credit primarily into housing, education, and agricultural markets.

Federal GSEs include:

- Federal National Mortgage Association (Fannie Mae), created in 1938 to assist buyers of home mortgages
- Federal Home Loan Mortgage Corporation (Freddie Mac), created in 1970 to aid buyers of home mortgages
- Federal Home Loan Bank System created in 1932 to provide funds for thrifts
- Federal Agricultural Mortgage Association (Farmer Mac), established in 1988 to facilitate the buying of agricultural mortgages
- Student Loan Marketing Association (Sallie Mae), created in 1972 to promote student loans
- College Construction Loan Insurance Association (Connie Lee), established in 1986 to facilitate new construction and renovation of college buildings

---

[19] We should also remember that, in principle, these policies do not necessarily misallocate resources. When private markets overestimate risk of demanders of insurance, policies may lead to a more efficient allocation of resources. For example, if the private sector charges an unwarranted risk premium to those who wish to build along flood plains, provision of public insurance may yield a more efficient allocation of resources. Remember, however, that this scenario requires that policies base premiums on true risk, which somehow effectively deals with the problem of moral hazard.

[20] This figure comes from Pennie Bennie as reported in "Shortfall in Pension Funds Rises Sharply to $50 Billion, U.S. Says," *Los Angeles Times*, December 13, 1992, A30. See also Congressional Budget Office, *Controlling the Losses of the Pension Benefit Guaranty Corporation*, January 1993.

Table 10-4 shows the credit market activities of four of the largest GSEs.

Although privately owned, GSEs make loans by selling debt that carries an *implicit* federal guarantee that the government will pay both principal and interest if the GSEs are unable to repay their investors. GSEs therefore act as financial institutions, and because they carry this implicit guarantee, their debt should be considered a potential liability of the public sector. Experiencing the largest percentage increase (4,091 percent in outstanding loan commitments since 1970) of credit and insurance programs, GSEs demonstrate the rapidly growing role of the federal government in U.S. financial markets.

The GSEs enjoy many legal benefits.[21] They are authorized to borrow, within specified limits, from the U.S. Treasury; they are, for the most part, exempt from regulation by the Securities and Exchange Commission; and their corporate earnings are exempt from federal, state, and local income taxes. In return for these benefits, GSEs are restricted in the assets they can purchase and are allowed to operate only in markets that meet the specific purpose for which Congress created them.

Implications of Implicit Federal Guarantee

Implicit federal guarantees are unstated or indirectly stated promises by the federal government to cover any losses in cases of default by government-sponsored enterprises.

The distinguishing characteristics of GSEs are their **implicit federal guarantees**; that is, the U.S. government backs their obligations in cases of default.[22] The implication for investors is that debt issued by GSEs is similar in risk to that of U.S. Treasury debt. This leads to lower risk, which translates into borrowing costs slightly higher than those of the U.S. Treasury, but below that of the AAA (lowest risk) debt of private corporations. The implicit federal subsidy is the difference in interest rates that GSEs must pay for funds versus what they would pay without the implicit guarantee.[23]

As with all credit and insurance programs, moral hazard is likely to be associated with the creation of GSEs. An implicit federal guarantee leads investors to scrutinize the fiscal health of GSEs less carefully. Because lending to GSEs carries little risk of default, lenders have little incentive to be concerned about exposure to risk. Investors in GSEs do not require higher risk-adjusted interest payments when risk rises; therefore, the implicit federal guarantee not only shifts risk to the public sector, but tends to raise risk taking as well.

Capital Requirements of GSEs

The ultimate incentive for GSEs to pursue prudent investment policies depends upon their level of capital and the resolve of the regulator, within legislated constraints, to oversee their investment portfolios. A recent U.S. Treasury Department study found

---

[21] While the following characteristics apply to all GSEs, there are some exceptions, and the interested reader should see Table 2 in Congressional Budget Office, *Controlling the Risks of Government-Sponsored Enterprises* (April 1991), 8.

[22] According to Congressional Budget Office, *Controlling the Risks of Government-Sponsored Enterprises*, April 1991, 9, there has been only one case where the Federal government did not immediately provide backing for a failing GSE; however, funds were eventually disbursed and therefore the implicit guarantee was upheld.

[23] Although no consensus exists on how to measure the size of this subsidy, it is commonly believed that the larger the GSE's risk exposure, the greater is the value of the subsidy. See, for example, Congressional Budget Office, *Controlling the Risks of Government-Sponsored Enterprises*, April 1991, 10.

TABLE 10-4
Outstanding Selected GSE Credit Market Borrowing
($Billions)

	1970	1980	1992
Fannie Mae	$15.2	$72.3	$543.0
Freddie Mac	—	4.6	427.0
Federal Home Loan Bank	10.5	74.4	85.0
Sallie Mae	—	—	50.0

Source: Table 2, *Report of the Secretary of the Treasury on Government Sponsored Enterprises*, May 1990; and *Budget Baselines, Historical Data, and Alternatives for the Future*, 1993.

that "some GSEs are among the most thinly capitalized of major U.S. financial entities."[24] Once again, the lower are capital requirements, the lower are the stakes of owners—and the greater are incentives to undertake higher-return, but riskier, investments. The Treasury study predicts that throughout the 1990s off-budget borrowing of GSEs will exceed federal on-budget borrowing.

Allocative and Distributive Effects

One effect of the implicit guarantee is to reallocate resources into markets served by GSEs. By being able to borrow more funds from investors who are attracted by the risk-free status of their investments, GSEs draw funds away from other markets that do not benefit from similar policies. By channeling funds into mortgage markets, for instance, Fannie Mae and Freddie Mac reallocate resources from nonhousing markets to housing markets.

The main purpose of GSEs is to channel funds to selected mortgage, agricultural, and educational markets. Created because private credit markets were believed to be inadequate to meet the social goals of providing all the credit needed in these markets, GSEs fulfill their purpose by borrowing large sums of funds from insurance companies, depository institutions, and pension funds, then lending these funds to borrowers or lenders. They may also buy loans made by other lenders in the secondary market. Thus a GSE could borrow $100 million from a pension fund and then channel these funds into the education market either by lending the $100 million to a commercial bank (lender) for education loans or to a university (borrower) for financing a new building. Some GSEs also direct resources by buying education loans of financial institutions, thereby channeling new liquidity into these firms so they can provide more education loans. Some GSEs also issue or guarantee securities backed by specific purpose loans. The operations of Fannie Mae and Freddie Mac, for example, are primarily devoted to issuing and guaranteeing mortgage-backed securities.

---

[24] *Report of the Secretary of the Treasury on Government-Sponsored Enterprises*, May 1990, 8.

The distributive effects of GSEs follow from their associated liabilities. At issue is: Who is responsible when a GSE cannot meet the demands of creditors? Although there are few causes for immediate concern over who would be called upon to bail out GSEs, this issue has been raised, and it is not clear what form a cleanup would take. The details would necessarily be worked out through the policy process; nevertheless, we might take some clues from the cleanup of the thrift industry in the 1980s.

GSEs and the Thrift Bailout

Consider the Financing Corporation (FICO), a GSE that was chartered by the Competitive Equality Banking Act of 1987. At that time, Congress granted FICO authority to issue $10.8 billion in debt to be used, by the FSLIC, to resolve insolvent thrifts. An off-budget government agency because it was created by Congress, FICO is operated by government appointees; further, it serves solely to finance a government activity (federal deposit insurance). Its activities do not show up on the on-budget books of the federal government, and therefore issuance of FICO debt has no net immediate effect on on-budget government spending.

There are at least three reasons for us to study FICO. First, because the issuance of $10.8 billion in debt implies an equal refunding of government activity in the form of deposit insurance, $10.8 billion is no longer available for other uses. Second, because FICO's debt carries a higher interest rate than that of U.S. Treasury debt, the cost of that $10.8 billion to U.S. taxpayers is estimated to be $3 billion higher (assuming 30 years in higher interest payments) than it would be if the U.S. Treasury directly funded this bailout.[25] Third, FICO is not unique. Consider REFCORP (Resolution Funding Corporation). Established in 1989, REFCORP was empowered to create another $31.2 billion in debt to perform essentially the same purpose as FICO: to refund the deposit insurance system. These funds are to be used by the Resolution Trust Corporation, established in 1989 by FIRREA, to dispose of insolvent thrifts.

New Role for GSEs?

We have shown that an important source of funds for the thrift bailout has been the activities of new GSEs. But new GSEs are not unique to the thrift industry. In 1988, the Federal Assistance Corporation (FAC) was created to bail out the Farm Credit System, a GSE created in 1917 to lend to farmers and farm cooperatives. The fact that we are now seeing the creation of GSEs to pay for the unfunded liabilities of disparate public programs suggests a new financing trend. If FICO and REFCORP were created to bail out federal deposit insurance policy, and FAC was created to bail out an existing GSE, an interesting question is raised: Will more GSEs be created if unfunded liabilities of other programs such as private pension insurance, flood insurance, and deposit insurance of commercial banks begin to surface?

Are GSEs the new budget gimmick of the 1990s?[26] As we saw in the previous chapter, rising budget deficits create incentives for policymakers to circumvent, to

---

[25] Congressional Budget Office, "The Savings and Loan Problem: A Discussion of the Issues," Staff Memorandum, February 1989.

[26] William G. Gale, "The Budget Gimmick of the 1990s?" *Wall Street Journal*, May 3, 1989, A15.

some degree, constraints imposed by the Gramm-Rudman-Hollings Act of 1985. In the case of unfunded liabilities associated with deposit insurance, policymakers could have paid off insurance claims by depositors who had invested their funds in insolvent thrifts. Unless spending in other areas was reduced (or general tax revenues raised), this budgetary move would have added to on-budget spending and therefore raised, dollar for dollar, the budget deficit for that year. By creating an off-budget GSE, policymakers may shift a portion of resolution costs off budget. While the on-budget deficit does not show an increase, the off-budget deficit rises as GSEs sell debt to finance resolutions that otherwise would have appeared on budget.

It is interesting that the Congressional Budget Office has admitted that "FICO's structure was developed for no other reason than to avoid any unified budget impact in the initial years of the refinancing program."[27] This suggests that a primary reason for creation of recent GSEs is to shield liabilities associated with government policies from voters.[28] It is not surprising that some analysts believe that new public programs are easier to fund through a GSE than through on-budget spending. For example recent proposals include new GSEs such as Dottie Mae to finance road-building loans for municipal governments and Vinnie Mac to finance mortgage insurance for veterans, neither of which has been approved by Congress.

Direct Loans, Guarantees, and Credit Policies

Loan guarantees represent 10 percent of federal credit and insurance outstanding and include Federal Housing Administration and Veterans Affairs mortgage loans, Small Business Administration loans, and guaranteed student loans. As Table 10-1 shows, these policies have grown by 419 percent since 1970. These credit policies lower the risk of lending to borrowers because, in cases of loan default, lenders receive some portion of principal and interest from the federal government. As our discussion of VA mortgages shows, such policies reallocate funds into markets where guarantees are offered and out of markets where guarantees are unavailable.

Direct loans, in contrast, are funds directly lent by the federal government to borrowers. They comprise the smallest category of all credit and insurance policies. In contrast to all other credit and insurance programs, direct loans show up directly on the books of the federal government. For example, when a direct loan is made to a farmer, the amount of the loan shows up directly as federal spending. When interest is received from the farmer, however, it shows up as income and is subtracted from the interest payments that the federal government pays on its debt. This subtraction yields the budgetary term called net interest payments, which we discussed in the previous chapter. Accounting for 3 percent of credit and insurance programs, direct loans are offered in such diverse areas as agriculture, rural electrification, and loans for

---

[27] Congressional Budget Office, "The Savings and Loan Problem: A Discussion of the Issues," Staff Memorandum, February 1989, 17.

[28] This is the thesis of James T. Bennett and Thomas J. DiLorenzo, *Underground Government: The Off-Budget Public Sector* (Washington, D.C.: Cato Institute, 1984). See also David Joulfaian and Michael L. Marlow, "The Relationship between On-Budget and Off-Budget Government," *Economics Letters* 35 (1991), 307–310.

exporters and importers of goods and services. This category has grown 241 percent since 1970, by far, the slowest growth of any federal credit and insurance program.

Federal Participation in Credit Markets

Federal participation in credit markets, defined as the sum of federal borrowing from the public, guaranteed borrowing, and borrowing of GSEs, is summarized in Table 10-5. Federal borrowing from the public is that portion of public borrowing by the U.S. Treasury to finance on-budget spending. Neither guaranteed borrowing nor GSE borrowing, however, show up as additional U.S. Treasury borrowing. Rather, their borrowing is considered to be off budget and accounts for roughly 41 percent of federal borrowing. The sum of on- and off-budget borrowing by the federal government has grown substantially since the 1960s, and accounted for 55.4 percent of net borrowing in U.S. credit markets in 1990. The 3.7-fold increase in federal participation demonstrates the growing role of the public sector in allocating resources in U.S. financial markets. This expansion of the federal role has, of course, led to a shifting of risk liability from the private sector to the public sector and to a higher level of risk taking in the overall economy.

Credit and Insurance Policy Reform?

Potential Costs of Federal Credit and Insurance Programs

With the exception of direct loan programs, all credit and insurance programs have the ability to create unfunded contingent liabilities for the off-budget public sector. Although many will not go into default or need a bailout, the rate of default and

TABLE 10-5
Federal Participation in the Credit Market ($Billions)

	1965	1970	1975	1980	1985	1990
Total net borrowing in credit market[a]	$67.2	$87.9	$164.0	$329.4	$743.3	$678.9
Federal borrowing from the public	$ 3.9	$ 3.5	$ 51.0	$ 69.5	$199.4	$220.1
Guaranteed borrowing	5.0	7.8	8.6	31.6	21.6	40.7
Government-sponsored enterprise borrowing	1.2	4.9	5.3	21.4	57.9	115.4
Total federal participation	$10.1	$16.2	$ 65.0	$122.5	$278.9	$376.2
Federal borrowing participation rate	15.0%	18.4%	39.6%	37.2%	37.5%	55.4%

[a] Total net funds borrowed in the credit market by domestic nonfinancial sectors, excluding equities. Financial sectors are omitted to avoid double counting, since financial intermediaries both borrow and lend in the credit markets.

Source: Table C-7, *Budget of the United States Government, Fiscal Year 1992.*

failure has undeniably risen. Spending on guarantees and insurance shows up only when defaults and insurance claims occur; it may therefore take many years for costs to show up on budget. In fact, when fees and insurance premiums are collected, federal budget deficits may initially fall, since these items are sometimes included as on-budget revenues of the government.

Over 1982–90, there has been a twelvefold increase in total costs of programs.[29] In 1982, loan write-offs and defaults totaled $3.7 billion, and insurance claims required on-budget expenditures of $4.6 billion. In 1990, loan write-offs were $2.9 billion, guaranteed loan defaults were $11.9 billion, and insurance costs were $93 billion, of which most covered losses of 433 failed banks and thrifts.

Table 10-6 shows estimates of potential federal costs of these programs. The first column shows estimates of outstanding values of loans and insurance in 1992. In terms of the present value of future obligations, a range of $178 billion to $266 billion is a recent estimate of the potential costs of these programs. In the future these estimates may change. They may drop, for instance, if higher down payments and collateral are required on loans. But they may rise if the opposite occurs.

The Office of Management and Budget has recently argued that

> *Historically, the Federal Government has given inadequate attention to managing the risk of these credit and insurance programs. Many of them were viewed as self-financing; credit was expected to be repaid, and the cost of insurance was assumed to be covered by premiums. To the extent that costs occurred, they were mostly "unexpected" and "uncontrollable."*
>
> *There has been a growing awareness in recent years that both the intended beneficiaries of these programs and the Nation are badly served when the principles of risk-management are not followed. The principle that the beneficiary should have a substantial stake has focused greater attention on the size of the borrower's downpayment and on banks' and businesses' capital. The principle that borrowers or insureds who take more risk should pay more has highlighted the need to relate premiums, fees, and interest rates to risk. Following these principles reduces the incentives that now exists for borrowers and insureds to take greater risks that may yield them larger gains, whereas the federal program would bear or share any losses without additional compensation for these additional risks. Putting programs on a sounder financial footing can expand, rather than reduce, their social benefits while cutting federal costs.*[30]

Proposals for reform of federal credit and insurance programs are usually of two general types: (1) improvements in ways in which programs affect risk taking and (2) better budgetary accounting of liabilities associated with programs.

Reforms

Accounting Methods

It has been recommended that costs of public insurance programs be measured as they occur, rather than later, when they must be paid.[31] Because insurance programs

---

[29] *Budget of the United States Government, Fiscal Year 1992*, Part 2, 203.
[30] *Federal Budget of the United States Government, Fiscal Year 1993*, Part 1, 269.
[31] *Budget of the United States Government, Fiscal Year 1993*, Part 1, 273.

TABLE 10-6
Potential Federal Costs ($Billions)

Program	Face Value (1992)	Range of Potential Costs (Present Value)
Deposit insurance	$2,763	—
Other insurance	2,026	$40–$63
GSEs	1,105	0–1
Guaranteed loans	671	57–82
Direct loans	93	42–56
TOTAL	$3,328	$179–$266

Source: Budget Baseline, Historical Data, and Alternatives for the Future, 1993.

commit the public sector to liabilities that are not estimated when insurance is provided, debate on the appropriateness of policy does not contain discussion of the true costs of policy.[32] Rather, as seen from the thrift crisis, policy costs tend to be greatly discounted in the early years of programs, and this practice may bias discussion in favor of provision of policy. Most costs, however, are recorded only when they must be paid, years or decades after the policies were enacted.

As argued by the Office of Management and Budget,

Cash budgeting for insurance programs thus delays the recognition of emerging problems. It does not help decision-makers to see what is occurring or what is ahead. As a result, they cannot act in time to ensure adequate resources or to reform the insurance system in ways that might limit costs. Under the current system, these are "sunk costs" by the time they appear in the budget. By that time, they are the Government's legal and moral responsibility, and little can be done to control them.[33]

The Omnibus Budget Reconciliation Act of 1990 (OBRA) requires that the federal government acknowledge the implicit cost of federal credit programs. Policymakers are required to base decisions on liabilities associated with credit programs when they discuss use of credit programs. Note, however, that although policymakers must discuss the issue of unfunded liabilities, there is still no requirement that reserve funds must meet future payouts of unfunded liabilities. This law also does not apply for deposit insurance policies or GSEs.

---

[32] The U.S. budget document has traditionally not prepared estimates of future liabilities that are being made today. However, since the early 1990s, the Office of Management and Budget has been spending more time detailing this information, and, although it was earlier discussed in the "Special Analyses" sections of the budget document, it now appears in the main budget book.

[33] *Budget of the United States Government, Fiscal Year 1993*, Part 1, 274.

Risk Adjustment

We have shown that credit and insurance programs do not base loan rates and insurance premiums on risk. Suggested reforms base loan rates and insurance premiums on risk and, at the same time, formulate policies that do not encourage additional risk taking in the economy. In the area of deposit insurance, for example, lowering the insurance ceiling may be one means of forcing depositors and stockholders to take a larger role in disciplining imprudent risk taking by institutions. The theory here is that the greater the risk that depositors and stockholders must bear, the greater are incentives to regulate risk taking. Application of this theory calls for higher capital requirements and risk-based insurance premiums.

The U.S. Treasury Department has recently offered the following recommendations for reforming regulation of GSEs:

1. All GSEs should be adequately capitalized, should meet high credit and operational standards, and should be subject to effective government supervision. If these conditions are not met, Congress should terminate all government ties with the GSE.

2. A private market mechanism should evaluate GSE risk. All GSEs should be required to obtain a AAA rating, absent any implicit federal guarantee, from at least two nationally recognized rating agencies.

3. The value of the government's financial support should be disclosed. Congress and the public should be aware of the size of the subsidy, as well as all the other advantages GSEs receive, to be able to analyze the true costs of GSE programs compared to the benefits the targeted beneficiaries actually receive. The administration recommends the amount of subsidy that results from a GSE's enhanced borrowing status be disclosed annually as a part of the President's budget.[34]

Bottom Line with Reforms

The bottom line of any set of reform proposals is whether programs do their job and promote the original goal of policy. While not always perfect substitutes, some degree of substitutability clearly exists between on-budget and off-budget policies; therefore, in general, rationales for using off-budget policies are identical to those for using on-budget policies. Questions, for instance, have been raised about certain GSEs that no longer serve their original purpose. Fannie Mae and Freddie Mac, for example, were created because it was believed that the private sector failed to provide an active secondary market in mortgages. While creation of these GSEs clearly speeded up development of an efficient, national, and standardized secondary market, it is probably true that if the implicit federal guarantee of GSE debt were eliminated, the secondary market would continue to exist in much the same form as it does today.

It is also useful to question why the profits of Fannie Mae, for example, go entirely to private investors when almost all risk is borne by taxpayers. Fannie Mae is now the fourth largest financial institution, is exempt from most taxes and regulation, and is commonly believed to have such political clout as to make it extremely

---

[34] Chapter 2, *Report of the Secretary of the Treasury on Government-Sponsored Enterprises*, May 1990.

difficult for the policy process to legislate higher capital standards or even allow the Securities and Exchange Commission to scrutinize its practices.[35] It is also interesting that many GSEs have their own lobbies which directly promote policies that allocate resources toward themselves. For example, Fannie PAC is Fannie Mae's Political Action Committee lobby. Policies may therefore serve the narrow self-interests of GSEs, thus raising the issue of political viability of reforms.

Final Thoughts

This chapter has provided an overview of the off-budget policy process. Policies allocate resources toward specific sectors of the economy and, in general, more resources are allocated toward higher-risk activities. Risk taking has also been shown to be promoted by moral hazard, regulatory forbearance, and adverse selection. While policies reallocate resources, taxpayers bear final liability for risk.

Expansion of off-budget policies may be understood only within a framework that models voters, special interest groups, and policymakers within the current institutional setting. The off-budget policy process is an alternative to the on-budget policy process. Expansion of off-budget policies may be the result of many factors, and one's view of which is correct is greatly influenced by one's view of what motivates behaviors of policymakers. One view is that expansion reflects the policymakers' belief that off-budget policies provide a reasonably cheap means of providing policies to voters. In this case, policymakers wish only to minimize costs of providing policies to voters. Some may argue, for instance, that policies regarding education and mortgage loans are cheaper when provided off budget than through on-budget spending programs. A related argument may be that because voters may not recognize the full beneficial implications of these programs, well-informed and paternalistic policymakers use these policies to provide their less-informed citizens with programs that would normally not be approved through the on-budget channel of the policy process.

An opposing view, however, is that off-budget expansion is a means by which narrowly self-interested policymakers attempt to hide policies from the scrutiny of voters. Proponents of this view argue that off-budget policies provide favors to special interest groups. A particularly intriguing issue is that of accountability of policymakers. If voters, for instance, do not recognize, or underestimate, future unfunded liabilities, narrowly self-interested policymakers may attempt to overexpand off-budget policies.

This discussion suggests a variety of views regarding the appropriateness of off-budget expansion, and it is up to the reader to form an opinion as to which view most accurately describes reality. It is appropriate to view expansion of these policies in much the same light as our discussion in Chapter 8 of the many hypotheses regarding the apparent natural tendency of government to expand. Various interpretations may be made on the issue of whether expansion is desirable, but we can be sure that the issue of off-budget expansion will gain importance in the ongoing debate over the size and role of government in the U.S. economy.

---

[35] See Kenneth H. Bacon, "Fannie Mae Expected to Escape an Attempt at Tighter Regulation," *Wall Street Journal*, June 19, 1992, A1; and "Fannie Mugs Again," *Wall Street Journal*, September 30, 1992, A16.

The Expanding Off-Budget Sector of State and Local Governments

Although we have focused on the federal off-budget sector, state and local governments have off-budget agencies as well. Special district governments are created to deliver goods and services in specific areas. Although the overall number of local governments has been falling rapidly, numbers of special district governments have almost tripled since 1952. There are now more than 33,000 special district governments. Although their primary sources of funding are property taxes and user fees, their activities appear on the books of state and local governments only in cases of default.

Major areas of involvement are flood control, mass transportation, toll roads, bridges, credit market lending, electricity, construction of school buildings, and cemeteries. Kansas, for example, has 655 cemetery districts, and Pennsylvania has 682 sewer districts. Special district governments vary greatly in size. The Addison Creek River Conservancy District in Illinois is rather small, with two employees, a budget of $88,000, and the task of keeping two miles of creek free from debris. The METRO subway in Washington, D.C., is one of the larger special districts.

Source: Kevin Johnson, "America's Forgotten Fiefdoms," Los Angeles Times, May 26, 1993, A1, A25.

Analysis

The diversity of views regarding special district governments echoes those expressed over government-sponsored enterprises. Advocates argue that by focusing on single tasks, they are more efficient than larger general-purpose governments. Ralph Heim, of the California Special Districts Association, says it this way: "I think the districts hold their own or do better than most other governments. . . . A vast majority of them do a good job and do it with less people."

An area of concern, however, is whether special districts are accountable to taxpayers. Jim Nolan, of the Taxpayers Federation of Illinois, believes that their large number make it difficult for taxpayers to monitor their activities, saying, "If we could somehow make the number of governments more manageable, we might clarify what's going on and promote a greater trust." Sam Randall, manager of a cemetery district in California with an annual budget of $1.6 million, states his belief: "I don't think the average person would know we exist. . . . I don't know that in my six years here that a public audience has been at our meetings." The role of special district governments is therefore as controversial as that of government-sponsored enterprises. This is not surprising since in addition to expanding rapidly in recent years, both influence resource allocation and the distribution of income. Both will surely come under increasing focus in public policy discussions.

Summary

- More than half of all U.S. borrowing is influenced by federal programs. The federal government is also the largest underwriter of risk. These policies are called *off-budget* because much of their costs do not immediately show up on the government accounting books, but they tend also to show up many years after legislation is enacted.

- Risk plays an important role in allocating resources in private credit and insurance markets. When credit and insurance programs alter the risk characteristics of individuals, resources are reallocated in credit and insurance markets, which are the target of off-budget policies. These policies channel funds into selected markets. Funds will therefore flow out of markets that are not subject to similar policies.

- Distributive effects occur as income is transferred to those able to take advantage of these policies, and income is taken away from those who participate in markets that experience outflow of credit and insurance resources. Taxpayers are also adversely affected when they bear unfunded liabilities of these programs.

- There are four general rationales for credit and insurance programs. First, creditors and insurance firms may overestimate risk characteristics and charge higher interest rates and insurance premiums than that implied by allocative efficiency. Second, private credit and insurance markets may not be fully developed. Third, these programs may foster equity and national priorities. Fourth, these programs may enhance allocative efficiency when externalities occur or when there are public goods.

- A moral hazard results from off-budget policies when an affected party increases risky behavior. The problem of moral hazard is commonly believed to be a major factor behind the surge in resolution costs of savings and loans that has occurred since the 1980s.

- Adverse selection refers to the phenomenon that high-risk individuals tend to be more interested in purchasing insurance and borrowing than low-risk individuals. Off-budget policies promote adverse selection because private firms have less incentive to base acceptance of insurance policies or loans on risk characteristics of customers.

- Various reforms of off-budget programs have been recommended. One recommendation is that costs of programs be measured as they occur, rather than when they are paid. Another is that programs base loan rates and insurance premiums on riskiness of beneficiaries. It has also been suggested that implicit federal guarantees be removed for those GSEs which no longer serve the original purpose of their creation.

Review Questions

1. What are the major differences between the on-budget and off-budget books of the federal government? Give examples of each.
2. What is meant by *risk* in credit and insurance markets?
3. What are four primary rationales for credit and insurance policies?
4. What is moral hazard? Give an example.
5. What is adverse selection?
6. What is regulatory forbearance?

Discussion Questions

1. What are the primary differences between on-budget spending and off-budget government policies?
2. We have argued that there is some substitutability between on-budget and off-budget policies. Explain how policies designed to increase the level

of pollution control in the economy could be provided through on-budget and off-budget means.

3. In the above question, what are the allocative and distributive effects of both types of policies designed to promote a greater level of pollution control in the economy?

4. Usury laws are one way by which the public sector may lower the rate of interest at which lenders charge borrowers in credit markets. Usury laws define maximum legal interest rates that lenders can charge borrowers. Use a demand and supply framework for mortgage funds to show how a usury law that lowers mortgage rates below equilibrium affects allocation of resources in mortgage markets. What are the distributive effects?

5. Some argue that VA loan programs are an essential form of compensation for veterans. Discuss how else compensation could be provided, and comment on how they differ in terms of their budgetary treatment, effects on resource allocation, and liabilities for taxpayers.

6. Who would tend to gain and lose if risk-based insurance premiums were established for deposit insurance? Do you believe that such a change is politically viable?

7. What incentives are there for special interest groups to lobby for GSEs? Give several examples.

8. It has been shown that direct loans are the slowest-growing federal credit and insurance program. Explain why this is the case.

9. Even though deposit insurance appeared to be in trouble only since the 1980s, some argue that the underlying unfunded liability was always there. Does this argument make sense?

10. Are off-budget policies a means of transferring wealth to special interests? Give several examples.

11. If it is true that many GSEs have outlived their usefulness, how would you propose to eliminate them? Comment on the allocational and distributional impacts of your policy.

Key Words

Redlining
Moral hazard
Adverse selection

Regulatory forbearance
Implicit federal guarantee

CHAPTER 11

Transfer Programs for the Poor

Social welfare policies are those which redistribute income among citizens.

The role of government in redistributing income among its citizens is one of the more contentious topics of public policy discourse. Redistribution occurs through transfers, defined as payments of cash, goods, and services to persons who render no service in return. Often called **social welfare policies,** income redistribution is the source of controversies over whether the public sector should engage in redistribution in the first place and heated disagreements over what form such policies should take if they are in fact justified. One thing is clear, however—the role of the public sector in income redistribution has expanded greatly over time.

In this chapter our study of income redistribution is organized by the distinction between two types of transfers: means-tested and social insurance policies. Means-tested programs, which include Aid to Families with Dependent Children (AFDC), public housing, and food stamps, are programs that benefit individuals and families who fail to meet a certain minimum means, usually defined in terms of income. These programs provide mainly for the poor and are often called safety net programs since they transfer basic, lifesaving necessities such as medical care, food, and housing. In contrast, social insurance programs are not means-tested and are not limited exclusively to the poor. These transfer programs compensate for income loss due to retirement, unemployment, illness, and disability. The three main social insurance programs are Social Security, Medicare, and unemployment insurance.

The evolution of spending on means-tested and social insurance programs is shown in Figure 11-1. In Figure 11-1a, we see the percentage of total federal spending devoted to social welfare, and in Figure 11-1b, the percentage of GDP. Both measures of welfare spending have roughly doubled since 1960: As a percentage of federal spending, it has expanded from 28 percent to 50 percent, and as a percentage of GDP, it has grown from 5 percent to 11 percent. And when we look at welfare spending less spending on social insurance, we see that social insurance spending is the fastest-growing category of welfare spending.

The following questions are examined in this chapter:

❏ What role should the public sector undertake in the redistribution of income?
❏ Who are the poor? How has the distribution of income changed over time?
❏ What are the means-tested programs of the federal government?
❏ What are the allocational and distributional effects of means-tested programs?

**FIGURE 11-1
Federal Social
Welfare
Expenditures**

*Source: Statistical
Abstract of the United
States,* 1993.

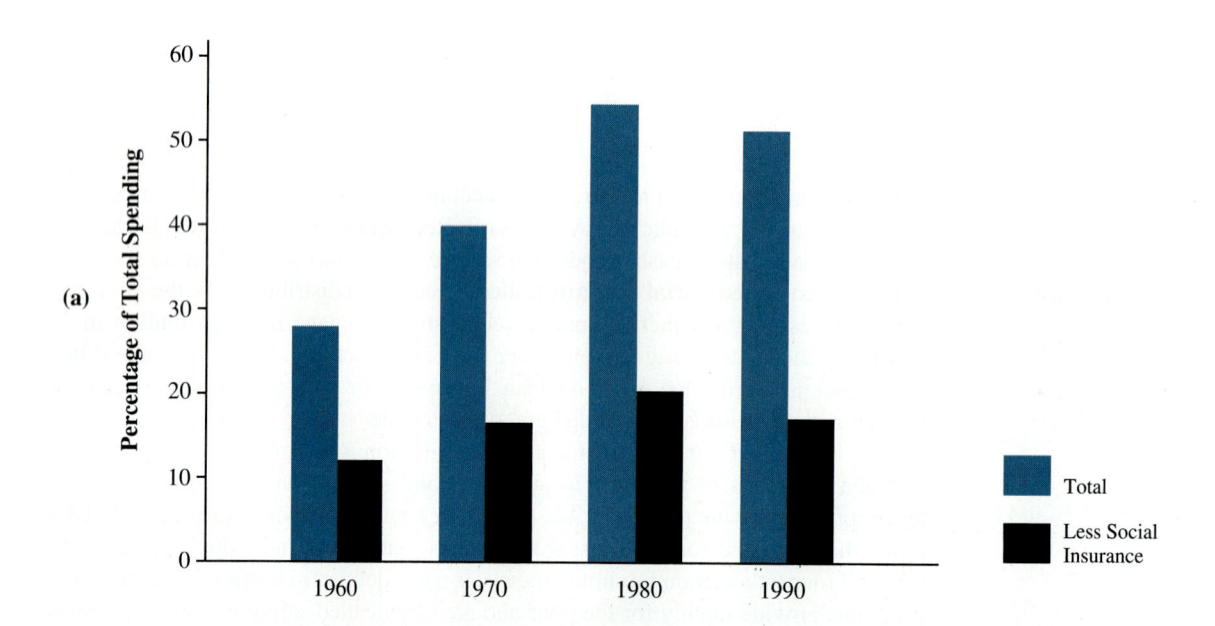

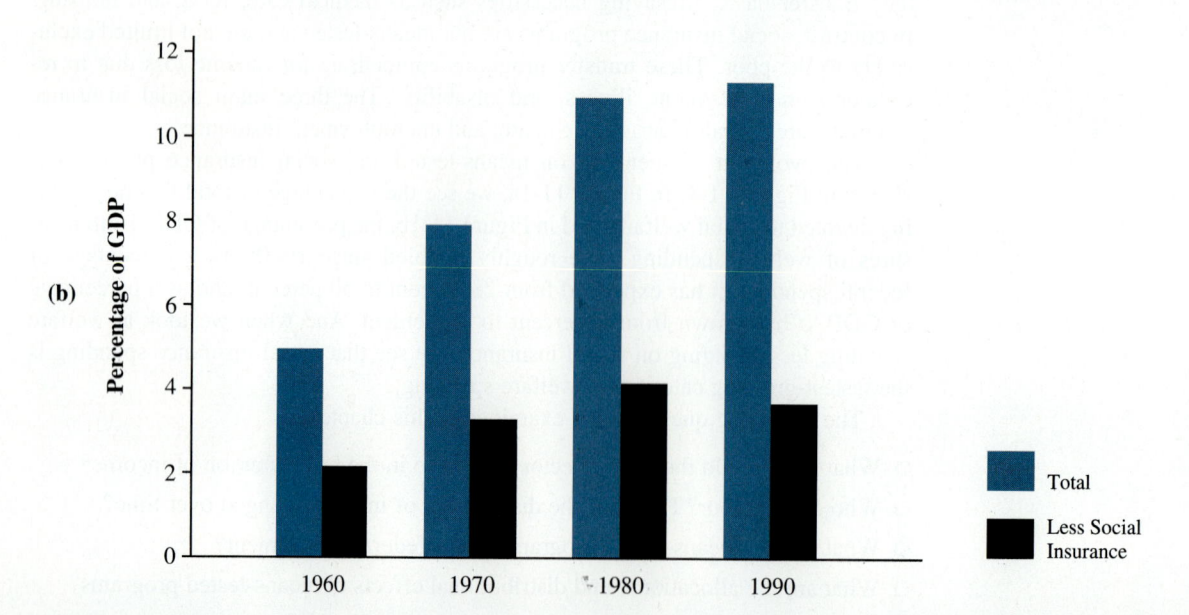

- Have means-tested programs reduced poverty?
- What policy reforms have been recommended to improve social welfare?

The Role of Government in Income Redistribution

Private Market Charity

Redistribution policies are motivated by a desire to improve upon the distribution of income that naturally occurs in private markets. The usual argument for intervention is that various market failures should be remedied through public policies. Discussion of the role of government in redistribution therefore requires examination of where market failures might occur.

It is useful to restate the argument for social welfare policies as an argument that the private sector allocates too few resources toward charity, the act of giving to the needy in society. From this restatement two obvious questions follow:

- How much private charity is there?
- What is the distribution of income in society?

We now address the first question, leaving the second for later in the chapter.

One measure of charity is derived from data on private philanthropic funds. In 1991, for example, these funds amounted to roughly 2.3 percent of GDP, which is slightly lower than the 3-percent figure shown in Figure 11-1 for federal means-tested programs as a percentage of GDP in 1990.[1] Private individuals may also engage in charity through volunteer work and other acts of generosity not measured under philanthropic funds.

Why might private markets fail to allocate an appropriate level of charity? Our chapter on externalities demonstrated that market failures may occur when private markets produce goods and services that exhibit positive externalities. An argument may be made, for example, that various charitable organizations, such as the Red Cross and the Salvation Army, offer positive externalities when they provide services to the needy and ill. Because private markets tend to underallocate resources in cases of goods that display positive externalities, various tax exemptions may correct this market failure. It is also often argued that free rider problems may cause some private individuals to redistribute too few of their resources to the poor. Direct public provision of welfare programs may be used to remedy the free rider problem.

It is also important to recognize that expansion of public transfer programs may alter private transfers to the poor. If public transfer programs crowd out private spending on charity, total transfers to the poor may increase, decrease, or remain the same. A case may be made, for example, that crowding out occurs when citizens believe that the public sector is the primary caretaker of other people's welfare. If individuals believe that public transfer programs are sufficient to meet the needs of the poor, they tend to reduce their own transfers to the poor. The implication is that when public

---

[1] *Statistical Abstract of the United States*, 1993.

transfers crowd out private transfers, total transfers expand by less than public transfers increase.

Goals of Redistribution Policy

It is easy to say that we want a better distribution of income in society. It is also easier to argue that our desire for redistribution policies arises from a need to help the less fortunate than it is to define what "less fortunate" means. Good intentions, however, say nothing about the goals that should be set for a redistribution policy. The determination of what constitutes a desirable income distribution involves subjective judgments on the part of analysts. And because society is a diverse collection of individuals, redistribution policy will necessarily be highly controversial.

Charity is usually modeled in terms of the *interdependent utility functions* of individuals.[2] That is, when the well-being of many individuals affects one's own utility, utility functions are said to be interdependent. In Chapter 6, we argued that the breadth of self-interest determines that interdependence, or the degree to which individuals wish to help, or be charitable to, others in society. It is often considered natural to wish to help relatives; beyond this, however, many citizens wish to transfer income to others. This observation suggests, by extension, that redistribution serves the broad self-interests of the public at large.

Charity may also be modeled as the product of fairly narrow self-interests on the part of its providers. It has been suggested, for instance, that welfare programs reduce the likelihood that poor individuals will engage in crime, rioting, and other forms of antisocial behavior. Here transfers by the well-off may be considered bribes, or payments, in return for a peaceful society. Whether narrow or broad self-interests—or both—motivate redistribution, it is clear that transfers are supported by many individuals in society.

The issue of what constitutes an optimal distribution of income is more difficult. One popular theory is that income is characterized by declining marginal utility and a more equal distribution of income will therefore increase total utility for society.[3] This theory implies that if policies transfer $1,000 from a rich individual to a poor individual, total utility for society will rise. When maximization of total social utility is the policy goal, this notion leads to the conclusion that an optimal distribution is characterized by uniformity of income.

The policy prescription that incomes should be equalized rests on the assumption that interpersonal comparisons of utility are possible. As discussed in Chapter 3, however, it is highly unlikely that such comparisons are possible in practice, so the idea loses much of its credibility. Two other problems associated with this theory warrant discussion.[4] First, a theory that assumes diminishing marginal utility of income also implies that policies increasing population raise total social utility as well. It is unlikely, however, that this prescription would be taken seriously by welfare economists,

---

[2] See, for example, Harry M. Hochman and James O. Rodgers, "Pareto Optimal Redistribution," *American Economic Review* 59 (September 1969): 542–557.

[3] See Abba Lerner, *The Economics of Control* (New York: MacMillan, 1944).

[4] See Gordon Tullock, *Economics of Income Redistribution* (Boston: Kluwer Nijhoff Publishing, 1983), 6.

thus casting further doubts on its credibility. Second, this approach implicitly assumes that all individuals have identical abilities to generate utility from a dollar's worth of income. Casual observation, however, suggests that not all people receive the same utility from identical activities. Some people appear to be happier than others. If they are, policies that promote a highly unequal income distribution may, in fact, lead to higher total social utility. Maximization of total social utility would require that higher income be awarded for efficient utility generators than for inefficient generators. It is clearly problematic to measure efficiency of utility generation, but it may not be more unrealistic than assuming that interpersonal utility comparisons can be made.

Another theory considers redistribution a form of insurance for members of society. If, for example, individuals place a "veil of ignorance" over themselves, shutting out any information about their future incomes, they might vote for redistribution policies to ensure against the possibility that their futures will turn bleak.[5] If voters knew that they had equal chances of being the poorest, the median, or the richest individual in society, they might vote for policies that would provide for them in the event that they were not to become the richest.[6] The veil of ignorance over voters forces their impartiality in their preferences for redistribution policies, so rational individuals might vote for policies for the same reasons that they purchase life, auto, and health insurance—to keep themselves from joining the poorest. It is doubtful that this risk-reducing behavior would generate consensus that a uniform distribution of income is optimal; nonetheless, this behavior supports some level of redistribution.

Many reasons, then, may motivate individuals to demand redistribution policies—broad self-interest, narrow-self interest, insurance, or any combination thereof. Despite this plethora of reasons, little consensus exists on what a desirable distribution of income should be. This is not surprising because the issues associated with optimal income distribution are *necessarily* subjective. Thus, even if the vast majority were to accept one definition of optimal distribution, considerable controversy over how to measure that distribution would remain. Fortunately, in this chapter we do not have to specify what an optimal distribution of income looks like; rather, we will examine the implications of alternative policies for the distribution of income.

Useful Distinctions

Equality of outcomes occurs when all individuals end up in identical circumstances (for example, with identical incomes).

Equality of opportunity occurs at such a time as all individuals have equal opportunities in life.

A useful distinction may be made between equality of outcomes and equality of opportunity. **Equality of outcomes** is the receipt by all individuals in society of equal incomes. **Equality of opportunity,** on the other hand, is an equal chance by all members of society to earn income; in practice, it may also mean that all individuals have the same opportunity to receive an education and enter all occupations. If the goal of policy is merely to create equal opportunity, there is no reason to expect that such policies will actually result in identical incomes for all members of society.

Various reasons account for the failure of equality of opportunity to lead inevitably to equality of income. Incomes differ for many reasons. A primary reason,

---

[5] John Rawls, *A Theory of Justice* (Cambridge, Mass.: Harvard University Press, 1971).

[6] See John C. Harsanyi, "Cardinal Welfare, Individualistic Ethics, and Interpersonal Comparisons of Utility," *Journal of Political Economy* 63 (August 1955): 309–321.

easy to observe in others, is differences in effort. Objectively, two workers with identical educations and abilities may earn different incomes. One may prefer to earn an annual income of $35,000 and live in a small town and take long vacations each year, but another may prefer to earn an annual income of $65,000 in a large city and take short annual vacations. The significant difference in these incomes stems from choices involving how much work to provide and where to live. The observed inequality of income does not therefore indicate a market failure that calls for correction by the public sector.

Income differences may also be the result of different educational choices. For example, although most individuals would prefer to have the income of a medical doctor, most individuals prefer not to spend the many years of preparation required to earn that position. Differences in ability also lead to income differences. Not all individuals have the natural ability to become a highly paid professional athlete or a highly paid doctor. Even though individuals may have sufficient motivation and desire, not all individuals have the natural ability to command high salaries.

Finally, income differences may be the result of different opportunities. Some individuals may not be able to earn income through hard work and effort because they may lack educational opportunities and therefore cannot enter high-paying occupations. If a local high school, for instance, does not provide adequate preparation for college, its graduates tend to have fewer income opportunities than those who attended better schools. Similarly, children whose parents lack sufficient resources to provide proper nutrition and health care cannot easily compete with children whose parents have greater resources. To address these differences, the public sector provides safety-net policies, education subsidies, and occupational training and placement, which help to equalize opportunity.

Little debate centers on the need to address inequality of opportunity. But whether these policies actually result in a more uniform income distribution remains debatable. When there is no reason to believe that effort and ability are identical among all members of society, there is also no reason to believe that equalization of opportunities inevitably results in greater equality of income. Furthermore, because it is difficult to assess the degree to which society provides equal opportunities, many analysts focus their attention on the degree to which incomes are equal—an unfortunate focus, as equality of opportunity and equality of income are different things and neither implies the other.

Distribution of Income

Measurement of Income

Poverty is usually defined in terms of income, and the most common measure is *money income,* which includes pretax earned and unearned income. This measure includes government cash transfers but excludes noncash transfers such as Medicaid, food stamps, or employer-provided fringe benefits such as health insurance. Because income is often shared among family members, we usually focus on incomes of families. *Families* are defined by the Census Bureau as groups of two or more people who live together and are related by birth, marriage, or adoption. An alternative designation, the *household,* is defined as all related and unrelated individuals living in the same housing unit.[7]

Real Median Family Income

In the range of incomes, the middle point—the income point at which equal numbers of families earn above and below—is the **real median family income.** Figure 11-2 plots the growth of real median income since 1960 and indicates how the midpoint of the income distribution of families has changed over time. A strong upward trend in real median family income is evident: Income was $10,670 higher in 1989 than in 1960, an increase of 45 percent. Expansion of income, however, has been uneven. Much of the expansion occurred during the 1960s, when median income rose from $23,543 to $31,534, an increase of 34 percent. From 1970 to 1985, however, median income rose from $31,534 to $31,962, an increase of only 1.3 percent. And the four-year interval from 1985 to 1989 saw income increase from $31,962 to $34,213, just 7 percent. Three reasons account for this uneven expansion.[8]

Real median family income is an inflation-adjusted income at which the number of families earning above it equals the number of families earning below it.

1. CHANGES IN FAMILY SIZE Between 1967 and 1990 average family size fell by 14 percent. During that time, then, a given value of median family income consequently was spread among a smaller number of individuals. This implies that the low rate of expansion of family income since the 1970s is understated, since it does not reflect expansion of income *per person* within the median family. Between 1967 and 1990, for example, average income per person rose by 62 percent, as opposed to 35 percent per family.

2. CHANGES IN FAMILY COMPOSITION As the average number of family members has fallen, single-parent families are becoming more prevalent. Between 1969 and 1989, for example, the proportion of female-headed families with children nearly doubled, from 11.3 percent to 21.7 percent. Moreover, by 1990, one-third of female heads of families were under 35 years old. These changes may be expected to alter median family income in at least three ways. (1) Even though the differential appears to be shrinking, females tend to earn less than males. (2) As the average age of heads of families falls, income tends to fall. Younger workers tend to earn less than older heads-of-households because they are still acquiring skills and lack job experience. (3) Some means-tested programs create incentives for lower income individuals to stay out of the work force, thereby increasing the number of low-income families headed by females who do not work outside the home. And the low incomes of female heads-of-families drive the median-income calculation down.

3. CHANGES IN THE BUSINESS CYCLE Gross domestic product and productivity tend to rise during economic expansions, when it is easier for individuals to find work and wages. During recessions, when employment is reduced and wages grow slowly,

---

[7] Under Census Bureau definitions, single persons living alone are counted as a single family or single household. Because most statistics described below are similar for definitions using households, we concentrate on those using families as the unit of observation.

[8] The analysis and data described here are primarily obtained from *Economic Report of the President,* February 1992.

**FIGURE 11-2
Median Family Income
(in 1989 Dollars)**

Source: Statistical Abstract of the United States, 1992

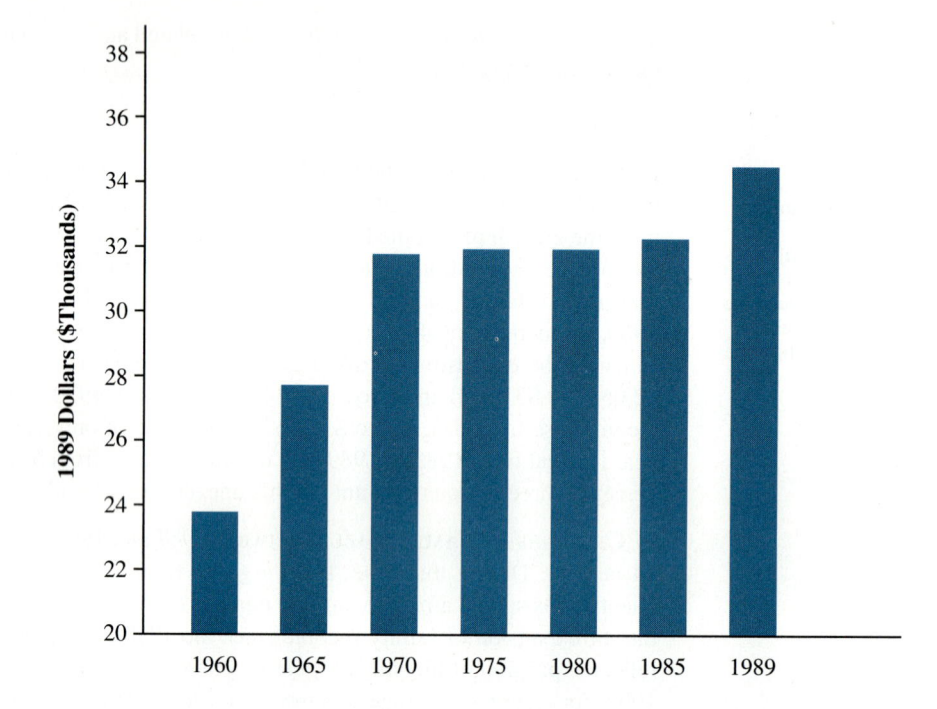

the economic opportunities of low-income workers are more severely limited than those of high-income workers. Although the immediate effects of the business cycle on median family income are mostly transitory, over time an obvious permanent upward trend income has become evident—as we can see in Figure 11-2. Consideration of the business cycle indicates that, because financial opportunities tend to grow during periods of expansion, long-term economic growth is one of the keys to alleviating poverty.

This discussion suggests that no single statistic, such as median family income, is a complete measure of the distribution of income. Changes in what constitutes the typical family generate other changes that cannot be interpreted from a simple statistic. We should also remember that the definition of money income omits in-kind government transfers to the poor (public housing and food stamps, for example) and therefore understates levels and improvements of income for lowest income groups.

Level versus Distribution of Income

A more important problem with using median family income as a measure of changes in poverty over time is that, by definition, only one family represents the median. What about incomes of nonmedian families? Although expansion of median income reflects a rising standard of living, it is clear that not all individuals share equally in this expansion. The distinction between the *level* and *distribution* of income allows us to see this point more clearly. Median income indicates one aspect of the level of income, but its distribution is an entirely different matter.

Figure 11-3, which shows the income levels of five individuals in a hypothetical society, illustrates the distinction between the level and distribution of income in tabular and graphical form. Three alternative income distributions (A, B, and C) are shown, each of which is characterized by an average and median income of $51,000. On the basis of median and average income, no differences are apparent among the three income distributions. More careful inspection, however, indicates vast differences under the three alternative distributions. Distributions A, B, and C show respective ranges of $25,0000–$79,000, $51,000–$51,000, and $3,000–$95,000. Whereas distribution B shows all individuals receiving identical incomes, distribution A reflects a wide range of individual incomes and distribution C has the largest range.

As Figure 11-3 clearly demonstrates, comparisons of median incomes do not necessarily offer useful comparisons of income distributions. We now introduce other methods of measuring the distribution of income.

**FIGURE 11-3
Comparative Income Distributions**

(a)

Individual	A	B	C
1	$25,000	$51,000	$ 3,000
2	35,000	51,000	16,000
3	51,000	51,000	51,000
4	65,000	51,000	90,000
5	79,000	51,000	95,000
Average	$51,000	$51,000	$51,000
Median	$51,000	$51,000	$51,000

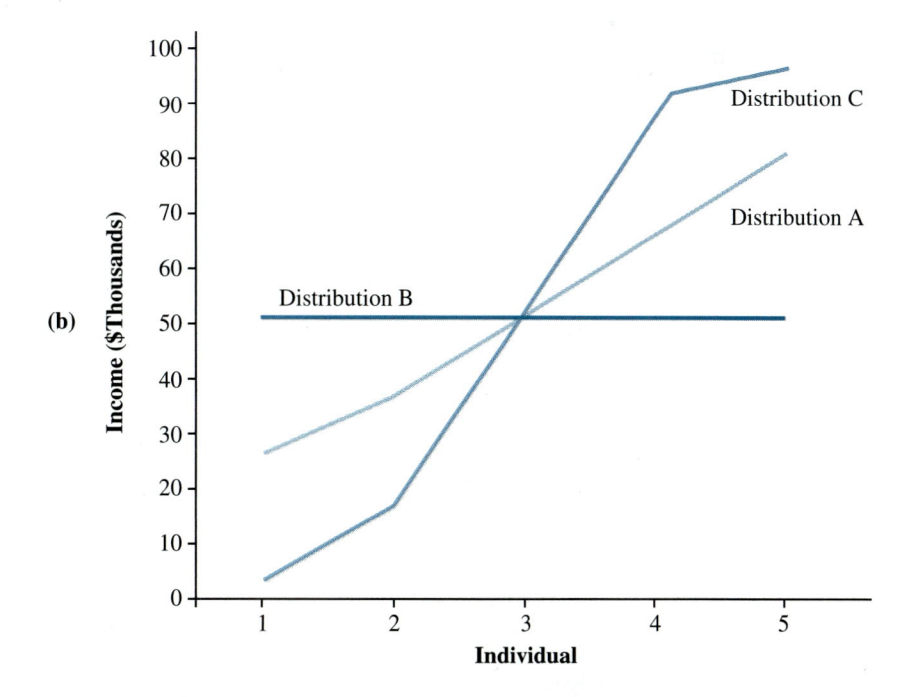

(b)

Poverty Thresholds

Poverty threshold is the minimum income level below which families must earn in order to be defined as poor.

One commonly used approach defines a **poverty threshold**—a minimum income level below which families must earn in order to be defined as poor. The Census Bureau uses this measure to define the poverty rate, which is the percentage of all families earning below the poverty threshold. Poverty thresholds are updated every year to reflect changes in the cost of living index. In Figure 11-4 those threshold values for families of varying size since 1970 are tabulated, and the percentages of families falling below threshold values of income are displayed graphically. Falling from 10 percent to 9 percent during the 1970s, the poverty rate peaked at 12.3 percent in 1983 and has since fallen to 10.3 percent. This pattern of peaks reflects changes in the economy: Significant increases in poverty rates occur during recessions. Recessions of the early 1980s, for example, were associated with large increases in poverty rates.

Remember that the definition of money income does not include fringe benefits and noncash transfers. Therefore, poverty rates overestimate poverty—a bias inherent in the measure, since noncash transfers account for a majority of means-tested programs. Another problem becomes obvious when we recognize that this approach does not indicate how families above the poverty threshold are faring. It is clear, then, that poverty rates, like median income, are not entirely adequate measures of income distribution, either.

The Middle Class

The **middle class** consists of persons whose earnings place them above the poverty threshold but below the point at which they could be considered wealthy.

Another approach is to show the distribution of income of all families, including those in the middle- and upper-income classes. Although no official definition of the **middle class** exists, an income range of $15,000 to $50,000 is often used to designate this segment of society. Figure 11-5 shows the percentages of families falling within three real income groups since the mid-1970s (in 1989 dollars): under $15,000, between $15,000 and $50,000, and more than $50,000. The percentage of families defined as poor—those earning less than $15,000—has remained fairly constant at about 20 percent over this time period. Falling from 62 percent in 1976, the percentage of middle class is now about 55 percent, a measure consistent with the widely held notion that the middle class is a falling proportion of families in the United States. The data also show that the direction of exodus from the middle class has been toward the highest income group.[9] The percentage of families in the upper income group has risen from 20 percent to about 30 percent.

Again, noncash transfers are not considered; therefore, since the lowest-income group receives the bulk of these transfers, this approach underestimates income of this group. We should not minimize the problems inherent in using money income to measure poverty. The Census Bureau has shown that for households in the lowest 20 percent of the income distribution, the estimated value of noncash transfers rose at nearly double the growth rate of money income over 1967–90.[10] Thus, if noncash transfers were included, a larger percentage of families would be defined as middle class.

---

[9] As noted in *Economic Report of the President*, February 1992, 120, changing the definition of middle class (for example, $25,000 to $75,000, or $25,000 to $50,000) preserves the basic results that the proportion of high-income families has increased.

[10] See *Economic Report of the President*, February 1992, 122.

**FIGURE 11-4
Poverty Thresholds**

Sources: Statistical Abstract of the United States, 1991 and 1993.

(a)

Size of Unit	1970	1980	1985	1991
1 Person	$1,954	$ 3,843	$ 4,974	$ 6,378
2 Persons	2,525	4,920	6,366	8,157
3 Persons	3,099	6,022	7,799	9,992
4 Persons	3,968	7,719	9,997	12,812
5 Persons	4,680	9,142	11,832	15,141
6 Persons	5,260	10,338	13,369	17,102

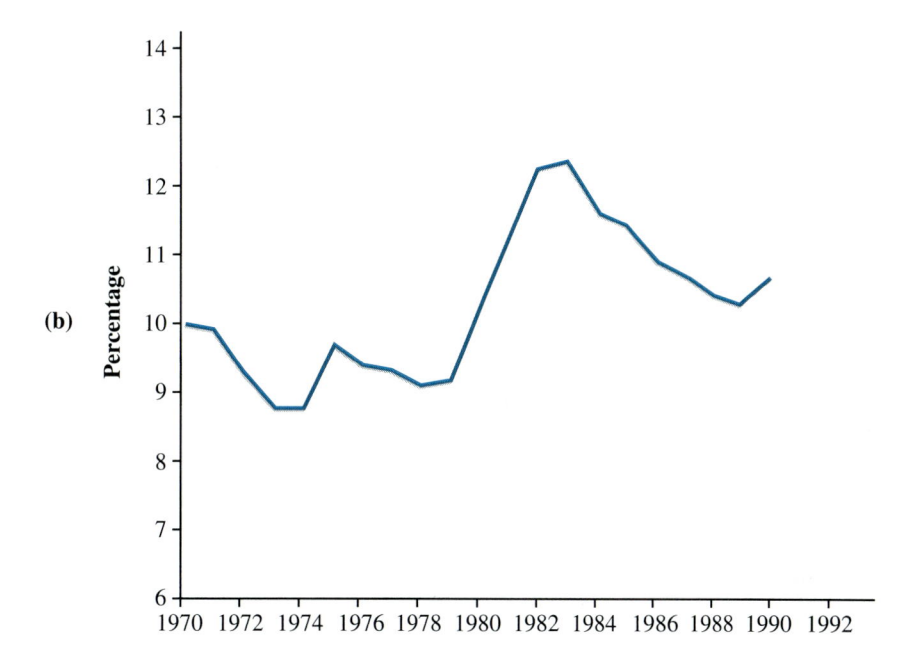

(b)

Cautionary Notes

Various approaches to measuring income distribution tell different stories.[11] In addition to the exclusion of noncash transfers in measures of income, three other factors suggest caution about reading too much into any of these measures.

1. TIME A focus on annual money income does not necessarily provide a useful approach to understanding changes in the distribution of income over time. Long-term income tends to be much less dispersed than annual income, and a focus on annual income therefore tends to overstate income dispersion. Many economists believe that long-term income, or *wealth,* is a more useful measure of the income distribution of society. Long-term income includes income earned from property and pensions, and

---

[11] Some economists prefer to use Gini ratios, which measure the dispersion of income from a range between 0 and 1. A value of 0 would indicate that every family had the same level of income, and higher values indicate increasing dispersion. A Gini ratio, however, does not measure how changes in income are changing for any group in the population.

**FIGURE 11-5
Income Groups**

Source: Joint Economic Committee, 1992.

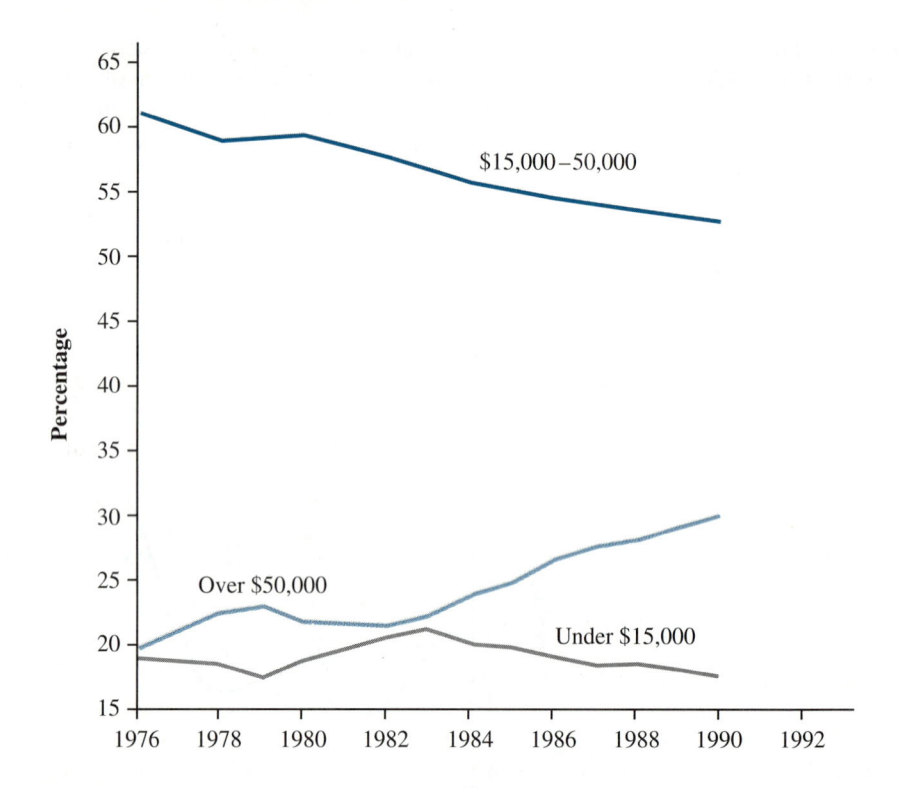

money earned over the working life of individuals. This point is clear, for example, when we consider the implications of changes in the average age of the working population for the distribution of income. Because earnings tend to rise with age, changes in the age composition of the labor force exert independent influences on income distribution. Younger work forces tend to produce lower annual incomes, but over time annual incomes rise, because the effects of longer experience and training result in higher wages.

2. CLASS MOBILITY Evidence clearly suggests considerable mobility across income classes from year to year.[12] In the mid-1980s, for example, one-third of all families moved from one quintile (one-fifth of families) to another each year. For the three lowest quintiles, roughly 18 percent of families moved to a higher quintile in the following year and, for the three highest quintiles, more than 20 percent of families moved to lower quintiles the following year. One study found that more than 75 percent of households are in a different decile (one-tenth of households) when ranked by long-term income than when ranked by annual income. While about 44 percent had annual income two or more deciles away from their long-term income, more than 50

---

[12] This evidence is discussed in *Economic Report of the President,* March 1992, 124–125. For a study of wealth mobility across generations, see Alan S. Blinder, "Inequality and Mobility in the Distribution of Wealth," *Kyklos* 29 (1976): 607–638.

percent in each of the lowest three deciles for annual income had long-term income in a higher decile. Moreover, more than 50 percent of households in the top three deciles for annual income had long-term income in a lower decile.

It is also important to recognize that because mobility also appears to increase over time, it is not necessarily true that a growing dispersion of income means that the poor get poorer and the rich get richer. Individuals who fall within various poor and rich classifications are part of an ever-changing mix; therefore, it is not correct to argue that the vast majority of the poor are in any sense the same individuals year after year.

3. TAX POLICY The distribution of income is heavily influenced by tax policy. The Census Bureau estimates that in 1990 the net effects of federal and state taxes and transfers raised the income of households in the bottom quintile by an average of more than $8,800, from about $2,100 to about $10,900.[13] Households in the top quintile paid $22,000 more in taxes than they received in transfers, reducing their average income from about $94,000 to under $72,000.

Description of Means-Tested Transfers

Cash transfers are transfer policies that give money to recipients.

Noncash transfers are transfer policies that provide goods or services, such as housing or food, rather than money.

Aid to Families with Dependent Children (AFDC) is a long-established transfer program that directly provides money to families with dependent children.

Eligibility for means-tested transfer programs requires that recipients fall below some minimum level of income or wealth. Programs come in two varieties: **cash transfers** and **noncash transfers.** Cash transfers directly deliver cash to recipients; noncash transfers, such as public housing and food stamps, provide in-kind benefits. Table 11-1 shows expenditures on selected means-tested programs. Expenditures are also broken down into cash and noncash transfers; cash transfers accounted for roughly 25 percent of all means-tested transfers. Many means-tested programs are funded jointly by the federal and state governments, but administered by state governments. Roughly 29 percent of funding is provided by state and local governments. The largest state programs are **Aid to Families with Dependent Children (AFDC)** and Medicaid.

Cash Transfers

- *Aid to Families with Dependent Children (AFDC)* provides money to families with dependent children and an absent parent or, in the case of two-parent families, a disabled or unemployed parent. Benefit levels and eligibility standards are set by states, and beneficiaries are eligible for federal job training. In 1990, AFDC transferred roughly $19.8 billion to 11.4 million people.

- *Supplemental Security Income (SSI)* transfers cash to elderly, disabled, and blind individuals. While this program is operated and funded by the federal government, many states offer supplements which vary considerably across states. In 1990, roughly 5 million recipients received SSI transfers that totaled $15.1 billion.

- The *earned income tax credit (EITC)* program was created in 1975 as a refundable federal tax credit for low-income working families with children. Roughly 11.9 million tax returners claimed deductions of $4.3 billion in 1990.

---

[13] *Economic Report of the President*, February 1992, 116.

TABLE 11-1
Expenditures on Selected Means-Tested Programs in 1990 ($Millions)

	Federal	State and Local	Total
Cash Transfers			
AFDC	$ 10,147	$ 9,691	$ 19,838
SSI	11,493	3,626	15,119
Earned income tax credit	4,354	0	4,354
Noncash Transfers			
Medicaid	41,103	31,033	72,136
Food stamps	14,992	1,185	16,177
Housing assistance	15,901	NA	15,901
Child nutrition	4,996	NA	4,996
Pell Grants	4,484	0	4,484
Job Training Partnership Act	3,784	0	3,784
Head Start	1,552	388	1,940
Energy assistance	1,314	122	1,436
TOTAL	$114,120	$46,045	$160,165

NA = not available.
Source: Table 4-1, *Economic Report of the President*, February 1992.

Noncash Transfers

❏ *Medicaid* is the largest means-tested transfer program and accounts for roughly 45 percent of spending on all programs. In 1990, roughly 25.3 million people received benefits totaling $72.1 billion. The general criterion is that recipients must be below age 65 and meet AFDC guidelines. This program is run by both federal and state governments, with the federal share determined by the economic resources of each state. (Medicaid is not to be confused with Medicare, which is discussed in Chapter 12, Social Insurance Programs.)

❏ *Food stamps* are vouchers redeemable for food and other items, not including alcohol, tobacco, and pet food. First widely offered in 1964, this federal program is administered by state governments, which are responsible for the administrative costs only. Household size and income determine benefits per family. In 1990, $16.1 billion worth of food stamps was transferred to 21 million people.

Two characteristics of the food stamp program are worth discussing. Recipients view food stamps as cash transfers, since their food budgets tend to be larger than the value of the vouchers they receive. Thus poor families who receive food stamps tend to replace, dollar-for-dollar, equal expenditures on food from available cash. In other words, upon receiving $50 in food stamps, recipients may spend $50 more on nonfood items. Second, a stigma appears to be attached to this program since many eligible recipients choose not to participate. While as many as 69 percent of AFDC-eligible families participate in AFDC, as few as 38 percent of food stamp–eligible families receive food stamps.[14] Using food stamps at grocery stores, for example, may embarrass welfare recipients more than collecting straightforward cash transfers.

- *Housing assistance* provides noncash transfers in the forms of rental subsidies, aid for construction/rehabilitation of low-income housing, and public housing. Largely begun in the 1930s, housing assistance programs have grown so that by 1990 the value of these noncash transfers amounted to $15.9 billion: Rental subsidies are at 80 percent of market value and public housing units in the United States number roughly 1.5 million. Unlike many other transfer programs, housing assistance programs are characterized by long waiting lists.

- *Child nutrition programs* offer food and nutritional educational programs for families with children. In 1990, this federal program transferred $5 billion to eligible recipients.

- *Pell Grants,* which subsidize undergraduate education, gave 3.4 million students subsidies of $4.5 billion in 1990.

- *The Job Training Partnership Act* of 1982 was responsible for transferring $3.8 billion in funds for the education and training of disadvantaged youths and adults in 1990.

- *Head Start* transfers noncash benefits to economically disadvantaged 3- and 4-year olds; in 1990, 541,000 children received nutritional, medical, educational, and social services totaling $1.9 billion.

- *Energy assistance* subsidizes energy bills; in 1990, $1.4 billion was transferred to eligible recipients.

Economic Effects of Transfers

Cash versus Noncash Transfers

Cash transfers allow recipients to increase consumption of any good or service they wish to purchase. In contrast, noncash transfers increase recipients' consumption in restricted designated areas such as food, housing, education, and medical services. Intuitively, then, we expect recipients to prefer cash transfers; we predict that because cash transfers come with no strings attached, they confer maximum flexibility and tend to generate higher utility than noncash transfers.

Case 1

Consider how a welfare recipient, Bill, reacts to two different transfer programs, cash and noncash, of equal value. Figure 11-6, which plots quantity of bread consumed per

---

[14] See Robert Moffit, "An Economic Model of Welfare Stigma," *American Economic Review* 73 (December 1983): 1023–1035, for the theory of welfare stigma as well as the studies of participation in AFDC and food stamp programs.

FIGURE 11-6
Cash versus Noncash Transfers

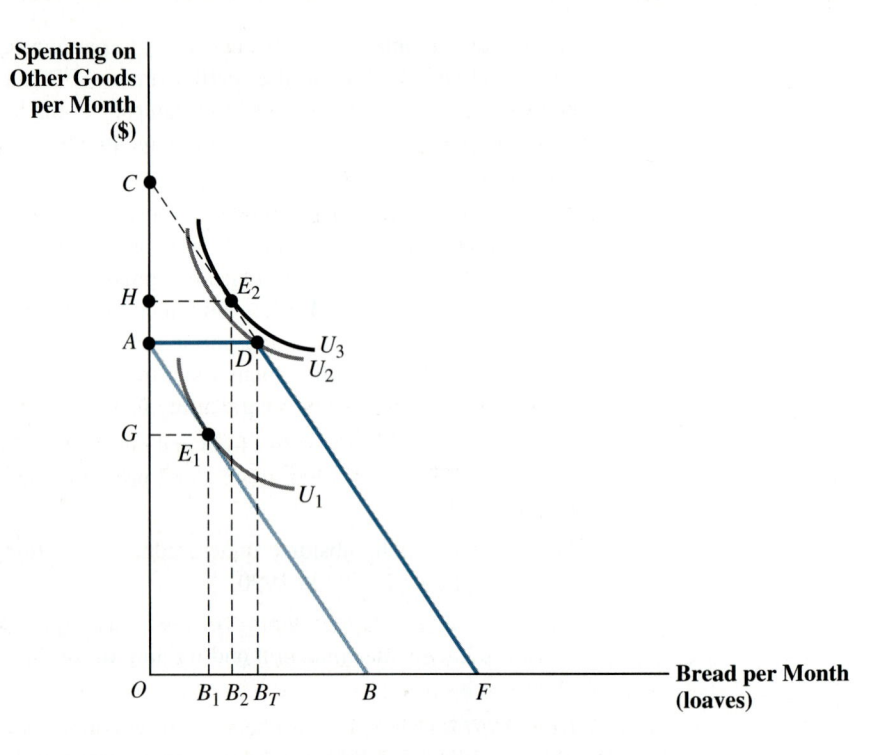

month against spending on other goods, shows that before transfers Bill maximizes utility by consuming on the highest indifference curve U subject to budget constraint AB.[15] Tangency point E_1 is characterized by OB_1 loaves of bread and OG spending on other goods.

Now assume that a noncash transfer provides Bill with OB_T loaves of bread. This transfer increases the maximum quantity of bread that Bill may purchase to OF loaves, which is equal to $OB + OB_T$ loaves. The new budget constraint is ADF because, even though Bill may now consume more loaves of bread at any level of spending on other goods, maximum spending on other goods remains at OA. Responding to the new budget constraint, Bill achieves equilibrium at point D on indifference curve $U2$. The noncash transfer therefore increases his consumption of bread and other goods.[16]

Would Bill prefer a cash transfer instead? An equivalent cash transfer would allow Bill to purchase the previous noncash transfer of OB_T loaves of bread. Substitution of an equivalent cash transfer creates a new budget constraint where the maximum consumption of bread increases to OF loaves and the ability to buy other goods rises to OC, an increase of AC (dollar value of cash transfer). With new budget

---

[15] See the appendix at the back of this book for a detailed description of indifference curves and budget constraints.

[16] Other examples show that noncash transfers lead to lower consumption of the noncash transfer. See, for example, Sam Peltzman, "The Effect of Government Subsidies-in-Kind on Private Expenditures: The Case of Higher Education," *Journal of Political Economy* 81 (January–February 1973), 1–27, which finds that noncash transfers of higher education lead to lower consumption of higher education.

constraint *CF*, Bill achieves equilibrium at point E_2 with bread consumption of OB_2 loaves and spending of *OH* on other goods. An equivalent cash transfer also increases Bill's consumption of bread and other goods.

Which transfer program does Bill prefer? His consumption of bread and other goods increases under both, but he achieves a higher indifference curve—that is, higher utility—in a cash program. And with a noncash program, Bill is compelled to consume more loaves of bread, and spend fewer dollars on other goods, than he would under an equivalent cash transfer. Logic suggests that Bill should therefore prefer the cash transfer. Cash transfers, however, are not always preferred over noncash transfers by welfare recipients, as Case 2 shows.

Case 2

Figure 11-7 shows that before any transfers, Bill maximizes utility at point E_1 where *U*1 is tangent to budget constraint *AB*; that is, he consumes OB_1 loaves of bread and spends OA_1 on other goods.

A noncash transfer of OB_T increases his maximum bread consumption to *OF* loaves, and because *OA* remains the maximum he may spend on other goods, the new budget constraint becomes *ADF*. Utility maximization occurs at point E_2, where Bill consumes OB_2 loaves of bread and spends OA_2 on other goods. As in Case 1, noncash transfers increase both consumption of bread and spending on other goods.

Now consider how Bill responds to an equivalent cash transfer. An equivalent cash transfer of *AG*—the dollars required to purchase *BF* loaves of bread—creates budget constraint *GF*. Maximizing utility at point E_2, Bill now consumes OB_2 loaves

FIGURE 11-7
Indifference between Cash and Noncash Transfers

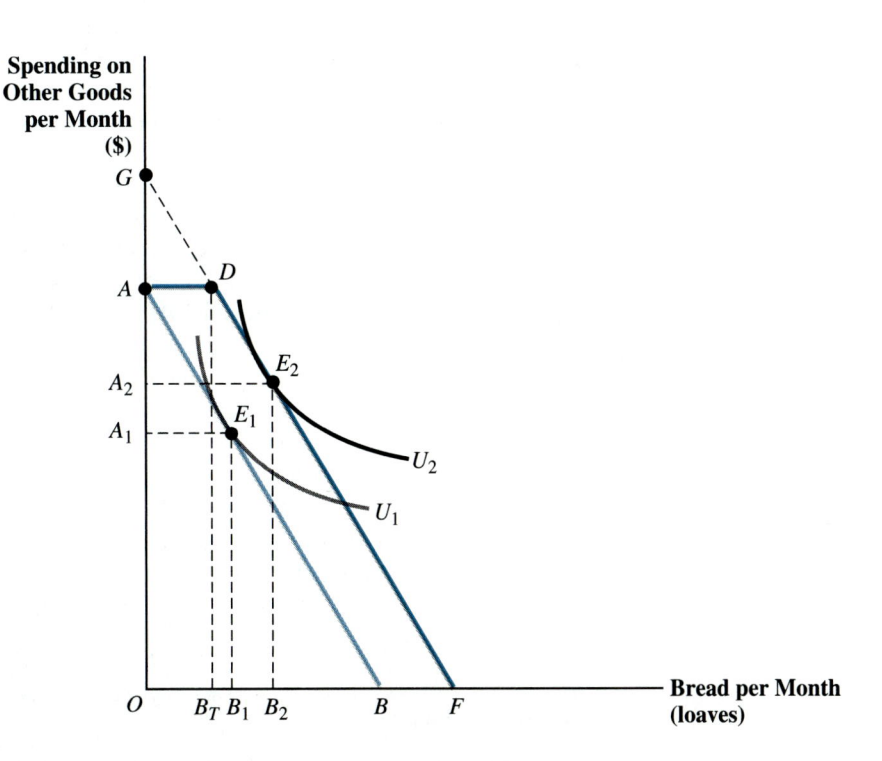

of bread and spends OA_2 on other goods. This equilibrium is identical to the one chosen under the noncash transfer and represents a situation in which Bill is indifferent between equivalent values of cash and noncash transfers.

Note that indifference occurs only when noncash transfers offer welfare recipients the same level of utility they can reach under an equivalent cash transfer. Whether this indifference can ever be a policy goal is doubtful, however. Among the millions of noncash transfer recipients, the chances that many share identical indifference curves or budget constraints are slim. It is extremely unlikely that many welfare recipients are indifferent to receiving cash or its equivalent value in a noncash transfer.

It is now reasonable to conclude that recipients prefer cash transfers to noncash transfers. This follows from the direct observation that, while some recipients may express indifference between the two types of transfer, few recipients express a preference for noncash transfers over equivalent cash transfers. And, to the extent that cash transfers carry less stigma than noncash transfers, they may be more effective as a means of redistributing income to the poor as well.

Welfare Costs

> **Welfare costs** occur when resource losses exceed taxes collected; also called excess burden.

Differences in utilities from the two transfer types indicate that dead weight losses, or **welfare costs,** occur with welfare policy. Welfare costs arise from the fact that cash transfers allow recipients to achieve higher utility than equivalent noncash transfers. We call this phenomenon a welfare cost because alternative policies are available—policies that offer recipients higher utility while lowering the costs to society. The solution to lowering welfare costs is simple: provide transfers in the form of cash.

This discussion leads to a very important question: Why do noncash transfers dominate welfare programs? Two factors may explain this. First, a case may be made for noncash transfers when goods exhibit characteristics associated with positive externalities. As discussed in Chapter 4, resources tend to be underallocated when private markets produce such goods. Because noncash transfers force recipients to consume certain goods, this policy may be more effective in channeling resources into goods with positive externalities than equivalent values of cash would be. For instance, if the poor could not be persuaded to use cash transfers to purchase inoculations for communicable diseases, noncash transfers of free inoculations would more likely increase allocative efficiency.

Second, it may be easier to use noncash transfers to increase consumption of specific goods that are not associated with positive externalities. If the ill or ill-housed tend to use cash transfers for consumption of goods other than health care or housing, then such noncash transfers as Medicaid and public housing may ensure that these groups receive more of these goods.

Notice that these factors necessarily imply the assumption that a certain group of individuals (policymakers or voters, for example) possesses better information about the needs of welfare recipients than they do themselves.[17] Rather than allow recipients to maximize what they believe are their own utility functions, proponents of this

---

[17] This assumption is used in James Tobin, "On Limiting the Domain of Inequality," *Journal of Law and Economics* 13 (1970): 263–277.

argument must assert either that welfare recipients do not really know their own utility functions or that their utility functions are improperly specified.

Excise Subsidies

Excise subsidies are subsidies given to the purchasers of particular goods or services.

Transfers may also be designed as subsidies that pay some portion of the price of a targeted good. While subsidy programs do not dictate usage, their primary goal is to expand consumption of targeted goods; they are therefore similar in nature to noncash transfers. **Excise subsidies** may be directed at many different types of goods, but all work along similar lines. Housing subsidies, for example, pay some portion of rent for those who qualify for the transfer program. Mortgage subsidies provide payment of some portion of monthly mortgage payments. The amount of rental subsidy usually depends upon family income and size and, as with all means-tested programs, recipients must meet minimal requirements, which are usually linked to income. The average rental subsidy is 80 percent of market value. If, then, Tiffany Washington had a monthly rental payment of $650, it would be split into a government payment of $520 and a payment of $130 by Washington.

Market Perspective

The effect of excise subsidies may be shown for the entire market in which they are directed. Let us consider how an excise subsidy for natural gas affects resource allocation when the industry is characterized as a long-run constant-cost industry. (The assumption of long-run constant cost rules out cases in which subsidies cause price increases, which would occur under an assumption of long-run increasing cost.) Figure 11-8 shows supply S and demand D curves in the natural gas market, and their intersection determines the presubsidy equilibrium of $.10 per thermal unit and Q_1 thermal units.

Now assume that a subsidy $.05 per thermal unit is offered to suppliers. (The subsidy could also be offered to consumers and would shift the demand curve up by the amount of the subsidy. The effect of this subsidy is identical to that of the case shown here.) The subsidy drops the market price from $.10 to $.05 per thermal unit and results in a drop in supply from S to S'. The new equilibrium is characterized by a lower price of $.05 and larger quantity Q_2. Therefore an increase in consumption of electricity results from this subsidy.

The subsidy clearly affects resource allocation, and it is appropriate to question whether it has influenced allocative efficiency, assuming no externalities, monopoly, or lack of information that might lead to inefficient allocation of resources. The presubsidy equilibrium reflects allocative efficiency, since $MB = MC$ at point B, the presubsidy equilibrium. Point E characterizes the postsubsidy equilibrium, and although it is true that $MB = MC'$, MC' does not reflect true marginal costs to society, but costs to natural gas firms only. The subsidy lowers the supply curve to S' for firms receiving subsidies, but true MCs remain those shown on the presubsidy supply curve S. Postsubsidy equilibrium is characterized by $MC > MB$. Therefore, from the standpoint of allocative efficiency, the subsidy causes too many resources to be allocated into this market and too few resources in other markets.

Let us now measure the gains received by recipients of subsidies. If we assume that recipients pay no taxes to support the subsidy program, gains consist of two components:

**FIGURE 11-8
Excise Subsidy: In the Natural Gas Market**

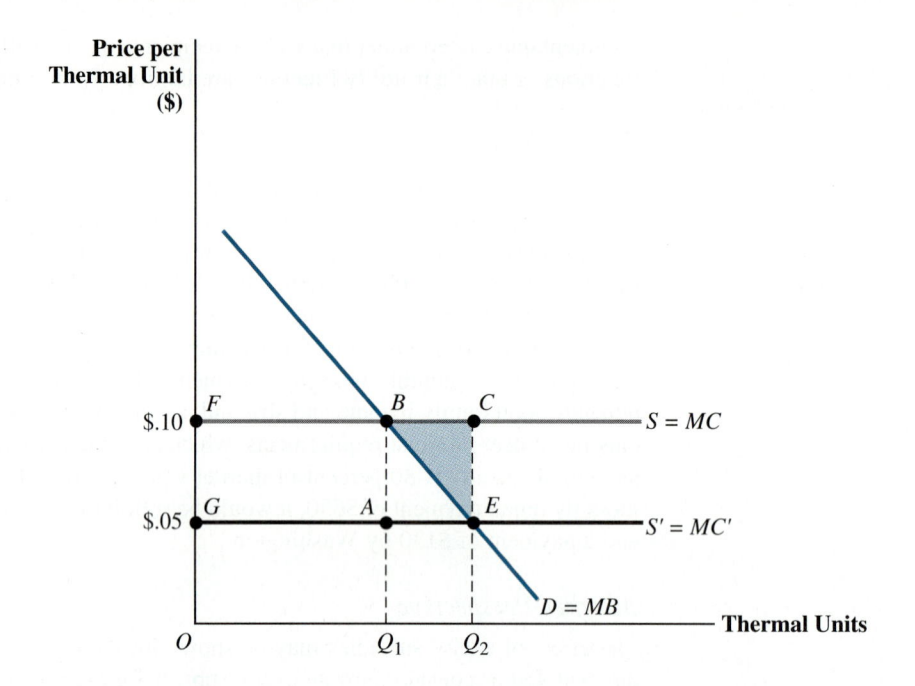

- *GFBA,* the per-unit subsidy multiplied by initial consumption Q_1
- *ABE,* the difference between *MB* and *MC* when the subsidy increases consumption from Q_1 to Q_2

The sum of these two components equals *GFBEA*.

Are welfare costs associated with excise subsidies? As previously defined, welfare costs occur when transfers cause costs to exceed benefits, which implies that an alternative policy may yield identical benefits, but at lower cost. This difference between benefits and costs is *BCE*, measured by cumulative differences between *MC* and *MB* over the range of increased production. The difference between benefits *ABE* and costs *ABCE* is *BCE*.

The welfare cost of this policy could be removed by substituting the excise subsidy of *GFCE* for a smaller cash transfer of *GFBEA*. This cash transfer equals net benefits received by beneficiaries of the excise subsidy, and because it eliminates *BCE* from the costs of the transfer program, completely eliminates the welfare cost as well.

Substitution of a cash transfer does not achieve allocative efficiency, however, since resources remain allocated where *MC* > *MB*. But substitution of the cash transfer is a Pareto superior move because it does not change recipient welfare but lowers costs for taxpayers. Taxpayers thereby achieve higher utility, as tax burdens fall by *BCE*, and welfare recipients suffer no loss in utility.

Individual Perspective

It is also useful to examine the welfare cost of the excise subsidy from Bill's perspective. In Figure 11-9 we see that before the excise subsidy, Bill maximizes utility by choosing point E_1 along budget constraint *AB*. Introduction of an excise subsidy

**FIGURE 11-9
Excise Subsidy:
From the Individual
Perspective**

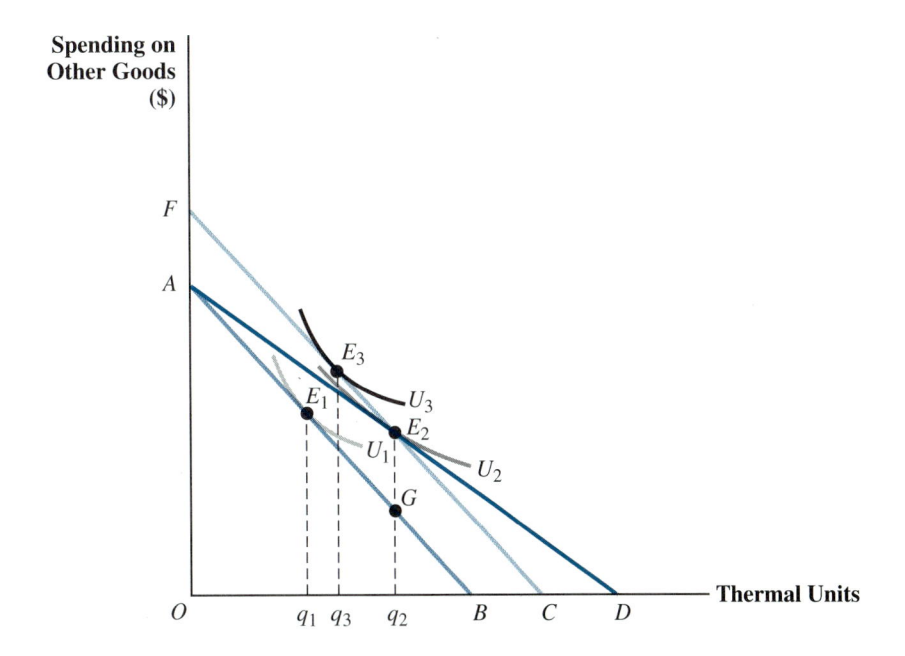

on natural gas results in flatter budget constraint AD, and Bill maximizes utility at point E_2. The excise subsidy causes Bill to increase natural gas consumption from q_1 to q_2. Note that the subsidy costs E_2G because if Bill were to purchase q_2 before introduction of the subsidy, he could spend only Gq_2 dollars on other goods. The subsidy, however, allows Bill to consume q_2 thermal units and spend E_2q_2 on other goods; E_2G is thus the subsidy provided when q_2 thermal units of natural gas are chosen.

A welfare cost occurs because an equivalent value of cash transfer allows Bill to achieve higher utility. An equivalent cash subsidy is E_2G, which equals distance AF on the vertical axis. Note that a cash subsidy of AF creates new budget constraint FC, which is parallel to initial budget constraint AB, but drawn so that it intersects point E_2. The new budget constraint intersects E_2 since, in order to show an equivalent transfer, Bill must be able to consume the bundle of goods chosen when he was given the excise subsidy. Bill achieves equilibrium at point E_3. This demonstrates that although he could have chosen bundle E_2, an equivalent cash transfer causes Bill to purchase less natural gas and to spend more on other goods. The difference in utility that results from equivalent values of cash and excise subsidies indicates the welfare cost of the excise subsidy from Bill's point of view. A welfare cost is associated with the excise subsidy since an equivalent cash transfer would yield higher utility for Bill. Alternatively, we could say that a welfare cost exists since a cash transfer that costs less than an equivalent excise subsidy provides equal utility.

Conclusion

Excise subsidies tend to be more successful in increasing consumption of targeted goods than equivalent increases in cash transfers. We have seen that excise subsidies result in greater consumption of natural gas than would occur under an equivalent cash transfer. Thus, policymakers who wish to target specific products for increased consumption tend to advocate excise subsidies over cash transfers.

Choice of Transfer Programs

In their choice of transfer programs policymakers are clearly influenced by what they believe about welfare recipients. Paternalistic policymakers tend to favor noncash transfers and excise subsidies, since these policies provide more control over the consumption patterns of welfare recipients than equivalent values of cash transfers. But policymakers who believe recipients know what is best for themselves tend to favor cash transfers.

All transfers may misallocate resources, but both excise subsidies and noncash transfers usually waste more resources than equivalent values of cash transfers. Substitution of cash transfers for noncash transfers tends to offer Pareto superior policy moves for welfare recipients and taxpayers alike. Welfare costs are also reduced when cash transfers are substituted for noncash transfers and excise subsidies.

Transfers and the Work–Leisure Trade-Off

The effects of welfare policies cannot be examined in a vacuum. Transfers not only provide income to recipients, but they may change behavior as well. No behavioral area has received more attention than that of the work–leisure choice of welfare recipients, called the **work–leisure trade-off.** It is often argued that two factors tend to reduce the incentives of welfare recipients to work. First, because they provide income, transfers reduce the financial need of welfare recipients to work. Second, welfare recipients tend to have diminished incentives to work, since earned income may reduce their welfare benefits. The AFDC program, for example, requires that after four months of work, earned income reduces, dollar for dollar, cash transfers. Similar rules apply to food stamp recipients. The fact that benefits are reduced when recipients work has been characterized as a tax on working, which tends to make work less attractive to welfare recipients.

Figure 11-10 shows the income–leisure trade-off for Brent, a representative welfare recipient. The budget constraint reflects the fact that hours spent consuming leisure cannot earn income and vice versa. The cost of additional hours of leisure is therefore lost income. Income per day is measured on the vertical axis and is determined by the hourly wage rate multiplied by the number of hours worked in a day. Thus, if the wage rate is $10 per hour an 8-hour day yields $80 in income earned. Assuming there is no nonwage income and that Brent is able to work 24 hours a day, maximum income per day is OW. Hours of leisure per day are measured on the horizontal axis, and OL is 24 hours of leisure. Brent maximizes utility at E_1 and earns OW_1 income and consumes Ol_1 hours of leisure.

How would a transfer of OW_2 income affect Brent's choice between income and leisure? This transfer does not require that Brent work; he is free to choose 24 hours of leisure if he so desires. This transfer changes the budget constraint facing Brent. If he chooses 24 hours of leisure, point A allows Brent to receive OW_2 in transfer

Work–leisure trade-off is the trade-off workers experience by either choosing to work or take time off.

FIGURE 11-10
The Income–Leisure Trade-Off

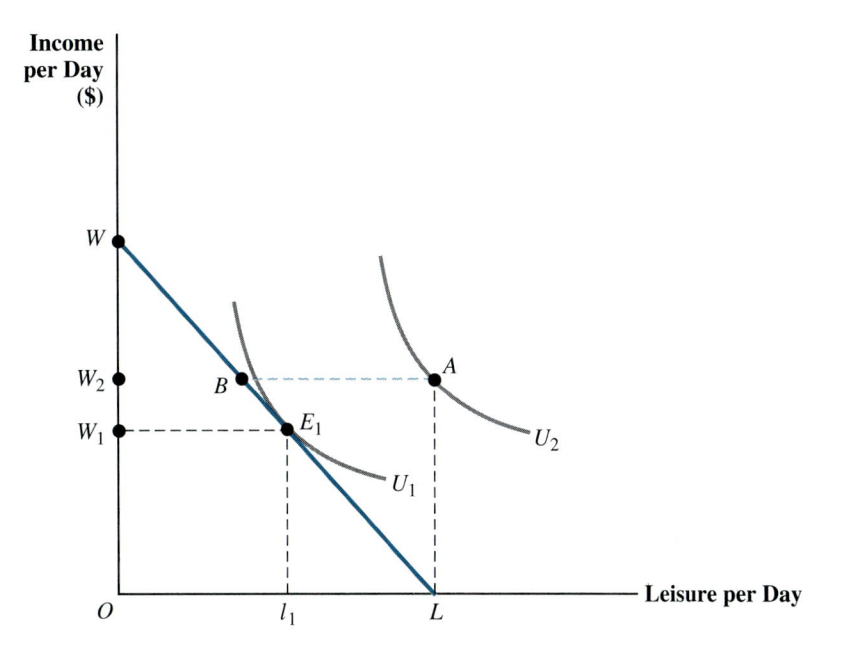

income. Assuming that each additional hour of work lowers the transfer dollar for dollar, the budget constraint shows no accompanying increase in income so long as earned income is below the value of the transfer. Leftward movements along the budget constraint are horizontal, as earned income substitutes for transfer income and demonstrates a 100 percent tax rate on earned income. At point *B*, however, additional hours of work raise earned income above the level of transfer; therefore, from this point on, the budget constraint follows the original one. The new budget constraint is therefore *ABW*.

What work–leisure trade-off does Brent now select? It is possible for him to react differently, but evidence suggests that transfers lower the incentives of recipients to work. Point *A*, which shows zero hours of work and 24 hours of leisure, shows this outcome. When point *A* reflects maximum utility, the welfare program creates no incentive for Brent to work. The welfare program therefore

❏ increases leisure from Ol_1 hours to *OL* hours, or 24 hours a day and
❏ raises Brent's utility by allowing him to consume along indifference curve *U*2.

Moral Hazard and Adverse Selection

In our discussion of off-budget policies in Chapter 10, we argued that moral hazard occurs when policies themselves tend to promote activities they are attempting to control or eliminate. We saw, for instance, that bank managers may undertake greater risks when they receive public deposit insurance. Adverse selection was also discussed as a problem when demanders of policies, such as flood insurance, tend to be those at greatest risk of collecting claims.

It has been argued that problems of moral hazard and adverse selection are likely to occur whenever the public sector transfers income toward the poor.[18] Moral hazard would exist, then, if policies that subsidize the incomes of the poor, promote activities that result in poverty. As our examination of the work–leisure trade-off demonstrates, this possibility arises with policies such as AFDC, which sets a 100 percent tax rate on earnings. If it is clear that low income levels result in transfers, some individuals may work less and enjoy greater hours of leisure than they would if transfers were not available. By thus promoting leisure, transfer policies create a moral hazard because they encourage behavior that lowers earnings for the poor. Even though there are ways around this problem, current welfare policies are probably characterized by such problems of moral hazard.

If applicants for welfare programs tend to be those with above-average preferences for leisure over work, problems of adverse selection may also arise. The selection of welfare recipients, then, may result in a relatively permanent class characterized by a greater tendency to become dependent upon transfers than the general population. An important implication here is that welfare policies carry a low probability of promoting work effort. Above-average preferences for leisure over work show up in indifference curves displaying preferences between earned income and hours of leisure, and welfare applicants tend to choose greater hours of leisure than would be chosen by the general population.

Negative Income Tax Policy

It is clear that many members of society do not advocate elimination of welfare transfers. It is also clear that many people favor reform of the welfare system. A negative income tax policy is a reform supported by many individuals holding a wide array of views regarding the welfare system.

Negative income tax policy is one that provides a minimum amount of income for all members of society.

A **negative income tax policy** would provide a minimum income for all members of society. Let us look at a few comparative examples of how such a policy would work.

Consider how a minimum income of $250 a month would influence the work effort of Jones P. Jones.

- ❏ If Jones earns zero income, she collects a cash transfer of $250 whether from a negative income tax or under a current welfare program.
- ❏ If Jones earns $50, only a fraction of those earnings would be used to reduce the cash transfer of $250 under a negative income tax. With a tax rate of, say, 20 percent, only $10 would be taken away from the transfer; therefore, take-home income would be $240 + $50 = $290. Current welfare programs (such as AFDC), however, set a tax rate of 100 percent of earnings below transfer levels; thus Jones' $50 in earned income would be used to reduce the transfer, thereby leaving Ms. Jones with a total income of $250.

---

[18] For this argument see Richard E. Wagner, *To Promote the General Welfare: Market Processes vs. Political Transfers* (San Francisco: Pacific Research Institute for Public Policy, 1989), 170.

❏ If Jones earns $400, she would pay $80 in taxes under a negative income tax, leaving a take-home income of $570. The value of transfer is therefore $170. Under the current system, her income would be $400, upon which she would have to pay taxes.

Under a negative income tax, then, increased work effort increases total income. Moreover, such a policy offers another benefit: Jones could continue to be eligible for cash transfers until she earns $1,250. This threshold income level would also define the point at which Jones must begin transferring income toward individuals who earn less than $1,250. With an income of $1,500, for example, Jones would collect no transfers; she would pay $50 in taxes and have a take-home income of $1,450. A negative income tax policy could also be designed with a progressive income tax rate wherein the tax rate would be higher for incomes above some threshold level.

What are the merits of a negative income tax policy? It is clearly consistent with the spirit of cash transfers since it tends to offer higher utility to welfare recipients than equivalent values of noncash transfers and excise subsidies. It exerts no adverse influence on work effort since it encourages individuals to work more than current transfer policies do. And it transfers more income to the poorest in society by not penalizing welfare recipients who wish to work. In addition, a negative income tax policy would avoid the short-term consequences associated with reform proposals that call for reduction or elimination of transfer payments. Although both types of policy reforms—negative income and reduction/elimination—would likely promote long-term increases in work effort, only the negative income policy does so without immediate reductions in the income of welfare recipients.

Various criticisms of a negative income policy have also been suggested. Such a policy, some argue, does not directly target such vulnerable groups as the elderly, children, or the disabled because it makes no distinctions among the poor. Others maintain, however, that this lack of discrimination is an advantage because it eliminates possible sources of inconsistencies associated with targeting benefits to specific groups. It is difficult, for example, to believe that all the elderly, families with dependent children, and disabled individuals require identical transfer payments. Moreover, under such a program, administrative costs associated with policing various means-tested requirements would be lower.

Another possible source of criticism may come from the welfare bureaucracy itself. This policy clearly eliminates the need for a large bureaucracy and therefore receives less-than-enthusiastic support from civil servants who administer current welfare programs. Moreover, the usual arguments for paternalism in policymaking may cause some to insist that noncash transfers and excise subsidies be maintained, thereby ensuring that the poor increase their consumption of various goods such as health care and housing assistance rather than use their income in any way they choose.

Alternative Views of Poverty

The underlying issues of welfare policy may be summarized as follows:

❏ Are the poor making rational choices to consume more leisure than the general population, or are they making no choice at all, subject to factors beyond their control?

❑ Do transfers cause certain individuals to become dependent upon welfare programs?

At one end of the debate are those who argue that most welfare recipients would prefer to work than to collect transfers; at the other end are those who maintain that most recipients prefer to collect transfers rather than work. This debate has at its center the following serious policy dilemma: *Most individuals want to transfer income to the poor but do not want, at the same time, to create incentives for recipients to become dependent upon transfers that ultimately reduce their overall self-sufficiency.*

The economic analysis of the work–leisure trade-off focuses on the rationality of decisions to become dependent upon transfer programs. That is, when problems of moral hazard and adverse selection occur, transfer policies encourage the creation of a permanent class of poor individuals. Within this framework, poverty may be viewed as a rational response to the transfer policies of the public sector.[19] Government failure is therefore believed to be responsible when the policy process approves incentives for the poor to remain poor. Proponents of this view observe that as transfer payments have risen in number and dollar value, such measures as poverty rates have not fallen commensurately. Rather, they predict that limiting transfers, or reducing the number of weeks that recipients may collect them, will diminish poverty in society.

Workfare, a policy that forces healthy welfare recipients to work eventually, has been a popular policy prescription among supporters of this view. An attempt to end dependence on welfare, workfare also requires that welfare recipients learn job-related skills until they find employment. At present, AFDC recipients, for example, must (with some exceptions) accept training and education or find work when their youngest child is over the age of three.

In contrast to the belief that poverty is the result of rational choices is the view that poverty is the result of factors beyond the control of most poor individuals. Proponents of this view therefore believe that private market failures, rather than government failure, is responsible for poverty. The argument that poverty is the result of inequality of opportunity is consistent with this viewpoint. Thus, transfers to the poor are justified on the basis of the notion that the poor have fewer opportunities to earn income than others and that, afforded more opportunities, they will eventually capture greater income through private initiative. Policies that improve the educational, nutritional, and medical opportunities for the poor are therefore seen as primary means of improving the probability that poor individuals will eventually escape poverty. In this view, limiting transfer payments is not considered a productive means of alleviating poverty. Because poverty is not rationally chosen, reduction or elimination of transfer payments would serve little purpose in the short or long run. In the short run, such a move would be disastrous and in the long run, pointless, as it would promote neither work nor the acquisition of skills.

Workfare is a policy requiring healthy welfare recipients to work in exchange for welfare benefits.

---

[19] Charles A. Murray is a chief proponent of this view; see his *Losing Ground: American Social Policy, 1950–1980* (New York: Basic Books, 1984).

Workfare: A Radical Proposal?

One of the more controversial proposals aimed at reforming welfare is the elimination of benefits after a set number of years. The theory behind this proposal is that strict time limits force able-bodied, but welfare-dependent, individuals to work. The Clinton administration backs this proposal as part of the campaign promise of "to end welfare as we know it." This is the most drastic action ever proposed by a U.S. president, and one that is gaining wider acceptance as more voters are increasingly critical of the welfare system. The plan is to stop payments for all able-bodied recipients after two years. If recipients still do not find employment after two years, they would be required to work for their benefits. At this point, welfare becomes workfare.

Though no state has gone so far as to set strict time limits, several states have gone in the direction of this proposal. Success stories in these states often come after welfare agencies provide job training and, in some cases, child care for welfare recipients. Margo Reeves of Wisconsin, for example, earned her high school equivalency degree while enrolled in a welding class. After collecting welfare for eight years, this mother of two has found a welding job and hopes never to need welfare again.

Source: Paulette Thomas, "Drawing the Line: Getting Families off Welfare and into Jobs Isn't as Easy as AFDC," *Wall Street Journal*, October 25, 1993, A1.

Analysis

Recent dramatic changes in numbers of welfare recipients suggest that radical policy reform is likely. During the 1980s, roughly 17,000 new welfare cases occurred each year. But new cases erupted to 305,000 per year between 1989 and 1992. Half of these cases are single mothers and, of these, roughly half are teenagers. While many reformers find it acceptable to exempt mothers with young children, and those who are completing high school as well, there is growing sentiment that exemptions be withheld for mothers who continue to have children while on welfare.

Some fear that this plan will lead to make-work jobs that the government somehow coughs up. Advocates, however, argue that teaching welfare recipients the ins and outs of conducting successful job searches will lead welfare recipients to many new private sector jobs. In addition to learning good interview techniques, they argue that classes showing which bus lines to take to job interviews have led to many new jobs. It is observable on many occasions how simple help may be, though we cannot minimize more complex needs.

One major obstacle to getting people off welfare will be removed if President Clinton's universal health coverage plan is approved. Currently publicly provided health benefits, such as Medicaid, are no longer available to those who leave the welfare rolls. Consider, for instance, Bonnie Oaks, who has collected welfare for twelve years in Cincinnati. Responsible for the support of her family, with a chronically ill husband and child, she lost her health benefits after accepting a job as a teacher's aide. Even though a nurse told her that she "was crazy to think about a job," Oaks was determined to get off welfare. She notes, however, that it is becoming increasingly difficult for her to stay off, as her health care costs accumulate.

Policy Reforms That May Attract a Wide Audience

Most citizens may believe that the public sector should provide equal opportunities as well as a substantial safety net of policies that meet the temporary needs of healthy, but poor, individuals. But there are many sources of disagreement as to what constitutes appropriate welfare policy reform. Even though the dichotomy of views just presented has been with us for a very long time, several reforms are likely to attract support from a wide audience.

ESCROW ACCOUNTS One reform is offered as a means of reducing the disincentives to work associated with AFDC and food-stamp programs.[20] You will remember that current policy sets a 100 percent tax rate on certain earnings received by welfare recipients. An attractive alternative to lowering benefits or eligibility is to allow welfare recipients to keep earnings in an escrow account. Such an account would save earnings for welfare recipients while they remain on the welfare rolls. After they succeed in working their way off the welfare rolls, welfare recipients could receive this account. Similar to a negative income tax policy in that it creates an incentive for welfare recipients to work, this policy is probably politically more viable than the negative income tax because it does not threaten to dismantle the current welfare bureaucracy.

An escrow account policy, however, may not appeal to reformers who recommend noncash transfers as a means of increasing consumption of targeted goods such as housing, food, education, and health care. Paternalism has been suggested as the attitude animating proponents of noncash transfer programs, and escrow-account reform is not paternalistic since it represents cash that may be used by former welfare recipients in any way they choose.

PRIVATIZATION Another reform that has received broad support is privatization of housing assistance programs. It has been argued that the key to adequate housing lies in the premise that private ownership of resources leads to good stewardship of resources. Advocates of privatization predict that when welfare recipients own equity stakes in their own housing units, their efforts to care for their properties will lead to improvements in overall housing quality. Equity stakes could be achieved by awarding low-interest mortgage loans or excise subsidies that pay some portion of monthly mortgage payments. In addition, public housing units could be sold outright to the poor at below-market prices.

ECONOMIC EXPANSION Economic opportunities for all members of society—poor and nonpoor alike—appear to be strongly related to the business cycle. Opportunities for employment, as well as increases in job training and wages, are much greater when the economy is strong than when it is weak. Along with the reform of transfer programs, policymakers who seek to alleviate poverty must not neglect macroeconomic policies that promote stable economic expansion.

---

[20] *Economic Report of the President*, February 1992, 148.

Summary

- The role of the public sector in transferring income to the poor has expanded since the 1960s. These policies are motivated by a desire to improve the distribution of income that naturally occurs in private markets. Determination of what constitutes a desirable distribution of income for society involves subjective judgments of analysts.
- Many transfer programs for the poor are means tested. In order to receive a transfer, an individual must earn income that falls below some minimum level. Programs come in two varieties: cash transfers, which directly deliver cash, and noncash transfers, which provide in-kind benefits. The majority of transfers are noncash.
- *Equality of outcomes* could be interpreted to mean that all individuals receive equal incomes. *Equality of opportunity* means that all members of society have equal opportunities to earn income and may, in practice, mean that all individuals have the same opportunities to receive education and enter all occupations. If the goal of policy is creation of equal opportunity, there is no reason to expect that policies will result in income equality.
- Poverty is usually defined in terms of income. This measure includes government cash transfers but excludes noncash transfers. Poverty is also measured in terms of income thresholds at which families that earn less than a minimum income level are classified as poor.
- Long-term income is less dispersed than annual income, and a focus on annual income overstates income dispersion. There is also considerable mobility across income classes over time, and the distribution of income is heavily influenced by tax policy.
- Recipients tend to prefer cash transfers over equivalent noncash transfers. From the viewpoint of utility maximization, cash transfers are a more efficient means of transfer. Some analysts, who exert a paternalistic influence on policy, believe that noncash transfers are preferable because noncash transfers allow policymakers greater control over the consumption of targeted goods by recipients. A welfare cost, however, occurs when an equivalent cash transfer results in higher utility for recipients.
- It is commonly believed that transfer policies tend to reduce the incentives of recipients to work. Two factors explain this effect: transfers reduce the need of recipients to work, and earned income usually reduces transfers. Negative income tax policies are often recommended as reforms because they do not create disincentives to work.

Review Questions

1. What are the major reasons for redistribution policies?
2. What is the distinction between equality of outcomes and equality of opportunities?
3. What is the difference between the level and the distribution of income?
4. What is a means-tested transfer program? Give two examples.
5. What is the difference between a cash transfer and a noncash transfer? Give examples of each.
6. What is a negative income tax policy?

Discussion Questions

1. Why might the public sector be called upon to redistribute income in society?
2. Explain what is meant by means testing of welfare programs.
3. Explain the difference between the level and distribution of income in society.
4. Explain the difference between equality of opportunity and equality of income. Would

equality of opportunity lead to equality of income? Explain why policy analysts tend to focus on income equality when they examine the effectiveness of welfare policies.

5. Do you believe that inheritances promote equality of opportunity in society?

6. Describe the primary allocational and distributional effects of transfer programs.

7. Why do welfare recipients generally prefer cash transfers over noncash transfers? Under what circumstances do policymakers prefer noncash transfers over cash transfers?

8. Explain why the negative income tax policy does not exert adverse effects on work effort. Do you believe that this policy has more or less welfare stigma than current welfare policies?

9. Our discussion of transfer policies suggests that the design of these policies exert important effects on work-leisure choices. What effects on macroeconomic growth might also be associated with different welfare policies?

10. Explain why, if public transfer programs crowd out private spending on charity, total transfers to the poor may increase, decrease, or remain the same.

Key Words

Social welfare policies
Equality of outcomes
Equality of opportunity
Real median family income
Poverty threshold
Middle class
Cash transfers
Noncash transfers
Aid to Families with Dependent Children (AFDC)
Welfare costs
Excise subsidies
Work–leisure trade-off
Negative income tax policy
Workfare

CHAPTER 12

Social Insurance Programs

Social insurance programs provide benefits to individuals and families for loss of income due to retirement, disability, illness, and unemployment. Although these programs are called insurance programs, they differ in one important respect from private insurance programs: social insurance programs are also transfer programs. Social insurance programs also differ from the transfer programs for the poor. Eligibility for transfers is not based on need but, rather, it is based on membership in groups such as the elderly, the disabled, and the unemployed. Social insurance programs are therefore not means tested and, in some instances, transfer income to the well-to-do in society.

This chapter focuses on the three major social insurance programs:[1]

Social Security
is a New Deal program that provides benefits to retired and disabled workers and their dependents.

Medicare
pays inpatient costs at hospitals and limited care at nursing homes.

Unemployment insurance
provides benefits to laid-off workers.

❏ **Social Security,** created in 1935, provides benefits to retired and disabled workers and their dependents.

❏ **Medicare,** introduced in 1965, pays inpatient costs at hospitals and limited care at nursing homes.

❏ **Unemployment insurance,** created in 1935, provides benefits to laid-off workers.

We can see the rapid expansion of social insurance programs in Figure 12-1. Social insurance spending is now roughly 33 percent of total federal spending (Figure 12-1a) and 7.5 percent of GDP (Figure 12-1b). Social Security is the largest social insurance program and accounts for roughly 21 percent of all federal spending, as Figure 12-2 shows. The share of spending devoted to Medicare has risen very rapidly since its creation in 1965 and now accounts for roughly 9.5 percent of all spending. Unemployment insurance averages about 1.5 percent of federal spending and, because it is mostly related to the business cycle, exhibits no significant long-term trends.

In our examination of social insurance programs, we raise the following questions:

❏ What are the rationales for social insurance programs?

❏ How do social insurance programs operate?

---

[1] There are also Workers' Compensation, Railroad Retirement, and Veterans' Disability Compensation social insurance programs.

331

**FIGURE 12-1
Social Insurance**

*Source: Budget of
the United States
Government, 1995.*

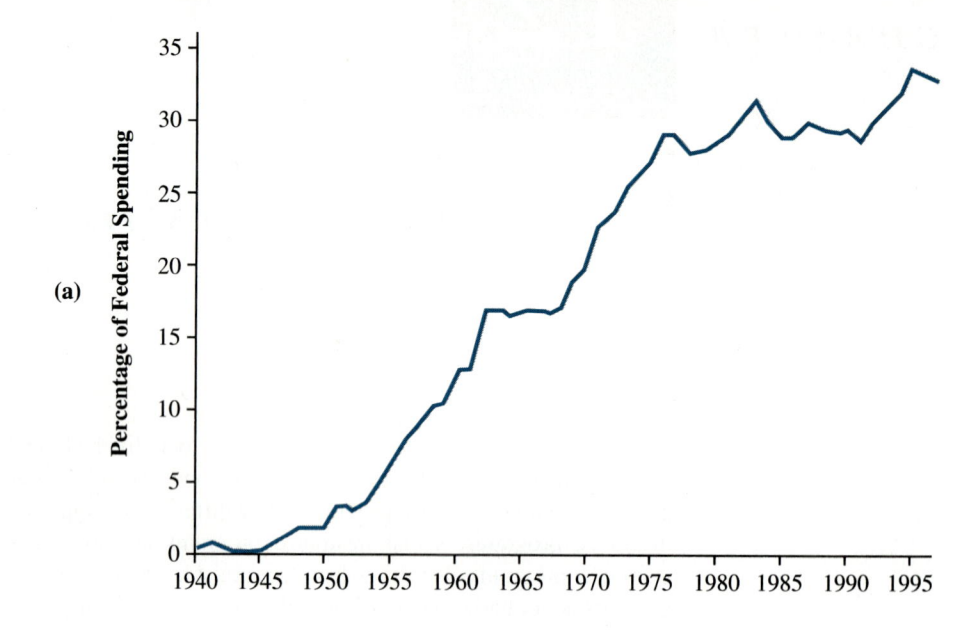

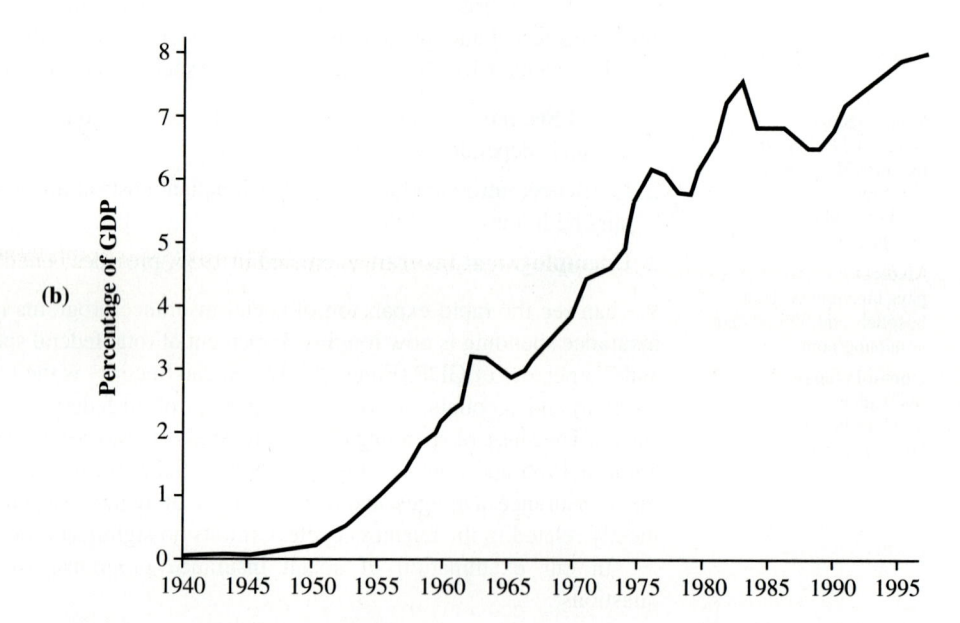

(a) Percentage of Federal Spending

(b) Percentage of GDP

❑ What effects on resource allocation and the distribution of income are exerted by social insurance programs?

❑ What implications for the future of the federal budget are drawn from our study of social insurance programs?

❑ What reforms might be introduced in the near future?

**FIGURE 12-2
Major Social
Insurance Programs**

Source: Budget of the United States Government, 1995.

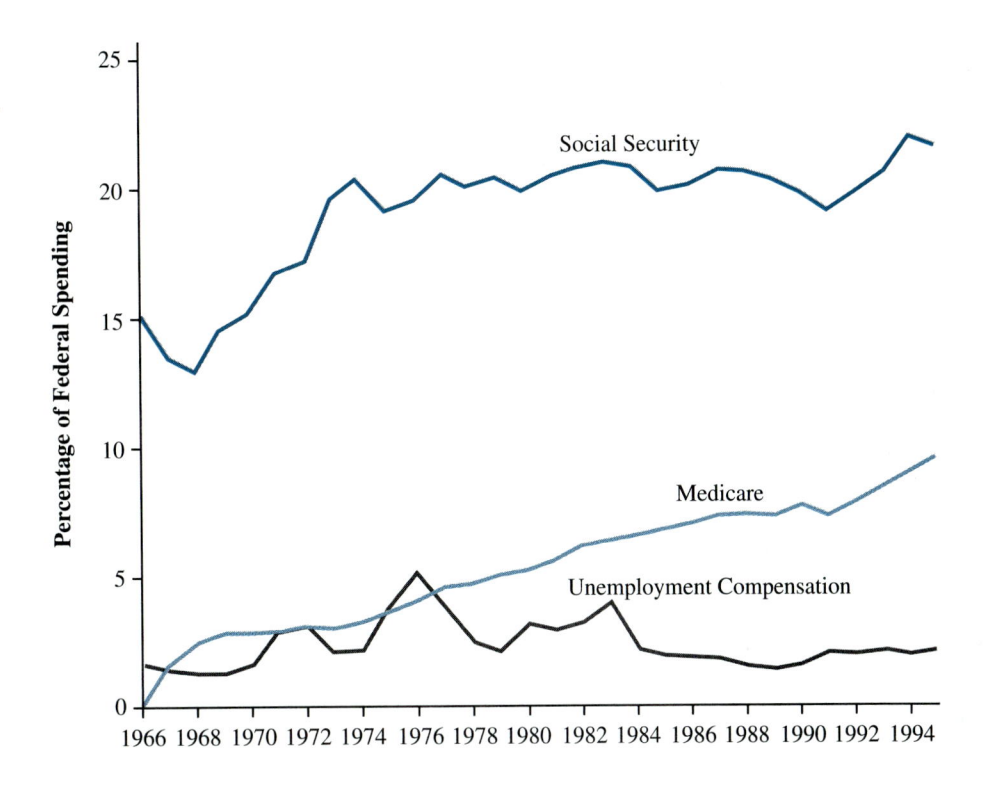

Major Social Insurance Programs: Social Security, Medicare, and Unemployment Compensation as percentage of federal spending, 1966–1994.

Historical Perspective

The creation of social insurance programs is historically significant for two reasons. First, the Social Security Act of 1935 was the first large-scale social program in the United States. Prior to the Great Depression, the government's role in the economy was principally one of providing for national defense and the protection of private property—a role consistent with an underlying belief that individuals themselves are chiefly responsible for their own economic security. At that time, the states were largely reluctant to accept a social security system. In fact, of the 21 states that created special commissions to study the question of whether states should offer social insurance programs, only one recommended a system of mandatory social insurance.[2] Economic collapse, however, was a powerful catalyst for change. The question became whether or not private individuals could be expected to provide for themselves in an economy that seemed highly unstable—one in which unemployment was high and the savings of many Americans had been wiped out. Because private markets appeared to have failed, support grew for a more active federal role in allocating economic resources.

Second, the Social Security program represented a break in the U.S. federalist tradition, concentrating power in the hands of the central government instead of the

---

[2] Carolyn L. Weaver, *The Crisis in Social Security* (Durham, N.C.: Duke University Press, 1982).

states or local governments. Until the 1930s, the notion of states' rights remained relatively intact; state governments, for example, had rarely been required to abide by the wishes of federal policymakers except in specific functions designated by the U.S. Constitution. Passage of the Social Security Act, however, signaled that the federal government could take responsibility for the welfare of citizens. This is not to say that the states offered concerted objections—there is no question that most state governments were in favor of Social Security. But it should be noted that the Social Security package approved by Congress contained relief funds for state and local governments, provisions that clearly helped remove some of the reluctance of state policymakers to transfer power to the federal government.

Rationales for Social Insurance Policies

We have seen many times that public policies are often based on perceived inadequacies of private markets and we will now discuss several rationales for public provision of insurance policies in the areas of health, retirement, and unemployment insurance.

Lack of Private Markets

Private markets may not evolve in every insurance area. Why might private insurance markets in the areas of retirement, health, disability, and unemployment not be fully developed? *Adverse selection* tends to occur in insurance markets in which those at greatest risk tend to demand more insurance than those at low risk. Consider unemployment insurance, which provides payments to insurees in the event of unemployment. Adverse selection would appear to occur: It is reasonable to expect workers who are likely to experience unstable employment to demand more insurance than workers who expect to have great employment stability. What problems might adverse selection pose for private insurance firms? One problem occurs when workers who want insurance are the ones who are most likely to collect benefits from insurance companies. Another problem exists when high rates of claims cause firms to charge relatively high premiums, thus discouraging applications from workers who experience stable employment. Adverse selection therefore creates a lopsided risk pool characterized by a relatively high percentage of high-risk workers.

A related problem is that of *moral hazard,* which occurs when policies tend to promote behaviors that they are supposed to control or prevent. Unemployment insurance may promote a moral hazard if, through its subsidization of unemployment, workers become unemployed more often or remain unemployed for longer periods of time.

For reasons of adverse selection and moral hazard, some argue that private insurance markets will tend to insure too few individuals or refuse to offer insurance to certain workers. This reasoning, however, tends to be less persuasive in the cases of retirement and health insurance, since both are characterized by well-evolved private markets. As proof of an active market in retirement insurance, consider that, over 1970–92, private pensions' share of total private financial assets doubled from 2 percent to 4 percent.[3] An active market in private health insurance is also evident and,

---

[3] *Statistical Abstract of the United States,* 1993.

from 1980–92, spending on private health insurance grew from 3 percent to 4 percent of GDP.[4] Many complaints have been lodged against private health insurers, but few would argue that lack of a private market for health insurance is a problem.[5] Expansion of social insurance policies has been mostly in Social Security and Medicare, which are areas in which private markets play an active role.

Promotion of Equity Goals of Society

Considerations of equity play an important role in social insurance programs. It has been argued that private market insurers set insurance premiums too high for various individuals in society. We saw in Chapter 10 that subsidies for educational loans are often based on the inability of low-income families to afford college for their children. Social insurance programs are designed to meet equity goals when they transfer income by subsidizing insurance programs for eligible individuals.

It is important to remember that private markets are not concerned with allocating resources on the basis of equity, and therefore private insurance markets will not provide this transfer function. Usage of the term *insurance* to characterize Social Security, Medicare, and unemployment insurance is therefore somewhat misleading and not entirely consistent with usage of the same term in private markets. For the purpose of clarification, it is important to distinguish between two very important, but different, characteristics of social insurance programs. One characteristic is the extent to which individual benefits are financed by payments of beneficiaries. This characteristic is the **insurance function** and is identical to the function performed by private insurers. The other characteristic is the extent to which individual benefits are paid by someone else. This characteristic defines the **transfer function** and is not performed by private insurers. The transfer function is unique to social insurance programs and, as we shall show, it is necessary to separate insurance and transfer functions when we examine social insurance programs.

> **Insurance function** occurs if a policy mimics a private insurance policy and therefore does not seek to transfer income.
>
> **Transfer function** occurs if a policy is designed to transfer income.

Paternalism

Paternalism is often a rationale for social insurance programs. It may be believed that some members of society will not voluntarily purchase private insurance, or save for their own retirement. It may also be believed that private individuals will not save for times when they are too ill to work or are laid off from work. Advocates of paternalism justify social insurance programs on the belief that policymakers better understand what is good for a certain proportion of individuals in society than the individuals do themselves.

Our discussion of paternalism raises an important issue concerning the difference between the insurance and transfer functions of social insurance programs. An individual may not wish to subscribe for reasons associated with either or both functions.

---

[4] Calculations made using data provided in Congressional Budget Office, *Projections of National Health Expenditures,* October 1992.

[5] Consideration of national standards may also argue for a federal government role in social insurance programs. It may, for example, be believed that all beneficiaries should be provided with similar benefits, and even though certain programs, such as unemployment insurance, are administered by the states, the federal government should set national guidelines for the states to follow.

It may be true, for example, that individuals do not choose to subscribe to social insurance programs because they do not believe that programs should perform a transfer function. This reason is very different from the case of individuals who do not wish to insure themselves for loss of income.

An assumption other than paternalism is also often used to recommend that all citizens contribute to social insurance programs. A negative externality may occur, for example, when uninsured individuals retire, become unemployed, disabled or ill, *and* they have not purchased or have been unable to purchase private insurance or some other means of providing for loss of income. When the public sector transfers income to uninsured individuals in these cases (for example, when they are treated at a public hospital), a negative externality is placed upon those who must pay for transfers. Universal coverage of all citizens would therefore reduce the extent of negative externality since all individuals would be covered under social insurance programs.

Social Security

Private Pensions

Private pension is a fund that accumulates contributions for the purpose of paying benefits upon a worker's retirement.

Before we discuss the mechanics of the Social Security system, it is useful to understand how a private market in retirement insurance, or a **private pension,** would operate. The mechanics of any pension fund may be thought of in terms of inflows and outflows. (For simplicity, we will assume there are no administrative costs.) Much as with a savings account, workers make contributions (inflows) to pension funds that provide the funds for future pension benefits (outflows) to workers during their retirement years. Pension funds invest pension contributions and, upon retirement, return to workers accumulated pension contributions plus interest earned while their contributions were invested.

Another way of viewing the inflow-outflow relationship is to recognize that liabilities of pension funds are projected promised future payments to contributors. The value of liabilities therefore depends upon the actuarial assessment of life expectancy, retirement age of contributors, and promised retirement benefits. The value of assets, however, depends on size and frequency of contributions and the expected rate of return on those funds. Understanding of assets and liabilities leads to the definition of a **fully funded pension fund.** When future pension payments are guaranteed by contributions that are invested, or saved, until recipients collect retirement benefits, pension funds are fully funded. Fully funded pension funds are therefore solvent at all times, and any private pension fund that cannot balance both sides of its balance sheet is termed not fully funded or, more commonly, insolvent.

Fully funded pension fund is a pension fund that has the financial resources necessary to meet future retirement benefits.

Would workers be willing to contribute to pension funds which are not fully funded? The answer is no, since private pension funds are only financially viable when they are fully funded. Note, however, that this does not imply that all pension funds offer identical rates of return to contributors. Differences occur when pension fund managers have different investment skills. The point remains, however, that there would be little or no demand by workers for pension funds that do not operate on a fully funded basis.

Social Security Taxes

Old Age, Survivors and Disability Insurance (OASDI) is the formal name of Social Security. Medicare, or Hospital Insurance (HI), is often considered a part of Social Security, but because of its distinctive characteristics, is discussed separately in this chapter. Social Security is financed through payroll taxes. Table 12-1 shows the history of **Social Security taxes.**[6] There are three important characteristics of Social Security taxes.

Social Security taxes are taxes paid by workers into the Social Security system.

1. Employers, as well as employees, pay Social Security taxes. Each is assessed an equal share and therefore our current (combined) tax rate of 15.3 percent consists of payments by both employee and employer of 7.65 percent each. Even though it may appear that the worker only pays a rate of 7.65 percent, economists generally believe that the employer's contribution is really paid by the worker. The employer's tax share is believed to lower, dollar for dollar, other salary or benefits that employees would receive if there were no payroll taxes. Since 1937, tax rates have grown over sevenfold.

2. Taxes are levied only up to an income threshold. Taxes are flat rate; that is, for every dollar of income up to the threshold, tax rates remain constant. Income thresholds have risen from $3,000 in 1937 to $60,600 in 1994 and increase each year by a cost-of-living index.

3. Maximum levels of taxes paid by workers are determined by the tax rate multiplied by income up to the threshold level.

Social Security Benefits

Social Security benefits are payments received by Social Security recipients whose contributions make them eligible.

Social Security benefits are administered by the Social Security Administration, which keeps records of earnings under the Social Security numbers and names of all workers. Benefits are based on earnings over work life, up to a maximum amount, and are only loosely based on the amount of tax payments by workers.[7] Benefits are based on average indexed monthly earnings (AIME), a calculation that averages monthly earnings and compares the earnings of workers against the national average wage from when beneficiaries started work until they reached the age of sixty, became disabled, or died, again only up to the threshold income. The AIME is then used to calculate the primary insurance amount, or PIA, a calculation of the base monthly benefit if the worker retired at the official retirement age. Until recently, age sixty-five was the age at which beneficiaries could receive full unreduced benefits; however, starting in 2000, the official retirement age is increased in monthly steps until, in 2027, it reaches age sixty-seven. Reduced retirement benefits, lower-benefit formulas applied to workers retiring before the official retirement age, are first available starting at age sixty-two.

---

[6] As is commonly done, Medicare taxes are included here as well. In 1994, these were set at the combined rate of 2.9 percent.

[7] Discussion of benefits is obtained from Social Security Administration, "Personal Earnings and Benefit Estimate Statement," 1989.

TABLE 12-1
Social Security: Rates and Maximum Contributions

Years	Annual Maximum Taxable Earnings ($)	Contribution Rate[a] (%)	Maximum Tax[b] ($)
1937–49	3,000	2	60
1950	3,000	3	90
1951–53	3,600	3	108
1954–56	4,200	4	168
1957–58	4,200	4.5	189
1959	4,800	5	240
1960–61	4,800	6	288
1962	4,800	6.25	300
1963–65	4,800	7.25	348
1966	6,600	8.4	554.4
1967	6,600	8.8	580.8
1968	7,800	8.8	686.4
1969–70	7,800	9.6	748.8
1971	7,800	10.4	811.2
1972	9,000	10.4	936
1973	10,800	11.7	1,263.6
1974	13,200	11.7	1,544.4
1975	14,100	11.7	1,649.7
1976	15,300	11.7	1,790.1
1977	16,500	11.7	1,930.5
1978	17,700	12.1	2,141.7
1979	22,900	12.26	2,807.54
1980	25,900	12.26	3,175.34
1981	29,700	13.3	3,950.1
1982	32,400	13.4	4,341.6
1983	35,700	13.4	4,783.8
1984	37,800	14	5,292
1985	39,600	14.1	5,583.6
1986	42,000	14.3	6,006
1987	43,800	14.3	6,263.4
1988	45,000	15.02	6,759
1989	48,000	15.02	7,209.6
1990	51,300	15.3	7,848.9
1991	53,400	15.3	10,246.6
1992	55,500	15.3	—
1993	57,600	15.3	—
1994	60,600	15.3	—

[a] Medicare tax rates are included in the contribution rates as well.
[b] There is no income threshold for Medicare.

Source: Table 12, Tax Foundation, *Facts and Figures on Government Finance*, 1991 Edition (Baltimore/London: The Johns Hopkins University Press, 1991).

Replacement rate
is the percentage of one's past salary met by retirement benefits.

The PIA is then adjusted for age at retirement, number of dependents, marital status, and other factors. One measure of benefit adequacy is the **replacement rate,** that portion of past income which is replaced in retirement by Social Security. Figure 12-3 plots, for various classes of workers, replacement rates for workers who retire at age sixty-five.[8] Three classes of workers are shown: *average, low,* and *high* income earners. The *average*-income earner is defined as one who earned the average income during each working year. *Low*-income earners are defined as those who earned roughly half of the average income, and *high*-income earners are those who always earned income equal to the threshold defined by Social Security. You will notice that replacement rates are highest for the low-income earners and lowest for high-income earners. Current replacement rates yield roughly 50 percent for low-income earners, 35 percent for average-income earners, and 25 percent for high-income earners. Be careful not to interpret these replacement rates as the rates of return provided to different classes of workers. As shown below, rates of return are a function of tax contributions paid during working life *as well as* benefits received in retirement.

Benefits are reduced if beneficiaries, between the ages of sixty-five and sixty-nine, earn income above $10,200 (1992$). Every $3 of income reduces benefits by $1. When workers under age seventy earn enough to reduce Social Security benefits to zero, benefits are delayed until retirement after seventy, which also leads to a slight increase in their AIME.

The issue of taxation of Social Security benefits is a highly controversial topic. Current law requires income taxation of 85 percent of benefits paid to couples with incomes over $44,000, and for individuals above $34,000.

Social Security also provides benefits other than retirement payments to disabled workers, their dependents, or their widows and widowers. Benefits are provided to spouses and to retired or disabled workers as early as age sixty-two. Benefits are available to widows and widowers who may collect benefits at age sixty, or fifty if disabled. Benefits are also available for unmarried children of deceased workers who are under age sixteen, or nineteen if in high school, or at any age if disabled before age twenty-two.

Trust Funds

Social insurance programs are funded through trust funds, which are specific funds set up to finance these programs. Two trust funds make up the **Social Security trust funds:** old-age and survivors insurance (OASI, established in 1939) and disability insurance (DI, established 1956).

Social Security trust funds
are comprised of IOUs provided by the federal government whenever Social Security taxes exceed payouts.

It may be inferred that the U.S. Treasury collects payroll taxes and then transfers them to the corresponding trust fund, but this is not how it works. The use of the term *trust fund* is somewhat misleading since all payroll taxes are sent to the general fund of the U.S. Treasury. Payroll taxes are indistinguishable from income taxes, corporate taxes, excise duties, and all other revenues of the federal government since they all reside in the general fund where they sustain operations of the U.S. government.

---

[8] Table 2-4, Henry J. Aaron, Barry P. Bosworth, and Gary Burtless, *Can America Afford to Grow Old? Paying for Social Security* (Washington, D.C.: Brookings Institution, 1989).

FIGURE 12-3
Replacement Rates for Retirement at Age 65 for Low, Average, and High Earners

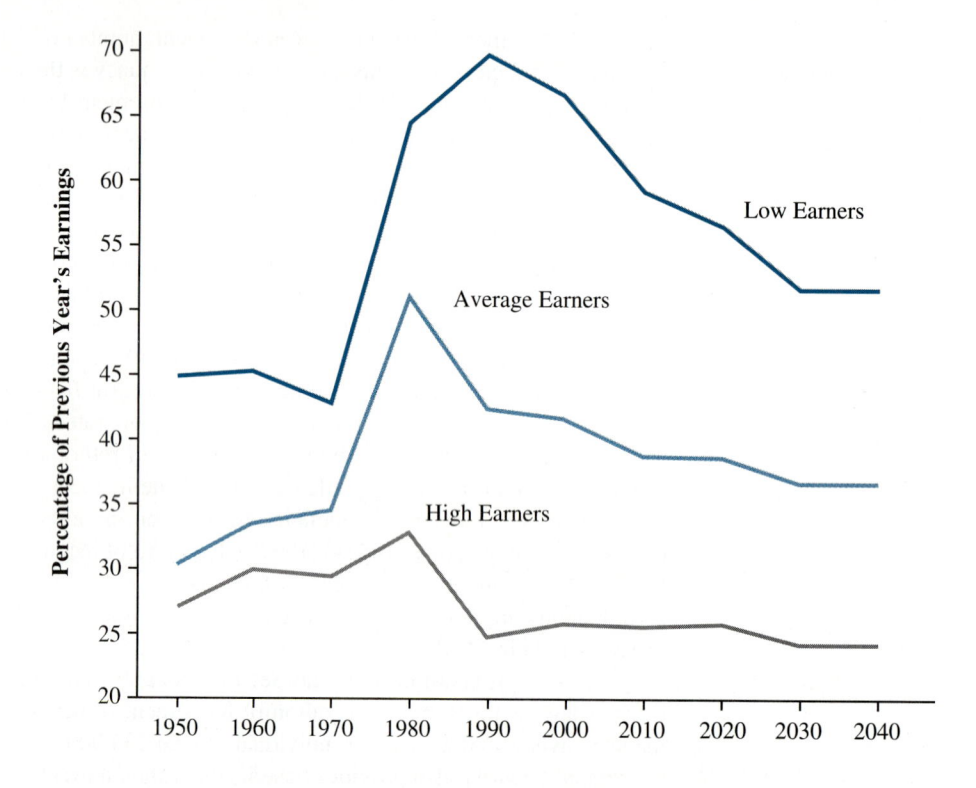

Payroll taxes are *not* directly deposited in any trust fund, but rather, as payroll taxes are collected, trust funds receive *credits* in the form of nonmarketable interest-earning Treasury securities. These securities, in effect, represent IOUs that the U.S. Treasury provides another government agency, the Social Security Administration. When the Social Security Administration pays benefits each month to Social Security recipients, the appropriate trust fund is debited by the amount of the payment.

An important, and probably much misunderstood, element of the financing of Social Security is its **pay-as-you-go** funding requirement.[9] In contrast to fully funded pension funds, the Social Security program is required only to have funds sufficient to meet its obligations in the current year; that is, it is required only to meet current payments to beneficiaries.

The pay-as-you-go funding constraint immediately raises two important issues. First, unlike fully funded private pensions, Social Security has no requirement that inflows must equal outflows over the life of the pension fund. In other words, it is not required to be able to meet its future obligations. The historical experience of this program has been to collect taxes that are far below those necessary to fund future benefit liabilities, and it is projected that long-term underfunding will continue.

Pay-as-you-go is a funding condition that requires current resources be sufficient only to cover current retirement benefits.

---

[9] It became pay-as-you-go in 1939. Some believe that the 1983 amendments to Social Security changed its funding requirements to a form that is now partially funded. This is not true in the sense that it is not required to invest current taxes for future payment of benefits.

Social Security surpluses arise whenever Social Security taxes exceed current payouts.

Social Security deficits occur whenever Social Security payouts exceed taxes collected.

Second, and possibly more important, is the issue surrounding what happens when annual inflows and outflows of the Social Security program are unequal. Whenever taxes exceed current claims, **Social Security surpluses** are said to occur, and whenever current claims exceed taxes, **Social Security deficits** are said to occur. In 1993, $419 billion in Social Security taxes were collected, and because benefits were only $305 billion, the $123 billion difference is a Social Security surplus. Surpluses are not required to be saved to provide funds to meet future liabilities of the Social Security program; in this way the program differs from a fully funded pension program. In fact, even if surpluses were saved in a separate account earmarked for future payments of Social Security benefits, there would be insufficient savings to meet future liabilities. Under the pay-as-you-go funding constraint, surpluses result in an equal crediting of IOUs that the U.S. Treasury delivers to the Social Security trust funds. These IOUs are pieces of paper that do not mean that the U.S. government promises that equivalent amounts of funds are being saved to trade for the IOUs in the future.

While the accumulated surpluses and deficits define the trust fund reserves, only IOUs, or paper credits owed by the U.S. Treasury, reside in the trust funds. In 1992, Social Security trust funds contained $335 billion in IOUs; by 1996, IOUs are projected to exceed $1 trillion.

Booming Trust Funds until 2050[10]

Table 12-2 shows actual and projected Social Security surpluses and deficits, 1960–2060, in both current and 1989 dollars. Surpluses are projected to reach a high of $494 billion in 2015, or $176 billion in 1989 dollars. Annual surpluses are projected to continue until 2030, when annual deficits become a permanent fixture of the program. Again, surpluses and deficits are *annual* balances of the Social Security program, and trust fund balances measure *accumulated* surpluses and deficits over time. Even though a surplus or deficit may occur in a given year, trust fund reserves in that same year may show either a positive or negative balance. A permanent series of deficits is projected to begin in 2030, but trust fund reserves turn negative around 2050 (2046 to be exact), with a projected value of −$6.3 trillion, or −$588 billion in 1989 dollars.

Demographics are an important contributing factor for these projected patterns of surpluses, deficits, and trust fund reserves. The elderly are not only an increasing percentage of the population, but they are also living longer. Figure 12-4 plots projected changes in numbers of Social Security beneficiaries and workers. Current projections show that benefits continue to expand, but workers will stop growing in number by 2010, when the baby boomers start to retire. These trends indicate that as long as numbers of workers continue growing, rising payroll tax revenues produce a continual stream of annual surpluses. But after 2010, when the number of workers stabilizes, growth in beneficiaries from roughly 50 million in 2010 to 80 million in 2040 will cause a permanent stream of annual deficits.

---

[10] Data in this section are obtained from Carolyn L. Weaver, ed., *Social Security's Looming Surpluses: Prospects and Implications* (Washington, D.C.: AEI Press, 1990).

TABLE 12-2
Annual Social Security Surpluses, Deficits, and Trust Funds ($Billions)

	Surplus/Deficit		Trust Fund Balance		
Year	Current Dollars	1989 Dollars	Current Dollars	1989 Dollars	% of GNP
1960	1	3	21	92	186
1970	4	12	34	114	103
1980	−4	−6	30	51	25
1990	69	66	195	195	77
1995	125	97	646	523	188
2000	203	130	1,428	952	312
2005	308	162	2,651	1,451	431
2010	431	187	4,473	2,012	522
2015	494	176	6,817	2,521	546
2020	448	131	9,276	2,819	505
2025	278	68	11,269	2,815	428
2030	−4	−1	12,182	2,501	336
2035	−372	−60	11,526	1,945	239
2040	−836	−112	8,894	1,234	143
2045	−1,558	−171	3,543	404	44
2050	−2,780	−250	−6,275	−588	−60
2055	−4,745	−351	−23,562	−1,815	−170
2060	−7,673	−467	−52,437	−3,319	−289

Source: Carolyn L. Weaver, ed., *Social Security's Looming Surpluses: Prospects and Implications* (Washington, D.C.: AEI Press, 1990). Reprinted with permission.

Figure 12-4b places the switch from surpluses to deficits in the perspective of the ratio of beneficiaries to workers. Over the century from 1960 to 2060, workers per beneficiaries are projected to fall from 5:1 to 2:1, causing a clear change in the mix of inflows and outflows in the Social Security program. Fewer workers will be paying payroll taxes and more beneficiaries will be collecting Social Security benefits. The figure also shows the percentage of population aged sixty-five and older, which is projected to more than double, from 9 percent to 22.5 percent over this same time period. The pattern of large annual surpluses being replaced by a series of large annual deficits is therefore not too surprising given projected demographic changes.

Implications of Changes in Trust Funds

Projected changes in trust funds lead to the following question: How will Social Security benefits be paid when deficits start to occur in 2030? Deficits force the Social Security Administration to cash in an equal amount of IOUs to the U.S. Treasury, but the federal government is not required to save what is promised in the trust fund

**FIGURE 12-4
Social Security
Beneficiaries**

Source: Carolyn L. Weaver, ed., *Social Security's Looming Surpluses: Prospects and Implications* (Washington, D.C.: AEI Press, 1990).

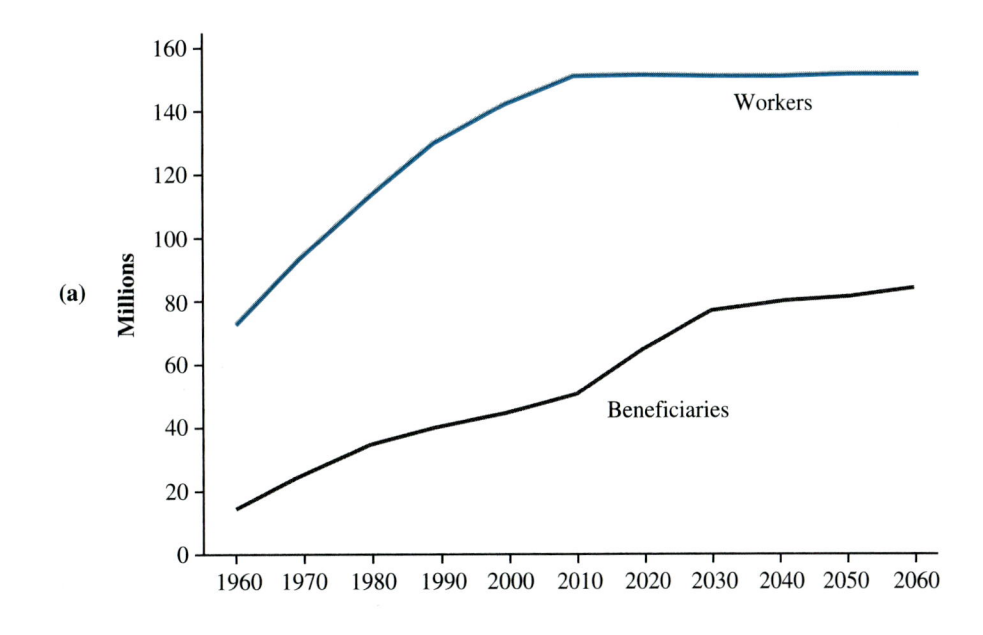

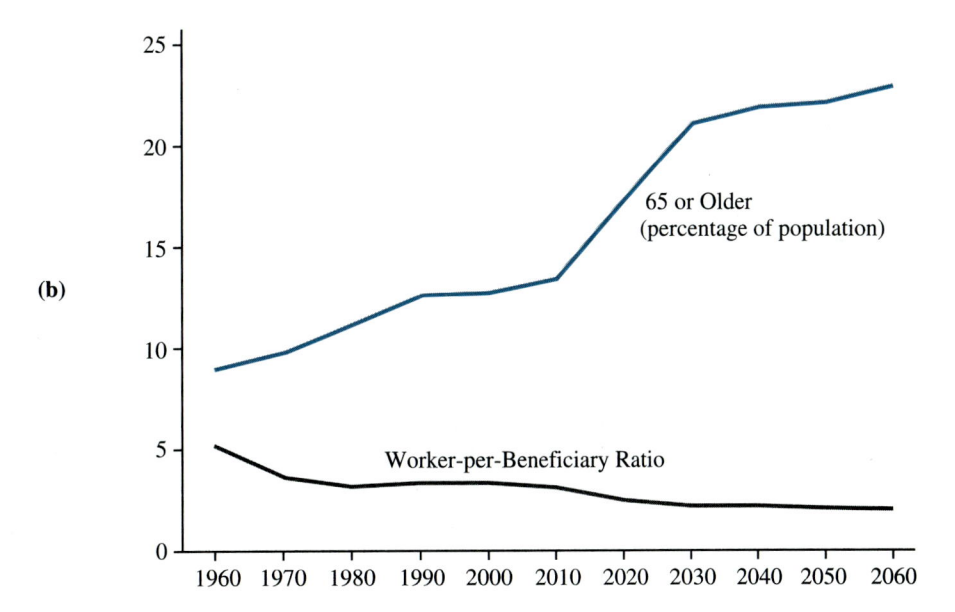

reserves, so there is considerable concern about where the cash will come from in 2030, when deficits are projected to arise. The annual deficits are projected to arrive before the trust funds begin to register negative balances, thus suggesting that the term *trust fund* may confer a false sense of security about the solvency of the Social Security program.

The IOUs sitting in trust funds represent a substantial unfunded, and long-term, liability of the federal government. It is not clear how this liability will be met, but at least three options are available. One is to raise payroll tax revenues, either by raising tax rates or the income threshold with which the payroll tax rate is applied. Inspection of Table 12-1 indicates that this option has been employed repeatedly over the years and leads many observers to predict that it is likely to be repeated in the future. It has also been projected that payroll taxes must rise from 15.3 percent to over 20 percent of taxable income if taxes are to keep up with projected benefit levels over the next 50 years.

A second possibility is to use nonpayroll taxes to fund Social Security benefits. Current Social Security benefits are always paid out of the U.S. Treasury's general fund and therefore, in practice, any tax may be used to finance current Social Security benefits. In contrast to the first option, this one requires that overall nonpayroll tax revenues be raised so that there would be no corresponding increase in the budget deficit or decrease in non-Social Security spending. Remember that every dollar in nonpayroll taxes funds a dollar of non-Social Security spending and that therefore using nonpayroll taxes to fund Social Security benefits results in a corresponding and equal increase in the budget deficit unless spending on programs other than Social Security is reduced.

A third option is to *directly* reduce Social Security benefits. A direct reduction in benefits would occur when, for example, all benefits are reduced by some fixed percentage. This option is often considered unlikely, because senior citizens are a powerful special interest group and Social Security benefits are entitlements, or benefits, that are perceived to be permanently available to beneficiaries. An *indirect* reduction in benefits may, on the other hand, be more politically viable, as has occurred when Congress raised the age at which full retirement benefits are first available from sixty-five to sixty-seven. Another indirect method by which benefits may be reduced is to reduce the cost-of-living formula that expands benefits each year.

It is important to emphasize at this point that since Social Security is not required to be fully funded, there is no reason to believe that any of these changes will necessarily alter the program from one that carries unfunded liabilities to one that carries fully funded liabilities. Changes in tax rates, benefit levels, income thresholds, and retirement ages have occurred in the past, and none of these has created a fully funded program. These changes merely postpone the date at which the permanent series of annual deficits arrives. Policies that replace the pay-as-you-go funding constraint with a fully funded constraint is another matter, which we will examine later.

Social Security Is a Transfer Program

The Social Security program is quite unlike any pension fund that would exist in the private market, for it serves both insurance and transfer functions. Private carriers serve only the insurance function, which characterizes programs that fund retirement benefits solely on the basis of contributions made during workers' earning years. Since Social Security benefits are only loosely tied to taxes paid, the program therefore should be only loosely considered an insurance program. Social Security transfers income in two fundamental ways, and the following discussion clearly shows how.

Intragenerational Transfers

Intragenerational transfers are transfers of Social Security benefits among members of the same generation.

One source of transfer occurs *within* a given generation. **Intragenerational transfers** occur because, within a given generation, different replacement rates face different Social Security beneficiaries. For example, consider two individuals who have contributed to Social Security during the same periods and whose income histories have always been above the income thresholds that define the ceilings under which payroll taxes are applied. Transfers are possible because even though they have contributed identical sums of Social Security taxes, their benefits will not necessarily be identical. When retirees, within a given generation, receive different benefit to tax ratios, transfers occur. Those with low benefit to tax ratios tend to transfer income to beneficiaries with high benefit to tax ratios.

The primary source of intragenerational transfers is from high-income to low-income individuals[11] The main reason that transfers flow in this direction is, as Figure 12-3 showed, current formulas for replacement rates are highest for low-income workers. Under current policy, for example, it takes 4.1 years for a married worker to recover (in benefits) all Social Security taxes when he or she retires at age sixty-five after working since age twenty-one at the federal minimum wage.[12] In contrast, if the same worker had always earned the income threshold, all taxes would be recovered only after 7.2 years. The difference, however, is probably smaller when it is recognized that lower-income recipients tend to face relatively higher mortality rates. Another study reported that households in the lowest income quintile received 20 percent of Social Security benefits and paid less than 2 percent of Social Security taxes in 1990.[13] Households in the top quintile, in contrast, paid 47 percent of all payroll taxes, but received only 11 percent of total benefits.

Intergenerational Transfers

Intergenerational transfers are transfers of Social Security benefits among members of different generations.

The other source of transfers occurs *across* generations. **Intergenerational transfers** occur because current benefits are paid by the taxes of today's workers. Workers of today therefore transfer income, in the form of payroll taxes, to current Social Security beneficiaries, who include retirees, survivors, and disabled individuals. While it is true that past payroll taxes of current beneficiaries paid for benefits of yesterday's beneficiaries, we have shown that taxes paid by current beneficiaries have not been saved in trust funds. Transfers flow from future generations of beneficiaries to current beneficiaries.

What accounts for intergenerational transfers? One reason is that, as shown in Table 12-1, tax rates and income thresholds have been greatly expanded over the life of the Social Security program. Consider, for example, an individual who retired in

---

[11] This is in contrast to the common perception that the payroll tax is regressive. However, such perceptions are based on the observation that taxes are paid proportionally only up to an income threshold and high-income individuals therefore tend to pay a smaller percentage of income in payroll taxes than low-income individuals. However, it is important to factor in the benefits received. Benefits to tax ratios tend to be highest for low-income individuals.

[12] As discussed in *Economic Report of the President,* February 1992, 142.

[13] *Economic Report of the President,* February 1992, 142.

1961 after paying taxes since 1937. Over this working life of twenty-four years, tax rates ranging from 2 percent to 6 percent were applied to income thresholds ranging from $3,000 to $4,800. A worker, however, who retired in 1991 after working the same number of years (since 1967) paid tax rates ranging from 8.8 percent to 15.3 percent on income thresholds ranging from $6,600 to $53,400. This comparison demonstrates that intergenerational transfers occur because earlier generations paid lower taxes than later generations. In other words, the current generation of Social Security beneficiaries paid lower taxes than does the current generation of workers, who are also funding the benefits of the current generation of beneficiaries.

In order to understand the extent of this transfer, we must consider both changes in taxes and benefits over time. One approach to understanding the degree to which transfers take place is to compare Social Security benefits to the value of payroll taxes paid by beneficiaries. One study estimates that roughly 80 percent of the benefits of current retirees are really transfers from the working population.[14] In other words, if tax payments of current beneficiaries had been invested at market interest rates, the value of taxes paid plus interest income would fund only about 20 percent of current benefits. This study therefore suggests that the mix between insurance and transfer functions is currently about 20 percent and 80 percent. This mix has been projected to continue until the early part of the next century when, under current tax and benefit rates, the transfer portion of benefits turns negative.

Another approach to the measurement of this transfer is to compare rates of return on taxes paid by beneficiaries of different generations. For married one-earner couples with median earnings histories who retired in 1970, the rate of return has been calculated to be 8.5 percent.[15] If, however, a comparable couple retired in 1980, the rate of return dropped to 5.9 percent and, for retirement in 1995, a 3.6 percent rate of return was determined. For retirement in 2025, the rate of return fell to only 2.2 percent.

Transfer Function of Government

The trends discussed in this section reflect the growing role of government in the area of income redistribution. While the early years saw Social Security solely as a system of retirement insurance, it has evolved into a primary source of transfer from the federal government to its citizens. Such transfers are dissimilar to those of means-tested programs in that the primary target of transfers are retirees, survivors, and disabled individuals. While some portion of transfers flow to low-income individuals, they are not the only recipients of transfers. Although intragenerational transfers are mainly from higher-income individuals to lower-income individuals, intergenerational transfers flow from future generations of beneficiaries (or current generations of workers) to current generations of beneficiaries (or past generations of workers).

---

[14] Michael J. Boskin, Marcy Avrin, and Kenneth Cone, "Modeling Alternative Solutions to the Long-Run Social Security Funding Crisis," in *Behavioral Simulation Methods in Tax Policy Analysis,* ed. Martin Feldstein (Chicago: University of Chicago Press, 1983).

[15] Table 4.1, panel B, in Michael J. Boskin, *Too Many Promises: The Uncertain Future of Social Security* (Homewood, Ill.: Dow Jones–Irwin, 1986).

Current Social Security Issues

Does Social Security Influence Saving?

Macroeconomics demonstrates the importance that investment plays in macroeconomic performance: In order for there to be investment, there must also be saving. One of the controversial issues surrounding Social Security is whether it affects saving behavior. Some economists believe that Social Security exerts an adverse effect on national savings; it is therefore important for us to question whether this program also exerts an indirect, and adverse, influence on macroeconomic growth.

Because Social Security provides benefits upon retirement, individuals may feel that they have a decreased need to save for their retirement. But we must also recall that some consider Social Security a necessary public program because some individuals will not or cannot voluntarily save for their retirement. To the extent that such individuals exist, there would appear to be little reason to believe that Social Security adversely affects saving behavior of individuals who are not believed to save any income for retirement in the first place.

We must also ask what effect Social Security might exert on the saving behaviors of individuals who, in its absence, would voluntarily save some portion of their income for retirement. If these individuals believed that Social Security was a substitute for their own saving, Social Security might exert a negative influence on their saving behavior. This influence may be described as a crowding-out effect whereby Social Security taxes crowd out some portion of workers' private savings.

Saving behavior is also believed to be linked with decisions regarding retirement. Social Security may influence these decisions because the program allows workers to collect benefits upon retirement. It may therefore create incentives for workers (as well as survivors and disabled individuals) to take earlier retirement than if it did not exist.[16] Moreover, since benefits are subject to income taxes after an income threshold is reached, Social Security may also create an incentive for workers to refrain from working after retirement; if this happens, it would tend to depress saving as well.

To the extent that Social Security crowds out private savings, this program increases saving by an amount smaller than payroll tax collections. The extent to which workers view Social Security benefits as substitutes for personal savings determines the degree to which total (private plus public) savings change as a result of the program. It should also be remembered that to the extent that personal savings are crowded out by Social Security taxes, total saving falls, since surpluses are not saved in the trust funds. Our discussion of the pay-as-you-go funding constraint suggests that surpluses do not represent net additions to national saving. It is ironic that if the program was established as a means of having the government save for the retirement of workers who could not or would not voluntarily undertake their own saving, the Social Security program does not save for the retirements of these workers either.

---

[16] One study attributes much of the decline in labor participation of the elderly during the 1970s to rising real benefit levels; see Michael J. Boskin and Michael Hurd, "The Effect of Social Security on Retirement in the early 1970s," *Quarterly Journal of Economics* (November 1984): 767–790.

One counterview that has attracted a great deal of controversy is that because Social Security provides a source of savings for parents, they will tend to be able to save more for their heirs.[17] If this effect were to offset the previously observed adverse effect of Social Security on saving behavior, then it is possible for the overall effect of the program to be neutral.

There appears to be fairly broad empirical support for the hypothesis that Social Security depresses national saving.[18] One of the problems with testing this hypothesis is that it is difficult to measure national saving. There will surely be much more investigation of this problem in the near future.

Effects on the Federal Budget

Where Do Surpluses Go?

While current definitions list the inflows and outflows of the Social Security program as separate items of the President's budget, for all practical purposes they are treated just like any other government spending and tax program.[19] We have shown that its tax revenues are treated just like any other tax collected by the federal government, and when the permanent string of deficits arrive in the next century, benefits may be funded through a wide variety of options, including changes in Social Security taxes or benefits, as well as increases in non–Social Security taxes or reductions in non–Social Security spending.

But Social Security differs from most other government programs in having its own trust funds. This distinction leads to an important policy issue: Where do surpluses go? We have shown that surplus monies do not actually flow into trust funds but, rather, pour into the general fund of the U.S. Treasury, where they are indistinguishable from any other tax revenue. No rules are placed on the ways in which these funds are used, although it is useful to list the possibilities. One option is to finance spending on programs other than Social Security. For instance, a new health care program could be funded, or an existing program could be expanded. Another option is to lower other taxes. For instance, a surplus of $85 billion could be substituted for $85 billion in income tax revenue. Still another option is to lower the overall budget deficit. There are no rules regarding which, or which combination, of these options is used in response to the long string of annual surpluses in Social Security. It is important, however, to recognize that only the last option, lowering the overall budget

---

[17] See Robert J. Barro, "Are Government Bonds Net Wealth?" *Journal of Political Economy* 82 (November–December 1974): 1095–1117.

[18] For a contrast of views on this issue see Martin S. Feldstein, "Social Security, Induced Retirement, and Aggregate Capital Formation," *Journal of Political Economy* 82 (September–October 1974): 905–926, which argues that Social Security has depressed personal saving by 50 percent; and Alicia H. Munnell, "The Impact of Social Security on Personal Saving," *National Tax Journal* (April 1974): 553–568, which finds a smaller, but significant, depressing effect on personal saving.

[19] For a history of the relationship of Social Security to the federal budget see Alicia H. Munnell, "Social Security and the Budget," *New England Economic Review* 27 (July–August 1985): 5–18. While Congress terms Social Security off-budget, this use of the term *off-budget* is not consistent with that developed in Chapter 10. *Off-budget* here means only that Social Security is excluded from the President's main set of budget figures but is still used in all federal budget calculations.

deficit, represents an overall increase in government saving. The first two options either expand overall spending of the federal government or reduce tax burdens in other areas of the budget.

Empirical evidence suggests that surpluses are used to finance overall expansion of federal spending.[20] The implication here is that so long as surpluses occur, the Social Security program has important stimulative effects on the size of government. Further, because surpluses do not expand government saving, the program does not add to the future productive capacity of the economy. Social Security surpluses appear to be simply borrowed by the government to finance current spending in other areas of the budget.

Measurement of Overall Budget Deficit

Under present law, surpluses and deficits of the Social Security program are included in computations of federal budget deficits. An important implication is that surpluses (deficits) reduce (increase), by an equal amount, sizes of federal budget deficits. To demonstrate the extent to which recent surpluses have influenced sizes of budget deficits, consider Figure 12-5, which plots two views of federal budget deficits—with and without inclusion of Social Security surpluses and deficits. Recent surpluses have clearly lowered federal budget deficits by substantial amounts.

Considerable controversy surrounds inclusion of surpluses in the definition of federal budget deficits. Debate centers on whether inclusion of surpluses provides a misleading picture of the budget deficit. One end of the debate is that surpluses should be excluded because they reflect unfunded liabilities of the federal government, and are not true surpluses. Since evidence suggests that surpluses are not saved, it is argued that current definitions of budget deficits are misleading and may even cause voters and policymakers to be less concerned over the size of current budget deficits than they would be if surpluses were excluded from the definition of the budget deficit.

People on the other end of this debate fear that exclusion of surpluses may lead to reductions in vital non–Social Security spending when the public observes that budget deficits are higher than they had been previously led to believe. As long as budget deficits continue to be a critical source of concern, targeted by deficit-reduction laws, exclusion of surpluses from the definition of the federal budget deficit would clearly lead to substantial increases in budget deficits that might be remedied through spending reductions in other areas of the budget.

Notice that this debate appears to center over the issue of the effects of budgetary definitions on perceptions of the fiscal affairs of the federal government. Clearly, different views exist on the question of whether it is appropriate to include Social Security surpluses in the definition of the budget deficit, but this debate clearly indicates that the Social Security program is intimately involved with all aspects of the federal budget. Social Security is not a separate entity of the federal government because its taxes and spending influence many other aspects of the overall budget, and budgetary definitions do appear to influence spending trends of the federal government.

---

[20] W. Mark Crain and Michael L. Marlow, "The Causal Relationship between Social Security and the Federal Budget," in *Social Security's Looming Surpluses: Prospects and Implications,* ed. Carolyn L. Weaver (Washington, D.C.: AEI Press, 1990).

**FIGURE 12-5
Federal Budget
Deficits with and
without Social
Security**

Source: Congressional Budget Office, *Economic and Budget Outlook*, 1994.

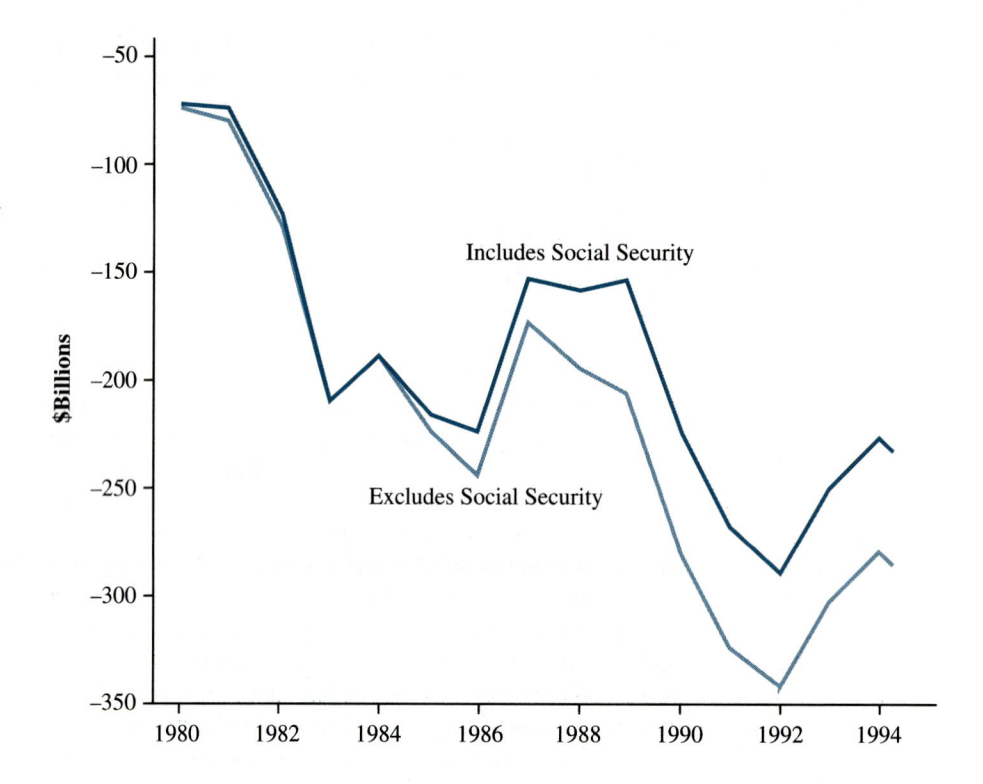

Reforming Social Security

Generational Accounting

Current accounting definitions do not provide a clear picture of the future liabilities of the Social Security program. It has been proposed that a system of generational accounts be set up that would describe the effects of today's Social Security policies on different generations.[21] Our previous discussion of income transfers within and across generations suggests that **generational accounting** would indicate increases in the wealth of today's generation and decreases in the expected wealth of future generations.

Such a revamping of the accounting system would clearly appeal to many economists, but serious political complications might make this reform politically inviable. Such a change not only creates an entirely new budgeting environment for policymakers but may also lead to a change in public perception of the Social Security program. Policymakers who promote fundamental changes in the Social Security program, if they do anything other than increasing benefits, tend not to win reelection.

Generational accounting is a method of recording long-term liabilities in order to measure their impact on future generations.

---

[21] For example, see Laurence J. Kotlikoff, "The Social Security 'Surpluses'—New Clothes for the Emperor?" in *Social Security's Looming Surpluses: Prospects and Implications,* ed. Carolyn L. Weaver (Washington, D.C.: AEI Press, 1990).

If a new accounting system caused voters to believe that they had been previously (and purposively) misled about the financing of the Social Security program, they might severely discipline incumbent policymakers. For example, if voters believed that it was only an insurance program, they might be upset to learn that their tax payments had never been saved for their retirement. The apparent high political costs to any politician who promotes significant changes in this program make it unlikely that a new accounting system will be approved in the near future.

Cutting the Payroll Tax

In the late 1980s, Senator Daniel Patrick Moynihan argued that the payroll tax should be rolled back until annual surpluses no longer exist. The primary rationale for this proposal was based on the argument that because surpluses are not saved in the trust funds, Social Security should become a true pay-as-you-go system whereby taxes equal benefits on an annual basis. The current system of projecting annual surpluses has been called a system of advance funding; when taxes exceed benefits in a given year, the U.S. Treasury places IOUs in the trust funds and uses the surplus cash for other purposes. Because these surpluses are not saved, Senator Moynihan argued that payroll taxes should be lowered annually until they equal Social Security benefits. A secondary rationale for this proposal was to lower tax burdens on workers.

An interesting aspect of the Moynihan proposal is how it dealt with the huge unfunded liabilities of the Social Security program. In order to maintain an equality of taxes and benefits during each budget year, tax rates were to be eventually raised when baby boomer retirements led to adverse changes in worker-beneficiary ratios. The proposal called for lowering the combined tax rate from 15.3 percent to 13.1 percent in 1992 and, after remaining constant until 2012, gradual increases to 19.1 percent by 2045 would create an equality between outflows and inflows in each budget year.

Congress met the Moynihan proposal with great opposition. This is not surprising, for his proposal would create some particularly difficult short-term problems for Congress. First and foremost, removal of annual surpluses would immediately lead to an equivalent increase in the federal budget deficit. For example, consider the projected surplus of $125 billion for 1995 as shown in Table 12-2. A cut in the payroll tax of $125 billion would raise the federal budget deficit by the same amount and might lead to substantial changes in other parts of the federal budget. Given the growing public sentiment against rising budget deficits, as well as the balanced budget rules discussed in Chapter 9, it is likely that increases in non–Social Security taxes or lowering of non–Social Security spending would result from the Moynihan proposal.

It is not surprising that members of Congress may prefer not to make the difficult budgetary choices that would surface under this plan. It should also be noted, however, that the proposal does directly deal with the unfunded liabilities of the current program since it calls for increasing payroll taxes in the future as adverse changes in worker to beneficiary ratios occur. This was clearly a bold step in the direction of dealing with this important and highly controversial policy issue. Note, however, that unlike a system of generational accounts, this proposal does not provide a means of reflecting future, although now funded, liabilities into today's annual budgetary measures.

Privatization

Another reform option is to privatize the Social Security system, allowing private markets to provide its services. There is, however, an important issue that must be addressed before this proposal can be seriously considered. We have shown that the two functions of this program are to provide retirement insurance and to transfer income. The private market, however, would not be inclined to undertake the latter function. Unless it somehow undertakes both functions, privatization would result in a fundamental redirection of the Social Security program. There are undoubtedly those who are happy to eliminate the transfer function, but there are also those who are adamantly opposed to dropping the transfer function. With this potential controversy in mind, we now proceed with various options for privatizing that do not eliminate both functions.

Let us concentrate on the insurance function first and remember that proponents of paternalism tend to believe that public provision of retirement insurance is necessary in order to make sure that all workers have retirement savings. Because some individuals will not voluntarily save for their retirement, mandatory participation in Social Security is often believed to be appropriate. The trick, then, is to devise a system whereby all workers save for their retirement. This could be accomplished by requiring that all workers invest some percentage of their salary in a private pension fund, such as an individual retirement (IRA) account.[22] For this reason, there should be little debate concerning this aspect of privatization and, in fact, the fact that private pension funds have greatly expanded in recent years suggests that private markets may easily take over the insurance function of the Social Security program. As a means of producing a standardized program, there is also no reason that the federal government could not set minimum standards for the insurance coverage.

The design of a private system of income transfers is more problematic. One simple solution would be to disengage the insurance function from Social Security, transforming it into a government program that only transfers income. The transfer function could also be simply transferred to another government agency, administered in much the same as way as the many means-tested transfers that were examined in the previous chapter. In this way, private firms would be responsible only for the insurance function. A more complex problem would be to require private pension funds to perform the transfer function. While in theory this could be accomplished by legislation requiring that firms provide a set mix of retirement insurance and transfers, advocates of privatization do not usually promote this option.

At this point, it is appropriate to ask what possible gains might occur under privatization. At least two important benefits might be realized through privatization. First, private pension funds might be expected to be fully funded. The importance of saving for economic growth has been discussed before, and there is much reason to believe that privatization would expand saving more than the current Social Security system has been able to accomplish. There may, however, be concerns as to whether policymakers could exert undue political pressure as to where private firms invest surplus funds.

---

[22] For example, see James M. Buchanan, "Social Insurance in a Growing Economy: A Proposal for Radical Reform," *National Tax Journal* 19 (December 1968): 386–395.

Second, privatization may be expected to expand program quality when it introduces competition into the market for retirement income. The Social Security system is currently a federal monopoly that commands mandatory participation of virtually every worker in the United States. The percentage of the civilian work force covered under Social Security was over 92 percent in 1991, and the 1983 amendments to the Social Security Act granted coverage to virtually every new hire in the work force.[23] Privatization of Social Security could lead to increases in competition in various ways. One is to allow all workers the option of contributing to the federal program or to a private one.[24] Under this system, it would be predicted that competition might lead to higher quality programs since when workers can withdraw their savings from one program to another, managers become more careful about the programs they offer to their customers. This would be similar to banking in that customers are free to choose the banks they feel are best suited to their needs.

Our discussion poses serious questions about the political viability of privatization. Removal of Social Security surpluses from the general tax fund would create a new budgetary environment, and it would not be supported by all policymakers or Social Security beneficiaries. Privatization would affect public perception of government performance in this area and, to the extent that voters were unhappy, policymakers might not desire changes in the status quo. Finally, privatization brings the distinction between insurance and transfer functions to the forefront of public discussion. If it is believed that many voters are unaware of the transfer portion of the program, policymakers may not wish to open themselves up to the possible criticism that would occur when public debate clarifies the distinction.

Medicare

Background on Health Care Costs

In 1992, 26.7 million individuals, or 14.1 percent of the U.S. population, were uninsured.[25] Projections have been made that by the year 2000, there will be 39.2 million uninsured individuals, constituting 14.6 percent of the U.S. population. To understand how rapidly health care costs are rising, consider Table 12-3, which shows that health care expenditures are projected to expand from 6 percent to 18 percent of GDP over 1965–2000. The role of the federal government in paying for health care is projected to roughly double from 24.7 percent to 48.3 percent over this same time span.

Introduced in 1965 and, as shown in Table 12-3, Medicare spending is projected to rise to 18.6 percent of all health care spending by 2000. The other major federal health care program is Medicaid, discussed in the previous chapter. Spending on Medicare and Medicaid programs rose from 8 percent of total federal spending in 1980 to 14 percent in 1994 and is projected to account for 23 percent of the budget by 2000.[26] Projected expansions of these programs suggest that, by 2000, Medicare and

---

[23] *Statistical Abstract of the United States,* 1993.

[24] Another option would be to allow the fifty state governments to provide their programs as substitutes for the federal program.

[25] Congressional Budget Office, "Projections of National Health Expenditures," October 1992.

[26] Congressional Budget Office, "Projections of National Health Expenditures," October 1992.

TABLE 12-3
Projections of National Health Expenditures

Year	Percent of Public Share	Percent of GDP	Percent Medicare of Total Health Expenditure
1965	24.7%	6.0%	0.0%
1980	42.0	9.2	14.0
1985	41.4	10.5	16.5
1990	42.4	12.1	16.1
1995[b]	46.5	15.1	16.8[a]
2000	48.3	18.0	18.6

[a] Value in 1992.
[b] Figures for 1995 and 2000 are projections.
Source: Table 2, "Projections of National Health Expenditures," Congressional Budget Office, October 1992.

Medicaid spending will exceed spending on Social Security, currently the largest federal program.

Rationales for Public Health Insurance

What sources of market failure may exist in the case of health insurance? One common argument is that private health insurance is subject to the problem of adverse selection whereby those at greatest risk of having health problems are those that have the highest demand for insurance. This being so, firms tend to raise premiums, thus discouraging applications from low-risk individuals. Private insurance may therefore be relatively expensive, as well as characterized by an unfavorable risk pool of insurees.

While there is some controversy concerning whether private insurance companies are able to set individual insurance premiums in line with the risk characteristics of applicants, many believe that private insurance markets fail to allocate resources efficiently. Even with coinsurance and deductibles, insurance coverage makes it cheaper for individuals to consume health care and to have less concern over controlling costs of medical care. Insurance coverage appears to increase the frequency with which individuals visit doctors and request expensive medical tests. From the point of view of individuals, the fact that there is little incentive to control one's health care costs may result in overallocation of resources into health care markets.

Remember, however, that social insurance programs are not necessarily interested in promoting allocative efficiency. Even if it were believed that private health insurance markets are efficient, there might be concerns over equity in those markets. For example, it may be believed that even though it is efficient for private insurance firms to charge relatively high premiums to high-risk, elderly individuals, public programs should subsidize costs of insurance for these individuals. This is similar to the reasoning for the transfer portions of Social Security. Medicare is really no different, since a substantial portion of this program serves a transfer function as well.

Characteristics of Medicare

There are two parts of the Medicare program:

❑ Hospital insurance (HI, or Part A)
❑ Supplemental medical insurance (SMI, or Part B)

Hospital insurance helps pay costs of inpatient hospital stays as well as post-hospital care of eligible individuals. Supplemental medical insurance pays a portion of doctor bills and outpatient health costs, and coverage only extends to those eligible for the hospital insurance portion and who pay a separate monthly premium. In 1989, Medicare coverage was expanded to include protection against catastrophic hospital bills that would wipe out the savings of beneficiaries.

All individuals are eligible for Medicare when they reach age sixty-five; however, under sixty-five, certain disabled individuals are eligible for hospital insurance. During 1992, 12.9 percent of the population was covered by Part A, and virtually all of these opted for the voluntary portion, or Part B, as well. Medicaid, in contrast, covered 8.3 percent of the population during this same year. By 2000, Medicare is projected to cover 13.3 percent, and Medicaid to cover 10.1 percent, of the population.[27]

Part A of Medicare is mostly funded through the payroll tax. As of 1994, the combined tax rate of 2.9 percent is applied against an unlimited income threshold. Roughly one-fourth of Part B is funded through insurance premiums, with remaining funds coming from the general tax fund of the federal government.

All signals point toward continued rapid expansion of costs of Medicare. While part of this expansion may be predicted by growth in the elderly population, more generous payment formulas are projected for the future. While several methods have been employed to attempt to control cost expansion of this program, there is a consensus that past remedies have not been entirely successful. For example, the prospective payment system (PPS) was introduced in the mid-1980s as a means of controlling the rapidly increasing costs of Part A of Medicare. The PPS was designed to better control hospital admissions and to pay a fixed fee to hospitals based on the illness of the individual, or what is called the diagnosis-related group (DRG). This system was also designed to prevent using this part of the Medicare program as a program of long-term care of the elderly. While PPS has been believed to have slowed the expansion of costs in the 1980s, it has been projected that Part A will expand at 9 percent to 10 percent a year in the 1990s as DRG payment rates and length of hospital stays expand.[28]

Medicare trust funds are comprised of IOUs provided by the federal government whenever Medicare collections of Social Security taxes exceed current Medicare spending.

Medicare Trust Funds

Part A of Medicare is financed through payroll taxes and **Medicare trust funds** (HI) were established at the time this program was approved in 1965, as had been done thirty years earlier with Social Security. Because Medicare operates under a pay-as-you-go operating constraint, many of the same concerns expressed over Social

---

[27] Congressional Budget Office, "Projections of National Health Expenditures," October 1992, 38.
[28] Congressional Budget Office, "Projections of National Health Expenditures," October 1992, 43.

Security also apply to Medicare. Transfers under this program are similar to those of Social Security and need not be discussed here. Medicare surpluses are also included in the definition of the federal budget deficit and lead to identical concerns to those expressed in our discussion of Social Security.

Table 12-4 displays actual and projected surpluses, deficits, and trust fund balances for Medicare. Current annual surpluses are projected to continue to roughly 2000, when a permanent string of rising annual deficits is projected to appear. Medicare is therefore projected to encounter serious financial problems much sooner than Social Security. Permanent annual deficits are projected by 2000, thirty years before those of Social Security. Trust fund balances of Medicare are projected to turn negative by 2005, or forty-five years before those of Social Security.

Differences in the timing at which the two programs are projected to run permanent annual deficits and operate under negative balances in the trust funds are undoubtedly due to a larger mismatch between tax inflows and benefit outflows for the

TABLE 12-4
Medicare: Surpluses, Deficits, and Trust Fund Balances ($Billions)

	Surplus/Deficit		Trust Fund Balance		
Year	Current Dollars	1989 Dollars	Current Dollars	1989 Dollars	% of GNP
1960	0	0	1	0	0
1970	1	−8	3	8	−7
1980	1	1	14	22	4
1990	13	13	85	85	10
1995	2	2	140	113	−14
2000	−24	−15	107	70	−65
2005	−68	−36	−71	−39	−130
2010	−153	−67	−550	−247	−198
2015	−297	−106	−1,557	−576	−247
2020	−557	−163	−3,508	−1,066	−281
2025	−997	−241	−7,108	−1,776	−316
2030	−1,680	−331	−13,383	−2,748	−359
2035	−2,676	−435	−23,665	−3,994	−415
2040	−4,095	−546	−39,746	−5,513	−485
2045	−6,111	−670	−64,048	−7,302	−561
2050	−8,996	−811	−99,335	−9,308	−631
2055	−13,126	−973	−151,980	−11,705	−705
2060	−19,029	−1,158	−228,585	−14,471	−780

Source: Carolyn L. Weaver, ed., *Social Security's Looming Surpluses: Prospects and Implications* (Washington, D.C.: AEI Press, 1990). Reprinted with permission.

Medicare program. When Medicare begins to run permanent annual deficits in 2000, policymakers have the following options. First, payroll taxes could be raised to support more inflows into the Medicare trust funds. Second, Medicare benefits could be reduced. Third, taxes could be raised or spending could be reduced in areas other than Medicare. It is quite possible, for example, that because the Social Security program is projected to operate under large annual surpluses for thirty years longer than the Medicare program, Social Security taxes may fund some of the shortfall in the Medicare program. This is not certain, however, since there will undoubtedly be many competing claims for those surplus funds by programs other than Medicare.

While many identical issues of concern arise in both Social Security and Medicare, several reasons suggest that fundamental changes in the Medicare program may occur long before changes in Social Security. *One* reason is purely financial and is based on the conventional wisdom that policy changes occur more readily when financial problems appear more immediate. As just discussed, the Medicare program is projected to operate under permanent annual deficits many years before Social Security. As with Social Security, however, there is no way of knowing which methods will be chosen to meet funding shortfalls. But it may be instructive to remember that when the Social Security system has run deficits in the past, surpluses were created by raising payroll tax rates. Clearly, these short-term adjustments have not solved the long-term mismatch between inflows and outflows, but tax increases temporarily postpone financing crises. Similar strategy may be employed in the Medicare program.

Another reason is that there is growing public sentiment for fundamental change in the health care industry. President Clinton, for example, campaigned on a pledge to reform health care, and only time will tell how these changes will affect Medicare.

Unemployment Insurance

Rationales for Public Unemployment Insurance

We have previously argued that private markets may not have an incentive to supply unemployment insurance. It may be reasonable to expect that adverse selection problems arise with unemployment insurance when workers who are likely to experience relatively high unemployment rates demand more unemployment insurance than workers who expect to have great employment stability. This behavior would not only raise premiums but would make insurance relatively unattractive to low-risk workers, those whom insurance firms find most attractive as insurees. Moral hazard problems may also arise if insurance coverage raises unemployment rates of insurees. Even without consideration of adverse selection and moral hazard problems, government may provide unemployment insurance when it is believed that public provision should transfer income as well as provide insurance to workers.

Characteristics of Unemployment Insurance

Unemployment insurance was part of the original Social Security Act of 1935, when unemployment was a national crisis. This social insurance program, which is operated by state governments within federal rules, provides benefits to unemployed workers. The program is mostly financed through payroll taxes, and coverage extends to over 90 percent of the civilian work force. While a tax rate is applied to a given threshold of taxable wages, this payroll tax is unlike Social Security and Medicare because taxes are only assessed on employers. The federal government collects the tax but generally releases all funds to state governments.

Benefits are only available for workers who have been laid off from work, and workers who have voluntarily quit their jobs are therefore not eligible to collect benefits. First-time workers are not eligible either; only workers with a work history may collect benefits. States usually allow a maximum of twenty-six weeks, during which unemployed workers may collect benefits. In 1989, recipients of this program spent an average duration of 13.3 weeks collecting unemployment benefits. There are, however, cases where the federal government extends the number of weeks of eligibility during periods of low economic growth and high unemployment.

Total spending on this program was $35.5 billion in 1993.[29] The average weekly benefit in 1991 was $170, with a high of $222 in Massachusetts and a low of $111 in Louisiana.[30] Benefit levels depend on a multitude of factors, such as previous income, size of family, which state the worker resides in, and many others. As shown in Figure 12-6, unemployment compensation, as a percentage of GDP, is strongly related to national rates of unemployment, since the higher the number of unemployed workers, the greater the number of claims for unemployment benefits. It is also apparent that, unlike Social Security and Medicare, the unemployment insurance program has not experienced rapid expansion. Rather, spending on the program buffers the economy during recessions by insuring incomes of unemployed workers.

How Unemployment Insurance Transfers Income

The principal means of transfer is from workers with stable employment histories to workers with frequent periods of unemployment. This transfer occurs as a result of the financing system, which is directly paid by employers, though the taxes lower other types of workers' compensation (for example, salaries and fringe benefits). Since all workers pay this tax, transfers flow from those that tend to collect benefits to those who do not. Even though tax rates are loosely based on the lay-off experience of firms, tax burdens are not entirely based on the likelihood that workers will collect benefits. Current tax structures have been found to provide large transfers, or subsidies, to workers in firms with relatively high lay-off experiences.[31] Transfers also tend to occur as a result of low-income workers tending to have higher replacement rates than high-income workers.

---

[29] *Budget of the United States Government,* 1995.

[30] *Statistical Abstract of the United States,* 1993, Table 598.

[31] Robert Topel, "Financing Unemployment Insurance: History, Incentives, and Reform," in *Unemployment Insurance: The Second Half-Century,* ed. W. Lee Hansen and James F. Byers (Madison, Wis.: University of Wisconsin Press, 1990).

FIGURE 12-6
Unemployment Compensation and the Unemployment Rate

Sources: Budget of the United States Government, 1995; and The Economic Report of the President, 1994.

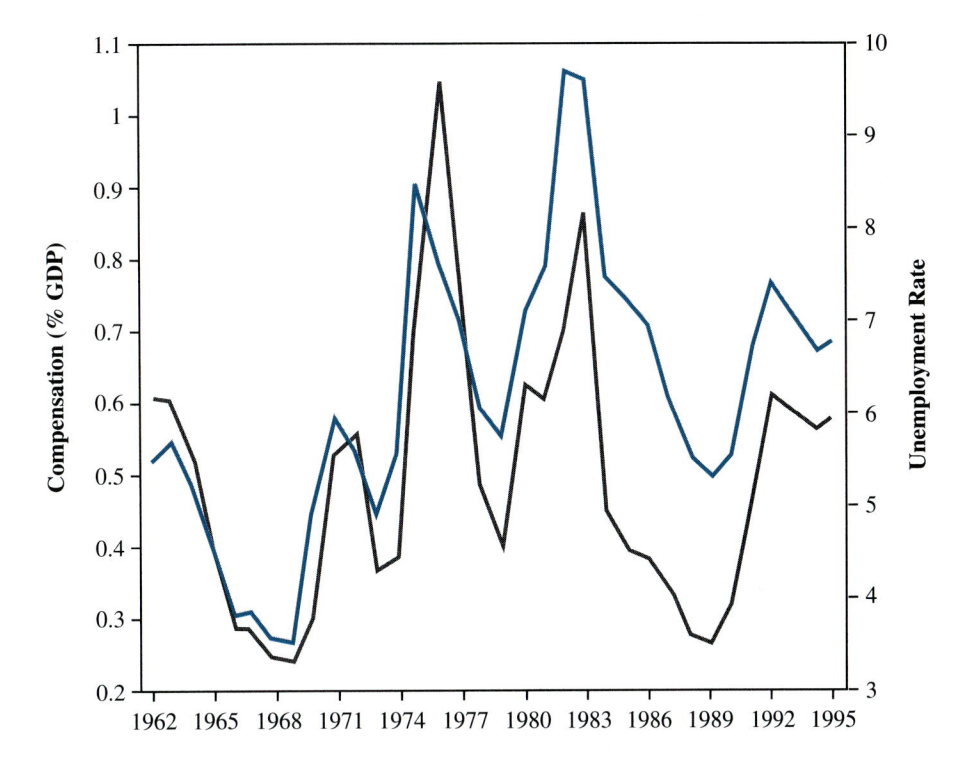

Economic Effects of Unemployment Insurance

There is strong empirical support for the hypothesis that insurance coverage extends the length of unemployment of beneficiaries.[32] One study finds that as much as 20 percent of unemployment of covered workers is caused by unemployment insurance.[33] It is important to recognize, however, that this is not necessarily an undesirable outcome. There is little argument among economists that there exists some optimal degree of unemployment in an economy, and therefore longer and more frequent periods of unemployment may be the result of workers attempting to search for jobs that better match their skills. Consider, for instance, a computer programmer who has just recently been laid off, through no fault of her own. Even if she is immediately offered another job, it is doubtful that first job offers represent good matches with her skills. Jobs may be offered in fields in which she has no interest or possibly in areas in which she has little aptitude. If several weeks in search for better jobs result in a job offer

---

[32] See Sheldon Danziger, Robert H. Haveman, and Robert Plotnick, "How Income Transfer Programs Affect Work, Savings, and the Income Distribution: A Critical Survey," *Journal of Economic Literature* 19 (September 1981): 975–1028, for a review of studies showing that higher unemployment compensation is associated with higher unemployment duration. For a study that takes a different view of the literature, see Anthony B. Atkinson and John Mickelwright, "Unemployment Compensation and Labor Market Transitions," *Journal of Economic Literature* 29 (December 1991): 1679–1727.

[33] Robert Topel, "Financing Unemployment Insurance: History, Incentives, and Reform."

that better matches her skills and interest, she would be better off not accepting first job offers. Because insurance subsidizes searches for better employment, evidence showing that unemployment is positively related to benefits may not imply that unemployment insurance misallocates resources.[34]

Another view is that higher incidence and duration of unemployment occur as a result of workers taking advantage of an insurance program that subsidizes unemployment. Under this view, raising benefit replacement rates, or extending the number of weeks in which benefits may be received, provides workers with higher incentives to remain unemployed and not seriously search for new, or better, employment opportunities. A recent study suggests that unemployment duration would rise an average of 1.5 weeks for an increase of ten percentage points in the replacement rate.[35] This finding raises the following important trade-off issue: We wish to provide adequate income replacement for those who are temporarily out of work and searching for new employment, but we do not wish to create an incentive for some workers to take undue advantage of the program.

Although concerns have been voiced that policies may have tended toward creating an incentive for individuals to stay out of work longer than is desirable, recent trends in benefits suggest that if this remains a problem, it is diminishing over time. Replacement rates have been falling for many years and, as recent as 1991, averaged only 36.5 percent of weekly wages.[36] If replacement rates continue to remain at this rate, or continue to fall, it would appear that incentives for idle unemployment are not particularly high. In fact, at these replacement rates, there may be legitimate claims that the program unduly reduces incentives for workers to undertake searches for reasonably good job matches.[37]

Concluding Observations

Our discussion so far has assumed that policymakers are solely motivated either to provide policies that enhance allocative efficiency or meet the equity goals of society. In Chapter 7, however, other assumptions about the behaviors of voters, special interest groups, and policymakers suggested otherwise and should not be ignored in examining social insurance policies. One important consideration, and its possible implications for future policy, is particularly interesting.

Special interests groups often persuade policymakers to provide policies that transfer income to themselves. We called this rent-seeking behavior and argued that there is

---

[34] Unemployment insurance may also encourage entry into the labor market. Because it reduces the costs of becoming employed, more individuals may therefore seek employment when provided with the security of knowing benefits are available should they become unemployed. See Milton Friedman's Nobel Lecture, "Inflation and Unemployment," *Journal of Political Economy* 85 (June 1977): 451–472.

[35] Bruce C. Meyer, "Unemployment Insurance and Unemployment Spells," *Econometrica* 58 (July 1990): 757–789.

[36] Table 597, *Statistical Abstract of the United States,* 1993.

[37] There also appears to be a growing interest in providing unemployment insurance programs that provide training for the unemployed as a means of permanently removing individuals from welfare rolls. See, for example, W. Lee Hansen and James F. Byers, "Unemployment Compensation and Restraining: Can a Close Link Be Forged?" in *Unemployment Insurance: The Second Half-Century,* ed. Hansen and Byers.

an incentive for special interest groups to form and lobby policymakers. Senior citizens are a powerful special interest group in this country, and it may not be surprising that they are also the main beneficiaries of social insurance programs. It should also be noted that as the elderly become a growing percentage of the population, their power in the policy process may grow in the future. Expansion of social insurance programs has been credited as the reason that the elderly have been the segment in society that has experienced the greatest growth in income. While in 1970, for example, 25 percent of all persons sixty-five years old and over had incomes at or below the poverty level, this percentage fell to 15.2 percent in 1979 and, in 1991, was at an all-time low of 12 percent.[38] It is therefore reasonable to question whether the theory of rent seeking provides us with a useful understanding of the ways that social insurance programs operate.

This issue of rent seeking is directed at the transfer portion of social insurance programs. Transfers occur within and across generations, and it is clear that social insurance programs are not directly aimed at transferring income to the poor. It has been estimated that, in 1990, roughly $30 billion in federal transfers were received by households with pretax, pretransfer income in the top fifth of all households.[39] It also appears that federal transfers increasingly have been provided to those who are not poor.[40] Means-tested transfers directed at the nonelderly poor are much smaller than the transfers that social insurance policies have sent to the elderly.[41] Given that much of the growth of transfer programs is in the form of social insurance programs, important questions about why transfers should not be more directly aimed at the poor are likely to surface in the future.

Summary

- Social insurance programs provide benefits to individuals and families for loss of income due to retirement, disability, illness, and unemployment. The three major programs are Social Security, Medicare, and unemployment insurance.

- Social Security operates on a pay-as-you-go funding requirement that is required only to meet the current year's outflow of benefits. When the current year's Social Security taxes exceed benefits, a surplus occurs. These surpluses are sent to the U.S. Treasury. The Social Security trust funds consist of accumulated surpluses.

- Social Security deficits arise when current Social Security taxes are less than current benefit payments. Shortfalls are remedied by calling upon the U.S. Treasury to make good on the IOUs in the Social Security trust funds. The IOUs residing in the Social Security trust funds represent a substantial unfunded, and long-term, liability of the federal government. At least three options are available to meet this liability. Social Security taxes may be raised; non-Social Security taxes could be raised; or Social Security benefits could be reduced. Under current tax and benefit policies,

---

[38] *Statistical Abstract of the United States,* 1993.
[39] *Economic Report of the President,* February 1992, 130.
[40] The major premise of Gordon Tullock, *Economics of Income Redistribution* (Boston: Kluwer-Nijhoff Publishing, 1983) is that the vast majority of redistribution policy is not aimed at the poor.
[41] See Isabel V. Sawhill, "Poverty in the U.S.: Why Is It So Persistent?" *Journal of Economic Literature* 26 (September 1988): 1073–1119.

- and demographic projections, continual and rising deficits are projected by the year 2030.
- Social Security provides two functions: insurance and transfer. The insurance function represents the extent to which individual benefits are funded by past tax payments. The transfer function represents the difference. Two types of transfer occur: intragenerational and intergenerational.
- Much controversy surrounds the question of whether Social Security exerts an adverse effect on saving. There is broad empirical support for the hypothesis that Social Security depresses national saving.
- Medicare costs are projected to rise to roughly 19 percent of all health care spending by the year 2000. Medicare is projected to operate under continual and rising deficits by the year 2000, thirty years before similar conditions occur under Social Security.

Review Questions

1. What are social insurance programs? What are the major social insurance programs?
2. What are the major rationales for social insurance programs?
3. How do the insurance functions differ from the transfer functions of social insurance programs?
4. What are the trust funds of the Social Security program?
5. What is meant by the pay-as-you-go funding requirement of Social Security?
6. What major Social Security reforms have been suggested?
7. In what sense is Medicare a social insurance program?

Discussion Questions

1. Distinguish between the insurance and transfer functions of social insurance programs.
2. Explain how means-tested programs and social insurance programs differ in their approach to transferring income to members of society.
3. Contrast the differences between fully funded and pay-as-you-go pension funds.
4. Explain the advantages and disadvantages to having Social Security on a pay-as-you-go basis. In your discussion, specifically address whether it is possible for Social Security to transfer income if it were forced to operate under a fully funded financing constraint.
5. Explain how a growing population may make the Social Security program appear to be more financially stable than it is.
6. Explain the differences between Social Security surpluses, deficits, and trust fund balances. Explain why deficits may appear long before balances in trust funds turn negative.
7. Describe how a system of generational accounts might change the public debate about the Social Security program.
8. Explain why an individual's rate of return from contributions to a social insurance program is positively related to the level of transfer received in the program.
9. Define what is meant by adverse selection and moral hazard. Give specific examples relating to unemployment insurance.
10. Explain why requiring all workers to contribute to unemployment insurance tends to reduce adverse selection problems. Explain why the same may not be true for problems associated with moral hazard.

Key Words

Social Security
Medicare
Unemployment insurance
Insurance function
Transfer function
Private pension

Fully funded pension fund
Social Security taxes
Social Security benefits
Replacement rate
Social Security trust funds
Pay-as-you-go

Social Security surpluses
Social Security deficits
Intragenerational transfers
Intergenerational transfers
Generational accounting
Medicare trust funds

CHAPTER 13

Health Care Policy

Introduction

Americans have access to the best health care providers and medical technology in the world. Gains in life expectancies are, in many respects, testimony in support of the many advances and breakthroughs we have experienced in health care. The downside, however, is that the United States devotes a significantly larger share of its national income to health care than do other industrialized countries. If present trends continue, that share will rise to roughly one-fifth of gross domestic product by the end of this century.

While public debate has only recently focused on the issue of health care, it is important to realize that the public sector has for many years played an active role in allocating resources in this market. Medicaid and Medicare programs are two major federal entitlement programs. Spending on these programs now constitutes roughly 45 percent of national health care expenditures. In response to growing concerns, various reforms to the health care system are currently under consideration. The growing number of Americans who lack health insurance is one recent concern, and because many of the uninsured are single parents and the unemployed, many question the fairness of the allocation of resources in the health care market. It is highly likely that fundamental reform of the health care system will occur in the near future.

Our examination of health care issues focuses on the following questions:

❑ How much do we spend on health care?
❑ What role does the public sector play in health care?
❑ What are the economic implications of rising health care expenditures?
❑ What factors underlie the expansion of health care expenditures?
❑ What are the major proposals for health care reform?

An Expanding Health Care Sector

How Much Do We Spend?

Trends in health care spending are often expressed in terms of shares of gross domestic product. As seen in Figure 13-1, health care spending, as a share of GDP, has rapidly expanded. In 1965, health care spending accounted for 6 percent of GDP.

**FIGURE 13-1
Current and
Projected Health
Care Expenditures**

Source: Congressional Budget Office, *Projections of National Health Care Expenditures,* 1992.

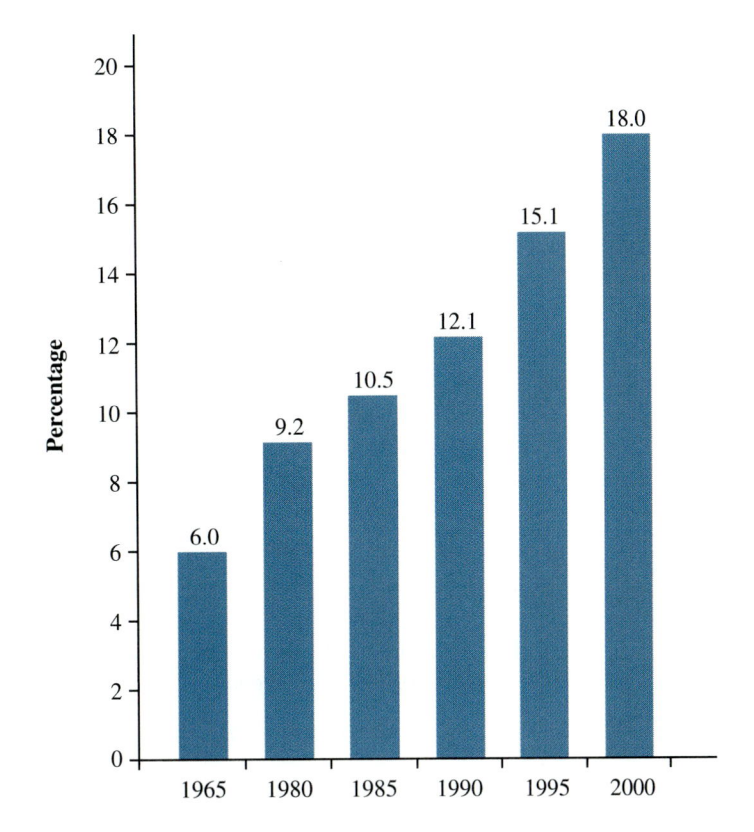

Year	Percentage
1965	6.0
1980	9.2
1985	10.5
1990	12.1
1995	15.1
2000	18.0

Spending is projected to rise to 15 percent of GDP by 1995. Congressional Budget Office (CBO) projects that, under current trends, health care spending will command 18 percent of GDP by 2000. Past and projected trends therefore indicate spending growth far in excess of GDP growth.

The health care sector employs 9 million people in the United States, of whom over 600,000 are physicians.[1] Figure 13-2 lists the major components of health care expenditures in the United States. Hospital-related spending is the largest component, at roughly 39 percent of total spending. There are about 6,500 hospitals, providing over 1 million hospital beds. The second-largest single component of total spending, at 19 percent, is physician services. Next are spending on nursing homes, at 8 percent, and on drugs and other nondurables (such as bandages and home health care products), at 7.3 percent of total spending.

The United States also claims what many believe to be the dubious honor of being the biggest spender on health care. A few comparisons indicate the order of difference. On a per capita basis, the United States spends 1.5 times as much as Canada, 1.7 times as much as Germany, and 2.6 times as much as the United Kingdom.[2] Even

---

[1] *Economic Report of the President,* 1993.

[2] *Economic Report of the President,* 1993.

**FIGURE 13-2
Components of
National Health Care
Expenditures, 1995
Projections**

Source: Congressional Budget Office, *Projections of National Health Care Expenditures,* 1992.

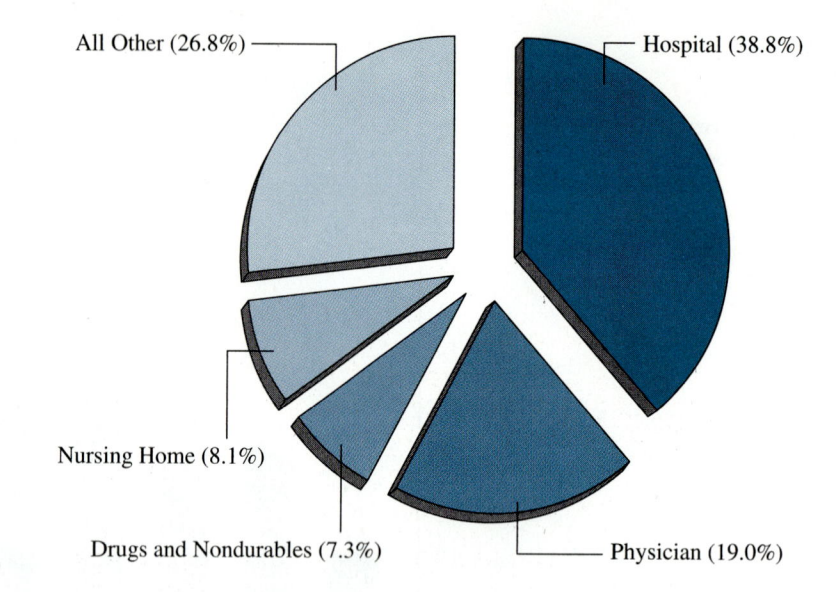

Hospital (38.8%)
All Other (26.8%)
Nursing Home (8.1%)
Drugs and Nondurables (7.3%)
Physician (19.0%)

so, all of these countries have experienced rapid expansion of health care spending since 1960, as Figure 13-3 shows.

Expansion of Public Health Care Spending

As shown in Figure 13-4 the public sector's involvement in the health care sector has expanded rapidly. The fastest growing components of national health care spending are the health entitlement programs, Medicaid and Medicare. They accounted for 26 percent of all national health care spending in 1965, but their share expanded to 45 percent by 1992, and the CBO projects that their share will climb to 48 percent by 2000.[3]

Medicare was created by the federal government to provide health insurance for most people over 65 or with disabilities. The two parts of the Medicare program are hospital insurance and supplemental medical insurance. During 1992, 12.9 percent of the population was covered by hospital insurance, and virtually all of this sector purchased the supplemental insurance portion of Medicare.

Hospital insurance helps pay costs of inpatient hospital stays and any subsequent posthospital care. In 1989, coverage was expanded to include protection against catastrophic hospital bills that would wipe out the savings of beneficiaries. Supplemental medical insurance pays a portion of doctor bills and outpatient health costs. Coverage, however, only extends to those who pay a separate monthly premium. In 1993, the monthly premium was $36.60, and although the premium originally funded one-half of the costs of supplemental insurance, premiums now cover less than one-fourth of costs.[4]

Medicare recipients often purchase **medigap insurance,** which is private insurance and covers insurance deductibles and insurance copayments not paid by

Medigap insurance is private insurance that covers deductibles and insurance copayments not paid by Medicare.

---

[3] Congressional Budget Office, *Projections of National Health Expenditures,* October 1992.
[4] *Economic Report of the President,* 1993.

**FIGURE 13-3
Growth in Health Care Expenditures**

Source: Congressional Budget Office, *Projections of National Health Care Expenditures,* 1992.

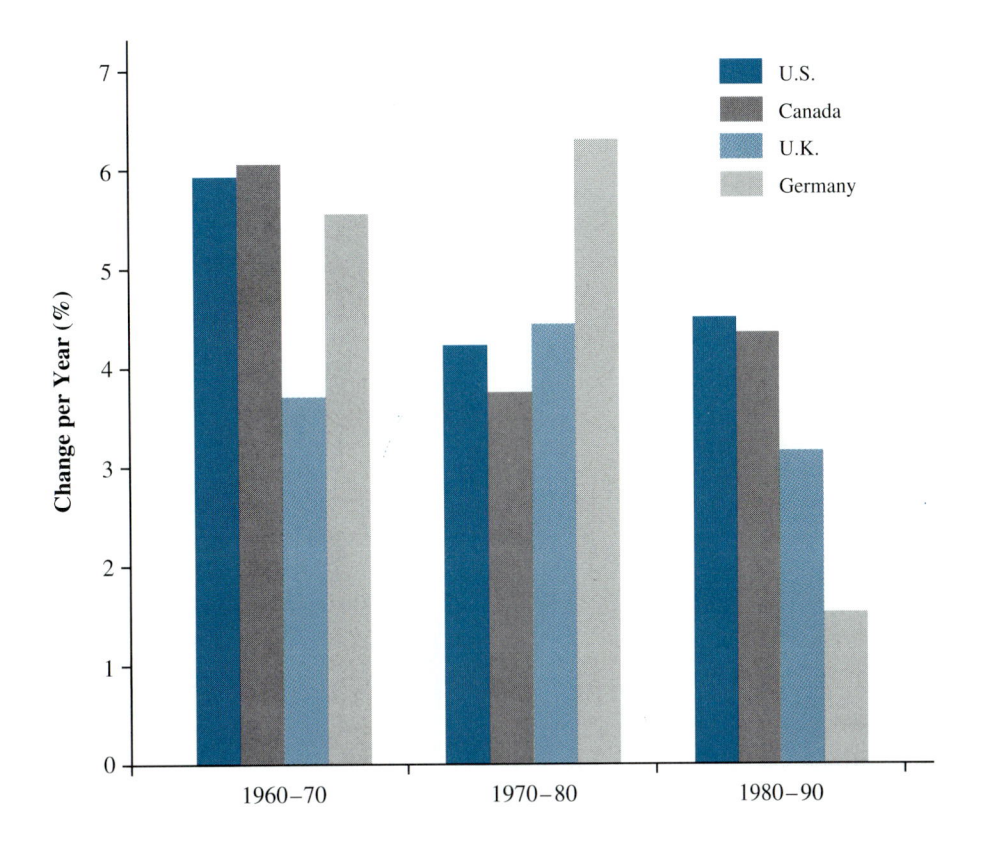

Insurance deductible is the dollar value of medical benefits that must be paid by patients before their insurance company pays for some of or all treatment costs.

Insurance copayment is that percentage of an insurance claim for which the insured is personally responsible.

Medicare. An **insurance deductible,** common in both private insurance and Medicare policies, is the dollar value of medical benefits that must be first paid by patients before their insurance begins covering treatment costs. A deductible of $200, for example, means that the first $200 worth of medical bills must be paid directly by the patient. An **insurance copayment** is the percentage of cost for which the insured is personally responsible. The insurance copayment is required after the insurance deductible is met. A 10 percent copayment, for instance, means that for a $100 health care bill the insured pays $10, and the insurance company pays $90.

Medicaid is the largest means-tested transfer program for the poor. Recipients must normally be below age sixty-five and meet requirements defined by the Aid to Families with Dependent Children program, and in certain cases, poor senior citizens are eligible to have Medicaid pay deductibles and copayments required by Medicare. In 1992, 8.3 percent of the population used Medicaid as their primary source of health insurance.[5] By 2,000, however, CBO projects that this percentage will rise to 10.1 percent—an increase of 22 percent.

Medicaid is operated by both federal and state governments, with the federal share determined by the economic resources of each state. States administer their own

---

[5] Congressional Budget Office, Projections of National Health Expenditures, October 1992.

**FIGURE 13-4
Current and Projected Sources of Health Care Funding**

Source: Congressional Budget Office, *Projections of National Health Care Expenditures*, 1992.

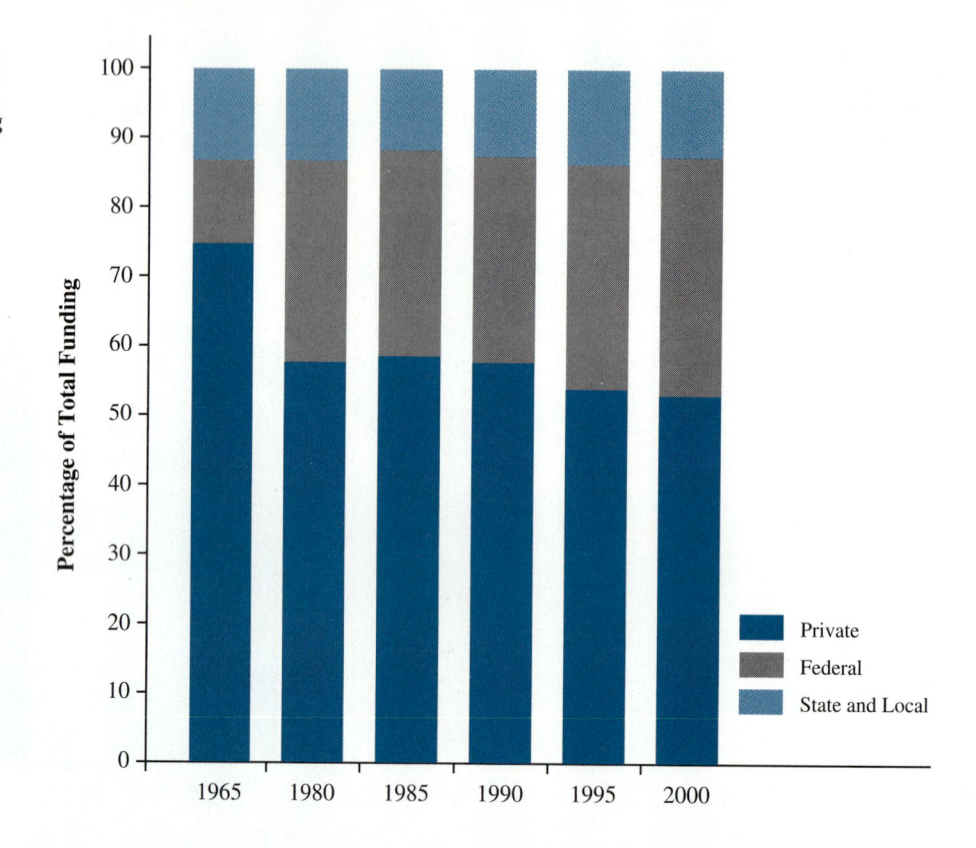

programs, but are subject to strict federal guidelines which outline benefit and eligibility rules. Currently, the federal government funds 43 percent of Medicaid costs but, depending upon the state, contributes from 50 percent to 70 percent of the costs of administering Medicaid programs.[6] While state and local governments also administer their own programs, Medicaid constitutes the single largest health expenditure of these governments.

Is There a Health Care Crisis?

It is difficult to argue that an expanding health care industry is all bad because, in part, rising spending indicates higher quality care that may result in higher quality of life for many individuals. New medical technology fosters some rapid gains in quality but is notoriously costly as well. While economists develop price indices to show how costs of a representative basket of health services, such as physician services, drugs, and hospital care, change over time, indices do not capture corresponding changes in quality. The knowledge of physicians, for example, rises over time, and therefore higher treatment costs are also associated with higher quality of treatments. Simple

---

[6] *Economic Report of the President*, 1993.

comparison of health care costs over time therefore does not indicate by how much or in which ways quality of care has changed.

The observation that quality increases with costs leads some to question whether there is really a health care crisis in the United States. Proponents of this view argue that the U.S. health care system is the envy of the world. Medical care is not only of the highest quality, but care is normally available upon demand, and many Americans have many choices in physicians and hospitals. Cost escalation is therefore the price of an excellent health care system. Proponents of a counterview argue that expansion in health care spending is more reflective of an inefficient system than of rising quality. We will examine, for example, several factors that many believe lead to overconsumption of health care.

It is of course difficult to know which view on cost escalation is correct. Both have merit. We will examine the many factors that lie behind the rise in health care costs, but there are strong indications that much of the rise is due to factors that increase the demand for medical care. In this way, higher consumption is associated with higher quality. It is also clear, however, that various factors lead to overallocation of health care resources, and the U.S. health care system is inefficient in this sense. The bottom line is that both views have some merit and explains why health care policy is a complex subject.

Implications of Rising Health Care Costs

Rising health care costs have important implications in many areas of our economy. This section examines three such implications.

Reduced Access to Health Insurance

Roughly 57 percent of all Americans receive health insurance through their employers.[7] Another 7 percent purchase insurance independently. Most senior citizens receive public health insurance through the Medicare program, often with supplements. Another 6 percent receive public health insurance through Medicaid programs, which currently service roughly one-half of poor Americans. More than 35 million Americans, or 14 percent of the population in 1992, did not have health insurance. The CBO predicts that the uninsured will rise to 39 million Americans by 2000.

Who are the uninsured? Single-parent families, unemployed individuals, and African-Americans constitute the bulk of the uninsured. Most minimum wage workers also have no access to employer-provided health insurance. While some uninsured Americans have the ability to purchase health insurance, others appear to lack access to either private or public insurance programs.

Why Are Some Americans Uninsured?

There are three primary reasons why many people are uninsured.[8] First, because employer-provided insurance is voluntary, some willingly forgo insurance when

---
[7] Congressional Budget Office, *Projections of National Health Expenditures,* October 1992.
[8] Congressional Budget Office, *Economic Implications of Rising Health Costs,* October 1992.

employers do not pick up the full costs of coverage. In some cases, they may be unable to afford insurance, but others may refuse it because they believe their health will remain excellent.

Second, the recent shifting from community rating to experience rating means that some individuals will not be offered insurance or will be required to pay premiums far in excess of the average. *Community rating* is insurance pricing that is based on averages of all insureds; all clients are therefore thrown into a single pool, and no distinction is made between risks of individual clients. *Experience rating,* in contrast, prices on the basis of a client's past history of claims; riskier clients therefore pay higher insurance premiums. Insurance firms may also decline coverage, or exclude various conditions from coverage, when one or more employees have costly health problems. Some of the uninsured certainly fall into this category.

Third, some uninsureds plan to use the subsidized medical care offered in emergency rooms of public hospitals. These people tend to seek medical attention only under medical emergencies, but a significant portion of the uninsured receive their medical care in this fashion.

Rising Costs Reduce Insurance Access

A growing concern is that rising health care costs will cause some employers to lay off full-time employees. Under current law, employers may legally exclude part-time workers from access to their insurance plans. Rising insurance costs therefore create an incentive for firms to lower overall costs through substitution of part-time employees for full-time employees. An incentive to subcontract work out is also a possibility as employers are increasingly burdened with rising health insurance costs.

Another concern is that rising health care costs will force many smaller firms to eliminate employer-provided insurance plans. Although part of this is because smaller firms have much higher administrative costs than larger firms, smaller firms are also less likely to self-insure. **Self-insuring** is the practice whereby firms create their own insurance programs. Roughly 65 percent of firms self-insured in 1991; but only 41 percent of firms with fewer than 500 employees did so.[9] Smaller firms tend to not self-insure because it is only viable under large and diverse risk pools. A few ill employees, for instance, cause a larger dent on health insurance reserves in a small firm than in a large firm. An advantage of self-insurance is that policies need not provide state-mandated benefits (for example, chiropractic, vision, or dental benefits). Such benefits must be provided when firms purchase from a state-regulated insurance firm. Self-insured firms therefore tend to offer less generous insurance packages; this may create hardships, but it also means that they are cheaper for employers to provide than packages available from insurance firms.

Self-insuring is a practice whereby firms create their own health insurance.

Health Cost Escalation: Slower Wage Growth?

Rising health care costs tend to dampen wage growth. Health insurance is not a free good, but rather, when offered through employers, constitutes part of the total compensation package. Consider, for example, a employer who experiences a 10 percent

---

[9] *Economic Report of the President,* 1993.

rise in health insurance costs.[10] One reaction would be for the employer to reduce health benefits by 10 percent through raising the employee's contribution toward health insurance or by lowering the numbers of allowed visits to physicians or days of covered hospitalization. Another reaction would be to simply lower wages by 10 percent.

Which option will be chosen? Workers are indifferent so long as they place equal values on additional dollars of health insurance benefits and wage income. (Actually, it is after-tax income because employer-provided health benefits are untaxed, and the appropriate comparison is therefore between untaxed health benefits and after-tax income.) Historically, workers have received higher health benefits at the expense of wage income. Over 1973–89, over one-half of all real gains in worker compensation came in the form of higher employer-provided health insurance benefits.[11] In contrast, other fringe benefits (for example, pensions) expanded by 15 percent, and real wage income hardly changed at all. Rising health care costs therefore tend to crowd out wage gains, as well as other job-related benefits, that would have otherwise become available.

Rising Costs Dampen Tax Revenues

Rising health care spending influences the revenue side of the federal budget. As we have discussed, employers have increasingly substituted rising health benefits for increases in wage income. This behavior dampens federal tax revenue growth because, unlike wage income, employer-provided health benefits are exempt from most taxation. Therefore, as rising health care costs push employers into raising health benefits (at the expense of higher wage income), the U.S. Treasury taxes a smaller proportion of workers' total compensation packages. Therefore, less income tax revenue is collected than otherwise would be the case. An implication is that larger federal budget deficits will occur unless losses in income tax revenue are accompanied by increases in other tax revenues or unless federal spending is lowered.

Why Such Rapid Growth?

There have been many attempts to explain the rapid expansion of health care costs. We now examine the major hypotheses.

An Aging Society

In 1965, 9.3 percent of the population was sixty-five and over and 3.4 percent was seventy-five and over.[12] By 1992, these percentages rose to 12.4 and 5.3 percent, respectively. Health costs can be expected to rise with an aging population because this segment of the population tends to demand more health care than its younger counterparts. It should also be recognized that although senior citizens spend relatively more on health care, improvements in medical technology and increased access

---

[10] For simplicity, we assume that no change in employee productivity has occurred.
[11] Congressional Budget Office, *Projections of National Health Expenditures,* October 1992.
[12] Congressional Budget Office, *Projections of National Health Expenditures,* October 1992.

to public insurance programs contribute to gains in longevity as well. In other words, while an aging population raises health care spending, higher health care spending tends to raise longevity, and one trend therefore reinforces the other.

Rising National Income

Many economists believe that the demand for health care is income elastic; that is, as national income rises, citizens increase spending on health care at a faster pace. Governments may also fund more health research and invest in more medical technology in a growing economy than in a stagnant one. A recent paper, which examines income elasticity coefficients in industrialized economies, reports estimates in excess of unity.[13] But even with these estimates, rising national income cannot explain more than one-fourth of the cost escalation we have experienced over the past 40 years.

Imperfect Information of Consumers

Although consumers never have perfect information in any market they participate in, it is commonly believed that informational problems are amplified in the health care market.[14] Patients, for instance, may delegate many decisions to physicians because of their overall lack of information regarding treatment options. Patients may rarely understand their choices in treatment, and once they no longer monitor their treatment alternatives, costs may no longer factor into choices over which treatments they receive. Rather, suppliers of health care make many of the decisions, and they may not be particularly cost conscious either.

Lack of competition may therefore characterize the health care industry because patients are not particularly concerned with locating low-cost providers of health care. Much of the competition in medical care is directed toward nonprice factors such as location and availability of appointments. There have also been laws restricting advertising in the health care market, as well as restrictions on the supply of physicians, other possible reasons that this market has not fully reaped the rewards of active competition and has been characterized by rapid increases in spending.

Third-Party Payments

Direct payments are those made directly by patients for health care.

A fundamental change in how we pay for health care has evolved over the years: *Patients directly pay for fewer and fewer of their health benefits.* The majority of **direct payments** are payments of insurance deductibles and copayments. Consumers directly paid one-half of all private insurance costs in 1965, but only 23 percent of costs by 1992.[15] By the year 2000, CBO projects that direct payments will fall to 20

---

[13] Joseph P. Newhouse, "Medical Care Costs: How Much Welfare Loss?" *Journal of Economic Perspectives* 6 (Summer 1992): 3–21. Estimates, however, for the United States are usually less than one; see, for example, David Parkin, Alistair McGuire, and Brian Yule, "Aggregate Health Care Expenditures and National Income: Is Health Care a Luxury Good?" *Journal of Health Economics* 6 (June 1987): 109–127.

[14] See, for example, Kenneth J. Arrow, "Uncertainty and the Welfare Economics of Medical Care," *American Economic Review* 53 (December 1963): 941–973.

[15] Congressional Budget Office, *Projections of National Health Expenditures,* October 1992.

Third-party payer is an insurer who makes payments to health care providers on behalf of the insured.

percent of total costs. Expansion of public insurance programs have also substantially lowered the direct costs of receiving medical treatment for a growing segment of the population. Increasingly, health care costs are therefore paid by a **third-party payer** that provides payments to health care providers on the behalf of the insured. That third party is either a private insurance firm or, in the cases of Medicaid and Medicare, the public sector.

An important implication of the rising importance of third-party payers is that the financial exchanges between consumers and producers of medical care are increasingly removed from one another. This separation is commonly believed to encourage a separation of costs from benefits of health care that ultimately leads to overconsumption of medical care.

How do third-party arrangements distort incentives to make efficient health care choices? Consider the costs facing a patient who is considering a medical procedure with a price tag of $1,000 and who has met his insurance deductible. With a copayment of 10 percent, the patient bears $100 in out-of-pocket expenses because his insurance company pays $900. As long as the procedure offers at least $100 in benefits, the patient will undergo the procedure. This is possibly inefficient, however, because its true cost is $1,000, not $100. The third-party arrangement therefore distorts choices and fosters overconsumption of health care resources because there is an incentive for consumers and producers to choose medical services with costs exceeding benefits. This behavior manifests itself when consumers undertake a greater number of doctor visits, purchase more medical prescriptions, and undergo more medical tests and procedures than would occur when patients directly pay for all medical costs. If the patient is responsible for the full $1,000, he would choose the procedure only as long as expected benefits were at least $1,000.

Implications of third-party payments for distortion of efficient medical choices may be easily seen in Figure 13-5. The demand for medical care, D, is downward sloping, indicating that, with all else remaining the same, there is an inverse relation between the price and quantity demanded of medical care. Marginal costs, MC, are assumed to be constant. Equilibrium occurs at quantity Q_1 and price $P_1 = \$100$ when there is no third-party payer. Notice that resources are efficiently allocated since, at Q_1, marginal costs and marginal benefits are equal at B.

A gap, however, exists between prices paid by consumers and costs when there is a third-party payer. Under a 10 percent copayment, such a gap occurs between the full price of $P_1 = \$100$ and the copayment price of $P_2 = \$10$. Since consumers directly pay only P_2, they purchase quantity Q_2 of medical care, which represents overconsumption, since marginal benefits, at E, fall far below marginal costs, at C. This represents an inefficient allocation of medical resources because total net benefits would rise when resources are shifted out of health care and into some other market.

Moral Hazard in Medical Insurance?

Moral hazard occurs when policies promote behaviors that the policies themselves are supposed to control or prevent. Unemployment insurance may promote a moral hazard if, through subsidization of unemployment, workers become unemployed more often or remain unemployed for longer periods of time. Automobile insurance may

**FIGURE 13-5
How Third-Party Payments Distort Choices**

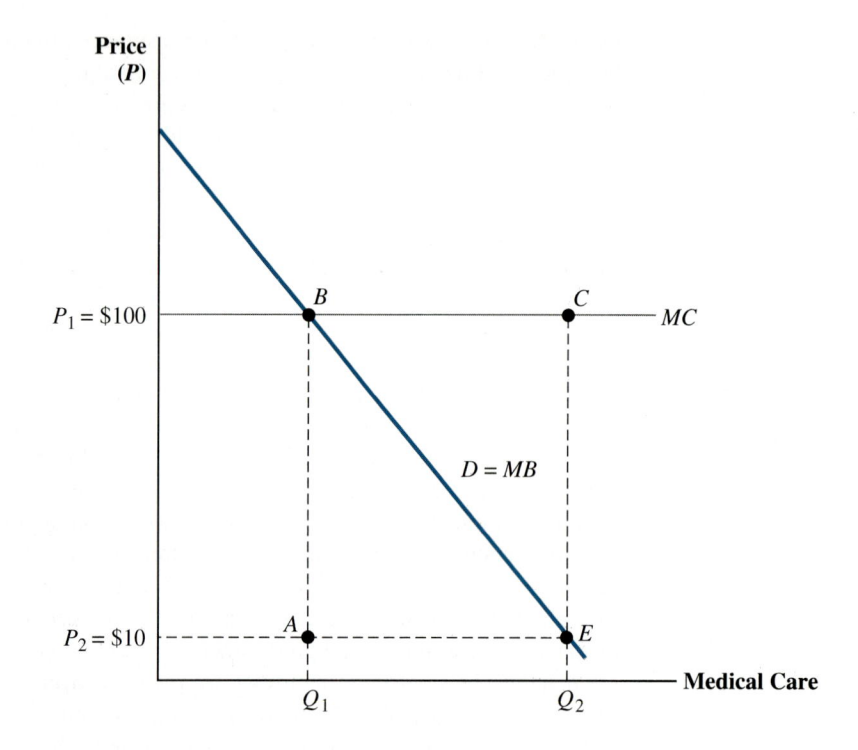

cause some drivers to drive faster and take other risks when insurance coverage makes them feel safer than they otherwise would.

Is there also a *moral hazard* in medical insurance? Few economists argue that medical insurance causes many consumers to undertake activities that raise their chances of illness or injury, but it is commonly believed that it fosters misallocation of health resources on the part of patients and health care providers.[16] Resource misallocation is considered evidence of a moral hazard in medical insurance and is widely believed to be a major factor behind the rapid expansion of health care costs.

Notice that moral hazard may be limited by raising insurance deductibles and copayments. However, as long as patients do not directly pay the full costs of their medical care, some level of moral hazard exists. Insurers may also limit their exposure to moral hazard when they define limits on the benefits that the insured may collect. For example, specialized medical care may be allowed only upon the advice of a primary care physician. Second opinions may also be required before the insured may undergo expensive surgeries. Insurance companies may also limit costs by

---

[16] See Martin Feldstein and Bernard Friedman, "Tax Subsidies, the Rational Demand for Insurance, and the Health Care Crisis," *Journal of Public Economics* 7 (April 1977): 155–178; and Mark Pauly, "Taxation, Health Insurance, and Market Failure in the Medical Economy," *Journal of Economic Literature* 24 (June 1986): 629–675.

Health maintenance organizations (HMOs) are health care providers that receive fixed sums for caring for patients.

Preferred provider organizations are health care providers that agree to limits on the fees they charge.

Tax expenditures are policies that exclude, defer, or exempt portions of income from taxation.

promoting preventive medical care through free seminars and newsletters that provide information on healthy lifestyles to their customers.

Greater use of coordinated care organizations is another way to limit exposure to moral hazard. Coordinated care organizations include **health maintenance organizations (HMOs)** and preferred provider organizations. Under an HMO, health care providers receive annual payments for each patient which do not vary with the quantity of services provided. The HMO approach gives health care providers a financial incentive to keep costs down and to promote more preventive care, because providers reap financial rewards when they lower treatment costs. HMOs have expanded rapidly in recent years, and many believe that this approach will generate long-term savings in health care costs.

Under a **preferred provider organization,** insurance firms contract with a select group of health care providers who agree to set limits on the fees that will be charged to patients. While patients may use non–preferred providers, doing so carries much higher out-of-pocket expenses than seeing a preferred provider. This approach therefore limits costs because it penalizes patients who go to higher-cost non-preferred providers.

Does Medical Technology Growth Push Demand?

A related hypothesis is that growth in medical technology raises the demand for more expensive medical treatment.[17] New technology allows earlier and more extensive treatment of many illnesses that were previously considered untreatable. Coupled with the incentives for demand expansion associated with third-party payers, cost explosion is argued to occur as patients increasingly demand more beneficial, but costly, medical treatment. It should nevertheless be recognized that this hypothesis indicates a possible reason for the expansion of medical costs, but it implies an expansion of health care quality as well. Remember, however, that expanding quality is cost effective only when marginal benefits equal or exceed marginal costs.

Tax Expenditures Promote Health Care Spending

Tax expenditures, which are also referred to as tax preferences or tax deductions, are policies that provide tax relief to taxpayers. Tax expenditures exclude, exempt, or deduct portions of income from taxation. One of the largest tax expenditures is the exclusion of employer contributions for medical insurance from income taxation. In 1994, this tax expenditure lowered income tax collections by $50.8 billion from what otherwise would have occurred.[18] There are several other tax expenditures for health-related activities, such as deductions allowed for certain medical expenses and the

---

[17] Note, however, that although new technology may raise the demand for medical care, the existence of medical insurance also promotes the expansion of new technology; see, for example, Burton A. Weisbrod, "The Health Care Quadrilemma: An Essay on Technological Change, Insurance, Quality of Care and Cost Containment," *Journal of Economic Literature* 29 (June 1991): 523–552.

[18] Table 2-1, *Budget Baselines, Historical Data, and Alternatives for the Future,* Office of Management and Budget, January 1993.

**FIGURE 13-6
Effect of Tax Expenditures on Health Insurance Consumption**

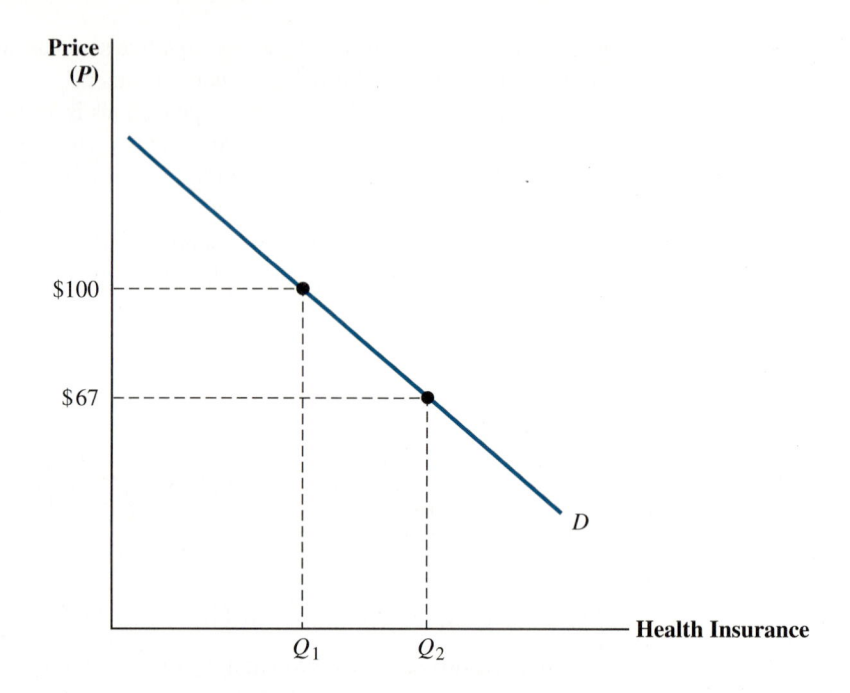

untaxed portions of medicare benefits, but these provide much less tax relief than the exclusion of employer-provided health contributions.

The effect of tax expenditures on the health care market may be seen in Figure 13-6. The demand for health insurance, D, is downward sloping, reflecting the law of demand. Before the tax expenditure policy, quantity Q_1 is the quantity of insurance demanded by consumers when they face a price of $100. Now suppose that tax expenditures are provided for employer-provided health insurance. At a marginal tax rate of 33 percent, the price of insurance now falls by 33 percent to $67 and leads consumers to expand consumption of insurance to Q_2.

Employers have an incentive to provide workers with insurance policies because the tax expenditure allows them to lower their total compensation costs. When compensation shifts from wage income to insurance, total compensation costs fall. To show this, consider that, in order to purchase Q_1 of insurance by themselves, consumers would have to pay $100. But its price falls to $67 when provided through their employer. Notice, however, that workers place identical values on Q_1 of insurance under either price. It is clearly cheaper for employers to give their employees an insurance policy, which is valued at $100, but costs only $67, than it is to provide them $100 in wage income (the price that workers would be charged for purchasing their own insurance).

This tax expenditure subsidizes health insurance purchases and therefore promotes inefficient resource allocations when marginal costs exceed marginal benefits. Also notice that as it promotes greater consumption of insurance, it also promotes expansion of health care spending through the incentives for overconsumption stemming from third-party payment arrangements.

Health Care Reform Proposals

Managed Competition

Managed competition is competition that would theoretically lower health care costs through the creation of competing, and regulated, health insurance firms.

Managed competition is aimed at expanding the availability of employer-provided insurance through health insurance purchasing cooperatives, or HIPCs.[19] A national health board in Washington, D.C., which would define a standardized package of health benefits that must be provided by all private and public insurers, would monitor HIPCs. Competition among all insurers would therefore focus on the same standardized health package and would, in theory, minimize the informational difficulties that characterize the current system whereby all insurance plans offer different health benefits.

Most managed competition proposals recommend that insurance coverage be extended to all Americans. All full-time employees could be offered employer-provided plans, and all employers would be required to contribute, for each employee, between 50 and 100 percent of the cost of the minimum benefit package offered by the lowest-priced HIPC. Part-time workers, and the unemployed, would be subsidized by taxes imposed on full-time workers as well as from other sources.

This plan allows individuals to choose any HIPC insurance policy as long as it includes the minimum benefit package. But insurance premiums for benefits that exceed this minimum package would not be tax deductible. This feature is believed to promote cost-effective policies, since without the tax deduction consumers facing the true cost of additional insurance would search for plans that have costs more in line with their benefits.

A potential problem is that HIPCs have an incentive to discourage high-risk consumers from purchasing their insurance. Some plans may not contract with physicians who treat more costly illnesses and would in this way discourage applications from those who tend to make more frequent and costlier claims. This problem may be avoided, however, by specifying that all medical specialties be provided within the minimal health package requirement.

Advocates believe that radical reform of the health care system is a necessary step toward extending insurance coverage to all Americans. Some advocates believe that the savings from introducing competition (and lowering costs) will be more than sufficient to cover the additional costs of extending health insurance to the more than 35 million Americans who currently lack insurance. Proponents of this view therefore believe that the government sector is able to jump-start competition in a health care market that, for years, has had little or no competition and to use cost savings to cover the costs of extending insurance to the uninsured.

Critics of managed competition voice many objections. One is that it is wishful thinking to believe that the government can appropriately manage resources in the health care market and point to the introduction of Medicare in 1966 as one important factor behind rapid escalation of health care costs. In other words, these critics believe that it is more likely that greater government control over health care resources will

---

[19] For a more detailed discussion of managed competition, see Congressional Budget Office, *Managed Competition and Its Potential to Reduce Health Spending,* May 1993.

result in higher health care spending. The tendency to raise spending through policy may be fostered when, in order to overcome the incentives of insurance firms to exclude those with histories of health problems, minimal benefits packages may be overly generous and result in greater consumption of health resources than exists today. Under these conditions, it becomes less likely that any cost savings through greater competition will actually result in an overall reduction in health care spending. Costs may also be expected to expand as all Americans will now have access to third-party payers and, as previously discussed, this payment method leads to overconsumption of health care.

Another criticism is that when managed competition mandates additional benefits in some employer-provided health plans, workers will experience slower wage growth as employers adjust total compensation packages to the change. Mandating that health plans be provided to all employees is predicted to result in layoffs or substitution of part-time workers for full-time workers. Another criticism involves the issue of who will pay for extending insurance coverage to the uninsured. As just argued, critics downplay the possibility that managed competition will create cost savings. As we shall show, the economic incidence of taxes is an important issue in assessing who gains and who loses from any public policy.

Play-or-Pay

Play-or-pay is a proposal requiring that employers provide insurance to employees and their dependents (play) or be charged a payroll tax to fund a public health plan (pay).

The **play-or-pay** proposal requires employers either to provide a basic health plan to employees and their dependents ("play") or be charged a payroll tax that provides participation in a public health plan ("pay"). Subsidies would be provided to the unemployed and, under some proposals, would be funded through general tax revenues.

While this proposal would result in greater insurance access, one downside is that to the extent that more workers are provided health plans through their employers or are provided more generous plans, slower wage growth will occur as employers adjust total compensation packages to the change. Mandating that health plans be provided to all employees is also likely to result in layoffs or part-time work for formerly full-time workers.

Notice that since this plan would increase access to insurance, there will be a tendency for this plan to raise overall health care spending as well. Moreover, policymakers would have to be careful not to set insurance premiums too low, since this would result in a huge public insurance program, and unless associated constraints are imposed on cost escalation, there is little reason to expect that it will successfully control costs to a greater extent than does the present system.

Rate Setting: A Cure for Cost Escalation?

Rate setting is the practice of setting price controls on medical procedures that may be charged to public and/or private insurance plans.

Sometimes recommended as a remedy for controlling the potential for cost escalation, **rate setting** is the practice of setting price controls on medical procedures that may be charged to public and/or private insurance plans. The economic implications of rate setting may be seen in Figure 13-7, which displays the demand D and supply S of medical care. In the absence of a price control, market equilibrium at b occurs where demand and supply curves intersect. An important characteristic of market equilibrium is that, at equilibrium price P_e and quantity Q_e, there is no surplus or shortage in the health care market.

FIGURE 13-7
Effect of Rate Setting on the Health Care Market

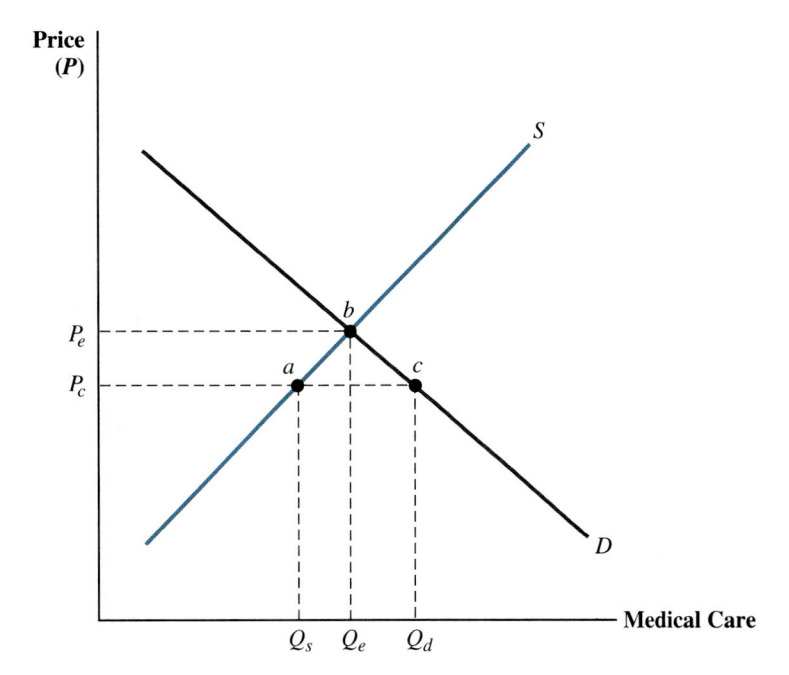

[Figure: Supply and demand graph with Price (P) on vertical axis and Medical Care on horizontal axis. Supply curve S slopes upward, Demand curve D slopes downward, intersecting at point b at price P_e and quantity Q_e. A horizontal line at P_c (below P_e) intersects the supply curve at point a (quantity Q_s) and the demand curve at point c (quantity Q_d).]

Now suppose that a maximum price of P_c is imposed on this market. While consumers wish to purchase Q_d medical care, suppliers are only willing and able to provide Q_s. The resulting mismatch is shortage ac. The immediate symptom of a shortage of medical care will be waiting lists, and if the maximum price lies far below equilibrium, they will be fairly long as well. While policymakers may attempt to raise the maximum price to shorten the length of the line, notice that this practice goes against the reason that the control is imposed in the first place: to reduce consumption of medical care.

While rate setting may appear to be an effective way of limiting cost escalation in medical care, there are several significant problems with this policy. One problem concerns rationing since some mechanism must replace the price mechanism for rationing medical care. The private market rations through price and, as seen in Figure 13-7, an equilibrium price of P_e rations medical care by removing any previous shortage or surplus. The shortage that would accompany the price control P_c, however, requires either health care providers or policymakers to determine who receives medical care—and who does not. If it is unclear that appropriate choices are made by either party, serious doubts will arise over the fairness of outcomes. Concerns may also arise over service quality as health care providers are forced to charge lower prices than they would otherwise charge.

It should also be recognized that health care providers will likely circumvent rate setting policies by raising the frequency of office visits and medical procedures. For example, a price control on office visits may cause physicians to require that their patients come in twice for medical procedures that previously were conducted within one visit. Office visits will tend to be more frequent, and shorter, as physicians work

National Health Insurance

National health insurance is health insurance provided by one insurer, the federal government.

Most proposals for **national health insurance** recommend the complete replacement of the current system with one national insurer: the federal government. Insurance would then either be funded entirely through general tax revenue or partially through a system of deductibles and copayments, as under Medicare and Medicaid. The immediate advantage is that all Americans would have access to health insurance. Another advantage is that, unlike managed competition and play-or-pay proposals, this approach to health care has been used elsewhere. All Canadians have been covered by public insurance plans since 1971. Plans are administered by each province and are funded primarily through general tax revenues. The United Kingdom adopted the National Health Service (NHS) in 1948, which provides all residents with health care as well as directly employing most health care providers. Private insurance alternatives are available, but all residents pay taxes to support the NHS.

A fundamental problem, however, is that with low direct costs and access to all citizens, a potential for rapid expansion of health care spending exists. For this reason, other countries that have adopted a national health insurance program, such as the United Kingdom, have resorted to strict controls on certain benefits. For example, some medical procedures are no longer performed on patients when it is no longer considered cost effective; that is, after they reach a certain age. Kidney dialysis, for example, is usually denied to people over age fifty-five in the United Kingdom. Another control is to have waiting lists, which means that health care is rationed on the basis of time rather than price. Such controls appear to be unavoidable since, with a fixed national budget for medical care, there must be some means to control demand for medical care. However, as shown in the case of price controls, all controls have serious disadvantages.

Summary

- Two trends are evident in the health care market: Americans are devoting more resources to health care, and the public sector is allocating more of our health care resources.
- The fastest growing components of national health care spending are the health entitlement programs Medicaid and Medicare. While they accounted for 26 percent of all national health care spending in 1965, their share expanded to 45 percent by 1992. By 2000, CBO projects their share at 48 percent.
- An insurance deductible is the dollar value of medical benefits that must first be paid by patients before their insurance company pays for treatment costs. An insurance copayment defines the percentage of a given insurance claim that the insured is personally responsible for.
- An expanding health care industry is not necessarily all bad because, in part, rising spending indicates higher quality care and clearly translates into longer life spans and improved quality of life for many Americans. A counterview is that expansion in health care spending is more reflective of an inefficient system than of rising quality.
- Major implications of rising health care costs are that fewer people have access to health insurance, and that wage income growth tends to slow down.

- The major reasons for the rapid expansion of health care spending are an aging society, rising national income, imperfect consumer information, third-party payments, and tax expenditures.
- A moral hazard in medical insurance exists when insurance fosters misallocation of health resources on the part of patients and health care providers.
- Many economists believe that the moral hazard is a major factor behind the rapid expansion of health care costs. Moral hazard may be limited by raising insurance deductibles and copayments and using HMOs and preferred provider plans.
- Three major reform proposals are managed competition, play-or-pay, and national health insurance.

Review Questions

1. In what sense has health care spending expanded over the last forty years?
2. What is the difference between an insurance deductible and an insurance copayment?
3. In what sense do rising health care costs restrict access to health insurance?
4. What are the major factors behind the rapid expansion of health care costs?
5. What is a third-party payer? How have third-party payments influenced spending on health care?
6. In what sense does the managed competition proposal increase competition in the health care industry?

Discussion Questions

1. Health care spending has clearly been rising rapidly. Discuss whether this expansion necessarily indicates that this is an undesirable trend.
2. Does the presence of third-party payers inhibit the incentives of consumers to search for low-cost medical care? Are the incentives of health care providers influenced by the third-party payment system?
3. Is it ever rational that someone be uninsured? Explain.
4. Some of the uninsured take advantage of subsidized medical services in the emergency rooms of not-for-profit hospitals. Who bears the costs of this behavior?
5. In what ways do tax expenditures influence the quantity of health insurance and health care demanded by consumers? Is it possible for tax expenditures to promote overconsumption of health care?
6. Explain how an increase in a copayment rate would foster greater allocative efficiency.
7. Explain what is meant by the following statement: Employees must pay for rising health care costs in one way or another.
8. If one believes there is a health care crisis, does this necessarily mean that the public sector should allocate more of the resources in the health care market? Explain.

Key Words

Medigap insurance
Insurance deductible
Insurance copayment
Self-insuring
Direct payments

Third-party payer
Health maintenance organizations (HMOs)
Preferred provider organizations
Tax expenditures

Managed competition
Play-or-pay
Rate setting
National health insurance

CHAPTER 14

Cost-Benefit Analysis

Policymakers study thousands of spending proposals each year. Each proposal has its supporters, and because the public sector is subject to scarce resources, not all projects can be funded. Supporters of various projects must compete against supporters of other projects for public funding. An obvious means by which policymakers judge the usefulness of the many spending proposals is through comparison of costs and benefits. In a sense, all of economic analysis is about cost-benefit analysis, and we have argued, for instance, that allocative efficiency occurs whenever other resource allocations that provide greater total net benefits to society do not exist. Cost-benefit analysis of public projects is therefore the application of the principles developed so far in this text.

Why does discussion of cost-benefit analysis merit an entire chapter? One principal reason is that, in practice, it is difficult to assign values to the costs and benefits of public projects. For example, what are the benefits and costs derived from building a new bridge or buying a new school bus? It is relatively easy to draw hypothetical total benefit and total cost curves for either project, but it is unquestionably a more difficult matter to assign dollar values to these curves. Application of cost-benefit analysis therefore provides some direction on how to go from theory to application in measuring costs and benefits of public projects.

Another reason that cost-benefit analysis merits detailed examination is immediately evident after values have been assigned to costs and benefits of public projects. How do we compare the usefulness of competing projects when their distributions of costs and benefits differ over time? It could be the case, for instance, that a new bridge might produce benefits over 100 years, and a new school bus might have a useful life of only ten years. Cost-benefit analysis provides a framework with which to compare competing projects characterized by dissimilar distributions of costs and benefits over time.

Our task in this chapter may be summarized by the following questions:

❏ What are the fundamentals of cost-benefit analysis?
❏ How does cost-benefit analysis deal with projects whose costs and benefits are distributed over long periods of time?
❏ What role can cost-benefit analysis play in public allocation of resources?

❑ What are the limitations of cost-benefit analysis?
❑ What role does cost-benefit analysis actually play in public allocation of resources?

Cost-Benefit Analysis and Allocative Efficiency

Allocative Efficiency

The fundamental rule of cost-benefit analysis is to allocate resources to their most efficient uses. Efficiency in resource allocation occurs whenever no other allocations exist that offer greater total net benefits to the collection of individuals who comprise society. Total net benefits equal total benefits minus total costs. We measure benefits associated with goods by the prices that consumers are willing to pay for various quantities of goods. The higher the prices consumers are willing to pay, the higher the social benefits associated with allocating resources toward production of goods. Social costs are measured by the concept of opportunity cost; they measure what consumers lose when resources are not allocated in the next best alternative. Consider, for example, production of street lamps. If the next best resource allocation is production of five more stop signs, opportunity costs of one more street lamp are the benefits that consumers would receive with production of five more stop signs.

Panels of Figure 14-1 show, in different frameworks, what constitutes an efficient quantity of street lamps for society. (We assume away the problems associated with market failure, for example, imperfect information, public goods, and externalities.) Figure 14-1a, which displays hypothetical total benefit *(TB)* and total cost *(TC)* curves for street lamps, shows that although total benefits rise as more resources are devoted to their production, total costs rise as well. Allocative efficiency occurs at the maximum distance between *TC* and *TB*, which occurs at L^*. Figure 14-1b shows total net benefits *(TNB)*, which is simply $TB - TC$. Allocative efficiency remains at L^* because only at this quantity will reallocation not result in higher total net benefits to society.

Figure 14-1c shows that L^* occurs at the intersection of the marginal benefit *(MB)* and marginal cost *(MC)* curves.[1] To remember why $MB = MC$ implies allocative efficiency, consider production of L_1 where $MB > MC$. If, for example, $MB = \$35$ and $MC = \$10$, then one additional street lamp increases total benefits by $35 but costs only an additional $10. It is efficient to expand production because benefits ($35) placed on an additional street lamp outweigh opportunity costs ($10); therefore, at L_1, no better use exists than to produce one *additional* street lamp. The opposite occurs at L_2, where $MB < MC$. If, for example, $MB = \$5$ and $MC = \$30$, benefits ($5) placed on one more street lamp are less than its opportunity cost ($30), and allocative efficiency requires that resources be moved out of street lamps and into the next best alternative market, where, at the margin, consumers place greater values on that good. Only when $MB = MC$ can resource allocation not be altered in a way that increases total net benefits.

---

[1] We have previously defined these concepts as $MB = \Delta TB/\Delta A$ and $MC = \Delta TC/\Delta A$, where MB = marginal benefit, MC = marginal opportunity cost, Δ = "change in," and A = quantity of good or service.

FIGURE 14-1
Efficient Quantity of Street Lamps

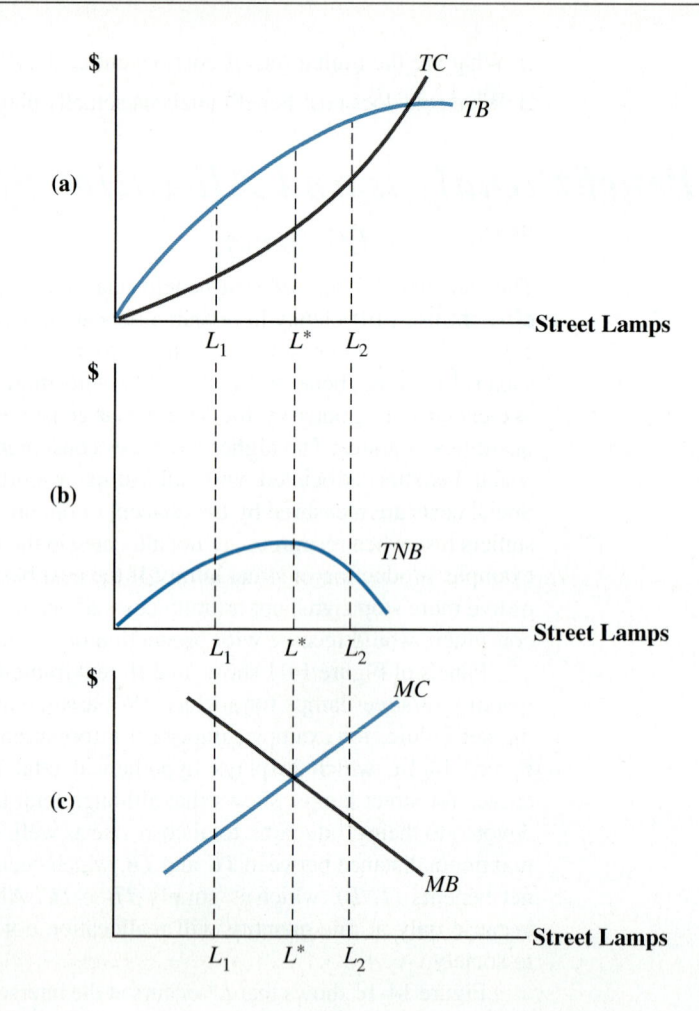

(a) TC, TB curves vs Street Lamps, with L_1, L^*, L_2 marked

(b) TNB curve vs Street Lamps, with L_1, L^*, L_2 marked

(c) MC and MB curves vs Street Lamps, with L_1, L^*, L_2 marked

We have just demonstrated that when net benefits are maximized, resources are allocated efficiently. While our application of this principle has focused on private markets, this same principle applies to allocative efficiency in public markets. Questions regarding such diverse issues as: How many miles of highway should be funded? or How many public housing projects should be built? or How many dollars should be allocated to research and development of new weapons systems? may be answered by this principle. By allocating resources until net benefits of each project are maximized, allocative efficiency is achieved in public markets. In this sense, we have been using cost-benefit analysis throughout this book.

Alternative Time Frameworks for Cost-Benefit Analysis

Our framework so far has been static in the sense that we have assumed that all benefits are provided and costs are borne during one period of time. Most public projects, however, have benefits and costs distributed over time. While one project, for instance, yields benefits of $50 million over 10 years, we would tend to rank it below another project of similar cost that yields $50 million immediately. Benefits are often long-lived as, for instance, street lamps, which provide services over many years to residents of neighborhoods. Costs are also long-lived since, after initial purchase and installation, maintenance and bulb replacements occur over time.

Present Value Framework

What Is Present Value?

We have often heard that time is money and that a dollar today is worth more than a dollar tomorrow. (For the time being, we disregard the problem of inflation, which also results in a dollar today being worth more than a dollar tomorrow.) These are simply expressions about **present value,** or what dollars received in the future are worth to us today. A helpful way to understand this concept is to consider the value of depositing money in your local bank. Deposits are investments that yield benefits in the form of interest income. An appropriate question is: How much is this investment worth to you today? Alternatively, you may ask: How much would you be willing to pay today for an investment that yields some level of future returns?

Present value is today's value of dollars received in the future.

If you deposit $1,000 today, you earn $50 in one year when the interest rate is 5 percent. The dollar value of this investment is therefore $1,050, receivable one year from today. In general, this result may be expressed as

$$A_1 = A_0 + rA_0 = A_0(1 + r) \tag{14-1}$$

where A_0 is the initial deposit, r is the interest rate, and A_1 is the future value of the initial investment. Following equation (14-1), we see that $A_1 = A_0 + rA_0 =$ ($1,050) = ($1,000) + .05($1,000). The future value of A_0 ($1,000) is therefore A_1 ($1,050). We also see that A_1 equals the initial investment of $1,000 ($A_0$) times 1.05 $(1 + r)$.

It is useful to rearrange equation (14-1) as

$$A_0 = \frac{A_1}{1 + r} \tag{14-2}$$

which means that the initial investment (A_0) equals the future sum (A_1) divided by $1 + r$. While this clearly shows that $1,000 equals $1,050 divided by 1.05, it is important to see the intuition behind this result. The initial sum of $1,000 is the present value of $1,050 one year ahead when the interest rate is 5 percent. Because the future value of this investment (A_1) is divided by the interest rate term $(1 + r)$, the interest rate is said to *discount* the value of future dollars into what those dollars are worth today. Following convention, we refer to the interest rate as the **rate of discount.**

Rate of discount is the interest rate used to calculate present value.

Our example demonstrates that $1,050 in the future is not worth $1,050 to us today. The present value of the investment is less than $1,050, or $1,000 to be exact. When we apply a discount rate of 5 percent, a future return of $1,050 yields a present value of $1,000. We can think of present value, therefore, as a means of expressing what claims to future dollars are worth to us today.

An application of the present value concept is to determine what an investor would be willing to pay for an investment that yields future benefits. For example, an investor would not be willing to pay $1,050 today for a future claim on $1,050 one year from today. Rather, because that future claim to $1,050 is worth only $1,000 today, the present value of the investment defines the *maximum* price an investor is willing to pay for any investment.

Two-Year Analysis

We may easily extend our present value framework to evaluate investments that yield returns over two years. Because interest is collected for an additional year, the future value of our initial investment becomes

$$A_2 = A_0 + rA_0 + r(A_0 + rA_0) \qquad (14\text{-}3)$$

where A_2 is the future value of our investment after two years, A_0 is the initial investment, rA_0 is interest earned in first year, and $r(A_0 + rA_0)$ is interest earned in the second year. A_2 is therefore the future value of A_0 when A_0 grows at rate r for two years.[2]

By rearrangement of equation (14-3), we see the future value of an initial investment of A_0 after two years at discount rate r is[3]

$$A_2 = A_0(1 + r)^2 \qquad (14\text{-}4)$$

If, for example, $A_0 = \$100$ and earns $r = .05$ over two years, A_0 grows into $A_2 = (\$100)(1.05)^2 = \$110.25$.

Alternatively, the present value of receiving $110.25 two periods from now is $100 and is determined by rearrangement of equation (14-4):

$$A_0 = \frac{A_2}{(1 + r)^2} \qquad (14\text{-}5)$$

An investment yielding $110.25 in two years has a present value of $100 when $r = .05$.

n-Period Analysis

For investments with maturity of n periods in the future[4]

$$A_0 = \frac{A_n}{(1 + r)^n} \qquad (14\text{-}6)$$

where A_n is the future value of A_0 at discount rate r over n years. Alternatively, A_0 is the present value of A_n, receivable n periods from now. This framework also shows that, for investments producing immediate returns of A_i, present value $A_0 = A_i/(1 + r)^n$, which

---

[2] Note, that because deposit A_0 stays at the bank for two years, the addition to the future value in the second year $[r(A_0 + rA_0)]$ is the sum of two parts: (1) rA_0, which is interest on another year of investment and (2) $r(rA_0)$, which is "interest on interest."

[3] Because $A_2 = A_0 + rA_0 + rA_0 + r^2A_0$, we see that $A_2 = A_0(1 + r)^2$.

[4] This follows from $A_n = A_0 + rA_0 + r(A_0 + rA_0) + \cdots + rA_0(1 + r)^{n-1}$, which may be rewritten as $A_n = A_0(1 + r)^n$, or as $A_0 = A_n/(1 + r)^n$.

equals A_i when $n = 0$. In other words, there is no need to discount dollars received today; therefore, dollar for dollar, increases in A_i increase the present value of returns.

For convenience, we now refer to A_0, the present value of future sums of money, as *PV*. That is,

$$PV = \frac{A_n}{(1 + r)^n} \qquad (14\text{-}7)$$

Comparing Projects Using the Present Value Framework

We can clearly see the versatility of the present value framework when we use it to compare the attractiveness of many projects or investments. Consider a public sewer project that returns $3,000 per year over three years. The present value of returns, at a discount rate of 5 percent, is

$$PV = \frac{\$3000}{(1.05)} + \frac{\$3000}{(1.05)^2} + \frac{\$3000}{(1.05)^3} = \$2857 + \$2721 + \$2591 = \$8169$$

Because the three $3,000 sums are received over three different years, each sum is discounted separately: The first period return of $3,000 is discounted by 1.05, the second by 1.05^2, and the third by 1.05^3. This example demonstrates that $9,000 in the future is not worth $9,000 today; that is, the present value of $3,000 in each of three successive years is less than $9,000, or $8,169 to be exact.

Contrast this example with a project that plants trees in a city park and yields a return of $9,000 three years from now. Assuming $r = .05$ once again and that expenditures are identical to those of the sewer project, we have

$$PV = \frac{\$9000}{(1.05)^3} = \$7774.54$$

We can now compare two projects yielding the same nominal returns, but whose benefits arrive under two very different time frames. Policymakers value the sewer project more highly since its present value of $8,169 is larger than the present value of $7,774.54 associated with planting trees.

Two Implications of Present Value Analysis

1. *The more remote are returns, the lower are present values.* To show this important result, reconsider the sewer project and compare present values of receiving $3,000 per year over three years: $2,857 (first year), $2,721 (second year), and $2,591 (third year). Because $3,000 three years from now has a smaller present value ($2,591) than $3,000 due in one year ($2,857), we have shown that present values of future returns decline the further in the future are returns.

    To understand the intuition behind this result, consider Table 14-1, which shows the present values of $1 at different discount rates. Think of this table as displaying present values of alternative returns, each earning $1 in some future period. This result is easily shown by looking along any column, which holds constant the rate of discount applied to the calculation of the present value of $1 receivable at some future date. For example, $1 deferred for 10 years is worth $.385 today with

TABLE 14-1
Present Value of $1 at Various Rates

		r (%)	
Year	1%	5%	10%
1	.990	.952	.909
2	.980	.907	.826
5	.951	.783	.621
10	.905	.614	.385
20	.819	.377	.149
30	.741	.231	.057
40	.672	.142	.022
50	.608	.087	.009
100	.370	.008	.0001

a discount rate of 10 percent, and when a $1 return is deferred for 20 years, present value falls to $.149. For any rate of discount, then, present value of returns is inversely related to the length of time one must wait for returns. This is intuitively plausible since it means the longer the wait, the less attractive returns become. Figure 14-2 shows this same result for deferred payment of $1 over each of 100 years at three different rates of discount. As the date of future payment rises, the present value, for any rate of discount, falls continuously.

2. *The higher the rate of discount, the lower the present value of returns.* From Table 14-1 again, it is clear that as rate of discount rises, the lower are present values of receiving $1 in the future. For example, for payment received in 10 years, present value of a $1 falls from $.905 ($r = 1\%$), to $.614 ($r = 5\%$), and to $.385 ($r = 10\%$). This same result is also shown in Figure 14-2, which shows that for any date of future delivery the present value of $1 falls as the rate of discount rises.

This result follows easily from the present value formula. Because $PV = A_n/(1 + r)^n$, we see that r is in the denominator; hence, increases in r must lead to decreases in PV. It is important to understand the intuition of this result as well: The higher is r, the greater the opportunity cost (or rate of discount) attached to spending (or lending) funds over a given time period. If, for example, you deposit $1,000 in a bank for five years, you incur a higher opportunity cost at a rate of discount of 10 percent than when it is 5 percent. The higher the opportunity cost, the lower the present value of returns: This is just another way of saying that the higher the rate of discount, the lower the present value of returns.

Application: Present Value of a Professional Athlete's Salary

We have all heard of professional football, basketball, and baseball players receiving multimillion dollar contracts, and most of us have dreamed about winning a lottery worth millions of dollars. But the fine print of most contracts and winnings is that payment occurs over many years and, therefore, because income is not received

FIGURE 14-2
Present Value of $1

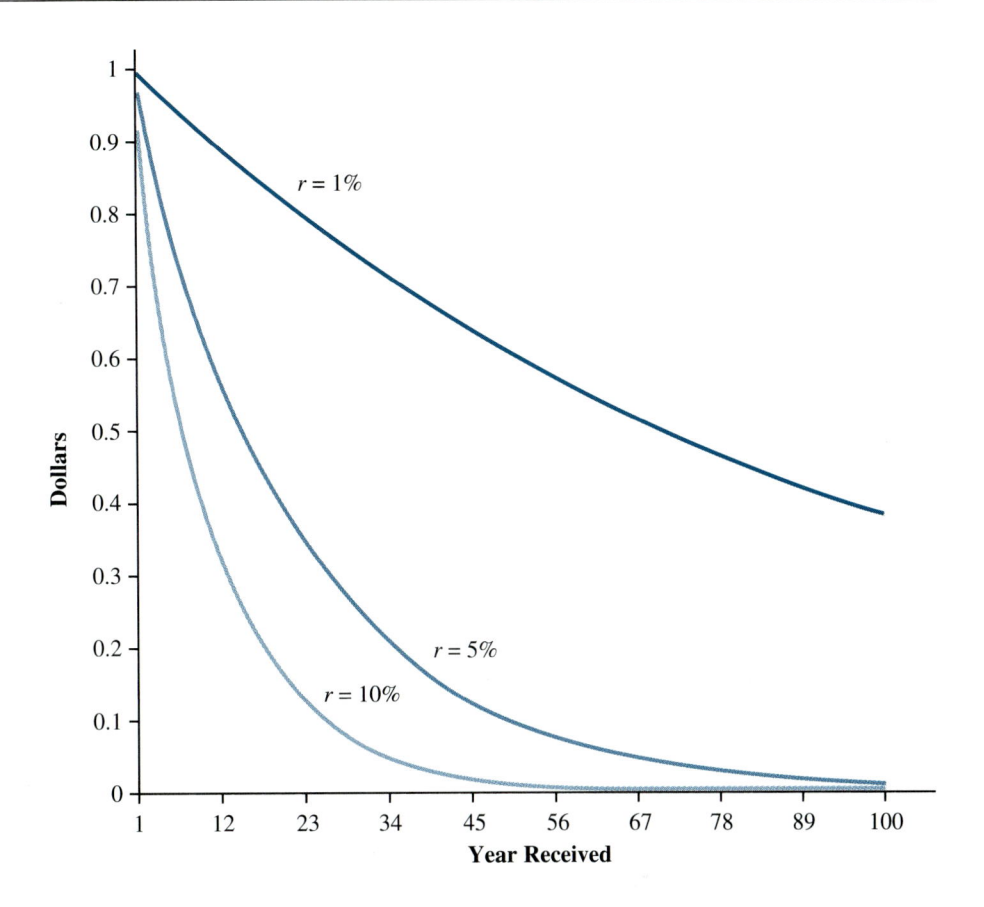

immediately, calculation of the present value of these contracts places them in perspective of today's dollars.

Consider Table 14-2, which shows, at a rate of discount of 10 percent, the present value of a $5 million contract offered to a professional ballplayer. Also assume that income is to be received in twenty equal annual installments. Notice that the further ahead are payments, the lower is present value: The present value of the first payment of $250,000 is $227,272.70 and, by the twentieth installment, the present value of $250,000 falls to $37,160.90. Summing up individual present values for each of twenty installments of $250,000, the present value of the $5 million contract is $2,128,391.

Figure 14-3 plots this same information. In Figure 14-3a, the contract payment is a constant $250,000, but present value of each annual payment declines continuously over the life of the contract. Figure 14-3b shows that the sum of annual payments accumulates to $5 million, but accumulates to a present value of only $2,128,391.

Another way of placing this contract in the perspective of today's dollars is to note that this ballplayer would be indifferent between receiving $5 million in twenty equal annual installments and receiving payment of $2,128,391 after the first year. Therefore, while ballplayers are well paid, present values of contracts are much lower than their stated value. This is one reason that such contracts often involve signing bonuses that offer additional sums of money when players sign contracts. Bonuses are

TABLE 14-2
Present Value of $5 Million Received in Twenty Equal Annual Installments
($r = 10\%$)

Year	Contract Amount	Present Value
1	$ 250,000	$ 227,272.7
2	250,000	206,611.6
3	250,000	187,828.7
4	250,000	170,753.4
5	250,000	155,230.3
6	250,000	141,118.5
7	250,000	128,289.5
8	250,000	116,626.8
9	250,000	106,024.4
10	250,000	96,385.8
11	250,000	87,623.5
12	250,000	79,657.7
13	250,000	72,416.1
14	250,000	65,832.8
15	250,000	59,848.0
16	250,000	54,407.3
17	250,000	49,461.2
18	250,000	44,964.7
19	250,000	40,877.0
20	250,000	37,160.9
SUM	$5,000,000	$2,128,391.0

paid immediately and discounting is therefore not necessary. A signing bonus of $500,000, for example, has a present value of $500,000.

Effects of Inflation on Present Values

Inflation affects many dimensions of our economic lives and is therefore a possible factor influencing our evaluations of projects. A sustained rise in the average price level over time, inflation erodes the purchasing power of money. An annual inflation rate of 5 percent, for example, means that the meal that cost $10 last year requires a payment of $10.50 this year.[5] Inflation erodes the purchasing power of money, and it

---

[5] To control for the influence of inflation on calculations, economists often distinguish between nominal and real values. Nominal, or face, values of the same meal in two adjoining years are $10 and $10.50. The real value, however, may be measured as either the meal itself (which has been assumed to be identical between the two years) or $10 measured in the base, or initial, year.

FIGURE 14-3
Value of a $5 Million Contract over Twenty Years

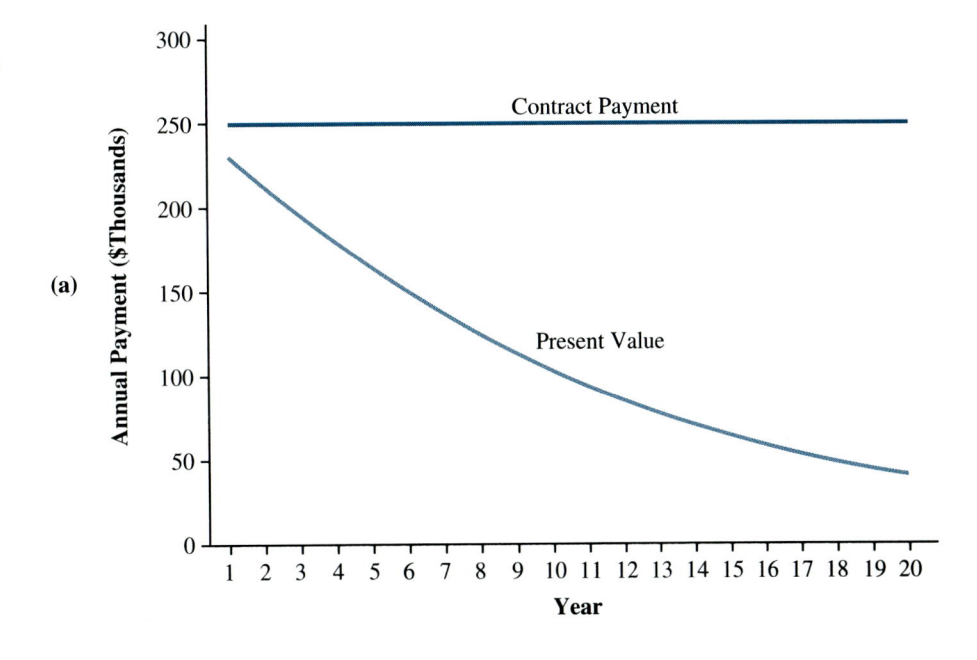

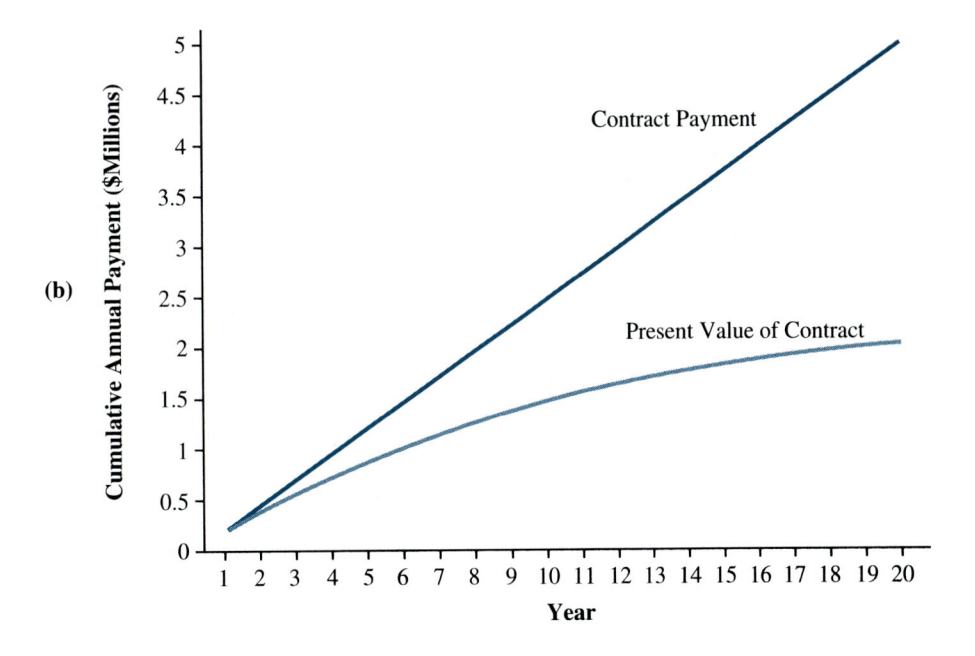

(a)

(b)

is only natural that investors will attempt to maintain the real purchasing power of their returns when they evaluate the present values of alternative projects yielding returns over time.

Present Value When There Is Inflation

Consider a project that builds a new public library and is expected to generate $300 per year in net benefits over the next three years. *Without inflation,* the present value of this project is

$$PV = \frac{\$300}{(1+r)} + \frac{\$300}{(1+r)^2} + \frac{\$300}{(1+r)^3}$$

With inflation, it will no longer be true that each of the $300 sums has equal purchasing power. In order to maintain purchasing power after one year, $300 must grow by the amount of inflation, π, or $300(1 + \pi)$, which at $\pi = .05$, equals $315. In other words, in order to be able to purchase the same goods that cost $300 in the first year, the purchaser must allow for inflation, which raises the prices of those goods to $315. Therefore, even though the sum has increased by $15 over the first year, purchasing powers of those two sums ($300 and $315) are equal.

After two years of inflation of 5 percent, $300 grows to $300(1 + \pi)^2$, or $330.75.[6] The general correction is therefore to add an inflation factor of $(1 + \pi)^n$ in each of n years. In our example, $300(1 + \pi) + 300(1 + \pi)^2 + 300(1 + \pi)^3$ are appropriate adjustments that maintain purchasing power over three consecutive years.

Inflation can be expected to change the purchasing power of interest income as well, and savvy investors will require that adjustments be made to the rate of discount. Note that because both r and π are expressed as rates of change, increases (decreases) in π directly lower (raise) the purchasing power of interest income associated with any r. An inflation rate of 5 percent, for example, lowers the rate of return on an investment by a like amount; thus funds invested at 12 percent yield a gain of only 7 percent in real purchasing power. To maintain constant purchasing power, investors add inflation rates to interest rates. An inflation rate of 5 percent causes investors to seek a return of 12 percent when they seek an inflation-adjusted return of 7 percent.

The inflation rate enters our calculation of present values when we multiply $(1 + r)^n$ by $(1 + \pi)^n$. For example, at $n = 1$, $r = 7\%$, and $\pi = 5\%$, we have $(1 + .07)(1 + .05) = 1.12$, or 12%.[7] An increase in return equal to the inflation rate, or (roughly) $r + \pi$, becomes the rate at which interest income on investments maintains constant purchasing power over time. After two years, $(1 + r)^2(1 + \pi)^2$ becomes the appropriate denominator in the present value framework.

Returning to the new library project, the influence of inflation on both returns and the discount rate yields the following present value calculation:

$$PV = \frac{\$300(1+\pi)}{(1+r)(1+\pi)} + \frac{\$300(1+\pi)^2}{(1+r)^2(1+\pi)^2} + \frac{\$300(1+\pi)^3}{(1+r)^3(1+\pi)^3}$$

---

[6] Note that this is identical to the way we generated the present value formula (eq. 14-4) $A_2 = A_0 + rA_0 + rA_0 + r^2A_0 = A_0(1 + r)^2$, where A_2 is the future value of an initial investment of A_0 after two years at discount rate r. In our present case, substitute π for r and we obtain the future value of $300 after two years of inflation, or $300(1 + .05)^2$.

[7] Actually, $(1 + r)(1 + \pi) = 1 + r + \pi + r\pi$, which, in this example, results in 1.1235. However, since $r\pi$ is usually very small (e.g., in our case .0035), it is usually left out of calculations.

Cancellation of like terms in the numerators and denominators therefore allows us to calculate present values with the same formula we developed before we introduced inflation.

Implications of Inflation for Present Value Calculations

We have just shown that, because of cancellations of $(1 + \pi)^n$, present value calculations are unaffected by inflation. It is reasonable to ask why we went through this exercise if inflation does not influence the way in which we calculate present values. The important point is that *present value calculations do not require that inflation be considered*.[8] This is fortunate because it is extremely difficult, in a world of highly variable inflation, to predict inflation with a great deal of accuracy.

There is considerable room for error when, for example, one must predict inflation over a period of 20 years. If, in 1960, policymakers were evaluating a water project that was estimated to generate net benefits over 20 years, what inflation rate would policymakers have included in their present value calculation? This would clearly be a difficult problem, and choices may have led to serious miscalculation of present values. As a general rule, it is important not to include inflation rates in our calculations of present values of projects. While, in theory, it is possible to accurately account for influences of inflation on present values, it is unlikely that we will make accurate predictions of inflation rates for projects that yield future returns.

Our discussion also suggests an important rule about inflation that we must follow if we wish to include predictions of inflation within the present value framework. It is essential that, when left out, $(1 + \pi)^n$ should be left out of both the numerator and denominator, or when left in, $(1 + \pi)^n$ be left in both the numerator and denominator. It is worth investigating what happens when this rule is not followed. In fact, federal government policy has, for many years, been to include $(1 + \pi)^n$ in the denominator and to exclude $(1 + \pi)^n$ in the numerator of present value calculations.[9] To see the effect of this policy on the calculation of present values, consider Table 14-3, which displays net returns for a hypothetical dam project.

Because returns flow over five years, it is appropriate to discount net benefits. Assuming a discount rate of 5 percent and an inflation rate of 5 percent, correct present value calculation of that stream of benefits shows a sum of $1,378. As we have shown, this sum does not require that the inflation rate term $(1 + \pi)^n$ be included in our calculation. However, when the inflation term is included only in the denominator, an incorrect estimate of $1,155.50 causes it to be understated by $222.68 and, therefore, provides policymakers with a misleading guide to project value.

Methods for Choosing between Projects

It is common sense that only projects that have positive net benefits should be considered for funding in either the private or public sector. Remember, though, that

---

[8] An exception to this statement occurs when rates of inflation for returns and discount rates differ. In this case, two different rates, π_a = inflation rate of returns and π_b = inflation rate of discount rate, should be included.

[9] Edward M. Gramlich, *A Guide to Benefit-Cost Analysis,* 2d ed. (Englewood Cliffs, N.J.: Prentice Hall, 1990), 98.

TABLE 14-3
Net Benefits from Dam Project

		Present Values	
Year	Net Benefits	Correct	Incorrect
1	$ 100	$ 95.24	$ 90.70
2	200	181.41	164.54
3	350	302.34	261.18
4	400	329.08	270.74
5	600	470.12	368.35
SUM	$1,650	$1,378.18	$1,155.50

positive net benefits mean only that total benefits exceed total costs and that this is a useful rule of thumb for evaluating usefulness of projects, but the fact that thousands of projects meet this criterion means that it does not tell us very much about which of these projects should be funded in a world of resource scarcity. It is important, therefore, to extend the analysis to determine a priority list that ranks projects according to their value to society.

Maximum Present Value of Net Benefits

Assume that a city government has two projects competing for $400 of tax revenues and that policymakers will choose the project with the highest present value of net benefits. Table 14-4 compares, for three rates of discount (1%, 5%, and 10%), the present values of two mutually exclusive projects that yield returns over five years. For simplicity, all numbers have been rounded off to the nearest dollar:

- Project A restores a 30-year-old arboretum.
- Project B builds a new dugout for the city's public baseball field.

Both projects require an initial expenditure of $400, and therefore net benefits for period 0 equal −$400. For restoration of the arboretum, zero net benefits occur in the first and second years and are followed by net benefits of $150, $200, and $250 in subsequent years. Over the course of five years, the (nondiscounted) sum of net benefits is $200. In contrast, the new dugout yields positive net benefits (in excess of $0) in all years, and over the course of five years, they grow from $15 to $225, and sum to $190.[10]

Although both projects yield positive net benefits over five years, there are important differences in year-to-year magnitudes of net benefits, as well as the sum of net benefits over five years. Our present value framework demonstrates that it is

---

[10] Note that for both projects the simple sum of net benefits could be obtained by using the present value framework with $r = 0$.

appropriate to discount net benefits before we decide, on the basis of present values, which of the two projects is preferable.

When $r = 1\%$, present values of net benefits for projects A and B are:

$$PV^A = -400 + \frac{0}{(1+r)} + \frac{0}{(1+r)^2} + \frac{150}{(1+r)^3} + \frac{200}{(1+r)^4} + \frac{250}{(1+r)^5}$$
$$= -400 + 0 + 0 + 146 + 192 + 238$$
$$= \$176$$

$$PV^B = -400 + \frac{15}{(1+r)} + \frac{75}{(1+r)^2} + \frac{125}{(1+r)^3} + \frac{150}{(1+r)^4} + \frac{225}{(1+r)^5}$$
$$= -400 + 15 + 74 + 121 + 144 + 214$$
$$= \$168$$

At $r = 1\%$, the present value of project A ($176) exceeds the present value of project B ($168), and city policymakers place highest priority on project A. Examination of Table 14-4 shows that because present values of both projects are identical ($90) when $r = 5\%$, policymakers are indifferent between the two projects, and without any other criteria, the choice may be made by a coin toss. However, when the rate of discount rises to 10 percent, a change in priority is prompted because the present value of project B ($12) exceeds that of project A ($5).

At first it might appear to be a curious outcome that choice of project changes when the rate of discount changes. However, the present value framework shows that the relative attractiveness of projects depends on distribution of net benefits *and* rates of discount.

Remember that project A does not yield positive net benefits until the third year. Project B, in contrast, immediately produces positive net benefits, and even though net benefits expand over time, increases do not occur as *abruptly* as in the case of project A. Remember also that the further in the future are returns, the lower are the present

TABLE 14-4
Net Benefits for Projects A and B

	Net Benefit Project		Present Values					
			$r = .01$		$r = .05$		$r = .10$	
Year	A	B	A	B	A	B	A	B
0	−$400	−$400	−$400	−$400	−$400	−$400	−$400	−$400
1	0	15	0	15	0	14	0	14
2	0	75	0	74	0	14	0	14
3	150	125	146	121	130	108	113	94
4	200	150	192	144	165	123	137	102
5	250	225	238	214	196	176	155	140
SUM	$200	$190	$176	$168	$ 90	$ 90	$ 5	$ 12

values of those returns. Calculation of present values lowers the relative attractiveness of projects that defer net benefits further into the future. Why do *increases* in the rate of discount improve the relative attractiveness of project B, the new dugout? Higher rates of discount lower the relative attractiveness of project A because a greater proportion of its returns are further in the future than those of project B.

Distribution of net benefits and the rate of discount are important ingredients into which project yields the highest present value. Higher rates of discount tend to favor projects with immediate returns, and lower discount rates tend to favor projects with longer-term returns.

Internal Rates of Discount

Internal rates of discount are the discount rates at which the present values of projects are zero.

Calculation of **internal rates of discount** requires knowledge of the present value and distribution of net benefits over time for different projects. For example, consider a project that yields $550 in one year and requires an initial outlay of $500. To solve for this project's internal rate of discount (i), we use the following equation:[11]

$$\$500 = \frac{\$550}{1 + i}$$

Solving for i, we see that $500(1 + i) = 550$, and because $1 + i = 550/500$, $i = 550/500 - 1 = .10$, or 10 percent.

If comparison of the internal rate of return (i) with the opportunity costs of funds (r) finds $i > r$, then the project yields positive net benefits and should be considered for funding against other alternative projects. For example, $r = 6\%$ means that this project should be funded.

Now consider a project that provides net benefits of $100 for each of two years and requires an initial expenditure of $150. Solving for i requires determining the solution to the following equation:

$$150 = \frac{100}{(1 + i)} + \frac{100}{(1 + i)^2}$$

Here, $i = .215$, or 21.5 percent, and, when compared to a competing project yielding $i = 10\%$, is a better candidate for funding. It should be noted, however, that solutions are not always so neat and tidy.[12] For this reason, comparison of present values is the preferred means of distinguishing between alternative projects.

Benefit-Cost Ratios

We have shown that total benefits must outweigh total costs in order for a project to be considered valuable. When projects are characterized by a stream of benefits over time $TB = (B_1 + B_2 + \cdots + B_n)$ and costs $TC = (C_1 + C_2 + \cdots + C_n)$, a desirable

---

[11] Alternatively, we can set $PV = 0$ and solve for i when using the present value formula $PV = -500 + 550/(1 + i)$.

[12] Quadratic equations have two solutions, both of which may make economic sense. But sometimes one solution may be a negative or imaginary number. Projects yielding returns over three or more years introduce even more problems.

Benefit-cost ratio is the ratio of the present value of benefits over the present value of costs.

benefit-cost ratio means that the present value of benefits should exceed the present value of costs. Note that this is the same as saying that the present value of net benefits, $NB = (B_1 - C_1) + (B_2 - C_2) + \cdots + (B_n - C_n)$, must exceed one before it can be a candidate for public funding.

A difficulty arises, however, in application of this criterion for gauging usefulness of public projects. While it may be concluded that alternative projects may simply be ranked in order of benefit-cost ratios, this is not always an effective system in practice. Consider, for example, Table 14-5, which compares benefits and costs of two projects: constructions of a new bridge and tennis courts in a local community. Assuming a discount rate of 5 percent, we see that present values of benefits exceed present values of costs for both projects, and therefore both projects meet this criterion. Based on the magnitude of their benefit-cost ratios, the bridge project (4.1) is ranked over tennis courts (2.8).

Inspection of present values of net benefits, however, yields a different verdict. Note that the bridge project yields a lower present value of net benefits ($361) than the tennis court project ($742); therefore, when the criterion is maximization of present value of net benefits, tennis courts are awarded higher social priority. This criterion is superior since, unlike benefit-cost ratios, it considers the *magnitude,* or scale, of net benefits associated with projects. It should be clear that the community would be better served with a project with a present value of net benefits of $742 versus $361, and because comparison of benefit-cost ratios does not result in this verdict, maximization of present values of net benefits remains a better criterion for assigning priority.

Application of Cost-Benefit Analysis

It would be incorrect to assume that the real world is as simple as what we have presented so far. There is little or nothing in our discussion that is particularly controversial; nothing has even hinted at possible problems in gathering data with which to apply cost-benefit analysis. We have simply ranked projects on the basis of present values of net benefits. The real world of policymaking, however, is a very different world. Much of cost-benefit analysis must be spent in three areas:

- measuring benefits
- measuring costs
- choosing an appropriate discount rate

Policymaking involves filling in the data with which to calculate present values of net benefits of alternative projects. Costs, benefits, and rates of discount are the heart of present value calculations, and in some cases public finance economists must collect this data from scratch. In other cases, they must evaluate data supplied by various parties with interests in the policy process.

Measuring Benefits

Quantification of benefits of proposed projects is a major part of cost-benefit analysis. Benefits are both direct and indirect. Consider, for example, a project which builds a

TABLE 14-5
Benefits and Costs of Two Projects

Project: Bridge

Year	B	C	NB	Present Values (r = 5%) B	C	NB
1	0	100	−100	0	95	−95
2	100	25	75	91	23	68
3	125	0	125	108	0	108
4	150	0	150	123	0	123
5	200	0	200	157	0	157
SUM	$575	$125	$450	$479	$118	$361

B-C Ratio = $479/$118 = 4.1

Project: Tennis Courts

Year	B	C	NB	Present Values (r = 5%) B	C	NB
1	0	300	−300	0	286	−286
2	200	100	100	181	91	91
3	300	50	250	259	43	216
4	400	0	400	329	0	329
5	500	0	500	392	0	392
SUM	$1,400	$450	$950	$1,161	$420	$742

B-C Ratio = $1,161/$420 = 2.8

---

new road. Direct benefits include reduced commuting time for drivers and indirect benefits include higher property values (that are unrelated to the fall in commuting costs) for certain neighborhoods. Is some cases, market prices provide useful information with which to estimate benefits. Figure 14-1 displayed total benefits associated with the market for street lamps. Since demand curves represent marginal benefit curves, estimation of demand curves allows calculation of total benefits. This method works fairly well for goods and services produced by both private *and* public sectors. Garbage collection and building of roads are two obvious cases in which there are active private and public markets. When there are private counterparts, total benefits may be estimated by information provided by demand curves. Benefits associated with a public water project may also be measured by estimating water demand supplied by a private company. Absence of a private market poses problems for estimation of demand since it is not always clear how to measure the demand for goods supplied by governments.

Consider the case of education. There is an active market in private education, and benefits surely flow to students, as well as to their parents. Private tuition rates are one possible measure of benefits associated with education. Significant differences between such diverse characteristics as SAT scores or rates of graduation imply differences in benefits provided in private versus public markets. If, for example, a local private school charges tuition of $3,500 and delivers a significantly higher SAT score than the local public school, private tuition may serve as a proxy for increased benefits associated with spending an additional $3,500 on education.

There are cases, however, such as air traffic control and national defense, with no private markets against which to calculate benefits. In these examples, their public goods characteristics create an added problem in measuring benefits. If, for example, the analyst took a survey that asked citizens to place a dollar amount on the benefits they receive from national defense programs, the free rider problem would likely emerge, thus resulting in underreporting of true benefits.

Indirect benefits, often called intangibles, are often difficult to measure as well. A critical issue is valuation of human life. We often hear, for example, of programs that educate the public about the health risks of using illegal drugs or the benefits in terms of saved lives that led to laws requiring that drivers use seat belts. But what dollar value can we place on saving a human life? While a common approach has been to predict lost earnings due to premature death, it is clearly more difficult to place a dollar figure on lost leisure and other intangibles associated with living. Lost time spent with children, for instance, is an extremely important part of many peoples' lives, and it is not clear how to place a dollar figure on this loss.

There are, however, private market counterparts that may be used to estimate value of life. For example, evidence is mounting that customers want air bags in their cars. By measuring the difference between the price of a car with and without air bags and observing whether air bags are purchased, we can obtain information on how much value buyers place on life. Along with estimates of the degree to which risk is lowered when air bags are in use, analysts may estimate the dollar figure that individual car buyers place on lower probabilities of death. Though this information is imperfect, it clearly provides more knowledge on the perceived value of life than when it is not considered.

Common Errors in Measuring Benefits

One common error is to double count benefits. It is incorrect, for instance, to count improvements in a local school and, at the same time, higher property values that stem from improvements in the local school. Since they tend to equal one another, one or the other should be counted. Another example is the benefits associated with a new public park. To the extent that benefits show up in higher property values for adjoining neighborhoods, these should be reflected in direct benefits associated with the new park.

Another common error is failure to distinguish between net benefits and transfers. An improved highway, for instance, may be expected to lead to higher income to motel owners. However, to some extent, higher income comes at the expense of travelers, who are charged higher rates and from other bypassed owners who now experience lower occupancy rates. Transfers result when higher benefits are associated with higher costs for other parties and should not be counted as improvements in net benefits; this effect is often called a pecuniary effect. Only changes in net benefits should be counted within the present value framework.

Valuing Life

Placing a value on life is one of the most difficult tasks of cost-benefit analysis, but this issue is at the heart of questions such as how safe a road or bridge must be. We need to answer these questions because we need to place values on lives lost or saved through chosen projects. Putting a cash value on a life is not as cold-hearted as one might think. We make comparable calculations whenever we go for a swim, drive, ride in an airplane, or smoke cigarettes. All of these activities have inherent risks, and calculations of their expected costs and benefits determine whether and to what extent we engage in these risky activities.

A common method of calculating the value of life is called the *human capital approach*. Under this method, value is calculated in terms of lost potential income. While this is fairly easy to calculate for those already in the work force, it is extremely difficult for those who have never worked outside the home. On another plane, critics argue that the human capital approach greatly underestimates the value of life because pain, grief, and suffering are not included in calculations. But how should these be included in the estimated value of life? The German government simply calculates the value of life by taking the undiscounted value of lost earnings. This clearly raises the estimated value of life but has not been followed by other governments.

Such governments as Sweden, Britain, the United States, and New Zealand no longer use the human capital approach. They measure the value of life by estimating the willingness to pay for additional safety measures such as safer cars or less flammable clothing, generally using two approaches. One approach simply asks individuals how much they are willing to pay for additional safety measures. This approach, however, assumes that individuals can easily calculate risks in many cases where risks are fairly small to begin with. The other approach calculates differences from market data. For example, if individuals are willing to pay $500 more for better brakes in their automobiles, this information is evaluated in terms of how much they are willing to pay for the associated greater safety. Pay differentials between high-risk jobs (e.g., coal mining) and low-risk jobs (e.g., college teaching) may also be used to calculate the prices that individuals are willing to pay for greater safety.

An interesting issue arises over whether values placed on lives saved vary with the type of risk. For instance, should a life saved from an auto accident be identical to one saved from a train wreck? While the U.S. government recognizes no difference, two British economists argue that the type of death does matter to individuals. They report that individuals are willing to pay more for saving lives on mass transit, such as subways, than on highways. They suggest that this reflects the belief that individuals have better chances of avoiding accidents when they are driving their own cars than when they are at the mercy of public transportation.

An interesting outcome of the willingness to pay method is that different governments report significant differences in estimated values of life. The highest value is that of $2.6 million in the case of the United States. Similar calculations in Sweden and Britain, however, estimate values of $1.2 million and $1.1 million, respectively, for each life saved.

Source: "The Price of Life: Why an American's Life Is Worth Twice as Much as a Swede's," *The Economist*, December 4, 1993, 74.

Measuring Costs

To build a new playground takes labor, concrete, land, machinery, and many other materials. Cost-benefit analysis must include initial costs as well as maintenance costs. The appropriate measurement is that of opportunity costs. Since both private and public sectors compete for resources, it is usually fairly easy to obtain good estimates of costs of such factors as labor and machinery. If, for example, the private market determines a price of $3,500 for playground equipment, then it is reasonable to conclude that this amount reflects the opportunity costs for resources used to produce this equipment. Information on costs of maintenance contracts can similarly be obtained by canvassing a number of private maintenance firms and determining the prices they charge for maintenance.

Several problems require elaboration. When a new playground is built, it is possible that various negative externalities are produced, lowering the welfare of various parties. For example, neighbors may not appreciate the increased street traffic and noise associated with a new playground. This, however, can be measured if property values fall after production of the new playground and should be included in calculation of changes in net benefits.

There are also problems in estimating costs of resources when markets are not perfectly competitive. Microeconomic theory shows that monopolists pay inputs below their marginal value, and when public projects hire resources in monopolistic markets, costs therefore tend to be underestimated. Other biases are evident as well when resources are hired from publicly subsidized industries in which resources tend to be paid in excess of their marginal value. These issues are likely to be difficult to deal with and are commonly disregarded in cost-benefit analysis.

A common error is to underestimate the costs of using previously unemployed resources. Some studies have even argued that unemployed labor has a zero cost. This may appear to be reasonable at first glance, but consider how many workers you could hire for a wage of zero dollars. Although it is not always clear what cost to place on unemployed resources, it is clearly not zero. The controversy therefore is over what cost to attach and as with benefits, clear, precise estimates are not always apparent.

Many issues surround the fact that taxes are generally used to fund public programs. Costs of collecting taxes are costs associated with public programs and therefore should be measured in cost-benefit analysis. Taxation also produces an *excess burden,* which is defined as the lower well-being of taxpayers that results from distortions in choices after taxes are levied. Many indirect effects also result when taxes reduce disposable consumer income. When taxes are raised to fund a new playground, some taxpayers may reduce other activities and thus affect the well-being of other members of society who do not benefit from the playground. If higher taxes, for instance, reduce maintenance of homes, resulting lower property values are an added cost associated with a new playground.

Measurement Problems and Cost-Benefit Analysis

It may appear impossible to measure benefits and costs when private market counterparts do not exist, when there are positive or negative externalities, or projects have public goods characteristics. But various rules of thumb are often useful in the real world. A rough estimate of indirect benefits, for example, may be implied by estimating what indirect benefits must equal to justify a certain level of direct benefits and costs. For example, suppose that it is possible to measure all direct benefits and costs for a new highway project and that net benefits are estimated to be −$150 million. Unless it can be argued that indirect benefits, such as saved lives, exceed $150 million, then it is implied that the project produces negative net benefits and is no longer a candidate for public funding. This is obviously not a precise technique, but it nonetheless deals with an issue that by its very nature is difficult to measure.

Another technique is to provide several estimates of benefits and costs. For example, there may be high and low estimates for how many campers will use a new campground or for how many citizens will use a new public library. This is one commonly used method for evaluating projects when there is some uncertainty over benefit and cost streams.

What Discount Rate Should Government Use?

Opportunity Cost of Not Allowing Private Sector to Allocate Resources

Public sector funding of any project means that resources are taken from the private sector. An obvious means of defining the public sector discount rate is therefore to measure opportunity costs as employment of those resources in the private sector. Alternatives may, for example, include a rate of 10 percent offered for deposits in a local bank and a return of 9 percent when those resources are used to construct a new building or purchase a computer.

Income Taxes and the Discount Rate

Much of private investment activity is financed by borrowing. Note that corporate income taxes influence the rates at which corporations borrow from investors. If, for example, the corporate income tax rate is 50 percent, then rates of return to investors are one-half of the interest paid to them by corporations. In a world in which investors see no risk differences between corporate and government debt, corporations must double the rate of return on their debt in order to compete against debt sold by governments. If, for instance, government debt offers 5 percent and corporations offered 5 percent as well, it would be extremely difficult, if not impossible, for corporations to attract investors. To be on equal footing, corporations must offer investors 10 percent since the after-tax return to investors is only 2.5 percent when 5 percent is offered by private corporations. In the presence of a corporate income tax rate of 50 percent and a government borrowing rate of 5 percent, the appropriate discount rate for government is 10 percent, not 5 percent. Ten percent represents the opportunity costs, or value of investment activity lost to society, as measured by lost private investment. *Pretax* rates of return therefore measure opportunity costs when the public sector displaces resources previously employed in private investment activity.

The problem here, however, is that resources taken from the private sector would normally have been devoted to both investment and consumption activities. The discount rate should be based on the *after-tax* rate of return to saving when private consumption is displaced by public projects. That is, if individuals save $100 at an annual rate of 6 percent, only $3 in *post-tax* interest income is earned when the tax rate is 50 percent. Since $3 measures lost earnings, the appropriate discount rate is 3 percent for public projects. *After-tax* rates of return therefore measure the opportunity costs of lost consumption.

It has been suggested that a weighted average of the returns on displaced investment and consumption be used to measure public discount rates. This approach is difficult to implement because tax rates are not uniform among businesses and individuals. Another complication is that it is not always clear which resources represent displaced investment and which represent displaced consumption.

Risk and the Discount Rate

There is no question that public debt tends to carry lower interest rates than debt sold in the private sector. This difference is often attributed to lower risk associated with investment by the public sector. As we saw in our examination of off-budget credit and insurance policies, risk is an attribute related to probability of loan default or untimely payback of debt. Risk associated with private investment is often measured by a risk premium that, for example, equals 2 percent when debt of the U.S. Treasury offers 8 percent and debt of a AAA-rated corporation offers 10 percent.

At first glance it may appear that risk premiums should be excluded from the opportunity costs of public projects since when resources are shifted from the private to the public sector, risk is somehow removed from investment projects. This thought implies that public projects are risk free, since there is virtually no likelihood that the United States government would go bankrupt and renege on its debt obligations. Two factors, however, suggest that private risk premiums should remain in public discount rates.

First, if the public discount rate is to measure the true opportunity costs of resources displaced in the private sector, then risk is very much a part of those costs and should therefore be included in the public discount rate. Second, it is incorrect to believe that risk is absent when the public sector allocates resources. Risk is not magically removed when resources are shifted from private to public uses. Our discussion of off-budget public programs in Chapter 10 showed that risk is shifted from private market participants to taxpayers. Even though it is true that risk of bankruptcy is virtually zero, taxpayers do bear the risks associated with public projects.

Our discussion of off-budget policies also showed that problems associated with moral hazard and adverse selection occur when the public sector allocates resources in credit and insurance markets. In some cases, risk rises when the public sector allocates resources previously employed in the private sector. Even in these cases, however, there is no reason to raise the risk premiums when resources are transferred from the private to the public sector since the discount rate measures risk associated with lost private sector uses, *not* public sector uses. Moreover, the extent that public programs do, in fact, raise overall risk, should be reflected in higher costs (tax burdens) in the cost-benefit calculations. This will lower the estimated present value of those projects and therefore their attractiveness as well.

A Lower Discount Rate for Public Projects?

Some economists argue that public projects should be discounted at a lower rate of discount than private sector projects. Two effects on our present value framework occur when the discount rate is lowered. One effect is that lower public discount rates raise present values of projects undertaken by the public sector and therefore may be expected to result in more projects undertaken by the public sector. The other effect is to change the distribution of short-run versus long-run policies of the public sector. We have previously demonstrated that the lower the discount rate, the more attractive are benefits that are further deferred into the future. When the discount rate is lowered, a shifting from shorter- to longer-term policies may be predicted to result.

Shortsighted Policies?

Some economists argue that public policies have an inherent tendency to be shortsighted. This may occur even though policies directed toward education, child care, research, and health care are often promoted on the basis of their long-term beneficial effects on the well-being of society. The policy process, however, may be biased against longer-run policies. An often-cited reason is that current generations are too narrowly self-interested and, therefore, undervalue benefits that current policies exert on future generations. This problem may be remedied by lowering the rate of discount that promotes greater numbers of longer-term policies.

Policies Addressing Market Failures

Our discussions of negative externalities and public goods have suggested various methods for public sector intervention to improve allocative efficiency. Because it may be argued that benefits or costs are improperly measured when market failures exist, one way of righting this wrong is to adjust discount rates accordingly. If, for example, benefits associated with an environmental cleanup program are believed to be underestimated, a lowering of the discount rate raises the project's present value of net benefits.

Note, however, that if an analyst believed that benefits were underestimated, the benefit stream used in the cost-benefit framework could be raised as well. In fact, it would appear to be more appropriate to raise estimated benefits, since this would be a direct adjustment to the present value framework rather than a change of the discount rate as an indirect method of righting of wrongs associated with underestimation of benefits. The point here is that if information exists on the extent to which costs or benefits are mismeasured, it is more appropriate to directly change benefits and costs than to adjust discount rates indirectly in hopes of achieving allocative efficiency. Note, as well, that if benefits and costs cannot be accurately measured, it is also impossible to know appropriate changes in public discount rates.

Redistributional Arguments

Arguments are also made that a lower public discount rate will better promote the public sector's ability to meet various equity goals. If, for example, it is believed that the private sector underallocates resources toward housing, food, and education for the poor, it may not be appropriate to use public discount rates for these programs that are based on the opportunity costs of resources in the private sector. One approach is to use cost-benefit analysis to analyze the distribution of benefits and costs over various classes of individuals or regions of the country.[13] Applications may include lowering discount rates on projects which redistribute resources from rich to poor so as to make them more appealing within the present value framework.

---

[13] See Arnold C. Harberger, "On the Use of Distributional Weights in Social Cost-Benefit Analysis," *Journal of Political Economy* 86 (April 1978): S87–S120.

The Policy Process and Cost-Benefit Analysis

So far, we have implicitly assumed that the policy process will approve only those policies that are justified on the basis of careful cost-benefit analysis. But it is appropriate to ask whether this is a good characterization of the policy process.

Incentives to Use Cost-Benefit Analysis

There are important differences between incentives of different parties to utilize cost-benefit analysis. Actions or projects undertaken today exert effects on profitability over many years. In the private market, firms are often assumed to maximize, in an *ex ante* sense, the present value of their firms, which are the discounted values of all future profits.[14] Owners of firms are therefore believed to undertake cost-benefit analysis as a means of promoting long-term profits. Government, in contrast, does not operate under similar long-term goals. When goals other than allocative efficiency (for example, income redistribution) are present, achievement of goals may not be dependent on undertaking careful cost-benefit analysis.

Voters, Interest Groups, and Cost-Benefit Analysis

Marketing Orders of the U.S. Department of Agriculture

It is instructive to examine the role that special interest groups may play in the use of cost-benefit analysis in the public sector.[15] As an example of a policy that does not stand the test of cost-benefit analysis, consider the U.S. Department of Agriculture's marketing orders, which were first introduced some sixty years ago, as part of President Franklin Roosevelt's New Deal during the Great Depression. These orders eventually restricted supply in markets for lemons, oranges, and other crops. For example, the marketing order for California-Arizona navel oranges was introduced in 1953, under President Dwight Eisenhower; it establishes the maximum quantity each supplier may ship to the domestic fresh market on a weekly basis. (This order was once temporarily suspended, by President George Bush, on December 14, 1992.) Once the quota is reached, oranges must be sold abroad or to the domestic processing industry. The result of the marketing order is simple: The limitation on supply in the fresh market raises revenues of growers as orange prices rise. Marketing orders have caused price increases by farmers that have then led to an annual disposal of as many as 50 million lemons, 2 billion oranges, 100 million pounds of raisins, 7 million pounds of filberts, millions of plums and nectarines, and so on.[16]

There are also price support policies through which the government guarantees the purchase of unlimited quantities of a crop at the price support level. Because farmers have no incentive to sell crops at prices lower than they can sell them to the

---

[14] See Michael Jensen and William H. Meckling, "The Theory of the Firm: Managerial Behavior, Agency Costs and Ownership Structure," *Journal of Financial Economics* 3 (October 1976): 305–360.

[15] *Economic Report of the President,* February 1992.

[16] See James Bovard, "Lost in the American Agricultural Swamp," *Economic Affairs* (December–January 1990): 1–9.

government, support prices become minimum prices for U.S. consumers. Sometimes price supports for sugar and rice have been four times the world price and, for butter, three times the world price. In 1986, the federal government paid farmers $4.35 a bushel for wheat and then sold some of this to the Soviet Union for less than $2 a bushel.

It has been estimated that agricultural policies result in roughly $10 billion in higher prices for food as well as $20 billion in federal transfers to farmers.[17] Producers gain income and losses are borne by consumers and taxpayers. Let us examine marketing orders within a cost-benefit framework.

The Department of Agriculture estimates that elimination of marketing orders for oranges would cost producers about $13 million annually and save consumers about $30 million.[18] Because benefits clearly are outweighed by costs, we can appropriately ask why these policies are approved in the policy process. The commonly cited rationales for these policies are to stabilize prices, control quality, and maintain a tradition of small farms in the United States, but these policies have over the years clearly led to income transfers for farmers, as evidenced by the growth of average farm family income as a percent of all family incomes: While 88 percent in 1960, this statistic grew to 139 percent in 1987.[19]

Special interest groups are united by a common interest, and often that interest is the pursuit of income transfers. You will recall that this phenomenon has been called rent seeking, attempts by special interest groups to win favors, or rents, from policymakers through the policy process. There are inherent incentives in democracy for special interest groups to lobby policymakers to transfer income from the many to the few. Redistribution occurs because policies generally confer substantial benefits on relatively small groups while at the same time distributing costs widely over the population. In the example of marketing orders for orange producers, benefits are estimated at $3,150 for each producer and costs average only $.12 per consumer; costs are clearly spread thinly across all orange consumers.[20]

Benefits and costs for supporting or fighting this program are quite different for producers than consumers. While the individual orange consumer has little financial incentive to gain $.12 a year, every orange producer has a substantial incentive to maintain or increase the annual transfer of $3,150. Given differences in incentives, it is predictable that policymakers are likely to respond to powerful rent seeking signals of orange producers.

The Audit Function of Policymakers

In theory, policymakers may police, or in some way block and discourage, rent seeking efforts of special interests. The judicious use of cost-benefit analysis would contribute to blocking programs that transfer income in the way just described. In fact,

---

[17] See Bovard, "Lost in the American Agricultural Swamp."

[18] *Economic Report of the President,* January 1992, 169.

[19] From Table 3-2 (and references cited therein) in James Bovard, *The Farm Fiasco* (San Francisco: ICS Press, 1991).

[20] *Economic Report of the President,* February 1992, 169.

this function of oversight is the responsibility of the executive branch of government, the branch with the largest and most diverse constituency of elected policymakers. It is therefore more probable that the incentive of the executive branch to require careful use of cost-benefit analysis is greater than it is for members of Congress. While farmers, for example, may represent a substantial portion of the constituency of a member of Congress, they necessarily represent a much smaller portion of the President's constituency.

At least two reasons, however, suggest limited potential for executive oversight. One is that it may be difficult for the executive branch to convince the public of the need to introduce a more rigorous requirement of cost-benefit analysis in all policies of the public sector when specific concerns are at issue. The public seems able to recognize that the overall scale of spending (or transfers) may be too large, but when a specific policy, which affects individuals, is isolated as being too far out of line with prescriptions of cost-benefit analysis, it is unlikely that the executive branch can overrule the organized actions of the special interest group who gains from the policy.[21] As we have argued, it is difficult to remove policies that spread costs thinly over the population, but transfer relatively large benefits to a small, but well-organized, special interest group.

A second reason for difficulties is the nature of the process through which policies are debated. Congress is the agent for legislation and spending, and therefore we must know the institutional nature of Congress and its operations in order to understand how policies are approved. Prior to legislation, policies are routinely discussed and reviewed in various committees. As we have discussed, cost-benefit analysis requires careful discussion of costs, benefits, and appropriate rates of discount. However, it has been recently argued that Congress conducts hearings that award a one-sided bias to proponents of policies. If this is true, then cost-benefit analysis is not properly used, since testimony and debate focus on benefits and neglect costs of programs.

A recent study has investigated the list of witnesses that provide input into congressional hearings.[22] A compilation of congressional witnesses before fourteen hearings shows that, of 1,060 witnesses, 96 percent, or 1,104, spoke in favor of programs (and usually higher spending); 39, or 3.7 percent, were neutral or mixed and 7, or less than 1 percent, opposed programs or spending. As one example, six witnesses, all in favor, spoke before a congressional committee on job training; they included an economics professor, the Labor Department official in charge of the program, and officials of the private companies that operated training facilities for the program. The discussion was not suspenseful. Another hearing was on "Private Sector Initiatives to Feed America's Poor," and eight of eleven witnesses were supporters of an expanded private sector role in antipoverty programs; many of the private sector programs, however, were themselves federally funded programs, and as for the one dissenter who provided testimony, he appeared at the end of the session, when all the senators had left for the day, and a staff member concluded the session. The same study finds that

---

[21] *Economic Report of the President,* January 1989, 169.

[22] James L. Payne, *The Culture of Spending: Why Congress Lives beyond Our Means* (San Francisco: ICS Press, 1991).

a majority of congressional witnesses are federal administrators (47 percent), followed by lobbyists (33 percent), state and local government officials (10 percent), members of Congress (6 percent), and representatives of business firms and consultants (4 percent).

Does Cost-Benefit Analysis Lead to Pareto Efficient Policies?

An implicit assumption of most cost-benefit analysis is that it is not necessary that individual losers be compensated when policies are approved. But, from the Pareto efficiency criterion, such policies are not efficient unless they compensate losers adequately so that no individual suffers a net loss. We argued in Chapter 3 that it is often impossible to provide full compensation for all losers, but it is worth remembering that use of criteria other than Pareto efficiency does not provide unambiguous net gains to societies composed of large and diverse collections of individuals. There have been some attempts to introduce equity considerations into cost-benefit analysis of public projects, but these necessarily involve interpersonal utility comparisons, which, from a policy point of view, tend to introduce more problems than they remove.

Cost-Benefit Analysis in an Imperfect Public Sector

Cost-benefit analysis provides a potentially valuable means of assessing the usefulness of public policies. It measures costs, benefits, and discount rates, and, provided that these measures are valid, alternative policies and projects may be accurately compared and evaluated.

In an imperfect public sector, three fundamental issues require further consideration. First, is it possible to correctly measure costs, benefits, and rates of discount? Second, measurement problems aside, can the policy process be relied upon to follow through on the careful recommendations of cost-benefit analysts? Third, is it correct to believe that maximization of the present value of net benefits actually provides a means of evaluating usefulness of public projects? Because cost-benefit analysis rejects the Pareto efficiency criterion, it is appropriate to question whether recommended policies unambiguously enhance social welfare.

This discussion may seem hard on the cost-benefit framework. It is, for example, unreasonable to assess the usefulness of cost-benefit analysis against the standard of perfect information or a perception of an ideal policy process. Improvements in analysis are surely to be the focus of the research agendas of many economists for years to come. But even with its present observable faults, careful use of the cost-benefit framework does effectively challenge policy advocates to provide a rigorous and systematic case for their policies. Some advocates may feel comfortable with assertions that their policies improve social welfare; cost-benefit analysis requires them to justify their policies on the basis of evidence that can be compared against the competing claims for those same resources by proponents of other programs. In this way, and assuming away previously discussed problems associated with special interest groups and the policy process, cost-benefit analysis provides a competitive process that in many ways mirrors the ways in which resources are allocated in the private sector.

Summary

- Cost-benefit analysis provides a framework for evaluating the usefulness of alternative public projects. Cost-benefit analysis allows for comparison of alternative projects characterized by dissimilar distributions of costs and benefits over time.
- The fundamental rule of cost-benefit analysis is to allocate resources to their most efficient uses. Present value analysis measures costs and benefits in terms of what future dollars are worth to us today. The rate of discount is the interest rate used to calculate present value.
- There are two primary implications of present value analysis. First, the more remote are returns, the lower are present values. Second, the higher the discount rate, the lower the present value of returns.
- The three major methods for choosing between projects on the basis of the present value framework are: maximum present value of net benefits, internal rates of discount, and benefit-cost ratios. Problems with using internal rates of discount and benefit-cost ratios indicate that maximum present value of net benefits is the best criterion for assigning priority to projects.
- Cost-benefit analysis is not easy to implement. Benefits are both direct and indirect and, in many cases, there are no private market counterparts from which to estimate benefit levels. Costs are difficult to estimate as well. There are problems in estimating costs in noncompetitive markets, there are external effects that are difficult to quantify, and there are excess burdens that arise when taxes are collected to pay for public programs. It is also not always clear which rate of discount to use.

Review Questions

1. What is cost-benefit analysis?
2. What is present value?
3. What is the relationship between the rate of discount and the present value of returns?
4. What are the major methods for choosing between projects? Is any method preferred over the others?

Discussion Questions

1. Explain why a program that offers total benefits in excess of total costs may not be recommended for funding by a cost-benefit analyst.
2. Suppose you are a policymaker and a local civic organization comes to your committee on parks and recreation and argues that a public expenditure of $250,000 will greatly enhance the welfare of the local community. What questions would you ask in terms of a careful cost-benefit study?
3. Suppose there are two mutually exclusive projects competing for funds of a local government. Project A builds a new swimming pool, and project B is a road extension. What benefits and costs are likely to be associated with these projects?
4. Below are the net benefits associated with the previously-mentioned public projects: Project A builds a new swimming pool and project B is a road extension. Calculate, for $r = 0$, $r = .05$ and $r = .10$, the present values of net benefits for these two projects. Discuss how (and why) choice of the discount rate affects which project is given first priority for funding.

	Net Benefit Project	
Year	A	B
1	−$500	$ 10
2	−350	40
3	10	50
4	500	100
5	950	150
SUM	$610	$350

saw what happened when public policy requires cost-benefit analysts to include the factor of inflation $(1 + \pi)^n$ in the denominator but to exclude it in the numerator of present value calculations. Explain what happens when the opposite rule is imposed. What bias would such a rule impose on the framework for choosing among public projects?

6. It has been shown that public policies may increase the risk associated with resource allocation when they promote moral hazard. Explain whether this possibility argues for a higher rate of discount for public projects versus private projects.

7. A potential problem applying cost-benefit analysis in the public sector is that governments have so many policies and, inevitably, some may conflict at times with one another. For example, the public sector subsidizes tobacco farmers and, at the same time, expends resources to make people quit smoking. Explain the precautions that could be used to prevent such problems in application of cost-benefit analysis.

8. Do you believe that public policy has an inherent tendency to be shortsighted? If so, what factors might explain this behavior, and what changes would you suggest to increase the proportion of projects with longer-term benefits?

9. How likely do you believe it is to expect the policy process to make judicious use of cost-benefit analysis in selections of projects to fund? Are there any changes that might be introduced into the policy process that might insure a greater respect for cost-benefit analysis?

10. Which of the following two contracts would you prefer? Contract A: Payment of $500,000 today or Contract B: $2 million deferred for 20 years? Assume $r = .10$.

Key Words

Present value
Rate of discount
Internal rates of discount
Benefit-cost ratio

PART 5

Financing Government Activities

Chapter 15
Financing Public Expenditures: An Introduction

Chapter 16
Principles of Tax Analysis

Chapter 17
Financing Expenditures through Budget Deficits

CHAPTER 15

Financing Public Expenditures: An Introduction

In President William Jefferson Clinton's inaugural address of January 20, 1993, his reference to taxes as "sacrifices" was widely observed as an attempt to remind voters that in order to provide public programs, governments must collect tax revenues. Taxes have been with us a long time; according to Benjamin Franklin they are one of life's two certainties. And the Boston Tea Party, as long ago as it was, may pretty well sum up many Americans' attitude toward taxes today.

Every public budget has two sides: expenditures and the financing of those expenditures. Taxation and budget deficits are the primary methods of public finance. When tax collections are less than public expenditures, a budget deficit occurs, and the difference is funded through sale of public debt. Although a budget surplus is also possible when tax collections are greater than public expenditures, the federal government has operated under a budget deficit in every year since 1969. Because of the federal government's persistent reliance on budget deficits, we devote an entire chapter on this important topic of public finance.

A wide range of taxes funds expenditures. Taxes may be applied to incomes of individuals or corporations; they may be levied on the purchase of goods such as gasoline, cigarettes, and groceries. Even casual observation of political debates and campaigns demonstrates a national preoccupation with linking tax policy to the issue of fairness. Everyone seems to agree that the ultimate objective of tax policy is fairness. But we are going to see evidence of many disagreements about what constitutes a fair system of taxation.

First, we begin with the basic issues:

❏ Which taxes are used to finance expenditures?
❏ What are the general trends of tax policies in the United States and other countries?
❏ What are the primary issues about the taxpayers' burdens?
❏ To what degree are tax policies substitutes for expenditure policies?
❏ What role does the policy process play in determining tax policy?

Financing Trends

We examine two primary characteristics of financing trends. We will first focus on aggregate tax receipts and examine the ways in which taxes as a share of the economy have evolved over time. We then turn our attention to the types of taxes that underlie the aggregate level of taxation and study how tax sources have changed over time.

Aggregate Financing Trends

Figure 15-1 shows federal tax revenues as a share of GDP in the United States since 1935. Starting at roughly 5 percent, tax revenues grew rapidly during World War II (1941–45) where, at its highest level, tax revenues were almost 22 percent of GDP. Although tax revenues fell in the aftermath of World War II, tax revenues have never come close to pre–World War II levels. Tax revenues fell to 15 percent of GDP in 1950 and have remained within the relatively narrow range of 17 to 20 percent since the early 1950s.

Changing Tax Sources

Taxation takes many different forms. Taxes may be levied on income and wealth, for example, or on specific goods such as gasoline and tobacco. Historically, the federal government has received tax income from five tax sources:

- *Individual Income*—taxation of the personal income of individuals. The largest category of taxation, this source accounts for 40 to 45 percent of total federal tax revenues.
- *Corporate Income*—taxation of the income of corporations. This tax source reached a high of 32 percent of total taxes in the 1950s, but it now provides roughly 10 percent of all collections.
- *Social Insurance*—payroll taxes collected for Social Security, Medicare, and unemployment compensation. This tax source has grown rapidly from roughly 10 percent in the 1950s to 37 percent of all tax collections.
- *Excise*—taxes on goods, such as alcohol and tobacco, and services, such as telephone, highway, waterway, and airport usage. Since 1950, this source has fallen from 20 percent to roughly 5 percent of tax collections.
- *Other*—estate and gift taxes, custom duties, fees and deposits of earnings made by the Federal Reserve System. This source has provided a fairly stable 5 percent of collections.

Figure 15-2 plots the histories of these tax sources since 1950.

Tax reform is the vehicle through which all major changes in the tax system occur. The issue of who should bear burdens of taxation must be a *normative* issue since there is no way of knowing with perfect certainty what constitutes a fair and just tax system. What is believed to constitute a fair tax system is subject to continual reappraisal as evidenced by the many changes in tax laws each year. This should not be surprising, since the same reappraisal also occurs each year on the expenditure side of the budget. Questions about how much to spend on welfare and national defense are, in many respects, no different than questions on the type of tax policy we should

Tax reform
is a process whereby major changes in the tax system occur.

Chapter 15   Financing Public Expenditures: An Introduction   415

**FIGURE 15-1
Federal Tax Receipts as a Percentage of GDP**

Source: Budget of the United States Government, 1995.

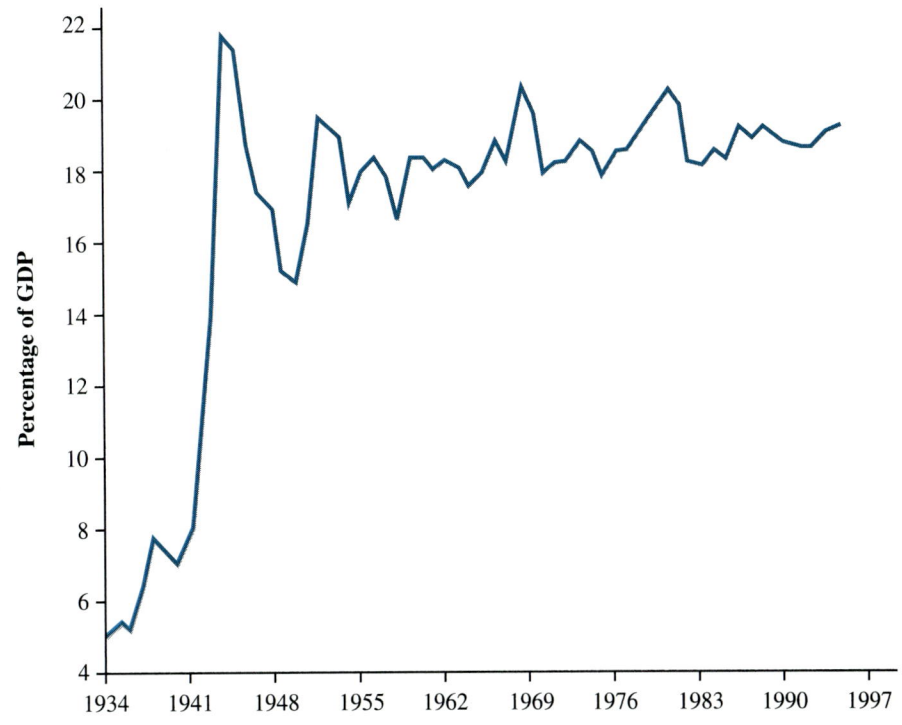

**FIGURE 15-2
Composition of Federal Tax Receipts**

Source: Budget of the United States Government, 1995.

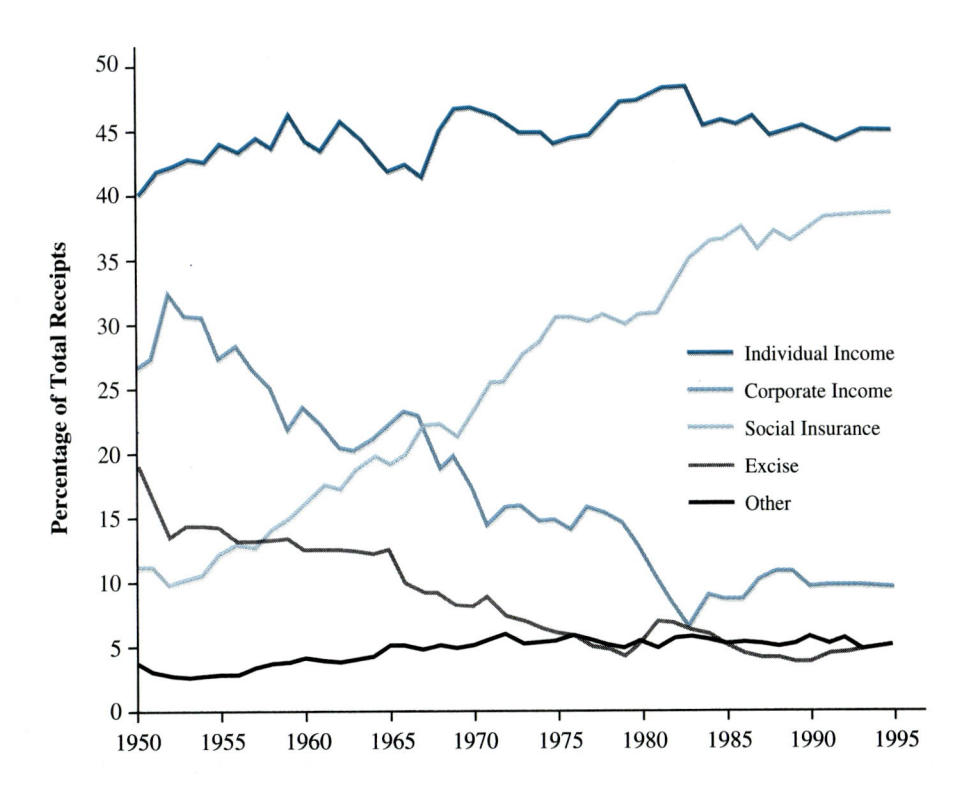

undertake. One fundamental change has been that as taxes on corporations have accounted for a notably smaller percentage of total collections, there has also been a significant increase in the percentage of taxes collected through social insurance programs.

Tax Trends of Other Countries

It is useful to compare U.S. tax trends with those of other countries.[1] Figure 15-3 compares the U.S. experience with that of the OECD countries.[2] Although there was little difference between tax revenues as shares of GDP in 1965, a widening gap is evident in intervening years. All these countries have experienced rising tax revenues, but the upward trend in the United States has been far more gentle than in the OECD countries. In 1990, for example, tax revenues were 40 percent of GDP in the OECD countries, but 30 percent in the United States.

Figure 15-4 indicates a substantial difference in tax sources as well.

- *PI* refers to personal income taxes; roughly 36 percent of tax collections in the United States are from this source, but the average for all OECD countries is roughly 30 percent of tax revenues.
- *TGS* refers to tax collections from excise taxes on specific goods (such as tobacco and alcohol) and on general sales. The combined OECD countries (22 percent of all tax collections) clearly rely on this tax much more than does the United States (16 percent of tax collections).
- *TSS* refers to Social Security tax collections; they comprise 29 percent of all tax collections in the OECD countries and in the United States as well.
- *PROP* refers to taxation of property. Primarily the province of state and local governments, this tax source accounts for 10 percent of tax revenues in the United States and for 8 percent of all OECD tax revenues.
- *CI* refers to taxes on corporations, and it accounts for roughly 8.5 percent of tax collections in the United States and in all OECD countries.

Benefits as a Principle of Tax Policy

Benefit Principle in Private Markets

We have said that private markets allocate resources efficiently, though exceptions occur in cases of imperfect information, monopoly, externalities, and public goods. Private markets maximize net social benefits when prices reflect marginal social costs and marginal social benefits. One way of viewing allocative efficiency is to

---

[1] The percentages in the next two graphs are not entirely compatible with earlier graphs. Unlike our earlier graphs, which focus on the federal government, we now compare tax policies of all governments (local, state, and federal) in these countries.

[2] The OECD countries are Australia, Austria, Belgium, Canada, Denmark, Finland, France, Germany, Greece, Ireland, Italy, Japan, Luxembourg, the Netherlands, New Zealand, Norway, Portugal, Spain, Sweden, Switzerland, Turkey, the United Kingdom, and the United States. Since the United States is a member of the OECD, it is included in the OECD average of tax collections.

**FIGURE 15-3
Tax Revenues as a Percentage of GDP**
OECD Average versus the United States

Source: Significant Features of Fiscal Federalism, February 1992.

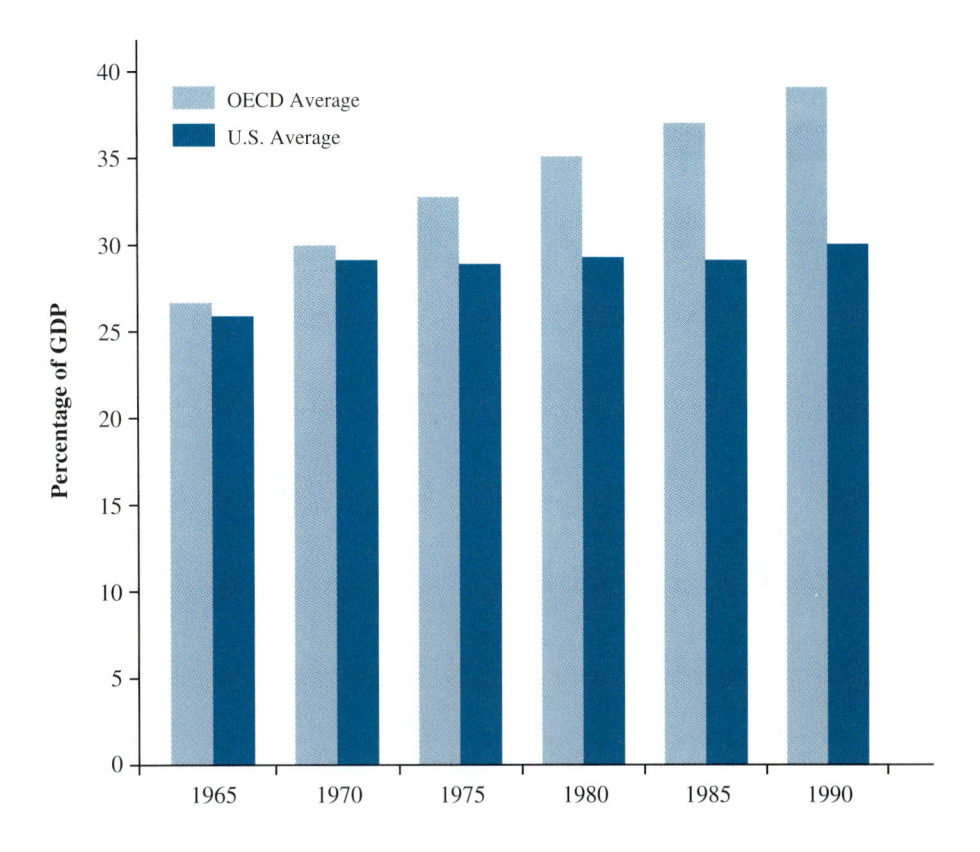

Benefit principle is a taxation principle whereby taxes are assigned on the basis of benefits received.

remember that pricing corresponds to a **benefit principle.** This principle characterizes transactions that meet the following two conditions.

- Only those who receive benefits are charged for use of resources used to provide goods. In other words, if Ken decides not to purchase season tickets to the local ballet company this year, he does not have to contribute to the ballet company. Michiko, however, contributes to the local football team every time she buys a ticket and watches a game.

- Prices charged by suppliers reflect benefits received by those who purchase their products. Recall that since prices equal marginal social benefits, this characteristic occurs when resources are allocated efficiently.

Notice that application of the benefit principle is synonymous with equity in some respects, when *fairness* is defined as charging consumers for the resources they consume. Those who receive benefits from goods are charged for the resources used to produce those goods, and those who receive no benefits are charged nothing. Application of the benefit principle is also sensitive to the frequency with which individuals consume goods. If, for instance, at the market equilibrium price of $1 per apple, Kendra chooses three apples, she contributes $3 toward the resources used to produce apples. When Manuel chooses four apples, he contributes $4 toward

**FIGURE 15-4
Percentage Distribution of Taxes in 1989**
OECD Average versus the United States

Source: *Significant Features of Fiscal Federalism,* 1992.

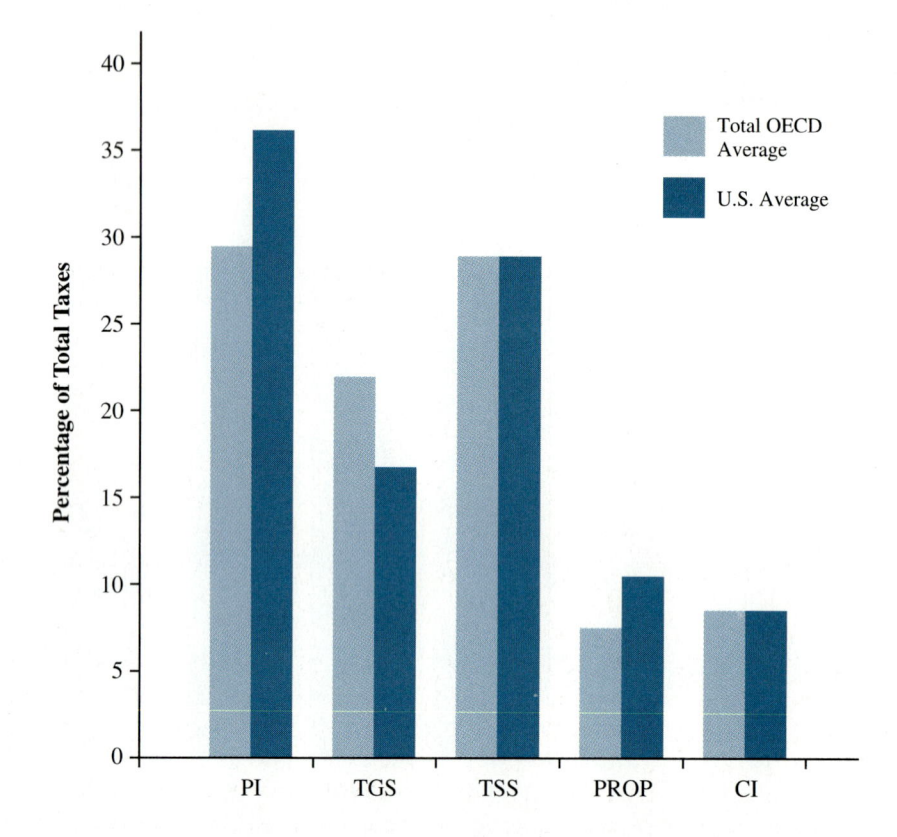

resources used by suppliers of apples. In this way, application of the benefit principle is sensitive to the use of resources by different consumers.

Benefit Principle in Public Markets: Application to Private Goods

There is considerable agreement that application of the benefit principle leads to desirable outcomes in private markets. This agreement leads us to consider whether this principle may be applied in the public sector. Since taxes are to the public sector what prices are to the private sector, cases arise where the benefit principle may be extended to tax policy.

Our discussion assumes for the time being that the public sector provides only *private goods,* which are characterized by rivalry in consumption and an environment in which suppliers may easily exclude nonpayers from enjoying their benefits. A soda, for instance, can be consumed by only one individual at a time, and if no shoplifting occurs, sellers can easily collect payment from all customers. *Public goods,* in contrast, are nonrival in consumption and characterized by lack of exclusion. National defense is commonly considered a public good, since consumption by one citizen does not ordinarily keep any other citizen from enjoying the benefits of a well-protected nation, and it is difficult or impossible to exclude nonpaying citizens from enjoying these benefits.

Application of the benefit principle in the public sector requires that citizens be taxed according to the benefits they receive from goods. If, for instance, Mary enjoys camping in a public campground, her tax bill should be directly related to her benefits. When both Manual and Kendra enjoy camping, higher taxes should be levied on the individual who receives the greatest benefits.

User charges, or fees, are tax policies consistent with the benefit principle. Charges are often levied on users of public toll roads, bridges, museums, parks, and campgrounds. Only users pay charges and fees. It is important to understand that coercion is not involved since, as in private markets, nonusers are not required to pay for any resources used to produce these services. Tax bills of users, however, rise with frequency of consumption.

Tax Earmarking

Tax earmarking is a tax principle whereby revenues are directed toward payment of specific programs.

The benefit principle is consistent with the practice of **tax earmarking,** which directs the proceeds from a tax source to the payment of a specific public program. For instance, taxes on gasoline consumption are often earmarked for funding public highways and in this way are very similar to user charges. Since drivers pay taxes on gasoline purchases, taxes are levied on those who benefit from public roads. Tax bills also rise with usage, since those who drive more tend to purchase more gasoline.

In principle, user charges and tax earmarking are applications of the benefit principle, but their application is often not entirely consistent in practice. When tax earmarking fails to raise revenues that cover total program costs, other funding sources make up the difference. If, for instance, the annual operating cost of a toll road is $11 million, but annual toll collections raise only $8 million, $3 million in other funding sources must make up the difference. When other tax sources are used, however, it is likely that nonusers, or infrequent users, will subsidize frequent users of the toll road. This is often the case in practice. For instance, most public parks do not cover operating costs through user fees, and to the extent that the general tax-paying population pays the difference, subsidies (or transfers) are awarded to users of public parks. This is clearly inconsistent application of the benefit principle, which requires that only those who benefit from public programs should be required to pay for operating costs.

Benefit Principle in Public Markets: Application to Public Goods

Private markets will tend to misallocate resources in cases of *public goods*. We now show that it is difficult to design tax policies for public goods that successfully adhere to the benefit principle.

Recall what constitutes optimal provision of public goods (assume only pure public goods here). Although market demand curves for private goods are derived by *horizontal* summation of individual demand curves, market demand curves for public goods are derived by *vertical* summation of individual demand curves. This difference stems from the fact that public goods, by definition, cannot be characterized by rivalry in consumption and therefore, once the market produces a given quantity, all consumers may equally enjoy benefits that flow from that quantity. One more consumer of national defense, for instance, does not reduce benefits for any other consumer.

Efficient output of a public good occurs when marginal social benefits equal marginal social costs, or where the market demand curve intersects the supply curve. Lindahl prices are prices that equal the marginal benefits of each consumer when the efficient output of a public good is provided. When Lindahl prices are charged, prices bear a perfect correspondence with the benefit principle. As long as tax policy is based on Lindahl pricing, public goods may, in theory, be taxed according to the benefit principle.

Problems, however, may prevent Lindahl pricing from guiding tax policy in practice. Recall that the *free rider effect* describes the natural tendency for some individuals to want to pay nothing for public goods they consume. If individuals are able to enjoy the benefits of a well-protected nation and are not required to pay for its costs, many individuals would choose to pay nothing. Those who choose to be free riders may continue to benefit from provision of the public goods since, by their very nature, it is difficult or impossible to exclude nonpayers from receiving their benefits. Sellers, however, will not base resource allocation on benefits received by free riders, but, rather, only on benefits received by paying customers. Private markets therefore underestimate social benefits when they exclude benefits enjoyed by free riders and result in too little production for society.

The free rider effect suggests an obvious problem with applying the benefit principle in cases of public goods. Policymakers may never know the true benefits received by all who consume public goods. Tax agents may request that beneficiaries report the level of their benefits, but the free rider effect suggests an inherent tendency of some beneficiaries to underreport levels of benefits.

When the free rider problem is considered within the context of the requirements of Lindahl pricing, it becomes highly improbable that policymakers will ever be able to provide efficient levels of public goods and, at the same time, tax users according to the benefit principle. Even if tax agents somehow knew the true marginal benefits of hundreds, thousands, or millions of users of public goods, the transactions costs of applying such a differential tax scheme would be considerable. And it is improbable that voters would support a tax system that charges a multitude of different taxes to different individuals since, in some respects, it could be perceived as unfair and capricious.

Even with these problems in application, tax policy does approximate Lindahl pricing and the benefit principle when public goods are financed through tolls and user fees. Toll booths provide natural impediments to free riders and, at the same time, collect taxes from those who benefit from usage of roads. More frequent users also pay more than infrequent users. Few programs are entirely self-financing, though, and they therefore reflect imperfect applications of the benefit principle.

The Benefit Principle Is Often Incompatible with Public Policy

Possible Inconsistencies

It should not be surprising that our tax system is not based on the benefit principle, since public policy has many other goals. Consider the case for providing a new road at an annual cost of $100,000 in a community of 10,000 individuals. Would the private sector tend to allocate resources and build a toll road? A private supplier would set price according to the benefit principle. Only those who benefit from the road would be asked to pay for the new road, and individual toll collections would be directly related to the magnitude of benefits received by individual users. But what if only 2,500 individuals would use the road, and annual revenue was estimated to be only $60,000? This project would fail the normal criteria of cost-benefit analysis that were developed in Chapter 14, and therefore the toll road would never be built in the private sector.

Even though this project fails a cost-benefit analysis, it is likely that one or more citizens believes that the project should be undertaken by the public sector. We have previously shown that the public sector often engages in activities that the private sector does not find worthwhile, and there are also examples of activities that the private sector does provide, but in fewer units than that associated with allocative efficiency. Instances of *market failure* may be claimed to exist whereby it is argued that the road is a public good or a good characterized by substantial positive externalities. Imperfect information may also lead to arguments that consumers or producers underestimate the value of the road to society. Finally, we have also seen that redistribution of income motivates many public policies and may lead various citizens to believe that the public sector should provide the road. Policies could also be designed that subsidize a private firm, or a law could be passed that requires that all citizens use the road on a daily basis, thus providing sufficient revenues for a private firm to build and operate the road.

Many policies could be used, but let us simply assume that the public sector provides the road and funds operating costs through taxation. Two tax policies may ensure that the road is self-financed: (1) tax those who benefit from the road at a rate higher than that suggested by the benefit principle or (2) tax users—frequent and infrequent—and nonusers alike. The first option is inconsistent with tax policy in practice, and we will not consider it a viable option. Rarely are public programs financed solely through taxes on users. The second option was previously shown to result in transfers from nonusers to those who use the road. When, for instance, an individual receives $40 in benefits and is assigned a tax burden of $5, a transfer of $35 occurs. Sizes of transfers are determined by differences between benefits received and tax payments.

The Benefit Principle and Cost-Benefit Analysis

Having established that transfers are inconsistent with a tax system based on the benefit principle, we now demonstrate that when tax policy deviates from the benefit principle, public programs will not necessarily meet the criteria of cost-benefit analysis. What does our discussion suggest about why investors in public projects tend to attach less risk to public bonds that are guaranteed by the general fund of the tax jurisdiction, than to bonds for which repayment is attached solely to the revenues from operation of the public project? The first type of bond, often called a **general obligation bond,** promises that payment of principal and interest comes from all taxpayers in the issuing government's jurisdiction. The second type of bond, referred to as a **revenue bond** or **nonguaranteed bond,** makes no such promise; payment of principal and interest may come solely from proceeds from the project funded by the bond, such as tolls on roads or bridges.

General obligation bond is a bond that guarantees that all taxpayers will be responsible for the bond's principal and interest payments.

Revenue bond (nonguaranteed bond) is a bond whose principal and interest payments are derived from revenues earned from projects funded by the bond.

Interest rates on general obligation bonds are usually lower than those of revenue bonds. Investors in revenue bonds must be concerned about whether a project will be self-financing: The lower the probability that projects funded will be self-financing, the higher interest rates will be. But private investors generally do not have to consider the likelihood that projects funded by general obligation bonds will be self-financing; as long as the issuing government's tax base is secure, investors have few worries about collecting interest and principal on their bond holdings. Unlike nonfederal governments, most U.S. government debt is financed through general revenue bonds backed by the "full faith and credit" of U.S. taxpayers. It is not surprising, then, that interest on debt issued by the U.S. Treasury is always below that of state and local governments.

Our discussion suggests that when projects are funded through revenue bonds, private market investors have a greater incentive to apply the tools of cost-benefit analysis to assess productivity of public projects than for projects funded through general obligation bonds. Benefits associated with proposed projects are directly related to projected revenues since the greater are benefits, the more revenue generated through tolls and other user fees. Higher revenues raise the likelihood that projects will generate revenues sufficient to cover payment of principal and interest due investors. In sum, private market investors purchase revenue bonds only when projects meet the criteria of cost-benefit analysis.

Private investors have no corresponding incentive to perform cost-benefit analysis of projects funded through general obligation bonds. Investors receive payment as long as the issuing government is able to collect sufficient taxes from the general population of taxpayers. This also suggests that private investors cannot be counted on to provide outside discipline that requires these public projects to meet the criteria of cost-benefit analysis. While cost-benefit analysis is very important to economists, the policy process often determines that other goals, such as income redistribution, are more important purposes of public policy. However, when cost-benefit analysis (and, hence, allocative efficiency) remains the guiding principle behind determination of which public projects to fund, voters and policymakers must take over the discipline that is generally exercised by private investors when projects are funded through revenue bonds.

Ability to Pay: An Alternative Principle

Overview

Ability-to-pay principle is a taxation principle whereby taxes are levied on the basis of the financial resources of individual taxpayers.

The notion of what constitutes a just and equitable tax system is normative in nature. The benefit principle marries tax burdens to benefits and therefore views the equity of existing tax policies in terms of how closely policy mirrors the benefit principle. A competing notion of equity is based on the **ability-to-pay principle** that taxes should be levied on the basis of personal resources of individuals. Simply stated, this principle states that the greater an individual's command over resources, the greater the burden that should be placed on the individual.

This principle represents a pivotal departure from the benefit principle, since its application results in tax policies that usually bear no relation to benefits received by individual taxpayers. To some extent, it can be argued that there is a correspondence between the benefit principle and the ability-to-pay principle. For example, the larger one's income or wealth, the greater the benefits that one receives from certain government services such as national defense and protection of personal property. In these cases, there would appear to be some correspondence; there is certainly less correspondence, however, for other government programs such as transfers.

To understand the logic behind this view of equity in taxation, consider its application to our previous example of a publicly provided road. Tax assignments are solely a function of resources available to individual taxpayers; there is no focus on taxing only those who use the road. It is conceivable that some citizens who are frequent users of the road are not taxed at all when they are believed to be poor. Infrequent users may also be taxed heavily when they are considered to be rich. Public education is an example that clearly demonstrates application of this principle. Even though parents with school-age children are the primary beneficiaries of public education, tax policy makes it irrelevant that some families have many school-age children, and others have few or none. (We assume that there are no significant positive externalities associated with education and therefore all benefits are received solely by families with children. Otherwise, a case could be made that the ability-to-pay principle is one way to subsidize these families and promote allocative efficiency in the education market.) In contrast, parents are charged for each child they send to private schools.

It comes as no great surprise that practical application of the ability-to-pay principle is a difficult, and often perplexing, matter. Remember that society is a diverse collection of individuals; at times, this uniqueness makes it difficult to formulate public policies.

Defining Ability to Pay: Horizontal Equity

Horizontal equity
is a concept whereby all individuals with identical abilities to pay are assigned identical tax burdens.

Horizontal equity is the concept that individuals with identical abilities to pay should be assigned identical tax burdens. Although income appears to be a useful yardstick for comparison of differences in ability to pay among taxpayers, it becomes less so when it is recognized that even when two individuals have identical incomes, they may exhibit substantial differences in age, health, family size, and personal property. One individual may have significant health care costs and a long list of overdue bills associated with caring for an elderly parent, and the other may have no dependents and no outstanding debt. Income, by itself, is therefore not always a dependable guide to differences in ability to pay.

Tax systems often deal with the issue of disparity by allowing deductions for such items as dependents, medical expenses, and moving costs. Even though two individuals may have identical incomes, the individual with a greater number of dependents and higher medical expenses is viewed as having lower ability to pay than someone with fewer dependents and lower medical expenses. The goal of horizontal equity is that tax burdens fall more heavily on the latter individual, who is perceived to have higher ability to pay.

A fundamental problem with using income to measure ability to pay—in other words, a deficiency in the horizontal equity concept—arises when we remember that two individuals may have equal opportunities and abilities to earn identical annual incomes of, say, $125,000, but there is no reason to believe that each individual will choose to earn $125,000. Ellen, for instance, may earn a medical degree and decide to work only one day a week—or work full time in a clinic for pubic housing residents—and earn $30,000. Anne, Ellen's classmate, who has equal aptitudes and abilities, chooses to work seven days a week in an expensive specialty or area of the country and earn $125,000. Based on income, Anne will be perceived to have much higher ability to pay than Ellen and, therefore, under the ability-to-pay principle, will be assigned a higher tax bill than Ellen.

The concept of horizontal equity also does not define tax assignments that should be placed on individuals with identical abilities to pay; rather, it backs the position that only those of identical abilities to pay be assigned identical tax bills. Although it may represent a laudable policy goal, the notion of horizontal equity offers no substantive direction for assigning tax bills to citizens; it is not within the power of this principle to assign tax burdens.

This lack is evident in the following example. Assume an economy with two types of individuals:

- individuals earning $100 per week
- individuals earning $5,000 per week

Assuming that incomes, by themselves, are useful indicators of abilities to pay, consider the case where tax assignments of $50 are placed on those individuals earning $100 per week, and tax assignments of $51 per week are placed on those with weekly earnings of $5,000. These tax assignments do provide horizontal equity, but it is likely that many individuals who believe in the ability-to-pay principle will also believe that these tax assignments are far from equitable. Fortunately, the other dimension in which the ability-to-pay principle may be applied proves more useful.

Defining Ability to Pay: Vertical Equity

Vertical equity is a concept whereby tax burdens rise with the ability to pay.

The basis of the concept of **vertical equity** is that tax burdens should rise with ability to pay. There is considerable disagreement about what constitutes vertical equity in tax policy. The basic issue is how much more should those with greater abilities to pay be assigned to pay in taxes.

Three systems may tie tax burdens to ability to pay within the concept of vertical equity.

A **progressive tax system** is a system in which tax bills rise faster than increases in income.

- A **progressive tax system** is one in which tax bills rise faster than increases in income. For example, a tax system is progressive when an individual with an income of $20,000 pays $2,000 in taxes (10 percent of income), but an individual earning $30,000 pays $4,000 in taxes (13.3 percent of income).

A **regressive tax system** is a system in which tax bills rise more slowly than increases in income.

- A **regressive tax system** is one in which tax bills rise more slowly than increases in income. For example, a tax system is regressive when an individual with an income of $20,000 pays $2,000 in taxes (10 percent of income), but an individual earning $30,000 pays $2,500 in taxes (8.3 percent of income). While the higher-income individual pays more tax, taxes as a share of income are less than those of the lower-income individual.

A **proportional tax system** is a system in which tax bills are a fixed percentage of income.

- A **proportional tax system** is one in which tax bills are a fixed percentage of income. A tax system, for example, is proportional when an individual with an income of $20,000 pays $2,000 in taxes (or 10 percent of income), and an individual earning $30,000 pays $3,000 in taxes (or 10 percent of income).

The United States uses a progressive system of income taxation.

Our ability to determine the degree to which a tax system is progressive, regressive, or proportional is allied with several issues. **Tax shifting,** in which individuals shift some portion of their tax burdens onto other individuals, is a complication. When taxes are placed on sellers of gasoline, for example, some portion of the tax may be shifted onto buyers.

Tax shifting is the moving by taxpayers of some portion of tax assignments onto others.

Another complication is that a regressive tax is, to some extent, consistent with the vertical equity concept. For example, consider two individuals, Django and Gloria, who earn $25,000 and $50,000, respectively. Assuming all other factors that affect ability to pay are constant (for example, number of dependents, health, wealth, and so on), this principle argues that Gloria should pay more taxes than Django. Note that under certain circumstances, this principle holds under a regressive tax system as well. If Django pays $2,000 in taxes (8% of income) and Gloria pays $3,000 in taxes (6 percent of income), then Gloria, the individual with the higher ability to pay, is assigned a higher tax bill. As long as Gloria is assigned a tax bill in excess of $2,000 (more than 4 percent of her income), a regressive income tax meets this requirement of the ability-to-pay principle. This example demonstrates the difference between absolute dollars paid in taxes and the ratio of taxes paid to income. Since it is not clear which definition of tax burden is more appropriate under the vertical equity concept, an ambiguity in applying the principle in practice is a clear problem.

Another complication arises when we remember that the ability-to-pay principle disregards the benefits that taxpayers receive from public policies. Without knowing which benefits taxpayers receive, it is difficult to assess vertical equity of a tax system. A rich person, for instance, may be assigned a tax payment of $45,000 on an income of $90,000 (or 50 percent of income) and receive $50,000 in benefits from public policies. A poor individual, in contrast, may pay $1,000 in taxes on an income of $8,000 (or 12.5 percent of income) and receive $1,000 in benefits, suggesting that transfers flow to those who receive benefits in excess of their tax assignments. We now develop a framework by which we can examine taxes and benefits together.

Transferring Income through Tax Policy

Application of the ability-to-pay principle results in changes in the distribution of income in society, and this is not surprising, since it is a major motivation underlying public policy. This motivation appears in much of our earlier discussions of expenditure policies. A few of them are as follows:

- ❏ Off-budget credit and insurance programs (Chapter 10), in which transfers occur when policies lower interest rates on loans and premiums on insurance policies in financial, agriculture, and education markets, among others.
- ❏ Welfare programs that transfer income to the poor (Chapter 11), among them food stamps, AFDC payments, and Medicaid. These programs are means tested; thus the transfers are directed toward those with limited resources.

❏ Social insurance programs, such as Social Security and Medicare (Chapter 12), which unlike means-tested programs, are not solely intended for those with limited resources but, nonetheless, often transfer income to beneficiaries.

Positive and Negative Transfers

Transfers may occur through tax policies as well as expenditure policies. Returning to our previous discussion of the public sector decision in a community to build a new road, we can trace the impact of different tax assignments on the economic well-being of one citizen, Roberto, who is assumed to receive $100 in benefits from this project. (The transfer issue is correctly examined in terms of the *marginal* use of road. That is, at the margin, what are the benefits received and taxes collected? While we do not explicitly state it each time, we assume that all the following benefit and tax scenarios are examined at the margin.) Consider the implications of the following three alternative tax assignments for the transfers that might be awarded Roberto.

Positive transfer occurs whenever individual tax payments are less than benefits received.

❏ Assigned a tax payment of $20, Roberto receives a **positive transfer** of $80. This transfer of $80 represents benefits for which Roberto does not bear corresponding costs.

Negative transfer occurs whenever individual tax payments exceed benefits received.

❏ Roberto is assigned a tax payment of $150 and therefore receives a transfer of −$50. A **negative transfer** is the assignment of a tax payment greater than benefits received.

❏ Assigned a tax payment of $100, Roberto receives no transfer. This tax assignment is consistent with the benefit principle and, as suggested before, transfers do not appear under application of this principle of taxation.

Tax assignments under the ability-to-pay principle are unrelated to benefits received; therefore any of the three scenarios may occur in practice. Tax assignments bear no relation to benefits, and the particular assignment depends only on Roberto's ability to pay. The first case above defines Roberto as having the lowest ability to pay and the second characterizes him as having the highest. Although the ability-to-pay principle does not process information about benefits when it assigns tax assignments, it does, nonetheless, enter into the issue of which transfers result from different tax assignments. Transfers occur whenever benefits are unequal to assignments of tax payments.

What does a negative transfer mean, as in the second case listed above, in which tax assignment exceeds benefits received? The tax assignment of $150 placed on Roberto enables a transfer of $50 to another individual, who is perceived to have a lesser ability to pay. The presence of negative transfers indicates that positive transfers are possible, and in order for positive transfers to occur, tax policy must assign a mix of positive and negative transfers.

Application of the ability-to-pay principle therefore opens the door for using the tax system to transfer income in society. Since transfers do not normally occur in private markets (with the notable exception of private charity), it is not difficult to understand why application of the ability-to-pay principle is consistent with the view that the public sector should transfer income through tax policy. Private markets price according to the benefit principle, and since transfers do not normally occur in them, application of the benefit principle is inconsistent with a public sector that undertakes the responsibility to redistribute income of its citizens.

Assessing the Performance of Transfer Policies

One implication that follows from our discussion is that although it is relatively easy to keep track of transfers that result from funding of a public road, it becomes increasingly difficult to keep track of the many transfers that occur when the public sector funds an increasing number of projects. While Roberto may receive a transfer of −$50 in the case of the public road, he may receive a transfer of +$75 when the public sector provides a pool since, as an avid swimmer, Roberto receives relatively high benefits from the pool.

Net transfers are the differences between taxes paid and benefits received.

The value of (aggregate) **net transfers** measures the final tally of how all transfers affect the well-being of Roberto. While in theory it is conceivable that all taxpayers know their final value of net transfer, this is most probably not the case in practice. The federal government has thousands of programs, and it is unlikely that each individual evaluates the individual benefits that flow from each of these programs. A more important complication, however, is that the tax system does not assign each taxpayer an itemized tax bill that clearly shows what each program is costing those individuals. Most public spending is financed by a general tax fund whose tax dollars may be used to finance any spending program approved through the policy process. For example, when an individual pays income tax of $1,200, the taxpayer is not presented with an itemized tax bill that shows $300 going toward national defense, $20 to education, $150 to interest on the national debt, and so on. While taxpayers may in theory perform their own research and determine how their own tax dollars are spent, it is not clear that many taxpayers find this a useful endeavor.

This discussion indicates why public finance textbooks have traditionally separated discussion of the topics of public expenditures from discussion of the funding of those expenditures. This separation is necessitated by the simple fact that most public spending programs are not funded on an individual basis. It is not like the private sector in which individuals easily recognize what individual goods and services cost them. Contrast public sector spending with payments made for goods and services in the private sector. In private markets, payments by individuals for utility bills, hamburgers, cars, vacations, and clothes each involve an itemized bill that directly links payment to a specific good or service. A monthly payment of $650 for rent, for instance, clearly links expenditure with payment for housing. In the public sector, however, an income tax payment of $1,200 does not clearly link individual expenditures with this payment. This difference follows from the fact that private markets price according to the benefit principle, and primarily tax according to the ability-to-pay principle.

This is simply a restatement of an earlier point. Although one advantage of the benefit principle is that tax assignments are clearly linked with benefits received, it does not allow for transfers to take place. Although transfers are an important role of the public sector, when transfers occur through tax policy, it becomes difficult to assess the performance of this important government function. As we have pointed out, individual citizens will not normally know how their tax assignments compare with the benefits they receive from the thousands of programs funded through the general tax fund. Policymakers as well can be expected to have similar difficulties since in order to assess how public policies affect income distribution, they must estimate how tax assignments of each individual taxpayer compare with the benefits that flow from the thousands of expenditure programs.

Who Receives Transfers?

Although it is commonly believed that application of the ability-to-pay principle results in lower tax burdens for the poor, this does not always happen. Economists may present their views on the ways to assign tax payments in conformity with various applications of horizontal and vertical equity, but actual tax assignments may not always transfer income to the poor, since tax policy is determined within the policy process and tax assignments are therefore chosen by voters and special interest groups as well as policymakers.

Let us return to our new road example, under the circumstance that Roberto is expected to receive benefits of $100 when the road is finished. An intelligent individual, Roberto certainly recognizes that his well-being is affected by his tax assignment. Assuming that he prefers a larger transfer over a smaller transfer, he prefers to pay as few dollars in taxes as possible and may, for instance, successfully lobby his local policymakers for a tax code that assigns him a relatively small tax payment. In such ways, the public sector will transfer income to individuals who are not necessarily poor. If, for instance, Roberto would ordinarily be classified as an individual with a sizable ability to pay, a low tax assignment results in a sizable positive transfer to an individual who is not poor.

Tax Expenditures

Tax expenditures are policies that exclude, defer, or exempt portions of income from taxation.

Many of us who have filled out tax forms know that various deductions and exclusions are provided that lower taxable income. Exclusions from taxation comprise the **tax expenditures** side of a public budget. While the term *tax expenditure* seems oxymoronic, it refers to policies that provide tax relief to taxpayers. Tax expenditures are also sometimes referred to as *tax preferences* or *tax deductions* and include all tax policies that result in revenue losses for the public treasury. In addition to excluding, exempting, or deducting portions of income from taxation, tax expenditures also provide preferential rates of taxation, tax credits, and deferred taxation for various economic activities. It should also be noted that there is some controversy over whether we should argue that tax expenditures represent revenue losses. Critics of the notion of a revenue loss suggest that this terminology implies that tax expenditures are gifts from the tax authorities to taxpayers in the form of lower tax bills. In other words, the notion of a tax expenditure leads some to suggest that the government has the right to tax all income sources and that taxpayers should be thankful to government for tax expenditure policies.

A sampling of a few of the more than 130 tax expenditures include the following:

❏ Housing and meals for military personnel are excluded from income taxation.
❏ Corporate research and experimentation projects are excluded from taxation.

- A 10 percent tax credit of up to $10,000 annually is allowed for corporations that clear land and plant trees for the eventual production of timber.
- Credit union earnings that are not distributed as dividends or interest to members are exempt from income taxation.
- A tax credit of 10 percent is provided for those who rehabilitate buildings built before 1936 and which are not used for residential purposes.
- Certain farmers are allowed to deduct various feed and fertilizer expenses.[3]

One of the largest tax expenditures is the allowance of interest on mortgage loans that homeowners deduct from income used to calculate personal income tax bills. This tax expenditure resulted in an estimated loss, in 1994, of $48 billion for the U.S. Treasury.[4] Revenue losses of other major tax expenditure programs include exclusion of employer-contributions for medical insurance and health care from income taxation ($50.8 billion), deductibility of charitable contributions from income taxation ($16.8 billion), and deductibility of medical expenses from income taxation ($3 billion). Aggregate losses in 1994 are estimated at $420 billion in individual income taxes and $56 billion in taxes on corporate income.

Important Distinction: Tax Rate versus Tax Base

Tax rates are specified levels of tax collection based on given levels of income.

Tax bases are the portion of income subject to taxation.

The important distinction between **tax rates** and **tax bases** helps us understand the role of tax expenditures in tax policy. We previously defined tax rates in terms of how many dollars in taxes are collected from a given level of income. (For the time being, we will focus on average tax rates.) If an individual with an income of $20,000 pays $2,000 in taxes, then the corresponding tax rate is 10 percent of income. The tax base is defined as that portion of income, or some other measure such as value of personal property, that is subject to the tax rate. The tax collection of $2,000, for instance, is determined by multiplying the tax rate, 10 percent, by the tax base, $20,000.

This distinction makes it clear that many different combinations of tax rates and tax bases will generate a given level of tax collection. A tax collection of $500 could, for example, result when a tax rate of 5 percent is applied against a tax base of $10,000 or when a tax rate of 10 percent is applied against a tax base of $5,000. Tax bills may therefore be increased or decreased, either through changes in tax rates or changes in the definition of tax bases.

Tax expenditures affect the definition of tax bases. For instance, when mortgage interest may be deducted from taxable income, this tax expenditure lowers the tax base and, without a corresponding increase in the tax rate, results in a lower tax bill for mortgage holders.

This distinction also indicates that without consideration of both tax rates and tax bases, the classification of a tax system as progressive, regressive, or proportional is a complex matter. For instance, when various individuals are able to take greater

---

[3] *Budget Baselines, Historical Data, and Alternatives for the Future,* Office of Management and Budget, January 1993.

[4] Table 2-1, *Budget Baselines, Historical Data, and Alternatives for the Future,* Office of Management and Budget, January 1993.

advantage of available tax expenditures than other individuals, definitions of tax bases are not uniform across individuals. Although tax rates may easily be computed, comparison of tax rates does not directly correspond to differences in tax burdens. One individual may be allowed tax expenditures of $1,000 (5 percent of income), the result being a tax base of $19,000. Another individual, who earns income of $30,000 and is allowed tax expenditures of $11,000 (37 percent of income), may have a tax base of $19,000 as well. While we can compare these two individuals' tax rates, we cannot compare them directly because each has different percentages of income subject to taxation. Assessment of the progressivity of a tax system that provides many tax expenditures is clearly a difficult matter.

Additional complexities for assessing tax burdens arise when both tax rates and tax bases are changed. When the tax rate on certain individuals is raised and, at the same time, additional tax expenditures are provided, total tax collection from individuals may rise, fall, or stay the same. This ambiguity can occur even if there is no corresponding change in income, only the definition of which portion of income is taxable.

Allocational Effects

Analysis of allocational effects is an important dimension of the study of expenditure policies. We analyze the allocational effects of tax expenditure policies in much the same way. A tax expenditure that allows home mortgage interest to be deducted from tax bases of individuals provides a straightforward example with which to study allocational effects. The primary effect of this policy is to lower the cost of financing a home. If, for instance, a monthly mortgage payment of $1,200 contains an interest payment of $1,000, $12,000 in interest payments are now deductible from the homeowner's annual tax base. If this mortgage holder's average tax rate is 25 percent, total tax liability falls by $3,000, or 25 percent of $12,000. (Marginal tax rates and their important effects on economic behavior are discussed in Chapter 19.) As tax bills of mortgage holders fall, this tax policy directs resources into mortgage markets. Other beneficiaries of this tax policy include real estate agents, home builders, and financial institutions, because lowering the after-tax cost of holding mortgages increases the demand for housing. Tax expenditure policies are also written with the explicit purpose of promoting, or directly subsidizing, various activities such as environmental cleanup, solar energy, and research and development of corporations.

It is inevitable that when tax expenditures direct resources into particular activities, resources are also redirected out of other areas of the economy. More resources in the home mortgage market means fewer resources in—to name only a few—education, health care, defense, and transportation markets. As we have seen many times, there is always an opportunity cost when resources are scarce, and tax expenditure policies have opportunity costs. The opportunity costs of the home mortgage interest deduction are the lost opportunities in the next best alternative use for the resources redirected as a result of the policy.

Distributional Effects

Tax expenditures also exert important effects on income distribution. This point may be shown by considering a hypothetical economy composed of five citizens, each of whom is currently assigned an annual tax bill of $100. Assume that one individual, Karen, is awarded a tax expenditure which lowers her tax bill to $75. This tax expenditure could, for instance, allow her to deduct grocery or gasoline bills from her tax base. As long as there is no corresponding change in benefits received by Karen, the tax expenditure provides a positive transfer to her.

As pointed out above, a positive transfer must be balanced out by one or more negative transfers. This may be shown by examining the ways in which this tax expenditure changes the relative tax liabilities of all five citizens.

- Before the tax expenditure, total tax collection in this community was $500, and because each citizen was assigned a tax of $100, each citizen was responsible for 20 percent (or $100/$500) of the total tax bill.
- After the tax expenditure, and assuming that total tax collection remains $500, Karen's share of the total tax burden is lowered to 15 percent (or $75/$500). Burdens of each of the four other citizens rise to 21.25 percent (or $106.25/$500) when they are equally responsible for paying the revenue loss caused by the tax expenditure.[5]

The tax expenditure affects the distribution of tax burdens across citizens since, for a given level of public expenditures, Karen's tax bill falls at the expense of the other four citizens. Negative transfers are borne by the other four citizens, who must now pay $5 more in taxes but receive no additional benefits in return.

Even though tax deductions for dependents, health care costs, and other items are attempts to conform to the ability-to-pay principle, considerable criticism asserts that too few tax expenditures are provided to those with limited resources. For instance, many critics question the appropriateness of the home mortgage interest deduction: Many poor individuals do not own houses and therefore cannot take advantage of this tax expenditure. A recent study has found that at least half of the benefits of tax expenditures flow to those in the top 20 percent of family income, and less than one-fifth flow to those families in the lowest two income quintiles.[6]

Substitutability with Expenditure Programs

Tax expenditure policies provide lower tax burdens to individuals and, in this sense, the well-being of these individuals is improved in much the same way as when they are beneficiaries of expenditure policies. Another way of demonstrating the distributional consequences of a tax expenditure policy is to recognize the similarity between tax expenditures and public expenditure programs. A cash grant of $25, an expenditure program, can be shown to provide Karen with benefits similar to those gained

---

[5] We assume that the expenditure program is not financed through debt creation which, unlike imposition of higher taxes, may affect intergenerational tax liabilities.

[6] Daniel H. Weinberg, "The Distributional Implications of Tax Expenditures and Comprehensive Income Taxation," *National Tax Journal* 40 (December 1987): 237–253.

through a tax reduction of $25.[7] The act of awarding Karen a cash grant of $25 also endows Karen with an additional $25 in benefits. Assuming that all five citizens share equally in providing the new $25 expenditure program and that prior to this policy all five citizens received $100 in benefits from public expenditure programs, Karen now receives $125 in benefits at a cost of $105. The other four citizens, however, continue to receive $100 in benefits but now face higher tax burdens of $105 each. In this way, we see that an expenditure program could be used to transfer income to Karen in much the same way as a tax expenditure policy. Income is transferred away from the other four citizens and toward Karen and, in either case, positive transfers require that one or more citizens bear negative transfers.

This resource reallocation, however, could also be accomplished through other policies. Off-budget credit or insurance policies could also be provided, such as loan guarantee or insurance programs. Let us return to the tax expenditure that allows mortgage holders to deduct interest from taxable income. The following expenditure programs may produce similar allocative effects: cash grants to mortgage holders, cash grants to home builders, or expenditure programs that fund one month's mortgage payment for every mortgage holder. There are many possibilities for expenditure programs that substitute for this tax expenditure policy.

Tax Expenditure Estimates Are Imperfect

Tax expenditures clearly are an important component determining a government's budget. It is now appropriate to question the degree to which the federal government uses these tax policies. It would appear that if a tax expenditure resulted in a lower tax bill of $50 for an individual, this would also equal the government's gain in revenue if the tax expenditure were taken away from that individual. For many reasons, however, estimation of revenue losses is far more complex.[8]

- ❏ *Tax expenditures may have incentive effects that alter economic behavior.* Our discussion of the mortgage interest deduction demonstrated that this tax expenditure directs resources into mortgage markets. If this tax expenditure were reduced, say by providing an annual maximum ceiling of $5,000 worth of deduction, fewer resources would be allocated into this market. Mortgage loans would also tend to be smaller than under current policy, which places no limit on the value of this deduction. As reduction in the value of the tax expenditure (from the point of view

---

[7] Note that we are abstracting away from the difference between tax rates and tax bases here, since we are focusing on total tax bills. Under most tax systems, the amount of tax reduction stemming from a tax expenditure is determined by multiplying the appropriate tax rate times the change in the tax base that comes from the tax expenditure. Also note that whether there is a one-for-one correspondence between the dollar values of tax expenditures and cash grants depends on which activities are allowed under the tax expenditure. As shown in our analysis of welfare programs for the poor, Karen would tend to favor cash grants when the activities covered by tax expenditures are activities that she either does not prefer to engage in or, when she does engage in them, she does not meet the full amount of tax deduction. For instance, the tax expenditure may cover spending on apples, which she does not like to eat. On the other hand, if the tax expenditure relates to spending on groceries and Karen always spends more than the revenue fall stemming from the tax expenditure, then the tax expenditure is similar to being awarded a cash grant of an equivalent amount.

[8] *Budget Baselines, Historical Data, and Alternatives for the Future,* Office of Management and Budget, January 1993.

of the taxpayer) causes fewer individuals to undertake mortgages and those in the market to undertake smaller loans, the tax revenue loss (from the point of view of the government) attributable to this tax expenditure falls, as fewer and smaller mortgages are created. In other words, if there were fewer and smaller mortgages, the increase in tax revenues that stems from the reduction of the value of tax expenditure would be smaller than the previous revenue loss associated with a greater number of mortgages, which on average were larger as well.

❏ *Tax expenditures are interdependent.* Changes in one tax expenditure may lead to revenue losses of other tax expenditures. If the interest deduction on mortgages were reduced, individual taxpayers are pushed into higher tax rates under progressive income tax systems, with the effect of increasing the value of other tax expenditures that have not undergone policy changes, such as those associated with charitable contributions and medical expenses. For example, the value to the taxpayer of deducting another dollar of charitable contribution from an individual tax base rises with the tax rate. Since this increases the charitable contributions of taxpayers, there is an associated rise in the revenue loss associated with charitable contributions. This effect does not require that the taxpayer increase charitable contributions since, when the tax base is changed by the reduction in the value of the mortgage interest deduction, a corresponding change in the relative value of all other tax expenditures occurs under a progressive income tax system. Revenue losses associated with a change in the value of one tax expenditure therefore may also change revenue losses from other tax expenditures.

❏ *Repeal of some tax expenditures may change rates of economic growth.* Changes in economic growth affect aggregate tax collections. Recessions are associated with falling tax collections and booms with rising collections. If, for example, reduction or elimination of the mortgage interest deduction resulted in a change in economic growth, aggregate tax collections would change as well.

Outlay Equivalence of Tax Expenditures

Outlay equivalents are the dollar values of public expenditures that would provide equal benefits to recipients of tax expenditures.

A convenient means of summarizing the importance of tax expenditures to the overall federal budget is to calculate their value in terms of **outlay equivalents.** Tax expenditures have been shown to be similar in nature to public expenditures, and it is therefore appropriate to compare them directly with expenditure policies. An outlay equivalent calculates, for a given tax expenditure, what dollar value of public expenditure would provide equal benefit to the recipient of the tax expenditure.

A mortgage holder who lowers her tax bill by $6,500 may, for instance, be indifferent between receiving this tax expenditure or a cash grant of $6,500 and, in this case, the outlay equivalent of this tax expenditure is exactly $6,500. There is, however, no reason to believe that a dollar-for-dollar correspondence exists between tax reductions and cash grants. There are incentive effects, as well as interdependencies between tax expenditure policies, which complicate estimation of revenue losses associated with tax expenditures. It may be the case, for instance, that deductibility of mortgage interest causes a homeowner to undertake a larger mortgage than she would undertake without the tax expenditure. In this case, the outlay equivalent for this tax expenditure might be $5,800 or some other dollar value less than $6,500.

It is, however, commonly believed that the relationship between the value of a tax expenditure and its outlay equivalent is remarkably close. The outlay equivalent for all tax expenditures, in 1993, has been estimated to be $518 billion—a considerable sum when we compare this with total federal expenditures of $1,475 billion in the same year.[9] For every $1,000 in federal spending, $350 of tax expenditures, measured in terms of outlay equivalents, took place.

Despite the similarity between tax expenditures and expenditure policies, they are not awarded equal status in the federal budget. It has been required that revenue losses associated with tax expenditures be accounted for only since 1974, when the Congressional Budget Act required their annual listing. Although listed in annual budget documents, they are published in an appendix of the budget document and, in this way, are treated more like off-budget credit and insurance policies that are also relegated to an appendix of the federal budget document.

Summary

- A wide range of taxes fund expenditures and include taxes on individual and corporate income and social insurance and excise taxes. Taxes on individual income are the largest category.

- Application of the benefit principle requires that citizens be taxed according to the benefits received from goods and services. It is often difficult to apply the benefit principle in practice. Policies aimed at furthering equity are also incompatible with the benefit principle.

- The ability-to-pay principle is that taxes should be levied on the basis of individual resources. Two approaches may be used. Horizontal equity is a concept whereby individuals with identical abilities to pay should be assigned identical tax burdens. Vertical equity is a concept whereby tax burdens should rise with ability to pay.

- A progressive tax system is one in which tax burdens rise faster than increases in income. Under a regressive tax, burdens rise more slowly than increases in income. A proportional tax creates tax burdens as a fixed percentage of income.

- A positive transfer occurs when benefits received from expenditure policies exceed taxes paid. A negative transfer occurs when tax payments exceed benefits received from policies. The value of net transfers measures the effect of transfers on the well-being of a taxpayer.

- Tax expenditures occur when policy excludes, defers, exempts, or allows deductions from taxation. Estimates of outlay equivalents calculate, for a given tax expenditure, the dollar value of public expenditure that would provide equal benefit to the recipient of the tax expenditure.

- An important distinction between tax rates and tax bases is that tax rates define the rate at which taxes are collected against a tax base, and the tax base defines what is subject to taxation.

Review Questions

1. What are the major sources of tax revenue?

2. What is the benefit principle?

3. What is the ability-to-pay principle?

4. What is the difference in tax policy between horizontal equity and vertical equity?

5. What are the differences among progressive, regressive, and proportional tax systems?

---

[9] *Budget Baselines, Historical Data, and Alternatives for the Future,* Office of Management and Budget, January 1993.

6. What are tax expenditure policies? Give two examples.

7. What is the difference between the tax rate versus the tax base?

Discussion Questions

1. Tax policy could focus on making people pay for benefits received, as in the *benefit principle,* but much of its focus centers on the *ability-to-pay principle.* Explain why this is true.
2. Explain the different notions of equity implicit in the *benefit principle* and the *ability-to-pay principle.*
3. Suppose that two individuals, Abdul and Benjamin, pay $5,000 and $6,000, respectively, in taxes. Can you tell if the tax system is regressive, proportional, or progressive?
4. Explain the differences between the concepts of horizontal and vertical equity.
5. Is the Social Security tax a good example of an earmarked tax that conforms to the benefit principle?
6. List three tax expenditures that might be used to promote the automobile industry. List three direct expenditure programs that would achieve the same result.
7. Show how reductions in tax rates reduce the value of most tax expenditures.
8. What changes in the types of policies funded by the federal government might occur if all debt were sold as revenue bonds rather than guaranteed bonds?
9. Explain within the model of the policy process what motivates tax reform.

Key Words

Tax reform
Benefit principle
Tax earmarking
General obligation bond
Revenue bond (nonguaranteed bond)
Ability-to-pay principle
Horizontal equity
Vertical equity
Progressive tax system
Regressive tax system
Proportional tax system
Tax shifting
Positive transfer
Negative transfer
Net transfers
Tax expenditures
Tax rates
Tax bases
Outlay equivalents

CHAPTER 16

Principles of Tax Analysis

This chapter presents the basic principles of tax analysis. Two general issues characterize the analysis: tax incidence and excess burden. Analysis of tax incidence examines who really bears burdens of taxation and therefore studies the process of tax shifting where some or all of a tax is passed onto another party. For example, although the government may impose a tax on firms, some of the tax may be passed on to consumers of their products. While it may look as if firms pay the taxes, they merely collect them from consumers and send them to the government Treasury. Excess burden describes the degree to which tax policies result in a greater burden on taxpayers than is absolutely necessary. All taxes, by definition, place burdens on one or more parties, but we shall show that an efficient tax system minimizes excess burden.

Tax incidence and excess burden provide our framework for understanding the resource allocative and distributive implications of tax policy. These are a few of the issues we analyze using this framework:

❏ Does statutory incidence (legal assignment) indicate who bears the burden of taxation?

❏ How do elasticities of supply and demand influence tax incidence?

❏ Do tax collections underestimate the true costs of taxation? What other costs are associated with tax policy?

❏ What implications for the policy process are suggested by the topics covered in this chapter?

Tax Incidence: General Issues

Statutory incidence is the indication of who is liable for payment of taxes.

Economic incidence indicates who actually bears the burden of taxation.

Tax shifting is the examination of the degree to which statutory incidence and economic incidence of taxes diverge. **Statutory incidence** indicates the person or firm judged legally liable for payment of a tax. A sales tax, for instance, requires that sellers of goods collect taxes on their general sales. **Economic incidence** indicates the person or firm who *actually* bears the tax. Economic analysis demonstrates that there are cases in which the seller pays all the tax and others in which consumers pay some or all of it. An important result is that statutory incidence reveals little useful information about economic incidence and, for this reason, economists are mostly interested in the economic incidence of taxes, since this indicates who actually bears the burden of taxation.

Balanced budget incidence evaluates the incidence of both taxation and the spending it finances.

The study of tax incidence may proceed in several directions. One is the study of the incidence of both taxation and spending and is called **balanced budget incidence.** For example, when $100 million is collected through a tax on gasoline consumption, there is also $100 million in spending for which the tax provides funding. Economic incidence when the $100 million in taxes fund public road maintenance would clearly differ from when taxes fund a new bike path. This is an interesting theoretical exercise, but there is a major inconsistency with applying this examination in practice. Tax revenues are rarely *earmarked* for the funding of specific programs. Most tax revenues flow into the government's general fund and any tax dollar may, in practice, fund any of a thousand or more programs. (We must also recall that the federal government has not operated under a balanced budget for more than twenty-five years, thereby adding deficit finance as a complication to consider when we study who bears the burdens of a given expenditure program.)

Differential tax incidence evaluates the incidence of taxation under the assumption that public spending does not change.

It is more common to study **differential tax incidence,** which assumes an unchanged level of public expenditures. An advantage of this approach is its elimination of the expenditure side of the public budget from the analysis of tax incidence. An examination of how tax incidence changes when a tax on natural gas is substituted for a tax on gasoline, liquor, or income is an example of differential tax incidence. This is the primary mode of analysis taken in this chapter.

Excise taxes are those levied on particular goods or services.

Unit taxes are those levied as a fixed amount per unit of a good or service purchased.

Ad valorem taxes are those levied as a percentage of product price.

Many different taxes could be used for our study of tax incidence, but in this chapter we concentrate on **excise taxes,** which are taxes levied on specific goods such as gasoline, cigarettes or liquor. Federal excise taxes (in 1994) include levies of 24 cents per pack of cigarettes, $2.14 per 750 milliliter bottle of distilled spirits, 33 cents per six-pack of beer, and 21 cents per 750 milliliter bottle of table wine.

Two types of excise taxes are considered in this chapter: **unit taxes** (or per unit taxes) and *ad valorem* **taxes** (or sales taxes). Unit taxes are taxes charged per unit of a good, such as per gallon of gasoline or per pack of cigarettes. Tax revenues are therefore determined by the quantity of units sold. An *ad valorem* tax, in contrast, is based on dollar volume, such as 6 percent on sales, a collection of $6 per $100 of sales.

Unit Taxes

Unit Tax on Suppliers

We begin our study of tax incidence by examining Figure 16-1, which shows the impact of a unit tax placed on suppliers of coffee cups. Pretax equilibrium price P_e and quantity exchanged Q_e are determined by the intersection of demand D and supply S. Assume that per unit tax T is levied on suppliers. Since the cost of each coffee cup goes up by the amount T, the supply curve rises vertically by T. The logic behind this vertical rise may be seen if we recall that supply curves represent *minimum* prices that suppliers must receive in order to produce various quantities. The minimum price for producing Q'_e, for example, is P, which is also equal to b. When producers must pay a per unit tax of T, the minimum price that suppliers must receive must rise by the

FIGURE 16-1
Tax Incidence
Unit Tax Levied on Suppliers

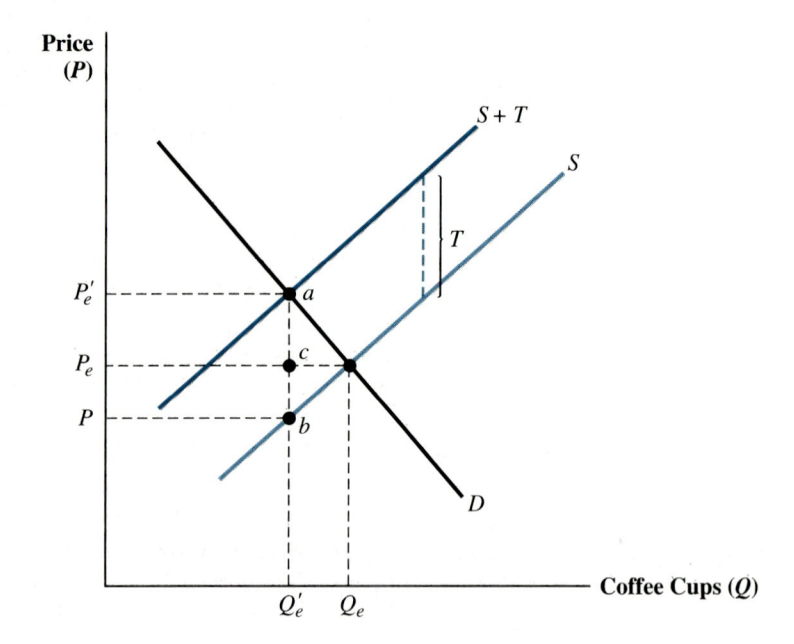

amount of the tax. For quantity Q'_e, $P + T = P'_e$, which is also associated with point a. Similar logic indicates that T is added to all minimum prices shown along S and results in new supply curve $S + T$, which is parallel to S.

The new equilibrium, determined by the intersection of D and $S + T$, is characterized by a higher price P'_e, and a smaller quantity of coffee cups exchanged Q'_e. Since the tax causes consumers to pay a higher price, it is important to question whether sellers pay any part of the tax. Note that, at the new quantity exchanged Q'_e, the increase in price from P_e to P'_e is less than the tax, which may be measured as the difference between S and $S + T$ at Q'_e, or PP'_e. The portion of the unit tax T borne by consumers is $P_e P'_e$. The rest is borne by producers. Since the post-tax price received by sellers is P, the portion borne by sellers is PP_e. Consumers and sellers therefore share the payment of tax T since, at Q'_e, PP_e is borne by sellers and $P_e P'_e$ is borne by consumers.

We have just demonstrated that a unit tax levied on suppliers is partially shifted onto consumers. The statutory incidence is a unit tax of T placed on suppliers. Economic incidence, however, differs from statutory incidence, since sellers shift a portion of the tax onto consumers. Tax revenues equal rectangle $PP'_e ab$, the unit tax multiplied by the number of units sold. Consumers contribute $P_e P'_e ac$ and sellers pay $PP_e cb$.

Unit Tax on Demanders

Would economic incidence change if the unit tax were imposed on consumers of coffee cups? To answer this question, consider Figure 16-2, which shows the effect of imposing the previous unit tax T on consumers. Pretax equilibrium is characterized by P_e and Q_e, which are the same as when the tax is imposed on sellers. But because the tax is imposed on consumers, the tax causes demand to shift downward by the amount of the tax, or $D - T$. To understand this change, remember that a demand curve reflects *maximum* prices that consumers are willing to pay for various quantities. For example, at Q'_e, consumers are willing and able to pay, at most, P per coffee cup. Although consumers remain willing to pay P, they must now pay an additional T per cup. Notice that, from the viewpoint of sellers, P'_e is the price they receive at Q'_e. Applying this logic to all other quantities, $D - T$ becomes the demand curve facing sellers.

Post-tax equilibrium is characterized by a lower price P'_e (received by sellers) and a smaller quantity, Q'_e, sold to consumers. Because the tax lowers the price paid to sellers from P_e to P'_e, part of the tax is shifted from consumers to sellers. Consumers now pay P'_e to producers, but are responsible for the tax as well which, at Q'_e, is equal to $P'_e P$. Because this total payment, or P per unit, made by consumers is higher than the original per unit price (P_e), this difference, or $P_e P$, measures the per unit burden placed on consumers. The per unit burden on sellers is $P'_e P_e$, the difference between the original price (P_e) and the new price P'_e they receive.

Once again, tax burdens are shared by consumers and sellers. Although statutory incidence has been transferred from sellers to consumers, tax shifting results when consumers shift part of the tax onto sellers. Tax revenues equal rectangle $P'_e Pab$, or the per unit tax multiplied by the number of units purchased by consumers. The share of revenues borne by consumers is $P_e Pac$, and the share borne by sellers is $P'_e P_e cb$.

Economic Incidence Is Unrelated to Statutory Incidence

We have shown that tax shifting causes economic incidence to differ from the statutory incidence of unit taxes. An interesting question is whether it matters to consumers or sellers who is assigned statutory incidence. Surprisingly, the answer is no.

FIGURE 16-2
Tax Incidence
Unit Tax Levied on Consumers

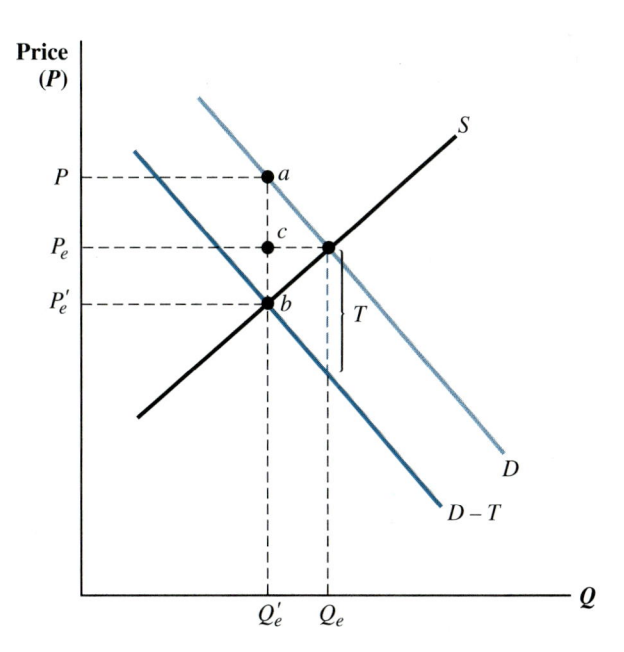

To see this important result, consider Figure 16-3, which compares economic incidences of unit tax T of our two previous examples. As before, the pretax equilibrium is characterized by P_e and Q_e, as determined by intersection of S and D.

Recall that supply curve $S + T$ results when statutory incidence is placed on sellers. The post-tax equilibrium price is P_2 and quantity exchanged is Q_1. At Q_1, the increase in price from P_e to P_2 is less than the per unit tax, which equals ab, and therefore, while $P_e P_2$ is borne by consumers, sellers bear $P_1 P_e$.

Also recall that unit tax T results in $D - T$ being the demand curve facing sellers when statutory incidence is assigned to consumers. Sellers receive P_1 per unit from consumers at the equilibrium quantity Q_1, the same quantity that results when the tax is placed on sellers. At Q_1, consumers pay more per unit when T is added to the price (P_1) they pay sellers. Therefore, consumers bear $P_e P_2$ and producers bear $P_1 P_e$ of the new tax and together these burdens equal T.

This comparison suggests two important implications for our study of tax incidence. One is that economic incidence is unrelated to statutory incidence. (Exceptions do occur when elasticities of demand or supply are perfectly elastic or inelastic.) The second is that tax collections are identical under either placement of statutory incidence. Tax revenue $P_1 P_2 ab$ is collected under both assignments, and shares borne by consumers and sellers are identical under either assignment.

An earlier chapter argued that much of tax policy is based on perceptions of fairness. Even though consumers and sellers are theoretically indifferent between the two assignments of statutory incidence, they may not be indifferent in practice. Our analysis shows that it really does not matter to either party, but notice that this conclusion is based solely on a world in which consumers and sellers have all the information summarized in Figures 16-1 through 16-3. But it is unlikely that all consumers or sellers are fully aware of the equivalence between either assignment of statutory

**FIGURE 16-3
Economic Incidence and Statutory Incidence**
Economic Incidence Does Not Depend on Statutory Incidence

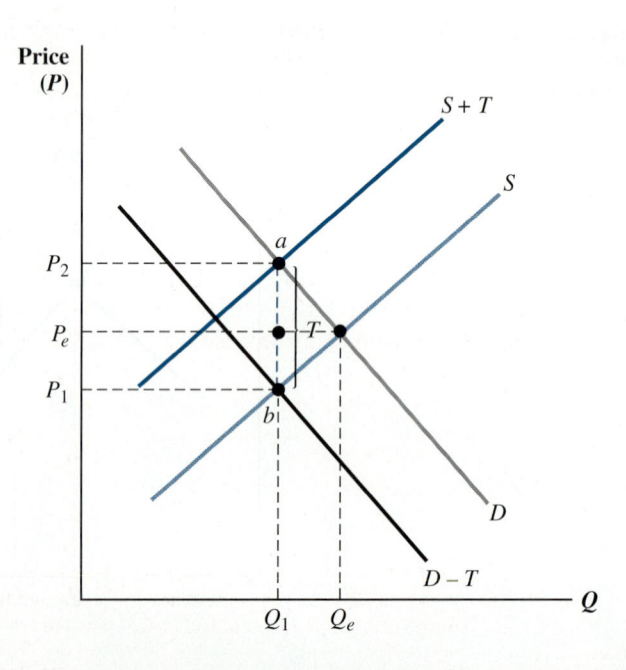

incidence, and it may therefore matter a great deal to consumers and sellers who is assigned statutory incidence. When, for example, consumers believe that assignment to sellers is fair, this perception is likely to lead them to prefer that statutory incidence be placed on sellers.

Incidence and Elasticities of Supply and Demand

Demand Elasticities

The term *demand elasticity* is used to describe how responsive consumers are to changes in price.[1] The more elastic the demand, the more responsive consumers are to price changes. Since we have shown that unit taxes change prices paid by consumers, demand elasticity indicates how responsive consumers are to tax policies. Although we have shown that economic incidence is unrelated to statutory incidence, this is not the same as saying that the economic incidence of a tax is independent of demand elasticity. We now show how demand elasticity influences economic incidence.

Figure 16-4 shows an initial equilibrium characterized by P_e and Q_e determined by intersection of D^{el} (a relatively elastic demand) and S. We have shown that a unit tax T levied on suppliers shifts supply upward to $S + T$.[2] The post-tax equilibrium is characterized by P_3 and Q^{el}. The unit tax equals P_1P_3 at Q^{el} and consumers bear P_eP_3 and producers bear P_1P_e, which together $(P_eP_3 + P_1P_e)$ equal the per unit tax (P_1P_3).

Relatively inelastic demand D^{in} offers an easy comparison with which to determine how demand elasticity influences tax shifting. Intersection of D^{in} and $S + T$ determines higher equilibrium price P_4 and quantity exchanged Q^{in}. At new quantity Q^{in}, the per unit tax equals P_2P_4, of which consumers bear P_eP_4 and producers bear P_2P_e.

In which case does the seller shift more of the tax? Because unit taxes are identical for either demand curve, simple comparison of the magnitudes borne by consumers reveals the case in which consumers bear the greatest incidence. Since P_eP_4 (inelastic case) > P_eP_3 (elastic case), it is clear that consumers bear a greater portion of the tax when demand is relatively inelastic.

This important result may be simply stated thus: *The more elastic (inelastic) the demand, the smaller (greater) the relative burden placed on consumers when a per unit tax is levied on a market.* The intuition behind this result is clear: The more elastic the demand, the more difficult it is for sellers to shift taxes onto consumers. We know, for instance, that highly elastic demands are often associated with goods for which there are many available substitutes. Consider assignment of a unit tax on one particular soft drink, Cola X. When consumers of Cola X believe that all other cola drinks, as well as all soft drinks, are good substitutes for Cola X, consumers will purchase many more of these substitutes as the tax on Cola X raises its price. In this case, sellers of Cola X have relatively little latitude to shift a sizable portion of the tax onto its consumers. In contrast, if all soft drink sellers were assigned the same unit tax, the range of substitutes is greatly diminished, and as the prices of all soft drinks rise in

---

[1] For a discussion of elasticity, see the appendix on microeconomic principles at the end of the book.
[2] Remember that economic incidence is not affected by statutory incidence; therefore the same results would occur if our example assigned incidence to consumers.

FIGURE 16-4
Tax Incidence and Demand Elasticity

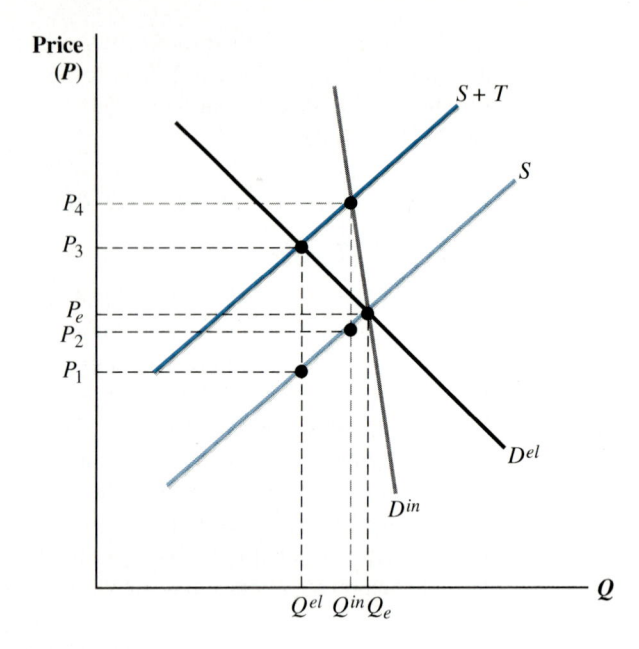

reaction to the tax, consumers have much less room to avoid the tax since fewer untaxed substitutes are available.

An important implication follows from this discussion: *When policymakers wish to place minimal tax burdens on consumers, taxes should be imposed on markets in which demands are relatively elastic.* Although statutory incidence is unrelated to economic incidence, economic incidence is influenced by demand elasticities. Our investigation of economic incidence is incomplete, however, since supply elasticity also influences economic incidence—an issue we now turn our attention to.

Supply Elasticities

Figure 16-5a shows the impact of a unit tax imposed in a market characterized by a perfectly inelastic supply. Assigning statutory incidence to consumers, the demand curve facing producers becomes $D - T$ after imposition of the tax. Intersection of $D - T$ and S determines the price received by sellers P_1. Note that P_1 is less than the pretax equilibrium price of P_e received by producers and that P_1P_e, the difference in price received by producers, is exactly equal to unit tax T. In other words, sellers bear the entire burden of the tax. To understand this, notice that consumers pay the same per unit price as before (P_e), but although they paid the entire P_e to producers before the tax, they now pay P_1 to producers and P_1P_e to the government.

In Figure 16-5b, the case of a perfectly elastic supply curve is examined. As before, a unit tax levied on consumers shifts the demand curve facing producers to $D - T$. The price received by producers, however, does not change and remains at P_e. This means that the entire burden is borne by consumers: At the new equilibrium quantity of Q_1, consumers pay P_1, of which P_e is paid to sellers and P_eP_1, the unit tax, is paid to the government.

FIGURE 16-5
Tax Incidence and
Supply Elasticity

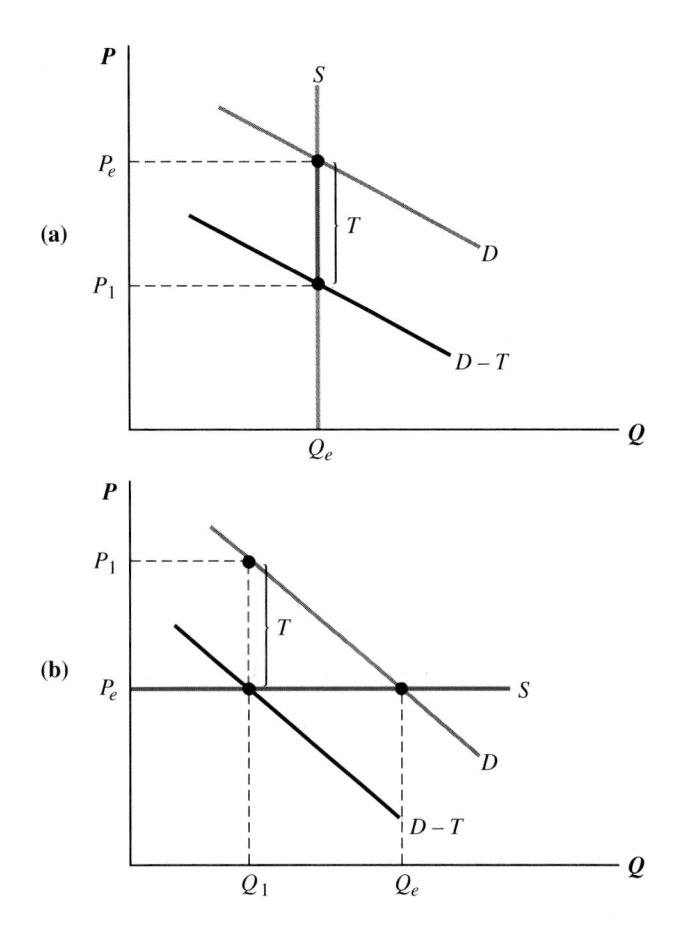

(a)

(b)

These important results may be simply stated: *The more elastic (inelastic) the supply, the smaller (greater) the relative burden placed on producers when a per unit tax is levied on a market.* When policymakers are interested in minimizing the relative burdens placed on consumers, they will tend to tax those markets characterized by relatively inelastic supplies. The intuition behind this result follows from the definition of supply elasticity. The more elastic is supply, the more responsive are suppliers to price changes. When tax policies lead to price changes, suppliers with more elastic supplies will also be those who are able to alter their output behavior more easily than those with relatively inelastic supplies.

Implications of Elasticity for Tax Policy

Our discussion suggests that consumers and sellers care which markets are taxed. Consumers bear less of a burden when taxes are imposed on markets with relatively elastic demands and relatively inelastic supplies. Sellers bear less of a burden when taxes are imposed on markets in which demands are relatively inelastic and supplies are relatively elastic. Citizens and special interest groups often use these facts in debating details and merits of proposed changes in tax policy.

Ad Valorem *Taxes*

An *ad valorem* tax is levied as a percentage of product price. Many states have sales taxes whereby a fixed percentage, such as 5 percent, is applied to sales of goods and services. Although statutory incidence is assigned to consumers, economic incidence differs from statutory incidence in many cases.

To examine economic incidence, assume that a 20 percent *ad valorem* tax is imposed on consumers in the market shown in Figure 16-6, where pretax equilibrium is characterized by P_e and Q_e. Remembering that a demand curve lists the *maximum* prices that consumers are willing to pay for various quantities, an *ad valorem* tax vertically lowers the demand curve facing producers by the amount of the tax. Unlike a per unit tax, however, an *ad valorem* tax is a percentage of sales price, and therefore the demand curve does not shift down in a parallel manner. For example, at a per unit price of $2, the new price received by firms is $1.60, or 80 percent of the original price. At price $1.50 per unit, the new price received by firms is $1.20 and, at price $.20, the new price is $.16. This logic plots out D' as the new demand curve facing firms and, as shown in Figure 16-6, the vertical distance between D and D' falls as price falls.

Post-tax equilibrium quantity falls to Q_1, and equilibrium price received by sellers falls to P_1. Consumers now pay a per unit price of P_2, of which P_1P_2 reflects the *ad valorem* tax. Burdens imposed on sellers are P_1P_e and, for consumers, P_eP_2, which together sum to P_1P_2, the tax evaluated at Q_1. As in our previous examination of unit taxes, the economic incidence of an *ad valorem* tax is a function of demand and supply elasticities. The reader should understand that the same relationships regarding elasticities apply to the case of *ad valorem* taxes.

Taxes on *Monopolists*

Our examples so far have only considered competitive markets. But what do we know about tax incidence when a unit tax is imposed on a monopolist? It is common, for example, to believe that monopolists may perfectly shift all taxes onto consumers. Let us investigate this common belief through Figure 16-7, which allows us to determine the economic incidence of a unit tax in a monopolistic market. Our analysis could also be extended to an *ad valorem* tax, but since results would be similar to those discussed here, we will concentrate on a per unit tax.

Microeconomic theory demonstrates that profit maximization requires that monopolists sell output where marginal revenue MR equals marginal cost MC. The MR curve lies below D and profit maximization occurs where $MR = MC$ at a. The highest price the monopolist may sell profit maximizing Q_M is P_M, which is determined by taking a vertical line up from a to the demand curve D.

Now suppose that a unit tax is imposed on this market. We have shown that economic incidence is usually unrelated to assignment of statutory incidence and, for simplicity, let us assign the tax to the consumer. As shown before, the demand curve facing the supplier changes when the statutory incidence of a unit tax falls on consumers. The new demand curve facing the monopolist is $D - T$ with its associated marginal revenue curve of $MR - T$.

Chapter 16 Principles of Tax Analysis 445

FIGURE 16-6
Tax Incidence of an *Ad Valorem* **Tax**

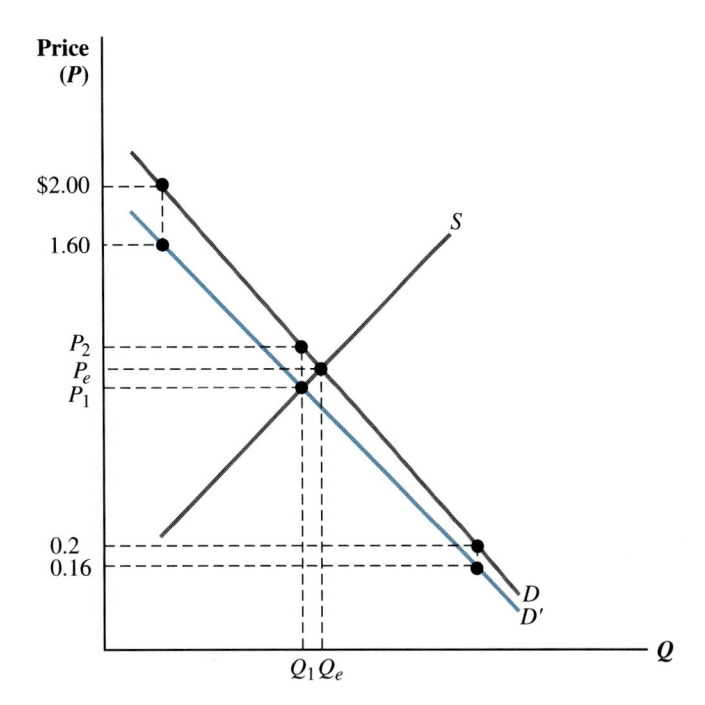

FIGURE 16-7
Tax Incidence in a Monopolistic Market

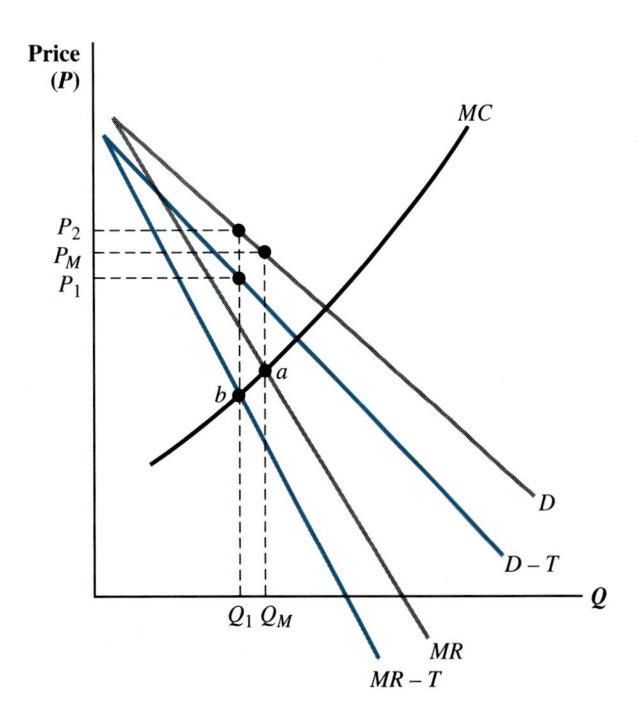

Equating $MR - T$ to MC, at b, we determine the post-tax profit maximizing output of Q_1. The consumer pays P_2 for Q_1, which is composed of two parts: P_1 paid to the monopolist and P_1P_2, which corresponds to the unit tax paid to the government. While the consumer now pays a higher price, a portion of the tax is clearly shifted onto the monopolist. P_1P_M is shifted onto the monopolist in the form of a lower price, and P_MP_2 is paid by the consumer in terms of a higher price.

Demand elasticity continues to play an important role in determining the ability of consumers to shift the burden of taxes onto sellers. Once again, the more elastic the demand, the greater the ability of consumers to shift some portion of the tax onto monopolists.

Several implications for tax incidence follow. From the point of view of consumers, the tax raises price and lowers quantity of product purchased. From the point of view of producers, price falls and profits fall. While we have not directly shown profits in Figure 16-7, we may infer that profits fall as a result of the tax. Since profits equal total revenues minus total costs, the tax, in effect, lowers the revenue possibilities facing the monopolist because total revenues are a function of demand curves. Costs are unaffected by the tax in our example, and the ability of the monopolist to earn profits is therefore adversely affected by a tax that lowers the demand facing the monopolist.

Taxes on Labor

Payroll taxes are levied on wage income. The major payroll taxes are levied through the Society Security and Medicare programs, which currently assign tax rates of 15.3 percent on payrolls, equally shared by employer and employee. (As discussed in our chapter on social insurance programs, this rate is applied up to a maximum income threshold in the case of Social Security. In 1993, the income threshold was removed for Medicare.) Statutory incidence therefore assigns both employer and employee tax rates of 7.65 percent. By now, however, we should suspect that statutory and economic incidence are two very different things.

Figure 16-8 shows a labor market where demand for labor D is from the point of view of firms, and the supply of labor S is from the point of view of workers. Because labor supply is commonly assumed to be inelastic, S is shown to be perfectly inelastic. Pretax wage rate w_e and labor quantity L_e characterize equilibrium in this labor market.

The payroll tax is an *ad valorem* tax on labor and therefore shifts demand to $D - T$. Intersection of $D - T$ and S determines new equilibrium wage rate w'_e. Notice, however, that this produces a lower wage rate for workers, but w_e remains the per unit price, or cost, of hiring L_e units of labor.

While the payroll tax does not affect the equilibrium quantity of labor, the wage received by laborers falls by the magnitude of the *ad valorem* tax. Even though the statutory incidence assigns employers an incidence equal to that of employees, the entire burden falls on workers. Employers therefore shift their share of the tax onto employees. This is ironic, since many people tend to believe that payroll taxes are fair, since they assign employers and employees equal tax shares. But other than differences in perceptions, this payroll tax would not be any fairer if either the employer or

FIGURE 16-8
Tax Incidence of a Payroll Tax

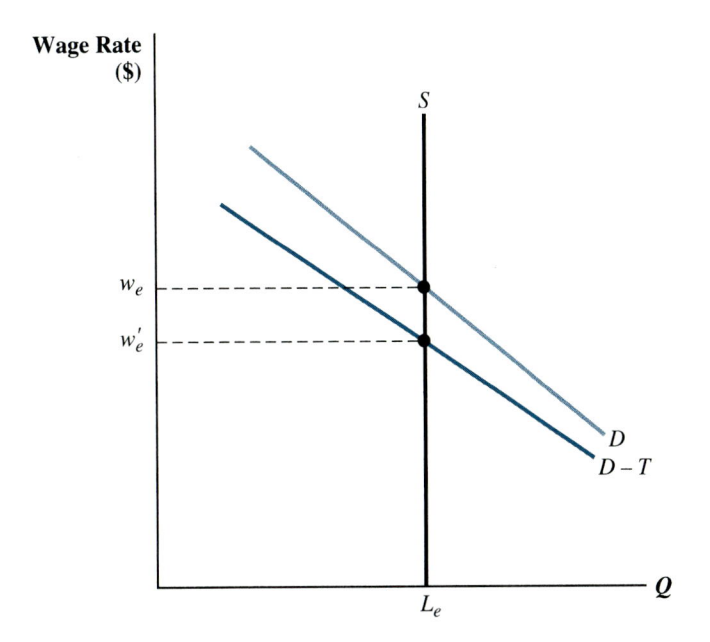

employee were assigned the entire statutory incidence of the tax. Workers pay all of the tax in either case and, once again, statutory incidence does not indicate economic incidence.

General Equilibrium Analysis of Tax Incidence

Two-Good World

So far, tax incidence has been examined within one market, and we have therefore implicitly assumed that all effects are exerted in the market subject to taxation. Such effects are primary effects. We live in an interdependent world, however, and tax policies imposed in one market may exert effects on other markets. Since tax policies have been shown to raise prices and reduce output in markets where taxes are imposed, resources tend to flow out of these markets and into other markets. These effects are considered secondary effects and, as we shall show, prices fall, and quantities exchanged increase, in these markets. **General equilibrium analysis of tax incidence** examines both primary and secondary effects.

Thousands of markets may be interrelated in reality, but assume for now that only two goods are produced in the economy: electric fans and chairs. In Figure 16-9, we show these two markets and, before imposition of a tax, intersection of supply (S) and demand (D) curves determines equilibrium in these markets. Now consider how a unit tax on suppliers of fans affects resource allocation in the market for fans. A unit tax T causes a parallel shift in supply to $S_f + T$ which increases equilibrium price to P'_f and decreases quantity exchanged to Q'_f. The analysis, so far, is no different than before. The tax is partially shifted onto consumers since, of the unit tax of $P_1 P'_f$ at Q'_f, $P_1 P_f$ is borne by producers, and $P_f P'_f$ is borne by consumers.

General equilibrium analysis of tax incidence is the study of tax incidence that considers interrelations between markets.

FIGURE 16-9
Tax Incidence
General Equilibrium Approach

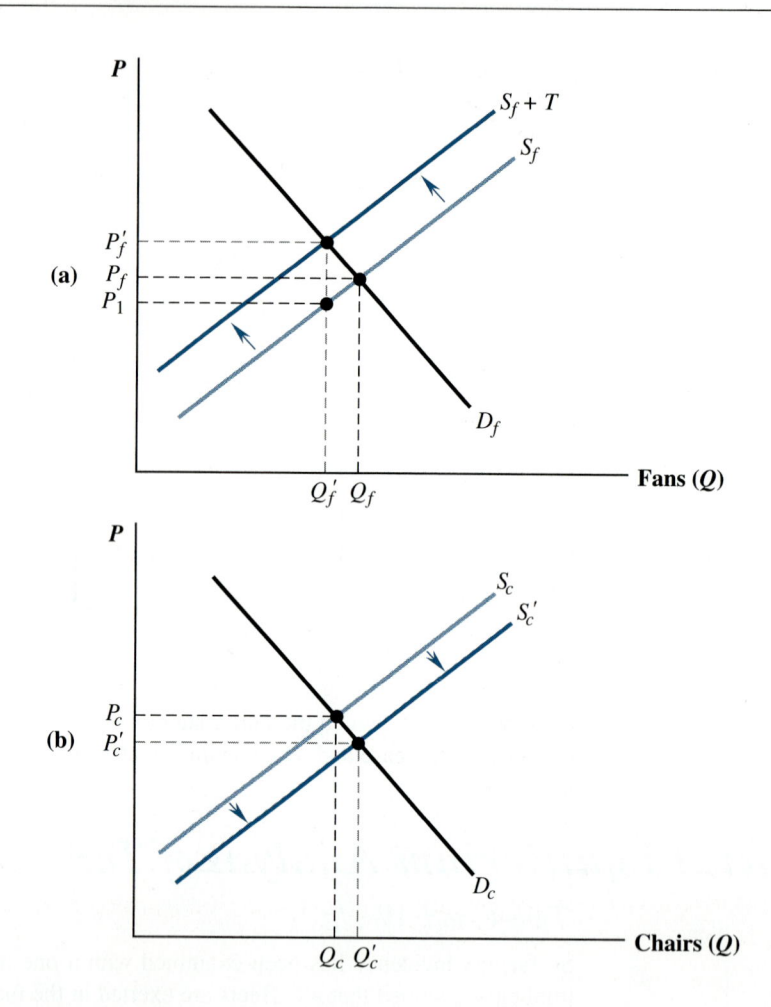

(a)

(b)

The next step is to consider how resource reallocation in the fan market influences the market for chairs. Fewer resources employed in the fan market means more resources are available for the chair market. This shifting of resources between markets leads to an increase in supply from S_c to S'_c. The price of chairs therefore falls from P_c to P'_c and quantity exchanged increases from Q_c to Q'_c; at the same time, $Q'_f Q_f$ electric fans are no longer produced.

Implications for Tax Incidence

This general equilibrium model of tax incidence is more complex since we see that although consumers now pay higher prices for fans, they also pay lower prices for chairs. The net effect for consumers is related to the relative shares of these two goods in their budgets. Consumers who spend relatively more on chairs than on fans tend to be better off after the tax and vice versa. Sellers with specialized resources in the fan market, however, will tend to lose since a tax on fans results in lower usage of resources in that market and therefore lower income for these owners of productive resources. Fewer resources are now employed in this market, and when lower value is attached to these resources, resource owners experience a reduction in income. If resources are not specialized, there are few effects on resource owners.

Complications

It is tempting to conclude that all analysis should follow the general equilibrium approach, but this is not necessarily true. Several complications make it difficult to undertake a full-scale general equilibrium analysis of tax incidence. One occurs because taxes, such as general sales taxes, are often applied to many markets at the same time. It is relatively easy to undertake a general equilibrium analysis in a two-good world in which taxes are only levied in one market, but tax policy is not so simple in reality. When a tax is imposed on the fan market, for example, a tax may be imposed on the chair market at the same time. When the same tax is applied in both markets, it may be expected that resources will not shift as much as in the case in which a tax is imposed on only one market. When different unit taxes are levied, it becomes relatively more complicated to trace all the possible ways in which resources will shift between markets. And when we expand our examination outside the two-good world and try to trace the effects on hundreds or thousands of markets, a complete analysis of all primary and secondary effects of taxes can be a daunting task.

When a tax is imposed on only one market, secondary effects may be rather minimal when resources are not highly specialized. For example, when a tax is imposed on the boat market, secondary effects may be exerted on thousands of other markets, such as clothing, food, housing, and vacation travel, each of which contain numerous submarkets. Secondary effects may be exerted on the market for vacations in Europe, Canada, the United States, South America, and so on. While inspection of the secondary effects of thousands of markets may result in a more complete analysis of tax incidence, the economist's extra effort is probably not justified on a cost-benefit basis.

Excess Burden of Taxation

What Is Excess Burden?

Excess burden
is a resource loss over and above taxes collected.

Excess burden of taxation is additional costs that arise when tax policies (beyond simple tax collections) cause resources to be misallocated. Economists also refer to excess burden as the welfare cost of taxation.

You will recall that allocative efficiency was defined in Chapter 3 as the condition whereby resources cannot be reallocated in a manner that increases total net social benefits. Allocative efficiency occurs whenever markets allocate resources until marginal social benefits (*MSB*) = marginal social costs (*MSC*). This condition has been shown to hold in private markets when supply and demand curves intersect. Remember, too, that certain caveats must hold as well, such as the absence of externalities and public goods.

To better understand what excess burden implies about tax policy, consider the market for books shown in Figure 16-10. Pretax market equilibrium is characterized by P_e and Q_e and, because *MSB* = *MSC*, resources are efficiently allocated.

FIGURE 16-10
Market Perspective of Excess Burden

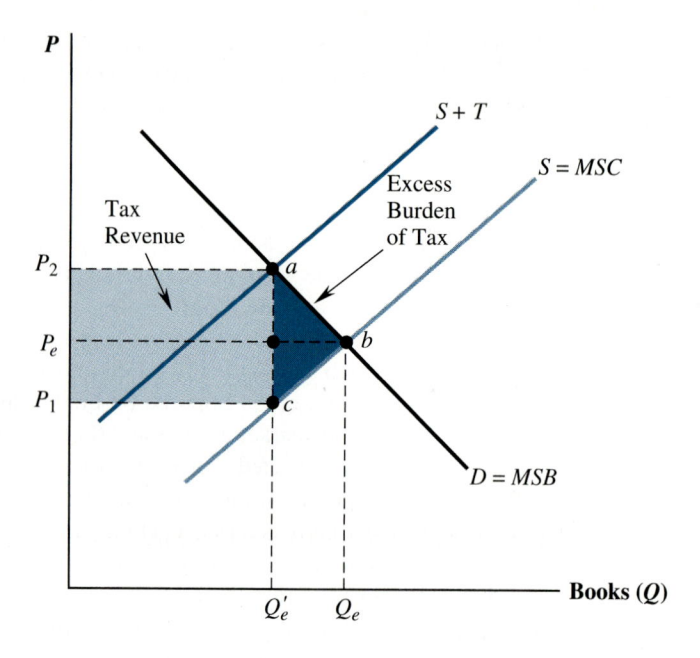

What effect on resource allocation occurs when a unit tax T is placed on suppliers of books? New supply curve $S + T$ causes a rise in equilibrium price to P_2 and a fall in quantity of exchange to Q'_e. Total tax collection equals $P_1 P_2 ac$, determined by multiplying the unit tax by the quantity of exchange.

The excess burden of this tax measures the degree to which the tax causes resources to be misallocated. At the new quantity of exchange (Q'_e), notice that $MSB > MSC$ which means that too few resources are now allocated in this market. In other words, further production up to Q_e would raise total net social benefits. Even though the new equilibrium is characterized by equality of demand and the new supply curve, this new supply curve $S + T$ does not reflect true MSCs since T does not reflect opportunity costs of production. Excess burden of this tax is measured by the difference between total net social benefits at Q_e (pretax production) and at Q'_e (post-tax production), a difference shown by triangle *abc*.

Excess burden reflects a welfare loss to society. Remember that tax revenues are used by the government either to purchase goods and services or to transfer income among members of society. Tax revenues may therefore be thought of as providing benefits in the form of government programs to citizens. The excess burden of taxation, however, reflects a different type of loss since these losses do not fund public programs. As just shown, a unit tax causes resources to be underallocated in the book market. Since this implies that resources are wasted, excess burden of taxation is sometimes called *deadweight loss* or *welfare loss*. An important implication is that tax collection underestimates true burdens of taxation whenever there are excess burdens.

Excess Burden and the Individual

Figure 16-11 allows us to understand the meaning of excess burden from the point of view of an individual who makes choices regarding two goods, X and Y. Before a unit tax on X is levied, the individual faces budget constraint *AB* and maximizes utility by choosing bundle *E*1 with *OE* units of Y and *OL* units of X.

The maximum amount of X that may be purchased falls when a unit tax is applied to its consumption. Such a change would be reflected in new budget constraint *AC*. This steeper budget constraint indicates that the maximum amount of Y that may be purchased is unchanged, but the maximum amount of X has fallen. Recall that the relative prices of the two goods determine the slope of the budget constraint.[3] A steeper budget constraint reflects the higher price of X that occurs after the unit tax is imposed on X. The individual now maximizes utility at point *E*2 and chooses *OF* of Y and *OJ* of X. The unit tax therefore leads the individual to consume more of Y and less of X.

Tax collections may be measured as *IE*2. This measurement follows from comparison of how much less Y may be purchased at any level of X after imposition of the tax. For example, at new equilibrium *E*2, the individual chooses *OJ* units of X. While *OJ* units could also have been chosen before imposition of the tax, note that *IE*2 represents the units of Y that are no longer available after the tax is imposed. A loss of *IE*2 units of Y therefore measures tax payments made by the individual. Although this does not reflect dollar value of taxation, it can easily be determined by multiplying the per unit price of Y times the quantity *IE*2.

Recall that excess burdens occur whenever taxes cause an inefficient allocation of resources. Misallocation would therefore occur whenever another tax of equivalent value would provide a higher level of utility for the individual. It is common to measure an equivalent tax in terms of a **lump sum tax,** any tax which collects a set sum and therefore does not vary with consumption of either good. For our purposes, the equivalent lump sum tax equals *IE*2.

An inward shift of the individual's budget constraint occurs, since a lump sum tax lowers the effective income of the individual. Such a shift causes budget constraint *AB* to shift back in parallel fashion by the distance *IE*2, the value of the equivalent lump sum tax. The new budget constraint is therefore *HD*, and because there is no relative price change under the lump sum tax, the slope of the new budget constraint equals that of the original budget constraint.

When confronted with new budget constraint *HD*, the individual maximizes utility at *E*3. Notice that since the individual reaches a higher indifference curve, the equivalent lump sum tax yields a higher level of utility than the unit tax. Excess burden arises since the equivalent lump sum tax allows the individual to attain higher utility. Excess burden may be simply measured as the difference between utilities achieved under the two tax policies.

If lump sum taxes may remove excess burdens, why are they not used more often in practice? A primary reason is that lump sum taxes are often perceived to be unfair. Tax policy is primarily based on the ability-to-pay principle. Because lump sum taxes

---

Lump sum tax is one that does not vary with units of goods purchased or sold.

---

[3] As shown in the appendix at the end of the book, the price ratio $-(P_X/P_Y)$ is the slope of the budget constraint.

FIGURE 16-11
Excess Burden of a Tax
Individual Perspective

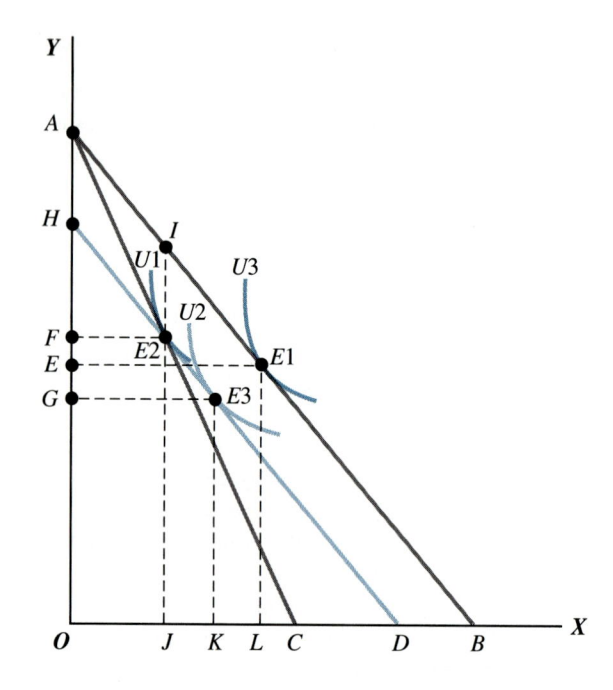

are not directly related to income of taxpayers, they often appear inequitable in comparison to other tax policies.

Excess Burden and Elasticity

We now return our focus to the market and demonstrate that the magnitude of excess burden is related to elasticity. Figure 16-12 compares excess burdens that result from two different demands: D^{el} is relatively elastic and D^{in} is relatively inelastic. Because it becomes easier to compare excess burden triangles, we assume a constant cost industry characterized by a horizontal supply curve such as S. Pretax equilibrium is described by P_e and Q_e.

A unit tax of T placed on sellers makes $S + T$ the new supply curve. Excess burden associated with inelastic demand D^{in} is *abc* and, for elastic demand D^{el}, it is *efc*. Simple inspection indicates that excess burden is highest in the case of the elastic demand.

The implication of this comparison may be stated thus: *For a given unit tax, the more elastic the demand, the higher the excess burden of the tax.*[4] What intuition lies behind this result? Recall that price elasticity of demand indicates the degree to which consumers are responsive to price changes. More elastic demands indicate more responsive consumers. Excess burden arises when taxes cause resource misallocations—

---

[4] Similarly, *holding the elasticity of demand constant, the more inelastic the supply, the smaller the excess burden associated with a given per unit tax.* This may be shown by analysis similar to that displayed above. The intuition is also similar. When supply is relatively inelastic, a given price change induces a relatively small response on the part of suppliers. Therefore, the smaller the output response, the smaller the excess burden associated with a given per unit tax.

FIGURE 16-12
Excess Burden and Demand Elasticity

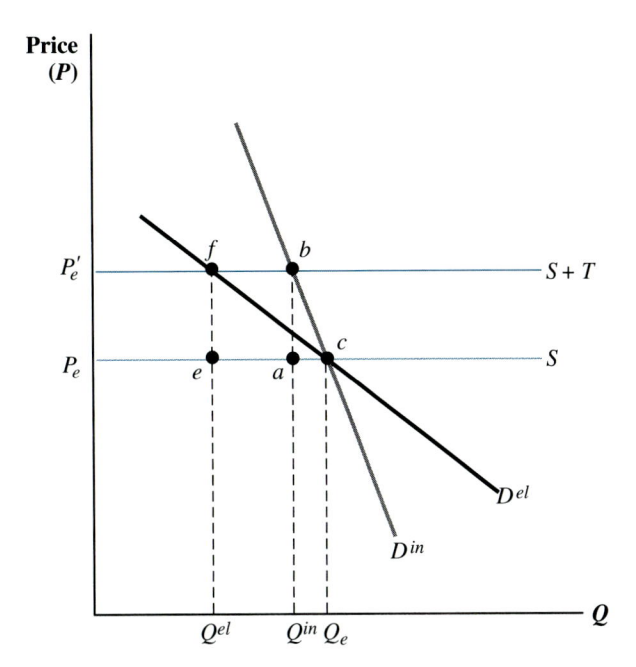

that is, when quantity of exchange drops below the level associated with allocative efficiency. Therefore, the more elastic is demand, the greater the reduction in quantity of exchange, and therefore the larger will be excess burden. In our example, excess burden is higher with the more elastic demand because quantity of exchange drops farther, from Q_e to Q^{el}, than in the case of the inelastic demand, from Q_e to Q^{in}.

Does the relationship between excess burden and demand elasticity indicate that tax policy should focus on taxing goods with relatively inelastic demands? Should minimization of excess burden be a primary concern of tax policy? Not necessarily, since even if it would lessen excess burden, we must remember that many goods characterized by inelastic demands are viewed as necessities. Food and housing are goods, for example, characterized by relatively inelastic demands, and targeting these goods for taxation may claim a substantial portion of the incomes of lower-income individuals.

But what about goods considered to be luxuries? These goods are often characterized by relatively elastic demands and may include yachts, mansions, and high-performance sports cars. It is not clear that high taxation of these goods is appropriate either, since taxation of these goods carries the price of high excess burden.

Measuring Excess Burdens of Unit Taxes

It is a fairly simple matter to derive a formula for measuring excess burden. As we saw in Figure 16-12, excess burden associated with unit taxes for constant cost industries may be measured by the area of a triangle, or

$$EB = \frac{(\Delta P \Delta Q)}{2}$$

where the base of the triangle is ΔQ, or the change in quantity exchanged that results from the tax and ΔP is the unit tax. Recall that we have previously shown that the size of excess burden is a function of the price elasticity of demand, which is defined as

$$e = \frac{\Delta Q}{\Delta P}\left(\frac{P}{Q}\right)$$

Solving for ΔQ

$$\Delta Q = \frac{\Delta P Q e}{P}$$

we substitute this into the *EB* formula

$$EB = \frac{\Delta P^2 Q e}{2P}$$

This formulation demonstrates two primary results. First, excess burden rises with the magnitude of the coefficient of price elasticity of demand. The more elastic the demand, the higher the excess burden arising from a unit tax. Also note that when demand is perfectly inelastic, or $e = 0$, excess burden is zero. Second, excess burden rises with the square of the price change.

Let us apply this formula to a hypothetical example in which a unit tax is applied on lawn chairs. If 500,000 lawn chairs were sold before the tax at a price of $50 per chair, and the price elasticity of demand is 0.5, the excess burden that occurs with a unit tax of $5 per chair is

$$EB = \frac{5^2(500{,}000)(0.5)}{2(50)} = \$62{,}500$$

This example allows us to demonstrate two previous points. Our first point was that excess burden rises with the coefficient of elasticity. Raising the coefficient to 1.5, for instance, raises excess burden to

$$EB = \frac{5^2(500{,}000)(1.5)}{2(50)} = \$187{,}500$$

Our second point was that excess burden rises with the square of the tax. This may be demonstrated by doubling the above tax to $10 per chair (in our initial example of $e = 0.5$), which raises excess burden to

$$EB = \frac{10^2(500{,}000)(0.5)}{2(50)} = \$250{,}000$$

Notice that a doubling of the unit tax quadruples excess burden. That is, doubling the unit tax from $5 to $10 increases excess burden from $62,500 to $250,000, a fourfold increase.

At this point, it is important to question: How much excess burden is associated with our tax system? While different researchers have used different methods of estimation, it is clear that excess burden constitutes a fairly sizable magnitude. Estimates, for example, are affected by which estimates of demand elasticity are assumed, which taxes are examined, as well as which time periods are covered by studies. Studies estimate the extent of excess burden associated with an additional dollar of tax collection. Edgar K. Browning estimates that for every additional dollar of tax collected on labor earnings, an additional 32 cents to 47 cents of excess burden occurs.[5] Charles Stuart found an excess burden of roughly 24 cents on an additional dollar of tax collected from labor earnings.[6] In a study of all taxes, Charles Ballard, John Shoven, and John Whalley estimated an excess burden of roughly 33 cents on an additional dollar of tax collection.[7]

Minimization of Excess Burden

Ramsey pricing is a method for minimizing excess burden for a given level of tax revenue.[8] We have previously shown that, for a given unit tax, excess burdens are higher for elastic demands than for inelastic demands. What this result suggests is that in order to minimize excess burden for a given tax revenue goal, it is desirable to set higher taxes on more inelastic demands than for elastic demands. In the case of two goods, the **Ramsey rule** is stated as:

$$\frac{T1}{T2} = \frac{e2}{e1}$$

where $T1$ and $T2$ refer to different unit tax rates, and $e2$ and $e1$ refer to price elasticities of demand for two different goods. This rules states that minimization of total excess burden, as measured by the sum of excess burdens in the two markets, occurs when tax rates are set in inverse relation to the price elasticities of the two goods.

The intuition behind this simple rule may be shown in the following way. Assume that all markets initially have identical tax rates. Since the more elastic the demand, the larger the excess burden from a given tax rate, higher tax rates should be set on inelastic demands, since they will produce smaller excess burdens than the same tax on an elastic demand. Since minimizing total excess burden will be accomplished at the margin, this rule may be restated thus: Tax rates should be varied until, *at the margin,* the fall in excess burden from lowering tax rates in an elastic market just equals, again *at the margin,* the rise in excess burden from raising tax rates in an inelastic market. When this condition holds, total excess burden is minimized.

Notice that application of the Ramsey rule results in tax rates that vary substantially across different markets. This is not often the case, so it is reasonable to question why there is great uniformity of tax rates across different markets. We have already suggested one important reason for this: Many necessities have relatively

> The **Ramsey rule** states that, in order to minimize total excess burden, tax rates should be set in inverse relation to price elasticities of demand.

---

[5] Edgar K. Browning, "On the Marginal Welfare Cost of Taxation," *American Economic Review* 77 (March 1987): 11–23.

[6] Charles Stuart, "Welfare Costs per Dollar of Additional Tax Revenue in the United States," *American Economic Review* 74 (June 1987): 352–362.

[7] Charles L. Ballard, John B. Shoven, and John Whalley, "General Equilibrium Computations of the Marginal Welfare Costs of Taxes in the United States," *American Economic Review* 75 (March 1985): 128–138.

[8] For the original proposition, see Frank P. Ramsey, "A Contribution to the Theory of Taxation," *Economic Journal* 37 (1927): 47–61.

inelastic demands, and although this rule indicates that these goods should be highly taxed, many argue that doing so would place undue burdens on the poor, who must allocate a relatively high percentage of their budgets to necessities. Another reason is that it may not be viewed as equitable for tax policy to set differential tax rates across markets. As we have seen many times before, just because an economist may show that such a policy is efficient, tax policy concerns of the public may not revolve around the issue of efficiency in taxation. Equity often takes a commanding lead as the most important factor behind tax policy.

Other Costs of Taxation

Excess burden is a hidden cost of taxation and, as we have shown, should be considered alongside the more direct costs as measured by tax collections. Many other costs are associated with taxation, and we will now briefly describe some of the more important additional costs.

Administrative Costs

Administrative costs of taxation are costs related to administering the tax system.

Any tax system must be administered by a tax agency. All expenditures of these agencies show up as **administrative costs of taxation** on the budget documents of governments. The 1993 budget of the Internal Revenue Service (IRS), for instance, was $161 million.[9] These expenditures, however, underestimate true administrative costs since many other parties are involved in administrating and planning tax policy. At the federal level, for instance, tax policy consumes the energies of many staff members of Congress and the U.S. Treasury. Enforcement costs are also part of administration and include such activities as audits and litigation by tax agencies. Administrative costs are also borne by the private sector since taxes are often collected by sellers and firms. Payroll taxes, for instance, are collected by firms and sent to the U.S. Treasury. Sales taxes are collected at the point of sale by sellers of goods and services. These are costs of the U.S. tax system and should be included in any measures of the costs of tax policies.

Compliance Costs

Anyone who had paid taxes knows that records must be kept, tax forms obtained, read, understood and filled out and, in many cases, accountants, lawyers, and friends, called in to help complete all the necessary paper work. The Internal Revenue Service (IRS) distributed over 8 billion pages of tax forms in 1988.[10] There are many reports, for instance, that suggest that the amount of time that individual taxpayers must take to prepare their tax forms grows each year. The federal tax code has more than 5,000 pages, and it has been estimated that the average family spends over 17 hours a year in tax preparation.[11]

---

[9] *Budget of the United States Government,* 1993.

[10] James L. Payne, *Costly Returns: The Burdens of the U.S. Tax System* (San Francisco: ICS Press Institute for Contemporary Studies, 1993).

[11] "How to Simplify the Crazy Tax Code," *Time,* April 20, 1992, 49.

Compliance costs of taxation are costs taxpayers incur in order to comply with tax laws.

There is little question that as tax collection and complexity have grown, **compliance costs of taxation** have grown right along with them. Before the 1970s, it was estimated that compliance costs were 1 to 2.5 percent of income tax revenues, but, for the most part, costs were simply measured in terms of how long it took to fill out tax forms.[12] A recent study has estimated that 2.1 billion hours were used by individual taxpayers to comply with tax laws.[13] In other words, at an average opportunity cost of $10 per hour, compliance cost equals $21 billion. This figure would still be an underestimate since it does not include payments to tax preparers and lawyers or the costs to corporations of complying with tax laws.

Tax Shelters

The previous chapter defined tax expenditures as policies which exclude, exempt, or deduct portions of income from taxation as well as provide preferential rates of taxation, tax credits, and deferred taxation for various economic activities. Two of the larger tax expenditures are deductions of interest on mortgage loans and exclusion of employer-contributions for medical insurance and health care from income taxation.

Tax shelters are legal means by which taxpayers lower their tax bills.

Tax shelters, which are not consciously provided by policymakers, allow individuals and corporations legal means of lowering their tax burdens. A subtle difference exists between tax shelters and tax expenditures. Tax expenditures are tax reductions that are consciously approved by policymakers. The deduction for interest expenses on home mortgages, for instance, is a policy decision that reflects a deliberate attempt to direct more resources into housing markets. Tax shelters may lower tax burdens in ways that were not envisioned by tax policymakers. One example is the case of home equity loans used to finance purchases of automobiles. A home equity loan is simply a loan in which collateral is the equity in the homeowner's house. Even though the 1986 Tax Reform Act eliminated the interest deduction on auto loans, homeowners are allowed to deduct interest when these loans are financed through home equity loans. Home equity loans therefore gained great popularity after the 1986 Tax Reform Act eliminated the tax deduction for interest on consumer loans. Although tax expenditures and tax shelters have similar influences on resource allocations and income distribution, only the former are the result of conscious decision making by policymakers. However, it may be argued that because policymakers knew that borrowers were going to take advantage of this tax exemption, they tacitly approved it. This ambiguity, however, reinforces the notion that there is subtle difference between a tax expenditure and a tax shelter.

The search for tax shelters by taxpayers can be easily explained by the benefits associated with reducing one's tax liability. A resource cost occurs, however, since tax shelters make certain transactions more productive than would otherwise be the case. Tax laws divert resources from efficient uses to less efficient uses and, in this sense, waste resources. Tax laws create higher demands for accountants, lawyers, and, yes, economists, who develop expertise on shifting resources on the basis of tax

---

[12] Joel Slemrod and Nikki Sorum, "The Compliance Cost of the U.S. Individual Income Tax System," *National Tax Journal* 37 (December 1984): 461–468.

[13] Joel Slemrod and Nikki Sorum, "The Compliance Cost of the U.S. Individual Income Tax System."

avoidance. As one tax lawyer recently suggested, "the whole industry of tax specialists would not exist but for the complexity of the tax code. Otherwise, we would be doing something constructive like building bridges."[14] These resource costs are extremely difficult to quantify, but the search for tax shelters rises with higher tax burdens.

Lobbying Costs of Rent Seeking Activities

Lobbying costs are the expenses incurred by lobbyists seeking tax expenditures.

Lobbying costs for tax expenditures are another cost of the tax system. You will recall that this behavior has previously been referred to as rent seeking behavior. When, for instance, a special interest group spends $100 million in lobbying costs in an attempt to gain a tax expenditure of $150 million, lobbying costs can be considered a cost of the tax system.[15]

Tax Evasion and Amnesties

Tax Evasion

Tax avoidance is the legal action of paying less taxes than would otherwise be assessed.

Tax evasion is the illegal action of paying less taxes than one legally owes.

Few individuals enjoy paying taxes, and it is quite clear that many individuals attempt to evade legislated tax assignments. Reducing a tax burden by $500, for instance, results in a higher take-home income of $500.[16] **Tax avoidance** of this sort is quite different from **tax evasion.** Evasion is *illegal* actions that result in paying fewer taxes than required under current tax laws. Tax avoidance, in contrast, is the legitimate use of existing tax laws to one's legal advantage. An example of tax avoidance is a taxpayer who deducts interest paid on a home mortgage from taxable income.

Underreporting of income to tax authorities is a major way in which people try tax evasion.[17] The *underground economy* is a term used to describe people who illegally work (for example, drug trafficking) or underreport (or simply do not report) income to tax authorities; it is believed to be as large as 5 to 10 percent of GDP.[18] Using this estimate, the underground economy in 1993, for instance, was between $308 billion and $616 billion. A principal means of lowering tax evasion is through enforcement of the tax code by the Internal Revenue Service. While it is clear that some taxpayers would never consider cheating on their taxes, other taxpayers base the level of their cheating on two factors, the probability of detection and the penalties awarded to tax evaders. Together, these determine the expected cost of tax evasion.

---

[14] Peter Faber, as quoted in "How to Simplify the Crazy Tax Code."

[15] For a discussion of the losses associated with rent seeking activity, see Roger D. Congleton, "Evaluating Rent Seeking Losses: Do the Welfare Gains of Lobbyists Count?" *Public Choice* 56 (1988): 181–184.

[16] This, of course, assumes that no costs were incurred (e.g., lobbying costs) in obtaining the tax reduction. When such costs are incurred, these must be subtracted from the benefits of tax avoidance.

[17] Taxes are also evaded when excise taxes are not uniform across different tax jurisdictions. For example, some states have higher taxes on cigarettes and liquor than others. To combat this evasion, many states have set laws prohibiting or limiting the purchasing of certain products across state lines. For example, residents of a high-tax state may be subject to a law prohibiting purchase of more than one carton of cigarettes or a set number of ounces of liquor from other states.

[18] Vito Tanzi, *The Underground Economy in the United States and Abroad* (Lexington, Mass.: D. C. Heath, 1982).

Tax Law Instability: Another Cost of Taxation?

Tax reform is an ongoing process in the United States. In just the five years following the Tax Reform Act of 1986, there were 5,400 changes in the tax code. Reflecting issues of tax fairness and efficiency, a downside to frequent changes in the tax code is that it makes tax planning difficult. In the words of Larry Langdon, director of taxes and logistics at Hewlett-Packard Company, "You feel like you're always being jerked around." The result? "It makes long-term financial planning difficult," says Hank Barnette, chairman of Bethlehem Steel Corporation.

While all businesses admit to lobbying for tax expenditures, there is the overwhelming consensus that the main problem is not coping with a particular tax code, but the constant changing of the tax code that causes most problems. What is a profitable investment one year may become a financial disaster in a following year. Larry Langdon at Hewlett-Packard remarks that despite constant discussion with his tax advisers, "they're cautious about how much advice they give us because they know it's a moving target."

Major beneficiaries of the constant spate of tax changes are accountants, lawyers, and lobbyists who earn their livelihoods off their expertise. Hewlett-Packard employs fifty people in its tax department. Larry Langdon remembers his amazement during a visit to a Japanese firm when he learned that it employed only five people in its tax department— and the firm was five times as large as his. One attorney, Ernest Christian of Washington, D.C., believes that tax consultants earn more income than the combined incomes of the U.S. steel and auto industries.

There is little question that constant changing of the tax code is costly to the economy. It should therefore be included, along with excess burdens and costs of administration, compliance, tax shelters, and lobbying, in computing the indirect costs of tax policy.

Source: Rick Wartzman, "Whether or Not They Benefit, Companies Decry Instability in Tax Law as a Barrier to Planning," *Wall Street Journal,* August 10, 1993, A16.

The IRS enforcement of tax laws is done through auditing of individual tax returns. A recent study of the period 1977–86 has shown that when audit rates for individual taxpayers fell from 2.05 percent to 1 percent and, for corporations, from 9.5 percent to 3 percent, tax collections fell by $15 billion dollars.[19] Reductions in audit rates were associated with budget reductions in the tax enforcement divisions as well as greater reliance on other policies to locate tax evaders for the IRS.

Tax Amnesties

Tax amnesties allow taxpayers to pay overdue taxes without prosecution.

At least twenty-eight states have attempted to recover lost revenues through **tax amnesties,** which provide taxpayers with opportunities to pay previously evaded taxes under the promise that no future legal action will be taken. While few states

---

[19] Jeffrey A. Dubin, Michael J. Graetz, and Louis L. Wilde, "The Effect of Audit Rates on the Federal Individual Income Tax, 1977–1986," *National Tax Journal* 43 (December 1990): 395–409.

have recouped over $100 million in lost revenues, many states have raised less than $1 million through amnesties.[20]

Tax amnesties are highly controversial. Common claims are that amnesties are unfair to those who pay taxes and that tax officials should concentrate on locating and punishing tax evaders. Under this view, tax amnesties simply validate past illegal behavior and, by doing so, provide greater incentives for individuals to evade taxes in the future on the expectation that the amnesties will recur. Proponents say this predictable behavior is offset by the collection of tax revenues in the present.

Tax Principles and the Policy Process

Our study indicates that a substantial portion of costs of taxation escapes scrutiny in public debate of tax policy. The dominant issue of debate is over fairness, which centers on application of the ability-to-pay principle. Other issues, such as minimization of excess burden, are not commonplace topics of public discussion.[21] We have demonstrated that replacement of unit taxes with lump sum taxes may lower or eliminate excess burdens, but we have suggested that lump sum taxes are unpopular because they are viewed as inequitable. Excess burden is costly to society, but represents a relatively obscure concept to most taxpayers.

Costs associated with compliance, administration, tax shelters, and lobbying are more visible than costs of excess burden. **Tax simplification** is policy changes that seek to reduce or eliminate many of these costs and is a recurring promise of elected policymakers. The 1986 Tax Reform Act was motivated in many respects by a desire to simplify the federal tax system. A recent study by Marsha Blumenthal and Joel Slemrod, however, has concluded that compliance costs climbed upward after its passage.[22]

In order to spend a dollar, the government must use up more than a dollar in economic resources. If, at the margin, these additional costs were 50 cents for each dollar of tax collection, one dollar in spending requires that $1.50 in resources be expended. A recent study has estimated that, in 1990, all of the additional costs associated with taxation summed to roughly $500 billion, or 65 percent of federal tax collections.[23] In other words, the payment of $30,000 in salary to a civil servant requires the use of $49,500 in total resources. While it is clear that is extremely difficult to

Tax simplification are those policies that seek to lessen the complexity of tax laws and collection.

---

[20] James Alm, Michael McKee, and William Beck, "Amazing Grace: Tax Amnesties and Compliance," *National Tax Journal* 43 (March 1990): 23–37.

[21] An efficient tax system may be viewed as one in which there is not an alternative method of taxation which, for the same level of tax collection, uses fewer resources. If such an alternative exists, then the present tax system misallocates resources.

[22] Marsha Blumenthal and Joel Slemrod, "The Compliance Cost of the U.S. Individual Income Tax System: A Second Look after Tax Reform," *National Tax Journal* 45 (March 1992): 185–202. Part of the rise in the compliance cost of individual income taxation is probably due to more individuals becoming self-employed, declaring capital gains and receiving pension, rental, and annuity incomes. For the view that the Tax Reform Act of 1986 did not substantially simplify the taxation of individuals, see Joel Slemrod, "Did the Tax Reform Act of 1986 Simplify Tax Matters?" *Journal of Economic Perspectives* 6 (Winter 1992): 45–57.

[23] James L. Payne, *Costly Returns: The Burdens of the U.S. Tax System* (San Francisco: ICS Press Institute for Contemporary Studies, 1993).

arrive at a noncontroversial sum of the costs of taxation, the point remains that a simple focus on tax collections underestimates the resource costs of taxation.

The fundamental rule of cost-benefit analysis is to allocate resources to their most efficient uses. Along with tax collection, total costs include excess burdens and costs associated with administration, compliance, lobbying, and tax shelters. Inclusion of these additional costs of taxation is likely to lower the number of projects that meet the criteria of cost-benefit analysis. Our previous discussion of cost-benefit analysis demonstrates the need for careful measurement of costs, benefits, and discount rates; provided that these measures are valid, alternative projects of varying length and of diverse goals may be accurately compared and evaluated. This chapter, however, suggests that when these other costs are added to dollars raised in tax collection, net social benefits associated with a given public policy fall.

It is worth remembering, however, that, while cost-benefit analysis assesses usefulness of public policies, it concentrates on efficiency in resource allocation, and not on the issue of equity.[24] The goal of cost-benefit analysis is maximization of the present value of net social benefits and, to the extent that policy decisions are made on other criteria, such as equity, the fact that the costs of taxation are higher than the dollars raised in tax collection may not dramatically alter decisions on which public projects are funded through the policy process.

Summary

- Tax shifting occurs when statutory incidence and economic incidence of taxation diverge. Statutory incidence refers to who is liable for payment of taxes. Economic incidence indicates who actually bears the burden of taxation.
- Economic incidence is unrelated to statutory incidence. A unit tax on suppliers imposes the same burden on suppliers and consumers as the same tax levied on consumers. The more elastic (inelastic) the demand, the smaller (greater) the relative burden placed on consumers when a tax is levied on a market. The more elastic (inelastic) the supply, the smaller (greater) the relative burden placed on sellers when a tax is levied on a market.
- Payroll taxes are levied on wage income; for example, Social Security and Medicare taxes assign equal tax liability to both the employer and employee. When the supply of labor is relatively inelastic, the majority of the tax burden is borne by employees.
- Excess burden of taxation is additional costs that arise when tax policies cause resources to be misallocated. Tax collections underestimate the true burden of taxation whenever there are excess burdens. For a given unit tax, the more elastic the demand, the higher are excess burdens. While minimization of excess burden might indicate that taxes should be placed on markets with relatively inelastic demands, this may not be desirable because such markets may represent substantial portions of the incomes of lower-income individuals.
- The Ramsey rule states that in order to minimize total excess burden, tax rates should be set in inverse relation to the price elasticities of goods.

---

[24] Tax policy may also be influenced by considerations of the macroeconomy. Keynesian macroeconomic models, for instance, hypothesize a relationship between taxes, deficits, and macroperformance. During recessionary periods, policymakers may recommend tax cuts or increases in budget deficits as means of stimulating employment and economic growth. Public finance normally does not address these important issues and debates concerning the macroeconomic implications of tax (and deficit) policies. The interested reader may consult one of the many textbooks in macroeconomics.

That is, higher taxes on inelastic demands and lower taxes on elastic demands. This rule is not usually applied because equity is often the most important force behind tax policy.

❏ Many other costs are associated with taxation. These include administrative costs, compliance costs, and lobbying costs of rent seeking activities.

Review Questions

1. What is the difference between statutory incidence and economic incidence of taxation? Is economic incidence related to statutory incidence?
2. What is meant by tax shifting?
3. How is demand elasticity related to the economic incidence of a unit tax placed on a consumer?
4. What is meant by the excess burden of taxation?
5. What is the Ramsey rule for setting tax rates?
6. What are the administrative and compliance costs of taxation?
7. What is the difference between tax evasion and tax avoidance?

Discussion Questions

1. Explain what is meant by the statutory and economic incidence of taxation. Why is there a difference?
2. Show how statutory and economic incidences differ when a per unit tax is placed on consumers of wine. How does economic incidence change when statutory incidence is placed on suppliers of wine?
3. From your discussion, explain whether consumers of wine would be indifferent between placement of statutory incidence.
4. In which market, gasoline or chocolate doughnuts, would you expect consumers to be able to pass on more of a unit tax?
5. Show, for an *ad valorem* tax on consumers, how demand elasticity influences the extent to which incidence is shifted from consumers to producers.
6. In our study of the payroll tax it was shown that the worker bears the entire tax when the supply of labor is perfectly inelastic. Perform a similar analysis for the case in which the supply of labor is not perfectly inelastic.
7. In which market would you expect secondary effects to occur when a unit tax is levied on the market for vacation travel?
8. Would you expect there to be a larger excess burden when a unit tax is placed on the market for insulin or a particular brand of over-the-counter cough medicine?
9. How would you introduce the concept of excess burden into public discussion of tax policy? What arguments and logic would you use for explaining why excess burden of tax policy should be understood by the public?
10. Explain how introduction of excess burden is likely to influence which public programs are chosen on the basis of cost-benefit analysis.

Key Words

Statutory incidence
Economic incidence
Balanced budget incidence
Differential tax incidence
Excise taxes
Unit taxes
Ad valorem taxes

General equilibrium analysis of tax incidence
Excess burden
Lump sum tax
Ramsey rule
Administrative costs of taxation
Compliance costs of taxation

Tax shelters
Lobbying costs
Tax avoidance
Tax evasion
Tax amnesties
Tax simplification

CHAPTER 17

Financing Expenditures through Budget Deficits

All politicians decry deficit finance and vow to enact policies that will balance the public budget. Several presidential campaigns have elevated the issue of budget deficits to one of national prominence.

Lively controversy over budget deficits is not the sole province of politicians. As budget deficits have become a permanent fixture of federal finance, controversy over this issue has increasingly erupted among the public, including economists. Public finance economists direct their attention to two general questions. First, what are the economic effects of budget deficits on the economy? Second, what, if anything, should be done to reduce or eliminate budget deficits? There is no consensus of answers. Theoretical and empirical differences among economists make the issue one of the most controversial in public finance.

A few of the various issues examined are:

❏ What role have budget deficits played in the history of federal finance?
❏ What measurement issues confound the study of budget deficits?
❏ What is the burden of public debt?
❏ What are the relationships between budget deficits and interest rates, savings and investment?
❏ Does deficit policy influence the growth of government?
❏ What do budget deficits imply about the fiscal health of governments?

Budget Deficits and the National Debt

What Are Budget Deficits?

It should not be surprising that, in general, there exists high correlation between tax revenues and public expenditures. Consider Figure 17-1a which plots federal tax revenues and expenditures as percentages of GDP since 1935. Tax revenues and expenditures rose rapidly during World War II and then fell immediately after the war

**FIGURE 17-1
Federal Budgets**
*(a) Federal Expenditures and Tax Revenues
(b) Federal Deficits (+) and Surpluses (−)*

Sources: *Budget Baselines, Historical Data, and Alternatives for the Future,* January 1993; and *Budget of the United States Government,* 1994.

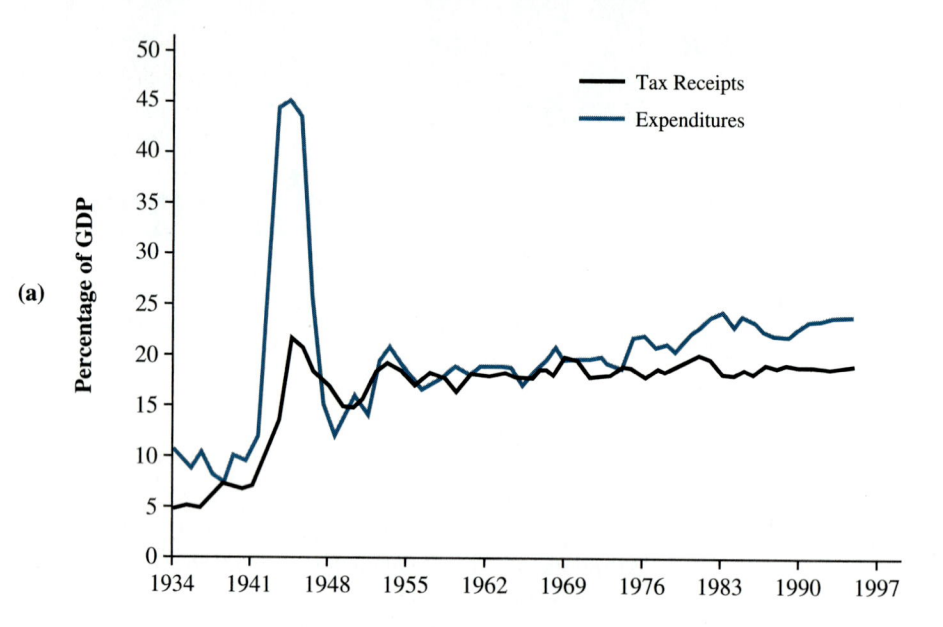

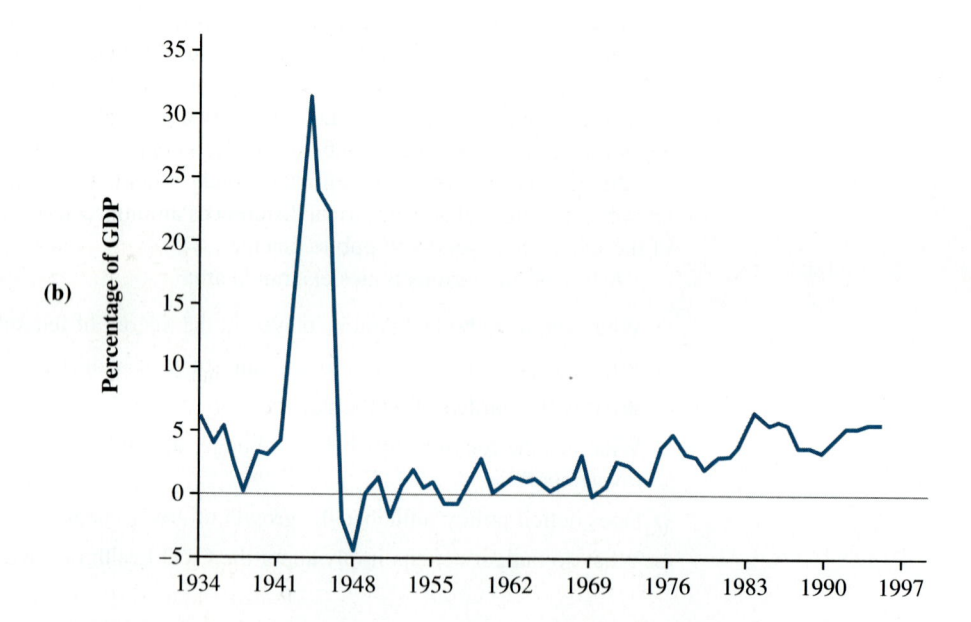

ended in 1945. Tax revenues have remained fairly steady at roughly 19 percent of GDP since the mid-1950s, but federal expenditures have experienced a gradual, but pronounced, rise to roughly 24 percent of GDP.

Budget deficits and surpluses occur whenever public expenditures and tax revenues diverge. Absence of budget deficits or surpluses, by definition, means that expenditures equal tax revenues. Budget deficits arise whenever expenditures exceed tax revenues, and surpluses occur whenever tax revenues exceed expenditures. Divergence between taxes and expenditures is easily seen by inspection of, in Figure 17-1b, our fiscal history. Rising to 31 percent of GDP in 1943, the World War II era was characterized by unprecedented levels of deficit finance since intervening years of deficit finance have not come close to these levels. The 1946–69 period, for example, saw seven years of surplus, sixteen years of deficit, and one year of budgetary balance. In nine of these sixteen deficit years, deficits were 1 percent or less of GDP.

The last year of budgetary surplus occurred in 1969, under President Richard Nixon and has been followed by a string of budget deficits which, as percentages of GDP, and as shown in Figure 17-1b, display an upward trend. This trend is apparent from the following comparison: Budget deficits averaged 1.5 percent of GDP over 1946–69, but averaged 3.4 percent since 1970.

National Debt

National debt is the sum of all unpaid public debt.

The terms *budget deficit* and **national debt** are often confused. Budget deficits, however, arise from the fact that a government, in order to be able to spend more than it receives in tax revenues, must sell debt. Budget deficits occur within a given budgetary year, and therefore a different dollar value exists in each year. The estimated value of the federal budget deficit in 1994, for instance, was $264 billion, which arose from the spending of $1,515 billion and tax revenues of $1,251 billion.[1] This simply indicates that payment of $264 billion of that year's spending was postponed to the future, and new public debt of $264 billion was sold that year.

The national debt, in contrast, measures the *sum* of all unpaid public debt. While a budget deficit reflects the extent to which one year's spending exceeds tax revenues, the national debt reflects the extent to which payment for all *past* deficit-financed spending remains postponed to the future. The national debt (net federal debt) was $3.6 trillion in 1994 and, in addition to the budget deficit of $264 billion of the same year, measures the magnitude of outstanding, or ongoing, federal debt. (There is some confusion as to whether the national debt should include debt that is sold to other federal agencies. Our discussion includes only debt held by the public.)

The historical pattern of the U.S. national debt (net federal debt) is displayed in Figure 17-2. Rising to almost 120 percent of GDP in 1946, the national debt fell after World War II to a low of 25 percent in the early 1980s. Since then, the national debt has climbed to over 50 percent of GDP.

The rapid rise in national debt since the mid-1970s is a result of the fact that budget deficits have been a permanent fixture of federal finance since 1970. Whenever the government operates under a budget deficit, the national debt must rise as well. (A rising ratio of budget deficits to GDP also indicates a rising ratio of national debt to GDP. Note, however, that rising deficits may lead to a falling ratio of national debt to GDP whenever the rate of GDP growth exceeds the rate of growth in the deficit.) Reduction of the national debt requires retirement of some portion of past public debt. The national debt, therefore, has continued to rise since 1970 since ensuing budget

---

[1] *Budget of the United States Government*, 1994.

**FIGURE 17-2
National Debt**

Source: Budget Baselines, Historical Data, and Alternatives for the Future, January 1993.

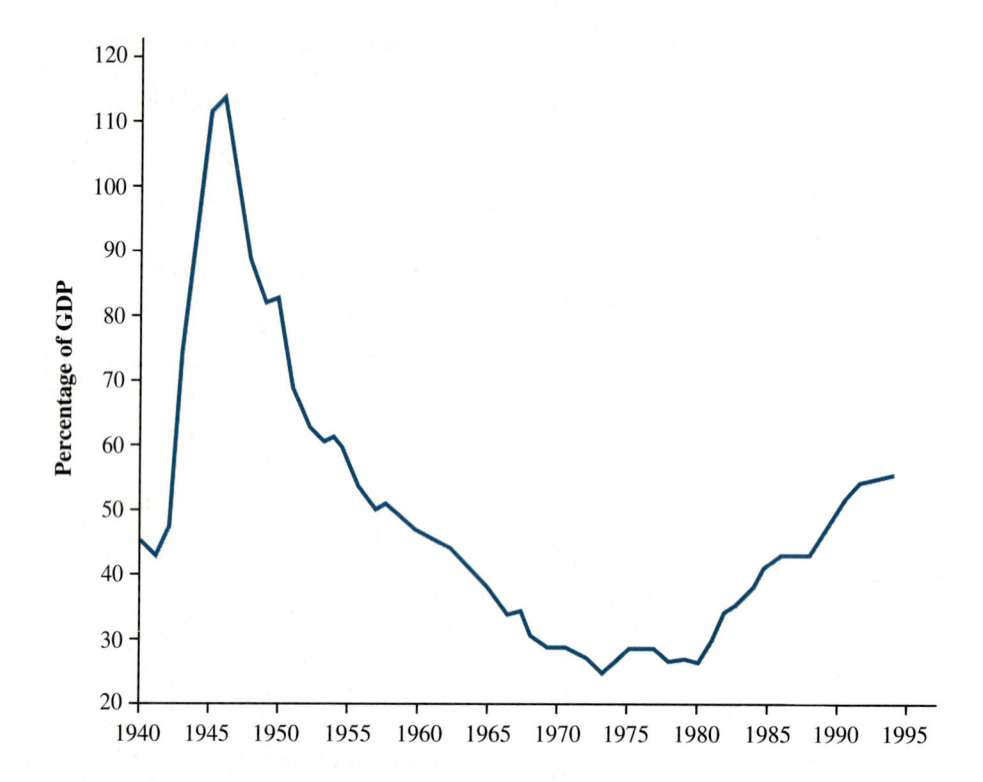

deficits have added to the national debt each year. Only tax revenues may be used to retire public debt, and only years of budget surplus can provide monies to retire the debt. The federal government has not retired a penny of past debts since at least 1969, the last year it operated under a budgetary surplus.

Components of the National Debt

Gross federal debt is the debt held by federal government agencies plus that held by the public.

Gross federal debt, which is all debt issued by the federal government, includes two broad categories: (1) debt held by federal government agencies and (2) debt held by the public. Roughly 75 percent of gross federal debt is held by the public, 25 percent by federal agencies. Gross federal debt in 1994, for example, was $4,778 billion, of which $1,203 billion was held by federal agencies, and $3,574 billion was held by the public.[2]

Much of the debt held by federal government agencies resides in federal trust funds for Social Security, Medicare, and the retirements accounts for civil service and military employees. When the Social Security program operates under a budgetary surplus, surplus funds are sent to the U.S. Treasury where, in return, IOUs are sent to the Social Security Administration. These IOUs are federal debt instruments, or securities, since the Treasury borrows from the Social Security Administration and

---

[2] *Budget of the United States Government,* 1994.

promises repayment when the Social Security program operates under budgetary deficits in the future.

Debt held by the public includes debt held by private banks, insurance companies, U.S. citizens, foreigners, the Federal Reserve banks, and foreign central banks. The vast majority of these debts are *marketable;* that is, they are traded on secondary markets. An active secondary market means that most Treasury bills, notes, and bonds are bought and sold many times before maturity. United States savings bonds, in contrast, are not marketable debt instruments, since they may not be sold to another individual after purchase.

> **Net federal debt** is gross federal debt minus debt held by federal agencies.

Analysts commonly use **net federal debt,** defined as gross federal debt minus debt held by federal agencies, as their measure of the national debt. The Congressional Budget Office has estimated in 1993 that without changes in federal spending and tax policies, net federal debt would rise to $4.8 trillion in 1998, and to $7.5 trillion by 2003.[3] The focus on net federal debt, as opposed to gross federal debt, is based on the notion that debt held by federal agencies merely reflects bookkeeping items and not actual debt transactions flowing through credit markets. Interest on debt owed to federal agencies is paid by one government agency to another, therefore reflecting an intergovernmental transfer of funds that does not directly contribute to the budget deficit. This debt is simply a promise of one agency to repay another agency at some point in the future.

Re-Funding of the National Debt

> **Re-funding of the national debt** occurs when maturing debts are replaced with new debts.

When budget deficits are run over many years, the public sector must engage in **re-funding of the national debt.** Re-funding is necessary since the public sector sells debt instruments of many different maturities. Treasury securities, for instance, are sold with maturities ranging from three months to more than twenty years. The Treasury borrows roughly three-fourths of its debt in securities with maturities from two to ten years.[4] The longest maturity of any debt instrument is thirty years.

A simple example demonstrates why the federal government must re-fund the national debt. Consider the alternatives available when, for example, a 2-year Treasury security matures. The government has two options:

❑ Pay off the security with funds received from current tax revenues.

❑ Pay off the security with funds received by issuing a new Treasury security.[5]

The first option retires the maturing IOU through current tax revenues. This is currently impossible: As long as the public sector operates under a budget deficit, current tax revenues are less than current spending, which claims all available tax revenues. As long as budget deficits occur, the public sector must not only continue

---

[3] Congressional Budget Office, *Federal Debt and Interest Costs, A CBO Study,* May 1993.

[4] Congressional Budget Office, *Federal Debt and Interest Costs.*

[5] Another option would be to renege on promises to pay off investors; this, however, is considered a most unlikely situation by all investors. Treasury debt has the lowest interest rates of any debt because investors perceive it as carrying the lowest risk of default.

postponement of payment for *past* spending but must postpone payment of some portion of *current* spending as well.

The second option is to re-fund maturing debt. This practice is called re-funding since it postpones, once again, payment of some portion of past spending. The federal government in 1980, for instance, re-funded roughly half of all net federal debt since, on average, one-half of all debt matured within a given year.[6] This meant that, for net federal debt of $710 billion, $355 billion in new Treasury debt was sold to refinance maturing debt. While in 1992 roughly 37 percent of all debt matured within a given year, expansion of net federal debt forced a much larger dollar volume—$1,109.5 billion—of re-funding to occur. One consequence of re-funding has been a rapid rise in interest expenses where nearly one in every seven federal spending dollars goes toward interest costs of servicing public debt.[7]

Measurement Issues

Budget deficits are defined, and estimated, by budget accountants. But what does this accounting measure really indicate about the fiscal affairs of a government? We now examine several measurement issues that suggest that budget deficits do not offer comprehensive representations of the fiscal affairs of governments.

Budget Deficit Is a Residual

A budget deficit is first and foremost a *residual:* the difference between public expenditures and tax revenues. A budget deficit estimate, by itself, is fairly meaningless unless we know which levels of expenditures and tax revenues lie behind it. This point is made clear when we consider how a budget deficit of, say, $200 billion is consistent with the following three situations:

- public expenditures of $200 billion and tax revenues of $0
- public expenditures of $500 billion and tax revenues of $300 billion
- public expenditures of $1,100 billion and tax revenues of $900 billion

Dissimilarities in the three fiscal behaviors suggest the importance of placing a given budget deficit within the fiscal circumstances that generate it. Viewing a budget deficit as a residual clearly indicates that budget deficits merely measure mismatches between public expenditures and tax revenues, an important concept to remember.

Inflation and the Real Value of Debt

Inflation causes a divergence between nominal and real values of debt. A mortgage holder with a monthly mortgage payment of $500, for instance, experiences a reduction in the real value of mortgage payments when there is inflation. This, of course, assumes that inflation is either unanticipated or underpredicted by the lender, so that the negotiated mortgage interest rate does not include an appropriate inflation premium.

---

[6] Congressional Budget Office, *Federal Debt and Interest Costs.*
[7] Congressional Budget Office, *Federal Debt and Interest Costs.*

Inflation allows the mortgage holder to make payments in dollars that are worth less than when the mortgage contract was created. While the *nominal* value of mortgage payments remain $500 per month, the *real* value of payments falls with inflation.

The same divergence between nominal and real values holds true for public debt. To understand why it is appropriate to measure public debt in real terms, consider the case in which the nominal value of national debt at the end of a given fiscal year is $200 billion, and inflation is 5 percent. The real value of public debt is reduced by $10 billion, or 5 percent of $200 billion. If a budget deficit of $25 billion is also incurred in the same year, the fall in the real value of public debt causes the budget deficit to only rise by $15 billion. The budget deficit falls in value because inflation lowers the real value of national debt by $10 billion. Notice that this effect on the budget deficit is identical to what would happen if tax revenue rose by the same amount. Inflation lowers the real value of debt in much the same way as would an increase in tax revenues. In effect, inflation acts as a revenue source to the U.S. Treasury.

The importance of this measurement issue is apparent when we observe that nominal measures of debt are the focus of most public debates concerning public debt. This focus, however, is misplaced when we realize that inflation has occurred during each and every year since rapid expansion of public debt began in the early 1970s. While it is true that nominal debt has rapidly expanded over this period, the real value of debt has risen at a slower pace. In fact, Robert Eisner and Paul J. Pieper have argued that adjustments for inflation turn many past nominal deficits during this period into budgetary surpluses.[8]

Capital and Noncapital Goods Are Not Separated

A *capital budget* is one that distinguishes between spending on short-lived and long-lived, or capital, assets. A new road, for instance, is a capital good since it yields benefits over many years. Spending on a transfer program, in contrast, provides most benefits in the year in which the transfer occurs and would not be considered a capital good. Some argue that a public budget should not simply add spending on short-lived and long-lived assets together since it underestimates net benefits, total benefits minus total costs, associated with purchasing capital assets. Although most costs of providing capital goods are borne in years projects are undertaken, benefits received in that year represent only partial accounting of benefits, since benefits are provided in future years as well. This suggests that budget deficit estimates provide myopic measures of fiscal imbalance because they are based on an accounting method that assumes that benefits from capital spending flow only in years in which projects are funded.

Although the theoretical distinction between capital and noncapital goods makes a strong case for a capital budget, problems arise with implementation of this concept. A principal problem lies with defining the useful lives of capital goods. For instance, how long are the useful lives of buildings, weapons, or roads? Another problem lies with measuring benefits received from capital goods. What dollar values should be placed on current and future benefits received by a new sewage system or school

---

[8] Robert Eisner and Paul J. Pieper, "A New View of the Federal Debt and Budget Deficits," *American Economic Review* 74 (March 1984): 11–29.

building? Errors in calculation that occur under a capital budget introduce new errors into budgetary accounting, which may be smaller or larger than errors present under current accounting definitions.

Possible advantages of distinguishing between capital and noncapital goods also appear to have diminished over time. Transfer programs have dominated expansion of public spending, suggesting that fewer advantages may be gained from a switch to a capital budget. As the share of federal spending devoted to capital goods falls, the switch to an accounting method that distinguishes between capital and noncapital goods yields fewer differences in estimates of budget deficits. A counterargument may be made, however, that greater capital expenditures would be undertaken under a capital budget since current accounting methods make capital goods appear to be relatively less useful than would be the case under a capital budget.

Unfunded Liabilities of Credit and Insurance Programs Are Not Reflected

Chapter 10 has shown that the public sector is heavily involved in credit and insurance markets. With the exception of direct loan programs, all credit and insurance programs have the ability to create unfunded contingent liabilities for the public sector. Current accounting methods do not include future contingent unfunded liabilities in today's measures since fiscal actions are recorded only in the year in which they come due, not in the year in which policies are legislated (creating the unfunded liabilities). While many programs will not go into default or require bailouts, we have witnessed rising rates of default and failure.

It is important to recognize that these are liabilities associated with current policies. When, for example, a policy guarantees twenty-year loans for farmers, costs may be incurred over the next twenty years. Under current accounting methods, the loan program may appear to be free of charge if defaults do not occur immediately. Costs, however, may occur in the future and will appear only in the budgetary year in which they incur and will necessitate either tax increases, spending reductions, or new public debt.

This example demonstrates that budget deficits underestimate long-term imbalances between public spending and tax revenues that stem from today's policies. Since budget deficits measure only differences between public spending and tax revenue in a *given* fiscal year, this short-term view of budgetary imbalance is increasingly myopic when we consider how rapidly loan defaults and insurance claims have risen in recent years. For example, a twelvefold increase in total costs of these programs occurred over 1982–90.[9] In 1982, under President Ronald Reagan, loan write-offs and defaults totaled $3.7 billion and insurance claims totaled $4.6 billion. In 1990, under President George Bush, loan write-offs and defaults were $14.8 billion and insurance costs were $93 billion, of which most of the latter covered losses of 433 failed banks and thrifts.

---

[9] *Budget of the United States Government,* 1992, Part 2, 203.

It is commonly argued that even though it would be useful to account for upcoming liabilities (stemming from today's policies) in today's budgetary measures, it is impossible to know future values of these liabilities. Estimates are available, however, that predict future loan defaults and insurance claims associated with policies in place today. A recent estimate places the present value of future obligations associated with these programs within a range of $179 billion and $266 billion.[10]

Unfunded Liabilities of Trust Funds Are Not Reflected

A substantial portion of the debt held by federal government agencies resides in Social Security and Medicare trust funds. By 1996, Social Security trust funds are projected to exceed $1 trillion. Trust fund balances represent unfunded liabilities, since the U.S. Treasury does not save for future repayments of IOUs. When annual deficits in the Social Security account begin in 2030, unfunded liabilities will be met by some combination of four options: higher payroll taxes, use of nonpayroll taxes to fund payments, reduction of Social Security benefits, or the sale of new public debt. No matter which combination is chosen, unfunded liabilities exist, and current accounting methods do not include them in current definitions of spending, taxation or, therefore, budget deficits.

Another measurement issue has recently been the subject of much controversy. Current accounting methods not only neglect future unfunded liabilities associated with trust funds, surpluses in the Social Security account lower, dollar-for-dollar, budget deficits of the same year! The budget deficit therefore appears to be smaller than it would be otherwise. Remember, however, that revenues associated with Social Security surpluses represent future unfunded liabilities, so that when they are used to fund today's spending, they may not be retrieved in the future, when unfunded liabilities come due. Considerable controversy surrounds this issue, but it is clear that inclusion of Social Security surpluses (by lowering the size of the budget deficit) does not provide an accurate picture of the present value of all future liabilities that are incurred through today's budgetary policies.[11]

Economic Effects of Public Debt

There is little question that public debt has expanded rapidly since the early 1970s. But is this a matter of concern? A highly controversial question concerns whether issuance of public debt places burdens on the economy. Issuance of debt, and payment of interest on debt, are potential burdens on many Americans. We now examine opposing viewpoints regarding what burdens, if any, are associated with public debt.

---

[10] *Budget of the United States Government,* 1993, Part 1, 273.

[11] Previous discussion examined a system of generational accounts as one means to describe the ways in which different generations are affected by today's policies. For example, see Laurence J. Kotlikoff, "The Social Security 'Surpluses'—New Clothes for the Emperor?" in *Social Security's Looming Surpluses: Prospects and Implications,* ed. Carolyn L. Weaver (Washington, D.C.: AEI Press, 1990). While such a revamping of the accounting system would clearly appeal to many economists, serious political complications might make this reform politically inviable.

Does the Foreign Share of the Debt Matter?

It has been argued that as long as the United States and its citizens hold the debt, there is little cause for concern. Proponents of this view argue that potential burdens should be measured in terms of payments of principal and interest on public debt. But burdens do not exist as long as Americans purchase the debt, since payment of principal and interest merely reflects redistribution of resources among themselves. In other words, the U.S. government and its citizens owe the debt to themselves, and therefore the claims on resources associated with debt issuance are merely redistributed among U.S. citizens. These people believe that because public debt does not cause resources to flow out of the country, public debt does not represent a burden on the economy.

But does an exception exist when we recognize that public debt may impose burdens on future generations? People who raise this kind of question maintain that even though future taxpayers are liable for payment of principal and interest, they are the principal recipients of these payments as well. Future taxpayers hold public debt directly when they own Treasury debt or indirectly when they invest in financial firms that include public debt in their asset portfolios. Future taxpayers therefore receive payment of principal and interest that offsets the higher taxes they pay when they retire public debt.

An obvious exception to this argument can be raised when foreigners own a portion of public debt. Foreign ownership may impose burdens on Americans since payment of principal and interest to foreigners may result in resource outflows that lower the U.S. capital stock. Since macroeconomic growth is positively related to the capital stock, future generations of U.S. citizens will experience slower macroeconomic growth and a lower standard of living than they would have if the **foreign share of debt** had not lowered the capital stock.

Foreign share of debt is that share of the national debt held by foreigners.

An additional concern associated with foreign ownership is the potential for increased capital market volatility in the event of serious economic or political crises. If, for example, foreigners found public debt less attractive, withdrawals of foreign funding might raise capital market volatility and disrupt the U.S. economy. Massive sell-offs of foreign debt holdings might result in lost jobs and interest rate volatility that could devastate the U.S. economy.

Is foreign ownership a cause of concern? The data in Table 17-1 suggest not. Foreign ownership has been remarkably stable for many years. Foreign ownership, as a share of all public debt, has remained within the fairly narrow range of 18 and 21 percent since 1976. It is true that the dollar value of foreign ownership has increased, but this is merely a result of rapid expansion in the national debt. Moreover, in 1992, the $39 billion paid in interest to foreign owners of our debt amounted to only 0.7 percent of GDP, or 2.8 percent of federal expenditures.[12] Payments to foreigners therefore do not presently represent substantial outflows of U.S. resources.

It should also be remembered that safety and profitability are the most important reasons that foreigners choose to purchase our public debt. Investors, whether

---

[12] Congressional Budget Office, *Federal Debt and Interests Costs,* 19.

TABLE 17-1
Estimated Ownership of Public Debt

	1976	1980	1990	1992
Commercial banks	25%	18%	8%	10%
Individuals	25	19	10	10
Insurance companies	4	3	6	7
Money market funds	0	1	2	3
Corporations	6	3	5	6
State and local government	10	15	22	19
Foreign	19	21	18	18
Other[a]	11	20	29	27

[a] Includes savings and loans, credit unions, nonprofits, mutual savings banks, corporate pensions funds, dealers and brokers, certain government deposit accounts.
Source: Economic Report of the President, January 1993.

domestic or foreign, assess safety and profitability of alternative investments. In addition to debt issued by the U.S. government and firms, investors consider debt of firms and governments of other countries. As long as the quality of U.S. debt does not experience a substantial downgrading vis-à-vis other investments, it is improbable that a substantial pullout of foreign investment will ever occur.

Intergenerational Burdens from Public Debt?

James M. Buchanan is a harsh critic of the view that the public debt does not impose burdens on future generations.[13] Buchanan argues that the conventional view implicitly assumes that public debt is the result of exchanges between today's buyers and sellers of the debt. But *future* taxpayers ultimately bear burdens associated with future payment of principal and interest, and unlike today's buyers and sellers, they do not enter into current agreements over issuance of today's public debt. This view represents the belief that the ability to sell public debt provides today's citizens the ability to force future generations to bear burdens of that debt. Today's citizens, in effect, promise that taxpayers of tomorrow will pay off public debt. Issuance of public debt, in effect, allows current generations to award themselves transfers by approving future spending with payments to be made by people unknown.

Today's taxpayers will be responsible, at most, for payment of interest on public debt as long as the debt continues to be re-funded by the U.S. Treasury. Future citizens not only inherit debt; they inherit other burdens, since, in order to pay off public debt, they experience lower standards of living as a result of a lower capital stock.

---

[13] See, for example, James M. Buchanan, *Public Principles of Public Debt* (Homewood, Ill.: Irwin), 1958.

Lower future living standards occur as public debt competes for the same loanable funds, or savings, as does the private sector.

For every additional dollar of public debt, there is one less dollar of savings available for private investors. This effect is commonly referred to as crowding out and is demonstrated in Figure 17-3, which shows the market for loanable funds. The private demand for loanable funds D takes the point of view of borrowers and is downward sloping since, as interest rates fall, it becomes more attractive to borrow funds. The supply of loanable funds S takes the point of view of savers, or lenders. While the federal sector may also borrow funds from state and local governments, as well as foreign governments, we will assume that the supply of loanable funds is derived entirely from private savers. It is upward-sloping since it becomes more attractive to save, as well as to lend, funds as interest rates rise. Equilibrium at a is characterized by i_1 and Q_1.

Now let us examine what occurs in this market when the public sector runs a budget deficit and borrows funds from private savers. The public sector competes with the private sector for funds, and this means that market demand rises from D to $D + BD$, where BD represents additional demand associated with the deficit. New equilibrium b is characterized by a higher interest rate i_2 and a larger quantity of loanable funds Q_2. This model therefore predicts that a budget deficit raises interest rates and the quantity of funds exchanged in the loanable funds market.

But savings and lending rise as well. Does this indicate crowding out? The answer is yes. As the interest rate rises from i_1 to i_2, the quantity of funds borrowed by the private sector falls from Q_1 to Q_3, as indicated by movement a to c along D. This fall in private sector investment measures the crowd out of private sector borrowing and will be reflected in lower loan volume in consumer markets for mortgages, refrigerators, automobiles, clothing, and so on, as well as, investment funds in private markets.

Since total borrowing rises, but private sector borrowing falls, borrowing by the public sector must make up the difference. Public sector borrowing of Q_3Q_2 (or at i_2, distance cb) equals the budget deficit.

An important implication of this model is that since creation of public debt raises interest rates, the reduction in private investment results in slower capital formation. Lower capital stocks lead to lower future productivity, and in this way public debt imposes burdens onto future citizens in the form of lower living standards. If the public capital stock were to rise, of course, some or all of the decrease in the private capital stock could be reversed. This is most unlikely, because transfers, not capital spending, have accounted for an increasing share of public spending.

The Ricardian Equivalence Proposition

Robert J. Barro provides a major departure from the view that budget deficits impose burdens on future citizens.[14] Barro argues that savings rise in anticipation of higher

---

[14] Robert J. Barro, "Are Government Bonds Net Wealth?" *Journal of Political Economy* 82 (November–December 1974): 1095–1117.

FIGURE 17-3
Conventional View of Budget Deficits

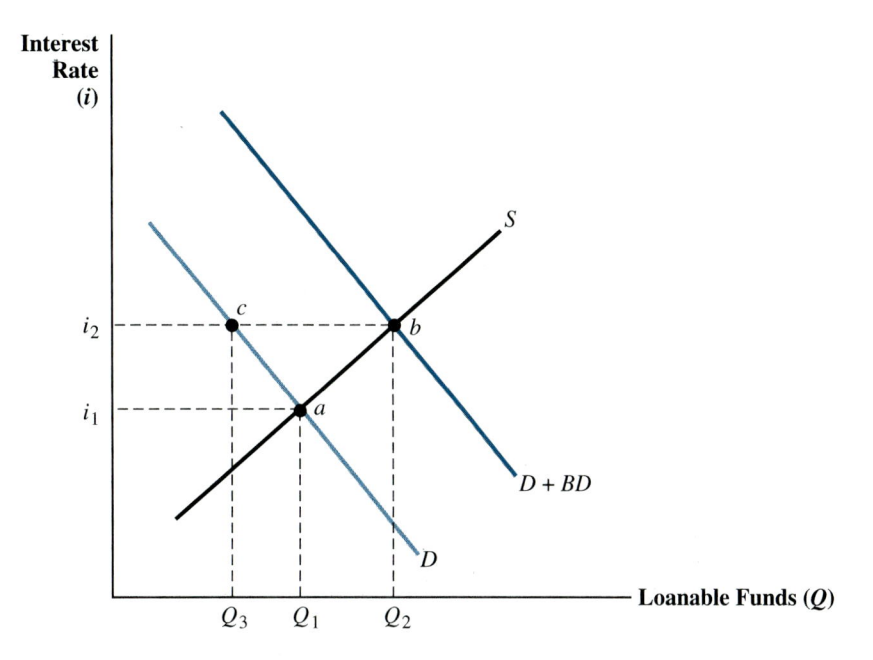

The **Ricardian equivalence proposition** theorizes that public debt and taxation exert equivalent effects on the economy.

future tax burdens implied by public debt. This is called the **Ricardian equivalence proposition,** its central thesis being that public debt and taxation exert equivalent effects on the economy.[15]

The following example demonstrates the proposition. Assume that, holding public spending constant, the government lowers taxes by the lump sum of $100 and borrows $100 for one year, at 5 percent interest. Issuance of public debt worth $100, in effect, pays for the tax reduction of $100. Notice, however, that taxpayers realize higher (take-home) income of $100 but also incur an obligation to repay the $100, with 5 percent interest, in the following year. This results in a trade-off of a tax reduction of $100 today for an increase in future taxes of $105. But the present value of next year's tax liability of $105 is $100 today and, in this sense, receiving $100 in lower taxes today is equivalent to paying $105 in higher taxes next year. Barro argues that since taxpayers recognize this equivalence between issuing public debt today and paying taxes tomorrow, they will save for tax payments of tomorrow.

This view also predicts that debt issuance does not alter net wealth of taxpayers because taxpayers are indifferent between having public spending financed through taxation or public debt. The present value of future tax obligations associated with public debt is equivalent to the value of taxes that would otherwise be collected today. Because public debt causes taxpayers to save for higher future taxes, this view predicts that public debt does not exert an effect on the capital stock any different from

---

[15] Named after the British economist David Ricardo (1772–1832), who argued that taxpayers would tend to save for future taxes required to pay off today's debt. Questions have been raised about whether Ricardo believed in this proposition; see Gerald P. O'Driscoll, "The Ricardian Nonequivalence Theorem," *Journal of Political Economy* 85 (February 1977): 207–210.

that when all public spending is financed through current tax revenues. Debt and tax finance therefore impose identical burdens on society.

Implications of this proposition for crowding out may be shown in a graph similar to the one used to describe the view that public debt imposes burdens on future generations. Figure 17-4 shows, like Figure 17-3, the demand and supply for loanable funds. Initial equilibrium is characterized by interest rate i_1 and quantity of savings and investment Q_1. Although a budget deficit raises demand to $D + BD$, taxpayers are believed to increase savings by an amount sufficient to cover the present value of future taxes implied by this budget deficit. Savings increases to S' since, for this budget deficit, this increase results in no change in the interest rate. As long as the interest rate does not change, crowding out of private investment does not occur.

Note that no change occurs in private borrowing (Q_1) or investment—another way of showing that savings rise to exactly offset the rise in demand caused by the budget deficit. Since budget deficits do not lower private investment, or capital formation, burdens are not passed on to future generations. Just as in the cases of taxation, the burden of the debt is borne solely by the generation that sells the debt.

Theoretical Criticisms of the Ricardian Equivalence Proposition

The Ricardian equivalence proposition represents a dramatic attack on the traditional view of deficits and, unsurprisingly, has many critics. A principal criticism is that because people's lives are finite, it is unlikely that they will live long enough to pay for all the public debt that has been incurred on their behalf. Barro, however, counters this objection with the argument that a **bequest motive** causes parents to transfer resources to their heirs that, in part, cover future bills heirs will receive when they are taxpayers.[16] The bequest motive therefore lowers burdens of public debt placed on future generations. But we can query the bequest motive: Consider the uncertain future tax rates, life spans, and incomes of heirs. These unknowns make it questionable whether bequests may be expected to perfectly meet future tax burdens of heirs. It has also been suggested that negative bequests may be rational behavior when parents predict that heirs will be better off financially than themselves.[17] Another obvious point is that not all citizens have heirs, in which case it becomes more difficult to believe that all citizens will bequest resources to future generations sufficient to cover upcoming tax burdens.

Another criticism focuses on the assumption of forward-looking behavior by today's citizens. Even though Barro's model assumes that it is rational for citizens to save for future tax payments associated with public debt, some question whether this is an accurate description of all citizens' behavior. Some citizens clearly have greater command over resources than others, and it is difficult to believe that lower-income individuals, especially those with heavy private debt burdens, have much ability, if

Bequest motive
is the passing by parents to children (or other heirs) of income to meet the burdens of higher future tax burdens implied by today's debt.

---

[16] Robert J. Barro, "Are Government Bonds Net Wealth?"

[17] See, for example, Allan Drazen, "Government Debt, Human Capital and Bequests in a Lifecycle Model," *Journal of Political Economy* 86 (1978): 337–342.

FIGURE 17-4
Ricardian View of Budget Deficits

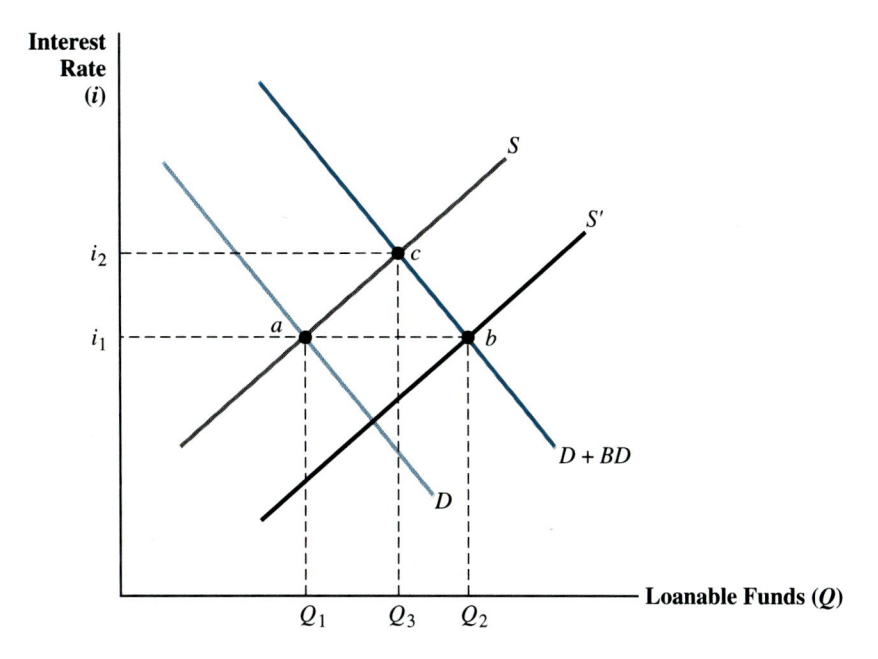

any, to save for upcoming tax burdens. There is also the issue of whether all citizens recognize the equivalence between public debt and future tax burdens. So long as some citizens are not forward looking, the prediction that public debt is *exactly* offset by private savings is questionable. If savings do not exactly offset future tax payments, the debt imposes burdens on future generations.

Lump sum taxes are another source of criticism. Barro's model shows that, for a constant level of public spending, there is an equivalence between lowering lump sum taxes and issuing pubic debt. Lump sum taxes are used in this model since it is known that they exert few, if any, effects on economic incentives to work, save, or invest. But because these taxes are unpopular, lump sum taxes are rarely used to finance public spending. Public debt is therefore likely to be funded through tax increases that may cause the economy to grow slower as incentives to work, invest, and save are lowered. A burden on future generations is therefore imposed by public debt when it leads to tax changes that distort economic incentives and result in lower future standards of living.

Evidence on Burdens Associated with Public Debt

Theoretical objections represent an important means of assessing the usefulness of the Ricardian equivalence proposition. Another avenue of assessment centers on empirical testing of the proposition. The fact that so much empirical research has been performed is testimony to the enormous attention that Barro's work has engendered in the economics profession. We now briefly summarize the important findings of the empirical literature on two major hypotheses associated with the Ricardian equivalence proposition.

An important empirical issue is whether taxpayers offset future tax payments, as implied by today's budget deficit through savings. Although results are mixed, savings do appear to rise as a result of budget deficits.[18] Despite a falling rate of national U.S. savings since the 1980s, support for the Ricardian equivalence proposition does appear to hold over very long periods of U.S. history.[19]

The hypothesis that budget deficits do not affect interest rates has also been widely examined. The traditional view is that budget deficits put upward pressure on interest rates as they raise the demand for loanable funds. The Ricardian equivalence proposition predicts no changes in interest rates since increases in the supply of loanable funds offset increases in demand for loanable funds. Empirical evidence indicates support for a positive effect on interest rates as well as no effect on interest rates.[20] The apparent contradictions presented by these empirical studies are most likely the result of inconsistencies in interest rate and public debt variables as well as time periods, an unsurprising outcome, since theoretical models provide no (or few) insights into issues regarding the interest rates to use in empirical testing. For example, should the 3-month Treasury bill rate, 30-year Treasury bond rate, 5-year certificate of deposit rate, or some other interest rate be used in empirical testing? Future empirical testing can be expected to provide more information on these issues.

Policy Issues

Budget deficits have dominated much of the recent public discussion over political leadership in the United States. The federal government has operated under a budgetary deficit in every year since 1970 and, as a result, net federal debt has risen from $283 billion to $3.6 trillion over 1970–94, over a twelvefold increase.[21] Budget deficits have been blamed for many economic ills, and we have discussed hypotheses showing links between public debt and interest rates, savings, investment, and economic growth. It is easy to argue that better control over budget deficits is a desirable goal of public policy, but many controversies remain over which policies will resolve problems, imagined or real, associated with a public sector that operates under a long and rising string of budget deficits.

---

[18] See, for example, Martin Feldstein, "Government Deficits and Aggregate Demand," *Journal of Monetary Economics* 9: (January 1982): 1–20; and James R. Barth, George Iden, and Frank S. Russek, "Do Federal Deficits Really Matter?" *Contemporary Policy Issues* 3 (Fall 1984–85): 79–95.

[19] Robert J. Barro, "The Ricardian Approach to Budget Deficits," *Journal of Economic Perspectives* 3 (Spring 1989): 37–54. It should also be noted that much of the decline in the U.S. savings rate is due to rising federal budget deficits which represent dissavings by the public sector.

[20] For arguments demonstrating the positive effect, see John H. Makin, "Real Interest, Money Surprises, Anticipated Inflation, and Fiscal Deficits," *Review of Economics and Statistics* 65 (August 1983): 374–384; and Khan H. Zahid, "Government Budget Deficits and Interest Rates: The Evidence since 1971, Using Alternative Deficit Measures," *Southern Economic Journal* 54 (January 1988): 725–731. For arguments demonstrating no effect, see Gerald P. Dwyer, "Inflation and Government Deficits," *Economic Inquiry* 20 (July 1982): 315–329; and W. Douglas McMillin, "Federal Deficits and Short-Term Interest Rates," *Journal of Macroeconomics* 12 (Fall 1986): 403–422.

[21] *Budget Baselines, Historical Data, and Alternatives for the Future,* Office of Management and Budget, January 1993.

Undertaxation or Overspending?

A budget deficit represents a residual that, by itself, carries few implications for the fiscal health of a government. For example, without knowing underlying levels of spending and tax revenues, it is extremely difficult to argue whether the budget deficit is, even relatively speaking, large or small. Comparison of a budget deficit with public spending is one way of determining whether a given budget deficit is small or large. A deficit of $10 billion, for instance, may be considered large when public spending is $50 billion or small when public spending is $500 billion.

Comparison to a benchmark of public spending demonstrates the three following options that may reduce or eliminate a budget deficit:

❏ increase taxes

❏ decrease public spending

❏ enact some mix of higher taxes and lower public spending

A budget deficit of $10 billion may be eliminated, in theory, by enacting a tax increase of $10 billion, reducing public spending by $10 billion, or combining a tax increase of $5 billion with a spending reduction of $5 billion.

Any of these options may be recommended, but each option suggests a very different view of what is the underlying *cause* of a budget deficit. Recalling that budget deficits are residuals, deficits must represent one of the following:

❏ undertaxation

❏ overspending

❏ some combination of undertaxation and overspending

Undertaxation is believed to occur when a budget deficit results from too little taxation.

Overspending is believed to occur when a budget deficit results from too much spending.

A tax increase is the logical policy recommendation when it is believed that a budget deficit represents **undertaxation.** Spending reduction is the logical recommendation when **overspending** is believed to be its cause. A mix of spending reduction and tax increases follows from the view that a deficit reflects both undertaxation and overspending.

We can easily present this discussion within our recent fiscal history. Figure 17-5 plots public spending and tax revenues as percentages of GDP since 1970. While spending and tax revenues were fairly close to each other in 1970, at respective levels of 19.9 percent and 19.6 percent, growing divergence characterizes recent history. For the 1970–94 period, an average difference of 3.4 percent occurred since spending averaged 22.1 percent and tax revenues averaged 18.7 percent of GDP. By 1994, spending and tax revenues were 24 percent and 18.9 percent, respectively.

It should be apparent that whether this divergence reflects undertaxation or overspending lies in the eyes of the beholder. If, for instance, 24 percent of GDP is believed to represent an appropriate level of spending, it is logical to recommend that taxes be raised to 24 percent of GDP. This policy recommendation would have entailed in 1994, for instance, a tax increase of $264 billion. Advocates of the view that the deficit represents overspending would argue that, in 1994, spending should have been reduced by $264 billion. Combination of tax increases and spending reductions that reduce the budget deficit by $264 billion would be advocated by those who believe that the deficit reflects both overspending and undertaxation.

**FIGURE 17-5
Federal Spending
and Tax Revenues**

*Sources: Budget
Baselines, Historical
Data, and Alternatives
for the Future, January
1993; and Budget of
the United States
Government, 1994.*

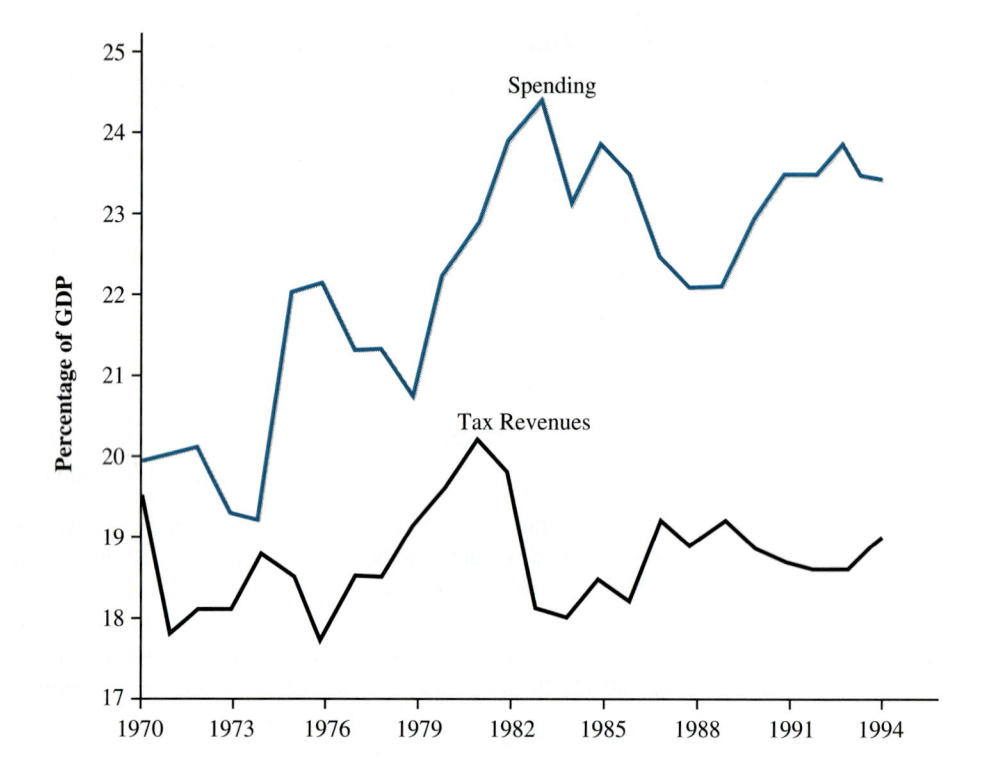

An appropriate solution requires introduction of the notion of an "appropriate" level of government spending, a fundamental issue in public finance. Those who believe that many cases of market failure exist, and that the policy process is a relatively efficient and equitable means of allocating resources, tend to advocate a relatively large public sector. The opposing viewpoint advocates a relatively small public sector since it is believed that government failure is a greater problem than market failure.

In debates during presidential campaigns, candidates at least indirectly argue the merits of increasing or decreasing public spending and tax collections. Various viewpoints are expressed in public debates as one political party generally argues for a stronger role for the public sector and the competing party argues for a weaker role for the public sector. It is unreasonable to expect that only one view is correct; rather, it is important to remember that each view is represented by various hypotheses and, to some degree, ideological influences as well.

Two Views of Budget Deficits and Government Expansion

Fiscal Illusion Hypothesis

It has been argued that budget deficits confuse taxpayers about the true nature of costs and benefits of public spending programs. The *fiscal illusion hypothesis* is that demanders tend to underestimate true costs associated with deficit finance, thereby creating the illusion that public program costs are less than their true costs.[22] This would imply, for example, that voters perceive that $10 billion of public spending costs less when financed through public debt than through taxation.

The implication of this hypothesis is that voters demand a higher quantity of spending since the cost that they perceive for that spending falls as governments rely more heavily on public debt. The ability to spend—but to have someone else pay for it—is believed to create an incentive for citizens to spend more than they would if they were also responsible for all tax burdens associated with public debt. Contrast the case of public debt with that of private debt incurred through use of credit cards. Private debt is the liability of the credit user and, even when the user dies before paying off all past debt, creditors have the right to secure payment from funds from that individual's estate. This is not true in the case of public debt since tax liabilities in the past, present, and future are not directly related to past, present, or future levels of public debt. No legal mechanism exists that forces taxpayers to repay public loans incurred during their lifetime.

James M. Buchanan and Richard E. Wagner argue that acceptance of Keynesian economics after the Great Depression opened the door for rapid expansion of deficit finance.[23] By advocating the use of deficit spending as a means of increasing aggregate demand during periods of slow economic growth, Keynesian economics removed the public's natural distaste for deficit finance, leaving a fiscal illusion that led to expanded public spending. What was previously considered an inappropriate means of financing public spending was awarded an academic seal of approval that Buchanan and Wagner argue provided spending-happy policymakers a new rationale for spending.

An important implication of this hypothesis is that some portion of spending expansion since the 1970s reflects overspending. This follows from the hypothesis that fiscal illusion causes voters to approve more spending than if expansion of public debt had not caused them to underestimate full costs of public spending. Under this view, public debt should be tightly controlled, and advocates of this view tend to be staunch supporters of balanced budget amendments that, under most circumstances, forbid issuance of public debt. As long as deficits finance some portion of spending, voters can be expected to approve overspending. Elimination of public debt removes the veil of fiscal illusion and allows voters to approve public spending on the basis of its true costs.

Ricardian Equivalence Proposition

Critics of the fiscal illusion hypothesis argue that voters are unlikely to systematically underestimate financing burdens and that expansion of public debt therefore exerts no

---

[22] A symmetrical argument is that fiscal illusion may also occur when voters *underestimate* the benefits of public policies. Under this expectation, voters tend to demand less government than is desirable, and the public sector is therefore predicted to expand less slowly than would be actually desired by voters who were not subject to this misperception.

[23] James M. Buchanan and Richard E. Wagner, *Democracy in Deficit* (New York: Academic Press, 1977).

significant influence on public spending.[24] This view is, of course, consistent with the Ricardian equivalence proposition that hypothesizes that voters recognize, for given levels of public spending, the equivalence between taxes and public debt. Under this view, public spending is unaffected by the tax-debt mix used to finance public spending. Voters do not operate under an illusion that public debt offers a cheaper alternative to taxation.

This view leads to the conclusion that public sector expansion is appropriate since voters fully realize costs of debt finance. It has been recently argued, however, that temporary budget deficits may serve a useful purpose. This argument is referred to as tax rate smoothing, and it suggests that tax increases should not always immediately rise in tandem with spending increases. We have previously argued that changes in tax rates may distort economic behavior associated with work, savings, and investment. Raising tax rates slowly over time may allow the economy to adjust to the adverse effects of tax increases. While the tax rate smoothing hypothesis does have a certain appeal, little evidence suggests that this policy has actively been used by the federal government.[25]

Do Tax Increases Lead to Deficit Reduction?

It is often proposed that tax increases will lead to lower budget deficits. The common perception is that whenever taxes rise, budget deficits fall, since deficits represent differences between public spending and tax revenues. Despite this common belief, economists have come to doubt that tax increases by themselves will necessarily lower budget deficits since public spending may change in response to changes in taxation.

The **budget constraint hypothesis** predicts that public spending rises whenever taxes are increased.[26] You will recall that microeconomic theory models consumers as subject to budget constraints that measure available resources. Increases in resources broaden spending opportunities, and decreases lessen spending opportunities. The budget constraint hypothesis applies the notion of the budget constraint to the public sector when it predicts that the government's ability to spend is constrained by its resources as defined by tax revenues and public debt.

Milton Friedman succinctly states the primary prediction of the budget constraint hypothesis: "Governments spend what governments receive plus whatever they can get away with."[27] This prediction follows from the view that there is always a public spending program that someone in the policy process wants to fund. There is no end—and has never been and probably never will be—to the problems and crises that might be remedied through the policy process; and this is particularly so in a country in

The **budget constraint hypothesis** predicts that government spending is primarily a result of the revenues received by policymakers.

---

[24] See, for example, Robert J. Barro, "Comments from an Unreconstructed Ricardian," *Journal of Monetary Economics* 4 (August 1978): 569–581.

[25] See, for example, David Bizer and Steven Durlauf, "Testing the Positive Theory of Government Finance," *Journal of Monetary Economics* 27 (August 1990): 123–141.

[26] Milton Friedman is often associated with this hypothesis; see, for example, Milton Friedman, *Tax Limitation, Inflation and the Role of Government* (Dallas: Fisher Institute, 1978). This hypothesis is also called the *tax-spend hypothesis*.

[27] Milton Friedman, *Tax Limitation, Inflation and the Role of Government*, 5.

which most governments have taken the taxpayers' problems as a genuine responsibility. Poverty, homelessness, AIDS, and education are just a few of the recent areas that have motivated public policy. Tax increases relax the budget constraint and make it easier for policymakers to enact spending programs aimed at solving one or more of these problems.

An implication of the budget constraint hypothesis is that a tax increase may cause a budget deficit to rise, fall, or remain the same. Consider, for instance, a budget deficit of $100 billion that occurs when a public sector collects $400 billion in tax revenue and spends $500 billion. The possible changes in the budget deficit that may occur when taxes are increased by $100 billion include these:

- The budget deficit falls to $0 when spending does not change.
- The budget deficit falls to $10 billion when spending rises by $10 billion.
- The budget deficit remains at $100 billion when spending rises by $100 billion.
- The budget deficit rises to $110 billion when spending rises by $110 billion.

These possibilities suggest that further study of the ways in which spending may change is warranted before we can predict how a budget deficit might change when taxes are increased.

Revenue-expenditure causality is the primary issue that must be resolved.[28] Four causal directions are possible:

Revenue-expenditure causality is the causal relationship between tax revenues and public spending.

- Taxes cause spending.
- Spending causes taxes.
- Taxes and spending cause each other.
- Taxes and spending are unrelated.

When *taxes cause spending,* tax increases lead to spending increases; a tax increase, therefore, may or may not lead to a reduction in the deficit. If a tax increase leads to a smaller increase in spending, the budget deficit falls by a smaller amount than the tax increase. If spending rises by more than the tax increase, the deficit rises. Finally, if spending rises by an amount equal to the tax increase, there is no change in the deficit.

When *spending causes taxes,* changes in taxes have no causal effect on spending and, therefore, tax increases lead to lower budget deficits. When *taxes and spending cause each other,* a tax increase results in an ambiguous effect on a budget deficit, since taxes and spending are interdependent. In other words, taxes tend to lead to spending changes, and spending changes lead to tax changes. Finally, when *taxes and spending are unrelated,* changes in taxes do not lead to any changes in spending and, in this case, tax increases lead to equal reductions in budget deficits.

---

[28] Causality is different from association or correlation. *Association* is merely a statement about whether a relationship exists between two or more variables. Or we may say, for instance, that money growth and inflation tend to rise and fall together and are therefore commonly believed to be correlated with each other. But the belief that money growth causes inflation is a statement of causality. Causality therefore involves a more informative statement about relationships between variables and, consequently, is a more difficult relationship to verify.

Federal policymakers are not legally constrained to act in one way or another; therefore any of the four possible causal directions may approximate reality. Granger causality tests have been used to empirically test which of these alternative hypotheses is most likely.[29] While a few studies do not find support for the budget constraint hypothesis,[30] many studies find partial support for the view that taxes cause spending.[31]

A reasonable assessment of the empirical evidence is that, without further information, a tax increase exerts an ambiguous effect on a budget deficit since some question exists as to whether spending changes as a result of a tax increase. It would follow that if one is interested in removing this ambiguity, legislation approving tax changes includes rules regarding the ways in which policymakers may use tax changes. For instance, a tax increase of $100 billion may be legislated with the stipulation that it not be used to finance additional spending. This stipulation would only make sense, of course, in the case of a Congress that believes that the tax increase should only be used to reduce a budget deficit.

Can Tax Legislation Increase Tax Collections?

Does it necessarily follow that tax increases result in higher tax collections? Despite numerous changes in tax laws over the last forty or so years, tax collections, as percentages of GDP, have remained remarkably constant.[32] Figure 17-6 shows that federal tax collections have hovered around 19 percent of GDP since the early 1950s. This apparent rigidity of tax collections presents an obvious dilemma for those who wish to lower budget deficits through tax increases.

You will recall that tax collections are a product of both tax rates and tax bases, and although both have been increased and decreased, tax collections show little change over these years. Several major overhauls of the tax code have instituted dramatic changes in tax policy, and income tax rates have varied widely over these years. Some tax reforms have sought to lower tax burdens (for example, the Revenue Act of 1964 and the Economic Recovery Act of 1981) and others have attempted to raise tax

---

[29] See Clive W. Granger, "Investigating Causal Relations by Economic Models and Cross Spectral Methods," *Econometrica* (July 1969): 424–438. Briefly, the concept of Granger causality is based on predictability of a variable over time and attempts to determine whether the forecasts of a variable Y, such as government spending, using both past values of itself and that of another variable X, such as tax revenue, yield better forecasts than those based solely on lagged values of Y alone. If so, then X is said to one-way cause Y. If it is found that X causes Y and that Y causes X, then there exists two-way causality between X and Y. If one-way causality exists in neither direction, the variables bear no causal relation to each other and are truly independent of each other.

[30] William Anderson, Myles S. Wallace, and John T. Warner, "Government Spending and Taxes: What Causes What?" *Southern Economic Journal* (January 1986): 630–639; and George M. von Furstenburg, Jeffrey R. Green, and Jin-Ho Jeogn, "Tax and Spend or Spend and Tax," *Review of Economics and Statistics* (July 1986): 179–188.

[31] Neela Manage and Michael L. Marlow, "The Causal Relation between Federal Expenditures and Receipts," *Southern Economic Journal* (January 1986): 717–729; Paul R. Blackley, "Causality between Revenues and Expenditures and the Size of the Federal Budget," *Public Finance Quarterly* (April 1986): 139–156; and Rati Ram, "Additional Evidence on Causality between Government Revenue and Government Expenditure," *Southern Economic Journal* (January 1988): 763–769.

[32] See, for example, W. Kurt Hauser, "The Tax and Revenue Equation," *Wall Street Journal*, March 25, 1993, A14; and "Return of the Tax Olympian," *Wall Street Journal*, May 7, 1993, A14.

**FIGURE 17-6
Tax Collection**

Tax Revenues as a Percentage of GDP

Sources: Budget Baselines, Historical Data, and Alternatives for the Future, 1993; and Budget of the United States Government, 1994.

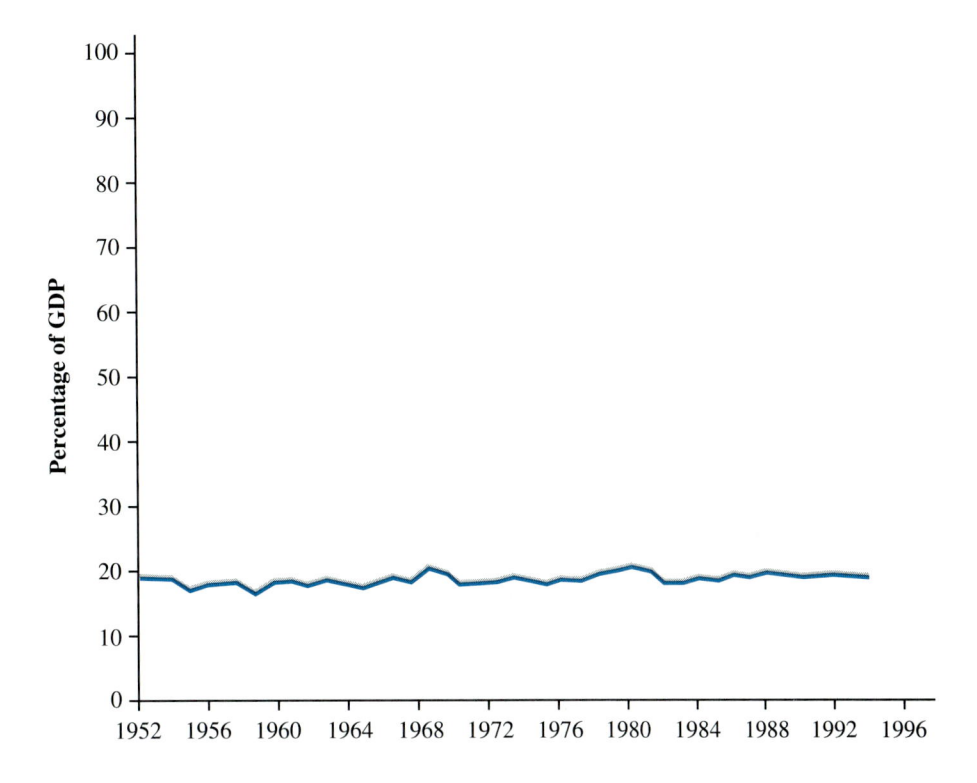

burdens (for example, Tax Equity and Fiscal Responsibility Act of 1982 and the Budget Omnibus Budget Reconciliation Acts of 1990 and 1993).

Several reasons have been suggested to explain the stability of tax collections. One argument is that projected tax increases tend to raise far less revenue than projected, and tax decreases tend to lower revenues by much less than projected. A new tax law, for example, which projects an additional $55 billion in tax revenue may raise only $25 billion. Or a projected tax decrease of $20 billion lowers revenues by only $12 billion.

Projected tax collections will differ from realized tax collections when projections are based on models that assume that taxpayers do not react to changes in tax laws. As previously suggested, changes in tax policy affect economic behavior, and projected and realized tax collections will diverge when projections are based on assumptions that taxpayers stand idly by as tax laws are changed. Taxpayers tend to be much more dynamic and energetic in response to new tax laws. Tax shelters prosper during periods of high tax rates as new incentives are created for shifting income away from higher-tax to lower-tax activities. Higher tax bills create incentives for taxpayers to hide and underreport income, lobby for tax expenditures, and substitute leisure for work activities. Projected increases in tax revenues will therefore overestimate realized revenues when taxpayers are assumed to be passive. Reductions in tax burdens may be expected to exert opposite incentives. Incentives to hide, underreport, and shift income into lower-tax activities falls with tax burdens. Realized reductions in tax collections therefore tend to fall below projected changes when taxpayers are assumed to be passive.

The business cycle may also be an underlying reason for the stability of tax collections over time. Despite changes in tax laws, tax collections rise and fall with the business cycle. Recessionary periods are characterized by falling tax revenues, since fewer people work and production slows. Booms have the opposite effect and are therefore associated with rising tax revenues.

Finally, the stability of tax collections may stem from the relationship between changes in tax laws and economic growth. All models of the macroeconomy predict, for various reasons, that tax increases (decreases) result in slower (faster) economic growth. In Keynesian models, for example, tax increases lead to reductions in aggregate demand and dampen economic growth. Supply-side models predict that rising tax rates result in a substitution of leisure for work and thus lower income tax revenue. These models accordingly predict that tax increases (decreases) lower (raise) economic growth and will generate a divergence between projected and realized tax revenues when projections are based on a model that assumes that changes in tax laws exert no influence on macroeconomic growth.

A Political Disequilibrium?

Political disequilibrium is an occurrence characterized by lack of consensus on political issues.

Persistent budget deficits may reflect a **political disequilibrium** whereby controversy lies over what constitutes an appropriate level of public spending. We have suggested that a budget deficit reflects undertaxation, overspending, or some combination of the two. At one side of the debate are those who believe that undertaxation is the cause of the budget deficit. This side will therefore propose that tax collections rise on the belief that current public spending levels are appropriate. Therefore, assuming away any possible problems in writing tax laws that result in higher tax collection, the analysts believe that deficits should be removed by tax increases. The other major view is that budget deficits reflect overspending. This view proposes that the budget deficit be removed by lowering spending down to current tax collections.[33]

A persistent disequilibrium may exist when discussion between advocates of these two positions fail to reach an accord over how to deal with the mismatch between public spending and tax revenues. A waiting game may ensue in which opponents wait for the other side to give in, pretty much as people do in a game of chicken. This may not be surprising when the policy process includes voters and policymakers who have firm, but opposed, beliefs regarding what constitutes an appropriate level of public spending. Although both sides may believe that budget deficits are bad, each may be committed to securing a role for the public sector consistent with a given public spending level. Advocates of the undertaxation argument may be willing to accept budget deficits when they believe that deficit-reduction negotiation with opponents will only result in spending reduction. Meanwhile, they may be content to wait out the budget deficit as they seek policy that eventually raises tax collections up to current spending levels. Advocates of the overspending view may accept budget deficits when they believe that deficit-reduction negotiation will only result in tax increases. These individuals may be willing to accept a budget deficit while they strive for future spending reductions.

---

[33] We have mentioned that another camp sees a mix between undertaxation and overspending, but for simplicity we will concentrate on those who see it as one or the other of these possibilities.

Substantial support for this disequilibrium view is offered by past deficit-reduction bills. As described in Chapter 9, Congress has passed the following deficit-reduction packages.

❏ The Balanced Budget and Deficit Reduction Act of 1985, often referred to as the Gramm-Rudman-Hollings Act, which placed the budget on a predetermined path toward budgetary balance by 1991.
❏ The 1987 Gramm-Rudman-Hollings Plan, which replaced the original 1985 plan and pushed a balanced budget out to the 1993 budgetary year.
❏ The Budget Enforcement Act of 1990 (and revisions in 1992 and 1993), which pushed a balanced budget out to an unspecified future date.

Figure 17-7 plots the history of these plans and demonstrates their lack of success in creating budgetary balance. Starting with the 1992 revision of the Budget Enforcement Act, the federal government no longer predicts a balancing of the budget within its planning horizon. In fact, the 1993 revision (also called the Omnibus Budget Reconciliation Act of 1993) planned that, after falling to a low of $201 billion in 1997, the budget deficit would begin rising again.

Each plan had its promises, but none explicitly stated *how* greater budgetary balance was to be achieved. Deficit reduction, however, arises only after tax increases, spending reductions, or some combination of the two, occur. A choice of one of these options, however, requires some consensus on what constitutes an appropriate level of

**FIGURE 17-7
Budget Deficit Reduction Plans**

Sources: Budget Baselines, Historical Data, and Alternatives for the Future, 1993; and Budget of the United States Government, 1994.

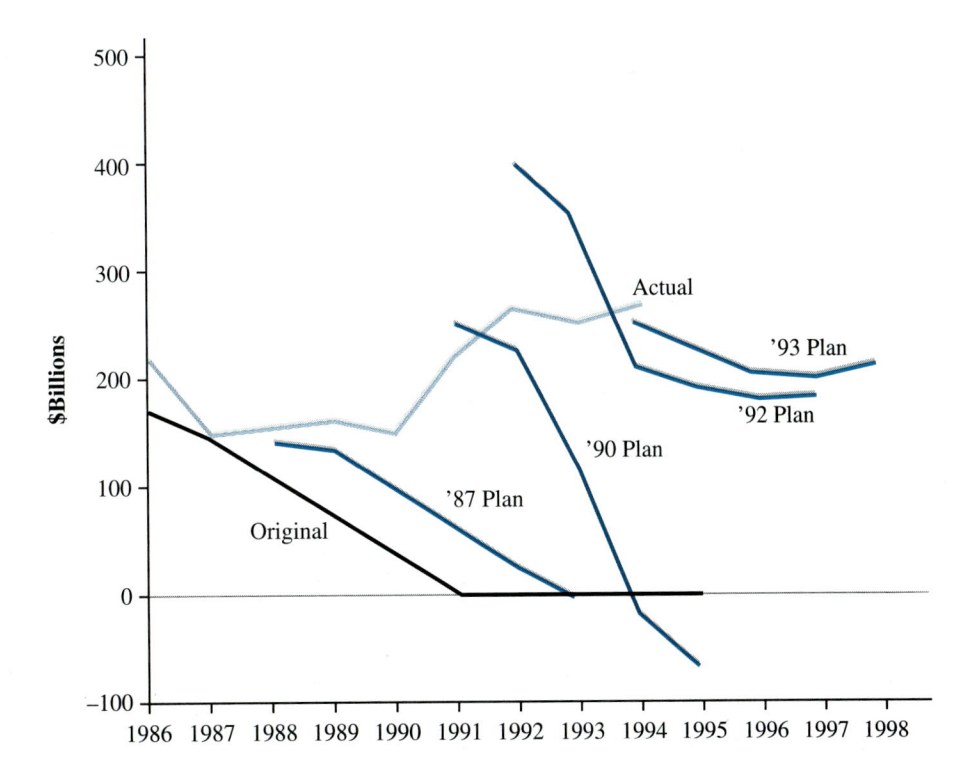

public spending. Without specification of how a budget deficit was to be eliminated or reduced, these rules avoided discussion of the crucial issue of whether the budget deficit was a result of undertaxation or overspending. We have discussed the opposing viewpoints regarding this issue. If neither side is willing to admit defeat, this fight should also be reflected in deficit-reduction rules approved by Congress. The hypothesis that persistent operation of budget deficits reflects a prolonged political disequilibrium suggests a reason for why the plans have failed to achieve greater budgetary balance.

Summary

- Budget deficits occur whenever public expenditures exceed tax revenues. Budget surpluses arise whenever tax revenues exceed public expenditures. The last year of federal budgetary surplus was 1969. It has since been followed by a string of budget deficits.
- National debt is the sum of all unpaid public debt. The national debt requires re-funding as long as the federal government continues to operate under budgetary deficit. There are two common definitions of national debt: gross federal debt and net federal debt. Gross federal debt includes debt held by federal government agencies and debt held by the public. Net federal debt is gross federal debt minus debt held by federal agencies.
- Definitions of deficits and national debt are imprecise measures of the fiscal situation of government. Definitions do not separate spending on capital goods from spending on noncapital goods and do not reflect unfunded liabilities of credit and insurance programs and trust funds.
- While some express concerns over foreign ownership of public debt, there has been little change in the share of foreign ownership since the mid-1970s.

- Another issue of concern is whether there are intergenerational burdens from public debt. One implication of the belief that burdens are created is that interest rates rise with debt creation, but empirical evidence on this hypothesis is mixed.
- An important policy issue is whether deficits reflect overspending or undertaxation. The overspending side of the debate argues that spending should be reduced. The undertaxation side argues that the solution is to raise taxes. Which of the sides is correct must be resolved through analysis of the question of what constitutes the appropriate size of government.
- There are two views regarding the relationship between budget deficits and government expansion. The fiscal illusion hypothesis predicts that demanders of government programs underestimate true costs of programs when there are deficits and thus create a demand for more spending than when the government operates under a balanced budget. The Ricardian equivalence hypothesis states that taxpayers are not deceived, do not underestimate the true costs of deficit finance, and therefore that deficits do not lead to overexpansion.

Review Questions

1. What are budget deficits? In what sense are budget deficits residuals?
2. What is the difference between a budget deficit and the national debt?
3. What is meant by re-funding of the national debt?
4. What is the Ricardian equivalence proposition?
5. What are the differences between the overspending and undertaxation views of budget deficits?
6. What is the fiscal illusion hypothesis?
7. What is the budget constraint hypothesis, and how does it relate to the issue of controlling the size of budget deficits?

Discussion Questions

1. Explain the difference between a budget deficit and the national debt.
2. Under what conditions will the national debt decline?
3. Explain why inflation causes the real value of public debt to decline.
4. It has been shown that budget deficits do not reflect unfunded future liabilities of the federal government associated with today's policies. Explain why it might be desirable to provide this information.
5. Explain how a surplus in the Social Security account will affect the value of a budget deficit. Discuss why this may provide a misleading measure of the state of fiscal finances.
6. Under what conditions might foreign ownership of public debt impose burdens on society? Under what conditions would it not?
7. Under what conditions might a budget deficit lead to higher interest rates? How will future economic growth be affected by higher interest rates?
8. In what sense are taxes and public debt equivalent under the Ricardian equivalence proposition?
9. Explain why policy recommendations aimed at reducing or eliminating budget deficits must have an underlying view of what an appropriate level of public spending is.
10. Assume that the federal budget deficit is currently $50 billion. What effect on the budget deficit would you expect when Congress passes a $50 billion tax increase?

Key Words

National debt
Gross federal debt
Net federal debt
Re-funding of the national debt
Foreign share of debt

Ricardian equivalence proposition
Bequest motive
Undertaxation
Overspending

Budget constraint hypothesis
Revenue-expenditure causality
Political disequilibrium

PART 6

The Practice of Taxation

Chapter 18
The Personal Income Tax

Chapter 19
Income Taxation and Behavior

Chapter 20
The Corporation Tax

Chapter 21
Taxation of Consumption and Wealth

CHAPTER 18

The Personal Income Tax

The federal income tax was created in 1913 through the Sixteenth Amendment to the Constitution, which granted Congress the right to "collect taxes on income, from whatever source derived." The federal income tax has evolved into the tax most commonly recognized by Americans, and very few people are unaware that tax bills are due by April 15 of each year. Many Americans gauge the overall fairness of tax policy through the income tax system. Discussion of income tax policy has also broadened in recent years from issues of fairness to questions regarding its relationship to economic growth and the federal budget deficit.

The history of the federal income tax is shown in Figure 18-1, which plots income tax receipts as percentages of total federal receipts and gross domestic product. It is clear that World War II was a catalyst in promoting rapid expansion of the income tax. Rising from roughly 15 percent of all federal receipts in the early 1930s, the income tax now collects 45 percent of all tax revenues. A similar trend characterizes its share of GDP: rapid expansion from 1 percent to 8 percent since the Second World War.

The focus of this chapter is as follows:

❏ How should income be defined?
❏ What is included in the taxable income base?
❏ Which tax rates are applied to the taxable income base?
❏ Which activities does income tax policy promote?
❏ How does tax policy influence the distribution of income?

Defining Taxable Income: Theory

What Is Income?

Haig-Simons criterion defines income as the change in the ability to consume during a given time period.

While the Sixteenth Amendment to the Constitution provides Congress with the power to collect income tax revenues, it does not define the income tax base. Economists call upon the **Haig-Simons criterion** to define income.[1] *The Haig-Simons criterion defines income as the change in the ability to consume during a given period; in practice, it is*

---

[1] Robert M. Haig, *The Federal Income Tax* (New York: Columbia University Press, 1921); and Henry Simons, *Personal Income Taxation* (Chicago: University of Chicago Press, 1938).

493

**FIGURE 18-1
Federal Income Tax Receipts**

Sources: Budget Baselines, Historical Data, and Alternatives for the Future, January 1993; and *Budget of the United States Government,* 1994.

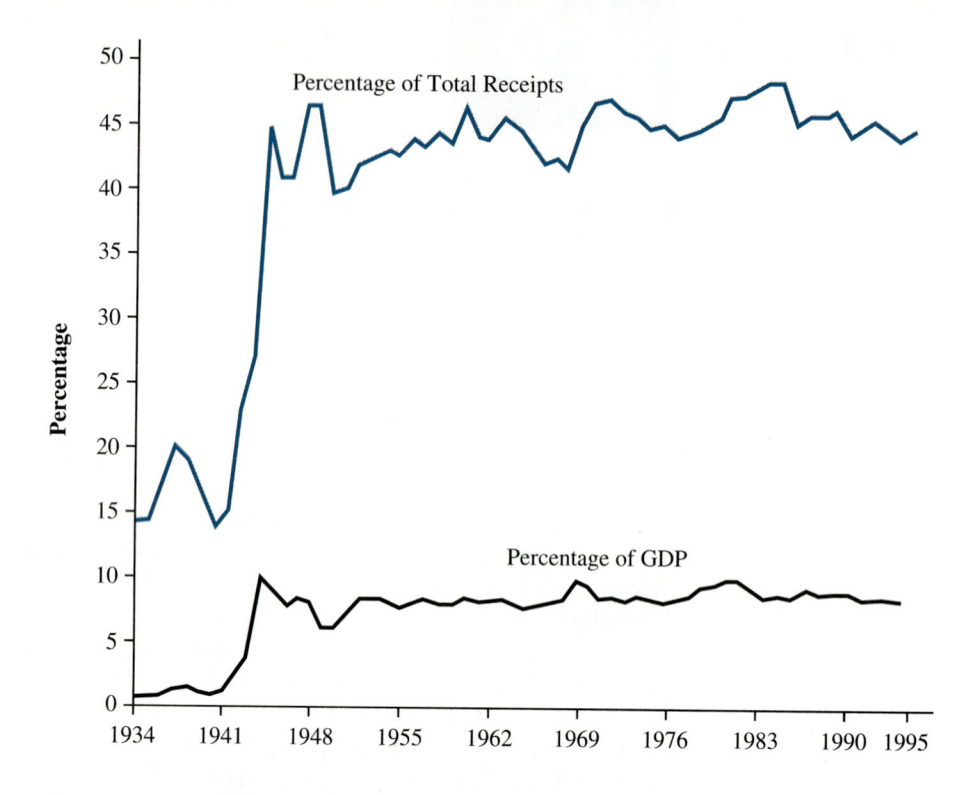

the monetary value of consumption plus changes in net worth over a given period. An individual's net worth equals the difference between the value of the person's assets and liabilities at any point in time. Consider, for instance, Sarah, who begins the year with a net worth of $50,000 and during the year receives a salary of $35,000. If at the end of the year Sarah's net worth rises to $90,000, her income for that year equals $75,000. If net worth remained at $50,000, she earned income of $35,000 over the year.

The example of Sarah makes it clear that although it is common to link income with salary and wages, doing the obvious causes an analyst to miss much of the income. Income is most commonly measured from the **source side of a budget,** which includes wages, salaries, government transfers, interest earnings, fringe benefits, and capital gains or losses. The **use side of a budget** shows where income goes. Uses include consumption, donations and gifts, savings and various costs that arise during the process of earning income. By definition, sources must equal uses, and in theory it is arbitrary whether we measure income from the source or use sides of budgets since taxes may be imposed against both sources and uses of income. The personal income tax and corporate income tax focus on sources, but taxes on uses, often called consumption taxes, may also raise revenue. A tax levied on cigarettes, for instance, is a consumption tax because it levies a tax on their sales.

Source side of budget
includes wages, salaries, government transfers, interest earnings, fringe benefits, and capital gains or losses.

Use side of budget
includes consumption, donations and gifts, savings, and various costs incurred during the process of earning income.

Defining a Comprehensive Measure of Income

The Haig-Simons criterion defines a comprehensive measure of income that bears little resemblance to what most taxpayers normally view as income. Not all income is received in monetary payments, as demonstrated by employer contributions to pensions, various public transfer programs (e.g., food stamps and public health services) and fringe benefits (e.g., free coffee, free parking, or subsidized meals). As every worker understands, benefits are understated by wages or salary. Salaried workers, for instance, may be willing to trade off more vacation time or shorter work weeks for less salary. Fringe benefits are forms of income and therefore should be included in a comprehensive measure of income.

While inclusion of fringe benefits in taxable income would encounter resistance from many taxpayers, other income sources would certainly be more controversial. The value of leisure, home gardening, lawn mowing, and baby-sitting generate **in-kind income,** since goods and services are the end products of these work activities. Time, effort, and materials are resources consumed in these activities in much the same way as when work is performed in the marketplace. Planting, fertilization, land use, and watering provide the in-home gardener with tomatoes, but since they are produced outside the marketplace, no monetary income is earned. The farmer also produces tomatoes but earns monetary income in the marketplace. Production of tomatoes therefore is a source of income for both the farmer and the backyard gardener, and both would be measured in a **comprehensive measure of income.**

Housing services received by homeowners are a major source of in-kind income since, in theory, homeowners may either use their homes themselves or rent them out to others. Services are received in either case, and whether services are received by owners (in-kind income) or renters (monetary income) is immaterial to the definition of comprehensive income. **Implicit rental income,** which is the value of potential rental income, is one measure of in-kind income earned by homeowners who choose to live in their houses.

Changes in net worth for most Americans occur through changes in the value of their homes. If the market value of a house, for instance, appreciates from $125,000 to $140,000, net worth rises by $15,000. (Capital gains should be measured in real, or inflation-adjusted, terms.) If this capital gain occurs over one year, comprehensive income rises by the capital gain. Similar changes in the value of other durable goods, such as boats, cars, and oriental carpets, would also be included in a comprehensive measure of income. Notice that since the Haig-Simons criterion defines income in terms of changes in the *ability* to consume over a given period, capital gains and losses should be included even when income changes are not evidenced through asset sales. In the language of the accountant, sales result in *realized* capital gains or losses, and *unrealized* capital gains or losses occur when assets do not change ownership. Even when assets are not sold, unrealized capital gains and losses influence the ability of owners to consume over the period during which income is measured.

One component of the tax treatment of capital gains receives wide criticism. Taxes are levied only when capital gains are realized, and this may cause some investors to hold onto their investments longer than they would if taxation were levied on accrued gains. This is called the **lock-in effect,** the encouragement by policy that makes investors tend to hold onto assets longer than they would if unrealized gains were taxed as well. In addition to discouraging investors from adjusting their portfolios in reaction to changing rates of return, the lock-in effect lessens resource shifting in these markets as well.

In-kind income is income in the form of goods and services rather than cash.

Comprehensive measure of income is income defined on the basis of the Haig-Simons criterion.

Implicit rental income is the value of potential rental income.

Lock-in effect occurs when a policy encourages investors to hold onto assets longer than they would if taxes were levied on accrued gains.

Finally, the costs of acquiring income should be subtracted from a comprehensive measure of income. Commuting costs, union dues, and all other costs incurred in the pursuit of earning income are not a final source of income but, rather, are costs of acquiring income.

Problems in Defining a Comprehensive Measure of Income

Legal definitions of income differ substantially from comprehensive definitions. The gulf between the two arises, in large part, from the problems inherent in measuring in-kind income derived from ownership of such durable goods as houses, boats, art, or swimming pools. Useful estimates of implicit income are hard to make unless appropriate standards are available for comparison. For example, the implicit rental income of a house may be measured against the recent selling price of a similar house in the same neighborhood; but when no such houses have sold in recent years, accurate comparisons are problematic. The same holds true for unrealized capital gains and losses of other durable goods.

But should all in-kind income be measured? Toasters and towels are durable goods, but measurement of their in-kind income hardly meets the criteria of cost-benefit analysis. Nor is it clear that, in practice, the values of in-kind income derived from home-grown tomatoes, carwashes, and furniture dusting merit separate lines on an income tax form.

Another issue is the measurement of the costs of acquiring income. While ownership of a car, for instance, may be required for commuting purposes, should all car expenses be deducted from taxable income? If, for instance, one derives pleasure from driving an expensive car to work, this results in in-kind income that should be included, not excluded, from a comprehensive definition of income. A fine line between pleasure and business is sure to exist in some cases, and this creates an area that complicates the measurement of the costs of acquiring income. Another issue arises over the question of whether full deductions should be allowed for an expensive car as for an economy car.

Why Economists Advocate a Comprehensive Definition

Economists tend to be strong advocates of defining the income tax base as broadly as possible, since it fosters **tax policy neutrality** which is the condition that occurs when tax policy does not distort the allocation of resources. Distortions will occur whenever various sources of income are excluded from the tax base. If, for instance, the income tax base is defined to include income earned by selling apples, but excludes income earned from selling bananas, tax policy tilts resource allocation toward bananas and away from apples. Tax policy distorts decisions that would normally emanate from the interactions of suppliers and demanders in the marketplace, and, in this sense, tax policy lowers allocative efficiency and creates an excess burden. Because tax policy encourages excluded sources and discourages included sources, allocative efficiency is fostered by defining income in a comprehensive manner.

This point is further clarified when we observe that exclusion of various fringe benefits, such as vacation time and free meals, from taxation, has led some workers to prefer increased fringe benefits over higher salaries. Fringe benefits and salary are

Tax policy neutrality occurs when a tax policy does not distort the allocation of resources.

Taxing Free Parking

One of the favorite perks of employment has just been attacked: free parking. The tax code now taxes, as ordinary income, the value of parking spaces over $155 per month, whether or not they are used by employees. All partners of corporations must also pay taxes on the entire value of their parking privileges. These rules lead one Washington lawyer to quip: "What's next? . . . Are they going to start taxing our desks and chairs?"

Why the new rule? One reason is to raise tax revenue. It has been predicted that complete removal of all tax exemptions for free parking will raise somewhere between $1.5 billion and $4.7 billion. Another reason is that raising the cost of commuting in your own car encourages workers to take mass transit.

Before the 1992 rule change, parking privileges were not taxed at all, but if employers provided mass transit fares to employees, these benefits were fully taxed as ordinary income.

Source: Paulette Thomas, "New Tax Means All Free Parking Won't Be Free," *Wall Street Journal,* January 10, 1994, B1.

Analysis

While its inclusion into the legal definition of taxable income is a step toward defining a more comprehensive definition of income, its inclusion also predictably influences resource allocation. Inclusion of parking privileges into taxable income will undoubtedly affect behavior in more ways than just coaxing some workers to take mass transit. One change is that firms may rearrange their parking spaces because, under the new law, free parking remains untaxed as long as parking spaces are shared between employees and customers. Another way of countering the new tax is for firms to convert from corporations to partnerships, since the latter may exclude $155 per month from taxation. One unintended change may bring bad news to large cities. The tax change now makes it more expensive to do business in expensive parking areas, such as many urban downtown locations. Strapped with higher costs of doing business, some businesses are likely to flee to lower-priced parking areas in the suburbs.

There are many other possibilities for avoiding the new tax, but it takes a lot of work on the part of firms to locate possible loopholes. In the words of one fringe benefits lawyer, Mary Hevener of Washington, D.C., "It's [the new tax law] very intricate. . . . If you don't have a lot of payroll people and high-priced tax lawyers, this is especially distressing."

both sources of income and would therefore be included in a comprehensive definition of taxable income. Tax policy, however, influences choices since when fringe benefits are excluded from the taxable income base, decisions regarding income sources are tilted toward fringe benefits and away from salaries and wages.

Economists also advocate comprehensive tax bases since, for a given level of tax revenue, they provide for lower tax rates. There is considerable agreement that tax rates influence labor supply, savings, and investment. Because lower tax rates promote economic growth and lead to higher standards of living, economists tend to advocate tax reform that would broaden tax bases and lower tax rates.

There are also concerns over the ways exclusions of income sources from taxable income are determined within the policy process. Tax expenditures, or exclusions of various income sources from taxation, are the product of taxpayers, special interest groups, and policymakers within the policy process. The benefit of having some portion of one's income excluded from the tax base is obvious. While in theory many exclusions could be rationalized on the basis of promoting various socially desirable activities, there are concerns that many are the product of rent seeking behavior. A more comprehensive measure of income would limit the ability of rent seekers to secure beneficial reductions in tax liabilities through securing exemptions of various income sources from taxable income.

Finally, concerns arise over applying the ability-to-pay principle to incomplete measures of income. If tax policy is to comply with horizontal or vertical definitions of equity, it is vital that a common, and broad, definition be applied to all taxpayers. Paul, for example, may earn much of his income from untaxed sources, but Kendra may earn most of her income from taxed sources. It may not be fair, however, to include only 45 percent of Paul's income, but 95 percent of Kendra's income, in the definition of the tax base. (Remember we are defining income in a comprehensive manner here.) It is clearly more difficult to apply the ability-to-pay principle as tax bases move further away from a comprehensive measure of income.

Defining Taxable Income: Practice

At its core, the tax code defines the taxable income base and assigns various tax rates that depend upon whether taxpayers are single, married, or single heads of households. Complexities arise over its many deductions, exemptions, and tax credits, as evidenced by the many thousands of pages which make up the tax code. We will take an overview of the tax code through the five basic steps of determining personal income tax liability.

Step 1: Calculation of Gross Income

Gross income is the sum of all income sources subject to taxation.

The first step is to calculate **gross income,** which is determined by adding up all income sources subject to taxation. A partial, but reasonably complete, listing of income sources includes:

❏ Wages, salaries, and tips
❏ Interest earned on accounts at financial institutions, loans, and most bonds
❏ Dividend income to stockholders
❏ Taxable refunds and credits of state and local income taxes
❏ Alimony received
❏ Noncorporate business income
❏ Capital gains or losses (when realized)
❏ Payments received from IRA accounts and income from private pensions and annuities
❏ 85 percent of Social Security income paid to couples with incomes over $44,000 and individuals above $34,000

- Income from rents, royalties, estates, and trusts
- Farm income or loss
- Unemployment compensation
- Prizes, rewards, and gambling earnings

Several departures from a comprehensive definition of income are noteworthy. Notice that most government transfers are excluded from the definition of gross income; AFDC payments, and in-kind transfers such as public housing, food stamps, and Medicaid benefits, are nontaxable income sources. Exceptions are unemployment benefits, which are fully taxed, and 85 percent of Social Security benefits when couples earn incomes over $44,000 and individuals above $34,000.

Another departure from a comprehensive definition of income is the exclusion of employer contributions into pension funds and health insurance. The exclusion of contributions for health insurance, for example, has been estimated to have reduced federal tax revenues by $75 billion in 1994.[2] Also excluded from taxable income are employer-provided child care, gyms, and other in-kind sources of income. Finally, as shown in a later chapter, transfers of wealth are assessed separate gift and estate taxes.

Step 2: Calculation of Adjusted Gross Income

Adjusted gross income (AGI) is gross income less allowable deductions.

The next step is to determine **adjusted gross income (AGI),** which deducts the following items from gross income:

- Contributions to an IRA Account: For individuals without an employer-provided pension plan, up to $2,000 per individual may be deducted from gross income. For those with employer-provided plans, and with adjusted gross income of less than $25,000, $2,000 may be deducted; but for incomes above $25,000 and below $35,000 (between $40,000 and $50,000 for married couples) only a portion of an IRA contribution may be deducted. For incomes above $35,000 (for individuals) or $50,000 (for married couples), no part may be deducted.
- One-half of self-employment tax for self-employed taxpayers[3]
- Penalties on early withdrawal of funds from a time savings deposit
- Alimony paid

Step 3: Calculation of Taxable Income

We now consider what determines taxable income.[4] Both exemptions and deductions are adjustment factors.

---

[2] Congressional Budget Office, *Reducing the Deficit: Spending and Revenue Options* (Washington, D.C.: February 1993).

[3] Recall that for those who are not self-employed, payroll tax (Social Security) liabilities are equally divided between employer and employee.

[4] The 1986 Tax Reform Act raised the values of both personal exemptions and the standard deduction; it also indexed them for inflation starting in 1989, a change that has been argued to have saved 4,800,000 poor individuals from paying income tax; see Joseph A. Pechman, "Tax Reform: Theory and Practice," *Economic Perspectives* 1 (Summer 1987): 11–28.

Exemptions

Exemptions reduce tax liability by lowering taxable income by roughly $2,300 for each exemption. (A phase-out of personal exemptions, expiring in 1997, applies to certain high-income taxpayers.) Exemptions are provided for the following:

- One per single adult or two for wife and husband
- One for each dependent child or relative

Deductions

Standard deduction is the maximum deduction allowed taxpayers who do not itemize deductions.

Itemized deductions are those deductions allowed taxpayers who do not take the standard deduction.

Two options are available: either use a **standard deduction,** which requires no documentation, or calculate **itemized deductions** on the basis of allowable deductions. The standard deduction specifies a fixed dollar amount, which in 1993 was $3,700 for a single taxpayer and for a married couple, $6,200 when they filed jointly. This option is commonly taken by lower-income taxpayers since itemizing tends to produce a lower level of deductions for them than provided by the standard deduction.

Major itemized deductions include the following:

- Medical and dental expenses (such as prescription medicines, medical visits and examinations, nursing help, hospital care, and travel costs) that exceed 7.5 percent of adjusted gross income
- State and local income, real estate and property taxes
- Interest paid on home mortgages and on money borrowed allocable to property held for investment[5]
- Gifts to charity in the form of cash, property, or out-of-pocket costs incurred during volunteer work
- Casualty (vandalism, fire, storms, and accidents) and theft losses
- Moving expenses incurred in connection with your job when a new workplace is at least 35 miles farther from your old home than the old home was from former place of employment
- Unreimbursed employee expenses for travel, transportation, and meal or entertainment expenses connected with your job

The Omnibus Budget Reconciliation Act of 1990 (OBRA90) created an itemized deduction phase-out for certain high-income taxpayers, and it is in effect until 1996. Deductions were lowered by 3 percent of the amount in which AGI exceeds $100,000. Though the markdown cannot exceed 80 percent of total itemized deductions, a taxpayer with an AGI of $150,000 and a mortgage interest deduction of $50,000, for example, must subtract 3 percent of $50,000, or $1,500, from itemized deductions and is therefore allowed to only deduct $48,500 from adjusted gross income.

---

[5] Various restrictions are introduced by the Omnibus Budget Reconciliation Act of 1990: The mortgage interest deduction was limited to $1 million and only on first and second homes; home equity loans were limited to $100,000.

Step 4: Calculating Tax Liability

Tax liability is total taxes owed by the taxpayer.

The next step is to determine **tax liability,** where the various tax rates are applied to taxable income. There are four income tax schedules:

- Single
- Married filing jointly
- Married filing separately
- Head of a household (single parent)

Each of these schedules has a different set of tax brackets that defines various tax rates over different taxable income levels. Table 18-1 displays tax rate brackets for single and married couples. Marginal tax rates are applied over various thresholds of taxable income and, as shown in the table, five **marginal tax rates** currently exist. The term *marginal,* as opposed to *average,* means that the tax rate changes over different ranges of taxable income. For a single taxpayer, for example, the following marginal tax rates are levied, with the exception of capital gains, a component of taxable income, which are taxed at the fixed rate of 28 percent:

Marginal tax rates are tax rates that change at various thresholds of income.

TABLE 18-1
Tax Rate Schedule, 1993

Single

Taxable Income	Marginal Tax Rate
$0–$21,450	15.0%
$21,451–$51,900	28.0
$51,901–$115,000	31.0
$115,001–$250,000	36.0
$250,001 and over	39.6[a]

Married Filing Jointly

Taxable Income	Marginal Tax Rate
$0–$35,800	15.0%
$35,801–$86,500	28.0
$86,501–$140,000	31.0
$140,001 and over	39.6[a]

[a] A surcharge of 10 percent on taxpayers with incomes above $250,000 makes the effective top rate 39.6 percent. But when deductions and exemptions are factored in, the effective top rate for some high-income taxpayers is actually 42 percent.

- 15 percent on taxable income from $0 to $21,450
- 28 percent on taxable income from $21,451 to $51,900
- 31 percent on taxable income from $51,901 to $115,000
- 36 percent on taxable income from $115,001 to $250,000
- 39.6 percent on taxable income in excess of $250,001[6]

Average tax rate is calculated by dividing tax liability by taxable income.

The **average tax rate,** in contrast, is determined by dividing tax liability by taxable income.

Let us determine the tax liability for Nicole, a single taxpayer, who, after claiming itemized deductions and her personal exemption, has taxable income of $75,000. Her combined tax liability is determined by adding tax liabilities over each relevant taxable income range:

- $3,217.50 (15 percent of the first $21,450)
- $8,526.00 (28 percent of $30,450, or income between $21,451 and $51,900)
- $7,161.00 (31 percent of $23,100, or income over $51,900)

Nicole's total tax liability is the sum of these numbers, or $18,904.50. Since taxable income is $75,000, she faces three different marginal tax rates (15, 28 and 31 percent). Her average tax rate is 25.2 percent, or $18,904.50/$75,000.

Notice that average and marginal tax rates are equal only when taxpayers face one marginal tax rate. For example, if Nicole had taxable income of $20,000, all income is subject to the marginal tax rate of 15 percent. Her tax liability, on taxable income of $20,000, is $3,000, indicating an average tax rate of 15 percent, or $3,000/$20,000.

When taxable income is subject to more than one marginal tax rate, the average tax rate falls below the highest marginal tax rate applied to taxpayers. With taxable income of $75,000, Nicole's average rate of 25.2 percent falls much below 31 percent, the highest marginal tax rate she faces.

Step 5. Lowering Tax Liability through Tax Credits

Tax credits are dollar-for-dollar reductions in tax liabilities.

Tax credits provide dollar-for-dollar reductions in tax liabilities. Recall that Nicole's tax liability, as determined in Step 4, was $18,904.50. A tax credit of $1,000 lowers her tax liability to $17,904.50. Tax credits, therefore, provide greater tax relief than an equal dollar of tax deduction. A tax deduction of $1,000 lowers taxable income by $1,000, but tax liability does not fall by $1,000. Nicole's taxable income, for example, would be lowered from $75,000 to $74,000 and her tax liability therefore falls by $310, as determined by multiplying the reduction in taxable income ($1,000) by the appropriate marginal tax rate (31 percent).

Earned income tax credits lower tax liabilities of poor taxpayers.

The **earned income tax credit,** which in 1994 allowed those with low incomes to claim a tax credit of up to $2,364, lowers tax liabilities of poor taxpayers; the credit

---

[6] The 39.6 percent rate was called a *surtax* in the Omnibus Budget Reconciliation Act of 1993, since it is an additional 10 percent added onto the top statutory rate of 36 percent. This allowed the tax writers to claim that despite the effective top rate of 39.6 percent, the top statutory marginal rate was 36 percent.

rises to $2,600 in 1995. The value of the credit rises with taxable income and is phased out after families reach a maximum income level. For those at the lowest income levels, this credit provides checks back to taxpayers and, in effect, assigns them negative tax liabilities. It has been argued that this program creates a greater work incentive for low-income individuals than other welfare policies and, for this reason, it is one of the more popular welfare programs among welfare analysts.[7] This program has been recently expanded. The 1993 budget increased this tax credit by roughly $20 billion over five years and for the first time made it available to working poor without children.

Other major tax credits include

- Child and dependent care expense credits for those who pay someone to care for their children or dependent adult in order to go to their jobs
- Credit for the elderly or the disabled for taxpayers age 65 or older, or under 65 with taxable disability income
- Other credits include payments of income tax to foreign governments, employment of people who are members of special targeted groups, use of alcohol for vehicular fuel, ownership of a low-income housing project, and expenses incurred in making your business accessible to the disabled

The Alternative Minimum Tax

In 1990, 779 taxpayers earning in excess of $200,000 did not pay any income tax—the highest number of non–income taxpaying taxpayers since 1977, when Congress ordered this information to be reported each year.[8] While this represents less than 0.1 percent of filers at this income level, federal tax policy has been criticized for allowing too many high-income individuals to avoid paying any income taxes.

Why do some high-income individuals who *do* file income tax returns escape income taxation? The primary means is through their use of various tax expenditures. The **alternative minimum tax (AMT)** limits the use of tax expenditures since it requires that high-income taxpayers pay a minimum of taxes that cannot be escaped through clever use of tax expenditures. The alternative minimum tax rate is 26 percent on "alternative minimum taxable income" (AMTI) in excess of $40,000 for a joint return or $30,000 for a single return. Since it seeks to limit the use of tax expenditures, the AMTI is defined more broadly than taxable income. In other words, it reduces the value of various itemized tax deductions (e.g., charitable deductions for appreciated property, itemized deductions of state and local taxes, and some tax-exempt interest) and therefore raises tax liabilities for some high-income taxpayers who claim many itemized deductions. Although there are many different provisions, the basic thrust of the AMT is to force high-income taxpayers to pay the larger of the AMT or the tax liability owed when the regular tax schedule is used.

Alternative minimum tax (AMT) is the least possible legal amount that must be paid by high-income taxpayers.

---

[7] C. Eugene Steuerle, "Tax Credits for Low-Income Workers with Children," *Journal of Economic Perspectives* 4 (Summer 1990): 201–212.

[8] "Life on EZ Street," *Los Angeles Times,* June 30, 1993, D1.

Income Tax Policy Reform

The basic thrust of tax reform is to change marginal tax rates and the tax base. Table 18-2 lists the major changes of the five principal overhauls of the personal income tax code since 1981. There have been hundreds of changes, but the major thrust of these changes may be observed by focusing on the changes listed in Table 18-2.

Economic Recovery Tax Act of 1981

Economic Recovery Tax Act of 1981 was a fundamental tax reform that, among other changes, lowered marginal tax rates 23 percent over three years.

The **Economic Recovery Tax Act of 1981** (ERTA81) fundamentally redirected tax policy by lowering marginal tax rates 23 percent over three years. The top marginal rate was lowered to 50 percent (from 70 percent), and it also reduced the number of separate marginal tax rates from fifteen to twelve. The top marginal tax rate on capital gains was lowered from 28 to 20 percent and, starting in 1985, personal exemptions and standard deductions were indexed for inflation.

The primary motivation behind ERTA81 was economic growth. Often associated with supply-side economics, President Ronald Reagan argued that economic growth would be enhanced by lowering marginal tax rates based on the argument that it would create greater incentives to work, save, and invest. This expectation is based on hypothesized relationships between marginal tax rates and economic behaviors of workers, savers, and investors. An interesting twist of this tax legislation was the claim that, by fostering economic growth, reduction of marginal tax rates would eventually raise tax revenue and lead to a falling budget deficit over time.

Social Security Amendments of 1983

Social Security Amendments of 1983 were the first to subject some Social Security benefits to taxation.

The **Social Security Amendments of 1983** subjected some Social Security benefits to taxation. Fifty percent of Social Security benefits were subjected to taxation for beneficiaries with income exceeding $25,000 (singles) or $32,000 (married couples). This tax change broadened the tax base since it taxed, as ordinary income, and for the first time, a portion of Social Security benefits.

Tax Reform Act of 1986

Tax Reform Act of 1986, perhaps the most ambitious tax reform ever, simplified many aspects of the tax code.

The **Tax Reform Act of 1986** (TRA86) was perhaps the most ambitious tax reform since income taxes were instituted in 1913. It was motivated by several factors. Simplification was an important factor and, possibly for this reason, the public voiced very strong support for TRA86. Simplification was a motivating factor behind the replacement of 14 tax rates, which ranged from 11 percent to 50 percent, to a simple tax structure with only two marginal tax rates, 15 percent and 28 percent. (See Table 18-2 for the bubble effect.) Base broadening was also an important simplifier since, when coupled with increases in values of standard deductions and personal exemptions, it greatly increased the number of taxpayers who filled out the so-called short tax form, not itemizing deductions. Fewer taxpayers claiming itemized deductions means less paperwork and lower compliance costs, factors that affect many taxpayers. Much of the base broadening was achieved through removal (over a period of five years) of the interest deduction on consumer debt and loans, deductions for state and

TABLE 18-2
Major Changes in Personal Income Taxation

Economic Recovery Tax Act of 1981

- Marginal tax rates lowered 23% over three years
- Twelve marginal tax rates ranging from 12% to 50% (down from 15 rates ranging from 14% to 70%)
- Top marginal tax rate lowered from 70% to 50%, effective in 1982
- Top marginal tax rate on capital gains lowered to 20% (from 28%)
- Personal exemption and standard deductions indexed for inflation, effective 1985

Social Security Amendments of 1986

- Tax 50% of Social Security benefits paid to individuals with incomes above $25,000 and, for couples, above $32,000

Tax Reform Act of 1986

- Top marginal tax rate lowered to 28%
- Replaced 14 tax rates (11% to 50%) with two tax rates (15% and 28%)[a]
- Standard deduction for married (filing jointly) increased to $5,000
- Personal exemption increased to $2,000
- Removed interest deduction on credit card debt and nonmortgage loans (after a phaseout period of five years)
- Limited deductions for business meals and entertainment to 80% of costs, limited medical deductions, raised floor for medical expenses from 5% to 7.5% of income
- Removed deductions for state and local sales taxes
- Counted realized capital gains as ordinary income
- Limited eligibility for deductions on IRA contributions to those without employer-provided pensions or those with incomes below various levels

Omnibus Budget Reconciliation Act of 1990

- Top marginal tax rate raised from 28% to 31%[b]
- Three tax rates (15%, 28%, 31%)
- Limited dollar value of tax deductions for those with adjusted gross incomes in excess of $100,000
- Maximum marginal tax rate on capital gains of 28%

Omnibus Budget Reconciliation Act of 1993

- Top marginal tax rate raised from 31% to 39.6%
- Four tax rates (15%, 28%, 31%, 36%, and 39.6%).[c] Taxed 85% of Social Security benefits paid to individuals with incomes above $34,000 and, for couples, above $44,000

---

[a] Actually a "bubble" was created whereby a 31 percent tax rate occurred for certain high-income taxpayers as a result of phaseout of exemptions and deductions for these taxpayers.

[b] As a result of limits on deductions and exemptions (expiring in 1997) for certain high-income taxpayers, some taxpayers faced effective marginal rates in excess of 31 percent.

[c] A surcharge of 10 percent on taxpayers with incomes above $250,000 raises the effective top rate to 39.6 percent. When their phaseout of deductions and exemptions is factored in, some high-income taxpayers' effective top rate is actually 42 percent.

local sales taxes, and limitations on deductions that could be claimed for medical expenses, business meals, entertainment, and IRA contributions.

Greater fairness, another motivating factor behind passage of TRA86, was primarily achieved through increases in standard deductions and personal exemptions that, in effect, led to substantial increases in tax-free income for low-income taxpayers. Base broadening was also promoted as a means of fostering greater fairness since there had been growing public sentiment that the wealthy were avoiding more tax liability through taking advantage of a growing number of tax expenditures. TRA86 lowered tax expenditures in two ways. First, it eliminated or reduced many of the previous tax expenditures. Second, reduction of marginal tax rates lowered the incentive for taxpayers to take advantage of tax expenditures retained by TRA86. For example, the value of the deduction for interest paid on a home mortgage falls as the marginal tax rate falls. A deduction of $12,000, for instance, lowers tax liability by $6,000 at a marginal tax rate of 50 percent. The same deduction is only worth $3,360 in lower taxes when the marginal tax rate is 28 percent.

Finally, economic growth was an important factor behind the changes introduced in TRA86. Returning to the theme introduced in ERTA81 that lower marginal tax rates would foster economic growth through expanding work effort, savings, and investment, TRA86 lowered the top marginal tax rate from 50 percent to 28 percent and lowered the number of marginal tax rates from fourteen to two (15%, 28%). Realized capital gains were also subjected to the marginal tax rates on ordinary income. Previous law allowed 60 percent of long-term capital gains to be deducted from gross income, leading at a top marginal tax rate of 50 percent, to a maximum effective rate of 20 percent.

Because the Congress, as well as many economists, were skeptical that lower tax rates would create additional tax revenues, TRA86 was easier to pass when the Reagan administration promised that it would be revenue neutral, a term that means that it would not lower tax collections below current levels. Revenue neutrality was to be achieved because base broadening provisions would tend to collect greater tax revenues that would offset tax revenue losses that resulted from lower marginal tax rates.

Omnibus Budget Reconciliation Acts of 1990 and 1993

Omnibus Budget Reconciliation Acts of 1990 and 1993 raised the numbers (and top brackets) of the marginal tax rates.

The **Omnibus Budget Reconciliation Act of 1990** (OBRA90) raised the top marginal tax rate from 28 percent to 31 percent and thereby raised the number of marginal tax rates from two to three (15%, 28%, 31%). As a result of temporary limits on deductions and exemptions (expiring in 1997) for certain high-income taxpayers (income in excess of $100,000), some taxpayers faced effective marginal rates in excess of 31 percent. OBRA90 reflected something of a compromise between President George Bush and Congress over the control of the rapidly rising budget deficit. Despite his campaign pledge of "no new taxes," President Bush agreed to raise taxes after Congress promised to restrain spending growth. This tax legislation therefore indicated a redirection from the tax legislations of the 1980s, which had lowered marginal tax rates on the theory that doing so would result in greater tax revenues as faster economic growth ensued.

The **Omnibus Budget Reconciliation Act of 1993** (OBRA93) was signed by President Clinton during his first year in office. The OBRA of 1993 raised the top marginal tax rate from 31 percent to 39.6 percent and replaced three marginal tax rates with five (15%, 28%, 31%, 36%, 39.6%). This tax bill also taxed 85 percent, instead of 50 percent, of Social Security benefits paid to individuals with incomes above $34,000 and, for couples, above $44,000. The rise in marginal tax rates under OBRA93 was promoted for two reasons: to make the tax system fairer by levying higher marginal tax rates on higher-income taxpayers and to raise tax revenues that would lower the budget deficit.

What Has Tax Reform Achieved?

Simplification?

Simplicity is clearly a rallying cry of taxpayers who desire a system that requires less documentation, easier and shorter tax forms, and less preparation time. Claims of greater simplicity were clearly important factors behind the public's broad acceptance of the TRA86. The blueprint for TRA86, in fact, was a report issued by the U.S. Treasury in 1984 entitled *Tax Reform for Fairness, Simplicity, and Economic Growth*. Interestingly, the blueprint proposed a system that was simple enough that nearly two-thirds of taxpayers would not be required to submit tax forms to the IRS since third parties (e.g., employers and banks) would provide the IRS with information sufficient to calculate taxpayer liabilities. Despite these ambitions, simplicity was eventually relegated to low priority in the rush to gain quick approval from a Congress that was greatly concerned that greater simplicity might lead to lower tax revenues.[9] Evidence, in fact, suggests that tax complexity continues to grow over time, since studies find that compliance time and costs have grown as a result of TRA86.[10]

Changes in Marginal Tax Rates

Both OBRA90 and OBRA93 represent fundamental redirections of tax policy since they reverse the falling trend of marginal tax rates, as well as the number of brackets, created by ERTA81 and TRA86. Much of the turnaround was due to the Clinton administration's rejection of two basic tenets of tax policy under the Reagan administration. First, the notion that higher marginal tax rates lead to significantly greater tax avoidance on the part of higher-income taxpayers was rejected. This rejection can be clearly seen in the following statement by Laura Tyson, chair of President Clinton's Council of Economic Advisers:

> *Overall, the historical record, appropriately interpreted, confirms that the higher tax rates on the wealthiest Americans proposed in the Clinton deficit-reduction plan will produce higher revenues. This is not to deny that these taxpayers will adjust to higher rates in a variety of often ingenious ways to minimize their tax obligations. But the degree to which tax avoidance will lower receipts has been greatly exaggerated.*[11]

Second, the Clinton administration rejected the belief that higher marginal tax rates cause taxpayers to lower work effort, savings, and investment. You will recall that

---

[9] Joel Slemrod, "Did the Tax Reform Act of 1986 Simplify Tax Matters?" *Journal of Economic Perspectives* 6 (Winter 1992): 45–57.

[10] See, for example, Slemrod, "Did the Tax Reform Act of 1986 Simplify Tax Matters?" 45–57.

[11] Laura Tyson, "Higher Taxes Do So Raise Money," *Wall Street Journal,* August 3, 1993, A14.

ERTA81 and TRA86 were based in large part on the hypothesis that these behaviors are highly responsive to marginal tax rates. Laura Tyson also clearly sees the rejection of this hypothesis when she states:

> Nor is it very likely that the wealthy will respond to higher tax rates by noticeable reductions in their labor supply.... This package will bring the benefits of long-term interest rates, increased national saving and investment, and higher living standards to all Americans, including the wealthiest Americans who are being asked to shoulder the burden of higher taxes.[12]

Base Broadening

Base broadening of the tax base eliminates or reduces tax expenditures.

Base broadening occurs when tax policy eliminates or reduces various tax expenditures. There are two different rationales for broadening the tax base. First, as our discussion of the Haig-Simons criterion indicates, a broader base provides for better application of the ability-to-pay principle since comprehensive measures of income allow for better comparisons of the resources available to different taxpayers. It should also be noted, however, that there is a cost to broadening the tax base because fairness may also dictate a less comprehensive measure of income when costs for health care, care for dependents, and so on may differ widely between different taxpayers. Deductions for health care costs, care for dependents, or commuting costs are factors that might lead to various adjustments to taxable income when the ability-to-pay principle is applied in practice.

A second—and, as shown above, more controversial—rationale for base broadening is that it allows for reductions in marginal tax rates without altering aggregate tax collection. In 1955, Joseph Pechman began publishing estimates of the personal income tax base under the Haig-Simons definition of income.[13] These calculations have suggested that the adoption of a broadened tax base makes it possible to significantly reduce tax rates and, at the same time, raise as much revenue as before, but with roughly the same degree of progression as before.

While elimination of various tax expenditures has been a central theme of tax reform (especially TRA86), it is commonly believed that substantial widening of the base has not occurred.[14] One reason appears to be that, as tax legislation broadens the base in some areas (e.g., removing deductions of interest on consumer debt and state and local sales taxes under TRA86), several areas that remain untaxed, such as employer-provided fringe benefits, have grown rapidly in recent years. Growth in these untaxed areas is commonly believed to be largely a factor of their tax-free status since, on a dollar-for-dollar basis, a dollar's worth of taxable income, such as salary, is worth less to an employee than an additional dollar of untaxed income in the

---

[12] Tyson "Higher Taxes Do So Raise Money," A14.

[13] Joseph A. Pechman, "The Individual Income Tax Base," *Proceedings of the Forty-Eighth Annual Conference in Taxation Sponsored by the National Tax Association,* 1955: 1–11. For an update, see Joseph A. Pechman and John Karl Scholz, "Comprehensive Income Taxation and Rate Reduction," *Tax Notes,* 17 (October 11, 1982): 83–93.

[14] See, for example, Joseph A. Pechman, "Tax Reform: Theory and Practice," *Journal of Economic Perspectives* 1 (Summer 1987): 11–28; and Richard A. Musgrave, "Short of Euphoria," *Journal of Economic Perspectives* 1 (Summer 1987): 59–71.

form of free health insurance, clothing, or meals. Moreover, as marginal tax rates have risen in recent tax legislation, incentives of taxpayers to lobby for additional tax expenditures have risen as well; therefore, in the future, we may see a greater number of tax expenditures narrow the tax base even more.

Equity

Increases in the value of the standard deduction and personal exemptions have lowered tax burdens of lower-income taxpayers. There is, in effect, a zero marginal tax bracket for taxpayers with incomes below various levels of taxable income. In 1993, exemptions were valued at $2,350 per family member, the standard deduction for single individuals was $3,700 and, for married couples, $6,200. For a family of five, the first $17,950 in adjusted gross income is subject to a zero tax. Rising values of standard deductions and personal exemptions therefore lower tax burdens more for lower- than for higher-income taxpayers since they exclude from taxation a greater percentage of their income.

A common means of comparing tax burdens is through calculation of average tax rates, which are calculated by dividing tax liability by income. Table 18-3 displays average U.S. tax rates, as calculated by tax liability divided by adjusted gross income, since the mid-1950s. As means of comparison, average tax rates are shown for two different taxpayers: single, no dependents and married, two dependents. Average tax rates are sometimes negative at low-income levels because of the refundable earned income credits that provide cash transfers for qualifying taxpayers.

Inspection of average tax rates indicates that the income tax system is progressive. Progressivity occurs when taxpayers are subjected to average tax rates that rise with income. The conclusion that may be drawn, therefore, is that after the many tax reforms, tax progressivity remains a characteristic of the tax code. It may be tempting to simply compare changes in average tax rates, but this is not an appropriate way of determining whether the tax system is more or less progressive than before. The problem with this comparison is that such data, as in Table 18-3, do not indicate the proportions of taxpayers earning incomes within the displayed ranges.

Figure 18-2 tackles this problem by showing, since 1980, and on the basis of adjusted gross income, how tax collections vary by income groups. The category top 1 percent of income earners, for instance, represents the share of tax collections that was paid by taxpayers earning the highest 1 percent of income. The top end of income earners therefore shouldered a growing share of tax collection: Their share rose from roughly 19 percent to 26 percent of total tax collections over this period. The stories for taxpayers earning the top 5 percent, 20 percent, and 25 percent of income are similar. Taxpayers earning the bottom 50 percent of income, in contrast, experienced a slight reduction in their burdens, which fell from 7 percent to 5.6 percent of income tax collections.

We conclude this section by noting that two issues complicate our ability to measure how tax reform has influenced the equity of the U.S. tax code. The first follows from our discussion in Chapter 16 of the sometimes great differences between statutory and economic incidence of taxation. Just as excise taxes may be shifted from one taxpayer to another, income taxes may be shifted as well. While the extent to which

TABLE 18-3
Federal Individual Income Tax: Average Tax Rates[a]

Single, No Dependents

AGI	1954–63	1965	1970	1975	1979–80	1985	1990
$ 5,000	12.0%	7.5%	4.0%	3.9%	5.0%	5.6%	4.9%
10,000	15.5	13.8	11.4	10.9	11.8	10.5	10.0
20,000	19.3	17.0	16.7	17.9	19.2	16.6	15.3
25,000	21.0	18.7	19.0	20.9	21.9	18.7	17.3
35,000	24.4	21.1	23.2	24.9	26.3	22.6	19.6
50,000	29.6	24.8	27.7	30.0	32.1	27.1	22.6
75,000	36.7	30.2	34.4	37.5	39.1	32.5	25.3

Married, Two Dependents[b]

AGI	1954–63	1965	1970	1975	1979–80	1985	1990
$ 5,000	0.0%	0.0%	−10.0%	−10.0%	−10.0%	−8.7%	−12.1%
10,000	6.1	5.8	1.4	1.4	3.7	4.7	−0.9
20,000	12.2	11.4	10.3	10.3	11.3	10.4	8.5
25,000	13.7	12.9	12.8	12.8	14.0	12.9	9.8
35,000	16.1	15.3	17.4	17.4	18.8	16.7	13.4
50,000	19.0	18.3	22.8	22.8	24.2	21.3	16.9
75,000	23.6	23.3	29.4	29.4	31.2	26.6	20.5

[a] Tax liability ($1980)/Adjusted gross income ($1980).
[b] Assumes that only one spouse works outside home.
Negative average tax rates refer to refundable earned income credits.

Source: Advisory Commission on Intergovernmental Relations, *Significant Features of Fiscal Federalism* 1, February 1992.

income tax shifting occurs is controversial, the possibility of shifting of income taxes introduces complications into our ability to interpret the data presented above.

The second complication is that a focus on tax burdens tells an incomplete story of the ways in which tax policy distributes the burdens of financing public programs. Sole focus on tax burdens neglects benefits that flow from public programs that are clearly important determinants of taxpayer welfare. Positive transfers were shown to occur whenever tax payments were less than benefits received from public programs. It has been estimated, for instance, that taxpayers in the lowest income quintile earned an average income of $2,096 and paid an average of $51 in income taxes, but they also received an average public transfer of $8,859.[15] Income, after taxes and transfers, therefore averaged $10,904 for these taxpayers. For the highest quintile, in contrast, average income was $93,966, which, after taxes and public (negative) transfers,

---

[15] *Economic Report of the President,* February 1992.

**FIGURE 18-2
Share of Total
Federal Income
Taxes (by Share of
Adjusted Gross
Income)**

Source: Joint Economic Committee, 1991.

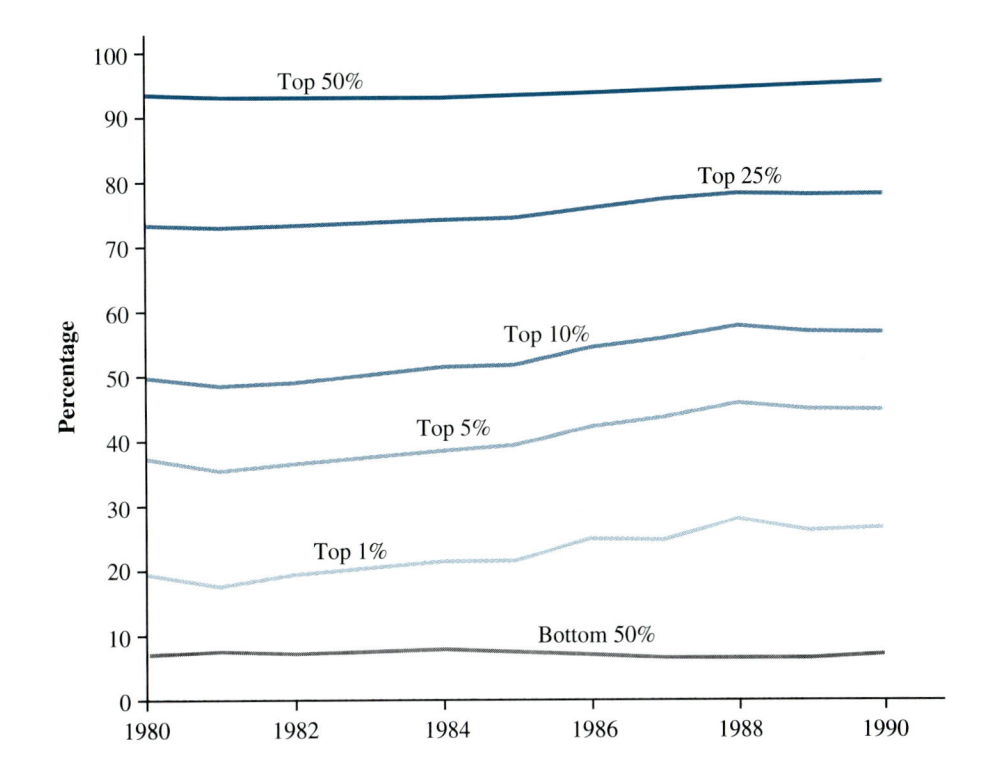

produced an average income of $71,944. Interpretation of these numbers is debatable in the area of whether they indicate the degree to which the income tax is progressive. Quite simply, it is difficult to assess this important issue.

Marriage Tax

Marriage tax
is the additional tax a married couple pays over and above the combined tax bills they would pay if they were unmarried.

As one writer recently quipped, "many married couples can save hundreds or thousands more dollars on their taxes. There's just one hitch: They have to get divorced."[16] A **marriage tax** is built into the income tax system, created by income splitting, the method used by the IRS to calculate the tax liabilities of married couples who file jointly. Under this method, combined income of couples is split evenly between husband and wife when tax liability is computed.

First, the good news for married taxpayers. It can be easily seen that income splitting greatly benefits high-income one-earner married couples. If, for example, Mary Smith earned $80,000 and Bob Smith earned $0, the tax code would determine their tax bill on the assumption that each earned $40,000. Suppose that a two-tier system exists, in which the first $25,000 is taxed at the rate of 15 percent and all additional income at the rate of 25 percent. In this case, the tax bill for this married couple is

---

[16] Kathy M. Kristof, " 'Til Death Do We Pay: Under New Tax Plan, Marriage Costs More Than Ever," *Los Angeles Times,* August 13, 1993, D1.

$15,000—far less than the $17,500 if the tax bill was computed on the basis of a single earner. The reason that the married couple pays fewer dollars in taxes is that income splitting allows the higher-income spouse to move a portion of her income to a lower marginal tax bracket. In our example, income splitting allowed Mary Smith to shift some income from a marginal tax rate of 25 percent to 15 percent. Being married therefore lowers the tax burden by $2,500 in this case and shows a financial incentive for the couple to remain married.

Let us now compute the actual tax burden that would have been imposed on Mary and Bob under the 1992 tax schedule. If single, Mary would have been assessed a tax liability of $20,462 on a taxable income of $80,000. Since Bob would not have been liable for taxes on zero income, their combined tax bill would have been $20,462. If married, however, their combined tax bill would have fallen to $17,753, a difference of $2,709! The income-splitting method is therefore beneficial in this case.

When incomes of both spouses are closer, however, a marriage tax begins to develop. In 1992, for example, the combined taxable income of $80,000 for the Smith family would have resulted in an income tax bill of $17,753. If Mary and Bill each earned $40,000 and were unmarried, their combined tax bill would have been $16,838, a difference of $915. In contrast to the previous example, in which there were substantial income differences between Mary and Bob, this example shows an economic incentive for them to divorce!

Differences in standard deductions show the presence of a marriage tax as well. In 1992, for instance, the standard deduction for single taxpayers was $3,600—but $6,000 for married couples filing jointly. Mary and Bob therefore lose $1,200 in standard deductions when they are married and, if this income falls in the 25 percent tax bracket, an additional tax liability of $300.

The Economic Recovery Tax Act of 1981 initiated a reform (Two Earner Deduction) that partly removed the marriage tax. Married couples were allowed to deduct 10 percent of the earnings of the lower-income spouse, and since those with more equal incomes would receive larger deductions, this reform was targeted at those most subject to the marriage tax. If Mary Smith earned $80,000 and Bill nothing, they were not eligible for this deduction. However, if Mary earned $50,000 and Bill earned $30,000, this deduction totalled $3,000, which at a marginal tax rate of 35 percent, for example, lowered their tax bill by $1,050. The Tax Reform Act of 1986 eliminated this deduction, however, on the theory that other changes (such as lower marginal tax rates) would provide sufficient relief from the marriage tax. As we have seen above, however, the marriage tax is still alive and well and an ongoing experience for married couples who earn roughly the same income.

We end this discussion by examining one other characteristic of the tax code that has received considerable criticism. You will recall that "head of household" is one of the four tax schedules. It is designed for single parents, most of whom are women, who have at least one dependent under the age of eighteen. As of 1992, heads of household earning beyond roughly $25,000 of taxable income pay more income tax than married couples with the same number of dependents. At taxable income of $30,000, for example, married taxpayers who file jointly owe $4,504 in taxes and heads of households owe $4,670, a difference of 4 percent. The difference rises to 15 percent, however, on taxable income of $35,000. A married couple owes $5,254, but a head of household owes $6,070. The difference falls thereafter, bu a substantial difference at taxable income of $80,000 remains; married taxpayers owe $17,753, but a head of household owes $18,846, a difference of 6.1 percent.

It has been suggested that inconsistencies are inevitable in a system with as many complexities as the U.S. tax code. It is clearly difficult to design a "fair" tax system when there are so many different taxpayers, each with different characteristics. There is no real "average" taxpayer. When officials try to fine tune the tax code, its various inconsistencies inevitably arise. This is not to argue that the tax system is "fair" in its treatment of married couples or single parents, but that it is unrealistic to expect that the tax code will ever be ideal for every taxpayer. Moreover, tax reforms try to correct the more obvious inconsistencies. Preliminary data, however, indicate that the Omnibus Budget Reconciliation Act of 1993 raises the marriage tax. This is probably not a desirable situation, and it suggests the immensity of the problems that cling to the tax code.

Inflation and Tax Burdens

Labor Income

Inflation causes nominal values to differ from real values. An income of $25,000 in year 1, for example, has the same purchasing power in year 2 only when there is no inflation. In this case, nominal and real income are equal. If, however, the average price level is 5 percent higher in year 2, an income of $26,250 would have the same purchasing power as $25,000 in year 1.

Consider, for example, a proportional income tax system that taxes all income at the rate of 20 percent. Suppose that, in year 1, a taxpayer with taxable income of $25,000 has a tax bill of $5,000 and, in year 2, the taxpayer has taxable income of $26,250 and pays taxes of $5,250. What implications for tax burdens arise when prices are 5 percent higher in year 2 than in year 1? In this case, the taxpayer experiences no increase in real income, but her tax bill rises by $250. Note, however, that this does not reflect a higher tax burden since the average tax rate is 20 percent in both cases. Inflation therefore poses no significant problems for taxpayers under a proportional tax system.

Under a progressive tax system, however, tax bills rise faster under inflation. Let us suppose that the first $25,000 is subject to a tax rate of 20 percent, and all other income is taxed at a rate of 50 percent. The first year's tax bill is $5,000, the same as before. But the tax bill in year 2 rises to $5,625, an increase of $375 over the previous example because of the inflation push to a higher marginal tax bracket. Her real income is no higher than before, but she must pay $625 in additional taxes. Despite no change in real income, her tax burden rises to 21.4 percent of income. This is **bracket creep,** the push by inflation of taxable income into higher marginal tax rates. Bracket creep may occur even when inflation does not push the taxpayer into higher tax rates. For example, if the tax rate changes from 20 percent to 50 percent at the threshold of $15,000, the tax bill in year 1 is $8,000 (32 percent of taxable income) and, in year 2, $8,625 (33 percent of income). This occurs because a higher percentage of income in year 2 is taxed at a higher marginal rate than in year 1.

Bracket creep occurs when increases in nominal income result in higher marginal tax rates.

Interest Income and Interest Expenses

Inflation affects the measurement of taxable interest income. This may be shown by the following example. Suppose Mary de Vita invests, at a rate of 10 percent, $10,000 in a certificate of deposit. Taxable interest income in the first year is $1,000, and so long as there is no inflation, this reflects a real increase in income of $1,000. But what if inflation of 5 percent occurs during this period? Real and nominal values of her interest income diverge, but the tax system does not recognize this difference. The nominal value of interest income is still $1,000, but its real value, in last year's dollars, is $952.38. The tax system, though, assigns tax bills on nominal values of interest income and therefore Mary's tax bill on the $1,000 of interest income will not change when the real value of that income falls with inflation. Savers such as Mary de Vita are therefore assessed higher tax burdens as a result of inflation.

Interestingly, the tax code works in the opposite direction for borrowers. As previously described, certain interest expenses may be deducted from taxable income. The most notable deduction is for interest expenses on home mortgages where, for example, if Mary de Vita incurs $12,000 in interest expenses each year, she is allowed to deduct this amount from her taxable income. At a marginal tax rate of 25 percent, this deduction would lower her tax bill by $3,000. Now let us introduce inflation, which, though leaving the nominal value of her interest expense at $12,000, lowers the real value of her expenses. It is easy to see why high rates of inflation benefit mortgage holders: Inflation allows borrowers to repay lenders in dollars worth less over time. The tax system, however, does not recognize this change in value and allows borrowers to deduct the nominal value of interest payments, therefore lowering tax bills by larger amounts than if the tax system allowed them to deduct only the real value of interest payments.

Capital Gains

Capital gains are increases in the value of assets realized at the time of their sale.

Capital gains occur when the price of an asset rises over the period in which the asset is held. Notice, however, that prices are nominal measures of value and a divergence between nominal and real values occurs in the event of inflation. Suppose, for instance, that Mary de Vita purchases $5,000 worth of stock and sells it the following year for $6,500. Under the rules of capital gains taxation, she must pay tax on the gain of $1,500. If, however, the price level has risen over the period in which she held the stock, the real value of that gain is something less than $1,500. Even though the real value of the capital gain represents Tina's real increase in income, the tax system taxes the nominal value of the capital gain and, in this way, the tax system imposes a tax burden on Mary that rises with inflation.

Political Responses

High and rising rates of inflation during the 1970s pushed the issue of bracket creep into public discussion when what had previously been a fairly slow and hidden form of rising taxation became a most visible cause of higher bills for most Americans. The tax reforms of the 1980s introduced indexation of personal exemptions, standard deductions, and income tax brackets for inflation, thus removing a substantial portion of bracket creep for most taxpayers. But there has been no similar success at solving the distortions that inflation imposes on taxation of interest expenses and income from capital gains.

While the budget deficit problem has led various members of Congress to call for the removal of indexation, little support has followed their attempts. It has been estimated by the Congressional Budget Office that, assuming an average inflation rate of 2.7 percent, elimination of indexation would raise tax revenues of $112 billion over 1994–98.[17] Although repeal of indexation might lead to some deficit reduction, burdens of higher taxation would fall more heavily on lower-income taxpayers since it would lower the value of personal exemptions and standard deductions more, as a percentage of their income, than for higher-income taxpayers. The Congressional Budget Office has also suggested that "another reason for retaining indexing is that it requires the Congress to decide explicitly on tax increases. Without indexing, inflation would cause the average income tax rate to increase without any legislative action."[18]

Summary

- The federal income tax was created in 1913. The income tax now collects roughly 45 percent of all federal tax revenues. The two important characteristics of the federal income tax are tax rates and the tax base. The tax rate is the rate at which taxes are collected against taxable income. The tax base is the definition of taxable income.

- The Haig-Simons criterion defines (comprehensive) income as the change in the ability to consume during a given time period, which in practice is the monetary value of consumption plus changes in net worth over a given period. Net worth equals the difference between the value of assets and liabilities.

- Income is commonly measured (in a comprehensive sense) from the source side of a budget, which includes wages, salaries, government transfers, interest earnings, fringe benefits, and capital gains or losses. The use side, in contrast, shows where income goes and includes consumption, donations, and gifts, savings, and various costs that arise during the process of earning income.

- The comprehensive measure of income includes many income sources not normally included in taxable income. Fringe benefits and in-kind income are not included. Issues relating to fairness and complexity in accounting for all sources of income indicate why there is a substantial difference between taxable income and a comprehensive measure of income.

- Economists advocate use of a comprehensive measure of income because it promotes tax policy neutrality. Neutrality occurs when tax policy does not distort the allocation of resources. Comprehensive tax bases also allow, at a given level of tax revenue, a lower tax rate that is also believed to promote economic growth.

- Tax reform changes tax rates and tax bases. These changes are usually motivated by factors related to simplification, equity, and base broadening.

---

[17] Congressional Budget Office, *Reducing the Deficit: Spending and Revenue Options* (Washington, D.C.: February 1993).

[18] Congressional Budget Office, *Reducing the Deficit,* 341.

Review Questions

1. What definition of income is consistent with the Haig-Simons criterion?
2. In what sense should implicit rental income be included in a comprehensive definition of income?
3. What is meant by tax policy neutrality?
4. What is the difference between the standard deduction and the itemized deduction?
5. What is the marriage tax?

Discussion Questions

1. Explain why tax liability is a function of both the taxable income base and tax rates.
2. Evaluate the following statement: Tax policy discourages taxed income sources and encourages untaxed income sources when the tax base is less than comprehensive.
3. Baby-sitting provides in-kind income when it is produced by parents. When parents hire a day care provider, it results in monetary income and is measured as such in the marketplace. Explain whether both should be included in a comprehensive definition of income.
4. Which would you prefer: a tax credit of $1,000 or a tax deduction of $1,000?
5. What are capital gains, and how are they treated in the personal income tax code? Explain how current policy encourages the lock-in effect, whereby investors tend to hold onto assets longer than otherwise would be the case.
6. What were the major characteristics of tax reform in the 1980s?
7. It has been argued that bracket creep allows "taxation without representation." Do you agree?
8. Explain why a standard deduction that does not rise with inflation will be of less value to taxpayers when there is inflation. Will lower-income or higher-income taxpayers be more adversely affected by inflation in this case?
9. Explain why economists often advocate broadening the income tax base. Discuss the implications of base broadening for tax expenditures.
10. What is the difference between the average tax rate and the marginal tax rate? Give examples of each and explain why this distinction is important.

Key Words

Haig-Simons criterion
Source side of budget
Use side of budget
In-kind income
Comprehensive measure of income
Implicit rental income
Lock-in effect
Tax policy neutrality
Gross income
Adjusted gross income (AGI)
Standard deduction
Itemized deductions
Tax liability
Marginal tax rates
Average tax rate
Tax credits
Earned income tax credit
Alternative minimum tax (AMT)
Economic Recovery Tax Act of 1981
Social Security Amendments of 1983
Tax Reform Act of 1986
Omnibus Budget Reconciliation Acts of 1990 and 1993
Base broadening
Marriage tax
Bracket creep
Capital gains

CHAPTER 19

Income Taxation and Behavior

Most economists agree that taxpayers avoid higher taxation. The degree to which they seek tax avoidance, however, is a subject of substantial controversy. In this chapter, we examine the theory and evidence on the relationship between income taxation and economic behavior. Models of labor supply and personal saving are developed that provide us with testable hypotheses on tax rates and individual behavior. Among the questions addressed through these hypotheses are the following:

- ❑ How do changes in tax rates influence the choice between work and leisure?
- ❑ Do workers shift income taxes on labor income onto other parties?
- ❑ Must aggregate tax collections fall when tax rates are reduced?
- ❑ How do tax rates on interest income influence saving behavior?
- ❑ Do savers shift income taxes on interest income onto other parties?
- ❑ Are income taxes on labor and interest income subject to excess burden?

Income Taxation and Labor Supply

Income–Leisure Model

The income–leisure trade-off was introduced in Chapter 11 on transfer programs for the poor. Figure 19-1 shows the income–leisure trade-off for Karla, a taxpayer with budget constraint ZL, which reflects the fact that hours spent consuming leisure cannot earn income, and hours in work cannot be used for leisure. The cost of an additional hour of leisure may therefore be measured in terms of income lost by not working. Income per day is measured on the vertical axis and is determined by the hourly wage rate multiplied by the number of hours worked in a day. If the wage rate w is $10 per hour and 8 hours are worked, $80 equals income earned that day. Assuming Karla is able to work 24 hours a day, OZ represents maximum income of $240 per day.

Measuring leisure hours per day on the horizontal axis, OL represents 24 hours of leisure. From our discussion of comprehensive income, remember that many sources of in-kind income, such as growing your own tomatoes, washing your car, and painting your house, are not taxed; we assume that these income sources fall under leisure activities. All untaxed income sources therefore fall under leisure.

517

FIGURE 19-1
How an Income Tax Lowers Work Effort

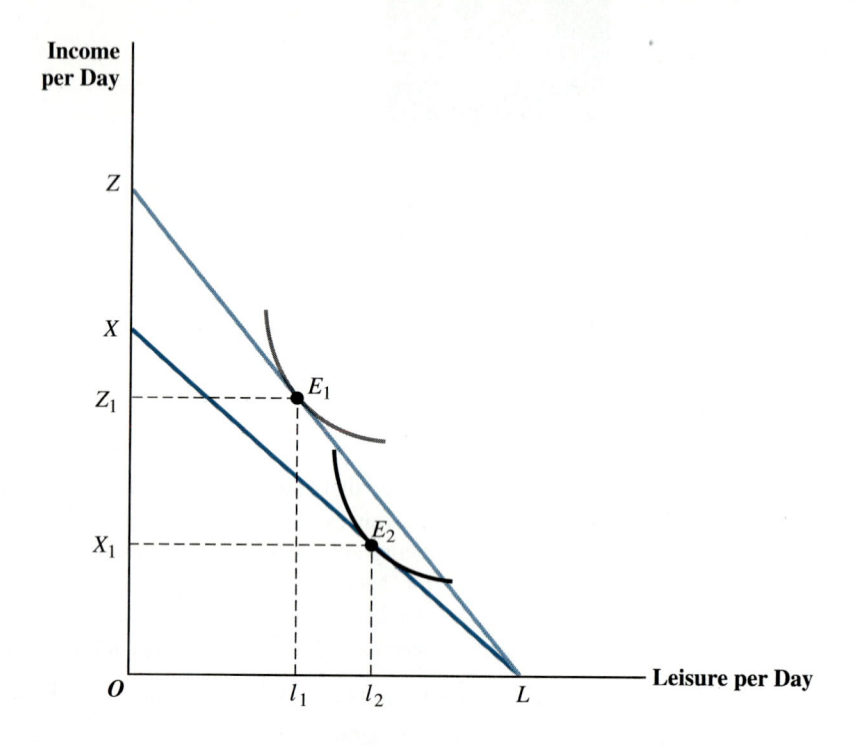

The slope of budget constraint ZL equals wage rate w. (For simplicity, we show the absolute value of the slope throughout this chapter.) Any point along ZL defines a combination of work and leisure that sums to 24 hours, since hours not spent in leisure must be spent working. If, for example, Karla chooses Ol_1 hours of leisure, the remaining portion of OL, or l_1L, measures hours devoted to working. Any point along the horizontal axis therefore characterizes a unique combination of hours spent working and in leisure.

Karla's preferences for work versus leisure are revealed by the slopes of indifference curves shown in Figure 19-1. We assume that Karla has conventional preferences and indifference curves are therefore convex to the origin.

Karla maximizes utility at $E1$ and earns OZ_1 income and consumes Ol_1 hours of leisure. Notice that Karla spends Ol_1 hours in leisure and devotes l_1L hours to work.

We now examine whether an income tax levied on Karla's labor income influences her choice between income and leisure. Assume that a proportional tax of t per hour provides her with an after-tax wage rate of $(1 - t)w$. If, for instance $t = 0.20$ and pretax $w = \$10$, the after-tax hourly wage is \$8, or $(1 - 0.2)\$10$. Taxation lowers the reward for working and therefore flattens the budget constraint facing Karla. Budget constraint XL, drawn with slope of $(1 - t)w$, is one such possibility.[1] Because Karla

---

[1] Progressive taxation would create various kinks in the new budget constraint in which each segment reflects the applicable tax rate. For example, consider two tax rates: t_1 applied to the first \$10,000 of income and a higher marginal rate t_2 applied to all income in excess of \$10,000. The first segment, for income up to \$10,000, would have slope of $(1 - t_1)w$ and, for all income in excess of \$10,000, slope would be $(1 - t_2)w$. Note, that since $t_2 > t_1$, the budget constraint becomes flatter when the tax rate rises to t_2.

may no longer choose $E1$, she experiences lower utility.[2] Karla now chooses $E2$, where she devotes Ol_2 hours to leisure and earns income of OX_1. Work hours are reduced from l_1L to l_2L, and therefore income taxation lowers Karla's labor supply as she substitutes leisure for work.

This will not always be the case. Figure 19-2, which uses the same budget constraints as in Figure 19-1, shows Karla increasing work hours in response to the same tax. Karla's choice of Ol_2 leisure hours and l_2L work hours reflects a different behavioral response and demonstrates the importance that individual behavior plays in the relationship between tax policy and labor supply.

Why the opposite behavioral responses? The conflict may be resolved by consideration of substitution and income effects.[3] You will recall that a *substitution effect* represents the extent to which a relative price change influences choices. A decrease in the price of ice cream, for example, makes consumers purchase more ice cream and fewer candy bars. For Karla, taxation lowers the reward for working and therefore raises the relative attractiveness of leisure. The substitution effect therefore causes Karla to substitute leisure hours for work hours. The *income effect* occurs when the after-tax wage reduction causes after-tax income to fall. Karla's hourly after-tax wage falls from $10 to $8 and, for example, an 8-hour day generates only $64, not $80, in after-tax income. The income effect exerts a positive effect on labor supply since Karla works additional hours to recoup some of her lost after-tax income.

The net change in work hours is determined by which effect dominates since each works opposite from the other. If, for example, the substitution effect lowers work effort by 3 hours, but rises 2 hours because of the income effect, work effort falls by 1 hour. Figure 19-1 illustrates such a story. The opposite story, as shown in Figure 19-2, results in more work effort, since the income effect dominates the substitution effect. A third possibility, of course, would be for neither effect to dominate, in which case an income tax does not influence work hours.

Incidence of Income Taxation on Labor Income

Recall that statutory and economic incidence of taxation are often two very different issues and that we are primarily interested in economic incidence. Sales taxes on candy bars, for instance, might be partially shifted from consumers to producers. Similarly, income taxes may be partially shifted from workers onto employers or consumers. Greater shifting causes a wider divergence between statutory and economic incidence, and this may reduce the case for using income to measure the ability to pay for public programs.

Since the tax is levied on suppliers of labor, shifting might result in higher wage rates. When assessed a tax on labor income, workers may attempt to recoup the resulting loss in after-tax income. Another possibility is that workers will attempt to recover lost after-tax income by demanding more income from untaxed sources such as free

---

[2] We abstract away from the issue of whether the income tax provides tax revenue that eventually returns benefits to Karla in the form of public programs. It could be the case, for example, that annual taxation of $4,000 provides public programs that benefit her more than if she had spent that money herself. Of course, the opposite is possible as well. Since we are interested in issues regarding taxation and labor supply here, and not whether or not taxation improves her overall level of utility, we do not consider this issue.

[3] See the Appendix at the end of the book for a general discussion of substitution and income effects.

FIGURE 19-2
How an Income Tax Raises Work Effort

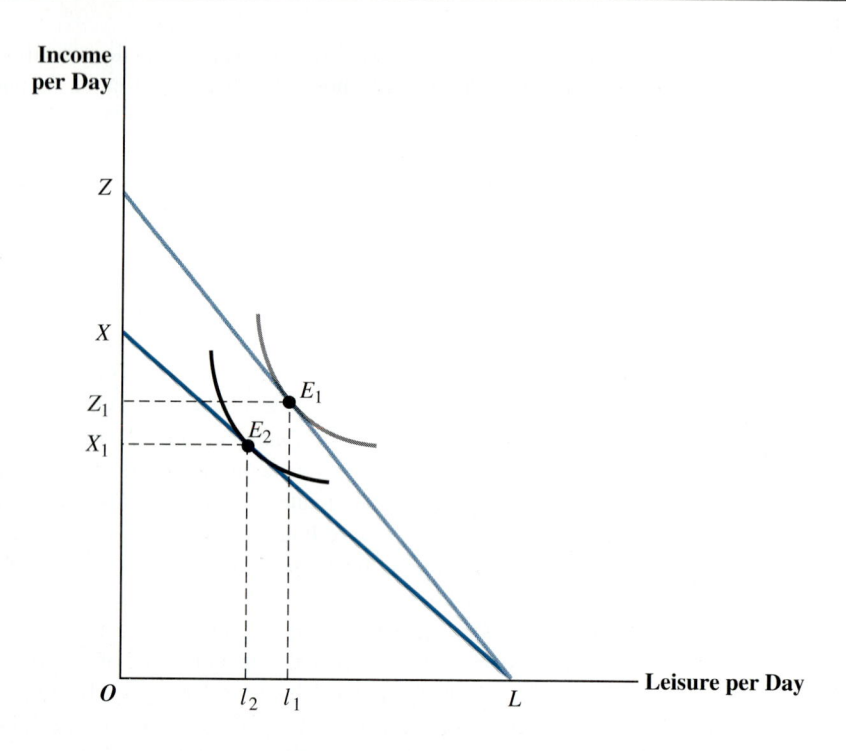

lunches, longer coffee breaks, plusher offices, and employer-provided health care contributions. Employer contributions for health care, for example, averaged over $400 a month for workers with families and, for individual workers, $165 a month in 1994.[4] Workers may also avoid income taxation by working in the underground economy or by lobbying for tax expenditures. Despite the importance of untaxed sources of labor income, we assume that all income sources are taxed and therefore workers may not escape taxation by substituting untaxed sources for taxed sources. In other words, for our purposes tax burdens can only be lowered through working less and spending more hours in leisure.

The various ways in which taxation may affect work effort are represented in the supply curves displayed in Figure 19-3. Supply of labor indicates the relationship between wage rates and hours worked while the demand for labor presents the relationship between wage rates and quantity of hours demanded by employers. We now show how tax shifting possibilities vary with the elasticity of labor supply.

Vertical Labor Supply

Vertical supply curve S, which is perfectly inelastic, represents the case in which substitution and income effects cancel each other out since work hours do not change

---

[4] Congressional Budget Office, *Reducing the Deficit: Spending and Revenue Options* (Washington, D.C.: February 1993).

FIGURE 19-3
Incidence of Taxation of Labor Income

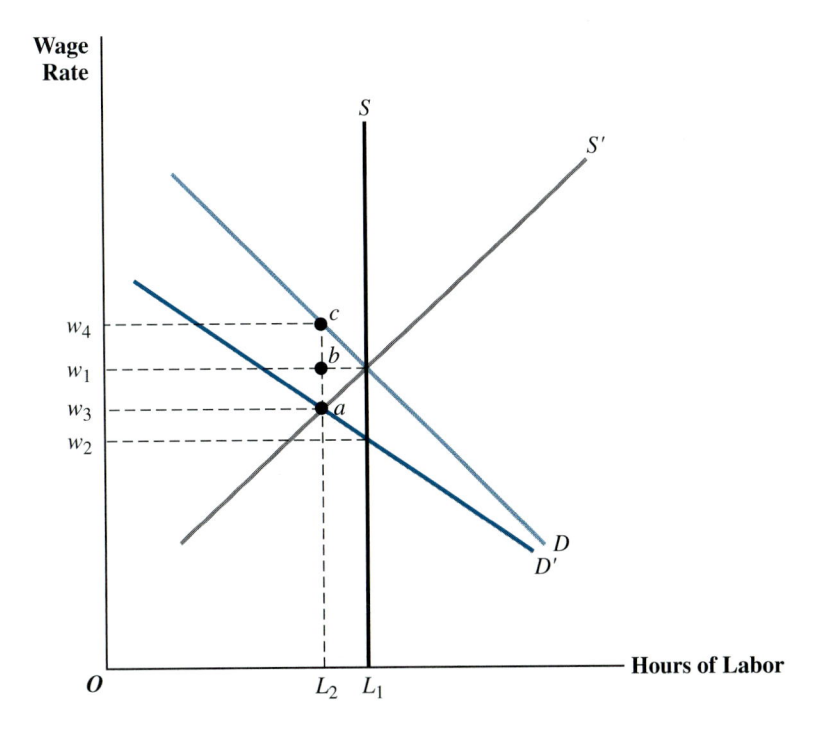

when after-tax wage rates fall. Market pretax equilibrium in this case is characterized by wage rate w_1 and L_1 hours of labor.

Now suppose a proportional income tax is imposed on this labor market. After-tax wage rates fall by the amount of the tax and the new demand curve therefore pivots downward to D'. This is not a parallel shift since, for a 20 percent tax rate, a pretax wage of $10 becomes an after-tax rate of $8; a pretax wage of $5 becomes an after-tax wage of $4, and so on. At L_1 work hours, after-tax wage rate w_2 equals $(1 - 0.2)w_1$.

The new equilibrium is characterized by a lower after-tax wage rate of w_2 when S is the supply of labor. Notice that, although the market, or pretax, wage rate remains w_1, workers receive an after-tax wage of only w_2 since workers pay the difference, or $w_2 w_1$, to the government. At an hourly wage of $10, $8 goes to the worker and $2 to the government. *Therefore, in the case of a perfectly inelastic supply of labor, workers cannot shift any of the income tax.*

Upward-Sloping Labor Supply

The story changes substantially when the supply curve is not perfectly inelastic, as occurs whenever substitution effects dominate income effects; such as S' in Figure 19-3. As income tax rates rise, work effort falls in response to lower after-tax wage rates.

Workers will now partially shift the same income tax as before onto employers, or, in some cases, onto customers through higher product prices. Market equilibrium is now characterized by L_2 work hours. Although the after-tax wage rate falls to w_3, workers receive market wage rate w_4, which is higher than before. Part of the tax is therefore borne by others since, at L_2, the tax equals ac, but only ab is borne by workers. Employers or consumers bear bc, the difference.

The elasticity of labor supply determines how much of the tax is borne by others. *The more (less) elastic is supply, the larger (smaller) the portion of tax paid by others.* This result may be easily demonstrated by noticing that, since S' is more elastic than S, the portion of the tax paid by others is larger when supply is more elastic. Although substantial controversy surrounds the issue of labor supply elasticity, many economists believe that it is fairly inelastic and that workers therefore bear most of the burden of an income tax.

Excess Burden of Income Taxation on Labor Income

Vertical Labor Supply

Excess burdens occur whenever taxes shift resources into less efficient allocations and will therefore occur whenever income taxation changes work efforts. It may appear that income taxation creates no excess burden when labor supply is inelastic, but this is not so. The key to understanding excess burden is to separate income and substitution effects that result from income taxation. Notice that all taxes, whether lump sum or not, have income effects, since resources are always transferred from taxpayers to governments. All taxes must therefore have income effects; this then indicates that income effects are not sources of excess burden. Excess burdens are therefore connected to substitution effects.

Now notice that just because work efforts are unaffected by income taxation when labor supply is inelastic, this does not mean that substitution effects do not occur. Rather, income and substitution effects merely cancel each other out. To determine excess burden, it then follows that income effects should be removed from labor supply curves. Such a curve, often called a **compensated supply curve,** holds income constant, and therefore all quantity changes represent substitution effects. Since income taxation results in substitution effects that lead to less work effort, compensated supply curves are upward sloping.

Figure 19-4 shows, for the perfectly inelastic supply curve of Figure 19-3, compensated supply curve S_{com}. When income taxation lowers the after-tax wage rate from w_1 to $(1-t)w_1 = w_2$, workers lower work effort from H_1 to H_2 as the result of the substitution effect.[5]

Upward-sloping labor supply curves have flatter compensated supply curves than vertical supply labor curves. This follows easily from the observation that because upward-sloping (uncompensated) supply curves are characterized by substitution effects dominating income effects, their corresponding compensated supply curves will tend to be more elastic as well since they also tend to have relatively larger substitution effects. Such a case is shown in Figure 19-4 where S'_{com} (which corresponds

> **Compensated supply curve**
> holds income constant, and therefore all quantity changes reflect substitution effects.

---
[5] In Chapter 16 we discussed the measurement of excess burden which, in our case, equals $0.5(tw_1)(H_1 - H_2)$.

**FIGURE 19-4
Compensated Labor Supply Curves**

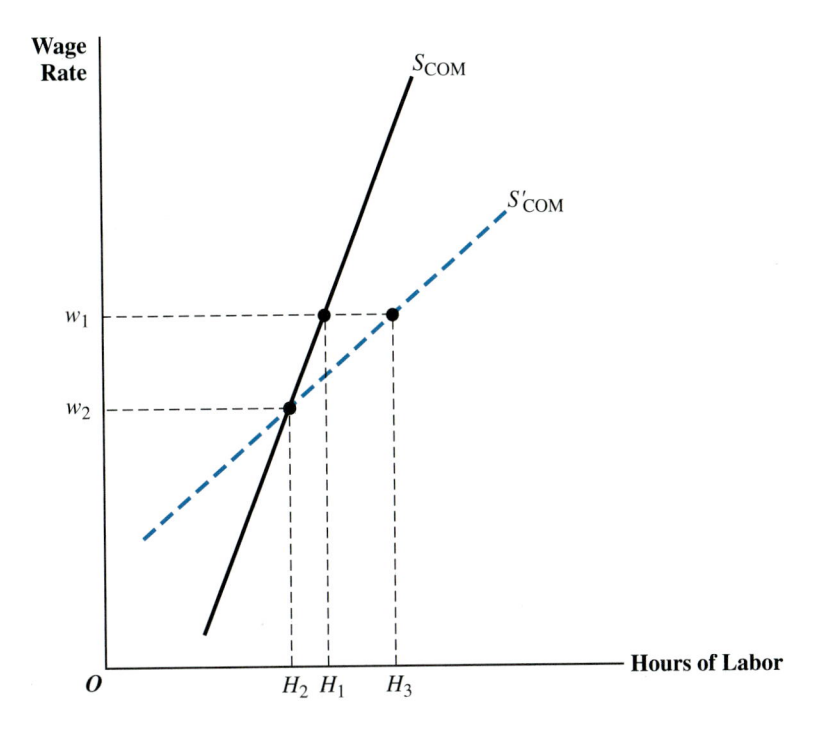

to S' in Figure 19-3) is flatter than S_{com} (which corresponds to S in Figure 19-3). Excess burden rises with the flatness of the compensated supply curve since flatter curves indicate that, for a given income tax, larger changes in work effort occur. In other words, excess burdens rise with supply elasticity and are highest when workers are most responsive to changes in after-tax wage rates. As shown in Figure 19-4, a fall in the after-tax wage rate from w_1 to w_2 results in a relatively larger shift in labor supply: from H_3 to H_2 in the case of elastic supply versus from H_1 to H_2 in the case of perfectly inelastic supply.

Empirical Evidence

We have just shown that the more elastic is labor supply,

- The more an income tax lowers work effort
- The greater the ability of workers to shift income taxes
- The larger are excess burdens

Much of the controversy surrounding the ways in which taxation influences economic behavior surrounds the degree to which individuals respond to tax rates. In other words, these three relationships are not controversial, but the magnitudes of each relationship are subject to controversy.

Since controversy hinges on labor supply elasticities, the next logical step in our examination is to question how elastic is labor supply. Empirical evidence suggests that labor supply is fairly inelastic and, as a consequence, workers have little ability to shift income taxation onto other parties. In a study of the impact of the Tax Reform Act of 1986, Jerry Hausman and James Poterba estimate that, for a husband earning $45,000 (in 1985 dollars), reductions in marginal tax rates from 33 percent to 28 percent raised work effort by 1.5 percent.[6] The labor supply of wives was predicted to increase by 2.64 percent under tax reform. Although much of this increase was believed to be due to higher labor force participation, not increased work hours, it is consistent with other studies, which generally find a more elastic labor supply for females. All workers therefore tend to operate under inelastic supply curves and therefore have limited abilities to shift income taxes onto other parties.

Much of the controversy over empirical evidence, however, is directed toward the issue of excess burden. You will recall that just because labor supply is fairly inelastic does not imply that excess burden is absent. Several studies report fairly large substitution effects that indicate relatively large excess burdens as well. Hausman, for example, found that, under the pre-1981 tax system, excess burden was 21.8 percent for the average married man.[7] This estimate suggests that for every additional dollar of tax revenue, an additional 22 cents of resources are wasted as a result of excess burden. In the same study, excess burden was found to be 54 cents for all taxpayers. Hausman and Poterba estimate that excess burden fell from 33 cents (on the dollar of tax increase) to 26 cents as a result of the 1986 Tax Reform Act.[8]

It should be pointed out that in addition to changes in income tax rates, many other factors that are not generally considered in empirical studies of labor supply may influence labor supply elasticity. A few of these are changes in decisions regarding occupational choice and retirement, as well as changes in the ratio of taxed to untaxed income earned by workers. Barry Bosworth and Gary Burtless have recently argued, for instance, that although labor supply grew rapidly during the tax reform years of the 1980s, most increases in labor supply cannot be attributed to tax reform, since gains in work efforts were concentrated among poor households that were mostly unaffected by tax changes.[9]

Labor Supply and the Laffer Curve

Theory

Laffer curve shows a hypothetical relationship between tax rates and tax revenues.

Perhaps no issue in tax policy received as much attention during the 1980s as the relationship between changes in tax rates and tax revenues. This relationship forms the basis of the **Laffer curve,** which many credit as the guiding principle behind reductions in marginal tax rates during the Reagan presidency. This curve is the brainchild of economist Arthur Laffer, who first drew it, the story goes, on a cocktail

---

[6] Jerry A. Hausman and James M. Poterba, "Household Behavior and the Tax Reform Act of 1986," *Journal of Economic Perspectives* 1 (Summer 1987): 101–119.

[7] Jerry A. Hausman, "Labor Supply," in *How Taxes Affect Economic Behavior,* ed. Henry Aaron and Joseph Pechman (Washington, D.C.: Brookings Institution, 1981): 27–72 (note that this refers to all taxes, not just income taxes).

[8] Hausman and Poterba, "Household Behavior and the Tax Reform Act of 1986."

[9] Barry Bosworth and Gary Burtless, "Effects of Tax Reform on Labor Supply, Investment, and Saving," *Journal of Economic Perspectives* 6 (Winter 1992): 3–25.

Does the Tax Code Influence a Couple's Wedding Date?

Andrew Fox and his fiancée, Cathy Cornett, "thought it would be a great thing to have a party around" their wedding on New Year's Eve. *Bridal Bargains,* a book written by Alan Fields, confirms that, New Year's Eve, ranking just behind the last Saturday in June, may be the most popular date for nuptials.

But two factors make this date one of the most expensive days on which to get married. First is cost. Competition for all the wedding necessities—chapel, band, tuxedo rentals, hall and hotel bookings, and limousines—all cost more on New Year's Eve. One wedding specialist estimates that a premium of at least 20 percent accompanies this popular day for parties.

Then there is the income tax code, which does not recognize that couples are married only for one day of the year. When they tie the knot, they become subject to the same tax rates they would face if they had been married on January 1. In other words, they confront the marriage tax, which, for an average two-income couple, amounts to $1,300 in higher federal income taxes.

Even though the only way that Andrew and Cathy may legally avoid the marriage tax is to remain unmarried, they can save a substantial sum of money by simply deferring their wedding date to the first day of the new year. The tax saving is not lost on Andrew and Cathy. As Andrew says, "We're not going to change the date. But we're probably going to wait until 12:01 to say 'I do.'"

Source: Kathy M. Kristof, "Hitch to Year-End Nuptials: Higher Taxes, Costs Make December 31 Vows Expensive," *Los Angeles Times,* December 29, 1993, D1.

---

napkin while dining in a posh restaurant next door to the White House. Controversy naturally follows the Laffer curve because it indicates that lowering tax rates may, under certain circumstances, raise tax revenues.

Recall that tax revenues equal tax rates multiplied by taxable income. For example, a tax rate of 20 percent on taxable income of $100 million leads to tax collection of $20 million. Under traditional analysis, increases in tax rates generally lead to increases in tax revenues. An increase in the tax rate to 25 percent, for example, would simply lead to $25 million in tax collection. Such revenue forecasts are *static* in the sense that changes in tax rates are assumed to not alter taxable income.

The Laffer curve is a rejection of the traditional analysis because it hypothesizes that changes in tax rates lead to changes in taxable income. This is a *dynamic* model of tax collection, so called because it rests on the theory that taxable income varies with changes in tax rates. When the tax rate is raised to 25 percent, for example, taxable income may fall from $100 million to $90 million, yielding revenues of $22.5 million. Tax collection rose in this example, but notice that a static revenue forecast would have overpredicted the gain in revenue.

The Laffer curve, as shown in Figure 19-5, shows a dynamic relationship between tax revenues and the tax rate. Tax revenues are plotted along the vertical axis, and tax rates are plotted along the horizontal axis. At a tax rate of 0 percent, tax

FIGURE 19-5
The Laffer Curve

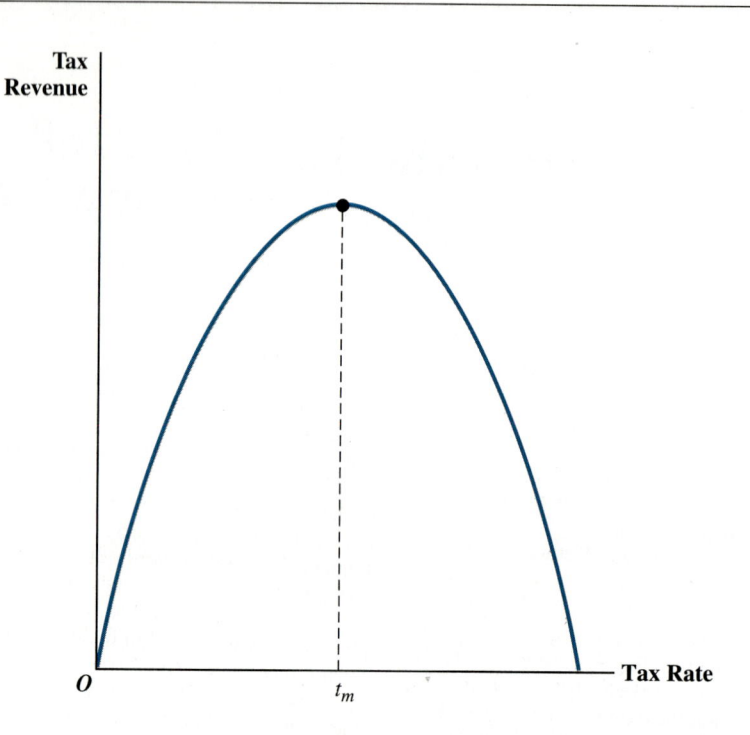

revenues are $0 since there are no taxes to collect. As tax rates rise from 0 percent to t_m, tax revenues rise; therefore either taxable income does not change (static forecast), or reductions in taxable income do not overturn rises in tax rates (dynamic forecast). For tax rates above t_m, tax rate increases lead to falling tax collections since reductions in taxable income are assumed to overturn increases in tax rates. At a tax rate of 100 percent, tax revenues fall to $0 on the assumption that taxable income turns to $0.

The Laffer curve follows easily from our earlier discussion of tax rates and labor supply since, under elastic labor supplies, increases in tax rates lead to reductions in labor supply. This linkage between tax rates and labor supply suggests that tax revenue forecasts should rise and fall with legislation that changes tax rates. For tax rates below t_m, the Laffer curve indicates that labor supply is relatively inelastic since increases in tax rates do not generate substantial reductions in labor supply, and therefore reduction in taxable income does not overturn rising tax rates. For tax rates above t_m, labor supply is assumed to be fairly elastic since rising tax rates lead to relatively larger reductions in labor supply, which lead to reductions in taxable income, which overturn rising tax rates.

Our discussion emphasizes only the linkage between tax rate changes and labor supply. Other linkages could also be hypothesized to show the same relationship between tax rates and tax revenues. Rising tax rates, for example, could also lead to greater use of existing tax expenditures, lobbying for new tax expenditures, and greater evasion of taxation through underreporting of income or moving into the underground economy.

Policy Implications

The theory behind the Laffer curve proved to be a critical factor behind tax reduction legislation of the 1980s. Because it hypothesizes that maximum tax collection occurs at t_m, much discussion centered on the issue of whether current rates of taxation were located to the left or right of t_m. If, for instance, current rates of taxation were located to the right of t_m, as many economists in the Ronald Reagan administration believed, tax reduction would raise tax revenues and lower the budget deficit. (This, of course, assumes that increases in tax revenues do not cause increases in public spending.) Lowering tax rates also had the endorsement of many economists since lower marginal tax rates also have the added benefit of lowering excess burdens.

Empirical Evidence

The empirical validity of the Laffer curve rests on two factors: labor supply elasticity and time. As we have shown before, the relationship between tax rates and labor supply is dependent upon labor supply elasticity. Notice that most economists would believe that, at a tax rate of 99 percent, labor supply is virtually nonexistent, since few workers would be willing to turn over 99 percent of labor income to their government. Controversy, however, surrounds the location of the threshold point described by t_m. One study concludes that because of relativity inelastic labor supply, t_m may be as high as 80 percent, clearly much higher than marginal tax rates currently in place for the average worker.[10]

Time is the other factor.[11] Specifically, how long does it take for the full effects of tax rate changes to work through the economy? Most economists believe that labor supply elasticity is higher when it is measured over longer time periods than for shorter time periods. It could be true, for instance, that although reductions in tax rates may not lead to significant and immediate changes in labor supply, substantial increases in work effort may surface several years after tax rate reduction. Notice how static revenue forecasts, which assume no changes in taxable income, would outperform dynamic revenue forecasts, which assume changes in taxable income, in the years immediately following tax reduction. While it may appear, in this case, that tax cuts lead to tax reduction, this may only be true in the interim period before labor supply fully responds to reductions in tax rates. In the long run, dynamic forecasts would outperform static revenue forecasts.

The point is that, when one empirically examines the empirical validity of the Laffer curve, it is not clear what time period it should be examined over. It may appear to have little empirical validity in the years immediately following tax cuts, but this is not an appropriate time frame for testing a dynamic relationship in which workers may take many years to fully adjust to reductions in tax rates. This also suggests the added complication that, although tax legislation of the 1980s reduced marginal income tax rates, other changes were introduced at the same time that may also affect

---

[10] Don Fullerton, "On the Possibility of an Inverse Relationship between Tax Rates and Government Revenues," *Journal of Public Economics* 19 (October 1982): 3–22.

[11] James M. Buchanan and Dwight R. Lee, "Politics, Time, and the Laffer Curve," *Journal of Political Economy* 90 (August 1982): 816–819.

tax revenues. Changes in other tax rates, such as increases in payroll taxes, as well as changes in the definition of the tax base, also occurred, making testing of the Laffer curve a difficult exercise.

In conclusion, the Laffer curve remains a public finance issue with many critics and many advocates. Arguments over labor supply elasticity, the location of t_m, and what constitutes an appropriate time period for testing are sure to be continued as the Laffer curve continues to attract debate.

Income Taxation and Saving Behavior

Interest on savings is one source of income, and much of this income is subject to personal income taxation. Saving behavior is an important area of study in public finance because of its implications for the capital stock and future living standards.

A Model of Intertemporal Choice

Since saving means the forgoing of present consumption, we examine the saving decision within a two-period **intertemporal choice model** of consumption behavior. This model examines available choices between consumption and saving. We assume that (non-interest) income is fixed at Y at the start of the first period and therefore ignore complications that arise when tax rate changes influence labor supply. Our model simply addresses this question: How much of Y will be consumed today versus tomorrow?

Intertemporal choice model is a model illustrating the various choices between consuming or saving income.

Two fundamental issues inform the saving decision. First, since income saved today means that tomorrow's consumption is higher by the sum of savings plus the interest on those savings, the market interest rate determines the cost of consuming income today. Second, the time rate of discount influences personal saving decisions. The rate of discount indicates preferences of individuals for consuming income today versus tomorrow and is influenced by such personal characteristics as patience and age. Patient individuals place relatively high values on benefits derived from consuming more tomorrow as a result of interest earnings on today's savings. Age is also an important factor: Middle-aged individuals tend to save more for future consumption than do the elderly who, on average, have fewer years in which to consume future income.

Figure 19-6 shows a model of intertemporal choice since it displays a trade-off between present and future consumption. Recall that all (non-interest) income is fixed at Y in the first period and therefore present consumption, as measured in dollars on the horizontal axis, is, at most, equal to Y. If all of Y is consumed in the first period, no interest may be earned, and future consumption therefore equals zero as well.

If all of Y is saved, maximum future consumption equals $(1 + r)Y$, where r is the market interest rate on saving. For example, if $r = 0.05$ and $Y = \$15,000$, maximum future consumption is $\$15,750$, which consists of beginning period income of $\$15,000$ plus interest earnings of $\$750$ ($0.05 \times \$15,000$). A point such as Z then describes maximum future consumption.

Line ZY is the intertemporal budget constraint facing an individual for given levels of Y and r. We now describe the importance that Y and r play in saving behavior:

FIGURE 19-6
Intertemporal Model of Savings Behavior

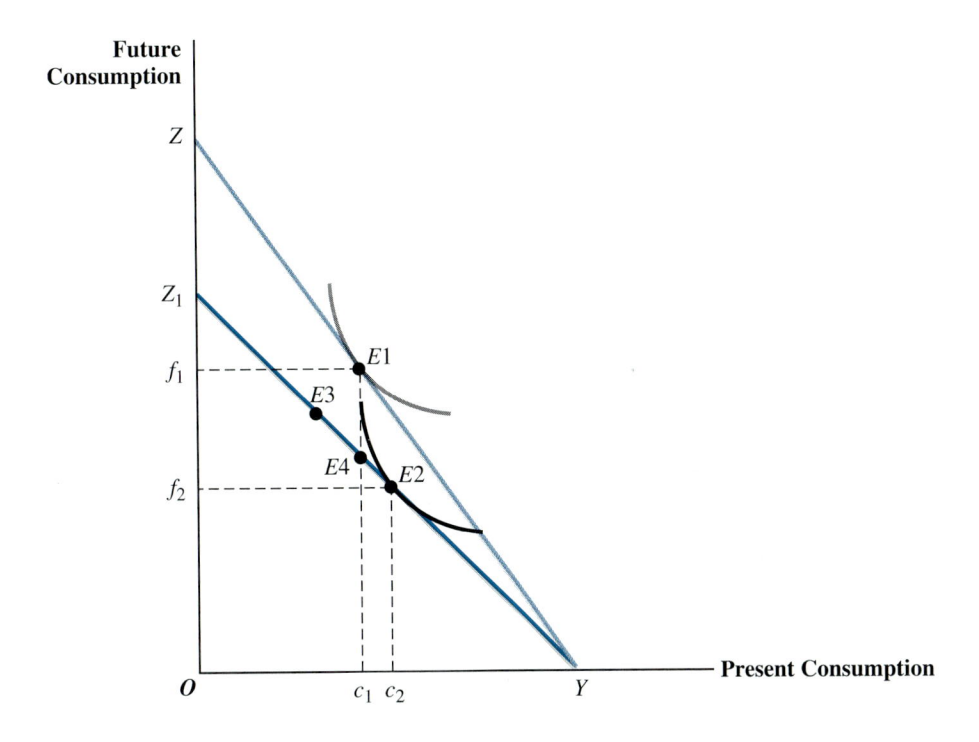

[Figure: Graph with Future Consumption on vertical axis and Present Consumption on horizontal axis. Budget constraint ZY rotates to Z_1Y. Points E1 (at c_1, f_1), E3, E4, and E2 (at c_2, f_2) shown with indifference curves.]

- Changes in Y change consumption opportunities of today and tomorrow. Increases in Y, for example, allow for increases in both today's consumption and saving; along with higher interest earnings, this provides for greater consumption tomorrow.[12]

- Changes in r influence consumption opportunities since, for any level of savings, interest earnings change in the same direction. As interest earnings rise, for example, consumption opportunities of tomorrow rise in tandem. Reductions in r exert opposite effects since, for a given level of savings, interest income falls. Such a fall may be from r to r_1, which causes a rotation of budget constraint ZY to Z_1Y.[13] The new budget constraint shows, for a given Y, a lower maximum level of future consumption. If $r_1 = 0.03$ and Y = $15,000, maximum consumption tomorrow is $15,450.00 (1.03 × $15,000).

Figure 19-6 also shows individual preferences for choosing between consumption today versus tomorrow. Preferences are shown through indifference curves, and this individual maximizes utility at E1 by choosing to consume c_1 today and f_1 tomorrow. Note that consumption of c_1 today means that $Y - c_1$ is saved which, at the market interest rate of r, leads to consumption of $(Y - c_1)(1 + r) = f_1$ tomorrow.

---

[12] It may be easily shown that higher values of Y lead to rightward, and parallel, shifts in the budget constraint. As shown shortly, the slope does not change when Y is changed since the slope of the budget constraint is equal to $(1 + r)$ and, since r is not changed, the slope will not change either.

[13] Rotation of the budget constraint occurs because its slope $(1 + r)$ falls as r falls.

Taxation of Interest Earnings and Intertemporal Choice

Our model of intertemporal choice can easily show how taxation of interest earnings influences saving decisions. Taxation of interest income lowers the reward to saving since, for a given savings level, it lowers future consumption. Taxation lowers the after-tax rate of return to saving from r to $(1 - t)r$. At tax rate $t = 33$ percent and $r = 5$ percent, for example, the after-tax return falls to 3.3 percent, or $(1 - t)r = 0.67 \times 0.05$. Taxation, therefore, creates a divergence between the market rate of return and the after-tax rate of return.

Notice that taxation of interest earnings exerts the same effect on the intertemporal budget constraint, as does a fall in the market interest rate. Maximum future consumption falls with taxation and results in rotation of the budget constraint from ZY to Z_1Y. The crossing point on the vertical axis falls since taxation lowers after-tax interest earnings. If $Y = \$15,000$, for example, maximum after-tax interest earnings fall from $750 to $502.50 when a tax rate of 33 percent is levied on a market interest rate of 5 percent. Taxation, however, does not affect Y and therefore the point at which the budget constraint crosses the horizontal axis does not change.

Savers may respond in various ways to lower after-tax returns. Figure 19-6 shows one possible response. Given a flatter intertemporal budget constraint, utility is maximized at $E2$, where she chooses to consume c_2 today and f_2 tomorrow.[14] Taxation, therefore, results in higher present consumption and, because this means fewer savings, lower future consumption as well.

Substitution Effects

This is only one possible response and, as seen in our discussion of tax rates and labor supply, final consequences of tax changes depend upon the interaction of substitution and income effects. The *substitution effect* of a lower after-tax return on saving results in lower saving and increased present consumption. In effect, future consumption now requires savers to forgo more present consumption. For example, future consumption of $105 is created on savings of $100 at $r = 5$ percent but requires $101.64 of savings when after-tax returns fall to 3.33 percent. As the price of future consumption rises, the substitution effect results in lower saving. Another way of stating this is to say that the opportunity cost to present consumption falls when interest earnings are taxed, and taxation therefore encourages taxpayers to consume more of their income.

Income Effects

The *income effect* lowers present consumption since savers attempt to recoup the drop in interest earnings that result from lower after-tax rates of return. If $1,000 was saved, at $r = 5$ percent, $50 in interest earnings were created for future consumption. An after-tax return of 3.35 percent, however, produces only $33.50 in future consumption—a drop of $16.50. The saver may choose to recoup the entire $16.50 through saving more today. Full recouping requires $492.54 in additional savings that,

---

[14] Note that, since c_2 means savings of $Y - c_2$, $f_2 = (Y - c_2)[1 + (1 - t)r]$.

of course, requires an identical reduction in present consumption. Savers may also recoup part of the loss by raising savings by less than $492.54.

Net Effect on Saving

How savers react to the income tax depends upon whether substitution or income effects dominate behavior. The substitution effect lowers saving, and the income effect promotes saving. The story shown in Figure 19-6 assumes that the substitution effect dominates, since present consumption increases from c_1 to c_2. The opposite story, whereby the income effect dominates the substitution effect, could easily be shown as well. For instance, equilibrium on budget constraint Z_1Y could be drawn at point $E3$ where present consumption falls below c_1. Equilibrium could also be shown at point $E4$, where the two effects cancel each other out and present consumption remains at c_1.

In theory, income taxation of interest earnings could result in higher, lower, or no change in saving. What actually occurs is determined by the interaction of substitution and income effects. But it is important to remember that these effects are themselves functions of personal behavior. In other words, the crucial linkage between taxation and saving is dependent upon decisions of savers. Economists may indicate which decisions lead to which outcomes, but empirical work is required to determine the decisions that characterize actual behavior.

Empirical Evidence

Many researchers find that personal saving behavior is fairly sensitive to changes in after-tax rates of return.[15] Others conclude that little sensitivity exists.[16] It must be recognized, however, that empirical testing must control for factors other than taxation in the examination of saving behavior. Many other factors influence saving decisions. Changes in demography, for instance, are believed to affect saving rates, one example is the growth of the elderly population, which may be expected to lead to reductions in national savings. There are also difficulties in calculating real after-tax rates of return to saving since inflation creates differences between nominal and real rates of return. Problems in controlling for demography and inflation, as well as other factors, have created considerable controversy over testing methodologies.

Tax Shifting by Savers

We now examine the possibility that savers shift some portion of taxation onto other parties by considering Figure 19-7, which displays the demand D and supply S for saving and investment. Remember that the supply curve takes the point of view of savers and the demand curve that of borrowers. Equilibrium occurs at $E1$ and is characterized by a market interest rate r_1 and savings S_1.

---

[15] See, for example, Michael Boskin, "Taxation, Saving, and the Rate of Interest," *Journal of Political Economy* 86 (April 1978): S3–S27; and Lawrence H. Summers, "The After-Tax Rate of Return Affects Private Savings," *American Economic Review* 74 (May 1984): 249–253.

[16] See, for example, Bosworth and Burtless, "Effects of Tax Reform on Labor Supply, Investment, and Saving."

FIGURE 19-7
Incidence of Taxation of Interest Income

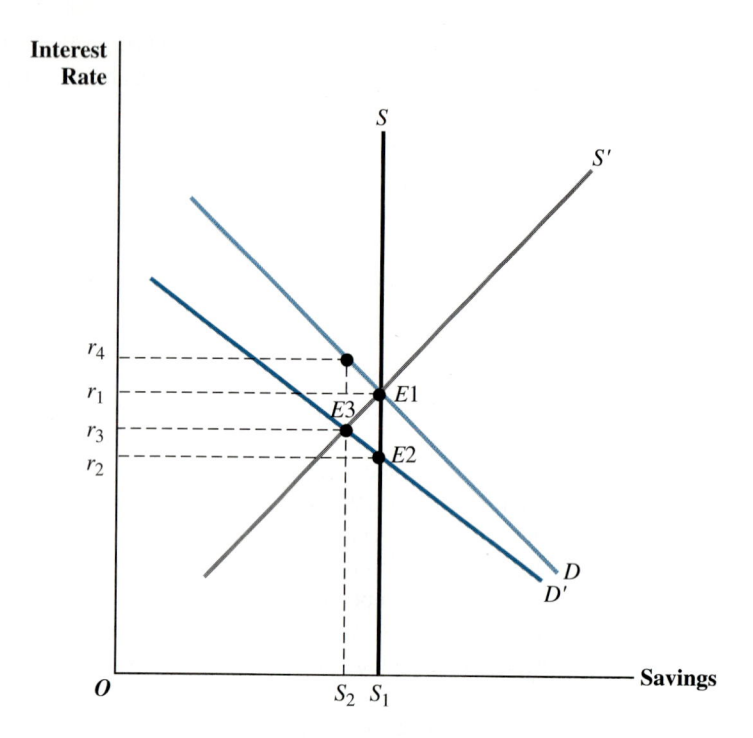

Suppose that interest earnings are assessed income tax rate t. As we saw with taxation of labor income, after-tax returns fall below market returns. D' describes the relationship between after-tax returns and quantity demanded. Taxation lowers the return from r to $(1 - t)r$ and, with $t = 33$ percent, a market interest rate of 9 percent becomes an after-tax rate of 6.03 percent; an interest rate of 7 percent becomes an after-tax rate of 4.7 percent; a 2 percent interest rate becomes an after-tax rate of 1.34; and so on. In other words, the tax causes a pivoting of demand from D to D'.

Inelastic Savings Supply

After-tax equilibrium $E2$ is characterized by an after-tax return of r_2, which is lower than the previous rate of r_1, which occurred prior to taxation. Savers are assumed to not change saving decisions since S is perfectly inelastic. Savers cannot shift any of the income tax when supply is perfectly inelastic. Even though the market rate remains r_1, savers receive only r_2, the after-tax rate. The difference, r_2r_1, is the portion of interest taxed away by the government. With a market rate of 5 percent and a tax rate of 33 percent, 3.35 percent would go to the saver and 1.65 percent to the government.

Upward-Sloping Savings Supply

Can savers shift some of the tax when supply is not perfectly inelastic as in the case of S' in Figure 19-7? After-tax equilibrium occurs at $E3$ with after-tax return r_3. Savers no longer bear the full brunt of the income tax since the tax equals r_3r_4 at S_2, but savers bear distance r_3r_1, and borrowers bear the difference, or r_1r_4.

Implications of Savings Supply Elasticity

Tax shifting is therefore related to the elasticity of savings. Savers are unable to shift taxation when supply is perfectly inelastic since they are completely unresponsive to changes in after-tax returns to saving. Upward-sloping supply curves, in contrast, correspond to savers who are somewhat responsive to after-tax returns and therefore may shift some portion of taxation onto other parties. Higher market interest rates, for instance, are one vehicle for shifting burdens onto others. Let us return to our example, $r = 5$ percent and $t = 33$ percent. If tax shifting results in a rise in the market interest rate from 5 percent to 6 percent, this produces an after-tax return of 4 percent and clearly imposes a smaller burden on savers than when the after-tax return falls to 3.35 percent in the case of perfectly inelastic supply.

An important implication of our analysis is that when savers are responsive to after-tax returns, taxation of interest income discourages saving. Notice that this could also be phrased in terms of encouraging present consumption since lower savings today also means higher present consumption. We have shown that the extent to which this occurs is dependent on the degree of elasticity, and as previously indicated, empirical evidence on this issue is mixed and highly controversial.

Excess Burdens

Examination of excess burdens closely follows our previous analysis of taxation of labor income. Reexamination of this issue is not necessary here, except to make the following points. We should recall that income and substitution effects should be separated through use of compensated supply curves, since excess burdens arise from the substitution effects of taxation. Excess burdens may then be shown to occur when tax policy causes too little savings and too much present consumption.

Behavior When There Are Interest Expense Deductions

Our model of intertemporal choice has considered saving decisions but can easily be extended to borrowing decisions. Interest expenses fall on borrowers and are the flipside to our study of interest income earned by savers. Borrowers are individuals who choose present consumption over future consumption when they forgo consumption of some portion of future income. Although our model of intertemporal choice assumes that income is received only at the beginning of period 1, extension to borrowing decisions requires that income be received in period 2 as well. Borrowing is only possible when resources are available tomorrow with which to repay loans.

In general, consumption of $D(1 + r)$ future income must be forgone to repay borrowing D in our two-period model. For example, if $D = \$1,000$ and $r = 5\%$, then future income of $1,050 (principal plus interest) is forgone since this amount is owed at the beginning of the second period. With deductions of interest expenses from taxable income, $50 may be deducted from taxable income. At a tax rate of 33 percent, deduction of $50 in interest expenses lowers tax liability by $16.50, to $33.50.

When interest expenses are deducted from taxable income, future consumption of $D[1 + (1 - t)r]$ income is forgone when money is borrowed during the first period. (The term $(1 - t)r$ refers to the after-tax interest rate on borrowing.) With $r = 0.05$, $t = 0.33$, and $D = \$1,000$, consumption in the second period is reduced by $1,033.50, or $1,000[1 + (1 - 0.33)0.05]$. The interest expense deduction lowers the after-tax cost of borrowing from $1,050 to $1,033.50, which also equals the reduction in future income that provides for present borrowing of $1,000.

The final result of interest expense deductibility centers, as before, on the interaction of substitution and income effects. The substitution effect of interest expense deductions is to raise borrowing since the relative price of borrowing falls in terms of forgone future consumption. Income effects decrease borrowing since borrowers' income is effectively increased as the real cost of borrowing has been reduced.

Allocation of Saving Activities

We have shown some of the controversies over the sensitivity of saving to changes in after-tax rates of return. But it is not controversial that exemption of interest income or expenses from taxation influences the allocation of saving or borrowing dollars. Even if aggregate saving or borrowing were unaffected by changes in tax rates, savers are influenced by policies that, by excluding interest income from taxation, narrow the definition of taxable income. Similarly, borrowing is influenced by policies that deduct interest expenses from taxable income.

Interest earnings are not always taxed and, in some instances, taxation is deferred to the future. Interest earnings, as well as contributions, on employer-contributions to pension plans are not taxed. For savers eligible to take advantage of IRA accounts, taxation of contributions and the interest they earn are deferred until they are cashed in. The Congressional Budget Office has estimated that, in 1991, tax expenditures associated with IRA contributions resulted in tax relief of $9 billion.[17] When all saving outlets are not taxed equally, resources flow into areas receiving preferential treatment. The logic behind this prediction follows easily from our model of intertemporal choice. Tax policy lowers only the after-tax return to those saving activities subjected to taxation and, in effect, raises the relative attractiveness of activities granted preferential treatment in the tax code.

Similarly, when tax policy allows interest expenses to be deducted from taxable income, borrowing costs of those activities fall relative to those not granted similar treatment. When the Tax Reform Act of 1986 disallowed interest expense deductions on car loans, student loans, charge accounts, and credit cards, effective borrowing costs rose relative to those areas that continued to receive preferential treatment. You will recall that in most cases current tax law continues to allow deductions of mortgage interest expenses from taxable income. The Congressional Budget Office has estimated that elimination of this deduction would have raised tax liabilities of 29 million homeowners by an average of $1,600 in 1994 and resulted in higher tax revenues of $213 billion over the 1994–98 period.[18]

Housing is an area that receives many other preferential tax policies.[19] You will recall from our previous chapter that capital gains are subject to personal income

---

[17] Congressional Budget Office, *Reducing the Deficit: Spending and Revenue Options* (Washington, D.C.: February 1993).

[18] Congressional Budget Office, *Reducing the Deficit: Spending and Revenue Options*.

[19] For example, current tax law provides a one-time exclusion of the first $125,000 in capital gains for taxpayers over age fifty-five. Capital gains, however, are not indexed for inflation; this leads to an overstatement of real income that to some extent may balance out the preferential tax treatments offered for housing.

taxation. Realized capital gains are taxed in the year in which an asset is sold. But an exception occurs in the case of housing since current tax law allows the seller to roll over gains when they are reinvested in another house within two years. Taxation of capital gains may therefore be deferred to the future, thus lowering the present value of tax liabilities associated with capital gains from housing.

Preferential treatment of housing is of conscious design by policymakers who want to encourage resources into housing markets. Preferential policies are controversial since they raise the issue of whether tax policies encourage overallocation of resources into housing markets. At issue is whether tax policy should be neutral in the sense of not causing inefficient resource shifting between markets. Broadening of the tax base results in greater neutrality, for tax policy encourages fewer activities and was one of the rationales for eliminating interest expense deductions for consumer loans and credit cards in the Tax Reform Act of 1986. It has been argued that activities still subject to interest expense deductions were also discouraged when marginal tax rates were reduced. That is, the value of the tax expenditure falls when marginal tax rates fall since a given dollar of deduction results in a smaller reduction of tax liability. It should nevertheless be recognized that the elimination of these deductions also served to raise the relative attractiveness of remaining preferred activities, such as housing, and, as a consequence, probably resulted in greater resource shifting into housing markets.

Summary

- ❏ An income–leisure model demonstrates how income taxation may affect labor supply. Behavioral responses to an income tax are determined through substitution and income effects. When the substitution effect dominates, work effort falls. When the income effect dominates, work effort rises. When neither effect dominates, there is no change in work effort.

- ❏ With a perfectly inelastic labor supply, workers cannot shift any of an income tax and therefore bear full incidence of the tax. The more (less) elastic is labor supply, the larger (smaller) is the portion of tax paid by someone other than workers. Many economists believe that labor supply is fairly inelastic and that workers therefore bear most of the burden of an income tax. The more elastic is labor supply, the larger are excess burdens associated with income taxation.

- ❏ The Laffer curve represents a dynamic model of tax collection because it theorizes that taxable income varies with changes in tax rates. The empirical validity of the Laffer curve rests on labor supply elasticity and time. The more elastic is labor supply, the greater are changes in labor supply—and therefore tax collections—that result from a given change in the tax rate. Time is also important, because changes in tax rates will not normally result in immediate changes in work effort and tax collection.

- ❏ A model of intertemporal choice demonstrates the possible relationships between income taxation of interest income and saving behavior. Income and substitution effects determine the relationship. The net effect depends upon which of these effects dominates. The empirical evidence on this issue is mixed.

- ❏ Savers may shift some portion of taxation onto other parties. Tax shifting is determined by the elasticity of saving. No tax shifting is possible when savings supply is perfectly inelastic. Shifting possibilities rise with elasticity of savings supply. Empirical evidence is mixed on this issue. Excess burdens arise when tax policy causes too little savings and too much present consumption.

Review Questions

1. What is the income–leisure model?
2. What is the substitution effect associated with an income tax?
3. What is the income effect associated with an income tax?
4. What is the Laffer curve?
5. What trade-off is shown in an intertemporal model of savings behavior?
6. What is the substitution effect associated with an income tax on interest income?
7. What is the income effect associated with an income tax on interest income?

Discussion Questions

1. We have shown that rising income tax rates may lead to reductions in work effort. Show how a reduction in income tax rates may affect work effort. Describe income and substitution effects in your answer.
2. Statutory tax incidence most closely resembles economic incidence when little tax shifting occurs. Explain why substantial tax shifting may reduce the case for using income to measure the ability to pay for public programs.
3. Explain why a vertical supply of labor curve has income and substitution effects that cancel each other out.
4. Would it be more difficult when labor supply is elastic or inelastic to forecast how tax revenues change when income tax rates are increased?
5. Explain the theory behind the Laffer curve. Under what conditions might tax rate reductions lead to increases in tax revenues?
6. Explain why the relationship between tax policy and saving is a function of the behavior of taxpayers.
7. In what way does income tax policy distort saving decisions?
8. Explain why preferential treatment of certain types of saving activities influences the allocation of saving in the economy.
9. In what sense do tax policies regarding housing create excess burdens?

Key Words

Compensated supply curve
Laffer curve
Intertemporal choice model

CHAPTER 20

The Corporation Tax

Corporations
are legal entities created by states, which approve charters submitted by founders.

Corporations are legal entities created by states, which approve charters submitted by founders. Ownership is vested in stockholders, who purchase transferable stock certificates. A stockholder with 500 shares of stock, for example, owns 5 percent of a corporation with 10,000 shares outstanding. In addition to limiting liability to the number of shares owned, corporate charters allow corporations to litigate, own property, and incur debts.

There are many criticisms of the corporation tax. For example, because income of corporations is subject to double taxation, it has been argued that the corporation tax discourages the corporate form of business. There is also widespread agreement that the corporation tax distorts business investment decisions of all firms, corporate or otherwise, in the economy. Perhaps these criticisms explain the rapid decline in the importance of the corporation tax to the overall tax collection effort. Figure 20-1 plots the history of corporation tax revenues as shares of total federal revenues and GDP. Since 1950, corporation tax revenues have fallen from 27 percent to just 9 percent of total federal revenues—a threefold decline. Substantial reduction is also evident when corporation tax revenues are compared to GDP: Revenues have declined from roughly 4 percent to 2 percent of GDP over this same period.

The corporation tax code is highly complex, and full of subtleties and provisions. Fortunately, an overview provides ample coverage of the important policy issues. The following issues form the foundation of our examination:

❏ What is the tax base for corporations?
❏ What tax rates are levied on the income of corporations?
❏ How does the corporation tax influence corporate behavior?
❏ Who bears the burden of the corporation tax?
❏ Should the corporation tax be integrated into the personal income tax?

Defining Taxable Income: Deductions

Gross Income

This section provides a quick examination of the corporation tax code. The first step is to calculate the gross income, or what might be called sales revenue, of

**FIGURE 20-1
Corporate Tax Revenues**

Sources: Budget Baselines, Historical Data, and Alternatives for the Future, January 1993; and Budget of the United States Government, 1994.

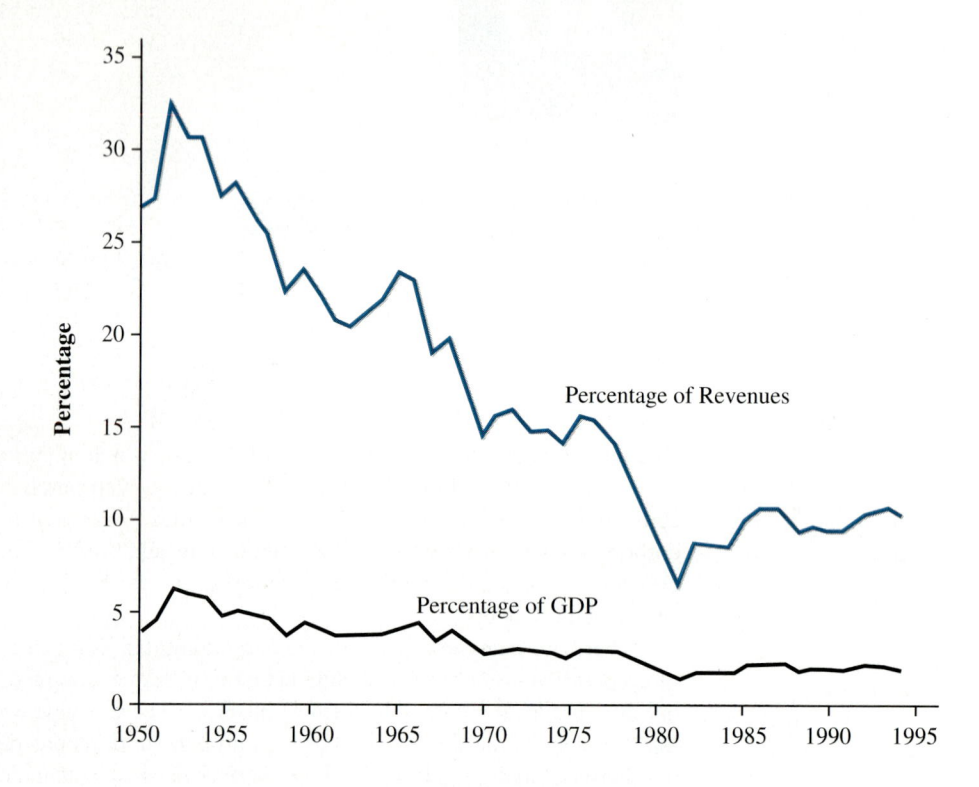

corporations. If Corporation Y sells 10,000 computer modems at a per unit price of $85, gross income equals $850,000. The next step is to deduct allowable costs of operation.

Wages

Wages are a deductible expense since they clearly represent a cost of doing business and earning income. Wages of all workers are deductible because managers are not owners of corporations. This is a benefit of incorporation. In cases of noncorporate business, most managers are owners themselves, and the personal income tax does not allow them to deduct their wage costs from taxable income. The ability to subtract all labor costs from taxable income is therefore an advantage of the corporate form of organization; for owners, or stockholders, hire managers to run corporations.

Interest Costs

Dividends are payments made to owners of corporations.

Double taxation is the taxing of income when it is earned by corporations and again when it is distributed to stockholders.

Interest costs are a cost of earning income since corporations fund some portion of investment activities through issuing debt in bond markets. Dividends, however, are not considered deductible expenses. **Dividends** are payments made on stock holdings and, in this respect, represent returns on investments to stockholders. Notice that dividends are subject to **double taxation.** Dividends are first taxed at the corporate level: Since they are not deducted from taxable income, corporations are taxed on the

Depreciation

Short-lived resources are assets with a useful life of one year or less.

Long-lived resources are assets with a useful life of one year or more.

The tax code distinguishes between short-lived and long-lived resources. **Short-lived resources,** such as packing cartons, boxes, and light bulbs, tend to be consumed within a year of purchase; therefore, their costs are fully deductible in the year of purchase. **Long-lived resources,** such as buildings, trucks, and machinery, are usually not replaced within a year of purchase. Because they do not wear out quickly, the costs of long-lived resources (often called *capital resources*) are distributed over many years during which depreciation takes place. A building, for instance, may have an economic life of 30 years—that is, a useful period of 30 years over which depreciation costs may be deducted as expenses. Thus only portions that become obsolete or wear out—that is, are genuinely consumed—each year should be deducted from taxable income. One rationale for distributing depreciation costs over the economic lives of capital resources is to provide firms with tax relief which, in theory, may be saved in funds that eventually replace worn or obsolete capital resources. This explains why depreciation is often called a *capital consumption allowance.*

Economic depreciation is the process by which capital resources are actually consumed or made obsolete.

Statutory depreciation specifies the rates at which capital resources may be deducted from taxable income over designated tax lives.

Tax life is the period over which statutory depreciation is allowed.

So far, we have focused on **economic depreciation,** which is the process by which capital resources are consumed or made obsolete over time. The tax code, however, defines **statutory depreciation** schedules, which specify rates at which capital resources may be deducted from taxable income over designated tax lives. We use the term *depreciation schedule* to signify underlying rates and methods of depreciation as well as tax lives of capital resources. The **tax life** of a capital resource is the allowable period over which depreciation may be claimed. While the economic life of a building may be 30 years, the tax code may assign tax lives as short as 10 years or as long as 40 years.

We can easily demonstrate that shorter tax lives and higher rates of depreciation in the early years of tax lives provide the most tax relief to firms. Suppose that a corporation purchases a machine that costs $5,000 and that the corporation tax rate is 35 percent, which, as shown later, is the rate that applies to most corporations.

Expensing

Expensing allows for the depreciation of the entire cost of an asset during the first year of its purchase.

At one extreme, the tax code could allow depreciation of the entire cost in the first year. This is called **expensing,** since the capital asset is assumed to be fully worn out in the first year of use. With a tax rate of 35 percent, tax liability falls by $1,750, or 35 percent of $5,000, in the year in which the machine is purchased.

Straight-Line Depreciation

Straight-line depreciation is the deduction of a uniform percentage of costs over each year of an asset's tax life.

Another method is called **straight-line depreciation,** which, for example, may allow an annual deduction of $1,000 over 5 years. At a tax rate of 35 percent, deductions of $1,000 lower tax liabilities by $350 per year. Recall, however, that money, or tax relief in this case, is worth more today than tomorrow, and so it is appropriate to calculate, as in Chapter 14, the present value of tax relief. Assuming a discount rate (r)

of 10 percent, and also assuming that the first deduction occurs at the end of the first year, the present value of tax relief equals

$$\frac{\$350}{(1+r)} + \frac{\$350}{(1+r)^2} + \frac{\$350}{(1+r)^3} + \frac{\$350}{(1+r)^4} + \frac{\$350}{(1+r)^5} = \$1,326.80$$

Notice that tax policy, in effect, lowers the price of the machine since the machine costs $5,000 today, but tax deductions lower its price by $1,326.80, the present value of tax relief.

We may easily show that changes in tax life alter values of tax relief. Dropping tax life to 2 years, tax deductions of $875 (35 percent of $2,500) in each of 2 years provides a present value of

$$\frac{\$875}{(1+r)} + \frac{\$875}{(1+r)^2} = \$1,518.59$$

Raising tax life to 10 years, annual tax deductions of $175 (35 percent of $500) in each of 10 years yields a present value of

$$\frac{\$175}{(1+r)} + \frac{\$175}{(1+r)^2} + \frac{\$175}{(1+r)^3} + \cdots + \frac{\$175}{(1+r)^{10}} = \$1,075.30$$

Shorter tax lives therefore provide greater tax relief than longer tax lives.

Depreciation Rates and Tax Lives

An important component of the Economic Recovery Tax Act of 1981 was its Accelerated Cost Recovery System (ACRS), which lowered tax lives of most equipment to 5 years and, for structures, to roughly 15 years. The Deficit Reduction Act of 1984 raised tax lives of structures to 18 years. Tax law currently assigns tax lives of roughly 3 to 30 years. On the low end are machines and equipment. Most buildings are on the high end.

We have presented examples of expensing and straight-line depreciation, but many capital resources are subject to slightly more complex depreciation schedules. The **double-declining balance** is a variant of the straight-line method that concentrates a majority of depreciation in the early years of tax life. Under this method, and assuming a tax life of 5 years for a machine that costs $5,000, double the deduction, or $2,000, of the straight-line method is deducted from taxable income. In each following year, the undepreciated balance is again subjected to double the deduction that would have been allowed under the straight-line method. The second year's deduction is therefore $1,2000, or double $600 (20 percent of $3,000) under the straight-line method. The firm continues this calculation until the double-declining balance method no longer yields greater tax relief than the straight-line method. At this point, they switch to the straight-line method.

It can easily be demonstrated that higher rates of depreciation in the early years of a given tax life yield greater tax relief than lower rates. A policy, for example, that grants 80 percent of resource cost as deductible during the first year provides greater tax relief than a policy that grants only 10 percent during the first year. To show this, compare present values of tax relief for a machine costing $5,000 where tax lives are

Double-declining balance is a variant of straight-line depreciation whereby the majority of depreciation is deducted in the early years of an asset's tax life.

2 years in both cases. Also assume once again that the discount rate is 10 percent. In our first case, 80 percent of $5,000 is deducted in the first year, thus lowering tax liability by $1,400 (35 percent of $4,000); in the second year, 20 percent of $5,000 is deducted, lowering tax liability by $350 (35 percent of $1,000). Present value of tax relief is therefore

$$\frac{\$1,400}{(1+r)} + \frac{\$350}{(1+r)^2} = \$1,561.99$$

In our second case, 10 percent of $5,000 is deducted in the first year, tax liability is lowered by $175 (35 percent of $500); in the second year, 90 percent of $5,000 is deducted, and tax liability is lowered by $1,575 (35 percent of $4,500). Present value of tax relief is therefore

$$\frac{\$175}{(1+r)} + \frac{\$1,575}{(1+r)^2} = \$1,460.75$$

Holding tax lives constant, quicker rates of depreciation therefore provide greater tax relief than slower rates of depreciation.

Depreciation and Inflation

A major criticism of statutory depreciation schedules is that they do not control for the way that inflation raises costs of replacing capital resources.[1] Standard deductions and personal exemptions within the personal income tax were indexed for inflation under the Economic Recovery Tax Act of 1981, but indexation has never been extended to the corporation tax.

Depreciation schedules are based on initial capital costs and, when the price level rises over tax lives, initial costs understate replacement costs. Inflation therefore results in tax relief based on past expenses rather than future expenses incurred when capital is replaced. A simple example demonstrates inflation's raising of capital replacement costs. Suppose that a machine that cost $5,000 is assigned a tax life of 5 years. Assuming a discount rate of 10 percent, the deduction of $5,000 from taxable income over 5 years yields a present value of tax relief of $1,326.80 under the straight-line method. Tax relief is therefore based on replacement of a $5,000 machine. If, however, prices have doubled over the tax life, replacement cost rises to $10,000; inflation therefore causes the value of tax relief to drop by half. Inflation lowers the value of tax relief as well, since depreciation schedules are based on initial costs, not replacement costs of capital. Since the value of tax relief falls with inflation, taxable income of corporations is higher than would occur if inflation-adjusted replacement costs were depreciable.

Apart from lowering the value of tax relief associated with depreciation schedules, inflation also benefits firms when it lowers the real value of their debt, assuming that inflationary premiums are not fully included in nominal interest rates at the time debt was sold by firms. Inflation lowers the real value of payments made to creditors

---

[1] For a discussion of this issue, see Robert Hall and Dale Jorgenson, "Tax Policy and Investment Behavior," *American Economic Review* 57 (June 1967): 391–414.

when there is general erosion in the purchasing power of dollars, thereby raising the value of deductions awarded to interest expenses and resulting in lower tax liability than otherwise would occur.

While this effect clearly benefits firms, evidence suggests that the net effect of inflation is to raise tax liabilities of corporations.[2] For this reason, many economists recommend that all aspects of the corporation tax be indexed for inflation.

Tax Rates and Tax Credits

Statutory Tax Rates

Statutory tax rates are tax rates defined by the tax code.

Taxable income is defined as gross income less allowable deductions. The next step in determining tax liability is to multiply taxable income by the appropriate **statutory tax rate.** As we saw in our study of the personal income tax, corporate taxable income is subject to several tax rates:

- 15 percent on the first $50,000 of taxable income
- 25 percent on taxable income between $50,000 and $75,000
- 35 percent on taxable income over $75,000

A surtax of 5 percent is added on to income between $100,000 and $335,000, raising its rate to 40 percent. The surtax is applied as a means of phasing out benefits of lower marginal tax rates for richer corporations. Once taxable income exceeds $335,000, the average rate returns to 35 percent and, because most corporations fall under this category, most are subject to a proportional tax rate of 35 percent.[3]

Effective Tax Rates

Effective tax rates are tax rates calculated by dividing tax liability by a comprehensive measure of income.

There is no reason to expect that statutory tax rates and effective tax rates are identical. **Effective tax rates** are calculated by dividing tax liability by a comprehensive measure of income. Discussion of the Haig-Simons criterion showed that comprehensive income is more extensive than the definition of personal taxable income. The same is true for the corporation income tax base. As just shown, inflation lowers the value of tax relief associated with depreciation schedules and therefore causes taxable income to exceed inflation-adjusted values. It is also generally believed that economic lives exceed tax lives, and therefore taxable income is much less than under a comprehensive definition, which uses economic depreciation as the criterion for deducting costs of capital resources. Furthermore, since dividends are double taxed, the corporation tax rate also understates effective tax rates.

Despite the many complications in determining effective tax rates, careful estimates are available. One study estimates that the Tax Reform Act of 1986, which is

---

[2] Martin Feldstein and Lawrence Summers, "Inflation and the Taxation of Capital Income in the Corporate Sector," *National Tax Journal* 32 (December 1979): 445–470.

[3] Although it has been estimated that roughly 90 percent of all corporations are taxed at rates below 35 percent, they earn roughly 10 percent of aggregate corporate income. See, for example, Congressional Budget Office, *Reducing the Deficit: Spending and Revenue Options,* February 1993.

the most recent and major tax reform of the corporation tax system, created the following effective tax rates on debt-financed investments:

- 29.9 percent for trucks, buses and trailers
- 38 percent for general industrial machinery
- 37 percent for industrial buildings[4]

Differences in effective tax rates are the result of different assumptions regarding inflation, tax lives, and depreciation schedules. Despite their differences, effective rates are fairly close to the top statutory corporation rate of 35 percent. As discussed later, however, tax policy encourages corporate managers to purchase those capital resources with lower effective tax rates and discourages those with higher effective tax rates.

Effective corporate tax rates exceed effective tax rates on personal income paid by most individual taxpayers. Higher tax rates on corporate income raises concerns about the fairness of the tax system since it is not clear that owners of corporations should be assessed higher tax rates than owners of noncorporate businesses. (Exceptions are S corporations, which, in addition to having fewer than 35 owners and being subjected to other requirements, are exempt from the corporation tax and, therefore, pay taxes only on personal taxable income.) Moreover, the higher tax rate on corporate income is widely believed to influence the form of business organization since current tax policies discourage the corporate form of organization.

Tax Credits

Tax credits provide dollar-for-dollar reductions of corporation tax liabilities. A credit for 20 percent of the cost of a capital resource, for instance, provides tax relief of $10,000 when the purchase price is $50,000. A $10,000 tax credit may result in a tax liability of $100,000 for a corporation that otherwise would have been responsible for $110,000.

The Research and Experimentation Tax Credit was created in 1981 to encourage increased investment in research and development. Although this credit has never been made permanent, it has been renewed many times in recent years. Another tax credit is offered to U.S. corporations operating in Puerto Rico or in any other U.S. protectorate. After meeting various requirements, corporations may offset taxes on income derived from operations in U.S. possessions by claiming a Foreign Tax Credit (FTC) for any tax paid on U.S. possessions. Many corporations take advantage of the FTC, and it has been estimated that the value of this credit is $18.8 billion over 1994–98.[5]

Tax Policy and Corporate Behavior

Corporation tax policy influences resource allocation in many areas of the economy. These influences are commonly referred to as distortions, since tax policy encourages

---

[4] Alan J. Auerbach, in "The Tax Reform Act of 1986 and the Cost of Capital," *Journal of Economic Perspectives* 1 (Summer 1987): 73–86, assumes a 4 percent real interest rate and an inflation rate of 3 percent.

[5] Congressional Budget Office, *Reducing the Deficit: Spending and Revenue Options*, February 1993.

corporate managers to allocate resources on the basis of after-tax rates of return rather than on market returns that would prevail in the absence of tax policy. The areas in which tax policy distorts corporate decisions include the following:

- Whether new investments should be financed with debt or equity
- Whether income is distributed as dividends or retained within the corporation
- Which capital resources to invest in

Financing through Debt versus Equity

Corporations may use three options to fund new investments: issue debt, sell new ownership shares, or use retained earnings. (Taking out a bank loan is a fourth option that here may be considered identical to selling debt.) While new debt carries the responsibility of payback of interest and principal to debt holders, corporate managers are in most cases under no obligation to distribute dividends to stockholders.

The corporation tax does not alter an obvious, fundamental criterion: Managers choose low-cost financing methods. Tax policy, however, biases corporate decisions in the direction of financing through debt over equity and retained earnings. Recall that interest expenses on corporate debt are fully deductible from taxable income, but dividends are not. *Preferential tax treatment is awarded to debt finance since it is cheaper, on an after-tax basis, than financing through equity or retained earnings.*

The following example demonstrates how tax policy lowers the after-tax cost of debt. Suppose that a corporation must choose whether to finance a $20,000 truck through selling debt or issuing new equity shares. Under debt finance, interest payments are fully deductible and, if annual interest expenses are $3,500, for example, annual tax relief of $1,225 occurs when the marginal tax rate is 35 percent. The deduction of interest expenses therefore lowers the price of the truck by $1,225 each year. Note that one could calculate the present value of tax relief by discounting future reductions in tax liability.

Compare this to financing the truck through new corporate equity. No tax relief occurs because there are no interest expenses to deduct. Furthermore, because dividends are not deducted from taxable income and, when distributed to stockholders, are taxed again under the personal income tax, income generated by corporate equity is taxed twice. Stockholders therefore pay more for investments that are equity financed than debt financed. The corporation tax therefore biases financing decisions in the direction of debt finance.

Why don't corporations finance all investments through debt? One reason is that they consider it judicious to finance investments through a mix of debt and equity. Firms that finance a majority of investments through debt are referred to as **debt heavy.** Higher debt burdens raise the likelihood that firms will have difficulties meeting payments of interest and principal. Risk of default therefore rises along with debt burdens, and if these conditions are not reversed, bankruptcy may result, in which case all outstanding stock carries a zero value. Remember that stockholders are owners of corporations and are unlikely to allow managers to finance all new investments through debt since stockholders maximize the value of corporations, as measured by

Debt heavy is the condition that results when firms carry large debt burdens; they are called debt-heavy firms.

the market value of outstanding stock.[6] There is, however, considerable agreement that tax policy fosters overutilization of debt finance. Tax policy is therefore believed to create a corporate sector whose performance is more vulnerable to macroeconomic downturns since, in both good and bad times, corporations service debt burdens that are larger than otherwise would be the case.

Dividends versus Retained Earnings

> **Retained earnings** are corporate earnings not distributed to stockholders.

Earnings on capital investments of stockholders may be distributed as dividends or reinvested in the corporation as **retained earnings.** In contrast to dividends, which are taxed twice, retained earnings are not assessed a corporation tax. Retained earnings, however, are indirectly taxed to the extent that they result in higher capital gains, which are taxed upon realization by stockholders. In other words, dividends are subject to immediate taxation, but taxation of retained earnings is deferred to the future.

Stockholders are only interested in after-tax rates of return and therefore tend to prefer retained earnings over dividends. This may be shown by remembering that a tax dollar costs more if it is owed today versus tomorrow. When distribution of dividends, for instance, results in a tax liability of $1,200, an opportunity cost arises when the stockholder is no longer able to invest and earn interest on that $1,200. This opportunity cost does not occur when earnings are retained within the corporation. Tax policy therefore encourages corporations to retain earnings.

Tax policy misallocates capital when stockholders would have gained greater return on their income when distributed in dividends rather than retained earnings. Rates of return on income reinvested in the corporation may, at times, exceed those available elsewhere, but tax policy biases decisions toward reinvestment of income within the corporation. This bias results from favored tax treatment and is unrelated to whether or not reinvestment in the corporation is a more productive use of income. In some cases, it would be more productive, as gauged by market returns, for stockholders to reinvest dividends in other corporations or businesses. Tax policy therefore distorts investment decisions and lowers the productivity of the nation's capital stock.

Our discussion raises the following question: Why do corporations distribute dividends to stockholders? There is controversy over the answer to this question, but many believe that frequent distribution of dividends serves as a useful advertisement that encourages investment by new investors. Frequent distribution of dividends may also provide valuable public relations to current stockholders who question whether corporate management has their best interests in mind.

Depreciation and the Choice of Capital Resources

Economic depreciation and statutory depreciation differ in most cases. The Internal Revenue Service simplifies the tax code by specifying identical depreciation schedules for broad groups of capital resources. All buildings, for instance, are assigned

---

[6] For a discussion of the ability of stockholders to control managers, see Michael C. Jensen and William H. Meckling, "Theory of the Firm: Managerial Behavior, Agency Costs and Ownership Structure," *Journal of Financial Economics* 3 (1976): 305–360.

identical tax lives and depreciation rates, even though one firm may build a sturdy building which lasts for a hundred years and another may build a rickety building that lasts only ten. The tax code recognizes no difference between the two buildings.

Capital is misallocated when broad groups of capital resources are subject to uniform depreciation schedules. Rather than base cost recovery on actual reductions in their value, all resources within broad categories are assumed to wear out at the same rate. Trucks driven 125,000 miles a year or 10,000 miles a year receive identical depreciation schedules. A conveyor belt operated nonstop is assigned the same depreciation schedule as one operated only on weekends.

Tax policy distorts investment decisions because they are based, to some degree, on how generous or miserly are depreciation schedules. Misallocation occurs because costs of replacing capital resources that wear out the fastest should be recovered more quickly than resources lasting much longer. The truck driven 125,000 miles per year depreciates in value much faster than the truck driven only 10,000 miles, but both are assigned identical depreciation schedules. The tax code therefore favors capital resources for which depreciation schedules are most generous. A less productive capital stock results from this distortion since tax law makes some capital resources more attractive only because they can be written off more quickly than other resources. It is possible, in theory, to eliminate this distortion by setting depreciation schedules that are more in line with true economic depreciation. For example, the truck that is driven only 10,000 miles per year could be given a slower rate of depreciation in each year of a longer tax life than the truck driven 125,000 miles. Such fine tuning of depreciation schedules, however, is likely to entail excessive monitoring and bookkeeping for firms and tax authorities and is unlikely to win much support from a public that demands a simplified tax system.

Incidence of the Corporation Tax

Statutory incidence of the corporation tax is assigned to stockholders as the owners of corporations. Recall, however, that statutory and economic incidence of taxation are not necessarily identical. We now examine whether stockholders bear all burdens of the corporation tax. We shall show that although corporate owners bear full burdens of taxation in the short run, shifting of capital resources in the long run causes partial shifting onto capital owners of noncorporate businesses.

Short-Run Incidence

The corporation tax may be viewed as a tax on the rate of return to capital. Corporate capital is a fixed input in the short run. This means that stockholders are unable to lower tax burdens through shifting capital resources in response to changes in after-tax rates of return to corporate capital. Stockholders, however, may shift burdens when they are able to alter prices and output but, as we now show, this is not possible in the short run.

Short-run average cost *(AC)* and marginal cost *(MC)* cost curves are shown in Figure 20-2 for a representative corporation in a competitive market. Recall that price *(P)* and marginal revenue *(MR)* are identical for competitive firms as reflected in

FIGURE 20-2
Short-Run Incidence of a Corporation Tax

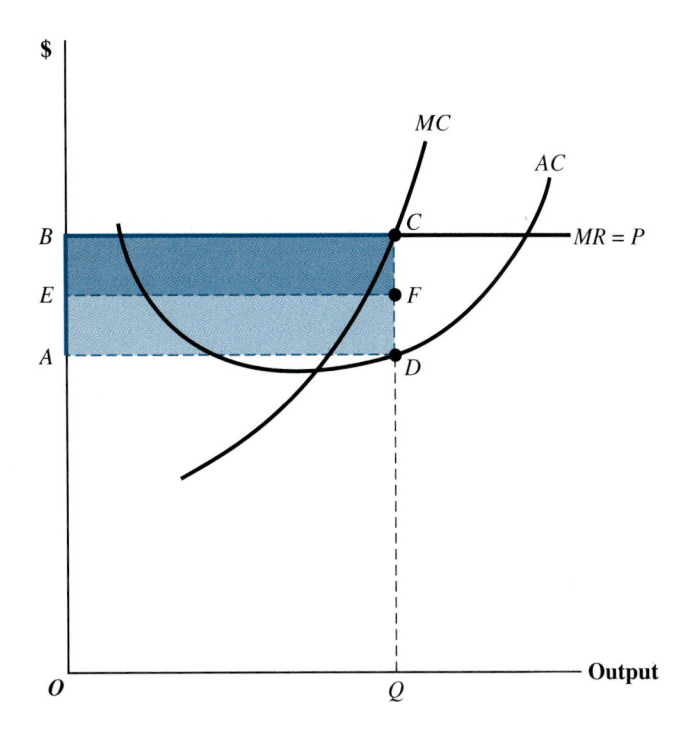

horizontal line $MR = P$. Profit maximization occurs where $MR = MC$ and this firm earns positive economic profit of *ABCD*. Note that stockholders earn rates of return that exceed their opportunity costs, but positive economic profits can only occur in the short run since they are driven to zero by entry of competing firms in the long run.[7]

Now suppose that a tax of *t*, which equals 50 percent, is imposed on corporate economic profit. Such a tax, which seizes one-half of *ABCD*, or *EBCF*, leaves an economic profit of *AEFD*. Notice that this tax does not alter marginal revenue or marginal cost and therefore neither price nor profit maximizing output are affected. The firm continues selling output *Q* at price *P* and, consequently, the burden of taxation falls entirely on stockholders in the form of a lower after-tax rate of return on their capital investments.

Controversy over this conclusion may arise when one rejects the assumption that corporate managers maximize short-run profits. A controversial issue is whether stockholders exert much short-run control over corporate managers who may alter prices and output in the short run and thereby shift some portion of the tax burden onto customers. The empirical evidence is mixed on the shifting issue. One study finds

---

[7] Recall that a normal profit occurs at $P = AC$ since the opportunity costs of capital owners are included in the definition of costs. In other words, any profit that exceeds zero is above normal since it rewards capital owners with a return above their opportunity cost of capital.

Short-run corporate tax incidence occurs before stockholders shift capital resources in response to corporate taxation.

Long-run corporate tax incidence occurs after stockholders shift capital resources in response to corporate taxation.

shifting of more than 100 percent, but others find no evidence of shifting.[8] **Short-run corporate tax incidence** is an important issue, but long-run incidence is even more controversial and receives greater attention in the literature.

Long-Run Incidence[9]

In the long run, stockholders adjust their capital holdings in response to lower after-tax rates of return and therefore short-run tax incidence is likely to differ from **long-run corporate tax incidence.** Assume that two sectors, corporate and noncorporate, exist and that only the corporate sector is subject to an income tax. (We could just as easily assume that, as in the present system, the corporate sector is taxed at a higher rate than the noncorporate sector.) This is a general equilibrium model, one that allows changes in one sector to lead to changes in another sector. We also retain the assumption of perfectly competitive markets. Finally, the supply of all capital inputs is assumed to be fixed at T, and thus the supply of savings is perfectly inelastic.

The supply (S) and demand (D) for loanable funds are plotted in Figure 20-3, where Figure 20-3a shows the corporate sector and 20-3b shows the noncorporate sector. Since this is a general equilibrium model, it shows how capital resources are shifted between sectors in the long run.

Economic theory predicts that returns to saving and investment in both sectors are equalized at a rate of return such as r_1. If this were not true, funds would flow from the lower-return sector to the higher-return sector. Outflows from the lower-return sector would result in higher rates of return, and inflows would depress rates of return in the higher-return sector. Absent transactions costs, funds would continue shifting until rates of return are equalized across sectors.

It is important to understand that, in equilibrium, all capital is distributed between the two sectors. At rate r_1, fixed supply T equals $C_1 + N_1$, which means that C_1 capital is invested in the corporate sector, and N_1 capital is invested in the noncorporate sector.

Now suppose that an income tax of t percent is imposed on the corporate sector. Recalling that a corporation tax lowers the after-tax rate of return to capital, the demand for loanable funds shifts downward from D to D' in the corporate sector. Since the tax rate is a percentage of the market rate of return, the shift is not parallel. In other words, a market return of r becomes an after-tax return of $(1 - t)r$. For example, with $r = 0.10$ and $t = 0.50$, $(1 - t)r = 0.05$; with $r = 0.05$, $(1 - t)r = 0.025$; and with $r = 0.01$, $(1 - t)r = 0.005$. By demonstration, therefore, we have shown that the vertical distance between the demand curves falls for movements down demand curves. For sake of convenience, we refer to r as the market rate of return and $(1 - t)r$ as the after-tax return to investment. Also note that, since the noncorporate sector is not subject to taxation, market and after-tax returns are equal in this sector.

---

[8] The study that demonstrates over 100 percent shifting is Marion Krzyzaniak and Richard Musgrave, *The Shifting of the Corporation Income Tax* (Baltimore: Johns Hopkins Press, 1963). For an example of a study showing no shifting, see John G. Gregg, Arnold C. Harberger, and Peter Mieszkowski, "Empirical Evidence on the Incidence of the Corporation Income Tax," *Journal of Political Economy* 75 (December 1967): 811–821.

[9] This section follows the model introduced in Arnold C. Harberger, "The Incidence of the Corporation Income Tax," *Journal of Political Economy* 70 (June 1962): 215–240.

(a) Corporate Sector

(b) Noncorporate Sector

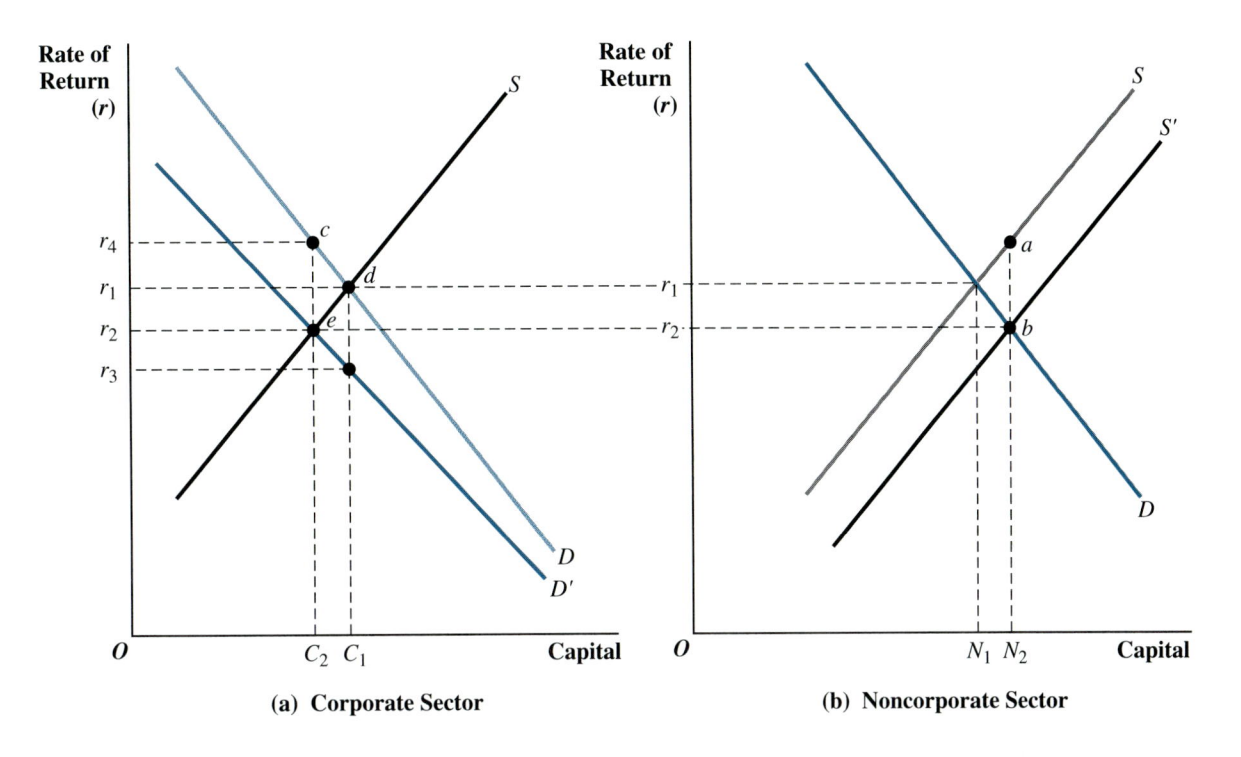

FIGURE 20-3
Long-Run Incidence of Corporation Tax

We first show the short-run response to the corporation tax. Corporate owners are unable to withdraw capital in the short run, so after-tax returns on corporate capital fall to r_3 at the initial capital level of C_1. As shown previously, owners bear the full burden of the corporation tax in the short run. This burden equals the vertical difference between D and D', or r_1r_3, and represents the difference between market and after-tax rates of return.

The tax lowers the after-tax rate of return to corporate capital to r_3, but the noncorporate sector retains a higher return of r_1. This, however, is not a stable outcome since stockholders will shift capital out of the corporate sector and into the noncorporate sector. Funds continue to shift in the long run until returns in both markets are again equalized.

Remember that capital resources are fixed, and shifting of capital out of the corporate sector and into the noncorporate sector therefore causes supply to rise from S to S' in the noncorporate sector. The rate of return on capital falls in this sector from r_1 to r_2 as capital investment rises from N_1 and N_2. An identical change must occur in the corporate sector. Corporate investment falls from C_1 to C_2 and, since its after-tax rate of return rises to r_2, its after-tax rate of return equals that of the noncorporate sector.

Our discussion implies that long-run shifting of capital resources is rapid and easy, but this is not usually the case in practice. Many machines and buildings are designed to handle fairly specific tasks and, in these cases, capital will not flow as easily as when machines and buildings are readily adapted to many different uses. This does not at all suggest that the model is not useful; rather, it simply states the realistic case that what may appear to be a rapid process of capital shifting is more likely to take many years. In cases where capital is designed for unique applications, or for declining industries, worn-out or obsolete capital is just not replaced and, over time, is removed from the capital stock.

Implications for Long-Run Incidence

Our analysis indicates that, *in contrast to the short-run impact, which is felt only in the corporate sector, rates of return in both sectors decline after imposition of a tax on corporate income.* After-tax returns in both sectors fall from r_1 to r_2. In other words, with $t = 0.50$, after-tax returns in both markets fall by 50 percent! The corporate tax is, in effect, a tax on owners of corporate and noncorporate capital alike. Notice that although the market rate of return rises to r_4 in the corporate sector, investors earn only an after-tax rate of $(1 - t)r_4$, which, in this case, equals r_2. The difference, or $r_2 r_4$ here, is the rate of corporate return taxed away by government.

So far we have considered the corporation tax from the point of view of individual investors. It is also important to understand how the tax forces corporate managers to raise market rates of return on their investments. Note that a market return of r_4 is required before managers may attract capital with after-tax returns of r_2. Contrast this with noncorporate managers who, because of equality between market and after-tax returns, need only generate market rates of return of r_2. The corporation tax therefore places corporate managers at a competitive disadvantage in the race for securing capital investment.

Although both corporate and noncorporate managers offer after-tax rates of return of r_2, the corporate manager must achieve higher market rates of return in order to attract capital. This is one reason why the corporation tax is considered a tax on the corporate form of business because it forces corporate capital to generate higher market rates of return than noncorporate capital. The following example demonstrates this point. An after-tax return of 6 percent requires that corporate managers earn 12 percent market returns on investments when the corporation tax rate is 50 percent. In contrast, noncorporate managers need to earn a market return of 6 percent since their earnings are not subject to the corporation tax. Of course, this means that corporations must cut back on lower-return investments and also explains why corporate investment activity falls from C_1 to C_2. As capital is shifted out of the corporate sector, other sectors, such as housing and noncorporate forms of business, receive more capital.

There are also effects exerted on consumers of these markets. As capital flows out of the corporate sector, output falls as well, and this raises prices of corporate goods. But prices will fall as well in the noncorporate sector as its capital investment rises and increases output in these markets. For individual consumers, the net effect on these opposing price changes depends upon the size of the price changes and the relative shares of corporate and noncorporate goods in their budgets. Many believe that the two effects wash each other out and therefore conclude that the corporation tax imposes little burden on consumers.

Burdens could also be placed on labor and suppliers of other inputs. For instance, if we relax the assumption of a fixed capital stock, the corporation tax could reduce the capital stock as after-tax rates of return fall in all sectors of the economy. A lower capital stock would lower wages since the marginal product of workers is positively linked to the level of capital investment in their industries. One study finds evidence of this effect and therefore concludes that a large share of the corporation tax is ultimately borne by workers.[10] It is safe to say, however, that much controversy exists over this conclusion.

In sum, there is no consensus on who ultimately bears the burden of corporation taxation. Many believe that owners of capital bear the burden, but this conclusion does not easily indicate how tax burdens are distributed across different taxpayers. It may be convenient to assume that most capital owners are wealthy, but this is a gross generalization. Remember, many lower-income individuals are hidden owners of capital. For instance, much of the capital stock is owned by pension funds, a fact that means they are ultimately owned by lower-income, as well as higher-income, workers. And we have shown that the burden of the corporation tax does not discriminate between corporate and noncorporate sectors. There is no reason to believe that it will discriminate between high-income and low-income individuals either, and therefore it is difficult to gauge the progressivity of burdens across a wide and diffuse population of capital owners.

Excess Burden

Excess burden of taxation refers to additional costs that arise when taxation causes misallocation of resources.[11] This may be easily shown by reinspection of Figure 20-3. At investment of C_2 in the corporate sector, marginal social return is r_4, but marginal social cost is only r_2.[12] This divergence means that there is too little corporate investment since additional investment to C_1 would yield gains in net social benefits. Pretax corporate investment was C_1 and, because it is consistent with allocative efficiency, indicates that taxation creates an excess burden when corporate investment falls below C_1. Too little investment in the corporate sector also means too much investment in the noncorporate sector. This may be shown by noting that, at N_2, marginal social benefit (*b*) falls below marginal social cost (*a*); therefore net social benefits would rise with less investment in the noncorporate sector.

Triangle *cde* measures excess burden in the corporate sector. (Similar analysis can also be done in the noncorporate sector.) Excess burden has been estimated to be roughly 12 percent of tax revenues generated by the corporation tax.[13] In other words, for every dollar raised in corporate tax collection, another 12 cents is consumed in the process of taxation.

---

[10] J. Gregory Ballentine, "The Incidence of a Corporation Income Tax in a Growing Economy," *Journal of Political Economy* 86 (October 1978): 863–876.

[11] Allocative efficiency is the condition whereby resources cannot be reallocated in a manner that increases total net social benefits. Allocative efficiency is consistent with intersection of supply and demand curves in private markets since resources are allocated until marginal social benefits are equal to marginal social costs. Private markets, however, do not usually achieve allocative efficiency when taxes are placed on consumers or producers.

[12] Note that taxation caused the downward shift in demand from D to D', but demand D still corresponds to the marginal social benefit of investment. Demand D', in contrast, refers to the after-tax rate of return and is plotted from the point of private individuals only.

[13] John B. Shoven, "The Incidence and Efficiency Effects of Taxes on Income from Capital," *Journal of Political Economy* 84 (December 1976): 1261–1283.

The capital stock, however, is probably responsive to changes in after-tax rates of return and therefore the corporation tax also lowers the national capital stock or encourages capital to flow to other countries in search of higher after-tax rates of return. There is fairly broad support for this proposition, and the corporation tax therefore creates additional distortions. Aggregate excess burdens are believed to be many times larger than the 12 percent figure just described. One study, for instance, estimates that aggregate excess burdens are as much as 33 percent of tax revenues; such an outcome would mean that, in order to raise $100 million in corporate tax collections, $133 million in resources would have been consumed.[14]

Reform of the Corporation Tax

Why Tax Corporations?

A popular argument for the corporation tax is that it forces corporations to pay taxes. This argument is often based on the notion that retained earnings are not taxed, and this is true. It should be remembered, however, that it is only true under a short-term definition of corporate income. Retained earnings are actually granted deferred taxation since they contribute to capital gains that, when realized by stockholders, are taxed at the time when stock is sold. Retained earnings therefore escape taxation only when income is measured on a year-to-year basis.

It is important to remember that policy can only tax individuals, and it may therefore appear that abstract entities such as corporations are subject to separate taxation, but incidence ultimately falls on individuals, not corporations. Our discussion of tax incidence has shown that long-run progressivity of the corporation tax is not entirely clear-cut either. In addition, the corporation tax is believed to create relatively high excess burdens when compared against other taxes.

The tone of this discussion indicates that many economists believe that reform, if not elimination, of the corporation tax is long overdue. Unsurprisingly, they have also proposed various reforms.

Which Directions for Reform?

Very few proposals suggest complete elimination of the corporation tax even though many economists believe that it should be completely integrated into the personal income tax. Most proposals recommend an improved linkage between economic depreciation and depreciation schedules, reducing the differential between effective tax rates on personal income and corporate income, indexing depreciation schedules for inflation, and eliminating the double taxation of corporate dividend income. In 1992, for instance, the U.S. Treasury Department recommended elimination of the double taxation of corporate income by reforming the corporation tax code so that it

---

[14] J. Gregory Ballentine, *Equity, Efficiency, and the U.S. Corporation Income Tax* (Washington, D.C.: American Enterprise Institute, 1980).

would no longer tax dividends at the level of personal income, but rather only at the level of the corporation.[15]

Transition problems with revising a tax system is one reason that many of these recommendations have not been approved. Current and past investment decisions have been driven by existing tax laws, and a comprehensive overhaul of our current tax system is sure to produce many winners and losers. Many of these transition problems may be avoided or lessened by slowly, but clearly, phasing in reforms over time. The 1986 Tax Reform Act, for example, eliminated interest expense deductions on consumer loans and credit cards over a number of years. Phase in of reforms is certain to attract wide support from many critics of the current corporation tax, and it will be interesting to see whether many of their recommendations appear in the near future.

Summary

- Corporate dividends are subject to double taxation. They are first taxed at the corporate level since, by not deducting them from taxable income, corporations pay tax on them. They are also taxed when stockholders receive them as a source of personal taxable income. Interest expenses, however, on corporate debt are deductible expenses and therefore are exempt from the corporation tax.
- Economic depreciation is the process by which capital resources are consumed or made obsolete over time. Statutory depreciation schedules specify rates at which capital resources may be deducted from taxable income over designated tax lives. Expensing allows depreciation of all costs during the first year of purchase of capital resources. Straight-line depreciation allows for a uniform percentage of costs to be deducted over each year of a tax life.
- Shorter tax lives provide greater tax relief than longer tax lives. Holding tax lives constant, quicker rates of depreciation provide greater tax relief than slower rates of depreciation.
- Statutory tax rates and effective tax rates normally differ. Effective tax rates are calculated by dividing tax liability by a comprehensive measure of income. Statutory tax rates are calculated by dividing tax liability by taxable income.

- Preferential tax treatment is awarded to debt finance since it is cheaper, on an after-tax basis, than financing through equity or retained earnings. The corporation tax therefore biases financing decisions in the direction of debt finance.
- Dividends are subject to immediate taxation, but taxation of retained earnings is deferred to the future. Tax policy misallocates capital when stockholders would have gained greater return on their income when distributed in dividends rather than retained earnings.
- Capital is misallocated when broad groups of capital resources are subject to uniform depreciation schedules. Tax policy distorts investment decisions because they are based, to some degree, on how generous or miserly are depreciation schedules.
- Statutory incidence of the corporation tax is assigned to stockholders since they are owners of corporations. In the short run, it is commonly believed that economic incidence falls on stockholders. Long-run incidence falls on all owners of capital because after-tax rates of return fall by the same amount in both corporate and noncorporate sectors. Excess burden arises because the corporation tax encourages too much investment in the noncorporate sector and too little investment in the corporate sector.

---

[15] U.S. Department of the Treasury, *Restructuring the U.S. Tax System for the 21st Century: An Option for Fundamental Reform,* December 1992. For a discussion of many of its proposals, see R. Glenn Hubbard, "Corporate Tax Integration: A View from the Treasury Department," *Journal of Economic Perspectives* 7 (Winter 1993): 115–132.

Review Questions

1. What is straight-line depreciation?
2. What are the major ways to finance corporate expansion?
3. What is the difference between receiving earnings in the form of dividends versus receiving them as retained earnings?
4. What are the major arguments against corporation taxation?
5. What are the major arguments in favor of corporation taxation?
6. What are the major proposals for reform of the corporation tax?

Discussion Questions

1. Explain how a comprehensive measure of personal income would include the income earned by corporations.
2. What are dividends? In what way are dividends subject to double taxation?
3. Why is depreciation a deductible expense of corporations? Would a firm favor a longer or short tax life when calculating deductions for depreciation? Is it true that more rapid depreciation would favor longer-term investments?
4. Explain why there is an inverse relation between tax lives and tax relief. Provide an example that demonstrates your answer.
5. In what way does inflation decrease the ability of firms to replace capital through capital consumption allowances?
6. Explain why corporation taxes must be paid by individuals. Does this imply that burdens of the corporation tax are fully borne by owners of corporations?
7. Explain how the corporation tax distorts the firm's choices regarding the financing of new investment. Explain how this might raise the likelihood of corporate bankruptcy.
8. Explain why the entire short-term burden of the corporation tax falls upon its owners.
9. Discuss why the long-term effect of the corporation tax is to lower the after-tax rates of return to all capital owners.
10. Would corporations be less vulnerable to economic downturns if a higher percentage of financing came through equity rather than debt?
11. Explain why it is difficult to determine how the burdens of the corporation tax are distributed among the population.
12. Why does the corporation tax create an excess burden? What policies might reduce the excess burden of corporate taxation?

Key Words

Corporations
Dividends
Double taxation
Short-lived resources
Long-lived resources
Economic depreciation
Statutory depreciation
Tax life
Expensing
Straight-line depreciation
Double-declining balance
Statutory tax rates
Effective tax rates
Debt heavy
Retained earnings
Short-run corporate tax incidence
Long-run corporate tax incidence

CHAPTER 21

Taxation of Consumption and Wealth

In this final chapter on taxation we examine taxation of consumption and wealth. Although these are important sources of revenue—especially for state and local governments—they are also believed to encourage desirable behavior on the part of citizens. Because consumption taxes, including sales taxes and value-added taxes, apply only to income that is consumed, they encourage saving and investment. Taxes on wealth, which include estate, gift, and property taxes, apply to transfers and ownership of property

We raise the following questions in our examination of consumption and wealth taxation:

❑ How would the tax base of a consumption tax differ from that of the income tax?
❑ What advantages do consumption taxes offer over income taxes?
❑ How does a VAT tax operate? What are its advantages over income taxes?
❑ Why should transfers of wealth be taxed?
❑ What are the economic effects of property taxation?

Consumption Taxes

Sales Tax Collections

In our discussion of tax incidence and excess burden in Chapter 16 we focused on consumption taxes, applying these basic principles of tax analysis to unit and *ad valorem* taxes. Unit taxes are consumption or excise taxes levied on a per unit basis. Gasoline, for example, is assessed on the basis of gallons purchased, and cigarettes on the basis of packs purchased. Unit tax revenues are calculated by multiplying the tax rate by the number of units purchased. Thus, if the federal gasoline tax rate is 18.4 cents per gallon, it generates tax revenue of $0.184 \times 10 = \$1.84$ for every 10-gallon purchase.

Ad valorem taxes, in contrast, are based on sales volume. The state sales tax in Virginia, for instance, is 3.5 percent, so $3.50 in tax revenue is collected on each $100 of sales. Although *ad valorem* taxes may be assessed on specific goods and services, such as cigarettes or gasoline, they are more commonly levied on all sales of goods and services. This probably explains why most people think of a sales tax when they think of an *ad valorem* tax. Only five states (Alaska, Delaware, Montana, New Hampshire, and Oregon) do not levy a general sales tax.

At the federal level, most sales tax revenues come from taxes on purchases of gasoline, cigarettes and alcoholic beverages, and on usage of telecommunications, electricity, and water. These are examples of unit taxes since they are levied on units of consumption. Federal *ad valorem* taxes are also imposed on such items as sport fishing equipment (10 percent), air passenger tickets (10 percent), local telephone service (3 percent), and bows and arrows (11 percent). Recent, and highly controversial, *ad valorem* taxes were legislated by Congress in 1990. Dubbed luxury taxes, they collected 10 percent on the amount of price over $30,000 on automobiles, $100,000 for boats, $250,000 for airplanes, and $10,000 for furs and jewelry. With the exception of the tax on automobiles, these taxes were rescinded in 1993.

Table 21-1 presents sales tax collections since 1950 for all levels of government. The top portion of the table shows that tax collections have grown for each level of government. The lower portion shows the importance of sales tax revenues in tax collection efforts. The following trends are indicated over this period:

❑ Federal sales tax collections have fallen from roughly 18 percent to 5 percent of total tax collections.

TABLE 21-1
Sales Tax Collections by Government

	$Billions of Revenues		
Year	Federal	State	Local
1950	$ 7.8	$ 4.1	$ 0.4
1960	12.6	10.5	1.3
1970	18.3	27.2	3.1
1980	32.0	68.2	12.1
1990	54.0	147.0	31.0

	Percentage of Total Revenues		
Year	Federal	State	Local
1950	18.3%	51.9%	5.0%
1960	12.7	58.3	7.2
1970	8.8	56.7	7.9
1980	5.6	49.8	14.0
1990	4.8	49.0	15.4

Source: Advisory Commission on Intergovernmental Relations, *Significant Features of Fiscal Federalism,* vol. 2, September 1992.

- ❏ State sales tax collections have remained fairly stable at roughly 50 percent of total tax collections.
- ❏ Local sales tax collections have risen from 5 to 15 percent of total tax collections.

These trends indicate that sales taxes are most important for state governments. Although much less important, sales taxes have become increasingly important as a revenue source of local governments. By comparison, sales taxes are a fairly small revenue source for the federal government and one whose relative importance has also declined rapidly since 1950.

National Consumption Taxation

Arguments in Favor

By definition, *sources* of income must equal *uses* of income. Income sources include salaries, wages, interest income, and dividends earned on ownership of stock. *Income uses* is a term used to define the ways in which income is spent or saved; it therefore includes consumption and savings. Unit taxes on cigarettes or gasoline, for instance, are consumption taxes, since they are levied on uses of a taxpayer's income. The personal income tax, in contrast, is not a consumption tax: Tax liability does not change when a taxpayer spends little or much of income on goods and services. Income tax liability, for instance, does not change when a taxpayer stops smoking or driving a car.

It may seem that since sources must equal uses, the decision to tax income sources or income uses is an arbitrary one. But many economists conclude that national taxes on income uses, or **national consumption taxes,** have significant advantages over taxes on income sources.[1] A principal advantage of a national consumption tax is that, unlike present income tax policy, it does not discourage saving. Sales taxes are paid only when taxpayers choose to consume, rather than save, some portion of their income. When income is saved, therefore, it is not subjected to taxation. For this reason, consumption taxes are commonly advocated as a cure for the national savings shortfall that many believe to be a serious problem area in the United States.

A comprehensive consumption tax, which is often called an **expenditure tax,** would tax all income less genuine, or allowed, saving. This is quite different from the present income tax system, which exempts, or defers, only a few savings sources for taxation. Contributions into Individual Retirement Accounts, which are subject to ceilings and available to only a portion of workers, are one of the few cases in which the income tax system encourages taxpayers to save. Most forms of interest income are subject to income taxation and tax liability is unaffected by decisions made about whether to reinvest interest earnings or raise present consumption. The current income tax system therefore distorts saving and investment choices.

Under a comprehensive consumption tax, taxation of all saving is deferred until savings are cashed in by taxpayers. Similarly, interest earned on savings is subject to taxation only when it leads to consumption. A comprehensive consumption tax is therefore argued to promote a larger capital stock since it encourages saving.

National consumption taxes are federal taxes levied on the consumption of goods and services.

Expenditure tax is a comprehensive consumption tax.

---

[1] See, for example, David F. Bradford, *Untangling the Income Tax* (Cambridge, Mass.: Harvard University Press, 1986).

How Well Do We Really Want "Sin" Taxes to Work?

Past calls for higher sin taxes, mainly on tobacco and alcohol, have been primarily motivated as measures that lower the budget deficit by raising tax revenues. Higher sin taxes have also been forwarded as a policy to lower consumption of tobacco and alcohol. But are the two goals compatible? On the one hand, tax revenue collections are positively related to the number of users of tobacco and alcohol. The extent to which a given tax increase yields higher revenues is therefore dependent upon consumption levels. Simply put, higher consumption yields higher tax revenues. On the other hand, higher taxes discourage consumption and therefore result in lower tax revenue gains. This is simply the result of the law of demand, which states that, with all else remaining the same, an inverse relation exists between the price of a good and its quantity of consumption.

Sources: Rick Wartzman, "Clinton's Proposal for 'Sin Taxes' May Stumble by Turning Too Many Americans into Saints," *Wall Street Journal*, April 20, 1993, A16; and Pierre Lemieux, "Canada's Taxing Pols Outwitted by Underground Economy," *Wall Street Journal*, April 8, 1994, A15.

Analysis

Advocates of higher sin taxes argue that jobs—tending bar, waiting tables, selling tobacco products, farming—are lost as alcohol and tobacco consumption are discouraged, but various benefits of higher taxes are believed to occur in the areas of lower health costs, fewer traffic accidents and fatalities, and lower law enforcement costs. In addition, Kenneth Warner, an economist at the University of Michigan, argues that "by increasing price, we can avoid having people addicted in the first place . . . while generating enormous revenues."

A major criticism of higher sin taxes comes from those who argue that it is more regressive than most other taxes. Another criticism is that higher taxes encourage the underground economy whereby consumers of tobacco and alcohol are more tempted to purchase from sellers who do not report their income to the IRS. This was certainly an effect of prohibition of alcohol sales in the 1920s and 1930s in the United States. Further, crime fighting became another by-product of the policy.

Perhaps the recent experience of Canada holds some clues as to the effects of higher sin taxes in the United States. As higher taxes have raised the price of a pack of cigarettes from $1.74 (U.S.) to $4.43, smoking has fallen by 40 percent. But this figure is quite deceiving because it is based on retail sales of Canadian merchants. Higher cigarette prices led to an enormous expansion of smuggling. It has recently been estimated that 40 percent of all cigarettes were purchased across the border in the United States where prices were half those in Canada. This led the Canadian government to cut the tax in half on February 8, 1994, as it became apparent that the underground economy had won the battle over higher cigarette taxes.

Another advantage of a national consumption tax is seen by those who believe that the federal government should play an active role in controlling the consumption habits of its citizens. Sales taxes discourage consumption when they raise prices of goods and services subjected to taxation. There are several possible rationales for controlling consumption through sales taxes. One is that certain behaviors, such as smoking and drinking of alcoholic beverages, may be socially undesirable, not so much from a personal view (obnoxiousness) as from a social one (risks to health, safety, and life). Consumption taxes may also be used to control negative externalities that arise when private and social costs of certain activities diverge. Externalities arise, for example, when roads become congested or air becomes polluted and, for this reason, sales taxes lower externalities by discouraging activities that generate externalities.

Finally, it is also argued that tax administration is often simpler under national consumption taxation than it is under income taxation. A consumption tax is simple to collect because, in most cases, it is collected at the point of sale—for example, when a driver purchases gasoline from a gas station or a family dines in a restaurant. You will recall that previous discussion of personal and corporate income taxation concluded that, despite recent attempts at simplification, the income tax code has become increasingly complex. With its many forms to fill out, records to keep and various deadlines to meet, taxation of income is often believed to be more complex than consumption taxation.

Arguments Against

There are obvious problems in administering consumption taxes at the national level. Every state that has a sales tax allows various exemptions. California, for instance, exempts food, prescription drugs, consumer electric and gas utilities, custom computer programs, repair charges, and installation services from taxation. Even within broad categories of exemptions, there are various exceptions. In most states, for example, food is exempted only when it is not purchased for on-premise consumption. A doughnut, for example, is subject to a consumption tax when it is consumed in a diner, but not if the consumer buys it at the local grocery and eats it in the car or at home. Policy decisions concerning which goods and services to exempt from taxation may raise concerns that a national consumption tax is often arbitrarily imposed.

Another problem in administration is that sales tax rates tend to be uniform in practice. You will recall, however, that the Ramsey pricing principle demonstrates that for a given level of tax revenue, minimization of excess burden requires that higher tax rates be assigned to more inelastic demands than for elastic demands.[2] Application of this principle therefore requires that tax rates be set in inverse relation to price elasticities of demand, a condition that implies that tax rates will vary substantially across markets.

Sales tax rates, however, tend to be uniform for several reasons. A primary reason is that many of the so-called necessities have relatively inelastic demands and therefore would require relatively high tax rates under Ramsey pricing. Many would argue, however, that this places undue burdens on the poor, who must allocate a relatively high percentage of their budgets to necessities. It may also be argued that it is unfair to set differential tax rates across markets and, as we have seen many times before, the public may not be particularly interested in designing an efficient tax code.

---

[2] This follows from the fact that excess burdens are higher for elastic demands than for inelastic demands.

Perceptions of equity often takes a commanding role in setting tax rates, as is entirely consistent with application of the ability-to-pay principle.

Assessment of the Issues

Many of the arguments for and against consumption taxes are based on comparisons between an idealized consumption tax versus the current income tax system. It is true that current income tax policy discourages saving because it does not index capital gains for inflation and double taxes corporate dividends, once as corporate income and again as personal income. But in principle, saving could be encouraged through a national sales tax as well as through substantial reform of the income tax system. Recent proposals, for instance, have recommended that capital gains be indexed for inflation and that corporate income be taxed only once. To imply that saving may only be fostered through substitution of a consumption tax for an income tax is an empty argument that presumes that the current income tax system cannot be reformed in a way that encourages saving.

It is also unrealistic to assume that a national consumption tax will not be designed with many exemptions and, in this way, it would be no different from the federal income system, which has a long and complex list of tax exemptions, tax deferrals, and tax credits. Exemptions on the use side of income are no different in principle from those that exist on the source side of income. These are all tax expenditures that provide tax relief to taxpayers. When various uses, such as food consumption, are exempted from taxation, or when taxation is deferred, tax expenditures are created in the consumption tax code.

Tax expenditures may easily promote various social policies. For instance, oat bran may be exempted from consumption taxation because it is believed to provide many health benefits. Housing could just as easily be promoted by exempting all mortgage payments from taxation. Note, however, that as more exemptions are provided, the tax base falls and may lead to higher tax rates that, in addition to raising excess burden, may lessen tax simplicity—which, you will recall, is one of the attractions of a consumption tax.

It should also be kept in mind that many policymakers who advocate a national consumption tax are not proposing that the consumption tax replace the existing income tax system. Rather, they view the national sales tax as a means of generating additional tax revenues that will lower the federal budget deficit.[3] Although it may be true that, at the margin, it is more desirable to raise revenues through a national consumption tax than through an income tax, this argument presumes that raising additional tax revenues is an appropriate end to itself. We must be careful, therefore, to separate these two issues: (1) Is a national consumption tax more desirable than a national income tax? (2) Should a national consumption tax be used to expand aggregate tax collection? These are not identical questions.

Finally, perceptions of equity are important factors in the choice between a national consumption tax and an income tax, and it is therefore appropriate to question

---

[3] Recall, however, the discussion of the tax-spend relation in Chapter 17, which indicated that substantial controversy surrounds the ability of a tax increase to lower a budget deficit.

whether the public perceives either tax system to be a better application of the ability-to-pay principle. Many people appear to assess ability to pay in terms of income, and a national consumption tax may therefore be perceived to be less equitable than the present income tax. This observation appears well founded in light of the many controversies that arose when President Bill Clinton first proposed a broad energy tax in his 1994 budget. It was predicted that this tax increase would raise $70 billion over five years by taxing consumption of all energy uses, but it was quickly scrapped for a more modest increase in gasoline taxes when sharp opposition arose on all sides of the voting public. Consumption taxes are traditionally viewed as regressive in nature, and this explains much of the opposition to President Clinton's proposal.

Are Consumption Taxes Regressive?

A cornerstone of tax policy is the concept of vertical equity, which is the belief that burdens of taxation should rise with ability to pay. One criticism of consumption taxes is that they are believed to be regressive; that is, tax burdens rise more slowly than increases in ability to pay. This belief follows from the observation that the poor tend to consume most of their income and therefore tend to pay taxes on a larger proportion of their income than do higher-income taxpayers who save a larger proportion of their income.

While, in principle, consumption taxes could promote greater progressivity by basing tax rates on income, this would greatly complicate the system. For example, an individual simply trying to buy some gasoline or groceries may be required to show the merchant an official statement of personal income level before the merchant knows which tax rate to levy on the previously simple purchases. This could presumably lead to greater tax burdens on higher-income taxpayers but would also require a cumbersome tax system as well.

Several issues complicate the question of whether consumption taxes are regressive. First, you will recall that tax shifting describes cases in which taxpayers shift, onto other individuals, some portion of their tax burdens. When taxes are placed on buyers of clothing, for example, some portion of the tax may be shifted onto sellers. Many taxes, whether levied on income or consumption, are subject to some shifting, and therefore determination of tax incidence is a much more difficult matter than provided by a simple knowledge of statutory incidence. This may be especially true when many goods are exempted from consumption taxation.

Another problem is that tax liabilities are usually compared against annual, rather than lifetime, income. It is well accepted, for example, that individuals tend to save more, and therefore consume less, during middle age than during their youth or retirement. A principal reason for this is that they reach their earnings peak during middle age. Moreover, young people just getting started tend to need high-ticket items such as furniture, appliances, and housing. The elderly tend to have to spend heavily on health care and retirement housing. For a given individual, therefore, consumption habits will change dramatically over a lifetime, and a simple snapshot taken at one point in time offers an incomplete picture of this person's consumption and savings behavior. When people's expenditures are measured in their early working or retirement years, the ratio of consumption to income is much larger than in their middle years. Therefore, burdens imposed by a consumption tax appear higher during these years than during the middle years. This discussion demonstrates that regressivity is better measured on the basis of lifetime, rather than annual, income. A recent study of consumption taxation in Canada has indicated that burdens are less regressive when calculated on the basis of lifetime income.[4]

A final consideration is that most studies of tax incidence do not consider the benefits that taxpayers receive from public expenditure policies. It is clear, however, that conclusions about tax equity should not be entirely based on tax bills. A rich taxpayer, for instance, may pay consumption taxes of $100,000 on an income of $350,000 (or 29 percent of income) and receive $50,000 in benefits from public expenditure policies. A poor individual, in contrast, may pay $1,000 in consumption taxes on an income of $3,000 (or 33.3 percent of income) and receive $5,000 in benefits. Therefore simple consideration of tax bill–income ratios need not convey much information on how regressive or progressive a national consumption tax would be; this problem complicates the issue for income taxation as well.

Value-Added Taxes

Value-added tax (VAT) is tax collected at various stages during the production of goods and services.

The **value-added tax,** or **VAT,** is a major revenue source in more than 50 countries. A VAT operates like a retail sales tax, except that it is collected at the various stages of production of goods and services. Taxes collected at each production stage are normally determined by the value added by labor, land, and capital. Although the VAT is not used in the United States, it is a major revenue source in 20 of the 25 OECD countries.

Support for introducing the VAT into the tax system of the United States is growing. Advocates base their recommendation on several arguments. One argument—and probably the least persuasive—is that the United States should adopt it because so many other countries have. This is clearly not a compelling argument, but nonetheless one that is heard frequently. It is also argued that a VAT promotes saving and a larger capital stock, since it taxes consumption rather than saving. Another argument is that the VAT is a fairly simple method of collecting substantial revenues, which would, in turn, lead to substantial savings for tax authorities. Critics of the VAT are fearful of its superior ability to raise revenue and predict that its fairly hidden nature would promote overexpansion of the public sector. Before we examine these arguments, we first discuss how a VAT operates.

Mechanics of a VAT

The most common way to operate a VAT is to tax goods as they travel among stages of production. By taxing the value added at each stage, the final value of the good is eventually taxed. Most VATs are based on the same principles, and the following

---

[4] James Davies, France St-Hilaire, and John Whalley, "Some Calculations of Lifetime Tax Incidence," *American Economic Review* 74 (September 1984): 633–649.

example, which uses the credit method, conforms to VATs used by most OECD countries.[5]

Table 21-2 shows how a VAT of 10 percent works in the simple case of a three-stage production process that flows from the manufacturer to the wholesaler and ends at the retailer.[6] The particular good being produced could be cookies, bicycles, or any other good. We assume that the manufacturer purchases nothing from any other firm and then sells only to the wholesaler. Retailers are also assumed to purchase only from wholesalers and then to sell only to consumers. For comparison purposes, the bottom of Table 21-2 shows how a retail sales tax of 10 percent would operate.

The key to the VAT is that invoices are created at each production stage. Firms are liable only for the difference between VAT paid on purchases and VAT charged on sales. Invoices keep track of which credits firms are allowed. Firms subtract the VAT paid on purchases (the credit) since it represents the tax liability in the previous stage of production. Taxes are therefore collected only on values added at each stage of production.

Now back to our example. The manufacturer collects $50 in VAT on sales of $500 (10 percent) to the wholesaler and can claim no credits, since there have been no purchases from another firm. In other words, the manufacturer occupies the first position in the production process and is liable for the entire $50 in VAT. The wholesaler then collects $80 in VAT on sales of $800 to the retailer but can claim a credit of $50, which represents the VAT paid on purchases from the manufacturer. The net VAT paid by the wholesaler is therefore $30, the difference between VAT paid on sales and VAT paid on purchases. The retailer occupies the final position and may collect $100 on sales of $1,000 to consumers. But since the retailer claims a credit of $80 for VAT paid on its purchases, the retailer's net tax liability is only $20. When the value of net VAT liabilities is added up over all three stages of production, the government receives $100 in VAT revenue.

Notice the similarity between the VAT of 10 percent and a general sales tax of 10 percent. The government collects $100 in tax revenue in either case, since both generate revenues equal to 10 percent of final sales. One difference, however, is that a VAT is levied on firms, and a sales tax is levied on consumers. Despite these obvious differences in statutory incidence, we must remember that economic incidence is unaffected by who is legally responsible for collecting the tax for the government.

Advantages of a VAT

An important advantage of a VAT over a general sales tax is that it presents fewer tax evasion concerns. Much of retail sales is conducted through cash transactions that are relatively easy to conceal from tax authorities. Our example of the VAT, however, shows that a large portion of tax revenue is collected before production reaches the retail level. There is also an incentive for firms to monitor payments of taxes made by other firms since they wish to claim as large of a VAT credit as possible when they

---

[5] Other methods, such as the subtraction method and addition method, are also used; see, for example, Congressional Budget Office, *Effects of Adopting a Value-added Tax,* February 1992.

[6] This discussion closely follows that in CBO's *Effects of Adopting a Value-Added Tax.*

TABLE 21-2
Taxing Consumer Purchases: VAT versus Retail Sales Tax

	Production Stage		
	Manufacturer	Wholesaler	Retailer
1. Sales (excluding VAT)	$500	$800	$1,000
2. Purchases (excluding VAT)	0	500	800
3. Tax on sales (10%)	50	80	100
4. Credit on purchases	0	50	80
5. VAT Owed (3 to 4)	50	30	20	$100
	Retail Sales Tax		
1. Sales (excluding sales tax)	500	800	1,000
2. Sales tax owed (10%)	0	0	100	$100

Source: A slight variation of a table presented in Congressional Budget Office, *Effects of Adopting a Value-Added Tax,* February 1992.

calculate the final value of their net VAT liability. Finally, in comparison to the present income tax system, the VAT encourages saving and investment since it is a tax on consumption, not on saving.

The VAT's Taxable Base

At least two reasons suggest the importance of designing as broad a taxable base as possible. One reason is that a broad-based tax does not unduly burden those who consume much of their income within the tax base. A tax base that excludes all purchases of automobiles except for station wagons may unduly discriminate against large families, who are more apt to purchase station wagons than small families or single individuals. Another reason is that a broader base allows for lower tax rates. The higher are tax rates, the higher are excess burdens, which arise when tax policy distorts consumption and saving choices made by taxpayers. A recent study estimates that replacing part of the personal income tax system with a broad-based VAT would lower annual excess burden in the economy by roughly 1 percent of national output.[7]

It is highly improbable, however, that the tax base for a VAT would include all consumption goods. We have seen that tax bases for retail sales and income contain many tax expenditures, and there is no reason to believe that this would not be the case for a VAT. Tax expenditures could simply be offered either through exemptions from paying VAT or by lowering tax rates to certain firms. The Congressional Budget Office has recently suggested that the broadest base would most likely include three-fourths of total consumption which, at a tax rate of 5 percent, would have raised $101 billion in revenue in 1988.[8]

---

[7] Charles L. Ballard, John K. Scholz, and John B. Shoven, "The Value-Added Tax: A General Equilibrium Look at Its Efficiency and Incidence," in *The Effects of Taxation on Capital Accumulation,* ed. Martin Feldstein (Chicago: University of Chicago Press, 1987).

[8] CBO, *Effects of Adopting a Value-Added Tax,* February 1992.

Several factors are likely to determine tax expenditure policies under a VAT. First, it is likely that the same reasons that generally exclude food, prescription drugs, consumer electric and gas utilities, and other such items from the general sales tax would also exclude them from the taxable base of the VAT. The usual reason for these exclusions is that they represent relatively large percentages of incomes of the poor, and their exclusion from the taxable base is therefore based on equity considerations. Second, certain areas, such as housing, are likely to be excluded to encourage their consumption. One often sees government policy encouraging various socially desirable activities; there is little question that this would be continued under a VAT.

Notice, however, that as more tax expenditures are legislated, the VAT's relative advantage in raising national savings falls. Remember that a VAT may promote saving over consumption only so long as consumption stays in the tax base and saving stays out of the tax base. But as more consumption activities are exempted, more consumption activities are encouraged. In other words, a VAT creates few distortions of saving decisions only when it includes all consumption activities in the tax base. When a VAT contains many tax expenditures, it may tend to discourage saving indirectly when it encourages more consumption than would otherwise occur under a comprehensive consumption tax base.

Little Support for a VAT in the United States

Despite many apparent advantages, the VAT has never received consistent support in the United States. The U.S. Treasury, for instance, did not include it in the 1986 Tax Reform Act. While it has been recently reintroduced within the public debate over financing of health care reform, the Clinton administration quickly dropped it when it drew intense criticism by all ends of the political spectrum.[9]

Two principal criticisms of the VAT endure in the United States. The first is that the VAT is a regressive tax, since tax bills take a larger share of lower-income taxpayers' incomes than they take from higher-income taxpayers. Recall, however, that regressivity tends to be overstated since it may be more appropriate to calculate tax burdens over lifetime income rather than on an annual basis. The Congressional Budget Office finds that, on the basis of annual income, families in the bottom quintile of income would bear burdens of a VAT that are three times larger than burdens on families in the top quintile of income.[10] The VAT, however, is found to be less regressive when lifetime income is substituted for annual income.

The other major criticism is that the VAT's superior revenue-generating capabilities would lead to overexpansion of the public sector.[11] There is some evidence that

---

[9] Michael K. Frisby, "VAT Possibility Is Reconsidered at White House," *Wall Street Journal,* April 15, 1993, A2.

[10] Congressional Budget Office, *Reducing the Deficit Spending and Revenue Options,* February 1993.

[11] There is also the issue of administrative and compliance costs. The Congressional Budget Office estimates that adoption of a European-style VAT would cost $750 million to $1.5 billion per year in administrative costs and another $4 billion to $7 billion in compliance costs; see CBO, *Reducing the Deficit.*

tax revenues grow more rapidly in countries that adopt the VAT.[12] When, for instance, many European countries adopted the VAT in the late 1960s, taxes as shares of national income in those countries rose much more rapidly than in countries that did not adopt the VAT.

There are two views, however, about the VAT's apparent ability to expand tax collections. The view held by critics of the VAT is that because the VAT is a hidden tax that escapes the notice of taxpayers, voters underestimate true tax burdens and therefore support additional spending made possible by expansion of tax revenues. There are legitimate questions, for instance, regarding the visibility of the VAT compared against taxes on retail sales or income. Consumers receive itemized sales receipts listing sales taxes paid at points of sale. Similarly, income tax bills are fully detailed on tax forms. The VAT, however, is paid at each stage of production, and it is unlikely that consumers will have ready access to the many invoices that a VAT normally creates through each stage of production. In some cases, there may be hundreds of production stages, many of which are unknown by any particular firm along the production line. As Ronald Reagan once put it, the VAT "gives the government a chance to blindfold the people and grow in stature and size."[13] This suggests the reason that the VAT receives such a hostile reception by those who believe that the government tends to overexpand.

The other view is that the VAT would provide much-needed revenue in a country that has problems raising sufficient revenue to meet spending. You will recall that the United States government has operated under budget deficits in every year since 1969; that is, increases in revenues have been outpaced by increases in public spending. Recent predictions testify to the substantial revenue-raising abilities of a broad-based VAT: A 5 percent VAT would generate $417 billion in tax revenues over 1995–98.[14]

You will also recall that our chapter on budget deficits described alternative viewpoints about the mismatch between spending and taxation. One view is that budget deficits result from undertaxation. It is easy to understand that advocates of this view tend to admire the revenue-raising abilities of the VAT. In contrast, critics of the VAT tend to believe that budget deficits result from overspending and therefore predict that a VAT would only fuel overexpansion of public spending by making it too easy for the government to raise additional tax revenues.

Wealth Taxation: Estate and Gift Taxes

Much of the support for the taxation of wealth rests on the notion that it provides a more comprehensive measure of ability to pay for public programs. Wealth is a *stock concept* in that its value is defined at a particular point in time. *Flow concepts,* such as annual income, refer to values defined over a particular period of time. Income, for

---

[12] See, for instance, Bruce Bartlett, "Not VAT Again!" *Wall Street Journal,* April 16, 1993, A10. An earlier study, however, argued that the VAT does not cause government spending growth; see J. A. Stockfish, "Value-Added Taxes and the Size of Government," *National Tax Journal* 38 (December 1985): 547–552.

[13] Quoted in Bartlett, "Not VAT Again!"

[14] CBO, *Reducing the Deficit.*

Wealth taxation is taxation imposed on the accumulated net value of assets at a particular point in time.

instance, is a flow concept, since we measure it on a weekly, monthly, or yearly basis. **Wealth taxation** levies taxes on the stock of accumulated net value of assets at a particular point in time.

Another reason for taxing wealth is to discourage sustained concentrations of wealth across generations.[15] Wealth taxation, in principle, offers a broader tax base than income through which tax policy may transfer income from one taxpayer to another.

A separate wealth tax is also claimed to be necessary because much of income escapes taxation upon the death of taxpayers. Unrealized capital gains, say from real estate or stocks, escape taxation under current tax law when taxpayers bequeath capital assets to others in their estates. A separate tax on estates therefore recoups some of the revenues lost by this tax provision. It should be recognized, however, that wealth taxation discourages saving, since capital investments are assessed greater tax liabilities than otherwise would occur.[16]

Federal estate and gift tax collections were estimated to be $12.6 billion in 1994 and, since this is only 1 percent of total tax revenues, they are a fairly minor revenue source. Despite its minor role in federal revenue collection, property taxation, which is another tax on wealth, raises considerable revenues for state and local governments.

Estate and Gift Taxation

Gift taxes are taxes imposed on the transfer of wealth while a taxpayer is living.

Estate taxes are taxes imposed on the transfer of wealth after the death of a taxpayer.

The difference between **gift taxes** and **estate taxes** is that the former is a tax on transfers of wealth that occur while the taxpayer is living, whereas the latter is a tax levied upon death. In 1994, tax rates on estates and gifts ranged from 18 percent on the first $10,000 to 50 percent on more than $2.5 million. However, generous tax credits exempt the first $500,000 from taxation in most cases, and most estates face a 37 percent tax rate on the first $150,000 over $600,000.[17] A 5 percent surtax is levied on estates between $10 million and $18.3 million.

Recall that one of the arguments for wealth taxation is that current tax law does not tax unrealized capital gains held at death. While, in most cases, taxes on capital gains are paid when assets are sold, this is not the case when assets are held by owners until death. Current law allows beneficiaries of the decedent's estate to claim a new tax basis for assets, so that all previous capital gains are erased. In other words, calculation of the cost basis of capital gains is advanced to the date at which the beneficiary receives the asset.

A simple example indicates how tax liabilities are determined when assets are transferred through disposition of estates. Suppose that an asset was purchased in 1980 at a cost of $1,000 and, upon the death of its owner in 1995, has a value of $10,000. While this would normally create a capital gain of $9,000, the capital gain

---

[15] Recall, however, our discussion (Chapter 11) of the important distinction between equality of opportunity and equality of outcomes. It complicates the ability of government to create greater equality among its citizens.

[16] For empirical support, see Michael J. Boskin, "Estate Taxation and Charitable Bequests," *Journal of Public Economics* 5 (January 1976): 27–56.

[17] CBO, *Reducing the Deficit,* 378.

becomes zero when this asset is transferred to a beneficiary. Only when the beneficiary sells the asset will subsequent capital gains be taxed. For instance, if the asset is sold in 1996 at a price of $11,000, the beneficiary is liable for paying taxes on a capital gain of only $1,000. If, however, the current holder of the asset leaves it in the estate, the capital gain is once again erased to zero upon transfer to a new owner. Our example indicates how the estate tax encourages taxpayers to hold assets until their death and then bequeath them to heirs. If the asset had been sold prior to the owners' death in 1995, that owner would incur a tax liability on capital gains of $9,000. By transferring the asset to a beneficiary upon the owner's death, substantial tax liability is eliminated.

It is widely believed that exempting capital gains held until death encourages taxpayers to hold onto assets longer than would otherwise be the case. This is just another example of tax avoidance. In this instance, tax policy promotes what is referred to as a *lock-in effect* whereby tax policy impedes the natural flow of investment funds in capital markets.

Wealth Taxation: The Property Tax

Property tax is a tax levied on personal property wealth.

While not levied at the federal level of government, taxation of property provides roughly 20 percent of the tax collections of state and local governments.[18] The **property tax** is the primary source of funds for local governments and is often designated for the financing of public schools. The property tax is a tax on wealth since it is levied on the value of property at a point in time. While in principle it may include all types of property, such as automobiles, boats, and jewelry, it is principally a tax on real estate. For the sake of convenience, we will focus on real estate and therefore assume that this is the only form of property held by taxpayers.

The property tax is an *ad valorem* tax, levied as a fixed percentage of property value. For example, a 5 percent tax on a property valued at $100,000 yields $5,000 in property tax revenue. The taxable base usually consists of two parts: land and its improvements, which include structures, landscaping, and anything else that improves its overall value.

A Uniform Property Tax

Property is really just one form of capital, and property taxation may therefore be examined in much the same way as taxes on corporate income. We see this when we recognize that the taxation of the value of property is similar to taxing the income from it. For instance, a rate of return of 20 percent characterizes a property valued at $100,000 that earns $20,000 in annual income for its owner. This suggests that since it yields a rate of return to its owner, property is just a form of capital investment. Notice that this property also generates $5,000 in annual tax revenue when the property tax rate is 5 percent. But $5,000 in annual tax revenue could also be collected when a tax rate of 25 percent is levied on annual income generated by this property.

---

[18] Advisory Commission on Intergovernmental Relations, *Significant Features of Fiscal Federalism,* vol. 2, September 1992.

Both tax policies therefore yield tax revenues of $5,000 and, in this respect, are identical.

Since a tax of 25 percent on income generated by property raises the same revenue as a property tax of 5 percent, the property tax may be modeled as a tax on the rate of return to capital. It is convenient to analyze the property tax in this way since this parallels our earlier discussion of the corporation tax.

Our model assumes two capital markets, property and nonproperty, and that all property capital is taxed at the same proportional rate. For the time being, nonproperty capital is not subject to taxation. (This closely parallels our model of corporate taxation where we assumed that two types of capital existed, corporate and noncorporate, and that only capital in the corporate sector was subjected to taxation.) Note that this is a general equilibrium model since the effects of a tax on two markets, property and nonproperty, are examined. Markets are assumed to be perfectly competitive and the capital stock (property + nonproperty) is fixed at T. A fixed capital stock means that, in equilibrium, inflows into one capital market must be offset by equal outflows from the other capital market.

Figure 21-1 plots the supply (S) and demand (D) for loanable funds in both capital markets. Panel a shows the property capital market, and panel b shows the nonproperty capital market. Economic theory predicts that, absent transaction costs, rates of returns to capital investment in both markets will be equalized at a return such as r_1. If one market had a rate of return higher than the other, funds would flow from the lower-return market into the higher-rate market until returns are equalized. General equilibrium is characterized by a distribution, such as P_1 in the property market and O_1 in the nonproperty market, which together sum to T, the fixed capital stock.

Now suppose that a property tax rate of t percent is levied on the income generated by property capital. Taxation causes its demand to rotate downward from D to D' as the after-tax rate of return to property falls. We refer to r as the market rate of return and $(1 - t)r$ as the after-tax rate of return to capital.

The short-run response to the property tax occurs as long as property owners are unable to shift out of property capital. After-tax returns fall to r_3 as long as owners hold P_1 in property capital; they therefore bear the full burden of the property tax, as measured by $r_1 r_3$. Notice that although property owners earn a lower after-tax return of r_3, nonproperty capital continues to yield r_1. This is an unstable situation, however, since property owners will shift investments from property to nonproperty capital until after-tax returns are equalized across capital markets.

This shifting of capital causes the supply of nonproperty capital to rise from S to S' and, consequently, its after-tax rate of return falls from r_1 to r_2 as investment rises from O_1 to O_2. Since the capital stock is fixed, investment in property falls by the same amount, or from P_1 to P_2. Lower property investment also means that its after-tax rate of return rises from r_3 to r_2. This analysis indicates that, in contrast to the short-run impact felt only by property owners, after-tax rates of return in *all* capital markets decline (from r_1 to r_2) as a result of the property tax.

Although after-tax rates of return are equalized across capital markets, property owners must earn higher market rates of return than owners of nonproperty capital. A simple example demonstrates this. An after-tax return of 6 percent requires that property owners earn 12 percent market returns when the property tax rate is 50 percent.

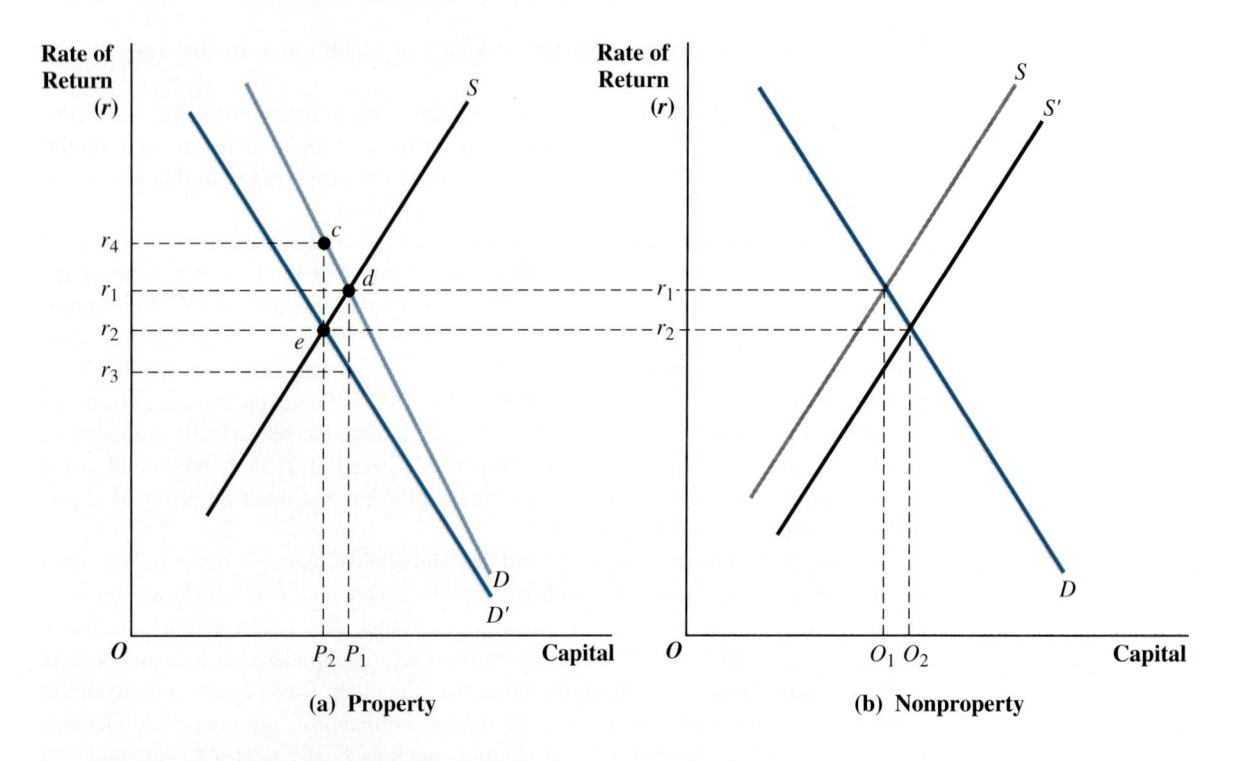

FIGURE 21-1 Incidence of a Property Tax

(a) Property

(b) Nonproperty

Owners of nonproperty capital, in contrast, need only earn a market return of 6 percent to receive a 6 percent after-tax rate of return. This difference places property owners in a competitive disadvantage and, as just shown, results in a capital outflow from property to nonproperty markets.

Excess burden arises here because property taxation encourages investment in nonproperty capital and discourages investment in property. Note that, at property investment of P_2, marginal social return is r_4, but marginal social cost is only r_2. In other words, too little property investment is undertaken since additional investment to P_1 (the pretax level of investment) would yield higher net social benefits. This also implies that too much investment is undertaken in the nonproperty capital market. Triangle cde measures the excess burden in the property market.

As we saw with the corporation tax, it is not entirely clear who ultimately bears the burden of taxes on capital income. While capital owners bear burdens, our analysis does not precisely indicate how tax burdens are distributed across owners of capital.

Consumers in these markets are likely to be affected as well. As property investment falls, housing prices are likely to rise. Note, however, that greater investment in nonproperty assets is likely to lower prices in those markets and, if the two effects wash each other out, the property tax may impose little burden on consumers. Other effects are expected to arise with relaxation of the assumption of a fixed capital stock. Lower after-tax returns in all capital markets may lower national savings as taxpayers consume more of their income or capital flight to other countries occurs. Moreover, workers will receive lower wages as their marginal productivities fall as a consequence of a smaller national capital stock.

Extension to a System of Nonuniform Property Taxes[19]

Property tax rates vary substantially across local governments. For example, in 1991, property values in Detroit were taxed at a rate of 4.4 percent, but a rate of 0.63 percent was levied on property values in Los Angeles.[20] It is incorrect, however, to directly compare property tax rates since tax bills vary by assessment ratios as well. Assessment ratios measure the percentage of market price that defines the property tax base. The assessment rate in Detroit, for example, was 49.4 percent; in Los Angeles, it was 61.2 percent.

We can easily demonstrate how tax rates and assessment rates together determine tax bills by seeing how tax bills would differ on a $75,000 house in either city. In Detroit, only 49.4 percent ($37,050) of property value is taxed, at a rate of 4.4 percent, yielding a tax bill of $1,630.20. Similar analysis yields a tax bill of $289.17 for the same property value in Los Angeles. (The tax burden differential is overstated here since average market values of homes are much higher in Los Angeles and therefore its tax base will be larger as well.) For simplicity, we will assume that assessment ratios are identical between jurisdictions, and we may therefore simply focus on the ways in which differences in property tax rates influence allocation of capital in the property market.

Our model of property taxation easily adjusts to the case of differential property tax rates when we assume that the supply of property capital is fixed.[21] In other words, capital may no longer flow between property and nonproperty markets, but property capital may flow between geographic locations. It is also convenient to analyze the effects of differential tax rates by discussing differentials in terms of differences from the average tax rate levied across all jurisdictions. In this way, all jurisdictions have the average tax rate in common, and locations with above-average tax rates are therefore designated as high-tax jurisdictions, and locations with below-average rates are referred to as low-tax jurisdictions.

Introduction of high-tax and low-tax jurisdictions means that property capital shifts from high-tax to low-tax jurisdictions in the long run. As shown before, shifting continues until after-tax rates of return are equalized across high-tax and low-tax markets. Therefore, just as in the previous model of uniform tax rates, all property owners earn lower after-tax returns and bear burdens of property taxation. Notice, as well, that property taxation still creates an excess burden since taxation discourages investment in high-tax jurisdictions and encourages investment in low-tax jurisdictions.

---

[19] The seminal article modeling the effect of nonuniform property taxes, and the article which is commonly referred as presenting the "new" view of property taxation, is Peter M. Mieszkowski, "The Property Tax: An Excise or a Profits Tax?" *Journal of Public Economics* 1 (April 1972): 73–91.

[20] U.S. Department of Commerce, *Statistical Abstract of the United States, 1993,* Washington, D.C.

[21] A more complex analysis would show differential property tax rates and retain the untaxed "other capital" sector. Analysis would show that as capital moves into the "other capital" market, capital flight would be highest for those locations with relatively high tax rates. While all capital owners will experience lower after-tax rates of return, owners of capital in high-tax locations will experience larger increases in market rates of return than those in low-tax locations.

Notice that capital flows force high-tax jurisdictions to earn higher market rates of return as taxation lowers their after-tax returns. This indicates that tax burdens are shifted, to some degree, to consumers in high-tax markets, since prices of goods will tend to rise when they use capital inputs. Higher housing prices are likely to develop that cause rental prices to rise as well. In addition, workers in high-tax jurisdictions may also experience lower wages as smaller local capital stocks reduce their marginal productivity. Landowners are likely to lose as well, since land is perfectly inelastic in supply, but capital outflows decrease its value as fewer improvements result from a smaller local capital stock.

The opposite occurs in low-tax jurisdictions. Prices of consumer goods fall as capital input costs fall as a result of a larger local capital stock. Rental prices of housing would also fall as capital is pulled out of high-tax markets and flows into low-tax markets and, as a larger local capital stock raises labor productivity, local wages tend to rise as well. Landowners are likely to gain higher land values since land is perfectly inelastic in supply, but the inflow of capital increases its value as capital inflows result in more improvements on the land.

In sum, our model of differential taxation demonstrates that all capital owners bear the burden of lower after-tax returns on capital. But, local effects differ from those in the aggregate; this is not so in the case of uniform taxation. Some consumers, workers, and landowners experience higher prices and wages, and others experience lower prices and wages. High-tax jurisdictions experience higher consumer prices, lower wages and lower land prices, and low-tax jurisdictions experience lower prices, higher wages and higher land prices. Although it may be true that in the aggregate these effects wash one another out, this analysis indicates that these effects vary across local jurisdictions.

Summary

- Unit taxes are consumption taxes that are levied on a per unit basis. *Ad valorem* taxes, which are based on sales volume, are consumption taxes as well. Most consumption tax revenues are collected by state and local governments.
- An advantage of a national consumption tax is that it does not discourage saving. Sales taxes are only paid when taxpayers choose to consume, rather than save, some portion of their income. Such a tax may also be simpler to administer than an income tax.
- A national consumption tax has several disadvantages. Uniform tax rates may hinder the pursuit of various equity goals. A national consumption tax would probably include many exemptions that would rival the number already in place under the income tax system. Exemptions would therefore shift resources into various consumption areas.

There are also concerns over regressivity; however, long-term regressivity of a national consumption tax is probably less than that of the present income tax system.

- The value-added tax (VAT) is a major revenue source in more than fifty countries. The United States currently has no VAT, though its supporters argue that it would promote saving and a larger capital stock. Opponents argue that it is a hidden tax that would promote tax growth and overexpansion of public spending.
- Much of the support for taxation of wealth rests on the notion that this tax provides a more comprehensive measure of the ability to pay for public programs. Taxation of wealth may also be used to discourage the accumulation and concentration of wealth across generations.

❏ The property tax is a major revenue source of state and local governments. The property tax is an *ad valorem* tax because it is levied as a fixed percentage of property value. Property tax rates vary substantially across governments. All capital owners bear the burden of property taxes because they lower the after-tax return to all capital. There are, however, local effects that differ from the aggregate effects of taxation. High-tax jurisdictions experience higher consumer prices, lower wages, and lower land prices; and low-tax jurisdictions experience lower prices, higher wages, and higher land prices.

Review Questions

1. What are consumption taxes?
2. What are the major arguments in favor of consumption taxes?
3. What are the major arguments against consumption taxes?
4. What is a VAT?
5. Why is there relatively little support for a VAT in the United States?
6. What are the major arguments in favor of wealth taxation?

Discussion Questions

1. Explain how sales taxes may be used by governments to control the consumption decisions of citizens.
2. In what sense are consumption taxes regressive? What policies could be used to make them less regressive?
3. Evaluate the following statement: Consumers would prefer a VAT over a general sales tax since producers pay the VAT along the stages of production while consumers pay the general sales tax at points of sale.
4. Explain why one of the advantages of a VAT is that it distorts saving decisions to a lesser degree than the current income tax.
5. Assess the following statement: The only way to improve the U.S. capital stock is through adoption of a VAT.
6. Discuss the various views regarding the use of a VAT to lower the budget deficit of the United States government.
7. Explain why some argue that it is appropriate to tax wealth because current tax law does not tax unrealized capital gains held at death.
8. In what sense is a property tax a tax on the rate of return to capital?
9. Explain how a change in the property tax rate in one jurisdiction affects the rate of return to owners of capital in other jurisdictions.
10. Explain how property taxation creates excess burden.

Key Words

National consumption taxes
Expenditure tax
Value-added tax (VAT)
Wealth taxation

Gift taxes
Estate taxes
Property tax

PART 7

Intergovernmental Finance

Chapter 22
Fiscal Federalism

CHAPTER 22

Fiscal Federalism

Fiscal federalism is the study of the structural organization of the public sector.

Fiscal federalism is the study of the structural organization of the public sector. The structure of the public sector refers to the way in which governmental activities are organized into political jurisdictions. Under a federal system, more than one government delivers public programs to citizens. The Constitution of the United States created a federal system of three layers of the public sector: federal, state, and local. The roads we drive on, the schools we attend, and the protection we receive from law enforcement officers are mostly provided by state and local governments. In addition to the fifty state governments, there are over 83,000 local governments in the United States.[1] During the course of a typical day, it is not uncommon for many of us to live in one jurisdiction, eat in another, and commute to work in another.

Optimal fiscal structure is the fiscal structure that meets the various efficiency and equity criteria of a society.

Much of our interest in federalism concerns the theory of **optimal fiscal structure,** which focuses on designing a system of governments that meets the efficiency and equity goals of society. Primary issues addressed in this theory include the appropriate numbers of governments and which responsibilities each should shoulder. Fiscal structure, for instance, may be characterized by many small governments or few large governments. Questions on which governments should provide roads, education, public health services, garbage collection, and all other goods and services are examined within optimal fiscal structure theory.

This chapter on federalism focuses on these questions:

❏ How are the responsibilities of governments divided in the United States?
❏ What are the advantages and disadvantages of federalism?
❏ Does taxpayer mobility result in a more efficient public sector?
❏ Does fiscal structure influence the size of the public sector?
❏ What roles do intergovernmental grants play in federalism?

---

[1] The Tax Foundation, *Facts and Figures on Government Finance* (Baltimore: Johns Hopkins University Press, 1991).

577

Trends in Fiscal Structure

Numbers of Governments

An important characteristic of fiscal structure is the degree to which it is dominated by the central government. The federal government of the United States, located in Washington, D.C., is the central U.S. government when we focus on the fiscal structure of the entire nation, although state governments are also central governments in the study of the fiscal structure of the fifty individual states. Domination of fiscal structure by the central government is often measured in terms of **fiscal centralization.** The greater the role of the central government, the more centralized is fiscal structure.

> **Fiscal centralization** is the degree to which government responsibilities are borne by the central government.

Table 22-1 displays numbers of governmental units underlying the fiscal structure of the United States. There are more than 83,000 individual governments, the vast majority of them local; that is, they are composed of counties, municipalities, townships, school districts, and special districts. County governments are typically found throughout the United States. Louisiana, where counties are called parishes, and Alaska, where they are called boroughs, are exceptions. Municipal governments—also commonly called towns, villages, and cities—are political subdivisions within which corporations provide local government functions aimed at specific population centers. Township governments, which are most commonly located in the Northeast and the Midwest, provide local governmental functions without regard to population concentrations. School district governments provide the vast majority of public education in the United States. Special district governments are independent, limited-purpose governments with substantial administrative and fiscal independence from other, more general-purpose governments.

The overall fiscal structure in the United States in this half-century has become increasingly centralized, and the number of governmental units has fallen sharply, from 155,116 in 1942 to 83,217 in 1987. The primary cause of increased centralization is the rapid consolidation of school districts, as evidenced by their decline from 108,579 to 14,741 over this same period.

Special districts, which have expanded from 8,299 to 29,487 since 1942, are the only category of governments experiencing rapid growth. In contrast to general-purpose governments, special districts are limited-purpose governments. They are created by state and local governments to provide specific public programs such as flood control, mass transportation, toll roads, bridges, credit market lending, electricity, and funding for construction of school buildings. Boundaries of special district governments often overlap many general-purpose governments. The expansion in their number has been controversial since much of their growth is explained by the many tax and expenditure limitations placed on most local governments. Since the early 1970s, nearly every state has operated under balanced budget rules and deficit limitations. Such budgetary constraints are imposed on counties, municipalities, townships, and school districts, but they generally do not constrain special districts. Growth in the number of special districts therefore appears to be mainly linked to the fact that their spending is easier to expand than more general-purpose governments.[2]

---

[2] See, for example, James T. Bennett and Thomas J. DiLorenzo, "Off-Budget Activities of Local
continued on next page

TABLE 22-1
Number of Governmental Units in the United States

	All Governmental Units	Counties	Municipalities	Townships	School Districts	Special Districts
Total Units for Selected Years, 1942–87						
1942	155,116	3,050	16,220	18,919	108,579	8,299
1952	116,807	3,052	16,807	17,202	67,355	12,340
1962	91,237	3,043	18,000	17,142	34,678	18,323
1972	78,269	3,044	18,517	16,991	15,781	23,885
1982	81,831	3,041	19,076	16,734	14,851	28,078
1987	83,217	3,042	19,205	16,691	14,741	29,487
Units for Selected States, 1987						
Arizona	577	15	81	NA	227	253
California	4,332	57	442	NA	1,098	2,734
Florida	966	66	390	NA	95	414
Georgia	1,287	158	532	NA	186	410
Idaho	1,066	44	198	NA	118	705
Illinois	6,628	102	1,279	1,434	1,029	2,783
Kentucky	1,304	119	437	NA	178	569
Louisiana	453	61	301	NA	66	24
Michigan	2,700	83	534	1,242	590	250
New Jersey	1,626	21	320	247	551	486
New York	3,303	57	618	929	720	978
North Carolina	917	100	495	NA	NA	321
North Dakota	2,788	53	366	1,355	310	703
Ohio	3,378	88	940	1,318	621	410
Pennsylvania	4,957	66	1,022	1,548	515	1,805
South Carolina	708	46	269	NA	92	300
Texas	4,416	254	1,156	NA	1,113	1,892
Virginia	431	95	229	NA	NA	106
Wisconsin	2,720	72	580	1,268	433	366

NA: None.

Source: Table A2, Tax Foundation, *Facts and Figures on Government Finance,* 1991 Edition (Baltimore/London: The Johns Hopkins Press, 1991).

Numbers of governments are also displayed for selected states in 1987. Great diversity clearly exists in fiscal structures of states. For example, California's population is roughly 41 times that of North Dakota and 4.7 times that of Virginia, but

---

Government: The Bane of the Tax Revolt," *Public Choice* 39 (1982): 333–342; and David Joulfaian and Michael L. Marlow, "The Relationship between On-Budget and Off-Budget Government," *Economics Letters* 35 (1991): 307–310.

California has 4,332 governments within the state, whereas there are 2,788 in North Dakota and only 431 governments in Virginia.[3] Substantial diversity in the composition of these governments is also evident. Special district governments, for instance, make up 63 percent of governments in California, but only about 25 percent in North Dakota and Virginia.

Centralization of Spending Policy

Table 22-2 presents centralization as defined by the federal government's share of total public spending. As numbers of governments have decreased, so has public spending become more centralized. Since 1902, federal spending has risen from 34.5 percent to 59 percent of total public spending. Spending patterns of state and local governments have therefore shifted as well. State governments have doubled, from 11 percent to 22 percent, their share of total spending. The share of total spending by local governments, in contrast, has sharply dropped from 54.8 percent to 18.7 percent since 1902.

Centralization by Spending Area

Table 22-3 splits, by spending area, state, local, and federal government spending. Only the federal government undertakes spending on national defense and international relations. The federal government is also the major provider in the areas of natural resources (e.g., national parks and environmental regulation) and insurance trusts (primarily Social Security). State governments are primary providers of spending policies directed toward highways, public welfare, and unemployment compensation. Local governments are primary providers of spending policies on education, utilities, and liquor stores. Questions concerning which governments should provide each spending area are, like governmental number and design, addressed by the theory of optimal fiscal structure.

Revenues of State and Local Governments

State and local governments fund their expenditures through many different tax sources. Figure 22-1 plots the percentage distribution of major tax sources since 1960. Here is a brief description of the importance of these tax sources to overall tax collection efforts.

- ❑ *Federal grants,* which are tax revenues collected by the federal government and distributed to state and local governments, have risen from 14 percent to 16 percent of tax revenues.
- ❑ *Individual income taxes,* which are collected on personal income, have risen from 5 percent to 12.5 percent of revenues.
- ❑ *Sales taxes,* which are primarily collected on general sales, have fallen slightly, from 23.5 percent to 21 percent of revenues.

---

[3] Population numbers for 1987 from U.S. Department of Commerce, *Statistical Abstract of the United States: 1991* (Washington, D.C.: Government Printing Office, 1991).

TABLE 22-2
Shares of Government Spending

Year	Percentage Distribution		
	Federal	State	Local
1902	34.5	10.8	54.8
1913	30.2	11.6	58.3
1922	40.5	13.6	46.0
1927	31.5	16.8	51.7
1932	34.3	20.6	45.1
1936	54.7	18.8	26.5
1940	49.3	22.3	28.5
1944	91.4	3.7	4.9
1950	63.7	18.2	18.1
1955	66.3	15.7	18.0
1960	64.3	16.5	19.1
1965	63.3	17.4	19.4
1970	62.5	19.4	18.1
1975	60.8	21.8	17.4
1980	64.2	20.0	15.8
1985	65.2	19.3	15.5
1990	59.0	22.4	18.7

Source: Table A10, Tax Foundation, *Facts and Figures on Government Finance,* 1991 Edition (Baltimore/London: The Johns Hopkins Press, 1991).

❏ *Property tax revenues,* which are primarily assessed on real estate, have dropped steeply, from 32 percent to 18 percent of revenues.

❏ *Other revenues* are primarily raised through social insurance taxes and have fallen from 11 percent to 7 percent of total tax revenues.[4]

❏ *Charges and fees,* which include admission charges to government-owned parks and museums, have risen from 15 percent to 25 percent of total revenues.

The same conclusions that we have drawn in earlier examination of federal policy pertain to state and local tax policy as well. We have yet, though, to analyze the implications of intergovernmental grants for resource allocation and the distribution of income.

---

[4] This also includes taxes on corporate income which, in 1990, accounted for only 2.3 percent of total revenues (Advisory Commission on Intergovernmental Relations, *Significant Features of Fiscal Federalism,* vol. 2, 1992).

TABLE 22-3
Distribution of Spending by Area and Level of Government

	Federal	State	Local	Total
National defense and international relations	100%	0%	0%	100%
Education	6	25	69	100
Highways	1	60	39	100
Public welfare	25	58	17	100
Hospitals	16	38	46	100
Health	32	36	32	100
Police	15	13	72	100
Natural resources	89	9	3	100
Housing and urban renewal	47	6	46	100
Air transportation	44	5	51	100
Water transport and terminals	53	12	34	100
Social insurance administration	60	40	0	100
Financial administration	25	31	44	100
Interest on general debt	78	10	12	100
Other[a]	44	17	39	100
Utility and liquor stores	0	12	88	100
Insurance trust	87	11	2	100

[a] Includes postal service, space research and technology, corrections, sewers, libraries, sanitation, fire, parking facilities, local parks, state and local public buildings, and unallocable services.

Source: Table A6, Tax Foundation, *Facts and Figures on Government Finance,* 1991 Edition (Baltimore/London: The Johns Hopkins Press, 1991).

Advantages of Federalism

Economic theory demonstrates that, in many cases, government programs should not be provided by one government. The choice is between a federal system of many governments and a unitary system of one government. Within optimal fiscal structure theory, analysts seek to design a system of governments that balances the advantages and disadvantages of both systems,[5] and we will now assess the many advantages of a federal system of government.

Better Correspondence to Demand Variations

Voters tend to have diverse preferences, and some variation in the programs of governments is therefore to be expected. Some voters, for example, want their government

---

[5] For early discussions of optimal fiscal structure, see Gordon Tullock, "Federalism: Problems of Scale," *Public Choice* 6 (1969): 19–30; and Wallace E. Oates. *Fiscal Federalism* (New York: Harcourt Brace Jovanovich, 1972).

**FIGURE 22-1
Sources of State and Local Revenue**

Source: Advisory Commission on Intergovernmental Relations, *Significant Features of Fiscal Federalism*, vol. 2, 1992.

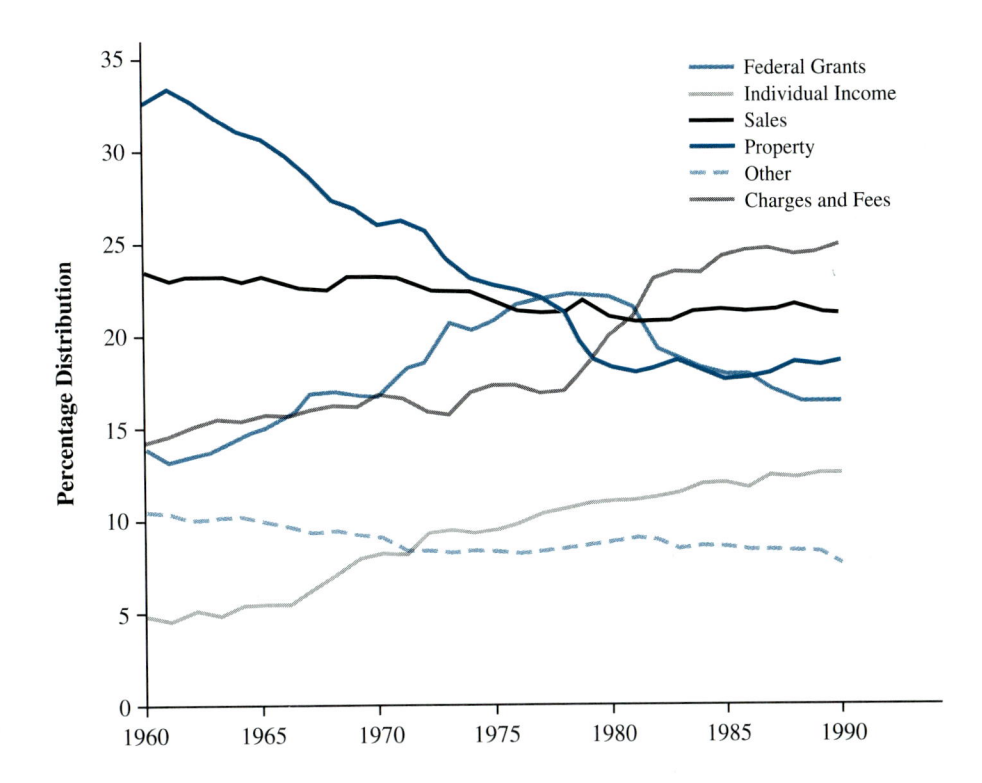

to provide jogging paths and tennis courts, and other voters want outdoor theaters, well-stocked libraries, and frequent community festivals. Figure 22-2, for instance, shows the demands of seven voters for a publicly provided jogging path that can be provided at a constant marginal cost (*MC*). The relevant policy issue may be stated thus: How long should the public jogging path be? Voters 1 and 2, as indicated by D_1 and D_2, prefer a relatively short path, and voters 6 and 7, as indicated by D_6 and D_7, prefer a relatively long path. Voters 3, 4, and 5, as indicated by D_3, D_4, and D_5, prefer a jogging path that is somewhere between the two extremes.

Suppose that all voters reside within the same political jurisdiction; only one government, therefore, provides the jogging path. The median voter model predicts that the preferences of the median voter dominates decisions made in the public sector under majority rule. In our example, the median voter displays demand D_4, and therefore a length of Q_4^* is chosen under majority rule. Notice that, even though all voters are provided the same jogging path, only the median voter receives a path consistent with (individual) maximum net benefits. That is, only the voter with demand D_4 consumes where $MB = MC$. In contrast, for all demands to the left of D_4, $MB < MC$ and, for all demands to the right of D_4, $MB > MC$. All voters except for the median voter consume a shorter or longer jogging path than they prefer. An important implication is that the greater are differences in preferences among voters, the less satisfaction voters, as a group, receive from their government.

Notice that for some voters satisfaction may be enhanced by relaxing the assumption that only one government provides the jogging path. Suppose, for instance, that

FIGURE 22-2
Demands for a Jogging Path

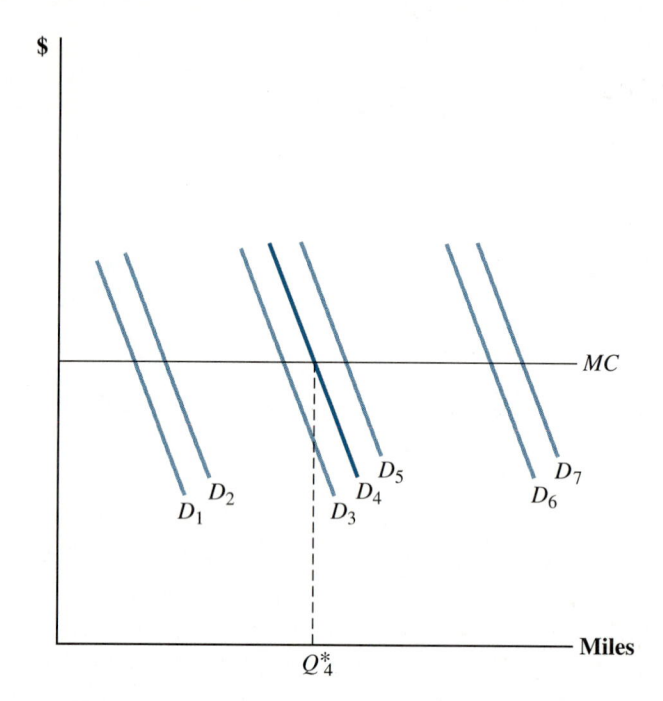

a federal system is designed whereby voters of like interests are assigned into one of three political jurisdictions. Voters 1 and 2 could be assigned to a jurisdiction that provides a short jogging path, voters 6 and 7 could be assigned to a jurisdiction that provides a long jogging path, and voters 3, 4, and 5 could be assigned to a jurisdiction that provides a path with a length somewhere in between.

Only in the jurisdiction assigned to voters 3, 4 and 5 will public decisions be dominated by voter 4, the same median voter when there was only one government. Voters 3, 4, and 5 therefore experience no change in welfare under the federal system since they continue to receive a jogging path of distance Q_4^*. Since they now receive jogging paths more in line with their preferences, however, all other voters gain higher utility. Voters 1 and 2 receive a shorter jogging path, and voters 6 and 7 receive a longer jogging path under the federal system. This example indicates that a federal system results in greater voter satisfaction than in the case of all voters being assigned to the same political jurisdiction. By allowing governments to tailor output to preferences of local constituents, differences in voter preferences are diminished within each jurisdiction.

Our discussion of a federal system evokes our earlier examination of the theory of clubs. This, of course, is a theory of voluntary cooperation between individuals seeking mutual advantage. Private clubs arise when club members share costs of providing goods such as swimming pools and golf courses. Sharing of goods arises between individuals with common interests and—in theory—is no different from our example of a system of local governments providing jogging paths. Local governments, in effect, are clubs through which local governments (clubs) provide jogging paths to local voters (club members).

The analogy between clubs and local governments helps us answer the question of what number of local governments will provide optimal correspondence to voter demands. The theory of clubs demonstrates that the more easily congested are activities of clubs, the smaller is optimal membership size, and the greater the number of clubs there should be.[6] The same conclusion applies to the optimal number of local governments. Because congestion arises at different rates for different goods, the optimal number of governments is greater than one in most spending areas. Police protection, for example, is easily congested, since officers can respond quickly only to calls when they are responsible for a limited service area. Moreover, preferences of voters for police protection will also widely differ if different neighborhoods have unequal crime rates and population densities. The optimal number and size of police forces will therefore vary across the country. Similar issues arise for other public programs as well and therefore, when preferences of individual voters are not uniform and congestion costs vary, an optimal fiscal structure is characterized by many governments of varying size.

This conclusion may be stated another way: *With all else remaining equal, a larger number of smaller governments should provide public programs when preferences of citizens are more heterogeneous than homogeneous.* In other words, communities with greater variation in preferences should have a larger number of smaller governments than those areas with less variation. Evidence, in fact, suggests that these differences occur in the U.S. federal system since greater numbers of local governments occur in those communities with greater differences in preferences of local voters.[7]

Can an Optimal Federal System Be Designed?

How might an optimal federal system be designed that correctly matches the preferences of a large and diverse group of citizens? Policymakers may certainly attempt to design an optimal federal system, but three complications cast serious doubts on their ability to design an optimal fiscal structure. One complication is the demand revelation problem. Information on preferences of all voters is in scarce supply, and policymakers therefore have limited ability to correctly assign like-minded voters to the many political jurisdictions that make up a federal system. Policymakers could simply ask all voters individually to state their marginal benefits associated with public goods, but the free rider problem suggests that many voters will underreport their true marginal benefits when they believe that an admission of higher marginal benefits raises their tax bills. In theory, policymakers may correctly measure preferences of voters in a single area, such as jogging paths or libraries, but it is highly improbable that accurate information could be uncovered on the thousands of programs provided

---

[6] This result follows from the fact that when expanded membership creates greater congestion costs, marginal costs rise rapidly. When we refer to rising marginal costs of provision, we are also saying that the activities of clubs become more similar to private goods, suggesting rivalry in consumption. When rivalry in consumption characterizes rising membership, club activities take on the properties of private goods, and optimal membership size is less than infinity. In contrast, pure public goods are characterized by zero marginal costs and the implication is that optimal membership size approaches infinity.

[7] Michael A. Nelson, "Decentralization of the Subnational Public Sector: An Empirical Analysis of the Determinants of Local Government Structure in Metropolitan Areas in the U.S.," *Southern Economic Journal* 57 (October 1990): 443–457.

by governments. In other words, it is unlikely that policymakers could correctly match voters to different political jurisdictions on the basis of their preferences for public programs.

A second problem is that even if policymakers could correctly assess preferences, all nonmedian voters receive either too many or too few government goods and services. Therefore, when policymakers assign voters to different political jurisdictions, they are also determining the extent to which nonmedian voters receive too much or too little government. It is unclear how policymakers would make these important judgments.

A third difficulty arises from the fact that most local governments offer a large array of programs. Child nutrition, health care, welfare programs, senior citizen centers, libraries, physical and mental therapy, transportation, sewer and water, fire stations, and law enforcement are just a few of the many programs offered by local governments. Each program, at least in theory, may merit its own single-function government, but this is too costly in practice. Many citizens must therefore be matched with other citizens who do not share similar preferences for the programs offered by their local government. Again it is unclear how policymakers could decide how to assign citizens to different local governments on the basis of their preferences for so many programs.

Tiebout Model: A Solution

Fortunately, these problems are substantially mitigated by the very nature of a federal system. The primary difference between a unitary system of one government and a federal system is that only in the latter can citizens move from one political jurisdiction to another when they are dissatisfied with policies provided by their local governments. A federal system offers citizens the right to reject public policies (through exit options) by moving from one local government to another. In contrast, rejection of unpopular policies (through exit options) may only be accomplished by leaving the country when one government provides all programs.

In Chapter 7, we showed that voters communicate their preferences to policymakers through available *voice* and *exit* options. The exercise of voice options occurs, for example, when citizens write to policymakers, vote in elections, and work in political campaigns. We argued, however, that voice options do not normally provide voters with complete control over public policies received in the policy process. The exercise of exit options is the ultimate threat that dissatisfied citizens may wield against policymakers, who would potentially lose their tax base and their viable public positions in large population shifts. This option has serious consequences for voters as well. Exiting is clearly a last resort, exercised after citizens conclude that available voice options in one place do not yield desired policies. Exiting political jurisdictions has been described as voting with your feet.

This model of voter behavior was developed by Charles Tiebout and is referred to as the **Tiebout model**.[8] This model predicts that because citizens search for desired packages of government programs, like-minded citizens tend to assemble in the same political jurisdiction. The end result of this search process is that residents of local

Tiebout model is a demonstration of interjurisdictional mobility whereby taxpayers search for desirable packages of government programs.

---

[8] Charles Tiebout, "A Pure Theory of Local Expenditures," *Journal of Political Economy* 64 (October 1956): 416–424.

governments tend to be fairly uniform in their preferences for public programs. Families, for instance, may congregate in communities where governments provide many swimming pools, good schools, and playgrounds. Senior citizens, in contrast, may congregate in communities where there are many adult education classes, adult recreation centers, and stringent noise ordinances. Yuppies tend to congregate in cities, their neighborhoods being upscale condominiums or gentrified old sections and their recreations in restaurants, theaters, and specialty shops.

Two beneficial consequences of citizen mobility are suggested by the Tiebout model. *First,* voters are able to locate in communities served by governments that offer their preferred assortment of public policies. There is a considerable literature demonstrating that under certain conditions mobility leads to a Pareto-efficient equilibrium whereby no citizen may leave a community and, at the same time, gain higher utility.[9] Citizens voluntarily sort themselves when they flee jurisdictions to relocate in jurisdictions offering policies more consistent with their preferences. Even though an initial assignment of citizens to local jurisdictions may be inefficient, mobility allows citizens the ability to transform inefficient assignments to efficient assignments when they may, with relative ease, relocate within a system of many governments.

Second, policymakers are more responsive to preferences of constituents when unhappy citizens have the ability to relocate. In effect, the ability to flee governments empowers citizens and increases their leverage in the policy process. Policymakers who fail to provide policies that correspond to demands of local citizens will observe exiting by their citizens. The consequence can be severe: With fewer citizens, erosion of tax bases jeopardizes the finances of governments.

At this point, we must note that it is unreasonable to conclude that a federal system results in a world in which all voters are content with *every* policy of their local government. A family, for instance, may be happy with local public schools, but unhappy with road maintenance. But, on balance, the Tiebout model predicts that citizens will be content to the extent that they are unable to gain higher satisfaction by relocating to another jurisdiction. Moreover, many other factors, such as climate, geographical preferences, and proximity to family, play a role in locational decisions and are considered as well.

Intergovernmental competition is a fiscal structure characterized by many competing governments.

The Tiebout model is a model of **intergovernmental competition.** Tax collections are clearly required to fund public programs, and policymakers therefore have an incentive to keep taxpayers happy under a federal system of many governments. When one government attracts a new taxpayer, another government loses a taxpayer. The incentive to gain new taxpayers is clearly seen when we observe that many state governments provide relocation services that lower moving costs for citizens who wish to move into their state. Governments often engage in substantial courting of businesses as well, since a new business generates considerable tax revenues and jobs for their jurisdictions.

---

[9] Various assumptions (e.g., absence of interjurisdictional externalities, absence of free riders, costless mobility, perfect information) have led to debates as to the relevance of this hypothesis. For a recent discussion of the Tiebout hypothesis, see Bruce W. Hamilton, "Tiebout Hypothesis," in *The New Palgrave: The World of Economics,* ed. John Eatwell, Murray Milgate, and Peter Newman (London: W. W. Norton, 1991).

Local Communities as Clubs

The ability to exit strengthens the comparison between private clubs and local governments within a federal system. Club members may quit whenever they are dissatisfied with club policies, just as citizens may relocate to other political jurisdictions. Like membership in private clubs, residence in a particular jurisdiction is based on benefits and costs. So long as many governments offer different policies, citizens have substantial freedom to choose jurisdictions that offer programs that closely match their preferences.

State and Local Governments as Laboratories

State and local governments that test innovative new public policies are considered **governments as laboratories.** A policy of **school choice,** for example, provides public funds for parents who choose to send their children to private schools. The Education Vouchers Initiative (Proposition 174), which was put to the vote of Californians in 1993, provided parents with annual vouchers worth about $2,600. These vouchers were to be funded out of public monies that had previously been set aside for funding of public schools. The school choice issue has clearly arisen out of widespread dissatisfaction with the quality of public schools, but there is considerable disagreement over whether it is appropriate for parents to use public funds to send their children to private schools.

Opponents of school choice policies argue that the quality of public education should be raised through improving school facilities and breadth of course offerings, improving security in the schools, and providing higher teacher salaries. Opponents also believe that school choice policies result in lower educational quality as the funding base for public schools is eroded when parents take advantage of vouchers. In other words, problems with public education may be fixed by higher funding levels, but only if funds are available to the public's schools. Opponents also argue that since vouchers do not normally cover full costs of private tuition, most poor or even middle-class parents will remain unable to afford private schools. School choice policies are therefore predicted to foster a mass exodus of children of upper-middle-income and higher-income parents to private schools. Meanwhile, the public school system will primarily educate children of lower-income parents.

Advocates of school choice policies respond that local school officials are unresponsive to demands for higher-quality education. These people believe that the only effective means of improving educational quality is through imposing a credible threat of exit on local school officials. Higher public funding, they think, would only be wasted on higher salaries and the hiring of too many administrators. Notice that this view follows directly from the Tiebout model. Vouchers, in effect, lower mobility costs for parents who desire good or excellent education for their children. Mobility costs fall, since, rather than requiring that parents move to communities with better public schools, parents now find it more affordable to send their children to private schools within their own communities. In other words, parents may now exit public schools without moving to another public school district when there are higher-quality private schools somewhere in their local community. School choice policies are therefore predicted to raise competition for students and result in higher educational quality.

Governments as laboratories are state and local governments that test new and innovative public policies.

School choice is a policy that makes public funds available to parents who choose to send their children to private schools.

Just How Mobile Are Americans?

We have argued that in order for the Tiebout model to work well, citizens must be willing to relocate. Just how mobile are Americans? This is a hard question to answer, but we may find some information from the rates at which Americans change jobs. Twenty-five years ago, for example, the average American changed jobs at least four times in a lifetime. This has now risen to seven, indicating that Americans are much more mobile than before. The conclusion that one may draw from the evidence is that Americans are willing to move when there are economic reasons involved.

Greater regional differences in unemployment rates is one factor behind growing mobility because workers are more likely to change jobs by relocating to other areas of the country. Over a three-month period in 1991, for instance, 41.5 million Americans, or roughly 17 percent of the population, moved to another home. A full 7 million moved out of state. In contrast, the average Briton moves half as often.

Similar differences exist between the United States and Continental Europe. One result of the wide difference between the moving patterns of Americans and Britons is predictable: Regional differences in unemployment rates persist for much longer periods of time in Britain than in the United States.

Source: "In Search of Stability," *Economist*, October 16, 1993, 25–26.

A recent study provides substantial support for the view that higher competition for students fosters higher educational quality.[10] When controlling for many factors, such as per capita spending on public school students, poverty, and educational attainment of parents, public school quality was determined to be positively related to the degree of competition provided by neighboring private schools. An important implication of this study is that when school vouchers create a more competitive environment between private and public schools, public school quality will improve.

It should also be recognized that school choice policies represent significant reversals from past policies that have raised mobility costs of parents. Recall from Table 22-1 that substantial centralization of public education has occurred in this country. The number of school districts has fallen from 108,579 to 14,741 over the forty-five years between 1942 and 1987.[11] Consolidation limits the ability of parents to search for alternative public suppliers of education and, consistent with the Tiebout model, is predicted to result in falling educational quality as it lowers the number of competing public school districts.

Our discussion does not imply that opponents of school choice policies reject the underlying prediction of the Tiebout model that parents will search for high-quality schools. They clearly understand that when vouchers lower mobility costs, some

---

[10] See Jim F. Couch, William F. Shughart II, and Al L. Williams, "Private School Enrollment and Public School Performance," *Public Choice* 76 (1993): 301–312. Performance was measured by test scores of a standardized algebra test given to all public school students in North Carolina.

[11] Much of this consolidation has been motivated by the argument that scale economies would result from consolidation. The issue of scale economies is examined later in this chapter.

parents will reject public schools when they believe that private schools are a better choice. Opponents may reject the view that public school officials are unresponsive to demands for higher quality, but both opponents and advocates predict that school choice policies will cause some parents to flee public for private schools.

The school choice issue clearly has many facets, but the point remains that it is easier for experiments in government policies to arise under a system of many governments than under only one government. An entire state, such as California, or even just one school district may experiment with a school choice policy; it is less likely that the entire country would undergo this experiment. Not all trials will be unmitigated successes, but successful school plans will tend to be adopted by other governments.

Controls Rent Seeking

Another advantage of a federal system is that it may discourage rent seeking by special interest groups. Recall that rent seeking occurs when special interest groups lobby policymakers for income transfers. Special interest groups are able to secure transfers when government policies confer substantial benefits on relatively small groups, at the same time distributing costs widely over the population. Income transfers are therefore easier to secure when only one government exists because costs may be more thinly spread across more taxpayers than is possible under many governments. Thus, for any one policy, burdens imposed on the average taxpayer are much lower under one government than under a federal system of many governments.

The following example demonstrates that fiscal structure influences the ability of special interest groups to secure preferential policies. Suppose that 500 swimmers lobby for a swimming pool to be built, at a cost of $25 million, in their local community of 50,000 citizens. Also suppose that there are 10 million citizens in their state. When the tax base is 50,000 citizens, the average cost per taxpayer is $500. However, if costs are spread over the entire population of their state, average cost per taxpayer falls to $2.50. It is likely that swimmers would encounter less resistance from taxpayers when costs are shared by all state taxpayers than when only local taxpayers bear the costs. Average tax increases of $2.50 are obviously much less of a burden than average tax increases of $500; therefore taxpayers have substantially less incentive to fight the pool construction. Notice that extension of the cost-sharing group to all citizens in the nation would result in even lower resistance.

There is yet another reason that a federal system lowers the ability of special interests to use the political system to transfer income to themselves. Citizens can shield themselves from burdensome policies simply by moving to another political jurisdiction; the federal system promotes voting with your feet. Therefore, the ability to force citizens to pay for policies that transfer income is kept in greater check by their mobility in a federal system. The Tiebout model therefore predicts that transfer policies that survive under a federal system are essentially voluntary in nature.

Disadvantages of Federalism

Economies of Scale

When goods and services are characterized by economies of scale, average costs drop with output expansion. As long as average costs continue to fall with greater production, it is cheaper to have one large government, rather than two or more smaller governments, produce goods and services. Centralization of government can therefore exploit economies of scale, in theory resulting in cost savings that flow to taxpayers. Government activities characterized by substantial economies of scale are therefore believed to be best performed by a few large governments.[12] National defense is commonly believed to be a public good that experiences substantial scale economies since it is cheaper to provide a secure nation by joining a nation's resources together rather than, in the case of the United States, having each of the fifty states supply their own programs. Water and electric utilities are believed to be subject to substantial scale economies, and it is therefore cheaper, on a per capita basis, for 1 million citizens to share costs than for two or more governments to provide these services.

Complications

Two factors suggest that the economies of scale argument has severe practical limitations. *One* complication is that economies of scale are eventually exhausted in most cases as diseconomies of scale appear. We should not conclude that costs continue to fall forever because average costs fall at first. The key is to determine when falling average costs are replaced by rising average costs. For instance, it may be cheaper, on a per capita basis, for garbage collection to be provided for 2,000 residences than for 200 residences, but it may become more expensive when service is extended to 20,000 residents. In this case, two or more governments may more cheaply provide this service.

Another complication is that centralization of government creates greater monopolization of production, and under the Leviathan view of policymakers may result in overexpansion of government. This view is entirely compatible with the Tiebout model, which predicts that exit options enable citizens to flee those governments which do not provide policies consistent with their preferences. We have shown that government centralization restricts exit options, and the Leviathan view therefore predicts that policymakers will pursue narrow self-interests to a greater extent under a more centralized fiscal structure. The major counterview goes under the assumption that policymakers are benevolent in nature and therefore rejects the Leviathan prediction that policymakers exploit monopoly power arising from greater centralization. Allocative efficiency will simply be enhanced under this view since scale economies may be better exploited when there are fewer governments supplying public programs.

These opposing viewpoints indicate a trade-off question: Do the cost savings that flow from economies of scale outweigh any spending expansion that may result from greater monopoly power when government spending becomes more centralized? These two effects are opposite one another, so which effect dominates is an empirical issue. Spending rises (falls) when greater centralization promotes spending expansion that exceeds (falls short of) cost savings.

---

[12] For a recent discussion of the view that a large number of small governments is often inefficient, see David L. Chicoine and Norman C. Walzer, *Governmental Structure and Local Public Finance* (Boston: Oelgeschlager, Gunn and Hain, 1985).

Two approaches have been used to test the relationship between centralization and government spending. One examines the relationship between centralization, as defined by the share of spending undertaken by state governments, and spending of local and state governments. Empirical evidence indicates that either no relationship exists or that greater centralization promotes higher public spending.[13] Findings of no relationship suggest that cost savings from economies of scale are exactly offset by any spending expansion that may result from expansion of monopoly power. Empirical evidence therefore suggests that greater centralization does not lower overall spending of state and local government.

Other theorists define centralization as the federal government's share of total public spending, arguing that the federal government influences intergovernmental competition between state and local governments. The *incentive* of citizens to flee state and local governments that do not provide programs consistent with their preferences is argued to be directly related to what proportion of all public spending the federal government undertakes. Unless they leave the country, citizens may not escape federal policies. Therefore, the greater the proportion of policies provided by the federal government, the smaller the potential gain from moving from one state or local government to another.

This important point may be clearly seen by contrasting the following two examples of total government spending of $100 billion.

❑ Case A, in which the federal government spends $80 billion and the difference, or $20 billion, is spent by state and local governments

❑ Case B, in which the federal government spends $25 billion and state and local governments spend $75 billion

The role of state and local governments is clearly much more important in Case B. When citizens are dissatisfied with government policies, there is a higher likelihood that migration to another state or local government provides greater correspondence with preferences in Case B. Voting with your feet simply cannot change 80 percent of government policies under Case A, but under Case B only 25 percent of policies are unaffected by migration. The Tiebout model predicts that policymakers are more unresponsive to citizen mobility when the federal government plays a more major role in spending policies. Empirical literature supports the hypothesis that centralization at the federal level is positively related to total public spending.[14] The implication is, therefore, that whatever cost savings arise from economies of scale are more than offset by the spending expansion that results from greater monopoly power.

---

[13] Wallace E. Oates, "Searching for Leviathan: An Empirical Study," *American Economic Review* 75 (September 1985): 748–757; and Kevin F. Forbes and Earnest M. Zampelli, "Is Leviathan a Mythical Beast?" *American Economic Review* 79 (June 1989): 587–596 provide examples of the no-relationship theory. For examples of evidence that increased centralization causes higher public spending, see John J. Wallis and Wallace E. Oates, "Does Economic Sclerosis Set in with Age? An Empirical Study of the Olson Hypothesis," *Kyklos* 41 (1988): 397–417; and Jeffrey S. Zax, "Is There a Leviathan in Your Neighborhood?" *American Economic Review* 79 (June 1989): 560–567.

[14] See, for example, Michael L. Marlow, "Fiscal Decentralization and Government Size," *Public Choice* 56 (1988): 259–269; and David Joulfaian and Michael L. Marlow, "Government Size and Decentralization: Evidence from Disaggregated Data," *Southern Economic Journal* 56 (April 1990): 1094–1102.

Interjurisdictional Externalities

We have demonstrated that resources are misallocated if there are externalities in private market transactions. When there are negative externalities, too many resources are allocated, and too few resources are allocated when there are positive externalities. **Interjurisdictional externalities** arise when governments fail to fully account all costs or benefits imposed on citizens of other governments. Consider public provision of education. When Utah, for example, educates a college student who, upon graduation, moves to Maine, taxpayers in Utah are less able to reap benefits from that student's education. An interjurisdictional externality occurs, as well, when one government's pollution control activity is based on benefits and costs of its citizens, even though costs and benefits spill across state lines. Therefore, what is an efficient level of pollution control for one government is likely to be an inefficient level from the viewpoint of all individuals who bear costs and receive benefits from controlling pollution.

Another example is local law enforcement. Externalities may spill over to other communities when local governments provide vastly different levels of local law enforcement.[15] When criminals are mobile and sensitive to differential enforcement of local laws, criminals tend to migrate to those government jurisdictions with low law enforcement and, in this way, high-enforcement jurisdictions export crime to low-enforcement jurisdictions.

Centralization of government is one way to internalize interjurisdictional externalities since, in effect, larger and more centralized governments develop policies on the basis of larger populations. Policies may be able to allocate resources more efficiently since fewer individuals who experience externalities live outside government jurisdictions where externalities are imposed.

> **Interjurisdictional externalities** are those that arise when governments fail to fully account for costs and benefits imposed on citizens of other governments.

Uniformity of Provision

Central governments provide greater uniformity of policies than do governments within a multitiered federal system. For example, rather than have fifty different pension funds provided by the fifty states, one program, such as Social Security, may be provided by the federal government. Air traffic control is one example of a policy that is uniform across the nation because the federal government provides it. State governments may also provide all road signs or safety standards when it is apparent that these policies should be uniform across a state for the safety of its citizens.

The Tiebout model demonstrates that the goal of policy uniformity will not normally be advanced through a federal system. Citizens search for local governments that deliver combinations of policies with the best correspondence to their preferences. High policy diversity results, therefore, when the nation is populated by a diverse group of individuals. When all citizens are not alike, a federal system results in a world in which not all policies are alike.

The issue of which policies should be standardized is, in many cases, highly controversial. Many people may believe that air traffic control should be uniformly

---

[15] See, for example, Stephen L. Mehay, "Interjurisdictional Spillovers of Urban Police Services," *Southern Economic Journal* 43 (January 1977): 1352–1359.

provided across the nation, but controversy clearly exists over the merits of requiring uniformity in the provision of transportation, welfare, and recreational programs. Note, however, that even if it is believed that a particular program should be standardized across the nation, such agreement does not necessarily imply that it must be directly provided by the federal government. Uniformity in most areas may be promoted by placing federal requirements on state and local governments. This, in fact, occurs in many welfare programs where the federal government mandates that certain benefit levels be provided by state governments.

Redistribution

Fiscal structure also influences abilities of governments to redistribute income. We have shown that a federal system allows citizens to move from one jurisdiction to another when they are dissatisfied with policies provided by their current government. Transfer policies can clearly be an important source of dissatisfaction that results in movement of citizens from one government to another within a federal system. Notice, however, that citizen mobility thwarts the ability of local governments to transfer income from the "rich" to the "poor." Transfer policies are self-defeating since when one local government transfers income, the poor tend to enter its jurisdiction as the rich leave. Exiting by rich citizens therefore lowers the ability to transfer income since, in an area with a now-smaller tax base, more generous transfers may raise the percentage of citizens who are entitled to transfers. Even when citizens care only about the welfare of poor citizens residing within their own community, lower than optimal levels of transfers have been shown to occur under a federal system.[16] Centralization of transfer policies is therefore often viewed as an appropriate device that restricts the adverse effects of citizen mobility on transfer policy.

Avoidance of Tax Wars

Tax wars are competitions between (or among) two or more governments on the basis of lowering taxes.

It has recently been argued that a federal system promotes **tax wars** whereby state and local governments compete with one another on the basis of tax burdens. Tax wars have been argued to result in suboptimal tax collections.[17] When governments are fearful of losing businesses and citizens to governments that impose lower tax burdens, they may set tax rates lower than what is required for high-quality public programs. When only one government exists, no other governments compete, and policymakers can therefore set higher tax rates, enabling a higher level of public spending.

It has been proposed that one way to eliminate "tax wars" and, at the same time, maintain a quasi-federal system, is to adopt a system of common shared taxes, under which all noncentral governments would share a common sales tax rate, applied to the same types of transactions. If, for example, a rate of 5 percent is set for all states, taxpayers would no longer be able to lower state tax burdens by moving (or driving for

---

[16] Charles Brown and Wallace E. Oates, "Assistance to the Poor in a Federal System," *Journal of Public Economics* 37 (April 1987): 307–330.

[17] Alice M. Rivlin, *Reviving the American Dream: The Economy, the States and the Federal Government* (Washington, D.C.: Brookings Institution, 1992).

commodities) to another state. A system of common shared taxes has also been argued to advance the transfer functions of governments. The federal government, for example, could collect tax revenues and be responsible for returning the proceeds back to the states. When poorer states receive a proportionately larger share of tax receipts, tax policy would transfer income from richer to poorer states.

Notice that this view rejects the prediction that mobility of citizens within a federal system results in efficient government policies. That is, voting with your feet is not perceived to result in tax policies that better correspond to preferences of constituents. But it is important to understand that the Tiebout model predicts that tax rates vary with the preferences of local communities. When constituents want a "large" public sector, they will tend to support higher tax rates than when constituents want a "small" public sector. The system of common shared taxes, however, eliminates the ability of citizens to choose state tax rates through freedom of movement between state governments.[18]

Stabilization Policies

One of the roles of the public sector is to provide macroeconomic policies that control the business cycle. It is widely accepted that stabilization policies are the province of central governments. Few economists, for instance, would argue that each state should control its own money supply. Similarly, countercyclical fiscal policy is believed to be most effective when performed at a national level and therefore is commonly argued to be the appropriate province of the federal government.

Intergovernmental Grants

Trends

Intergovernmental grants are monies flowing from one government (grantor) to another government (recipient).

Conditional grants are grants accompanied by stipulations imposed by grantor governments as to how revenues are to be spent by recipient governments.

Intergovernmental grants are revenue transfers from one government to another in a federal system. Grants flow from grantor governments, who collect the revenues, to recipient governments. As seen from Table 22-4, grants usually flow from higher-level governments to lower-level governments. Grant dollars received by state governments, for example, are primarily received from the federal government. Federal grant dollars totalled $226.1 billion in 1994, and although federal grants have been as high as 17 percent of total federal outlays (in 1978), they now roughly represent 15 percent of total federal outlays.[19] Although the vast majority of grant dollars received by local governments are distributed by state governments, a substantial portion of these grant dollars are merely passed along from federal grants received by state governments.

There are two general types of grants. **Conditional grants** are the most common; they are disbursed when the grantor government indicates how recipient governments

---

[18] Recent evidence, however, indicates that state and local tax differentials have fallen over the 1929–86 period, and therefore the extent to which tax wars are being waged is falling as well. See Gerald W. Scully, "The Convergence of Fiscal Regimes and the Decline of the Tiebout Effect," *Public Choice* 72 (1991): 51–59. Whether this spatial convergence of tax rates is the result of Tiebout moves in a federal system or due to collusion within a more centralized system is subject to debate.

[19] *Budget of United States Government,* 1994.

TABLE 22-4
Percent of Revenues Derived from Grants

	State Governments		Local Governments	
	Federal	Local	Federal	State[a]
1952	13.8%	1%	1.2%	26.0%
1962	19.0	1	1.8	25.2
1972	23.8	1	4.0	30.6
1980	22.3	1	8.2	31.5
1990	18.7	1	3.2	29.7

[a] Includes significant amounts of federal grants that are passed through by state governments to local governments.

Source: Table 41, *Advisory Commission on Intergovernmental Relations,* September 1992.

Unconditional grants are grants carrying no restrictions on the ways in which revenues are to be spent by recipient governments.

are to spend the revenues. **Unconditional grants,** which do not specify how revenues are to be used by recipient governments, account for a very small proportion of grants. Unconditional grants are also called block grants.

Roughly 66 percent of federal grants in 1994 were specified to be spent on health and income security programs of state and local governments.[20] A substantial proportion of these grants were directed at programs, such as Aid to Families with Dependent Children and Medicare, in which state and local governments share the costs of federally mandated programs. Grants for physical capital, which are directed at projects such as highways, airports, and sewage treatment plants, account for roughly 16 percent of federal grants and are the second largest category of federal grants.

Rationales

Intergovernmental grants are primarily a means by which higher-level governments influence the spending decisions of lower-level governments. It is for this reason that most grant dollars flow from higher- to lower-level governments.

A brief review of the disadvantages of federalism indicates the various areas in which intergovernmental grants may increase efficiency or equity of resource allocation in a federal system. One disadvantage is that when interjurisdictional externalities are present, state or local governments making spending decisions tend to do too much or too little spending. Benefits that follow from spending on education and medical research, for instance, tend to cross over to other local jurisdictions and therefore, when a state or local government considers only the benefits received by its citizens, it underfunds these activities. Costs that arise from activities that generate pollution and congestion are underestimated when state and local governments consider only costs imposed on their constituents and therefore tend to allocate too many resources

---

[20] *Budget of United States Government,* 1994.

to these activities. Conditional grants that specify that grant dollars be spent on increasing activities that generate positive externalities, or decreasing activities that generate negative externalities, increase overall efficiency of resource allocation in the economy.

Conditional grants may also further the goals of program uniformity when grant dollars must be spent on upgrading government programs. For example, grant dollars may be directed toward improving reading levels of fourth-grade students. Grants may also be directed at equity goals when grant dollars are distributed in the direction of local governments of states or municipalities with high percentages of poor citizens.

Economic Effects of Unconditional Grants

Figure 22-3 shows the effects of unconditional grants on local government spending. As defined previously, unconditional grants require only that grant dollars be spent by the recipient government; therefore, no requirements are placed on which public programs are to be promoted. Community indifference curves are also displayed that, in theory, indicate local preferences for consuming two types of goods: private sector goods and public sector goods. The vertical axis measures units of private sector goods. Units of public sector goods are on the horizontal axis. The budget constraint for our local community is AB and, given preferences, combination $E1$, with private sector goods of S_1 and public sector goods of P_1, are chosen by this community.

When the local community receives an unconditional grant from a higher-level government, its budget constraint shifts outward to a new budget constraint such as CD. Notice that the uppermost point of this new budget constraint is C (and not F) because the grant is to be used only to fund additional public sector goods and therefore does not increase the level of private sector goods that may be purchased. The size of the grant, in effect, is AC, which measures the additional level of public sector goods that may be consumed after the grant. The new equilibrium occurs at $E2$, where private sector goods of S_2 and public sector goods of P_2 are consumed. The grant therefore raises consumption of both private and public sector goods.

Why, though, is the increase in consumption of public sector goods (which equals P_1P_2) smaller than the grant (which equals AC)? Since the entire grant must be spent on public sector goods, this result implies that the community lowers its own funding of public sector goods after receiving the grant. In other words, the recipient government now offers tax relief to its citizens.

In general, unconditional grants exert influences similar to those seen when local governments receive lump sum grants that do not stipulate that all grant dollars be spent on public sector goods. This occurs as long as grant dollars are less than the amount communities want to spend on public sector goods before receiving grants. Recall our discussion of transfers (Chapter 11), which demonstrated that food stamps are commonly viewed as cash transfers by recipients. Food budgets of recipients tend to be larger than the value of foods stamps they receive, and recipients therefore replace their own expenditures on food with food stamps. In other words, when $50 in foods stamps are received, recipients may spend $50 more on non–food items. Similarly, intergovernmental grants tend to be smaller than local government expenditures and, in this way, there is little difference whether grants must be spent on public sector goods or may be used to provide tax relief to citizens.

FIGURE 22-3
Economic Effects of Unconditional Grants

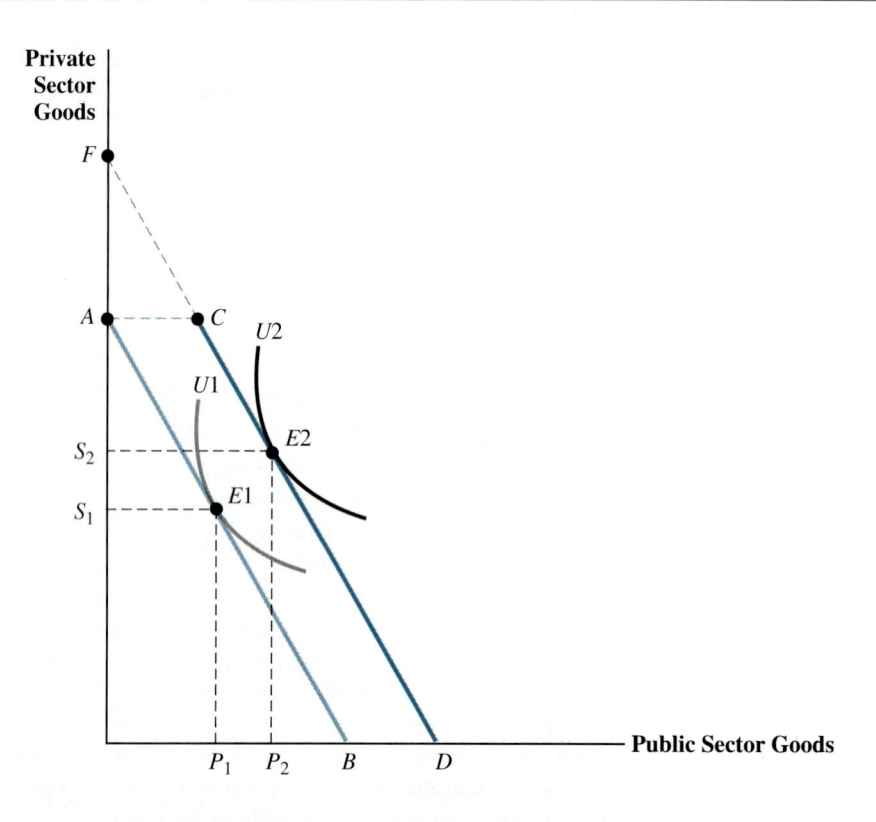

Matching and Nonmatching Conditional Grants

Nonmatching conditional grants are transfers of fixed sums of revenue to recipient governments.

Matching conditional grants are transfers of revenues whereby grantor governments match recipient governments' funds.

Conditional grants specify, in some detail, which public programs the grants are to be spent on. **Nonmatching conditional grants** transfer fixed (lump) sums of revenue to recipient governments. For **matching conditional grants,** grantor governments specify some rate, usually from 5 to 50 percent, at which they match funding by recipient governments. A match rate of 35 percent, for example, means that, for every dollar of spending, the grantor government provides 35 cents to the recipient government. The additional 65 cents is the responsibility of the recipient government.

We can analyze differences in the ways in which matching and nonmatching grants influence spending decisions of recipient governments in much the same way as we examined the economics of excise subsidies on transfer programs for the poor. Consider Figure 22-4, which contrasts the cases of matching and nonmatching conditional grants. Before any grants are received, the community is constrained by budget constraint AB and, given its preferences, chooses $E1$ where P_1 of public sector goods are consumed. A matching grant flattens the budget constraint to AC since the grant subsidizes consumption of public sector goods. The new equilibrium is $E2$, and therefore the matching grant increases consumption of public sector goods to P_2.

If an *equivalent* nonmatching grant had been offered, the budget constraint would shift, in a parallel manner, out to DF, since this intersects the equilibrium attained with the matching grant. This grant is *equivalent* in the sense that it allows

**FIGURE 22-4
Matching versus
Nonmatching
Conditional Grants**

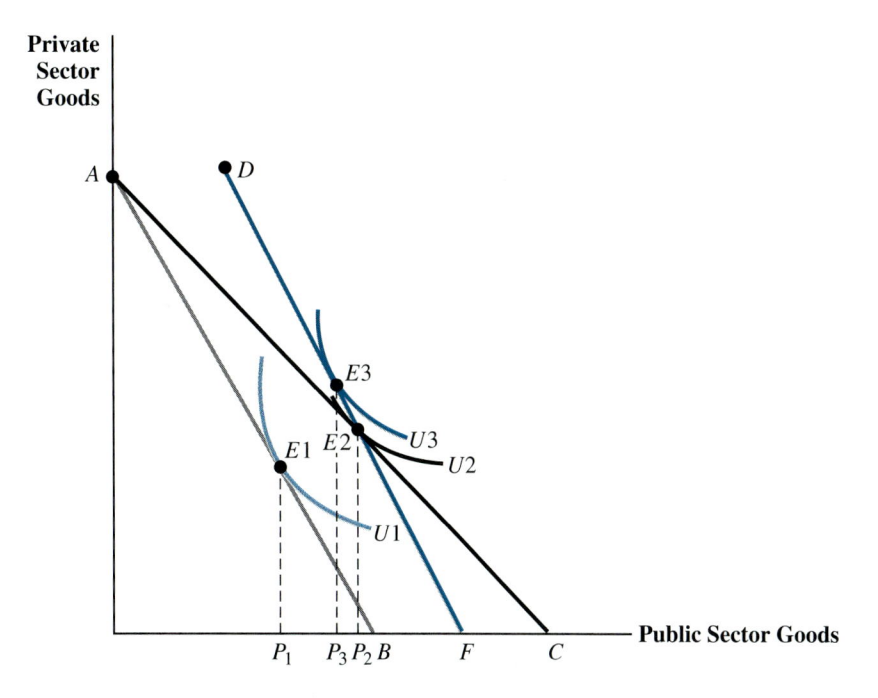

the community to consume the combination of goods that are chosen under the matching grant. The new equilibrium is $E3$, and the *equivalent* nonmatching grant results in consumption of public sector goods of P_3.

This comparison demonstrates that the community reaches higher utility, as indicated by a higher indifference curve, when a nonmatching grant, of equivalent value, replaces a matching grant. Notice that the matching grant causes the community to consume more public sector goods than it would consume under an equivalent nonmatching grant. An excess burden therefore occurs, since a policy that generates higher utility (nonmatching grant) could replace a current policy (matching grant) of equivalent value. The excess burden will exist as long as the matching grant is not replaced with an equivalent nonmatching grant.

Grant Policy

Why Offer Matching Grants?

Why would matching grants be used over nonmatching grants? An obvious reason is for grantor governments to force recipient governments to consume more public sector goods than they would otherwise prefer to consume. This reason is similar to our argument on welfare programs that excise subsidies, for such goods as housing or natural gas consumption, induce recipients to consume more of these goods than when they receive equivalent cash transfers. Grant policy may therefore be influenced by paternalism, with grantor governments believing they should directly alter the consumption habits of recipient governments.[21] Matching conditional grants, for instance, could be directed toward child nutrition programs, health care facilities, or rental housing assistance and, as demonstrated in Figure 22-4, recipient governments tend to spend more on programs when they are funded through matching grant programs. The Department of Housing and Urban Development, for example, is budgeted to fund 215 such grants at a projected cost of $990 million over 1994–98.[22]

Although matching grants promote more consumption of targeted goods than equivalent nonmatching grants, remember that nonmatching grants promote higher welfare for citizens of recipient governments. Therefore, nonmatching grants are more appropriate than matching grants when their primary purpose is to raise community welfare.

Equalization of the Income Distribution

Grants may be used to equalize the distribution of income in society. Sizes of many grants, for instance, are based on such factors as community income and urban density. Poorer communities therefore tend to receive larger grants than wealthier communities. Values of grants, however, tend to be based on characteristics of so-called average citizens residing in local communities, even though some poor communities may include a sizable population of higher-income citizens. Even though a local community may contain many poor citizens, higher-income individuals therefore receive transfers as well when grants are sent to local governments. It may be difficult, for instance, for local communities to distribute grant monies only to poor individuals when grantor governments provide conditional grants for such broadly used programs as sewage systems, roads, and mass transit. Economists therefore generally believe it is preferable to send transfers directly to poor individuals than to poor communities.

Another important concern is whether grant dollars are really distributed on the basis of income inequality among eligible lower-level governments. A study of the distribution of federal grants has found that, although grants were to be distributed on the basis of economic need, there was in fact no connection between grant dollars and such variables as poverty rates, per capita income, and urban density of recipient governments.[23] Various measures of political powers of recipient governments, however, were found to be significant determinants of the distribution of grants. For example, federal grant dollars awarded to state governments were positively influenced by the degree of seniority of U.S. Senators, percentages of congressional representatives in the majority party, and the degree to which elected members of Congress served on influential House and Senate committees. In other words, the stated intentions of grants may be to equalize incomes of citizens of recipient governments, but the policy process does not always yield policies that serve this purpose.

---

[21] For a recent counterview, arguing from evidence of the 1930s that matching grants allowed recipient governments greater discretion over their spending than unconditional grants, see John J. Wallis, "The Political Economy of New Deal Federalism," *Economic Inquiry* 24 (July 1991): 510–524.

[22] Congressional Budget Office, *Reducing the Deficit: Spending and Revenue Options,* February 1993.

[23] Randall G. Holcombe and Asghar Zardkoohi, "The Determinants of Federal Grants," *Southern Economic Journal* 48 (October 1981): 393–399.

Summary

- Fiscal federalism studies the structural organization of the public sector. Public spending has become increasingly centralized at the federal level of government. The theory of optimal fiscal structure focuses on designing a system of governments that meets the efficiency and equity goals of society.
- The major sources of state and local government revenues are fees and charges. Sales tax and property tax revenues are the second- and third-largest revenue sources, respectively.
- There are many advantages to having a federal system of government. A fundamental one is that it allows better correspondence to demand variations of local residents.
- The Tiebout model solves the problem of determining an optimal system of governments by allowing citizens to use their mobility to search for jurisdictions that meet their policy preferences. This search process creates an environment whereby governments compete for citizens. This model predicts that, because citizens search for desired packages of government programs, like-minded citizens tend to assemble in the same political jurisdictions.
- Federalism has several disadvantages. If public programs are subject to substantial economies of scale, then costs of providing these programs may rise with fiscal decentralization. Interjurisdictional externalities may prove difficult to control when there are many competing governments. Decentralization makes it more difficult for public programs to have national standards and to transfer income. It has also been suggested that tax wars erupt under federalism.
- Intergovernmental grants are a means of allowing grantor governments greater control over recipient governments. Grants are revenue transfers from one government to another. Conditional grants are the most common and occur when grantor governments indicate how revenues are to be spent by recipient governments. Unconditional grants do not specify how revenues are to be spent.
- In general, the influences of unconditional grants are similar to what happens on those occasions when local governments receive lump sum grants that carry no stipulation that all grant dollars be spent on public sector goods. Matching grants tend to cause communities to consume more public sector goods than they would consume under equivalent nonmatching grants. An excess burden occurs in this case because a policy that generates higher utility could replace another policy of equal cost. Matching grants are preferred, however, when grantor governments believe that recipient governments should be forced to consume more public sector goods than they otherwise would prefer to consume.

Review Questions

1. What is the subject matter of fiscal federalism?
2. What is meant by fiscal centralization? How can centralization be measured?
3. Which government functions are primarily carried out by the federal government? Which functions are more commonly carried out by state and local governments?
4. What are the major advantages of federalism?
5. What are the major disadvantages of federalism?
6. What is the Tiebout model?
7. What are the major types of intergovernmental grants?

Discussion Questions

1. Has the fiscal structure of the United States become more or less centralized over time? Discuss the two different approaches to measuring centralization.

2. We have shown that both centralized and decentralized fiscal structures have advantages and disadvantages. Explain how the theory of optimal fiscal structure incorporates the advantages of both.

3. In what sense does a decentralized public sector allow governments to tailor their services to the preferences of their citizens for public programs? Will a decentralized system create much uniformity in government programs across the nation?

4. Explain how the Tiebout model solves the problem of preference revelation since an efficient public sector does not require that policymakers determine what an optimal fiscal structure looks like.

5. It is widely believed that public goods are appropriately provided on the basis of who benefits from them. That is, it is optimal for programs, such as a local symphony or park, which provide benefits for relatively few citizens, to be provided by local governments. Provision by a central government is believed to be appropriate for programs such as national defense or health research with national benefits. Explain the logic behind these arguments.

6. Discuss the various assumptions that underlie the argument that school choice policies will damage only the public school system since such policies do not offer solutions to current problems with public education. Explain how this view differs from that of people who favor school choice policies.

7. We have argued that federalism allows state and local governments to conduct experiments that would not normally be pursued by the federal government. Name some areas in which federalism may promote experiments.

8. Explain why it is easier for special interest groups to secure preferential policies under relatively large governments.

9. What are the differences between conditional and unconditional grants? Explain why grantor governments may prefer to use one over the other.

10. If the purpose of grants is to help recipient governments, why not offer tax relief to recipient governments instead? Under what circumstances would tax relief be preferable over grants?

Key Words

Fiscal federalism
Optimal fiscal structure
Fiscal centralization
Tiebout model
Intergovernmental competition
Governments as laboratories
School choice
Interjurisdictional externalities
Tax wars
Intergovernmental grants
Conditional grants
Unconditional grants
Nonmatching conditional grants
Matching conditional grants

APPENDIX

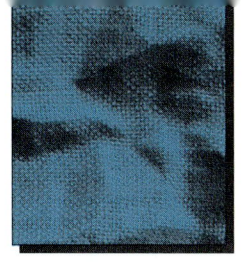

Review of Microeconomic Theory

This appendix contains a brief summary of the important microeconomic concepts used in public finance. Readers who have recently taken a microeconomics course may use this appendix to refresh their memories quickly, but beginning students may wish to consult an introductory or intermediate textbook for a more detailed presentation of microeconomic theory.

Exchange in Private Markets

Microeconomic theory analyzes the ways in which consumers and producers allocate the scarce resources of land, capital, and labor to produce goods and services. Without scarcity of resources, consumers and producers would always be able to completely satisfy their many needs and wants. But resource scarcity is a fact; therefore, microeconomics studies the ways in which consumers and producers make decisions about the many choices in consumption and production available to society. Microeconomics includes **consumer theory,** which studies the behaviors of consumers, and **producer theory,** which studies the behaviors of producers in the private market economy. Together, consumer and producer theories examine the exchange process that takes place between consumers and producers in private markets.

Consumer Theory

Utility Theory

Consumer theory rests on the **law of demand:** *An inverse, or negative, relationship exists between the price of a good and its quantity demanded by consumers.* An inverse relationship between two variables occurs when one variable rises as another variable falls. Thus if the quantity of apples demanded rises (falls) as the price of apples falls (rises), an inverse relationship exists between quantity demanded and price. Consumer theory demonstrates that the law of demand is a product of **utility-maximizing behavior,** where utility is a measure of the satisfaction that consumers receive from goods. By subjectively determining how much utility is derived from consumption, consumers choose which goods to purchase with their limited incomes.

In Figure A-1a we see the relationship between **total utility, *TU*,** and quantity of consumption. Kathy is a consumer who enjoys candy bars (*CB*); thus, as she begins

FIGURE A-1
Total Utility and the Law of Diminishing Marginal Utility

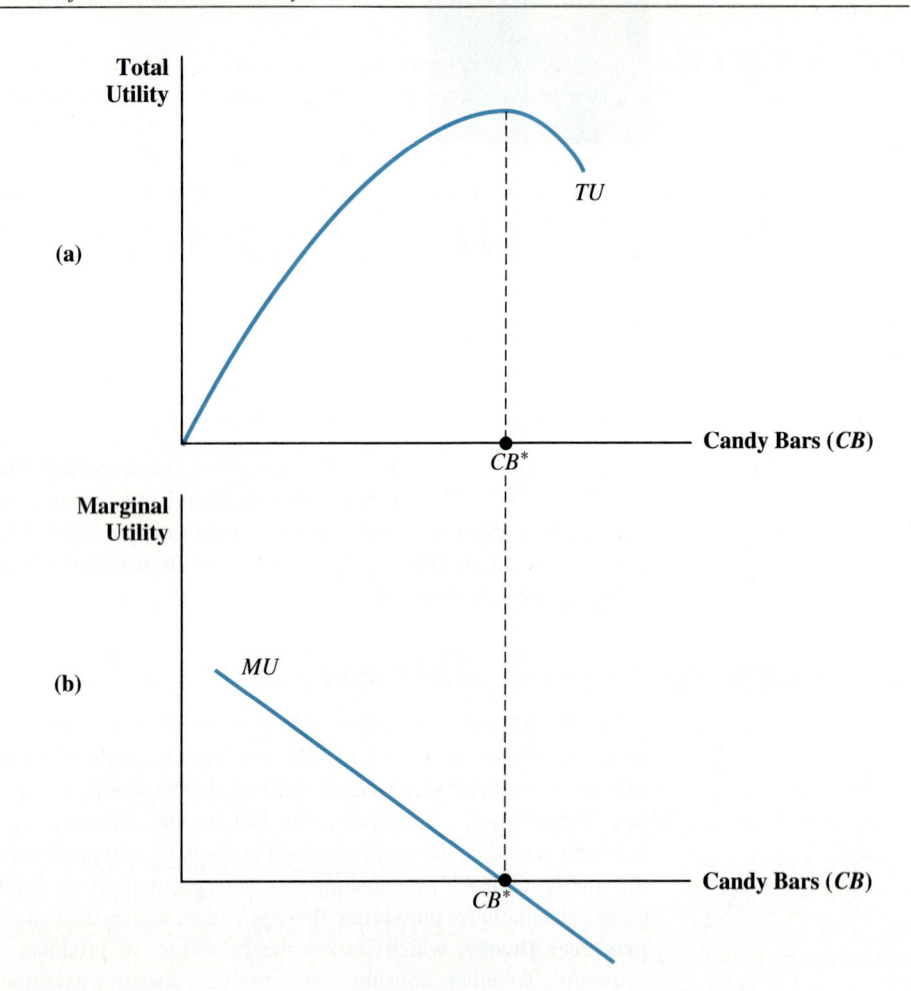

(a)

[Graph showing Total Utility (TU) curve rising, peaking at CB*, then falling, with Candy Bars (CB) on the x-axis]

(b)

[Graph showing Marginal Utility (MU) as a downward-sloping line crossing the x-axis at CB*, with Candy Bars (CB) on the x-axis]

to consume more candy bars, *TU* rises. However, after one or more candy bars, the additional utility she derives from eating more tends to diminish. Changes in total utility that occur with additional consumption of goods are termed **marginal utility,** *MU,* defined as $\Delta TU/\Delta Q$, where Δ (delta) means "change in" and Q is the quantity of consumption.

The fact that marginal utility tends to fall with repeated consumption of a good is so common that this behavior is called the **law of diminishing marginal utility:** *With repeated consumption, a point occurs at which further consumption is associated with falling marginal utility.* In Figure A-1b, for example, we see from *MU* that the first candy bar is the one that delivers the highest marginal utility to Kathy. As she eats additional candy bars, additional pleasure, as measured by marginal utility, starts to fall. Two reasons account for falling marginal utility. One reason is that consumers tend to receive the most satisfaction from the first uses of a good. For example, even if Kathy is a chocoholic, the first candy bar may satisfy her "sweet tooth." While still pleasurable, additional candy bars are bound to deliver less pleasure than the first bar. The other reason stems from physical limits or constraints. Kathy can consume just so many candy bars, for example, before becoming ill.

By itself, however, falling marginal utility does not indicate whether total utility is rising or falling. The issue of whether total utility is rising or falling rests on the relationship of marginal utility to zero. In Figure A-1, we see that total utility rises whenever further consumption yields positive (greater than zero) marginal utility. Only when marginal utility turns negative (less than zero) does total utility begin to fall with further consumption. Negative marginal utility means that Kathy becomes worse off with additional consumption; thus Kathy will not consume additional candy bars after marginal utility becomes negative.

How many candy bars will Kathy consume? Total utility is maximized at quantity CB^*, which is the number of candy bars where marginal utility becomes zero.[1]

Preference Orderings between Goods

Several factors influence Kathy's consumption of candy bars and these need to be examined within the utility framework. For example, Kathy's resources are undoubtedly limited and she purchases goods other than candy bars. Consumer theory examines how her income, the price of candy bars, and the prices of many other goods influence her overall behavior as a consumer.

If Kathy wishes to consume many goods, it is reasonable to assume that she ranks her preferences. Suppose then that her choices include three goods: candy bars (CB), milk shakes (MS), and green beans (GB). Kathy's preference orderings are assumed to be *transitive*. This means that, if Kathy prefers candy bars to milk shakes and milk shakes to green beans, then she also prefers candy bars to green beans. Kathy may also experience indifference between goods. This means that, given choices between two consumption opportunities, she does not care which good she consumes. Indifference orderings are also assumed to be transitive. Therefore, if Kathy is indifferent between candy bars and milk shakes and between milk shakes and green beans, then she is also indifferent between candy bars and green beans.

Indifference Schedules and Curves

Indifference schedules are lists of combinations, or bundles, of two goods such that consumers are indifferent between all combinations in the schedule. Consider the following two indifference schedules, $I1$ and $I2$, which characterize Kathy's tastes for candy bars and milk shakes:

---

[1] In mathematics, a function is maximized (or minimized) when its slope is zero. Because the slope of the total utility curve TU is equal to marginal utility, $MU = \Delta TU/\Delta Q$, total utility is maximized when $MU = 0$.

	Schedule $I1$		Schedule $I2$
Candy Bars *(CB)* (Units)	Milk Shakes *(MS)* (Units)	Candy Bars *(CB)* (Units)	Milk Shakes *(MS)* (Units)
10	0	12	0
7	1	10	1
5	2	8	2
4	4	6	4

Along $I1$, Kathy is indifferent between four *(CB,MS)* combinations, which also means that all four combinations—(10, 0), (7, 1), (5, 2), and (4, 4)—are equally desirable. While $I1$ also lists four combinations that Kathy is indifferent between, she prefers each combination in $I2$ to each combination in $I2$. This preference follows from the fact that, for any quantity of milk shakes, $I2$ provides more candy bars than does $I1$, as seen, for example, in the *(CB, MS)* bundle (5, 2) on $I1$ versus bundle (8, 2) on $I1$.[2]

Plots of indifference schedules are called **indifference curves.** In Figure A-2, for example, we see two indifference curves in which quantities of candy bars and milk shakes are plotted on each axis. Indifference curves have four general characteristics.

❑ *Indifference curves have negative slopes.* Indifference curves have negative slopes because consumers tend to prefer larger quantities of all goods. Economists call the slope of indifference curves the **marginal rate of substitution (MRS)**. The formula for the *MRS* of indifference curves shown in Figure A-2 is $-(\Delta MS/\Delta CB)$, where *MS* is the quantity of milk shakes and *CB* is the quantity of candy bars. A negative *MRS* indicates that, if Kathy consumes fewer milk shakes, she can maintain her utility level only by consuming more candy bars. The *MRS* measures the rate at which Kathy is willing to trade milk shakes for candy bars and, at the same time, remain equally satisfied with all combinations along the indifference curve. Indifference, then, is indicated by movements along a negatively sloped indifference curve.

❑ *Utility is positively related to distance from origin.* Consumers prefer combinations of goods lying on indifference curves that are farthest from the origin. While any bundle along $I1$ yields identical utility, any bundle on $I2$ is preferred to any bundle on $I1$. To demonstrate this, compare point *a*, which contains combination (MS_1, CB_1), to point *b*, which contains combination (MS_1, CB_2). Because *a* and *b* contain identical quantities of milk shakes (MS_1), *a* and *b* may be differentiated by quantities of candy bars. Because *b* contains more candy bars than *a*, Kathy prefers *b* to *a*. Furthermore, because Kathy is indifferent between any bundle along one indifference curve, all bundles on $I2$ are preferred to all bundles on $I1$. Utility is therefore positively related to distance from the origin.

---

[2] We are assuming that marginal utilities of all goods are always greater than zero. This is a common assumption since it is reasonable to expect that utility-maximizing consumers never consume where marginal utility is negative.

FIGURE A-2
Indifference Curves

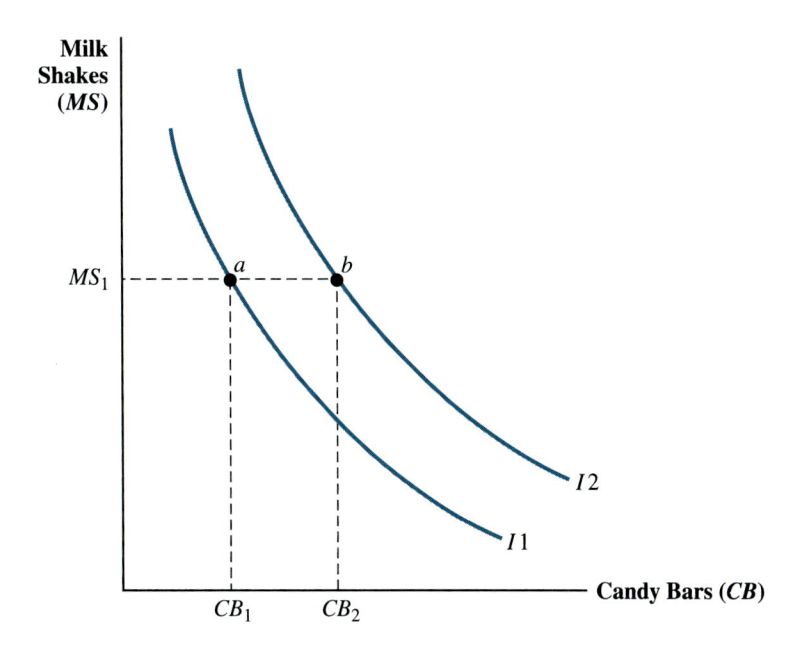

- *Indifference curves are nonintersecting.* Examine the logic implied by the intersection of $I1$ and $I2$ at bundle a in Figure A-3. Because c lies on the same indifference curve as a, and b also lies on the same indifference curve as a, Kathy must be indifferent between c and a and between b and a. Thus, by the transitive property of preference orderings, Kathy must also be indifferent between c and b. But how could she be indifferent between c and b when, for identical levels of candy bars, c offers a greater number of milk shakes than b? This logic violates the assumption that more of a good is preferred to less; therefore, indifference curves do not intersect.

- *Indifference curves are convex to the origin.* Convexity means that the slope (MRS) of an indifference curve falls with movements down I. The implications of a falling MRS are demonstrated in Figure A-4 where $MRS = -\Delta MS/\Delta CB$. Now consider moving down $I1$ in equal increments (ΔMS) of milk shakes and observe what happens to ΔCB. A movement from a to b shows that, as the number of milk shakes falls from MS_5 to MS_4, Kathy increases her consumption of candy bars from CB_1 to CB_2. MRS is then $-(MS_5 - MS_4)/(CB_1 - CB_2)$. Next, movement from b to c shows that, for an identical reduction of milk shakes (MS_4 to MS_3), Kathy increases her consumption of candy bars from CB_2 to CB_3. The MRS is now $-(MS_4 - MS_3)/(CB_2 - CB_3)$, and because $MS_5 - MS_4 = MS_4 - MS_3$ and $CB_1 - CB_2 < CB_2 - CB_3$, the slope of $I1$ falls when moving from a to b. Similar observations may be made for movements to c, d and e and demonstrate that $I1$ is convex to the origin.

**FIGURE A-3
Indifference Curves
Do Not Intersect**

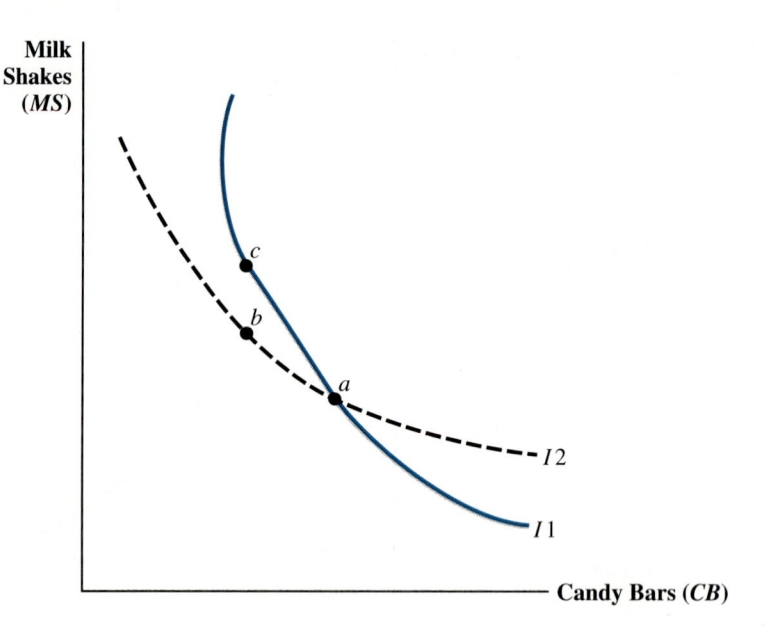

**FIGURE A-4
Indifference Curves
Are Convex to the
Origin**

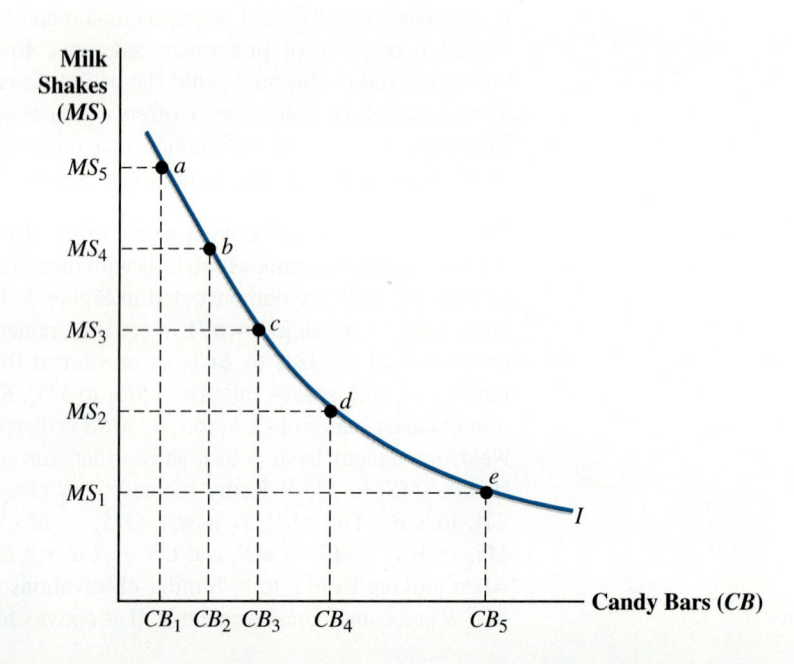

What intuition explains the convexity of indifference curves?[3] While Kathy's indifference between *a* and *b* implies that both offer identical utility, movement from *a* to *b* means that the marginal utilities of candy bars and milk shakes are changing. Following the law of diminishing marginal utility, Kathy's high consumption of milk shakes at *a* is associated with relatively low marginal utility and her low consumption of candy bars is associated with relatively high marginal utility. In other words, one less milk shake does not greatly reduce Kathy's overall utility; so, as compensation for one less milk shake, Kathy is willing to accept a relatively small increase in candy bars. This is also true because, at *a*, Kathy is consuming relatively few candy bars and therefore one more candy bar yields a relatively high increase in total utility. As candy bars are substituted for milk shakes, the decrease in overall utility caused by the lower consumption of milk shakes (MS_5 to MS_4) is relatively small; therefore, as compensation for that decrease in overall utility, Kathy is willing to accept a relatively small increase in candy bars (CB_1 to CB_2).

The story changes as we move from *b* to *c*. While there is the same reduction in milk shakes as from *a* to *b*, milk shakes are becoming relatively more scarce and candy bars are becoming relatively less scarce. Compensation for the same reduction in milk shakes now requires a larger increase in candy bars if Kathy is to experience no change in overall utility. This is true because higher marginal utility of milk shakes requires more candy bars as compensation for the larger reduction in overall utility

---

[3] A more technical discussion of falling *MRS* follows from equation (1), which is the equation for an indifference curve:

$$TU_T = TU_{MS} + TU_{CB} \qquad (1)$$

where TU_T is Kathy's overall total utility level, TU_{MS} is her milk shake utility level, and TU_{CB} is her candy bar utility level. Equation (1) shows that overall utility is a function of the separate utilities associated with consuming each of the two products. For a movement down an indifference curve, we can rewrite (1) as

$$\Delta TU_T = \Delta TU_{MS} + \Delta TU_{CB} = 0 \qquad (2)$$

Equation (2) is equal to zero since, for movements down an indifference curve, overall total utility does not change. That is, in order for total utility to be unchanged, movements along an indifference curve must be met with equal changes in the utility levels associated with each of the two products. We can rewrite (2) as

$$MU_{MS}\,\Delta Q_{MS} + MU_{CB}\,\Delta Q_{CB} = 0 \quad \text{or} \quad -MU_{MS}\,\Delta Q_{MS} = MU_{CB}\,\Delta Q_{CB} \qquad (3)$$

Equation (3) shows that the change in utility associated with fewer units of milk shakes is equal to $-MU_{MS}\,\Delta Q_{MS}$, which is the marginal utility of milk shakes multiplied by the reduced number of milk shakes. The change in utility associated with more units of candy bars is equal to $MU_{CB}\,\Delta Q_{CB}$, which is the marginal utility of candy bars multiplied by the increased number of candy bars. We can rewrite (3) as (4) to arrive at the *MRS*, or the slope of an indifference curve:

$$\frac{\Delta Q_{MS}}{\Delta Q_{CB}} = \frac{-MU_{CB}}{MU_{MS}} \qquad (4)$$

The *MRS* of milk shakes for candy bars is identical to the ratio of the marginal utility of candy bars to the marginal utility of milk shakes; therefore, *MRS* falls along an indifference curve because of what is happening to MU_{CB}/MU_{MS}. As candy bars are substituted for milk shakes, the marginal utility of candy bars tends to fall and the marginal utility of milk shakes tends to rise, as indicated by the law of diminishing marginal utility. Therefore, as the numerator falls and the denominator rises, the ratio MU_{CB}/MU_{MS}, which is *MRS*, falls.

stemming from fewer milk shakes. In addition, each additional candy bar is associated with falling marginal utility, and therefore more candy bars are required as compensation for decreases in milk shakes. The story continues for movements farther down I as more and more candy bars are required as compensation for the increasing scarcity of milk shakes. Therefore, changes in marginal utilities that occur as milk shakes are traded for candy bars explain why falling *MRS* is a characteristic of indifference curves.

Budget Constraints

Two factors influence consumption opportunities: prices of products and the incomes of consumers. Suppose, for example, that Kathy has $10 and that the prices of candy bars and milk shakes are, respectively, $1 and $2 per unit. If Kathy uses her income to purchase only one of the products, she could purchase 5 milk shakes or 10 candy bars. In Figure A-5, these maximum consumption opportunities occur at points *A* and *B* on the two axes where the quantities of milk shakes and candy bars are measured. The straight line *AB* formed by these points includes all combinations that may be purchased for $10 and is called a **budget constraint.** For example, bundle *b* on *AB* contains 3 milk shakes and 4 candy bars and costs $10.

What about bundles not included on *AB*? Bundle *a*, which lies below *AB*, contains 2 milk shakes and 2 candy bars and costs only $6. Therefore, all bundles below constraint *AB* cost less than Kathy's budget. In contrast, bundle *c*, which contains 4 milk shakes and 6 candy bars, costs $14. Therefore, all bundles above constraint *AB* lie beyond Kathy's budget of $10.

The ratio of prices, $-P_{CB}/P_{MS}$, is the slope of *AB* and, in our example, is equal to $-1/2$. This means that for every milk shake Kathy gives up, she can buy 2 candy bars.[4] The slope then indicates the rate at which Kathy may exchange candy bars for milk shakes and remain within her budget.

What happens to the budget constraint when the price of candy bars changes?[5] Intuitively, higher prices mean that fewer goods may be purchased. Figure A-6 shows that when the price of candy bars rises from $1 to $2, the maximum number of candy bars Kathy may purchase is 5. If the price of milk shakes remains the same, the slope of the new budget constraint *AC* is $-2/2$, or -1, which is steeper than *AB*, the old budget constraint. This steeper slope reflects fewer consumption opportunities. In

---

[4] That the slope is equal to the ratio of product prices follows from the budget constraint equation

$$I = P_{MS}Q_{MS} + P_{CB}Q_{CB} \qquad (1)$$

where I = income, P = product prices, and Q = quantities of goods. A movement along the budget constraint (1) does not change income and therefore may be shown as

$$\Delta I = P_{MS}\Delta Q_{MS} + P_{CB}\Delta Q_{CB} = 0 \qquad (2)$$

Rearrangement of (2) shows that the slope of the budget constraint is

$$\frac{\Delta Q_{MS}}{\Delta Q_{CB}} = \frac{-P_{CB}}{P_{MS}} \qquad (3)$$

[5] The price of milk shakes can be changed as well; and, using the formula for its slope, $-P_{CB}/P_{MS}$, we can easily determine if the resulting budget constraint becomes flatter or steeper.

FIGURE A-5
Budget Constraint

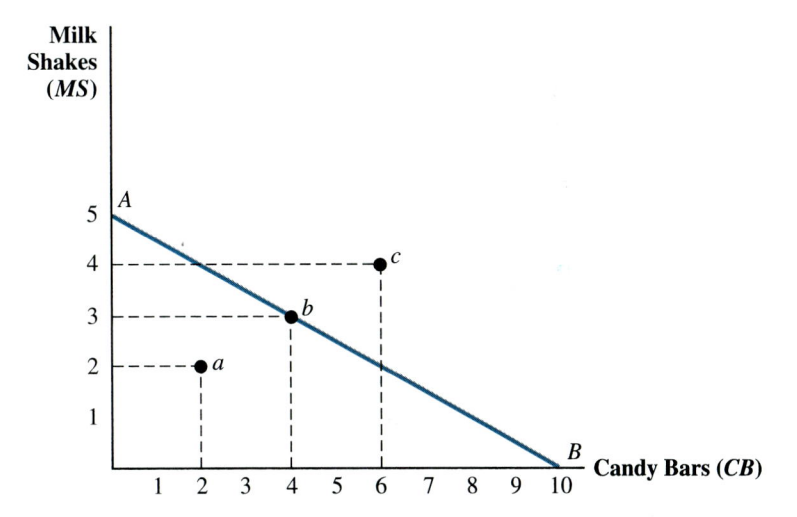

FIGURE A-6
Price Changes and Budget Constraints

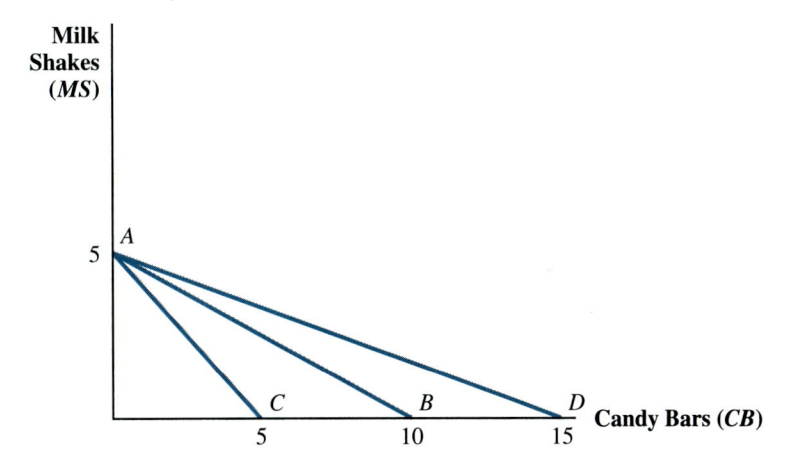

other words, for every milk shake Kathy now gives up, she may purchase only one more candy bar. In contrast, a fall in the price of candy bars to $0.67 flattens the budget constraint, as indicated by AD. The slope of AD is $-(0.67/2) = -0.33$, which indicates that, for every milk shake she gives up, Kathy may purchase three more candy bars.

What happens to Kathy's budget constraint when prices hold constant but her income changes? Higher income means greater consumption opportunities. Budget constraint CD in Figure A-7 reflects a doubling of income to $20, so that when all income is spent on one good, 10 milk shakes or 20 candy bars may be purchased. Because product prices have not been changed, the slopes of AB and CD are identical.

Consumer Equilibrium

Indifference curves and budget constraints are the tools necessary to place consumers in equilibrium. Indifference curves convey information about tastes for goods

**FIGURE A-7
Income Changes and Budget Constraints**

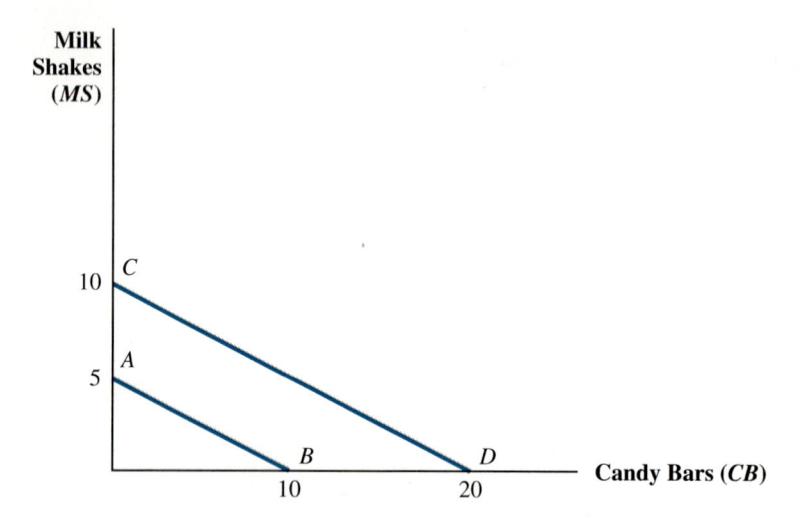

[Graph showing Milk Shakes (MS) on vertical axis and Candy Bars (CB) on horizontal axis. Two parallel downward-sloping budget lines: inner line AB from A (MS=5) to B (CB=10); outer line CD from C (MS=10) to D (CB=20).]

consumers *wish* to consume and budget constraints indicate which combinations of goods they *can* consume. Figure A-8 shows Kathy's budget constraint and a few of the many indifference curves that reflect her tastes for candy bars and milk shakes. Which combination of goods will she choose?

Although all bundles of candy bars and milk shakes on *AB* are candidates for using all of her income, each bundle yields different levels of utility. Because the farther an indifference curve is from the origin, the higher its associated utility, Kathy maximizes utility by choosing a bundle on *AB* that lies on the indifference curve farthest from the origin. Utility is not maximized along *I*1 since Kathy can afford many bundles along *I*2. But bundles *d* or *c* on *I*2 are not chosen—even though they yield higher utility than any bundle on *I*1—because other bundles with higher utility may still be purchased. Bundle *f* along *I*4 yields higher utility but cannot be selected because it lies outside of her income. Inspection reveals that bundle *e* with combination (CB^*, MS^*) is just right: It lies on the budget constraint and, at the same time, yields the highest utility.

Consumer equilibrium occurs only when a consumer has no reason to change consumption. Bundle *e* is a point of consumer equilibrium because, when Kathy chooses that bundle, she cannot afford another combination of candy bars and milk shakes that yields higher utility. In other words, bundle *e* is the only one at which she has no reason to change her combination of milk shakes and candy bars because she cannot increase her utility and, at the same time, remain within her budget.

An important characteristic of consumer equilibrium is that it occurs at the point where an indifference curve is tangent to a budget constraint. A *tangency* occurs when the slopes of two lines are equal. Therefore, at *e*, $MRS = -P_{CB}/P_{MS}$.[6] At any bundle

---

[6] More technically, the equality of slopes of budget constraints and indifference curves means that $-P_{CB}/P_{MS} = MU_{CB}/MU_{MS}$; therefore, $MU_{CB}/P_{CB} = MU_{MS}/P_{MS}$ at consumer equilibrium. The latter condition indicates that utility is maximized when the utility from spending an additional dollar on each good is equal.

**FIGURE A-8
Consumer
Equilibrium**

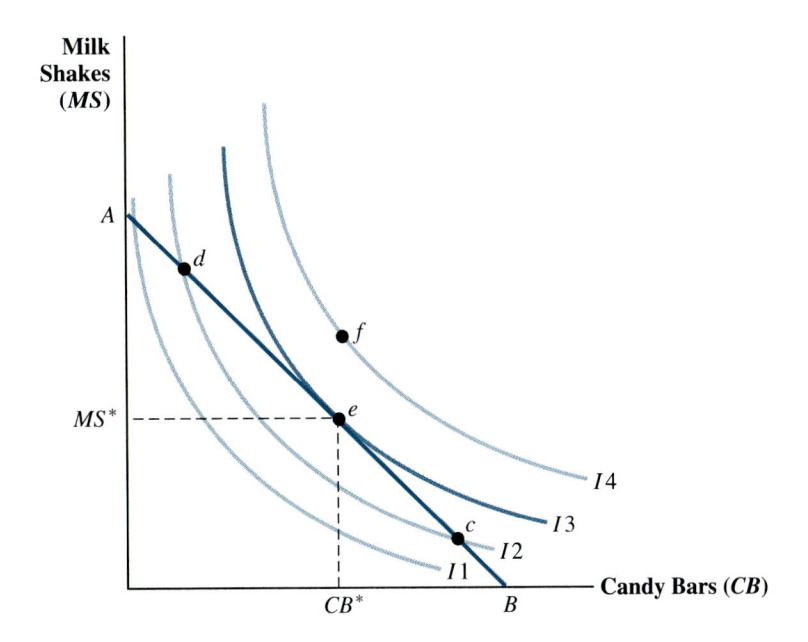

other than e, $MRS \neq -P_{CB}/P_{MS}$. To understand why equality of slopes is a characteristic of consumer equilibrium, consider bundle d. If by trading milk shakes for candy bars, Kathy moves onto higher indifference curves, then gains in utility from more candy bars more than offsets losses in utility associated with decreased consumption of milk shakes. Since the MRS at d is relatively high, Kathy is eager to exchange many milk shakes for candy bars. The MRS at d is also higher than the slope of the budget constraint ($MRS > -P_{CB}/P_{MS}$) which indicates that the rate at which she is *willing* to trade milk shakes for candy bars (MRS) is greater than the rate at which she is *able* to trade these products (P_{CB}/P_{MS}). When $MRS > -P_{CB}/P_{MS}$, utility is increased by choosing fewer milk shakes and more candy bars.

As Kathy purchases more candy bars and fewer milk shakes, she becomes less enthusiastic about the trade, as indicated by falling MRS. At bundle c, for example, the MRS of the indifference curve is lower than the slope of the budget constraint ($MRS < -P_{CB}/P_{MS}$), which indicates that Kathy's willingness to substitute more candy bars for milk shakes is lower than the market price trade-off between the two goods. Here, utility is improved by consuming more milk shakes and fewer candy bars. Only at bundle e where $MRS = -P_{CB}/P_{MS}$ can Kathy not substitute between the two goods and increase utility.

Changes in Income and Consumer Equilibrium

In Figure A-9 we see the effect of higher income on Kathy's equilibrium purchase of candy bars and milk shakes. As income rises, budget constraints shift outward and parallel to AB, as budget constraints CD and EF show. Kathy adjusts to higher incomes by choosing bundles that lie at the tangencies of indifference curves and budget constraints. The path of her equilibrium bundles, $e1e2e3$, which is called an

**FIGURE A-9
Income Consumption
Curve**

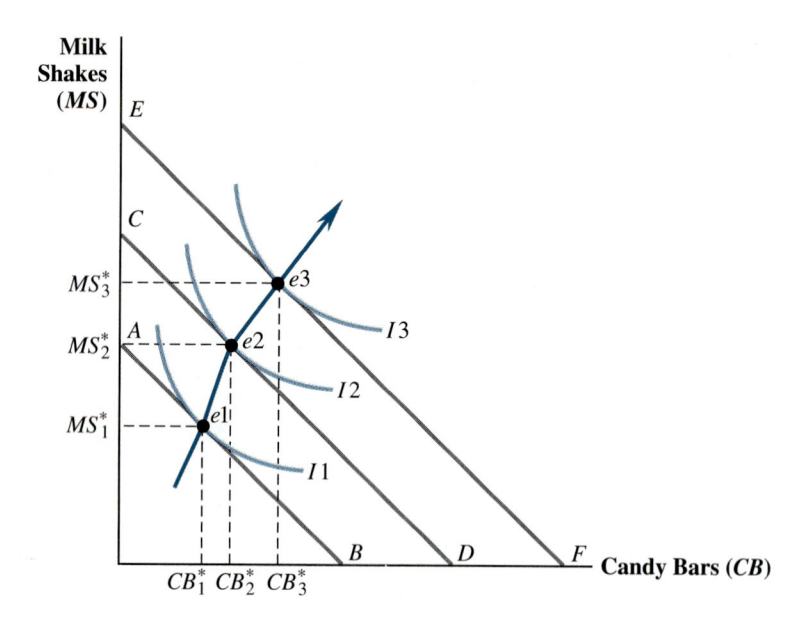

Figure: Income consumption curve with Milk Shakes (MS) on vertical axis and Candy Bars (CB) on horizontal axis, showing equilibrium points e1, e2, e3 on indifference curves I1, I2, I3 with budget lines AB, CD, EF.

income consumption curve, defines the equilibrium path that consumption follows as income changes. In this case candy bars are normal goods. **Normal goods** are goods whose consumption increases as income expands. Thus, as we see in Figure A-9, income consumption curves of normal goods have positive slopes. In Figure A-10, however, we see a negatively sloped income consumption curve for the case in which candy bars are **inferior goods;** that is, goods whose consumption decreases when income expands. Tastes of consumers are a major determinant of whether goods are normal or inferior.[7] Differences in tastes, for example, explain the different behaviors of consumers who, if given higher incomes, reduce their consumption of a good—say, hamburgers—and others, who increase their consumption of the same good.

Changes in Prices and Consumer Equilibrium

Figure A-11a shows the effect of lower prices of candy bars on consumer equilibrium. Lower prices flatten slopes of budget constraints as shown, for example, by the change from *AB* to *AC*. Flatter budget constraints indicate that, for every milk shake given up, Kathy may purchase a greater number of candy bars. Bundle *e*1 no longer represents consumer equilibrium since rearrangement of candy bars and milk shakes (along the flatter budget constraint) increases utility. New equilibrium bundle *e*2 is characterized by (1) more of each good (MS_1^* to MS_2^* and CB_1^* to CB_2^*) and (2) higher utility (*I*1 to *I*2). Figure A-11a shows only three equilibrium bundles, but we can conceive of many equilibrium bundles corresponding to each possible price of candy bars.[8] A line drawn

---

[7] It is also possible to have both positive and negative segments to the slopes of income consumption curves. This means that, at some income levels, a good is normal and, at other segments, it is inferior.

[8] Figure A-11a shows the case of a positively sloped price consumption curve. Other cases exist, however, and the slopes of price consumption curves depend upon price elasticity of demand. Intermediate microeconomic textbooks show the details of the differences implied by price elasticities.

FIGURE A-10
Inferior Good

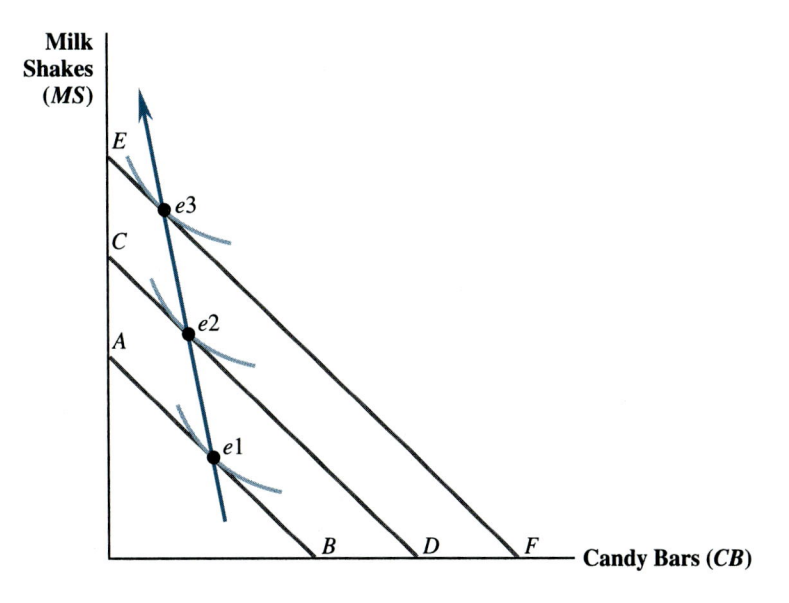

FIGURE A-11
Demand Curve Derived from the Price Consumption Curve

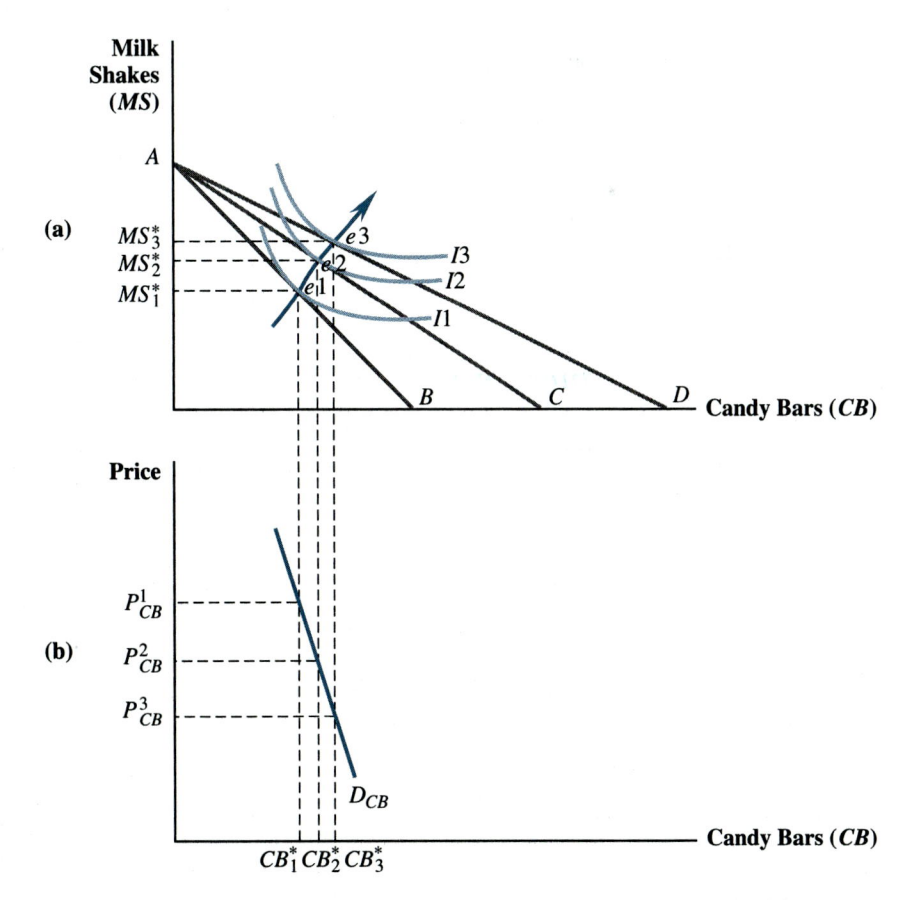

(a)

(b)

through all corresponding points of consumer equilibrium (outlined here by $e1e2e3$) is called a **price consumption curve,** which indicates how consumption of goods changes with prices.

Deriving Demand Curves from Price Consumption Curves

Demand curves are derived from price consumption curves. Four factors influence demands for goods:

- *Price.* Decreases in the prices of goods—houses, cars, lobsters—increase buyers' *enthusiasm* for goods.
- *Income.* Income is an important determinant of *purchasing ability;* for normal goods, higher incomes expand consumption, and for inferior goods, higher incomes reduce consumption.
- *Tastes.* Consumers' subjective preferences are important determinants of *demand.* Some individuals enjoy eating broccoli and other individuals can think of very few vegetables they enjoy less than broccoli. Broccoli-lovers can be expected to have relatively strong demand and broccoli-haters have weaker, or no, demand for the vegetable.
- *Prices of Closely Related Goods and Services.* When two goods are **substitutes** for each other, a higher price of one good causes the consumer to purchase more of the other. Candy bars and ice cream are substitutes when higher candy bar prices lead consumers to purchase more ice cream and fewer candy bars. When two goods are **complements** of each other, a higher price of one causes consumers to consume less of the other. Movie-going and candy bars are complements when increases in ticket prices decrease movie-goers' consumption of candy bars (since fewer tickets purchased results in fewer candy bars consumed).

In Figure A-11b, we use the price consumption curve in Figure A-11a to construct Kathy's **demand curve** for candy bars. At price P^1_{CB}, Kathy maximizes utility by consuming CB^*_1 candy bars. Price P^1_{CB} is obtained from the numerator of the price ratio that determines the slope of budget constraint AB. If price is lowered to P^2_{CB} (as obtained from the flatter budget constraint AC), Kathy maximizes utility by consuming CB^*_2 candy bars. In other words, as the price of candy bars is lowered, Kathy consumes a greater number of candy bars. This behavior, as described by the price consumption curve in Figure A-11a, is plotted in Figure A-11b. The only difference between the upper and lower portions of Figure A-11 is that the vertical axis in Figure A-11a measures quantity of milk shakes and the vertical axis in Figure A-11b measures the price of candy bars. The relationship between price and quantity demanded, which is plotted in Figure A-11b, is the demand curve for candy bars.

Note the following three points about demand curves.

1. *Demand curves have negative slopes.* As price falls, quantity demanded rises. This inverse relationship is a result of utility-maximizing behavior on the part of consumers and indicates that, when prices are lowered, consumers choose more of those goods and, at the same time, achieve higher utility.

2. *Price changes do not shift demand curves.* In order to isolate the relationship between price and quantity demanded by consumers, the *ceteris paribus* (which is Latin for "other things being equal") assumption holds constant all other determinants of demand. These other determinants are income, tastes, and prices of closely related goods. For movements along a given demand curve, there can be no change in these other determinants; therefore, demand cannot change. For example, in Figure A-11b, as long as income, tastes, and the prices of closely related goods do not change, D_{CB} is the demand for candy bars. Changes in prices of candy bars cause movements along that demand curve and are called **changes in quantity demanded.** A drop in price for P_{CB}^1 to P_{CB}^2, for example, causes an increase in the quantity demanded of candy bars from CB_1^* to CB_2^*.

3. *When the other determinants of demand change, demand curves shift.*[9] When the *ceteris paribus* assumption is relaxed, demand curves shift. Figure A-12 demonstrates two possible shifts: an increase from D_{CB} to D_{CB}'' and a decrease from D_{CB} to D_{CB}'. To understand why these movements are called **increases in demand** and **decreases in demand,** consider the positions of these demand curves with respect to P_{CB}. Going from D_{CB} to D_{CB}'', the quantity consumed at P_{CB} is larger on D_{CB}'' ($CB_3 > CB_1$); therefore, this change reflects an increase in the demand for candy bars. Going from D_{CB} to D_{CB}', the quantity consumed at P_{CB} is smaller on D_{CB}' ($CB_2 < CB_1$) and therefore reflects a decrease in the demand for candy bars.

Substitution and Income Effects

Figure A-13 shows that two separate effects—substitution effects and income effects—occur when a fall in the price of candy bars causes Kathy to increase consumption of candy bars from CB_1 to CB_3. **Substitution effects** indicate how price changes affect the attractiveness of products to consumers; such effects suggest the degree to which consumers substitute into and out of other goods when the price of one good changes. In other words, a decrease in the price of ice cream, for example, makes consumers purchase more ice cream and fewer cookies. **Income effects** indicate how, in response to a change in the price of a good, consumers respond to changes in the purchasing power of their income. Suppose at a price of $1 per orange, Pat buys 3 oranges for a total expenditure of $3 on oranges. When the price falls to $0.25 per orange, Pat need spend only $0.75 if he purchases the same number of oranges. With $2.25 left over, however, Pat may decide to purchase additional oranges—this would be a result of the income effect.

Substitution Effects

Substitution effects measure the change in consumption that stems from the lower relative price of a good—*not* to any other factor that might influence the consumption of that good. Thus, in Kathy's case, substitution effects would measure a change in her

---

[9] The word "other" is used here because it reflects all determinants of demand other than price of the product. As just discussed, changes in price cause "changes in quantity demanded" and not "changes or shifts in demand."

FIGURE A-12
Changes in Demand

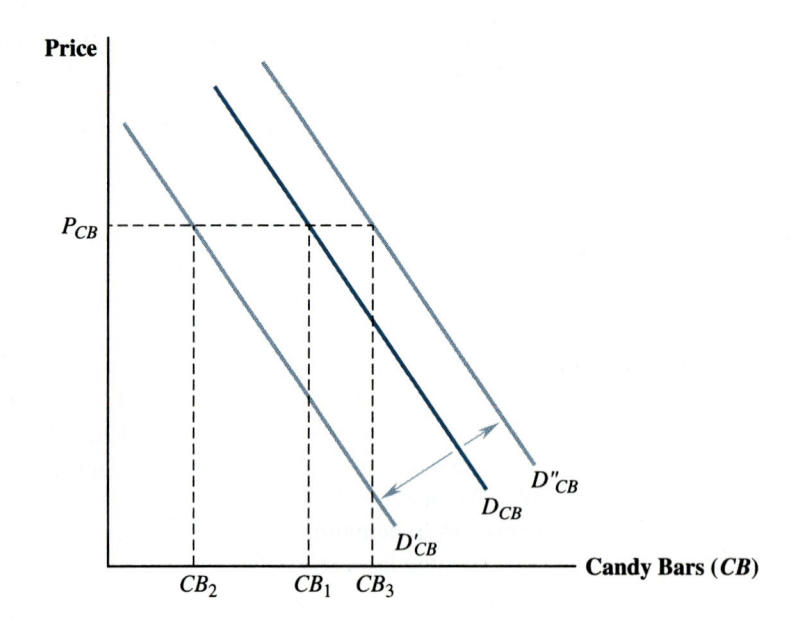

FIGURE A-13
Substitution and Income Effects

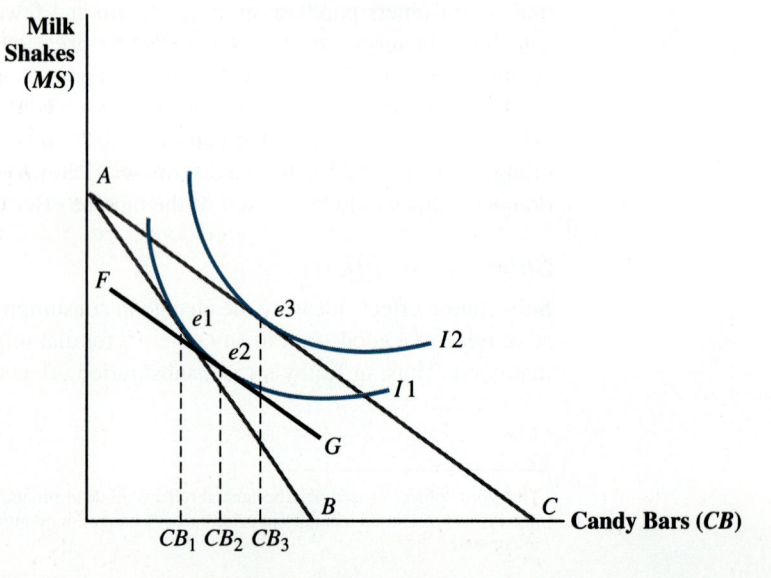

consumption arising solely from the lower relative price of candy bars.[10] To determine this substitution, we ask the following question: If Kathy remains on indifference curve $I1$, how many more candy bars will she purchase when prices are lower? The answer to this question comes from determining where consumer equilibrium would lie on $I1$ when Kathy discovers the lower relative price of candy bars. Budget constraint FG, drawn parallel to AC, is tangent to the original indifference curve $I1$ at point $e2$; thus, its slope represents the new lower relative price of candy bars. Distance CB_1CB_2 is the substitution effect that results from the drop in the price of candy bars since, by holding utility constant along $I1$, Kathy is no better off than before the change in the relative price of candy bars. Kathy would purchase CB_2, and not CB_1, candy bars solely as a result of the lower relative price.

Income Effects

Income effects measure the extent to which changes in consumption are due to the higher purchasing power of income that follow from price changes. For example, an individual with $100 can purchase more compact discs at $10 each than at $20 each. In our example, the income effect measures how many more candy bars Kathy buys when her purchasing power rises. Distance CB_2CB_3 is the income effect since the parallel shift from FG to AC allows the consumer to move from equilibrium bundle $e2$ to $e3$. Because the relative price of candy bars does not change when the budget constraint shifts from FG and AC, this effect is unrelated to the substitution effect. (Note carefully that, while this discussion of parallel shifting of budget constraints is similar to our discussion of income consumption curves, income levels are not changing; only the purchasing power of the initial income has changed[11])

The total change in consumption CB_1CB_3 then comprises two components: substitution effect CB_1CB_2 and income effect CB_2CB_3.

Market Demand Curves

Market demand curves are constructed by aggregating the demands of all individuals in a specific market. Figure A-14 exhibits the demand curves of three individuals for movies: D_C^M (Chan), D_M^M (Manuel) and D_V^M (Veda). Assuming the market comprises these three individuals, the market demand curve is constructed by horizontally summing the demand curves of each individual. At price P_1^M, Chan chooses 2, Manuel chooses 3, and Veda chooses 4 movies, so market quantity demanded is 9 movies. Summing quantities for each individual and for each price, market demand is therefore D_{C+M+V}^M.

---

[10] The term *relative* is used here since it is the price of candy bars, relative to the price of milk shakes, that matters to Kathy.

[11] We cannot consider a change of income here since it is being held constant within the *ceteris paribus* assumption. However, if it were to change, then the demand curve would shift and therefore invalidate our price consumption curve, which is defined by $e1$ and $e3$.

**FIGURE A-14
Market Demand Curves**

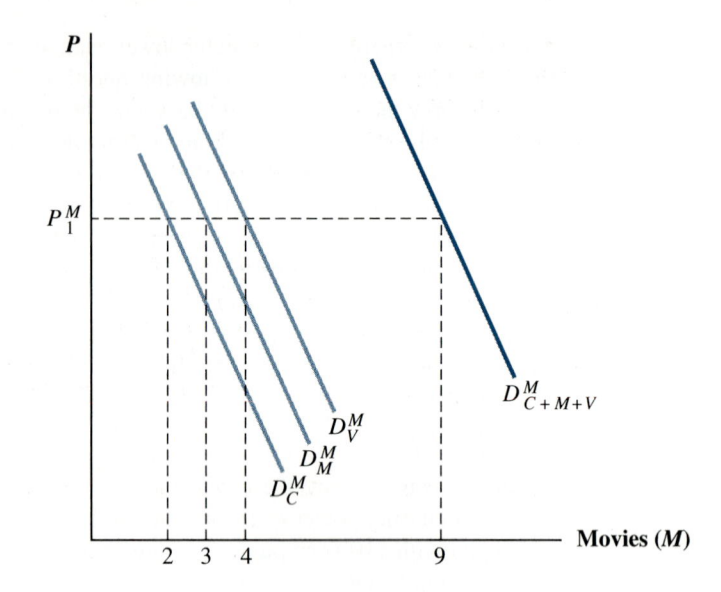

(Figure: Market demand curves plotted on axes P vs Movies (M); curves labeled D_C^M, D_M^M, D_V^M, and D_{C+M+V}^M; at price P_1^M, quantities 2, 3, 4, and 9 are indicated.)

Producer Theory

Role of Profits

Producer theory models the role of suppliers in delivering products to consumers. Producers are assumed to be profit-maximizers where profits are defined as total revenues minus total costs. To calculate total revenue, we use the price and quantity information summarized by demand curves. Total revenues are determined by multiplying product price by quantity sold to consumers: Thus, for example, if consumers purchase 1,000 oranges at $0.50 each, total revenues are $500. If total production costs for 1,000 oranges are $400, producers earn a profit of $100.

Production Costs and Supply Curves

Supply curves summarize the behavior of producers in private markets and show the relationship between the prices of goods and the quantities producers are willing to provide at those prices. Profits are enhanced whenever costs are minimized; therefore, profit-maximization behavior requires minimization of production costs. Supply curves have three important characteristics.

1. *Supply curves have positive slopes.* Figure A-15 shows a hypothetical market supply curve (S^A) for apples.[12] On the vertical axis is price per bushel (P) and, on the horizontal axis, is the number of bushels produced (A). Supply S^A has a positive slope, which indicates that, at higher prices, producers are willing to produce more bushels of apples. For example, at P_1^A, producers are willing to supply A_1 bushels

---

[12] As in the case of market demand, market supply is constructed by summing horizontally the supply curves of all firms in the market.

FIGURE A-15
Supply Curve

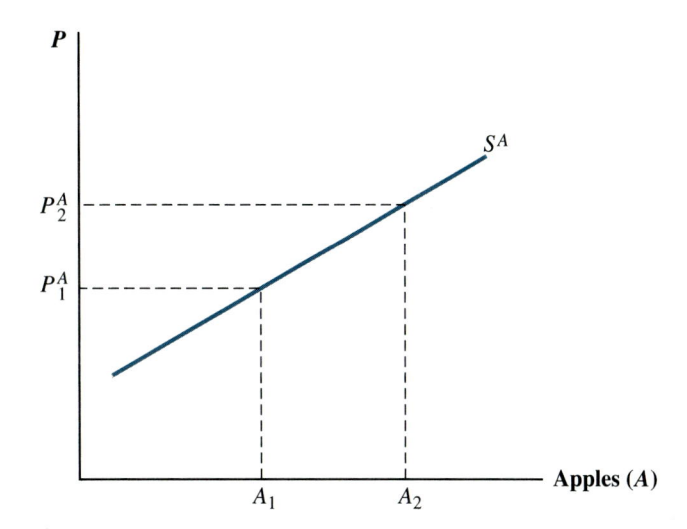

and, at P_2^A, producers are willing to supply A_2 bushels of apples. This positive relationship between price and quantity results from diminishing marginal productivity. That is, because resources are scarce and heterogeneous, increases in production generally result in higher costs of production. Heterogeneity of resources means that not all resources are of equal quality. To produce more apples, producers may be able to increase farmland only by adding acreage not as well suited to producing apples as the acreage they are currently farming. While this increased farmland may allow the seller to produce more apples, each additional bushel produced on inferior farmland will cost more. Because resources are both scarce and heterogeneous, producers must incur higher costs to produce more output; thus price and quantity of supply are positively related.

2. *Changes in product prices do not shift supply curves.* Economists isolate the relationship between product price and quantity supplied by invoking the *ceteris paribus* assumption that holds constant all other factors that might influence supply. Two factors are held constant along any given supply curve:

❏ *Prices of resources:* Resource prices are costs of using the scarce resources land, labor and capital to produce goods. Because higher (lower) resource prices mean higher (lower) production costs, changes in resource prices influence how producers allocate resources. When labor costs rise, for example, producers often reduce labor resources and expand usage of capital equipment.

❏ *Technology of production:* Technology is the way in which resources are transformed into products. It determines how many resources, and what combinations, are required to produce goods. Advances in technology arising from research and development result in fewer or better combinations of resources necessary to produce goods. Thus, as in the obvious cases of pocket calculators and personal computers, improved technology and technological advances lower production costs.

For movements along supply curves, no change in resource prices and technology occur, and therefore supply curves do not shift when product price changes. In Figure A-15, a drop in price from P_2^A to P_1^A causes a movement along the supply curve which is called a **decrease in quantity supplied** from A_2 to A_1. A rise in price from P_1^A to P_2^A causes a movement along the supply curve which is called an **increase in quantity supplied** from A_1 to A_2.

3. *Supply curves shift in response to changes in resource prices and technology.* Relaxation of the *ceteris paribus* assumption leads to shifts in supply curves. Figure A-16 demonstrates the two directions in which shifts in supply curves of apples may occur. Rightward shifts (S_1^A to S_2^A) are **increases in supply,** and leftward shifts (S_1^A to S_3^A) are **decreases in supply.** The logic behind this terminology can be seen by considering the quantities of apples forthcoming at P_1^A and observing that, on S_2^A, a larger quantity of apples (A_2) is produced than on S_3^A (A_3).[13]

Market Equilibrium: Supply and Demand Analysis

By themselves, market demand and supply curves do not describe final outcomes of the exchange process between consumers and producers. Demand and supply curves describe what actions consumers and producers are willing to undertake at different prices. Given that consumers care about maximizing utility and producers care about maximizing profits, how do their different interests allow them to agree on a price and quantity? To determine the final outcomes of private markets, we must understand how consumers and producers feel about different prices.

Figure A-17 shows market supply (S^B) and demand curves (D^B) for books. At a relatively high price, such as P_1^B, consumers wish to buy a relatively small number of books (B_1) and producers are willing to supply a relatively large number of books (B_3). This situation is called a **surplus,** or excess supply, and occurs whenever quantity supplied is greater than quantity demanded at the going price. Here, suppliers produce more books than they can sell and therefore experience a surplus of B_1B_3 books. Consumers are unwilling to purchase any more books at P_1^B and producers understand that, to remove surpluses, prices must fall.

At a relatively low price, such as P_2^B, consumers want to purchase a large number of books (B_2), but producers will supply only a relatively small number of books (B_4). This situation is called a **shortage,** or excess demand, and occurs whenever quantity demanded is greater than quantity supplied at the going price. Additional books that consumers wish to purchase are equal to the shortage of B_4B_2 books. To buy more books, consumers must pay higher prices.

Price and quantity combination (P_e^B, B_e) is a **market equilibrium** and occurs at the intersection of the demand and supply curves at point e. At equilibrium e, the number of books purchased is equal to the number produced. At any other quantity or price, shortages or surpluses develop, which would result in either price increases or decreases.

---

[13] Increases in resource prices and decreases in technology lead to decreases in supply. Decreases in resource prices and increases in technology lead to increases in supply.

FIGURE A-16
Changes in Supply

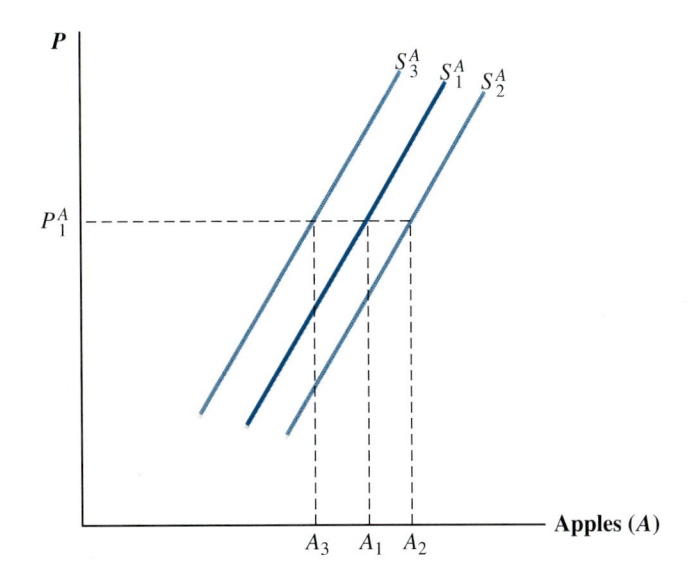

FIGURE A-17
Market Equilibrium

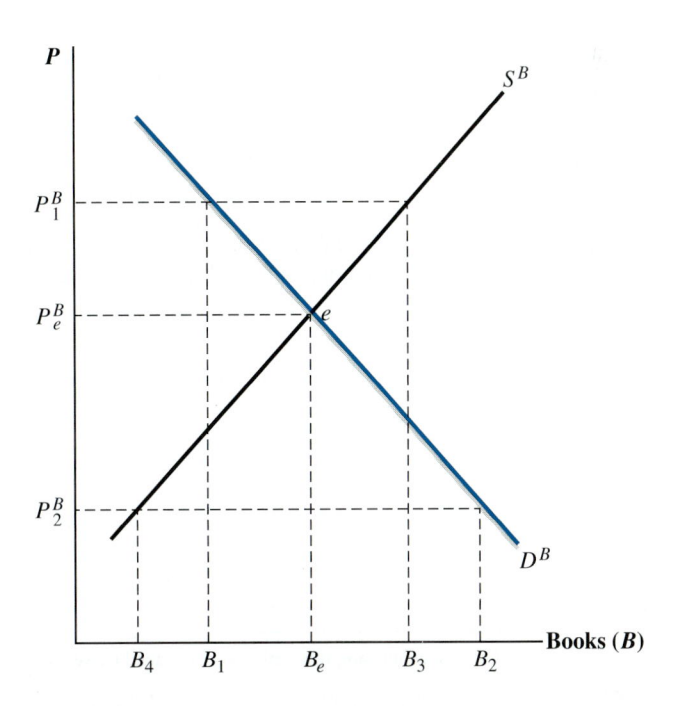

Price Elasticity of Demand and Supply

Price Elasticity of Demand

Even though demand curves have negative slopes, demand curves come in many varieties. Demands differ because all individuals have different tastes, incomes, and views regarding what constitutes complementary and substitute goods. At the level of markets, demand for housing should be quite different from demand for candy bars, toothpicks, or apples. Economists use the concept of **price elasticity of demand,** ϵ_d, to measure responsiveness of consumers to price changes and is defined as

$$\epsilon_d = \frac{\text{Percentage change in quantity demanded}}{\text{Percentage change in price}} = \frac{\Delta Q^d/Q^d}{\Delta P/P} \qquad (A\text{-}1)$$

Estimates of price elasticity result in negative numbers due to the inverse relationship between quantity demanded Q^d and price P. Demands that are relatively elastic are those that undergo relatively large changes in quantity demand when prices change. Relatively inelastic demands undergo relatively little change in quantity demand when price changes occur.

Figure A-18 shows, for the candy bar market, a relatively elastic demand ($D1$) and a relatively inelastic demand ($D2$).[14] To demonstrate differences in price elasticity between different demand curves, consider a price change from P_1 to P_2. For identical price changes, changes in quantity demanded are relatively large (CB_1CB_3) for $D1$ and relatively small (CB_1CB_2) for $D2$. Demand $D1$ is elastic since consumers purchase a great many more candy bars, and $D2$ is inelastic since the same price drop results in relatively little change in consumption of candy bars.

Price Elasticity of Supply

Price elasticity of supply, ϵ_s, measures the responsiveness of producers to price changes and is defined as

$$\epsilon_s = \frac{\text{Percentage change in quantity supplied}}{\text{Percentage change in price}} = \frac{\Delta Q^s/Q^s}{\Delta P/P} \qquad (A\text{-}2)$$

Supply curves that are relatively elastic (inelastic) undergo relatively large (small) changes in quantity supplied when price changes occur. Consider how the supply curves in Figure A-19 respond to a price increase from P_1 to P_2. $S1$ undergoes a relatively large increase in production (A_1A_3) and $S2$ undergoes a relatively small increase in production (A_1A_2); therefore, $S1$ is relatively price elastic and $S2$ is relatively price inelastic.

---

[14] Our discussion simplifies this issue: Demand curves often display both elastic and inelastic segments.

**FIGURE A-18
Price Elasticity
of Demand**

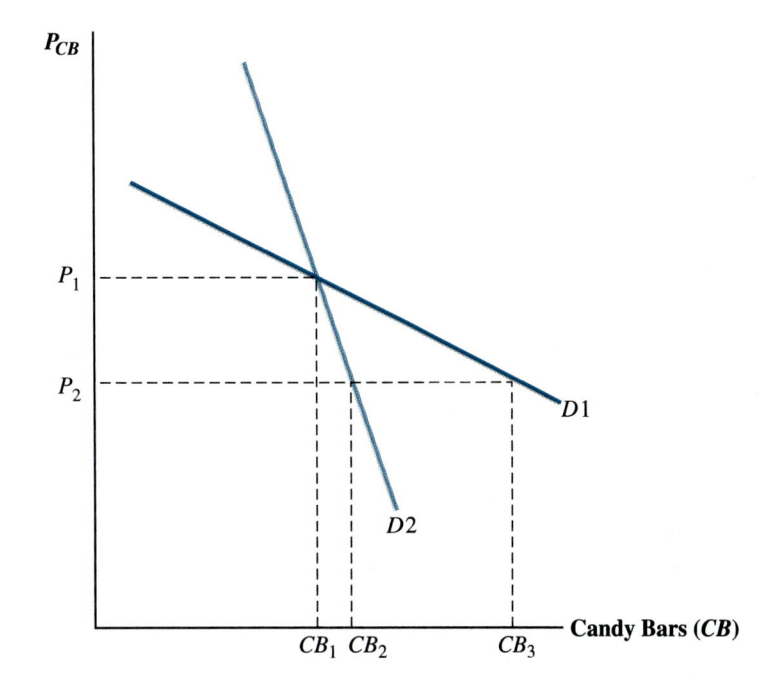

**FIGURE A-19
Price Elasticity
of Supply**

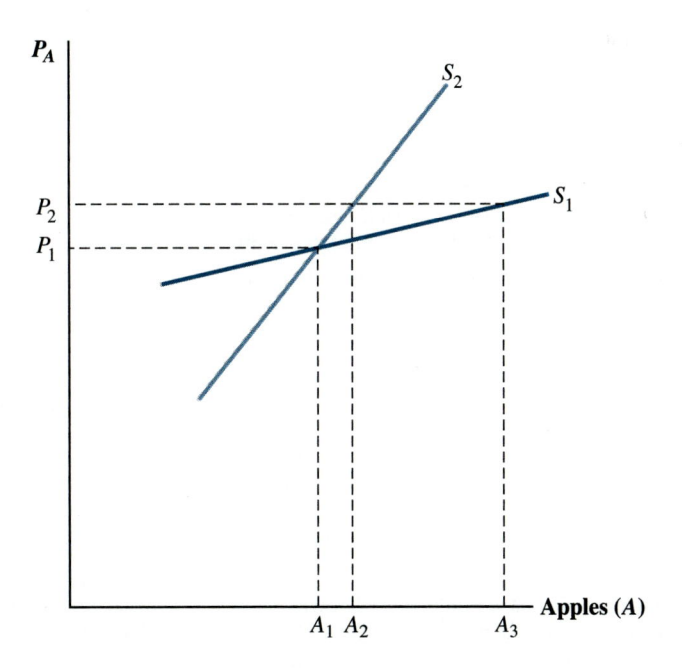

References

Aaron, Henry J., Barry P. Bosworth, and Gary Burtless. *Can America Afford to Grow Old? Paying for Social Security.* Washington, D.C.: Brookings Institution, 1989.

Abney, G., and T. Lauth. "The Line Item Veto in the States: An Instrument for Fiscal Restraint or an Instrument for Partisanship?" *Public Administration Review* 45 (1985): 372–377.

Abrams, Burton A., and Russell F. Settle. "The Effects of Broadcasting on Political Campaign Spending: An Empirical Investigation." *Journal of Political Economy* 84 (October 1976): 1095–1108.

Abrams, Burton A., and William R. Dougan. "The Effects of Constitutional Restraints on Governmental Spending," *Public Choice* 49 (1986): 101–116.

Abramson, Paul R., and John H. Aldrich. "The Decline of Electoral Participation in America." *American Political Science Review* 76 (1982): 502–521.

"Adios, Gerrymander." *Wall Street Journal,* December 20, 1991, A10.

Advisory Commission on Intergovernmental Relations. *Significant Features of Fiscal Federalism* 2, September 1992.

Ahlbrandt, R. S., Jr. "Efficiency in the Provision of Fire Services." *Public Choice* 16 (Fall 1973): 1–15.

Alm, James, Michael McKee, and William Beck. "Amazing Grace: Tax Amnesties and Compliance." *National Tax Journal* 43 (1990): 23–37.

Anderson, Terry L., and Donald R. Leal. *Free Market Environmentalism.* Boulder, Colo.: Westview Press, Inc., 1991.

Anderson, William, Myles S. Wallace, and John T. Warner. "Government Spending and Taxes: What Causes What?" *Southern Economic Journal* 52 (January 1986): 630–639.

Angello, Richard J., and Lawrence P. Donnelley. "Property Rights and Efficiency in the Oyster Industry." *Journal of Law and Economics* (October 1975): 521–533.

Arrow, Kenneth J. "Uncertainty and the Welfare Economics of Medical Care." *American Economic Review* 53 (December 1963): 941–973.

Aschauer, David A. "Fiscal Policy and Aggregate Demand." *American Economic Review* 75 (March 1985): 117–127.

———. "Is Public Expenditure Productive?" *Journal of Monetary Economics* 25 (March 1989): 177–200.

———. "Public Investment and Productivity Growth in the Group of Seven." *Economic Perspectives.* Federal Reserve Bank of Chicago 8 (September–October 1989): 17–25.

Atkinson, Anthony B., and John Mickelwright. "Unemployment Compensation and Labor Market Transitions." *Journal of Economic Literature* 29 (December 1991): 1679–1727.

Auerbach, Alan J. "The Tax Reform Act of 1986 and the Cost of Capital." *Journal of Economic Perspectives* 1 (Summer 1987): 73–86.

Bacon, Kenneth H. "Fannie Mae Expected to Escape an Attempt at Tighter Regulation." *Wall Street Journal,* June 19, 1992, A1.

Ballard, Charles L., John B. Shoven, and John Whalley. "General Equilibrium Computations of the Marginal Welfare Costs of Taxes in the United States." *American Economic Review* 75 (March 1985): 128–138.

Ballard, Charles L., John K. Scholz, and John B. Shoven. "The Value-Added Tax: A General Equilibrium Look at Its Efficiency and Incidence." In *The Effects of Taxation on Capital Accumulation*, edited by Martin Feldstein. Chicago: University of Chicago Press, 1987.

Ballentine, J. Gregory. "The Incidence of a Corporation Income Tax in a Growing Economy." *Journal of Political Economy* 86 (October 1978): 863–876.

———. *Equity, Efficiency, and the U.S. Corporation Income Tax.* Washington, D.C.: American Enterprise Institute, 1980.

Barro, Robert J. "Are Government Bonds Net Wealth?" *Journal of Political Economy* 82 (November–December 1974): 1095–1117.

———. "Comments from an Unreconstructed Ricardian." *Journal of Monetary Economics* 4 (August 1978): 569–581.

———. "A Free Marketeer's Case against Term Limits." *Wall Street Journal,* December 24, 1991, A6.

———. "The Ricardian Approach to Budget Deficits." *Journal of Economic Perspectives* 3 (Spring 1989): 37–54.

Barth, James R. *The Great Savings and Loan Debacle.* Washington, D.C.: AEI Press, 1991.

Barth, James R., Joseph J. Cordes, and Anthony M. Yezer. "Federal Government Attempts to Influence the Allocation of Mortgage Credit: FHA Mortgage Insurance and Government Regulations." In *Conference on the Economics of Federal Credit Activity,* Congressional Budget Office, part 2, 1980.

Barth, James R., George Iden, and Frank S. Russek. "Do Federal Deficits Really Matter?" *Contemporary Policy Issues* 3 (Fall 1984–85): 79–95.

———. "Government Debt, Government Spending, and Private Sector Behavior: Comment." *American Economic Review* 76 (December 1986): 1158–1167.

Bartlett, Bruce. "Not VAT Again!" *Wall Street Journal,* April 16, 1993, A10.

"The Battle of the Pastry Cooks." *The Economist,* May 18, 1991, 27–28.

Baumol, William J. "The Macroeconomics of Unbalanced Growth: The Anatomy of Urban Crisis." *American Economic Review* 57 (June 1967): 415–426.

Baumol, William J., and Wallace E. Oates. *Economics, Environmental Policy, and the Quality of Life.* 2d ed. New York: Harcourt Brace Jovanovich, 1982.

Becker, Gary S. "Public Policies, Pressure Groups, and Dead Weight Losses." *Journal of Public Economics* 28 (1985): 329–347.

Bennett, James T., and Manuel H. Johnson. "Tax Reduction without Sacrifice: Private-Sector Production of Public Services." *Public Finance Quarterly* 8 (October 1980): 363–396.

Bennett, James T., and William P. Orzechowski. "The Voting Behavior of Bureaucrats: Some Empirical Evidence." *Public Choice* 41 (1983): 271–283.

Bennett, James T., and Thomas J. DiLorenzo. *Underground Government: The Off-Budget Public Sector.* Washington, D.C.: Cato Institute, 1984.

———. *Destroying Democracy: How Government Funds Partisan Politics.* Washington, D.C.: Cato Institute, 1985.

———. "How (and Why) Congress Twists Its Own Arm: The Political Economy of Tax-Funded Politics." *Public Choice* 55 (1987): 199–213.

———. *Unfair Competition: The Profits of Nonprofits.* Lanham: Hamilton Press, 1989.

Bergstrom, Theodore C., and Robert P. Goodman. "Private Demands for Public Goods." *American Economic Review* 63 (June 1973): 280–296.

Bizer, David, and Steven Durlauf. "Testing the Positive Theory of Government Finance." *Journal of Monetary Economics* 27 (August 1990): 123–141.

Black, Duncan. "On the Rationale of Group Decision Making." *Journal of Political Economy* 56 (February 1948): 23–34.

———. *The Theory of Committees and Elections.* Cambridge: Cambridge University Press, 1958.

Blackley, Paul R. "Causality between Revenues and Expenditures and the Size of the Federal Budget." *Public Finance Quarterly* (April 1986): 139–156.

Blinder, Alan S. "Inequality and Mobility in the Distribution of Wealth." *Kyklos* 29 (1976): 607–638.

Blumenthal, Marsha, and Joel Slemrod. "The Compliance Cost of the U.S. Individual Income Tax System: A Second Look after Tax Reform." *National Tax Journal* 45 (1992): 185–202.

Borchard, William M. "Trademark Piracy at Home and Abroad." *Wall Street Journal,* May 7, 1991.

Borcherding, Thomas E. "The Causes of Government Expenditure Growth: A Survey of the U.S. Evidence." *Journal of Public Economics* 28 (1985): 359–382.

Borcherding, Thomas E., and Robert T. Deacon. "The Demand for the Services of Non-Federal Governments." *American Economic Review* 62 (December 1972): 891–901.

Borcherding, Thomas E., Winston C. Bush, and Robert M. Spann. "The Effects of Public Spending on the Divisibility of Public Outputs in Consumption, Bureaucratic Power, and the Size of the Tax-Sharing Group." In *Budgets and Bureaucrats: The Sources of Government Growth,* edited by Thomas E. Borcherding. Durham, N.C.: Duke University Press, 1977.

Borcherding, Thomas E., and Gary W. Dorosh. *The Egg Marketing Board.* Vancouver: Fraser University, 1981.

Boskin, Michael J. "Estate Taxation and Charitable Bequests." *Journal of Public Economics* 5 (January 1976): 27–56.

———. "Taxation, Saving, and the Rate of Interest." *Journal of Political Economy* 86 (April 1978): S3–S27.

———. *Too Many Promises: The Uncertain Future of Social Security.* Homewood, Ill.: Dow Jones-Irwin, 1986.

Boskin, Michael J., Marcy Avrin, and Kenneth Cone. "Modeling Alternative Solutions to the Long-Run Social Security Funding Crisis." In *Behavioral Simulation Methods in Tax Policy Analysis,* edited by Martin Feldstein. Chicago: University of Chicago Press, 1983.

Boskin, Michael J., and Michael Hurd. "The Effect of Social Security on Retirement in the Early 1970s." *Quarterly Journal of Economics* 7 (November 1984): 767–790.

Bosworth, Barry, and Gary Burtless. "Effects of Tax Reform on Labor Supply, Investment, and Saving." *Journal of Economic Perspectives* 6 (Winter 1992): 3–25.

Bovard, James. "Lost in the American Agricultural Swamp." *Economic Affairs (*December–January), 1990.

———. "Billbord Ban: Road to Ruin for Property Rights." *Wall Street Journal,* April 2, 1991.

———. *The Farm Fiasco.* San Francisco: ICS Press, 1991.

Bowen, Howard R. "The Interpretation of Voting in the Allocation of Economic Resources." *Quarterly Journal of Economics* 58 (November 1943): 27–48.

Bradford, David F. *Untangling the Income Tax.* Cambridge: Harvard University Press, 1986.

Brady, Gordon L., and Michael L. Marlow. "The Political Economy of Endangered Species Management: The Case of Elephants." *Journal of Public Finance and Public Choice* (1991): 29–39.

Brennan, Geoffrey, and James M. Buchanan. *The Power to Tax: Analytical Foundations of a Fiscal Constitution.* Cambridge: Cambridge University Press, 1980.

Brown, Charles. "Minimum Wage Laws: Are They Overrated?" *Journal of Economic Perspectives* 2 (Summer 1988): 133–145.

Brown, Charles, and Wallace E. Oates. "Assistance to the Poor in a Federal System." *Journal of Public Economics* 37 (April 1987): 307–330.

Browning, Edgar K. "On the Marginal Welfare Cost of Taxation." *American Economic Review* 77 (March 1987): 11–23.

Buchanan, James M. *Public Principles of Public Debt.* Homewood, Ill.: Irwin, 1958.

———. "Constitutional Economics." In *The World of Economics,* edited by John Eatwell, Murray Milgate, and Peter Newman. New York: W.W. Norton & Company, Inc., 1991 (first published in *The New Palgrave: A Dictionary of Economics,* The Macmillan Press Limited, 1987).

———. "The Domain of Constitutional Economics." *Constitutional Political Economy* 1 (1990): 1–18.

———. "An Economic Theory of Clubs." *Economica* 32 (February 1965): 1–14.

———. "Notes for Economic Theory of Socialism." *Public Choice* 8 (Spring 1970): 29–43.

———. "Social Insurance in a Growing Economy: A Proposal for Radical Reform." *National Tax Journal* 19 (December 1968): 386–395.

Buchanan, James M., and Gordon Tullock. *The Calculus of Consent: Logical Foundations of Constitutional Democracy.* Ann Arbor: University of Michigan Press, 1962.

———. "The Expanding Public Sector: Wagner Squared." *Public Choice* 32 (1977): 147–150.

———. "Polluters' Profits and Political Response: Direct Controls versus Taxes." *American Economic Review* 65 (March 1975): 139–147.

Buchanan, James M., and Richard E. Wagner. *Democracy in Deficit: The Political Legacy of Lord Keynes.* New York: Academic Press, 1977.

Buchanan, James M., and Dwight R. Lee. "Politics, Time, and the Laffer Curve." *Journal of Political Economy* 90 (August 1982): 816–819.

Bush, Winston C., and Arthur T. Denzau. "The Voting Behavior of Bureaucrats and Public Sector Growth." In *Budgets and Bureaucrats: The Sources of Government Growth,* edited by Thomas E. Borcherding. Durham: Duke University Press, 1977.

Cheung, Steven N. S. "Roofs or Stars: The Stated Intents and Actual Effects of a Rents Ordinance." *Economic Inquiry* 13 (March 1975): 1–21.

Chicoine, David L., and Norman C. Walzer. *Governmental Structure and Local Public Finance.* Boston: Oelgeschlager, Gunn and Hain, 1985.

Church, George J. "Gorezilla Zaps the System: Al Gore Seeks to 'Reinvent Government,' but Beware the Bureaucracy's Seasoned Heel Draggers." *Time,* September 13, 1993, 25–28.

Coase, Ronald H. "The Nature of the Firm." *Economica* 4 (1937): 386–405.

———. "The Problem of Social Cost." *Journal of Law and Economics* 3 (October 1960): 1–44.

Collender, Stanley E. *The Guide to the Federal Budget, Fiscal 1993.* Washington, D.C.: Urban Institute Press, 1992.

Congleton, Roger D. "Evaluating Rent-Seeking Losses: Do the Welfare Gains of Lobbyists Count?" *Public Choice* 56 (1988): 181–184.

Congressional Budget Office. *Balancing the Federal Budget and Limiting Federal Spending: Constitutional and Legislative Approaches.* Washington, D.C.: U.S. Government Printing Office, 1983.

———. *Controlling the Losses of the Pension Benefit Guaranty Corporation.* Washington, D.C.: U.S. Government Printing Office, January 1993.

———. *Controlling the Risks of Government-Sponsored Enterprises.* Washington, D.C.: U.S. Government Printing Office, April 1991.

———. "The Cost of Forbearance during the Thrift Crisis." Washington, D.C.: U.S. Government Printing Office, June 1991.

———. *The Economic and Budget Outlook: An Update.* Washington, D.C.: U.S. Government Printing Office, August 1991.

———. *The Economic Effects of Reduced Defense Spending,* March 1992.

———. "The Economic Effects of the Savings and Loan Crisis." Washington, D.C.: U.S. Government Printing Office, January 1992.

———. *Economic Implications of Rising Health Costs."* Washington, D.C.: U.S. Government Printing Office, October 1992.

———. *Effects of Adopting a Value-Added Tax.* Washington, D.C.: U.S. Government Printing Office, February 1992.

———. *Federal Debt and Interest Costs.* Washington, D.C.: U.S. Government Printing Office, May 1993.

———. *Fiscal Outlook.* Washington, D.C.: U.S. Government Printing Office, January 1993.

———. *Managed Competition and Its Potential to Reduce Health Spending.* Washington, D.C.: U.S. Government Printing Office, May 1993.

———. *Projections of National Health Expenditures.* Washington, D.C.: U.S. Government Printing Office, October 1992.

———. *Reducing the Deficit: Spending and Revenue Options.* Washington, D.C.: U.S. Government Printing Office, February 1993.

———. "The Savings and Loan Problem: A Discussion of the Issues." Washington, D.C.: U.S. Government Printing Office, February 1989.

Conway, M. Margaret. *Political Participation in the United States.* Washington, D.C.: Congressional Quarterly Press, 1985.

Couch, Jim F., William F. Shughart II, and Al L. Williams. "Private School Enrollment and Public School Performance." *Public Choice* 76 (1993): 301–312.

Crain, W. Mark, and Brian L. Goff. *Televised Legislatures: Political Information Technology and Public Choice.* Norwell, Mass.: Kluwer Academic Publishers, 1988.

Crain, W. Mark, and Michael L. Marlow. "The Causal Relationship between Social Security and the Federal Budget." In *Social Security's Looming Surpluses: Prospects and Implications,* edited by Carolyn L. Weaver. Washington, D.C.: The AEI Press, 1990.

Crain, W. Mark, and James C. Miller III. "Budget Process and Spending Growth." *William and Mary Law Review* (Spring 1990).

Dahl, Robert A. *Polyarchy Participation and Opposition.* New Haven, Conn.: Yale University Press, 1971.

Dales, J. H. *Pollution, Property, and Prices.* Toronto: University of Toronto Press, 1968.

Danziger, Sheldon, Robert H. Haveman, and Robert Plotnick. "How Income Transfer Programs Affect Work, Savings, and the Income Distribution: A Critical Survey." *Journal of Economic Literature* 19 (September 1981): 975–1028.

Davies, D. G. "The Efficiency of Public versus Private Firms: The Case of Australia's Two Airlines." *Journal of Law and Economics* 14 (April 1971): 149–165.

———. "Property Rights and Economic Efficiency: The Australian Airlines Revisited." *Journal of Law and Economics* 20 (April 1977): 223–226.

Davies, James, France St-Hilaire, and John Whalley. "Some Calculations of Lifetime Tax Incidence." *American Economic Review* 74 (September 1984): 633–649.

Davis, Bob. "Bush Plans to Unveil a 90-Day Moratorium on New Regulations." *Wall Street Journal,* January 20, 1992, A1.

Demsetz, Harold. "Toward a Theory of Property Rights." *American Economic Review* 57 (May 1967): 347–359.

Dougan, William R., and Daphne A. Kenyon. "Pressure Groups and Public Expenditures: The Flypaper Effect Reconsidered." *Economic Inquiry* 26 (January 1988): 159–170.

Downing, Paul B. *Environmental Economics and Policy.* Boston: Little, Brown and Company, 1984.

Downing Paul B., and James N. Kimball. "Enforcing Pollution Control Laws in the United States." *Policy Studies Journal* 11 (September 1982): 55–64.

Downs, Anthony. *An Economic Theory of Democracy.* New York: Harper and Row. 1957.

———. "Why the Government Budget Is Too Small in a Democracy." *World Politics* 12 (1960): 541–563.

Drazen, Allan. "Government Debt, Human Capital and Bequests in a Lifecycle Model." *Journal of Political Economy* 86 (1978): 337–342.

Dubin, Jeffrey A., Michael J. Graetz, and Louis L. Wilde. "The Effect of Audit Rates on the Federal Individual Income Tax, 1977–1986." *National Tax Journal* 43 (1990): 395–409.

Dwyer, Gerald P. "Inflation and Government Deficits." *Economic Inquiry* 20 (July 1982): 315–329.

Economic Report of the President. Washington, D.C.: U.S. Government Printing Office, 1989.

———. Washington, D.C.: U.S. Government Printing Office, 1990.

———. Washington, D.C.: U.S. Government Printing Office, 1991.

———. Washington, D.C.: U.S. Government Printing Office, 1992.

———. Washington, D.C.: U.S. Government Printing Office, 1993.

Eisner, Robert, and Paul J. Pieper. "A New View of the Federal Debt and Budget Deficits." *American Economic Review* 74 (March 1984): 11–29.

"Fannie Mugs Again." *Wall Street Journal,* September 30, 1992, A16.

"Farming: A Soft Touch." *The Economist,* January 23, 1993, 26–27.

Feige, Edgar L. *The Underground Economies: Tax Evasion and Information Distortion.* Cambridge: Cambridge University Press, 1989.

Feldstein, Martin S. "Social Security, Induced Retirement, and Aggregate Capital Formation." *Journal of Political Economy* 82 (September–October 1974): 905–926.

———. "Government Deficits and Aggregate Demand." *Journal of Monetary Economics* 9 (January 1982): 1–20.

Feldstein, Martin, and Bernard Friedman. "Tax Subsidies, the Rational Demand for Insurance, and the Health Care Crisis." *Journal of Public Economics* 7 (April 1977): 155–178.

Feldstein, Martin, and Lawrence Summers. "Inflation and the Taxation of Capital Income in the Corporate Sector." *National Tax Journal* 32 (December 1979): 445–470.

Fiorina, Morris P. *Congress: Keystone of Washington.* 2d ed. New Haven: Yale University Press, 1989.

Fischer-Menshausen, H. "Entlastung des Staates durch Privatisierung von Aufgaben." *Wirtschaftsdienst* 55 (1975): 545–552.

Fitzgerald, Randall, and Gerald Lipson. *Pork Barrel: The Unexpurgated Grace Commission Story of Congressional Profligacy.* Washington, D.C.: Cato Institute, 1984.

Forbes, Kevin F., and Earnest M. Zampelli. "Is Leviathan a Mythical Beast?" *American Economic Review* 79 (June 1989): 587–596.

Freeman, A. M. III, *The Benefits of Environmental Improvement.* Baltimore: Johns Hopkins Press, 1979.

Frey, Bruno. "Why Do High Income People Participate More in Politics?" *Public Choice* 11 (Fall 1971): 101–105.

Frey, Bruno S., Werner W. Pommerehne, Friedrich Schneider, and Guy Gilbert. "Consensus and Dissension among Economists: An Empirical Inquiry." *American Economic Review* 74 (December 1984): 986–994.

Friedman, Benjamin. *Day of Reckoning.* New York: Random House, 1988.

Friedman, Milton. "Inflation and Unemployment." *Journal of Political Economy* 85 (June 1977): 451–472.

———. "The Methodology of Positive Economics." In *Essays in Positive Economics.* Chicago: University of Chicago Press, 1953.

———. *Tax Limitation, Inflation and the Role of Government.* Dallas, Tex.: Fisher Institute, 1978.

Friedman, Milton, and Anna J. Schwartz, *A Monetary History of the United States, 1867–1960.* Princeton, N.J.: Princeton University Press, 1963.

Friedman, Milton, and Rose Friedman. *Free to Choose.* New York: Harcourt Brace Jovanovich, 1980.

———. *Tryanny of the Status Quo.* New York: Harcourt Brace Jovanovich, 1983.

Frisby, Michael K. "VAT Possibility Is Reconsidered at White House," *Wall Street Journal,* April 15, 1993, A2.

Fritz, Marshall. "Protectionist Plum Ripens in California." *Wall Street Journal,* January 7, 1994, A10.

Fullerton, Don. "On the Possibility of an Inverse Relationship between Tax Rates and Government Revenues." *Journal of Public Economics* 19 (October 1982): 3–22.

Gale, William G. "The Budget Gimmick of the 1990s?" Wall Street Journal, May 3, 1989, A15.

———. "Economic Effects of Federal Credit Programs." *American Economic Review* 81 (March 1991): 133–152.

"Government by the Nice, for the Nice." *The Economist,* July 25, 1992, 25–26.

Gramlich, Edward M. *A Guide to Benefit-Cost Analysis.* 2d ed. Englewood Cliffs, N.J.: Prentice Hall, 1990.

Gramlich, Edward M., and Daniel L. Rubinfeld. "Voting on Public Spending: Differences between Public Employees, Transfer Receipts, and Private Workers." *Journal of Policy Analysis and Management* 1 (1982): 516–533.

Granger, Clive W. "Investigating Causal Relations by Economic Models and Cross Spectral Methods." *Econometrica* 37 (July 1969): 424–438.

Greene, Kevin V., and Vincent G. Munley. "Generating Growth in Public Expenditures: The Role of Employee and Constituent Demand." *Public Finance Quarterly* 7 (1979): 82–109.

Gregg, John G., Arnold C. Harberger, and Peter Mieszkowski. "Empirical Evidence on the Incidence of the Corporation Income Tax." *Journal of Political Economy* 75 (December 1967): 811–821.

Grossman, Phillip J. "Federalism and the Size of Government." *Southern Economic Journal* 55 (January 1989): 580–593.

———. "Fiscal Decentralization and Government Size: An Extension." *Public Choice* 62 (1989): 63–70.

Groves, Theodore, and J. Ledyard. "Optimal Allocation of Public Goods: A Solution to the 'Free Rider' Problem." *Econometrica* 45 (1977): 783-809.

Haig, Robert M. *The Federal Income Tax.* New York: Columbia University Press, 1921.

Hall Robert, and Dale Jorgenson. "Tax Policy and Investment Behavior." *American Economic Review* 57 (June 1967): 391–414.

Hamilton, Bruce W. "Tiebout Hypothesis." In *The New Palgrave: The World of Economics,* edited by John Eatwell, Murray Milgate, and Peter Newman. London: W.W. Norton, 1991.

Hansen, W. Lee, and James F. Byers. "Unemployment Compensation and Retraining: Can a Close Link Be Forged." In *Unemployment Insurance: The Second Half-Century,* edited by W. Lee Hansen and James F. Byers. Madison, Wis.: Wisconsin University Press, 1990.

Harberger, Arnold C. "The Incidence of the Corporation Income Tax," *Journal of Political Economy* 70 (June 1962): 215–240.

———. "On the Use of Distributional Weights in Social Cost-Benefit Analysis." *Journal of Political Economy* 86 (April 1978): S87–S120.

Harsanyi, John C. "Cardinal Welfare, Individualistic Ethics, and Interpersonal Comparisons of Utility." *Journal of Political Economy* 63 (August 1955): 309–321.

Hauser, W. Kurt. "The Tax and Revenue Equation." *Wall Street Journal,* March 25, 1993, A14.

Hausman, Jerry A. "Labor Supply." In *How Taxes Affect Economic Behavior,* edited by Henry Aaron and Joseph Pechman. Washington, D.C.: Brookings Institution, 1981.

Hausman, Jerry A., and James M. Poterba. "Household Behavior and the Tax Reform Act of 1986." *Journal of Economic Perspectives* 1 (Summer 1987): 101–119.

Higgs, Robert. *Crisis and Leviathan: Critical Episodes in the Growth of American Government.* New York: Oxford University Press, 1987.

Hirschman, A. O. *Exit, Voice and Loyalty.* Cambridge: Harvard University Press, 1970.

Hochman, H. M., and J. O. Rodgers. "Pareto Optimal Redistribution." *American Economic Review* 59 (September 1969): 542–557.

Hoffman, Elizabeth, and M. L. Spitzer. "Experimental Tests of the Coase Theorem with Large Bargaining Groups." *Journal of Legal Studies* 15 (January 1986): 149–171.

Holcolmbe, Randall G., and Asghar Zardkoohi. "The Determinants of Federal Grants." *Southern Economic Journal* 48 (October 1981): 393–399.

Hotelling, Harold. "Stability in Competition." *Economic Journal* 39 (March 1929): 41–57.

"How to Simplify the Crazy Tax Code." *Time,* April 20, 1992, 49.

Hunter, William J., and Michael A. Nelson. "Interest Group Demand for Taxation." *Public Choice* 62 (1989): 41–61.

"In Search of Stability." *The Economist,* October 16, 1993, 25–26.

Jensen, Michael, and William H. Meckling. "The Theory of the Firm: Managerial Behavior, Agency Costs and Ownership Structure." *Journal of Financial Economics* 3 (October 1976): 305–360.

Johnson, Kevin. "America's Forgotten Fiefdoms." *Los Angeles Times,* May 26, 1993, A1, A25.

Joulfain, David, and Michael L. Marlow. "Centralization and Government Competition." *Applied Economics* 23 (October 1991): 1603–1612.

———. "Government Size and Decentralization: Evidence from Disaggregated Data." *Southern Economic Journal,* April 1990.

———. "Incentives and Political Contributions." *Public Choice* 69 (1991): 351–355.

———. "The Relationship between On-Budget and Off-Budget Government." *Economics Letters* 35 (1991): 307–310.

Kaldor, Nicholas. "Welfare Propositions of Economics and Interpersonal Comparisons of Utility." *Economic Journal* 49 (September 1939): 549–552.

Kalt, Joseph, and Mark Zupan. "Capture and Ideology in the Economic Theory of Politics." *American Economic Review* 74 (June 1984): 279–300.

Kau, James B., and Paul H. Rubin, "The Size of Government." *Public Choice* 37 (1981): 261–274.

———. "Self-Interest, Ideology and Logrolling in Congressional Voting." *Journal of Law and Economics* 22 (October 1979): 365–384.

Kelman, Steven. *Making Public Policy: A Hopeful View of American Government.* New York: Basic Books, 1987.

———. "Public Choice and Public Spirit." *The Public Interest* 87 (1987): 80–94.

Kihlstrom, Richard E., and Mark V. Pauly. "The Role of Insurance in the Allocation of Risk." *American Economic Review* 61 (May 1971): 371–379.

Kormendi, Roger C. "Government Debt, Government Spending, and Private Sector Behavior." *American Economic Review* 71 (December 1983): 994–1010.

Kosters, Marvin H., ed. *Fiscal Politics & the Budget Enforcement Act.* Washington, D.C.: AEI Press, 1992.

Kotlikoff, Laurence J. "The Social Security 'Surpluses'—New Clothes for the Emperor?" In *Social Security's Looming Surpluses: Prospects and Implications,* edited by Carolyn L. Weaver. Washington, D.C.: AEI Press, 1990.

Kristof, Kathy M. "Hitch to Year-End Nuptials: Higher Taxes, Costs Make December 31 Vows Expensive." *Los Angeles Times,* December 29, 1993, D1.

———. "'Til Death Do We Pay: Under New Tax Plan, Marriage Costs More Than Ever." *Los Angeles Times,* August 13, 1993, D1.

Krzyzaniak, Marion, and Richard Musgrave. *The Shifting of the Corporation Income Tax.* Baltimore: Johns Hopkins Press, 1963.

Laband, David N. "Is There a Relationship between Economic Conditions and Political Structure?" *Public Choice* 42 (1984): 25–37.

LaGanga, Maria L. "Firms Can Earn Pollution Credits by Buying Old Cars." *Los Angeles Times,* January 9, 1993, A1.

Landes, William M., and Richard A. Posner. "The Independent Judiciary in an Interest-Group Perspective." *Journal of Law and Economics* 18 (December 1975): 875–901.

Lauter, David. "President Delivers Health Care Pep Talk." *Los Angeles Times,* January 4, 1994, A14.

Lerner, Abba. *The Economics of Control.* New York: Macmillan, 1944.

Lewis-Beck, Michael. "Agrarian Political Behavior in the United States." *American Journal of Political Science* 21 (1977): 543–565.

"Life on EZ Street." *Los Angeles Times,* June 30, 1993, D1.

Lindahl, Erik. "Just Taxation—A Positive Solution." (1919) In *Classics in the Theory of Public Finance,* edited by Richard A. Musgrave and Alan T. Peacock. London: Macmillan, 1958.

Lindsey, Lawrence B. *The Growth Experiment: How the New Tax Policy Is Transforming the U.S. Economy.* New York: Basic Books, 1990.

Littlechild, S. C., and Jack Wiseman. "The Political Economy of Restriction of Choice." *Public Choice* 51 (1986): 161–171.

Logan, Robert R. "Fiscal Illusion and the Grantor Government." *Journal of Political Economy* 96 (1986): 1304–1318.

Mackay, Robert J., and Carolyn L. Weaver. "Agenda Control by Budget Maximizers in a Multi-Bureau Setting." *Public Choice* 37 (1981): 447–472.

Makin, John H. "Real Interest, Money Surprises, Anticipated Inflation and Fiscal Deficits." *Review of Economics and Statistics* 65 (August 1983): 374–384.

Manage, Neela, and Michael L. Marlow. "The Causal Relation between Federal Expenditures and Receipts." *Southern Economic Journal* 52 (January 1986): 717–729.

Marlow, Michael L. "The Economics of Enforcement: The Case of OSHA." *Journal of Economics and Business* 34 (1982): 165–171.

———. "Fiscal Decentralization and Government Size." *Public Choice* 56 (1988): 259–269.

———. "Intergovernmental Competition, Voice and Exit Options and the Design of Fiscal Structure." *Constitutional Political Economy* 3 (Winter 1992): 73–87.

Marlow, Michael L., John P. Link, and Robert P. Trost. "Market Structure and Rivalry: New Evidence with a Nonlinear Model," *Review of Economics and Statistics* 66 (November 1984): 676–682.

Mayhew, David R. *Congress: The Electoral Connection.* New Haven: Yale University Press, 1974.

McCallum, John. "Government, Special Interest Groups, and Economic Growth." *Public Choice* 54 (1987): 3–18.

McClosky, Herbert, and John Zaller. *The American Ethos: Public Attitudes toward Capitalism and Democracy.* Cambridge: Harvard University Press, 1984.

McDowell, Jeanne. "Fighting for Yosemite's Future." *Time,* January 14, 1991, 46.

McMillan, W. Douglas. "Federal Deficits and Short-Term Interest Rates," *Journal of Macroeconomics* 12 (Fall 1986): 403–422.

Mehay, Stephen L. "Interjurisdictional Spillovers of Urban Police Services." *Southern Economic Journal* 43 (January 1977): 1352–1359.

Meltzer, Allan H., and Scott F. Richard. "A Rational Theory of the Size of Government." *Journal of Political Economy* 89 (October 1981): 914–927.

Meyer, Bruce C. "Unemployment Insurance and Unemployment Spells." *Econometrica* 58 (July 1990): 757–789.

Mieszkowski, Peter M. "The Property Tax: An Excise or a Profits Tax." *Journal of Public Economics* 1 (April 1972): 73–96.

Miller, James C., III. "Cut Federal Spending—Limit Congressional Terms." *Wall Street Journal,* August 19, 1991, A8.

Mills, Edwin. "Has the United States Overinvested in Housing?" *Business Review,* Federal Reserve Bank of Philadelphia, April 1987.

Moffit, Robert. "An Economic Model of Welfare Stigma." *American Economic Review* 73 (December 1983): 1023–1035.

Moore, Stephen. "Crime of the Century: The 1990 Budget Deal after Two Years." *Policy Analysis* no. 182. Washington, D.C.: Cato Institute, October 1992.

Mueller, Dennis C. *Public Choice II.* Cambridge: Cambridge University Press, 1989.

Mueller, Dennis C., and Peter Murrell. "Interest Groups and the Size of Government." *Public Choice* 48 (1986): 125–145.

Munnell, Alicia H. "The Impact of Social Security on Personal Saving." *National Tax Journal* (April 1974): 553–568.

Murray, Charles A. *Losing Ground: American Social Policy 1950–1980.* New York: Basic Books, 1984.

Musgrave, Richard A. "Short of Euphoria." *Journal of Economic Perspectives* (Summer 1987): 59–71.

Muth, Richard F. *Public Housing: An Economic Evaluation.* Washington, D.C.: American Enterprise Institute, 1973.

Nardinelli, Clark, Myles S. Wallace, and John T. Warner. "Explaining Differences in State Growth: Catching Up versus Olson." *Public Choice* 52 (1987): 201–213.

Nelson, Michael A. "Decentralization of the Subnational Public Sector: An Empirical Analysis of the Determinants of Local Government Structure in Metropolitan Areas in the United States." *Southern Economic Journal* (October 1990): 443–457.

Newhouse, Joseph P. "Medical Care Costs: How Much Welfare Loss?" *Journal of Economic Perspectives* 6 (Summer 1992): 3–21.

"New York's Taxis." *The Economist,* March 9, 1991, 28.

Niskanen, William A., Jr. *Bureaucracy and Representative Government.* Chicago: Aldine-Atherton, 1971.

———. "Bureaucrats and Politicians." *Journal of Law and Economics* 18 (December 1975): 617–643.

Nutter, G. Warren. *Growth of Government in the West.* Washington, D.C.: American Enterprise Institute, 1978.

Oates, Wallace E. *Fiscal Federalism.* New York: Harcourt Brace Jovanovich, 1972.

———. "Searching for Leviathan: An Empirical Study." *American Economic Review* 75 (September 1985): 748–757.

O'Driscoll, Gerald P. "The Ricardian Nonequivalence Theorem." *Journal of Political Economy* 85 (February 1977): 207–210.

Oelert, W. "Reprivatisierung des Offentlichen Personalverkehrs." *Der Personenverkehr* 4 (1976): 108–114.

Office of Management and Budget. *Budget Baselines, Historical Data, and Alternatives for the Future.* Washington, D.C.: U.S. Government Printing Office, January 1993.

———. *Budget of the United States Government.* Washington, D.C: U.S. Government Printing Office, 1991.

———. *Budget of the United States Government.* Washington, D.C.: U.S. Government Printing Office, 1992.

———. *Budget of the United States Government.* Washington, D.C.: U.S. Government Printing Office, 1994.

Olson, Mancur. *The Logic of Collective Action: Public Goods and the Theory of Groups.* Cambridge: Harvard University Press, 1965.

———. *The Rise and Decline of Nations,* New Haven: Yale University Press, 1982.

Ornstein, Norman J., Thomas E. Mann, and Michael J. Malbin. *Vital Statistics on Congress, 1991–1992.* Washington, D.C.: Congressional Quarterly, Inc., 1992.

Parker, Glenn, R. "Competition in Congressional Elections." In *Studies of Congress,* by Glenn R. Parker, Washington, D.C.: Congressional Quarterly Press, 1985.

Parkin, David, Alistair McGuire, and Brian Yule. "Aggregate Health Care Expenditures and National Income: Is Health Care a Luxury Good?" *Journal of Health Economics* 6 (June 1987): 109–127.

Pauly, Mark V. "Income Redistribution as a Local Public Good." *Journal of Public Economics* 2 (February 1973): 35–58.

———. "Taxation, Health Insurance, and Market Failure in the Medical Economy." *Journal of Economic Literature* 24 (June 1986): 629–675.

Payne, James L. *Costly Returns: The Burdens of the U.S. Tax System.* San Francisco: ICS Press, Institute for Contemporary Studies, 1993.

———. *The Culture of Spending: Why Congress Lives beyond Our Means.* San Francisco: ICS Press, 1991.

Peacock, Alan T., and Jack Wiseman. *The Growth of Public Expenditure in the United Kingdom.* Princeton, N.J.: Princeton University Press, 1961.

Pechman, Joseph A. "The Individual Income Tax Base." *Proceedings of the Forty-Eighth Annual Conference in Taxation Sponsored by the National Tax Association,* 1955.

———. "Tax Reform: Theory and Practice," *Journal of Economic Perspectives* 1 (Summer 1987): 11–28.

Pechman, Joseph A., and John Karl Scholz. "Comprehensive Income Taxation and Rate Reduction." *Tax Notes* (October 11, 1982): 83–93.

Peltzman, Sam. "An Economic Interpretation of the History of Congressional Voting in the Twentieth Century." *American Economic Review* 75 (September 1985): 656–675.

———. "The Effect of Government Subsidies-in-Kind on Private Expenditures: The Case of Higher Education." *Journal of Political Economy* 81 (January–February 1973): 1–27.

———. "The Growth of Government," *Journal of Law and Economics* 23 (October 1980): 209–288.

"Perk City" *Time,* October 14, 1991, 18–20.

Perry, James, M. "Movement to Limit Lawmakers' Terms Revs Up and Heads toward Congress." *Wall Street Journal,* July 17, 1991, A10.

"Political Pornography." *Wall Street Journal,* September 9, 1991, A12.

"Political Pornography—II," *Wall Street Journal,* February 4, 1992, A14.

"Pollution Control: Unshackling the Invisible Hand," *The Economist,* January 4, 1992, 66.

President's Commission on Privatization. *Privatization: Toward More Effective Government,* March 1988.

"The Price of Life: Why an American's Life Is Worth Twice as Much as a Swede's," *The Economist,* December 4, 1993, 74.

Ram, Rati. "Additional Evidence on Causality between Government Revenue and Government Expenditure," *Southern Economic Journal* (January 1988): 763–769.

———. "Wagner's Hypothesis in Time-Series and Cross-Section Perspectives: Evidence from 'Real' Data for 115 Countries." *Review of Economics and Statistics* 69 (May 1987): 194–204.

Ramsey, Frank P. "A Contribution to the Theory of Taxation." *Economic Journal* 37 (1927): 47–61.

Ratner, Jonathan B. "Government Capital and the Production Function for U.S. Private Output." *Economics Letters* (1983): 213–217.

Rawls, John. *A Theory of Justice.* Cambridge, Mass.: Harvard University Press, 1971.

"Real House Reform." *Wall Street Journal,* October 30, 1993, A18.

"Return of the Tax Olympiad." *Wall Street Journal,* May 7, 1993, A14.

Riker, William H., and Peter C. Ordeshook. "A Theory of the Calculus of Voting." *American Political Science Review,* 1968.

Rivlin, Alice M. "Economics and the Political Process." *American Economic Review* 77 (March 1987): 1–10.

———. *Reviving the American Dream: The Economy, the States and the Federal Government.* Washington, D.C.: Brookings Institution, 1992.

Samuelson, Paul. "Diagrammatic Exposition of the Theory of Public Expenditure." *Review of Economics and Statistics* 37 (November 1955): 350–356.

———. "The Pure Theory of Public Expenditure." *Review of Economics and Statistics* 36 (November 1954): 387–389.

Sandler, Todd, and John T. Tschirhart. "The Economic Theory of Clubs: An Evaluative Survey." *Journal of Economic Literature* 18 (December 1980): 1481–1521.

Sawhill, Isabel V. "Poverty in the United States: Why Is It So Persistent?" *Journal of Economic Literature* 26 (September 1988): 1073–1119.

Scitovsky, T. "A Note on Welfare Propositions in Economics." *Review of Economic Studies* 9 (November 1941): 77–88.

Scully, Gerald W. "The Convergence of Fiscal Regimes and the Decline of the Tiebout Effect." *Public Choice* 72 (1991): 51–59.

Scully, Gerald W., and Daniel J. Slottje. "Ranking Economic Liberty across Countries." *Public Choice* 69 (1991): 121–152.

"Sell the Whale." *The Economist,* June 27, 1992, 16.

Senat, Hamburger *Abschlubbericht des Beauftragten zur Gebaudereinigung.* Hamburg, 1974.

"Shortfall in Pension Funds Rises Sharply to $50 Billion, United States Says," *Los Angeles Times,* December 13, 1992, A30.

Shoven, John B. "The Incidence and Efficiency Effects of Taxes on Income from Capital." *Journal of Political Economy* 84 (December 1976): 1261–1283.

Simons, Henry. *Personal Income Taxation.* Chicago: University of Chicago Press, 1938.

Slemrod, Joel. "Did the Tax Reform Act of 1986 Simplify Tax Matters?" *Journal of Economic Perspectives* 6 (Winter 1992): 45–57.

Slemrod, Joel, and Nikki Sorum. "The Compliance Cost of the U.S. Individual Income Tax System." *National Tax Journal* 37 (December 1984).

Smith, Adam. *The Wealth of Nations,* edited by Andrew Skinner. England: Penguin Books, Ltd., 1974.

Smith, Anthony. "Mass Communications." In *Democracy at the Polls: A Comparative Study of Competitive National Elections,* edited by David Butler, Howard R. Penniman, and Austin Ranney. Washington, D.C.: American Enterprise Institute, 1981.

Smith, Vernon. "Experiments with a Decentralized Mechanism for Public Good Decisions." *American Economic Review* 70 (September 1980): 584–599.

Social Security Administration. "Personal Earnings and Benefit Estimate Statement." 1989.

Steuerle, C. Eugene. "Tax Credits for Low-Income Workers with Children," *Journal of Economic Perspectives* (Summer 1990): 201–212.

Stigler, George J. *Memoirs of an Unregulated Economist.* New York: Basic Books, 1988.

———. "The Theory of Economic Regulation." *The Bell Journal of Economics and Management Science* 2 (1971): 3–21.

Stockfish, J. A. "Value-Added Taxes and the Size of Government." *National Tax Journal* 38 (December 1985): 547–552.

Stokes, Donald E. "What Decides Elections." In *Democracy at the Polls: A Comparative Study of Competitive Elections,* edited by David Butler, Howard R. Penniman, and Austin Ranney. Washington, D.C.: American Enterprise Institute, 1981.

Stuart, Charles. "Welfare Costs per Dollar of Additional Tax Revenue in the United States." *American Economic Review* 74 (June 1984): 352–362.

Summers, Lawrence H. "The After-Tax Rate of Return Affects Private Savings." *American Economic Review* 74 (May 1984): 249–253.

Tanzi, Vito. *The Underground Economy in the United States and Abroad.* Lexington, Mass.: D.C. Heath, 1982.

Tatom, John A. "Public Capital and Private Sector Performance." *Review* 73, Federal Reserve Bank of St. Louis (May–June 1991): 3–15.

Tax Foundation. *Facts and Figures on Government Finance,* 1991 edition. Baltimore: Johns Hopkins Press, 1991.

Taylor, Jeffrey. "Smog Swapping: New Rules Harness Power of Free Markets to Curb Air Pollution." *Wall Street Journal,* April 14, 1992, A1, A9.

Thomas, Paulette. "Drawing the Line: Getting Families off Welfare and into Jobs Isn't as Easy as AFDC." *Wall Street Journal,* September 25, 1993, A1.

———. "New Tax Means All Free Parking Won't Be Free." *Wall Street Journal,* January 10, 1994, B1.

Tideman, T. Nicolaus, and Gordon Tullock. "A New and Superior Process for Making Social Choices." *Journal of Political Economy* 84 (December 1976): 1145–1160.

Tiebout, Charles M. "A Pure Theory of Local Government Expenditures." *Journal of Political Economy* 64 (October 1956): 416–424.

Tobin, James. "On Limiting the Domain of Inequality." *Journal of Law and Economics* 13 (1970): 263–277.

Tollison, Robert D., W. Mark Crain, and Paul A. Paulter. "Information and Voting: An Empirical Note." *Public Choice* 24 (1975): 43–49.

Topel, Robert. "Financing Unemployment Insurance: History, Incentives, and Reform." In *Unemployment Insurance: The Second Half-Century,* edited by W. Lee Hansen and James F. Byers. Madison, Wis.: Wisconsin University Press, 1990.

Tucker, William. "A Model for Destroying a City." *Wall Street Journal,* March 12, 1993, A10.

Tullock, Gordon. *The Politics of Bureaucracy.* Washington, D.C.: Public Affairs Press, 1965.

———. *Autocracy.* Dordrecht: Martinus Nijhoff Publishers, 1987.

———. "Dynamic Hypothesis on Bureaucracy." *Public Choice* 19 (1974): 127–131.

———. *Economics of Income Redistribution.* Boston: Kluwer Nijhoff Publishing, 1983.

———. "Federalism: Problems of Scale." *Public Choice* 6 (1969): 19–30.

———. "The Transitional Gains Trap." *Bell Journal of Economics* 6 (Autumn 1975): 671–678.

———. "The Welfare Costs of Tariffs, Monopolies and Theft." *Western Economic Journal* 5 (June 1967): 224–232.

———. *Welfare for the Well-to-Do.* Dallas: The Fisher Institute, 1983.

Tyson, Laura. "Higher Taxes Do So Raise Money." *Wall Street Journal,* August 3, 1993, A14.

U.S. Department of Commerce. *Statistical Abstract of the United States.* Washington, D.C.: U.S. Government Printing Office, 1990.

———. *Statistical Abstract of the United States.* Washington, D.C.: U.S. Government Printing Office, 1991.

———. *Statistical Abstract of the United States.* Washington, D.C.: U.S. Government Printing Office, 1992.

U.S. Department of Treasury. *Report of The Secretary of the Treasury on Government Sponsored Enterprises.* Washington, D.C.: U.S. Government Printing Office, May 1990.

Von Furstenburg, George, Jeffrey R. Green, and Jin-Ho Jeong. "Tax and Spend or Spend and Tax?" *Review of Economics and Statistics* 67 (May 1986): 179–188.

Wagner, Adolph. *Finanzwissenschaft* (1883) partly reproduced in Richard A. Musgrave, and Allan T. Peacock, eds. *Classics in Public Finance.* Macmillan: London, 1958.

Wagner, Richard E. *To Promote the General Welfare: Market Processes vs. Political Transfers.* San Francisco: Pacific Research Institute for Public Policy, 1989.

———. *Public Finance: Revenues and Expenditures in a Democratic Society.* Boston: Little, Brown and Company, 1983.

———. "Revenue Structure, Fiscal Illusion, and Budgetary Choice." *Public Choice* 25 (1976): 45–61.

Wallis, John J. "The Political Economy of New Deal Federalism." *Economic Inquiry* 24 (July 1991): 510–524.

Wallis, John J., and Wallace E. Oates. "Does Economic Sclerosis Set in with Age? An Empirical Study of the Olson Hypothesis." *Kyklos* 41, no. 3 (1988): 397–417.

Ward, Benjamin. "Taxes and the Size of Government." *American Economic Review* 72 (May 1982): 346–350.

Wartzman, Rick. "Clinton's Proposal for 'Sin Taxes' May Stumble by Turning Too Many Americans into Saints." *Wall Street Journal,* April 20, 1993, A16.

———. "Whether or Not They Benefit, Companies Decry Instability in Tax Law as a Barrier to Planning." *Wall Street Journal,* August 10, 1993, A16.

Weaver, Carolyn L. *The Crisis in Social Security.* Durham, N.C.: Duke University Press, 1982.

———. ed. *Social Security's Looming Surpluses: Prospects and Implications.* Washington, D.C.: AEI Press, 1990.

Webber, Carolyn, and Aaron Wildavsky. *A History of Taxation and Expenditure in the Western World.* New York: Simon & Schuster, 1986.

Weinberg, Daniel H. "The Distributional Implications of Tax Expenditures and Comprehensive Income Taxation." *National Tax Journal* 50 (1993): 237–253.

The World Almanac and Book of Facts 1990. New York: World Almanac, 1989.

Glossary

Ability-to-pay principle is a taxation principle whereby taxes are levied on the basis of the financial resources of individual taxpayers. (p. 422)

Adjusted gross income (AGI) is gross income less allowable deductions. (p. 499)

Administrative costs of taxation are costs related to administering the tax system. (p. 456)

Ad valorem **taxes** are those levied as a percentage of product price. (p. 437)

Adverse selection is the tendency whereby those at the greatest risk of collecting insurance are also those most likely to purchase insurance. (p. 281)

Agenda control arises when voters or committee members order voting on issues in such a way as to secure a favorable outcome. (p. 194)

Aid to Families with Dependent Children (AFDC) is a long-established transfer program that directly provides money to families with dependent children. (p. 313)

Allocational effects are the ways in which policies influence the use of resources. (p. 237)

Allocation function is the shifting of resources into preferred (and out of non-preferred) areas. (p. 13)

Alternative minimum tax (AMT) is the least possible legal amount that must be paid by high-income taxpayers. (p. 503)

Average tax rate is calculated by dividing tax liability by taxable income. (p. 502)

Balanced budget amendment is a law that under most circumstances prohibits policymakers from running a budget deficit. (p. 263)

Balanced budget incidence evaluates the incidence of both taxation and the spending it finances. (p. 437)

Base broadening of the tax base eliminates or reduces tax expenditures. (p. 508)

Behavioral assumptions are predictions of voters' and policymakers' interactions in the policy process. (p. 152)

Benefit-cost ratio is the ratio of the present value of benefits over the present value of costs. (p. 397)

Benefit principle is a taxation principle whereby taxes are assigned on the basis of benefits received. (p. 417)

Benevolent view of government is the belief and theory that policymakers are motivated to maximize the well-being of society. (p. 203)

Bequest motive is the passing by parents to children (or other heirs) of income to meet the burdens of higher future tax burdens implied by today's debt. (p. 476)

Bracket creep occurs when increases in nominal income result in higher marginal tax rates. (p. 513)

Broad self-interest is the desire to enhance one's own well-being as well as that of others with whom one recognizes some literal or figurative kinship. (p. 154)

The **budget constraint hypothesis** predicts that government spending is primarily a result of the revenues received by policymakers. (p. 482)

Budget deficit occurs when public spending exceeds tax revenues. (p. 22)

The **Budget Enforcement Act of 1990** extended the Gramm-Rudman-Hollings budget deadline to 1994. (p. 258)

Budget surplus occurs when tax revenues exceed public spending. (p. 22)

Bureaucracy theory rests on the assumption that civil servants are primarily motivated by the power, pay, and prestige associated with being a government employee. (p. 205)

Capital budgets are budgets that distinguish between short-lived and long-lived assets. (p. 264)

Capital gains are increases in the value of assets realized at the time of their sale. (p. 514)

Cash transfers are transfer policies that give money to recipients. (p. 313)

Centralization is the degree to which policies emanate from central governments. (p. 135)

Coase theorem is a proposition that resources are allocated efficiently so long as there are well-defined property rights and transactions costs are negligible. (p. 86)

Coercion occurs when individuals are compelled, against their will, to receive and pay for public policies. (p. 141)

Common-pool problems occur when public stewardship of resources allocates resources inefficiently. (p. 146)

Compensated supply curve holds income constant, and therefore all quantity changes reflect substitution effects. (p. 522)

Compensation test is a test of resource reallocations based on measurable increases in net social benefits. (p. 54)

Compliance costs of taxation are costs taxpayers incur in order to comply with tax laws. (p. 457)

Comprehensive measure of income is income defined on the basis of the Haig-Simons criterion. (p. 495)

Conditional grants are grants accompanied by stipulations imposed by grantor governments as to how revenues are to be spent by recipient governments. (p. 595)

Consumer surplus is the difference between maximum possible expenditures and actual expenditures. (p. 45)

Corporations are legal entities created by states, which approve charters submitted by founders. (p. 537)

Corrective taxation is tax policy that forces market participants to account for the opportunity costs of all resources. (p. 92)

Credit and insurance policies reallocate resources in credit and insurance markets. (p. 26)

Credit claiming is declaring responsibility for a successful public policy. (p. 173)

Crisis displacement theory of government predicts that government expansion occurs as the result of significant adverse past events. (p. 223)

A **current services budget** allows for automatic spending increases to maintain past levels of service. (p. 255)

Debt heavy is the condition that results when firms carry large debt burdens; they are called debt-heavy firms. (p. 544)

Decision costs occur when resources are expended to persuade voters to agree on proposals. (p. 184)

Demanders of public programs are parties (for example, voters and special interest groups) who seek public policies. (p. 213)

Differential tax incidence evaluates the incidence of taxation under the assumption that public spending does not change. (p. 437)

Direct loans are made directly by the public sector. (p. 28)

Direct payments are those made directly by patients for health care. (p. 372)

Discretionary spending consists of disbursements subject to annual review and budgeting. (p. 251)

Distribution function is the changing of the final recipients of goods and services produced by the economy. (p. 14)

Distributional effects are the ways in which policies transfer income from one person to another. (p. 238)

Dividends are payments made to owners of corporations. (p. 538)

Double-declining balance is a variant of straight-line depreciation whereby the majority of depreciation is deducted in the early years of an asset's tax life. (p. 540)

Double-peaked preferences are a characteristic whereby, as voters move away from most preferred options, utility falls at first, but eventually rises. (p. 195)

Double-taxation is the taxing of income when it is earned by corporations and again when it is distributed to stockholders. (p. 538)

Earned income tax credits lower tax liabilities of poor taxpayers. (p. 502)

Economic depreciation is the process by which capital resources are actually consumed or made obsolete. (p. 539)

Economic incidence indicates who actually bears the burden of taxation. (p. 436)

Economic Recovery Tax Act of 1981 was a fundamental tax reform that, among other changes, lowered marginal tax rates 23 percent over three years. (p. 504)

Economies of scale occur when increased levels of production result in decreased average costs of production. (p. 134)

Effective tax rates are tax rates calculated by dividing tax liability by a comprehensive measure of income. (p. 542)

Elected policymakers are chosen by voters for public office. (p. 165)

Entitlement programs are those which provide benefits to all who meet various eligibility requirements. (p. 260)

Equality of opportunity occurs at such a time as all individuals have equal opportunities in life. (p. 305)

Equality of outcomes occurs when all individuals end up in identical circumstances (for example, with identical incomes). (p. 305)

Equilibrium size of government is the size characterized by the intersection of the demand and supply of government. (p. 215)

Equity is a criterion for allocating resources on the basis of fairness. (p. 5)

Estate taxes are taxes imposed on the transfer of wealth after the death of a taxpayer. (p. 567)

Excess burden is a resource loss over and above taxes collected. (p. 449)

The **executive branch** of government is headed by the President of the United States. (p. 166)

Excise subsidies are subsidies given to the purchasers of particular goods or services. (p. 319)

Excise taxes are those levied on particular goods or services. (p. 437)

Exit options allow voters to reject policies by moving to other political jurisdictions. (p. 201)

Expenditure tax is a comprehensive consumption tax. (p. 557)

Expensing allows for the depreciation of the entire cost of an asset during the first year of its purchase. (p. 539)

External costs are those imposed by majorities on minorities. (p. 185)

Federal budget process represents the events, decisions, laws, and the influential people that determine federal spending. (p. 252)

Fiscal centralization is the degree to which government responsibilities are borne by the central government. (p. 578)

Fiscal federalism is the study of the structural organization of the public sector. (p. 577)

Fiscal illusion hypothesis theorizes that current policies are the result of incorrect perceptions by voters. (p. 222)

Fiscal rules are procedures, such as the line-item veto and balanced budget laws and amendments, that seek to control spending or budget deficits. (p. 261)

Foreign share of debt is that share of the national debt held by foreigners. (p. 472)

Free riders are individuals who let others pay for goods they themselves consume. (p. 121)

Fully funded pension fund is a pension fund that has the financial resources necessary to meet future retirement benefits. (p. 336)

General equilibrium analysis of tax incidence is the study of tax incidence that considers interrelations between markets. (p. 447)

General obligation bond is a bond that guarantees that all taxpayers will be responsible for the bond's principal and interest payments. (p. 421)

Generational accounting is a method of recording long-term liabilities in order to measure their impact on future generations. (p. 350)

Gerrymandering is the formation of political districts so as to favor one political party over another. (p. 202)

Gift taxes are taxes imposed on the transfer of wealth while a taxpayer is living. (p. 567)

Government failure occurs when a public policy results in an inefficient or inequitable outcome. (pp. 16, 61)

Glossary

Government purchases consist of tangible goods and services purchased by the government. (p. 242)

Governments as laboratories are state and local governments that test new and innovative public policies. (p. 588)

Government-sponsored enterprises (GSEs) are off-budget government agencies that reallocate resources in credit markets. (p. 27)

Government transfers redistribute income. (p. 242)

The **Gramm-Rudman-Hollings Act** called for automatic spending cuts in order to balance the budget of the federal government by 1991. (p. 258)

Gross federal debt is the debt held by federal government agencies plus that held by the public. (p. 466)

Gross income is the sum of all income sources subject to taxation. (p. 498)

Haig-Simons criterion defines income as the change in the ability to consume during a given time period. (p. 493)

Health maintenance organizations (HMOs) are health care providers that receive fixed sums for caring for patients. (p. 375)

Horizontal equity is a concept whereby all individuals with identical abilities to pay are assigned identical tax burdens. (p. 423)

Imperfect information is lack of complete information. (p. 60)

Implicit federal guarantees are unstated or indirectly stated promises by the federal government to cover any losses in cases of default by government-sponsored enterprises. (p. 289)

Implicit rental income is the value of potential rental income. (p. 495)

The **Impoundment Act of 1974** is a Congressional act that denies the President the power to impound funds. (p. 254)

Inframarginal externalities occur whenever externalities disappear at production levels consistent with private market allocations of resources. (p. 105)

In-kind income is income in the form of goods and services rather than cash. (p. 495)

Insurance copayment is that percentage of an insurance claim for which the insured is personally responsible. (p. 367)

Insurance deductible is the dollar value of medical benefits that must be paid by patients before their insurance company pays for some of or all treatment costs. (p. 367)

Insurance function occurs if a policy mimics a private insurance policy and therefore does not seek to transfer income. (p. 335)

Intergenerational transfers are transfers of Social Security benefits among members of different generations. (p. 345)

Intergovernmental competition is a fiscal structure characterized by many competing governments. (p. 587)

Intergovernmental grants are monies flowing from one government (grantor) to another government (recipient). (p. 595)

Interjurisdictional externalities are those that arise when governments fail to fully account for costs and benefits imposed on citizens of other governments. (p. 593)

Internal rates of discount are the discount rates at which the present values of projects are zero. (p. 396)

Internalization of costs is the allocation of resources by private markets on the basis of full social costs. (p. 88)

Intertemporal choice model is a model illustrating the various choices between consuming or saving income. (p. 528)

Intragenerational transfers are transfers of Social Security benefits among members of the same generation. (p. 345)

Itemized deductions are those deductions allowed taxpayers who do not take the standard deduction. (p. 500)

The **judicial branch** of government is the system of courts headed by the Supreme Court. (p. 167)

Lack of exclusion is a characteristic of public goods making it difficult or impossible to restrict the enjoyment of benefits to any individual. (p. 118)

Laffer curve shows a hypothetical relationship between tax rates and tax revenues. (p. 524)

The **legislative branch** of government in the United States is Congress, which consists of the Senate and the House of Representatives. (p. 166)

Leviathan view of government is the belief and theory that policymakers are motivated to maximize their narrow self-interests. (p. 203)

Lindahl prices are prices that equal the marginal benefits individuals receive when they consume optimal quantities of public goods. (p. 125)

Line-item veto allows the President or governors to eliminate individual spending items from an entire budget. (p. 261)

Loan guarantees are loans guaranteed by the public sector. (p. 28)

Lobbying costs are the expenses incurred by lobbyists seeking tax expenditures. (p. 458)

Lock-in effect occurs when a policy encourages investors to hold onto assets longer than they would if taxes were levied on accrued gains. (p. 495)

Logrolling occurs when voters further their well-being by trading votes (on multiple issues) with one another. (p. 196)

Long-lived resources are assets with a useful life of one year or more. (p. 539)

Long-run corporate tax incidence occurs after stockholders shift capital resources in response to corporate taxation. (p. 548)

Lump sum tax is one that does not vary with units of goods purchased or sold. (p. 451)

Majority rule of voting is a procedure that requires that a majority, simple or otherwise specified, must agree to policies before they are passed. (p. 184)

Managed competition is competition that would theoretically lower health care costs through the creation of competing, and regulated, health insurance firms. (p. 377)

Mandatory spending consists of disbursements not subject to annual review or budgeting. (p. 251)

Marginal benefits are the change in total benefits divided by the change in consumption. (p. 42)

Marginal opportunity costs are the change in total opportunity costs divided by the change in consumption. (p. 42)

Glossary

Marginal tax rates are tax rates that change at various thresholds of income. (p. 501)

Market equilibrium occurs when market demand and market supply intersect. (p. 43)

Market failure occurs when the private market fails to produce an efficient or equitable outcome. (pp. 8, 61)

Marriage tax is the additional tax a married couple pays over and above the combined tax bills they would pay if they were unmarried. (p. 511)

Matching conditional grants are transfers of revenues whereby grantor governments match recipient governments' funds. (p. 598)

Median voter theorem is the proposition that preferences of the median voter are chosen when several conditions, such as all preferences being single-peaked, are present. (p. 187)

Medicare pays inpatient costs at hospitals and limited care at nursing homes. (p. 331)

Medicare trust funds are comprised of IOUs provided by the federal government whenever Medicare collections of Social Security taxes exceed current Medicare spending. (p. 355)

Medigap insurance is private insurance that covers deductibles and insurance co-payments not paid by Medicare. (p. 366)

Methodological individualism is the concept that all choices over resource allocation rest with individuals in private markets and with collections of individuals in public markets. (p. 38)

The **middle class** consists of persons whose earnings place them above the poverty threshold but below the point at which they could be considered wealthy. (p. 310)

Monopoly government is a public sector characterized by a single government. (p. 142)

Moral hazard is the tendency of policies to exert perverse incentives on the behaviors of firms and individuals. (p. 278)

Narrow self-interest is the desire to enhance one's well-being without regard to the well-being of others. (p. 153)

National consumption taxes are federal taxes levied on the consumption of goods and services. (p. 557)

National debt is the sum of all unpaid public debt. (p. 465)

National health insurance is health insurance provided by one insurer, the federal government. (p. 380)

Negative externalities occur when private markets fail to allocate resources on the basis of full social costs. (p. 80)

Negative income tax policy is one that provides a minimum amount of income for all members of society. (p. 324)

Negative transfer occurs whenever individual tax payments exceed benefits received. (p. 426)

Net federal debt is gross federal debt minus debt held by federal agencies. (p. 467)

Net interest expenditures are the interest expenses from borrowing less the interest fees from lending. (p. 248)

Net transfers are the differences between taxes paid and benefits received. (p. 427)

NIMBY is the attitude of policymakers and voters characterized by the saying "not in my backyard." (p. 244)

Noncash transfers are transfer policies that provide goods or services, such as housing or food, rather than money. (p. 313)

Nonelected policymakers are not elected by voters. (p. 165)

Nonmatching conditional grants are transfers of fixed sums of revenue to recipient governments. (p. 598)

Normative analysis is analysis based on value judgments. (p. 11)

Off-budget policies are credit and insurance policies that do not directly show up on the government budget. (p. 28)

Omnibus Budget Reconciliation Acts of 1990 and 1993 raised the number (and top brackets) of marginal tax rates. (p. 506)

On-budget policies are spending and tax policies that show up directly on the government budget. (p. 28)

Opportunity cost is measured by what is lost by not pursuing the next-best alternative. (p. 6)

Optimal fiscal structure is the fiscal structure that meets the various efficiency and equity criteria of a society. (p. 577)

Optimal majority rule is one that results in the minimization of the sum of decision and external costs. (p. 184)

Outlay equivalents are the dollar values of public expenditures that would provide equal benefits to recipients of tax expenditures. (p. 433)

Overspending is believed to occur when a budget deficit results from too much spending. (p. 479)

Pareto efficiency characterizes resource allocation in which no individual can be made better off without making any other individual worse off. (pp. 8, 51)

Pareto inefficiency characterizes a resource allocation whereby another allocation exists that would make at least one individual better off and no individual worse off. (p. 53)

Pareto superior move is a resource reallocation in which one individual is made better off without making any other individual worse off. (p. 53)

Paternalism is a characterization of a belief that policies should be provided that would not necessarily be freely chosen by voters. (p. 15)

Pay-as-you-go is a funding condition that requires current resources be sufficient only to cover current benefits. (p. 340)

Play-or-pay is a proposal requiring that employers provide insurance to employees and their dependents (play) or be charged a payroll tax to fund a public health plan (pay). (p. 378)

Policy process is the interaction of voters and policymakers to determine public policies. (p. 8)

Political action committees (PACs) are special interest groups subject to limits on the amount of funds they may contribute to political candidates. (p. 132)

Political disequilibrium is an occurence characterized by lack of consensus on political issues. (p. 486)

Political participation is the act of contributing to the policy process. (p. 153)

Pollution permits are transferable property rights to pollute up to a specified maximum level of pollution. (p. 100)

Pork barrel spending consists of disbursements that solely benefit a particular locale or special interest group. (p. 246)

Position taking is declaring a particular position on a policy issue. (p. 173)

Positive analysis is analysis based on pure scientific prediction. (p. 10)

Positive externalities occur when private markets fail to allocate resources on the basis of full social benefits. (p. 80)

Positive transfer occurs whenever individual tax payments are less than benefits received. (p. 426)

Poverty threshold is the minimum income level below which families must earn in order to be defined as poor. (p. 310)

Preferred provider organizations are health care providers that agree to limits on the fees they charge. (p. 375)

Present value is today's value of dollars received in the future. (p. 385)

Price effects hypothesis theorizes that because the public sector is increasingly service-oriented and engaged in transfer policies, government grows more quickly than the economy. (p. 217)

Prisoners' dilemma is a situation in which two parties may gain from cooperation but are destined to act independently of each other. (p. 91)

Private costs are costs incurred by private parties. (p. 81)

Private goods are rival in consumption. (p. 118)

Private markets are characterized by resource allocation through the price system. (p. 37)

Private market structure consists of the institutions through which exchanges between consumers and producers take place. (p. 200)

Private pension is a fund that accumulates contributions for the purpose of paying benefits upon a worker's retirement. (p. 336)

Privatization occurs when government responsibilities are shifted to the private sector. (p. 144)

Progressive income tax is a tax system in which tax bills rise faster than income. (p. 5)

A **progressive tax system** is a system in which tax bills rise faster than increases in income. (p. 424)

Property tax is a tax levied on personal property wealth. (p. 568)

A **proportional tax system** is a system in which tax bills are a fixed percentage of income. (p. 424)

Protection function is the safeguarding of the personal property and rights of individuals by the public sector. (p. 13)

Public choice models the public-market exchanges between voters and policymakers much as exchanges between consumers and producers in private markets are modeled. (p. 151)

Public finance is the study of how spending and tax policies influence our economic lives. (p. 3)

Public goods are nonrival in consumption. (p. 118)

Public markets are characterized by resource allocation through the interaction of voters and policymakers in the policy process. (p. 37)

Public market structure consists of the institutions through which exchanges between voters and policymakers take place. (p. 200)

Public spirit is concern for pursuing policies that benefit all of society. (p. 12)

The **Ramsey rule** states that, in order to minimize total excess burden, tax rates should be set in inverse relation to price elasticities of demand. (p. 455)

Rate of discount is the interest rate used to calculate present value. (p. 385)

Rate setting is the practice of setting price controls on medical procedures that may be charged to public and/or private insurance plans. (p. 378)

Rational ignorance is the result of rational decision making when obtaining complete information is unreasonable, impractical, or unproductive. (p. 156)

Real median family income is an inflation-adjusted income at which the number of families earning above it equals the number of families earning below it. (p. 307)

Redlining is the process of denying credit and insurance to residents in certain (redlined) neighborhoods, usually those in high-risk areas. (p. 273)

Re-funding of the national debt occurs when maturing debts are replaced with new debts. (p. 467)

A **regressive tax system** is a system in which tax bills rise more slowly than increases in income. (p. 424)

Regulation is a form of command-and-control policy aimed at restricting, influencing, or defining behavior that produces negative externalities. (p. 98)

Regulatory agencies are government agencies that monitor and enforce Congressional regulations. (p. 30)

Regulatory forbearance occurs whenever a regulator does not enforce an existing rule. (p. 284)

Rent controls are the artifacts of public policies that set the maximum rents landlords may charge renters. (p. 47)

Rent seeking is that part of the policy process in which special interest groups try to win favors. (p. 208)

Replacement rate is the percentage of one's past salary met by retirement benefits. (p. 339)

Retained earnings are corporate earnings not distributed to stockholders. (p. 545)

Revenue bond (nonguaranteed bond) is a bond whose principal and interest payments are derived from revenues earned from projects funded by the bond. (p. 421)

Revenue-expenditure causality is the causal relationship between tax revenues and public spending. (p. 483)

The **Ricardian equivalence proposition** theorizes that public debt and taxation exert equivalent effects on the economy. (p. 475)

School choice is a policy that makes public funds available to parents who choose to send their children to private schools. (p. 588)

Self-insuring is a practice whereby firms create their own health insurance. (p. 370)

Self-interest is concern with one's own well-being. (p. 12)

Short-lived resources are assets with a useful life of one year or less. (p. 539)

Short-run corporate tax incidence occurs before stockholders shift capital resources in response to corporate taxation. (p. 548)

Simple majority rule is a procedure in which the greatest number of votes wins. (p. 184)

Single-peaked preferences characterize preferences when, as options move further away from a voter's most preferred option, those preferences or options become less desirable. (p. 194)

Social costs are those incurred by private parties in addition to any other costs borne by other members of society. (p. 81)

Social Security is a New Deal program that provides benefits to retired and disabled workers and their dependents. (p. 331)

Social Security Amendments of 1983 were the first to subject some Social Security benefits to taxation. (p. 504)

Social Security benefits are payments received by Social Security recipients whose contributions make them eligible. (p. 337)

Social Security deficits occur whenever Social Security payouts exceed taxes collected. (p. 341)

Social Security surpluses arise whenever Social Security taxes exceed current payouts. (p. 341)

Social Security taxes are taxes paid by workers into the Social Security system. (p. 337)

Social Security trust funds are comprised of IOUs provided by the federal government whenever Social Security taxes exceed payouts. (p. 339)

Social welfare function indicates the changes in a society's welfare as each member experiences changes in personal well-being. (p. 56)

Social welfare policies are those which redistribute income among citizens. (p. 301)

Source side of budget includes wages, salaries, government transfers, interest earnings, fringe benefits, and capital gains or losses. (p. 494)

Special interest groups are associations of voters linked by some common interest. (p. 129)

Stabilization function is the smoothing out of the ups and downs of the macroeconomy. (p. 15)

Standard deduction is the maximum deduction allowed taxpayers who do not itemize deductions. (p. 500)

Statutory depreciation specifies the rates at which capital resources may be deducted from taxable income over designated tax lives. (p. 539)

Statutory incidence is the indication of who is liable for payment of taxes. (p. 436)

Statutory tax rates are tax rates defined by the tax code. (p. 542)

Straight-line depreciation is the deduction of a uniform percentage of costs over each year of an asset's tax life. (p. 539)

Subsidies result from policies that pay firms for not producing negative externalities. (p. 96)

Suppliers of public programs are parties (for example, government employees and private contractors) who provide public policies. (p. 213)

Tax amnesties allow taxpayers to pay overdue taxes without prosecution. (p. 459)

Tax avoidance is the legal action of paying less taxes than would otherwise be assessed. (p. 458)

Tax bases are the portion of income subject to taxation. (p. 429)

Tax credits are dollar-for-dollar reductions in tax liabilities. (p. 502)

Tax earmarking is a tax principle whereby revenues are directed toward payment of specific programs. (p. 419)

Tax evasion is the illegal action of paying less taxes than one legally owes. (p. 458)

Tax expenditures are policies that exclude, defer, or exempt portions of income from taxation. (pp. 375, 428)

Tax liability is total taxes owed by the taxpayer. (p. 501)

Tax life is the period over which statutory depreciation is allowed. (p. 539)

Tax policy neutrality occurs when a tax policy does not distort the allocation of resources. (p. 496)

Tax rates are specified levels of tax collection based on given levels of income. (p. 429)

Tax reform is a process whereby major changes in the tax system occur. (p. 414)

Tax Reform Act of 1986, perhaps the most ambitious tax reform ever, simplified many aspects of the tax code. (p. 504)

Tax simplification are those policies that seek to lessen the complexity of tax laws and collection. (p. 460)

Tax shelters are legal means by which taxpayers lower their tax bills. (p. 457)

Tax shifting is the moving by taxpayers of some portion of tax assignments onto others. (p. 425)

Tax-spend hypothesis theorizes that spending rises in response to higher tax revenues. (p. 226)

Tax wars are competitions between (or among) two or more governments on the basis of lowering taxes. (p. 594)

Theory of clubs explains voluntary cooperation among individuals seeking mutual advantage. (p. 127)

Third-party payer is an insurer who makes payments to health care providers on behalf of the insured. (p. 373)

Tiebout model is a demonstration of interjurisdictional mobility whereby taxpayers search for desirable packages of government programs. (p. 586)

Total net benefits are total benefits less total costs. (p. 39)

Transfer function occurs if a policy is designed to transfer income. (p. 335)

Unanimity rule of voting is a procedure that requires that all individuals must agree to policies before they are passed. (p. 183)

Unanimity test is a test of resource reallocations based on approval by all parties. (p. 56)

Unconditional grants are grants carrying no restrictions on the ways in which revenues are to be spent by recipient governments. (p. 596)

Undertaxation is believed to occur when a budget deficit results from too little taxation. (p. 479)

Unemployment insurance provides benefits to laid-off workers. (p. 331)

Unit taxes are those levied as a fixed amount per unit of a good or service purchased. (p. 437)

Use side of budget includes consumption, donations and gifts, savings, and various costs incurred during the process of earning income. (p. 494)

Utility possibilities curve is a plot of the maximum utility for one individual, holding constant the utility of another individual. (p. 52)

Value-added tax (VAT) is tax collected at various stages during the production of goods and services. (p. 562)

Vertical equity is a concept whereby tax burdens rise with the ability to pay. (p. 424)

Voice options allow the expression of demands by voters to policymakers. (p. 201)

Voluntary agreements are arrangements under which all parties have reached mutual consent. (p. 142)

Voting cycles occur when no voting equilibrium exists. (p. 193)

Wagner's law is the theory that public spending increases more quickly than does national income. (p. 216)

Wealth taxation is taxation imposed on the accumulated net value of assets at a particular point in time. (p. 567)

Welfare costs occur when resource losses exceed taxes collected; also called excess burden. (p. 318)

Welfare economics is the study of the efficiency and equity of resource allocation. (p. 51)

Welfare state is a term used to describe a public sector heavily engaged in redistributing income among its citizens. (p. 246)

Workfare is a policy requiring healthy welfare recipients to work in exchange for welfare benefits. (p. 326)

Work–leisure trade-off is the trade-off workers experience by either choosing to work or take time off. (p. 322)

Zero marginal cost of provision occurs when one or more citizens may consume a good with zero additional costs. (p. 118)

Name and Subject Index

A

Aaron, Henry J., 339
Ability-to-pay principle, 422–425
Abney, G., 264
Abrams, B. H., 158
Abramson, Paul R., 164
ACME Energy, 104–105
Adjusted gross income (AGI), 499
Ad valorem taxes
　described, 437, 444–445
　introduction of legislated, 556
　property tax as, 568
Adverse selection, 281, 287, 323–324
Agenda control, 194
Aggregate financing, 414
Ahlbrandt, R. S., Jr., 144
Aid to Families with Dependent Children (AFDC), 301, 313
Air Quality Management District (AQMD), 102
Aldrich, John H., 164
Allocational effects, 237–238
Allocation function, 13–14
Allocative efficiency
　cost-benefit analysis and, 383–385
　of GSEs, 290–291
　negative externalities and, 81–82
　of nondeposit insurance programs, 288
　positive externalities and, 103–104
　property right assignment and, 88
　subsidies and, 104
　of tax expenditures, 430
Alm, James, 264, 460
Alternative minimum taxable income (AMTI), 503
Alternative minimum tax (AMT), 503
Anderson, Terry L., 146
Anderson, William, 484
Angello, Richard J., 83
Arrow, Kenneth J., 372
Aschauer, David A., 265–266
Atkinson, Anthony B., 359
Auerbach, Alan J., 543
Average indexed monthly earnings (AIME), 337
Average tax rate, 502
Avrin, Marcy, 346

B

Bacon, Kenneth H., 297
Balanced Budget and Deficit Reduction Act of 1985, 258–260, 263
Balanced budget incidence, 437
Ballard, Charles L., 455, 564
Ballentine, J. Gregory, 551, 552
Bank Insurance Fund (BIF), 282
Barro, Robert J., 166, 223, 348, 474, 476, 477, 478, 482
Barth, James R., 113, 115, 266, 281, 283, 478
Bartlett, Bruce, 566
Base broadening, 508–509
Baumol, William J., 93, 217
Becker, Gary S., 145
Beck, William, 460

Behavioral assumptions, 152
Benefit-cost ratios, 396–397
Benefit principle
　public policy and, 420–422
　within tax policy, 416–420
Benevolent view of government, 203
Bennett, James T., 130, 136, 143, 145, 164, 221, 292
Bequest motive, 476
Bergstrom, Theodore C., 218
Bizer, David, 482
Black, Duncan, 151, 183
Blackley, Paul R., 227, 484
Blinder, Alan S., 312
Blumenthal, Marsha, 460
Borchard, William M., 92
Borcherding, Thomas E., 208, 213, 217–218, 221, 223
Boskin, Michael J., 346–347, 531, 567
Bosworth, Barry P., 339, 524, 531
Bovard, James, 89, 405–406
Bowen, Howard R., 188
Bracket creep, 226, 513
Bradford, David F., 557
Brady, Gordon L., 83
Brennan, Geoffrey, 142, 203, 225
Broad self-interest
　of policymakers, 173–175
　of voters, 154–155
Brown, Charles, 49, 594
Browning, Edgar K., 455
Buchanan, James M., 38, 56, 98, 127, 136, 138, 142, 151, 183, 184, 186, 203, 222, 225, 352, 473, 481, 527
Buch, Winston C., 221
Budget and Accounting Act (1921), 253
Budget constraint hypothesis, 482–483
Budget deficits
　described, 22, 24, 463–465
　fiscal illusion hypothesis on, 480–481
　measuring, 468–471
　national debt compared to, 465–466
　policy issues of, 478–488
　political disequilibrium and, 486–488
　Ricardian equivalence proposition on, 481–482
　Ricardian view of, 474–477, 481–482
　tax increases and, 482–484
　See also Public debt
Budget Enforcement Act of 1990 (BEA), 258, 260–261, 263
Budget Omnibus Budget Reconciliation Acts of 1990 and 1993, 485
Budget surplus, 22, 24
Bureaucracy theory, 205–207
Burtless, Gary, 339, 524, 531
Bush, George, 99, 405
Bush, Winston C., 164, 221, 223
Butler, David, 154
Byers, James F., 358, 360

C

Capital budgets, 264–265, 469–470
Capital consumption allowance, 539

Capital gains, 514
Capital resources, 545–546
Cash transfers
　noncash vs., 315–319
　types listed, 313–314
Centralization
　decentralization and, 135
　fiscal, 578
　public sector, 225–226
　of spending policy, 580
Ceteris paribus, 215, 217
Changes in quantity demanded, 617
Cheung, Steven N. S., 49
Chicoine, David L., 591
Child nutrition programs, 315
Class mobility, 312–313
Clean Air Act (1990), 99, 100
Clinton, Bill, 265, 413
Clubs
　community associations as, 137, 588
　formation of, 127–129
　limited membership of, 136
　special interest groups as, 129–134
　theory of, 127
Coase, Ronald, 86
Coase theorem
　analysis of, 90
　described, 85–88
　implications of, 88–89, 108
Coercion, 141–142
Cold War, 244–246
Collections of individuals, 38
Collender, Stanley E., 260–261
Common-pool problems, 146
Compensated supply curve, 522–523
Compensation, 95–96
　See also Income
Compensation tests, 54
Competition
　intergovernmental, 587
　managed, 377–378
　perfect, 75–79
Competitive Equality Banking Act of 1987, 291
Comprehensive measure of income, 494–498
Conditional grants, 595–596
Cone, Kenneth, 346
Congleton, Roger D., 458
Connie Lee, 288
Consumer equilibrium, 611–613
Consumer Product Safety Commission (CPSC), 30
Consumer surplus, 45–47
Consumer theory
　budget constraints of, 610–611
　consumer equilibrium of, 611–613
　indifference schedules of, 605–610
　law of demand of, 603–605
　preference orderings of, 605
Consumption
　consumer theory on, 603–619
　defined by Haig-Simons criterion, 493–494

by free riders, 121
intertemporal choice model of, 528–529
of public goods, 128
public/private goods and, 118
taxation of, 555–573
Contract curve, 67–68
Conventional loans, 277
Conway, M. Margaret, 153, 159–161, 163
Cordes, Joseph J., 281
Corporation taxes
defining taxable income for, 537–542
excess burden of, 551–552
impact of policies of, 543–546
long-run incidence of, 548–551
rates/credits for, 542–543
reform of, 552
short-run incidence of, 546–548
Corrective taxation, 92–94
Cost-benefit analysis
allocative efficiency and, 383–385
alternative time frameworks for, 384–385
application of, 397–404
benefit principle and, 421–422
policy process and, 405–408
present value framework for, 385–393
selecting projects using, 393–397
value of life within, 400
within imperfect public sector, 408
Couch, Jim F., 589
Council of Economic Advisors, 253
Crain, W. Mark, 158, 162, 264, 349
Credit market, 270–273, 283
Credit policies, 273–275, 293–297, 470–471
Crisis displacement theory of government, 223–225
Current services budget, 255–258, 256–257

D

Dales, J. H., 100
Danziger, Sheldon, 359
Davies, D. G., 143
Davies, James, 562
Davis, Bob, 99
Deacon, Robert T., 218
Debt
financing through, 544–545
foreign share of, 472–473
gross federal, 466–467
national, 465–468
public, 472–482
Debt heavy, 544–545
Decentralization, 135
Decision costs, 184–186
Decreases in demand, 617
Deductions, standard/itemized, 500
Defense spending, 244–246
See also Public spending
Delinquency rate, 277
Demand
decreases in, 617
elasticities of, 441–443
market equilibrium and, 622–623
price consumption curves and, 616–617
public program, 215–217
tax policy and, 443
See also Supply and demand
Demanders of public programs, 213
Democracy, 189–192

Demsetz, Harold, 83
Denzau, Arthur T., 164, 221
Deposit insurance
described, 281–282
direct allocative effect on, 276
policy on, 281–288
See also Federal insurance
Depository Institutions Deregulation and Monetary Control Act (1980), 282
Depreciation
capital resource choices and, 545–546
corporate taxes, 539
expensing, 539
inflation and, 541–542
straight-line, 539–540
tax lives and rates of, 540–541
Depreciation schedule, 539
Dictatorships, 180–181
Differential tax incidence, 437
DiLorenzo, Thomas J., 130, 136, 145, 292
Direct loans, 28
Direct payments, 372–373
Discount rate
for public projects, 403–404
risk and, 403
used by government, 402–403
Discretionary spending, 251
See also Public spending
Distributional effects
of credit/insurance policies, 276–277
of deposit insurance, 286
described, 238–239
of GSEs, 290–291
on nondeposit insurance programs, 288
of tax expenditures, 430–431
Distribution function, 14
Dividends, 538, 545
Donnelley, Lawrence P., 83
Dorosh, Gary W., 208
Double-declining balance, 540–541
Double-peaked preferences, 195–197
Double-taxation, 538–539
Dougan, William R., 264
Downing, Paul B., 95, 99
Downs, Anthony, 151, 163, 229
Drazen, Allan, 476
Dubin, Jeffrey A., 459
Durlauf, Steven, 482
Dwyer, Gerald P., 478

E

Earned income tax credit (EITC), 313, 502
Eatwell, John, 56, 587
Economic depreciation, 539
Economic efficiency, 8
Economic incidence, 436–437, 439–441
Economic liberty, 177–178
Economic Recovery Tax Act of 1981 (ERTA81), 484, 504–506, 541
Economies of scale, 134–135, 590–591
Edgeworth–Bowley box, 65
Education
public spending on, 237–239
school choice issue, 588–590
shortsighted policies on, 404
Effective tax rates, 542–543
Efficiency
individual view of, 38

market conditions and, 44–45
market equilibrium and, 43–44
market incentives for, 99
overall, 72–74
production of goods, 71–72
resource allocation, 39–47
tax policy based on, 139–141
Efficiency in exchange, 64–69, 75–77
Efficiency in production, 64, 69–72, 75–77
Efficient production, 71–72
Eisner, Robert, 264, 469
Elected policymakers, 165–166
Elephant market analysis, 85
Energy assistance, 315
Entitlement programs, 260
Environmental Protection Agency (EPA), 30, 100
Equality of opportunity, 305–306
Equality of outcomes, 305
Equilibrium public sector size, 216
Equilibrium size of government, 215
Equity
financing through debt vs., 544–545
resource allocation and, 5, 8
sales tax rates and, 560
tax policy based on, 141, 509–511
vertical, 561
Equity goals, 60–61
Escrow account policy, 328
Estate taxes, 567–568
Excess burden
of corporate taxes, 551–552
elasticity and, 452–453
the individual and, 451–452
market perspective of, 449–450
minimization of, 455–456
saving behavior and, 533
unit taxes measured, 453–455
Excise subsidies, 319–321
Excise taxes, 437
Executive branch, 166–167
Exit options, 201–203
Expenditure policies
allocational effects of, 237–238
defense spending, 244–246
distributional effects of, 238–239
federal budget process of, 252–261
net interest, 248–252
pork barrel spending, 246–248
purchases vs. transfers as, 242–244
transfers as, 246
See also Governments
Expenditure tax, 557
Expensing, 539
External costs, 185–186
Externalities
common-pool problems of, 146
corrective subsidy of, 97
inframarginal, 105–106
interjurisdictional, 593
negative, 81–92
positive, 80–81
public goods characterized by, 135–136
reciprocal nature of, 87

F

Faber, Peter, 458
Fannie Mae, 288, 296–297

Farmer Mac, 288
Federal Assistance Corporation (FAC), 291
Federal budget process
  described, 252–253
  Impoundment Act of 1974 and, 254
  prior to 1974, 253
  reform of, 261–264
Federal budgets
  between 1934–94, 464
  Social Security impact on, 348–349
Federal credit, 26–28
Federal deficit
  GRHI impact on, 258–260
  Social Security impact on, 349–350
Federal Deposit Insurance Corporation (FDIC), 282
Federal Home Loan Bank System, 288
Federal insurance
  allocation effects on, 276
  described, 281–282
  economic impact of policy on, 285–288
  of GSEs, 288–293
  outstanding, 27
  policy and risk of, 283–284
  potential costs of, 293–297
  resource allocation and, 26–27
  types of social, 301
Federalism
  advantages of, 582–590
  disadvantages of, 590–595
  fiscal, 577
Federalist Papers (Madison), 208
Federal Savings and Loan Insurance Corporation (FSLIC), 112–113, 282
Federal spending, 21
  See also Public spending
Feige, Edgar L., 51
Feldstein, Martin, 348, 374, 478, 542
Financial Institutions Reform, Recovery, and Enforcement Act of 1989 (FIRREA), 282, 285
Financing Corporation (FICO), 291–292
Finanzwissenschaft, Adolph Wagner, 216
Fiorina, Morris P., 172–173
Fiscal centralization, 578
Fiscal federalism, 577
Fiscal illusion hypothesis, 222–223, 480–481
Fiscal rules, 261
Fiscal structure
  federalism model of, 582–595
  optimal, 577
  trends in, 578–582
Fiscal years, 19
Fischer-Menshausen, H., 143
Fitzgerald, Randall, 247–248
Food stamps, 314–315
Forbes, Kevin F., 592
Foreclosure rate, 277–278
Foreign share of debt, 472–473
Freddie Mac, 288, 296
Freeman, A. M., III, 95
Free parking tax, 497
Free riders
  benefit principle and, 420
  club benefits and, 128
  described, 121
  special interest groups and, 134
Frey, Bruno S., 11, 163

Friedman, Benjamin, 265
Friedman, Bernard, 374
Friedman, Milton, 153, 175, 206, 250, 282, 360, 482
Friedman, Rose, 175, 206, 282
Frisby, Michael K., 565
Full Employment Act of 1946, 253
Fullerton, Don, 527
Fully funded pension fund, 336

G

Gale, William G., 286, 291
Garn–St. Germain Act of 1982, 285
General Accounting Office (GAO), 253
General equilibrium analysis of tax incidence, 447–449
General obligation bond, 421–422
Generational accounting, 350–351
Gerrymandering, 202
Gift taxes, 567–568
Gilbert, Guy, 11
Goetze, Rolf, 50
Goff, Brian L., 158
Goodman, Robert P., 218
Gore Plan, 32–33
Government failure, 16, 61–62
Government purchases, 242
Governments
  benevolent view of, 203
  crisis displacement theory of, 223–225
  demand and supply of, 213–233
  employees, 26
  equilibrium size of, 215
  exit options and, 202–203
  expanding off-budget sector of, 298
  expansion due to monopoly, 228
  income redistribution role of, 303–306
  increase in demand/supply for, 219–220
  intergovernmental competition model of, 587
  intergovernmental grants between, 595–599
  intervention debate, 104–105, 109
  Leviathan view of, 203–204
  negative externalities and intervention by, 92–101
  number of U.S. units of, 579
  off-budget, 269–299
  per-capita spending of, 4
  privatization of services by, 144
  progressive taxation to expand, 230–231
  public process and branches of, 166–167
  public spending distribution of, 19–20, 581–582
  revenues of all, 25
  spending by area, 22
  tax expenditure estimates of, 432–433
  tax wars between, 594–595
  transactions costs and role of, 89–91
  transfer function of, 346
  uniformity of provision by, 593–594
  See also Expenditure policies; Federalism
Governments as laboratories, 588
Government-sponsored enterprises (GSEs), 27–28, 288–293
Government transfers, 242
Grace Commission, 247
Grace, J. Peter, 247

Graetz, Michael J., 459
Gramlich, Edward M., 221, 393
Gramm-Rudman-Hollings Act I (1985), 258–260, 263, 292
Gramm-Rudman-Hollings Act II, 260, 263
Grand utility possibilities curve, 74
Granger, Clive W., 484
Grants
  conditional, 595–596
  intergovernmental, 595–599
  nonmatching/matching conditional, 598–599
  policies on, 599–600
  unconditional, 596–598
Greene, Kevin V., 222
Green, Jeffrey R., 227, 484
Gregg, John G., 548
Gross domestic product (GDP)
  described, 7
  federal tax receipts portion of, 415, 484–485
  health care portion of, 364–368
  private spending portion of, 21
  public spending share of, 20, 213–214
Gross federal debt, 466–467
Gross income
  corporate, 537–538
  personal, 498
Groves, Theodore, 139
GSE loans, 27–28

H

Haig, Robert M., 493
Haig-Simons criterion, 493–494
Hall, Robert, 541
Hamilton, Bruce W., 587
Hansen, W. Lee, 358, 360
Harberger, Arnold C., 404, 548
Harsanyi, John C., 305
Hauser, W. Kurt, 484
Hausman, Jerry A., 524
Haveman, Robert H., 359
Head Start, 315
Health care sector
  crisis within, 368–369
  expansion of, 364–368
  reform of, 377–380
  rising costs within, 369–376
Health insurance
  debate over national, 9–10, 380
  rationales for public, 354
  reduced access to, 369–370
  as workfare issue, 327
  See also Medicare
Health maintenance organizations (HMOs), 375
Higgs, Robert, 223
High-tax jurisdictions, 571–572
HIPCs, 377
Hirschman, Albert O., 201
Hochman, Harry M., 304
Hoffman, Elizabeth, 185
Holcombe, Randall G., 600
Home equity loans, 457
Horizontal equity, 423–424
Hotelling, Harold, 190
Housing assistance, 315
Housing assistance programs, 328

Hubbard, R. Glenn, 553
Human capital approach, 400
Hurd, Michael, 347

I

Iden, George, 266, 478
Imperfect information, 60
Implicit federal guarantee, 289
Implicit rental income, 495
Impoundment Act of 1974, 254
Income
 additional factors impacting on, 311–313
 consumer equilibrium and changes in, 613–614
 defining comprehensive measure of, 494–498
 defining taxable, 498–503
 Haig-Simons criterion of, 493–494
 health costs and rising, 372
 human capital approach to, 400
 interest, 514, 530–532
 level vs. distribution of, 308–309
 measuring, 305–307
 middle class, 310–311
 payroll taxes on, 446–447
 poverty threshold of, 310
 purchasing ability and, 616
 real median family, 307–308
 taxable interest, 514
 tax liabilities compared to annual, 561–562
Income effect, 530–531, 618–619
Income–leisure model, 517–519
Income redistribution
 demands for, 221
 equality of outcomes/opportunity and, 305–306
 fiscal structure, impact on, 594
 grants used for, 600
 issues of, 95–96, 306–313
 policy goals of, 304–305
 public discount rate and, 404
 through private market charity, 303–304
 through special interest groups, 360–361
 through tax policy, 425–428
 See also Social insurance programs
Income taxes
 discount rate and, 402–403
 income criteria for, 493–498, 498–503
 income–leisure model and, 517–519
 inflation and, 513–515
 labor income and, 519–520
 marriage tax built into, 511–513, 525
 policy reform for, 504–511
 progressive, 5
 saving behavior and, 528–535
 vertical supply curve S and, 520–521
 See also Income; Taxes
Increases in demand, 617
Incumbents, 201–202
Indifference schedules/curves, 605–610
Individual retirement (IRA) account, 352
Inelastic savings supply, 532
Inferior goods, 614
Inflation
 depreciation and, 541–542
 impact on present value by, 390–393
 tax burdens and, 513–515

Inframarginal externalities, 105–106
Infrastructure provision, 265
In-kind income, 495
Innovations, regulation and, 99
Insurance copayment, 367
Insurance deductible, 367
Insurance function, 335
Insurance market
 adverse selection within, 281
 allocation effects on, 275–277
 role of risk in, 270–273
Insurance policies, 273–275, 293–297, 470–471
Interdependent utility functions, 304
Interest costs, 538–539
Interest income, 514, 530–532
Intergenerational transfers, 345–346
Intergovernmental competition, 587
Intergovernmental grants, 595–599
Interjurisdictional externalities, 593
Internalization of costs, 88
Internal rates of discount, 396
Intertemporal choice model, 528–529
Intragenerational transfers, 345
IOUs (Medicare), 355–357
IOUs (Social Security), 341, 344, 351
Irrational ignorance, 160
Itemized deductions, 500

J

Jaarsma, Bert, 164
Jensen, Michael C., 405, 545
Jeong, Jin-Ho, 227, 484
Job Training Partnership Act of 1982, 315
Johnson, Manuel H., 143
Jorgenson, Dale, 541
Joulfaian, David, 162, 292, 579, 592
Judicial branch, 167

K

Kaldor, Nicholas, 54
Kalt, Joseph, 175
Kau, James B., 175, 216, 227
Kelman, Steven, 156, 173
Keynesians, 61, 481
Keynes, John Maynard, 61, 230
Kihlstrom, Richard E., 278
Kimball, James N., 99
Kormendi, Robert C., 266
Kosters, Marvin H., 260
Kotlikoff, Laurence J., 350, 471
Kristof, Kathy M., 511
Krzyaniak, Marion, 548

L

Laband, David N., 181
Labor supply
 evidence on elasticities of, 523–524
 income taxes and, 517–524
 Laffer curve and, 524–528
 vertical/upward-sloping, 520–523
Labor taxes, 446–447
Lack of exclusion, 118–119
Laffer curve, 524–528
Landes, William M., 170
Lauth, T., 264
Law of diminishing marginal utility, 604–605

Law of increasing cost, 71
Leal, Donald R., 146
Ledyard, J., 139
Lee, Dwight R., 527
Legislative branch, 166–167
Lerner, Abba, 304
Leviathan view of government, 203–204
Lewis-Beck, Michael, 163
Liabilities
 calculating tax, 501–502
 generational accounting of, 350–351
 Haig-Simons criterion and, 493–494
 lowering tax, 502–503
 of major insurance program, 287, 470–471
 moral hazard and, 282
 moral hazard and risk, 277–279
 of trust funds, 471
Lindahl equilibrium, 126–127
Lindahl, Erik, 125, 126
Lindahl prices, 125–126, 129
Lindahl pricing
 taxation vs., 139–141
 tax policy guided by, 420
 unanimity rules of voting and, 183
Lindsey, Lawrence B., 226
Line-item vetoes, 261–262
Link, John P., 114
Lipson, Gerald, 247–248
Littlechild, S. C., 204
Loan guarantees, 28, 292–293
Lobbies, 129
Lock-in effect, 495, 568
Logrolling, 196–198
Long-lived resources, 539
Long-run tax incidence, 548–551
Low-tax jurisdictions, 571–572
Lump sum tax, 451–452

M

McCallum, John, 231
McClosky, Herbert, 216
McDowell, Jeanne, 92
McGuire, Alistair, 372
Mackay, Robert J., 194
McKee, Michael, 460
McMillin, W. Douglas, 478
Macroeconomic growth, 230–231
Madison, James, 208
Majorities, 185–186
Majority voting, 194–195
Majority voting equilibrium, 192–193
Majority voting rules, 184, 199–200
Makin, John H., 478
Malbin, Michael J., 133, 157, 159, 169, 201
Managed competition, 377–378
Manage, Neela, 227, 484
Mandatory spending, 251
Mann, Thomas E., 133, 157, 159, 169, 201
Marginal benefits *(MB)*, 42–43
Marginal costs *(MC)* of production, 70–71
Marginal opportunity costs, 42–43
Marginal private benefits *(MPB)*, 103–104
Marginal rate of substitution *(MRS)*, 66–67, 606
Marginal rate of transformation *(MRT)*, 70–71
Marginal social benefits *(MSB)*, 81–83, 103–104, 449–450

648 Index

Marginal social opportunity costs *(MSC)*, 81–83, 449–450
Marginal tax rates, 501–502
Marginal utility *(MU)*, 604
Market demand curves, 619–620
Market equilibrium
   efficiency and, 43–44
   supply and demand analysis of, 622–623
Market failure
   described, 8, 61–62
   policies addressing, 404
   public goods and, 120–122
   pure public goods and, 122–123
Market prices, 82–83
Marlow, Michael L., 83, 99, 114, 162, 202, 227, 292, 349, 484, 579, 592
Marriage tax, 511–513, 525
Matching conditional grants, 598–599
Maximization of social welfare, 57–58
Mayhew, David R., 172
Meckling, William H., 405, 545
Median voter model
   described, 188
   public goods provision of, 189
   representative democracy and, 189–192
   See also Voters
Median voter theorem, 187
Medicaid, 314
Medical technology, 375
Medicare
   characteristics of, 355
   cost expansion of, 366–368
   health care costs of, 353–354
   rationales for, 354
   as social insurance, 301, 331
   See also Health care sector
Medicare trust funds (HI), 355–357
Medigap insurance, 366
Mehay, Stephen L., 593
Meltzer, Allan H., 221
Methodological individualism, 38–39
Meyer, Bruce C., 360
Mickelwright, John, 359
Microeconomic theory
   consumer theory within, 603–619
   price elasticity of demand and supply, 624–625
   producer theory within, 620–622
   supply and demand analysis of, 622
Middle class, 310–311
Mieszkowski, Peter M., 548, 571
Milgate, Murray, 56, 587
Miller, James C., III, 264
Mills, Edwin, 108
Minorities, 185–186
Moffit, Robert, 315
Monopolies
   allocative efficiency and, 59–60
   efficiency in exchange/production and, 76–77
   perfect competition compared to, 77–79
   taxes on, 444–446
Monopoly government, 142–143
Moore, Stephen, 261
Moral hazard
   described, 114
   liabilities and, 282
   off-budget policies and, 280–281

risk liabilities and, 277–279
   as social insurance issue, 334–335
   of transfer programs, 323–324
   VA loan program and, 279–280
   within medical insurance, 373–375
Mortgage market, 272
Moynihan, Daniel Patrick, 351
Mueller, Dennis C., 143, 181, 183, 194, 217, 221
Munley, Vincent G., 222
Munnell, Alicia H., 348
Murray, Charles A., 326
Murrell, Peter, 221
Musgrave, Richard A., 126, 216, 548
Muth, R. F., 144
Mutual forbearance, 114

N

Nardinelli, Clark, 231
Narrow self-interest
   of policymakers, 171–172
   of voters, 153–154
National consumption taxes, 557–562
National debt
   components of, 466–467
   described, 465–466
   re-funding of the, 467–468
   See also Budget deficits
National health expenditures, 354
National health insurance, 380
   See also Health insurance
National Health Service (NHS), 380
National Science Foundation (NSF), 104
Negative externalities
   allocative efficiency and, 81–82
   controlled by regulation, 98–99
   described, 59, 80–81
   government intervention and, 92–101
   market prices and, 82–83
   prisoners' dilemma and, 91
   property right assignments as, 83–85
   special interest groups and, 135–136
   See also Externalities
Negative income tax policy, 324–325
Negative transfers, 426–427
Nelson, Michael A., 585
Net federal debt, 467
Net interest expenditures, 248–252
Net transfers, 427
Newhouse, Joseph P., 372
Newman, Peter, 56, 587
NHTSA, 30
NIMBY, 244
Niskanen, William A., Jr., 169, 205–206
Nixon, Richard, 253
Noncash transfers, 314–319
Nonelected policymakers, 165–166, 176–177
Nonfederal spending, 21
Nonguaranteed bond, 421–422
Nonmatching conditional grants, 598–599
Nonprofit associations, 130
Normal goods, 614
Normative analysis, 11
Nutter, G. Warren, 214

O

Oates, Wallace E., 92, 203, 592, 594
Occupational Safety and Health Administration (OSHA), 30, 99

O'Driscoll, Gerald P., 475
OECD countries, 30–31, 416, 418
Oelert, W., 143
Off-budget government
   allocative effects of, 275–277
   costs of credit/insurance programs, 293–297
   credit/insurance markets and, 270–273
   credit/insurance policies of, 273–275
   deposit insurance policy of, 281–288
   described, 269
   expanding nature of, 298
   GSEs policies of, 288–292
   impact on risk of, 277–281
   loan guarantees of, 292–293
Off-budget policies, 28
Old Age, Survivors and Disability Insurance (OASDI), 337, 339
Olson, Mancur, 129, 134, 231
Omnibus Budget Reconciliation Act of 1990 (OBRA), 260, 295, 500, 505–507
On-budget policies, 28
Opportunity cost, 6
Optimal federal system, 585–586
Optimal fiscal structure, 577
Optimal majority rules, 184–187
Ordeshook, Peter C., 162
Organization for Economic Cooperation and Development (OECD) countries, 30–31, 416, 418
Ornstein, Norman J., 133, 157, 159, 169, 201
Orzechowski, William P., 164, 221
OSH Act, 30
Outlay equivalents, 433–434
Overall economic efficiency, 72–74
Overproduction, 106–108, 190
Overseas Private Investment Corporation (OPIC), 286
Overspending, 479

P

Pareto efficiency
   allocations, 52–53
   conditions for, 66–67
   cost-benefit analysis impact on, 408
   as public policy criteria, 8
   public spending costs and, 239–241
   welfare economic context of, 51–52
Pareto inefficiency, 53
Pareto superior allocation, 53
Pareto, Vilfredo, 51
Parker, Glenn R., 201
Parkin, David, 372
Paternalism, 15, 335–336
Paulter, Paul A., 162
Pauly, Mark V., 203, 278, 374
Pay-as-you-go funding, 340–341
Payne, James L., 407, 456, 460
Payroll taxes, 446–447
Peacock, Alan T., 126, 216, 223
Pechman, Joseph A., 499, 508
Pell Grants, 315
Peltzman, Sam, 175, 221, 316
Penniman, Howard R., 154
Pension Benefit Guaranty Corporation (PBGC, or Pennie Bennie), 286, 288
Pepper, Claude D., 247–248
Perfect competition, 75–79

Perry, James M., 166
Pieper, Paul J., 264, 469
Pigou, Arthur C., 93
Play-or-pay proposal, 378
Plotnick, Robert, 359
Policy intentions, 156
Policymakers
 audit function of, 406–408
 broad self-interests of, 173–175
 elected/nonelected, 165–166, 176–177
 ideal vs. actual behaviors of, 173–174
 institutional factors, 166–167
 interest expenditures and, 251–252
 Leviathan/benevolent view of, 203–205
 members of Congress as, 167–171
 narrow self-interests of, 171–172
 NIMBY attitude of, 244–245
 public finance choices by, 11
 special interest groups and, 207–210
Policy process
 cost-benefit analysis and, 405–408
 described, 8
 implications of theories for, 228–230
 intentions vs. results of, 156
 modeling the, 152–153
 policymakers and, 165–177
 special interest groups and, 155
 tax principles and, 460–461
 voters and, 153–155
Policy results, 156
Political action committees (PACs), 132–133, 297
Political disequilibrium, 486–488
Political participation, 153
Political patronage, 176
Pollution permits, 100–101
Pommerehne, Werner W., 11
Pork barrel spending, 246–248
Positive analysis, 10–11
Positive externalities
 allocative efficiency and, 103–104
 described, 59, 80, 101, 103
 inframarginal, 105–106
 special interest groups and, 136
 See also Externalities
Positive transfers, 426–427
Posner, Richard A., 170
Poterba, James M., 524
Poverty threshold, 310
Power
 self-interest and, 175
 of special interest groups, 145–146
Preferred provider organization, 375
Present value, 385–386, 390–393
Present value framework
 application of, 388–390
 comparing projects using, 387
 described, 385–387
 implications of, 387–388
Pressure groups, 129
Price effects hypothesis, 217
Prices
 consumer equilibrium and, 614–616
 demand curves and, 616
 demand/supply and elasticity of, 624–625
 negative externalities and market, 82–83
 producer theory on, 621–622
 substitution effects and, 617

Primary insurance amount (PIA), 337, 339
Prisoners' dilemma, 91
Private costs, 81
Private goods
 benefit principle, application to, 418–419
 compared to public, 120
 described, 118
 market demand for, 123
 within public markets, 119–120
Private market charity, 303–305
Private markets
 benefit principle in, 416–418
 characteristics of, 37–38
 consumer surplus and equilibrium of, 45–47
 efficiency and adaptation of, 44–45
 lack of social insurance in, 334–335
 microeconomic theory of, 603–625
 public goods within, 119–120, 126–129
 public intervention in, 50–51
 resources within, 6–7
Private market structure, 200
Private opportunity costs (*MPC*), 81
Private pensions, 336
Private philanthropy funds, 155
Private sector
 majority voting rules of, 199
 optimal majority rule in, 186–187
 public goods within, 126–129
 special interest groups within, 130–131
 spending by, 20
Private Sector Survey on Cost Control, 247
Privatization
 described, 144
 of housing assistance programs, 328
 of Social Security, 352–353
Producer theory, 620–622
Production
 centralization of public, 135
 innovation and, 99
 monopoly government, 142–143
 supply curves and costs of, 620–622
Production possibilities curves, 69–70
Progressive income tax, 5
 See also Income tax
Progressive tax system, 425
Property right assignments
 allocative efficiency and, 88
 Coase theorem on, 85–88
 described, 83–85, 138–139
 geographical boundaries of, 92
 wealth distribution and, 88–89
Property tax, 568–572
Proportional tax system, 424–425
Protection function, 13
Public choice, 151–152
Public debt
 burdens associated with, 477–478
 foreign share of, 472–473
 intergenerational burdens from, 473–474
 Ricardian equivalence proposition of, 474–477, 481–482
 See also Budget deficits
Public exchange
 under dictatorships, 180–181
 voice/exit options of, 201–205
Public expenditures, 414–416, 428–434
 See also Expenditure policies

Public finance, 3–4, 16
Public goods
 benefit principle, application to, 419–420
 characterized by externalities, 135–136
 compared to private, 120
 described, 59, 118
 efficient quantities of, 123–125
 financing, 125
 lack of exclusion and, 118–119
 market demand for, 123
 market failure and, 120–122
 median voter model and, 189
 private market provision of, 119, 126–129
 produced in private/public markets, 120
 public sector provision of, 143–146
Public markets
 benefit principle in, 418–420
 characteristics of, 37–38
 institutional differences between, 177–178
 private goods within, 119–120
 public goods within, 120
 resources within, 7–8
Public market structure, 200
Public policies
 benefits of, 4–5
 costs of, 5–6
 Pareto efficiency criterion and, 8
Public programs, 215–217
 See also Social insurance programs
Public sector
 centralization of, 225–226
 changes in equilibrium size of, 217–220
 credit/insurance intervention by, 273–275
 debate over role of, 15–16
 economic growth and expansion of, 230–231
 employee demand, 221–222
 employment within, 26
 equilibrium size of, 215–220
 federal credit/insurance programs of, 26–28
 financing activities of, 21–25
 fiscal federalism of, 577–601
 of foreign countries, 30–31
 the Gore plan for, 32–33
 government spending on, 19–20
 infrastructure provision of, 265
 majority voting rules of, 199–200
 primary functions of, 13–15
 public goods within, 143–146
 pure public goods and, 134
 size/growth of, 19, 33
 welfare economics, role of, 58–61
Public spending
 annual government, 19–20
 areas of, 20–21
 centralization of, 227
 costs of, 239–242
 on education, 237–239
 GDP share of, 213–214
 for health care, 366–368
 Impoundment Act of 1974 and, 254
 infrastructure, 266
 social welfare, 302
 tax revenues and, 480
 Wagner's law on, 216
 See also Expenditure policies

Public spirit, 12
Purchasing ability, 616
Pure private good
 described, 120
 optimal provision of, 122–126
 public sector provision of, 134
Pure public good, 120

R

Ram, Rati, 215, 484
Ramsey, Frank P., 455
Ramsey rule, 455
Ranney, Austin, 154
Rate of discount, 385
Rate setting, 378–380
Rational ignorance, 156–159
Ratner, Jonathan B., 265
Rawls, John, 305
Reagan, Ronald, 99
Real median family income, 307–308
Recision power, 254
Redlining, 273–274
Reelection, 169
REFCORP (Resolution Funding Corporation), 291
Re-funding of the national debt, 467–468
Regressive tax system, 424
Regulation
 benefits of, 113–114
 costs of, 114–115
 innovation incentives and, 99
 negative externalities controlled by, 98–99
 of S&Ls, 112–113
Regulatory agencies, 30
Regulatory forbearance, 284–285
Regulatory policy, 115–116
Reinventing Government Plan, 32–33
Rent controls, 47–50
Rent seeking, 208, 590
Resolution Trust Corporation (1989), 291
Resource allocation
 Coase theorem of, 85–88
 common-pool problems within, 146
 with compensation, 55
 without compensation, 55–56
 cost-benefit analysis of, 383–385
 deposit insurance policy and, 285
 efficiency in, 39–47
 equity vs. efficiency in, 53–54
 within an imperfect world, 108–109
 importance of process of, 58
 off-budget policies of, 273–275
 Pareto efficiency criterion and, 8
 positive/normative analysis of, 11–12
 within private market, 6–7
 within public market, 7–8
 public sector choices on, 8, 10
 public sector role in, 58–61
 rent control and, 47–48
 risk and, 273
 tax expenditure programs for, 431–432
 See also Externalities
Retained earnings, 545
Revenue Act of 1964, 484
Revenue bond (nonguaranteed bond), 421–422
Revenue-expenditure causality, 483
Revenues
 derived from grants, 596
 sources of, 24–25
 of state/local governments, 580–581, 583
 See also Taxes
Ricardian equivalence proposition, 474–477, 481–482
Ricardo, David, 475
Richard, Scott F., 221
Riker, William H., 162
Risk
 adjusting GSEs, 296
 credit/insurance market, 270–273
 discount rate and, 403
 off-budget policies impact on, 277–281
 policy and, 283–284
 resource allocation and, 273
Rivlin, Alice M., 230, 261, 594
Rodgers, James O., 304
Rosentone, Steven J., 163
Rubinfeld, Daniel L., 221
Rubin, Paul H., 175, 216, 227
Russek, Frank S., 266, 478

S

St. John, Michael, 50
Sales taxes
 described, 555–557
 national, 557–562
 value-added (VAT), 562–566
Sallie Mae, 288
Samuelson, Paul, 118
Sandler, Todd, 127
Save the whale debate, 90
Savings Association Insurance Fund (SAIF), 113, 282
Saving behavior
 allocation of, 534–535
 interest earnings, taxation and, 530–531
 interest expense, deductions and, 533–534
 intertemporal choice model of, 528–529
 tax shifting, 531–532
Savings and loans institutions (S&Ls)
 crisis of insolvent, 114–115
 regulation of, 112–113
 regulatory forbearance and insolvent, 284–285
Sawhill, Isabel V., 361
Schneider, Friedrich, 11
Scholz, John K., 564
School choice issue, 588–590
Schram, Arthur, 164
Schwartz, Anna J., 250
Scitovsky, T., 54
Scully, Gerald W., 177, 177–178, 595
Self-insuring, 370
Self-interest
 constraints on, 175–176
 described, 12
 policymaker, 171–175
 voter, 153–155
Senat, Hamburger, 143
Sequestrations, 258
Settle, R. F., 158
Shortage, 622
Short-lived resources, 539
Short-run corporate tax incidence, 546–548
Shoven, John B., 455, 551, 564
Shughart, William F., II, 589
Simons, Henry, 493
Simple majority rule, 184
Simple majority voting rules, 187–192
Single-peaked preferences, 194–195, 197
"Sin" taxes, 558
Skinner, Andrew, 39
Slemrod, Joel, 457, 460, 507
Slottje, Daniel J., 177–178
Smith, Adam, 39, 151
Smith, Anthony, 157, 159
Smith, Vernon, 185
Social costs, 81
Social insurance programs
 costs of, 332–333
 described, 331
 historical perspective of, 333–334
 policy rationales for, 334–336
 Social Security as, 336–353
 See also Income redistribution
Social Security
 beneficiaries of, 343
 benefits of, 337–339
 compared to private pensions, 336
 current issues of, 347–350
 funded through trust fund, 339–344
 rates and maximum contributions to, 338
 reforming, 350–353
 as social insurance, 301, 331
 taxes for, 337
 as a transfer program, 344–346
Social Security Act of 1935, 333–334
Social Security Amendments of 1983, 504
Social Security Amendments of 1986, 505
Social Security deficits, 341
Social Security surpluses, 341
Social Security trust funds, 339–344
Social welfare, 57–58
Social welfare function, 56
Social welfare policies, 301, 303
Society
 as collection of individuals, 38–39
 corrective tax gains by, 94
 economic expansion within, 328
 equity goals of, 60–61
 health costs and aging, 371–372
 logrolling, impact on, 198
 optimal fiscal structure and, 577
 promotion of equity goals of, 335
 theory of clubs within, 127–129
 total net benefits *(TNB)* to, 39–40
 welfare economic constraints in, 58
Sorum, Nikki, 457
Source side of budget, 494
Spann, Robert M., 223
Special districts, 578
Special interest groups
 described, 129–130
 expansion as result of, 228–229
 impact on private sector, 130–131
 impact on public sector, 405–406
 incentives to form, 131
 income redistribution policies of, 360–361
 negative externalities and, 135–136
 PACs as, 132–133
 policymakers and, 207–210
 positive externalities and, 136
 power of, 145–146

public good nature of, 133–134
public policy process and, 155
rent seeking and, 208, 590
Spending cuts, 255–258
Spending. *See* Public spending
Spitzer, M. L., 185
Stabilization function, 15
Stabilization policies, 61
Standard deduction, 500
Statutory depreciation, 539
Statutory incidence, 437, 439–441
Statutory tax rates, 542
Steuerle, C. Eugene, 503
St-Hilaire, France, 562
Stigler, George J., 86
Stokes, Donald E., 154
Straight-line depreciation, 539–540
Stuart, Charles, 455
Subsidies
  allocative efficiency and, 104
  described, 96–97
  excise, 319–321
  on nonprofits, 145
  overproduction caused by, 106–108
Substitution effect, 530, 617–619
Summers, Lawrence H., 531, 542
Supplemental Security Income (SSI), 313
Suppliers of public programs, 213
Supply and demand
  elasticities of, 441–443
  impact on tax policy, 443
  market equilibrium analysis of, 622–623
  price elasticity of, 624–625
  public program, 215–217
Supply elasticities, 442–443
Surplus, 622

T

Tanzi, Vito, 458
Tatom, John A., 265
Tax amnesties, 459–460
Tax analysis
  of *ad valorem*, 444–445
  of excess burden, 449–450
  general equilibrium analysis of tax incidence, 447–449
  general issues of, 436–437
  on monopolists, 444–446
  of payroll taxes, 446–447
  of unit taxes, 437–443
Tax avoidance, 458
Tax bases
  broadening of, 508–509
  described, 429–430
  VAT's, 564–565
Tax bite in the eight-hour day, 5
Tax burdens, 5
Tax credits
  corporate, 543
  personal, 502
Tax deductions, 428–429
Tax earmarking, 419
Tax Equity and Fiscal Responsibility Act of 1982, 485
Taxes
  administrative costs of, 456
  ad valorem, 437, 444–445, 556
  behavior and income, 517–535

budget deficits and increase of, 482–484
changing sources of, 414–416
compared to foreign countries, 416
compliance costs of, 456–457
consumption, 555–566
corporation, 537–553
corrective, 92–94
discount rate and income, 402–403
estate/gift, 566–568
excess burden of, 449–450
excise, 437
expenditure, 557
gift/estate, 567–568
Lindahl pricing vs., 139–141
lobbying costs of, 458
lump sum, 451–452
on monopolists, 444–446
national consumption, 557–562
payroll, 446–447
personal income, 493–515
Pigouvian, 93–94
progressive income, 5
property, 568–572
public sector expansion through, 230–231
public spending and revenues, 480
reforming Social Security, 351
rising health costs and, 371
sales, 555–557
"sin," 558
Social Security, 337
tax shelters and, 457–458
tolls as, 6
unit, 437–439
U.S. collection of, 23
value-added (VAT), 562–566
Tax evasion, 458–459
Tax expenditures
  allocational effects of, 430
  described, 428–429
  distributional effects of, 430–431
  estimates of, 432–433
  health care spending and, 375–376
  lobbying costs of, 458
  outlay equivalents of, 433–434
  rate vs. base of, 429–430
  substitutability of, 431–432
  tax shelters compared to, 457
Tax freedom day, 5
Taxing free parking, 497
Tax liability, 501–502
Tax life, 539
Tax policies
  ability-to-pay principle, 422–425
  aggregate financing trends in, 414
  based on efficiency, 139–141
  based on equity, 141
  benefit principle within, 416–420
  equity within consumption, 561–562
  implementing, 96
  income redistribution through, 313, 425–428
  increased collections through, 484–486
  negative income, 324–325
Tax policy neutrality, 496
Tax preferences, 428–429
Tax rates
  average, 502
  average personal income, 510–511

described, 429–430
effective, 542–543
marginal, 501–502
statutory, 542
Tax reform
  for corporation taxes, 552
  for personal income tax, 504–511
  policy changes through, 414, 416
Tax Reform Act of 1986 (TRA86), 457, 504–508
Tax Reform for Fairness, Simplicity, and Economic Growth, 507
Tax shelters, 457–458
Tax shifting, 425
Tax simplification, 460–461
Tax-spend hypothesis, 226–227
Tax wars, 594–595
Taylor, Jeffrey, 100
Theory of clubs, 127–128, 136
Third-party payer, 373–374
Tideman, T. Nicolaus, 139
Tiebout, Charles M., 203, 586
Tiebout model, 586–587, 589
Tobin, James, 318
Tollison, Robert D., 162
Tolls, 6
Topel, Robert, 358, 359
Total benefits *(TB)*, 40–41
Total net benefits *(TNB)*, 39–42
Total opportunity costs *(TC)*, 40
Total utility *(TU)*, 603–604
Transactions costs, 89–91
Transfer function, 335
Transfer programs
  assessing performance of, 427–428
  economic effects of, 315–322
  means-tested, 313–315
  positive/negative, 426–427
  recipients of, 428
  Social Security as, 344–346
  work–leisure trade-off and, 322–325
  See also Income redistribution
Trost, Robert P., 114
Tschirhart, John T., 127
Tullock, Gordon, 86, 98, 139, 151, 180–181 184, 186, 206, 208, 222, 304, 361, 582
Tyson, Laura, 507–508

U

Unanimity rules of voting, 182–184
Unanimity test, 56
Unconditional grants, 596–598
Underground economy, 458
Undertaxation, 479
Unemployment insurance
  characteristics of, 357–358
  economic effects of, 359–360
  income redistribution through, 358–359
  rationales for, 357
  as social insurance, 301, 331
Unfunded (underfunded) program, 277
Uniformity of provision, 593–594
United States
  budget deficits/surpluses of, 224
  capital budget for, 265–266
  fiscal structure in the, 578–582
  progressive tax system used in, 424–425

652 Index

United States *(cont.)*
  public spending in, 20, 23
  social welfare expenditures in, 302
  tax collection in, 23
  tax distribution of, 418
  voting participation in, 164
Unit taxes
  on demanders, 438
  measuring excess burdens of, 453–455
  on suppliers, 437–438
Upward-sloping labor supply, 521–523
Upward-sloping savings supply, 532
Urbanization, 220
U.S. Agriculture Department, 225, 405–406
U.S. Congress
  budgetary fights between Nixon and, 253
  characteristics of, 167–171
  incoming mail to, 158
  legislative output of, 28–30
  line-item veto and, 261–262
  regulatory agencies of, 30
Use side of budget, 494
Utility-maximizing behavior, 603
Utility possibilities curve, 52, 68–69
Utility theory, 603–605

V

VA loan program, 279–280
Value-added tax (VAT), 562–566
Value on life, 400
Van Winden, Frans, 164
Vertical equity, 424–425, 561
Vertical labor supply curve S, 520–521
Voice options, 201–202
Voluntary agreements, 142
Von Furstenburg, George, 227, 484
Voter preferences, 191
Voters
  consideration of reallocations by, 58
  as demanders of spending programs, 215–217
  logrolling by, 196–198
  median voter model of, 188–192
  median voter theorem on, 187
  political participation of, 153, 160–161
  public finance choices by, 12–13
  rational ignorance of, 156–159
  self-interest of, 153–155
  as well-informed, 159–160
Voting
  behavioral factors within, 162–164
  correlation between age and, 132
  in foreign countries, 164
  institutional factors of, 160, 162
  majority rules of, 184
  optimal majority rule of, 184–186
  participation of, 160–161
  simple majority rules of, 187–192
  unanimity rules of, 182–184
  for U.S. Presidents, 192
  U.S. vs. other countries, 164–165
Voting cycles, 193–194
Voting Rights Act (1965), 202

W

Wages, 538
  See also Income
Wagner, Adolph, 216
Wagner, Richard E., 126, 140, 222, 324, 481
Wagner's law, 216
Wallace, Myles S., 231, 484
Wallis, John J., 592, 600
Walzer, Norman C., 591
Ward, Benjamin, 227
Warner, John T., 231, 484
Wealth distribution, 88–89
Wealth taxation, 567
Weaver, Carolyn L., 194, 333, 341, 349–350, 471
Webber, Carolyn, 246

Weinberg, Daniel H., 431
Weisbrod, Burton A., 375
Welfare costs, 318–319
Welfare cost of taxation, 449–450
Welfare economics
  described, 51–52
  equity vs. efficiency in, 53–54
  in practice, 58
  See also Pareto efficiency
Welfare policies
  policy reforms, 328
  underlying issues of, 325–328
  workfare and, 326–327
  work–leisure trade-off within, 322–323
Welfare state, 246
Whalley, John, 455, 562
Wicksell, Knut, 56
Wildavsky, Aaron, 246, 253
Wilde, Louis L., 459
Williams, Al L., 589
Wilson, James Q., 205
Wiseman, Jack, 203, 204, 223
Wolfinger, Raymond E., 163
Workfare, 326–327
Work–leisure trade-off, 322–323

Y

Yezer, Anthony M., 281
Yule, Brian, 372

Z

Zahid, Khan H., 478
Zaller, John, 216
Zampelli, Earnest M., 592
Zardkoohi, Asghar, 600
Zax, Jeffrey S., 592
Zero marginal costs of provision, 118, 122
Zupan, Mark, 175